Comparing Legal Cultures

SÖREN KOCH
JØRN ØYREHAGEN SUNDE (EDS.)

Comparing Legal Cultures

Revised and Extended 2nd Edition

FAGBOKFORLAGET

2. edition / 2. print run 2022
ISBN: 978-82-450-3394-6

Graphic production: John Grieg, Bergen
Cover design by Fagbokforlaget

Enquiries about this text can be directed to:
Fagbokforlaget
Kanalveien 51
5068 Bergen
Tel.: 55 38 88 00
email: fagbokforlaget@fagbokforlaget.no
www.fagbokforlaget.no

Preface

We are proud to present a second revised and extended edition of *Comparing Legal Cultures* containing eleven new chapters. Seven new introductions to the legal cultures of Australia, Belgium, Italy, Norway, Poland, Romania, and the USA have been added. That made it necessary to restructure the content of the current volume. The contributions contained in the first edition have been updated and amended in order to achieve a higher degree of structural and conceptual coherence. Based on years of experience teaching and applying a legal cultural approach to comparative law, both in Norway and abroad, we have extended and slightly amended the analytical framework. By adding four introductory chapters explaining in more detail our theoretical approach (and its limits), method, and how to use the information on the selected legal cultures, we intend to enhance the readers' understanding of the didactical purpose of this book and how to use it. Finally, a concluding chapter is intended to illustrate briefly how a comparison of different legal cultures may be conducted.

To give the reader direct access to the sources and information in the apparatus, we have chosen to use footnotes instead of endnotes.

Fagbokforlaget were immediately interested in publishing the second edition of this volume and provided excellent support along the way. All contributions to this book have undergone an intense and, at times, annoying editing process. We are very grateful for the authors' commitment and patience. PhD student Marius Mikkel Kjølstad has been (once again) our assistant and handyman in the final stage of the editing process of this second edition. In the final stages, student Marie Hatten provided valuable assistance. We are deeply grateful for all their efforts. The same applies for Dr. Adelyn Wilson, who critically evaluated the draft and contributed to enhance the quality of individual chapters and the book as a whole.

Bergen, 1 May 2020

Sören Koch *Jørn Øyrehagen Sunde*

Content

1. The Outset – How to Learn Sailing the Ocean of Legal Cultures

Sören Koch

> "Culture appears fundamental – a kind of lens through which all aspects of law must be perceived, or a gateway of understanding through which every comparatist must pass so as to have any genuine access to the meaning of foreign law."[1]

1. Introduction

Are legal cultures comparable? This book attempts to answer this question affirmatively. It establishes a framework for comparing and analysing selected key features of legal cultures. The proposed framework is based on an operationalised concept of legal culture, which is defined throughout the book as ideas of and expectations to law made operational by institutional(-like) practices.[2] On this account, the framework directs special attention to the interplay between institutional and intellectual structures inherent to almost all contemporary legal cultures.[3] Breaking legal cultures down into two institutional elements (institutions of conflict resolution and norm production) and four intellectual elements (ideal of justice, legal method, degree and attitude towards professionalisation, and internationalisation) allows the reader to *compare* particular features of legal cultures by *identifying* similarities and differences, and furthermore *explaining* and *analysing* them contextually. The proposed framework is based on a legal cultural model (LCM), capable of accommodating different approaches to law, be they socio-legal, positivistic, critical, or pluralist approaches (see *infra* Ch. 2 and Ch. 3). Further, the heuristic character of the LCM is meant to provide deeper understanding

---

1 Roger Cotterrell, 'Comparative Law and Legal Culture' in Mathias Reimann and Reinhard Zimmermann (eds), *The Oxford Handbook of Comparative Law* (2nd ed. Oxford University Press 2019) 711.

2 See Jørn Øyrehagen Sunde', 'Managing the Unmanageable – An Essay Concerning Legal Culture as an Analytical Tool' in this volume, Chapter 2, 27; Jørn Øyrehagen Sunde, 'Champagne at the Funeral – An Introduction to Legal Culture' in Knut Einar Skodvin and Jørn Øyrehagen Sunde (eds), *Rendezvous of European Legal Cultures* (Fagbokforlaget 2010) 11.

3 On the advantages and limitation of such an approach Mathias Siems, *Comparative Law* (2nd ed. Cambridge University Press 2018) 147 ff.; Cotterrell (2019) (n 1) 713 ff., 730 ff.

of the selected legal cultures. It invites the reader to study the structural elements and their interaction. In other words, this framework constitutes our *tertium comparationis*. Accordingly, all 15 national legal cultures presented in this book are roughly structured according to this framework.[4]

2. The aim of the book

Overall, the aim of this book is to enhance the reader's understanding of the historical embeddedness and unique nature of each legal culture. In addition, it provides a more holistic and sophisticated understanding of the legal culture in question.[5] Such a deeper understanding of legal cultures can be valuable, even essential, as a *point of departure* for conducting all kinds of legal comparative studies, on the macro[6] as well as on the meso and micro level.[7] Legal cultural knowledge and understanding can help to ask the right questions and choose a proper methodological approach suitable for the individual purpose and object of a comparative study. Fundamentally, it provides us with a tool to critically check our assumptions and put empirical observations into context. We aim to enhance the readers' ability to think and argue critically and reflectively, not only when encountering foreign lawyers, legal systems, and laws, but also with regard to their own national legal cultures. In a constantly more pluralistic and internationalised (legal) world, this is a skill crucial for both contemporary and future lawyers.[8]

---

4 For more detailed explanation of the framework and its intended function and limitations, see Sunde, Chapter 2 of this volume. However, it is important to emphasise that it was essential to grant the authors of each contribution the liberty to apply the framework in a way that suited the presentation of their native legal cultures. Their individual approaches but also writing styles and way of reasoning can be regarded as expression of the diversity of legal cultures included in this volume.

5 This has been emphasised as one of the main purposes of comparative law by several leading on critical approaches from scholars. Jaakko Husa, in *A New Introduction to Comparative Law* (Bloomberg 2015) n 3 further elaborated on from a macro perspective, see in particular Chapter 9-11; Esin Örücü, 'Developing Comparative Law' in Esin Örücü and David Nelken (eds), *Comparative Law –A Handbook* (Hart Publishing 2007) 44, 53 f. ('understanding law in context'; 'development of critical minds'); Esin Örücü, 'Methodology of Comparative Law' in Jan M. Smits (ed), *Elgar Encyclopedia of Comparative Law* (Edward Elgar 2006), 442–454, 445 f.

6 Recently Jaakko Husa, 'Macro Comparative Law – Reloaded' (2018) Vol. 131 No. 4 *Tidsskrift for Rettsvitenskap* 410.

7 Mark Van Hoecke, 'Deep Level Comparative Law' in Mark Van Hoecke (ed), *Epistemology and Method of Comparative Law* (Hart Publishing 2004), 165 ff.; Konrad Zweigert and Hein Kötz, *An Introduction to Comparative Law* (3rd ed. Clarendon Press 1998) 40.

8 On the impact of legal pluralism and globalization on law see, Husa (2015) (n 5), 55; Siems (2018) (n 3) 303 ff.; Michael Faure and André van der Walt (eds), *Globalisation and Private Law: The Way Forward* (Edward Elgar 2010); Paul Schiff Berman, *Global Legal Pluralism: A Jurisprudence of Law Beyond Borders* (Cambridge University Press 2012); David Kennedy, 'New Approaches to Comparative Law: Comparativism and International Governance' *Utah Law Review* (1997) 546–547.

3. The analytical framework

In order to achieve these aims the book introduces three analytical tools: First, the already mentioned legal cultural model, which helps to identify and analyse selected features in any given legal culture. We are using the metaphor of MAPPING to describe this process. Second, a model to illustrate the multi-layered nature of law. Using the metaphor of a LEGAL SEA, this tool allows us to study the extent and impact of changes in a legal culture over time and helps to explain the constant interaction between law and society. Both models are introduced in Chapter 2 and amplified in Chapter 3. From different perspectives, both chapters explain the methodological approach in more detail and provide the theoretical and conceptual framework. The purpose, subject and object of comparing legal cultures will be thoroughly examined in order to justify the operationalised concept of legal culture developed for this book. At the same time, we discuss delimitations from related concepts such as 'legal system', 'legal tradition' and 'legal family'. By explaining what a legal cultural perspective has to offer to comparative law, the purpose of comparing legal cultures is further refined. In this regard, we critically discuss the merits and limitations of traditional ways of classifications and taxonomies such as the distinction between common law, civil law and mixed legal systems.

Chapter 4 contains an innovation. In the last three decades countless articles, chapters, and books on the methods of comparative law have been published; however, systematic accounts on how to structure and conduct a comparative study in law are scarce. The COMPASS formula tries to remedy this deficiency. It provides a guideline on how to use the knowledge of national legal cultures presented in Chapters 5–19 when performing comparative analysis. Following its seven steps will help the reader navigating in the treacherous waters of comparative law. In other words, COMPASS enables the reader to use the legal cultural information systematically presented in this book to perform comparative analysis. Its scope of application is not exclusively limited to the comparative studies based on the legal cultural approach. Rather, COMPASS provides a blueprint or roadmap for all kinds of comparative studies, regardless of the comparatists' epistemological interest, the specific purpose and object of comparison, or the methodological approach chosen for the study. Furthermore, COMPASS describes a hermeneutical operation that aims to be effective on all levels of comparison (macro, meso, micro, surface or deep level). The different steps are presented in abstract terms but illustrated by several specific examples along the way. In addition, we actively use the insights of our contributions to enrich and illustrate this process.

In combination, these three tools enable the reader to *identify*, *explain*, *analyse*, and *compare* similarities and differences among legal cultures. The wide scope of applicability and dialectical merits of these tools render them interesting for all legal comparatists. Accordingly, this book addresses not only law students, but also judges, other legal professionals including administrators of justice, and those working on legislative projects.

4. Content and Structure

Subsequent to the introductory chapters, the book contains 15 chapters applying the legal cultural model to carefully selected national legal cultures. We attempt to resemble cultural diversity, particularly in Europe, but have also included the legal cultures of the United States of America, Australia, and China. Of old habit, we first structured the contributions according to the traditional civil and common law divide and added a third category – hybrid legal systems – for the misfits, which this very general taxonomy produces. When rethinking the chosen structure, we concluded that there are no reasons to use this orthodox general classification which, regardless of its didactical merits, has been increasingly criticised for being imprecise or even misleading.[9] The ongoing internationalisation of law in the age of globalisation has caused contemporary law in all modern legal cultures to be more or less pluralistic, meaning that overlapping legal regimes can be applied to solve conflict and govern social behaviour. To a certain extent, this has contributed to the convergence of transnational, supranational, extra-judicial, local and regional legal cultures, subcultures and law. The traditional classifications in legal traditions or legal families are not able (and do not intend) to display these developments.[10]

One of the blessings of using the LCM, which is the very spine of this book, is that it allows the reader to move beyond the general and often inaccurate distinction between civil and common law or the taxonomy of legal families. The LCM enables identifying and explaining similarities and differences of legal cultures regardless of whether they belong to a certain tradition or family.[11] Hence, instead of following any established classification or taxonomy, we presented the contributions as we would look them up on a globe: we start our journey in our own home country in the North and then read the globe from left to right, moving in stages south in Europe. Finally, we cross the Atlantic Ocean to the USA and continue from there to Australia and China, thus extending the perspective to the global level.

According to the established framework, each contribution discusses institutional and intellectual elements of the legal culture at hand and the interconnection among these elements. Further, all contributions contain a figure on the organization of the court system. At the end of each chapter the findings are summarised in a table containing all six elements of the legal cultural model. A bibliography is added to each contribution. All accounts of the national cultures start by providing some basic data on

9 Siems (2018) (n 3) 94 ff.; Margaret Fordham, 'The Experience of Civil Lawyers When Studying the Common Law' 8 *Asian Journal of Comparative Law* (2013) 1–20, 8. This becomes also obvious when analyzing the judicial law-making and statutory interpretation of law in civil and common law countries, see Esmeralda Colombo and Lars Kvestad, 'An Introduction to the Italian Legal Culture' in this volume, Chapter 15, 589; Martin Brenncke, *Judicial Law-Making in English and German Courts, Techniques and Limits of Statutory Interpretation* (Intersentia 2018); Stefan Vogenauer, *Die Auslegung von Gesetzen in England und auf dem Kontinent* (Mohr Siebeck 2001).

10 The concept legal family has been criticised as being biased; it tends to overemphasise similarities inside a legal family and differences to legal orders outside this family, cf. Siems (2018) (n 3) 94 ff. with further references.

11 We agree, however, with Husa (2018) (n 6) 418 and 445 f, who argues that the concept of legal families may be valuable when doing legal dogmatic comparison with a strong focus on 'law in books'. However, should the comparatist's epistemological interest concern 'law in action', Husa recommends a legal cultural approach.

geographical, economic, and political preconditions that form the general framework for legal cultures. Some authors have chosen to provide a brief historical introduction, others have used historical arguments explaining specific features or notions in their legal cultures.

Pursuant to the plan of this book, the contributions provide an 'inside-view' of the legal cultures encompassed therein. Accordingly, it was essential to grant the authors of each contribution the liberty to apply the framework in a way that suited them best for the presentation of their native legal cultures. These contributions are of course individual expressions, but to some extent, their approaches, writing styles, and way of reasoning can be regarded as an expression of the diversity of legal cultures as well. Our authors had to determine the content of each element of the legal cultural model. For example, each author had to consider what is regarded as a producer of legal norms or how best to define and describe crucial aspects of the prevailing ideal of justice. Sometimes it proved necessary to modify the structure or change the order of the framework, presented in more detail in Chapter 2 and 3, to describe and explain features in a legal culture contextually. In the chapter on the legal culture of England and Wales, Christian Franklin deemed it necessary to combine the institutional and intellectual elements of norm production and legal method.[12] Considering that courts traditionally have a highly important role in producing legal norms in England and that the way precedents are produced inevitably requires knowing how judges build their arguments, it becomes feasible to discuss legal method in conjunction with norm production. In the chapter on the legal cultures of the USA, Lloyd T. Wilson Jr. describes the ideal of justice by using the dichotomy of legal security and flexibility, which is related to, but not identical with the distinction between predictability and individual justice as highlighted by other authors in this volume.[13] Esmeralda Colombo and Lars Kvestad regard legal method as a crystallisation-point of the intellectual structure in the Italian legal culture by emphasising the impact that the ideal of justice, professionalisation and internationalisation have on the way lawyers apply the law.[14] Sören Koch, Lloyd T. Wilson Jr., Bruno Debaenst, and Tina Soliman Hunter had to address tensions between federal and state levels in their legal cultures.[15] Interestingly, they all emphasise very different natures and effects of federalism on the respective legal cultures.

Accordingly, individual considerations, styles and interpretation, which are caused by the authors' different cultural backgrounds, are the reason why both structure and terminology of the contributions in this volume can to some extent differ. This is something we were more than willing to accept in order to provide authentic maps of the cultures included in the volume. From our point of view, these nuances do not render

12 Christian N.K. Franklin, 'A Legal Cultural "Take" on the Legal System of England & Wales' in this volume, Chapter 11, 357.

13 Lloyd T. Wilson, Jr., 'A View of the Legal Culture of the United States of America' in this volume, Chapter 17, 665 f.

14 Colombo and Kvestad (2020) (n 9) 588 ff.

15 Sören Koch, 'An Introduction to German Legal Culture' in this volume, Chapter 8, 228 ff.; Wilson (2020) (n 13) 642; Bruno Debaenst, 'An Introduction to the Belgian Legal Culture' in this volume, Chapter 12, 463; Tina Soliman Hunter, 'Introduction to Australian Legal Culture' in this volume, Chapter 18, 708.

a comparison impossible. On the contrary, being aware of such nuances might help getting a better understanding of cultural particularities.

The concluding chapter illustrates how to use the knowledge provided in Chapters 5 to 19, when conducting a comparative study. It provides an example of a legal cultural comparison on the macro-level, demonstrating how to sail the ocean of legal cultures. It aims to verify the initial assumption of this introductory chapter: comparing legal cultures is possible and can provide interesting insights.

5. Bibliography

Berman PS, *Global Legal Pluralism: A Jurisprudence of Law Beyond Borders* (Cambridge University Press 2012)

Brenncke M, *Judicial Law-Making in English and German Courts, Techniques and Limits of Statutory Interpretation* (Intersentia 2018)

Cotterrell R, 'Comparative Law and Legal Culture' in Reimann M and Zimmermann R (eds), *The Oxford Handbook of Comparative Law* (2nd ed. Oxford University Press 2019)

Faure M and van der Walt A (eds), *Globalisation and Private Law: The Way Forward* (Edward Elgar 2010)

Fordham M, 'The Experience of Civil Lawyers When Studying the Common Law' (2013) 8 *Asian Journal of Comparative Law* 1

Husa J, *A New Introduction to Comparative Law* (Bloomberg 2015)

—— 'Macro Comparative Law – Reloaded' (2018) Vol. 131 No. 4 *Tidsskrift for Rettsvitenskap* 410

Kennedy D, 'New Approaches to Comparative Law: Comparativism and International Governance' (1997) *Utah Law Review*

Örücü E, 'Methodology of Comparative Law' in Smits JM (ed), *Elgar Encyclopedia of Comparative Law* (Edward Elgar 2006)

—— 'Developing Comparative Law' in Örücü E and Nelkan D (eds), *Comparative Law – A Handbook* (Hart Publishing 2007)

Siems M, *Comparative Law* (2nd ed. Cambridge University Press 2018)

Sunde JØ, 'Champagne at the Funeral – An Introduction to Legal Culture' in Skodvin KE and Sunde JØ (eds), *Rendezvous of European Legal Cultures* (Fagbokforlaget 2010)

Van Hoecke M, 'Deep Level Comparative Law' in Van Hoecke M (ed), *Epistemology and Method of Comparative Law (Hart Publishing 2004)*

Vogenauer S, *Die Auslegung von Gesetzen in England und auf dem Kontinent* (Mohr Siebeck 2001)

Zweigert K and Kötz H, *An Introduction to Comparative Law* (3rd ed. Clarendon Press 1998)

2. Managing the Unmanageable – An Essay Concerning Legal Culture as an Analytical Tool[1]

Jørn Øyrehagen Sunde

1. A first mapping and getting around the unmanageable concept of legal culture

Legal culture is all about mapping out and getting around the unknown. As an illustration, we can have a look at the copper engraving on the front page of this book. It is of the city Bergen in the western part of Norway and was published in Paris in 1683 in the five volumes *Description de L'Univers.* This specific version of the engraving was published in Frankfurt in 1719 in *Beschreibung des gantzen Welt-Kreysses.* At that time the artist, Alain Manesson Mallet, had been dead for over a decade. He was born in Paris in 1630, and had a career as an engineer, officer in the army and cartographer – a map maker. His description of the universe rested on the works of others that he rewrote in the book and turned into maps. The fifth volume is on *Das Alte und Neue Europa*, and

1 This essay is based on ideas developed in my articles 'Champagne at the Funeral – an Introduction to Legal Culture' in Jørn Øyrehagen Sunde and Knut Einar Skodvin (eds), *Rendezvous of European Legal Cultures* (Fagbokforlaget 2010); 'Legal Cultural Changes in Europe – Teaching Future Prospects on the Basis of Legal History and Comparative Law' in Kjell Å. Modéer and Per Nilsén (eds), *How to Teach European Comparative Legal History* (Juristförlaget 2011); and 'Live and Let Die – An Essay Concerning Legal-Cultural Understanding' in Maurice Adams and Dirk Hairbaut (eds), *The Method and Culture of Comparative law – Essays in Honour of Mark van Hoecke* (Hart Publishing 2014). The idea has further been developed in especially the book *Høgsteretts historie 1965–2015 – At dømme i sidste Instans* (Fagbokforlaget 2015); the articles 'Dissenting votes in the Norwegian Supreme Court 1965–2009: A legal cultural analysis' (2012) 1 *Rechtskultur – Zeitschrift für Europäische Rechtsgeschichte* 59; 'Daughters of God and counsellors of the judges of men – a study in changes in the legal culture in the Norwegian realm in the High Middle Ages' in Stefan Brink and Lisa Collinson (eds), *New Approaches to Early law in Scandinavia* (Turnhout 2014); and 'Legal Cultural Dependency of Norwegian Legal Method – and its future' in Ingvill Helland and Sören Koch (eds), *Nordic and Germanic Legal Methods* (Mohr Siebeck 2015); and in lectures held at the University in Regensburg (Germany), Beijing (Renmin/China), Milano (Bocconi/Italy), Budapest (the Academy of Sciences/Hungary), Tartu (Estonia), and Luleå (Sweden).

he starts in the north with the kingdom of Norway and the city of Bergen.[2] Mallet had never been to Bergen himself and seen the city, but he relied especially on a map of Bergen made by Hieronymus Scholeus and probably published for the first time in 1588.[3] That Mallet had never visited Bergen is evident from the map – for instance, the castle is too small compared to the Rosenkrantz-tower, and the St. Mary Church is too large compared to both of them. But if you disregard nuances of this kind, anyone studying the map would not only get a good impression of the city but be able to find their way from one part to the other, even though it is no street map.

This is, then, what legal culture is all about: mapping out and getting around. Drawing maps will always require a certain degree of abstraction. Considering the purpose of a map, that is to provide an overview, it seems not feasible to include all details. Even more, just like a map 1:1 is of no use to the traveller, a presentation of legal culture that carefully examines all nuances of every detail is of no use to a student or an applier of law. In both cases the aim is not an exact representation of the world as we perceive it, but to make a tool that can be used when navigating unknown terrain. The appropriate level of detail is dictated by the purpose of the map or of the presentation of legal culture. Mallet's map of Bergen was made to give a first glance of this northern harbour in Europe, and not to guide the reader of *Description de L'Univers* from house-to-house. This book on legal culture is aimed at giving the reader an introduction to legal culture that will be a useful backdrop when dealing with questions of law, for instance in understanding underlying structures and lines of argument, but not on such a detailed level that it will guide a lawyer through a case.

Mallet worked as a cartographer in a century when the art of map-making advanced rapidly. This was due to the new seafaring technology opening up new routes to new markets, which in return gave a boost to the market for maps. Legal culture has experienced an increased interest due to the same factors – new communication technologies have opened up new markets, in return creating a market for legal knowledge beyond the national, a market in which legal cultural insight has a part. The internationalisation of law is an ancient phenomenon, much older than the invention of the nation state during the 18th century. But the intensity has varied greatly and has increased rapidly after the fall of the Berlin Wall in 1989. In a European context the influence of the Council of Europe, with its European Convention on Human Rights and Court in Strasbourg, and the European Union, moving from a common market to a union with partly common politics in areas like currency and foreign affairs and a common court in Luxembourg, have played a central role in creating a transnational legal order in Europe.

In the present era of internationalisation of law, the purpose of applying legal culture as an analytical tool is, in short, to make different notions of law and how law operates in society understandable to such an extent that they do not form obstacles for cooperation. This applies to the lawyer advising a client, the judge passing a decision, the politician in

2 Alain Manesson Mallet, *Beschreibung des gantzen Welt-Kreisses: In sich begreifend verschiedene Vorstellungen der Welt, allgemeine und besondere Land-Charten der alten und neuen Erdbeschreibung* (Johan David Zunner 1683) 3–8.

3 Hallvard S. Bakken, 'Scholeus-stikket', available at https://spesial.w.uib.no/?page_id=1111 accessed 3 April 2020.

a national parliament voting on a new piece of legislation, the bureaucrat or politician in an international body preparing or voting for transnational legislation, or the scholar preparing a common frame of reference on an entire field of law. But they do not operate within the same timeframe, and within the same scale of consequences. From the lawyer advising a client to the scholar, the time available to investigate before acting increases dramatically, and so does the effect of their legal acts. And just like Mallet's map might bring you to Bergen but not lead you through every alley in the city, the introductions to different legal cultures in this book will not provide a complete guide, but instead give you the ability to get a basic understanding, and to act on the basis of this understanding.

This approach takes legal culture out of a purely academic setting and into the legal world outside the ivory tower. We are talking of taking legal culture out of books and into action. At the same time, this is no more dramatic than that we have taken legal philosophy and put it into action as legal methodology. Legal philosophy has studied and developed the sources of law and how to apply them in the most sophisticated manner. However, every application of law cannot rest on the thorough and in-depth analysis of legal philosophy, but instead on the reworked shape of legal method. Legal culture can also be most thoroughly studied in depth, but that is not the aim of this book. Instead, it aims to supply the reader with tools to operationalize legal cultural knowledge in the everyday operations of law. In other words, the book you are holding in your hands right now has been produced with the ambition of managing the unmanageable concept of legal culture, and by this making it applicable.[4]

2. Defining legal culture

Isidore of Seville, bishop on the Iberian Peninsula, already noted in the 7th century that good laws were those adjusted to local conditions and customs: "A law should be honourable, just, feasible, in agreement with nature, in agreement with the custom of the country, appropriate to the time and place".[5] The need for local adjustment of law, as expressed by Isidore of Seville, became a ruling idea within the Church in the Middle Ages. Hence, Canon Law was to a large degree throughout the Middle Ages generously adjusted to the local culture, including the legal culture, in which it was applied. The same idea was later expressed in *De l'esprit des lois*, published by Charles Montesquieu in 1748, where he (as did Isidore) advised the lawmaker to make law in accordance with the local natural and cultural conditions:

> "They [the laws] should be in relation to the climate of each country, to the quality of its soil, to its situation and extent, to the principal occupation of the natives (…) they should have relation to the degree of liberty which the constitution will bear; to the religion of the inhabitants, to the inclinations, riches, numbers, commerce, manners, and

4 On the unmanageable character of legal culture, see Peter Mankowski, *Rechtskultur* (Mohr Siebeck 2016).

5 *The Etymologies of Isidore of Seville* (Cambridge University Press 2006) 121 no. xxi.

> customs. In fine, they have relations to each other, as also to their origin, to the intent of the legislator, and to the order of things on which they are established; in all of which different lights they ought to be consider."[6]

In the aftermath, it can be claimed that legal culture for Montesquieu was a factor to take into consideration when legislating. And his ideas were of great importance to the emergence of the ideas of a close relationship between nation and law, as phrased by for instance Johann Gottfried von Herder and Friedrich Carl von Savigny.[7] However, Montesquieu, von Herder, von Savigny and others did not use the term 'legal culture' as a label on the effect on law of all these different factors shaping law. A notion of legal culture was there, but not the term. This was because until recently, the notion of legal culture was based on observation of actual practice and not a theoretical exercise. The term 'legal culture' emerged slowly in the legal literature in the second half of the 19th century,[8] but was applied merely as a reference or statement, and not to explore and achieve a deeper understanding of legal phenomena.

An important acknowledgement is that legal culture is a label we put on observations we make. That means that legal culture is a construct we make to be able to analyse and understand a social reality. In Norway, for instance, there is only one court hierarchy comprised of mostly general courts with judges who deal with civil, criminal, administrative, and constitutional cases on a regular basis. There are few specialized courts, only in large city courts one might find a low degree of specialisation within the general courts. Decisions from the Supreme Court are considered to have a binding effect as precedent, but no formal binding force beyond the case at hand. Decisions from the lower courts have no such effects. At the same time, there is no real civil code in Norway, and no other codes of law for that matter, but there are single statutes and loads of decrees governing society together with Supreme Court precedent and a series of other legal sources such as preparatory work, custom, and value-based considerations. The single court hierarchy, the generalist judges, the preference for statutes and decrees to codes of law, and the multiple sources of law are social realities that are part of what can be labelled the Norwegian legal culture. The notion of a Norwegian legal culture is hence based on observations that can be noted, measured, studied, and compared, and these influence how law operates in the Norwegian society, even though the notion of a Norwegian legal culture itself is a construct.

Legal culture is hence a construct made to come to terms with observations made in society. In this way, legal culture as a term is much like the maps drawn by Mallet. They are representations of observations made that make us able to study and gain a

6 Charles Montesquieu, *The Spirit of the Laws* (Batoche Books 2001) 23.

7 See Roger Cotterrell, 'Comparative law and legal culture' in Mathias Reimann and Reinhard Zimmermann (eds), *The Oxford Handbook of Comparative Law* (Oxford University Press 2019) 714–715.

8 See for instance Emory Washburn, 'The Relationship to the Civil and Common Law' (1873) Vol. 21 No. 11 *The American Law Register* 673, 679; Caroline A. Foley, 'Royal Commission on Labour. The Employment of Women' (1894) Vol. 4 No. 13 *The Economic Journal* 185, 186; Maurice Sheldon Amos, 'Some Reflections in the Philosophy of Law' (1927) Vol. 3 No. 1 *The Cambridge Law Journal* 31, 34.

higher level of understanding. We label these observations of law legal culture because they influence how law operates, and because they are normally governed by notions shared and manifested by actions done without much ado and analysis. Law shares these characteristics with other cultural products like language and taste. But unlike language and taste, law is an instrument of government. This again ties law more directly to power. The relationship between law and power is complex and has many facets. Here it is sufficient to say that law makes power more effective, because it makes it possible to govern without physical presence, and at the same time restrains power, because power not exercised in accordance with law appears illegitimate. In either way, the relationship between law and power directs law towards institutionalisation, even in the stateless society. This is a special characteristic of law being part of culture. On this background we can define legal culture as **ideas of and expectations to law made operational by institutional(-like) practices**.

There exist several definitions of legal culture. Lawrence M. Friedman was a pioneer in taking the notion of legal culture and turning it into an analytical tool to understand law and – not at least in – society. In his *The Legal System* from 1975, he defined legal culture as "ideas, values, attitudes and beliefs of a specific group of people towards law".[9] For instance in an article in 1990, he rephrased the definition: "ideas, attitudes, values, and opinions about law, the legal system, and legal institutions in some given population."[10] This definition can be taken as representative of a whole tradition within legal cultural research where the emphasis is on mentality rather than on institutions.[11] Different from this tradition, John Bell claims that "[T]he law is something more than simply a system of rules or legal standards. Those rules operate in a context of institutions, professions and values that form altogether a 'legal culture'."[12] Legal culture is not merely a question of ideas of and expectations to law, but also to the institutional practices that constitutes law. However, Bell is maybe overemphasising the latter.[13] By defining legal culture as ideas of and expectations to law made operational by institutional(-like) practices, we try to strike a fine balance between the two.

An alternative label to legal culture could have been legal system. But a legal system has connotations to the conscious construct of law through institutions, and hence does not direct the attention towards the role of shared and more or less unconscious notions that is an important part of the legal analysis that legal culture covers in this book. For example, a purely institutional approach cannot explain why there is hardly any specialisation within Norwegian courts. Yet another alternative term could be legal tradition. The problem with legal tradition is the opposite of legal system – it draws the attention

9 Lawrence Friedman, *The Legal System: A Social Science Perspective* (Russel Sage Foundation 1975) 223.

10 Lawrence M. Friedman, 'Some Thoughts on Comparative Legal Culture' in David S. Clark (ed), *Comparative and Private International Law. Essays in Honor of John Henry Merryman on his Seventieth Birthday* (Duncker & Humblot 1990) 53.

11 See the discussion in Cotterrell (n 7) 720–724.

12 John Bell, *Judiciaries within Europe* (Cambridge University Press 2006) 6, which is the definition he also uses in *French legal cultures* (Butterworths 2001).

13 Ibid 7.

to notions and not shared institutions. An analysis of notions of law does not fully explain why a series of legal sources are considered relevant in Norwegian law, among them preparatory works and precedent. The most relevant alternative term is legal family. This has been a favoured term of comparative law and does not have connotations towards either notions or institutions of law and should hence be terminologically an appropriate alternative to legal culture. But the term legal family indicates a hierarchy with origin and diversions and does not reflect the complex reality of influences and dialogue that shapes notions and directs actions within the legal sphere. A long, well established and highly regarded tradition of extensive legislation in a continental tradition in Norwegian law goes hand-in-hand with a similarly long, well established and highly regarded tradition of extensive use of precedent as a legal source in an English tradition. In whatever legal family you place Norwegian law, it hence becomes the black sheep because of its simultaneous reliance on both extensive legislation and extensive use of precedent. (At the same time, this is more or less a characteristic of many small jurisdictions and putting them all in the same legal family – the orphanage of comparative law – does not really have any clarifying effect).

3. Legal culture and legal change

The more direct power relation makes law somewhat different from other cultural elements, like language. At the same time, there are also many commonalities. The first is that the observations made of law, as of language, are better understood if we view them as parts of a layered phenomenon. Within legal philosophy, this has lately been propagated by Kaarlo Tuori in his *Critical Legal Positivism*.[14] In this part of his philosophy he has been inspired by the French Annales School of history, whose many offspring has been labelled history of mentalities, new history and cultural history.[15] If we take Tuori's model of a layered law and turn it into an image, we can view it as a legal sea split into three levels. On the surface level we have the actual, time-specific legal actions. A piece of case law passed by the Supreme Court will be found on this level of the legal sea. On a middle level we have the more enduring aspects of law. Here we would find the notion that precedent is a source of law. On the bottom level of the legal sea we have the treasure box of law. Here we find fundamental ideas like that there are sources of law.

If we now turn to language, as a related cultural element, we find on a surface level words, on a middle level we find grammar, and on the very bottom are the technologies of language, like speech, written document, digital document, etc. Words come and go, just like case law, provisions in legislation, customs, etc. As the terms 'personal computer' or 'mobile phone' emerge to describe new phenomena in society, new legislation or case law emerges to give functional answers to legal questions. But how we conjugate nouns

14 Kaarlo Tuori, *Critical Legal Positivism* (Ashgate 2002).

15 See the brief overview in Alfred J. Andrea, 'Mentalities in History' (1991) Vol. 53 No. 3 *The Historian* 605; and also Michael Harsgor, 'Total History: The Annales School' (1978) Vol. 13 No. 1 *Journal of Contemporary History* 1.

like 'computer' or 'phone' changes far less frequently, just like what is regarded as a legal source is far more constant than the content of legal sources. The very idea of legal sources, found on the bottom level of the legal sea, is in this relation the most constant. In a Norwegian context, the idea of legal sources emerged in the 13th century, the idea of a whole series of legal sources in the 18th century, while the idea of legal sources is challenged in the 21th century.

To view social phenomena as layered is not exactly rocket science. It is still an extremely important acknowledgement as concerns legal culture, because it enables us to deal with legal cultural change. Culture in general, and legal culture more specifically, is intuitively viewed as static – it is the rock raised above the sea of change. This is true and untrue at the same time. Legal culture is static at the same time as it is dynamic. Norwegian language and Norwegian law change all the time at the surface level, that is, on a word and legal rule level. It changes far less frequently on the middle level, and – as we have seen just above – hardly ever on the bottom level. This means that legal culture is ever changing and holding back change at the same time, just on different levels.

This is a very important acknowledgement. However, it is still not flying to the moon, even though it gives us a perspective on law and legal change. But there is more to the notion of law as layered. Next to viewing legal change as happening on different levels, the image of the legal sea helps us understand that legal change is a question of complex interactions between the different layers of law. Changes on the surface level do not change more than some of the appearances of a legal culture. But many constant and lasting changes might in the end change the ideas on the middle level. And many constant and lasting changes on the surface level might again change the ideas on the bottom level of the legal sea. The movement might also be the opposite: changes on the bottom level might trigger off changes in the higher levels of law. However, both this top-down and bottom-up model arc difficult to observe in legal history in pure form and are instead simultaneous movements. For instance, it neither seems that the idea of written law started with the writing of more and more single legal provisions, nor with the introduction of a written code, but with the notion of a written code and with the writing of single provisions and statutes much at the same time in the 12th century. Either way, we see by this that legal cultural change is not only tied to the different layers but takes place as a dialectical movement between them.

We have to keep in mind that the legal sea is a model created to describe part of the complex character of legal culture, and the complex legal cultural processes of change. It is not designed to encompass the important role historic events and individual actors play in a legal culture in general, in regard to legal cultural change. The German experience with the Nazi regime, or the legal theorist Torstein Eckhoff in Norway, are examples of historic events and individual actors that contributed to legal change in their legal culture.

We also have to keep in mind that the legal sea, as depicted above, only portrays the internal legal culture. Friedman stressed already in *Legal Systems* from 1975, that we have to differentiate between the internal and external legal culture.[16] However, this distinction has not been much developed in legal cultural studies. The internal legal culture is the legal culture dominated by legal actors, like lawyers, members in parliament legislating, or case handlers in public administration. The external legal culture is the legal culture constituted by all members of society. The internal legal culture is more easily definable and detectable, while the external is much vaguer. However, we must not forget that politics at large take place in the external legal culture. Law is a product of political processes, and the external legal culture must not be lost or out of sight, even though we are often forced to concentrate on the more accessible – at least for lawyers – internal legal culture. As we will soon see, the Legal Cultural Model that is essential for analysing legal cultures in this book, is aimed at deconstructing the internal legal culture.

4. Legal culture and communication

In short, a legal culture is created and upheld by communication. Again, we can turn to Mallet's map of Bergen from 1683 to understand this rather abstract phenomenon. There are few citizens depicted on this map. On one hand, a city is made up of individual citizens. On the other hand, a city is much more than the sum of individual citizens. The surplus is created through the interplay between the citizens. The same can be said of a legal culture. On one hand it is made up of individual actions and notions, on the other hand it is more than the sum of individual actions and notions, and this surplus is created through the interplay. This interplay creates a community in its notions and actions. There will still be individual variations, and at times direct opposition. But what is shared increases with the interplay. A legal culture is hence not an entity that erases differences, but one that creates community despite the differences. The homogenous character of a legal culture is therefore dependant on the degree of interplay and to what extent it manages to create community.

There will always be competing communication. If we return to Bergen in 1683, the city had, as Mallet wrote, citizens from many nations – "*Ihre Einwhoner seind viel und unterschiedlicher Nationen*."[17] Till the middle of the 19th century, it was said that to do business in Bergen you had to master six languages in addition to Norwegian. The Scots, English, French, Germans, Dutch, Danes, and Norwegians all had their language, spoken at home and in their own communities. For a long time, Germans were the most important, since Bergen was one of four *Kontor* that the Hanseatic league had outside the Holy German Empire. The German language influenced the Norwegian spoken especially in Bergen, but also in the entire western part of Norway. The same was the case with law. Each of these groups partly exercised their own business rules internally, and each of the warehouse that we see on Mallet's map along the harbour, had a neighbourhood court that exercised their own legal norms. But there was also a city court, which

16 Friedman (1975) (n 9) 223–224.

17 Mallet (1683) (n 2).

dealt with legal issues between members of the different groups. A German merchant at the Hansa *Kontor* would hence be part of both a German and a Norwegian legal culture. In the 16th century, the communication structures mastered by the Hansa *Kontor* would be the most extensive and effective, and therefore a German merchant would be most influenced by this. In the second half of the 18th century, the opposite was the case, and the German merchants were slowly pulled towards the Norwegian legal culture.

This is not solely a historical situation. In Norway today, for instance, the Sámi – the indigenous population in northern Norway, Finland, and Russia – have their own legal culture because they have their own communication structures within their community. At the same time, they have interacted with Norwegian society and have been influenced by and part of the legal culture communicated here. Even more, due to a nomadic lifestyle and for a while unsettled borders, they were also influenced by the Swedish and Russian legal cultures when interacting with these societies. On the other hand, we see that European communication of law has increased with European integration through the Council of Europe and the European Union. The adherence to a European legal culture has hence increased for both Norwegians and Sámi. The co-existence between legal cultures, and mutual influences, is a result of interplay and the legal communication resulting from it.

From this it could be deduced that the basic legal cultural unit is the national legal culture. This is not the case. Above, it was claimed that a German merchant in Bergen would have to relate to both a German and Norwegian legal culture. But then the matter is seen from a retro perspective, because in 1683 when Mallet drew his map of Bergen, there existed no unified German or Norwegian legal culture. The Holy German Empire was split into more than 300 jurisdictional units partly with their own legal norms and court hierarchies, and hence partly their own legal cultures. Norway had had a unified law and court hierarchy since the Middle Ages, but its unified character had been severely weakened during the 15th century. Therefore, it is fairer to say that the German merchant had to relate to both a Lübeck and Bergen legal culture. But for more than two centuries, the nation was developed as a political unit with strong and effective communication structures and came to totally dominate as a legal cultural unit in Europe. Still as we have seen, for instance the Sámi in Norway have partly had similar effective communication structures within parts of the ethnic group, and consequently survived as a legal culture. On a European level similar effective communication structures have emerged to such an extent that some feel these threaten the national legal culture.

5. The Legal Cultural Model

In his *Description de L'Univers*, Mallet not only gave the reader a map of Bergen, but also a description of the city to define it through central characteristics like a good harbour, that it was a Hansa city, that the houses were made of wood, and that the inhabitants came from many different nations.[18] To make legal culture a manageable concept, we

18 Ibid 6.

also have to identify its central characteristics. And just like the legal sea is a handy image to come to terms with legal change, the legal cultural model is handy when sorting out the characteristics of law and their relationships.

A problem with the term legal culture is that it at times is used in a concealing instead of a revealing manner. For instance, when asking why both statutes and precedent for several hundred years have been important sources of law in Norway, we can explain it by saying it is due to legal culture. But this is just putting a label on the unknown, without the label having any explanatory effect in itself. Labelling the phenomenon "legal culture" is just the beginning, and not the end of the process. For instance, when analysing why precedent has become an important source of law in Norway, it may be a good starting point to study books on legal methodology. However, we have to take into account institutional structural elements of the legal culture as well, in particular the organization of the court system. It is the interplay of these elements that provides an explanation. In other words, the label legal culture is not an explanation, but in need of one.

There is a long and rather varied tradition for splitting legal culture up into elements to make it more manageable as an analytical tool. In a pioneer article on 'Foundations of European Legal Culture', based on a speech held in 1983 and originally published in 1985, Franz Wieacker investigated 1) personalism, 2) legalism, and 3) intellectualism when explaining the European legal culture.[19] In the classic *An Introduction to Comparative Law*, first published in German in 1984 and in English in 1992, Konrad Zweigert and Hein Kötz defined and investigated 1) historical background, 2) mode of thought, 3) institutions, 4) legal sources, and 5) ideology as a group of elements that plays a key role in the style of a legal family (and not of a legal culture).[20] Later, Mark van Hoecke and Mark Warrington dealt with this in their 1998 article 'Legal Cultures, Legal Paradigms and Legal Doctrine: Towards a New Model of Comparative Law', which operated with 1) concept of law, 2) legal sources, 3) legal method, 4) argumentation, 5) legitimation, and 6) ideology.[21] Yet another approach was used by Cees van Damm in his article 'Who is afraid of Diversity' from 2009, where he investigated 1) individualism vs collectivism, 2) masculinity vs femininity, 3) uncertainty avoidance, 4) power distance, and 5) long-term vs short-term orientation.[22] As pointed out in Chapter one of this volume, there is no right and wrong in how legal culture is split up, only a question of what serves the purpose.[23] Wieacker did a legal historical survey, Zweigert and Kötz had a contemporary and more practical approach, van Hoecke and Warrington a more scholarly approach, while van Damm aimed to explain differences in European tort law.

---

19 Franz Wieacker, 'Foundations of European Legal Culture' (1990) Vol. 38 *The American Journal of Comparative Law* 1.

20 Konrad Zweigert and Hein Kötz, *An Introduction to Comparative Law* (Clarendon Press 1998) 68.

21 Mark van Hoecke and Mark Warrington, 'Legal Culture, Legal Paradigms and Legal Doctrine: Towards a New Model for Comparative Law' (1998) Vol. 47 *International Comparative Law Quarterly* 495.

22 Cees van Damm, 'Who is afraid of diversity – Cultural diversity, European co-operation, and European tort law' (2009) Vol. 20 *King's Law Journal* 281.

23 See Sören Koch, 'The outset – how to learn sailing the ocean of legal cultures' in this volume, Chapter 1, s. 21–22.

Based on my studies in Norwegian legal history, focusing on law as a social and cultural phenomenon more than on specific fields of law, and aiming to make legal culture an instrument applicable for students and appliers of law, law-makers, and scholars, we have chosen to construct a legal cultural model as an analytical tool to investigate legal culture.[24] In this model, legal culture is first split up into an institutional and intellectual structure, and focuses on especially the six structural elements 1) conflict resolution, 2) norm production, 3) ideal of justice, 4) legal method, 5) professionalisation, and 6) internationalisation. In sum, these structures and structural elements make up the Legal Cultural Model. On one hand, the model does not claim universal validity. On the other hand, it has proven applicable in surprisingly many different contexts. Not least because the model is flexible regarding how thorough a legal cultural investigation can be made.

The institutional structure of a legal culture is, in short, institutions where law is shaped through different practices. The most basic institutions are those that settle conflicts, simply because conflict resolution is society's most basic demand of its legal system. It is through conflict resolution that peace and security can dominate society. Norm production is an activity that has gradually been at least partly emancipated from conflict resolution. Originally, legal norms were produced by deciding cases; each time a conflict was resolved, a norm was produced. As time went by, these norms were reused in similar cases, and case law appeared. Case law could however also be systemised and developed by a lawmaker, who then could go on to legislate independently from court practice, and in doing so, create a new institutionalised practice within law. The last move in this process would be codifications of law. It is in this way legislation became a dominating method of producing legal norms. However, precedent was not superseded by legislation in all legal cultures and has continued to play a role in most. And this role is increasing in a period of internationalisation of law driven forward by transnational courts and their case law.

The production and application of legal norms does not take place in an intellectual vacuum. Rather, there are several intellectual factors that dictate how norms are made and applied. The most basic is the ideal of justice. As with conflict resolution, justice is a basic demand directed towards law. Conflicts resolved arbitrarily, for instance by drawing straws, are better than unsolved conflicts, and thus this has been a means of solving conflicts in desperate situations. However, conflict resolutions that are experienced as just have a much higher degree of legitimacy than those experienced as unjust or arbitrary and will therefore be accepted more often and extensively. There are many often conflicting perceptions of justice, such as distributive or corrective justice vs. commutative justice, collective vs individual justice, fairness vs predictability, etc. As a rule, all legal cultures try to balance the values encompassed by these abstract concepts of justice. However, how this balance is intended to be reached may vary from one legal culture to another. This is the point of departure when considering what is just.

To make an ideal of justice operative – that is, to solve a specific case in accordance with an ideal of justice – a legal methodology is required. A legal method is simply the

24 The presentation of the Legal Cultural Model was first presented in Sunde (2010) (n 1).

manner in which ideals of justice are transformed from values and various sources of law into legal rules used to settle a specific conflict. One task for legal method is also to create a fairly tight framework for the otherwise uncertain process of going from legal raw material to refined legal rules, making it intersubjective.

While lawyers and non-lawyers might share an ideal of justice, legal method appears with an increased professionalisation of law, and is more and more specialised. First, professionalisation means that those who handle law on behalf of society spend more and more of their time on legal issues. Second, it means that there are special criteria to fulfil before one can be trusted with the position of handling law. All kinds of professionalisation have the same effect: they afford lawyers an internal view of law. This implies that good law in the eyes of the professional becomes more and more a question of internal correlation, while good law for the non-professional is still a question of justice in the individual case. This implies that it is the attitude towards professionalisation inside the community of lawyers that determines this intellectual element of the LCM. The same applies for the last intellectual element of the model.

Internationalisation is here used in relation to all kinds of influence of legal material produced outside jurisdictional borders. As society changes, law must change to be able to fulfil its obligation in conflict resolution. Only in exceptional cases can law be changed based on mere experiment; normally, legal reforms are based on experience. The main sources for deriving knowledge from experience are history and comparative law. The extensive use of comparative law is when reforming law makes law a social and cultural nomad. However, when comparing legal cultures, we can observe variations regarding the degree and attitude towards internationalisation. In a Norwegian context, law has continuously been influenced by legal technologies and norms from outside the jurisdictional borders that exist at any given time. With change as the reason for this continuous internationalisation, it is no surprise that the internationalisation has contributed to changing how law is perceived inside the borders it has crossed. Other legal cultures have shown more reluctance to international impulses, or even regarded them as a threat for the national legal culture. The discussion around Brexit may serve as an example for such tendencies.

6. Applying the Legal Cultural Model

Even though a model is never more than the mere shadow of what it is supposed to reflect, this model of legal culture can be used as a point of departure for legal-cultural analyses and comparative studies. This applies both to the student of law and the legal practitioner.

Let us first apply the Legal Cultural Model as a student of law approaching law from a theoretical angle. Or, to link it to the Mallet's map of Bergen, like someone who wants to know what kind of city Bergen is. And let us do this by again looking at a question already posed in this chapter: why is precedent a source of law in Norwegian legal culture?

If we start by looking into conflict resolution as a structural element in the Norwegian legal culture, we find that there is only one court hierarchy with hardly any specialist courts at any level. Hence, there is an almost pyramidal court hierarchy formed with a Supreme Court on top that can pass down precedent to all the lower courts. If we then turn to norm production, we find that Norway is governed by about 700 statutes and 10,000 decrees, but no code of law. Efforts are definitely made to harmonize the statutes and decrees. But with no system of law of the kind you find in a continental codification to fall back on, the legislated law in Norway is in need of another kind of unifying force. That role is played by the Supreme Court, which makes an important contribution to the unification of law through precedent.

This is possible because the idea of justice in the Norwegian legal culture is not strict predictability, but that law should be adjusted through appliance to give an equitable result in the individual case. This is done by the courts. One instrument to keep this practice from becoming arbitrary, is Supreme Court precedent that unifies the adjustment. Since the ideal of justice is a fairly flexible predictability open to equitable adjustment through the application of law, the legal method is not a strict deductive method. Instead, it is a method where a variety of legal sources are used as sources to make the appliance flexible but not arbitrary.

This also fits well with the fact that lay judges still play an important role in criminal cases, but these days far less in civil cases. Their approach to law is often less focused on the predictability obtained by strict deduction from legislated law, and more on flexible application. Legal science in Norway has also not aimed at creating a system of law to replace the role of precedent. The internationalisation of law, especially human rights, has been partly court driven, with the Supreme Court taking the lead in unifying Norwegian legal norms produced within and outside Norwegian jurisdictional borders.

By this analysis, using the Legal Cultural Model, we have made sense of a central feature of the Norwegian legal culture. But the Legal Cultural Model could also be applied by a practitioner[25] – by someone who is planning to go to Bergen to do trade there, to continue the use of the map-metaphor. Imagine you are a judge on the European Court of Human Rights (ECtHR) in Strasbourg in 2012. Your chamber receives one of the rather rare Norwegian cases, this time concerning retroactive legislation and protection of property.[26] The question at stake is could the Norwegian Parliament issue an act that: 1) *de facto* makes perpetual all temporary land lease contracts already entered into, and in addition 2) severely limits the lessor's right to link land rent to the market value of the leased land? The judge begins her preparation by reading selected parts of the Norwegian Supreme Court decisions from 2007, that finally decided the case nationally.[27] The core legal question in the case as it appeared in the Norwegian court system, was whether or

25 This presentation of the usefulness of the Legal Cultural Model in practice is taken from Sunde (2014), 'Live and Let Die' (n 1).

26 *Lindheim and Others v Norway* App no. 13221/08 and 2139/10 (ECtHR, 12 June 2012).

27 Rt. 2007 p. 1281 and Rt. 2007 p. 1306.

not the law on land-leasing contracts was contrary to the Norwegian Constitution of 1814, and hence subject to judicial review.

The first thing she notices is that this question was dealt with within the ordinary court system, simply because in Norway there is no constitutional court, and few specialized courts. This means that at first, a single judge in one of the 60 first-level courts decided the case and performed the judicial review. Then the case would normally have been decided by three judges in one of the six courts of appeal, if it was not appealed directly to the Supreme Court using a "leapfrog" mechanism. The second thing she notices is that the ordinary courts are competent to perform judicial review if there is a conflict between the Constitution and an act of Parliament. Due to their political dimension, such cases are argued before all the 20 judges in a plenary session when the case reaches the Supreme Court.

As she keeps on reading the decisions from the Norwegian Supreme Court, she notices that there are explicit references to several sources of law. This is a feature of Norwegian legal culture that can be traced back at least to the mid-eighteenth century. The Constitution is treated as a living legal instrument, and hence as a source of law, as in the American constitutional tradition. There are also references to several single acts of Parliament, a quite obvious source of law. There are however no references to codes, because the last code for Norway, issued for the Norwegian kingdom by the Danish-Norwegian king, dates from 1687, and only six articles are still in force. There are also several references to preparatory works,[28] which are a source of law in Norway, as in all the Nordic countries. There are as well several references to decisions by the Supreme Court itself, which – as we have seen – is treated as precedent and the second most important source of law. The same applies to decisions from the ECtHR, which in Norwegian law is treated as precedent, whether or not Norway is a party to the decisions.[29] The references to legal literature are few, and even if these are regarded as a source of law, it is of minor importance. That does not apply to considerations of fairness, which play a major role in the decisions you read. For instance, in Paragraphs 112 and 113 of the first Supreme Court decision, she finds a discussion of the retroactive effect of the act of Parliament. The argument is that since the lessor could imagine that the government one day would regulate land-leasing contracts in a way that affected the lessor's right to negotiate the land rent, "it must lie within the freedom granted to the legislator under Article 97 of the Constitution to regulate matters in this way" without the regulation being dismissed as retroactive, and hence unconstitutional and inapplicable in the case.[30] The discussion, then, is not on the principle of retroactive laws, but rather on fairness.

The vagueness of both the Norwegian Constitution of 1814 and the European Convention of Human Rights, and the specific character of the case law of the Norwegian Supreme Court and the ECtHR, leave room for fairness arguments. There is however

28 The preparatory works consist of all the official documents that prepare the ground for a new piece of legislation.

29 Ingvill Helland, *Rulings of the European Court of Human Rights as a Legal Argument – a Comparison between German and Norwegian law* (Ph.D. thesis, University of Bergen 2012) 411–412.

30 Here quoted from *Lindheim and Others v Norway* (n 26) Para. 16.

nothing extraordinary about the fairness arguments in this case, since value-based assessments are a relevant source of law.[31] The Norwegian Supreme Court uses the fairness argument quite often, and surprisingly often makes explicit references to it. In Norwegian legal theory, this group of arguments, together with system-based arguments, are embedded in the legal source "reelle hensyn", which is one of seven legal sources acknowledged in Norwegian law. Between 1996 and 2012,[32] the Supreme Court has made explicit references to this legal source in 223 of the 2,738 cases they have decided. The annual average of such references is 13 of 161 cases.[33] In criminal cases, value-based assessments are used less frequently since the Norwegian Constitution of 1814 § 96 states the rule of law principle in criminal cases: "reelle hensyn" were referred to in the actual votes in 55 of 1,361 cases. Between 1996 and 2012, the Norwegian Supreme Court has made explicit references to value-based arguments in the actual votes in 168 of 1,377 civil cases.[34] Next to the abundance of legal sources explicitly referred to, the rather extensive use of value-based assessments, even to some extent in criminal cases, is a striking characteristic of Norwegian legal culture.

As the judge in the ECtHR reads the decisions of the Norwegian Supreme Court, and notices these characteristics of Norwegian law, to which a Norwegian lawyer would pay scant attention, you venture into a legal-cultural landscape in which you will remain throughout the case. This is seen by the fact that characteristics of Norwegian law such as juridical review or the abundance of legal sources are not questioned by the ECHR. However, the judges on the Norwegian Supreme Court also ventured into a legal-cultural landscape in this case. Knowing that the cases could end up in Strasbourg, they based their argumentation partly on case law from the ECHR, and they avoided the strangest element of the Norwegian culture, which is the open and explicit reference to fairness through references to "reelle hensyn".[35] The lawyers appearing before the ECtHR had also taken legal culture into consideration and adjusted their argumentation by fitting fairness arguments into the balancing test, which they linked to the principle of proportionality so often exercised by the ECHR. Hence, all legal practitioners involved in this case ventured into a legal-cultural landscape.

---

31 "Reelle hensyn" literally means 'actual considerations' and includes a whole group of different kinds of arguments, the function of which in Norwegian law today is to secure a fair outcome of the case. See also Ingvill Helland and Sören Koch, 'Methodische Grundlagen der juristischen Entscheidungsfindung im norwegischen Privatrecht' (2013) No. 3 *Zeitschrift für Europäisches Privatrecht* 584, 610–614, who describe "reelle hensyn" as "vershiedene Würdigunsgeschichtpunkte, die oftmals wie reine Billigkeitswägungen mit Bezug auf den konkreten Fall wirken".

32 1996 is chosen as a breaking point, since the criminal procedure was changed by law. Since 1996, the Norwegian Supreme Court has decided about an equal number of civil and criminal cases every year; prior to this, the Court would decide more than three times the number of criminal cases.

33 In 1997, 1999, 2001, 2004, and 2007, the Norwegian Supreme Court made such explicit references to fairness in more than 10% of the cases it decided, while this was done in less than five percent of the cases in 2008 and 2010.

34 Sunde (2015), *Høgsteretts historie 1965–2015*, 291–292. If we also include references to value-based assessments in the introductory part of the Supreme Court decisions, the numbers are 70 of 1,361 criminal cases and 342 of 1,377 civil cases.

35 Gjermund Mathisen, 'From Rendezvous to Relationship' in Jørn Øyrehagen Sunde and Knut Einar Skodvin (eds), *Rendezvous of European Legal Cultures* (Fagbokforlaget 2010) 203.

<table>
<tr><th colspan="4">Legal Culture and its structures and structural elements</th></tr>
<tr><th colspan="4">Institutional structure</th></tr>
<tr><th colspan="2">Conflict resolution</th><th colspan="2">Norm production</th></tr>
<tr><td colspan="2">Unified court hierarchy with one Supreme Court on top</td><td colspan="2">A need for unifying law, also legislated law</td></tr>
<tr><th colspan="4">Intellectual structure</th></tr>
<tr><th>Ideal of justice</th><th>Legal method</th><th>Degree of professionalisation</th><th>Character of internationalisation</th></tr>
<tr><td>Predictability but flexibility to adjust law according to equity</td><td>A series of legal sources giving arguments for adjustment according to equity</td><td>Extensive use of lay judges and a legal science without ambitions of making a system of law</td><td>Partly court driven, with the Supreme Court taking the lead</td></tr>
</table>

We see from these examples that the legal cultural model can be used to split up and analyse a question which otherwise could easily be labelled legal culture without further explanation. What we have to keep in mind is, firstly, that not all legal structural elements are relevant in answering a question. Secondly, that there might be other structural elements that are not included in this simplified model. For instance, within the institutional structure we could have added legal education, and within the intellectual structure we could have added legal ideology, which in Norway is legal realism that promotes the adjustment of law through practice as an ideal. Thirdly, we must not forget that the legal cultural model only deals with the internal legal culture, which is the legal culture shared by those who work with law. The external legal culture, which is the legal culture that encompasses all subjects to a specific legal culture, is much wider and cannot be put into a model. Here we find factors like economy and religion, which may be relevant for the legal culture, but which are not legal in their character.

There is an obvious and necessary relation between the internal and external legal culture. It is like the relationship between the map of Bergen on the front of this book, and the map of Europe on the back of it. This map was also made by Mallet for his *Description de L'Univers* from 1683, while this specific version of the engraving was published in 1719 in *Beschreibung des gantzen Welt-Kreysses*. Bergen is only a tiny spot in Europe, just like the internal legal culture is only a tiny spot within the general culture in society. At the same time, if Bergen is where you are going, it is a map of Bergen that you need. And if it is a legal matter you are in need of mapping out and getting around, it is the kind of map of the internal legal culture that the legal cultural model offers that you need. This book provides such maps for 15 national legal cultures. The concluding chapters offer guidance on how to use the maps to conduct comparative legal studies, in other words how to compare legal cultures.

7. Bibliography

Amos MS, 'Some Reflections in the Philosophy of Law' (1927) Vol. 3 No. 1 *The Cambridge Law Journal* 31. DOI: https://doi.org/10.1017%2Fs0008197300103939

Andrea AJ, 'Mentalities in History' (1991) Vol. 53 No. 3 *The Historian* 605

Bakken HS, 'Scholeus-stikket' available at https://spesial.w.uib.no/?page_id=1111 accessed 3 April 2020

Bell J, *French legal cultures* (Butterworths 2001)

—— *Judiciaries within Europe* (Cambridge University Press 2006). DOI: https://doi.org/10.1017%2Fcbo9780511493829

Cotterrell R, 'Comparative law and legal culture' in Reimann M and Zimmermann R (eds), *The Oxford Handbook of Comparative Law* (Oxford University Press 2019). DOI: http://dx.doi.org/10.1093/oxfordhb/9780198810230.013.22

The Etymologies of Isidore of Seville (Cambridge University Press 2006)

Foley CA, 'Royal Commission on Labour. The Employment of Women' (1894) Vol. 4 No. 13 *The Economic Journal* 185. DOI: https://doi.org/10.2307%2F2955893

Friedman LM, *The Legal System: A Social Science Perspective* (Russel Sage Foundation 1977)

—— 'Some Thoughts on Comparative Legal Culture' in Clark DS (ed), *Comparative and Private International Law. Essays in Honor of John Henry Merryman on his Seventieth Birthday* (Duncker & Humblot 1990). DOI: https://doi.org/10.3790%2F978-3-428-06838-8

Harsgor M, 'Total History: The Annales School' (1978) Vol. 13 No. 1 *Journal of Contemporary History* 1. DOI: https://doi.org/10.1177%2F002200947801300101

Helland I, *Rulings of the European Court of Human Rights as a Legal Argument – a Comparison between German and Norwegian law* (Ph.D. thesis, University of Bergen 2012)

—— 'Methodische Grundlagen der juristischen Entscheidungsfindung im norwegischen Privatrecht' (2013) No. 3 *Zeitschrift für Europäisches Privatrecht* 584

Mathisen G, 'From Rendezvous to Relationship' in Sunde JØ and Skodvin KE (eds), *Rendezvous of European Legal Cultures* (Fagbokforlaget 2010) 203

Mallet AM, *Beschreibung des gantzen Welt-Kreisses: In sich begreifend verschiedene Vorstellungen der Welt, allgemeine und besondere Land-Charten der alten und neuen Erdbeschreibung* (Johan David Zunner 1683)

Mankowski P, *Rechtskultur* (Mohr Siebeck 2016)

Montesquieu C, *The Spirit of the Laws* (Batoche Books 2001)

Sunde JØ, 'Champagne at the Funeral – an Introduction to Legal Culture' in Sunde JØ and Skodvin KE (eds), *Rendezvous of European Legal Cultures* (Fagbokforlaget 2010)

—— 'Legal Cultural Changes in Europe – Teaching Future Prospects on the Basis of Legal History and Comparative Law' in Kjell Å. Modéer and Per Nilsén (eds), *How to Teach European Comparative Legal History* (Juristförlaget 2011)

—— 'Dissenting votes in the Norwegian Supreme Court 1965–2009: A legal cultural analysis' (2012) 1 *Rechtskultur - Zeitschrift für Europäische Rechtsgeschichte* 59

—— 'Live and Let Die – An Essay Concerning Legal-Cultural Understanding' in Maurice Adams and Dirk Hairbaut (eds), *The Method and Culture of Comparative law - Essays in Honour of Mark van Hoecke* (Hart Publishing 2014)

—— 'Daughters of God and counsellors of the judges of men – a study in changes in the legal culture in the Norwegian realm in the High Middle Ages' in Stefan Brink and Lisa Collinson (eds), *New Approaches to Early law in Scandinavia* (Turnhout 2014)

—— *Høgsteretts historie 1965–2015 – At dømme i sidste Instans* (Fagbokforlaget 2015)

—— 'Legal Cultural Dependency of Norwegian Legal Method – and its future' in Ingvill Helland and Sören Koch (eds), *Nordic and Germanic Legal Methods* (Mohr Siebeck 2015)
Tuori K, *Critical Legal Positivism* (Ashgate 2002)
van Damm C, 'Who is afraid of diversity – Cultural diversity, European co-operation, and European tort law' (2009) Vol. 20 *King's Law Journal* 281
van Hoecke M and Warrington M, 'Legal Culture, Legal Paradigms and Legal Doctrine: Towards a New Model for Comparative Law' (1998) Vol. 47 *International Comparative Law Quarterly* 495
Washburn E, 'The Relationship to the Civil and Common Law' (1873) Vol. 21 No. 11 *The American Law Register* 673. DOI: https://doi.org/10.2307%2F3303211
Wieacker F, 'Foundations of European Legal Culture' (1990) Vol. 38 *The American Journal of Comparative Law* 1
Zweigert K and Kötz H, *An Introduction to Comparative Law* (Clarendon Press 1998)

3. Legal Culture and Comparative Law – Diving into the Ocean

Sören Koch

1. Introduction

For almost ten years I have been applying the legal cultural model (LCM) presented in the previous chapter "Managing the Unmanageable" in both my research and my teaching.[1] In courses given to students domestically and internationally we have applied, evaluated, and discussed its merits and limitations. During these discussions I became aware of some more or less common misunderstandings and misperceptions related to the model and its intended function as an analytical tool for both legal historical and comparative studies. In this chapter, I aim to enhance the understanding of the methodological approach on which this second edition of *Comparing Legal Cultures* is based. It builds on the ideas presented in the introductory chapters in this volume[2] and the article "Champagne at the Funeral" by professor Sunde,[3] adding some minor adjustments relating to terminology, structure, and purpose of the analytical model when used for comparative legal studies. How to conduct a comparative legal study based on the legal cultural knowledge provided in this volume is explained in more detail below in a separate Chapter (*infra* Ch. 4).

In this chapter, I focus on the conceptual and methodological questions related to the analytical framework presented in the first two chapters of this book. A mentioned above, the aim of the book is to *identify*, *explain*, *analyse* and *compare* similarities and differences among legal cultures.[4] It is this purpose that frames our definition of legal

1 See e.g. Sören Koch, "Consequences of changing expectations to law and its institutions. Illustrated by the role and background of judges in Norway" (2015) Vol. 83 No. 3–4 *The Legal History Review* 461; Ingvill Helland and Sören Koch, "Comparing Legal Methods – an Analytical Framework" in Ingvill Helland and Sören Koch (Eds.), *Nordic and Germanic Legal Methods* (Mohr Siebeck 2014) 1–19.

2 Sören Koch, "The Outset – How to Learn Sailing the Ocean of Legal Cultures" in this volume, Chapter 1 and Jørn Øyrehagen Sunde, "Managing the Unmanageable – An Essay Concerning Legal Culture as an Analytical Tool" in this volume, Chapter 2.

3 Jørn Øyrehagen Sunde, "Champagne at the Funeral. An Introduction to Legal Culture" in Jørn Øyrehagen Sunde and Knut Einar Skodvin (Eds.), *Rendezvous of European Legal Cultures* (Fagbokforlaget 2010).

4 Koch (2020) "The Outset" (n. 2) Section 1.

culture. I will have a closer look at three determining factors: the objective, subject and object of the comparison and how they are merged into our operationalised concept of legal culture (Section 2). To enhance understanding for this approach we have to engage with the broader discourse on comparative law: its function, purposes and methods. Having set the scene, by briefly presenting the traditional approach to comparative law and its challenges, I discuss the advantages but also limitations of our legal cultural perspective (Section 3). In this connection the merits and limitations of classification and taxonomies are elucidated. Entering the complex universe of comparative law from this perspective will enable us to elaborate on how the LCM interacts with some other approaches and methods discussed by contemporary comparative legal scholars (Section 4).[5] Based on the broadly accepted idea that legal culture constitutes the context for the production and application of law, the final section discusses how to use legal cultural knowledge to systematically analyse the context of law (Section 5).

2. The Operationalised Concept of Legal Culture

What constitutes a legal culture?[6] For decades the reference to legal culture has become increasingly popular, not just in academic writings but also in court practice and in legislative preparatory works.[7] The idea of legal culture as something encompassing more than legal rules and institutions has coined scholarly debates about the nature and aims of comparative law ever since.[8] The powerful statement by Cotterrell at the beginning of the introduction bears evidence of the almost magical appeal the concept has on comparative lawyers.[9] Still, the concept seems intangible. Sally Merry observed that "legal culture is a very productive concept, as well as a very incoherent one. It means many different things to different scholars. Perhaps this is why it is so useful."[10] A great variety of entities have been labelled "legal cultures". Some com-

5 For an overview of the complexity of approaches towards comparative law see, Mathias Siems, *Comparative Law* (2nd ed. Cambridge University Press 2018); Jaakko Husa, *A New Introduction to Comparative Law* (Bloomberg 2015); Esin Örücü, "Developing Comparative Law" in Esin Örücü and David Nelken (Eds.), *Comparative Law – A Handbook*, (Hart Publishing 2007); Esin Örücü, "Methodology of Comparative Law" in Jan M. Smits (Ed.), *Elgar Encyclopedia of Comparative Law* (Edward Elgar 2006) 442–454; Mathias Reimann and Reinhard Zimmermann (Eds.), *The Oxford Handbook of Comparative Law* (2nd ed. Oxford University Press 2019); Esin Örücü and David Nelken, *Comparative Law – A Handbook* (Hart Publishing 2007); Jan M. Smits (Ed.), *Elgar Encyclopedia of Comparative Law* (Edward Elgar 2006).

6 For an early attempt to define the concept, see Henry W. Ehrmann, *Comparative Legal Cultures* (Englewoods Cliff 1976), building on Leon Friedman, "Legal Culture and Social Development" (1969) Vol. 6 *Law and Society Review* 19.

7 David Nelken, "Thinking About Legal Culture" (2014) Vol. 1 *Asian Journal of Law and Society* 255, 257.

8 Roger Cotterrell, "Comparative Law and Legal Culture" in Mathias Reimann and Reinhard Zimmermann (Eds.), *The Oxford Handbook of Comparative Law* (2nd ed. Oxford University Press 2019) 710.

9 Ibid. 711.

10 Sally Merry, "What is Legal Culture? An Anthropological Perspective" in David Nelken (Ed.), *Using Legal Culture* (Wildy, Simmonds and Hill 2012).

mentators see a global or European legal culture emerging.[11] Others spot legal culture inside legal institutions such as courts.[12] Religions have been said to have developed distinct legal cultures, such as a Christian, Islamic or Hindu legal culture.[13] Again others recognise that various fields of law have developed distinct legal subcultures.[14] Against this background, the concept of legal culture has been heavily criticised for its vagueness in legal literature.[15] Patrick Glenn challenges the very notion of culture.[16] Uwe Kischel concludes that there is no "idealtypus" of a legal culture.[17] Esin Örücü states that "there is no clear-cut definition of legal culture."[18] Others such as Lawrence Friedman, David Nelken, Mark Van Hoecke/Mark Warrington and Franz Wieacker have provided definitions of the concept.[19] Still, each of these commentators uses the

---

11 Lawrence Friedman, "The Place of Legal Culture in the Sociology of Law" in Michael Freeman (Ed.), *Law and Sociology* (Oxford University Press 2006), referring to a global legal culture based on values such as individualism, equality, and human rights. Franz Wieacker, "Foundations of European Legal Culture" (1990) Vol. 38 *American Journal of Comparative Law* 1; Genevieve Helleringer and Kai Purnhagen (Eds.), *Towards a European Legal Culture* (Nomos 2014); Martijn W. Hesselink, "The New European Legal Culture" in Martijn W. Hesselink (Ed.), *The New European Private Law: Essays on the Future of Private Law in Europe* (Kluwer Law 2002); critical to idea of a European legal culture Volkmar Gessner, "Global Legal Interaction and Legal Cultures" (1994) Vol. 7 *Ratio Legis* 132, 135 f. Åse B Grødeland and William L. Miller, "One European Legal Culture or Several?" in Åse B Grødeland and William L. Miller (Eds.), *European Legal Cultures in Transition* (Cambridge University Press 2015) 1 ff.

12 Nina Louisa Arold, *The Legal Culture of the European Court of Human Rights*, (Nijhoff 2007); Idem, "The Melting Pot or the Salad Bowl Revisited – Rendezvous of Legal Cultures at the European Court of Human Rights" in Knut Einar Skodvin and Jørn Øyrehagen Sunde (Eds.), *Rendezvous of European Legal Cultures* (Fagbokforlaget 2010) 61 ff; Christian Franklin, "The Melting Pot or the Salad Bowl Revisited (again) – Rendezvous of Legal Cultures at the European Court of Justice" in Knut Einar Skodvin and Jørn Øyrehagen Sunde (Eds.), *Rendezvous of European Legal Cultures* (Fagbokforlaget 2010) 77 ff.

13 James Q. Whitman, "Comparative Law and Religion" in Mathias Reimann and Reinhard Zimmermann (Eds.), *The Oxford Handbook of Comparative Law* (2nd ed., Oxford University Press 2019); Chibli Mallat, "Comparative Law and the Islamic (Middle Eastern) Legal Culture" in Mathias Reimann and Reinhard Zimmermann (Eds.), *The Oxford Handbook of Comparative Law* (2nd ed., Oxford University Press 2019); Grødeland and Miller (2015) (n. 11) 3.

14 Annelise Riles, "Comparative Law and Socio-Legal Studies" in Mathias Reimann and Reinhard Zimmermann (Eds.), *The Oxford Handbook of Comparative Law* (2nd ed. Oxford University Press 2019). Grødeland and Miller (2015) (n 11) 3, see also below Subsection 4.

15 Peter Mankowski, *Rechtskultur* (Mohr Siebeck 2016), 1 ff.; Roger Cotterrell, "The Concept of Legal Culture" in David Nelken (Ed.), *Comparing Legal Cultures* (Aldershot 1997) 13–31; skeptical also Nelken (2014) (n. 7); Patrick H. Glenn, "Legal Culture and Legal Traditions" in Mark Van Hoecke (Ed.), *Epistemology and Methodology of Comparative Law* (Hart Publishing 2004) 20.

16 Petrick H. Glenn, *Legal Traditions of the World* (Oxford University Press 2000) 45 f.

17 Uwe Kischel, *Rechtsvergleichung* (Mohr Siebeck 2015) § 4 para. 47.

18 Örücü (2007) (n. 5) 59.

19 Friedman (2006) (n. 11) 189 very broadly refers to patterns of behaviour, opinions or ideas regarding to the legal system. David Nelken, "Defining and Using the Concept of Legal Culture" in Esin Örücü and David Nelken (Eds.), *Comparative Law – A Handbook* (Hart Publishing 2007) 113 defines legal culture in the most general sense as "relatively stable patterns of legally orientated social behaviour and attitudes" and adds "Like culture itself, legal culture is about who we are, not just what we do"; Mark Van Hoecke and Mark Warrington, "Legal Cultures, Legal Paradigms and Legal Dogmatics: Towards a New Model for Comparative Law" (1998) Vol. 47 *The International and Comparative Law Quarterly* 495, 498; Mark Van Hoecke, "Methodology of Comparative Research" in Mark Van Hoecke (Ed.), *Law and Method* (2015) 22 fn. 30: "Legal Culture in a broad sense, encompassing tradition, usages, world view, paradigmatical framework and anything which is not law in the strict sense but influences legal

concept of legal culture, albeit often not uncritically, to meet very different cognitive interests and purposes. One invariable notion of legal culture seems to be a mooring in society. The interaction between law and society is crucial for sociological approaches and can be particularly valuable to explain change in law and legal systems. From a legal doctrinal perspective, legal culture can serve as the context in which rules and institutions have been developed and are applied. Jaakko Husa observed that "legal culture may be defined so that it contains elements of multiple fields that study law – not just doctrinal studies, but sociology, philosophy and history."[20] In his textbook, *A new approach to comparative law*, which has a specific focus on legal culture, he describes legal culture as point of reference: "the system-specific way in which values and practice and legal concepts are integrated in the actual operation of the legal system".[21] This makes perfect sense for the aim of his textbook, which is "to acquaint the reader with the theoretical and methodological grounds of comparative law".[22] Nevertheless other authors with different outlooks and intentions have defined the concept differently.

This implies that the content of the concept is highly dependent on the analytical *purpose* it aims to serve.[23] In other words, an all-encompassing, correct or universal definition of legal culture is not at hand and is not even desirable.[24] On the other hand, for a systematic comparison of legal cultures it is not feasible to operate with an open ended concept of legal culture. Rather one has to consider the aim of comparing legal cultures by individually determining the elements under investigation and the entities included in the comparison. Because these constituent elements of a legal culture are in constant interaction, I call them here *subjects* of comparison. In order to be comparable, these elements must be phrased in a manner, allowing a comparison of features that are functionally sufficiently similar, but at the same time adequately broad enough to identify differences.[25]

---

thinking. Wieacker, (1990) (n. 11), 1–29, 5 regards legal culture as a product of history with three distinct features characterising the European legal culture: Individualism, Legalism and Intellectualism, see Cotterrell (2019) (n. 8) 714; Grødeland and Miller (2015) (n. 11) 2 (using Nelken's definition).

20 Jaakko Husa, "Macro Comparative Law – Reloaded" (2018) Vol. 131 No. 4 *Tidsskrift for Rettsvitenskap* 410, 433.

21 Husa (2015) (n. 5) 4.

22 Ibid. 2.

23 Nelken (2014) (n. 7) 260: "As many authors have pointed out, if we are to make use of the term for the purpose of carrying out empirical investigations, it is important to be able to operationalize it." See also David Nelken, "Puzzling out Legal Culture: A Comment on Blankenburg" in David Nelken (Ed.), *Comparing Legal Cultures* (Aldershot 1997); Lawrence Friedman, "The Concept of Legal Culture: A Reply" in David Nelken (Ed.), *Comparing Legal Cultures* (Aldershot 1997); Friedman (2006) (n. 11) 186 admits that the concept of legal culture is "troublesome" and that there is a "serious problem of definition." Van Hoecke and Warrington (1998) (n. 19) 495–536, 499; Wieacker (1990) (n. 11) 3 f.

24 This is also the conclusion of the comprehensive analysis of the term legal culture provided by Mankowski (2016) (n. 15), 533; almost all leading comparative scholars seem to agree on this. Nelken (2007) (n. 19) 127; Husa (2018) (n 20) 422: "[…] legal culture is awkward to place in a genuinely global definition." See also Helland and Koch (2014) (n. 1) 10.

25 Jaakko Husa, "Farewell to Functionalism or Methodological Tolerance" (2003) Vol. 67 No. 3 *Rabel Journal of Comparative and International Law (Rabel)* 419, 432: "The requirement of "some common elements" must be understood somewhat loosely in order to avoid a too-far reaching similarity assumption." Examples for such elements

Furthermore, the entities under comparison, the *research objects*, need to be identified when determining the concept's content for this specific analytical purpose. Considering both the *subjects of comparison* and the *research object* therefore seem necessary to establish the framework in which the concept is supposed to operate. Let's have a closer look at these three elements: purpose, subject and object of comparing legal cultures.

As mentioned above, the *purpose* of this volume is to enable the reader to *identify, explain, analyse* and *compare* similarities and differences of central features of selected national legal cultures in order to make them comparable to other legal cultures. For this purpose, it seems too narrow to focus on intellectual elements of a legal culture only, as has been done by legal sociologists and anthropologists.[26] Law is produced and applied in legal institutions, which in turn are framed in order to realise specific ideas of and expectations of law. The definition of legal culture as ideas and expectations of law made operation by institutional(-like) practice contains both dimensions: the institutional and intellectual.[27] However, this definition is still too abstract to be used as an analytical tool. Therefore, we distinguish further between subcategories such as norm production, conflict resolution, ideal of justice, legal method, degree and attitude towards professionalisation and internationalisation to capture *some* central (but very consciously not all) features of a legal cultures.[28]

Focusing on these features enables us to compare legal cultures. Moreover, it is the interplay of the internal elements that can explain and provide valuable insight into important characteristics of legal cultures. Consequently, this book provides a framework for comparative studies by conveying basic, but systematically structured legal cultural knowledge in order to facilitate understanding.[29] Hence the concept of "legal culture" does not explain similarities and differences, but instead, the analytical framework, which is entailed in the operational concept of legal culture, can do so.

According to our purpose, the *subject* of legal cultural comparison is *not* just the substantive law and the institutions producing and applying it, but also attitudes, mentalities, values, ideals and principles directly related to the production and application of law. Thus, this chapter and the remainder of this book are *not* primarily concerned with broader understandings of a legal culture as encompassing the atti-

---

are institutionalised ways of norm production or commonly recognise accepted principles of legal method which have been adopted by almost all contemporary legal cultures.

26 See e.g. Friedman (2006) (n. 11) or Nelken (2014) (n. 7).

27 In more detail on the function of the definition and the legal cultural model as an analytical tool, see Sunde (2020) (n. 2).

28 Sunde had originally planned to enclose another subcategory – legal ideologies, and one could easily think of other categories giving valuable insides, such as institutionalized values bases (constitutions, international treaties etc.), institutional ways of law enforcement, etc.

29 We therefore disagree with Franz and Keebet von Benda-Beckmann, "Why Not Legal Culture?" in David Nelken (Ed.), *Using Legal Culture* (Wildy, Simmonds and Hill 2012), who maintain that it is "difficult to reconstruct it [legal culture] as an analytical category." It is not the concept itself that enables meaningful analysis but understanding the interaction between its components that make an operationalized concept of legal culture a valuable tool to achieve knowledge and understanding. In order to avoid obscuring the interrelations between the elements, we have chosen to limit ourselves to six elements.

tudes, mentalities, values, ideals and principles of a specific population at large. This implies an important limitation towards our concept of legal culture. Legal culture is here understood in a narrow sense, as a culture dominated by professional actors (judges, advocates, legal scholars, legislators most generally legal professionals – in short lawyers).[30] However, law is not a closed system but is in constant and dynamic interaction with its surrounding society.[31] There are also some institutionalised overlaps between the two spheres, such as laymen participation in courts of law. Still, what distinguishes legal culture from other cultures is the *dominating* role of legal actors. In other words, the legal cultural framework presented and applied throughout this book relates to factors determining law, its institutions and the role and attitudes of the legal profession. Accordingly, other factors such as politics, economy, religion, communication techniques etc. which beyond doubt affect legal cultures are not constituent elements of our definition. Rather, these factors constitute the wider general cultural context for a legal culture in a narrow sense.

The research *object* in this volume is determined by the perception of those mainly shaping and operating in its boundaries, i.e. professional lawyers. Even in a globalised world, most practicing lawyers perceive themselves as lawyers of a particular national legal culture; they are Norwegian, Italian or Austrian lawyers. This applies as a rule also for lawyers working in international law firms. Against this background, it seems appropriate to focus on national legal cultures. However, we want to remind the reader that nation and state are necessarily opaque concepts. The operationalised concept of legal culture, provided above, is not limited to a comparison of legal culture on the level of sovereign states. Different legal cultures can exist both outside and inside states. The co-existence of a Scottish and English legal culture in the United Kingdom can serve as an example.[32] In his contribution, Lloyd Thomas Wilson Jr. points out that the USA consists of 50 legal cultures in the states, encapsulated by the legal culture of the federal state.[33] In contrast, in Germany despite its federal structure, the joint experience of lawyers and their perception of law allows it to speak of only one German legal culture.[34]

In addition, international or supra-national structures may fall into the scope of the narrow definition of the operationalised concept of legal culture. This requires that these entities have established mechanisms for conflict-resolution and norm production based on a more or less clearly defined purpose to regulate certain types of legal matters according to intersubjective procedural principles and driven by professional actors sharing some kind of common education and mentality. Furthermore, sub-cultures may emerge under the umbrella of the national legal culture. In France, and to a lesser

30 Friedman (2006) (n. 11) 189 distinguishes between internal and external legal culture. Critical to this distinction is Nelken (2012) (n. 10) 262.

31 Grødeland and Miller (2015) (n. 11) 3 ff.

32 Christian N.K. Franklin, "A Legal Cultural 'Take' on the Legal System of England & Wales" in this volume, Chapter 10, and Andrew R.C. Simpson, "An Introduction to Scottish Legal Culture" in this volume, Chapter 11.

33 Lloyd T. Wilson, Jr., "A View of the Legal Culture of the United States of America" in this volume, Chapter 17, 639.

34 Sören Koch, "An Introduction to German Legal Culture" in this volume, Chapter 8, 223.

extent in Sweden and Finland, a separate legal culture for public law, with its own institutions, procedures, method and education has emerged over time.[35] In Germany, some commentators regard labour law as such a subculture.[36] Besides labour law courts being organised into a separate court hierarchy, a rather fragmented legislation renders verdicts of the federal labour law Supreme Court (*Bundesarbeitsgericht*) a highly relevant source of legal argumentation for the expert-lawyers (*Fachanwälte*) dominating this field of law. Also, alternative dispute-resolution mechanisms (both nationally and internationally) may produce institutional and intellectual structures that comply with our definition of legal culture.[37] Lawyers may perceive themselves belonging to several legal cultures at the same time, e.g. a French judge at the ECtHR can perceive herself as being a French public and European lawyer.[38]

Accordingly, a legal cultural approach based on an operationalised concept of legal culture does not deny the existence of legal pluralism; nor does it reject the notion of convergence.[39] Quite the opposite, recognising that contemporary law is governed by overlapping and sometimes merging legal regimes is one of the most important *explanations* for the challenges and changes we can observe today in almost all national legal cultures particularly in Europe but also around the globe. Therefore, we decided to integrate the degree and attitudes towards internationalisation of law as a separate element of the intellectual structure. The institutionalised practice of implementing inter, supra and transnational law and lawyers' attitudes towards this process may provide interesting insights when comparing legal cultures.

Despite consciously acknowledging that legal cultures co-exist and often overlap, we still regard it as legitimate to focus on selected *national* legal cultures. This methodological choice seems appropriate for achieving the aim of this book: conveying basic, but systematically structured legal cultural knowledge in order to facilitate understanding and enable cross-cultural comparison. Accordingly, the relationship between and interaction among different legal cultures, *inter alia* in the form of legal transplants and reception of law, even though highly interesting topics of comparative research,[40] fall outside the scope of this volume. Instead of focusing on such external interrelations, the contributions in this book provide a systematically structured *internal* perspective. Presenting the internal structure and becoming aware of the dynamic interplay of the

---

35 Sunniva Cristina Bragdø-Ellenes, "An Introduction to French Legal Culture" in this volume, Chapter 13, 474, Anna Nylund, "An Introduction to Finnish Legal Culture" in this volume, Chapter 6, 160.

36 Bernd Rüthers, "Welcher Methodenkanon sollte für die Rechtsprechung verbindlich sein?" in Susanne Hähnchen (Ed.), *Methodelehre zwischen Wissenschaft und Handwerk* (Mohr Siebeck 2019). Mankowski (2016) (n. 15) 409 ff.

37 Laura Ervo, "Nordic Court Culture in Progress: Historical and Futuristic Perspectives" in Laura Ervo and Anna Nylund (Eds.), *The Future of Civil Litigation* (Springer 2014) 383 ff.

38 Arold (2010) (n. 12) 65.

39 For an interesting case of convergence see the comparative study by Martin Brennecke, *Judicial Law Making in English and German Courts, Techniques and Limits of Statutory Interpretation* (Intersentia 2018) 245, arguing that judicial style and judicial reasoning in both jurisdictions (concerning statutory interpretation) is "fundamentally uniform". See also Stefan Vogenauer, *Die Auslegung von Gesetzen in England und auf dem Kontinent* (Mohr Siebeck 2001) arriving at a similar conclusion.

40 Cotterrell (2019) (n. 8) 715 with further references.

legal cultural elements will enable the reader to achieve a deeper understanding of the legal cultures selected for this volume.

But what to do with this legal cultural knowledge and understanding? How do we use it when performing comparative analysis? In order to answer these questions, we have to engage with the wider field of comparative law. One of the biggest challenges for all comparative lawyers is that our perceptions of law are highly embossed by our education and experience in our native legal cultures. Engaging with foreign lawyers and communicating across boarders therefore requires understanding of foreign legal cultures. This becomes obvious when considering more traditional approaches to comparative law and the criticism raised against them.

3. Legal Culture and Functionalism

The traditional starting point for lectures on comparative law is what is called the functional approach. Let's assume that a comparatist wants to understand how a given problem occurring in society is solved in different legal orders. Functionalism has been considered, despite recent and legitimate criticism, a "legitimate form of comparative law" if applied in a *moderate version* that accepts the inherent limitations of this approach.[41] In the 20th century functionalism was a very common and almost uncritically accepted approach among comparative scholars. It became even more attractive in the attempt to identify a common core of European Private Law[42] or even a universally applicable (new) *ius commune* as a basis for the harmonisation and unification of law in Europe.[43] Such approaches were closely related to what can be labelled the traditional core of comparative law,[44] with a strong focus on the comparison of black letter law embedded in a legal scientific tradition dating back to the early 20th century.[45] This type of traditional comparative research focused on comparing specific legal rules or institutions: to wit, the way different jurisdictions handle unjustified enrichment, medical malice practice or consumer protection issues.[46] Black letter law such as legislation or court decisions were the main subjects of this kind of comparison. Previously, Gustav

---

41 Husa (2003) (n. 25) 421. Ralf Michaels, "The Functional Method of Comparative Law" in Mathias Reimann and Reinhard Zimmermann (Eds.), *The Oxford Handbook of Comparative Law* (2nd ed. Oxford University Press 2019) 380 f.

42 Wieacker (1990) (n. 11) 6. On the use of the functional approach in the common core project, see Van Hoecke (2015) (n. 19) 20.

43 Reinhard Zimmermann, "Savigny's Legacy: Legal History, Comparative Law and the Emergence of a European Legal Science" (1996) Vol. 112 *Law Quarterly Review* 576; Idem., *The law of Obligations: Roman Foundations of the Civilian Tradition* (Clarendon Press 1996).

44 Dagmar Schieck, "Comparative Law and European Harmonisation: A Match Made in Heaven or Uneasy Bedfellows?" (2010) Vol. 21 *European Business Law Review* 203.

45 Husa (2018) (n. 20) 434; Van Hoecke (2015) (n. 19) 10 ff.

46 A great variety of legal institutions are compared by Konrad Zweigert and Hein Kötz, *An Introduction to Comparative Law* (3rd ed., Clarendon Press 1998) in their still highly influential textbook on comparative law. It would be pointless waste of space here to refer to the great number of studies provided in this fashion over the last decades.

Radbruch,[47] but particularly Konrad Zweigert and Heinz Kötz argued that such research requires a functional approach.[48] The basic assumption, and at the same time the most criticised aspect of their methodological approach, is that all societies face similar social problems (universalism).[49] Comparing different legal solutions, which are supposed to solve the same problem, they argued, makes it possible to identify and evaluate rules that have the same or at least similar function. Accordingly, Zweigert and Kötz stated: "The basic methodological principle of comparative law is that of functionality. [...] Incomparables cannot usefully be compared, and in law the only things which are comparable are those which fulfil the same function."[50] The aim of such a comparison may be to critically evaluate different solutions and furthermore to provide normative considerations *de lege ferenda*; with other words arguing for the best or most efficient solution for a legal problem.[51] However, already Zweigert and Kötz recognised that such policy considerations have to be carried out by carefully evaluating the effects of legal rules in their respective legal cultural context.[52] To understand the legal cultural context of legal rules and institutions, legal history offers an apt tool. Legal historians have constantly indicated that legal institutions developed to solve a particular social problem in the past, have been adapted to solve new social problems. By doing so, they have deliberately attacked the notion of historical continuity.[53] Furthermore, legal historians have enriched our understanding of the unique development of legal institutions and rules in different legal cultures.

For example, the Roman Law institute of *negotiorum gestio* (benevolent intervention into another's affairs without mandate[54]), was introduced to facilitate necessary economic or legal interventions in favour of an absent neighbour or fellow citizen.[55] As no modern forms of long distance communication existed in the Ancient world, such an institution was regarded necessary by the Roman jurists, since no means to presume

47 Gustav Radbruch, *Einführung in die Rechtswissenschaft* (9th ed., Mohr Siebeck 1958), 194 ff.

48 Zweigert and Kötz (1998) (n. 46) 379.

49 For an overview on the great number of critical approaches see, Siems (2018) (n. 5) 45 ff., Husa (2003) (n. 25) 423 with further references.

50 Zweigert and Kötz (1998) (n. 46) 34.

51 Zweigert and Kötz (1998) (n. 46) 47, and a more reluctant but still affirmative Michael Bogdan, *Concise Introduction to Comparative Law* (Europe Law Publishing 2013) 65–67; Peter de Cruz, *Comparative Law in a Changing World* (2nd ed, Cambridge University Press 2007) 224; Husa (2003) (n. 25) 425; Walter Joseph Kamba, "Comparative Law, A Theoretical Framework" (1974) Vol. 23 *International Comparative Law Review Quarterly* 485, 517.

52 Mark Van Hoecke, "Deep Level Comparative Law" in Mark Van Hoecke (Ed.), *Epistemology and Method of Comparative Law* (Hart Publishing 2004)165 ff.; Van Hoecke, (2015) (n. 19) 9 f.

53 E.g. Sören Koch, *Unaufgeforderte Hilfeleistung in Notsituationen: Eine rechtshistorische und rechtsvergleichende Studie zu den zivilrechtlichen Aspekten der Nothilfe mit besonderer Berücksichtigung des Rechts der Geschäftsführung ohne Auftrag* (Peter Lang 2011) 424 ff.

54 This is the translation which has been chosen for the Draft Common Frame of Reference, a more precise translation has been offered by Nils Jansen, "Management of Another's Affairs without a Mandate" in Jürgen Basedow et al., *The Max Planck Encyclopedia of European Private Law,* Vol. II (Oxford University Press 2012).

55 Koch (2011) (n. 53) 21 ff.

a contractual relationship without previous consent were recognised.[56] In modern times, the institute was deprived of its original context and *inter alia* applied to "self-sacrifice" in cases of rescue operations,[57] which were not encompassed by the Roman law institute. A comparative analysis reveals that the content and application of the underlying principle, significantly depends on the treatment of the institute in legal doctrine, the reception of Roman law, the existence or lack of alternatives as functionally equivalent mechanisms and the degree of individualism in the respective legal cultures.[58] In Scotland, a rather narrow interpretation in accordance to the original scope of application prevails,[59] while countries like England and Norway (for very different reasons) have either not recognised the principle at all or accorded it almost no practical importance.[60] Interestingly, an institute based on an apparently consistent legal principle can prove to have rather different scopes of application and even different purposes; in other words, despite similar legal terminology it is difficult to establish whether there exists a common dogmatic principle serving a similar function (e.g., that of *negotiorum gestio*) in different European legal cultures.[61]

Thus, applying the functional method can reveal substantive differences despite terminological similarities.[62] As Michaels has put it, "the functional approach emphasises differences within similarities".[63] Consequently, functionalism does not depart from seemingly identical rules, but rather looks for comparable socio-economic problems demanding legal regulation or solution. Legal cultural understanding and knowledge can contribute to identifying those problems by taking into account the particular institutional and intellectual framework in which these problems are solved.

Another assumption the traditional functional approach is based upon, is that similar factual problems always will lead to similar practical results (*praesumtio similitudinis*). From a legal cultural perspective such an assumption is questionable.[64] This point can be explained by an example. Same sex partnerships or marriages might be subject to comprehensive legal regulation in one legal culture while another culture may subject these institutes to moral norms only or may altogether prohibit them. The same applies

56 Max Kaser, *Römische Rechtsquellen und angewandte Juristenmethode* (Böhlau 1986) 225 ff.; Zimmermann (1996) (n. 43) 435 f.; Samuel J. Stoljar, "Negotiorum Gestio" *International Encyclopedia of Comparative Law*, 17 Vol. X (1984) 6 ff.

57 Jansen (2012) (n. 54).

58 Ibid. concludes that the institute of negotiorum gestio has "transformed into a highly flexible, yet in the same time unstructured, means of restitution. Modern functional parallels are the law of unjustified enrichment and instances of subrogation, as found, for example, in insurance and labour law."

59 *Lord Advocate v. Rogers* (1978) SLT (St.CH) 31; Kenneth Reid and Reinhard Zimmermann, *A History of Private Law in Scotland* Vol. II (Oxford University Press 2001). On the other hand, the scope of application in modern Scots private law encompasses also cases of unjustified intervention in another's affairs, see Jansen (2012) (n. 54).

60 Koch (2011) (n. 53) 183, 217.

61 Jansen (2012) (n. 54) "those rules do not offer a fair comparative picture of the present state of European law, nor are they convincing as a proposal for a future law."

62 Michaels (2019) (n. 41) 381; similarly, Cotterrell (2019) (n. 8).

63 Ibid.

64 Based on this assumption Zweigert and Kötz (1998) (n. 46) 40, Critical Michaels (2019) (n. 41); Van Hoecke (2015) (n. 19) 9.

to adultery.[65] As Husa pointed out, "the hardcore of functional method in comparative law does not support the similarity presumption, on the contrary, it encompasses both similarities and difference."[66]

Many legal comparatists applying a functional approach are preoccupied with exploring similarities. Comparatists applying a cultural perspective often emphasise sustainable diversity.[67] Does that mean that these approaches are incompatible? Not necessarily. Again, the outlook of the comparatist is decisive. If one is interested in finding a common determinator for the harmonisation of law, the functional approach seems tempting. Still, without acknowledging the existence of cultural difference, the comparatist may remain ignorant of the fact that a similarly phrased rule may serve a very different function in a different legal culture. If one wants to describe law as a product of a particular culture, it may appear necessary to emphasis diversity.[68] Still, a meaningful comparison requires that we at least acknowledge that legal cultures have certain functions in common e.g. institutions that resolve legal conflicts or produce legal norms. Again, others promote the idea that the dynamic development of transnational and supranational regimes facilitates changes in and convergence between legal cultures. Cultural differences may, in their view, be regarded as an obstacle for legal pluralism and the globalisation of law. They might be tempted to downplay them.[69] However, they cannot analyse the impact of international law without recognising that conflicts arise because national and international regimes address the same function and attempt to regulate similar social problems.

Functionalism is thus not irrelevant for the comparison of legal cultures.[70] The question is rather *what* can be compared, more precisely *what can be regarded as sufficiently functionally equivalent*. An operational concept of legal culture transformed into a legal cultural model provides categories for such functionally equivalent elements. Such elements have been explained in-depth above (*supra* Ch. 2) but are worthy of some sketches to explain why the elements of the LCM are functionally equivalent.

While the functional approach tends to overemphasise similarities, postmodern theories on comparative law such as linguistic and pluralistic approaches tend to overemphasise differences, sometimes even rejecting the mere possibility of conducting any kind of meaningful comparison.[71] The legal cultural approach promoted in this volume, on the other hand, tries to establish a middle ground by acknowledging cultural diversity, but at the same time recognising that there are structural features common to all modern legal

65 Siems (2018) (n. 5) 46.

66 Husa (2003) (n. 25) 425.

67 Patrick H. Glenn, *Legal Traditions of the World: Sustainable Diversity* (5th ed., Oxford University Press 2014).

68 Cotterrell (2019) (n. 8) 712.

69 Glenn (2014) (n. 67) 14.

70 Husa (2003) (n. 25) 428: "For example the concept of legal culture makes it possible to compare legal systems even when the functions may differ; here functionalism has very little to say." In the same direction Van Hoecke and Warrington (1998) (n. 19) 521.

71 See above (n. 80).

cultures (in the narrow operational sense established above).[72] Almost all contemporary legal cultures have developed institutionalised mechanisms of conflict resolution (courts, ADR, mediation etc.) as well as institutional ways of norm production (legislation, case law). The way lawyers are educated, is to a certain degree regulated and institutionalised as well. For example, in Germany, even though the states, and to some extent the law faculties, enjoy the freedom to regulate the structure and content of law studies, a close cooperation among the states and universities has been established determining the formal requirements for lawyers. In order to be recognised a lawyer (*Volljurist*) requires in all states to pass two state examinations (*Staatsexamen*).[73] In these exams, candidates have to solve hypothetical cases based on substantive law in fields such as civil and criminal law, public law including constitutional law and EU law. These institutionalised aspects of legal education are inevitably linked to a core of legal sources (Basic Law, Civil and Criminal Code and other federal legislation) and a common understanding of the method that should be applied to legal problem solving.[74] Furthermore, the civil-law tradition and the particular scientific approach to law in Germany have contributed to making intersubjective and systematic predictability an ideal also in legal education.[75] Against this background, unified (and to some extent institutionalised) ways of educating lawyers are a result of the particular ideas and expectations of law prevailing in Germany. At the same time, they are important preconditions for the common cultural identity of German lawyers.[76] This is a reason, why we asked the contributors to focus on the degree and attitude towards professionalisation, rather than letting them describe how educational institutions are established, structured or financed. Against this background, professionalisation, despite being highly institutionalised in many legal cultures, can be regarded as an intellectual element.

The same applies for the rather open category of the "ideal of justice". Many legal orders have to some extent determined fundamental values and principles for the application of law in their respective constitutions. Human rights catalogues and the basic organization of the state, political system, structure and competences of the courts etc. can therefore be regarded as institutionalised. However, it is the application of these fundamental values and principles in legal practice and by legal actors that shapes a legal culture. The current constitutional crisis in Poland may serve as an example of the interaction between institutionalised values and changing expectations to law and its function in society.[77]

If the aim of comparing legal cultures is to achieve general knowledge and understanding one needs to explore both similarities *and* differences among functionally suf-

---

72 Grødeland and Miller (2015) (n. 11) 4 f. use legal culture as a basis for arguing for convergence; for this purpose they emphasis similarities.

73 Koch (2020), "An Introduction to German Legal Culture" (n. 34) 258.

74 Ibid. 259, see also 221 ff.

75 Ibid. 257, 266 ff.

76 Ibid.

77 See Anna Klimaszewka, Anna Machnikowska and Sören Koch, "An Introduction to Polish Legal Culture" in this volume, Chapter 9, 319 f.

ficiently similar elements in different legal cultures.[78] Interestingly, this volume proves that differences are not limited to legal cultures belonging to a different family or tradition, neither do similarities exclusively occur among legal cultures that belong to the same family or tradition.

For example, the use of precedents seems to be facilitated by a rather low number of supreme court judgments and a court structure with a single competent court on top. These preconditions are met for both the UK and Norwegian Supreme Court, but not for the *cour de cassation* and the *Bundesgerichtshof*.[79] The functions of all these courts in their legal cultures are similar in so far as they rule in last instance (they function as institutions of conflict resolution), but different regarding their effect and role in the practical application of law (their function as norm producers).

As long as the categories of the functional comparison are framed sufficiently abstract, it becomes possible to identify and explain cultural similarities *and* differences within functionally equivalent entities. Such a moderate assumption of functional similarity is a necessary precondition for a systematic comparison of legal cultures, but most importantly such an approach enables one to analyse law in different legal cultures contextually.

4. Contextual approaches and the role of legal culture

4.1 Context matters!

Today comparatists agree that it is meaningless to compare legal texts without taking their socio-legal function into account as well. In other words, not just the text but also the context matters. However, the questions about what the relevant context is, how the context can be studied and to what extent functional equivalents can be identified have been highly controversial. Pierre Legrand, one of the most prominent critics of the orthodox functional approach, has constantly attacked the idea that different legal cultures face universal challenges.[80] He therefore stressed that it is utterly impossible to identify any institution or legal norm that serves the exact same function in two legal orders. On this basis, he rejected the idea of finding the best or most efficient solution to a legal problem and regarded the very notion as fallacious.[81] Instead, Legrand suggested studying the legal mentalities or the deep structure of law as he calls it.[82] As other critics of the functional approach, he argued that the search for functional equivalents brings comparatists to emphasise similarities and disregard differences.[83] The problem with

78 See also Siems (2018) (n. 5) 143 advocating a similar claim: "A preferable position is to be open to both similarities and differences"; with further supporting references.

79 See the discussions in the respective chapters in this volume on England & Wales, Norway, Germany, and France.

80 Pierre Legrand, "European Legal Systems are not Converging" (1996) Vol. 45 Issue 1 *International and Comparative Law Quarterly* 52.

81 Ibid. 55.

82 Ibid. 56.

83 Ibid. 52.

Legrand's focus on the intellectual side of legal cultures is, as Husa correctly pointed out, that his "intriguing hermeneutical discourse on the subject does not offer a method."[84]

What is lacking in Legrand's vision is an operationalisation of the legal cultural framework for the *mentalité*; namely a method for analysing what is sufficiently comparable functionally. In addition, it seems inappropriate to entirely reject the existence of universal ideas and expectations towards the function and purpose of law.[85] Indeed, any radical cultural relativism renders legal comparison impossible. An operationalised concept of legal culture, transformed into a model that distinguishes between different aspects or elements of the institutional and intellectual structures respectively, may offer a way out of this methodological dead end. Such an approach can provide us with sufficient understanding to actually describe the context of rules and their application, which in turn is necessary to identify both functional similarities *and* differences.[86]

Mark Van Hoecke characterised postmodern and functionalism critical approaches to comparative law as epistemologically pessimistic while he labelled advocates of the traditional functional approach as optimists.[87] A legal cultural approach could be one way to overcome this pessimism without necessarily replacing it with a naive epistemological optimism.[88] Furthermore, such a perspective does not have a focus on positive law, but takes the application of law and the underlying ideals and attitudes into consideration as well. And this not just by looking at *which* institutions produce and apply law, but also asking *how* they do that and why. All contributions in this volume contain a description of institutional ways of conflict resolution, including a figure illustrating the organization of the court system, but also a section on legal method and on the degree and attitude towards professionalisation. All these factors must be taken into account when analysing how lawyers tend to solve cases in a legal culture.

Another important element of the context of law are institutionalised ways of norm production. These differ from culture to culture, too. Rodolfo Sacco characterises law as "an aggregate of various legal formants."[89] Legal formant is an umbrella concept encompassing legislation, courts practice and legal doctrine. All these actors contribute to shape the law, even though their impact on institutional ways of norm production varies considerably. This becomes particularly obvious regarding the role of legal doctrine.

84 Jaako Husa, "About the Methodology of Comparative Law – Some Comments Concerning Wonderland", http://www.law.unimaas.nl/maastrichtworkingpapers (accessed 17 April 2020) (2007) 13.

85 Husa (2003) (n. 25) 430: "[Universalism] must support an idea according to which human beings and their societies and legal systems have at least some common elements."

86 Many comparative lawyers have recognized the need for contextualization. But the traditional conceptualization in comparative textbooks is, according to Esin Örücü, "Family trees for Legal Systems: Towards a Contemporary Approach" in Mark Van Hoecke (Ed.), *Epistemology and Methodology of Comparative Law* (Hart 2004) 37, unfeasible when trying to classify legal systems.

87 Van Hoecke (2004) (n. 14) 172; see also Husa (2007) (n. 84) 17, Cotterrell (2019) (n. 8) 728.

88 In this direction Geoffrey Samuel, "What is Legal Epistemology" in Dirk Heirbaut and Maurice Adams (Eds.), *The method and culture of comparative law* (Hart Publishing 2014) 23 ff.

89 Rudolfo Sacco, "Legal Formants. A Dynamic Approach to Comparative Law" (1991) Vol. 39 *American Journal of Comparative Law* 1 and 343.

Except for the institutional writers in Scotland,[90] scholarly opinions, regardless of how thoroughly preformed, widely accepted or highly esteemed, are not formally binding for courts of law. Even in Germany legal doctrine is not perceived as a formal source of law.[91] However, in continental European legal cultures such as the German, the Italian and the French, legal scholars considerably helped to shape not only the substantive law but also the intellectual framework for its application. Consequently, it might be interesting to take a closer look at the role of legal scholarship. Many contributions in this book discuss the impact of legal doctrine and individual legal scholarship on the production of legal norms. In other words, depending on the culture in question, scholarly opinions may be regarded as a more or less important contextual factor. The same applies for institutional ways of conflict resolution. In some cultures, judges actively cite legal doctrine to underpin the legitimacy of their reasoning, in others this happens rarely or may even have been prohibited. Nevertheless, a lack of reference to academic works in court judgments is not necessary to prove that legal doctrine is irrelevant or not considered by judges. Recent studies have shown that English judges increasingly use academic works to form the argumentation on which a decision is based.[92] Mere empirical citation-studies may therefore render an incomplete or even misleading evaluation.

Understanding law in context requires, as stressed by many other comparative legal scholars, that we take deeper levels of law into consideration as well.[93] In Chapter 2, Sunde introduces a dialectical tool illustrating different layers of law by using the metaphor of a legal sea. He distinguishes between the surface layer (black letter law, law in books and legal institutions) from deeper levels of law.[94] As mentioned above, the application of law today is highly determined by professional lawyers, their attitudes, methods and professional ethics.[95] The often unwritten rules, principles and internal discourses in this societal subsystem contain therefore a layer of the law on a deeper level. These rules, principles and discourses are more difficult to pinpoint and to analyse. The presentation of the prevailing ideals of justice and legal method in the contributions of this book aim to provide the reader with a general knowledge regarding these principles and discourses and to invite further reading. People's ideas and expectations of law constitute *another* layer of the deep structure of law. Understanding a legal culture will always demand acknowledging that the application of law is based on values accepted (not necessarily shared) by considerable parts of the population. "Law in action" is therefore also an expression of and based on underly-

90 Simpson (2020) (n. 32).

91 Koch (2020) (n. 34) 253.

92 Brenncke (2019) (n. 39) 26.

93 Örücü (2007) (n. 5) 59; Siems (2018) (n. 5) 117 ff.; Van Hoecke (2004) (n. 52) 81; Van Hoecke (2015) (n. 19) 23 f.

94 Sunde, Chapter 2; Sunde (2010) (n. 2).

95 See above.

ing conceptions and perceptions of law and its function in society.[96] In contrast to the LCM and COMPASS formula, the legal sea model serves primarily illustrative purposes and is to a much lesser degree analytical. Often the transition between different layers is rather smooth, that is, no clear-cut distinction can be drawn between the layers. Accordingly, it makes more sense to talk about deeper levels of law than trying to place a notion at a specific level. As a rule of thumb, one could say that perceptions of law shared by the majority of the population (e.g. "do not kill", *pacta sunt servanda*, private property is a fundamental right etc.) are at a deeper level as are (often) unwritten principles of law (e.g. lex posterior or lex superior principle). The essential difference is that lawyers are deeply familiar with the latter, while those lacking a legal education are not. Again, as a rule of thumb, perceptions with deep roots in society change at a slower rate than legal principles, institutions or rules at the surface. However, as the "Me2" movement proves, changes in society can happen very fast, and in these cases the surface-level has to be adapted to new expectations towards law.

Hence, acknowledging the multilayer nature of law is another important precondition for understanding law in context. Displaying law as a legal sea is a dialectical tool that enables us to analyse the complex interplay between different social and legal actors and institutions when both applying and developing the law.[97] In addition, this tool allows us to analyse the intensity of changes in a legal culture over time. Changes impacting not just the surface, but deeper levels of law, indicate changes in the legal culture as a whole. As legal cultures are never static but rather dynamically changing all the time,[98] the model can help visualise and categorise the *degree* and *extent* of current and past developments. Deep-level analysis can thus contribute to explain the impact of, for instance, internationalisation of law, globalisation, legal pluralism or political developments in reaction to these challenges to the national legal cultures.

The contributions in this book can of course not be expected to provide such a deep-structure analysis for all the legal cultural elements.[99] This would require a multidisciplinary approach which exceeds the scope and purpose of their presentations. However, we believe that regarding law as a multi-layered phenomenon is an underlying assumption common to all theories on comparative law based on a cultural perspective.

A legal cultural approach thus tries to avoid a one-dimensional perception of *law-as-a-mirror-of history*,[100] recognising instead that legal cultures are, as Sunde puts it, in

96 On the importance of distinguishing "law in action" from "law in books", see Van Hoecke (2015) (n. 19) 22; stressing the impact of this distinction when comparing different approaches to legal method, Helland and Koch (2014) (n. 24) 1 ff.

97 Sunde (2020) (n. 2).

98 Siems (2018) (n. 5) flux, with reference to Sunde (2010) (n. 3).

99 Still, some interesting reflections on current developments caused by changes on different levels are made by Colombo and Kvestad in regard to Italy, and by Kimaszewska, Machnikowska and Koch concerning the ongoing constitutional crisis in Poland.

100 Siems (2018) (n. 5) 151.

a "constant flux."[101] To what extent society as a whole or the discourse inside the legal community facilitates legal cultural change has caused debates.[102] Often an interplay of both will be decisive. However, considering historical experiences and the role of legal professionals may explain differences between legal cultures. The traditionally strong focus on legal science (*Rechtswissenschaft*) and a more formalistic approach to law in Germany may constitute one of the reasons for a greater autonomy of law from society in Germany than in other continental legal orders.[103] In the Nordics, on the other hand, a traditionally low degree of scholarly impact on law combined with a unique legal realistic approach to law has facilitated a higher degree of adaptability to social change.[104] Another important factor is to what extent law is perceived an independent subsystem with an inherent logic and therefore to a lesser degree dependent on other discourses in society.[105] As the case of Poland shows, a certain constitutionally guaranteed detachment of law and politics might become an important safeguard for the rule of law in times of political and constitutional crisis.[106] On the other hand, losing contact with society may result in a loss of confidence in the judiciary causing equally devastating effects. The degree of societal confidence in the judiciary and law is another important contextual aspect that is discussed by several contributors in this book. Rather than being part of the legal culture, (in a narrow sense) this contextual factor can be said to be the link between the external and internal legal culture described by Friedman.[107]

To sum up: a functional approach aims to *identify* both functional equivalents and differences, but it is the historical, philosophical, social and legal cultural *context* that provides an *explanation* for the development of different legal solutions. In addition, other factors such as geography, political or economic preconditions can be of relevance when exploring a particular function of legal rules or institutions.[108] However, these contextual factors are not encompassed by the narrow cultural approach presented above and fall therefore outside the scope of this book. Instead it provides knowledge of the selected cultural elements and allows one to analyse their interplay thus establishing a cultural context of law.

101 Sunde (2010) (n. 3) 24.

102 Cotterrell (2019) (n. 8) 723 ff.

103 Thomas Lundmark, *Charting the Divide between Common and Civil Law* (Oxford University Press 2012) 96–128.

104 See Grødeland and Miller (2015) (n. 11) 90 ff. having found that English and Norwegian respondents tend to prefer principles or pragmatic approaches to law, while Bulgarian, Polish and Ukrainian respondents indicate to prefer detail legislation applied literally. The survey explores the attitudes and perceptions of the general public and law professionals in five European countries: England, Norway, Bulgaria, Poland and Ukraine.

105 Advocation such an intellectually-focused approach Glenn (2004) (n. 15) 66.

106 Klimaszewka, Machnikowska and Koch (2020) (n. 77) 317.

107 Friedman (2006) (n. 11).

108 Even though the latter factors are not included in our narrow definition of legal culture (cf. above), we have asked our contributors to provide some general information about these features in their introductions. These sections provide further reference in case these factors become relevant.

4.2 Limitations of the legal cultural approach

Where entities or subjects for comparative research do not comply with our narrow definition of legal culture, e.g. due to a lack of either common institutional or intellectual structures, our approach is not suitable. For instance, not all legal systems recognising Sharia law as a source of law share common legal institutions applying Sharia law consistently in all countries governed by Islamic law. Instead, institutions of norm production and conflict resolution are very differently organised at the state level. The lack of a common institution has caused considerable differences in the way Sharia law is interpreted and applied. Furthermore, the conflicting religious currents make it very difficult to trace a common legal mentality among lawyers applying Islamic law, nor is the legal education organised in a way that lawyers in Islamic countries perceive themselves as part of a common legal culture. Therefore, the term legal family or legal tradition might suit better, when trying to pinpoint certain similarities regarding the religious foundations of law.[109]

Speaking about a European Legal Culture can be problematic for other reasons. On one hand, the Union has produced quite a comprehensive body of substantive law. EU institutions are competent to produce norms and resolve conflicts arising for their interpretation. However, EU directives require implementation to be directly applied in the member states. This leaves room for different applications of legal provisions on the national level, although these norms are supposed to have identical effect in all member states and are based on common legislative intention(s).[110] Since the majority of lawyers are trained to apply the legal method prevailing in their national legal cultures, the application of these norms may differ, even though this should ideally not be the case.[111] In other words, one can argue that the EU still lacks a sufficiently coherent common ideology and legal methodology.[112] Despite some institutions offering a particular degree in EU law, few lawyers describe themselves as "European" lawyer.[113] As the contributions of this book illustrate, it is quite difficult to maintain that there exists one ideal of justice, one articulated legal methodology or specific attitudes towards professionalisation common to all lawyers in Europe. Wieacker correctly observed that we share some fundamental values and ideas on law due to our historical heritage dating back to Greek philosophy, the reception of Roman Law, Canon Law, the impact of

---

109 See also Husa (2018) (n. 5) 424, 438 ff.

110 Gunther Teubner, "Legal Irritants: Good Faith in British Law or How Unifying Law Ends Up in New Divergence" (1998) Vol. 61 *Modern Law Review* 11.

111 Helland and Koch (2014) (n. 24) 9; Gessner (1994) (n. 11) 135 points out: "As long as patterns of interpretation (values, attitudes) and behavioural routines with respect to law as well as social institutions which form part of the legal implementation process are not integrated, a common or even similar legal practice cannot be expected.".

112 This is also something Karl Riesenhuber, *European Methodology – Grundfragen der Methoden des Europäischen Privatrechts*, (De Gruyter 2006) has problems of explaining in his introductory chapter.

113 An early advocate of such a European legal Education is e.g. Mark Van Hoecke, "Für eine europäische Juristenausbildung" (1990) *Juristenzeitung* 991 ff. The college of Europe provides today such an education, but the numbers of lawyers educated there compared to the total number of lawyers in Europe is very small.

the Enlightenment and natural law.[114] This interaction shaped what is often called the "Western legal tradition".[115] Still, the national legal cultures, in our narrow sense, remain remarkably different.

Consequently regarding such entities, *our* narrowly constructed legal cultural approach does not provide a suitable conceptual framework for a comparative analysis.[116] Deliberately accepting such limitations helps to avoid fruitless or prolonged methodological discussions on incomparable research objects. The operationalised concept of legal culture transformed into a legal cultural model allows us to reconstruct the complex phenomenon of legal culture and at the same time to delimit it from other concepts, albeit related, such as the concept of legal systems, legal tradition or legal family. The concept of legal systems emphasises the institutional preconditions governing the application of law.[117] Its focus on substantive law and the institutions of law renders it narrower than our concept of legal culture. Legal tradition is a broader concept particularly emphasising similarities on the intellectual level such as a common perception of what constitutes a legal source or how to apply law in practice. Legal families are another related concept frequently used by legal comparatists. It highlights the idea of direct historical relationships between certain legal systems.[118] The concept has its values for macro-comparative research and can be used to explain the external impact and interaction across legal systems.[119] As mentioned above, describing these external relations is not the aim of this book. Instead, the LCM allows us to map the legal orders, without being bound by classifications into legal families or legal traditions.[120] In other words, the LCM serves as our *tertium comparationis.*[121] Being aware of its purpose, objective and object, this approach can provide us with new and sometimes surprising insights and perspectives.

4.3 The merits and limitations of classification and taxonomies

Still, classifications are not without merits.[122] They can be used to systematise legal systems in terms of institutional similarities and relationship of substantive law but most importantly, they enable us to understand the relationship between similarities and make

114 Wieacker (1990) (n. 11).

115 See Siems (2018) (n. 5) 42 ff.

116 For a different approach and a wider definition of legal culture see, Van Hoecke and Warrington (1998) (n. 19) 5 ff. who build on Franz Wieacker, "Grundlagen der Rechtskultur", in Stig Jørgensen (Ed.), *Tradition and Progress in Modern Legal Cultures* (Franz Steiner Verlag: Stuttgart 1985), identifying certain criteria (individualism and rationalism) for distinguishing Western legal culture from Asian and Islamic legal culture.

117 Glenn (2004) (n. 15) 6f.

118 Husa (2018) (n. 5) 427.

119 Jaakko Husa, "The Future of Legal Families" in Mathias Reimann and Reinhard Zimmermann (Eds.), *The Oxford Handbook of Comparative Law* (2nd ed. Oxford University Press 2019).

120 Zweigert and Kötz (1998) (n. 46) 63 ff.

121 The term "tertium comparationis" has been concisely summarized by Van Hoecke (2015) (n. 19) 27.

122 See for a comprehensive discussion of this topic Siems (2018) (n. 5) 85 ff.

it easier to identify differences. Another, more practical advantage of classification is that gaining knowledge and understanding of say, the French legal system makes it easier to analyse legal systems based on a French model like Argentina. A comparatist familiar with the English Common Law will have less problems of accessing the Australian or New Zealand legal systems or identifying differences between them. From a pedagogic and dialectic perspective, a classification may also contribute to establish taxonomies based on common philosophic theories of law, their functions and underlying values.[123] Indeed, members of the same legal tradition often share some basic perceptions regarding the intellectual elements of their respective legal cultures. As a rule, legal systems of the same tradition have rather similar ideas about how to identify and apply relevant legal sources. Legislators and courts seem to be less reluctant to adopt rules, principles and legal institutions from similar legal cultures, compared to a more remote legal culture.[124] For example in the Nordic countries, lawyers frequently take solutions advocated in another Nordic state into consideration, at least if the national law does not provide a sufficiently clear answer to a legal question.[125] Similar notions appear also on the institutional level. Legislative preparatory works have traditionally had a special importance in the Nordic countries and are regarded as sources of law in all Nordic countries.[126] However, that does not mean that transfer of legal knowledge and rules i.g. in form of transplants are limited to happening inside the same legal family or tradition.[127] Furthermore, legal transplants will often develop rather different functions and effects while merging with and adapting to the recipient's legal culture. Eirik Holmøyvik described this adaption process as the result of passing a legal cultural filter.[128] He argued that the legal cultural filter will be more permeable towards inspiration from members of the same legal tradition or family. Cultural similarities make legal transplants more likely, while the legal cultural filter may offer more resistance to legal transplants from geographically or ideologically more distant cultures. Nevertheless, lacking a pre-existing relationship does not make legal transplants impossible or shaky, to which the history of the German Constitutional Court (established with the American Supreme Court

123 Husa (2015) (n. 5) 254 ff.

124 E.g. the Norwegian supreme court frequently refers to the case law of the neighboring Scandinavian countries and much less frequently to judgments of other European supreme courts.

125 Ingvill Helland and Sören Koch, "Introduction to the Norwegian Legal Method" in Ingvill Helland and Sören Koch (Eds.), *Nordic and Germanic Legal Methods* (Mohr Siebeck 2014) 128.

126 See the contributions on the Norwegian and Finnish legal Culture in this book, and Helland and Koch (2014) (n. 125) 122 ff.; Sten Schauenburg-Müller, "On Danish Legal Method" 155 ff.; Johan Boucht, "Introduction to Finnish and Swedish Legal Method"167 f.; Ingvill Helland and Sören Koch, "Norwegian and German Legal Methods Compared" in Ingvill Helland and Sören Koch (Eds.), *Nordic and Germanic Legal Methods* (Mohr Siebeck 2014) 293.

127 Siems (2018) (n. 5) 231 ff.

128 Eirik Holmøyvik, "A little bit of This and a little bit of That – the Complexity of Legal Reception" in Knut Einar Skodvin and Jørn Øyrehagen Sunde (Eds.), *Rendezvous of Legal Cultures* (Fagbokforlaget 2010) argued that the likelihood of legal transfers depends on certain preconditions such as knowledge, communication, incentive, applicability and capability; (on p. 47 f.).

as a model) bears witness.[129] To this end, it is useful to recall that Lena Foljanty use the metaphor of cultural translation to describe the complex transition process foreign law undergoes when encountering a different legal culture.[130]

Even in countries with a shared political history, distinct legal cultures can be identified. Once again reference to the Nordic countries can illustrate this point. Due to common ethnic, religious, linguistic and social structures they traditionally share features such as a fragmented legislation based on narrowly construed statutes rather than systematic codifications, a pragmatic style of legal argumentation, a simple and stringent court hierarchy without constitutional courts, a cooperative rather than competitive style of conflict resolution, a high degree of confidence in courts and in alternative dispute resolution mechanisms.[131] A closer look at the respective legal cultures reveals interesting differences concerning institutional structures, legal methodology and the underlying doctrine of sources of law.[132] Denmark and Norway share 400 years of common government. Still, Norway has always kept its legal cultural identity, because it had never completely abandoned its own legal institutions, laws and customs.[133] Due to social, economic and not least geographical differences between the two parts of the Danish-Norwegian Realm (1397–1814), a complete merger was never achieved or even attempted.[134] The same applies for Finland and Sweden or Austria and Hungary in Central Europe.

An operationalised concept of legal culture transformed into a legal cultural model allows identification of differences also within closely related legal cultures and enables an explanation of them contextually.[135] In doing so, one can avoid some of the downsides of classifications such as an over-emphasis on similarities.[136] Even if certain countries have received their legal systems from a "mother" culture, their legal cultures can develop differently over time.[137] Let's take the USA and Australia, which were colonies of England and part of the Commonwealth, thus sharing common institutions with England (Westminster Parliament and the House of Lords). Nevertheless, they developed their own legal cultures, partially because both the USA and Australia adopted a federal sys-

129 Koch (2020), "An Introduction to German Legal Culture" (n. 34) 235.

130 Lena Foljanty, "Legal Transfer as Process of Cultural Translation: On Consequences of a Metaphor" in *Max Planck Institute for European Legal History Paper* Series No. 2015-09.

131 Cf. Marius Mikkel Kjølstad, Sören Koch and Jørn Øyrehagen Sunde, "Introduction to Norwegian Legal Culture" in this volume, Chapter 5, 114, 124; Nylund (2020) (n. 35) 154.

132 See e.g. contributions on the Norwegian, Swedish-Finnish and Danish approaches to legal methods in Helland and Koch (2014) (n. 24) and the contributions on Norway and Finland in this volume (cf. Ibid.).

133 Koch (2015) (n. 1) 469.

134 See Jørn Øyrehagen Sunde, *Speculum legale – rettsspegelen* (Fagbokforlaget 2005) 177 ff. for an overview of the legal situation in Denmark-Norway.

135 See Erhard Blankenberg, "Patterns of Legal Culture: The Netherlands Compared to the Neighboring Germany" (1998) Vol. 46 *American Journal of Comparative Law* 1.

136 Critical to approaches focused mainly on similarities e.g. Michaels (2019) (n. 41).

137 Siems (2018) (n. 5) 75.

tem with independent court systems on the federal and the territorial level.[138] This, in turn, requires a different way of arguing in court and consequently a different training for lawyers.[139] Further, their own legal cultures differ from one another, notwithstanding the similar origin in English law and the development of the state into a federal state.

4.4 Civil, Common Law and Mixed Legal Systems

The legal cultural approach, presented in this book, can be used to critically evaluate or even contest classifications one finds in traditional comparative law literature. The majority of textbooks on comparative law operates with the dichotomy between Civil law and Common law. The terminology is not always applied consistently. Depending on the specific focus of the author, some speak of civil/common law systems, others of traditions or families.[140] Nevertheless, this distinction has proven didactically highly valuable and is used by many authors in this volume as well.[141] On the other hand, the classification has been criticised as imprecise or even misleading.[142] A focus on different traditions may lead to an overemphasis on difference between members of different traditions, while at the same time downplaying differences between legal orders of the same tradition.[143] Indeed, all meta-classifications are possibly best suited to *identify* similarities and differences. However, comparative studies need to *identify* and *explain* similarities and differences (see *infra* Ch. 4). Therefore, the LCM presented in this book tries to avoid any reference to a specific tradition, family or other category used by comparative lawyers to classify legal systems. Today, there is a general agreement that the very label "common law" or "civil law" is not sufficient to *explain* similarities or differences.[144] Instead, the underlying institutional and intellectual context is crucial, particularly the socio-economic and legal theoretical preconditions which determine, for instance, the role of courts in a particular legal system, their style of argumentation or different functions of legal concepts.[145] Here, legal cultural knowledge can also provide important insights, helping the comparatist identify similarities and differences and explaining them contextually.

138 See Wilson (2020) (n. 33) 639 and Tina Soliman Hunter, "Introduction to Australian Legal Culture" in this volume, Chapter 18, 703.

139 Compare the contributions on England & Wales, USA, and Australia in this book.

140 Husa (2018) (n. 5) 25, Siems (2018) (n. 5) 51.

141 E.g. Esmeralda Colombo and Lars Kvestad, "An Introduction to the Italian Legal Culture" in this volume, Chapter 15, 547; Koch (2020), "An Introduction to German Legal Culture" (n. 34) 222; Franklin (2020) (n. 32) 333; Wilson (2020) (n. 33) 666; Bragdø-Ellenes (2020) (n. 35) 487.

142 Siems (2018) (n. 5) 74 ff. with further reference.

143 On the distinction between families, traditions and cultures, see Husa (2018) (n. 5) 418 ff.

144 Siems (2018) (n. 5) 74.

145 Illustrative Siems (2018) (n. 5) 61 ff., 70 ff.

Legal orders showing elements resembling both legal traditions are often labelled "mixed legal systems".[146] The term "mixed" relates as a rule to the dichotomy between civil and common law, but has recently been supplemented with notions of post-colonialism and legal pluralism.[147] From a legal cultural perspective, the term "mixed" is problematic as it indicates that elements originate from the one or the other tradition, or indicating that these features have been *adopted* from either a "pure" Common or Civil Law-system.[148] For the standard examples in comparative literature, Scotland, Quebec and South Africa,[149] this might be at least to a certain degree true, but this is not necessarily the case when considering the Nordic and many African and South American counties. In 1274 the Norwegian King Magnus the Law-mender enacted his Code of the Realm implementing a new ideal of social governance through royal legislation.[150] This ideal was received as part of a European intellectual movement.[151] The content of the code, however, was merely suited for the specific conditions of that time in Norway and shows little influence of Roman law or other external influence. Canon law had influenced the underlying perception of justice, but also in this regard the impact was rather of a remote nature.[152] Where such influence can be spotted, the impact was of rather indirect nature.[153] In contrast to other legislative projects of the late medieval period, the Code of the Realm provided the framework for the application of law for more than 400 years.[154] The result was a unique legal culture (concerning both the institutional and intellectual structures). Hence, in the case of Norway, having been labelled a mixed legal system, the "mixed" qualification *explains* very little: institutional resemblances with civil law and common law systems are more or less coincidental and often a result of more practical needs than based on conscious decisions to implement common or civil law elements into Norwegian Law.

The impression that the "mixed" qualification is a result of a very specific development and dynamic can be further supported by taking into account taking into account

146 Kenneth Reid, "The Idea of Mixed Legal Systems" (2003) Vol. 78 *Tulane Law Review* 5 ff.; Vernon Valentine Palmer (ed), *Mixed Jurisdictions Worldwide* (2nd ed., Cambridge University Press 2012); Ibid., "Mixed Legal Systems – The Origin of the Species" (2013) Vol. 28 *Tulane European and Civil Law Forum* 103; interestingly, Palmer does not count the Nordic Legal Systems among the "mixed systems".

147 Ibid. 112 ff. with further references.

148 Critical to the concept of "pure law", see Vernon Valentine Palmer, "Mixed Legal Systems … and the Myth of Pure Laws" (2006) Vol. 67 *LA. Law Review* 1205.

149 Palmer (2013) (n. 146) 105, referring to the Oxford-educated Scotsman and Dean of the McGill law faculty in Quebec as being the first to have shown particular interest in these systems.

150 Jørn Øyrehagen Sunde, "Daughters of God and the Counsellors of the Judges of Men: Changes in the Legal Culture of the Norwegian Realm in the High Middle Ages" in Stefan Brink and Lisa Collinson (Eds.), *New Approaches to the Early Law in Scandinavia* (Brepolis 2014) 131.

151 Sunde (2010) (n. 134) 103 ff.; Sunde, (2014) (n. 150) 133 ff.

152 Sunde, (2014) (n. 150) 168 ff.

153 Ibid.

154 The Code of the Realm by King Christian the V's New Norwegian Code of 1687 was formally abandoned. In 1604, King Christian IV had already enacted an officially revised Danish translation of the Code of 1274, which originally was written in the Old Norwegian language of the Vikings (*norrønt*).

the history of Scotland, another representative of a "mixed legal system".[155] Importantly, there is not necessarily a commonality among so-called mixed legal systems. This becomes obvious when comparing the very different legal cultures of Scotland, Norway and South Africa. In other words, the term "mixed legal systems" is a catch-all category that encompass all legal systems that cannot be explicitly located in the civil or common law tradition.[156] Siems suggests the term "hybrid systems" as potentially preferable.[157] Still, the term hybrid also had its origins in biology and indicates a interspecies relationship. As shown above, such relationships are often constructed rather than based on historical developments. Regardless of the label that one puts on legal systems, the discussion here and among legal comparatists illustrates the difficulties with and eventually limitations to all attempts to classify entities such as legal systems and legal cultures.

Another distinction, which has become more popular recently, is that of Western and Non-Western law including *inter alia* Oriental law, Islamic law and Hindu law.[158] Critics of the traditional functional approach have made us aware that comparative studies have long been dominated by researchers coming from the Western legal tradition and have therefore been biased by underlying ideas developed by Christian and Enlightenment thinkers based on a joint intellectual heritage dating back to Greek, Roman and Natural law philosophy, including concepts such as nation-state, democracy, capitalism, liberalism and individualism.[159] The elements of the legal cultural model, on the other hand, are not based on a specific tradition and do not depend on particular philosophical assumptions. Consequently, comparing legal cultures based on functional meta-categories or building blocks such as norm production or legal method might contribute to the avoidance of culturally biased perceptions of foreign law. The focus on the building blocks of the legal cultures included in this volume allows us to apply a more nuanced approach by showing that legal cultures often are impacted by or resemble features of different legal traditions. Further, despite members of legal families sharing intellectual and institutional structures, significant legal cultural differences can be identified among them as well.

Finally, the proposed approach allows us to take a reflective stand on questions of convergence, namely the merging of legal cultures due to international cooperation and transnationalisation of law. A high degree of internationalisation in combination with a positive attitude toward international impulses seem to facilitate these tendencies. Similarly, the cultural approach allows one to critically evaluate opposite tendencies related to cultural relativism and separatism, which emphasise the impossibility of legal transplants and convergence.[160]

155 Reid (2003) (n. 146) 7 ff.

156 Siems (2018) (n. 5) 101: "However, following the focus of traditional comparative law on common and civil law, the term "mixed legal systems" is often limited to legal systems which have been strongly influenced by both of these legal families."

157 Siems (2018) (n. 5) 101 ff. refers to hybrid as a broader concept compared to mixed legal systems, and distinguishes further between horizontally (104) and vertically (106) divided legal systems.

158 Van Hoecke (2015) (n. 19) 5 ff.

159 Siems (2018) (n. 5) 78 f.

160 See above.

5. Legal cultural knowledge as a point of departure

It is essential to realise that the articles published in this volume are just a point of departure, or as Sunde puts it, a very rough map which gives the reader an often-generalised impression of a given legal culture by describing some significant landmarks. This is the precondition for comparing these features. Accordingly, the LCM is an intellectual tool that helps to systematically collect and present information on legal cultures in a way that enables us to identify similarities and differences and more importantly, to explain them contextually by *inter alia* analysing the interplay between the legal cultural elements. For example, all legal cultures presented in this book emphasise that supreme court rulings are recognised as important for the way lawyers build their arguments. However, different styles of framing the underlying reasons for judgments impact the role of these rulings in legal argumentation.[161] The concise syllogism traditionally applied by the French *Cour de cassation* in combination with a high number of rulings this court produces each year, make its rulings less suitable for being recognised as strictly binding precedents compared to the more comprehensive account of both the underlying facts and reasons provided in the judgments of the UK Supreme Court or the Norwegian Supreme Court.[162] In addition, the latter two supreme courts hand down a considerably lower number of rulings each year,[163] which makes it easier to review the case law of these courts. The general competence of both courts to deal with all kinds of legal matters, compared to the higher degree of specialisation in continental supreme courts facilitates the binding nature of these judgments.[164] However, because no principle of *stare decisis* is recognised in Norway,[165] where Supreme Court rulings are recognised as one of several (in theory equally ranged) legal sources,[166] the method of distinguishing has a less prominent place in the Norwegian legal methodology.[167] Thus, the interplay between court structure, caseload of the court, style of reasoning, methodological approach, and degree of specialisation all impact and are at the same time a framework for the underlying theory of legal sources. Analysing a legal culture with

161 An analysis of the different structures and styles of court rulings in England, Germany and Norway resembling the different ideals of justice in these countries is provided in the following chapter.

162 See Bragdø-Ellenes (2020) (n. 35) 486; Franklin (2020) (n. 32) 352; Kjølstad, Koch and Sunde (2020) (n. 131) 111.

163 Franklin (2020) (n. 32) 347 f.; Kjølstad, Koch and Sunde (2020) (n. 131) 111.

164 On the high degree of specialization in German courts, see Koch (2020), "An Introduction to German Legal Culture" (n. 34) 229 ff. For a different type of specialization in France, see Bragdø-Ellenes (2020) (n. 35) 474.

165 Kjølstad, Koch and Sunde (2020) (n. 131) 253.

166 Ingvill Helland and Sören Koch, "Introduction to Norwegian Legal Method" in Ingvill Helland and Sören Koch (Eds.), *Nordic and Germanic Legal Methods* (Mohr Siebeck 2014) 123.

167 Kjølstad, Koch and Sunde (2020) (n. 131) 131; Ingvill Helland and Sören Koch, "Norwegian and German Legal Methods Compared" in Ingvill Helland and Sören Koch (Eds.), *Nordic and Germanic Legal Methods* (Mohr Siebeck 2014) 300 ff.

the help of the LCM can help to find an explanation for particular features and notions of a legal system and the law it produces.[168]

Furthermore, comparing legal cultures with the help of the LCM allows us to draw analytical conclusions based on empirical data rather than subjective experience when speaking about something as vague as a legal culture. The model enables us to explore central features of a foreign legal culture and their interplay, *without* requiring a complete immersion, which is to be assimilated by or at least deeply familiar with the foreign legal culture.[169] The LCM contributes to understanding legal cultures on their own terms and preconditions.[170] It thus produces general knowledge and understanding of how the law is applied (socio-legal comparative law),[171] which can be used to identify meaningful objects of comparison and to avoid biased assumptions or conceptual confusion. Still, this does not mean that a legal cultural perspective exclusively focuses on differences between legal cultures or even advocates a cultural relativism.[172] Instead, applying the LCM enables us to identify both similarities and differences *and* to explain them contextually.[173]

However, it would be misleading to assume that comparative analysis based on the LCM is limited to comparing similar general features in different legal cultures. This kind of macro-perspective is indeed very helpful for conducting comparative studies, but is as a rule not the overall objective of the comparatist. Often, the aim is to answer a specific question relating to the role, function or effect of legal rules, principles or institutions. Consequently, applying a legal cultural perspective by recognising similarities and differences among legal cultures, is not *exclusively* a choice of method, but rather a framework for the individual comparative study including the method applied therein. This framework allows to systematically enhance the knowledge and understanding of legal cultures, which in its turn is a necessary precondition for developing a critical and

168 A similar observation has been made by Mark Van Hoecke, *Law as Communication* (Hart Publishing 2002) 5 ff. emphasising the role of the way lawyers communicate law in institutional forms. John Bell, on the other hand, promotes the idea that law is a social institution, see "The Importance of Legal Institutions" in Maurice Adams and Dirk Heirbaut (Eds.), *The Method and Culture of Comparative Law* (Hart Publishing 2014) 207 ff. If we want to understand "the distinct features of a legal system, then we need to focus on the nature of law as a social institution", by emphasising that law is best seen not only as legal norms, but as part of the institutional context in which they are embedded – the organisations, procedures, personnel, and ethos which make it work. In other words, ideas and expectations of law made operational in an institutional (like) practice.

169 On immersion, see Vivian Grosswald Curran, "Cultural Immersion, Differences and Categories in U.S. Comparative Law" (1998) Vol. 6 Issue 1 *American Journal of Comparative Law* 43, who stated, however, that a complete immersion is, at least for lawyers educated in a different legal culture, almost impossible to achieve.

170 For John Bell, this is a necessary precondition to undertake comparative studies, see *Judiciaries Within Europe: A Comparative Review* (Cambridge University Press 2006) 41.

171 Emphasising the anthropological foundations of this approach, Siems (2018) (n. 5) 118; Sunde (2010) (n. 3) 26; Sally Engle Merry, "What is Legal Culture? An Anthropological Perspective" (2010) Vol. 5 Issue 2 *Journal of Comparative Law* 40, 42.

172 Warning against such a relativism, Mankowski (2016) (n. 15) 524 f. An example of a rather pessimistic view is Teubner (1998) (n. 110).

173 Örücü (2007) (n. 5) 50: "In order to fulfill the requirements of scholarly comparative research, both similarities and differences must be considered."

reflective attitude when conducting comparative legal studies. Regardless of whether the researcher's question concerns the micro, meso or macrolevel, a deeper understanding of a legal culture's general features helps us to conduct comparative analysis based on a proper inherent understanding or "Vorverständnis".[174] It allows to ask the right questions and can help, *inter alia*, to identify functional similarities or to plainly recognise that similarly phrased legal rules, principles and institutions can fulfil different functions.[175] At the same time, it helps to understand the limitation caused by differences in language, terminology and mentalities, which are inflicted upon all (legal) comparisons.

6. Conclusion

Summing up, comparing general features of legal cultures provides us with a better understanding for the institutional and intellectual *context* of law in the selected legal cultures. This allows to identify both similarities and differences and to analyse the internal interplay between the different, legal cultural elements and is an essential prerequisite for performing comparative analysis. However, the LCM does not provide a guideline on how to conduct and structure comparative studies. The COMPASS formula, which is presented in more detail the following chapter, is a suitable tool for this task. A sufficient degree of knowledge and understanding for the legal cultures under examination enables comparatists framing both the research question in accordance to their cognitive interest, choosing the object and determining the objective of the comparison as well as choosing the individual methodological approach to this end.

7. Bibliography

Arold, NL, *The Legal Culture of the European Court of Human Rights* (Nijhoff 2007).

Arold, NL, "The Melting Pot or the Salad Bowl Revisited – Rendezvous of Legal Cultures at the European Court of Human Rights" in Skodvin, KE and Sunde, JØ (Eds.), *Rendezvous of European Legal Cultures* (Fagbokforlaget 2010).

Bell, J, "The Importance of Legal Institutions" in Adams, M and Heirbaut, D (Eds.), *The Method and Culture of Comparative Law* (Hart Publishing 2014).

Bell, J, *Judiciaries Within Europe: A Comparative Review* (Cambridge University Press 2006).

Blankenberg, E, "Patterns of Legal Culture: The Netherlands Compared to the Neighboring Germany" (1998) 46 *American Journal of Comparative Law* 1.

Boucht, J, "Introduction to Finnish and Swedish Legal Method" in Helland, I and Koch, S (Eds.), *Nordic and German Legal Methods* (Mohr Siebeck 2014).

Brennecke, M, *Judicial Law Making in English and German Courts, Techniques and Statutory Interpretation* (Intersentia 2018).

174 Similarly, Van Hoecke (2004) (n. 52) 165 ff.

175 Siems (2018) (n. 5) 119 with reference to the research of Richard Hyland.

Cotterrell, R, "Comparative Law and Legal Culture" in Reimann, M and Zimmermann, R (Eds.), *The Oxford Handbook of Comparative Law* (2nd ed. Oxford University Press 2019).

Cotterrell, R, "The Concept of Legal Culture" in Nelken, D (Ed.), *Comparing Legal Cultures* (Aldershot 1997).

Curran, VG, "Cultural Immersion, Differences and Categories in U.S. Comparative Law" (1998) Vol. 6 Issue 1 *American Journal of Comparative Law* 43.

de Cruz, P, *Comparative Law in a Changing World* (2nd ed. Cambridge University Press 2007).

Ehrmann, HW, *Comparative Legal Cultures* (Englewoods Cliff 1976).

Ervo, L, "Nordic Court Culture in Progress: Historical and Futuristic Perspectives" in Ervo, L and Nylund, A (Eds.), *The Future of Civil Litigation* (Springer 2014).

Foljanty, L, "Legal Transfer as Process of Cultural Translation: On Consequences of a Metaphor" in *Max Planck Institute for European Legal History Paper* Series No. 2015-09.

Franklin, C, "The Melting Pot or the Salad Bowl Revisited (again) – Rendezvous of Legal Cultures at the European Court of Justice" in Skodvin, KE and Sunde, JØ (Eds.), *Rendezvous of European Legal Cultures* (Fagbokforlaget 2010).

Friedman, L, "Legal Culture and Social Development" (1969) Vol. 6 *Law and Society Review* 19.

Friedman, L, "The Concept of Legal Culture: A Reply" in Nelken D (Ed.), *Comparing Legal Cultures* (Aldershot 1997).

Friedman, L, "The Place of Legal Culture in the Sociology of Law" in Freeman M (Ed.) *Law and Sociology* (Oxford University Press 2006.)

Gessner, V, "Global Legal Interaction and Legal Cultures" (1994) Vol. 7 *Ratio Legis* 132.

Glenn, PH, "Legal Culture and Legal Traditions" in Van Hoecke M (Ed.), *Epistemology and Methodology of Comparative Law* (Hart Publishing 2004).

Glenn, PH, *Legal Traditions of the World* (Oxford University Press 2000).

Glenn, PH, *Legal Traditions of the World: Sustainable Diversity* (5th ed., Oxford University Press 2014).

Grødeland, ÅB, *European Legal Cultures in Transition* (Cambridge University Press 2015).

Helland, I and Koch, S, "Comparing Legal Methods – an Analytical Framework" in Helland, I and Koch, S (Eds.), *Nordic and Germanic Legal Methods* (Mohr Siebeck 2014).

Helland, I and Koch, S, "Introduction to the Norwegian Legal Method" in Helland, I and Koch, S (Eds.), *Nordic and German Legal Methods* (Mohr Siebeck 2014).

Helland, I and Koch, S, "Norwegian and German Legal Methods Compared" in Helland, I and Koch, S (Eds.), *Nordic and Germanic Legal Methods* (Mohr Siebeck 2014).

Helleringer, G and Purnhagen, G (Eds.), *Towards a European Legal Culture* (Nomos 2014).

Hesselink, MW, "The New European Legal Culture" in Hesselink, MW (Ed.), *The New European Private Law: Essays on the Future of Private Law in Europe* (Kluwer Law 2002).

Holmøyvik, E, "A little bit of This and a little bit of That – the Complexity of Legal Reception" in Skodvin. KE and Sunde, JØ (Eds.), *Rendezvous of Legal Cultures* (Fagbokforlaget 2010).

Husa, J, "About the Methodology of Comparative Law – Some Comments Concerning Wonderland", http://www.law.unimaas.nl/maastrichtworkingpapers (accessed 17.04.2020) (2007).

Husa, J, "Farewell to Functionalism or Methodological Tolerance" (2003) Vol. 67 No. 3 *Rabel Journal of Comparative and International Law (Rabel)* 419.

Husa, J, "Macro Comparative Law – Reloaded" (2018) Vol. 131 No. 4 *Tidsskrift for Rettsvitenskap* 410.

Husa, J, "The Future of Legal Families" in Reimann, M and Zimmermann, R (Eds.), *The Oxford Handbook of Comparative Law* (2nd ed., Oxford University Press 2019).

Husa, J, *A New Introduction to Comparative Law* (Bloomberg 2015).

Jansen, N, "Management of Another's Affairs without a Mandate" in Basedow, J. et al., *The Max Planck Encyclopedia of European Private Law*, Vol. II (Oxford University Press 2012).

Kamba, WJ, "Comparative Law, A Theoretical Framework" (1974) *International Comparative Law Review Quarterly* 23.

Kaser, M, *Römische Rechtsquellen und angewandte Juristenmethode* (Böhlau 1986).

Kischel, U, *Rechtvergleichung* (Mohr Siebeck 2015).

Koch, S, "Consequences of changing expectations to law and its institutions. Illustrated by the role and background of judges in Norway" (2015) Vol. 83 No. 3–4 *The Legal History Review* 461.

Koch, S, *Unaufgeforderte Hilfeleistung in Notsituationen: Eine rechtshistorische und rechtsvergleichende Studie zu den zivilrechtlichen Aspekten der Nothilfe mit besonderer Berücksichtigung des Rechts der Geschäftsführung ohne Auftrag* (Peter Lang 2011).

Legrand, P, "European Legal Systems are not Converging" (1996) Vol. 45 Issue 1 *International and Comparative Law Quarterly* 52.

Lundmark, T, *Charting the Divide Between Common and Civil Law* (Oxford University Press 2012).

Mallat, C, "Comparative Law and the Islamic (Middle Eastern) Legal Culture" in Reimann, M. and Zimmermann, R (Eds.), *The Oxford Handbook of Comparative Law* (2nd ed. Oxford University Press 2019).

Mankowski, P, *Rechtskultur* (Mohr Siebeck 2016).

Merry, SE, "What is Legal Culture? An Anthropological Perspective" (2010) Vol. 5 Issue 2 *Journal of Comparative Law* 40.

Merry, SE, "What is Legal Culture? An Anthropological Perspective" in Nelken, D (Ed.), *Using Legal Culture* (Wildy, Simmonds and Hill 2012).

Michaels, R, "The Functional Method of Comparative Law" in Reimann, M and Zimmermann, R (Eds.), *The Oxford Handbook of Comparative Law* (2nd ed., Oxford University Press 2019).

Nelken, D, "Defining and Using the Concept of Legal Culture" in Örücü, E and Nelken, D (Eds.), *Comparative Law – A Handbook* (Hart Publishing 2007).

Nelken, D, "Puzzling out Legal Culture: A Comment on Blankenburg" in Nelken, D (Ed.), *Comparing Legal Cultures* (Aldershot 1997).

Nelken, D, "Thinking About Legal Culture" (2014) Vol. 1 *Asian Journal of Law and Society* 255.

Palmer, VV (Ed.), *Mixed Jurisdictions Worldwide* (2nd ed., Cambridge University Press 2012).

Palmer, VV, "Mixed Legal Systems – The Origin of the Species" (2013) *Tulane European and Civil Law Forum* 28.

Palmer, VV, "Mixed Legal Systems … and the Myth of Pure Laws" (2006) Vol. 67 *LA. Law Review* 1205.

Radbruch, G, *Einführung in die Rechtswissenschaft* (9th ed., Mohr Siebeck 1958).

Reid, K and Zimmermann, R, *A History of Private Law in Scotland* Vol. II (Oxford University Press 2001).

Reid, K, "The Idea of Mixed Legal Systems" (2003) Vol. 78 *Tulane Law Review* 5.

Reimann, M and Zimmermann, R (Eds.), *The Oxford Handbook of Comparative Law* (2nd ed., Oxford University Press 2019).

Riesenhuber, K, *European Methodology – Grundfragen der Methoden des Europäischen Privatrechts* (De Gruyter 2006).

Riles, A, "Comparative Law and Socio-Legal Studies" in Reimann, M. and Zimmermann, R (Eds.), *The Oxford Handbook of Comparative Law* (2nd ed., Oxford University Press 2019).

Rüthers, B, "Welcher Methodenkonon sollte für die Rechtsprechung verbindlich sein?" in Hähnchen, S (Ed.), *Methodelehre zwischen Wissenschaft und Handwerk* (Mohr Siebeck 2019).

Sacco, R, "Legal Formants. A Dynamic Approach to Comparative Law" (1991) 30 *American Journal of Comparative Law* 1 and 343.

Samuel, G, "What is Legal Epistemology" in Heribaut, D and Adams, M (Eds.), *The method and culture of comparative law* (Hart Publishing 2014).

Schauenburg-Müller, S, "On Danish Legal Method" in Helland, I and Koch, S (Eds.), *Nordic and Germanic Legal Methods* (Mohr Siebeck 2014).

Schieck, D, "Comparative Law and European Harmonisation: A Match Made in Heaven or Uneasy Bedfellows?" (2010) Vol. 21 *European Business Law Review* 203.

Siems, M, *Comparative Law* (2nd ed., Cambridge University Press 2018).

Smits, JM (Ed.), *Elgar Encyclopedia of Comparative Law* (Edward Elgar 2006).

Stoljar, SJ, "Negotiorum Gestio" (1984) 17 Vol. X *International Encyclopedia of Comparative Law.*

Sunde, JØ, "Champagne at the Funeral. An Introduction to Legal Culture" in Sunde, JØ and Skodvin, KE (Eds.), *Rendezvous of European Legal Cultures* (Fagbokforlaget 2010).

Sunde, JØ, "Daughters of God and the Counsellors of the Judges of Men: Changes in the Legal Culture of the Norwegian Realm in the High Middle Ages" in Brink, S and Collinson, L (Eds.), *New Approaches to the Early Law in Scandinavia* (Brepolis 2014).

Sunde, JØ, *Speculum legale – rettsspegelen* (Fagbokforlaget 2005).

Teubner, G, "Legal Irritants: Good Faith in British Law or How Unifying Law Ends Up in New Divergence" (1998) Vol. 61 *Modern Law Review* 11.

Van Hoecke, M and Warrington, M, "Legal Cultures, Legal Paradigms and Legal Dogmatics: Towards a New Model for Comparative Law" (1998) Vol. 47 *The International and Comparative Law Quarterly* 495.

Van Hoecke, M, "Deep Level Comparative Law" in Van Hoecke, M (Ed.), *Epistemology and Method of Comparative Law* (Hart Publishing 2004).

Van Hoecke, M, "Für eine europäische Juristenausbildung" *Juristenzeitung* (1990).

Van Hoecke, M, "Methodology of Comparative Research" in Van Hoecke M (Ed.), *Law and Method* (2015).

Vogenauer, S, *Die Auslegung von Gesetzen in England und auf dem Kontinent* (Mohr Siebeck 2001).

Von Benda-Beckmann, F and Von Benda-Beckmann, K, "Why Not Legal Culture?" in Nelken, D (Ed.), *Using Legal Culture* (Wildy, Simmonds and Hill 2012).

Whitman, JQ, "Comparative Law and Religion" in Reimann, M and Zimmermann, R (Eds.), *The Oxford Handbook of Comparative Law* (2nd ed., Oxford University Press 2019).

Wieacker, F, "Foundations of European Legal Culture" (1990) Vol. 38 *American Journal of Comparative Law* 1.

Wieacker, F, "Grundlagen der Rechtskultur" in Jørgensen, S (Ed.), *Tradition and Progress in Modern Legal Cultures* (Franz Steiner Verlag 1985).

Zimmermann, R, "Savigny's Legacy: Legal History, Comparative Law and the Emergence of a European Legal Science" (1996) Vol. 112 *Law Quarterly Review* 576.

Zimmermann, R, *The law of Obligations: Roman Foundations of the Civilian Tradition* (Clarendon Press 1996).

Zweigert, K and Kötz, H, *An Introduction to Comparative Law* (3rd ed. Clarendon Press 1998).

Örücü, E, "Developing Comparative Law" in Örücü, E and Nelken, D (Eds.), *Comparative Law – A Handbook* (Hart Publishing 2007).

Örücü, E, "Family trees for Legal Systems: Towards a Contemporary Approach" in Van Hoecke, M (Ed.), *Epistemology and Methodology of Comparative Law* (Hart 2004).

Örücü, E, "Methodology of Comparative Law" in Smits, JM (Ed.), *Elgar Encyclopedia of Comparative Law* (Edward Elgar 2006).

Örücü, E and Nelken, D, *Comparative Law – A Handbook* (Hart Publishing 2007).

4. From mapping to navigation – a COMPASS formula for Conducting Comparative Analysis

Sören Koch

1. Introduction

So far, we have learned that it is possible to analyse features of a legal culture by applying an operationalised concept of legal culture transferred into a legal cultural model (LCM). The LCM is an intellectual tool that helps to systematically collect and present information on legal cultures in a way that enables us to identify similarities and differences and, more importantly, to explain them contextually by *inter alia* analysing the interplay between the legal cultural elements.[1] However, the LCM does not provide a guideline of how to compare features in different legal cultures.

So, how exactly do we conduct comparative analyses based on legal cultural knowledge and understanding? In the following section, I attempt to give a tentative answer by introducing a seven-step formula, organised in a hermeneutical circle. To keep with the analogy of navigating, let us use the acronym COMPASS.[2] Even though the formula has been developed to serve as a guideline for legal cultural comparison and will be illustrated by using examples from the contributions of this book, its scope of application is not limited to the comparative studies based on the legal cultural approach. COMPASS provides a blueprint or roadmap for all kinds of comparative studies, regardless of the

1 Jørn Øyrehagen Sunde', 'Managing the Unmanageable – An Essay Concerning Legal Culture as an Analytical Tool' in this volume, chapter 2; Sören Koch, 'Legal Culture and Comparative Law – Diving into the Ocean' in this volume, chapter 3; Jørn Øyrehagen Sunde, 'Champagne at the Funeral – An Introduction to Legal Culture' in Knut Einar Skodvin and Jørn Øyrehagen Sunde (eds), *Rendezvous of European Legal Cultures* (Fagbokforlaget 2010) 11 ff.

2 After working on my model for years, I became aware that the consulting-platform Hofstede Insights provides a service labelled "The Culture compass" (cf. https://hi.hofstede-insights.com/the-culture-compass accessed 12 April 2020). Purpose, function and the intended audience of this tool differs considerably form the compass-formula presented in this article. It tries to uncover differences in cultural-based behavior patterns in order to provide guidance in professional relations but has no particular focus on "legal culture". Still, it is noteworthy that a consulting firm regards analyzing cultural difference as a key factor for economic success. Consequently, there seems to be a demand for a cultural compass both in economic and legal relations.

comparatists' epistemological interest, the specific purpose and object of comparison or the methodological approach chosen for the study. Furthermore, COMPASS describes a hermeneutical operation that aims to be effective on all levels of comparison (macro, meso, micro, surface or deep level).

The way of conducting a comparative analysis is, as has been shown above,[3] highly dependent on the epistemological interest, purpose and interests of the comparatist.[4] However, this does not mean that we cannot give any form of generalised guideline.[5] If we acknowledge that such a guideline needs to be formulated in abstract categories, certain universal elements can be identified. These are presented here as 'steps' organised in a chronological order.[6] As a rule, all comparative investigations can be said to consist of seven basic steps.[7] These steps ought to be applied regardless of the individual epistemological interest, the specific purpose of the comparison or the person/institution conducting comparative studies. I will describe each step in rather abstract terms first. However, in order to move beyond a mere theoretical and abstract presentation, I have chosen to illustrate these steps with the help of specific examples. The question of lay participation in court, particularly in criminal proceedings, will frequently be referenced. Recently, this topic has been discussed and analysed comparatively by international and national courts, legislative bodies, and individual scholars alike.[8] In addition, several contributions in this volume have addressed the relationship between professional and lay judges.[9] My purpose is to show that the

---

3 See Sören Koch, 'The outset – how to learn sailing the ocean of legal cultures' in this volume, chapter 1.

4 Therefore, Jaakko Husa promotes a flexible understanding of comparative methodology and distinguishes between four ideal types of interests of knowledge, see 'About the Methodology of Comparative Law: Some Comments Concerning the Wonderland…', *Maastricht Working Papers* 2007 Issue 5, p. 19, available at http://works.bepress.com/jaakko_husa/3/ accessed 12 December 2019. See as well Esin Örücü, 'Developing Comparative Law' in Esin Örücü and David Nelken, *Comparative Law. A Handbook* (Hart Publisher 2007) 48.

5 Providing guidelines for legal comparative research is a rather common topic in textbooks or introductory articles on comparative law. See Konrad Zweigert and Hein Kötz, *An Introduction to Comparative Law* (3rd edn, Clarendon Press 1998) 11, proposing five steps; Mathias Siems, *Comparative Law* (2nd edn, Cambridge University Press 2018) 15, proposing a four-step approach, with somewhat more general guidelines; Husa (2007) (n 4) 19 f.

6 For a similar terminology see Örücü (2007) (n 4) 49. However, Örücü does not present a comprehensive analytical model.

7 An alternative approach has been presented by Peter de Cruz, *Comparative Law in a Changing World* (2nd edn, Cavendish Publishing Ltd 1999) 235–239: 1. Action plan for identifying the underlying social, legal or policy problem; 2. Choice of the jurisdiction and legal family it belongs to; 3. Choice of the primary sources of law; 4. Gathering and assembling the empirical material; 5. Systematizing the materials; 6. Using the findings (if possible) to answer the initial research question; 7. Critically analyzing the legal principles according to their intrinsic meaning; 8. Presenting the conclusion(s) if necessary with caveats concerning cultural differences.

8 In contrast to Mark Van Hoecke, 'Methodology of Comparative Legal Research' (2015) *Law and Method* 1, this chapter does not focus exclusively on scholarly comparative legal research but attempts to show that also other legal actors conduct comparative legal analyses.

9 Anna Nylund, 'An Introduction to Finnish Legal Culture' in this volume, chapter 6, 164; Lloyd T. Wilson, Jr., 'A View of the Legal Culture of the United States of America' in this volume, chapter 17, 652; Christian N.K. Franklin, 'A Legal Cultural "Take" on the Legal System of England & Wales" in this volume, chapter 11, 342 ff.; Sören Koch, 'An Introduction to German Legal Culture' in this volume, chapter 8, 235 f.; Bruno Debaenst, 'An Introduction to the Belgian Legal Culture' in this volume, chapter 12, 449; Marius Mikkel Kjølstad, Sören Koch and Jørn Øyrehagen Sunde, 'Introduction to Norwegian Legal Culture' in this volume, chapter 5, 112 f.; Anna Klimaszewka, Anna Machnikowska and Sören Koch, 'An Introduction to Polish Legal Culture' in this volume, chapter 9, 276.

legal cultural perspective, applied in accord with our theory, has been or could have been applied in order to enhance the validity and legitimacy of individual arguments and conclusions. Finally, other examples from the previous chapters will be employed to illustrate how legal cultural knowledge can be utilised in the analytical process described by the COMPASS-formula.

2. The COMPASS-formula

In short, the seven steps of the COMPASS-formula are:[10]

1. **C**reating a *research question* or *hypothesis* in concordance with the overall *epistemological interest of the research*, followed by defining both the
2. ***O****bjects* and *objectives* of the comparison, including the choice of jurisdictions, cultures, subcultures, institutions, rules, principles etc. under comparison. On this basis we need to design a suitable
3. ***M****ethod* for conducting a comparison serving the overall purpose, the specific problem which suits the objects and objectives of comparison.
4. **P**inpointing both *similarities* and *differences*,
5. ***A****ssessing* and *explaining* the observed similarities and differences,
6. ***S****ystematising* and critically *scrutinising* the comparative findings in order to answer the research question/verify or falsify the initial hypothesis.
7. **S**tarting all over again by *adapting* the research question and *critically reviewing* all other subsequent steps in light of the findings.

The first three steps constitute the preparatory stage, while the following steps are part of the application stage. Note that all dialectical models are always idealised reproductions or illustrations of a more complex reality.[11] This applies also to the COMPASS formula. Conducting comparative research is rarely a straight-forward process without setbacks. Often the researcher must go back and reinterpret or adjust initial assumptions or even dismiss or reformulate the research question. Jaakko Husa therefore spoke of a hermeneutical spiral and correctly observed that any "comparative study is in a continuous

10 These steps can also be formulated as questions: 1. What is my general research interest and what do I want to find out in particular? 2. Why and to what end will I use comparative analysis in my study and what is the object of my comparison, which jurisdictions/cultures/subcultures/institutions/field of law are relevant for the comparison? 3. What is the best methodological approach to reach my goal and what kind of materials should be included in the survey? 4. Comparing the objects selected, what are similarities and differences between the relevant legal entities under comparison? 5. How can the empirical findings be assessed, explained and contextualised? 6. How can we best systematise the findings. Taking into consideration the systemised empirical findings, what does this mean for the initial research question / does the material support the initial hypothesis? 7. Does the findings invite modifying the hypothesis, research-question or methodological approach?

11 See Sunde (2020) (n 1) 23 ff.

epistemological stir."[12] Consequently, conducting comparative research is a hermeneutical process. However, in order to present the different steps of the process in a structured and pedagogical manner, a hermeneutical circle seems a suitable illustration. COMPASS takes the imperfect and heuristic nature of comparative research into account as well. The last step invites the comparatist to critically re-consider all previous steps in light of the findings. The research-question (based on the epistemological interest) is the start and endpoint of this analytical operation. Experience shows that the outcomes of such an operation are very often the origin of new questions and hypotheses forcing the researcher to reconsider her initial assumptions and expectations.[13] Occasionally, the researcher will have to adjust her perceptions concerning own legal culture or law as well.[14]

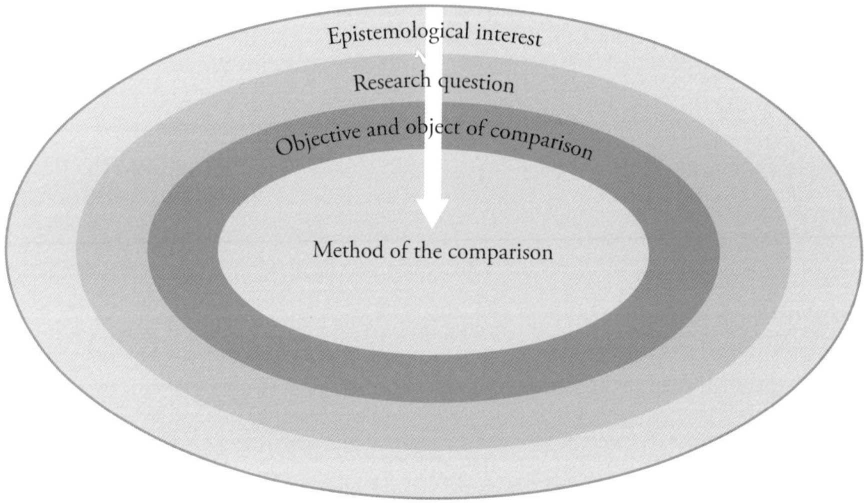

Fig. 1 The preparatory stage – epistemological and methodological considerations.

12 Jaakko Husa, 'Research Designs of Comparative Law – Methodology or Heuristics?' in Maurice Adams and Dirk Heirbaut (eds), *The method and culture of comparative law. Essays in honour of Mark Van Hoecke* (Hart Publishing 2014) 54.

13 See in more detail Step 7.

14 Emphasising the increasing importance of cross-border communication and the need for legal cultural understanding in order to facilitate communication Ingvill Helland and Sören Koch, 'Comparing Legal Methods – an Analytical Framework' in Ingvill Helland and Sören Koch (eds), *Nordic and Germanic Legal Methods* (Mohr Siebeck 2014) 2 f. and 8 ff.

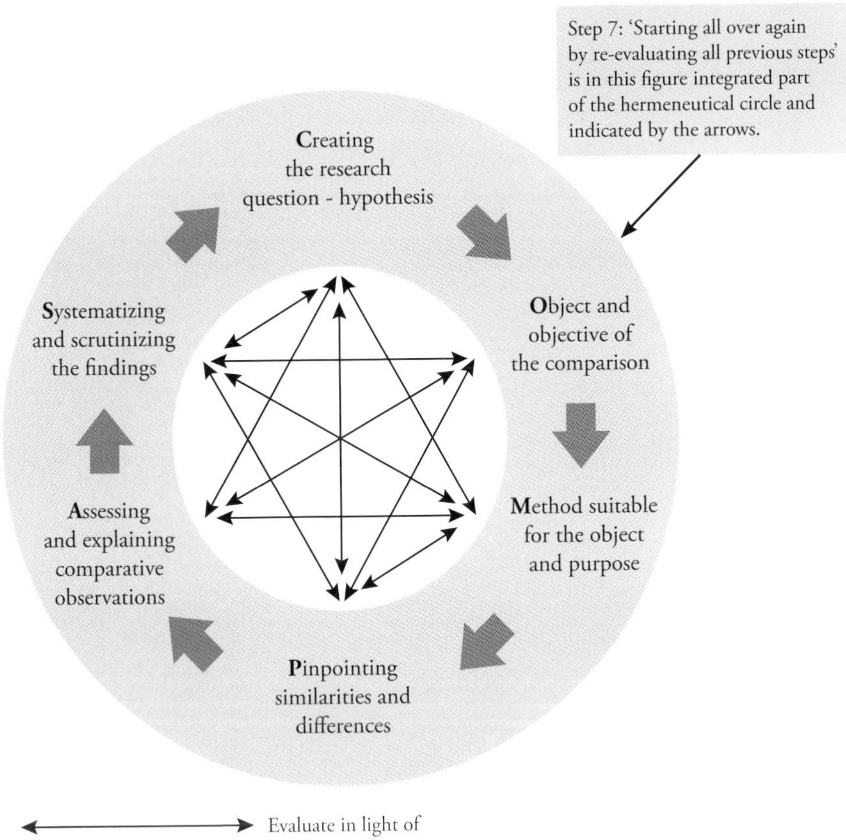

Fig. 2 The hermeneutical circle.

Step 1: Concretising the Research Question

In a constantly more globalised word, it is not difficult to find good reasons for analysing more or less any given legal topic comparatively,[15] at least if one wants to achieve a deeper understanding of the law, its intended and actual effects and its cultural embeddedness. However, this task requires that the researcher ask herself what *precisely* she wants to achieve – what is the comparatist's own epistemological interest.[16] Is the purpose to solve a specific legal dogmatic problem in the national legal order, to draft new or amend existing legislation, to harmonise the law in different legal orders, or to academically explain similarities and differences among them? Consequently, and common to all sci-

15 Örücü (2007) (n 4) 44: "It has become indispensable for all doctoral researchers, judges and legislators to consult foreign materials as a matter of routine."

16 Husa (2014) (n 12) 55.

entific surveys, the overall epistemological interest is the source from which a particular **research question** or **working hypothesis** emerges.[17] The question may concern the content and effect of domestic, international or even transnational law.[18] For example: can the victim of a negligently conferred tort claim compensation for frustrated expenses (e.g. the costs of a theatre ticket)? How is this legal problem solved in Germany, Austria, and Norway?[19] Are there legal grounds to claim compensation for expenses frustrated due to a general closedown caused by a pandemic? Or the researcher might be interested in the structure, work or efficiency of legal institutions[20] or their way of applying the law.[21] For instance, how do different legal jurisdictions handle access to justice[22] or use analogy to develop the law?

Neither the question nor the hypothesis has to be genuinely comparative in nature. For example, a legislator could use comparative analysis to consider whether to introduce, extend, abolish or limit lay participation in court in the national legal system. Particularly when looking for inspiration, a comparative perspective seems expedient to find a solution for a problem that is insufficiently regulated by national law. Such a question can be raised by an individual scholar or a group of scholars, but also a court or a legislative body.

If we use the problem of lay participation in criminal justice as an example, we can observe that both international and national courts as well as legislative bodies have used comparative observations in their reasoning.[23] Driven by the desire to involve citizens in the administration of justice,[24] many legal orders have established certain forms of lay participation. In several jurisdictions the question whether the accused is guilty or not

17 Zweigert and Kötz (1998) (n 5) 34.

18 E.g. Reinhard Zimmermann, *Comparative Foundations of a European Law of Set-Off and Prescription* (Cambridge University Press 2002).

19 Such a comparative study has been presented by Sören Koch, *Der Ersatz frustrierter Aufwendungen im norwegischen Recht* (Peter Lang 2011); Sören Koch, 'Erstatning for bortkastede utgifter' (2012) No. 05 *Tidsskrift for Rettsvitenskap* 581.

20 E.g. Anna Nylund, 'Comparing the Efficiency and Quality of Civil Justice in Scandinavia: The Role of Structural Differences and Definitions of Quality' (2019) Vol. 38 No. 4 *Civil Justice Quarterly* 427.

21 E.g. Ingvill Helland and Sören Koch, 'Norwegian and German Legal Methods Compared' in Ingvill Helland and Sören Koch, *Nordic and Germanic Legal Methods* (Mohr Siebeck 2014) 267–322; Stefan Vogenauer, *Die Auslegung von Gesetzen in England und auf dem Kontinent* (Mohr Siebeck 2001); Martin Brenncke, *Judicial Law-Making in English and German Courts – Techniques and Limits of Statutory Interpretation* (Intersentia 2018); Stefan Vogenauer, *Die Auslegung von Gesetzen in England und auf dem Kontinent*, (Mohr Siebeck 2001).

22 In 2013 the United Nations Principles and Guidelines on Access to Legal Aid in Criminal Justices Systems were published, see http://www.unodc.org/documents/justice-and-prison-reform/UN_principles_and_guidlines_on_access_to_legal_aid.pdf accessed 1 April 2020. To what extent these principles are implemented in different countries can be of interest for both NGO's, national governments, international or supranational organizations, academics, but also private investors wondering to what extent the rule of law has been implemented in various countries.

23 On the use of comparative law by courts see Ulrich Drobnig and Sjef van Erp (eds), *The Use of Comparative Law by Courts* (Kluwer 1999); Kanstantsin Dzehtsiarou, 'Comparative Law in the Reasoning of the European Court of Human Rights' (2010) Vol. 10 *University College Dublin Law Review* 104. On comparative law in the legislative process see David Louis Finnegan, 'Applied Comparative Law and Judicial Reform' (2006) Vol. 8 Thomas M. Cooley *Journal of Practical and Clinical Law* 97.

24 *Taxquet v Belgium* App no. 926/05 (ECtHR Grand Chamber, 16 November 2010) para. 83.

is decided by a jury. As a rule, the jury is under no obligation to provide reasons for its verdict. The jury simply answers "yes" or "no". In Europe, this gives rise to the question if and under which circumstances such a procedure constitutes a violation of the right to a fair trial pursuant to Article 6 of the European Convention on Human Rights. This question is of general academic interest but became highly relevant for "law in action" in the famous case *Taxquet v Belgium*.[25] The accused, Mr. Taxquet, claimed this procedure would render it impossible for him to understand why he was found guilty. Based on a comparative investigation of different ways of organising jury-systems and the relevant procedural rules in several countries, the Grand Chamber of the European Court of Human Rights (ECtHR) ruled that Belgium had violated the accused's basic right to a fair trial pursuant to Article 6 of the European Convention on Human Rights (ECHR) in this case.[26]

A different, though related question is whether the verdict of the ECtHR could be invoked by convicts who are sentenced based on a jury-decision in a third country, e.g. Norway before 2018. Despite the constitutional issue of the extent to which national courts are obliged to implement rulings of the ECtHR that do not directly concern their own legal subjects,[27] a comparative dimension became relevant here too. The question was, is the national criminal procedure organised in a way that does not violate ECHR Article 6 although the jury did not give reason for its decision in such a third country's jurisdiction. Answering this question requires comparing this country's jury system and criminal procedures with the Belgian one. The Norwegian Supreme Court was faced with this task a couple of years ago. We shall see how the court approached this task in more detail later.[28]

In the aftermath of the abovementioned decisions by the ECtHR and the Norwegian Supreme Court, a legislative committee was appointed to consider whether to recom-

---

25 On the background of the case and its effects on the Belgium legal culture, see Debaenst (2020) (n 9) 446.

26 In *Taxquet v Belgium*, the ECtHR expressly rejected this. The court states in para. 83: "The Court notes that several Council of Europe member States have a lay jury system, guided by the legitimate desire to involve citizens in the administration of justice, particularly in relation to the most serious offences. The jury exists in a variety of forms in different States, reflecting each State's history, tradition and legal culture; variations may concern the number of jurors, the qualifications they require, the way in which they are appointed and whether or not any forms of appeal lie against their decisions (see paragraphs 43–60 above). This is just one example among others of the variety of legal systems existing in Europe, and it is not the Court's task to standardise them. A State's choice of a particular criminal-justice system is in principle outside the scope of the supervision carried out by the Court at European level, provided that the system chosen does not contravene the principles set forth in the Convention."

27 On this see Ingvill Helland, *Rulings of the European Court of Human Rights as a Legal Argument – a Comparison between Norwegian and German Law* (PhD thesis, University of Bergen 2012) 149 ff.

28 See e.g. the judgment of the Norwegian Supreme Court in Rt. 2009 p. 750, especially para. 37 ff. and the parallel ruling of the same day in Rt. 2009 p. 773. Interestingly, this ruling came before the final Grand Chamber ruling cited above. However, the Supreme Court discussed at length the chamber ruling by the ECtHR in *Taxquet v Belgium* (n 24). On the reactions to this first ruling in favour of *Taxquet* in Norway, see Asbjørn Strandbakken, 'Juryen for fall? Noen refleksjoner etter Taxquet vs. Belgia' (2009) Vol. 35 No. 1 *Kritisk Juss* 101; Inge Lorange Backer, 'Feller Den europeiske menneskerettsdomstol juryen?' (2009) No. 3 *Tidsskrift for strafferett* 301; Magne Strandberg, 'Oversikt over empirisk forskning om lekdommere', published as a attachement to NOU 2011: 13 Juryutvalget: Når sant skal skrives.

mend the amendment or abolishment of the jury system in Norway.[29] This committee built on comparative considerations too, and so did scholars critically reviewing this legislative process.[30] Observing that lay participation in courts is organised differently in Belgium, Norway, France, England, Germany, and other jurisdictions can hence be relevant for international and national courts, in the legislative process, and in academic discourse. We shall see that all these institutions and actors have used comparative analysis to provide arguments for answering very different **questions** related to the same topic.

Step 2: Object and objective of the comparison

Once the overall aim of the individual investigation has been defined, the second step is to identify thoroughly the **object and objective of the comparison** as part of the research design. This can of course be regarded as a methodological choice. However, for pedagogical reasons, it may be useful to distinguish between the choice of object (what do I want to compare?), purpose or objective (why do I want to compare these objects?) and the comparative method applied in order to conduct a comparison (how do I compare these objects in order to achieve my objective?). Admittedly, there is a strong correlation between all these questions. The choice of object and objective is therefore an important methodological question and determines, but also limits, the choices of method(s) in a narrower sense considerably. For example, analysing the mentality of judges (objective/object) may require sociological or anthropological methods,[31] while comparing the efficiency of tax-regulations in selected countries (objective/object) probably will be best served by a law and economic approach.[32]

---

29 NOU 2011: 13 Juryutvalget: Når sant skal skrives. The committee was split: a majority was in favour of pursuing the jury-system with some amendments (*lagrettefraksjon*), whereas the minority recommended a system with co-judges (*meddomsrettsløsning*).

30 E.g. Anders Løvlie, 'En kort innføring i NOU 2011: 13 Juryutvalget – Når sant skal skrives' (2011) Vol. 37 No. 4 *Kritisk Juss* 252. Lars-Jonas Nygard, 'Juryen for fall?' (2011) Vol. 37 No. 4 *Kritisk Juss* 259. Svein Magnussen, Dag Erik Eilertsen, Karl Halvor Teigen, Ulf Stridbeck og Ellen M. Wessel, 'En kvantitativ studie av sikkerhet i bevisvurdering i straffesaker hos norske fagdommere og lekdommere' (2014) Vol. 127 No. 3–4 *Tidsskrift for Rettsvitenskap* 384. A critical response to these empirical observations is provided by Leif Petter Olaussen, 'Concordance between Actual Level of Punishment and Punishments suggested by Lay People – but with less use of Imprisonment' (2014) Vol. 2 No. 1 *Bergen Journal of Criminal Law and Criminal Justice* 69; Leif Petter Olaussen, 'Holdbart – utover rimelig tvil? Noen kommentarer til en enkeltstudie' (2016) Vol. 129 No. 1 *Tidsskrift for Rettsvitenskap* 74.

31 E.g. using interviews, Sir Basil Markensis, 'Judicial Mentality: Mental Disposition or Outlook as a Factor Impeding Resource to Foreign Law' (2006) 80 *Tulane Law Review* 1325; James L. Gibson, 'Judges' Role Orientations, Attitudes, and Decisions: An Interactive Model' (1978) Vol. 72 No. 3 *The American Political Science Review* 911; Brian Flanagan and Sinéad Ahern, 'Judicial Decision-Making and Transnational Law: A Survey of Common Law Supreme Court Judges' (2011) Vol. 60 No. 1 *International and Comparative Law Quarterly* 1; Nina-Louisa Arold, 'The Melting Pot or the Salad Bowl Revisited – Rendezvous of Legal Cultures at the European Court of Human Rights' in Jørn Øyrehagen Sunde and Knut Einar Skodvin (eds), *Rendezvous of European Legal Cultures* (Fagbokforlaget 2010) 61 ff.; Christian Franklin, 'The Melting Pot or the Salad Bowl Revisited (again) – The meeting of Legal Cultures at the European Court of Justice' in Knut Einar Skodvin and Jørn Øyrehagen Sunde (eds), *Rendezvous of European Legal Cultures* (Fagbokforlaget 2010) 77 ff.

32 N. H. D. Foster, 'Comparative Commercial Law' in Esin Örücü and David Nelken (eds), *Comparative Law: A Handbook* (Hart Publisher 2006).

Mathias Siems distinguished between three main objectives of comparative studies: 1. knowledge and understanding, 2. practical use at the national level, and 3. practical use at the international level.[33] Other scholars such as Patrick Glenn and Esin Örücü have presented distinctions that are more sophisticated, but that basically contain the same elements.[34] In the abovementioned example, comparative observations were used by the ECtHR to solve the jury case according to international law, the Norwegian Supreme Court used comparison to solve a case on the national level, while legal scholars and the legislative body mainly built on a comparative knowledge to enhance the understanding of the national criminal procedure and its relationship to international law regimes.

Taking a closer look reveals that knowledge and understanding are important preconditions for the practical use both on the national and international level too.[35] Enhancing knowledge and understanding is therefore, in my view, the purpose of all legal comparison, regardless of the particular function it is supposed to serve and regardless of who performs it. For all kinds of comparative studies, comparative knowledge is essential, while its use may differ according to the specific purpose of the comparison.

Knowing how many European countries have adopted a jury system may be interesting but is of little help when trying to solve the abovementioned questions legal scholars, legislative committees or national and international courts had to address. Understanding the historical and socio-cultural context of the jury, its establishment and function, on the other hand, allows the comparatist to draw reflected conclusions, e.g. when considering variables comparing the Norwegian jury to institutions in other countries such as Belgium, England, or the US. The functions of a body of layman may differ depending on the institutional and intellectual preconditions in different legal cultures.[36] One may ask how jury members are appointed and by whom. Moreover, the competences of a jury may vary rather considerably. In some legal orders juries are used both in civil and criminal matters and have comprehensive competences regarding even the application of law.[37] In other legal cultures the competences of a jury are strictly lim-

33 Siems (2018) (n 5) 2.

34 H. Patrick Glenn, 'The Aims of Comparative Law' in Jan M. Smits (ed), *Elgar Encyclopedia of Comparative Law* (Edward Elgar 2006) 58–60 distinguishes between: 1. Comparative law as instrument of learning and knowledge; 2. Comparative Law as an instrument of evolutionary and taxonomic science; 3. Contributing to one's own legal system; 4. Harmonisation of law. Örücü (2007) (n 4) 53–56 lists: 1. Improvement and consolidation of knowledge; 2. Grouping of legal systems in order to understand changes that take place during the moving of institutions; 3. Broadening the minds of students and development of tolerance; 4. Using comparative law research in legislative law reforms; 5. Interpretation-tool for judges by making them aware of foreign solutions to similar problems; 6. Helping to interpret international conventions and agreements; 7. Harmonisation of law by identifying the 'better law'.

35 Similarly, Van Hoecke (2015) (n 8) 16–18.

36 See Wilson (2020) (n 9) 652 ff., emphasising the constitutional embeddedness of institution of juries in the US Constitution.

37 Ibid.

ited, or its verdict can be revoked by professional judges.[38] Some countries have chosen to opt for a cooperative solution where layman and professional judges rule together on facts,[39] but sometimes on the legal aspects of the case as well.[40] In this case it may be important to consider the relationship between layman and professional judges. Does the professional or layman have the majority and does this proportion change depending on the character of the crime or whether the case is treated in first instance or by an appellate court?[41] It is often the comparatist's task to identify such differences when determining the object of comparison. The LCM is a tool that helps to find answers to all of these questions, and more importantly to connect the dots helping to achieve a deeper understanding of the legal cultural context.

Another important choice the researcher must make at this stage is which jurisdictions to include in the survey.[42] This is an essential part of selecting the object of comparison. Picking jurisdictions is once again highly dependent on what the researcher tries to achieve and what the initial research question is. If the aim is to study the possibility of harmonisation of a law in Europe,[43] it seems redundant to include case law or legal doctrine from non-European jurisdictions in the research. Accordingly, the research object holds an important limitation regarding the empirical material. However, the legal discourse outside of Europe may be an important source of inspiration, as long as the researcher is conscious of differences related to the cultural context in which legal ideas are developed and operate.

Still, conducting a comprehensive survey on relevant regulations, case law, doctrinal works, and other fields than law throughout Europe may prove difficult if not impossible for an individual researcher. This difficulty, not only due to the variation of languages and legal systems within the territory of the EU/EEA but also due to the fact that such a comprehensive investigation would require enormous financial and human resources. Such comparative projects therefore often require research networks or teams of researchers. Alternatively, the researcher can limit the research to selected jurisdictions using the findings to elaborate on a provisional model, which in a second step can be

38 This was the case in Norway before the abolishment of the jury system in 2018. Cf. Lov 1981-05-22-25 om rettergangsmåten i straffesaker (straffeprosessloven) [the Criminal Procedural Act] §§ 352 ff., amended by Lov 2017-06-16-58 om endringer i straffeprosessloven mv. (oppheving av juryordningen) [Act on the Abolishment of the Jury], in force since 1 January 2018.

39 E.g. in England, cfr. Franklin (2020) (n 9) 342 f.

40 See e.g. in Germany, cfr. Koch (2020), 'German Legal Culture' (n 9) 234.

41 Comparing the situation in Norway and Germany after the abolishing the jury-system in 2018 shows interesting differences in this regard. In both countries the legislator has opted for a cooperation model, but in Germany, lay judges are in the minority in the appellate court and in cases which are treated by a *Schöffengericht* in first instance. In Norway, with its strong tradition for lay participation in criminal proceedings, the legislator has made sure that the number of laymen in the relevant procedures always exceeds the number of professional judges in the appellate courts as well. However, there are no lay judges in the Supreme Courts in both countries.

42 Siems (2018) (n 5) 17.

43 E.g. John Bell and David Ibbetson, *European Legal Development: The Case of Tort* (Cambridge University Press 2012).

tested in other jurisdictions and against other fields than law.[44] However, when developing such a provisional model, the researcher must carefully select the jurisdictions included in the pilot study.[45] Comparing only jurisdictions with similar socio-economic preconditions or based on a common legal tradition may render biased results. Consequently, taking the wider cultural context into consideration is already important at this early stage. The basic information on the economic, political, and social situation as well as the geographical position of each legal culture at the beginning of each chapter of this book may provide a point of orientation, helping the researcher to explore further information necessary to make her choice.

On the other hand, there may be good reasons to limit the comparison to just one or very few jurisdictions, or jurisdictions with rather similar legal cultures.[46] In the Nordic countries it is quite common for legal scholars to take the neighbouring countries' solutions for legal dogmatic problems into account when systematising and developing their own legal doctrine. Almost all legal dogmatic dissertations submitted in Bergen from 1969 until 2018 contain these kinds of comparative remarks.[47] As a rule, the authors did not spend considerable energy in explaining the historical, cultural or economic context, but focused on a more traditional black-letter-law comparison.[48] This could be regarded as acceptable due to the rather similar legal cultural structures in the Nordics. Still, as can be witnessed by reading the chapters on Finland and Norway,[49] the lack of an administrative court hierarchy in Norway and differences in the ideal of justice and the legal methodology may render it necessary to take a closer look if the comparison is related to these notions.

Another question is which entities and sources shall be included into the comparison.[50] Often the laws of different nations will be feasible choices (not necessarily states – e.g. Scotland and England are [still] part of the United Kingdom but have distinct legal systems and laws).[51] Also here referring to legal cultures may be a more appropriate and precise distinction. However, international and supra-national laws, institutions or legal

44 Sören Koch, *Compilation as a Technique for Disseminating Legal Knowledge in the Early Modern Period* (Olin Foundation, forthcoming).

45 Ibid. suggesting that a comparison of legal cultures such as Norway and Scotland would be an ideal starting point for developing an analytical framework for studying the nature and impact of legal compilations in the early modern period.

46 This has been stressed particularly for functional studies with the purpose of harmonising the law, see Örücü (2007) (n 4) 55. Husa (2014) (n 12) 58 distinguished between bilateral and multilateral comparative law. However, a limitation to rather similar legal cultures may be feasible whenever one wants to identify differences based on structural and terminological rather than different cultural preconditions, cf. Nylund (2019) (n 20) 427.

47 Sören Koch, 'Den "moderne resepsjonen" – Internasjonaliseringen i undervisning og forskning mellom 1969 og 2003' in Johan Giertsen, Berte-Elen Reinertsen Konow, Erling Johannes Husabø and Øystein L. Iversen (eds), *Rett i vest – Festskrift til 50-årsjubileet for juristutdanningen ved Universitetet i Bergen* (Fagbokforlaget 2019) 74 f.

48 Ibid.

49 Chapter 5 and 6 in this volume.

50 Örücü (2007) (n 4) 56 noted that distinguishing between macro and micro level is highly important in this regard.

51 Therefore, this volume contains separate chapters on England & Wales (Chapter 11) and Scotland (Chapter 10).

actors and their attitudes can also be included or the main object of comparison.[52] Furthermore, the researcher has to decide whether the object of comparison is exclusively contemporary law or shall include historical sources as well.[53]

In many cases, external limiting factors can be decisive such as language, accessibility of information, and funding but not least the interest of the comparator.[54] Once again the objective of the comparison is decisive. Finding the "best" or "most efficient" solution for a social problem requires the researcher to compare rules and legal institutions that serve a more or less similar function.[55] If the purpose is to analyse the meaning of an abstract concept such as "ownership", doctrinal and philosophical works or court and administrative practice seem relevant objects in addition to legislative regulations.[56] Such analytical approaches to comparative law will often benefit from considering the historical and philosophical discourse.[57]

Precisely identifying the object of comparison also helps to avoid ending up comparing incomparable things. When comparing legal norms, the functional approach may serve as an appropriate point of departure. However, when the objective of comparison is to evaluate the role of specific legal institutions and their place in a given legal culture, the functional approach may prove insufficient. For example, the question could be raised whether a narrow functional comparison of different jury systems for severe criminal cases in different legal orders would be sufficient to find arguments for or against a violation of the fair trial principle or the amendment or even abolishment of such a jury system in a national legal system. The ECtHR indirectly acknowledges this when accepting legal cultural differences as a reason to limit the scope of its own

---

52 This has become particularly important for those analyzing the emergence of a transnational legal order and those analyzing the impact of international and supra-national institutions on the national legal cultures and legal systems see e.g. Paul Schiff Berman, *Global Legal Pluralism: A Jurisprudence of Law Beyond Borders* (Cambridge University Press 2012); Gralf-Peter Callies and Peer Zumbansen, *Rough Consensus and Running Code: A Theory of Transnational Private Law* (Hart Publishing 2010).

53 Siems (2018) (n 5) 17 further mentioned the comparison between contemporary and past law (diachronic comparison). See also Husa (2014) (n 12) 59 f.

54 Siems (2018) (n 5) 19.

55 Örücü (2007) (n 4) 55.

56 Van Hoecke (2015) (n 8) 12; T. K. Ahn, Loukas Balafoutas, Mongoljin Batsaikhan, Francisco Campos-Ortiz, Louis Putterman and Matthias Sutter, 'Securing property rights: A dilemma experiment in Austria, Mexico, Mongolia, South Korea and the United States', (2016) Vol. 143 *Journal of Public Economics* 115; Aikaterini Mandalaki, 'Critical Comments on the Ownership of Lands and Agricultural Laws in Ancient Greece', (2019) 8 *Legal Roots: the International Journal of Roman Law, Legal History and Comparative Law* 43; Judith Schacherreiter, *Das Landeigentum als Legal Transplant in Mexico* (Mohr Siebeck 2014); Eva-Maria Kieninger, 'Sachenrechtliche Prinzipien und Grundbegriffe als Gegenstand der Rechtsvergleichung' in Reinhard Zimmermann (ed), *Zukunftsperspektiven der Rechtsvergleichung* (Mohr Siebeck 2016).

57 Very early Wesley Newcomb Hohfeld, *Fundamental Legal Conceptions as applied in Judicial Reasoning* (Yale University Press 1919; reprint Greenwood Press 1978) 15 ff.; More recently Masha Antokolskaia, *Harmonisation of Family Law in Europe: A Historical Perspective* (Intersentia 2006). From a historical perspective Sören Koch, 'Consequences of changing expectations to law and its institutions. Illustrated by the role and background of judges in Norway' (2015) Vol. 83 No. 3–4 *The Legal History Review* 461 ff.

jurisdiction.[58] Here, our legal cultural perspective may help in establishing an alternative basis for a fruitful comparison.

By acknowledging that juries are part of the institutional mechanism of conflict resolution in some countries such as the US, England, Belgium, and Norway (before 2018),[59] but not or no longer recognised in the legal orders of e.g. Germany, Romania, and Norway (since 2018),[60] it might be necessary to extend the object of comparison to other forms of lay participation in court. The ECtHR did such an investigation in the *Taxquet* judgment. In the ruling, the court identified three types of countries: those with a jury system, those acknowledging other types of lay participation, and those where only professional judges rule in ordinary courts of justice. However, such an empirical observation is of little help when considering the question whether the mere existence of a jury constitutes a violation of Article 6 ECHR or whether the jury should be abandoned e.g. in Norway. Simply counting the number of legal orders acknowledging a jury in criminal cases and comparing it to the number of those who have not, is hardly any reasonable basis for a policy decision.[61] More interesting from a policy perspective is the question *why* different legal cultures have developed different types of lay participation. Is the institutionalised practice founded on a particular legal mentality and is the institutional framework similar to or rather different from the jurisdiction under investigation? However, before answering these questions one must analyse the extent to which the solutions in different legal cultures actually vary.

Step 3: Methodological Approach (in a narrow sense)

This requires that the comparatist choose his or her **methodological approach** for identifying and explaining similarities and differences, that is, the way the comparison will be conducted. Again, this approach must be chosen by considering the initial epistemological interest and precise question, as well as the objective and the object of comparison. As explained above, these can vary considerably. Therefore, it is not reasonable or even possible to speak about '*the* method of comparative law'.[62] There are countless

58 See *Taxquet v Belgium* (n 24) para. 83.

59 Cf. Wilson (2020) (n 9) 652; Franklin (2020) (n 9) 342; Debaenst (2020) (n 9) 445; Kjølstad, Koch and Sunde (2020) (n 9) 111 ff.

60 Cf. Koch (2020), 'German Legal Culture' (n 9) 231; Cosmin Dariescu, 'An Introduction to Romanian Legal Culture' in this volume, Chapter 16, 612; Kjølstad, Koch and Sunde (2020) (n 9) 112 f.

61 However, looking at the work of the Study Group on a European Civil Code one sometimes gets the impression that the sheer quantitative measurement was regarded decisive in order to consider a legal institute such as the Roman law-based principle of *negotiorum gestio* (Benevolent Intervention into Another's Affairs) a necessary part of the soft law instrument of the Draft Common Frame of Reference, cf. Book V Chapter 1 of the DCFR.

62 Arguing for methodological pluralism Örücü (2007) (n 4) 52 ff.; Husa (2007) (n 4) 18; Van Hoecke (2015) (n 8) 8; Husa (2014) (n 12) 56. Today, this can be described as the mainstream in scholarly textbooks on comparative law. Explicitly Michele Graziadei, 'The functionalist heritage' in Pierre Legrand and Roderick Munday (eds), *Comparative Legal Studies: Traditions and Transitions* (Cambridge University Press 2003) 101; Jaakko Husa, 'Farewell to Functionalism or Methodological Tolerance?' (2003) Vol. 67 No. 3 *Rabel Zeitschrift für ausländisches und internationales Privatrecht* 446.

approaches, from the more traditional functional approach to empirical and numerical ones.[63] Mark Van Hoecke distinguished between these methods: functional, structural, analytical, law in context, historical, and common core-method.[64] Geoffrey Samuel further acknowledged that there are different epistemological approaches[65] or "schemes of intelligibility" as he calls them: causal, functional, structural, hermeneutical, actional, and dialectical.[66] In addition, postmodern, contextual, gender, transnational, global, universal or regional perspectives have recently been introduced to the comparative discourse.[67] Siems provided a comprehensive overview of many different approaches, their advantages and also their shortcomings.[68] An important methodological challenge is the question of how to identify and measure similarities and differences empirically.[69] Quantitative methods are suitable for identifying and measuring both similarities and differences on the institutional and intellectual level.[70] In particular, they may be feasible for analysing the impact of foreign legal ideas,[71] function and changes of legal transplants,[72] or the quality and efficiency of legal rules and institutions.[73] Interestingly, the methodological approach applied in a comparative study is often not made explicit, either because this seems obvious, or because the comparison also lacks a clear meth-

63 Siems (2018) (n 5) part II, 113 ff.

64 Van Hoecke (2015) (n 8) 8–21 with several examples.

65 On the question of epistemology of comparative law, see Mark Van Hoecke, 'Deep Level Comparative Law', in Mark Van Hoecke (ed), *Epistomology and Method of Comparative Law*, (Hart Publishing 2004) 165 ff.; Geoffrey Samuel, 'What is Legal Epistemology?' in Maurice Adams and Dirk Heirbaut (eds), *The Method and Culture of Comparative Law* (Hart Publishing 2014) 23.

66 Geoffrey Samuel, *An Introduction to Comparative Law Theory and Method* (Hart Publishing 2014) 81.

67 Comprehensive overviews can be found in Siems (2018) (n 5); Uwe Kischel, *Comparative Law* (Oxford University Press 2019) Chapter 3; Husa (2014) (n 12) 60 ff.

68 Siems (2018) (n 5) 31–49; 113–146; 156–179.

69 Siems (2018) (n 5) 182 ff. and with several examples 52 ff.; Stefan Vogenauer, *Civil Justice Survey* (2008); Stefan Vogenauer, 'Regulatory Competition Through Choice of Contract Law and Choice of Forum in Europe: Theory and Evidence' (2013) Vol. 21 No. 1 *European Review of Private Law* 13; Naomi Creutzfeldt, 'How Important is Procedural Justice for Consumer Dispute Resolution? A Case Study of an Ombudsman Model for European Consumers' (2014) Vol. 37 *Journal of Consumer Policy* 523.

70 Madhav S. Aney, Shubhankar Dam and Giovanni Ko, 'Jobs for Justice(s): Corruption in the Supreme Court of India', 2017, available at https://papers.ssrn.com/sol3/papers.cfm?abstract_id=3087464 accessed 29 March 2020.

71 Antokolskaia (2006) (n 57) 27 emphasised that there is a perceived subjectivity of comparative observations, which can best be countered by applying empirical research methods. A method that can be used is cross-citation practice between courts, see Mathias Siems, 'Citation Patterns of the German Federal Supreme Court and of the Court of Appeal of England and Wales' (2010) Vol. 21 *King's Law Journal* 152.

72 For a summary on the debate on legal transplants, see Mathias Siems, 'The Curious Case of Overfitting Legal Transplants' in Maurice Adams and Dirk Heirbaut (eds), *The Culture and Method of Comparative Law* (Hart Publishing 2014) 136 ff.; David Cabrelli and Mathias Siems, 'Convergence, Legal Origins, and Transplants in Comparative Corporate Law: A Case-Based and Quantitative Analysis' (2015) Vol. 63 No. 1 *American Journal of Comparative Law* 109. An interesting cultural perspective was applied by Lena Foljanty, 'Legal Transfers as Processes of Cultural Translation: on the Consequences of a Metaphor' *Max Planck Institute for European Legal History Research Paper Series* No. 2015-09.

73 See e.g. Nylund (2019) (n 20); Mathias Siems, 'Numerical Comparative Law: Do we need Statistical Evidence in Law in Order to Reduce Complexity?' (2005) Vol. 13 *Cardozo Journal of International & Comparative Law* 521; Siems (2018) (n 5) 207 ff. with further references.

odological framework. Furthermore, a lack of knowledge concerning the structural and institutional practices may cause the investigation to go astray when analysing efficiency and quality of civil justice based on formal definitions and criteria, which do not resemble the diversity of institutionalised practices.[74]

For example, applying a functional approach to the question concerning lay juries stated above would exclusively require focusing on institutions including laypersons deciding serious criminal cases. The observation that juries in the US often decide on *civil matters*[75] or that lay judges are commonly used in proceedings related to *minor* criminal offences in England[76] and Germany[77] are irrelevant from a mere functional perspective. If one applies a cultural perspective by actively taking the cultural context into account as well, e.g. by extending the comparative research to the broader topic of lay participation in ordinary courts and their constitutional, historical and socio-legal preconditions, this might give us some indication of the general attitude towards lay participation in these legal cultures. Lloyd T. Wilson Jr. emphasised in his contribution to this volume the strong constitutional embeddedness of lay participation and the underlying perception of a strong democratic legitimisation as two main factors for the particular role of this institution in the US legal culture.[78] In Romania[79] and Italy,[80] with their strong roots in the civilian legal tradition and a highly professionalised judiciary, or in Germany with a high degree of specialisation of judges and a strong focus on intersubjectivity of law, we can register a more reluctant attitude towards lay participation in court.[81] This allows us to *explain* contextually why a certain legal culture is more open or reluctant to the idea of letting laypersons judge on the facts of a case or even on the law itself. Taking into account other cultural factors such as confidence in the courts,[82] the prevailing ideal of justice and the methodological approach or the attitude towards democratic elements in the judici-

74 Nylund (2019) (n 20) 438. In this direction also Erhard Blankenburg, 'Patterns of Legal Culture: The Netherlands Compared to the Neighboring Germany' (1998) Vol. 46 Issue 1 *The American Journal of Comparative Law* 1, who applied a concept of legal culture that does not include institutional elements. However, the differences he observed are mainly due to structural differences, and to a lesser degree to difference in mentality. Challenges of numerical comparison are also addressed by Marco Fabri, 'Methodological Issues in the Comparative Analysis of the Number of Judges, Administrative Personnel, and Court Performance Collected by the Commission for the Efficiency of Justice of the Council of Europe' (2017) Vol. 7 No. 4 *Oñati Socio-Legal Studies* Series 616.

75 See Wilson (2020) (n 9) 652.

76 See Franklin (2020) (n 9) 342.

77 See Koch (2020), 'German Legal Culture' (n 9) 231 f.

78 See Wilson (2020) (n 9) 652 f.

79 See Dariescu (2020) (n 60) 613.

80 See Esmeralda Colombo and Lars Kvestad, 'An Introduction to the Italian Legal Culture' in this volume, Chapter 15, 481.

81 See Koch (2020), 'German Legal Culture' (n 9) 232.

82 The European Network of Councils for the Judiciary (ENCJ), 'Public Confidence and the Image of Justice', ENJC Report 2017–2018 provided empirical data on the European levels on public confidence in the courts. Available at https://www.encj.eu/node/480 accessed 25 January 2020. This volume's contributions on the Norwegian on the one hand and the French and the Polish legal cultures on the other hand provide a legal cultural explanation for the different degrees of confidence in the judiciary in these countries.

ary and balance of power, will enable us to better understand the complex interplay between intellectual and institutional structures of a legal culture. Such an in-depth understanding of law based on its historical, social, economic, and political context is especially important for academics and legislative bodies when developing policy considerations or discussing the law *de lege ferenda*. This example highlights again the intrinsic interdependency between purpose, object and method.

When deciding individual cases, such a contextual understanding seems at first glance of limited importance. In *Taxquet*, the Grand Chamber of ECtHR made initially clear that it is outside the scope of its jurisdiction to evaluate the member states' choice of a particular criminal justice system.[83] Furthermore, the Court emphasised that it is not its task to standardise these systems. Concerning the establishment of a jury (with or without the obligation to provide an explanation for the verdict), the Court held that the states have a rather broad margin of appreciation.[84] Nevertheless, the reason for such a statement was founded on an empirical comparison of institutional differences between the member states and other jurisdictions provided earlier in the judgment.[85] Based on this material the Court concluded in its final assessment that the court recognises "a legitimate desire to involve citizens in the administration of justice, particularly in relation to the most serious offences." More importantly, however, the court expressly recognised the existence of variations, "reflecting each State's history, tradition and legal culture, […]."[86] In other words, the ECtHR chose to focus on institutional variations (research object), stating that a member state's choice of establishing a jury does not *per se* violate the Convention. Intellectual structures of the member states' legal cultures, such as the prevailing ideal of justice or the attitude towards professionalisation, especially regarding the administration of justice in court, were not the object nor the objective of the comparative observations in the judgment.

The Norwegian Supreme Court's challenge was slightly different. Tacitly accepting that the institution of a jury itself posed no violation of the Convention,[87] it had to find reasons why the institutional ways under which a jury operated in Norway differed considerably from the procedure that was used in the *Taxquet* case in Belgium. Accordingly, the object of the comparison was the specific procedure applied in the relevant case heard by the Supreme Court and the procedure in cases where the ECtHR had found the jury verdict violated Article 6.[88] In contrast to the ECtHR, the task of the Norwegian Supreme Court thus required a focus on quite a *different* object of comparison and accordingly a different method. The court had to consider whether the Norwegian jury system provided sufficient mechanisms to satisfy the requirements outlined by the

83 *Taxquet v Belgium* (n 24) para. 83.
84 Ibid. para. 84.
85 Ibid. para. 43–60.
86 Ibid. para. 83.
87 Rt. 2009 p. 750, especially para. 83.
88 Ibid. para. 62 ff., 77 and 83.

ECtHR in the *Taxquet* case.[89] Consequently, the judges looked for functional and legal similarities and differences in the institutionalised procedures in Norway and Belgium. The legislative committee in Norway was interested in the historical development of juries and alternative forms of lay participation in courts in different legal cultures and applied a historical and contextual approach. However, neither the ECtHR, the Norwegian Supreme Court nor the legislative committee were explicit about their methodological agenda and approach. In academic analysis it seems necessary to describe and legitimise the methodological choices.

Step 4: Pinpointing and identifying similarities and differences

The next step in the process is to **pinpoint** and **identify similarities and differences** according to the methodological approach chosen previously. With this step, the researcher establishes the empirical basis for the comparative analysis. Identifying similarities and differences is often the most time-consuming part of the study. However, the more precise the object of comparison has been defined, and the more precise the comparative method is formulated, and the less the risk of comparing apples and oranges. Depending on the researcher's epistemological position (pessimistic or optimistic)[90] and the purpose of the research (distinguishing, classification or harmonisation) the emphasis of the comparison can be identifying similarities or differences, or both. Generally, a preoccupation with one of the two should be avoided as this may give rise to the objection of a biased approach, lacking intersubjectivity and scientific objectivity.[91] The legal cultural approach presented in this book aims to enhance understanding for both the uniqueness of legal cultures and the differences between them. At the same time, the LCM allows the comparatist to identify institutional and intellectual similarities. These can appear in the form of legal transplants,[92] hybrid-institutions[93] but also as a result of the interaction and convergence of legal cultures.[94] The operationalised elements in the

89 Ibid. para. 62.

90 Husa (2018); Van Hoecke (2015) (n 8).

91 Örücü (2007) (n 4) 50.

92 E.g. the Federal Constitutional Court in Germany was established with the US Supreme Court as a role model. This does not, however, mean that the legal transplant was an exact copy of the US institution nor that the court developed identically functions, attitudes or position in the German legal culture. Rather, the FCC functions in a modified way suitable for the particular preconditions and demands of the German legal culture. See Lena Foljanty, *Recht oder Gesetz. Juristische Identität und Autorität in den Naturrechtsdebatten der Nachkriegszeit* (Mohr Siebeck 2013).

93 An example of that is the institutionalized legislative cooperation between the Nordic counties in the 20th century, resulting in harmonized legislation such as the Nordic Sales of Goods Acts. See Ole Lando, 'Nordic Uniform Act on the Law Applicable to International Sales of Goods' (1966) Vol. 15 Issue 4 *The American Journal of Comparative Law* 806.

94 Franklin (2020) (n 9) 363 emphasised the increasing importance of statutory law in the English legal culture, while Colombo and Kvestad (2020) (n 80) 554 maintained that in Italy, due to the increasing importance of case law, an attenuated 'stare decisis principle' has been acknowledged. In many other contributions of this book we find further

legal cultural model enable us to identify notions of a common origin, similar effects, or functional equivalents despite dogmatic or conceptual differences.[95] Furthermore, it can help to identify elements (e.g. similar/identical terminology, institutional frameworks, substantive principles, constitutional values, etc.) that seem similar but in fact have a different content, function or effect. Recognising such hidden differences is crucial for conducting a valid functional comparison of for example substantive legal rules of constitutional law[96] or a legal doctrinal institution such as the principle of *negotiorum gestio*/benevolent intervention into another's affairs.[97]

The role of lay participation in court may illustrate this. All states in the US have a jury system inspired by the English jury model. As the American jury system has its roots in the English legal system, this is not surprising. However, comparing the rules governing juries in the US and England *today* reveals rather significant differences regarding the competences and functions of juries.[98] Indeed, taking the wider context and historical development of the juries into account enables us to understand when changes occurred and most importantly why that happened. Considering the impact and effect of these changes on both the intellectual and institutional level of the LCM may provide us with an even deeper understanding of the development of particular features in different legal cultures. However, such considerations belong to the next step in the hermeneutical process.

Turning our attention back to identification of similarities and differences, a more general question arises. To what extent is it at all possible to speak of similarities? The answer to this question depends on the individual comparatist's approach to comparative law. Cultural relativists or pessimists, as they are sometimes labelled,[99] such as Pierre Legrand and his followers, maintain that cultural diversity makes it literally impossible to identify similarities.[100] Their intention is to rather emphasise and explore the mental

---

examples for convergence often as a result of increasing globalisation and internationalisation of law. On convergence in general, see Francis Fukuyama, *The End of History and the Last Man* (Free Press 1992). On the convergence of law, see Lawrence Friedman, 'Borders: On the Emerging Sociology of Transnational Law' (1996) Vol. 32 *Stanford Journal of International Law* 65, 72 ff.; Siems (2018) (n 5) 262 ff. Mathias Siems, 'Convergence in Corporate Governance: A Leximetric Approach' (2009–2010) *Journal of Corporation Law* 729; Jan Smits, 'Convergence of Private Law in Europe: Towards a New Ius Commune?' in Esin Örücü and David Nelken (eds), *Comparative Law. A Handbook* (Hart Publishing 2007).

95 E.g. concerning different understandings of the fundamental concepts "legal rule", "*Rechtsregel*" or "*rettsregel*", see Helland and Koch (2014) (n 21) 270 ff.

96 Perceived similarities in the framing of constitutional provisions does not necessarily mean that the interpretation of these norms is similar. Recent research has shown that even almost identically framed provisions are interpreted rather differently by constitutional courts, tribunals or court with the competence to conduct constitutional review.

97 See Sören Koch, *Unaufgeforderte Hilfeleistung in Notsituationen* (Peter Lang 2009); Nils Jansen, 'Negotiorum Gestio and Benevolent Intervention in Another's Affairs: Principles of European Private Law?' (2007) Vol. 15 *Zeitschrift für Europäische Privatrecht* 958.

98 Wilson (2020) (n 9) 653 and Franklin (2020) (n 9) 341.

99 Van Hoecke (2004) (n 65) 172 ff.; Husa (2007) (n 4) 16.

100 Pierre Legrand, 'The Impossibility of Legal Transplants' (1997) Vol. 4 No. 2 *Maastricht Journal of European and Comparative Law* 111. Pierre Legrand, 'European Legal Systems are not Converging' (1996) Vol. 45 Issue 1 *International and Comparative Law Quarterly* 52.

preconditions and the deep structures of law.[101] Less radical approaches acknowledge that even though features, institutions or rules due to their cultural embeddedness are never entirely identical, they may still be regarded as similar in terms of socio-legal function, their intention or effect.[102] Those who believe in convergence of legal cultures or who advocate for a harmonisation of law in a particular field of law (optimists),[103] will probably be more interested in identifying similarities in order to establish e.g. a common core of legal principles or at least a common ground for the harmonisation of law.[104] Their challenge is to avoid downplaying or ignoring differences.[105] Particularly, when making policy-considerations it is the task of the comparatist to identify both similarities and differences. Accepting that a complete harmonisation of law does not seem possible or even desirable, the comparatist must develop solutions which take the existence of differences into account, and if necessary, develop completely new legal solutions or simply acknowledge that in a particular field, cultural differences make any attempt of harmonisation meaningless.

Regardless of the individual attitude towards comparative law, the comparatist must be sure that the identified similarities and differences resemble the object of the comparison. As shown above, this object can vary even if the overall topic of the comparative research is identical. The task of the ECtHR was to determine whether the specific procedure applied in the trial against *Taxquet* in Belgium violated Article 6 of the Convention. The comparative observations were used to illustrate that "the jury exists in a variety of forms in different states, reflecting each State's history, tradition and legal culture."[106] Hence the court focused on empirical **differences** such as the number of jurors, their qualification and appointment and whether it was possible to appeal their verdict etc.

When the Norwegian Supreme Court had to consider a violation of Article 6 of the Convention by Norwegian courts, the judges had a different focus. They held that the *Taxquet* ruling did not support a conclusion that all court decisions based on a jury verdict, provided without an explanation, constitute a violation of the fair trial principle.[107] The court therefore deliberately focused on comparing the Norwegian and Belgian criminal procedures applied in jury cases in order to evaluate whether the shortcomings of the Belgium system had functional **equivalents** in Norway or whether the procedure in Norway was organised in a way that would satisfy the minimum standards of the Convention according to the ECtHR's interpretation of Article 6.[108] Since the judges

101 Legrand (1997) (ibid.) 117. Critical to Legrand's focus on differences, Siems (2018) (n 5) 142; Husa (2014) (n 12) 64; Husa (2007) (n 4) 12.

102 Esin Örücü, 'Method of Comparative Law' in Jan M. Smits (ed) *Elgar Encyclopedia of Comparative Law* (Edward Elgar 2006) 443; Van Hoecke (2015) (n 8) 16 ff.; Husa (2007) (n 4) 13.

103 E.g. in constitutional, but also in private law, see Jörg Fedtke, 'Constitutional Transplants: Returning to the Garden' (2008) Vol. 61 *Current Legal Problems* 49; Jan M. Smits, 'Convergence of Private Law in Europe: Towards an New Ius Commune', in Esin Örücü and David Nelken (eds), *Comparative Law: A Handbook*, (Hart Publishing 2007).

104 Siems (2018) (n 5) 38; Ugo Mattei et al (eds), *Schlesinger's Comparative Law* (7th edn, Foundation Press 2009) 99.

105 Örücü (2007) (n 4) 50.

106 *Taxquet v Belgium* (n 24) para. 83.

107 Rt. 2009 p. 750 para. 53.

108 Ibid. para. 62 ff., 77 and 83.

were convinced that the Norwegian system as such was not violating these standards, they had to emphasise to what extent the Norwegian proceedings were structurally and legally **different** from the Belgian one.[109]

Again, another focus on similarities and differences can be found in the final report of the legislative committee that evaluated the future of the Norwegian jury order. The committee stated that the purpose of the comparative inquiry was to be inspired by the solutions in other countries.[110] As a consequence, the report focused on **jurisdictions having adopted** a jury system. Objects of comparison are types of cases treated by a jury, number of jury members, allocation of competences between lay and professional judges, to what extent lay judges are instructed and provided with an abstract of the evidence presented in court, whether there is a demand for a majority vote, whether professional judges can overrule the verdict of the jury, whether the jury has a duty to provide reasons for their decision and to what extent the anonymity of the jury members is guaranteed.[111] In addition, the report encompasses comparative observations concerning legal orders that have opted for a collaborative court model of lay adjudication as well.[112] Both similarities and differences between the Norwegian and the foreign systems were identified and highlighted.

Legal scholars participated in the discussion concerning the future of the Norwegian jury system, and they too used comparative observations. An interesting difference to the legislative committee was that they were mostly interested in the relationship between international and national law, particularly to what extent the verdict of the ECtHR would impact the national legal system and the particular way of reasoning preferred and practiced by Norwegian lawyers.[113] Consequently, they identified structural **differences** in the argumentation and the legal sources on which the ECtHR and the Norwegian Supreme Court based their verdicts.[114] In other words, they were particularly interested in legal methodological preconditions and effects an international judgment had on an institution with a long tradition in the national legal culture (the jury), but also discussed to what extent the legislator should consider changing the law based on the experience from the Belgian case. Pinpointing similarities and differences may therefore be a first step in the comparative *analysis*, but without an assessment and explanation, this process is incomplete.

---

109 Cf. e.g. ibid. para. 77, where the court refers to the argumentation in the *Taxquet*-case and concludes that: "This is a different situation compared to the one in the *lagrett* [the jury in the Norwegian court] where the court is provided separate questions [...]" (my translation: "Dette er en annen situasjon enn der lagretten er forelagt separate spørsmål [...]"). The UN Human Rights Committee accepted both the outcome and the argumentation of the Norwegian Supreme Court, when dismissing the claim by one convict who had appealed his case to the Supreme Court (cf. Rt 2009 p. 773), see *T.L.N. v Norway* Communication No. 1942/2010 (HRC, views adopted 16 July 2014, published 25 August 2014).

110 NOU 2011: 13 Juryutvalget – Når sant skal skrives 47.

111 Ibid. 48.

112 Ibid.

113 E.g. Strandbakken (2009) (n 28) 258 ff.; Jon Petter Rui, 'Fra menneskerettighetsdomstolen' (2012) No. 1 *Tidsskrift for strafferett* 110.

114 Ibid.

Step 5: Assessment and Explanation of identified differences and similarities

The assessment and explanation of the empirical observations is the essential part of the analysis.[115] Without assessing and explaining similarities and differences the comparison is incomplete and of little value. Assessing empirical data often requires interpretation. Here the context becomes particularly relevant.[116] Collecting the number of members of juries in different countries may be interesting in order to understand what is regarded as a critical mass of jurors necessary to minimise the chance for arbitrary results or reduce it to an acceptable level. However, sometimes mere economic considerations (juries are expensive) were decisive when the legislator regulated the number of jurors. Therefore, it might be feasible to establish subcategories or to interrelate empirical observations such as GDP and number of jurors in one state compared to GDP and number of jurors in another country. The survey may show a significant correlation between such factors or demonstrate that such a correlation is lacking. Regardless of the outcome, in both cases we have gained new knowledge.

Very often political, geographical, historical, philosophical, and other cultural factors are relevant when interpreting and explaining observed similarities and differences as well. A legal cultural perspective based on legal historical knowledge and understanding can make the difference between educated guessing and intersubjective fact-based correlations.

For example, some legal cultures have developed a legalistic approach to law, demanding a rather strict adherence to the wording of relevant provisions in statutory law. The contributions in this book reveal that the reasons for such an approach to law can vary considerably. In Finland, such a perception of law was furthered as a result of protecting the Finnish legal culture from being merged with or absorbed by the Russian legal culture during the time of occupation.[117] In Poland, on the other hand, a quite similar approach to written sources of law was for a long time promoted due to the lack of a sufficiently elevated national legislation.[118] In contemporary Poland, some scholars and judges regard a strict application of the wording of legislation a safeguard against political attempts to undermine the rule of law.[119] Yet another explanation for a legalistic

115 Rudolf B. Schlesinger, 'The Past and Future of Comparative Law' (1995) Vol. 43 No. 3 *The American Journal of Comparative Law* 447, 447: "To compare means to observe and *explain* similarities and differences." (my emphasis). Maurice Adams and John Griffiths, 'Against "Comparative Method": Explaining Similarities and Differences' in Maurice Adams and John Bomhoff, *Practice and Theory in Comparative Law* (Cambridge University Press 2012) 279 ff.

116 Husa (2014) (n 12) 66 f. with reference to the methodological concept of "thick description" developed by the ethnographer Geertz pointing out: "In this case, it means a thick description of the legal cultures under study. Legal Cultures here as systems that are constructed of an established 'system of meanings': these systems are epistemological frame of legal cultures (written or unwritten) where various actors (legislator, judges, researchers) are in interaction with legal norms."

117 Nylund (2020) (n 9) 152.

118 Klimaszewka, Machnikowska and Koch (2020) (n 9) 274 ff. with further reference.

119 Ibid. 317 f. with further reference.

approach can be found in France. Here, the traditionally low degree of confidence in the courts has contributed to limit the courts' impact on norm production.[120] As a result, syllogism as a form of deduction of legal consequences from legislation became the ideal style of legal reasoning in the Cour de cassation.[121] In Germany, the constitutional obligation to respect legislation and law (*Gesetz und Recht*) in Article 20 III of the Basic Law, as well as the particular scientific focus on law, limits the possibility of deviating from the clear wording of a relevant Act of Parliament.[122] An interpretation *contra legem* is therefore in principle prohibited, except for the situation where constitutional values require an adjustment (cf. e.g. the *Soraya* case).[123]

Accordingly, there may be several, often cumulative reasons why a legal culture has adopted a particular notion that seems quite similar to notions in another legal culture. However, as shown above, the similarity on the surface (legalistic approach), may have very different historical, political, economic or cultural foundations and can thus be explained differently when considering the deeper levels of law.[124]

Explaining similarities and differences often requires a multidimensional approach. One should at least consider two dimensions: the historical (*vertical*) and cultural (*horizontal*) dimension.[125] Historical analysis can help to explain why a legal culture has developed specific features or rejected others. Considering the interplay within the elements on the legal cultural model allows the comparatist to explain certain features as a result of a culture's internal structure.

Analysing the development and theoretical foundations of general legal cultural features by using the LCM on the *macro* level will enable the comparatist to identify nuances and minor deviations that may become relevant when conducting comparative analysis on the *meso* or *micro* level. For example, a researcher might be interested in finding out to what extent it is possible to speak about a common legal method in Europe,[126] to what extent children born out of wedlock are treated legally equal to children born in marriage,[127] or how the international rules on the sale of goods (CISG

120 An empirical study provided by Marc A. Loth, 'Courts in a Quest for Legitimacy: A comparative Approach' in Nick Huls, Maurice Adams and Jacco Bomhoff (eds), *The Legitimacy of Highest Courts' Rulings. Judicial Deliberations and Beyond* (TMC Asser Press 2009) 268, supported this observation.

121 Sunniva Cristina Bragdø-Ellenes, 'An Introduction to French Legal Culture' in this volume, chapter 13, 499.

122 Koch (2020), 'German Legal Culture' (n 9) 252.

123 Decision of the Federal Constitutional Court (BVerfGE 34, p. 269 ff.)

124 On the demand for deep-law comparison, see Van Hoecke (2004) (n 65) 165 ff.

125 The term 'dimension' has been used in a comparable way by William Ewald, 'Legal History and Comparative Law' (1997) Vol. 7 *Zeitschrift für Europäisches Privatrecht* 553: "For legal history comparative law across the dimension of time, just as comparative law (in the narrow sense of the term) compares law across the dimension of space, from country to country." An illustrative example is Ruth Katharina Weber, *Der Begründungsstil von Conseil constitutionnel und Bundesverfassungsgericht. Eine vergleichende Analyse der Spruchpraxis* (Mohr Siebeck 2019), part 2, 149 ff. ("Justizkultureller Hintergrund") und part 3, 243 ff. ("Institutionelle Erklärungsmuster").

126 See e.g. Andreas Schwartze, 'Die Rechtsvergleichung' in Karl Riesenhuber (ed), *Europäische Methodenlehre. Handbuch für Ausbildung und Praxis* (3rd edn, De Gruyter 2015).

127 Antonia Schnitzler, *Rechtskulturvergleich zur Gleichstellung nichtehelicher Kinder. Eine Untersuchung zur rechtlichen Anpassung an gesellschaftliche Veränderung in Deutschland und England* (Mohr Siebeck 2019).

– UNCITRAL) are implemented and applied in two or several jurisdictions.[128] For all these research questions, a legal cultural perspective may provide contextual information that can prove essential for understanding the existing written and unwritten rules, their application, and furthermore the identification and analysis of similarities and differences. The researcher may choose to focus on either relevant legislation, or the works of legal scholars ("law in books"), or the argumentation in European courts, international courts of justice or national courts, as well as private, constitutional and administrative practice ("law in action").[129] Calling all these factors "legal formants", Sacco has suggested combining of all of them.[130] However, without a proper understanding of the legal methodology applied in these countries and the way the judiciary is organised and works in practice, just reading e.g. the judgments or doctrinal works, can cause misunderstanding concerning the arguments used by different actors. Accordingly, a qualitative analysis of legal arguments in case law requires consideration of the relevant text and context of legal provisions, such as the preparatory works, the intention of the historical legislator, the underlying legal doctrine, etc.[131] In addition, other factors such as religious beliefs, economic considerations, ideologies, etc. may be relevant.[132] In order to assess and explain the varying meanings of concepts like "free will" or "consent", it is highly relevant to consider other disciplines such as philosophy and medicine. The discussion in both disciplines have affected the perception of these concepts quite differently in various cultures.[133] Consequently, a multidisciplinary approach seems feasible or even necessary. A comparative study may therefore require inter or even multidisciplinary approaches and methods as well.[134] As a rule, a single researcher cannot accomplish such studies. Instead, an interdisciplinary and international team of researchers is required.[135] The LCM can provide both the analytical framework for an interdisciplinary coopera-

128 E.g. Angelo Chianale, 'The *CISG* as a Model Law: A Comparative Law Approach' (2016) *Singapore Journal of Legal Studies* 29. José Angelo Estrella Faria, 'The Influence of the UNIDROIT Principles of International Commercial Contracts on National Laws' (2016) Vol. 21 Issue 2–3 *Uniform Law Review* 238.

129 The importance of distinguishing between 'law in books' and 'law in action' for comparative research has been emphasized by Maurice Adams and Jacco Bomhoff, 'Comparing law: practice and theory' in Maurice Adams and Jacco Bomhoff (eds), *Practice and Theory in Comparative Law* (Cambridge University Press 2012) 3 ff. See also Örücü (2007) (n 4) 61.

130 Rodolfo Sacco, 'Legal Formants: A Dynamic Approach to Comparative Law' (1991) Vol. 39 *American Journal of Comparative Law* 343 (Issue 1, part I) and 1 (Issue 2, part II). See also Graziadei (2003) (n 62) 116. The concept of legal formants resembles to some extent the Norwegian term 'legal source factors' (*rettskildefaktorer*) which became particularly influential through the writings of the legal realist Torstein Eckhoff in the 1970s, see Kjølstad, Koch and Sunde (2020) (n 9) 126 ff.

131 Sacco (1991, II) (n 130) 23 ff.

132 Siems (2018) (n 5) 130; Örücü (2007) (n 4) 61 speaking of 'contextual formants'.

133 E.g. J. O. A. Tan and J. R. McMillan, 'The discrepancy between the legal definition of consent and the British Medical Association's guidelines' (2004) Vol. 30 *Journal of Medical Ethics* 427.

134 In favour of multidiciplinary approaches, Siems (2018) (n 5) 404 ff. Particularly, in relation to a legal cultural approach, Örücü (2007) (n 4) 59.

135 A call for interdisciplinarity was recently promoted by Stephan Kirste (ed), *Interdisziplinarität in den Rechtswissenschaften. Ein interdisziplinärer und internationaler Dialog* (Duncker & Humblot 2016).

tion by breaking down communication challenges despite differences concerning the methodological point of departure.

A contextual explanation of identified similarities and differences considering all these perspectives by using the LCM, will allow the researcher(s) to identify certain patterns, which then can be transferred into categories and specific analytical models.[136] This categorisation will promote conducting a systematic and less biased survey of relevant formants and the legal arguments included therein.[137] Furthermore, such a survey can be used to evaluate the extent to which any doctrinal or conceptual incoherence is caused by an underlying disagreement about e.g. the philosophical, economic, ideological, political, geographical or other factors of relevance. Systematically reconstructing a *neutral terminology* can be the foundation for a new conceptual framework independent from biased perceptions in different scientific fields on the national as well as the international level. In other words, a contextual explanation of empirical data (such as legal arguments used in courts) can be a precondition for developing an unbiased terminology and the *tertium comparationis*,[138] or as Nils Jansen calls it, a second-order language.[139] Such a second-order language can prove particularly important where legal concepts are essential subjects of the comparison.

However, creating a research matrix for analysing and explaining the comparative observations must carefully be distinguished from the final step of the process: systematising the findings and applying them to answer the initial research question/hypothesis.

Step 6: Systematising the findings and answering the research question

Depending on the nature of the comparison and the methodological approach, the process of analysing the empirical findings may vary considerably. However, as a rule a good starting point is to **systematise** the collected and contextually explained data. Establishing categories and subcategories is often a good strategy. In this regard sociological and mathematical models can become important. Particularly if the researcher tries to establish correlations between empirical facts or their impact on other facts, lawyers (also comparative lawyers) are often reluctant to use methods developed in social or natural science.[140] The purpose of such methods is to scientifically substantiate highly significant correlations.[141]

136 Koch (forthcoming) (n 44).

137 Sacco (1991, II) (n 130) 2 ff.

138 For definitions and explanations of the term, see Örücü (2007) (n 4) 48; Husa (2014) (n 12) 60.

139 On the notion of *tertium comparationis* and the limits of finding an objective standard developed independently from the established terminology in certain legal cultures, see Zweigert and Kötz (1998) (n 5) 35; Husa (2014) (n 12) 60; Van Hoecke (2015) (n 8) with reference to the approach promoted by Nils Jansen, 'Comparative Law and Comparative Knowledge' in Mathias Reimann and Reinhard Zimmermann (eds), *The Oxford Handbook of Comparative Law* (Oxford University Press 2006) 330.

140 Nylund (2019) (n 20) 426 ff.

141 George Kanire, *Social Science Research Methodology* (Grinn 2012) Chapter 6, 75.

An often-underestimated challenge is to recognise the existence of alternative explanations. It seems tempting to assume that a low number of mortal traffic accidents in Norway[142] is significantly correlated to the strict speed limits (on highways and out of town as a rule 80 km/h). How significant the relation between the two facts is, becomes questionable when considering that there are alternative explanations at hand. Many Norwegian roads are not suited for driving faster than the speed-limit allows. Furthermore, Norway has very severe penalties for driving while intoxicated (unconditioned imprisonment in cases of blood alcohol content of 1.2 or more, including a considerable fine and the loss of the driving licence for at least a year).[143] Over the last few decades, this deterring effect has caused a considerable change in attitude towards drinking and driving.[144] As a significant number of fatal traffic accidents are caused by intoxicated drivers,[145] decreasing social and legal acceptance of driving under the influence of alcohol is an alternative explanation for the comparatively low numbers of fatal accidents in Norway.[146] The rapidly increasing security standard of the automobile fleet in a wealthy country like Norway may be another relevant factor particularly when comparing with developing countries.

The conclusion that a low number of fatal traffic accidents (relative to population size etc.) is (exclusively) caused by speed limit regulations may be misleading because other factors may have contributed to the same result. Consequently, it would be a tenuous statement that reducing the speed limit is the most effective legislative measure to achieve the aim of avoiding fatal traffic accidents. Once again, a lack of social and cultural contextualisation may cause misconceptions. A comparative survey aiming to find the most effective legal solution to avoid fatal traffic accidents would have to consider alternative explanations such as geography, rules and attitudes towards intoxicated driving or wearing safety belts, standard of cars involved in such accidents, etc. As a rule, the engagement with a foreign culture creates the awareness of the relevant factors which must be considered. Assessing the empirical findings contextually can therefore help to find new categories or relevant variables that must be taken into account in the survey as well.

---

142 See Statistics Norway, 'Road traffic accidents involving personal injury' (updated 4 October 2019), available at https://www.ssb.no/transport-og-reiseliv/statistikker/vtu/aar accessed 3 March 2020.

143 Cf. Lov 1965-06-18-4 om vegtrafikk (vegtrafikkloven) [the Road Traffic Act] §§ 31 and 33.

144 In a survey among 4,000 Norwegians, 75% answered the question whether they could think of driving after having had one unit of alcohol in Southern Europe, where this would be legal, by stating that this would be unthinkable to them. See Øystein B. Fossum, 'Vesentlig mer liberale til promillekjøring', *Dinside.no* 26 June 2019, available at https://www.dinside.no/motor/vesentlig-mer-liberale-til-promillekjoring/71213768 accessed 3rd March 2020.

145 In 2018, 34% of all fatal traffic accidents were caused by intoxicated drivers. For the period 2015–2018, the average number was 22%. See Statens Vegvesen, 'Dybdeanalyser av dødsulykker i vegtrafikken 2018' 14. Available at https://www.vegvesen.no/_attachment/2784246/binary/1339801?fast_title=Dybdeanalyser+av+d%C3%B8dsulykker+i+vegtrafikken+2018.pdf accessed 3 March 2020.

146 The abovementioned example also proves that legal regulation alone might not change realities – a change in attitudes might prove as important. However, changes in the intellectual structure of cultures usually take time. Legislative initiatives can contribute and support such changes but rarely enforce them against the will of the citizens.

When considering how to systematise the empirical material, the comparatist often needs to be creative. However, being part of the analytical process, the purpose of the study and the object(s) of comparison must be constantly considered. The judges in the ECtHR distinguished three categories of legal systems: "those without any form of jury trial or any model of lay adjudication in criminal matters; those using a collaborative court mode of lay adjudicators sitting and deliberation alongside with professional judges in criminal matters, and those which have opted for the 'traditional' jury model in criminal matters."[147] In order to consider whether the existence of a jury is already a violation of the ECHR, this may be a reasonable starting point.

The legislative committee evaluating the jury system in Norway did not devote any attention to systems without a form of lay adjudication in criminal matters. They distinguished, in concordance with the policy question they had to decide, between collaborative and exclusive forms of lay adjudication.[148] They organised the empirical data according to the consideration which had been identified as particularly relevant for the Norwegian context and for the mandate of the committee.[149] Differences and similarities were analysed for each aspect separately.

Yet another form of systematisation is to use or create objective criteria which enable us to measure functions or effects of legal norms, institutions, etc. The field of law and economics has been a forerunner in developing such criteria and analytical models based on economic or political theories. In comparative studies on civil justice and constitutional law, the choice of criteria has become a prominent issue.[150] Terminological or systematic considerations may serve as additional rubrics. It seems once again important to emphasise that the hermeneutical nature of the analytical process may require empirical data to be systematised before it can be assessed. In this case the systematisation can contribute to identifying similarities and differences or to explain them. This may be particularly necessary if the researcher has collected a comprehensive amount of empirical material. A systematisation may become necessary already when developing the research question and design. However, to avoid biased assumptions in these cases, the chosen categories or other types of systematising factors must be reviewed and if necessary reconsidered in the light of the contextual assessment and explanation provided in Step 5.

Finally, the explained, critically evaluated, tested, and systematised comparative findings can be used to answer the initial research question. The faction of the Norwegian jury committee in favour of adopting a cooperative system (*meddommerfraksjon*), that is, a system where layman and professional judges collaborate and decide on all aspects of a criminal case, made frequent use of these observations, emphasising the advantages of such a model compared to the established jury model in Norway at that time.[151]

147 *Taxquet v Belgium* (n 24) para. 44.

148 NOU 2011: 13 Juryutvalget: Når sant skal skrives 65.

149 Ibid. 66.

150 E.g. Nylund (2019) (n 20) 438 f.

151 NOU 2011: 13 Juryutvalget: Når sant skal skrives 168 ff.

Members of both factions (those in favour of a jury and those in favour of a cooperation model) used identified similarities and differences with other legal cultures in their argumentation. Nevertheless, both factions can be blamed for having done this in a rather uncritical way. The legal cultural and historical context was not considered thoroughly. This is surprising because the socio-legal conditions under which the jury system was established in Norway in 1887 had changed considerably compared to the early 21st century. The main argument for letting lay judges decide on the facts of criminal cases independent from professional judges was that the latter were recruited from an intellectual and social elite in a socially much more divided (class) society. Today, a high degree of confidence in the courts and in a highly egalitarian society are prominent features of the Norwegian legal culture. The increased complexity of criminal cases particularly in the field of economic crimes has contributed to make it challenging for lay judges to evaluate the facts of such cases. Considering the rather similar societal development in Denmark would have provided good arguments to look even closer towards the neighbouring county and the historical reasons for the institutionalisation of the jury.

Step 7: Starting all over again

As pointed out previously, the COMPASS formula is organised in a hermeneutical circle. This implies that the explained, critically evaluated, tested, and systematised comparative findings of the survey should be used not just to answer but also to **critically review** the initial research questions and the underlying assumptions. For example, the outcome of a comparative analysis can give rise to doubts as to whether almost identically framed legal norms, which may even be based on a common legal institution historically speaking, have developed different functions or have a different scope of application in different legal cultures. This would indicate that an assumption of similarity can be falsified and any hypothesis such as the idea that we can harmonise the law (in this particular field) on the European level along the lines of a common core of principle, would prove invalid.[152] Another example, based on my own experience, relates to hidden conceptual differences. Working on an edited volume on comparing legal methods in Nordic and Germanic legal cultures, a Norwegian colleague and I built on the assumption that the semantical related concepts of '*Rechtsregel*' and '*rettsregel*' (literary translated legal rule) had the same content for German and Norwegian lawyers.[153] Driven by the desire to identify and explain similarities and difference in both countries' legal methodology, our research question was: how do German and Norwegian lawyers apply legal rules in order to solve particular legal problems? In our conversations it eventually became clear

152 One example for such an analytical conclusion can be found in Koch (2011) (n 19) 440 ff., where I argue that applying the Roman law based principle of *negotiorum gestio* to solve rescue cases or even making these types of cases the new paradigm of a European principle of Benevolent Intervention into Another's Affairs (cf. DCFR Book V) can hardly be justified by regarding the institute as part of a common core of European private law because it had a rather different social foundation and function in Roman law and the *ius commune*, and because it lacks recognition in all European legal cultures.

153 On this discussion in detail and with further references, Helland and Koch (2014) (n 21) 270 ff.

that we had a very different idea in mind when we used the term legal rule. In Germany, a '*Rechtsregel*' refers to the legal norm contained in a legislative provision or a specific customary rule. Accordingly, *Rechtsregel* is an abstract norm in need of interpretation. Solving a case with the help of this norm requires that it is applied to the case at hand (this process is called *Subsumption*). In other words, the legal rule is the **starting point** of the application of law in Germany. In contrast, the Norwegian concept of *rettsregel* is used when a lawyer refers to the **outcome** of this process. *Rettsregel* equals what Wolfgang Fikentscher in German refers to as '*Fallnorm*'.[154] In light of this rather surprising discovery, we had to adapt our research question. Furthermore, the whole research design had to be put to the test. We naturally assumed that semantical related concepts of 'Rechtsregel' and 'rettsregel' had an identical content. Our culturally determined perception prevented us from detecting this crucial difference. Only by accumulating deeper cultural knowledge were we able to detect the communication obstacle and adjust the comparative design accordingly.

Note, however, that it is not necessary to mechanically follow all the steps presented here before adjusting or changing the research question, the methodological approach, or the objective of the comparative analysis. Conducting comparative research is, as the abovementioned examples have shown, a hermeneutical process that requires a critical and reflective attitude on all stages. It further requires the willingness to react flexible if the initial assumptions seem inadequate or incomplete. A basic knowledge and understanding of the involved legal cultures on a meta-level may help to identify and solve such challenges when conducting comparative research on the micro or meso level.

3. Conclusion

Sailing the high seas requires both experience and guidance. The same applies to navigating in the ocean of comparative law. This chapter provides a compass formula for conducting comparative studies. Examples based on the contributions in this volume explain how the structured accounts of different legal cultures can be used as a *starting point* and *background* for comparative legal studies. Applying an operationalised concept of legal culture transferred into the LCM aims to enable the reader to gain a deeper structural understanding of foreign law in context. Such an understanding is, in our view, an essential precondition for all kinds of comparative studies. We have argued that the analytical core task of comparative legal studies is to *assess* and *explain* identified similarities and differences.[155] Assessing and explaining the context of law may require interdisciplinary and multidimensional approaches. Considering both the historical and legal cultural dimension can provide interesting insights. Still, the individual epistemological interest and specific research question determine the purpose, object, and method suitable for the comparison. It is beyond the scope and intention of this chapter

154 Wolfgang Fikentscher, *Methoden des Rechts in vergleichernder Darstellung*, Vol IV (Mohr Siebeck 1977) 190 ff.

155 See also Husa (2014) (n 12) 53 f. with reference to Schlesinger (1995) (n 115).

to give an account of the extensive international discussion on comparative law or any specific approach to legal comparative method. Rather, its purpose is to enable the reader to critically reflect on the interplay between the institutional and intellectual structures inherent in all legal cultures and to systematically compare them both vertically (historically) and horizontally (intra/intercultural).[156] This chapter in particular and this book in general provide the necessary tools and materials for preforming comparative studies based on a comparison of legal cultures.

4. Bibliography

Adams M and Bomhoff J, 'Comparing law: practice and theory' in Adams M and Bomhoff J (eds), *Practice and Theory in Comparative Law* (Cambridge University Press 2012). DOI: https://doi.org/10.1017%2Fcbo9780511863301.001

Adams M and Griffiths J, 'Against "Comparative Method": Explaining Similarities and Differences' in Adams M and Bomhoff J (eds), *Practice and Theory in Comparative Law* (Cambridge University Press 2012)

Ahn TK, Balafoutas L, Batsaikhan M, Campos-Ortiz F, Putterman L and Sutter M, 'Securing property rights: A dilemma experiment in Austria, Mexico, Mongolia, South Korea and the United States', (2016) Vol. 143 *Journal of Public Economics* 115. DOI: https://doi.org/10.1016%2Fj.jpubeco.2016.08.015

Aney MS, Dam S and Ko G, 'Jobs for Justice(s): Corruption in the Supreme Court of India', 2017, available at https://papers.ssrn.com/sol3/papers.cfm?abstract_id=3087464 accessed 29 March 2020

Antokolskaia M, *Harmonisation of Family Law in Europe: A Historical Perspective* (Intersentia 2006)

Arold NL, 'The Melting Pot or the Salad Bowl Revisited – Rendezvous of Legal Cultures at the European Court of Human Rights' in Sunde JØ and Skodvin KE (eds), *Rendezvous of European Legal Cultures* (Fagbokforlaget 2010)

Backer IL, 'Feller Den europeiske menneskerettsdomstol juryen?' (2009) No. 3 *Tidsskrift for strafferett* 301

Bell J, *Judiciaries Within Europe: A Comparative Review* (Cambridge University Press 2006). DOI: https://doi.org/10.1017%2Fcbo9780511493829

—— 'The importance of legal Institutions' in Adams M and Heirbaut D (eds), *The Method and Culture of Comparative Law* (Hart Publishing 2014). DOI: https://doi.org/10.5040%2F9781474201636.ch-015

—— and David Ibbetson, *European Legal Development: The Case of Tort* (Cambridge University Press 2012). DOI: https://doi.org/10.1017%2Fcbo9781139128988

Berman PS, *Global Legal Pluralism: A Jurisprudence of Law Beyond Borders* (Cambridge University Press 2012). DOI: https://doi.org/10.1017%2Fcbo9781139028615

Blankenburg E, 'Patterns of Legal Culture: The Netherlands Compared to the Neighboring Germany' (1998) Vol. 46 Issue 1 *The American Journal of Comparative Law* 1. DOI: https://doi.org/10.2307%2F841077

Brenncke M, *Judicial Law-Making in English and German Courts – Techniques and Limits of Statutory Interpretation* (Intersentia 2018). DOI: https://doi.org/10.1017%2F9781780687902

Cabrelli D and Siems M, 'Convergence, Legal Origins, and Transplants in Comparative Corporate Law: A Case-Based and Quantitative Analysis' (2015) Vol. 63 No. 1 *American Journal of Comparative Law* 109. DOI: https://doi.org/10.2139%2Fssrn.2629847

---

156 Studies on the field of comparative legal history often will need to combine both. See Heikki Pihlajamäki, 'Comparative Context in Legal History: Are we all Comparatists Now?' in Maurice Adams and Dirk Heirbaut (eds), *The Culture and Method of Comparative Law* (Hart Publishing 2014) 121 ff.

Callies GP and Zumbansen P, *Rough Consensus and Running Code: A Theory of Transnational Private Law* (Hart Publishing 2010). DOI: https://doi.org/10.5040%2F9781472565112

Chianale A, 'The *CISG* as a Model Law: A Comparative Law Approach' (2016*) Singapore Journal of Legal Studies* 29

Creutzfeldt N, 'How Important is Procedural Justice for Consumer Dispute Resolution? A Case Study of an Ombudsman Model for European Consumers' (2014) Vol. 37 *Journal of Consumer Policy* 523. DOI: https://doi.org/10.1007%2Fs10603-014-9269-x

Curran VG, 'Cultural Immersion, Differences and Categories in U.S. Comparative Law' (1998) Vol. 6 Issue 1 *American Journal of Comparative Law* 43. DOI: https://doi.org/10.2307%2F841078

De Cruz P, *Comparative Law in a Changing World* (2nd edn, Cavendish Publishing Ltd 1999)

Drobnig U and van Erp S (eds), *The Use of Comparative Law by Courts* (Kluwer 1999)

Dzehtsiarou K, 'Comparative Law in the Reasoning of the European Court of Human Rights' (2010) Vol. 10 *University College Dublin Law Review* 104. DOI: https://doi.org/10.2139%2Fssrn.1703120

Engle Merry S, 'What is Legal Culture? An Anthropological Perspective' (2010) Vol. 5 Issue 2 *Journal of Comparative Law* 40

Estrella Faria JA, 'The Influence of the UNIDROIT Principles of International Commercial Contracts on National Laws' (2016) Vol. 21 Issue 2–3 *Uniform Law Review* 238. DOI: https://doi.org/10.1093%2Fulr%2Funw013

Ewald W, 'Legal History and Comparative Law' (1997) Vol. 7 *Zeitschrift für Europäisches Privatrecht* 553

Fabri M, 'Methodological Issues in the Comparative Analysis of the Number of Judges, Administrative Personnel, and Court Performance Collected by the Commission for the Efficiency of Justice of the Council of Europe' (2017) Vol. 7 No. 4 *Oñati Socio-Legal Studies* Series 616

Fedtke J, 'Constitutional Transplants: Returning to the Garden' 61 *Current Legal Problems* (2008)

Fikentscher, W, *Methoden des Rechts in vergleichernder Darstellung*, Vol IV (Mohr Siebeck 1977)

Finnegan DL, 'Applied Comparative Law and Judicial Reform' (2006) Vol. *8 Thomas M. Cooley Journal of Practical and Clinical Law* 97

Flanagan B and Ahern S, 'Judicial Decision-Making and Transnational Law: A Survey of Common Law Supreme Court Judges' (2011) Vol. 60 No. 1 *International and Comparative Law Quarterly* 1. DOI: https://doi.org/10.1017%2Fs0020589310000655

Foljanty L, *Recht oder Gesetz. Juristische Identität und Autorität in den Naturrechtsdebatten der Nachkriegszeit* (Mohr Siebeck 2013)

—— 'Legal Transfers as Processes of Cultural Translation: on the Consequences of a Metaphor, *Max Planck Institute for European Legal History Research Paper Series* No. 2015-09

Foster NHD, 'Comparative Commercial Law' in Örücü E and Nelken D (eds), *Comparative Law: A Handbook* (Hart Publisher 2006)

Franklin C, 'The Melting Pot or the Salad Bowl Revisited (again) – The meeting of Legal Cultures at the European Court of Justice' in Sunde JØ and Skodvin KE (eds), *Rendezvous of European Legal Cultures* (Fagbokforlaget 2010)

Friedman L, 'Borders: On the Emerging Sociology of Transnational Law' (1996) Vol. 32 *Stanford Journal of International Law* 65

Fukuyama F, *The End of History and the Last Man* (Free Press 1992)

Gibson JL, 'Judges' Role Orientations, Attitudes, and Decisions: An Interactive Model' (1978) Vol. 72 No. 3 *The American Political Science Review* 911. DOI: https://doi.org/10.2307/1955111

Glenn HP, 'The Aims of Comparative Law' in Smits JM (ed), *Elgar Encyclopedia of Comparative Law* (Edward Elgar 2006). DOI: https://doi.org/10.4337%2F9781847200204.00010

Graziadei M, 'The functionalist heritage' in Legrand P and Munday R (eds), *Comparative Legal Studies: Traditions and Transitions* (Cambridge University Press 2003). DOI: https://doi.org/10.1017%2Fcbo9780511522260.005

Helland I, *Rulings of the European Court of Human Rights as a Legal Argument – a Comparison between Norwegian and German Law* (PhD thesis, University of Bergen 2012)

—— and Koch S, 'Comparing Legal Methods – an Analytical Framework' in Helland I and Koch S (eds), *Nordic and Germanic Legal Methods* (Mohr Siebeck 2014)

—— and Koch S, 'Introduction to Norwegian Legal Method' in Helland I and Koch S (eds), *Nordic and Germanic Legal Methods* (Mohr Siebeck 2014)

—— and Koch S, 'Norwegian and German Legal Methods Compared' in Helland I and Koch S (eds), *Nordic and Germanic Legal Methods* (Mohr Siebeck 2014)

Hohfeld WN, *Fundamental Legal Conceptions as applied in Judicial Reasoning* (Yale University Press 1919; reprint Greenwood Press 1978)

Husa J, 'Farewell to Functionalism or Methodological Tolerance?' (2003) Vol. 67 No. 3 *Rabel Zeitschrift für ausländisches und internationales Privatrecht* 446. DOI: https://doi.org/10.1628%2F0033725033631996

—— 'About the Methodology of Comparative Law: Some Comments Concerning the Wonderland…', *Maastricht Working Papers* 2007 Issue 5, available at http://works.bepress.com/jaakko_husa/3/

—— 'Research Designs of Comparative Law – Methodology or Heuristics?' in Adams M and Heirbaut D (eds), *The method and culture of comparative law. Essays in honour of Mark Van Hoecke* (Hart Publishing 2014). DOI: https://doi.org/10.5040%2F9781474201636.ch-004

Jansen N, 'Comparative Law and Comparative Knowledge' in Reimann M and Zimmermann R (eds), *The Oxford Handbook of Comparative Law* (Oxford University Press 2006). DOI: https://dx.doi.org/10.1093/oxfordhb/9780199296064.013.0010

—— 'Negotiorum Gestio and Benevolent Intervention in Another's Affairs: Principles of European Private Law?' (2007) Vol. 15 *Zeitschrift für Europäische Privatrecht* 958

Kanire G, *Social Science Research Methodology* (Grinn 2012)

Kieninger EM, 'Sachenrechtliche Prinzipien und Grundbegriffe als Gegenstand der Rechtsvergleichung' in Zimmermann R (ed), *Zukunftsperspektiven der Rechtsvergleichung* (Mohr Siebeck 2016)

Kirste S (ed), *Interdisziplinarität in den Rechtswissenschaften. Ein interdisziplinärer und internationaler Dialog* (Duncker & Humblot 2016). DOI: https://doi.org/10.3790%2F978-3-428-54823-1

Kischel U, *Comparative Law* (Oxford University Press 2019). DOI: https://doi.org/10.1093%2Foso%2F9780198791355.001.0001

Koch S, *Unaufgeforderte Hilfeleistung in Notsituationen* (Peter Lang 2009)

—— *Der Ersatz frustrierter Aufwendungen im norwegischen Recht* (Peter Lang 2011)

—— 'Erstatning for bortkastede utgifter' (2012) No. 05 *Tidsskrift for Rettsvitenskap* 581

—— 'Consequences of changing expectations to law and its institutions. Illustrated by the role and background of judges in Norway' (2015) Vol. 83 No. 3–4 *The Legal History Review* 461. DOI: https://doi.org/10.1163%2F15718190-08334p06

—— *Compilation as a Technique for Disseminating Legal Knowledge in the Early Modern* (Olin Foundation, forthcoming)

Lando O, 'Nordic Uniform Act on the Law Applicable to International Sales of Goods' (1966) Vol. 15 Issue 4 *The American Journal of Comparative Law* 806. DOI: https://doi.org/10.2307%2F838379

Legrand P, 'European Legal Systems are not Converging' (1996) Vol. 45 Issue 1 *International and Comparative Law Quarterly* 52. DOI: https://doi.org/10.1017%2Fs0020589300058656

—— 'The Impossibility of Legal Transplants' (1997) Vol. 4 No. 2 *Maastricht Journal of European and Comparative Law* 111. DOI: https://doi.org/10.1177%2F1023263x9700400202

Loth MA, 'Courts in a Quest for Legitimacy: A comparative Approach' in Huls N, Adams M and Bomhoff J (eds), *The Legitimacy of Highest Courts' Rulings. Judicial Deliberations and Beyond* (TMC Asser Press 2009). DOI: https://doi.org/10.1007%2F978-90-6704-519-3_18

Løvlie A, 'En kort innføring i NOU 2011: 13 Juryutvalget – Når sant skal skrives' (2011) Vol. 37 No. 4 *Kritisk Juss* 252

Magnussen S, Eilertsen DE, Teigen KH, Stridbeck U og Wessel EM, 'En kvantitativ studie av sikkerhet i bevisvurdering i straffesaker hos norske fagdommere og lekdommere' (2014) Vol. 127 No. 3–4 *Tidsskrift for Rettsvitenskap* 384

Mandalaki A, 'Critical Comments on the Ownership of Lands and Agricultural Laws in Ancient Greece', (2019) 8 *Legal Roots: The International Journal of Roman Law, Legal History and Comparative Law* 43

Mankowski P, *Rechtskultur* (Mohr Siebeck 2016)

Markensis B, 'Judicial Mentality: Mental Disposition or Outlook as a Factor Impeding Resource to Foreign Law' (2006) 80 *Tulane Law Review* 1325

Mattei U et al (eds), *Schlesinger's Comparative Law* (7th edn, Foundation Press 2009)

Meier J, *Das Subjektive System der Geschäftsführung ohne Auftrag* (Mohr Siebeck 2019). DOI: https://doi.org/10.1628%2F978-3-16-156447-5

Nygard LJ, 'Juryen for fall?' (2011) Vol. 37 No. 4 *Kritisk Juss* 259

Nylund A, 'Comparing the Efficiency and Quality of Civil Justice in Scandinavia: The Role of Structural Differences and Definitions of Quality' (2019) Vol. 38 No. 4 *Civil Justice Quarterly* 427

Olaussen LP, 'Concordance between Actual Level of Punishment and Punishments suggested by Lay People – but with less use of Imprisonment' (2014) Vol. 2 No. 1 *Bergen Journal of Criminal Law and Criminal Justice* 69

—— 'Holdbart – utover rimelig tvil? Noen kommentarer til en enkeltstudie' (2016) Vol. 129 No. 1 *Tidsskrift for Rettsvitenskap* 74.

Örücü E, 'Method of Comparative Law' in Smits JM (ed) *Elgar Encyclopedia of Comparative Law* (Edward Elgar 2006)

—— 'Developing Comparative Law' in Örücü E and Nelken D (eds), *Comparative Law. A Handbook* (Hart Publishing 2007)

Pihlajamäki H, 'Comparative Context in Legal History: Are we all Comparatists Now?' in Adams M and Heirbaut D (eds), *The Culture and Method of Comparative Law* (Hart Publishing 2014). DOI: https://doi.org/10.5040%2F9781474201636.ch-009

Rui JP, 'Fra menneskerettighetsdomstolen' (2012) No. 1 *Tidsskrift for strafferett* 110

Sacco R, 'Legal Formants: A dynamic Approach to Comparative Law' (1991) Vol. 39 *American Journal of Comparative Law* 1 (Issue 1, part I) and 343 (Issue 2, part II). DOI. https://doi.org/10.2307%2F840669

Samuel G, 'What is Legal Epistemology?' in Adams M and Heirbaut D (eds), *The Method and Culture of Comparative Law* (Hart Publishing 2014). DOI: https://doi.org/10.5040%2F9781474201636.ch-002

—— *An Introduction to Comparative Law Theory and Method* (Hart Publishing 2014). DOI: https://doi.org/10.5040%2F9781849468442

Schacherreiter J, *Das Landeigentum als Legal Transplant in Mexico* (Mohr Siebeck 2014). DOI. https://doi.org/10.1628%2F978-3-16-153047-0

Schlesinger RB, 'The Past and Future of Comparative Law' (1995) Vol. 43 No. *3 The American Journal of Comparative Law* 447. DOI: https://doi.org/10.2307%2F840650

Schnitzler A, *Rechtskulturvergleich zur Gleichstellung nichtehelicher Kinder. Eine Untersuchung zur rechtlichen Anpassung an gesellschaftliche Veränderung in Deutschland und England* (Mohr Siebeck 2019). DOI: https://doi.org/10.1628%2F978-3-16-157672-0

Schwartze A, 'Die Rechtsvergleichung' in Riesenhuber K (ed), *Europäische Methodenlehre. Handbuch für Ausbildung und Praxis* (3rd edn, De Gruyter 2015). DOI: https://doi.org/10.1515%2F9783110915259.75

Siems M, 'Numerical Comparative Law: Do we need Statistical Evidence in Law in Order to Reduce Complexity?' (2005) Vol. 13 *Cardozo Journal of International & Comparative Law* 521. DOI: https://doi.org/10.2139%2Fssrn.514142

—— 'Convergence in Corporate Governance: A Leximetric Approach' (2009–2010) *Journal of Corporation Law* 729. DOI: https://doi.org/10.2139%2Fssrn.1444860

—— 'Citation Patterns of the German Federal Supreme Court and of the Court of Appeal of England and Wales' (2010) Vol. 21 *King's Law Journal* 152. DOI: https://doi.org/10.1080%2F09615768.2010.11423698

—— 'The Curious Case of Overfitting Legal Transplants' in Adams M and Heirbaut D (eds), *The Culture and Method of Comparative Law* (Hart Publishing 2014). DOI: https://doi.org/10.5040%2F9781474201636.ch-010

—— *Comparative Law* (2nd edn, Cambridge University Press 2018). DOI: https://doi.org/10.1017%2F9781316856505

Smits J, 'Convergence of Private Law in Europe: Towards a New Ius Commune?' in Örücü E and Nelken D (eds), *Comparative Law. A Handbook* (Hart Publishing 2007)

Strandbakken A, 'Juryen for fall? Noen refleksjoner etter Taxquet vs. Belgia' (2009) Vol. 35 No. 1 *Kritisk Juss* 101

Strandberg M, 'Oversikt over empirisk forskning om lekdommere', attachement to NOU 2011: 13 Juryutvalget: Når sant skal skrives

Sunde JØ, 'Champagne at the Funeral – An Introduction to Legal Culture' in Sunde JØ and Skodvin KE (eds), *Rendezvous of European Legal Cultures* (Fagbokforlaget 2010)

Tan JOA and McMillan JR, 'The discrepancy between the legal definition of consent and the British Medical Association's guidelines' (2004) Vol. 30 *Journal of Medical Ethics*

Teubner G, 'Legal Irritants: Good faith in British Law or how Unifying Law ends up in new Divergence' (1998) Vol. 61 No. 1 *Modern Law Review* 11. DOI: https://doi.org/10.1111%2F1468-2230.00125

Van Hoecke M, *Law as Communication* (Hart Publishing 2002)

—— 'Deep Level Comparative Law' in Mark Van Hoecke (ed), *Epistemology and Method of Comparative Law*, (Hart Publishing 2004). DOI: https://doi.org/10.5040%2F9781472559586.ch-009

—— 'Methodology of Comparative Legal Research' (2015) *Law and Method*. DOI: https://doi.org/10.5553%2Frem%2F.000010

Vogenauer S, *Die Auslegung von Gesetzen in England und auf dem Kontinent* (Mohr Siebeck 2001)

—— *Civil Justice Survey* (2008)

—— 'Regulatory Competition Through Choice of Contract Law and Choice of Forum in Europe: Theory and Evidence' (2013) Vol. 21 No. 1 *European Review of Private Law* 13

Weber RK, *Der Begründungsstil von Conseil constitutionnel und Bundesverfassungsgericht. Eine vergleichende Analyse der Spruchpraxis* (Mohr Siebeck 2019). DOI: https://doi.org/10.1628%2F978-3-16-156895-4

Zimmermann R, *Comparative Foundations of a European Law of Set-Off and Prescription* (Cambridge University Press 2002). DOI: https://doi.org/10.1017%2Fcbo9780511495113

Zweigert K and Kötz H, *An Introduction to Comparative Law* (3rd edn, Clarendon Press 1998)

5. An Introduction to Norwegian Legal Culture

Marius Mikkel Kjølstad, Sören Koch and Jørn Øyrehagen Sunde

1. Introduction

Norway is a country at the northern periphery of Europe with a population of 5.3 million inhabitants.[1] Even though Norway has one of the fastest growing populations in Europe,[2] the population density is relatively low. On average, there are approximately 15 inhabitants per square kilometre.[3] The low population density is mainly due to the geographical shape of the country. The land-surface of the country is at 385,000 square kilometres, but only 2.2 % is cultivated land.[4] Historically, the high mountains and the sea have been important to survival next to agriculture. The Norwegian coastline stretches more than 2,500 km from the very north (Hammerfest) to the most southern point (Lindesnes). The territory governed by Norwegian law includes parts of the Atlantic Ocean up to 200 nautical miles from the coastline.

"Norway" means "the way/route to the north" and was a functional name of the Norwegian coastline along the North Sea as a sailing route for trade. In the Early Middle Ages, the Norwegian realm was divided into several small kingdoms. Before the first attempts were made to establish a centralized power, the law territories Gulating and Frostating, situated along the Norwegian coast and facing the North Sea, were established. Their origin is unknown, but they were operative latest in the early 10th century. Eidsivating and Borgarting were established in the 11th and 12th centuries in the eastern part of Norway. These territories were named after the regional assemblies where free men gathered to solve conflicts of all kinds. Hence, there was not a centralized power

---

1 5,367,580 persons were registered as Norwegian inhabitants per 1 January 2020. See Statistics Norway, "Population. Annually, per 1 January", available at https://www.ssb.no/en/befolkning/statistikker/folkemengde/aar-per-1-januar accessed 26 March 2020.

2 According to Statistics Norway, the Norwegian population increased by 39,368 persons in 2019. See ibid.

3 See FN-sambandet, "Norge", available at https://www.fn.no/Statistikk?country=306#group-by-letter accessed 26 March 2020.

4 Ibid.

that enacted law and established means of conflict resolution, but instead there were law and conflict resolution that lay the foundation for the emergence of a centralized power.

The kinship (*ætt*) was of essential importance in the social organization in the Norwegian realm.[5] However, during the High Middle Ages this kinship-society fell apart at the same time as a centralized government emerged. A factor spurring the tempo and character of this development was the civil wars between 1130 and 1217. As they ended, a unified and effective reign was established with the crowning of King Håkon IV Håkonsson.[6] The king and the church became central governing institutions in the realm. A major event in Norwegian political and legal history was when King Magnus the Law Mender issued his Code of the Realm in 1274, Code of the Cities in 1276, his administrative code in 1277, and a code of law for Iceland in 1281, indicating the strength of central power in the Norwegian realm at the end of the 13th century.[7]

In the 13th and early 14th century, Norway was a flourishing realm with a prospering cultural and economic life. The devastating Black Plague that struck the country in 1349 changed this for several centuries to come. The country had entered into a personal union with Sweden in 1319, and in 1397 the union of Scandinavian kingdoms was expanded to include Denmark. Sweden left the Kalmar Union in 1523. Norway was downgraded from an independent realm to a Danish province after the Lutheran reformation was introduced in 1536.[8] This situation lasted until absolutism was established in 1660. Then Norway was announced as an independent kingdom once again. Whatever the formal status, Norway had on the one hand some independence – for instance its own code of law and court system – while on the other hand, all central institutions were in Copenhagen, from which the Danish-Norwegian realm was governed.[9]

A first brief period of political independence was achieved as a result of Napoleon's defeat and the peace treaty of Kiel in 1814.[10] One condition for peace was that the Danish King, who had supported France and Napoleon, would transfer the sovereignty over Norway to the Swedish King, who had fought with the United Kingdom, Russia, and the other allies. In Norway, which was not even involved in the negotiations, a national assembly was mustered and a constitution drafted in the spring of 1814. After a short war and negotiations, Norway entered into a personal union with Sweden with a common king but otherwise independent. Therefore, Norway could maintain its own

---

5 Jørn Øyrehagen Sunde, *Speculum legale – rettsspegelen. Ein introduksjon til den norske rettskulturen si historie i eit europeisk perspektiv* (Fagbokforlaget 2005) 53–55.

6 Ibid. 40.

7 Jørn Øyrehagen Sunde, "Daughters of God and Counsellors of the Judges of Men: Changes in the Legal Culture of the Norwegian Realm in the High Middle Ages" in Stefan Brink and Lisa Collinson (Eds.), *New Approaches to Early law in Scandinavia* (Brepols 2014) 139–141.

8 This has caused that some Norwegians even until today regard the reformation as a national tragedy that led to irrecoverable loss regarding both the native Norwegian language and culture.

9 Regarding the influence of absolutism in Norway, see Knut Mykland, Anders Bjarne Fossen, John Herstad and Bjørn Utne, *Norge under enevelde 1660–1720* (Fagbokforlaget 1975).

10 On the constitutional history and the context for the independence of 1814, see Dag Michalsen and Eirik Holmøyvik, *Lærebok i forfatningshistorie* (Pax 2015); Ola Mestad (Ed.), *Frihetens forskole. Professor Schlegel og eidsvollmennenes læretid i København* (Pax 2014) 1 f.

Parliament, Bank, University, and even Military. But most importantly, Norway kept its constitution. In contrast to the political union with Denmark, the union with Sweden had little effect on law and legal thinking in Norway.[11]

In 1884 – still in union with Sweden – the parliamentary system was introduced, following a prominent impeachment case. The personal union with Sweden ended in 1905, and Norway gained its complete political independence after more than 500 years of being in a union of some kind. Despite several political attempts and two referenda in 1972 and 1994, Norway has never become a member of the European Union (EU). However, as part of the European Economic Area (EEA) and the Schengen Agreement, Norway is economically – and to a lesser degree also politically and institutionally – bound to the EU. In addition, Norway has signed and implemented the European Convention on Human Rights and major United Nations human rights conventions.[12]

Today, Norway is a constitutional monarchy based on the second oldest constitution (*Grunnloven*) still in force in the world.[13] The country is administratively divided into 11 counties, headed by an elected county parliament. Each county is again divided into municipalities, governed by an elected local parliament and a mayor appointed by the majority of the local parliament. All together there are 356 Norwegian municipalities, with the smallest having a population of about 200 and the largest, which is the capital Oslo, more than 650,000 inhabitants.[14]

Norway is still a predominantly Lutheran country, even though the state church was dissolved in 2012. While Norway was one of the poorer countries in Europe at the beginning of the 20th century, the situation has changed dramatically, not the least triggered by the exploitation of Norwegian oil and gas resources since the early 1970s. In 2018, Norway was one of the riches countries in the world with a GDP of 434,167 million USD.[15] Another figure of importance is the gender equality index, showing that Norway is among the states with the highest gender equality-rate.[16]

Some general characteristics of the Norwegian culture are: an egalitarian structured society with a comparably low degree of social hierarchies, a rather short distance between the elite and the people accompanied by a high degree of confidence in the state

11 Dag Michalsen, "Structural-Historical Features in 'The Norwegian Legal Method'" in Ingvill Helland and Sören Koch (Eds.), *Nordic and Germanic Legal Methods* (Mohr Siebeck 2014) 76.

12 Lov 1999-05-21-30 om styrking av menneskerettighetenes stilling i norsk rett [The Human Rights Act].

13 The Constitution has, however, been amended several hundred times since 1814, see Malcolm Langford and Beate Kathrine Berge, "Norway's Constitution in a Comparative Perspective" (2019) Vol. 6 No. 3 *Oslo Law Review* 198, 223.

14 Erik Bolstad, "Kommuner i Norge" in Store norske leksikon (2016) https://snl.no/Kommuner_i_Norge accessed 27 March 2020.

15 See The World Bank, "Gross domestic product 2018", available at https://databank.worldbank.org/data/download/GDP.pdf. GDP per capita was approximately 81,700 USD in 2018, see The World Bank, "GDP per capita (current US$)", available at https://data.worldbank.org/indicator/NY.GDP.PCAP.CD. Both links accessed 27 March 2020.

16 Statistics Norway, "Indicators for gender equality in municipalities, 2019" http://www.ssb.no/en/befolkning/statistikker/likekom/aar accessed 27 March 2020.

authorities but at the same time allowing a high degree of self-governance.[17] The attempt to reduce differences between groups and individuals in the Norwegian legal culture over centuries has caused a certain aversion to conflicts and a rather uncompetitive attitude (with the except of sports). As a consequence of the egalitarian nature of the Norwegian culture in combination with the geopolitical and historical preconditions of the country, pragmatic solutions are favoured over principled ones.[18] A common feature with other Nordic countries is that social welfare has been state policy since the 1930s. Relatively high taxes are one result of this policy, but also comparably high standards of social security, as well as in the health and labour sector.

2. Conflict Resolution

2.1 Ordinary conflict resolution

The ordinary Norwegian courts are organized into a three-level court hierarchy, typical for all Nordic courts.[19] Judges in these courts are provided with a general jurisdiction. Altogether there were 376 district judges in Norway in 2018,[20] handling about 14,500 civil cases and 64,500 criminal cases.[21] Among the civil cases also administrative cases will be counted, i.e., review of administrative decisions. A common feature of all Nordic countries is that there is no separate constitutional court. Consequently, this figure also includes constitutional cases.

The Norwegian three-level court hierarchy was established with the Code of 1274 issued by Magnus the Law Mender and has since been considered an ideal structure. Nevertheless, the historical traces are mainly to be found in the terminology and basic structure, and do not mirror continuity in their function.[22] Originally, the assemblies consisted of a gathering of free men deciding cases according to local customs and often mitigating conflicts rather than judging strictly according to law. However, the Code of 1274 strengthened the institutional procedures. The King would now safeguard that the verdicts of the assembly were followed, and royal officials gradually started to achieve

---

17 Anna Nylund, "The Many Ways of Civil Mediation in Norway" in Laura Ervo and Anna Nylund (Eds.), *The Future of Civil Litigation – Access to Court and Court Annexed Mediation in the Nordic Countries* (Springer 2014) 104.

18 Ibid.

19 Jørn Øyrehagen Sunde, "From Courts of Appeal to Courts of Precedent—Access to the Highest Courts in the Nordic Countries" in Cornelis Hendrik (Remco) van Rhee and Yullin Fu (Eds.), *Supreme Courts in Transition in China and in the West* (Springer 2017) 59–60.

20 Domstolsadministrasjonen, "Årsrapport 2018 Om domstolene i Norge", available at https://www.domstol.no/Enkelt-domstol/arsrapport/om-domstolene-i-norge/ accessed 4 December 2019. There were also 161 deputy judges temporarily employed.

21 Domstolsadministrasjonen, "Årsrapport 2018. Saksavvikling i domstolene", available at https://www.domstol.no/Enkelt-domstol/arsrapport/aktiviteterogresultater/saksavvikling/ accessed 12 March 2020.

22 With some more details on terminological continuities and functional discontinuities in the Norwegian legal system, see Sören Koch, "Consequences of changing expectations to law and its institutions. Illustrated by the role and background of judges in Norway" (2015) 83 *The Legal History Review* 461.

judge-like competences. Still, as a rule, a jury of free men (*lagrette*) ruled on the facts.[23] Through a royal decree from 1590, an appellate system was introduced and in 1797 the court system was fundamentally restructured.[24] From that point on the elements of lay participation in the appellate courts were considerably reduced. Nevertheless, in the district courts at the first level, lay participation has been an immanent part since time immemorial. At the same time, an extrajudicial mechanism of conflict resolution was introduced in which local laymen would help the parties to settle the case.[25] Lay participation in court was re-established in criminal cases in 1887 and in civil cases in 1915.[26] In many of the criminal cases, lay participation took the form of a co-operational model where the panel consisted of both lay and professional judges (*meddomsrett*), but in certain cases before the second instance courts, a jury was given the exclusive competence to rule on the facts of the case.[27] Due to continuous criticism of the jury system, the Criminal Procedural Act was changed in 1933, and the professional judges could overrule the verdict of the jury if they were convinced that the verdict was based on a wrongful evaluation of evidence presented in court.[28] After many decades of public and scholarly discussion, the jury was finally abolished in 2018, and the cases formerly decided under the jury system are now decided under a co-operational model as well.[29] But even though the jury's competence to rule exclusively on the facts of criminal cases was removed, the lay judges still maintain a majority over the professional judges.[30] Lay judges have played a less important role in civil cases, but the parties have a right to request to have the judge in their case supplemented by two lay judges.[31] In the Supreme Court, laymen have never been involved. Compared to other European legal cultures, the lay element in criminal proceedings remains relatively strong in Norway.

---

23 Sunde (2014), "Daughters of God" (n. 7).

24 On these reforms and their historical context see Koch (2015) (n. 22) 475 ff.

25 Anna Nylund emphasises that the lay members have limited power to decide the case, see Nylund (2014) (n. 17) 103: "Conciliation boards are still part of the court system, although they are not formally defined as courts. According to the Dispute Act, general civil cases start in the Conciliation boards, although they have only limited powers to decide cases."

26 The Civil Dispute Act that was enacted in 1915 did, however, only enter into force several years later – in part in 1927 and in its entirety in 1936.

27 On the history and development of the jury system, see e.g. NOU 2011: 13 Juryutvalget – Når sant skal skrives Chapter 5; NOU 2002: 11 "Dømmes av likemenn" Chapter 3; NUT 1969: 3 Innstilling om rettergangsmåten i straffesaker fra Straffeprosesslovkomiteen 73 ff.

28 See NUT 1969: 3, 75.

29 For the preparatory works, see Prop. 70 L (2016–2017) Endringer i straffeprosessloven mv. (oppheving av juryordningen).

30 In the district courts, the panel is as a main rule set up with two lay judges and one professional judge, cfr. Lov-1981-05-22-25 om rettergangsmåten i straffesaker (straffeprosessloven) [The Criminal Procedure Act] § 276. In the appellate courts, the panel consists of five lay judges and two professional judges, cfr. § 332. However, it is worth mentioning that not all cases are decided under the co-operational model.

31 Lov 2005-06-17-90 om mekling og retterganger i sivile tvister (tvisteloven) [the Civil Dispute Act] § 9-12.

At the first level of courts, there are 60 district courts of first instance (*tingretter*).[32] More than one third of the district courts are staffed with three FTE judicial posts or less,[33] whereas the largest, situated in the capital of Oslo, has more than 70 judges and 40 deputy judges.[34] In smaller courts the judge or the judges have to handle all kinds of cases. But even in rather small courts, an informal and partial specialization is possible through court assignment. This means that judges with special competence are assigned cases where this competence is relevant.[35] The problem is that such a practice can easily be in conflict with the principle of random case assignment.[36] In Oslo district court, this informal and partial specialization is taken to the level of moderate specialization. Here, approximately half of the judges spend 25 % of their workload on cases from one or a few specific fields of law.[37] Oslo district court also deals with all intellectual property cases in Norway, a task the court can only fulfil to a satisfactory extent by a moderate specialization within the court. In 2019, an expert commission proposed to reduce the number of district courts to 22, one of the arguments being that larger organizations will enhance the possibility for moderate specialization and thereby improve the quality of the courts' work.[38] The political authorities will most likely choose a different approach, but a reorganization with the aim of creating larger jurisdictional units is the most likely outcome.[39]

On the second level there are six courts of appeal (*lagmannsretter*). The only access to the court of appeal is through appeal from the district courts. The only two exceptions are appeals from The National Insurance Court (*Trygderetten*) and the Norwegian Complaints Board for Public Procurement (*Klagenemnda for Offentlige Anskaffer*), which are both administrative organs with court-like functions.[40] In 2018, the Norwegian courts of appeal employed 180 judges altogether, handling annually about 2,000 civil cases and

32 See NOU 2019: 17 Domstolstruktur 32. An NOU (abbr. for *Norges offentlige utredninger*) is an Official Norwegian Report, that is, a report drawn up by an expert commission on the basis of a mandate from the Government. The NOUs form a key part of Norwegian politics and legislative procedure. All NOUs can be accessed at https://www.regjeringen.no/no/dokument/nou-ar/id1767/.

33 Ibid. 23.

34 See https://www.domstol.no/en/Enkelt-domstol/Oslo-District-Court/om-domstolen/virksomheten/organisasjon/ accessed 28 March 2020.

35 See NOU 2017: 8 Særdomstoler på nye områder? 38–39.

36 Ibid. 37.

37 See https://www.domstol.no/en/Enkelt-domstol/Oslo-District-Court/om-domstolen/virksomheten/moderat-spesialisering/ accessed 28 March 2020.

38 See NOU 2019: 17 Domstolstruktur 78–81. More precisely, the commission has proposed to reduce the number of jurisdictional entities (*rettskretser*) to 22, but some of these will, just like today, have several offices (*rettssteder*) due to geographical distances. The commission suggested a reduction from 69 to 30 offices.

39 In March 2020, the Government presented the report for public consultation, together with an alternative structure proposed by the Government. The Government's proposal is to reduce the jurisdictional entities to 22 but to keep all of the 69 offices that exist today, see e.g. Aud Darrud, "Regjeringen vil beholde antall domstoler, men slå sammen administrasjonene", *NRK.no* 2 March 2020, available at https://www.nrk.no/norge/domstolsstrukturen-pa-horing_-regjeringen-vil-beholde-antall-domstoler_-men-kutte-i-administrasjon-1.14925415 accessed 3 April 2020.

40 Lov 1966-12-16-9 om anke til Trygderetten [Appeals to the National Insurance Court Act] § 26; and Lov 2004-03-05-12 om konkurranse mellom foretak og kontroll med foretakssammenslutninger [Competition Act] § 39.

1,300 criminal cases.[41] There are no special chambers within the appeal courts. However, Borgarting Court of Appeal in Oslo is the only court that deals with appeals in cases concerning intellectual property, while Gulating Court of Appeal in Bergen is the only appellate court to deal with competition law cases. To take on this role, there has to be a moderate specialisation within these courts, meaning that some judges specialize in these kinds of cases by simply taking more than their mathematical share of a specific kind of cases.

On top of the pyramidal court hierarchy is the Norwegian Supreme Court, with the same general jurisdiction as the lower courts, concerning all fields of law including civil, criminal, administrative, and constitutional matters. In contrast to most of the continental legal cultures, but in accordance with the Nordic tradition, the Supreme Court has the competence to examine both the facts and the application of the law, with the exception that in criminal cases, it cannot evaluate the evidence.[42] The Supreme Court is divided into two chambers.[43] The members of each chamber are rotating. Consequently, these chambers do not consist of permanent bodies of staff with specialist insight in certain fields of law and cannot develop a case law distinct from the other chamber. In other words, the aim is to avoid specialisation and diverging case law, thus securing legal unity.[44]

Under certain circumstances, especially in cases concerning deviation from established Supreme Court practice and questions regarding review of Norwegian law in relation to the Constitution or international law, a grand chamber consisting of 11 judges has to decide. A plenary session of 19 judges decides extraordinary cases.[45] This plenary function of the Norwegian Supreme Court makes it also a *quasi*-constitutional court,[46] which is a feature common to all Scandinavian countries. Hence, the Norwegian Supreme Court has been a member of the Conference of European Constitutional Courts since 2003.[47]

The right to exercise judicial review is a right enjoyed by all courts at all levels. Hence, a single district court judge might rule an act of Parliament invalid. In Norway this

41 Domstolsadministrasjonen, "Årsrapport 2018. Nøkkeltall 2018", available at https://www.domstol.no/Enkelt-domstol/arsrapport/nokkeltall2018/ accessed 4 December 2019.

42 See the Civil Dispute Act §§ 30-3 and 29-3 and the Criminal Procedure Act § 306.

43 See Lov 1915-08-13-5 om domstolene (domstolloven) [the Court Act] § 4.

44 For details regarding the implementation of the two chambers and their function, see Jørn Øyrehagen Sunde, *Høgsteretts historie 1965–2015 – At dømme i sidste Instans* (Fagbokforlaget 2015) 165–167.

45 See the Court Act § 5 (4). Recent examples of cases decided in plenary session include a case concerning the constitutional prohibition of retroactive effect (Rt. 2010 p. 143), the lawfulness of a workers' union's boycott under EEA law (HR-2016-2554-P), and land rights for a Sámi community (HR-2018-456-P). The latter two cases can be read in English here: https://www.domstol.no/en/Enkelt-domstol/supremecourt/rulings/2019/supreme-court-criminal-cases/hr-2019-282-s/ and https://www.domstol.no/en/Enkelt-domstol/supremecourt/rulings/2018/hoyesterett-sivil/hr-2018-456-p/ accessed 27 March 2020.

46 Arnfinn Bårdsen, "De nordiske høyesterettene som konstitusjonsdomstoler: Noen nyere utviklingslinjer i Norges Høyesterett", speech held at a seminar for the Nordic supreme courts, Stockholm 23 and 24 March 2015, available at https://www.domstol.no/globalassets/upload/hret/artikler-og-foredrag/nordiske-konstitusjonsdomstoler---stockholm-mars-2015.pdf accessed 9 March 2020.

47 See https://www.vfgh.gv.at/cms/vfgh-kongress/en/geschichte.html accessed 20 April 2017.

happened last in 2010.[48] This might be explained by the influence from USA, especially through the work of Alexis de Tocqueville in the first half of the 19th century, giving the US court a far more prominent place in government than what was known from the European continent.[49] But even more important are the geographical distances within Norway (see above). Appeals from one edge of the country to the Supreme Court in the centre, would be time consuming due to travel distances alone. In Norway a culturally founded notion that it was the duty of a district judge to pass a decision like the Supreme Court to save appeal and travel seems to have developed already in the 18th century.

If the Parliament (*Stortinget*) disagrees with a specific ruling of the court, the only way to handle the situation is to enact new legislation, which then is binding for the judiciary in future cases, or to amend the Constitution.[50] A strict separation of powers in the French tradition was thus never realised or intended in Norway, and Norwegian courts have exercised a right to review administrative decisions since 1818, and performed constitutional review since 1822.[51] The courts' right and duty to review was finally codified in 2015.[52]

2.2 Miscellaneous mechanisms of conflict resolution

There are three main exception to the general jurisdiction of Norwegian first instance courts, meaning that the specialized court are a separate administrative unit and the decisions are appealed directly to the Appeal Court. First of all there is the Land Consolidation Courts, handling property related cases.[53] These courts can trace their roots far back into the 19th century, and were labelled a specialised court from 1882, but first in 2004 made a part of the general court administration.[54] There are today 34 Land Consolidation Courts in Norway, and here 80 judges[55] handled 1,288 cases in 2017.[56] There also used to be Land Consolidation Appeal Courts, but from 2016 the ordinary courts of appeal also deal with the appeals in land consolidation cases.

---

48 HR-2010-2057-P; https://lovdata.no/artikkel/dom_i_hoyesterett_i_plenum_-_forbrytelse_mot_menneskeheten_og_krigsforbrytelse/254 accessed 10 April 2017.

49 Martin Sunnquist, *Konstitutionellt kritiskt dömande – Förändringar av nordiska domares attityder under två sekel* (Jure 2014) 132–133, 156–157 and 174.

50 An example is the *Finanger* case (Rt. 2001 p. 1811).

51 Eirik Holmøyvik, "Utviklinga av prøvingsretten i Norge" in Dag Michalsen and Eirik Holmøyvik, *Lærebok i forfatningshistorie* (Pax 2015). For a general account of the development of judicial review, see also Anine Kierulf, *Judicial Review in Norway. A Bicentennial Debate* (Cambridge University Press 2018).

52 Kongeriket Norges Grunnlov [The Norwegian Constitution] § 89.

53 On these courts, see https://www.domstol.no/en/the-land-consolidation-courts-of-norway/ accessed 26 April 2017.

54 Hans Sevatdal and Eirik Wannebo, "Utviklingen av jordskifteretten sett i lys av matrikkelsystemet, forvaltningen og de ordinære domstoler" in Øyvind Ravna (Ed.), *Areal og eiendomsrett* (Universitetsforlaget 2007) 391–414.

55 The Land Consolidation Courts also employed 8 deputy judges in 2018, see https://www.domstol.no/Enkelt-domstol/arsrapport/nokkeltall2018/ accessed 9 March 2020.

56 See https://www.domstol.no/domstoladministrasjonen/publikasjoner/arsrapport/tema-13/domstolene-i-2017/#-jordskifterettene accessed 9 March 2020. The abovementioned expert commission has suggested to reduce the number of jurisdictional entities for the Land Consolidation Courts to 13 and keep 20 offices, see NOU 2019: 17 Domstolstruktur 166.

There is also a Norwegian Labour Court, established in 1915. As in the other Nordic countries, the Norwegian Labour Court originates from the specific organization of the labour market, where collective agreements play a central role as a regulative instrument. It is therefore disputes arising from collective agreements that fall within the jurisdiction of the labour court in Norway.[57] In 2018, this court decided 16 cases by judgment of a panel of seven judges, where three are permanent judges with a training as lawyers, and 26 cases were decided by instruments other than judgment.[58]

In Oslo, there is a special district court, dealing with bankruptcy and several traditional notary tasks.[59] In other cities these specialised courts merged with the district courts during the last court reform in 2006.

A special position within the Norwegian court system, is the district court in the inner part of the County Finnmark, the Sis-Finnmárkku diggegoddi. This is not a specialized court, but one of the districts courts. However, it is a district court with special language requirements and partly a different hierarchy of legal sources, established to ensure the Sámi – the indigenous population in northern Norway – access to court. Cases with Sámi parties are heard in Sámi, and Sámi customs are given a special priority.[60] When cases are appealed to Hålogaland Court of Appeal and the Supreme Court, these special features still apply.

When considering conflict resolution in Norway today, one must distinguish between the ordinary court hierarchy and quasi-judicial organs of conflict resolution. The ordinary courts with general jurisdiction organized in a pyramidal court hierarchy, with the few exceptions described above, are on one hand significantly different from what we find in other European countries. On the other hand, the general jurisdiction and the organization of the ordinary courts is possible because of the flora of quasi-judicial organs surrounding the court hierarchy.

Different kinds of boards (*nemnder*) are an important part of this flora.[61] These bodies are either public, like The Patients' Injury Compensation Board (*Pasientskadenemnda*), or semi-public, like the Financial Services Complaints Board (*Finansklagenemnda*), which is set up by the industry itself in co-operation with public authorities. These boards might treat rather few cases annually, or thousands of cases every year, like the Immigration Appeals Board (*Utlendingsnemnda*). They might be court-like with an oral procedure, like the County Social Welfare Boards (*Fylkesnemndene for barnevern og sosiale saker*), or operate more like an administrative complaint board, like the Norwegian Compensation Board for Victims of Violent Crime (*Erstatningsnemnda for voldsof-*

57 See http://www.arbeidsretten.no/engelsk.php accessed 20 April 2017.

58 See the 2018 annual report of the Norwegian Labour Court p. 6, available (in Norwegian) at https://www.arbeidsretten.no/dv-cms/resources/virksomhetsrapport-2018.pdf accessed 9 March 2020.

59 See https://www.domstol.no/en/Enkelt-domstol/Oslo-County-Court/ accessed 27 March 2020. The abovementioned expert commission has proposed to merge the special district court and the ordinary district court in Oslo, see NOU 2019: 17 Domstolstruktur 65–66.

60 See https://www.domstol.no/Enkelt-domstol/indre-finnmark-tingrett/om-indre-finnmark-tingrett/samisk-dimensjon/ accessed 9 March 2020.

61 For a concise overview, see Nylund (2014) (n. 17).

fer). The more than 50 public Norwegian complaint boards handled more than 30,000 cases both concerning civil and administrative law in 2014.[62] That was about twice as many cases as was handled by the ordinary courts at all levels.[63] These specialised boards have taken over many of the cases which were originally treated by the conciliation boards (*forliksråd*) which have roots back to the late 18th century.[64] The conciliation boards are a municipality-based, mediation-like conflict resolution board with three lay judges appointed by the municipality council, which hear and decide petty cases locally. In 2017, more than 350 conciliation boards, one for each municipality, decided a little over 77,000 cases.[65]

In addition, mediation is becoming increasingly important and popular in Norway.[66] More than 10 % of all civil claims filed in the Norwegian first instance courts in 2014 were mediated in court by a judge, with a success rate of about 65 %.[67] It should also be noted that another 10 % of the civil cases are subject to a special small claims procedure within the ordinary courts, which is supposed to be less time consuming, less costly, and hence also less traditionally legal in form. Of criminal cases, almost 50 % are subject to summary proceedings on the basis of a guilty plea, which is also less time consuming, less costly, and also to a lesser degree governed by strict judicial procedures.[68]

The following figure contains an overview of the Norwegian system of conflict-resolution.

62 See the official report of the competent department: Difi-rapport 2014:2 "Viltvoksende nemnder? Om organisering og regulering av statlige klagenemnder" p. 14. Available at https://www.difi.no/sites/difino/files/difi-rapport-2014_2-viltvoksende-nemnder.-om-organisering-og-regulering-av-statlige-klagenemnder.pdf accessed 27 March 2020.

63 Domstolsadministrasjonen, "Domstolene i Norge. Årsrapport 2014" 16–18.

64 On the history of alternative dispute resolution with a particular focus on mediation in the Nordic countries, see Anna Nylund, Kaijus Ervasti and Lin Adrian, "Introduction to Nordic Mediation Research" in Anna Nylund, Kaijus Ervasti and Lin Adrian, *Nordic Mediation Research* (Springer 2019) 2.

65 See http://www.forliksraadet.no/index.php?page_id=30 accessed 9 March 2020.

66 See Camilla Bernt, *Meklerrollen ved mekling i domstolene* (Fagbokforlaget 2011).

67 Domstolsadministrasjonen, "Domstolene i Norge. Årsrapport 2014" 17.

68 Ibid.

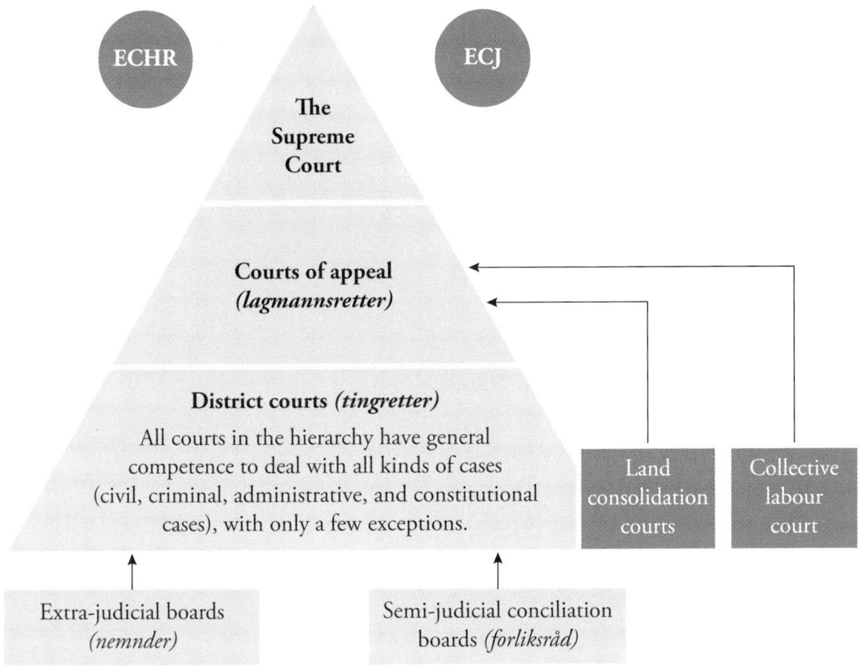

Fig. 1 The Norwegian Court System – an overview.

2.3 Perspectives

An open question is how to integrate the international courts of justice into this picture of the Norwegian court hierarchy. The European Court of Human Rights (ECtHR), the EFTA Court, and the European Court of Justice (ECJ) are in fact quite important for the resolution of conflicts in Norway. However, their jurisprudence is not directly binding on or applicable in the Norwegian courts. Norway is in principle governed by the dualistic approach, meaning that international and national law are two separate domains.[69] Accordingly, if an alteration of a legal provision proves necessary because it is regarded as violating the Convention or the EEA Agreement, it is the task of the Norwegian legislator to abolish or replace it, not the court's.[70] Consequently, the international courts of justice do not constitute an extra level of appeal in the ordinary court hierarchy of Norway. On the other hand, the dynamic way of applying the law in the European Courts is quite similar to the way the Norwegian courts work. Furthermore, due to the pragmatic approach to legal method, judgments of the ECJ or the EFTA Court are

69 See subsection on internationalisation below.

70 See e.g. Rt. 2010 p. 1500 and Rt. 2005 p. 1365 (the *Finanger II* ruling).

relevant as a legal argument base (*rettskildefaktor*).[71] The rulings of the European Courts are therefore often *de facto* treated as if they were precedents, even though they are not.[72]

3. Norm Production

3.1 Introduction

King Magnus the Law Mender's Code of 1274 introduced full scale law lawmaking as a norm producing method in Norway. However, in the Code of 1274 it was admitted that there were loopholes in the code, and that the code at times had to be abandoned because an application of it would give an unjust outcome. In both cases the judges were not just free but obliged to mend the shortcoming of legislated law.[73] Thus, an interplay between legislator and courts as norm producers became the norm in the Norwegian legal culture, even though attempts have been made several times to shift the balance in favour of the legislator.[74] Hence in present Norwegian law, Parliament's legislation, the Parliamentary authorised administrative norm production (delegated legislation), and courts making precedent are still the three major mechanisms of producing legal norms.

3.2 Norm production by Parliament and the executive branch of government

Norm production through legislation has a long tradition in Norway and Scandinavia. As stated above, Norway got its first code of law covering the entire realm in 1274. Only three other European countries did the same in the High Middle Ages.[75] In the Early Modern Period, new codes were enacted in Denmark (1683), in Norway (1687), and Sweden, which included Finland until 1809 (1734). The Norwegian Code of 1687 is still formally part of the applicable law, even though only six of the originally more than 1,800 articles still apply.

In the aftermath of the Code of 1274, a series of statutes were already produced to amend the law. After the Code of 1687 was issued, more than 4,500 statutes amended, replaced or supplied the articles in the code until 1814.[76] Since 1687, legislated law has been produced in the form of statutes – i.e. single acts, ordinances or decrees covering single fields of law – instead of continentally modelled codes. In the Norwegian con-

71 See the subsection on internationalisation below.

72 Sunde (2015), *Høgsteretts historie* (n. 44) 451–453.

73 Jørn Øyrehagen Sunde, "The Legal Cultural Dependency of the Norwegian Legal Method – and its Future" in Ingvill Helland and Sören Koch (Eds.), *Nordic and Germanic Legal Methods* (Mohr Siebeck 2014) 48–49.

74 Cf. King Christian the V's Norwegian Code of 1687 – Book I Section I Art. 2 in conjunction with Art. 4, stating that nobody but the King had the right to amend, abolish, dispend or even interpret the provision of this early modern law compilation. Advocates were at the same time prohibited to refer to precedents in the Supreme Court.

75 Armin Wolf, *Gesetzgebung in Europa 1100–1500* (C.H. Beck 1996) 47–48.

76 See Jørn Øyrehagen Sunde, "Fornuft og Erfarenhed" – framveksten av metodisk medvit i dansknorsk rett på 1700-talet (Ph.D. thesis, University of Bergen 2007) 39.

stitution it was decided that the independent Norway would adopt a civil and criminal code in the French tradition within a few years. A criminal code was issued in 1842 but abandoned and replaced by statutes in 1902. A civil code was drafted, but never completed, and in 1845, Parliament decided to dismiss the project.[77] Instead, the tradition of issuing statutes prevailed.

This means that Norway has never established a tradition of regulating law in the form of a civil code with a chapter on family law and a sub-chapter on cohabitation where a definition of cohabitation was given, where marriage and cohabitation were made alternative forms of partnership with equal legal consequences, and finally the exceptions of equal legal consequences. Instead, in Norway separate statutes have been adopted: regulating for instance marriage or the relationship between children and parents,[78] while cohabitation was a subject in 52 statutes and 677 decrees in 2017,[79] with several definitions that do not seem to be related to each other.[80] Due to this tradition of legislation, Norwegian legislation appears *fragmentary*, which is one of the reasons why court practice plays an important role in unifying the law. We will return to this important notion of the Norwegian legal culture, when analysing intellectual elements.

The tempo in and extent of the legislative activity has varied up through history and are at present very high. Since the turn of the millennium, the Norwegian Parliament has annually passed about 120 legislative acts. Most of them – usually more than 80 % – are acts amending already existing statutes. However, they can still be quite extensive. The rest is new legislation either replacing existing statutes, or filling loopholes in legal regulation. Altogether, Norway has a little more than 600 statutes.[81] Some might be very brief, like the statute from 1999 with only four paragraphs turning five major human rights conventions into Norwegian law.[82] Others are extensive, like the statute on civil procedure from 2005, which could have been labelled a code in its own right.[83]

Already in the fall of 1814 we find that the Norwegian Constitution of 1814 was applied in the courts as positive law.[84] This is one of the reasons for the early develop-

77 Hilde Sandvik, "Hvorfor lyktes kriminalloven, men ikke sivilloven i Norge?" in Hilde Sandvik and Dag Michalsen (Eds.), *Kodifikasjon og konstitusjon – Grunnloven § 94s krav til lovbøker i norsk historie* (Pax Forlag 2013). See also Dag Michalsen, *Rett – En internasjonal historie* (Pax 2011) 356–358.

78 Lov 1991-07-04-47 om ekteskap [the Marriage Act], and Lov 1981-04-08-7 om barn og foreldre [the Act on Parents and Children].

79 Based on searches in the Lovdata database conducted 20 April 2017, see https://lovdata.no/sok?q=samboer&filter=LOVER and https://lovdata.no/sok?q=samboer.

80 See e.g. Lov 1972-03-03-5 om arv m.m. [the Inheritance Act, to be replaced 1 January 2021 by Lov 2019-06-14-21] § 28a; Lov 1986-02-28-8 om adopsjon [the Adoption Act] § 5a; Lov 1992-06-26-86 om tvangsfullbyrdelse [the Enforcement Order Act] § 7–13; Lov 1996-06-07-32 om gravplasser, kremasjon og gravferd [the Funeral Act] § 9; and Lov 2008-05-15-35 om utlendingers adgang til riket og deres opphold her [the Immigration Act] § 41.

81 NOU 2012: 2 Utenfor og innenfor – Norges avtaler med EU, 126 footnote 11.

82 The Human Rights Act § 2 (see n. 12).

83 The Civil Dispute Act (see n. 31).

84 Frode Ulvund, *Fridomens grenser 1814–1851. Handhevinga av den norske "jødeparagrafen"* (Spartacus Forlag/Scandinavian Academic Press 2014) 141–173.

ment of a right to review legislation, despite the fact that the Constitution itself did not contain anything about such a right until 2015.[85]

The Norwegian Parliament amends the constitution and produces statutes. However, the executive branch of government is also a major norm producer, providing decrees. In Norway there are more than 10,000 decrees. Some of them are short-lived, like decrees on seasonal fishery,[86] while some last for years and years.[87] Some decrees are fairly short,[88] while some are as long as a statute.[89] At times there can be a blurred borderline between what can be regulated by the executive through decrees, and what has to be regulated by statutes by the legislator.[90]

The legislator does not only produce legislation with a normative effect, but also preparatory works. Preparatory works are the documented investigations, discussions, and statements from the legislative process by expert commissions, by government ministries, by parliamentary Standing Committees, etc.[91] In Norway the values and principles a statute is based upon can be found here, as well as the rationale behind and meaning of the different provisions discussed and explained. They make it possible to keep the legislation rather short and readable, because details and digressions can be put into the preparatory work. In many ways, the preparatory works in Norway fill a comparable function to that of commentaries on legislation in several European legal cultures. However, an essential difference is that they, in contrast to commentaries provided by legal scholars, have at least a remote democratic foundation. Having this in mind it becomes comprehensible that preparatory works are regarded a source of law in their own right, a unique feature Norway shares with the other Nordic countries.

Preparatory works have two main functions. First, a legal question might be solved according to information that is only found in the preparatory work, i.e., they serve as a primary legal argument base (*primært rettsgrunnlag*).[92] Far more often they play a secondary role as a source used to interpret legislation. Second, they tie the single statutes to the system of law more in general. It has to be kept in mind that between these two functions, there is a quite unclear borderline.

As a result of abandoning the idea of a systematically coherent codification, the predominant legislative technique has remained until today to make statute-like laws on specific topics or amendments to existing legislation, accompanied by preparatory works. Despite the fragmentary character of legislation in the Nordics, the idea of legisla-

85 Cf. Norwegian Constitution § 89.

86 E.g. Forskrift om regulering av fisket etter blåkveite nord for 62° N (FOR 2016-12-21-1835), enacted in 2017.

87 E.g. Delegering av myndighet etter lov om konkurranse i ervervsvirksomhet (konkurranseloven) og lov om pristiltak fra Administrasjonsdepartementet til Konkurransetilsynet (FOR-1993-12-17-1314).

88 E.g. Delegering av Kongens myndighet til å sette lov 17. juni 2016 nr. 30 om EØS-finanstilsyn i kraft til Finansdepartementet (FOR-2016-06-17-714).

89 E.g. Forskrift til lov om gravplasser, kremasjon og gravferd (FOR-1997-01-10-16).

90 See e.g. https://www.stortinget.no/no/Saker-og-publikasjoner/Publikasjoner/Innstillinger/Stortinget/2013-2014/inns-201314-299/1/ accessed 21 April 2017.

91 The preparatory works are mostly digitalised and can be accessed via the database Lovdata.

92 Nils Nygaard, *Rettsgrunnlag og standpunkt* (2nd ed., Universitetsforlaget 2007) 103–104; Erik Monsen, *Innføring i juridisk metode og oppgaveteknikk* (Cappelen Damm Akademisk 2012) 86.

tion as a main source of norm production was never abandoned. In addition, Norwegian laws are as a rule formed abstract/general in character. Therefore, lawyers can deduce legal consequences from them. This has led some to the idea that Norway is a civil law system.[93] We cannot subscribe to such a statement. Instead, Norway can be labelled a hybrid legal system with features comparable to, but neither completely identical to nor received from either the common or the civil law tradition. Norway shares this with legal systems, which have been labelled "mixed legal systems".[94] The most prominent examples of such mixed legal systems are Scotland and South Africa. However, in contrast to Norway, tthe legal systems and the legal cultures of these countries have a more formal link to the common and civil law traditions than the Norwegian legal culture. An important factor resembling the common law tradition in Norway is the role of courts as norm producers.

3.3 Norm production by the Supreme Court

As we have seen, the Supreme Court is alone at the top of the Norwegian court hierarchy. Even in the Code of 1274, the King and his council were made the third and last instance in the court system, and their decisions would have the same effect as legislated law.[95] This system prevailed until the Code of 1687, which intended to abolish the court's norm-producing power. However, the Code itself, as well as the gradually increasing number of additional statutes, proved insufficient to regulate the Norwegian realm. Therefore, the Supreme Court would continue to produce norms by providing precedents until 1814. Inspired by the philosophy of Montesquieu, the constitutional assembly obliged the Parliament to enact a civil and criminal code.[96] Once again, one of the underlying intentions was to abandon precedent as a legal source. The idea was that this would secure legal unity, and hence predictability. However, as mentioned above, this aim was never achieved, and precedent remained the most important legal source in a Norwegian context next to legislation.

The present Norwegian Supreme Court was established with the enactment of the Constitution of 1814 and decided its first case the following year. Already in 1815, the court itself decided to keep a record of previous decisions. This was a signal to practicing lawyers that they would have some effect as precedent. For this reason, Supreme Court

---

93 E.g. Konrad Zweigert and Hein Kötz, *An Introduction to Comparative Law* (3rd ed., Clarendon Press 1998) 277, Jacob Sundberg, "Civil Law, Common Law and the Scandinavians" (1969) 13 *Scandinavian Studies in Law* 179, and Giuditta Cordero-Moss, "International Contracts between Common Law and Civil Law: Is Non-state Law to Be Preferred? The Difficulty of Interpreting Legal Standards Such as Good Faith" (2007) 7 No. 1 *Global Jurist Advances* 14.

94 Concerning the terminology of "mixed legal systems" and "legal hybrids", see Sören Koch, "Legal Culture and Comparative Law – Diving into the Ocean" in this volume, Chapter 3, 62 ff.

95 Sunde (2014), "The Legal Cultural Dependency" (n. 73) 53.

96 See Sandvik (2013) (n. 77).

decisions were published from 1836 by the Norwegian Bar Association.[97] From 1864, the decisions were published in full length with the reasoning, and with dissenting votes. This made the Supreme Court decisions accessible and suitable as precedent.[98] However, the main task of the Supreme Court was to decide the individual case as a last resort for appeal.[99] Hence, Supreme Court decisions would have the effect of precedent if it turned out that they were be used as a legal source in a later case. This was the situation until the early 1990s. At this time the number of court cases in general had proliferated dramatically, increasing the workload of the Supreme Court. The legislator, with important input from the Court, hence had to decide whether the Court should increase its caseload – which had at its peaks gone beyond 400 decisions annually – and the number of chambers and judges, or whether it should decrease the caseload and concentrate on producing precedent. Partly, the Parliament passed the necessary changes in the procedural legislation, and partly, it supplied the Supreme Court with the financial means to hire clerks,[100] and gradually the Court was transformed to a court of precedent without much political consideration and no political debate. In practice this means that the cases appealed to the Norwegian Supreme Court are filtered and 90 % of all appeals are denied access to the Supreme Court by a decision that is usually brief, and decided by three judges but mainly drafted by the Court's clerks.[101] The remaining 10 % are cases concerning legal issues that the Appeal Selection Committee finds need legal clarification or development, and the decision is aimed at this. Thus, today almost all decisions passed by the Supreme Court are precedents.[102] In practice this means that the decisions are lengthy, they have a thorough discussion of law, a clearer formulation of the legal rule produced, and individual votes and dissents that underline the individual responsibility of the judges when deciding the case and producing a legal norm for future application.

As in the rest of the Nordic countries, there is no *stare decisis* principle recognised in Norwegian law. Firstly, because precedent produced by the Norwegian Supreme Court is not formally binding. The factual binding character of precedent is instead first and foremost a product of legal cultural notions.[103] Secondly, only decisions passed by the Supreme Court are regarded as precedent in legal theory and treated as such by the

97 Today the database Lovdata provides full text versions of all Supreme Court decisions dating back to the 19th century. In addition, a great number of appellate court and district court decisions can be found here. Note, however, that these rulings do not have the same function and effect as precedent, see in more detail the subsection on legal method below.

98 Sunde (2015), *Høgsteretts historie* (n. 44) 243–245.

99 Cf. The Norwegian Constitution § 88: "The Supreme Court rules in last instance".

100 Gunnar Grendstad, William R. Shaffer, Jørn Øyrehagen Sunde and Eric N. Waltenburg, *Proactive and Powerful – Law Clerks and the Institutionalization of the Norwegian Supreme Court* (Eleven 2020) 173–179.

101 Ibid. 82–85.

102 See Jørn Øyrehagen Sunde, "Dissenting votes in the Norwegian Supreme Court 1965–2009: A legal cultural analysis" (2012) Heft 1 *Rechtskultur – Zeitschrift für Europäische Rechtsgeschichte* 59, 62–63 and 66–68.

103 It is possible to argue, however, that the role of Supreme Court precedent has been recognised by the legislator. According to The Court Act § 5 (4), a potential deviation from its own practice is one of the factors to be taken into account when the Court decides whether a case shall be relinquished from a chamber in favour of a grand chamber or plenary session. This procedure was first established with the Plenary Act of 1926.

courts themselves.[104] Decisions of district courts and courts of appeal are hence only relevant to the parties of the case and produce no effect *inter omnes*. But in some fields of law where legislation and precedent have been scarce, like tort law, decisions from lower courts traditionally have attracted some more attention.[105] However, in the aftermath of the Norwegian Supreme Court changing from a court of appeal to a court of precedent, the character of appeal court decisions has changed as well. The reason is that the Supreme Court has reduced its caseload to be able to produce decisions with more relevance to the legal system. In recent years, the court handles between 100 and 120 cases every year. The need for clarification and development of law by the courts is felt by practitioners to be larger than what these rather few decisions can fulfil.[106] Gradually, the decisions by the courts of appeal have gained what in the common law tradition is labelled "persuasive authority". This development has yet not influenced the teaching of legal method at the universities, but in 2016, the new role of appellate court decisions was partly recognised by the Supreme Court.[107]

The increased focus on precedent in the Norwegian Supreme Court from the early 1990s was possible mainly due to the Court's decisions being treated as an important legal source next to legislation in parts of Norwegian legal literature and the teaching of law. Legal literature in itself has not had any prominent role as a source of law. Its contribution to the norm production has been mainly through systematising legislation and Supreme Court decisions, and hence creating a system from which new norms might be deduced. In some fields of law with a scarcity of legislation and precedent, such as tort law, this has been a valuable, but not large, contribution to norm production.

3.4 Other kinds of norm production

Since the middle of the 19th century, there has been a very distinct separation between custom and customary law, where the latter is a legal source and the first only has the potential to be one. Customary law is custom recognised by the courts as a legal source. Hence, the production of norms through the making of customary law is shared between the legal subjects creating a custom, and the courts turning it into customary law. However in general, mainly due to the role of precedent, customary law plays a quite insignificant role in Norwegian law today. The exception is Sámi law. The Sámi are an indigenous people today found from the middle to the very north of Norway. Due to treaty obligations and the Constitution § 108, Sámi customs enjoy special relevance in Norwegian law. This is one of the reasons why the district court of Inner Finnmark

104 Sunde (2015), *Høgsterets historie* (n. 44) 245–256.

105 Nils Nygaard, *Skade og ansvar* (Universitetsforlaget 2007) 525–530; Peter Lødrup and Morten Kjelland, *Lærebok i erstatningsrett* (Gyldendal Akademisk 2009) 572–574.

106 Jørn Øyrehagen Sunde, "Norsk personskaderett i praksis" (2015) No. 2 *Tidsskrift for erstatningsrett forsikringsrett og velferdsrett, 77*, 78–80.

107 HR-2016-1803-A (para. 15).

County was established in 2005, with a special obligation to allow room for Sámi language and customs.

Furthermore, administrative organs may also produce legally relevant practice. The main rule is that administrative practice is only binding for the administration and can be reviewed by the courts if it concerns the relationship between state and citizen as well.[108] On the other hand, the Supreme Court pays attention to established administrative practice, even though it in no way is bound by it.

4. Ideal of justice

4.1 Introduction

The ideal of justice is on one hand a product of the institutional structures of the legal culture, and on the other hand it shapes the institutional structures. This dialectic relationship between the institutional and the intellectual structures of law is a key factor to understand the character of a legal culture. At the same time, it must be kept in mind that the institutional structures can be investigated empirically. For instance, the number of district courts and the number of Supreme Court decisions can be counted, and even the role of the courts of appeals' decisions can be empirically studied. One can argue that certain intellectual aspects or mentalities shape the legal cultural framework, but this can hardly ever be documented in the same way as the institutional structures. They are hence far more discursive; their relevance and importance for the understanding of a legal culture are still unquestionable.

4.2 Predictability as the main ideal of justice

In a legal context predictability became the dominating ideal of justice in the western world mainly during the 18th century, since predictability became an inherent part of the modern society emerging. Without predictability the citizens cannot enjoy protection of rights like freedom of speech and security of financial investments. But predictability is an expectation that governs almost every action in a modern society. For instance, we expect to be able in advance to know what the topic of a course taught at university is, what are the learning and reading requirements, what kind of participation is required, where and when the lectures and exam are held, etc.

Against this background, it is to be expected that predictability in general also serves as an ideal of justice in Norway. The best way to approach this issue is through the legal sources. As we have seen, legislation and precedent are the main legal sources in Norwegian law. Legislation is an instrument to produce legal norms that applies in general to cases yet to emerge and is hence a way to secure legal predictability. This is because the

108 Ingvill Helland and Sören Koch, "Introduction to Norwegian Legal Method" in Ingvill Helland and Sören Koch (Eds.), *Nordic and Germanic Legal Methods* (Mohr Siebeck 2014) 126.

legislation is made without the distraction of actual cases, with actual parties and actual destinies, that might move the norm producer emotionally. Instead the norm producer can make the norms to fit into a systematic and coherent body of law that has a general aim. In theory, and to a large extent in practice, this makes law more predictable. The idea is that the less subjective elements that influence the making of law are, the less subjective elements that influence the application of law will be.

Precedent is also produced for cases yet to emerge and secures legal predictability for these. This applies especially to Norwegian law where only the Supreme Court produces precedent, and where production of precedent has been the main task of the Supreme Court since the early 1990s. In other words, precedents can also provide predictability of law. However, the Norwegian Supreme Court makes precedent on the basis of actual cases, with actual parties that have the possibility to and often appear in court before the judge, with different specific circumstances to take into consideration. Hence, the making of precedent is characterised by a framework of subjective elements that is more or less absent from the making of legislation. This brings the legal norm produced closer to the adjustment of law to fairness, which is part of the role and function of Norwegian courts in general, and of the Supreme Court in particular.

4.3 Fairness as a supplementing ideal of justice

A very particular legal source in Norwegian law is value-based assessments or policy considerations (*reelle hensyn*).[109] It is very hard to define the source, and prevailing definitions do not necessarily match how it is applied in legal literature, legal teaching, and court practice. In this context, we will only put emphasis on the fairness component of value-based assessments as a legal source. It has to be kept in mind that also system-based assessments might be referred to as "reelle hensyn". However, it is rare that they are unless they are a part of a larger assessment that does also include the value-based assessments.

On one hand, the legal theory of Professor Torstein Eckhoff, who taught legal method and legal sources at the Faculty of Law in Oslo from the 1950s and published a textbook on the subject in 1971, facilitated that value-based assessments became recognised as a legal source.[110] On the other hand, such assessments had been an openly recognised source of law since the Code of 1274. This was changed with the Code of

109 This terminology is used by both Torstein Eckhoff and Jan Helgesen, *Rettskildelære* (5th ed., Tanum 2001) and Mads Henry Andenæs, *Rettskildelære* (2nd ed., Oslo 2009) 3 ff. However, they both point out that the choice of terminology is to some extent a matter of personal preference. As demonstrated more recently by Sverre Blandhol, "Pragmatismens aktualitet i rettsvitenskap og rettsanvendelse" (2004) No. 3. *Tidsskrift for Rettsvitenskap, 365*, on 366–371 ff., the label *reelle hensyn* may have been introduced by Eckhoff, but the elements it encompassed were already in active use in practical legal argumentation. In other words, the term *reelle hensyn* is simply a label applied to a number of previously existing phenomena and does not serve to distinguish argument bases that are relevant to legal argumentation from argument bases that are not. For further discussion, see also Blandhol, *De beste grunner. Reelle hensyn i juridisk argumentasjon* (Gyldendal 2014) (n. 109) 67–154 with further references. In this article, we will use the terms "value-based assessments" and "policy considerations" interchangeably.

110 Sverre Blandhol (2014) (n. 109) 150–153.

1687, when all other sources of law than legislation were officially abolished. As we have seen in relation to precedent, this abolishment was unsuccessful. And in legal theory in the 18th century, value-based assessments were among the legal sources listed. The present Norwegian term for value-based assessments, "reelle hensyn", was developed by the Supreme Court in the early 20th century. Eckhoff gave them a more prominent role in his legal theory than had been done before, partly inspired by American legal realism. However, at the same time Eckhoff placed himself in a long tradition in Norwegian law for treating value-based assessments as a relevant legal source.[111]

The role of value-based assessments as a legal source in Norwegian law has been to fill loopholes of law, but also to adjust law when it has been too strict or too lenient. This is the role of such assessments in many legal cultures. What is particular to the Norwegian legal culture, is how they openly are applied as a legal source and often even labelled a source of law (*rettskilde*) in court decisions, in legal literature,[112] and in legal teaching.[113] If we focus on the Supreme Court's decisions, value-based assessments were openly referred to in 12 % of the civil cases and 4 % of the criminal cases from 1996 until 2012.[114] This gives an empirical foundation for claiming that these kinds of arguments enjoy a high degree of legitimacy in the Norwegian legal culture. This again indicates that fairness and individual justice are part of the prevailing ideal of justice in the Norwegian legal culture, which occasionally have to be balanced against considerations of predictability. Even though predictability is the dominant ideal of justice, it is hence balanced against fairness, and in individual cases fairness will actually sometimes prevail.

Since value-based considerations are easily applied without being referred to, these figures do not reveal to what an extent fairness and individual justice is a part of the prevailing ideal of justice in the Norwegian legal culture. However, there are several indicators that this is a substantive part of the Norwegian ideal of justice. One is the already mentioned status of precedent as a legal source. Precedent does, as we have seen above, secure legal predictability, at the same time as it is a legal source that is less tied to law as a system, and more to law as a living force in society. This also indicates that fairness and individual justice is a part of the prevailing ideal of justice in the Norwegian legal culture.

Yet another indication of this is the character of Norwegian legislation. As stated above, the production of legal norms by making statutes instead of having a code, leaves legislation more fragmented. The interpretation and the filling of loopholes is therefore less dictated by a system of law, and more open to the influence of value-based assessments.

---

111 Sunde (2014), "The Legal Cultural Dependency" (n. 73) 58–59; and Sunde (2012) (n. 102) 69–70.

112 Carl August Fleischer, *Rettskilder og juridisk metode* (Ad Notam Gyldendal 1998) 70; Alf Petter Høgberg, "Reelle hensyn" in Alf Petter Høgberg and Jørn Øyrehagen Sunde (Eds.), *Juridisk metode og tenkemåte* (Universitetsforlaget 2019) 343 (but see 346–347 for nuances).

113 Ragna Aarli and Synne Sæter Mæhle, *Fra lov til rett* (2nd ed., Gyldendal 2017); Monsen (2012) (n. 92) 47 f.

114 Sunde (2015), *Høgsteretts historie* (n. 44) 293–295. It has to be remembered that *reelle hensyn* might be referred to when performing system-based assessments as well. However, system-based assessments are usually not referred to as *reelle hensyn* if they operate alone and are not supported also by value-based assessments.

4.4 Perspectives

Even though the most extreme consequences of strict predictability were attenuated during the 19th century, the focus on legal certainty and predictability has remained strong in the western world in general, and in Norway more particular, until today. However, even if predictability is still important, in a post-modern society one has to admit that this ideal has to be adapted to the complexity of our world. Law has become a field that is cultivated by educated specialists – called lawyers. For these specialists the idea of predictability is still essential. Providing legal certainty is still regarded as highly important for social peace, economic stability and progress. At the same time the notion of predictability is an essential precondition for the principles of legality and equality before the law.

However, in some contrast to continental Europe, the notion of *corrective justice* remained as a strong position in Norway as well. This idea has been presented by different Norwegian legal scientists with different conceptions of law, which, despite ideological differences, have one thing in common, and that is the idea that law consists of more than the black-letters of legislation. Almost all of them have emphasised the pragmatic dimension of the Norwegian law as well.[115] One consequence of this pragmatic approach to law is that some scholars argue that under certain circumstances there might be more than one legitimate solution to a legal question.[116] Taking into consideration the fragmentary character of Norwegian legislation and the prominent role of policy considerations in legal argumentation, such statements are closely related to the legal realistic approach to law that had become popular in the second half of the 20th century.[117]

This turn to legal realism could not remain without consequences for the perception of the concept of predictability and the ideal of justice. Today, predictability in Norway concerns mainly a specific form of applying the law by using more or less institutionalised practises in order to legitimise the outcome of a legal dispute. Consequently, predictability no longer refers exclusively to the specific outcome of a case, but to the predictability of procedure. Taken in conjunction with the comparably very high

115 Gerd Fredrik Malt, "To glemte linjer i tradisjonell rettsfinningslære" (1992) No. 1–2 *Tidsskrift for Rettsvitenskap* 48, 80.

116 Erik Monsen, "En kommentar til Høyesteretts bruk av 'tause forarbeider' i Rt. 2015 s. 1324" (2016) No. 3 *Jussens Venner* 159: "Den juridiske metodelæren åpner for at det i en rekke tilfeller kan tenkes flere legitime løsninger på et rettsspørsmål."

117 However, the legal realistic approach to law is no longer uncontested in Norway today. Recently, some scholars refrained from the notion that law is defined exclusively by looking at what the judges of the Supreme Court are doing. First and foremost, professor Nils Nygaard and Jan Fridthjof Bernt have emphasised the idea that the Court is bound by the surrounding legal, constitutional and cultural framework.

degree of confidence in the Norwegian institutions of conflict-resolution,[118] a sufficient degree of legal security can be achieved without feeling the need to regulate every detail in comprehensive and systematic codes. The courts in their turn are as a rule cautious not to take advantage of the wide scope of discretion often bestowed on them by the legislator.[119] This form of judicial self-restraint in combination with the high degree of confidence in the judiciary enables the Norwegian courts to provide a degree of legal certainty that is regarded as sufficient, allowing at the same time for pragmatic adjustments where a too formal application of the law seems inappropriate.[120]

As modern society becomes increasingly more complex and, accordingly, the law governing social relations does so as well, one may wonder whether this Norwegian model is fit for future challenges. Still, as long as the confidence in the legitimacy of the courts' work remains at the current high level and judges continue to exercise their wide competences restrictively, the balanced Norwegian ideal of justice may also in the future provide a sufficient framework for the application of law.

5. Legal method[121]

5.1 Introduction

Legal method, understood as the way lawyers tend to apply law to solve legal problems, can be considered a manifestation of the prevailing ideal(s) of justice. The Norwegian understanding of legal method has been heavily influenced by the historical and cultural context within which the current Norwegian law developed. Two characteristics of its institutional structures have proven particularly important. First, there is the fragmentary character of the legislation, which leaves more room for the discretion of the judiciary as well as arguments derived from other legal argument bases. Second, there is the structure of the court system, which is constructed as a single hierarchy headed by the Supreme Court. This means that the Norwegian courts, in contrast to continental courts, are not specialised to the same degree. These preconditions, among others, have allowed for the development of a legal method that is rather different from those applied in continental Europe, both in terminology and also partly in substance.

---

118 An annual survey on the public confidence in Norwegian courts published by the Norwegian Court Administration shows that since 2010, the percentage of respondents with very high (*svært stor*) or quite high (*ganske stor*) confidence in the courts has been higher than 80 % every year, and close to 90 % in 2014 and 2017. For 1998–2003, the numbers were between 60 and 70 % annually. It is worth mentioning, however, that 2019 was the year with lowest percentage reporting a very high confidence since 2010 (down 10 percentage points from 2018). The 2019 survey was conducted after the "NAV scandal" was made known to the public (on this, see the section on internationalisation below). See Iwar Arnstad, "Fortsatt stor tiltro til domstolene, men lavere enn i 2018", available at https://www.domstol.no/nyheter/nyhetsarkiv/2019/fortsatt-stor-tiltro-til-domstolene-men-lavere-enn-i-2018/. See also https://www.domstol.no/nyheter/nyhetsarkiv/2019/tiltro/. Both links accessed 3 April 2020.

119 Ingvill Helland and Sören Koch, "Norwegian and German Legal Methods Compared" in Ingvill Helland and Sören Koch (Eds.), *Nordic and Germanic Legal Methods* (Mohr Siebeck 2014) 312.

120 For a similar but more detailed conclusion, see ibid. 312 ff., 316 f.

121 This subchapter is based on Helland and Koch (2014), "Introduction to Norwegian legal Method" (n. 108) 99–140.

5.2 Norwegian legal realism and the legal theory of Torstein Eckhoff

The theory on legal method in Norway was heavily influenced by the works of Torstein Eckhoff, especially his textbook on the subject from 1971.[122] Through an extensive analysis of Supreme Court case law, Eckhoff successfully demonstrated that the established theory of legal sources only partially described and explained the actual argumentation patterns of the Supreme Court.[123] In reality, Eckhoff observed, the Court's argumentation was not based solely on the traditionally acknowledged sources of law, but included other types of arguments as well.[124] For example, the Supreme Court may on occasion construct a primary legal basis from general legal principles.[125]

Eckhoff's theory has its roots in the Nordic legal realism,[126] and is based on the pragmatic idea that the argumentation pattern of the highest court ought to be considered a benchmark for all practitioners of law.[127] This understanding has won an almost unconditional acclaim in the Norwegian legal literature, and subsequent authors have contributed to its continued development.[128] The applicable law in a concrete case, in other words the applicable legal rule(s), often depends on a combination of different

---

122 Torstein Eckhoff, *Rettskildelære*, (1st ed., Tanum 1971). Despite the title of this book (which could be translated as "theory of legal sources") he argued against the traditional concept "source of law", which he found misleading. See also Torstein Eckhoff and Jan Helgesen, *Rettskildelære* (5th ed., Tanum 2001) 23.

123 The traditional concept "sources of law" is still in active use in Denmark, as seen in Jens Evald, *Retskilderne og den juridiske metode* (Jurist- og Økonomforbundets Forlag 1997) 35 ff.; Jens Evald, *At tænke juridisk – juridisk metode for begyndere* (4th ed., Nyt Juridisk Forlag 2011) 18; Peter Blume, *Juridisk Metodelære* (5th ed., Jurist- og Økonomforbundets Forlag 2009) 57 ff.

124 Eckhoff and Helgesen (2001) (n. 109) 22 ff.

125 A prominent example is the hospital journal judgment (*Sykejournaldommen*, Rt. 1977 p. 1035). Here, a patient wished to access his medical journal, since he considered filing a claim for damages against the hospital. The Supreme Court rejected the hospital's argument that the journal was intended for internal use only and as such was exempted from the right to access pursuant to the Administration Act (*Forvaltningsloven*). Finding that the right to access administrative documents was not exhaustively regulated in existing legislation, the patient was granted access on the basis of general legal principles (*alminnelige rettsgrunnsetninger*). This legal argument base belongs to the category policy considerations.

126 Alf Petter Høgberg and Morten Kinander, "Det formelle legalitetsprinsippet og rettskildelæren" (2011) No. 1 *Tidsskrift for Rettsvitenskap* 15, 43 f.; The Nordic legal realism is based on an approach to the question of what constitutes law that is similar to the American, compare Oliver Wendell Holmes, "The Path of the Law" (1897) Vol. 10 *Harvard Law Review* 457, 460 f: "The prophecies of what the courts will do in fact, and nothing more pretentious, are what I mean by the law."

127 The considerable influence of Eckhoff's theory on legal method may be due to the fact that it is based on an extensive analysis of jurisprudence from the Supreme Court, something which affords the theory a high degree of legitimacy. See Knut Martin Tande, "Individuelle valg og vurderinger i rettsanvendelsesprosessen" (2011) No. 1 *Jussens Venner* 1, 4.

128 See e.g. Carl August Fleischer, *Rettskilder* (Ad Notam Gyldendal 1995); Nygaard (2007), *Rettsgrunnlag og standpunkt* (n. 92); Jan Fridthjof Bernt and Synne Sæther Mæhle, *Rett, samfunn og demokrati* (Gyldendal Akademisk 2007); Andenæs (2009) (n. 109); Erik Magnus Boe, *Grunnleggende juridisk metode – En introduksjon til rett og rettstenkning* (3rd ed., Universitetsforlaget 2012); Tande (2011) (n. 127).

arguments that must be derived from specific legal argument bases[129] in order to be accepted as legitimate.[130] In Norwegian law, these are referred to as *rettskildefaktorer* ("source of law factors"). The concept is markedly different from the previously used term *rettskilde* ("source of law"). First, the new terminology reflects how law is constructed from a number of factors; it cannot be found in one single source. Second, the term encompasses everything that constitutes a part of the law – in other words, everything that is relevant for legal argumentation – including factors that were previously merely considered convincing arguments.[131] Consequently, all arguments that cannot derive from one of the legal argument bases are not considered relevant for legal argumentation.

This terminology is still criticised for its misleading reference to the expression "source of law",[132] but within the Norwegian legal community there is hardly any disagreement regarding the basic idea behind the concept.[133] Only arguments that may be deduced (or induced) from a *rettskildefaktor* (or a combination of them) may constitute normative parts of the law. Everything else is irrelevant to legal argumentation. The readiness with which the legal community accepted Eckhoff's idea, that law cannot be found in any one specific source, but rather is a product of a balancing of a considerable number of factors, may in part be due to the fragmentary Norwegian legislation:

129 This approach clearly resembles the argumentation theory described by Theodor Viehweg, *Topik und Jurisprudenz* (5th ed., Munich 1974). This structural parallel between Viehweg's theoretical approach on the one hand and the pragmatic theories on legal method in the Scandinavian legal systems on the other has been highlighted by Bjarte Askeland, "Prinsipp og pragmatisme i erstatningsretten" in Gudrun Holgersen, Kai Krüger and Kåre Lilleholt (Eds.), *Nybrott og odling, Festskrift til Nils Nygaard* (Fagbokforlaget 2002) 24, as far as Norwegian law is concerned and, with regard to Swedish law, by Håkan Andersson, *Skyddsändamål och adekvans* (Uppsala 1993) 216–239, especially on 231.

130 Norwegian law essentially recognises three legitimising factors which serve to explain the principles of relevance. First and foremost, law is legitimised through its democratic basis. However, a democratic basis is neither an absolute requirement nor necessarily sufficient for law to be recognised as legitimate. Other legitimising factors are predictability or legal certainty and justice or fairness. A legitimate legal rule must strike a balance between these factors. The scope of this article does not leave room for a more detailed description of the system of legitimacy. See for this purpose Nygaard (2007), *Rettsgrunnlag og standpunkt* (n. 93) 43 ff.; Bernt and Mæhle (2007) (n. 128) 142 ff. and 177 ff., compare 109 ff. An introduction in English is also given by Ingvill Helland, "The permissibility and (conditional) recommendability of contra legem interpretations in Norwegian law" (2014) No. 1 *Retfærd* 17, 26 f.

131 Compare the distinction made by Thomas Henninger, "Legal Culture and Common Principles of European Legal Methods" in Ingvill Helland and Sören Koch (Eds.), *Nordic and Germanic Legal Methods* (Mohr Siebeck 2014). According to this definition, Norwegian law has no sources of law whatsoever, but is made up entirely of secondary argument bases. Even the wording of an Act of Parliament, despite its central importance in the practical application of the law, is only convincing. There is no unconditional obligation to arrive at the result indicated by the wording.

132 Critical with regard to the term, Nygaard (2007), *Rettsgrunnlag og standpunkt* (n. 92) 29 ff.; Fleischer (1995) (n. 128) 64 ff.; Bernt and Mæhle (2007) (n. 128) 218 f.

133 See, however, Bjarte Askeland, "Eckhoffs rettskildelære under press" (1999) *Kritisk Juss* 115, 121, who is of the opinion that institutionalising the normative effects of policy considerations by recognising *reelle hensyn* as one of the seven legal argument bases may lead to unpredictable and even unjust results.

several legal issues are not, or only in part, regulated through legislation.[134] In addition, the legislative regulation consists of a number of provisions in various statutes, neither of which sufficiently regulate the issue when taken on its own.[135] Despite the increased activities of the legislator over the last few decades and even with the aid of unwritten customary law, a number of legal issues remain unregulated.

At the same time, the Supreme Court is obligated to find a solution in each case brought before it.[136] In so doing, the Court cannot rely on the coherency of a legal system supported by a highly developed system of concepts. Rather, it must find a different foundation for its decisions. While not stated expressly in the Constitution of 1814, Norwegian judges are nevertheless bound by the framework set up by the legislator and the legal order in consequence of the constitutional separation of powers. However, as a result of its competence to rule in the final instance, the determination of the currently applicable law is ultimately up to the Supreme Court itself.[137] Furthermore, its decisions enjoy a high degree of acceptance in both Norwegian society in general and within the jurisprudence in particular. To Eckhoff, it therefore made sense to analyse the argumentation patterns of the Supreme Court, in order to identify the types of arguments that are recognised as legitimate in juridical discourse, and to deduce general principles of legal argumentation from them. He argued that these principles may then be applied to cases thus far unregulated, and thereby contribute to a higher degree of predictability and legal certainty.[138] The obvious practical value of this kind of empirical analysis of Supreme Court case law has contributed to the ground-breaking success of Eckhoff's theory on legal method.[139] As a result, a distinct focus on the argumentative style and content of the case law of the Supreme Court is notable in the applied legal method of Norwegian lawyers, in all fields of legal education, science, practice and adjudication alike.

134 Lov 1969-06-12-26 om skadeserstatning (skadeserstatningsloven) [The Norwegian Compensatory Damages Act] is an example of the latter. The Act contains provisions on liability in tort under certain special conditions, such as parents' liability for damages caused by their children and owners' liability for damages caused by pets, but the general rules on liability remain customary law.

135 There are no codifications either in private or in public law. In criminal law, however, the basis in legislation required by the strict principle of legality contained in § 96 of the Constitution led to the adoption of a Penal Code in 1842, later replaced first by the Penal Act of 1902 and then by the Penal Act of 2005. On the fragmentary legislative technique common in all other areas of law, see for example Nygaard (2007), *Rettsgrunnlag og standpunkt* (n. 92) 29. Up until 2019, a chronologically ordered compilation of Acts of Parliament was published annually, titled *Norges Lover*.

136 Cf. the Constitution § 88.

137 The Constitution § 88 literally only states that the Supreme Court rules in the final instance. This is, however, understood as both a prohibition of denial of justice *and* an empowerment to give rulings on all legal issues, whether covered by legislation or not. The legitimacy of the Court's development of the law beyond the scope of legislation is consequently not seen considered a constitutional problem. Presumably, this is also in part due to the high degree of confidence which the Supreme Court traditionally enjoys among the Norwegian population; for the documentation of this confidence, see n. 118.

138 Eckhoff and Helgesen (2001) (n. 109) 23.

139 Tande (2011) (n. 127) 23.

Eckhoff identified seven groups of legal argument bases. Although later authors have suggested other approaches to the systematisation of these,[140] in the following we will take Eckhoff's system as a starting point, as this system remains the most commonly accepted in Norway today.

According to Eckhoff, the legal argument bases recognised as legitimate encompass, in addition to legal texts like the Constitution, Acts of Parliament and administrative regulations (*lov*), preparatory works (*forarbeider*) and subsequent statements by the legislator regarding the understanding of an Act (*etterarbeider*),[141] case law (*rettspraksis*), the practice of other state organs including the administration (*andre myndigheters praksis*), the practice of private subjects of the law (*privates praksis*), prevailing views on law, including legal science (*rettsoppfatninger*), and finally the abovementioned policy considerations or value-based assessments (*reelle hensyn*). In addition, Eckhoff also refers to certain foreign and international legal argument bases. The law of other countries is primarily relevant in the area of uniform legislation – Acts of Parliament resulting from the legislative cooperation between the Nordic countries from the late 19th century – or where there is a legal void, that is a shortage of national sources.[142] Analysing the case law of the Supreme Court closely reveals that the court almost never adopts particular legal rules but rather looks for the underlying legislative intentions and basic principles. As a rule, foreign law is merely used as a supportive argument.

Eckhoff's theory on legal method is built around the so-called balancing model (*avveiningsmodell*).[143] According to this model, the applicable legal rule for the concrete case is established by applying three steps.[144] First, the relevant legal argument bases must be identified. Second, arguments must be drawn from them by means of interpretation. Finally, these arguments must be harmonised, or balanced against each other.[145] The applicable legal rule is the *outcome* of this balancing process,[146] and describes the law that is to be applied to the case in question. All steps of this process are regulated by

---

140 Nygaard (2007), *Rettsgrunnlag og standpunkt* (n. 92) 29 ff.; Fleischer (1995) (n. 128) 64 ff.; Bernt and Mæhle (2007) (n. 128) 218 f.

141 These later elaborations on the understanding of legislation are, however, only allotted limited weight, since they are considered to be lacking democratic legitimacy. The preparatory works gain a measure of democratic legitimacy by means of the adoption of the Act, something which in the absence of statements to the contrary is considered an implicit approval of the information contained in the motives, but this implicit approval is of course lacking in the case of subsequent elaborations on interpretation. However, even such statements are not wholly irrelevant, and their weight may vary depending on the type of statement as well as the concrete circumstances of a case. On the varying weight of subsequent statements, see Eckhoff and Helgesen (2001) (n. 109) 99 f.

142 Eckhoff and Helgesen (2001) (n. 109) 288 ff.

143 This term was not employed by Eckhoff himself, but is commonly employed by subsequent authors to describe his methodological approach, compare for example Knut Bergo, *Tekst og virkelighet i rettskildelæren* (Cappelen Akademisk 2002) 39; Bjarte Askeland, "Rettskildelærens utvikling i rettsteoretisk belysning", (2003) No. 1 *Jussens Venner* 8, 13 ff.

144 Bernt and Mæhle (2007) (n. 128) 200 f., 204 f. and 206 ff.

145 Eckhoff and Helgesen (2001) (n. 109) 20 ff.; Nygaard (2007), *Rettsgrunnlag og standpunkt* (n. 92) 31.

146 On the difference between the concepts "legal rule" in Norway and Germany respectively, see Helland and Koch (2014), "Norwegian and German Legal Methods Compared" (n. 119).

principles for the application of law (*rettskildeprinsipper*).[147] An inherent characteristic of this balancing model is that each argument, having been deduced from either of the abovementioned argument bases, may fulfil more than one function. A later legal theorist, Nils Nygaard, identified three functions, depending on the concrete context. First, a legal argument base may constitute a primary legal basis.[148] The primary legal basis outlines the conditions that must be fulfilled in order for the desired legal consequences to take effect. Depending on the circumstances, the primary legal basis may be found in a single type of argument base such as a provision in an Act of Parliament or may have to be construed from a number of bases. This is the case with customary law, which is the product of consistent, long-standing practice, legal conceptions, and value-based assessments. Or, as a consequence of the fragmentary technique favoured by the Norwegian legislator, it may be necessary to construct a primary legal basis from a combination of legal provisions.[149]

The second function of Norwegian legal argument bases is their contribution to the interpretation of the primary legal bases. The technique to use various legal argument bases to interpret an unclear wording is, despite minor deviations, recognised in all modern courts in Europe and constitutes thus no unique feature of the Norwegian legal culture.

Finally, a legal argument may be utilised as a so-called supporting argument (*støtteargument*). This is an argument that is not necessary for the result as such, but which favours the same conclusion and therefore strengthens the impression that this conclusion must be experienced as correct, thus also reinforcing the legitimacy of the result. Supporting arguments may be useful in the interpretation of a primary legal basis, in the sense that they support the understanding the interpreter has arrived at by other means, or they may support a specific end result – for example, where more than one legal rule is applicable to the same facts, but would produce the same result.

More interesting in terms of comparing legal cultures is the way collisions between legal arguments are treated in Norway. One obvious way to resolve collisions between arguments in order to arrive at a single legal rule in a consistent, predictable fashion would be to organise the arguments into a hierarchy according to different types of argument base. Unlike sources of law in other legal systems, however, the Norwegian legal argument bases are in principle all ranged equally.[150] Their relationship to one another must instead be assessed in each individual case, since the factors are balanced against

147 Helland and Koch (2014), "Introduction to Norwegian legal Method" (n. 108) 112 ff.

148 The concept of primary legal basis (*primært rettsgrunnlag*) was introduced by Nygaard (2007), *Rettsgrunnlag og standpunkt* (n. 92) 100.

149 This is no different in German, where it may be necessary to combine several provisions in order to establish the legal basis for a claim (*Anspruchsgrundlage*). For example, a claim for restitution of damages does not follow from § 823 (1) of the BGB alone; rather, this provision must be seen in conjunction with BGB §§ 249 ff. and 254, as well as the unwritten principles of factual and adequate causation. Another example is the chain of norms building the primary legal basis for claims arising from a defect discovered in a purchased object, see BGB §§ 433 and 434 (1) 1 no. 2 taken in conjunction with §§ 437 and 439.

150 Very clear on this feature of Norwegian legal method Eckhoff and Helgesen (2001) (n. 109) 23.

each other according to principles of weight.[151] The only exception is the hierarchy inherent in different types of written norms, based on rules of competence (here apply the widely accepted principles of *lex superior, lex posterior*, etc.).[152]

This lack of a hierarchy between different types of argument bases means that although Acts of Parliament are normally of fundamental importance for the determination of concrete cases due to their strong democratic legitimacy as well as their contributions to generally predictable decisions, the interpreter is in principle free to deviate from the wording in favour of other arguments, provided that these are sufficiently strong.[153] Even an interpretation that directly contradicts an unambiguous wording may under certain circumstances be considered legally permissible.[154] However, this is only possible provided strong arguments, derived from the other relevant legal argument bases, favour a different solution.[155] A typical and uncontroversial example is cases where the scope of the wording after a natural understanding encompasses situations which, according to the preparatory works, were not supposed to fall under the provision. In Norwegian law, even an intuitive assessment of what is just may in principle outweigh the wording

151 Andenæs (2009) (n. 109) 21.

152 The Constitution is *lex superior* to ordinary legislation, which in its turn takes precedence over administrative regulations in case of conflict. Pursuant to clauses of precedence (contained in ordinary legislation), certain human rights conventions and also EEA law take precedence over (other) ordinary legislation but yield to the Constitution in case of conflict. This position in the hierarchy of written law has been referred to as "semi-constitutional" in recognition of the legal consequences of the precedence clauses, but the rules remain formally on the level of ordinary legislation, and the precedence clauses may be revoked by the Norwegian parliament at any time (although this is highly unlikely in the current political climate).

153 On the discretion of the courts, see Synne Sæther Mæhle, *Grenser for rettsanvendelsesskjønn: Om rettslig legitimitet i et spenningsfelt mellom flertallsmakt og rettighetsvern* (Gyldendal Akademisk 2005). For an overview in English of the weight of the wording and the possibility to deviate from this, see also Helland (2014), "The permissibility" (n. 130) especially 30–31.

154 See the *Fatherhood I* ruling (Rt. 1916 p. 648). A man was sued for fatherhood of a child born about nine months after he had intercourse with the mother but sought to defend himself by proving that he was sterile and therefore could not possibly be the father in a biological sense. The Act regulating fatherhood and (perhaps most importantly for the mother) the obligation to pay child support did not allow for any kind of defence provided the legal conditions – namely sexual intercourse at the relevant time – were fulfilled. According to the preparatory works (Ot.prp. no. 10 (1892) p. 80), alleged sterility was explicitly not accepted as a defence, both because the reliability of such proof was questionable, and because of the "disgusting" trials of evidence which might then have been required to take place before the courts. Faced with seemingly conclusive evidence of sterility, the majority of the court found themselves unable to uphold a legal rule which nevertheless named the sterile plaintiff as father to the child, as such a rule was found to be "in itself unreasonable". When the relevant legislation was reviewed in 1915, Parliament explicitly chose to retain the previous regulations. Nevertheless, the result from 1916 was repeated and evidence of sterility accepted as defence when the problem next arose in the *Fatherhood II* ruling (Rt. 1921 p. 406), in contradiction not only of the wording of the Act, but also of the recently confirmed, express will of the legislator. For further examples see Hans Petter Graver, *Hva er rett* (Universitetsforlaget 2011) 21 ff. For a more recent example, see HR-2018-2241-U, where the Appeal Selection Committee concluded that a DNA test collected in a criminal case could be used as evidence in civil cases concerning clarification of paternity, despite § 12 (6) of the Police Register Act prescribing that the police's DNA register shall only be used in criminal cases.

155 Eckhoff and Helgesen (2001) (n. 109) 23. In the case of the abovementioned *Fatherhood II* ruling, the wording was set aside primarily for self-evident reasons of justice and legal certainty.

of an Act of Parliament[156] – although this will only be considered in extreme cases, and efforts are currently being made in Norwegian legal science to reduce the intuitive aspect of value-based assessments.[157]

5.3 Perspectives

Whether this balancing model is still suited as an approach to the increasingly complex national and international legal problems that legal practitioners today come up against on a regular basis, seems at best uncertain.[158] When Eckhoff developed his methodological approach in lectures in the 1950s and 1960s, lawyers in Norway had mainly received their education by the same professors based on a very limited number of textbooks. This led to a relatively speaking highly homogenous body of legal practitioners applying law in Norway. Despite the inherent flexibility and intuitive elements of Eckhoff's balancing model, this homogenous education enabled the legal practitioner to resolve legal conflicts in keeping with the fundamental, but often unspoken values of the legal order.

Over the last few decades, however, both the societal and legal framework within which the legal method functions have changed, in part considerably.[159] Legal education has diversified as a greater selection of literature has become available to students at the now seven educational institutions.[160] Furthermore, Norwegian society and the background of judges are no longer as homogenous, and the law, the legal community and society at large have all become subject to an increasing number of international (or, more precisely, extra-national) influences. This opens up an influx of foreign legal materials and values into national legal argumentation. The coming generation of lawyers will therefore be faced with other challenges than were the students of Eckhoff's time. These tendencies are also evident in the legal discourse. Slogans such as globalisa-

156 Eckhoff and Helgesen (2001) (n. 109) 27 f. Compare the Supreme Court's reasoning in the *Fatherhood II* ruling.

157 Tande (2011) (n. 127) 16 ff with further references.

158 Critical already Jan Fridthjof Bernt and David R. Doublet, "Norsk rettsvitenskap mellom rettspositivisme og ny-normativisme" in Peter Blume and Hanne Petersen (Eds.), *Retlig polycentri: til Henrik Zahle på 50-årsdagen* (Akademisk Forlag 1993) 145, who predicted a paradigm shift in the form of a deviation from the legal realism which, however, has yet to materialise in mainstream Norwegian legal dogmatics. On this topic, see Askeland (2003) (n. 143); see also Kai Krüger, "Komparativ rettsmetode – observasjoner vedrørende prinsipper for rettsanvendelse i Europa nord og sør – illustrert ved tilfelle i Norge og Italia" (1996) *Jussens Venner* 281; Tande (2011) (n. 127) 27.

159 Bernt and Mæhle (2007) (n. 128) 225 f.

160 For details see subsection 6.

tion, internationalisation, pluralism, polycentrism, and postmodern jurisprudence have become increasingly prominent in the Norwegian debate on legal method.[161]

At the same time, the legislator has become exponentially more active since Eckhoff developed his model, adopting and updating ever more legislation, often prompted by the EEA cooperation or similar international initiatives. The lawyer must take into account an ever-growing amount of often very technical legal texts, administrative regulations, court rulings, and legal opinions. Combined with the weakening of the preconditions for a common intuition, this calls for stronger normative guidelines and more transparency in the balancing process.[162] The reasoning of the decision-maker would then become more easily accessible to the entire legal community, thus reinforcing the legitimacy of the outcome of the interpretative process.[163] Nygaard made a first step in this direction.[164] According to his methodological approach, the principles that govern the interpretative process derive from certain fundamental values inherent to the legal system. The extent to which each legal argument base furthers these values, is in principle decisive for its relevance as well as its argumentative weight. Recently, more legal scientists have joined the call for a turn to a more objective legal method,[165] with clearer normative guidelines and objectively ascertainable limits.[166]

Despite variations in the methodological preconditions, Norway is not the only country having to deal with methodological challenges as a result of, *inter alia*, the ongoing globalisation process and the accessory internationalisation of the law. However, the flexibility of the Norwegian methodological approach may turn out to be an advantage. As a result of the scarcity of national legal sources, the Nordic legislative cooperation and other historical circumstances, Norwegian law is not foreign to the idea of taking

---

161 Jørn Jacobsen, "Law, Legal Science and Methodological Pluralism" in Johan Giertsen, Berte-Elen Reinertsen Konow, Erling Johannes Husabø and Øystein L. Iversen (Eds.), *Rett i vest – Festskrift til 50-årsjubileet for juristutdanningen ved Universitetet i Bergen* (Fagbokforlaget 2019) 355–356; Finn Arnesen and Are Stenvik, *Internasjonalisering og juridisk metode* (Universitetsforlaget 2015) 11 ff. and 49 ff.; Askeland (2003) (n. 143) 12; Askeland (1999) (n. 133) 115 with further references. A study of the doctoral theses defended at the Faculty of Law in Bergen since its foundation in 1969 documents that the number of candidates reflecting upon or problematizing fundamental notions of legal methodology has increased the last decades, see Marius Mikkel Kjølstad, "Det rettsvitenskapelige kloster. Doktorgradsutdanning og avhandlinger ved Det juridiske fakultet i Bergen 1969–2018" in Giertsen et al. (Eds.) 52.

162 Mæhle (2005) (n. 153).

163 Hans Petter Graver, "I prinsippet prinsipiell – om rettsprinsipper" (2006) No. 2–3 *Tidsskrift for Rettsvitenskap* 189. See also Askeland (2003) (n. 143) f.

164 Nygaard (2007), *Rettsgrunnlag og standpunkt* (n. 92) 61, 159 ff. Nygaard was not the first to discuss the values that constitute the normative basis of the legal system, see Jan Fridthjof Bernt and David Roland Doublet, *Juss, samfunn og rettsanvendelse – en introduksjon til rettsvitenskapen* (Ad Notam Gyldendal 1996), particularly 200 f. However, his was the first textbook on legal method that sought to establish a normative basis for Eckhoff's balancing model.

165 Bernt and Mæhle (2007) (n. 128) 226; Askeland (2003) (n. 143) 21 f.; Morten Kinander, "Trenger man egentlig 'reelle hensyn'? – To betydninger, noen problemer" (2002) *Lov og rett* 234. Against a more formalistic approach and stricter adherence to principles, Sverre Blandhol, "Er rettsanvendelsen i EU-domstolen og Menneskerettsdomstolen vesensforskjellig fra norsk rettskildelære?" (2005) No. 5–6 *Lov og Rett* 316, 326 f.

166 Mæhle (2005) (n. 153); Tande (2011) (n. 127) 23.

non-national sources into account when interpreting and developing the national law.[167] This is not seen as a challenge to the normative values of the legal system, nor to the constitutional order. Rather, the open argumentative style of the Norwegian legal method allows for the seamless integration of new legal material into the interpretative process while maintaining the balance of fundamental values in the legal order.

To sum up, the practice of the Norwegian Supreme Court serves as role model for the legal method, which lawyers are supposed to apply when solving a legal problem. The Court's approach to legal sources is horizontal and not vertical. The legitimacy of the argumentation plays a central role and determines which arguments are relevant and how much an argument weighs in relation to other relevant arguments. As evidenced by the fragmentary character of Norwegian legislation, the idea that the system of general and abstract rules must be both comprehensive and universally coherent was never generally recognised in Norway. Rather, a pragmatic approach to legal method is still prevailing but may be to some extent be challenged by the ongoing internationalisation.

6. Professionalisation

6.1 Introduction

The specific requirements regarding Norwegian lawyers are closely interconnected with the prevailing idea of legal method and the specific institutionalized way of solving conflicts in Norway. The broad competence of the courts concerning all fields of law requires a general approach to legal methods including a uniformly applicable theory of the sources of law as well as their application to a specific case. It is this generalized method of applying the law that still forms the backbone of legal education in Norway and thus provides the basic prerequisite for any legal professional.

To safeguard a correct and predictable application of the law it is regarded necessary that this is a task of legal professionals. However, this contains not (yet) a demand for specialisation; rather, the ideal remains to educate professional generalists. Consequently, a high degree of legal-generalist-professionalisation is a precondition and a very important feature of the Norwegian legal culture today.

6.2 The generalist approach to law

A legal exam is a requirement to practice law in Norway, which has been the case since 1736. In the 18th century, many Norwegian students got private tutoring instead of travelling to Copenhagen to study, where the main university in the Danish-Norwegian

167 Jørn Øyrehagen Sunde, "Der organische Zusammenhang des Rechts: How the reception of Savigny came to influence legal reception in Norwegian law in the 19th and first part of the 20th century" in Volker Lipp and Halvard Haukeland Fredriksen (Eds.), *Reforms of Civil Procedure in Germany and Norway* (Siebeck Mohr 2011) 7–18.

realm was situated.[168] The first teaching of law on Norwegian soil at a university level came with the establishment of the University of Oslo in 1811. In Bergen, and probably other major Norwegian cities, students still got private tutoring until 1968. In 1969, teaching of law began at the University of Bergen, and a law faculty was established in 1980.[169] Seven years later, teaching of law started at the University of Tromsø, and a faculty of law was established there in 1997. Since 2005, it usually takes five years of studying to obtain a master's degree in law. From the turn of the millennium, a three-year bachelor study in law has been established at the universities in Agder and Stavanger, and at the colleges in Drammen and Lillehammer.

Since a law degree became a requirement for practicing law in 1736, the annual number of graduating lawyers was fairly low for a long time. In 1955 there were 50 law students that graduated. Ten years later there were 90. In 1972 this number surpassed 200 and continued to increase. In 1990 the number of law students graduating surpassed 500, in 1995 it was more than 800 for the first time, in 2000 about 900 students graduated from the law study, and the number has mainly been between 800 and 900 students graduating since then.[170] As society is getting more complex, the demand for lawyers is constantly increasing. For instance, the number of members of the Norwegian Bar Association increased from about 2,800 in 1987 to about 9,000 thirty years later, which is an increase of over 300 %. To study law is hence much desired by young Norwegians. Very good high school grades are required to become a lawyer due to a *numerus clausus* system, limiting the number of applicants admitted to the study of law.

It was also at the beginning of the 1990s that the number of PhD students started to increase. In 1994, 100 Norwegians had achieved a doctoral degree in law. The number surpassed 200 in 2005, and 300 in 2010, and are now close to 400.[171] With an increase in the number of students and PhD students, the need for professors to teach and supervise also increased. In 1968 there were nine ordinary professors in law in Norway, which increased to 12 in 1969 with the establishment of a law study in Bergen. In the early 1990s there were still just above 20, but had passed 80 in 2012, and in 2017 there were more than 120 professors in law in Norway.

These numbers display the quite insignificant size of Norwegian legal scholarship for most of Norwegian legal history. It can also be added that between 1716 – when the first textbook in law in Danish was published by Ludvig Holberg – and 1950, not more than about 150 persons staying for a longer period in Norway published legal literature, and

168 The other university in the Danish-Norwegian realm was in Kiel in present day Germany, then in the dukedom of Schleswig-Holstein.

169 On the history of the law faculty, see the introductory chapters in Johan Giertsen, Berte-Elen Reinertsen Konow, Erling Johannes Husabø and Øystein L. Iversen (Eds.), *Rett i vest – Festskrift til 50-årsjubileet for juristutdanningen ved Universitetet i Bergen* (Fagbokforlaget 2019) 1–130.

170 Jørn Øyrehagen Sunde, "Å skunda seg langsamt" in Johan Giertsen, Berte-Elen Reinertsen Konow, Erling Johannes Husabø and Øystein L. Iversen (Eds.), *Rett i vest – Festskrift til 50-årsjubileet for juristutdanningen ved Universitetet i Bergen* (Fagbokforlaget 2019) 134–135.

171 Kjølstad (2019) (n. 161) 48.

several of these legal authors were judges.[172] The traditional lack of a significant impact of legal scholars on the Norwegian legal culture can to some extent explain the reluctance to adopt a systematic approach to law. Focusing on legal practice also in legal education has facilitated a pragmatic approach to law, a legal realistic instead of a scientific legal methodology, and acceptance of policy considerations as legitimate legal argument bases. Law students are trained in a generalist approach to law which aims to provide procedural rather than outcome predictability.

A law degree qualifies to work as a lawyer in general, and with one exception there are no further qualifications required. This exception is for getting a licence to practice as a lawyer. The Organ for Supervision of Legal Practitioners (*Tilsynsrådet for advokatvirksomhet*) has the authority to decide the requirements and to reward licences.[173] The requirement is, in short, a two years period as a paid trainee in a law firm (or as an assistant judge, in a position with the public prosecutor, or at a faculty of law), to pass some theoretical courses, and to litigate three cases in court.[174] A licence to practice as a lawyer is no requirement to become a judge. This applies to judges at all three levels of the court hierarchy.

Norwegian judges are hence non-specialized in two different ways. First, they are not especially trained to be a judge. Second, they normally do not deal with special kinds of cases. Norwegian courts are also non-specialized in yet another way – lay judges are most extensively used. In 2016 there were 856 lay judges per 100,000 inhabitants in Norway, which is by far the absolutely highest number in Europe; Monaco has 394, Denmark 174, Slovenia 167, and Germany 112.[175] Lay judges are used in civil cases in the district and appeal courts if requested by the parties. This quite rarely happens. However, in some specific civil cases, for instance child custody cases and cases concerning dismissal, lay judges are required. The use of lay judges is most intense in criminal cases. In all criminal cases before the district court, the court is set with one professional and two lay judges, increased to two professional and three lay judges if the case is more severe. In the courts of appeal, appeals concerning evidence submitted to prove guilt or, in cases that might result in more than six years of imprisonment, appeals related to the sentencing, are decided by a body of two professional and five lay judges which rule in cooperation on both the facts and the law.[176]

---

172 Sunde (2015), *Høgsteretts historie* (n. 44) 242.

173 See https://tilsynet.no/.

174 See https://www.advokatforeningen.no/om/om-medlemskapet/english/working-as-a-trainee-lawyer-advokatfullmektig-in-norway/ accessed 21 April 2017.

175 European Commission for the Efficiency of Justice, "European judicial systems – Efficiency and quality of justice", CEPEJ Studies NO. 26, 2018, p. 103. Available at https://rm.coe.int/rapport-avec-couv-18-09-2018-en/16808def9c accessed 9 March 2020. Monaco has 394 lay judges per 100,000 inhabitants, Denmark 174, Slovenia 167, and Germany 112.

176 See the Criminal Procedure Act (n. 30) §§ 276 and 332.

6.3 Perspectives

Even though the education is still focused on producing legal generalists, specialization in specific fields of law is becoming increasingly important particularly for attorneys. This is not least caused by the constantly increasing complexity of the law and the surrounding society. In the light of the ideal of justice and a generally applicable legal method this may cause problems in the future. On the one hand, judges in courts with general competence are in principle obliged to decide all kinds of cases. On the other hand, one can observe that attorneys are often a specialist in one or two fields of law. This may cause an imbalance in the knowledge between judges and attorneys.[177]

Another quite unsolved and somewhat underestimated problem is the constantly increasing number of legal sources applicable in Norway, reducing the traditional wide discretion of those applying the law in many fields of law. This may make it necessary to adjust both the way lawyers apply the law but also the education of legal professionals. Implementing a bachelor's degree in law may be regarded as a first step to a new form of legalistic professionalisation with a strong focus on the formal application of legislation. The underlying problem will nevertheless remain. The multiplicity of relevant legal sources calls for specialisation, but specialisation requires change in the system of conflict resolution and in legal methods. If and to what extent these changes will take place depends strongly on the impact and pace of internationalisation of law in Norway.

7. Internationalisation[178]

Internationalisation of law is a phenomenon that concerns, at least to a certain extent, all modern legal cultures. One may therefore question whether internationalisation can be characterized as a structural element of a specific legal culture. When talking about internationalisation as a specific feature of a legal culture, we refer here to the impact of internationalisation on the specific culture at hand and the attitude towards these impacts and the phenomena of internationalisation of law in general. In other words, how do lawyers, judges, politicians, but also citizens respond to challenges and consequences of internationalisation? Is the national legal system capable of implementing foreign legal materials? To what extent do legal transplants and international impulses cause major disturbance in a specific legal culture? It seems difficult to answer these

177 A recent decision of the Supreme Court (HR-2017-33-A – *Forusstranda*) can be used as an illustrating example. The judges had to decide on a very difficult legal dogmatic question regarding fundamental aspects of contract, bankruptcy and company law. It can be argued that the judges were not able to consider properly the complexity of the legal argumentation put forward by the representatives of both parties. This decision will therefore presumably not lead to the clarification of the law but may cause further litigation since the law seems less clear than prior to the ruling. For a criticism of the judgment, see Hans Fredrik Marthinussen, "'Forusstranda': Kreditorvern ved fisjon og fusjon, rettsvernhevd og formuerettslige metodespørsmål" (2017) Vol. 52 No. 2 *Jussens Venner* 67.

178 The chapter is partly based on findings published in Ingvill Helland and Sören Koch, "International influences in Norwegian legal method" in Ingvill Helland and Sören Koch (Eds.), *Nordic and Germanic Legal Methods* (Mohr Siebeck 2014).

questions on a general basis as there are often conflicting interests in society responding differently to these challenges. When talking about the impact of internationalisation on a legal culture, we limit our observation to the traceable impacts international law has on the Norwegian legal system, especially its institutions, and the way international law affects, or is perceived to affect, the application of law.

In Norway we can observe a major change in the perception regarding the internationalisation of law in the last two decades. The first sign of a desire to harmonize Norwegian and EU law can be found in the Product Liability Act from 1988.[179] More important was that Norway became part of the EEA Agreement in 1994, and implemented the European Convention on Human Rights in 1999.[180] In the 21st century the internationalisation of law has become a constantly growing challenge both for legal practitioners and academics.[181] Today more than 30 % of law in action might be derived from legal sources produced outside the Norwegian jurisdictional borders.[182] However, despite the perception of internationalisation as something new, a closer look at the Norwegian legal history reveals that internationalisation has been a rather constant factor in the Norwegian legal culture. What has changed over time is the intensity, quality and visibility of international influences.

Being an active member of the international community, Norway is party to an extensive number of treaties, several of which place obligations upon the state regarding the content of national law.[183] Because Norway is a dualistic state, the fact that Norway has taken an obligation upon itself on the international level is generally not sufficient

179 Lov 1988-12-23-104 om produktansvar [the Product Liability Act], in relation to Council Directive 85/374/EEC of 25 July 1985 on the approximation of the laws, regulations and administrative provisions of the Member States concerning liability for defective products.

180 Being a party to the EEA Agreement, Norway is obliged to implement EU directives and regulations into national law. Cf. the EEA Agreement Art. 1 (2) and 3 taken in conjunction with Art. 7. The EEA Agreement has been incorporated into Norwegian law by means of the EEA Act (Lov 1992-11-27-109 om gjennomføring i norsk rett av hoveddelen i avtale om det Europeiske økonomiske samarbeidsområde (EØS) m.v.) and takes precedence over other national legislation in case of conflict due to the precedence clause in § 2. For an overview of Norway and the EEA agreement, see Fredrik Bøckman Finstad, "Norway and the EEA" in Finn Arnesen, Halvard Haukeland Fredriksen, Hans Petter Graver, Ola Mestad and Christoph Vedder (Eds.), *Agreement on the European Economic Area. A Commentary* (C.H. Beck/Hart/Nomos 2018).

181 On the changing attitudes towards internationalisation at the law faculty in Bergen, see Sören Koch, "Den 'moderne resepsjonen' – Internasjonaliseringen i undervisning og forskning mellom 1969 og 2003" in Johan Giertsen, Berte-Elen Reinertsen Konow, Erling Johannes Husabø and Øystein L. Iversen (Eds.), *Rett i vest – Festskrift til 50-årsjubileet for juristutdanningen ved Universitetet i Bergen* (Fagbokforlaget 2019).

182 Sunde (2015), *Høgsteretts historie* (n. 44) 405–406.

183 The European Convention on Human Rights as well as the other Conventions listed in § 2 of the Human Rights Act are perhaps among the most important, besides the European Economic Agreement (EEA).

to make a treaty directly applicable in national law.[184] The practical consequence for legal argumentation is that international law may generally not constitute the basis of an independent legal rule, unless it has been specifically implemented into national law by the Norwegian Parliament.

International law is, however, not only relevant as the primary legal basis of an independent legal rule. Pursuant to the principle of presumption, it may also be relevant for the interpretation of national sources of law. The principle of presumption states that national law is presumed to be in accordance with those rules of international law Norway is contractually or by custom bound to follow.[185] Accordingly, national law is supposed to be interpreted in light of Norway's international obligations, regardless of whether or not the international law in question has been incorporated.[186]

This is especially important regarding the cooperation with the EU. As a consequence of § 2 of the EEA Act, all national provisions that are adopted for the purpose of meeting Norway's obligations under the EEA Agreement take precedence over other legislation. The purpose of such a provision is that the EU legislation itself becomes relevant, at least as a factor for interpretation, and so do the decisions of the EFTA Court, which is responsible for overseeing the EEA Agreement. An important mechanism here is the possibility for Norwegian courts to request the EFTA Court to give an advisory opinion on the interpretation of the EEA Agreement, a procedure that has been used more frequently by the courts in recent years.[187] The decisions of the ECJ are also relevant, despite the fact that Norway has no legal standing before this court.[188] Because legal uniformity is an important rationale behind the EEA agreement, Norwegian courts will generally try to follow the ECJ's interpretation of EU law, and interpret Norwegian

184 Unlike the consent of the German Parliament pursuant to Art. 59 Grundgesetz (GG), the consent of the Norwegian Parliament pursuant to § 26 of the Norwegian Constitution only takes effect in international law. That the consent is not simultaneously an incorporation is clearly evident from its form. At a time when legislation required the separation of the Parliament into two chambers, both of which were required to adopt a legislative proposal in order for it to become law, the proposition for consent to ratification of the international conventions was put to the Parliament as such in a *Stortingsproposisjon* (see for example St.prp. nr. 83 (1951) as regards consent to the ratification of the ECHR), and the Parliament gave its consent in a plenary session.

185 See Rt. 1984 p. 1175, on p. 1180, although in this judgment it was applied as a standard in the absence of clear guidance from either legislation or preparatory works. See also St.prp. nr. 100 (1991–1992) p. 319 concerning the EEA Act; Arnesen and Stenvik (n. 161) 59 ff.; Morten Ruud and Geir Ulfstein, *Innføring i folkerett* (4th ed., Universitetsforlaget 2011) 63 ff. A similar principle applies in Germany, see BVerfGE 74, 358 (para. 35). See Robert Uerpmann, *Die Europäische Menschenrechtskonvention und die deutsche Rechtsprechung: ein Beitrag zum Thema Völkerrecht und Landesrecht* (Berlin 1993) 112 for further references.

186 The Supreme Court judgment HR-2016-2591-A offers an example of the limits of applying the principle of presumption.

187 See Article 34 of the Agreement between the EFTA States on the Establishment of a Surveillance Authority and a Court of Justice. The increasing number of referrals is documented by Per Christiansen, "Article 34 [Advisory opinions]" in Finn Arnesen, Halvard Haukeland Fredriksen, Hans Petter Graver, Ola Mestad and Christoph Vedder (Eds.), *Agreement on the European Economic Area. A Commentary* (C.H. Beck/Hart/Nomos 2018) 1038.

188 Erik Magnus Boe, *Rettskildelære under debatt* (Universitetsforlaget 2012) 384, see also n. 194 below. However, judgments handed down *after* the adoption of the EEA agreement are not *binding* on Norway, not even under international law, cfr. Article 6 of the EEA Agreement; Knut Bergo, *Høyesteretts forarbeidsbruk* (Cappelen Akademisk 2000) 401.

law accordingly as dictated by the principle of presumption.[189] In consequence, the legal order's openness towards international influences may better be described as a form of soft dualism.[190] The extent of this soft dualism is perhaps best shown by the fact that even the interpretation of several human rights provisions in the Constitution – the highest ranking legal source – is to a great extent influenced by case law from international human rights bodies.[191]

Due to the quite comparable methodological approach in the European Courts and the way the Supreme Court judges argue, it is possible for Norwegian lawyers to adapt dynamically to the international case law. The flexible and dynamic approach to legal methods – with its strong focus on the practice of the Norwegian Supreme Court – seems to facilitate the use of international case law as a legal argument. At the same time Norwegian lawyers are used to deduce legal norms from abstract legislation, and in this way, the legal culture is well equipped to handle EU directives and regulations.

One particular challenge posed by the internationalisation is, however, the increased complexity of law. As already mentioned, more than 30 % of law in action today might be derived from legal sources produced outside the Norwegian jurisdictional borders.[192] In the field of human rights law – which encompasses more and more areas of life – many issues are regulated by several international regimes, sometimes with diverging and non-coordinated approaches to the same material human right.[193] Within the EEA system, a similar problem may arise – and has indeed arisen – in cases of different interpretations of EEA law by the EFTA Court and the ECJ.[194] Heterarchical structures like these are particularly demanding for a legal culture that has traditionally been based on a one-tiered and centralized court hierarchy. Moreover, the sheer quantity of legal material has been amplified following the accession to the EEA. The recent "NAV scandal" indicates that Norway is still struggling to come to grips with this situation. In brief, it turned out in 2019 that the Norwegian Labour and Welfare Administration (NAV) has

189 Nygaard (2007), *Rettsgrunnlag og standpunkt* (n. 92) 38; Jens Edvin A. Skoghøy, "Dommerrollen gjennom de siste 50 år – noen utviklingstrekk" (2011) No. 1–2 *Lov og Rett* 4; Halvard Haukeland Fredriksen, "Hvem avgjør tolkningen av EØS-avtalen? – noen betraktninger om størrelsen 'gjeldende EØS-rett'" (2010) No. 2 *Tidsskrift for Rettsvitenskap* 247; Boe (2012), *Rettskildelære under debatt* (n. 188) 386. See also the debate by both the majority and the minority in Rt. 2000 p. 1811 (*Finanger I*).

190 Helland and Koch (2014), "International influences" (n. 178) 364.

191 See in particular Rt. 2015 p. 93 (para. 57).

192 See n. 182.

193 An illustrative example is how the European Court of Human Rights in 2014 concluded that a French general ban on full face veils, i.e. niqab and burqa, did not violate the right to freedom of religion, whereas the United Nations Human Rights Committee arrived at the opposite conclusion in 2018. Compare *S.A.S. v France* App no 43835/11 (ECtHR, 1 July 2014) and *Sonia Yaker v France* Communication no 2747/2016 (HRC, decided 17 July 2018, published 7 December 2018). But frequently, actors at the international level try to coordinate their approaches, see for instance the ECtHR's "Bosphorus presumption", establishing a (rebuttable) presumption that a state will not violate the ECHR by implementing EU law. Cfr. *Bosphorus Hava Yolları Turizm ve Ticaret Anonim Şirketi v Ireland* App no 45036/98 (ECtHR, 30 June 2005) (para. 155–156 and 165).

194 See in particular HR-2013-496-A (*STX*), where the Supreme Court disregarded an advisory opinion from the EFTA Court (E-2/11), based in part on the view that the opinion diverged from the ECJ's practice (see, *inter alia*, para. 100).

refused for years to grant various social benefits to persons if they have been travelling abroad. The NAV case is many-faceted, and at the time of writing, several legal and political questions remain to be clarified. But at least, the fact that a restriction on the free movement of workers could go on for years without almost no one questioning the legality of such a restriction or the relation to relevant secondary law suggests that the general level of knowledge about EEA law is too limited.

Lesson learned from legal history is that the extent and tempo of internationalisation is equivalent to the flow of law students, and the sources of it equal to where the law students go to study.[195] If we look at the flow of students at the Faculty of Law in Bergen, and where they go to study, we see that more than 50 % of the students study abroad for half a year or a full year, and that they go to study all over the world, even though the large majority go to different European countries. The faculty also receives almost as many students as it sends abroad, and from as many countries. It is hard to predict the future, also when it comes to the internationalisation of law. However, by taking the pulse of the student flow, we get an idea of where things are going. And with the high numbers of outgoing students, it might be that the Norwegian legal culture will be better equipped in some years to handle the complexity that follows from an increased internationalisation of law.

8. Conclusion

The Norwegian legal culture is a part of the Nordic legal tradition, and often appears as a hybrid of elements that can be linked to the civil law tradition on the European mainland, and elements that can be linked to the common law tradition. Other legal cultures, such as Scotland, have also been impacted by these two legal traditions. However, as the chapter on the Scottish legal culture in this volume demonstrates, the institutional or intellectual structures of the legal culture in Scotland and Norway are far from identical or even similar. Furthermore, the reasons for the mixed character of Scots law are quite different and were *inter alia* a result of changing political influences. For Norway, and the other Nordic countries, it has been rather a product of historical circumstances, and not politics.

In the High Middle Ages, Norway had already established a court hierarchy in three levels, which has remained the ideal court structure. There are only two specialized courts at the first level, but some moderate specialization on both the first and the second level of the court hierarchy. This is partly made possible by the extensive use of conflict resolving boards handling the majority of all civil cases outside the court system. However, this leaves the Norwegian court hierarchy quite exceptionally stringent and unified in a European context, and hence very fit for passing down precedent.

Norway has a long tradition of legislation, even for making codes of law. However, since 1687 legislation has been adopted in the form of/as statutes and decrees. This leaves

195 Sunde (2005) (n. 5) 326.

legislated law rather fragmentary, even though the use of the constitution as positive law, and the use of preparatory work as a legal source, supplies it with systematic structures. However, there is still a great deal of room for the Supreme Court to manoeuvre when filling loopholes and attempting to create legal unity. The pyramidal structure of the court system is perfect for passing down precedent to lower courts.

The idea of justice in a modern society has been predictability. Norway is no exception to this rule. But assessments of fairness and individual justice are both legitimate and quite frequently used by judges and legal practitioners. Such assessments have quite some weight, even if the proposed solution, at least from a formal or dogmatical point of view, is less predictable. This ties in with the rather pragmatic nature of the Norwegian culture in general and the Norwegian approach to legal methodology in particular and explains why precedent is an important legal source next to legislation. In other words, to some extent courts adjust prescribed law to fairness and individual justice.

The Norwegian legal method is based on a realist and pragmatic approach. That means that it is to a lesser degree characterized by a hierarchy of norms and a strict deduction from positive legal sources. The application of law is instead based on a balancing process, in which relevant legal argument bases are used in different functions to legitimise the specific outcome of the case at hand. The generalist approach to legal method provides procedural predictability, which in turn furthers the ideal of balancing legal security and individual justice. The rather varied flora in the legal landscape caused by the fragmentary character of legislation, provides the courts with an essential degree of discretion, which in turn facilitates the expectation that law is fair next to being predictable.

The degree of legal professionalisation in Norway was for a long time very low. There was only one faculty of law until 1980, few students of law, few law doctorates, few professors of law, and comparably little legal literature produced. This changed especially during the 1990s, caused by an increasing demand for lawyers since the 1980s. Also for a long time, the generalist character of Norwegian courts and approach to method has held back specialisation among lawyers. At the same time, there is a quite extensive use of lay judges in Norwegian courts, adding to the moderate professional character of Norwegian law. Legislation is framed in a rather nontechnical manner. The intention is to also make law easily accessible for laypersons.[196] This contributes to the fact that in Norway, law is to a lesser degree regarded a closed (scientific or bureaucratic) subsystem than in many other legal cultures, where law is the domain of a highly professionalised elite of lawyers and legal scholars.

Norway has traditionally been exposed to a high degree of international impulses. The intensity and nature of this impact has varied over time, but despite the peripheral position of the country was never completely absent. On one hand, Norway subscribes to a dualistic system. Internationally produced law has to be implemented into Norwe-

196 At the Faculty of Law in Oslo, a project focusing on clear and understandable language in legal research and teaching was launched in 2016, see https://www.jus.uio.no/forskning/prosjekter/klarsprak/index.html accessed 29 March 2020.

gian law by the legislator to be directly applicable. On the other hand, it is presumed that obligations deriving from international custom and treaties of which Norway has signed, apply unless they are in conflict with Norwegian law. At the same time, the culture of precedent has made Norwegian law very open to direct influence of international law as interpreted by the ECtHR, the EFTA Court, and the ECJ. The case law of these courts is used as *quasi* precedent by Norwegian courts. As a consequence, internationally produced law has some direct effect on Norwegian law despite the dualistic system.

The Norwegian Legal Culture and its structures and structural elements					
Institutional structure		**Intellectual structure**			
Conflict resolution	*Norm production*	*Ideal of justice*	*Legal method*	*Degree of professionalisation*	*Character of internationalisation*
One hierarchy of ordinary courts, some moderate specialisation through case assignment in the first and second level courts, two specialized courts in the first instance, and a whole series of public and *quasi*-public boards handling civil cases outside the court system.	Legislation through statutes and decrees, precedent from the Supreme Court is important but not formally binding, case law from the courts of appeal have increasingly persuasive authority. Limited influence of scholarly writings. Increasing impact of law produced outside Norway.	Predictability is the starting point but modified through court practice also aimed at securing fairness and individual justice. The aim of balancing these two ideals facilitates a rather pragmatic expectation of procedural predictability promoting a heuristic rather than legalistic approach to law.	Pragmatic approach to legal argumentation based on a flexible balancing model taking into account a variety of legal argument bases, including legislation, preparatory works, case law, legal opinions, private and administrative practice, and policy considerations.	A 5-year master's degree in law is required to practice as a lawyer, a large increase in the output of law graduates and a large increase in the job market for lawyers especially the last three decades, for a long time a quite insignificant legal scholarship, and consequently a strong focus on court practice. Legal education has an unusually strong focus on the general approach on legal method.	Traditionally high degree and rather open attitude towards international impulses, varying in intensity and nature over time, momentarily very high intensity due to increasing inter, supra, and transnationalisation. Moderate dualistic system – implementation required. Exception: judgments from ECtHR, EFTA Court and ECJ, which are used as *quasi* precedent in courts.

9. Bibliography

Aarli, R and Mæhle, SS, *Fra lov til rett* (2nd ed., Gyldendal 2017).

Andenæs, MH, *Rettskildelære* (2nd ed., Oslo 2009).

Andersson, H, *Skyddsändamål och adekvans* (Uppsala 1993).

Arnesen, F and Stenvik, A, *Internasjonalisering og juridisk metode* (Universitetsforlaget 2015).

Askeland, B, "Eckhoffs rettskildelære under press" (1999) *Kritisk Juss* 115.

Askeland, B, "Prinsipp og pragmatisme i erstatningsretten" in Holgersen, G, Krüger, K and Lilleholt, K (Eds.), *Nybrott og odling, Festskrift til Nils Nygaard* (Fagbokforlaget 2002),

Askeland, B, "Rettskildelærens utvikling i rettsteoretisk belysning", (2003) No. 1 *Jussens Venner* 8.

Bårdsen, A, "De nordiske høyesterettene som konstitusjonsdomstoler: Noen nyere utviklingslinjer i Norges Høyesterett", speech held at a seminar for the Nordic supreme courts, Stockholm 23 and 24 March 2015, available at https://www.domstol.no/globalassets/upload/hret/artikler-og-foredrag/nordiske-konstitusjons-domstoler---stockholm-mars-2015.pdf.

Bergo, K, *Høyesteretts forarbeidsbruk* (Cappelen Akademisk 2000).

Bergo, K, *Tekst og virkelighet i rettskildelæren* (Cappelen Akademisk 2002).

Bernt, C, *Meklerrollen ved mekling i domstolene* (Fagbokforlaget 2011).

Bernt, JF and Doublet, DR, "Norsk rettsvitenskap mellom rettspositivisme og ny-normativisme" in Blume, P and Petersen, H (Eds.), *Retlig polycentri: til Henrik Zahle på 50-årsdagen* (Akademisk Forlag 1993).

Bernt, JF and Doublet, DR, *Juss, samfunn og rettsanvendelse – en introduksjon til rettsvitenskapen* (Ad Notam Gyldendal 1996).

Bernt, JF and Mæhle, SS, *Rett, samfunn og demokrati* (Gyldendal Akademisk 2007).

Blandhol, S, "Pragmatismens aktualitet i rettsvitenskap og rettsanvendelse" (2004) No. 3 *Tidsskrift for Rettsvitenskap* 365.

Blandhol, S, "Er rettsanvendelsen i EU-domstolen og Menneskerettsdomstolen vesensforskjellig fra norsk rettskildelære?" (2005) No. 5–6 *Lov og Rett* 316.

Blandhol, S, *De beste grunner. Reelle hensyn i juridisk argumentasjon* (Gyldendal Juridisk 2014).

Blume, P, *Juridisk Metodelære* (5th ed., Jurist- og Økonomforbundets Forlag 2009).

Boe, EM, *Grunnleggende juridisk metode – En introduksjon til rett og rettstenkning* (3rd ed., Universitetsforlaget 2012).

Boe, EM, *Rettskildelære under debatt* (Universitetsforlaget 2012).

Christiansen, P, "Article 34 [Advisory opinions]" in Arnesen, F, Haukeland Fredriksen, H, Graver, HP, Mestad, O and Vedder, C (Eds.), *Agreement on the European Economic Area. A Commentary* (CH Beck/Hart/Nomos 2018). DOI: https://doi.org/10.5771%2F9783845275796-1032

Cordero-Moss, G, "International Contracts between Common Law and Civil Law: Is Non-state Law to Be Preferred? The Difficulty of Interpreting Legal Standards Such as Good Faith" (2007) 7 No. 1 *Global Jurist Advances* 1. DOI: https://doi.org/10.2202%2F1934-2640.1189

Eckhoff, T, *Rettskildelære*, (1st ed., Tanum 1971).

Eckhoff, T and Helgesen, J, *Rettskildelære* (5th ed., Tanum 2001).

Evald, J, *Retskilderne og den juridiske metode* (Jurist- og Økonomforbundets Forlag 1997).

Evald, J, *At tænke juridisk – juridisk metode for begyndere* (4th ed., Nyt Juridisk Forlag 2011).

Finstad, FB, "Norway and the EEA" in Arnesen, F, Haukeland Fredriksen, H, Graver, HP, Mestad, O and Vedder, C (Eds.), *Agreement on the European Economic Area. A Commentary* (C.H. Beck/Hart/Nomos 2018). DOI: https://doi.org/10.5771%2F9783845275796-59

Fleischer, CA, *Rettskilder* (Ad Notam Gyldendal 1995).

Fleischer, CA, *Rettskilder og juridisk metode* (Ad Notam Gyldendal 1998).

Graver, HP, "I prinsippet prinsipiell – om rettsprinsipper" (2006) No. 2–3 *Tidsskrift for Rettsvitenskap* 189.

Graver, HP, *Hva er rett* (Universitetsforlaget 2011).

Grendstad, G, Shaffer, WR, Sunde, JØ and Waltenburg, EN, *Proactive and Powerful – Law Clerks and the Institutionalization of the Norwegian Supreme Court* (Eleven 2020).

Haukeland Fredriksen, H, "Hvem avgjør tolkningen av EØS-avtalen? – noen betraktninger om størrelsen 'gjeldende EØS-rett'" (2010) No. 2 *Tidsskrift for Rettsvitenskap* 247.

Helland, I, *Rulings of the European Court of Human Rights as a Legal Argument – a Comparison between Norwegian and German Law* (PhD thesis, University of Bergen 2012).

Helland, I, "The permissibility and (conditional) recommendability of contra legem interpretations in Norwegian law" (2014) No. 1 *Retfærd* 17.

Helland, I and Koch, S, "International influences in Norwegian legal method" in Helland, I and Koch, S (Eds.), *Nordic and Germanic Legal Methods* (Mohr Siebeck 2014).

Helland, I and Koch, S, "Introduction to Norwegian Legal Method" in Helland, I and Koch, S (Eds.), *Nordic and Germanic Legal Methods* (Mohr Siebeck 2014).

Helland, I and Koch, S, "Norwegian and German Legal Methods Compared" in Helland, I and Koch, S (Eds.), *Nordic and Germanic Legal Methods* (Mohr Siebeck 2014).

Henninger, T, "Legal Culture and Common Principles of European Legal Methods" in Helland, I and Koch, S (Eds.), *Nordic and Germanic Legal Methods* (Mohr Siebeck 2014).

Holmes, OW, "The Path of the Law" (1897) Vol. 10 *Harvard Law Review*. DOI: http://dx.doi.org/10.2307/1342108

Holmøyvik, H, "Utviklinga av prøvingsretten i Noreg" in Michalsen, D and Holmøyvik, E, *Lærebok i forfatningshistorie* (Pax 2015).

Høgberg, AP, "Reelle hensyn" in Høgberg, AP and Sunde, JØ (Eds.), *Juridisk metode og tenkemåte* (Universitetsforlaget 2019).

Høgberg, AP and Kinander, M, "Det formelle legalitetsprinsippet og rettskildelæren" (2011) No. 1 *Tidsskrift for Rettsvitenskap* 15.

Jacobsen, J, "Law, Legal Science and Methodological Pluralism" in Giertsen, J, Konow, BER., Husabø, EJ and Iversen, ØL (Eds.), *Rett i vest – Festskrift til 50-årsjubileet for juristutdanningen ved Universitetet i Bergen* (Fagbokforlaget 2019).

Kierulf, A, *Judicial Review in Norway. A Bicentennial Debate* (Cambridge University Press 2018). DOI: https://doi.org/10.1017%2F9781108617727

Kinander, M, "Trenger man egentlig 'reelle hensyn'? – To betydninger, noen problemer" (2002) *Lov og rett* 234.

Kjølstad, MM, "Det rettsvitenskapelige kloster. Doktorgradsutdanning- og avhandlinger ved Det juridiske fakultet i Bergen 1969–2018" in Giertsen, J, Konow, BER, Husabø, EJ and Iversen, ØL (Eds.), *Rett i vest – Festskrift til 50-årsjubileet for juristutdanningen ved Universitetet i Bergen* (Fagbokforlaget 2019).

Koch, S, "Consequences of changing expectations to law and its institutions. Illustrated by the role and background of judges in Norway" (2015) 83 *The Legal History Review* 461. DOI: https://doi.org/10.1163%2F15718190-08334p06

Koch, S, "Den 'moderne resepsjonen' – Internasjonaliseringen i undervisning og forskning mellom 1969 og 2003" in Giertsen, J, Konow, BER., Husabø, EJ and Iversen, ØL (Eds.), *Rett i vest – Festskrift til 50-årsjubileet for juristutdanningen ved Universitetet i Bergen* (Fagbokforlaget 2019).

Krüger, K, "Komparativ rettsmetode – observasjoner vedrørende prinsipper for rettsanvendelse i Europa nord og sør – illustrert ved tilfelle i Norge og Italia" (1996) *Jussens Venner* 281.

Langford, M. and Berge, BK, "Norway's Constitution in a Comparative Perspective" (2019) Vol. 6 No. 3 *Oslo Law Review* 198.

Lødrup, P and Kjelland, M, *Lærebok i erstatningsrett* (Gyldendal Akademisk 2009).

Malt, GF, "To glemte linjer i tradisjonell rettsfinningslære" (1992) No. 1–2 *Tidsskrift for Rettsvitenskap* 48.

Marthinussen, HF, "'Forusstranda': Kreditorvern ved fisjon og fusjon, rettsvernhevd og formuerettslige metodespørsmål" (2017) Vol. 52 No. 2 *Jussens Venner* 67. DOI: https://doi.org/10.18261/issn.1504-3126-2017-02-01

Mestad, O (Ed.), *Frihetens forskole. Professor Schlegel og eidsvollmennenes læretid i København* (Pax 2014).

Michalsen, D, "Structural-Historical Features in 'The Norwegian Legal Method'" in Helland I and Koch S (Eds.), *Nordic and Germanic Legal Methods* (Mohr Siebeck 2014).

Michalsen, D and Holmøyvik, E, *Lærebok i forfatningshistorie* (Pax 2015).

Monsen, E, *Innføring i juridisk metode og oppgaveteknikk* (Cappelen Damm Akademisk 2012).

Monsen, E, "En kommentar til Høyesteretts bruk av 'tause forarbeider' i Rt. 2015 s. 1324" (2016) No. 3 *Jussens Venner* 159. DOI: https://do.org/10.18261/issn.1504-3126-2016-03-03.

Mykland, K, Fossen, AB, Herstad, J and Utne, B, *Norge under enevelde 1660–1720* (Fagbokforlaget 1975).

Mæhle, SS, *Grenser for rettsanvendelsesskjønn: Om rettslig legitimitet i et spenningsfelt mellom flertallsmakt og rettighetsvern* (Gyldendal Akademisk 2005).

Nygaard, N, *Rettsgrunnlag og standpunkt* (2nd ed., Universitetsforlaget 2007).

Nygaard, N, *Skade og ansvar* (Universitetsforlaget 2007).

Nylund, A, "The Many Ways of Civil Mediation in Norway" in Ervo, L and Nylund, A (Eds.), *The Future of Civil Litigation – Access to Court and Court Annexed Mediation in the Nordic Countries* (Springer 2014). DOI: https://doi.org/10.1007%2F978-3-319-04465-1_6

Nylund, A, Ervasti, K and Adrian, L, "Introduction to Nordic Mediation Research" in Nylund, A, Ervasti, K and Adrian, L, *Nordic Mediation Research* (Springer 2019). DOI: https://doi.org/10.1007%2F978-3-319-73019-6_1

Ruud, M and Ulfstein, G, *Innføring i folkerett* (4th ed., Universitetsforlaget 2011).

Sandvik, H, "Hvorfor lyktes kriminalloven, men ikke sivilloven i Norge?" in Sandvik H and Michalsen D (Eds,), *Kodifikasjon og konstitusjon – Grunnloven § 94s krav til lovbøker i norsk historie* (Pax Forlag 2013).

Sevatdal, H and Wannebo, E, "Utviklingen av jordskifteretten sett i lys av matrikkelsystemet, forvaltningen og de ordinære domstoler" in Ravna, Ø (Ed.), *Areal og eiendomsrett* (Universitetsforlaget 2007).

Skoghøy, JEA, "Dommerrollen gjennom de siste 50 år – noen utviklingstrekk" (2011) No. 1–2 *Lov og Rett* 4.

Sundberg, J, "Civil Law, Common Law and the Scandinavians" (1969) 13 *Scandinavian Studies in Law* 179.

Sunde, JØ, *Speculum legale – rettsspegelen* (Fagbokforlaget 2005).

Sunde, JØ, *"Fornuft og Erfarenhed" – framveksten av metodisk medvit i dansknorsk rett på 1700-talet* (PhD thesis, University of Bergen 2007).

Sunde, JØ, "Der organische Zusammenhang des Rechts: How the reception of Savigny came to influence legal reception in Norwegian law in the 19th and first part of the 20th century" in Lipp, V and Haukeland Fredriksen, H (Eds.), *Reforms of Civil Procedure in Germany and Norway* (Siebeck Mohr 2011).

Sunde, JØ, "Dissenting votes in the Norwegian Supreme Court 1965–2009: A legal cultural analysis" (2012) Heft 1 *Rechtskultur – Zeitschrift für Europäische Rechtsgeschichte* 59.

Sunde, JØ, "Daughters of God and Counsellors of the Judges of Men: Changes in the Legal Culture of the Norwegian Realm in the High Middle Ages" in Brink, S and Collinson, L (Eds.), *New Approaches to Early law in Scandinavia* (Brepols 2014). DOI: https://doi.org/10.1484%2Fm.as-eb.1.101969

Sunde, JØ, "The Legal Cultural Dependency of the Norwegian Legal Method – and its Future" in Helland, I and Koch, S (Eds.), *Nordic and Germanic Legal Methods* (Mohr Siebeck 2014).

Sunde, JØ, *Høgsteretts historie 1965–2015 – At dømme i sidste Instans* (Fagbokforlaget 2015).

Sunde, JØ, "Norsk personskaderett i praksis" (2015) No. 2 *Tidsskrift for erstatningsrett forsikringsrett og velferdsrett* 77.

Sunde, JØ, "From Courts of Appeal to Courts of Precedent—Access to the Highest Courts in the Nordic Countries" in van Rhee, CH and Fu, Y (Eds.), *Supreme Courts in Transition in China and in the West* (Springer 2017). DOI: http://doi.org/10.1007/978-3-319-52344-6_4

Sunde, JØ, "Å skunda seg langsamt" in Giertsen, J, Konow, BER, Husabø, EJ and Iversen, ØL (Eds.), *Rett i vest – Festskrift til 50-årsjubileet for juristutdanningen ved Universitetet i Bergen* (Fagbokforlaget 2019).

Sunnquist, M., *Konstitutionellt kritiskt dömande – Förändringar av nordiska domares attityder under två sekel* (Jure 2014).

Tande, KM, "Individuelle valg og vurderinger i rettsanvendelsesprosessen" (2011) No. 1 *Jussens Venner* 1.

Uerpmann, R, *Die Europäische Menschenrechtskonvention und die deutsche Rechtsprechung: ein Beitrag zum Thema Völkerrecht und Landesrecht* (Berlin 1993).

Ulvund, F, *Fridomens grenser 1814–1851. Handhevinga av den norske "jødeparagrafen"* (Spartacus Forlag/Scandinavian Academic Press 2014).

Viehweg, T, *Topik und Jurisprudenz* (5th ed. Munich 1974).

Wolf, A, *Gesetzgebung in Europa 1100–1500* (C.H. Beck 1996).

Zweigert, K and Kötz, H, *An Introduction to Comparative Law* (3rd ed., Clarendon Press 1998).

6. An Introduction to Finnish Legal Culture

Anna Nylund

1. The framework of Finnish legal culture

1.1 Finnish legal culture – some introductory remarks

This chapter discusses the main hallmarks of Finnish legal culture, the interconnections between these and the legal cultural shift Finland has witnessed in the past decades. In this chapter, legal cultures are defined as "ideas of and expectations to law made operational by institutional(like) practices".[1] To operationalise the elusive concept of legal culture, the legal cultural model as it has been developed by Jørn Øyrehagen Sunde will be employed: this chapter discusses both the institutional elements – norm production and conflict resolution – and intellectual elements – the ideal of justice, legal method, professionalisation and internationalisation.[2]

Before we start to discuss the specifics of Finnish – or for that matter, any – legal culture, we should bear in mind that while each national legal culture is unique, the distinctness should not be overestimated. Often, a single element, or part of an element, of the legal culture is similar to what we will find in many other countries. Hence, it is seldom the single element that makes a legal culture unique, rather the specific combination of elements. Furthermore, the extent to which a legal culture is distinct, is often highly relative. For a comparatist this entails the challenge of a balanced account where neither the particular nor the "generic" aspects of the legal culture dominate. Finnish legal culture can be identified as a part of Nordic legal culture:[3] the legal cultural ele-

1 Jørn Øyrehagen Sunde', 'Managing the Unmanageable – An Essay Concerning Legal Culture as an Analytical Tool' in this volume, chapter 2, s. 27.

2 Ibid, 2.

3 The term "Nordic" will be used in this text instead of Scandinavian. Although Scandinavia is often used to describe the Nordic countries, it is misleading in a geographical sense, in terms of both physical and cultural geography. In physical geography, Scandinavia refers to the Scandinavian peninsula, which is shared by only two – Norway and Sweden – of the five Nordic countries, whereas Denmark, Finland and Iceland are not included. In a cultural, more precisely a linguistic perspective, Finland and the Sami population in the north, are not Scandinavian, since Finnish and the Sami languages are not Scandinavian languages.

ments have the same general traits in all Nordic countries.[4] Nonetheless, each country exhibits a specific flavour. In this contribution, Nordic elements of the Finnish legal culture will be discussed, in particular the strong ties to Swedish law will be highlighted.

Before analysing the institutional and intellectual elements of Finnish legal culture, a brief introduction to Finnish (legal) history and to present-day Finnish society will be given. The overviews will serve as a background for understanding historical and societal context and enable us to identify traits that it shares with the other Nordic countries and traits that distinguish it from the other Nordic legal cultures.

1.2 The historical development of Finland's legal culture

Although Finland has been populated since the end of the last ice age, there was no state formation until the high medieval period. During the 12th and 13th centuries Swedish kings gradually invaded Finland in the Northern Crusades, and Finland became successively a fully consolidated part of Sweden. As a consequence, Swedish was the language of administration and education, and Swedish laws were in force. In Finnish legal history the central codes enacted in 1734 form a milestone despite the fact that the acts were compilations of early modern law and not a result of the Enlightenment.[5] Some of these are still formally law, although most of the provisions have been amended or repealed. The turn to absolutism resulted in the enactment of constitutional acts vesting the king with almost unlimited powers in the 1770s and 1780s. Parliament was assembled only at the King's will and the King could influence the decisions of the executive and judiciary branch.[6]

The Napoleonic war, which the Finnish War fought between Sweden and Russia in 1808–09, was a part of, are a turning point in Finnish history. Sweden lost the war and had to relinquish Finland to Russia. Finland became an autonomous Grand Duchy (*Suomen suurruhtinaskunta, Storfurstendömet Finland*)[7] in the Russian empire. In 1809 the Russian Tsar assembled the four Estates (nobility, clergy, burghers and peasants all with hereditary seats, each group having a fourth of the vote) at the Diet of Porvoo (*Porvoon maapäivät, Borgå lantdag*) to pledge allegiance. The Tsar, in turn, guaranteed that the language, which at that time was officially Swedish, the Lutheran religion (Russia is Greek-Orthodox) and the laws were unchanged. The Tsar let Finland keep its Swedish laws partly because the absolutistic constitutional acts of the 1770s and 1780s gave the Tsar wide powers he desired, and thus, there was no pressing reason for repealing them.[8]

The first decades of the Russian period were a period of stagnation in terms of legal development. The Diet did not meet a single time between the Diet of Porvoo and the

4 For an introduction to Nordic law, see Pia Letto-Vanamo, Ditlev Tamm and Bent Ole Gram Mortensen (eds) *Nordic Law in European Context* (Springer 2019).

5 Göran Inger, *Svensk rättshistoria* (Liber 2010) 162–164.

6 Ibid 165–170.

7 The Finnish and Swedish terms are given in brackets.

8 Heikki Mattila, 'Språket och den nordiska rättsfamiljen' (2005) no. 1 *Tidskrift utgiven av Juridiska Föreningen i Finland* 43, 45–48.

Diet in Helsinki in 1963. Hence, no new laws were enacted and reforms necessitating legal change could not be implemented and the Swedish laws and language maintained their dominant position. The second half of the 19th century marked a period of economic growth, industrialisation, development of civil society and its institutions, tangible improvements of the educational system, and the burgeoning of a Finnish national identity.[9] In the mid-1800s, the Fennomanic movement gained momentum: Finnish became the official language of the country alongside Swedish and the Finnish language was increasingly used in public administration, courts, educational institutions and (legal) scholarship. Part of the Finnish nation building effort was to educate lawyers to fill the new administration with skilled persons and to introduce lawyers to the forefront of legal thinking of the time, despite the fact that the ideas could not be manifested in legislation and legal institutions at that time.[10] Finland followed the German humanistic tradition, which stressed the role of academic education and the study of the national culture. Therefore, the university and academics had an important role in nation building.[11]

During this time, Finland renewed its ties to the Nordic countries. The Finnish economy and social structures were very different from their Russian counterparts; hence, it was not natural to adopt Russian laws. Finnish lawyers joined the Pan-Scandinavian legal movement and the Nordic Lawyers' Meetings, and legal reforms were a direct effect of Nordic co-operation or Nordic influences.[12] As a consequence of the relatively autonomous position of Finland and the orientation towards the Nordic countries and Germany, the Russian period left few direct traces on Finnish legal language and legislation.

Some members of the Russian elite disliked what they witnessed: the blossoming of a distinct Finnish legal culture. The tide turned against the Finnish efforts of moulding the Finnish society as a result of Russification in the 1890s and early years of the 20th century. Prominent Russian politicians wanted to tie Finland closer to the Russian empire, to abolish Finnish autonomy, and to resist the growing tendencies of nation building within the Russian empire. A central method was to try to make Finnish legislation more Russian. Old laws giving Finnish citizens the exclusive right to hold important positions in society were abolished, and Finnish judges were threatened with prison if they discriminated against Russian citizens. Still, Russification left few permanent marks

9 Pentti Virrankoski, *Suomen historia 1 & 2* (2nd rev edn, Suomalaisen Kirjallisuuden Seura 2009) 497–520; Eino Jutikkala and Kauko Pirinen, *A History of Finland* (6th rev edn, Werner Söderström Osakeyhtiö 2003) 299–349.

10 See e.g. Heikki Pihlajamäki, 'Translating German Administrative Law: The Case of Finland' (2011) *Rechtsgeshcichte* vol. 19, 267.

11 Henrik Meinander, *A History of Finland* (Hurst & Company 2011) 83–87. The situation in Finland can be compared to the situation in Norway at this time: both countries were happily divorced from their earlier mother-land, respectively Sweden and Denmark, both had the opportunity to build their own institutions, from the mid-1850s advance their own language and culture, and both kept many of their old Swedish and Danish laws respectively and enacted new laws.

12 Anna Nylund, 'Mixing Past and Future – the Making of a Nordic Legal Culture 1850–2050' in Jørn Øyrehagen Sunde and Knut Einar Skodvin (eds), *Rendezvous of European Legal Cultures* (Fagbokforlaget 2010).

on legislation.[13] However, the impact on the intellectual elements, in particular the legal method and the ideal of justice in the form of legalism, is still visible.

The Russo-Japanese war in 1904–1905 temporarily weakened the Russian empire, briefly halting Russification efforts. Finnish politicians seized the opportunity by reforming the Finnish Diet in 1906: overnight it transformed from one of the most outdated, to the most advanced Parliaments of the period. As the first country in the world, Finland introduced universal suffrage to all citizens – men and women – above the age of 24.

In the second Russification period, members of the parliament, civil servants, and judges resorted to passive opposition to prevent Russians from exerting influence on the Finnish legal system and society. Another tool that civil servants and judges employed is strict legalism, viz., a method that stresses strict adherence to the laws, in particular the Constitution. A prerequisite for resorting to legalism, particularly in a country with many outdated statutes, is having many civil servants and politicians with a thorough understanding of the law.[14] As a result, the political elite consisted of many lawyers. During this period, the role of judicial review as a method for combatting Russification was debated. Some maintained that judicial review would enable the courts to disqualify statutes for formal reasons, sometimes even based on substantive reasons. Other commentators regarded judicial review as a potential threat: by making the courts political organs, the czar could be tempted to use them as a vehicle for intensifying Russification.[15]

Finland declared itself independent on 6 December 1917, in the midst of the First World War. During the first months of the independence, Finland drifted into a civil war dividing the nation into socialists (the Reds) and conservatives (the Whites) with atrocities committed by both sides. The Whites won the war in May 1918 and the population was left divided and bitter. Finland was still a largely rural, poor, comparably unindustrialised country in need of economic modernisation, and the war had only acerbated the problems. However, the civil war had made the elite aware of the economic and social problems of the poor, and the acute need to strengthen the economy and welfare reforms. Law was used as a tool to build confidence in the country and across the dividing lines by stressing strict adherence to the wording of the law and equal treatment. Land reforms and labour law reforms strengthened the economic and social position of the poor landless rural population, and thus lessened tension between the social strata and the factors that had contributed to the civil war. The new nation needed new institutions and laws, and once again lawyers to serve as civil servants. During the 1920s, the organisation of the state could be relatively quickly modernised, since the foundational concepts and values of the modern state had already been taught to law students for

13 Russification is a process by which non-Russian minorities were assimilated and acculturated in Imperial Russia and the Soviet Union. Russian nationals were given leading positions in institutions, the Russian language was promoted in business, administration and education, and Russian national symbols were presented to alter the self-identity and language of the people.

14 Virrankoski (n 8) 582–611 and 697–707; Jutikkala and Pirinen (n 8) 350–394.

15 Martin Sunnqvist, *Konstitutonellt kritiskt dömande. Förändringen av nordiska domares attityder under två sekel* (Jure 2014).

some decades.[16] The Great Depression of the 1930s harmed modernisation, economic and social development, and industrialisation.[17]

The Finnish economy had slowly recovered from the Great Depression, when the Soviet Union in November 1939 waged war on Finland. The Finns fought back the Soviet army despite the lack of proper equipment and poor organisation of the troops. After the war in 1944, Finland was forced to relinquish 10% of its territory, and as a result it lost 20% of the industry and had to replace 11% of its inhabitants. Additionally, Finland had to pay heavy reparations to the Soviet Union. Despite a wrecked economy and loss of many lives, the war was a relative success: unlike many other countries, Finland had kept its independence and restrained Soviet influence over the country and its institutions.[18]

The post-war years were a period of rapid urbanisation, industrialisation and modernisation. This was also the true beginning of the Finnish welfare state, a few decades after the other Nordic countries. However, legal modernisation was still quite slow partly due to the fact that economic and societal reformation projects were considered more important than reforming legal structures. Another reason was the political situation. Although Finland was formally a neutral country, it had strong official ties to the Soviet Union, which were offset by unofficial – and strong economic – ties to the West as well. The balancing act required maintaining the image of friendship with the Soviet, while still seeking Western influences. This led to self-censorship of anti-Soviet opinion, often referred to as "Finlandisation".[19] Politics was considered "dangerous" for lawyers, as this might involve stepping on the sore toes of the Soviet Union and the political elite. Thus, lawyers stressed their role as legal technicians, stressing the legislation as the primary source of law, and downplaying any law-making activities. In addition, international activities were considered suspicious, except maintaining ties to the other Nordic countries.[20]

During the 1980s, Finland was finally transformed to a modern, industrial, urban and wealthy nation. Emigration turned to net immigration, criticism of government and the Soviet Union became more approved, and Finland opened its doors to the world. Finland faced rapid Europeanisation in the 1990s through membership in the European Convention on Human Rights (ECHR) in 1990, and membership in the European Union (EU) in 1995.

16 Pihlajamäki (n 9).

17 Virrankoski (n 8) 932–966; Jutikkala and Pirinen (n 8) 456–478.

18 Virrankoski (n 8) 932–966; Jutikkala and Pirinen (n 8) 456–478.

19 See e.g. Tuomas Forsberg & Matti Pesu (2016) 'The "Finlandisation" of Finland: The Ideal Type, the Historical Model, and the Lessons Learnt' (2016) Vol. 7 No. 3 *Diplomacy & Statecraft* 473.

20 Jutikkala and Pirinen (n 8) 473–474.

1.3 The contemporary Finnish society

Today, Finland is a modern, technology savvy nation that can be characterised as a Nordic welfare state. Finland is the north-eastern outpost of Western Europe and geographically the eight-largest country in Europe. In the east, Finland shares 1,340 kilometres border with Russia, in the north Finland shares a 740 kilometres-long border with Norway, and in the west Finland and Sweden share a border on land and water. In the south, the Finnish gulf separates Finland and Estonia.

The population of Finland is about 5,500,000 and with only 18 inhabitants per square kilometre, has the third lowest density of population in Europe, far below the EU median of 117.[21] In addition to the Finnish-speaking majority making up about 90% of the population, there is a Swedish-speaking minority with extensive rights and small Sami and Gypsy minorities. Finnish and Swedish are the official languages.[22] All statutes and government bills exist in two parallel versions. Swedish is a compulsory language in school, and in the Swedish-speaking areas, public services are available in both languages. The use of the Swedish language has even up till today contributed to strong ties to Swedish law. The majority of the population is Lutheran.

Finland is a highly industrialised, technology-based nation, with a Gross Domestic Product per capita of 42,076 € in 2018, making it the 11th most prosperous country in Europe.[23] The economy is often described as mixed, i.e. a capitalistic economy with significant state regulation and a corporate structure. The labour organisations and their respective counterparts from the industry are powerful, as in the other Nordic countries. The main products exported are electrotechnical goods, metal products, machinery, transport equipment, wood and paper products, and chemicals.[24]

Finland is a republic with a parliamentary democracy. The 200 members of the one-chamber parliament (*eduskunta*, *riksdagen*) are elected every four years. The President has mostly a ceremonial role but has some official powers in foreign relationships. The President is elected directly by popular vote every six years. Most of the political, administrative, economic, and cultural power is concentrated in the capital Helsinki.

---

21 See http://ec.europa.eu/eurostat/tgm/table.do?tab=table&init=1&language=en&pcode=tps00003&plugin=1 accessed 30 December 2019. Only three European countries have a lower population density: Norway, Russia, and Iceland.

22 The number of Swedish-speaking people is approximately 300,000 and there are more than 7,000 Sami and 5,000-6,000 Finnish Gypsies. The immigrant population amounts to about 5% of the population. Estonians, Russians, Swedes, and Somali are the largest groups of immigrants. About 75% of the population are a member of the Lutheran National Church and about 1% are a member of the National Greek Orthodox Church. See http://www.stat.fi/tup/suoluk/suoluk_vaesto_en.html accessed 30 December 2019. Finland and Greece have the only indigenous Orthodox Churches in Western Europe. The Finnish National Orthodox Church is a national Church and has the same status in society as the National Lutheran Church.

23 See http://www.stat.fi/til/vtp/2018/vtp_2018_2019-06-20_tau_001_en.html and http://statisticstimes.com/economy/countries-by-projected-gdp-capita.php both accessed 30 December 2019.

24 See http://finland.fi/Public/default.aspx?contentid=160032&nodeid=44491&culture=en-US accessed 30 December 2019.

2. Conflict resolution in Finland

2.1 The court structure and court reform in Finland

The Finnish court system is based on the Swedish court system, which in turn has been influenced by the French and German legal systems. The court system is divided into two branches: general courts and administrative courts.

The three-tiered general courts have competence for all matters except for administrative cases. Almost without exception all civil, criminal and family law cases start in one of the 20 District Courts (*käräjäoikeus, tingsrätt*).[25] The case can be appealed to one of the five Courts of Appeal (*hovioikeus, hovrätt*). A leave to appeal (called leave for continued consideration) for the Courts of Appeal is required for all civil cases and criminal cases where the sanction is less than eight months of imprisonment. Leave to appeal is granted mainly if there is reason to suspect that the judgment of the District Court might be erroneous. The Court of Appeal can also grant leave if the case raises an important question of law significant for similar cases or if there is another important reason for doing so. A leave is granted in about half of all cases; the other half of cases are subject to simplified written proceedings. The Supreme Court (*Korkein oikeus, Högsta domstolen*) hears second-tier appeals. A leave to appeal is needed for all cases for the Supreme Court, as the primary task of the Supreme Court is to ensure uniform application of the law, to clarify the law and contribute to filling lacunae. The court does not give any grounds for the cases it rejects. Additionally, the Supreme Court has the jurisdiction to hear extraordinary appeals to annul final decisions of courts because of significant new evidence or a clearly erroneous outcome or procedure.

District courts are quorate with a single professional judge in civil, family and petty criminal cases. In criminal cases, where the accused person risks at least 4 years of imprisonment for one of the crimes, a panel consisting of one professional judge and two lay judges hears the case. The Courts of Appeal are quorate with a panel of three professional judges and the Supreme Court with a panel of five professional judges. The Supreme Court has 19 justices in total.

The use of lay judges has declined markedly in recent decades. Until the reforms in the 1990s, a panel consisting of a professional judge and number of lay judges heard most civil and criminal cases in general courts. Today, lay judges are practically never used in civil cases and the number of lay judges on the panel in criminal cases has been reduced from three to two. The diminished used of lay judges is a partially a matter of cost, partially due to the increasing complexity of law and society.[26] Nevertheless, lay judges are still considered to be pivotal for maintaining a coherent understanding of justice, the functioning of the courts and the justice system among citizens, for building trust in the justice system and for exercising democratic control of courts. Lay judges

25 Only criminal matters on treason and high treasons, as well as certain offences committed by a public official will be treated in first instance by the Court of Appeal.

26 Pia Letto-Vanamo, 'Finnish Judges Between Tradition and Dynamism' in Sophie Turenne (ed), *Fair Reflection of Society in Judicial Systems – A Comparative Study* (Springer 2015) 160–163.

can also contribute by bringing in experience of life, knowledge of the local community and ensuring that the courts uphold "folksy" characteristics.[27]

The administrative court system is two-tiered. Administrative decisions made by public authorities can be appealed to one of the six Administrative Courts (*hallinto-oikeus, förvaltningsdomstol*). Often one must first seek self-rectification from the authority making the decision before one can appeal the case to the courts. In some cases, the first recourse is to an administrative body and one can file a lawsuit only after having exhausted administrative recourse processes. The Administrative Courts have jurisdiction on questions of expediency, although they generally refuse to decide such issues. General principles of administrative law, such as the principles of proportionality, equality and protection of legitimate interests, give courts the power to investigate whether the authority has complied with these when exercising discretionary powers.[28] In cases concerning municipal decisions, courts can only decide on questions of law and the court procedure is of a cassatory nature.[29] This reflects the tradition for a strong legal independence of municipalities. The Administrative Courts are normally quorate with a panel consisting of three professional judges. The rulings are subject to appeal to the Supreme Administrative Court (*Korkein hallinto-oikeus, Högsta förvaltningsdomstolen*). A leave to appeal is required for some matters, including inter alia most tax cases and immigration law cases. The Supreme Administrative Court is quorate in a panel of five justices. The court has currently 21 justices, two of which are on a leave of absence, and seven interim justices.

There is no judicial specialisation within the general and administrative courts, but the judges at larger courts form chambers. However, the chambers are not permanent; a certain number of judges rotate from one chamber to another each year, and judges must change chamber after a number of years. Therefore, judges are generalists. In land, water, environmental and intellectual property rights cases, courts are quorate with a panel consisting of both professional judges with legal training and judges with expertise in environmental or technical matters.

In the appellate courts and the administrative judicial branch, court procedure relies on the use of referendaries (*esittelijä, föredragande*). Referendaries are (junior) lawyers who have qualifications as a judge. Their task is to prepare the case by writing a memorandum summarising the case and relevant legislation, court practice and bases for legal arguments. The referendary presents the case and a suggestion for the judgment to the panel of judges deciding the case. The panel is not bound by the suggestion. In Admin-

27 Oikeusministeriö, *Tuomioistuinlaitoksen kehittämistoimikunnan mietintö*. KM 2003:3 (Oikeusministeriö 2003) 176 ff.

28 Kaarlo Tuori, 'Tuomarivaltio – uhka vai myytti?' in Marjut Heikkilä (ed), *Säädöksiä, systematiikkaa vai ihmisoikeuksia?* (Acta Universitatis Lappeenrantaensis 2004) 22–24 and Olli Mäenpää, 'Deference to the Administration in Judicial Review in Finland' in G. Zhu (ed), *Deference to the Administration in Judicial Review* (Springer 2019) 181.

29 Olli Mäenpää, 'Administrative Law' in Juha Pöyhönen (ed), *An Introduction to Finnish Law* (Kauppakaari 2002) 459.

istrative Courts, the referendaries actively collect information and statements from the relevant authorities.[30]

There are four special courts in Finland. The Market Court (*markkina oikeus, marknadsdomstolen*) hears cases on unfair trading practices, consumer cases where the Consumer Ombudsman is the claimant, competition law cases, public procurement law cases, and intellectual property rights cases. Cases where a single consumer or a group of consumers have suffered direct losses are under the jurisdiction of the general courts.[31] The Labour Court (*työtuomioistuin, arbetsdomstolen*) deals with the interpretation and contents of collective bargaining agreements. General courts have jurisdiction over disputes arising from individual labour contracts. The Labour Court has a full-time president and vice-president, the rest of the members are appointed part-time and represent either employers or employees. The Insurance Court (*vakuutusoikeus, försäkringsdomstolen*) decides cases relating to social benefits such as pensions, unemployment benefits, housing allowance, student grants, matters related to the mandatory public health insurance, and compensation of work-related injuries. The Insurance Court is the only court dealing with these cases, and the cases can generally not be appealed. The High Court of Impeachment (*valtakunnanoikeus, riksrätten*) deals only with very special cases where charges for unlawful conduct in office are brought against a member of the Government, the President of Finland or members of the highest courts. The judges consist of the chief justices of the Supreme Court, Supreme Administrative Court, the three most senior chief judges of the Courts of Appeal, and four members elected by the parliament. The Court has heard only four cases since it was founded in 1922. In sum, the special courts generally do not deal with classic civil, commercial and criminal law cases; most of the courts are specialists in different areas of administrative law and in regulatory law. There is no constitutional court.

The Finnish court system has gone through a process of consolidation, streamlining and professionalisation during the last few decades.[32] The Water Courts (*vesioikeus/vattendomstol*) were abolished and integrated into administrative bodies, and the Water High Court was integrated into the Vaasa Administrative Court. Although the Water Courts were courts by name, their functions were mainly related to granting permissions to build constructions such as waterpower plants and banks, to grant the right to environmental emissions and to float goods. Land Courts (*maanoikeus/jordrätt*), which had jurisdiction in matters concerning land cadastral survey matters, in 2001 were integrated into selected District Courts. The interaction of three main factors contributed to the abolition of Water and Land Courts. First, the consolidation of courts entails less expenditure on court administration through fewer small administrative units. Second, a strong belief in general courts and generalist judges. Although one or a few judges at each of the general courts in question specialise in land cases and one division of the

30 See https://oikeus.fi/tuomioistuimet/hallintooikeudet/en/index/asionti.html accessed 23 March 2020.

31 Most of these cases are solved by Consumer Boards. The majority of businesses follow the non-binding decisions of the Consumer Boards.

32 Oikeusministeriö (n 27).

administrative court hears all water cases, the judges will also hear a range of other cases. Hence specialisation is only partial. Third, the removal of Water Courts reflects a trend towards transferring non-adjudicative matters from courts to administrative organs and, in reverse, concentrating adjudicative functions in court.[33]

For land and water cases – cases that are in essence entangled with environmental law – the discontinuation of Land and Water Courts as separate units coincides with the influx of a massive body of EU environmental law and, in general, a period of stricter environmental regulation. Intuitively, one could conclude that the increased density of environmental regulation would call for more specialisation – not less – and hence, special courts, rather than integrating courts. The abolition of these courts illustrates how the idea of the advantages of general courts prevailed over developments that signified a momentum for specialisation.

The organisation of how recourse against decisions on social security benefits is sought is the paramount example of how adjudicative functions have been consolidated and professionalised. Until the late 1990s, recourse was sought within Kela, the Social Security Institution of Finland. The internal appeals board was transformed into the Social Security Appeal Board (*Sosiaaliturva-asioiden muutoksenhakulautakunta, Besvärsnämnden för social trygghet*), a *de facto* court established in 2016. The Board is fully economically, legally and organisationally independent from administrative organs; the judges have permanent, full-time positions, rules regarding judges apply fully to them, and the Administrative Judicial Procedure Act (*laki oikeudenkäynnistä hallintoasioissa, lag om rättegång i förvaltningsärenden*) governs the proceedings.[34] The judges in administrative appeals boards are often appointed for a limited time, have part-time positions and the Administrative Procedure Act (*hallintolaki, förvaltningslag*) governs the proceedings. As will be explained below, Europeanisation of law has not been the primary incentive for these changes. Instead, much of it can be attributed to a shift in the ideas of the view of the Constitution and the rule of law have had in demanding that the fundamental rights must be protected and that citizens must be able to efficiently enforce their rights through recourse to independent and highly professional organisations. Furthermore, the Social Security Appeal Board is a manifestation of the generalist judge: it was formed as a merger of two separate bodies, thus unifying adjudication of social security rights into the hands of a single body.

The most recent development is the concentration of uncontested pecuniary claims into nine District Courts as of 1 September 2019. Court staff handle and decide the claims unless the claim becomes contested. When applicable, contested claims are transferred to the District Court that has territorial jurisdiction based on the general rules. By concentrating the cases to a limited number of courts, the staff becomes highly specialised, which is likely to increase both quality and efficiency. The centralisation has

33 Anna Nylund, 'Klima, miljø og domstoler i et komparativt perspektiv' in Ole Kristian Fauchald and Eivind Smith (eds), *Mellom jus og politikk: Grunnloven § 112* (Fagbokforlaget 2019) 94.

34 Anna Nylund, 'Comparing the Efficiency and Quality of Civil Justice in Scandinavia: The Role of Structural Differences and Definitions of Quality' (2019) Vol. 38 *Civil Justice Quarterly* 427.

arisen at least partly from EU law. The Court of Justice of the European Union (CJEU) requires national courts to apply part of EU consumer law on their own motions. Many uncontested claims are, in fact, consumer claims where the unpaid debt stems from consumer goods or services. In its ruling KKO 2015:60, the Finnish Supreme Court held that Finnish courts are obliged to investigate the fairness of a clause in a consumer contract whenever the court has a sufficient legal and factual basis for it, i.e., whenever there is an indication that a clause could be unfair and the court has or can obtain information about the contract clause by ordering the claimant to provide a copy of the contract.[35] The ruling revealed that many District Courts did not have adequate processes and expertise to comply with the requirements of EU law as manifested in the Supreme Court ruling. Professionalisation through the means of centralisation had to be put in place.

This account of the Finnish court system would make it tempting to classify Finland as having a civil law-type judiciary. However, there are several traits that do not match the "ideal" model of civil law. First, there are few special courts and judges are not specialists apart from the general court/administrative court division. The special courts deal mainly with questions beyond the private law/public law division. Only the Insurance Court is a traditional special court. The discussion on the demarcation of the jurisdiction of the court systems is almost non-existent. Second, there is no constitutional court; the supreme courts perform judicial review. The Ministry of Justice suggested that the Supreme Court and Supreme Administrative Court merge to form a single unified Supreme Court with two branches of courts under it.[36] The Supreme Administrative Court and other organisations dealing with administrative law were highly sceptical to the suggestion.[37] Hence, the Ministry has not moved forward with the project.

35 KKO 2015:60, para. 22–24.

36 'Korkeimpien oikeuksien organisatorinen yhdistäminen – Hyötyjen ja haittojen arviointi', *Oikeusministeriön julkaisu 1/2015* (the Finnish Ministry of Justice 2015). See https://julkaisut.valtioneuvosto.fi/bitstream/handle/10024/76569/om_1_2015_korkeimp_oikyhdist_154.pdf?sequence=1&isAllowed=y accessed 30 December 2019.

37 'Korkeimipien oikeuksien organisatorinen yhdistäminen. Lausuntotiivistelmä', *Mietintöjä ja lausuntoja 33/2017, Oikeusministeriö* (the Finnish Ministry of Justice 2015).

2.2 The Finnish Court system

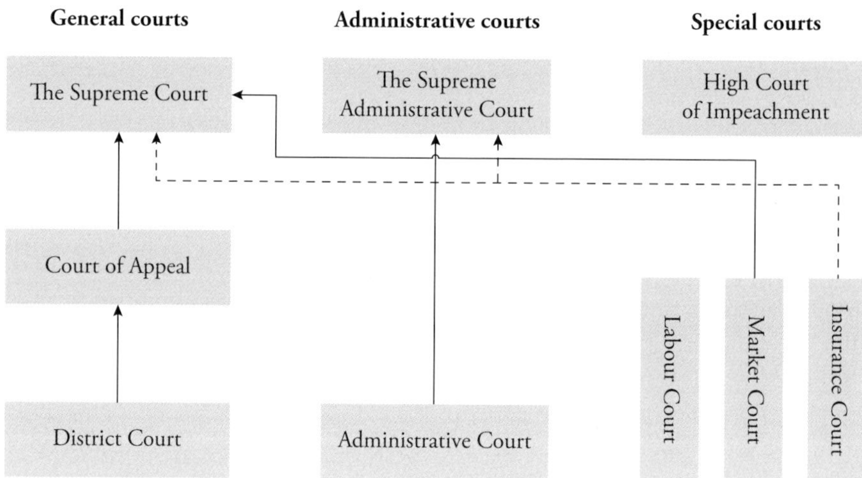

Fig. 1

2.2.1 Court procedure in Finland

When Finland became independent in 1917, the Code on Judicial Procedure (*oikeudenkäymiskaari, rättegångsbalken*) from 1734 was still in force, albeit with some amendments. Several persistent but unsuccessful attempts were made to draft a new code based on the procedural laws of Austria and Germany, and later Sweden.[38] As a result, rules originating from 1734 formed the backbone for court proceedings until the early 1990s. The poor organisation and funding of courts and prosecutors exacerbated the problem until the organisational reforms in the late 1970s. Court procedure was lengthy, bureaucratic and based on written documents. As there were few trained lawyers in the rural areas, the judge was the central actor in the court room.[39]

In 1993, the general rules of procedure and rules governing civil procedure in the Code of Judicial Procedure ware completely refurbished and in 1997 the Criminal Procedure Act (*laki oikeudenkäynnistä rikosasioissa, lag om rättegång i brottmål*) was enacted to modernise the rules of criminal procedure. Both reforms were heavily influenced by Swedish law and marked a significant change from written proceedings to oral proceedings with a concentrated, oral main hearing as the centrepiece. In civil proceedings, the emphasis is on the preparatory stage of proceedings where the judge has a central role

38 See also Maria Astrup Hjort, 'Sources of inspiration of Nordic procedural law: Choices and objectives of the legal reforms' in Laura Ervo, Pia Letto-Vanamo and Anna Nylund (eds), *Rethinking Nordic Courts* (Springer, forthcoming).

39 Pia Letto-Vanamo, 'Internationella idèer och den nationella realiteten' in Jukka Kekkonen and others (eds), *Norden, rätten, historia. Festskrift till Lars Björne* (Suomalainen lakimiesyhdistys 2004) 124–128.

in sorting out key issues, what the parties disagree about, which legal arguments are relevant, and which pieces of evidence may be significant. The active role of the judge is similar to the role of the judge in Swedish and German civil procedure.[40] During the main hearing the parties present the case, the evidence and their arguments directly to the court. The criminal procedure is also oral, but preliminary hearings are rare and written preparation is very limited. Court procedure is based on a notion that citizens do not need legal representation. However, almost all parties have some kind of legal representation in civil cases today.[41]

In Finnish legal culture, the function of oral hearings is primarily the hearing of evidence and promoting dialogue between the parties, not to serve as a forum for complex legal or factual argumentation. In civil cases, the preparatory hearing has a pivotal function in defining the legal and factual ambit of the dispute by separating disputed and undisputed issues. Additionally, it enables the judge to facilitate mutual understanding and dialogue between the parties and thus to facilitate full or partial settlement.[42] Although oral proceedings are the norm in District Courts, proceedings in other courts are mainly written. The Courts of Appeal have an oral hearing only in about one third of the cases.[43] The Supreme Court rarely hears oral arguments and relies mainly on written evidence when deciding the case. The Administrative Courts and the Supreme Administrative Court almost exclusively use written proceedings.[44] The rules of administrative judicial procedure mandate the court to aid the parties inter alia by ordering evidence to be presented and by not being as strictly bound by the circumstance and arguments the citizens provide in support of their case. Referendaries, i.e., court clerks, have a central role in the proceedings in all courts except for District Courts. They oftentimes draft a summary of the case and ensure all written materials (documents) are included in the case file and finally draft a suggestion for the ruling. In written proceedings, the referendary presents the case to the panel of judges making the final ruling. Written proceedings are related to an ideal of law as a coherent, logical system where predictability and equal application of law is the paramount concern and where the role of courts is to provide for the rule of law by diligently applying legal rules.

---

40 Anna Nylund, 'Structure of Civil Proceedings – Convergence through the Main Hearing Model?' (2018) Vol. 9 No. 2 *Civil Procedure Review* 13. Although England and Norway have seemingly similar rules on the preparatory stage of civil proceedings, judges perceive their role differently and many tasks allocated to the judge in Finland, is allocated to the parties.

41 Satu Saarensola, 'The Risk of Legal Costs and Its Effects on Access to Court' in Laura Ervo and Anna Nylund (eds), *The Future of Civil Litigation. Access to Courts and Court-annexed Mediation in the Nordic Countries* (Springer 2014) 234.

42 Anna Nylund, 'Europeanisation of Nordic Civil Procedure – Does the Map Match the Terrain?' in Laura Ervo, Pia Letto-Vanamo and Anna Nylund (eds), *Rethinking Nordic Courts* (Springer, forthcoming); Laura Ervo, 'Swedish-Finnish Preparatory Proceedings: Filtering and Process Techniques' in Laura Ervo and Anna Nylund (eds), *Current Trends in Preparatory Proceedings* (Springer 2016) 32–37.

43 Data is collected from annual reports of the courts on http://www.oikeus.fi/ accessed 30 December 2019.

44 Data on the prevalence of oral hearings and granting of leaves to appeal (leave for continued consideration), are collected from Annual Reports of the courts found on www.oikeus.fi accessed 30 December 2019.

Nevertheless, one should not draw the conclusion that Finnish procedural law is quintessentially civil law based. The procedural rules are far less detailed than in for example Germany, and the process is less formal and formalistic. Although the court and the parties address each other in a formal way, both the preparatory stage and the main hearing are conducted in a flexible rather than formalistic way. Courts have plenty of discretion to tailor the proceedings to each case.

Moreover, assisting the parties to settle has increasingly become a task for courts. Although settlement has been culturally preferred to litigation, the 1993 reform accentuated and formalised the role of the judges in promoting settlement, with the introduction of court-connected settlement in 2006 amplifying the shift to judges having a dual function. These reforms can be seen as a continuation of the role of the (Country Court) judge as the provider of pragmatic, equitable solutions.[45] Today many judges actively promote settlement by encouraging parties to negotiate, by summarizing what the parties agree and disagree on, and the costs of fully-fledged litigation. Judges can help parties draft a settlement. These activities are in many ways typical for the Nordic countries, where amicable solutions within the court procedure have long traditions.[46] Today, approximately 15 percent of all civil cases are directed to court-connected mediation.[47] The presence of mediation has shifted and diversified the role of judges, particularly in District Courts: their role is to resolve disputes by using techniques from both adjudication and mediation. The outcome can reflect the predictability and rule of law through application of legal norms in litigation proceedings, equity and pragmatism through a process of mediation where the preferences of the parties determine the outcome, or even a mixture of these.[48] Since settlement efforts and court-connected mediation are based on discussion and active party participation, they form a sharp contrast to most other types of court proceedings, which are written.

2.2.2 Case load

The number of incoming litigious civil cases is among the lowest per capita in Europe:[49] Finnish District Courts hear only about 8,500 general civil cases and about 2,000 fam-

45 Ervo (n 42) 44.

46 Anna Nylund, 'Conclusions on the Future of Civil Litigation in the Nordic Countries' in Laura Ervo and Anna Nylund (eds), *The Future of Civil Litigation. Access to Courts and Court-annexed Mediation in the Nordic Countries* (Springer 2014) 416.

47 See https://oikeus.fi/fi/index/ajankohtaista/tiedotteet/2016/09/tuomioistuinsovittelulisaantynythuomattavasti10vuodenaikana.html accessed 17 February 2020.

48 Jukka Siro and Mikko Aaltonen, 'Riita-asiat tuomioistuimissa 2000-luvulla' (2019) Vol. 117 *Lakimies* 758, 774; Riikka Koulu, Risto Koulu and Sanna Koulu, *Tuomarin roolit tuomioistuimissa* (Alma Talent 2019) 340–341; Laura Ervo, 'Swedish-Finnish Preparatory Proceedings: Filtering and Process Techniques' in Laura Ervo and Anna Nylund (eds), *Current Trends in Preparatory Proceedings. A Comparative Study of Nordic and Former Communist Countries* (Springer 2016) 51.

49 The 2019 EU Justice Scoreboard, available at https://ec.europa.eu/info/sites/info/files/justice_scoreboard_2019_en.pdf accessed 30 December 2019.

ily cases annually.[50] The number of criminal cases (58,000) is more than five-fold compared to civil cases. In addition to general civil cases, courts decide non-litigious matters (44,000 cases), which consist, *inter alia*, of divorce cases and insolvency proceedings. The number of uncontested pecuniary claims, i.e., claims relating to the collection of debt where the debt itself is not disputed, is high (400,000 cases) compared to general civil cases. The Courts of Appeal hear approximately 8,200 cases annually. The Supreme Court decides annually about 110–130 cases, approximately 7% of all cases where appeal is sought. In addition, the Supreme Court decides about 180 cases, including extraordinary appeals, and cases where the proceedings in the lower courts were erroneous or unfair, or where the outcome was clearly wrong.

The six Administrative Courts decide about 20,000 cases annually. The Supreme Administrative Court has a caseload of about 6,200 cases annually, but only about 100 cases are published. Each year, the Market Court has approximately 700 cases, the Labour Court has about 200 cases, and the Insurance Court has about 5,500 cases.

The number of civil cases is generally considered to be too low.[51] Only half of the civil cases are resolved after a court hearing, of these approximately half were solved by a final judgment and the other half were settled. This means that there is an average of less than two main hearings in each of the 20 District Courts each week. Most main hearings are limited to two or three days, which means that on average, each District Court would only need one courtroom to deal with all litigious civil cases.[52] Yet, the average case disposition time for contentious civil cases is almost twice as high as in other Nordic countries.[53] So far, no plausible explanation has been offered to account for this difference. Perhaps some of the problems could be attributed to late professionalisation, the historic lack of funding of courts, slow court reforms and the relative "weakness" of courts as the third state power. As a remedy for delays in justice, citizens and companies whose case has been unreasonably delayed can apply for a compensation, currently 1,500 euro per year of delay. Despite the relatively slow proceedings, the public opinion and trust in courts is high.[54]

---

50 All data are from 'Tuomioistuinten työtilastoja vuodelta 2018', *Oikeusministeriön julkaisuja, Toiminta ja hallinto 2019:8* (the Finnish Ministry of Justice 2019). See http://julkaisut.valtioneuvosto.fi/bitstream/handle/10024/161460/OMTH_2019_8_Tuomioistuinten_ty%c3%b6tilastoja_vuodelta_2018.pdf?sequence=4&isAllowed=y accessed 30 December 2019.

51 See e.g. Anna-Liisa Autio, 'The Main Problems in Access to Court Regarding the Dispute Resolution of Finnish Companies' in Laura Ervo and Anna Nylund (eds), *The Future of Civil Litigation. Access to Courts and Court-annexed Mediation in the Nordic Countries* (Springer 2014).

52 'Tuomioistuinten työtilastoja vuodelta 2018', *Oikeusministeriön julkaisuja, Toiminta ja hallinto 2019:8* (the Finnish Ministry of Justice 2019). See http://julkaisut.valtioneuvosto.fi/bitstream/handle/10024/161460/OMTH_2019_8_Tuomioistuinten_ty%c3%b6tilastoja_vuodelta_2018.pdf?sequence=4&isAllowed=y 34–35, accessed 30 December 2019.

53 The 2019 EU Justice Scoreboard. See CEPEJ Statistics, see http://www.coe.int/t/dghl/cooperation/cepej/evaluation/2016/STAT/03.asp. accessed 30 December 2019

54 See Saarensola (2014) (n 41); Laura Ervo and Amie Dahlqvist, 'Delays in Civil Proceedings: Comparative Studies between Finland and Sweden' in Laura Ervo and Anna Nylund (eds), *The Future of Civil Litigation. Access to Courts and Court-annexed Mediation in the Nordic Countries* (Springer 2014).

2.3 Alternative dispute resolution

The relatively low number of cases in Finnish courts stems partly from consumers using out-of-court dispute resolution mechanisms. In 2017, 6,431 cases were filed with the Consumer Disputes Board (*kuluttajariitalautakunta, konsumenttvistnämnden*)[55] and 979 cases were filed with The Finnish Financial Ombudsman bureau (FINE, *Vakuutus- ja finanssineuvonta, Försäkrings- och finansrådgivningen*).[56] Consumer dispute resolution is free of charge or entails only limited costs for the consumer and are hence often used although the boards' decisions are not binding.[57] Additionally, the Consumer Ombudsman (*kuluttaja-asiamies, konsumentombudsmannen*) is a powerful actor in consumer law. In addition to persuading traders to comply with consumer law voluntarily, the Ombud has the right to impose a prohibition reinforced with a penalty payment on traders who refuse to comply, or even initiate a class action on behalf of citizens. So far, the Ombud has taken steps towards filing the first class-action case in Finnish legal history.[58] Consumer law is only one example. Out-of-court procedures are put in place in other fields as well, which reduces the need to file lawsuits.

Another example of alternative dispute resolution is victim-offender mediation in criminal cases and civil cases related to a crime, for instance claims for damage arising from a criminal act, that the Finnish institute for health and welfare (*Terveyden ja hyvinvoinnin laitos, Institutet för hälsa och välfärd*) coordinates and monitors. Mediation is either parallel to or in minor cases a replacement to court proceedings. The number of mediated criminal cases was 14,789 in 2018. In addition, 737 civil cases related to a crime were mediated.[59] Municipalities offer mediation services in child custody, residence, contact and relocation cases. Mediation is free of charge for the parties.

3. Norm production

3.1 Norm production through legislation

Statutory law is the most important method of norm production in Finnish law. As in the other Nordic countries, systematically coherent codifications have never been adopted: the prevailing legislative technique is to enact statutes, each of which covers

---

55 Kuluttajariitalautakunta, *Toimintakertomus 2017*. See https://www.kuluttajariita.fi/material/attachments/kuluttajariitalautakunta/liitteet_kuluttajariitalautakunta/gwq7VQXgt/Toimintakertomus_2017.pdf accessed 17 February 2020.

56 FINE Vakuutus- ja finansineuvonta. *FINEn vuosikertomus 2018*. See https://www.fine.fi/media/julkaisut-2019/finen-vuosikertomus-2018_verkkosivut.pdf accessed 17 February 2020.

57 There are other consumer dispute bodies as well, but these have a limited case load compared to the Consumer Disputes Board and FINE.

58 See https://www.kkv.fi/ajankohtaista/Tiedotteet/2019/23.10.2019-kuluttaja-asiamies-puuttuu-pikaluottojen-kohtuuttomiin-kustannuksiin/ accessed 23 March 2020. Class actions are considered to be a draconian measure, the use of which should be avoided as long as other measures could be effective.

59 See https://thl.fi/fi/tilastot-ja-data/tilastot-aiheittain/sosiaalipalvelut/rikos-ja-riita-asioiden-sovittelu accessed 17 February 2020.

a relatively limited area of law, e.g., marriage, parental responsibility and inheritance are regulated in different statutes. Language of the statutes is relatively simple and fairly easily comprehensible for a lay person.[60]

The Government submits about 260 new bills to the Parliament per year. In 2018, 74 new acts of Parliament, or amendments of an existing act, were published in the Statutes of Finland. Two publishers offer currently a collection of acts of parliament supplied with statutes of lower rank and relevant EU law.[61] The acts are arranged thematically, not chronologically, making laws easy to find for a trained lawyer. Thus, the books of statutes mimic the systematisation of codes. Central EU regulations and directives were published in a separate volume of the book of statutes during the first years of Finnish EU membership. Now they are integrated into the systematic presentation of Finnish legislation, which is logical, since they are of equal importance as national law is.[62]

Decrees (*asetus, förordning*), i.e. statutory law with a lower rank than acts of parliament, ordinances and other types of binding guidelines issued by government agencies by far exceed the number of laws. In 2018 more than 1,300 decrees, ordinances and guidelines were published. They are hence in practice an important form of norm production.

3.2 Courts as producers of norms

Finnish courts have traditionally been unpolitical institutions trying to live up to the ideal of the judge as only the mouthpiece of the law. Until the late 1970s, law-making was not considered to be a task of the courts. The seminal reform in 1980 transformed the role of the Supreme Court from serving private interests, i.e., solving the case at hand, to serving public interests by selecting cases based on their importance for future cases. Serving private interests requires hearing many cases to provide justice to as many citizens and enterprises as possible, serving public interests requires the court to select a limited number of cases to enable the legal community to keep track with case law and to enable the court to deliberate hard questions.[63] Since 1980, the primary task of the Supreme Court has been and is to ensure equal and uniform application of law and to provide clarification when several different interpretations are possible, when the content of the law is ambiguous and when it must fill a lacuna. The Supreme Court selects 100–120 cases annually, which are published in the yearbook of the court.

60 Letto-Vanamo, Tamm and Mortensen (2019) (n 3); Jukka Kekkonen, *Johdatus kontekstuaaliseen oikeushistoriaan* (Helsingin yliopiston oikeustieteellisen tiedekunnan julkaisuja 2002) 84–85.

61 Edilex publishes «Lakikirja» and Talentum «Suomen Laki». Talentum also publishes the Swedish-language version «Finlands Lag», see http://www.editapublishing.fi/ and www.talentumshop.fi both accessed 30 December 2019.

62 Pekka Timonen, 'Sources of law and material on the sources of law' in Juha Pöyhönen (ed), *An Introduction to Finnish Law* (Kauppakaari 2002) 24–28. The President may also issue decrees relating to foreign policy.

63 For a discussion of the public and private role of supreme courts, see Aleš Galič, 'Civil Law Perspective on the Supreme Court and its Functions' (2019) *Studia Iuridica LXXXI* 44; Per Henrik Lindblom, 'The Growing Role of the Courts and the New Functions of Judicial Process – Fact or Flummery?' and 'The Role of the Supreme Court in Scandinavia', both in Per Henrik Lindblom, *Progressive Procedure* (Iustus 2017).

As the Supreme Court admits only a limited number of cases, Courts of Appeals have also gained a role as norm-producers by providing cases that illustrate how vague concepts, such as "unfair" or "gross neglect" are to be interpreted. In 2016, a provision enabling the Court of Appeals to hear cases raising issues of principle in a grand chamber of seven judges or in a plenary session was enacted to enhance the role of courts as producers of norms.

The Supreme Administrative Court serves primarily public functions. However, since the administrative court system is only two-tiered, the Supreme Administrative Court has a mixed function as a regular appellate court and a court that produces case law. Annually, the court selects approximately 100 cases for publication based on the extent to which they provide clarification of law and enhance unity.

Internationalisation in the 1990s, in particular EU membership and ratification of the European Convention on Human Rights (ECHR), has been instrumental in strengthening the role of the supreme courts as producers of law by requiring courts to assess whether national law is compatible with supranational law, and when necessary, give preference to supranational law. Hence, courts have an important role in aligning national law with supranational law through interpretation. Both producing precedent and interpreting European law require that the court explains the issue at hand and gives extensive grounds weighing different arguments. Therefore rulings, particularly the part explaining the argumentation of the court, have become longer. The length of the ruling also depends on whether it was unanimous or not. Despite the fact that judges have individual votes, judges seek to find common ground and to make unanimous rulings. The result is sometimes vague or slightly incoherent argumentation.[64]

The role of the ECHR and EU law has been instrumental in making courts guardians of constitutional rights. Until the constitutional reform in 2000, Finnish courts had no right to review acts of parliament and until 1995, provisions on human rights were few, fragmentary and outdated in the Finnish Constitution, leaving no room to manoeuvre for the courts. Today, courts shall give primacy to the Constitution only when an Act of Parliament is in evident conflict with the Constitution. Statutes of a lower level shall not be applied by courts or other public authorities if they are unconstitutional. Thus, courts have a mandate to perform judicial review. Nonetheless, Finnish courts are still reluctant to exercise their powers and openly challenge the legislator.

The two-tier mechanism for review of constitutionality is the key explanation. When the Finnish parliament enacts statutory law, it transfers the bill to the Constitutional Law Committee whenever it finds that the constitutionality of the bill must be investigated. The Committee assesses constitutionality abstractly *ex ante* and authors a report with a recommendation to the parliament after having heard experts on the subject matter and on constitutional law. The reports are similar to court rulings with the argumen-

64 Heikki Pihlajamäki, 'Kansalinvälistymisen aika 1980–2018' in Heikki Pihlajamäki (ed), *Lainkäyttöä läpi vuosisadan. Näkökulmia Korkeimman Oikeuden historiaan 1918–2018* (Edita 2018) 223–230. See also Martin Sunnqvist, 'The Changing Role of Nordic Courts' in Laura Ervo, Pia Letto-Vanamo and Anna Nylund (eds), *Rethinking Nordic Courts* (Springer, forthcoming).

tation building on interpretations set out in earlier reports, thus creating coherency in interpretation of the Constitution. The reports are considered *de facto* binding.[65] When the Committee has found the proposed bill unconstitutional, the parliament rejects the bill, amends the bill or makes an exceptive enactment, i.e., to enact the bill despite it being unconstitutional. An exceptive enactment requires a 2/3 majority of votes in the Parliament in two consecutive sessions, or that the bill is declared urgent with a majority of 5/6 of the votes and that the bill is subsequently accepted with a majority of 2/3 of the votes. Between 1919 and 2000, a total of 888 exceptive enactments were adopted.[66] Today, exceptional enactments are seldom used. Instead, the Parliament is expected to ensure that statutes comply with the Constitution.[67]

Finnish lawyers have shared the belief that moral questions should be left to the Parliament, more precisely, its Constitutional Law Committee, and that courts should therefore not interfere with the political considerations of the Parliament. *Ex ante* review by the Parliament has been, and still is, the primary method of review of constitutionality and the Constitutional Law Committee is a powerful organ.[68] Since statutes of a lower level have not passed through the Constitutional Law Committee, courts have had more leeway in disapplying them. The combined effect of constitutional reform and Europeanisation have resulted in a gradual shift towards courts increasingly and more overtly reviewing acts of parliament.[69]

3.3 Legal scholarship as a producer of norms

During the Russian period in the 19th century, legal scholars desired to advance Finnish legal culture by systematising and analysing Finnish law, as discussed above. Because the courts and the legislator were weak and not able to keep track with the modernisation of the Finnish society and economy, legal scholarship contributed to filling the void. Borrowing from German law, legal scholarship could create a system behind fragmentary and obsolete statutes, by developing a hierarchy of concepts and by creating general doctrines of law (*yleiset opit, allmänna läror*). Old laws could be adapted to new situa-

65 Juha Lavapuro, Tuomas Ojanen and Martin Scheinin, 'Intermedia constitutional review in Finland: promising in theory, problematic in practice' in John Bell and Marie-Luce Paris (eds), *Rights-Based Constitutional Review: Constitutional Courts in a Changing Landscape* (Edward Elgar Publishing 2016); Outi Suviranta, 'Viranomaisen jatkovalitusoikeus, perustuslaki ja lainsäädännön kehittäminen' in Samuli Hurri (ed), *Demokraattisen oikeuden ehdot* (Tutkijaliitto 2008); Martin Scheinin, 'Constitutional Law and Human Rights' in Juha Pöyhönen (ed), *An Introduction to Finnish Law* (Kauppakaari 2002) 40–42 and 45–50.

66 Lavapuro, Ojanen and Scheinin (2016) (ibid) 220–221.

67 Ibid.

68 See also Jaakko Husa, 'Panorama of World's Legal Systems – Focusing on Finland' in Kimmo Nuotio, Sakari Melander and Merita Huomo-Kettunen (eds), *Introduction to Finnish Law and Legal Culture* (Publications of the Faculty of Law University of Helsinki 2012) 9.

69 Juha Karhu, 'Lakien perustuslainmukaisuuden jälkivalvonta, perustuslain 106 § ja "Iijoki II" tapaus (KKO2006:71)' in Samuli Hurri (ed), *Demokraattisen oikeuden ehdot* (Tukijaliitto 2008); Jukka Viljanen, 'The European Convention on Human Rights and the Transformation of the Finnish Fundamental Rights System' (2007) vol. 52 *Scandinavian Studies in Law* 299, 317.

tions by careful analysis of concepts and the use of general doctrines thus enabling partial modernisation without new legislation. The ideal was to keep the law free from values and to abide strictly by the law, by only resorting to arguments found in legal texts and not including arguments related to the society at large.[70] Although German legal thinking has been consequential, there is no concept of *herrschende Meinung* as in German law, where the scholars would have a direct influence on what the law is.[71]

Today, the role of legal scholarship has changed. Many scholars do not attempt to primarily describe what the law is; the aim is to create coherence within the legal system or to deliver a critical, sometimes normative, analysis of what the law should be or how the law is practiced. The questions are, if the law fulfils its purpose, and how the law should be interpreted or changed in order for it to fulfil its purpose. Creating a more coherent system is reserved for emerging areas of law such as communications law, or areas of law going through a metamorphosis, such as environmental law.[72]

4. Ideal of justice

4.1 Legalism and predictability

Finnish legal culture can be characterised as legalistic, viz., statutory law is the only true source of law, and all legal arguments should be derived from statutory law supplied with arguments from preparatory works. Extra-legal arguments, such as references to morals, general principles in society or the practicability of the result, were not accepted in legal argumentation. During the Russian period, the courts were hesitant to resort to other arguments than the statutes that had been enacted during the Swedish era, as doing so could enable the Czar to use a less legalistic and freer argumentation to strengthen his position.[73] Some have attributed the aversion towards judicial review, and other "rigid" characteristics of the Finnish legal culture, to tensions between social classes and other socio-political tendencies in the 1910s and their aftermath.[74] In the post-war period, "Finlandisation" contributed to upholding the idea of pure sovereignty of the Finnish state by rigid application of statutory law: the legislator – the Parliament – and the executive – the government – reign in the country, not lawyers. The practice of exceptional acts is the paramount example of the "absolute" powers of the legislator and how constitutional law could be circumvented in Parliament. The courts and the executive branch must apply and adhere to the law and to a formalistic idea of the rule of law and

70 Lars Björne, *Den konstruktiva riktningen. Den nordiska rättsvetenskapens historia. Del III 1871–1910.* (Institutet för rättshistorisk forskning 2002) 170–171; Kaarlo Tuori, *Ratio and Voluntas: The Tension Between Reason and Will in Law* (Ashgate 2011) 129–131; Aulis Aarnio, 'Introduction' in Juha Pöyhönen (ed), *An Introduction to Finnish Law* (Kauppakaari 2002) 9–11; Raimo Siltala, *Oikeustieteen tieteenteoria* (Suomalainen lakimiesyhdistys 2003) 508–511 and 520.

71 Sören Koch, 'An Introduction to German Legal Culture' in this volume, Chapter 8, 247.

72 For a discussion of quality in legal scholarship, see a set of short writings in *Lakimies* 2019 no. 2.

73 Björne (2002) (n 70) 169–171.

74 Lavapuro, Ojanen and Scheinin (2016) (n 65).

should not be involved in weighing and balancing rights and legal principles.[75] Respecting the law, or at least the will of the democratic legislator, is respecting the sovereignty of the Finnish people. Predictability has thus been the key ideal of justice. The legalistic attitude is reflected in the Finnish saying "maa on lailla rakennettava", "the country shall be built by using laws".

Legality and predictability can also be traced to the strong peasant culture and late professionalisation. Since the first laws were recorded, the language used has been simple, in the beginning even vernacular. The influence of Roman law, Canon law and legal scholarship was very limited, and hence, there were few clearly defined legal concepts. Due to late professionalisation – few lawyers and few professional judges – lay people were among the main users of statutory law. By reading, the one should (at least ideally) be able to predict one's legal position. Despite the formidable development of legal scholarship and introduction of complex legal concepts and terminology, the ideal of an accessible law nonetheless remains an ideal and requires adherence to the law.[76]

Moreover, legal scholarship maintained the epitome ideal of law as pure in the sense that it should not be contaminated by social or ethical perspectives. Legal argumentation should consist of an analysis of the words and concepts used in statutory law and be unaffected by the personal views and values of the person interpreting the law. Many legal scholars advocated the ideal of one single right answer to a legal question also well into the 1960s.[77]

Until the 1970s, country court judges contributed to the ideal of one single right solution by not glancing through the book of statutes or referring to a specific provision of law for justifying the outcome, they simply pronounced the judgment like an oracle uttering what the law is. The structure of the court proceedings enabled the judge to do so. Prior to the final hearing, the judge read the court files including all the relevant information from previous hearings and documents related to the case and could therefore prepare the ruling before the final hearing. Rulings were short, and the judge could memorise the key issues.[78] Nowadays court proceedings, particularly the preparatory hearings, consist of dialogue between the court and the legal counsel, and the court pronounces its ruling a few weeks after the oral main hearing has been closed.

75 Tuomas Ojanen, 'EU Law and the Response of the Constitutional Law Committee of the Finnish Parliament' (2007) Vol. 52 *Scandinavian Studies in Law*.

76 Ditlev Tamm, 'Courts, law, language and culture' in Laura Ervo, Pia Letto-Vanamo and Anna Nylund (eds), *Rethinking Nordic Courts* (Springer, forthcoming).

77 Lars Björne, *Realism och skandinavisk realism. Den nordiska rättsvetenskapens historia. Del IV 1911–1950.* (Institutet för rättshistorisk forskning 2007) 223–227; Susanna Lindroos-Hovinheimo, 'Finnish Legal Theory in the Twentieth Century' in Kimmo Nuotio, Sakari Melander and Merita Huomo-Kettunen (eds), *Introduction to Finnish Law and Legal Culture* (Publications of the Faculty of Law University of Helsinki 2012) 22.

78 Letto-Vanamo (2004) (n 39).

4.2 Equity in the shadow of legalism

Is there no room for equity in the Finnish legal culture? Finns regard themselves as pragmatic and Finnish politics is flooded with examples of a down-to-earth approach. Equity is important in Finnish and Swedish legal culture and is expressly mentioned in "The Rules for Judges" written by Olaus Petri in the 16th century. Although the rules have never been formal law or formally approved, since 1635 they have been printed as a preamble in statute books in both Finland and Sweden. The rules are based on old Nordic legal culture mixed with influences from German legal thought, Greek philosophy, Roman law, and Hebrew law. The rules reflect a two-fold ideal of justice: one stressing that decisions may not be arbitrary and random (predictability), and the other stressing that law must be fair and promote equality (equity).[79] Paragraphs nine and ten of the rules illustrate the importance of equity and fairness: "What is not just and fair cannot be law either; for it is on account of the fairness which dwells in the law that the law is accepted." "All law is to be wielded with wisdom because the greatest right is the greatest wrong; and there must be mercy in justice as well." According to a Finnish saying the law is as it is read (*laki on niinkuin sitä luetaan*), which implies a highly contextual approach to law and legal interpretation.

The Rules for Judges capture a mind-set and ideology that has co-existed with legalism. Although the statutes cannot be set aside when they are found to be unjust or unfair, many cases involve an interpretation of statutes or filling of lacunae. When different interpretations, or different ways of filling lacunae, arise, a judge should choose the just and fair alternative. The Rules for Judges also stress that the greater good of society should be promoted: thus, a solution that captures the aim or rationale of the law is better than the one fulfilling the letter of the law. The greater good of society can be interpreted to be the equitable solution in the case.[80]

Until modernisation of the court system and court procedure in the 1990s, the Country Court judges embodied the dualism of legalism and equity. The citizens had great respect for the educated people and for authorities in their field, and a belief in the law as the guardian of an egalitarian society. Therefore, judges were highly respected, and citizens came to the country court judge expecting him to decide their case according to the law, which they perceived as just. The solemnity of the court process underlined the significance of the law. However, it is possible that the judges often perceived their role as the wise judge, who will rather use equity and fairness than the letter of the law, to decide the case.[81] The appearance of the judge as an oracle served this purpose as well as the ideal of legality: when the judge makes no references to a specific provision, controlling whether the judge employed a literal interpretation of the law or resorted to equity, or perhaps a mixture of these, is arduous, or even an insurmountable task.

---

79 Jarkko Tontti, 'Olaus Petri and The Rules for Judges' (2000) 4, no. 1 *Associations – Journal for Social and Legal Theory 113*.

80 Aulis Aarnio, 'Värdena och domarreglerna. Tankar om förhållandet mellan rätt och moral' in Ulf Bernitz, Bill W Dufwa and others (eds), *Festskrift till Jan Hellner* (Norstedt 1984).

81 Letto-Vanamo (2004) (n 39) 124–126.

In Nordic law, general clauses on good faith are ubiquitous. Only actions done in good faith are worthy of receiving the protection of law. In commercial law, there are many references to literally "good manners" ("*hyvä tapa*", "*god sed*") meaning, that marketing, trademarks and commercial activities may not be against public policy or accepted principles of morality. Morality and good faith are easy to use as common points of reference in a society where the level of social stratification is relatively low, and where there is a coherent, national culture.[82]

Europeanisation has shifted the balance slightly in favour of equity, since EU law stresses teleological interpretation. However, developments in the legal method have also particularly been instrumental in the turn towards equity, as will be explained below. Simultaneously, the view of sovereignty as a rejection of outside influence in constitutional law has been replaced by a more benign view of supranational law that embraces 'international co-operation for the protection of peace and human rights and for the development of society', as the Finnish Constitution Section 1 Subsection 3 states. This also entails a paradigmatic shift in regarding the rule of law and the Constitution as being primarily instruments to protect and promote human rights.[83] Hence, in legal decision-making, be it legislative, administrative or adjudicative, general principles of law and human rights occupy the centre stage, at least in the hard cases, requiring the solutions to be equitable and fair.[84]

5. Legal method

5.1 Sources of law and bases for legal arguments

Until the 1990s, legal arguments were generally divided into three categories: strongly obligating sources of law, weakly obligating sources of law and permissible arguments. According to Aulis Aarnio, strongly obligating sources of law had to be used, otherwise the legal community would not approve of the argumentation. Weakly obligating sources should be used in legal argumentation, but they could be set aside for a good reason, and permissible arguments were accepted by the legal community, but one did not have to use them.[85]

Acts of Parliament (*laki, lag*) and customary law (*maan tapa, sedvanerätt*) were the strongly obligating sources of law. As Acts of Parliament cover almost all aspects of life, the role of customary law is negligible. Weakly obligating source of law consisted of case law (from the supreme courts) and preparatory works (*esityöt, förarbeten*). Legal literature, policy considerations, legal principles and arguments from comparative law

82 Juha Pöyhönen, 'The Law of Obligations' in Juha Pöyhönen (ed), *An Introduction to Finnish Law* (Kauppakaari 2002) 60–63.

83 Ojanen (2007) (n 75).

84 E.g. Lavapuro, Ojanen and Scheinin (2016) (n 65).

85 Aulis Aarnio, *Essays on the Doctrinal Study of Law* (Springer 2011) 150–151.

are the main types of permissible sources. Legal literature and legal principles have in practice the highest rank.

The 1990s marked a paradigm shift in the legal method primarily due to internationalisation as Finland ratified the ECHR and became an EU Member State. Today, legal reasoning is openly considered to be interpreting, weighing and harmonising different sources of law. The hierarchy of legal sources is considered dynamic and contextual, not static.[86] The most important legislation of the EU and the Finnish Constitution are the most important sources of law. They are followed by precedents from the Court of Justice of the European Union (CJEU) and European Court of Human Rights (ECtHR), and Finnish legislation, preparatory works, and Finnish precedents. Additionally, general legal principles are important. Decisions by government agencies, European principles of law, legal scholarship, and comparative law arguments are acknowledged as bases for legal arguments. Arguments relating to morals and the general good of society have increased in weight, as have arguments stressing coherence in the legal system.[87]

5.2 Statutory law

Linguistic interpretation of the relevant provision in a statute is the starting point of legal decision-making and argumentation in Finland. Acts of Parliament are the most important type of statutory law. Decrees (*asetus, förordning*), that is general norms issued by ministries and the government of Finland, are also important in containing often detailed and highly technical rules. However, decrees are not subject to direct democratic control by the Parliament.[88] As explained above, Finnish courts seldom set aside statutes; whenever possible, conflicts are solved by interpretation or by resorting to general norms of collision, such as *lex specialis* and *lex posterior.*

Acts of Parliament do not form one coherent entity and concepts might have a different meaning in the acts. For instance, there is no equivalent to the German Civil Code (*Bürgerliches Gesetzbuch*) since the content is included in many short statutes regulating only one specific area. Compared to countries with codification, the Finnish statutes will seem fragmentary, lacking a coherent framework and terminology. Legislation is pragmatic, statutes are written in fairly simple language, and they are not based on large-scale theoretical systems.[89] The opening sections of many acts define the purpose of the Act of Parliament and the main terminology used.[90]

86 Timonen (2002) (n 62) 22–25; Hannu Tolonen, *Pääsykoekirja 1/2003* (Turun yliopisto 2003) 128–134; Juha Karhu, 'Perusoikeudet ja oikeuslähdeoppi' (2003) no. 5 *Lakimies* 789.

87 Siltala (2003) (n 70) 247–284; Tuori (2011) (n 70) 161–172; Karhu (2003) (ibid).

88 Johan Boucht, 'Introduction to Finnish and Swedish Legal Method' in Ingvild Helland and Sören Koch (eds), *Nordic and Germanic Legal Methods* (Mohr Siebeck 2014) 172–174.

89 In Finland, the ideal is that ordinary people should be able to understand what the law is by reading the law. Therefore, the language used in the law must be simple. See Husa (2012) (n 68).

90 See for example the Consumer Protection Act defining consumer, consumer goods and services, and business, and the Personal Data Act, defining the objectives of the act, the scope of application and important terminology in the first three sections of the Act.

5.3 Preparatory works

Preparatory works, *travaux preparatoires*, are an important source of law in Finland. The weight of preparatory works is derived directly from the legislative powers of the Parliament. In lack of systematic codifications, the Government bill (*hallituksen esitys, regeringens proposition*) helps to connect a specific act to the body of statutory law by describing the aims of the law, the leading principles, the relationship to other statutes, and the relationship between different parts of the law. This information gives valuable input for interpreting the law. Sometimes the Government bill gives examples of situations that are covered by a provision in the law. The preparatory works often include background information needed when interpreting laws, for instance.

Preparatory works transform societal values and goals, and thereby also fairness and equity, to a source of law. The rationale of the Act of Parliament or provision can be derived from the preparatory works, either directly or by resorting to a reconstruction of the hypothetical rationale. When circumstances change, courts might argue that a provision should be interpreted differently to accomplish the objective purpose (*ratio legis*) of the act and thus contribute to upholding the presumed will of the Parliament – and the Finnish people – even amidst societal change.[91] The solution might not be obvious when reading the text of the statue, but it can be justified by referring to the preparatory works. In contrast to other Nordic countries, the Finnish government seldom uses broadly based commissions with a wide mandate to investigate an issue to produce a voluminous report. Instead, the government forgoes this step and uses reports from other Nordic countries, primarily Sweden, as a source of information, and supplies it with investigations authored by government employees.

Europeanisation has lessened to some degree the value of preparatory works. The case law of the ECtHR and the CJEU usually trump preparatory works as a source of law, since preparatory works are considered to be less important than statutory law. The courts must do an independent analysis of compatibility with European legislation and cannot rely on the opinion of the Government and Parliament. However, the CJEU has recognised that preparatory works can be used as a means for implementation of EU law in the Nordic countries.[92] The language in a provision may be general if the preparatory works specifies it by, for instance, listing examples or explaining the rationale and basic principles to be applied in interpretation of the provision. Further, the Parliament can explain why a particular solution has been chosen and why that solution complies with EU law, the ECHR and other international human rights conventions. The national, and European, courts may use the information when assessing if the law and the interpretation of the law is compatible with supranational law.

---

91 Timonen (2002) (n 62) 28; Boucht (2014) (n 88).

92 Case C-478/99 *Commission v Sweden* [2002] ECR I–04147.

5.4 Case law

The traditional role of courts has been to provide interpretations, not to create law. In practice, however, the courts have always created law and courts have considered fairness and practicability of the result, not just the text of the statute, when deciding a case.[93] Case law from the supreme courts published in the courts' yearbooks is considered a source of law and as *de facto* precedent. The Supreme Court publishes virtually all the cases it has admitted on the basis of their value as precedents, i.e. approximately 100–120 cases annually. The Supreme Administrative Court publishes additionally about 100 other cases in full length. These cases clarify or develop the law or are of a general interest in other ways.[94]

Since the turn of the millennium, the supreme courts have explicitly created new legal rules and principles in their precedents.[95] Although precedent is not formally binding, lower courts will depart from it only if there is a weighty reason. Such reasons might be new case law from European courts, that the ruling is old, new or amended statutes, or significant societal changes. The supreme courts are only allowed to depart from their own precedent when ruling in an enlarged chamber or in full court.[96] Factors influencing the weight of a precedent are *inter alia* whether the ruling was unanimous, the content of any dissenting votes, and whether the ruling reinforces a previous line of argumentation or marks a shift in argumentation.[97] The supreme courts write a summary indicating the key issues in the case, but often do not describe the outcome. The short summary of the case identifies the binding norm. Traditionally, the opinions of the judges have been short, but during the last few decades, they have become longer to make the argumentation more transparent and to provide sufficiently detailed arguments to assist lower courts and lawyers in interpreting the cases.

Europeanisation and increased focus on human rights in the Finnish Constitution has enhanced precedent as a source of law. Section 1 of the Constitution of 1999 explicitly states that the Constitution guarantees human rights and that Finland is an EU member and participates in European and international cooperation. This section gives courts the right and duty to guarantee both national and international human rights as stated in treaties ratified by Finland and to ensure the efficient application of EU law. The Constitution states explicitly that courts may perform judicial review. Since case law from the European courts and EU regulations are not directly implemented in national law, courts must step in to interpret these in a Finnish context and to ensure that Finnish law is compatible with EU law and the ECHR. Precedents from the European courts have become important sources of law, since much of the development of supranational law comes directly from the case law of the ECtHR and the CJEU. Their considerable

---

93 Timonen (2002) (n 62) 29; Aarnio (2002) (n 70) 13–15 and 18–19.

94 See https://www.kho.fi/en/index/decisions.html accessed 14 February 2020.

95 Pihlajamäki (2018) (n 64) 220–221.

96 Ibid 219–221.

97 Mika Huovila, 'Oikeuslähdeoppi ja oikeudellinen argumentaation rikostuomion perusteluissa' (2004) *Lakimies* 42.

weight and importance as sources have been partly transmitted to the case law from the Finnish supreme courts.[98]

The increasing role of the courts has affected the administrative branch of courts to a larger extent than general courts. Earlier the demarcation between questions of law and questions of discretion (policy) were far clearer marked. Today, many administrative decisions have a legal dimension in addition to free discretion, as a consequence of EU law, the ECHR and other binding international human rights conventions, constitutional law, new legislator techniques where the Act of Parliament states its purpose, and legalisation (meaning that an increasing part of society is regulated by law).[99]

5.4.1 Decisions of government bodies

The practice of governmental and other public bodies is also a basis for legal arguments. The Parliamentary Ombudsman of Finland oversees that public authorities and officials obey the law – especially the Constitution – and the principles of good administration. Citizens can file a complaint directly with the Parliamentary Ombudsman. The Chancellor of Justice of the Government has parallel powers in monitoring the lawfulness of the Government, the ministries, and the President. An individual can file a complaint with the Chancellor of Justice if a civil servant or an authority has acted in an unlawful manner or has not fulfilled their legal duties. Although the decisions of the Parliamentary Ombudsman and the Chancellor of Justice do not revoke the administrative decision as such, administrative organs do comply by amending the decision at hand, their practices in future cases and sometimes even provide some kind of a remedy directly or indirectly. The decisions also influence other authorities and the interpretation of law, since they are used as a source of law in the same vein as court rulings.[100]

Furthermore, decisions and guidelines from ministries are important in practise, since they influence a large number of the administrative decisions that are made each day. In addition, government practice is also a legal argument. Consistent practices are important to ensure equality before the law and predictability and are therefore often respected.

98 Laura Ervo, 'The Finnish Way of Understanding Procedural Autonomy: A Practical Approach to Implementing EU Civil Procedural Law' in Bart Krans and Anna Nylund (eds), *Procedural Autonomy across Europe* (Intersentia 2020) 60–62; Markus Kari, 'Korkein hallinto-oikeus, oikuesvalitotuomioistuin' in Markus Kari (ed), *Oikeusvaltion rakentaja. Korkein hallinto-oikeus 100 vuortta* (Edita 2018) 36; Pihlajamäki (2018) (n 64) 249–255. See also Sunnqvist (forthcoming) (n 64).

99 Olli Mäenpää, 'Tarkoituksenmukaisuus – vallanjaon rajapyykki?' in Samuli Hurri (ed), *Demokraattisen oikeuden ehdot* (Tutkijaliitto 2008); Tuori (2004) (n 28) 22–24.

100 Markus Kari, 'Syyttäjästä kehittäjäksi. Eduskunnan oikeusasiamiehen kehitys kansalais- ja perusoikeuskeskeiseksi' in *Eduskunnan oikesuasiamies 1920–2020. Satavuotta laillisuusvalvontaa ja oikeusturvaa* (Edita Publishing 2020) 140–161.

5.4.2 Legal scholarship and legal principles

Finnish courts seldom refer directly to legal scholarship, and preparatory works have usually few references to doctrine. Yet, legal scholarship is *de facto* often used as a central source of information and arguments.[101] Earlier, legal scholarship helped counterbalance outdated and inadequate statutes, providing insight to how the rationale of the law – the will of the legislator – could be interpreted in a new situation, and how new situations should be systematised and conceptualised.

Modernisation of statutory law has not made legal scholarship redundant. On the contrary, in grappling with an immense body of law – national, supranational, statutory, case law – legal scholarship has an essential role in organising arguments from different sources of law condensing the main ideas, principles, concepts and doctrines, and amalgamating these into a coherent system. Legal scholarship and textbooks are the main source of information for law students and students are taught to use scholarship to solve legal problems. Many justices, and some referendaries, as well as many leading employees in ministries and government agencies have doctorate degrees in their field of law. There are approximately 550–600 persons in Finland holding a doctoral degree in law, two thirds of which are occupied outside of academia.[102] A significant number of lawyers drift between academia and central government agencies and/or courts, thus they are prone to use a method resembling that of legal scholarship in their reasoning.[103]

In the 1980s, legal principles came into fashion among legal scholars. Scholars endeavoured to uncover existing principles and to introduce new principles, as well as discuss how legal principles should and could be used in legal argumentation and what their weight as legal sources should be. This lay the groundwork for embracing the principle-oriented changes resulting from codification of human rights in the Constitution, ratification of the ECHR and EU membership, and contributed to a shift in the legal method, as will be explained below.[104] Legal scholarship is the foremost source of information on legal principles and general legal doctrines.

Legal scholarship is published in one of four legal journals, and in a few legal journals edited by students, books and webpages. In 2016, more than 80 books that could be classified as legal literature were published. These were books published primarily for lawyers or other law professionals. There is no tradition of distinguishing between textbooks, handbooks and scholarly work. Often the same book serves all purposes, at least to some degree.

101 Pihlajamäki (n 60) 228–229.

102 The number of persons holding a doctoral degree in law from a Finnish university were 498 at the end of 2015, see Heikki Halila and Ville Pönkä, 'Neljäsataayhdeksänkymmentäviisi – eräitä tietoja suomalaisista oikeustieteen tohtoreista 31.12.2015' (2016) vol. 114 no. 5 *Lakimies* 765. Since then, 70–75 new degrees have been earned.

103 Timonen (2002) (n 62) 30; Pia Letto-Vanamo, 'Autonomy and heteronomy of the judiciary – a historical approach' (2011) vol. 1 no. 8 *Oñati Socio-Legal Series*; Boucht (2014) (n 88).

104 Lindroos-Hovinheimo (2012) (n 77); Tolonen (2003) (n 86) 175 ff.; Siltala (2003) (n 70) 247–284; Karhu (2003) (n 86).

5.4.3 The methods of law: from legalism and the ideal of deduction…

As mentioned above, legalism gained a strong foothold in Finnish legal culture during the 1800s and maintained its strong position until the 1980s. During the first post-war decades, what was called analytical scholarship was in favour. The method still emphasised statutory law as a legal source, but allowed the use of other legal arguments, such as case law. Elements of external character, e.g., social and economic arguments, were not accepted as a basis for legal argumentation. The list of sources was hierarchical, and limited, as explained above. Legal interpretation meant uncovering a meaning, not creating a meaning.[105]

In contrast to other Nordic countries, legal realism did not get a strong foothold in Finland. Legal realism focuses on how judges uses the law, how judges will decide a case when answering the question "what is law". A norm is only valid if judges believe it is moral and good, and thus apply it. In Finland, the question "what is law" was still primarily a normative question; the law is what written sources say it is. The goodness or morality of a norm does not impact the validity of the norm, as long as the legislator has accepted the norm. Minimum criteria of acceptability must, however, still be met, i.e., the norm must be acceptable to most citizens, the courts (or the Supreme Court) must accept it by applying it, or the majority of the legal scholars must accept it.[106] The criteria of acceptability demonstrate that the Finnish ideal of legalism was far from absolute – and how legal scholarship and courts are recognised as norm producers.[107]

Why has Finland been so different? One explanation is that in Finnish history, strict obedience to statutory law has been important in order to create and protect an independent Finnish society from external political influences. After World War II, engaging in political activities was not the proper task of the judge or the legal scholar, hence positivism and deduction was considered safe. Another factor is that the method reflected the ideal of justice, norm production, conflict resolution and professionalisation. If statutory law is the key institution for norm production, predictability is accentuated and professionalisation is weak, legalism with simplified deduction fits as a method. Further, internationalisation is important for the development of methods: where do scholars travel, whose writings have served as inspiration? Finnish legal scholars have travelled to Germany. Because Finland was not occupied by Germany, Finns did not have a general aversion against Germans after the war. "Finlandisation" reduced scholarly influences from the United States. Finally, the Finnish legal system was archaic: modernisation of law was slow, as it was not a priority on a societal level. The level of professionalisation of lawyers was low, and the welfare state was developed far later than in the other Nordic

105 Aarnio (2002) (n 70) 6–7.

106 Pekka Timonen, 'Doctrine of the source of law of a scholar and of a judge' (1990) 34 *Scandinavian Studies in Law* 262, 269.

107 Jaakko Husa, Kimmo Nuotio and Heikki Pihlajamäki, 'Nordic Law – Between Tradition and Dynamism' in Jaakko Husa, Kimmo Nuotio and Heikki Pihlajamäki (eds), *Nordic Law – Between Tradition and Dynamism* (Intersentia 2007).

countries. The need for lawyers to engage in building the welfare state, and thus using an instrumentalist, not formalist, method of argumentation came far after the pinnacle of legal realism.[108]

The strong focus on German legal thinking was not unproblematic. In contrast to Germany, Finland has single statutes, which are more fragmentary than codes and result in more lacunae; thus, legislation is not easily amenable to deductive reasoning. Additionally, single provisions in the statutes are often amended rather than making overall amendments, creating even more fragmentary statutes. Lawyers have had to resort to creative interpretation in the process of modernizing law without modernisation of legislation and to make law more coherent. Statutory interpretation is required in practise analysis of several different sources of law and bases for argument, including the preparatory works, case law and legal scholarship.

5.4.4 ...to weighing, balancing and harmonising

The legalist approach to law came under siege in the 1980s when legal scholars increasingly argued for acceptability, predictability and morality as the core values of law, rather than the pedigree of a norm. The novel approach allowed a wider range of legal arguments. For instance, case law, particularly supreme court rulings, is valid law, because case law enhances foreseeability and often the greater good of society. This might be true even if it departs from the clear wording of statutory law as long as the grounds for the ruling reflect the legal culture and general ideas of fairness or important policy goals as these are expressed in the initial parts of the act or its preparatory works. Arguments of principle are also valid, since they reflect the moral or value-based element of law and enhance predictability.[109]

Using acceptability, morality and predictability as the predicaments of law engender the internal criticism of law: a provision in an act of Parliament can be formally valid law, but it must be disapplied if strong arguments suggest so. The development culminated in Kaarlo Tuori's theory on the levels of the law and the importance of the subsurface level of legal arguments.[110] The subsurface level legal arguments are not a complete break from the legalistic tradition, as they are clearly *legal* arguments, not arguments external to the law. Moral and practical arguments can only be included as they are embedded in the legal culture and to the extent they can be extracted from bases for legal arguments.

The static list of sources of law and legal arguments needed to be replaced by a flexible, contextual doctrine of sources that reflects the multitude of sources. Similarly, the ideal of a coherent, entirely foreseeable legal outcome, and the existence of one single,

---

108 Tuori (2011) (n 70) 128–129; Toni Malminen, 'So You Thought Transplanting Law is Easy? Fear of Scandinavian Legal Realism in Finland, 1918–1965' in Jaakko Husa, Kimmo Nuotio and Heikki Pihlajamäki (eds), *Nordic Law: Between Tradition and Dynamism* (Intersentia 2007); Pia Letto-Vanamo, 'Rättsvetenskap och framsteg – de allmänna lärorna som verktyg för de finska juristerna' (2009) *Tidskrift utgiven av juridiska föreningen i Finland,* 400–410; Björne (2007) (n 77) 223–227; Letto-Vanamo (2004) (n 39).

109 Lindroos-Hovinheimo (2012) (n 77); Aarnio (2011) (n 85) 162–163.

110 Kaarlo Tuori, *Critical Legal Positivism* (Ashgate 2002).

right answer was abandoned in favour of an approach stressing the quality of argumentation over finding the correct outcome at least in the hard cases. In hard cases, arguments derived from different sources will require harmonising, weighing and balancing to find an acceptable outcome. Therefore, legal interpretation is about determining the relative weight of legal sources in the case at hand, starting in the general rank of sources and legal arguments.[111] Several factors have contributed to the emergence of a new legal method, *inter alia*, the emergence of new or significant developments within legal fields such as environmental law and communications law where elements of public and private law are combined; the increasing recognition of legal principles as a source of law; and, not least, Europeanisation.[112] In a polycentric legal system where law emanates from several independent regimes, harmonising the legal rules from different systems is a fundamental part of the legal method and consequently far from static deduction. The distinction between uncovering meaning and creating meaning can no longer be strictly upheld.[113]

As the role of the courts has traditionally been weak both in the institutional and intellectual structure of the legal culture, Finnish law has not needed a clear method of distinguishing. Since case law has only been considered a 'weakly' obliging source of law, and the method allowed in practice arguments from several different sources, courts could draw on or bypass a ruling based on other arguments than the degree of factual similarity between the ruling and the case at hand. Another reason for the absence of distinguishing is that a theory for identification of the *ratio decidendi* is a prerequisite for distinguishing. In absence of clear rules for high quality judicial argumentation, many supreme court rulings do not explicitly state the *ratio decidendi.* Instead, it is left to the reader to identify the precise rule that the court applied, often by 'reverse-engineering' the argumentation of the court. It can hence be difficult to establish whether the *ratio decidendi* is very specific, which would make it easily amenable to distinguishing, or a general rule, from which it would be difficult to deviate even when the circumstances of the cases are alike. In hard cases, the courts harmonise and balance arguments derived from different sources, so the *ratio decidendi* could be a formula for harmonising, weighing and balancing, setting out a method for argumentation rather than the outcome.[114] A third factor is that the summary of the case, which contains very limited factual information and often frames the issue at hand in an abstract manner, is the most important part of the ruling.[115] The summary in itself is not amenable to distinguishing, and it guides the reader to focus on the line of argumentation rather than the factual background of the case. Since precedents have become more central and case law from the

111 Karhu (2003) (n 86).

112 Tuori (2011) (n 70) 161–172.

113 Aulis Aarnio, 'On the Source of Law' in Kimmo Nuotio, Sakari Melander and Merita Huomo-Kettunen (eds), *Introduction to Finnish Law and Legal Culture* (Publications of the Faculty of Law University of Helsinki 2012).

114 For a more detailed discussion, see Christina Ramberg, *Prejudikat som rättskälla i förmögenhetsrätten* (Wolters Kluwer 2017) and for a brief discussion in English, see Sunnqvist (forthcoming) (n 64). Both authors write from a Swedish perspective, but the discussion is relevant for Finland as well.

115 Raimo Siltala, 'Prejudikaateista ja tuomarin prejudikaatti-ideologisasta' (1999) no. 5 *Lakimies* 674

European courts must be applied directly by Finnish courts, the legal method for using precedents probably has to be developed.[116] In the future, a clearer distinction between *ratio decidendi* and *obiter dicta*, and an improved method for distinguishing cases, may be required to determine which legal arguments are the most important and to foresee the future developments in case law.[117]

6. Professionalisation

6.1 Legal education and legal publishing

University education in law started in 1640 when the predecessor of the University of Helsinki – the Royal Academy of Turku – was founded. However, for the first 200 years, the number of students and scholars was very modest. The situation changed from the 1860s, when a need for civil servants, particularly those with legal education, emerged as a result of growing modernisation, industrialisation and urbanisation. Simultaneously, evolving nationalism, the conception of a Finnish people, speaking the Finnish language living in an independent, or at least autonomous, country, elicited a need for lawyers to build strong Finnish institutions.[118]

Today, lawyers are trained at four universities: the University of Helsinki, the University of Turku, the University of Lapland and the University of Eastern Finland. In addition, Åbo Akademi University has programmes in law. The University of Helsinki has by far the largest enrolment, enrolling almost half of the total approximately 5,100 students in the Bachelor of Laws and Master of Laws programmes in the country. Annually, about 300 students receive their Master of Laws in Helsinki, 160 in Turku, 120 in Lapland, and 120 in Eastern Finland. Between 20 and 30 students receive a doctorate degree in law.[119] The four law schools have about 115–120 professors and associate professors, and many researchers with a doctorate degree in law. In addition, other universities have programmes with a significant component of law, for instance tax law, company law or public law. Several university colleges offer paralegal education as a specialisation for the Bachelor of Business Administration degree. These students gain knowledge in many areas of law and in legal methods, preparing them for careers with a substantive legal component.

Legal education is based primarily on students reading legal literature. Case law is discussed in legal textbooks, and the statute book has references to important case law in the footnotes. However, law students seldom read case law in the yearbooks of the supreme courts. In more advanced courses requiring the students to write papers or do

116 Siltala (1999) (n 115).

117 Ramberg (2017) (n 114) and Sunnqvist (forthcoming) (n 64).

118 Aarnio (2002) (n 70) 7–8.

119 See https://vipunen.fi/fi-fi/_layouts/15/xlviewer.aspx?id=/fi-fi/Raportit/Yliopistokoulutuksen%20tutkin-not-n%C3%A4k%C3%B6kulma-yliopisto.xlsb accessed 30 December 2019.

independent legal research, precedents are more salient. This reflects the method where legal scholarship has a noticeable role and the role of case law is comparably weak.

The main task of legal education has been to educate legal generalists. The first three years of study are essentially the same for all students, the fourth year consists of electives, and the final year consists of studies related to the master's thesis, including studies in legal writing, legal research and legal methods. However, after finishing their studies, lawyers tend to specialise in a specific field of law, such as labour law or tax law. Only judges and country lawyers, the number of which is decreasing, are true generalists.

Earlier, almost all books were in Finnish or Swedish.[120] Because of internationalisation, part of the syllabus is in English in relevant subjects. Finnish Law Schools also offer English-speaking Master's programmes. Today practically all legal areas have some European content and many of them require knowledge of applying EU law, the ECHR and other binding human rights conventions, and comparing supranational and national law. Many students study abroad for a longer or shorter period of time or take a Master's Degree at a foreign university.

6.2 The legal profession

A Master's Degree in law is required for practicing law. Legal education consists nevertheless of two parts: first students must complete a Bachelor's Degree in law and then continue to earn their Master's Degree in general law. However, a student can also pursue a specialised degree programme, e.g., in commercial or public international law, but these degrees do not qualify for employment as a lawyer. Competition among lawyers is fierce before law school: Only about 10% of the applicants pass the entrance examinations and are admitted to study at the University of Helsinki. The other law schools have marginally higher admittance rates. There is, of course, fierce competition for the most attractive jobs after graduation, although unemployment figures are relatively low among law graduates. The procedures for the selection of students will change starting in 2020, which might engender cultural changes among law students in the long run.

Annually, about 150 lawyers receive court training as a Trainee District Judge. The training lasts one year and consists of working as a judge in the District Court, or first in a District Court and then in a Court of Appeal or Administrative Court. After the training period is completed, the trainee receives the highly esteemed honorary title Master of Laws with court training (trained at the bench) (*varatuomari, vicehäradshövding*). As the number of trainee positions is about one fourth of the number of law school graduates, positions in the larger cities are sought-after. The court training is the primary method of recruiting judges, still most trainee judges seek employment outside courts.

120 Because Swedish is an official language in Finland, legal education is offered in Swedish at the University of Helsinki. Some legal books are originally written in Swedish; others are translated into Swedish. However, only a small part of all legal books is available in Swedish. There are several professorships designated as Swedish-speaking in Helsinki, and those professors teach mostly in Swedish. Swedish-speaking students can submit papers, exams and theses in Swedish, and exam questions are available in Swedish.

After the trainee period, prospective judges usually find employment as referendaries or lower rank judges at a District Court. Junior judges often switch jobs and work on short contracts. Many are appointed permanently when they are in their 40s, despite having been employed in the court system since their late 20s.

Today there are more than 16,000 lawyers in Finland. The Finnish Bar Association has only 2,100 members that can use the title advocate (*asianajaja, advokat*). In addition to the 2,100 advocates, some 600 associate lawyers work under the supervision of advocates. Membership in the Bar is open by application to lawyers providing legal services on a professional basis and who are either self-employed or work at a law firm. Additionally, to qualify for membership one must have at least four years of work experience as a lawyer, two of which must be as an advocate in an advocate's office, at the Legal Aid office or as a sole practitioner. Lawyers employed by companies, private or public organisations may not be members of the Bar. Thus, the number of potential advocates is low. Members of the Bar have privileges relative to the courts, for instance only advocates are appointed as defence counsel in criminal cases.

Until 2013, there were practically no restrictions on legal representation in courts: Parties could choose anybody to represent them in court. Accordingly, many lawyers offering legal services are not members of the Bar Association, since membership costs money and requires compliance with the Code of Conduct and the Disciplinary Board. In order to ensure better quality of legal representation in courts, and better access to justice, restrictions have been applied to non-advocate representatives. Today, legal representatives must either be advocates or they must register as licenced counsel (*luvan saanut oikeudenkäyntiavustaja, rättegångsbiträde med tillstånd*). The licenced counsels are subjected to similar rules, regulations and disciplinary procedure as advocates. In 2018, there were approximately 1,600 licensed counsels.[121] It is still premature to assess the impact of the reform on Finnish legal culture. However, the reform is likely to contribute to further professionalisation, since the independent lawyers and non-lawyers offering legal services will face a dramatic reduction of their market.

Civil servants were until recently the backbone of the Finnish legal profession. Courts were quite weak, and judges were not well paid, the prosecutors were poorly organised and professionalised, and there were few advocates. Only recently has the position of civil servants become less prominent, but the percentage of lawyers occupied as legal counsel is still low.

7. Internationalisation

7.1 Law, language and legal culture

Until the 1990s, Swedish law was the main source of inspiration for Finnish law and Swedish reports were a highly influential source of inspiration and information, ena-

121 Oikeudenkäyntiavustajalautakunnan toimintakertomus 2018. See https://oikeus.fi/material/attachments/yhteiset/yhteiset/Pr5TC9ms5/toimintakertomus_verksamhetsberattelse_2018.pdf accessed 5 March 2020.

bling the Finnish legislator to forego the expensive and time-consuming stage of drafting a report.[122] The legislator has also relied on Nordic cooperation and enacted many laws based on Nordic draft laws. It is hardly surprising that the Swedish heritage is still omnipresent in Finnish law. In the early years of the 2000s, the Finnish legislator turned also to Norway for influences on inter alia drafting rules on court-connected mediation in civil cases and in parental responsibility cases.[123]

Swedish and German law and legal thinking have been the main sources of inspiration for legal scholars. Throughout the 1900s, scholars, and even students writing their master's thesis, have been expected to have thorough knowledge of Swedish legal literature. The growing body of Finnish legal scholarship has reduced the need to resort to Swedish, and Nordic, scholarship. German legal thought has had a significant impact particularly on the general development of doctrine, and the theoretical and philosophical study of law. One reason for German dominance was probably that both Finland and Germany had weak states where neither the courts nor the legislator could dominate norm-production. Thus, legal scholarship filled a void. As explained above, German legal thought rather than Scandinavian realism resonated with the prevailing ideas among Finnish legal scholars, and continental (legal) philosophy has continued to be a main source of inspiration.[124]

In the last few decades, common law countries and the English language have increasingly exerted influence on Finnish law, although the impact is still only weakly perceptible. Today, approximately a third of all doctoral dissertations are written in English. However, dissertations with a primarily national focus still use relatively few sources in other languages than Finnish and Swedish.[125] The English legal culture, and common law thinking in general, have so far had very limited influence on Finnish law.

Despite close economic and cultural ties, Nordic cooperation has been diminishing. The Nordic countries often opt for different paths in their relations to the EU and have employed different strategies in their endeavours to influence European policymaking and the European courts.[126] New influences are often supranational, European. However, many scholars have extensive Nordic networks, government officials use the other Nordic countries for benchmarking and inspiration, and many large companies, including large law-firms, are often Nordic.[127]

122 Laura Ervo, 'Comparative Analysis between East-Scandinavian Countries' (2015) vol. 61 *Scandinavian Studies in Law* 135.

123 Kirsikka Linnanmäki, 'Mediation: A Change in Finnish Court Culture?' in Laura Ervo, Pia Letto-Vanamo and Anna Nylund (eds), *Rethinking Nordic Courts* (Springer, forthcoming).

124 Lindroos-Hovinheimo (2012) (n 77).

125 Pia Letto-Vanamo, 'Eurooppalainen oikeus Suomen oikeuden haasteena' in Veli-Pekka Viljanen (ed), *Oikeudenalojen rajat ja rajattomuus* (Turun yliopisto 2002).

126 Päivi Leino-Sandberg, Samuli Miettinen and Liisa Leppävirta, 'Har det nordiska rättsliga samarbetet en framtid i Europeiska unionen?' (2016) Vol. 19 No. 3 *Europarättslig tidskrift* 399; Nylund (2010) (n 11); Ulf Bernitz, 'What is Scandinavian Law? Concepts, Characteristics, Future?' (2010) Vol. 50 *Scandinavian Studies in Law* 13.

127 Anna Nylund, 'European Integration and Nordic Civil Procedure' in Laura Ervo and Anna Nylund (eds), *The Future of Civil Litigation. Access to Courts and Court-annexed Mediation in the Nordic Countries* (Springer 2014).

7.2 Europeanisation – limited impact or transformation of Finnish legal culture?

Until the 1990s, Finnish lawyers seldom had to work with transnational law. Finnish ratification of the ECHR in 1990 and the EU membership in 1995 were significant events; within a few years, EU law permeated many areas of Finnish law, such as environmental law and consumer law. Argumentation based on human rights went from almost non-existent to being an integral source of law. As a consequence, the legal sources and the legal method had to be radically changed to enable weighing and balancing arguments derived from different sources.[128] As explained above, the genesis of the transition from a strict hierarchy of sources and the idea of a single correct solution to a looser, more contextual ranking of sources and a method emphasising transparent, more detailed argumentation and a process of amalgamating arguments from different sources to create an acceptable outcome, can be traced to the 1980s. However, Europeanisation has been instrumental in bringing about the change, as discussed above.

Moreover, Europeanisation has also contributed to the shift from legalism to equity and pragmatism in particular through increased use of legal principles in legal argumentation and as a source of law. Again, national developments that preceded the influx of European law, laid a fertile ground for principle-based argumentation and for using legal principles and teleological arguments as a source of law, in particular in hard cases. Similarly, the combined effect of a tradition of courts providing pragmatic solutions in parallel with enforcement of legal rights, a shift towards privatisation of dispute resolution on a global level, and introduction of the EU mediation directive[129] has resulted in Finnish courts increasingly merging pragmatism and adherence to the law.[130]

Europeanisation has also had a tangible influence on the role of courts. As a result of Finnish EU membership in January 1995, courts were suddenly mandated to openly review whether Finnish law complied with EU law and the ECHR, and in consequence, forced to perform judicial review.[131] One could expect the courts eagerly embracing their new powers. However, Finnish courts have proceeded cautiously in applying their powers and to avoid open conflicts whenever possible, such as setting aside Finnish law that does not comply with EU law.[132] The prudent, gradual transition from a prohibition of exercising judicial review to supreme courts openly reviewing whether statutory law is congruent with the Constitution, and the obligations arising from the ECHR and EU law, nonetheless signify a palpable legal cultural shift in the role of courts and have given courts increased powers.

---

128 Pihlajamäki (2018) (n 64) 249–252; Lavapuro, Ojanen and Scheinin (2016) (n 65).

129 Parliament and Council Directive 2008/52/EC of 21 May 2008 on certain aspects of mediation in civil and commercial matters. OJ L 136/3.

130 Linnanmäki (forthcoming) (n 123).

131 To be precise, the change took place already in January 1994 when the Agreement on the European Economic Area entered into force. The duties arising from the ECHR had a slightly more gradual impact, and thus it is more difficult to pinpoint the exact timing of the change, apart from the fact that it coincided with EU-Europeanisation.

132 Lavapuro, Ojanen and Scheinin (2016) (n 65) 239–241.

The fact that Finnish courts seldom request preliminary rulings from European courts, and the supreme courts make the vast majority of the requests, illustrates a cautious approach to Europeanisation.[133] References to EU law and the ECHR are relatively few in Finnish court rulings. Nevertheless, Finnish courts apply EU law and the ECHR diligently and have clearly embraced key doctrines as they have been developed by the CJEU and the ECtHR.[134] The same applies to statutory law; Finns pride themselves on diligently implementing EU directives and regulations in statutory law. However, one can question the quality of implementation and the extent to which EU law has influenced the content of the law, legal concepts and legal thinking. EU law permeates some areas of law, such as environmental law and consumer law, and consequently, the content of law is highly European. In other areas of law, such as family law and procedural law, the influence of EU law is barely discernible.

8. Conclusion

The last decades have been a period of transformation for Finnish legal culture. Internationalisation, particularly Europeanisation, have had a profound impact on norm production, the ideal of justice and the legal method by augmenting the role of courts and case law, the weighing and balancing of sources to find a predictable yet equitable solution to each case. Yet, one should not overemphasise the role of internationalisation; the transformation started in the late 1970s when the supreme courts became courts of (non-binding) precedent and the organisation and funding of courts was improved. Simultaneously, the importance of legal principles and the necessity of including arguments relating to morality and goodness of the outcome gained foothold in legal thinking. In their combined effect, these developments produced changes in norm production, legal method and the ideal of justice, augmenting the role of courts as norm-producers and shifting the balance from legality and formal predictability to equity. Internationalisation in the 1990s was pivotal in this transformative process, but the relatively rapid and smooth transition can be attributed to developments in other areas of legal culture that contributed to a fertile ground for introducing principled-based argumentation on human rights, teleological argumentation of EU law, the enhancing the role of courts as norm-producers, the shift from legalism to more equity based ideal of justice, and a legal method mixing deducting, weighing and balancing and some distinguishing.

How can Finnish legal culture be characterised today? Finnish legal culture, like Nordic countries in general, escapes the dichotomy between civil law and common law; the hallmarks of neither systems match. Characterising the Finnish legal culture as a mixed legal system can also be misleading since it is not a mixture of elements from common law and civil law, instead, the elements that place it somewhere half-way between the two

133 Ervo (2015) (n 122) 59; Anna Nylund 'Norway: An Insider Outside – or an Outsider Inside – European Civil Justice' in Anna Nylund and Bart Krans (eds), *The European Union and National Civil Procedure* (Intersentia 2016) 110.

134 Ervo (2015) (n 122); Lavapuro, Ojanen and Scheinin (2016) (n 65) 241.

have developed organically and most of these traits are also found in the other Nordic legal cultures.[135] The most fertile approach to any attempt at classification of the Finnish legal culture would be to call it a Nordic or Scandinavian legal culture, and adding that the Nordic legal cultures escape a dichotomous taxonomy of European or Western legal systems.

Polycentric norm production, pragmatism and low level of specialisation characterise contemporary Finnish legal culture. The three are interconnected and could partly arise from a relatively small population that is spread over a large territory, which cannot be easily combined with specialisation and an abstract method of creating norms. Hence, one method is one of weighing and balancing information from different sources, the ideal of justice is one of balancing predictability with finding pragmatic outcomes, and most lawyers and judges are generalists.

The Finnish Legal Culture and its structures and structural elements					
Institutional structure		**Intellectual structure**			
Conflict resolution	**Norm production**	**Ideal of justice**	**Legal method**	**Degree of professionalisation**	**Character of internationalisation**
Two parallel hierarchies of courts: general courts and administrative courts, a few special courts. Many conflicts are solved by boards.	Legislation through statutes is the main method. Non-binding precedent from supreme courts is important as well. Legal scholarship is also important.	Predictability through strict application of laws has been the ideal. Equity has also a long tradition and is applied alongside predictability.	Deduction from statutes, use of legal constructions created by legal scholarship, some use of principles, and no refined method of differentiation.	Increasing claims for professionalisation. 5-year Master's Degree in law is required. Focus on legal science. Further training through practice to become a barrister/solicitor or judge is required.	Dualistic system – implementation required. Exception: judgments from ECtHR and CJEU are directly applied in courts. Law received from continental Europe. Students are increasingly mobile: foreign students come to Finland, and Finnish students study abroad.

135 See Jaakko Husa, *A New Introduction to Comparative Law* (Hart 2015) 228–229; Husa, Nuotio and Pihlajamäki (2007) (n 107); Jørn Øyrehagen Sunde, 'The Art of Internationalisation, or What is Nordic Law' in Jaakko Husa, Kimmo Nuotio and Heikki Pihlajamäki (eds), *Nordic Law – Between Tradition and Dynamism* (Intersentia 2007); Jan M. Smits, 'Nordic Law in a European Context: Some comparative observations' in Jaakko Husa, Kimmo Nuotio and Heikki Pihlajamäki (eds), *Nordic Law – Between Tradition and Dynamism* (Intersentia 2007); Bernitz (2010) (n 126).

9. Bibliography

Aarnio A, 'Värdena och domarreglerna. Tankar om förhållandet mellan rätt och moral' in Bernitz U, Dufwa B W and others (eds), *Festskrift till Jan Hellner* (Norstedt 1984)

—— 'Introduction' in Juha Pöyhönen (ed), *An Introduction to Finnish Law* (Kauppakaari 2002)

—— *Essays on the Doctrinal Study of Law* (Springer 2011). DOI: http://dx.doi.org/10.1007/978-94-007-1655-1

—— 'On the Source of Law' in Nuotio K, Melander S and Huomo-Kettunen M (eds), *Introduction to Finnish Law and Legal Culture* (Publications of the Faculty of Law University of Helsinki 2012)

Autio A-L, 'The Main Problems in Access to Court Regarding the Dispute Resolution of Finnish Companies' in Ervo L and Nylund A (eds), *The Future of Civil Litigation. Access to Courts and Court-annexed Mediation in the Nordic Countries* (Springer 2014)

Bernitz U, 'What is Scandinavian Law? Concepts, Characteristics, Future?' (2010) Vol. 50 *Scandinavian Studies in Law* 13

Björne L, *Den konstruktiva riktningen. Den nordiska rättsvetenskapens historia. Del III 1871–1910.* (Lund: Institutet för rättshistorisk forskning 2002)

—— *Realism och skandinavisk realism. Den nordiska rättsvetenskapens historia. Del IV 1911–1950.* (Stockholm: Institutet för rättshistorisk forskning 2007)

Boucht J, 'Introduction to Finnish and Swedish Legal Method' in Helland I and Koch S (eds), *Nordic and Germanic Legal Methods* (Mohr Siebeck 2014)

Ervo L, 'Swedish-Finnish Preparatory Proceedings: Filtering and Process Techniques' in Ervo L and Nylund A (eds), *Current Trends in Preparatory Proceedings* (Springer 2016). DOI: http://dx.doi.org/10.1007/978-3-319-29325-7

—— 'The Finnish Way of Understanding Procedural Autonomy: A Practical Approach to Implementing EU Civil Procedural Law' in Krans B and Nylund A (eds), *Procedural Autonomy across Europe* (Intersentia 2020)

—— 'Comparative Analysis between East-Scandinavian Countries' (2015) vol. 61 *Scandinavian Studies in Law* 135

—— and Dahlqvist A, 'Delays in Civil Proceedings: Comparative Studies Between Finland and Sweden' in Ervo L and Nylund A (eds), *The Future of Civil Litigation. Access to Courts and Court-annexed Mediation in the Nordic Countries* (Springer 2014)

Forsberg T and Pesu M, 'The "Finlandisation" of Finland: The Ideal Type, the Historical Model, and the Lessons Learnt' (2016) Vol. 7 No. 3 *Diplomacy & Statecraft* 473

Galič A, 'Civil Law Perspective on the Supreme Court and its Functions' (2019) *Studia Iuridica LXXXI*

Halila H and Pönkä V, 'Neljäsataayhdeksänkymmentäviisi – eräitä tietoja suomalaisista oikeustieteen tohtoreista 31.12.2015' (2016) vol. 114 no. 5 *Lakimies* 765

Hjort MA, 'Sources of inspiration of Nordic procedural law: Choices and objectives of the legal reforms' in Ervo L, Letto-Vanamo P and Nylund A (eds), *Rethinking Nordic Courts* (Springer, forthcoming)

Huovila M, 'Oikeuslähdeoppi ja oikeudellinen argumentaation rikostuomion perusteluissa' (2004) *Lakimies* 13

Husa J, 'Panorama of World's Legal Systems – Focusing on Finland' in Nuotio K, Melander S and Huomo-Kettunen M (eds), *Introduction to Finnish Law and Legal Culture* (Publications of the Faculty of Law University of Helsinki 2012)

—— 'Panorama of World's Legal Systems – Focusing on Finland' in Nuotio K, Melander S and Huomo-Kettunen M (eds), *Introduction to Finnish Law and Legal Culture* (Publications of the Faculty of Law University of Helsinki 2012)

—— *A New Introduction to Comparative Law* (Hart 2015)

——, Nuotio K and Pihlajamäki H, 'Nordic Law – Between Tradition and Dynamism' in Husa J, Nuotio K and Pihlajamäki H (eds), *Nordic Law – Between Tradition and Dynamism* (Intersentia 2007)

Inger G, *Svensk rättshistoria* (Liber 2010)

Jutikkala E and Pirinen K, *A History of Finland* (6th rev edn, Werner Söderström Osakeyhtiö 2003)

Karhu J, 'Perusoikeudet ja oikeuslähdeoppi' (2003) no. 5 *Lakimies* 789

—— 'Lakien perustuslainmukaisuuden jälkivalvonta, perustuslain 106 § ja "Iijoki II" tapaus (KKO2006:71)' in Hurri S (ed), *Demokraattisen oikeuden ehdot* (Tutkijaliitto 2008)

Kari M, 'Korkein hallinto-oikeus, oikuesvalitotuomioistuin' in Kari M (ed), *Oikeusvaltion rakentaja. Korkein hallinto-oikeus 100 vuortta* (Edita 2018)

—— 'Syyttäjästä kehittäjäksi. Eduskunnan oikeusasiamiehen kehitys kansalais- ja perusoikeuskeskeiseksi' in *Eduskunnan oikesuasiamies 1920-2020. Satavuotta laillisuusvalvontaa ja oikeusturvaa* (Edita Publishing 2020)

Kekkonen J, *Johdatus kontekstuaaliseen oikeushistoriaan* (Helsingin yliopiston oikeustieteellisen tiedekunnan julkaisuja 2002)

Koulu R, Koulu R and Koulu S, *Tuomarin roolit tuomioistuimissa* (Alma Talent 2019)

Lavapuro J, Ojanen T and Scheinin M, 'Intermedia constitutional review in Finland: promising in theory, problematic in practice' in Bell J and Paris ML (eds), *Rights-Based Constitutional Review: Constitutional Courts in a Changing Landscape* (Edward Elgar Publishing 2016)

Leino-Sandberg P, Miettinen S and Leppävirta L, 'Har det nordiska rättsliga samarbetet en framtid i Europeiska unionen?' (2016) Vol. 19 No. 3 *Europarättslig tidskrift* 399

Letto-Vanamo P, 'Eurooppalainen oikeus Suomen oikeuden haasteena' in Viljanen V-P (ed), *Oikeudenalojen rajat ja rajattomuus* (Turun yliopisto 2002)

—— 'Internationella idèer och den nationella realiteten' in Kekkonen J and others (eds), *Norden, rätten, historia. Festskrift till Lars Björne* (Suomalainen lakimiesyhdistys 2004)

——'Rättsvetenskap och framsteg – de allmänna lärorna som verktyg för de finska juristerna' (2009) no. 3–4 *Tidskrift utgiven av juridiska föreningen i Finland* 400

—— 'Autonomy and heteronomy of the judiciary – a historical approach' (2011) vol. 1 no. 8 *Oñati Socio-Legal Series*

—— 'Finnish Judges Between Tradition and Dynamism' in Turenne S (ed), *Fair Reflection of Society in Judicial Systems – A Comparative Study* (Springer 2015)

——, Tamm D and Mortensen BOG (eds), *Nordic Law in European Context* (Springer 2019)

Lindblom PH, 'The Growing Role of the Courts and the New Functions of Judicial Process – Fact or Flummery?' *Progressive Procedure* (Iustus 2017)

—— 'The Role of the Supreme Court in Scandinavia' in Lindblom PH, *Progressive Procedure* (Iustus 2017)

Lindroos-Hovinheimo S, 'Finnish Legal Theory in the Twentieth Century' in Nuotio K, Melander S and Huomo-Kettunen M (eds), *Introduction to Finnish Law and Legal Culture* (Publications of the Faculty of Law University of Helsinki 2012)

Linnanmäki K, 'Mediation: A Change in Finnish Court Culture?' in Ervo L, Letto-Vanamo P and Nylund A (eds), *Rethinking Nordic Courts* (Springer, forthcoming)

Mäenpää O, 'Administrative Law' in Pöyhönen J (ed), *An Introduction to Finnish Law* (Kauppakaari 2002)

—— 'Tarkoituksenmukaisuus – vallanjaon rajapyykki?' in Hurri S (ed), *Demokraattisen oikeuden ehdot* (Tutkijaliitto 2008)

—— 'Deference to the Administration in Judicial Review in Finland' in Zhu G (ed), *Deference to the Administration in Judicial Review* (Springer 2019)

Malminen T, 'So You Thought Transplanting Law is Easy? Fear of Scandinavian Legal Realism in Finland, 1918–1965' in Husa J, Nuotio K and Pihlajamäki H (eds), *Nordic Law: Between Tradition and Dynamism* (Intersentia 2007)

Mattila H, 'Språket och den nordiska rättsfamiljen' (2005) no. 1 *Tidskrift utgiven av Juridiska Föreningen i Finland* 43

Meinander H, *A History of Finland* (Hurst & Company 2011)

Nylund A, 'Mixing Past and Future – the Making of a Nordic Legal Culture 1850–2050' in Sunde JØ and Skodvin KE (eds), *Rendezvous of European Legal Culture* (Fagbokforlaget 2010)

—— 'European Integration and Nordic Civil Procedure' in Ervo L and Nylund A (eds), *The Future of Civil Litigation. Access to Courts and Court-annexed Mediation in the Nordic Countries* (Springer 2014)

—— 'Conclusions on the Future of Civil Litigation in the Nordic Countries' in Ervo L and Nylund A (eds), *The Future of Civil Litigation. Access to Courts and Court-annexed Mediation in the Nordic Countries* (Springer 2014). DOI: http://dx.doi.org/10.1007/978-3-319-04465-1_20

—— 'Norway: An Insider Outside – or an Outsider Inside – European Civil Justice' in Nylund A and Krans B (eds), *The European Union and National Civil Procedure* (Intersentia 2016)

—— 'Structure of Civil Proceedings – Convergence through the Main Hearing Model?' (2018) Vol. 9 No. 2 *Civil Procedure Review* 13

—— 'Comparing the Efficiency and Quality of Civil Justice in Scandinavia: The Role of Structural Differences and Definitions of Quality' (2019) Vol. 38 *Civil Justice Quarterly* 427

—— 'Klima, miljø og domstoler i et komparativt perspektiv' in Fauchald OK and Smith E (eds), *Mellom jus og politikk: Grunnloven § 112* (Fagbokforlaget 2019)

—— 'Europeanisation of Nordic Civil Procedure – Does the Map Match the Terrain?' in Ervo L, Letto-Vanamo P and Nylund A (eds), *Rethinking Nordic Courts* (Springer, forthcoming)

Oikeusministeriö, 'Korkeimpien oikeuksien organisatorinen yhdistäminen – Hyötyjen ja haittojen arviointi', *Oikeusministeriön julkaisu 1/2015* (the Finnish Ministry of Justice 2015), available at https://julkaisut.valtioneuvosto.fi/bitstream/handle/10024/76569/om_1_2015_korkeimp_oikyhdist_154.pdf?sequence=1&isAllowed=y accessed 30 December 2019

—— 'Korkeimipien oikeuksien organisatorinen yhdistäminen. Lausuntotiivistelmä', *Mietintöjä ja lausuntoja 33/2017, Oikeusministeriö* (the Finnish Ministry of Justice 2015).

—— Tuomioistuinlaitoksen kehittämistoimikunnan mietintö. KM 2003:3 (Oikeusministeriö 2003)

Ojanen T, 'EU Law and the Response of the Constitutional Law Committee of the Finnish Parliament' (2007) 52 *Scandinavian Studies in Law*

Pihlajamäki H, 'Translating German Administrative Law: The Case of Finland' (2011) Vol. 19 *Rechtsgeshcichte* 267

——'Kansalinvälistymisen aika 1980–2018' in Pihlajamäki H (ed), *Lainkäyttöä läpi vuosisadan. Näkökulmia Korkeimman Oikeuden historiaan 1918–2018* (Edita 2018)

Pöyhönen J, 'The Law of Obligations' in Pöyhönen J (ed), *An Introduction to Finnish Law* (Kauppakaari 2002)

Ramberg C, *Prejudikat som rättskälla i förmögenhetsrätten* (Wolters Kluwer 2017)

Saarensola S, 'The Risk of Legal Costs and Its Effects on Access to Court' in Ervo L and Nylund A (eds), *The Future of Civil Litigation. Access to Courts and Court-annexed Mediation in the Nordic Countries* (Springer 2014)

Scheinin M, 'Constitutional Law and Human Rights' in Pöyhönen J (ed), *An Introduction to Finnish Law* (Kauppakaari 2002)

Siltala R, 'Prejudikaateista ja tuomarin prejudikaatti-ideologisasta' (1999) no. 5 *Lakimies* 674

—— *Oikeustieteen tieteenteoria* (Suomalainen lakimiesyhdistys 2003)

Siro J and Aaltonen M, 'Riita-asiat tuomioistuimissa 2000-luvulla' (2019) vol. 117 *Lakimies* 758

Smits JM, 'Nordic Law in a European Context: Some comparative observations' in Husa J, Nuotio K and Pihlajamäki H (eds), *Nordic Law – Between Tradition and Dynamism* (Intersentia 2007)

Sunde JØ, 'The Art of Internationalisation, or What is Nordic Law' in Husa J, Nuotio K and Pihlajamäki H (eds), *Nordic Law – Between Tradition and Dynamism* (Intersentia 2007)

Sunnqvist M, *Konstitutonellt kritiskt dömande. Förändringen av nordiska domares attityder under två sekel* (Jure 2014)

—— 'The Changing Role of Nordic Courts' in Ervo L, Letto-Vanamo P and Nylund A (eds) *Rethinking Nordic Courts* (Springer, forthcoming)

Suviranta O, 'Viranomaisen jatkovalitusoikeus, perustuslaki ja lainsäädännön kehittäminen' in Hurri S (ed), *Demokraattisen oikeuden ehdot* (Tutkijaliitto 2008)

Tamm D, 'Courts, law, language and culture' in Ervo L, Letto-Vanamo P and Nylund A (eds) *Rethinking Nordic Courts* (Springer, forthcoming)

Timonen P, 'Doctrine of the source of law of a scholar and of a judge', (1990) 34 *Scandinavian Studies in Law* 361

—— 'Sources of law and material on the sources of law' in Pöyhönen J (ed), *An Introduction to Finnish Law* (Kauppakaari 2002)

Tolonen H, *Pääsykoekirja 1/2003* (Turun yliopisto 2003)

Tontti J, 'Olaus Petri And The Rules For Judges' (2000) Vol. 4 No. 1 *Associations – Journal for Social and Legal Theory* 113

Tuori K, *Critical Legal Positivism* (Ashgate 2002)

—— 'Tuomarivaltio – uhka vai myytti?' in Heikkilä M (ed), *Säädöksiä, systematiikkaa vai ihmisoikeuksia?* (Acta Universitatis Lappeenrantaensis 2004)

—— *Ratio and Voluntas: The Tension Between Reason and Will in Law* (Ashgate 2011)

Viljanen J, 'The European Convention on Human Rights and the Transformation of the Finnish Fundamental Rights System' (2007) vol. 52 *Scandinavian Studies in Law* 299

Virrankoski P, *Suomen historia 1 & 2* (2nd rev edn, Suomalaisen Kirjallisuuden Seura 2009)

7. An Introduction to Estonian Legal Culture

Merike Ristikivi, Andreas Kangur, Irene Kull, Katre Luhamaa, Marin Sedman, Hesi Siimets-Gross, Age Värv

1. Introduction

The Republic of Estonia, in Estonian *Eesti*, is a country in Northern Europe, located in the Baltic region. The territory of Estonia covers 45,227 km^2,[1] it has 3,794 km of coastline and is bordered by the Baltic Sea and the Gulf of Finland. The neighbouring countries in the North are Finland and Sweden, in the South Latvia and in the East the Russian Federation.[2]

The history of Estonia is strongly influenced by the general history of Europe.[3] During the Northern Crusades, Estonia became a battleground for centuries. By the 13th century, Estonia was converted to Christianity and ruled by the Teutonic Order and the Danes. The Germans became landed gentry and wielded substantial influence over Estonia for the next 700 years. Territories of Estonia and Latvia became Medieval Livonia and the main towns were official members of the prosperous Hanseatic League. Tallinn, the capital of Estonia,[4] was granted Lübeck city rights in 1248,[5] under which also many local towns were governed until the end of the 19th century. The German invasion was followed by the rule of neighbouring kingdoms who were looking to expand their geographical influence and by the 19th century, Estonia had been governed by the kings of

---

1 The Tartu Peace Treaty of 1920 defined 47,549 km^2. The treaty between Estonia and Soviet Russia was signed on 2 February 1920, ending the Estonian War of Independence (1918–1920), and establishing the border between Estonia and Russia. From 1920–1945, the border with Russia extended beyond the Narva River and town of Petseri in the East. This territory (ca. 2,300 km^2) was incorporated into Russia at the end of World War II and remains today under Russian control.

2 The distance from Tallinn to Helsinki is 85 km, to Stockholm 405 km, to Riga 307 km, and to St. Petersburg 395 km.

3 On the historical development of Estonia, see Mati Laur, Tõnis Lukas, Ain Mäesalu and others, *History of Estonia* (Avita 2000); Andres Kasekamp, *A history of the Baltic states* (Palgrave Macmillan 2010).

4 Historically also known as Reval.

5 For more about Lübeck city law in Tallinn, see Tiina Kala, *Lübecki õiguse Tallinna koodeks 1282 / Der Revaler Kodex des Lübischen Rechts 1282* (Tallinna Linnaarhiiv 1998).

Denmark, Sweden, Poland and the Russian czar. In the middle of the 19th century, as a response to Russification, Estonians' national awakening began, laying the foundation to Estonian high culture and political self-determination.[6]

In the aftermath of World War I and the Russian revolutions, the Estonian Declaration of Independence was issued on 24 February 1918. The two-year War of Independence against Soviet Russia and German forces that followed came to an end in 1920 when Russia was also forced to recognize the Republic of Estonia as an independent nation. In 1940, Estonia was annexed by the Soviet Union as a result of the Molotov-Ribbentrop Pact. During World War II, Estonia was occupied by Nazi Germany in 1941, then reoccupied by the Soviet Union in 1944. On 20 August 1991, the Supreme Council of the Republic of Estonia adopted the Resolution on the National Independence of Estonia, reconstituting the pre-1940 state. On 28 June 1992, the Constitution of the Republic of Estonia was adopted by a referendum.[7] Estonia joined NATO on 29 March 2004 and the European Union on 1 May 2004.[8]

Estonia is a parliamentary democracy. The head of state is the president who is elected by the parliament (*Riigikogu*) or the electoral college for a term of 5 years. The president has mainly representative functions, although he still retains a number of executive powers. The president may veto a parliamentary bill and have it sent back for revision, and his signature is required when appointing the ministers of the government (*valitsus*). The president is also the supreme commander of the armed forces.

National legislative authority is vested in the parliament with 101 members elected for a term of four years. The executive power is exercised by the government headed by the prime minister. The parliament is empowered to appoint and recall the prime minister. As a counterweight, the government can make a proposal to the president to call new elections if the parliament expresses no confidence in the government. With cyber security and internet freedom at its core, Estonia's progress includes the development of the e-state, e-government and i-voting, a system that allows voters to cast their ballots from any internet-connected computer, anywhere in the world. In 2005, Estonia became the first country in the world to hold nationwide elections using this method, and in 2007, it made headlines as the first country to use i-voting in parliamentary elections. In the 2019 parliamentary elections, internet voting accounted for 43.7 percent of the votes cast.[9]

---

6 More about this political and cultural turn, see Toomas Karjahärm, 'The Awakening of the Estonian Nation: From its Origins to Independence' (2007) 3 *Revue d'Histoire Nordique = Nordic Historical Review*.

7 The Constitution of the Republic of Estonia (hereinafter referred to as "the Constitution"), Riigi Teataja (State Gazette), 1992, 26, 349. An unofficial translation of the consolidated Constitution is available at https://www.riigiteataja.ee/en/eli/530102013003/consolide accessed 13 April 2020.

8 Treaty of Accession of the Czech Republic, Estonia, Cyprus, Latvia, Lithuania, Hungary, Malta, Poland, Slovenia and Slovakia, European Union, OJ L 236, 23.9.2003.

9 The main bodies in charge of telecommunications regulatory issues are the Ministry of Economic Affairs and Communications (https://www.mkm.ee) accessed 13 April 2020, the Consumer Protection and Technical Regulatory Authority (http://www.ttja.ee/en) accessed 13 April 2020, and the Estonian Competition Authority (https://www.konkurentsiamet.ee) accessed 13 April 2020.

Estonia is divided into 15 counties and 79 local government units among which there are 15 cities and 64 rural municipalities. Each city and rural municipality (*omavalitsus*) have their own elected local representative and executive bodies.[10] Estonia's population is 1.328 million people, with a density of 30 inhabitants per square kilometre. The capital of Estonia is Tallinn with 445,175 inhabitants making up approximately 30% of the total population. Other large cities are Tartu with 95,334 inhabitants, Narva with 56,459, Kohtla-Järve with a population of 33,709, and Pärnu with 51,271 inhabitants. The municipal election term is four years. All permanent residents over 18 years old, regardless of citizenship, are eligible to vote in municipal elections.

Before World War II, Estonia was a relatively homogeneous society, and ethnic minorities constituted only about 12% of the total population. The migrant population was brought in during the Soviet rule from other parts of the Soviet Union. Today, more than 100 different nationalities and ethnic groups are represented in Estonia. The largest ethnic groups beside Estonians are Russians with 26%, Ukrainians 2%, and Belarusians and Finns each making up 1% of the Estonian population. Altogether about 420,000 people, or 31.4% belong to various ethnic groups other than Estonians.[11] All minorities living in Estonia have the right to preserve their language and cultural distinctiveness.

The official language in Estonia is Estonian, spoken by about 1.1 million people throughout the world. About 950,000 of them live in Estonia. The Estonian language belongs to the Finno-Ugric language family and is closely related to Finnish language. Although the rulers of Estonia changed several times during the 700 years of foreign occupations (Denmark, Germany, Poland, Sweden, and Russia), the strongest influence on the Estonian language was exerted by Low and High German.[12] The roots of about a quarter of the words that form the present day Estonian vocabulary can be traced back to Low German.

The oldest written records of the Estonian language date from the 13th century. The Chronicle of Henry of Livonia (*Heinrici Chronicon Lyvoniae*) contains Estonian place names, words, and fragments of sentences. The Reformation reached Estonia in 1523, the first known Estonian language book was printed in Lübeck in 1525 and had Lutheran texts in it. The oldest Estonian-language book of which actual fragments have been preserved is Wanradt and Koell's Catechism dated 1535. During the national awakening in the mid-19th century, the Estonian language rapidly advanced from being the spoken idiom of the peasants to becoming a cultural language; it began to be used in literature and science. During the Soviet Occupation (1940–1941 and 1944–1991), use of the Estonian language became one of the most powerful forms of Estonian identity, opposing the Soviet ideology.[13] After restoring the independence of the Republic of

10 For more about the local government system in Estonia, see https://www.rahandusministeerium.ee/en/local-governments-and-administrative-territorial-reform accessed 13 April 2020.

11 For more data, see the Statistics Estonia: https://www.stat.ee accessed 13 April 2020.

12 Especially strong was the influence of the Middle Low German that was the *lingua franca* of the Hanseatic League, spoken in the North Sea and Baltic Sea region.

13 For more about the development of the Estonian literary language, see Mati Erelt, *Estonian language* (Eesti Teaduste Akadeemia Kirjastus 2007).

Estonia (1991), Estonian is the only official language in the country's local government and state institutions.

Estonia can be considered a highly secularized country. Most Estonians do not belong formally to any religious organization. According to the census data of 2011, 9.91% of the adult population in Estonia considered themselves Lutherans and 16.15% considered themselves Orthodox. The Orthodox community in Estonia is divided between the Estonian Apostolic Orthodox Church and the Estonian Orthodox Church of Moscow Patriarchate. The relations between the two Orthodox Churches, one under the canonical jurisdiction of the Ecumenical Patriarchate and the other under the canonical jurisdiction of the Moscow Patriarchate, are complicated due to historical and legal/canonical reasons. All other Christian churches and religious associations have adherents comprising less than 1 percent of the population.[14]

Flexibility and openness are the characteristics of Estonia's economic policy. Balanced state budget, e-government services and liberal trade and investment laws have ensured Estonia's economic success. Since January 2011, Estonia has been a member of the Eurozone and the currency in Estonia is the euro. Estonia became the OECD's 34th member country on 9 December 2010.

GDP at current prices as of 2019 was 28 billion euros. Approximately 79% of Estonia's total trade was with EU member countries. Estonia's main trade partners are Finland, Sweden, Latvia, Russia and Germany. Main export articles are machinery and appliances, timber and wood products, mineral products, metals, transportation equipment, chemical products, textiles, and medical devices. Estonia is among the leading countries in Central and Eastern Europe in terms of foreign direct investments. The largest direct investments come from Sweden (28%) and Finland (22%). The most preferred fields of activity for foreign direct investment in Estonia are finance and insurance (29%), real estate activities (18%), and wholesale and retail trade (13%).

Estonia has become one of the most advanced e-societies in the world, often referred to as "e-Estonia".[15] For citizens of Estonia, e-services have become routine: e-elections, e-taxes, e-police, e-healthcare, e-banking, and e-school. In addition to its physical use, the ID card is also used to effect digital signatures. Moreover, one can also use a mobile-ID to identify oneself for online services. Estonia is the first country to offer e-residency, a government-issued digital identity and status that provides access to Estonia's transparent digital business environment. There are already 62,000 e-resident entrepreneurs using their digital rights to manage business from anywhere, entirely online.[16]

14 Merilin Kiviorg, *Law and Religion in Estonia* (2nd ed, Kluwer Law International 2016).

15 See https://www.e-estonia.com/ accessed 13 April 2020.

16 For detailed data, see https://e-resident.gov.ee/ accessed 13 April 2020.

2. Conflict resolution

In 1990, the administration of justice on Estonian territory was separated from the judicial power of the USSR and given into the sole competence of Estonian courts.[17] In October 1991, the Supreme Council of the Republic of Estonia passed the Republic of Estonia Courts Act and the Status of Judges Act.[18] These Acts were the foundation for the creation of a three-tier court system that was later included in the Constitution. Today, Estonia has a unified court system organized into a three-tier hierarchy.[19] The Estonian court system is comprised of district courts (*maakohtud*) and administrative courts (*halduskohtud*)[20] acting as trial courts, the circuit courts of appeal (*ringkonnakohtud*), and the Supreme Court (*Riigikohus*).[21] The specific regulations for all of these courts can be found in the Courts Act,[22] Code of Administrative Court Procedure,[23] Code of Criminal Procedure,[24] Code of Misdemeanour Procedure,[25] Code of Civil Procedure,[26] and Constitutional Review Court Procedure Act.[27] Although the Constitution provides the possibility of creating specialized courts for the adjudication of specific types of legal disputes, no specialized courts have been created. The creation of emergency courts is prohibited by the same constitutional article. City courts (also provided for in the Constitution) ceased to exist with the court reform of 2006, and district courts are the courts of first instance in both criminal and civil cases. Consequently, the organization of Estonian courts is quite simple.

District courts hear all civil, criminal and misdemeanour matters. There are four district courts in Estonia with approximately 150 judges and courthouses located in each county. In most courthouses the judges are specialized in either civil or criminal and misdemeanour matters. The code of criminal procedure, however, provides that

17 Principles of Temporary Procedure of Estonian Government Act, 16.05.1990 https://www.riigiteataja.ee/akt/24030 accessed 13 April 2020.

18 The Republic of Estonia Courts Act, Riigi Teataja 1991, 38, 472, and the Status of Judges Act, Riigi Teataja 1991, 38, 473, see https://www.riigiteataja.ee/akt/30561 accessed 13 April 2020.

19 Ülle Madise, Berit Aaviksoo, Hent Kalmo and others, *Eesti Vabariigi Põhiseadus. Kommenteeritud väljaanne* (Juura 2012) Art. 149 commentary no. 3.

20 On the establishment and development of Estonian administrative procedure, see Ivo Pilving, 'Die Schaffung und Entwicklung der Verwaltungsgerichtsbarkeit in Estland' (2014) no. 21 *Juridica International* 46.

21 The fact that the Constitution names the specific courts that exist in the court system is quite rare. This was found necessary due to the lack of legal tradition. See Madise and others (n 19) Art. 149 commentary no. 1.

22 Courts Act, Riigi Teataja 2002, 64, 390. An unofficial translation is available at https://www.riigiteataja.ee/en/eli/527032019003/consolide accessed 13 April 2020.

23 Code of Administrative Court Procedure, Riigi Teataja 23.02.2011, 3. An unofficial translation is available at https://www.riigiteataja.ee/en/eli/521032019005/consolide accessed 13 April 2020.

24 Code of Criminal Procedure, Riigi Teataja 2003, 27, 166. An unofficial translation is available at https://www.riigiteataja.ee/en/eli/515052019002/consolide accessed 13 April 2020.

25 Code of Misdemeanour Procedure, Riigi Teataja 2002, 50, 313. An unofficial translation is available at https://www.riigiteataja.ee/en/eli/508042019014/consolide accessed 13 April 2020.

26 Code of Civil Procedure, Riigi Teataja 2005, 26, 197. An unofficial translation is available at https://www.riigiteataja.ee/en/eli/512042019002/consolide accessed 13 April 2020.

27 Constitutional Review Court Procedure Act, Riigi Teataja 2002, 29, 174. An unofficial translation is available at https://www.riigiteataja.ee/en/eli/508042019015/consolide accessed 13 April 2020.

a criminal offense and the civil action arising from that criminal offense can be adjudicated in the same proceedings. Administrative courts hear all administrative law matters as a first instance court. There are two administrative courts in Estonia with a total of 28 judges and 4 courthouses.

A circuit court or a court of appeal is the court of second instance. Circuit courts hear all appeals against judgments and appealable orders of district courts and administrative courts. There are two circuit courts in Estonia, with 29 judges serving in Tallinn Circuit Court and 16 in Tartu Circuit Court. Circuit courts are divided into specialized civil, criminal and administrative law chambers.

According to the Constitution, the Supreme Court is the highest court in the country and as such it is both the court hearing appeals from the circuit courts, as well as the court of constitutional review.[28] The lower courts can initiate constitutional review at the Supreme Court when they find that a piece of legislation is not in compliance with the Constitution. Similarly, certain higher public officials can initiate constitutional review proceedings at the Supreme Court.[29] In the European context, the Estonian system of constitutional review is quite rare since the highest court of general jurisdiction also serves as the constitutional court.[30] There are 19 justices on the Supreme Court and the court is divided into Civil, Criminal and Administrative Law Chambers; the Constitutional Review Chamber is composed of the Chief Justice and rotating members of the other chambers.

Figure 1 shows the structure of the Estonian Court system:

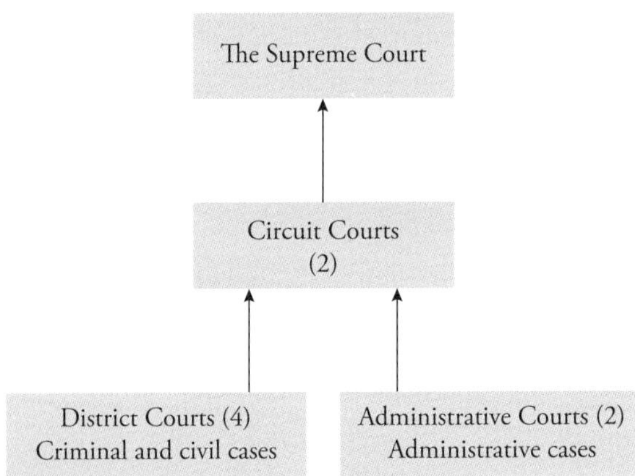

Fig. 1 The Estonian court system.

28 Julia Laffranque, 'The Judicial System of Estonia and European Union Law' (2005) vol. 33 issue 2 *International Journal of Legal Information* 227.

29 See Peeter Roosma, 'Constitutional Review Under 1992 Constitution' (1998) no. 3 *Juridica International* 25; Berit Aaviksoo, 'Judicial activism in constitutional review decisions of the Supreme Court of Estonia' (2007) no. 13 *Juridica International* 60.

30 Thilo Marauh, 'Supreme Court or separate constitutional court: the case of Estonia' (1999) no. 2 *European Public Law* 301.

For trial courts, the statistical data includes four types of cases: civil, administrative, criminal and misdemeanour matters.

Table 1 Caseload figures of trial courts[31]

Type of case	Number of cases 2016	Number of cases 2017	Number of cases 2018
Civil	30,048	30,068	29,134
Criminal	16,635	17,136	15,092
Misdemeanour	10,628	7,380	6,771
Administrative	3,123	2,967	2,477
Total	**60,434**	**57,551**	**53,474**

The total number of cases decided in the district courts has slightly declined during the years 2016–2018. Most of the district courts' caseload is made up of civil cases. Cases counted under "criminal" also include various pre-trial matters such as search warrants, wiretap warrants or pre-trial detention, as well as post-trial matters such as release on parole or probation violations.

Table 2 Circuit Courts

Type of case	Number of cases 2016	Number of cases 2017	Number of cases 2018
Civil	2,896	2,800	2,820
Criminal	2,273	2,097	1,935
Misdemeanour	214	171	138
Administrative	1,731	1,679	1,447
Total	**7,114**	**6,747**	**6,340**

Compared to cases originating in district courts, administrative law cases clearly stand out with a much higher percentage of the total docket in the appellate courts. Between 2016 and 2018, an average of 58% of administrative cases were appealed to the Circuit Courts from the courts of first instance. There are two main reasons for this. Firstly,

31 The data is based on the statistical information published by the Ministry of Justice: http://www.kohus.ee/et/eesti-kohtud/kohtute-statistika accessed 13 April 2020.

the filing fees in administrative matters are much lower than they are in civil matters.[32] Higher filing fees probably discourage appeals in civil cases. Secondly, according to the Ministry of Justice, 94% of all criminal and misdemeanour convictions result from proceedings not involving a trial (either a guilty plea or a blanket evidentiary stipulation). In those proceedings, the grounds for appeal are limited by law. Also, since the charges are essentially uncontested, the resultant conviction and sentence are the expected outcome readily accepted by both the defendant and the state.

The Supreme Court collects statistical data characterizing the work of the court with regard to the petitions filed with the Supreme Court in all four types of cases, and additionally constitutional review proceedings.[33]

Table 3 Supreme Court

Type of case	Number of cases 2016	Number of cases 2017	Number of cases 2018
Civil	172	194	155
Criminal	73	72	49
Misdemeanour	29	21	10
Administrative	97	85	76
Constitutional review	10	43	8
Total	**381**	**415**	**298**

The Supreme Court has discretionary jurisdiction and appeals to the Supreme Court can be taken on points of law only. There are two reasons why the Supreme Court might grant a leave for appeal:

1) if the circuit court has evidently applied a provision of substantive law incorrectly or has committed a material procedural error, and this could have resulted in an incorrect judgment, or
2) if the adjudication of the appeal by the Supreme Court has fundamental importance with respect to guaranteeing legal certainty and developing a uniform judicial practice.

All cases, regardless of their value or their complexity, start from district or administrative courts, except constitutional review proceedings not originating in the courts, or

32 State Fees Act, Riigi Teataja 30.12.2014, 1. An unofficial translation of the consolidated State Fees Act is available at https://www.riigiteataja.ee/en/eli/504062019006/consolide accessed 13 April 2020.

33 The data is based on the statistical information published by the Supreme Court of Estonia: http://www.riigikohus.ee/et/riigikohus/statistika accessed 13 April 2020.

petitions to review election results.[34] No proceedings begin in a circuit court, which is solely an appellate court. Such structure of the court system is quite rare in Europe, because in many countries, cases that are more complex begin from second instance courts, and in some cases the highest court solves the case as the first and last instance. Estonian constitution does not allow such flexibility.[35] The main reason for this is that the Supreme Court only reviews points of law and does not accept or review evidence. This in turn means that in order to secure the fairness of judicial proceedings, at least one court instance, the Circuit Court, should also review the fact-finding by the courts of first instance.

The rules for each type of case are different and set forth in the five relevant procedural codes. There is thus no single form of procedure for all courts or court cases. Because of specialization of lower court judges and the division into chambers of appellate courts and the Supreme Court, the seemingly unified court system actually works as three separate specialized three-tiered systems with the Supreme Court *en banc* topping the pyramid on rare occasions.

The proceedings in civil and administrative law cases at the trial level may but do not necessarily include holding a hearing. Depending on the nature of the case and sometimes contingent on the parties' consent, the disposition of civil and administrative law cases in first instance courts may be entirely by written proceedings. The same is true regarding appellate courts and while trial courts hold oral hearings in nearly all contested cases, circuit courts prefer to proceed in writing and have more latitude in denying litigants' motions for oral hearing. In criminal cases, district courts must always hold a hearing in order to ensure that criminal defendants are guaranteed a fair trial, or when they waive their right to trial, that the waiver is voluntary and informed. In criminal appeals, the appellate courts may proceed on briefs only, unless oral arguments or taking of supplemental evidence have been requested by any of the parties. As a rule, when a hearing is held, it will be in open court unless the matter is one where the Constitution allows for closed hearings (e.g. pertaining to minors, family relations, mental health or state secrets).

Since 2012, the Supreme Court has the right, in all five case types, to decide whether oral hearing is necessary. Oral arguments in the Supreme Court now only take place once or twice a year.

At the trial level, most cases are adjudicated by a judge sitting alone. Lay judges flank the trial judge in serious criminal cases; in especially complex or important administrative law disputes, the chief judge of the administrative court may assign the case to a three-judge panel. At the appellate level, appeals are decided by a panel of three judges. Similarly, the Supreme Court usually works in panels composed of three justices unless there is a reason to involve the entire chamber or assign the case to the court *en banc*.

All evidence as well as legal issues must normally be introduced at the trial level. Circuit Courts review lower court judgments and orders only to the extent specified in

34 Art. 4 section 2 of the Constitutional Review Court Procedure Act.

35 Madise and others (n 19) Art. 149 commentary no. 3.

the appeal (exceptions apply) and rely on the facts as established by trial courts unless the appeal alleges that the trial court's findings of fact are clearly erroneous. Where the appellant has successfully argued that the lower court incorrectly excluded or rejected evidence, the circuit court may also accept evidence that had been incorrectly rejected. In criminal matters, the circuit court will reverse appealed trial court judgment regardless of the scope of appeal if it determines that the trial court has committed a material error of procedure (such as when the criminal defendant was left without legal counsel or the case was decided by a judge who was not authorized to adjudicate the matter). The Supreme Court does not take evidence and only reviews questions of law; however, it occasionally engages in indirect fact-finding stating that lower courts have committed an error of procedure by drawing incorrect conclusions from the evidence.

In addition to courts, some disputes may be resolved by extra-judicial tribunals and in certain cases, an extra-juridical procedure is mandatory before the matter can be taken to court. The decisions of these extra-judicial tribunals are subject to judicial review. For example, the administrative review foreseen in the Public Procurement Act[36] is mandatory. If an applicant in public procurement has not contested the actions and decisions of the contracting authority with the Public Procurement Review Committee, a court will not accept the complaint.

In addition, parties in civil disputes can opt for mediation as provided for in the Conciliation Act.[37] Rules of court procedure also provide for referring a case to mediation if the court and the parties agree that mediation may facilitate a more expeditious resolution of the dispute. The Conciliation Act contains rules regulating and promoting recourse to mediation in civil law disputes. In the course of mediation, an impartial person (conciliator or mediator) helps the parties resolve their conflict in a series of meetings and other communications. The mediator may put forward his own proposal to the parties.

3. Norm production

Article 146 of the Constitution states that the courts administer justice in accordance with the Constitution and the laws. "Laws" do not mean only "statutes" but must be interpreted to include also other sources, which can be binding to a greater or lesser degree.[38] Legislative acts include laws that are passed by the legislative branch (such as statutes adopted by the Parliament or decrees of the President); legislative acts given by the executive branch (regulations of the Government and the ministers, regulations of the universities and regulations of the Bank of Estonia); and legislative acts (regulations) of the municipal governments.

36 Public Procurement Act, Riigi Teataja 15.03.2019, 1. An unofficial translation of the consolidated Conciliation Act is available at https://www.riigiteataja.ee/en/eli/525032019011/consolide accessed 13 April 2020.

37 Conciliation Act, Riigi Teataja 01.01.2010, 1. An unofficial translation of the consolidated Conciliation Act is available at https://www.riigiteataja.ee/en/eli/530102013028/consolide accessed 13 April 2020.

38 Madise and others (n 19) Art. 146 commentary no. 22.

The Estonian legal system was fully revised in the 1990s. In many cases, Germanic family of law was chosen as a model for the new laws.[39] In the field of private law this entailed drafting the civil code based on the pandect system consisting of the general part, property law, family law, law of succession, and law of obligations.[40]

Because of the urgent need for new law, the Soviet Civil Code of 1965 was gradually replaced with these five separate parts of the civil code. For that reason, it has been said that Estonia has an *imaginary* civil code, consisting of five parts made as separate acts.[41] The order in which the different parts of the civil code were adopted was determined by the urgency for regulation in respective areas. Thus, it was not the General Part of the Civil Code Act from 1994 which was issued first, but the Law of Property Act from 1993. This can be explained by the need to establish legal regulation covering immovable property ownership and other real rights.[42] The Family Law Act was adopted in 1994, the Law of Succession Act in 1996 and the Law of Obligations Act in 2002. Legal literature has promoted the idea of unifying these acts into a single code, but this view has not been supported since these legal acts function *de facto* as a single code.[43] Similarly, Estonia has a Commercial Code from 1995 which regulates the establishing, dissolution and activities of commercial undertakings, and the activities of sole proprietors. The tradition of codes is followed in other areas of law as well. As an example, the substantive criminal law is codified in the Penal Code of 2002, which has been influenced by German and French criminal law.[44] In 2011, the General Part of the Economic Activities Code Act was adopted, which regulates economic activities that require permits and registration. In 2007, codification of environmental law was initiated with the aim of systematizing the existing law, filling the gaps, abolishing discrepancies, and introducing necessary amendments.[45] In August 2014, selected provisions of the General Part of the Environmental Code Act came into force. In addition, codification projects have been initiated in the field of intellectual property law[46] and social security law.

At the same time, there are still many areas of law – such as state administration, taxation, agriculture, culture, sports, consumer protection, etc. – that are regulated by statutes. In 2017, the Parliament adopted or amended 122 statutes; in 2018, it passed

39 Paul Varul, 'Legal Policy Decisions and Choices in the Creation of New Private Law in Estonia' (2000) no. 5 *Juridica International* 107; Harri Mikk, 'Tsiviilõiguse reformist Eestis' in *Kinnistusraamatu- ja, notaripäevad 13.–15. mai 1999* (Justiitsministeerium 2000) 114.

40 Varul (n 39) 108.

41 Irene Kull, 'Reform of Contract Law in Estonia: Influences of Harmonisation of European Private Law' (2008) no. 1 *Juridica International* 124.

42 Paul Varul, 'The Creation of New Estonian Private Law' (2008) vol. 16 no. 1 *European Review of Private Law* 101.

43 Varul (n 39) 118.

44 For details, see Jaan Sootak and Priit Pikamäe, 'Estonian Criminal Law: Reform as a Path to Independence' (2000) vol. 8 no. 1 *European Journal of Crime, Criminal Law and Criminal Justice* 70.

45 Hannes Veinla, 'Basic Structures of the Draft General Part of the Environmental Code Act' (2010) no. 1 *Juridica International* 131.

46 This project has the objective to review the copyright act and draft the industrial property code. See Aleksei Kelli, 'Intellektuaalse omandi kodifitseerimine: vajadused, võimalused ja töökorraldus' (2012) no. 7 *Juridica* 483.

or amended 148 statutes; and in 2019, the respective number was 83.[47] All legislative instruments are published in the official online publication Riigi Teataja (State Gazette).[48]

Article 2 of the Constitution of the Republic of Estonia Amendment Act provides that when Estonia has acceded to the European Union, the Constitution of the Republic of Estonia is applied without prejudice to the rights and obligations arising from the Accession Treaty. This means that EU law is viewed as part of Estonian legal system.[49]

Historically developed general principles of law are also a source of law, which serve as guidelines for implementation and interpretation of legal norms, and as a filler of possible gaps in regulation.[50] Article 3 of the Constitution states that generally recognized principles and rules of international law are an inseparable part of the Estonian legal system whereas Article 123 states that Estonia cannot enter into international treaties which are in conflict with the Constitution, and when laws or other legislation of Estonia are in conflict with an international treaty ratified by the Parliament, provisions of the international treaty apply. It follows that the Constitution distinguishes between two types of binding international law: general principles of international law, and international treaties. The purpose of such an approach is to stress that a norm of international law may be binding for Estonia even in the absence of a specific treaty.[51] The Supreme Court has confirmed the duty to follow the norms of international law.[52]

Estonian legal system recognizes custom (*tava*) as a source of civil law. Article 2 of the General Part of the Civil Code Act provides *expressis verbis*: "(1) The sources of civil law are legislative instruments and custom. (2) Custom arises from long-term usage of a type of conduct if the persons involved in commerce consider it legally binding. A custom shall not override legislative instruments." It has been discussed in Estonian legal literature if rules of conduct laid down by representatives of one profession may be regarded as a source of law.[53] There is some Supreme Court case law supporting this position. For example, the court has found that since there is a special body that investigates and adjudicates allegations of ethical violations by the Estonian press, the rules under Code of Ethics of the Press are binding.[54]

In some cases, the binding nature of a custom is implied. As an example, the Law of Obligations Act (LOA) recognizes *lex mercatoria* and stipulates in Article 25 Section 2 that parties who enter into contracts with respect to their economic or professional activ-

---

47 https://www.riigikogu.ee/tegevus/tooulevaade/statistika/ accessed 20 March 2020.

48 See www.riigiteataja.ee accessed 20 March 2020.

49 Madise and others (n 19) Art. 146 commentary no. 23.

50 Ibid Art. 3 commentary no. 43.

51 Ibid Art. 3 commentary no. 42.

52 Judgment of the Constitutional Review Chamber of the Supreme Court of Estonia from 21.12.1994 no. III-4/A-10/94.

53 Irene Kull, 'Eesti tsiviilõiguse allikate tugev ja nõrk kohustuslikkus' (2010) no. 7 *Juridica* 463.

54 Judgment of the Civil Chamber of the Supreme Court of Estonia from 13.05.2005 no. 3-2-1-17-05. Based on the arguments of the Supreme Court in that case, it has been suggested that the code of ethics of the Estonian Bar Association can be viewed as another example of legally binding conduct rules, see Kull (n 53) 466.

ities are bound by any usage that persons who enter into contracts in the same field of activity or profession generally consider applicable and take into account. The exception is when application of such usage would be contrary to law or would be unreasonable under the circumstances. The LOA also awards binding nature to the practice that the contracting parties have established between themselves. There are several other statutes which expressly give normative meaning to custom in specific areas. For example, the Credit Institutions Act refers to "principles of sound banking management"; Article 65 Section 3 of the Railways Act mentions "good rail transport practices", and the Securities Markets Act talks about "good business practices".

In the 1990s, some jurists favoured the idea of expressly establishing court precedent as a source of law.[55] Initially , this idea did not find full support.[56] As an exception, Article 2 of the Code of Criminal Procedure (CCrP) stipulates that the sources of criminal procedure include judgments of the Supreme Court on issues, which are not regulated by other sources of law of criminal procedure, but which have arisen in the application of the relevant legislation. While it has been suggested in the scholarly writing that this provision should be interpreted to mean a limited binding force in line with the continental tradition[57], the Supreme Court in 2007 made clear that the principle of legal certainty dictates not only the binding nature of Supreme Court case law in procedural issues but a "factually binding force" with regard to substantive law issues as well.[58] The Supreme Court has explained that their legislative competence under CCrP Article 2 does not entail the right to create new coercive measures or to restrict fundamental rights in any other way that would be contrary to Article 11 of the Constitution.[59]

Supreme Court case law does not have such strong binding authority in any other area. The judgments of the Supreme Court are considered "weakly binding sources", since lower courts in fact take Supreme Court practice into account and usually follow it.[60] This means that the legal principle contained in the Court's reasoning may be considered part of legal doctrine and thus of the law.[61] A judge should consider following the holding of an earlier court judgment not so much due to the formal aspect but rather due to the persuasive character of its legal content. At the same time, it is undisputed that the courts have an important role in developing the law. This was especially true in the 1990s when the judges sometimes had to decide matters that were not yet precisely regulated. Legal literature shows that court judgments of that period have been an important basis for drafting new legislation.[62]

---

55 Rait Maruste, 'Kohtupretsedendist' (1994) no. 5 *Juridica* 116.

56 Raul Narits, Õiguse entsüklopeedia (Juura 2007) 69.

57 Meris Sillaots, 'Decisions of Supreme Court as a Source of Estonian Law of Criminal Procedure' (2001) no. 2 *Juridica* 142.

58 Judgment of the Supreme Court of Estonia from 01.04.2008 no. 3-1-1-101-07.

59 Judgment of the Criminal Chamber of the Supreme Court of Estonia from 25.10.2006 no. 3-1-1-17-68-06.

60 Kull (n 53) 471.

61 *Ibid*, 467.

62 Varul (n 39) 109; Irene Kull, Janno Lahe, Jaanus Ots, Maarja Torga, 'Riigikohtu tsiviilkolleegiumi praktika seadusandja mõjutajana' (2009) no. 8 *Juridica*.

Preparatory work of statutes is not a binding source of law. However, minutes of parliamentary discussions and explanatory letters accompanying the bills are considered helpful tools in interpreting the law as they help to identify intentions of the legislator.[63] The statutes drafted in the 1990s sometimes resemble textbooks because of their didactical style and a large number of legal definitions. After regaining independence, there was no tradition of publishing preparatory materials in Estonia, and this may have been the reason that actual texts of legislative instruments often contain references and explanations, that could have been left to the realm of explanatory memoranda.[64] Nowadays, the availability of preparatory materials has improved considerably: materials prepared by the drafters, including explanatory letters, research reports, opinions given by different institutions and records of parliamentary discussions are available on the web page of the parliament.[65]

The Estonian legal system has developed quickly under the influences of the ideas coming from other legal systems, and by receiving legal transplants. The Supreme Court has stated in several judgments that foreign legal acts, court practice, and legal doctrines can be taken into account when interpreting Estonian law. This requires, however, that the following conditions are met: 1) there is no Estonian case law and 2) the rules or legal system of the model country are similar to those in Estonia.[66] Such an approach makes the Estonian legal system open to the influences from other legal systems and facilitates the harmonisation of law in Europe. On the other hand, the Supreme Court has cautioned judges against uncritical referencing of foreign law and stressed that foreign law and legal literature can serve as a source of inspiration and information animating the court's reasoning but cannot take the place of domestic law. The court explained that the similarity of Estonian law to German law does not in any way legitimate abstaining from the principle that in Estonia the state power, including judicial power, is exercised solely on the basis of the Constitution and the laws of Estonia in conformity therewith.[67]

Scholarly writings are not considered a source of law in Estonia. Their function is to facilitate interpretation of statutes, i.e. they are used in finding the purpose and meaning of statutory language.[68] Nevertheless, scholarly writings can have a strong impact on court practice by suggesting arguments that can be used in the reasoning of judgments.[69] Until not too long ago, explicit references to legal literature in Supreme Court case law were scarce, but in recent years the Court has resorted to academic literature, especially statutory commentary, more frequently.

---

63 Narits (56) 155.

64 Marju Luts (now Luts-Sootak), 'Textbook of Pandects or New Style of Legislation in Estonia?' (2001) no. 1 *Juridica International* 158.

65 See https://www.riigikogu.ee/ accessed 20 March 2020.

66 See Judgments of the Supreme Court of Estonia from 21.12.2004 no. 3-2-1-145-04 and from 13.09.2005 no. 3-2-1-72-05, from 09.12.2008 no. 3-2-1-103-08 and from 12.10.2011 no. 3-2-1-90-11.

67 Order of the Criminal Chamber of the Supreme Court of Estonia from 13.06.2018 no. 1-17-11509.

68 Kull (n 53) 465.

69 Ibid.

4. Ideal of justice

The preamble of the Constitution summarizes that the Estonian state is founded on universal principles of "liberty, justice and rule of law" supporting the idea of universal liberty. On the other hand, the main aim of the Estonian state is according to the preamble, to preserve the Estonian people, the Estonian language, and the Estonian culture.[70] This aim presupposes the creation and development of a legal order which honours the principles of human dignity and social and democratic rule of law as required by Article 10 of the Constitution.[71] The Constitution contains a catalogue of rights, which reflects the basic values of Estonian society and legal system. As will be further discussed in Subchapter 7, such basic values accepted in Estonian legal culture derive, among others, from the European Convention on Human Rights and the Charter of Fundamental Rights of the European Union.[72]

Article 10 of the Constitution includes the principle of legal certainty, which entails both the clarity of the content of the law as well as the security that the established norms remain in force (the principle of legitimate expectation).[73] Legal certainty serves as the central principle according to which laws are made, interpreted and applied. The Supreme Court has pointed out in several judgments that the principle of legal certainty demands that a person must be able to adequately predict the legal consequences of his actions.[74]

The transformation to democracy and market economy that started in 1991 forced Estonia through rapid changes in all parts of the legal system within a relatively short time. Despite the relatively consistent and coherent system of written rules, which was achieved in most areas of law in cooperation between legislature, legal scholars and practitioners, the interpretation of legal rules was rather unpredictable. The courts were mostly criticized for methodological weaknesses, formalistic application of law, failure to apply the general principles of law and ignorance in using the concept of justice.[75] This Soviet legacy was gradually driven out by the introduction of a new legal culture through new laws. Predictable results in application and enforcement of legal rules as

70 Lauri Mälksoo comments on these two tensions (universal principle and preservation of national values) as expressions of Kantian-universal and Herder-patriotic ideas. See Lauri Mälksoo, 'Põhiseaduspatriotism – kas ka Eesti jaoks?' (2009) 10–11 *Vikerkaar*.

71 According to the commentary on Art. 10 of the Constitution, this article provides the basic values applicable to the whole legal system. The rights, freedoms and duties set out in that chapter do not preclude other rights, freedoms and duties which arise from the spirit of the Constitution or are in accordance therewith, and which are in conformity with the principles of human dignity, social justice and democratic government founded on the rule of law. Madise and others (n 19) Art. 10.

72 See more Julia Laffranque, 'European Human Rights Law and Estonia: One- or Two-way Street?' (2015) no. 23 *Juridica International* 4.

73 See Judgments of the Supreme Court of Estonia from 02.12.2004 no. 3-4-1-20-04; from 10.03.2008 no. 3-3-2-1-07; from 17.04.2012 no. 3-4-1-25-11; and from 12.04.2016 no. 3-3-1-35-15.

74 See Judgments of the Supreme Court of Estonia from 02.12.2004 no. 3-4-1-20-04; from 10.04.2012 no. 3-1-2-2-11, p. 67; from 16.03.2010 no. 3-4-1-8-09; and from 12.11.2016 no. 3-1-1-65-16.

75 Frank Emmert, Administrative and Court Reform in Central and Eastern Europe, (2003) vol. 9, issue 3 *European Law Journal*, 288.

one of the purposes of the legal system is directly related among others to the method used in drafting statutes. Namely, borrowing has been the main method of drafting new legislation and is still widely practiced.[76] Comparison of relevant laws of countries with similar legal systems in drafting legislation is often used as the starting point for both domestic legislative needs as well as transposition of EU legal initiatives into Estonian legal system. Relatively uncritical transposition of European law was characteristic during the transformation process[77] and has been replaced by a more critical attitude in recent years.[78]

The style of legislative instruments in Estonia can be described in general as rather detailed. This has an explanation; to a certain extent, it was caused by rapid changing of society and lack of legal literature and case law normally supporting and explicating the legislative text. Today, when Estonia has a developed tradition of jurisprudence and comprehensive case law, the didactic function of private law acts has lost its importance.[79] At the same time, judges obtained skill and knowledge how to use normative principles that have been incorporated into the legal system such as the principles like freedom of contract, reliability, reasonableness or good faith and fair dealing.[80] Today, the principle of good faith and fair dealing is considered one of the most important private law principles through which constitutional values and basic principles appear in private law. Through this principle, respect for fundamental rights and freedoms, justice, fairness, order, good faith, reasonableness and other values set out in the Constitution and arising from its substance can be protected.

Thus, Estonian legislation is a peculiar combination of extensively detailed rules together with definitions, open concepts, and broad terminology. The combination of the two styles in the early years of independence led the courts to use general principles rather than specific regulations of the law. After 20 years of court practice and legal scholarship, comprehensive doctrine and case law in many areas, the tradition in Estonian

76 For more about transplants in private law, see Varul (n 39) 104; Martin Käerdi, 'Estonia and the New Civil Law' in Hector L. MacQueen, Antoni Vaquer and Santiago Espiau Espiau (eds), *Regional Private Laws and Codification in Europe* (Cambridge University Press 2003) 250–251; Irene Kull, 'Codification of Private Law in Estonia' in Julio César Rivera (ed), *The Scope and Structure of Civil Codes* (Springer 2013) 133; Irene Kull, 'European and Estonian Law of Obligations – Transposition of Law or Mutual Influence?' (2004) no. 9 *Juridica International* 32; Villu Kõve, 'Draft Common Frame of Reference and Estonian Law of Obligations Act: Similarities and Differences in the System of Contractual Liability' (2008) no. 14 *Juridica International* 208.

77 On comparison with German lawyers, see more in Joachim Sanden, 'Methods of Interpreting the Constitution: Estonia's Way in an Increasingly Integrated Europe' (2003) no. 8 *Juridica International* 128, 139.

78 Assessment given by Hent Kalmo in 'Euroopa Liidu õiguse ootamatud mõjud' (2015) no. 2 *Juridica* 71.

79 Marju Luts-Sootak describes it as follows: "The Estonian reform laws generally stand out by their unusual text-book-like style. Firstly, it is evident in numerous legal definitions. The attempt to formulate legal definitions becomes apparent in all areas of law, not in private law only. Secondly, Estonian legislation stands out by the detailed nature of regulation." See also Marju Luts-Sootak, 'The certainty/stronghold of law, the world of yesterday and today's weather', speech delivered at the celebration of the 90th anniversary of the Supreme Court of Estonia, 14 January 2010. (https://www.riigikohus.ee/sites/default/files/elfinder/dokumendid/prof_marju_luts-sootak_2010.pdf) accessed 13 April 2020.

80 Principle of reasonableness is defined in Art. 7 of the LOA, principle of good faith in the Art. 6 of the LOA.

courts to apply general principles has produced more legal certainty and predictability in terms of both the outcome and legal method.

One of the possibilities to ensure legal certainty (sometimes also predictability) is *obiter dicta* of the judgments of the Supreme Court that can provide thorough explanations of a relevant area of law, hypothetical set of facts and explanations of how the court believes the law would apply to those facts, and even legislative proposals. These parts of the judgments are not officially binding but are regarded as a reflection of custom that contribute to the predictability of law.[81]

When trying to balance predictability and individual justice, the courts are ready to use a number of different interpretive methods to achieve justice between parties.[82] Particularly, the Civil Law Chamber of the Supreme Court has been willing to prioritize fairness over other policy considerations. There is extensive practice where principles of good faith and fair dealing are applied with the purpose of doing justice in individual cases without reference to earlier case law. The legislator has afforded the courts a fairly broad competence to ensure justice in individual cases under private law. It is still unclear whether and how far the courts can deviate from the explicit legislative intent in order to achieve a fair (but unpredictable) result. During the last 10 years, Estonian court practice moved from a relatively extensive application of the principle of good faith[83] including arguments of justice and fairness[84] to a more reluctant approach to the use of general principles and fairness considerations. On the other side, recent court practice shows that the general principle of objective good faith applies not only in contractual relations to protect the freedom of contract but also in other fields of private law (company law, labour law, property law, etc). One of the reasons might be that with some 25 years of legal tradition and case law under our belts, not too many completely unprecedented situations arose, and we have a reasonably fair solution ready in either statutory or case law. Finally, the application of the principle of good faith and fair dealing has created also preconditions for a better protection of constitutional values in private law.[85] This also demonstrates that legislation that contains numerous definitions, examples, and explanations, does not prevent courts from developing law by interpretation and application of general principles for the purposes of fair and equitable disposition of individual cases.

---

81 Irene Kull, 'Comparative Law in Developing Court Practice in Small Jurisdictions – Mission Possible' (2013) no. 43 *R.D.U.S.* 20.

82 Maarja Torga, 'Characterisation in Estonian Private International Law — a Proper Tool for Achieving Justice between the Parties?' (2011) no. 18 *Juridica International* 84.

83 For example, during recent years, in cases where consumers have difficulties providing evidence of usurious nature of a credit contract, courts tend to refer to the general principle of good faith, which could be applied *ex officio* and without any issues of the burden of proof. See more Karin Sein and Urmas Volens, 'Legal Problems and Regulations related to Easy-access Nonsecured Consumer Loans in Estonia' (2014) no. 22 *Juridica International* 131.

84 See Irene Kull and Sander Kärson, 'Consequences of implementing EU legislation: an Estonian experience' in James Devenney and Mel Kenny (eds), *The Transformation of European Private Law. Harmonisation, Consolidation, Codification or Chaos?* (Cambridge University Press 2013) 196.

85 Irene Kull, 'Unfair Contracts of Suretyship – a Question about the Horizontal Effect of Fundamental Rights or about the Application of Contract Law Principles' (2007) no. 12 *Juridica International* 36.

In conclusion, defining the ideal of justice in Estonian legal culture is not an easy task due to the short history of having a legal system based on the principles of rule of law. According to the case law and legal scholarship, legal certainty serves as one of the fundamental principles of the Estonian legal system. As in any other legal system, general principles become important interpretative tools in ascribing meaning to vague norms and as such play a crucial role in the development of the Estonian legal system. In addition, legislation provides courts a reasonable flexibility to adjust and develop legal practice that would guarantee both individual justice and predictability.

5. Legal method

Article 3 of the Constitution provides that in Estonia:

> "The state authority shall be exercised solely pursuant to the Constitution and laws, which are in conformity therewith. Generally recognized principles and rules of international law are an inseparable part of the Estonian legal system."

This provision forms the basis for the hierarchy of sources of law along with Article 146 that reads as follows: "Justice shall be administered solely by the courts. The courts shall be independent in their activities and shall administer justice in accordance with the Constitution and the laws." Article 104 in the Estonian Constitution provides a list of statutes that can be adopted and amended only by the majority vote of the entire parliament. The courts are also vested with the competence of constitutional review, i.e. courts refrain from applying statutory law that is in some respect unconstitutional, and the Supreme Court can declare any act void for unconstitutionality. This combination of constitutional provisions effectively establishes a hierarchy of legal norms where the constitution itself is at the top of the pyramid, followed by international law instruments, the constitutionally enumerated statutes enacted by the qualified majority vote, regular statutes, and executive regulations.

Estonian judges phrase their judgments and opinions impersonally and where a case is decided by a panel of judges, the opinion is always *per curiam*. In the Supreme Court (and in exceptional cases, also circuit courts), dissenting and concurring opinions are sometimes added to the majority judgment. Judges in Estonia prefer literal interpretation of statutory language where possible. However, when a legal problem is presented that does not have an immediate solution spelled out in the statutory law or the existing case law of higher courts, trial judges must get creative. Then judges first resort to the original explanatory letters accompanying the statute, and scholarly legal commentaries of the pertinent statute if available. If needed, they turn to the provisions of the Constitution. Where an immediate literal solution presents itself, trial courts rarely examine the underlying principles or constitutionality of a piece of legislation on their own without parties first raising the argument that something may be amiss. There may be several reasons for this, the most obvious are the heavy caseload of trial courts and the notion that courts primarily resolve disputes, thus where no dispute exists, there is no need for the courts to act.[86]

The Supreme Court is more inclined to engage in discussions about principles, especially where issues that are being adjudicated are novel and the court has set out to provide guidance for future cases.[87] Those opinions can feature lengthy discussions not only on the legislative intent but also on theoretical concepts and principles animating the law.[88]

Principles of substantive law are sometimes invoked as interpretive tools as well as primary sources of law in the absence of clear rules, at times with no reference to any statutory or other authority and one can only guess out of which hat they were pulled. Usually their true origin is German legal doctrine that the judges tend to use as an interpretive aid and inspiration for their arguments. The legitimacy of the statements of principle is somewhat redeemed by the fact that in Estonia, Supreme Court justices often tend to be involved in the legislative process as experts and the advisory opinions by the Supreme Court on proposed legislation are generally followed. The Supreme Court, especially its Criminal Law Chamber, also makes frequent references to the case law of the European Court of Human Rights (ECtHR) and the principles emanating from it.

Whereas judges and legal practitioners are generally well aware of case law and its significance, the technique of using it in legal reasoning is less refined than in common law countries. Case law is usually invoked after the statutory provision purporting to pertain to the dispute at hand has been located or found to be absent. One factor contributing to the lack of finesse in handling case law may be that the existence of case law in Estonia had been denied or ignored in legal education for many years. This in spite of the fact that for some 20 years the Supreme Court has been signalling that lower courts should heed the higher courts' case law. The Criminal Law Chamber of the Supreme Court even explicitly admonished lower courts and called it an unacceptable affront to legal certainty when lower courts ignore the Supreme Court's case law.[89]

Positive citations to case law in trial court judgments used to be rare but have become more common in recent years.[90] Where such citations are found, the argumentation rarely touches upon the specifics of the earlier case or engages in a methodical comparison of the facts in order to legitimise applying it as a precedent. This can be attributed to the writing style of the Supreme Court itself where the Court often abundantly cites its

86 In procedural sense, this notion has its limits, of course – certain actions would be initiated and adjudicated by the courts *sua sponte*.

87 In some instances, the Court offers guidance in loosely related issues as well, sometimes explicitly prefacing these notes as *obiter dictum*.

88 See, for example, Judgment of the Supreme Court of Estonia from 25.03.2004 no. 3-1-1-17-04, where the Supreme Court explained the law of self-defense or Judgment of the Supreme Court of Estonia from 30.04.2013 no. 3-1-2-3-12 where the Court created the legal framework for bridging civil law and criminal law in forfeiture of property cases.

89 Judgment of the Supreme Court of Estonia from 01.04.2008 no. 3-1-1-101-07.

90 I.e. where the court follows or extends earlier precedent. For practical approach on how to use precedent in Estonia, see Andreas Kangur, *Kohus ja Kohtulahend. Mõtteid ja soovitusi kohtulahendi kirjutajale* (Riigikohus 2012) 76.

earlier cases but usually does not explain why the facts are sufficiently similar. Unfavourable precedent is sometimes simply deliberately overlooked by the litigants, possibly in the hopes that the adverse party is not aware of the precedent due to insufficient research. The courts rarely spend time distinguishing precedent on their own but may explain based on the facts why the *ratio* of an earlier case is not applicable when the earlier case has been alluded to by one of the parties. The Supreme Court has also explicitly overruled its earlier precedent based on the finding that it is unsound.[91]

Estonian legal theory knows several different kinds of gaps or voids in regulation. Where there is a true gap, the reasoning process resorts to analogy or induction, which in essence boils down to the court creating the norm for the judgment, either based on a similar situation already covered by existing law or based on the goals and values as discerned from the current legal order. The courts usually have a duty to hear and decide pending legal conflicts unless the dispute is one that is not even supposed to be governed by law.[92]

Whereas analogy and induction are both generally valid routes towards resolving the legal matter in the absence of existing law, there are some generally recognised principles containing prohibitions against such forms of reasoning. Public authorities cannot induce norms permitting them to act. Substantive criminal law must also be confined to its literal meaning and actions cannot constitute crimes based on analogy or teleological induction.[93]

Where analogy or induction is resorted to, courts often go to great lengths to guise their creative exploits as mere interpretation of existing statutory law or precedent. This also means that often the policy goals underlying the choices made by the courts are not explicitly spelled out in judicial writing. Where the parties to litigation perceive there to be a legislative void or more often a contradiction tending to produce an absurd result, they are much more explicit about policy objectives in urging the court to support their position.

In most legal actions, the courts are bound by the facts alleged in the pleadings: while the court is free to apply any norm it deems applicable regardless of whether the parties relied on it or not, courts are usually not permitted to extend their fact-finding mission to facts not pleaded. Much more interesting is the issue of whether the courts consider the long-term implications of their judgments and whether the interpretation of the law is swayed by considerations of justice in the particular case. In many instances, the courts are explicitly directed to take the circumstances of the particular case into account. For

91 One of the examples is the Judgment of the Supreme Court of Estonia from 05.12.2014 no. 3-1-1-52-14, where the Court found that a person who is the sole shareholder and the director of a limited liability company cannot be convicted of embezzling his company's funds, and thus overruled its earlier precedent based on changes in the statutory law that had taken place and caused the earlier precedent to be no longer befitting the legal environment.

92 These days, the sphere of those disputes not meant to be regulated has shrunk to only a limited array of interactions between persons and just a bit broader area of activities of a person in relation to his surrounding environment.

93 This does not necessarily mean that courts apply the interpretation that is most favorable to the defendant. The inquiry regarding mistakes of law turns on whether the mistake was unavoidable for a reasonable person in the defendant's situation.

example, where the application of statutory law would result in breach of the good faith principle in civil matters, a court may, according to the Supreme Court, apply the good faith principle instead of the statutory provisions. Similarly, due to the hierarchy of the sources of law, international law instruments can at times play a pivotal role in reaching the judgment since they rank above national statutory law. The role of international and European law is further discussed under the section on Internationalisation below.

6. Professionalisation

The general attitude towards legal professionalisation in education is governed by two distinct features. First, there is a strong focus on a technically highly progressive and pragmatic application of law, still based on and valuing a positivistic and doctrinal approach to law. Second, legal education conveys a positive but not uncritical attitude towards international law, in particular EU and German law.

In 2019, there were three law schools in the public universities of Estonia that awarded Bachelor's and Master's degrees in law.[94] The oldest and most renowned for legal studies is the School of Law of the University of Tartu (*Tartu Ülikool*), which also has a campus in Tallinn since 2002.[95] The University of Tartu is the only university in Estonia that offers three levels of law programmes that cover all fields of law. The Tallinn campus offers bachelor's and master's level law programmes. The bachelor programme is taught in Estonian. Regular master's level studies are also in Estonian but there is an Information Technology Law programme offered in Tartu and a master's programme in International Law and Human Rights offered at Tallinn campus that are taught in English.[96] In 2019, there were 1,312 law students at the law school in Tartu and in Tallinn, including 52 doctoral students. The University of Tartu School of Law has 17 professors (including 4 visiting professors), 17 associate professors and 8 lecturers.[97]

The Tallinn University School of Governance, Law and Society was created in 2010[98] and has stayed an independent and autonomous academic institution of Tallinn University.[99] Since 2012, it has provided an opportunity to study law at the bachelor's level and international business law (2012–2018) at the master's level in Helsinki. In 2019,

94 Tallinn School of Economics (Tallinna Majanduskool) offers a legal services curriculum for legal assistants and specialists in legal matters for the enterprises which is a 3-year programme at the bachelor's level. See the English homepage of Tallinn School of Economics: https://tmk.edu.ee/en/ accessed 28 March 2020.

95 'Teaduskonnast', Homepage of School of Law of University of Tartu: https://oigus.ut.ee/et/teaduskonnast accessed 14 April 2020.

96 'About us', Homepage of School of Law of University of Tartu: https://oigus.ut.ee/en/about-us and 'Admissions', Homepage of School of Law of University of Tartu: https://oigus.ut.ee/en/admissions accessed 28 March 2020.

97 The 30 visiting lecturers for IT Law are not included in this number. 'Osakonnad', Homepage of School of Law of University of Tartu: https://oigus.ut.ee/et/teaduskonnast/osakonnad accessed 28 March 2020. The number of students is based on information provided to the authors by the Ministry of Education (on 4 November 2019).

98 Law School Nord was founded in 1991 and until 1998 called Private Bachelor School of Tallinn.

99 'Õigusteadus', Homepage Tallinn University School of Governance, Law and Society: https://www.tlu.ee/yti/oigusteadus#oppekava-ja--ained- accessed 28 March 2020.

there was a bachelor's level law programme in English with a possibility to specialize in International and European Law and Finnish law.[100] At the master's level, it is possible to study Human Rights in the Digital Society (LLM) in Tallinn.[101] In 2019, there were three professors, three associate professors, and twelve lecturers teaching around 440 law students.[102]

TalTech also has a Department of Law (*Tallinna Tehnikaülikooli Õiguse instituut*),[103] which offers programmes taught in English and specializing in Law and Technology and European and International Law. TalTech offers both bachelor's and master's programmes.[104] In 2020, the institute had 302 law students[105], two professors, two adjunct professors, three associate professors and eight senior lecturers.[106]

The nominal duration of a bachelor's programme in law is three years, a general master's in law takes two years to complete. A specialized master's programme such as the IT law programme at the University of Tartu may last only one year.

There is no specific requirement that a student must complete practical training or internship for a bachelor's degree in law. For a master's, the curriculum includes an obligatory practical training period of at least 6 weeks.[107] Nevertheless, bachelor's students of the University of Tartu law school have the option of choosing an internship lasting at least four weeks as part of their coursework.[108] In the Tallinn University School of Governance, Law and Society, the period of practical training at the bachelor's level can be 2–3 weeks and 4–5 weeks for master's level studies.[109] In the TalTech law school,

100 'Welcome to Study in TLU Law School in Helsinki', Homepage Tallinn University School of Governance, Law and Society: https://www.tlu.ee/en/yti/law#course-outline accessed 28 March 2020.

101 'Human Rights in the Digital Society', Homepage Tallinn University School of Governance, Law and Society: https://www.tlu.ee/en/yti/human-rights-digital-society#course-outline accessed 12 April 2020.

102 'Kontakt', Homepage Tallinn University School of Governance, Law and Society: https://www.tlu.ee/en/yti/human-rights-digital-society#academic-staff. The number of students is based on information provided to the authors by the Ministry of Education (on 4 November 2019).

103 The TalTech law school was first founded as a private university: the Concordia International University Estonia (CIUE) in 1996. Then CIUE merged with Audentes University in 2003. In July 2008, IUA merged with Tallinn School of Economics and Business Administration (TSEBA) of Tallinn University of Technology and from 2018 it has a new international acronym TalTech.

104 'Academic programs', Homepage of Department of Law of Tallinn University of Technology (TalTech): https://www.ttu.ee/?id=149472 accessed 12 April 2020.

105 The number of students is based on information provided to the authors by the Ministry of Education (on 4 November 2019).

106 'Staff', Homepage of Department of Law of Tallinn University of Technology (TalTech): https://www.ttu.ee/institutes/department-of-law/department-2/contacts-37/ accessed 12 April 2020.

107 'Menetluspraktika', Tartu Ülikooli õigusteaduskond: https://oigus.ut.ee/et/praktika/menetluspraktika accessed 12 April 2020.

108 'Õppepraktika', Tartu Ülikooli õigusteaduskond: https://oigus.ut.ee/et/praktika/oppepraktika accessed 12 April 2020.

109 'Praktikajuhend', Tallinna Ülikooli Ühiskonnateaduste Instituut: https://www.tlu.ee/yti/opingud/dokumendid-ja-juhendid#uldised-dokumendid accessed 12 April 2020.

a 4-week internship is optional at the bachelor's level and is mandatory at the master's level.[110]

A master's or a four-year bachelor's degree in law is required for Bar admission or an appointment as a public prosecutor, a notary or a judge.[111] In order to be admitted to the Bar, one must be sponsored by a fully licensed attorney-at-law and pass the bar exam. This confers upon the candidate the title of assistant attorney-at-law which is essentially an apprenticeship under the sponsoring attorney's guidance. An exam to become fully licensed can be taken after 3 years. Similarly, one must pass a qualifying examination in order to be eligible for appointment as a prosecutor or a judge. There is no common legal practice exam but mobility between the judiciary, private bar and the prosecutor's office is facilitated by mutual recognition of prior work experience in lieu of the exam.

In Estonia, one does not have to be an attorney in order to represent others in trial courts, however the same educational requirements still apply. As of 2020, the Estonian Bar Association had 1075 members. The number of non-licensed freelance practitioners is unknown. As a notable exception from the education requirement, the court may allow an in-house counsel in civil and administrative matters to appear regardless of law degree. Thus, even persons who have not completed their degree (e.g. law students) can be employed in private sector positions ordinarily reserved for people holding law degrees. In public sector, educational requirements are more stringent.

There are five law journals that are published in Estonia. The School of Law of the University of Tartu publishes the most influential Estonian law journal *Juridica* in Estonian,[112] and its English edition, *Juridica International*,[113] that introduces the Estonian legal system and development of legal thought to foreign readers. The Estonian Parliament publishes in Estonian their journal *Riigikogu Toimetised* (Acts of the Estonian Parliament), providing a forum for discussing the constitutional tasks of the Parliament and other public law matters. It is oriented towards politicians and everyone interested in politics, modern society, and governance.[114] In addition, there is a magazine *MaksuMaksja* (The Taxpayer) published monthly since 1997 in Estonian by the Estonian Taxpayers' Association. It includes instructive and educational articles and information by professionals in various fields.[115] The journal *Õiguskeel* (Legal Language) could also be classified as a legal journal since it deals with the problems of legal language and is a communal platform for lawyers and linguists.[116] In addition, 3,110 books were classified as

110 'Praktika üldine korraldus TalTechis', Homepage Department of Law of Tallinn University of Technology (TalTech): http://www.ttu.ee/tudengile/oppeinfo/praktika/ accessed 12 April 2020.

111 For example, according to Art. 15 (1) of the Prosecutor's Office Act, public prosecutors are required to have at least a master's degree or equivalent. The same requirement is imposed by the Courts Act Art. 47.

112 The journal and English summaries are available at https://www.juridica.ee/ accessed 13 April 2020.

113 The full name is Juridica International. Law Review. University of Tartu, available at http://juridicainternational.eu/ accessed 13 April 2020.

114 See the homepage of the Parliament: Ajakirjast: http://www.riigikogu.ee/rito/?id=10643 accessed 13 April 2020.

115 See the Estonian Taxpayers Association's homepage: 'Activities of ETA'. The journal is available at http://www.maksumaksjad.ee/modules/emlajakiri/index.php?op=mod&CID=1 accessed 13 April 2020.

116 See the journal at the webpage http://www.just.ee/et/oiguskeele-numbrid-2007 accessed 13 April 2020.

legal literature in the National Bibliography in the period 1991–2019; this number also includes editions of legal acts in book form.[117]

The degree of professionalisation in the Estonian legal culture is generally speaking high. Even though representing parties in court does not necessarily require a law-degree, court procedures are dominated by professional lawyers as are the institutions producing legal norms.

7. Internationalisation

As discussed above, Estonian legal culture, the Constitution and its institutions have a positive attitude towards international human rights law, international practice and the internationalisation of law. International human rights treaties have played an important role during Estonia's transition to democracy at the end of the 1980s and early 1990s.[118] First amendments to the Estonian Soviet Socialist Republic's constitutional documents in 1988 were based on international human rights instruments – the International Covenant on Civil and Political Rights,[119] and the International Covenant on Economic, Social, and Cultural Rights.[120]

Estonia was also looking for support from the international community and applied for membership in central international organizations like the United Nations, the Council of Europe, and the Organization for Security and Co-operation in Europe. The UN accepted Estonia as a member in 1991.[121] The same year Estonia signed the ICCPR and the ICESCR as well as numerous other UN human rights instruments.[122] The new Constitution was adopted in 1992;[123] international human rights treaties, and international experts, were of great influence in its drafting process. Estonia then joined the Council of Europe in 1993,[124] and the judgments by the European Court

117 According to the database of National Bibliography, available at https://erb.nlib.ee/ accessed 13 April 2020.

118 See e.g. Katre Luhamaa, 'Estonia: Transition Through Human Rights' in Vinodh Jaichand and Markku Suksi (eds), *60 Years of the Universal Declaration of Human Rights in Europe* (Intersentia 2009) 325. Generally, on the continuity arguments of Estonia, see e.g. Lauri Mälksoo, *Illegal Annexation and State Continuity: Case of the Incorporation of the Baltic States by the USSR: A Study of the Tension between Normativity and Power in International Law* (Martinus Nijhoff Publishers 2003).

119 ICCPR, United Nations General Assembly, United Nations, Treaty Series, vol. 999, p. 171 and vol. 1057, p. 407.

120 ICESCR, United Nations General Assembly, GA Res 2200A (XXI).

121 General Assembly of the UN, "Admission of the Republic of Estonia to membership in the United Nations", A/RES/46/4.

122 Eesti Vabariigi ühinemisest rahvusvaheliste lepingutega, mille depositaariks on ÜRO peasekretär, Riigi Teataja 1991, 35, 428, available at www.riigiteataja.ee/akt/13031565 accessed 13 April 2020.

123 See also Markku Suksi, *On the Constitutional Features of Estonia* (Åbo Akademi 1999); Caroline Taube, *Constitutionalism in Estonia, Latvia and Lithuania: A Study in Comparative Constitutional Law* (Iustus Förlag 2001) 79.

124 For a personal account on the accession to the Council of Europe, see Lennart Meri, 'Euroopa kui eesmärk', speech in the Council of Europe, Strasbourg on 26 November 1991, in *Presidendikõned, Eesti mõttelugu 9* (Ilmamaa 1996) 268.

of Human Rights have been binding for Estonia since 1996.[125] Estonia entered the European Union in 2004.

Article 3 of the Constitution stipulates that principles of international law form an inherent part of the Estonian legal system[126] thus making Estonia a monist country. Article 123 of the Constitution establishes international treaties as hierarchically situated below the constitution but above the domestic legislation. In 1998, the Supreme Court stated that if Estonian laws are in conflict with international agreements ratified by the parliament, the provisions of the international agreement apply.[127] This is especially true in relation to international human rights treaties since Article 10 of the Constitution expands the catalogue of basic rights with other rights, freedoms and obligations, which are in conformity with the Constitution and the principles of human dignity, social justice and democratic government founded on the rule of law. Thus, international human rights treaties can and have supplemented the non-exclusive list of basic rights included in Chapter 2 of the Constitution with other rights such as the right to good governance. Already in 1994, the Supreme Court observed:

> "When creating the general principles of Estonian law, the general principles of law developed by the institutions of the Council of Europe and the European Union should be taken into consideration alongside the Constitution. These principles have their origin in the general principles of law of the highly developed legal cultures of the member states."[128]

Estonian courts, including the Supreme Court, frequently use international human rights law arguments and instruments together with the case law.[129] The ECHR, the International Covenants and the European Charter of Fundamental Rights and practice of the relevant supervisory bodies are, therefore, the Court's main instruments that help to elucidate and interpret basic rights or support the court's argumentation.[130] In an individual matter, when the international treaty is clearer than the Constitution, the ratified

---

125 ECHR, Council of Europe, CETS No. 5. ECHR, Consolidated text in Riigi Teataja II 2010, 14, 54, available at www.riigiteataja.ee/akt/13320295 accessed 13 April 2020.

126 For an overview of the Government system of Estonia see e.g. Jüri Põld, Berit Aaviksoo and Rodolphe Laffranque, 'The Governmental System of Estonia' in Nóra Chronowski (ed), *Governmental Systems of Central and Eastern European States* (Oficyna Wolters Kluwer Polska 2011) 235.

127 Judgment of the Constitutional Review Chamber of the Supreme Court from 27.05.1998 no. 3-4-1-4-98, translation available at www.nc.ee/?id=461 accessed 13 April 2020.

128 Judgment of the Constitutional Review Chamber of the Supreme Court from 30.09.1994 no. III-4/A-5/94, translation available at www.nc.ee/?id=482 accessed 13 April 2020.

129 Eve Rohtmets, 'Case law of the European Court of Human Rights in Decisions of the Supreme Court of Estonia' (January 2012), available at www.riigikohus.ee/vfs/1364/Article%20by%20Estonian%20Supreme%20Court.pdf accessed 13 April 2020. On constitutional review see e.g. Roosma (n 29) 3.

130 René Värk and Carri Ginter, 'Estonia' in Leonard M. Hammer and Frank Emmert (eds), *The European Convention on Human Rights and Fundamental Freedoms in Central and Eastern Europe* (Eleven International Publishing 2012) 183, 188–90. See also e.g., *en banc* Judgment of the Supreme Court of Estonia from 04.02. 2014 no. 3-4-1-29-13, available at www.riigikohus.ee/?id=1499 accessed 13 April 2020; Judgment of the Constitutional Review Chamber of the Supreme Court of Estonia from 19.12.2019 no. 5-19-38.

treaty can be directly applicable. Direct implementation of an international treaty does not necessarily mean constitutional review; where domestic and international legislation are in conflict, the relevant court can bypass domestic legislation and apply the international treaty.[131] For an international law norm to be directly applicable, it must regulate internal relations, be clear enough and must not need additional national regulation.[132]

The supremacy of international treaties has been further crystallized with the accession to the European Union, when Estonia amended its Constitution with the following provision:

> "Estonia may belong to the European Union, provided the fundamental principles of the Constitution of the Republic of Estonia are respected. When Estonia has acceded to the European Union, the Constitution of the Republic of Estonia is applied without prejudice to the rights and obligations arising from the Accession Treaty."[133]

Accordingly, EU law takes precedence over national law as long as it is not in conflict with the basic principles of the Estonian Constitution. Since membership in the EU, the Estonian Courts have regularly applied both the EU legal acts as well as use the case law of the CJEU.[134] The Supreme Court has limited its rights in considering the constitutionality of the legal norms relating to EU law:

> "As a rule, the Supreme Court is not competent to review the constitutionality of a provision of an Estonian act of general application relating to EU law. Among other exceptions, the Supreme Court has this competence in a situation where EU law gives the Member States the right of discretion regarding the transposition and implementation of EU law, in the exercise of which the Member States are bound by their Constitutions and Constitutional principles. When EU law sets an objective to the Member States but leaves the measures for achieving it to be decided by the Member States, the measures chosen must conform both to EU law and the Estonian Constitution."[135]

In recent years, there has been some pushback from Estonian lawyers pointing out the need to clarify and limit the direct effect of EU law similar to "Solange-judgment" of

131 Translation by the authors. Judgment of the Administrative Law Chamber of the Supreme Court of Estonia from 02.10.2014 no. 3-3-1-47-14.

132 Judgment of the Administrative Law Chamber of the Supreme Court of Estonia from 20.12.2002 no. 3-3-1-58-02.

133 The Constitution of the Republic of Estonia Amendment Act, Riigi Teataja 2003, 64, 429, available at www.riigiteataja.ee/en/eli/530102013005/consolide accessed 13 April 2020.

134 See e.g. Carri Ginter, *Application of Principles of European Law in the Supreme Court of Estonia* (Tartu University Press 2008).

135 Judgment of the Constitutional Review Chamber of the Supreme Court of Estonia from 14.12.2010 no. 3-4-1-10-10, available at www.riigikohus.ee/?id=1215 accessed 13 April 2020.

the German Constitutional Court.[136] All this indicates that the Estonian legal culture in the last three decades has been impacted by an high degree of international impulses and internationalisation of law. In general, this implies a very positive attitude (though not entirely uncritical) towards internationalisation. The prominent place of German legal doctrine, EU-law and the case law of the ECJ and the ECtHR, in education, norm production and conflict resolution underlines this feature of the Estonian legal culture.

8. Conclusion

Estonia can be classified as a civil law country with strong Germanic influences, with codified legislation that serves as the primary source of law. In Estonia, case law has persuasive, but not formally binding authority. However, case law of the Supreme Court as well as of the CJEU and the ECtHR are increasingly regarded as precedents and applied at all national courts.

The Legal Culture and its structures and structural elements	
Institutional structure	
Conflict resolution	*Norm production*
Officially administrative and district courts serving as courts of first instance, two circuit courts of appeal and one supreme court make it look like a unified three-tiered court system. With the trend towards specialization at trial court level, and separate specialized chambers in the Supreme Court as well as circuit courts, it looks more like three separate hierarchies – administrative, civil and criminal court system with the Supreme Court 'en banc' occasionally acting as a common umbrella.	Statutory law is pervasive and its volume is increasing in spite of recent calls to curb norm production. Supreme Court case law is for practical purposes binding, especially in cases where no explicit statutory provision exists. General principles of law and scholarly writing are important interpretive tools, but not strictly binding sources of law. EU-law is a binding source of law, where directly applicable.

136 These views are best documented in Madis Ernits, Carri Ginter, Saale Laos, Marje Allikmets, Paloma Krõõt Tupay, René Värk, Andra Laurand, 'The Constitution of Estonia: The Unexpected Challenges of Unlimited Primacy of EU Law' in Anneli Albi, Samo Bardutzky (eds) *National Constitutions in European and Global Governance: Democracy, Rights, the Rule of Law* (T.M.C. Asser Press 2019) 887–950.

Intellectual structure			
Ideal of justice	*Legal method*	*Degree of professionalisation*	*Character of internationalisation*
Estonia is a country of rule of law and its legal system is based on the idea of legal certainty guaranteed by Art. 10 of the Constitution. Legal certainty means clarity of the content of the law in force (principle of legal clarity) as well as the security that established norms remain in force (principle of legitimate expectation). The principle of good faith is universally applicable, but due to a high value of legal certainty, courts are reluctant to apply it extensively.	Deduction from statutes and application of Supreme Court case law. Where no express statutory provision exists, courts use analogy and induce new norms for judgment based on general principles and legislative intent.	High degree of professionalisation. Legal education based on a positivistic and doctrinal approach, embedded in a progressive and pragmatic application of law. A 4-year bachelor's degree in law or 3-year bachelor's combined with 2-year master's is considered a basic qualification for admission to classical legal professions. No general law practice examination exists but mobility between different professions is encouraged through mutual recognition of entry examinations between judiciary, prosecutor's office and the Bar association. Bar membership is not required to represent others in trial courts.	High degree and positive attitude towards internationalisation of law and international impulses on the Estonian legal culture. Estonian legal order is monist, and, therefore, binding international law forms part of the domestic law. Both international treaties as well as the international court practice including the practice of the ECtHR and CJEU can be directly relied upon in domestic courts. National laws can be declared invalid by the Supreme Court if they conflict with international obligations.

9. Bibliography

Aaviksoo B, 'Judicial activism in constitutional review decisions of the Supreme Court of Estonia' (2007) no. 13 *Juridica* International

Emmert F, 'Administrative and Court Reform in Central and Eastern Europe', (2003) vol. 9, issue 3 *European Law Journal*

Erelt M, *Estonian language* (Eesti Teaduste Akadeemia Kirjastus 2007)

Ernits M, Ginter C, Laos S, Allikmets M, Tupay PK, Värk R, Laurand A, 'The Constitution of Estonia: The Unexpected Challenges of Unlimited Primacy of EU Law' in Albi A, Bardutzky S (eds) *National Constitutions in European and Global Governance: Democracy, Rights, the Rule of Law* (T.M.C. Asser Press 2019)

Ginter C, *Application of Principles of European Law in the Supreme Court of Estonia* (Tartu University Press 2008)

Käerdi M, 'Estonia and the New Civil Law' in MacQueen HL, Vaquer A and Espiau S (eds), *Regional Private Laws and Codification in Europe* (Cambridge University Press 2003). DOI: https://doi.org/10.1017%2Fcbo9780511495007.012

Kala T, *Lübecki õiguse Tallinna koodeks 1282 / Der Revaler Kodex des Lübischen Rechts 1282* (Tallinna Linnaarhiiv 1998)

Kalmo H, 'Euroopa Liidu õiguse ootamatud mõjud' (2015) no. 2 *Juridica*

Kangur A, *Kohus ja Kohtulahend. Mõtteid ja soovitusi kohtulahendi kirjutajale* (Riigikohus 2012)

Karjahärm T, 'The Awakening of the Estonian Nation: From its Origins to Independence' (2007) 3 *Revue d'Histoire Nordique = Nordic Historical Review*

Kasekamp A, *A history of the Baltic states* (Palgrave Macmillan 2010)

Kelli A, 'Intellektuaalse omandi kodifitseerimine: vajadused, võimalused ja töökorraldus' (2012) no. 7 *Juridica*

Kiviorg M, *Law and Religion in Estonia* (2nd ed, Kluwer Law International 2016)

Kõve V, 'Draft Common Frame of Reference and Estonian Law of Obligations Act: Similarities and Differences in the System of Contractual Liability' (2008) no. 14 *Juridica International*

Kull I, 'European and Estonian Law of Obligations—Transposition of Law or Mutual Influence?' (2004) no. 1 *Juridica International*

—— 'Unfair Contracts of Suretyship — a Question about the Horizontal Effect of Fundamental Rights or about the Application of Contract Law Principles' (2007) no. 12 *Juridica International*

—— 'Reform of Contract Law in Estonia: Influences of Harmonisation of European Private Law' (2008) no. 1 *Juridica International*

—— 'Eesti tsiviilõiguse allikate tugev ja nõrk kohustuslikkus' (2010) no. 7 *Juridica*

—— 'Codification of Private Law in Estonia' in Julio César Rivera (ed), *The Scope and Structure of Civil Codes* (Springer 2013). DOI: https://doi.org/10.1007%2F978-94-007-7942-6_6

—— 'Comparative Law in Developing Court Practice in Small Jurisdictions — Mission Possible' (2013) no. 43 *R.D.U.S.*

—— and Kärson S, 'Consequences of implementing EU legislation: an Estonian experience' in Devenney J and Kenny M (eds), *The Transformation of European Private Law. Harmonisation, Consolidation, Codification or Chaos?* (Cambridge University Press 2013). DOI: https://doi.org/10.1017/cbo9781139870559.012

—— and Lahe J, Ots J, Torga M, 'Riigikohtu tsiviilkolleegiumi praktika seadusandja mõjutajana' (2009) no. 8 *Juridica*

Laffranque J, 'The Judicial System of Estonia and European Union Law' (2005) vol. 33 issue 2 *International Journal of Legal Information*

—— 'European Human Rights Law and Estonia: One- or Two-way Street?' (2015) no. 23 *Juridica International*

Laur M, Lukas T, Mäesalu A and others, *History of Estonia* (Avita 2000)

Luhamaa K, 'Estonia: Transition Through Human Rights' in Jaichand V and Suksi M (eds), *60 Years of the Universal Declaration of Human Rights in Europe* (Intersentia 2009)

Luts M (now Luts-Sootak), 'Textbook of Pandects or New Style of Legislation in Estonia?' (2001) no. 1 *Juridica International*

—— 'The certainty/stronghold of law, the world of yesterday and today's weather', speech delivered at the celebration of the 90th anniversary of the Supreme Court of Estonia, 14 November 2019 (https://www.riigikohus.ee/sites/default/files/elfinder/dokumendid/prof_marju_luts-sootak_2010.pdf)

Madise Ü, Aaviksoo B, Kalmo H and others, *Eesti Vabariigi Põhiseadus. Kommenteeritud väljaanne* (Juura 2012)

Mälksoo L, *Illegal Annexation and State Continuity: Case of the Incorporation of the Baltic States by the USSR: A Study of the Tension between Normativity and Power in International Law* (Martinus Nijhoff Publishers 2003)

—— 'Põhiseaduspatriotism – kas ka Eesti jaoks?' (2009) 10–11 *Vikerkaar.*

Marauh T, 'Supreme Court or separate constitutional court: the case of Estonia' (1999) no. 2 *European Public Law* 301

Maruste R, 'Kohtupretsedendist' (1994) no. 5 *Juridica*

Meri L, 'Euroopa kui eesmärk', speech in the Council of Europe, Strasbourg on 26 November 1991, in *Presidendikõned, Eesti mõttelugu 9* (Ilmamaa 1996)

Mikk H, 'Tsiviilõiguse reformist Eestis' in *Kinnistusraamatu- ja, notaripäevad 13.–15. mai 1999* (Justiitsministeerium 2000)

Narits R, *Õiguse entsüklopeedia* (Juura 2007)

Pilving, 'Die Schaffung und Entwicklung der Verwaltungsgerichtsbarkeit in Estland' (2014) no. 21 *Juridica International* 46

Põld J, Aaviksoo B and Laffranque R, 'The Governmental System of Estonia' in Chronowski N (ed), *Governmental Systems of Central and Eastern European States* (Oficyna Wolters Kluwer Polska 2011)

Rohtmets E, 'Case law of the European Court of Human Rights in Decisions of the Supreme Court of Estonia' (January 2012) www.riigikohus.ee/vfs/1364/Article%20by%20Estonian%20Supreme%20Court.pdf.

Roosma P, 'Constitutional Review Under 1992 Constitution' (1998) no. 3 *Juridica International*

Sanden J, 'Methods of Interpreting the Constitution: Estonia's Way in and Increasingly Integrated Europe' (2003) no. 8 *Juridica International*

Sein K and Volens U, 'Legal Problems and Regulations related to Easy-access Non-secured Consumer Loans in Estonia' (2014) no. 22 *Juridica International*

Sillaots M 'Decisions of Supreme Court as a Source of Estonian Law of Criminal Procedure' (2001) no. 2 *Juridica*

Sootak J and Pikamäe R, 'Estonian Criminal Law: Reform as a Path to Independence' (2000) vol. 8 no. 1 *European Journal of Crime, Criminal Law and Criminal Justice.* DOI: https://doi.org/10.1163/15718170020519049

Suksi M, *On the Constitutional Features of Estonia* (Åbo Akademi 1999)

Taube C, *Constitutionalism in Estonia, Latvia and Lithuania: A Study in Comparative Constitutional Law* (Iustus Förlag 2001)

Torga M, 'Characterisation in Estonian Private International Law—a Proper Tool for Achieving Justice between the Parties?' (2011) no. 18 *Juridica International*

Värk R and Ginter C, 'Estonia' in Hammer LM and Emmert F (eds), *The European Convention on Human Rights and Fundamental Freedoms in Central and Eastern Europe* (Eleven International Publishing 2012)

Varul P, 'Legal Policy Decisions and Choices in the Creation of New Private Law in Estonia' (2000) no. 5 *Juridica International*

—— 'The Creation of New Estonian Private Law' (2008) vol. 16 no. 1 *European Review of Private Law*

Veinla H, 'Basic Structures of the Draft General Part of the Environmental Code Act' (2010) no. 1 *Juridica International*

8. An Introduction to German Legal Culture

Sören Koch

1. The framework of Germany's legal culture

1.1 Defining the German legal culture

From a historical point of view, it seems difficult to identify exactly what defines the German legal culture. In contrast to England, Norway or France it is not possible to determine the geographical boundaries of this culture more or less exactly. This is due to Germany's geographical position in the centre of Europe with just a few natural borders. Not even language can serve as a proper criterion to describe the frontiers of the German legal culture since both Switzerland and Austria have developed their own legal cultures. In addition, no real political unity was established until 1871. However, even after a central government was in place, the German *Reich* (Second Empire from 1871–1918) was still based on a federal structure, which left the different territories with wide-reaching legislative and political competences limiting the power of the central government. The federal character of its political and legal framework has been and still is a prominent characteristic of the German legal culture. In contrast to England and partly Norway, there has not been a consistent development regarding the institutions of conflict-resolution and norm-production until the late 19th century. The federal structure has consequences mainly for the institutional elements of the German legal culture. The complicated system of competences regarding norm-production and conflict resolution dealt with in Sections 2 and 3 of this chapter are a direct consequence of this feature. However, before we can go into details, it is necessary to take a look at the historical preconditions of the German legal culture.

From the Middle Ages until the early 19th century, the Holy Roman Empire provided a basic legal cultural framework.[1] However, it is not possible to draw a direct line from its institutions to the legal culture of Germany today. First, due to a lack of political power, the empire never managed to provide a comprehensive legal framework; no legal harmonisation or unity was gained in the territories. Besides the universal regimes of Roman law, canon law, and natural law, as well as a few statutes related to constitutional topics, there was almost no imperial legislation that had to be applied in all parts of the empire. In other words, one can hardly speak of a common norm-production. Second, the empire had never established an efficient institutional framework for conflict-resolution. Even though a supreme court (*Reichskammergericht*) was established in 1495, very few cases (relative to the number of cases solved in local and regional institutions all over the Empire) were actually decided there. In addition, the *Reichskammergericht* did not work efficiently most of the time.[2] Furthermore, several territories were given the privilege to decide cases related to the local laws in last instance (*privilegium de non appellando*).

However, from the end of the 19th century German legal culture can, more or less exactly, be identified as the culture related to the legal order of the German national state. Indeed, even the separation of Germany into two states in the period between 1948 and 1990 seems not to have had any lasting effect on the contemporary legal culture. In this survey I therefore refer to the culture of the territories in which German law is applied when speaking of German legal culture. This does not necessarily mean that the national borders are always completely identical with the cultural ones, especially when it comes to the intellectual elements of this culture.[3] However, regarding the institutional elements, the culture is so closely intermingled with the national state that the abovementioned limitation seems suitable.

On the other hand, taking into consideration that Germany is a federal state, one could question whether speaking of just one German legal culture is appropriate. Indeed, the states (*Länder*) have exclusive legislative competence in many fields of law. In addition, they are politically responsible for the education of lawyers and even have their own constitutional courts.[4]

Despite this diversion of competences and institutions, the most fundamental features of the German law are regulated on the federal level. The comprehensive codifi-

1 On the composition of the Holy Roman Empire, see Reinhard Zimmermann, 'Characteristic Aspects of the German Legal Culture' in Joachim Zekoll and Gerhard Wagner (eds), *Introduction to German Law* (3rd ed, Wolters Kluwer 2019) 2 f.; Hans-Peter Haferkamp, 'Holy Roman Empire' in Jürgen Basedow, Klaus J. Hopt, Reinhard Zimmermann and Andreas Stier (eds), *The Max Planck Encyclopaedia of European Private Law* (Oxford University Press 2012) 835 ff.

2 One can find an overview of the comprehensive legal historical research done on the *Reichskammergericht* in Peter Oestmann, *Ein Zivilprozess am Reichskammergericht* (Böhlau 2009) 1 ff.; Friedrich Battenberg and Bernd Schildt (eds), *Das Reichskammergericht im Spiegel seiner Prozessakten* (Böhlau 2010) 1 ff.

3 See Stephan G. Hinghofer-Szalkay, 'Twins or estranged Cousins? – Legal Methodology in Austria vis-à-vis Germany' in Ingvill Helland and Sören Koch (eds), *Nordic and Germanic Legal Methods* (Mohr Siebeck 2014) 223.

4 This does not apply for the state Schleswig-Holstein. All questions regarding the constitution of this state have to be solved by the Federal Constitutional Court (FCC) (*Bundesverfassungsgericht*). All other states have their own constitutional courts.

cations of civil, penal, constitutional, administrative, and procedural law, which are applicable anywhere in Germany, called the *Bundesrecht*, constitute a framework for the common legal culture. Federal legislation in these fields of law is furthermore required reading for law students all over Germany.

A first important observation concerning the nature of this culture is that federal legislation, structured in comprehensive codes, provides the basic principles of substantive law and the institutional framework for its application. Such elementary building-blocks of the legal system are rare to find in unwritten customs; for example, the prevailing opinion among constitutional lawyers is that there is no room for customary constitutional law.[5] Characteristic of the German way of legal thinking is a rather strong focus on written law as the main basis for conflict resolution. At the same time, this focus on written law is regarded as a prerequisite for legal certainty and equal treatment before the law.[6] The central significance of federal law as an accumulating and harmonising factor becomes even more evident when taking into account that the law of the *Länder* has to give way when it comes into conflict with law on the federal level.[7]

Finally, the question may arise whether European legal culture has become a part of the contemporary German legal culture to such an extent that it is no longer possible to separate them. It is certainly correct to claim that German law has in some areas lost almost all of its importance due to overriding EU law. However, so far this has not changed the character of the legal culture significantly. The ongoing process of internationalisation has apparently scratched neither the deeper levels of the national perception of law nor those of its legal cultural prerequisites. An increasing majority of lawyers in Germany consider law still a preponderant national issue. That Germany is one of the strongest supporters of the EU (but also one of its biggest beneficiaries) and that several proposals concerning the harmonisation of the law in Europe are based on initiatives of German scholars,[8] has not changed the prevailing scepticism regarding Union law in general. The particular object of criticism is the impact of EU law on the system of national law and its alleged coherence.[9] Still, compared to many other European countries, legal scholars have a quite positive attitude towards the ongoing Europeanisation of law.

---

5 Christian Tomuschat, *Verfassungsgewohnheitsrecht? – Eine Untersuchung zum Staatsrecht der Bundesrepublik Deutschland* (Carl Winter Universitätsverlag 1972). More open for the existence of unwritten constitutional law, Heinrich Amadeus Wolff, *Ungeschriebenes Verfassungsrecht unter dem Grundgesetz* (Mohr Siebeck 2000).

6 Ingvill Helland and Sören Koch, 'Norwegian and German Legal Methods Compared: Similarities and Differences, their Reasons and Consequences' in Ingvill Helland and Sören Koch (eds), *Nordic and Germanic Legal Methods* (Mohr Siebeck 2014) 277 ff. with further references.

7 The supremacy of federal law follows from the Basic Law (BL) (*Grundgesetz*) Art. 31: "Federal law shall take precedence over State law."

8 As an illustration, the Draft Common Frame of Reference (DCFR) is a project that is inseparably connected to Christian von Bar and his Study Group on a European Civil Code located in Osnabrück.

9 See e.g. Burkhard Hess, *Intertemporales Privatrecht* (Mohr Siebeck 1998); Roland Bieber, Astrid Epiney and Marcel Haag, *Die Europäische Union – Europarecht und Politik* (11th ed, Nomos 2015).

1.2 Historical, geographical and political preconditions

Now when we focus more thoroughly on the historical roots of this legal culture, it becomes clear how strong the link is between the contemporary legal culture and its historical preconditions. Because it was geographically positioned in the centre of Europe, other legal cultures occasionally gained influence over the whole or specific parts of the Holy Roman Empire and left their traces on the German legal culture.

Since the High Middle Ages, Roman law, as taught at the universities in northern Italy, became the object of reception. In the Empire, Roman law was even acknowledged a secondary source of law. It became quite usual for lawyers to study both the local laws and more general principles of Roman law. As this was a common feature in almost all of Europe, the contemporary interpretation of Roman law became known as *ius commune*. This *ius commune* held its central position in the German jurisprudence until the end of the 19th century.[10]

In the aftermath of the Thirty Years' War (1618–1648), parts of the Empire came under foreign control. In northeast Germany, the Swedish legal culture left its traces. In the early 19th century, in western parts of Germany, French legal thinking gained influence—especially after the Napoleonic Code was implemented in some areas west of the river *Rhein*. In addition, the different regions, territories and even some independent cities had their own customs, legislation, and judiciary. For many centuries, Germany was thus a melting-pot of different legal cultures rather than a unified one.

It was the self-imposed task of legal science, and not that of a legislature or a supreme court, to frame the law, legal unity, and eventually the national legal culture in Germany. The ideal of legal unity had strong roots in German legal theory ever since the 17th century. However, due to strong regional interests that prevailed then, even under the umbrella of the Holy Roman Empire, such a unity could not be achieved before the end of the 19th century. The rather unpolitical approach of the historical school (*Historische Rechtsschule*), with its main focus on the system and inherent logic of the law, made it possible to reconstruct a uniform law implementing solutions from different legal cultures. This approach may have been one of the reasons why German law became internationally so popular in the 19th and early 20th century. The German civil code called *Bürgerliches Gesetzbuch* (BGB) of 1900 was thus not just the creation of a prospering science focusing on Roman Law in its modern form (*Pandektenwissenschaft*), but at the same time can be regarded a product of legal harmonisation of different legal traditions

10 Jan Schröder, *Recht als Wissenschaft* (2nd ed, Mohr Siebeck 2012) 14 ff.

and legal cultures that existed in the former political independent territories united in the second German Empire (1871–1918).[11]

The same applies for a number of other codes that were enacted at the end of the 19th century. Already in 1877, a code on the organization of the court (*Gerichtsverfassungsgesetz*) and a civil and a criminal procedure code (*Zivil* and *Strafprozessordnung*) came into force. These codifications were shortly afterwards followed by a Code of Commerce (*Handelsgesetzbuch*) and a code on bankruptcy (*Konkursordnung*). All these codifications had one primary goal and that was to accomplish legal unity throughout the *Reich*. Legal science regarded itself as supervisor of this legislative process.[12] A complete systematisation of the law in all its different areas, based on logical deduction from universally applicable concepts (*Begriffsjurisprudenz*) was seen as the ideal.[13] Even though the enthusiasm regarding the jurisprudence of concepts faded rather quickly, the idea of the systematisation and inner logic of the law still has strong roots in German legal thinking, even though recently more hermeneutical approaches have also been discussed in Germany.[14]

Another important factor that has to be taken into account when considering the unique features of the German legal culture is the size of the population and – what is even more important – the population density.[15] Compared to Norway, there is an obvious difference in the total amount of inhabitants. Germany's population in 2019 was about 83 million, with a population density with an average of 232 persons per square

---

11 The situation of Germany before 1877 resembles in certain (but not all) aspects the situation of the European Union today. The diversity of legal systems within the borders of the newly established *Reich* had to be harmonised before a new unified legal order could be implemented. Since politics was not considered fit for this task, the construction of the law was mainly driven by an alleged unpolitical legal science that saw its task as reconstructing the whole legal order by identifying common features of the different legal orders involved by analysing their historical roots. A next step was adapting these features to the legal reality at hand and thus establishing a legal framework that was supposed to provide the necessary preconditions for a coherent legal system. Coherence of concepts in different codes and other legislation was regarded as such a precondition. In the 20th century this enterprise was often misleadingly described as jurisprudence of concepts ("*Begriffsjurisprudenz*"). The aim of most legal scholars in the 19th century was rather to establish a coherent framework from a multitude of overlapping legal orders than to deduce law mechanically from concepts. In the contemporary European debate concerning a common frame of reference in private law, some fairly identical ideas, approaches, and discussions can be observed. See on this the respective articles by Joachim Rückert, Hans-Peter Haferkamp, Ralf Seinecke, and others in Joachim Rückert and Ralf Seinecke (eds), *Methodik des Zivilrechts – von Savigny bis Teubner*, (3rd ed, Nomos 2017).

12 Hans-Peter Haferkamp, 'Historical Conditions for the Contemporary Understanding of Legal Method in Germany' in Ingvill Helland and Sören Koch (eds), *Nordic and Germanic Legal Methods* (Mohr Siebeck 2014) 88.

13 On the complex and often misleading label '*Begriffsjurisprudenz*', see Joachim Rückert and Ralf Seinecke, 'Zwölf Methodenregeln für den Ernstfall' in Joachim Rückert and Ralf Seinecke (eds), *Methodik des Zivilrechts – von Savigny bis Teubner*, (3rd ed, Nomos 2017) 42. See also Haferkamp (2014) (n 12) 87 f.

14 As a protagonist for this approach, Professor Gunther Teubner (born 1944) can be mentioned, see Philipp Sahm, 'Methode und (Zivil-)Recht bei Gunther Teubner' in Joachim Rückert and Ralf Seinecke (eds), *Methodik des Zivilrechts – von Savigny bis Teubner*, (3rd ed, Nomos 2017).

15 These elements refer to the wider concept of legal culture and are not part of the operationalised concept of legal culture as introduced by Jørn Øyrehagen Sunde, 'Champagne at the Funeral – An Introduction to Legal Culture' in Jørn Øyrehagen Sunde and Knut Einar Skodvin (eds), *Rendezvous of European Legal Cultures* (Fagbokforlaget 2010) 20; see also Jørn Øyrehagen Sunde, 'Managing the Unmanageable – An Essay Concerning Legal Culture as an Analytical Tool' in this volume, chapter 2, 27.

kilometre.[16] The population-density in Germany is thus more than 15 times higher than for example in Norway. One has to admit that this relationship is somehow misleading since the main part of the Norwegian population lives in just a few towns alongside the coastline. However, the significant deviation concerning population density may serve as an indicator of how close people live together and to which extent communication was and still has to be organised. Recognising that the contemporary legal culture is a product of a country's history, this is likely to have an influence on the culture of conflict resolution as well as other relevant factors in the legal culture.[17] Another significant factor may be the composition of the society. In Germany, one fifth of the population has an immigration background.[18] This makes Germany a country with a relatively high cultural divergence compared to many other countries in Europe.

Finally, the German legal culture has also been affected by the economic preconditions, requirements, and the specific structure of the federation's economic culture. Since the Second World War, this structure has changed drastically. While production and converting of raw materials were still dominant factors until the 1980s, this sector has lost much importance in favour of the constantly growing service sector. Today, the German economy rests mainly upon small and medium-sized businesses (*Mittelstand*). These businesses are often family enterprises that pass from one generation to the next. This implies that management as a rule not only tries to maximise the profit of the company, but is also interested in a sustainable development of the business that is supposed to be passed on to the next generation.[19] Predictability is thus seen as one of the most important values when it comes to all kinds of transactions. The legislature therefore seeks to provide a framework that is supposed to ensure the highest possible degree of legal certainty to support the basis of the German economy.

Thus, there are three specific extra-legal features of crucial importance when analysing the interplay of the different elements in the German legal culture in a comparative framework. These are: the federal structure, population density and composition, and the special economic and political position Germany traditionally has had in the centre of Europe and still has in the European Union.

16 Data based on the figures of the Federal Statistical Bureau (Statistisches Bundesamt) https://www.statistikportal.de/de/bevoelkerung/flaeche-und-bevoelkerung accessed 11 December 2019.

17 Furthermore, we have to bear in mind that just a few decades ago the population density in Norway was even much lower than today.

18 According to the Federal Centre for Political Education (Bundeszentrale für politische Bildung https://www.bpb.de/nachschlagen/Zahlen-und-fakten/soziale-situation-in-deutschland/61646/migrationshintergrund-i accessed 6 December 2019, the combined number of foreigners (9.9 million, 12.1%) and Germans with migration background (10.9 million 13.3%) is 25.5% of the total population of Germany.

19 Two of the most successful car-producers in Germany, VW and BMW, were family until recently enterprises.

2. Conflict resolution

2.1 Introduction

In this section, I will deal with the institutionalised mechanisms of conflict resolution. These are first and foremost organised in the ordinary court system.[20] In addition, there are other mechanisms of conflict resolution outside the judiciary. For the purpose of this section, the mechanisms of extra-legal conflict resolution are of minor interest and will therefore not be discussed in detail. However, it is worth mentioning that the German legislature has recently introduced and strengthened a number of instruments of mediation and arbitration. These are in some cases mandatory before a dispute can be brought to the ordinary courts.[21] The reason for the establishment of such instruments is to unburden the ordinary courts and to spare the parties the costs of the formal proceedings. In certain fields of law, such as commercial law, family law, and labour law, Alternative Dispute Resolution mechanisms have gained practical importance and are frequently used. Beyond this, the introduction of such extra-legal mechanisms of conflict resolution have not affected Germany's legal culture on a deeper level.

The court structure plays a significant role when it comes to explaining the specific features of the German legal culture. The structures of the court system are essential, for example when assessing the extent to which reliance on case law will produce predictable results or why case law is not recognised as a formal source of law except for some decisions made by the Federal Constitutional Court (FCC).[22] Furthermore, the construction of the system for conflict resolution – primarily the court system – will necessarily constitute an important part of the framework for providing legal security and by that have an effect on both the ideal of justice and the legal method applied in the different branches of the law.[23] In the following, I will therefore give a brief overview of the main characteristics of the German court system.

The graphic below gives a first impression about the complexity of the German judiciary.

20 For a brief overview of the German court system, see e.g., Udo Branahl, *Justizberichterstattung. Eine Einführung* (VS Verlag für Sozialwissenschaften 2005) 33–35, or Anke Freckmann and Thomas Wegerich, *The German Legal System* (Sweet & Maxwell 1999) 129 ff. Nigel Foster and Satish Sule give a more detailed introduction, see *German Legal System and Laws* (4th ed, Oxford University Press 2010) 66–88. In addition, there are some optional courts described in Art. 96 of the Basic Law. See Jörn Axel Kämmerer, *Staatsorganisationsrecht* (2nd ed, Vahlen 2012) 153–154.

21 On all forms of conflict resolution from a historical perspective and on a comparative basis, see Wim Decock and others (eds), *Handbuch der Geschichte der Konfliktlösung in Europa. Vol. I–III* (Frankfurt am Main, forthcoming).

22 Cf. Act on the Constitution of the Federal Constitutional Court (*Bundesverfassungsgerichtsgesetz*) § 31 (2).

23 Helland and Koch (2014), 'Norwegian and German Legal Methods Compared' (n 6) 267–322.

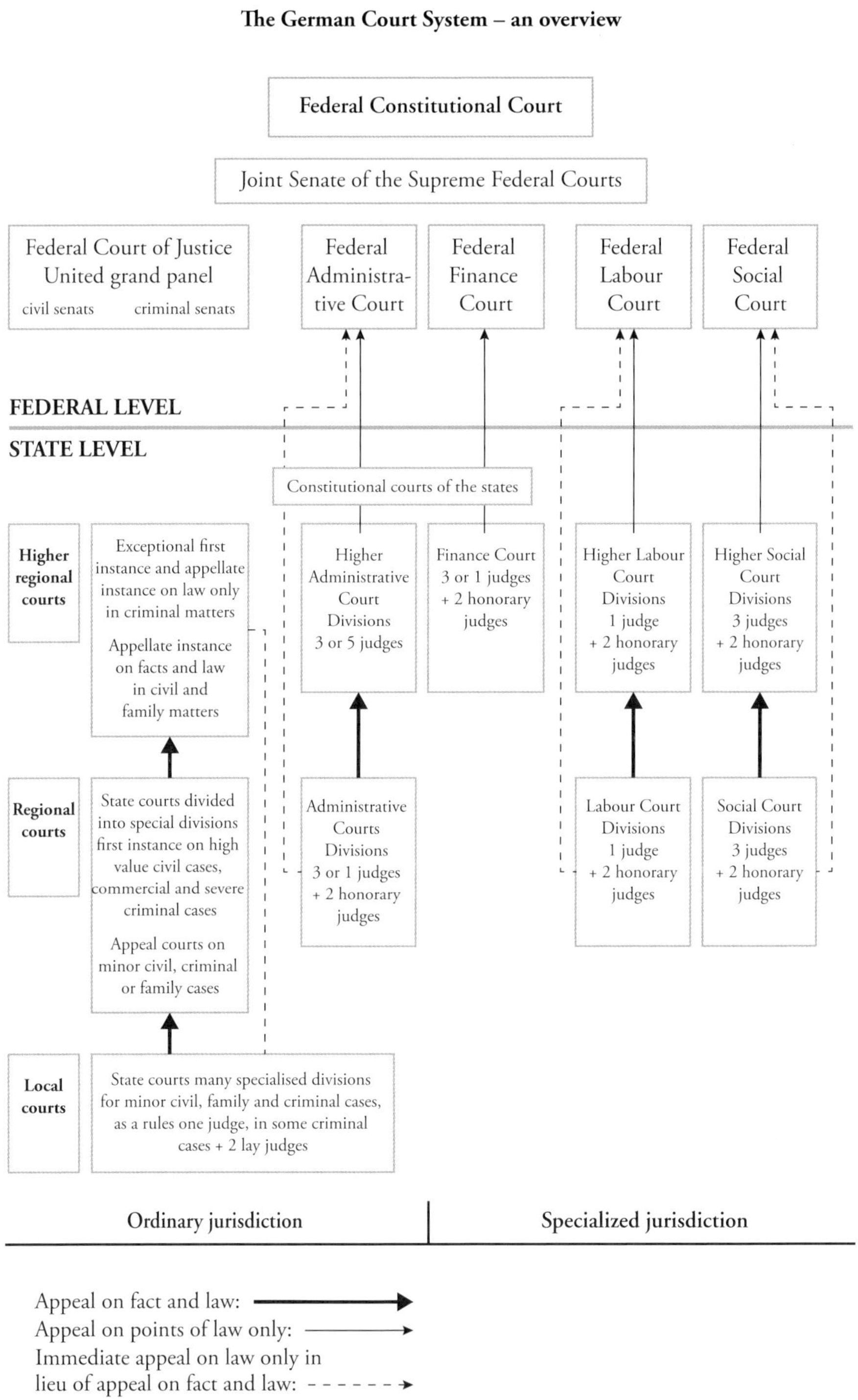

Fig. 1 The Courts of Law in the Federal Republic of Germany.

2.2 Ordinary courts

Article 20 (2) of the German the Basic Law (BL) – the *Grundgesetz* (GG) – states that the powers of the State come from the people, and shall be exercised by legislative, executive, and judiciary organs.[24] The basic principles governing the organization of the judiciary branch of government are described in Chapter 9 of the Basic Law, which entrusts the power of adjudication to judges, and states that it shall be exercised by the Federal Constitutional Court, the Federal Courts provided for in the Basic Law, and by the Courts of the States.[25] In other words, the competence of the courts has been divided vertically between the Federation and the States, and horizontally between several federal courts with their specific field of expertise.

The result is that unlike the US Supreme Court, the Swiss Bundesgericht, or indeed the Norwegian *Høyesterett*, there is no all-encompassing Supreme Court in Germany. Instead, there are five federal courts, each of which forms the head of its own hierarchy,[26] in addition to the Federal Constitutional Court.[27] Which court will act as the Supreme Court therefore depends on the area of law. In addition to the Constitutional Court, the Basic Law prescribes the establishment of separate courts for administrative law (*Verwaltungsgerichtsbarkeit*), labour law (*Arbeitsgerichtsbarkeit*), social welfare law (*Sozialgerichtsbarkeit*), and fiscal matters (*Finanzgerichtsbarkeit*), in addition to what is called the 'ordinary judiciary branch' (*ordentliche Gerichtsbarkeit*), which is headed by the Federal Court of Justice (*Bundesgerichtshof*) and deals with issues of civil and criminal law.[28]

Each court is further divided into chambers, senates, or divisions for the lower courts, whose competences may be divided further into specific areas of law in order to allow for specialisation of the judges. For instance, the *Bundesgerichtshof* (BGH) has ten senates dealing with civil law. Each Senate is responsible for a particular area of law within that field.[29] To name another example, the Federal Administrative Court has a senate especially dedicated to disciplinary cases.[30] This division of competences is not complete; competences may also be divided by other criteria such as the date the case was registered

24 BL Art. 20 (2): "All state authority is derived from the people. It shall be exercised by the people through elections and other votes and through specific legislative, executive and judicial bodies."

25 Translated into English by the author BL Art. 92: 'The judicial power shall be vested in the judges; it shall be exercised by the Federal Constitutional Court, by the federal courts provided for in this Basic Law, and by the courts of the states.'

26 See Basic Law Art. 95 (1).

27 The competences of the Federal Constitutional Court are outlined in Art. 93.

28 BL Art. 95.

29 See https://www.bundesgerichtshof.de/SharedDocs/Downloads/DE/DasGericht/Organigramm/organigramm.pdf?_blob=publicationFile&v=5 accessed 11 December 2019: I. Civil Senate: Intellectual property; II. Civil Senate Company Law; III Civil Senate: Liability of public Authorities and real estate agent law; IV Civil Senate: inheritance law; V Civil Senate: Real estate Law; VI Civil Senate: Tort Law; VII Civil Senate: Construction mandate law and Architect Law; VIII Civil Senate: Sales of goods law and lease of property; IX Civil Senate: Insolvency law; X Civil Senate: Patent Law; XI: Bank- and Security law; XII Civil Senate: Family law and Protection of industrial Property.

30 See http://www.bverwg.de/en/rechtsprechung/verwaltungsgerichtsbarkeit/aufbau-der-verwaltungsgerichtsbarkeit accessed 11 December 2019.

with the court, or the first letters of the parties' surnames.[31] The five senates which BGH has dedicated to criminal law have overlapping competences, since the cases are divided between them based on their geographical origins.

The introduction of a functional division in the court system on the federal level has a long history and can be traced back to 1873 when a special court for disciplinary (*Disziplinarhof*) matters was introduced.[32] Four years later, in 1877, the Constitution of Courts Act (*Gerichtsverfassungsgesetz* (GVG)) was enacted. Pursuant to GVG § 13, a Supreme Court (*Reichsgericht*) was established, competent to deal with all criminal and civil matters, including commercial law, in last instance. The internal organization of the Court resembles the idea of a functional specialisation since each chamber had its separate competences. A tradition for specialised courts mainly related to military jurisdiction[33] was continued by the establishment of a Supreme War Tribunal (*Reichsmilitärgericht*) in 1900.[34] Further supreme courts were introduced in 1918 (*Reichsfinanzhof*) and 1927 (*Reichsarbeitsgericht*).

Even though the Constitution of the Weimarer Republic (*Weimarer Reichsverfassung*) held provisions obligating the legislature to introduce a Supreme Administrative Court (*Reichsverwaltungsgericht*), due to political disagreements this Court was not established before 1941.[35] The official purpose for the introduction of a Supreme Administrative Court was to safeguard legal unity in the field of administrative law. However, another aspect was also emphasised by the constitutional committee in 1919: the establishment of a court with special competences was regarded as a necessary response to the increase and diversity of public responsibilities in the modern society. This implies indirectly that the judges in these courts would have a particularly high degree of expertise on the relevant field of law. A similar line of argumentation was applied regarding other specialised jurisdictions and it seems this opinion is still predominant in German legal literature today.[36]

Against this background, it is not surprising that the Basic Law was maintained in the German legal tradition even though a proposal to abandon all specialised courts

31 The *Geschäftsverteilungsplan* of the BverwG may be downloaded from this site: https://www.bverwg.de/rechtsprechung/geschaeftsverteilungsplan accessed 11 December 2019. The division of tasks is determined by the presidency of each court before the start of each professional year pursuant to the Court Constitution Act § 21.

32 Introduced by Reichsbeamtengesetz v. 31. 3. 1873 (RGBL p. 61).

33 Cf. § 176 of the Constitution of St. Paul's Church (*Paulskirchenverfassung*) enacted 28 March 1848 (which never entered into force).

34 Based on *Militärstrafgerichtsordnung* of 1 December 1898.

35 Based on the decree *Erlass des Führers und Reichskanzlers über die Errichtung des Reichsverwaltungsgerichts* 3 April 1941 (RGBL p. 201).

36 See the commentary on the Basic Law by Monika Jachmann-Michel, 'Art. 95' in Theodor Maunz and Günther Dürig (eds), *Bonner Kommentar zum Grundgesetz* (8th ed, C.H. Beck 2019) 88. EL August 2019 to Art. 95 para. 41: "Die Errichtung solcher Sondergerichte ist eng mit dem Wandel zum modernen Interventions- und Leistungsstaat verbunden, bedeutet die Herausbildung spezieller Gerichtsbarkeiten doch eine sachlich angemessene Reaktion auf die Zunahme von Staatsaufgaben. Im Interesse einer effektiven Wahrnehmung dieser vielfältigen Staatsaufgaben erschien es geboten, bestimmte Sachgebiete bzw. Personengruppen von vornherein einer bundeseinheitlichen Gerichtsbarkeit zu unterwerfen." See also Helmuth Schulze-Fielitz, 'Art. 96' in Horst Dreier (ed), *Grundgesetz Kommentar*, Bd. 3 (2nd ed, Mohr Siebeck 2008) para. 1.

and establish just one Supreme Court with an all-encompassing jurisdiction in accordance to the American model was discussed in the Constitutional Assembly (*Parlamentarischer Rat*). Because no agreement on this issue had been reached in this Assembly, the original version of the Basic Law still referred to just one Supreme Court (*Oberstes Bundesgericht*)[37]. This approach failed eventually because the majority of German lawyers regarded specialised courts to be a precondition for a sufficiently high degree of 'correct' application of the law. In addition, the members of the constitutional assembly had already been worried about the possible implications one Supreme Court would have on the authority of the newly established Federal Constitutional Court. Another objection was the *de facto* reduction of a three-level court hierarchy to a system that had only two regular instances. In 1950, the contemporary model with several parallel court hierarchies had already been re-established.[38]

Another interesting feature of the German legal culture becomes visible when we take a closer look at the caseload of the ordinary courts. In 2018, the *Bundesgerichtshof* decided 6,117 cases in the civil law and 3,651 in the criminal law branch. In addition, the Federal Administrative Court had to manage a caseload of approximately 1,300 cases, the *Bundessozialgericht* approximately 2,000 cases, the *Bundesarbeitsgericht* approximately 1,800 cases, and the *Bundefinanzgerichtshof* approximately 2,400 cases, altogether about 17,200 cases. These numbers have been more or less constant throughout the last years.[39]

The high degree of specialisation is accompanied by a high degree of professionalisation in the courts. In contrast to England and Norway, but also to France and Belgium, Germany has a comparatively low degree of lay participation in the judiciary. In 1924, the last remaining parts of a jury-system (*Schwurgericht*) were already abolished.[40] After the Second World War, lay-judges decided as co-judges together with their professional colleagues in certain proceedings before the labour-law courts[41] and commercial courts.[42] In these cases, the lay judges are as a rule representatives of special-interest organizations with specific knowledge of the respective fields (*Expertenricher*). In criminal proceedings,

37 The original wording of BL Art. 95 was still based on the assumption that the Federal Republic would have just one Supreme Court: "(1) Zur Wahrung der Einheit des Bundesrechts wird ein Oberstes Bundesgericht errichtet. (2) Das Oberste Bundesgericht entscheidet in Fällen, deren Entscheidung für die Einheitlichkeit der Rechtsprechung der oberen Bundesgerichte von grundsätzlicher Bedeutung ist. (3) Über die Berufung der Richter des Obersten Bundesgerichtes entscheidet der Bundesjustizminister gemeinsam mit einem Richterwahlausschuß, der aus den Landesjustizministern und einer gleichen Anzahl von Mitgliedern besteht, die vom Bundestage gewählt werden. (4) Im Übrigen werden die Verfassung des Obersten Bundesgerichts und sein Verfahren durch Bundesgesetz geregelt."

38 With an amendment of the Basic Law in 1968, the wording of Art. 95 was modified and the single Supreme Court also disappeared now officially. For further details on the amendments of Art. 95, see Jachmann (n 36) para. 56.

39 See https://www.destatis.de/DE/Themen/Staat/Justiz-Rechtspflege/Tabellen/gerichtsverfahren.html (updated 25 October 2019).

40 Emminger-Verordnung (Emminger ordinance) which changed the Criminal Procedure Code and abolished the so called '*Geschworenengerichte*'.

41 Cf. §§ 20 ff. Labour Law Court Act.

42 Constitution of Courts Act § 105.

lay judges (*Schöffen*) are included.[43] In the Higher Regional Courts (*Oberlandesgericht*) and at the federal level, no lay judges are recognised.[44] From a comparative perspective, it seems notable that lay judges in cases before the appellate courts are in minority.[45] However, a conviction cannot be based on the verdict of the professional judges alone.

2.3 The question of jurisdiction and legal unity

In principle, the procedure before the German courts is oral.[46] However, the legal reality is that written elements are often predominant in almost all fields of law. Details can be looked up in the procedural codes governing each branch of law.[47] These procedural codes also contain thorough provisions on the competences of the ordinary and specialised courts. The Courts Constitution Act (*Gerichtsverfassungsgesetz*) regulates the competence of each level of court. For example, some serious criminal cases are to be brought before a special chamber at the regional court (*Landgericht*),[48] which also has a second function as the court of appeal in minor criminal cases. These latter cases are dealt with by the local courts (*Amtsgericht*) in the first instance.[49] In civil law cases, the first instance is usually the local court, however if the value of the case (*Streitgegenstand*) exceeds Euro 5,000 the regional court has precedence.[50] Regardless of the value of the matter at hand, the local court has exclusive jurisdiction when a dispute concerns legal

43 See Constitution of Courts Act (Gerichtsverfahrensgesetz – GVG) §§ 29, 33a, 74 (2), 76.

44 Constitution of Courts Act § 122 and §§ 132, 139.

45 See figure 1 above.

46 Civil Procedure Code (Zivilprozessordnung – ZPO) § 128 (1): "The parties shall submit their arguments regarding the legal dispute to the court of decision orally."

47 Cf. for civil law the Civil Procedure Code (Zivilprozessordnung – ZPO) § 128 (2): "The court may give a decision without hearing oral argument provided that the parties have consented thereto; such consent may be revoked only in the event of a material change to the litigation circumstances. The court shall determine, at its earliest convenience, the deadline for written pleadings to be submitted, and shall determine the date of the hearing on which the decision is to be pronounced. A decision given without a hearing for oral argument is inadmissible should more than three (3) months have lapsed since the parties granted their consent." Also, for other types of resolutions oral proceedings are as a rule not necessary, cf. § 128 (4): "Unless determined otherwise, decisions of the court that are not judgments may be given without a hearing for oral argument being held." In addition, Civil Procedure Code §§ 253 contain the rules on filing a claim. This has to happen in writing.

48 Constitution of Courts Act § 74 (2); 74a; 74c.

49 Constitution of Courts Act § 24.

50 Constitution of Courts Act § 23 No. 1 in conjunction with Civil Procedure Code § 3, providing the Court with the right to rule on the value of the case on grounds of its own discretion.

issues with special connection to the local environment.[51] This applies e.g., to disputes concerning claims arising out of a lease of living accommodation or the existence of such a lease. On the other hand, the regional courts have exclusive jurisdiction regardless of the value of the matter concerning claims brought against the fiscal authorities on the basis of civil service regulations, tort claims against judges and civil servants, and several other specific actions.[52] Finally the Higher Regional Courts (*Oberlandesgericht*) have exclusive jurisdiction in the first instance for hearings and rulings on model case proceedings under the Act on Model Case Proceedings in disputes regulated by the Capital Markets Act.[53] In connection to the Volkswagen scandal, a new type of claim was established.[54] The so-called '*Musterfeststellungsklage*' (a variant of a class action) is based on a recommendation of the EU Commission from 2013.[55] It enables certain organizations to file class actions e.g., tort claims of a group of potential victims to be treated in a model trial. The procedure is highly controversial in Germany, because many lawyers perceive it incommensurable with the German legal culture. The powerful German Lawyers Association (*Deutscher Juristentag*) has disapproved the implementation.[56] One of the counter-arguments is that the German legal culture is not suited with 'American conditions' and a law-firm-driven culture of class action and punitive damages.[57] Others claim that such an instrument is necessary in any modern legal culture to efficiently handle specific types of claims that arise from the very conditions of globalised markets and the risks of damages affecting a high number of persons.[58]

Occasionally the questions of addressing the correct level in the court hierarchy are controversial or even decisive for the outcome of the lawsuit. The same applies when it comes to deciding potential conflicts of competence between ordinary courts and specialised courts or ordinary courts and administrative courts. For example, the question

---

51 Constitution of Courts Act § 23 Nr. 2. An exclusive jurisdiction of the local courts is established concerning the following disputes: disputes concerning claims arising out of a lease of living accommodation or concerning the existence of such a lease. The same applies for disputes between travelers and providers of food or lodging, carriers, shippers or passage brokers at ports of embarkation concerning bills for food or lodging, carriage charges, passage monies, carriage of travelers and their belongings and loss of or damage to the latter, as well as disputes between travelers and artisans arising on the occasion of travel; disputes pursuant to Section 43, Numbers 1 to 4 and 6 of the Condominium Act; disputes concerning damage caused by game and claims arising out of a contract for a life annuity, life endowment or life interest or for vacating of premises that is connected with the transfer of possession of a piece of land.

52 Courts Constitution Act § 71 (2).

53 Courts Constitution Act § 118.

54 See https://www.bmjv.de/SharedDocs/Gesetzgebungsverfahren/DE/Musterfeststellungsklage.html; https://www.bmjv.de/SharedDocs/Gesetzgebungsverfahren/Dokumente/BgBl_Musterfeststellungsklage.pdf;jsessionid=DC3B-3C50CBFBAB9642842F24A96FFA4B.2_cid324?__blob=publicationFile&v=1 accessed 11 December 2019.

55 Recommendation (2013/396/EU) of 26 June 2013 as part of the recent EU-policy "New Deal for Customers."

56 See the final statement here: https://www.djt.de/fileadmin/downloads/72/Beschluesse_gesamt_final.pdf accessed 11 December 2019.

57 See ibid para. C 15 and the underlying reasoning of the referent on this topic https://www.djt.de/fileadmin/downloads/72/72_thesen_180728.pdf accessed 11 December 2019.

58 For a comprehensive discussion of the legislative intentions and purposes as well as the underlying policy-considerations, see Martin Weimann, *Kollektiver Rechtsschutz – Ein Memorandum der Praxis [Collective Legal Protection: Notes from the Field]* (De Gruyter 2018) 14, 71 ff.

of whether a contracting party is an employee or an independent contractor will have consequences not just for the scope of the contractual obligations, but will also determine whether the case has to be decided by a labour court (*Arbeitsgericht*) or an ordinary court (*Amts-* or *Landesgericht*, depending on the value of the case).

A final interesting feature of the German court system is that the scope of a case depends on the specific level where the case is located in the hierarchy of courts. While the ordinary courts of first and second instance have to consider both evidence and law, the federal Supreme Courts' function is limited to consider whether the lower courts have applied the law correctly (*Revisionsinstanz*). The same applies usually for the High Regional Courts, except for cases where these courts are first or second instance. The system of ordinary courts thus primarily serves to provide for legally correct and predictable outcomes, safeguarded by a high degree of diversification and specialisation.

Diversification and specialisation can certainly contribute to safeguard legal unity within a relevant field of law. However, it may also contribute to the opposite outcome, when the case law of two courts or two chambers in the same court deviate. This may occur particularly where the competences of two or more subdivisions overlap. In this case, there is a risk of diverging jurisprudence, *inter alia* as a result of the courts' considerable caseload and the absence of a theory of precedent.[59] Diverging jurisprudence refers to the situation where two subdivisions of a court disagree on a matter of law over time, so that the outcome of individual cases vary depending on to which chamber or senate the case is assigned. A chamber may deviate from its own previous case law without particular justification, but should it wish to deviate from the case law of another chamber, a grand chamber must be called to settle the issue.[60] This presupposes, however, that the ruling chamber or senate is aware of the case law of the other chamber. Today, due to the thousands of rulings handed down annually by German courts, it is difficult to keep a complete overview of all potentially relevant case law. That one chamber or senate may on occasion come to deviate from the case law of another without immediately realising it, is therefore to be expected. The establishment of the Grand Senate is supposed to remedy this. However, pursuant to § 16 of the Federal Act on the unity of case law of the highest courts, the binding force of the judgment is explicitly limited to the case at hand. Accordingly, even the highest ordinary court on the Federal level has no competence to produce precedents. The very low number of cases actually decided by the Grand Senate,[61] seen in conjunction with the relatively high overall caseload of

---

59 Until the 1960s, the caseload of the courts was quite manageable. Diverging jurisprudence was therefore regarded as a minor problem and the idea to establish a special Supreme Court to handle those cases was rejected. Instead, a Grand Senate of all Federal Supreme Courts in Germany (*Gemeinsamer Senat der obersten Gerichtshöfe*) was introduced in 1968. The court was established by Federal Act (*Gesetz zur Wahrung der Einheitlichkeit der Rechtsprechung der obersten Gerichtshöfe des Bundes*) enacted 19 June 1968.

60 Constitution of Courts Act (*Gerichtsverfassungsgesetz*) § 132. The same applies for the highest courts on the state level (*Oberlandesgerichte*), in cases where they want to deviate from established case law of another high appeal court or of a federal supreme court. See Constitution of Courts Act (*Gerichtsverfassungsgesetz*) § 121 (2).

61 From 2000 till 2019 there have been only four rulings by the common Senate of all Federal Supreme Courts in Germany, this institution has therefore never gained the function of a Federal Supreme Court.

the Supreme Courts, indicate that the procedure before the Grand Chamber is of very limited practical importance. Consistency of case law is thus recognised as a legislative value, but the purpose is not to create a generally competent Supreme Court, but to avoid undesired side-effects of specialisation and diversification. This indicates that in Germany the value of specialisation is regarded even higher than that of legal unity.

2.4 The role of Constitutional Courts

Constitutional courts – on both the state and federal level – are relatively newly added institutions in the German legal system. They were introduced after the Second World War as a direct reaction to the total collapse of the former constitutional order of the Weimar Republic. When the National Socialist Labour Party (NSDAP) took office in 1933, the new government immediately began to abolish all democratic and fundamental rights without any noteworthy resistance from the established state organs, especially the judiciary.[62] It was mainly the influence of the Americans under the command of General Lucius D. Clay that led to the establishment of the federal order and constitutional courts in West Germany.[63] Both the competences of these courts and their internal organization show considerable similarities to the American Supreme Court. Lacking a tradition for such constitutional courts in German law, these institutions are based on a legal transplant. While the constitutional courts of the states have minor importance for the legal order today, quite the opposite is true when it comes to the Federal Constitutional Court. Considering the high esteem for this institution and its rulings, it may be justified to speak about an extremely successful example of a legal transplant.[64]

The Federal Constitutional Court's (FCC) main function is constitutional review of acts both by the legislature as well as the executive branch. It is no 'super revisions instance' (*Superrevisionsinstanz*) but controls exclusively whether an act of a state power is in concordance with the provisions of the Basic Law. By doing so, however, it sometimes changes the character of German law fundamentally, as, for example, was the case in the *Soraya* ruling.[65] The *Soraya* case concerned a claim for reparation of non-pecuniary damages suffered as a result of a grave and objectively serious violation of the plaintiff's right to privacy. Prior to this decision, German private law doctrine did not provide any remedies for non-pecuniary losses. Furthermore, the whole system of the Civil Codes was based on the assumption that tort law actions are limited to compensation of damages that can be measured economically. The Federal Court of Justice (*Bundesgerichtshof*) had nevertheless awarded a non-pecuniary compensation, relying on an analogy from

62 On this collapse from an inside perspective, see Sebastian Haffner, *Geschichte eines Deutschen – Die Erinnerungen 1914–1933* (Deutsche Verlags-Anstalt 2000).

63 Justin Collings, *Democracy's Guardians: A History of the German Federal Constitutional Court. 1951–2001* (Oxford University Press 2015) 71 ff.; Jutta Limbach (ed), *Das Bundesverfassungsgericht. Geschichte – Aufgabe – Rechtsprechung* (C. F. Müller 2000).

64 Concerning the debate on whether or not legal transplants are even possible, see Mathias Siems, *Comparative law* (2nd ed, Cambridge University Press 2018) 229 ff.

65 Bundesverfassungsgerichtsentscheidung (BVerfGE 34, p. 269 ff.)

§ 847 of the Civil Code. The FCC arrived at the same result, but argued that the right to privacy, as contained in Chapter 1 and 2 of the Basic Law, required a sufficient degree of protection by the civil law. Denying compensation for injuries of human dignity and honour was no longer regarded to be consistent with the Constitution's value system. The Court therefore interpreted the relevant provisions in the Civil Code in the light of these constitutional values.[66] Both the Federal Court of Justice and the majority of scholars[67] accepted this interpretation even though it was considered as an interpretation that was not in accordance to the wording of the Code, in other words an interpretation '*contra legem*'.[68] The system of the Civil Code seems to be flexible enough to sustain amendments contradicting the intentions of its draftsmen. Another contributory factor may be that the provisions of the Civil Code are highly abstract. They provide the legal practitioner with an opportunity and sometimes with a duty to interpret them in the light of values, which the legislator did not have had in mind when the Code was enacted. However, to adopt the law to changed social or political preconditions in such a radical manner requires the authority of the FCC. In the *Soraya* case, the Court's dynamic interpretation of the Basic Law's fundamental rights guarantees caused a paradigm shift in German tort law. In contrast to the ordinary courts of justice in Germany, the FCC is not bound by the constitutional limitation to legislation and law (*Gesetz und Recht*), which again underlines the court's political function.

That the FCC could gain such a central position in the legal system was facilitated by the constitutional principle obliging all other state powers to take the value system of the Basic Law into consideration.[69] The fundamental importance of these values gave rise to the argument that they also have an indirect horizontal effect on private relationships (*mittelbare Drittwirkung*).[70] Thus, the Basic Law is more than a mere framework of the state organization. It is not just a historical document but a living constitution and a dynamic instrument in the hand of the FCC and all other courts.[71] It has become a symbol for the Federal Republic of Germany, and a safeguard of democracy and freedom. The identity-creating function of the Basic Law was further facilitated by the reunification of the two German states in 1990. Despite the Basic Law's provisional nature, it became the constitution of the reunited Germany.[72]

---

66 BL Art. 2 (1) in conjunction with Art. 1 (1).

67 But there were critical voices as well, see e.g., Uwe Diedrichsen, 'Das Bundesverfassungsgericht als oberstes Zivilgericht – ein Lehrstück der juristischen Methodenlehre' (1998) Vol. 198 *Achiv für die Civilistische Praxis* 171, 172 ff.

68 For details on this case and its significance especially for the German legal method, see Helland and Koch (2014), 'Norwegian and German Legal Methods Compared' (n 6) 269 with further references. On *contra legem* interpretation in Norwegian law, see Ingvill Helland, 'The permissibility and (conditional) recommendability of *contra legem* interpretations in Norwegian law' (2014) Vol. 37 no. 1/144 *Retfærd* 17.

69 BL Art. 1 (3) and 20 (2).

70 This was established by the FCC in the *Lüth*-ruling BVerfGE 7, 198.

71 Interesting discussions on this topic contains Julian Krüper, Mehrdad Payandeh and Heiko Sauer (eds), *Konrad Hesses normative Kraft der Verfassung* (Mohr Siebeck 2019).

72 When the Basic Law was enacted in 1949, it was regarded as a provisional constitution, which was supposed to be replaced with a new constitution in case of a reunification of Germany and a final peace agreement with the Allies.

The FCC's core task is to safeguard the spirit of the new constitutional order in the German Federal Republic and at the same time to protect the free democratic basic order (*freiheitlich demokratische Grundordnung*).[73] As the watchdog over this national treasure, the FCC has won the respect of not just professional lawyers, but politicians and citizens alike.[74] No other political institution in Germany reaches a comparable degree of confidence in the population. Many of its decisions are made public and in addition are translated into English.[75] Being appointed a Federal Constitutional Judge is today regarded the highest award a lawyer can obtain.[76] As an illustration, the President of the FCC occupies the fifth highest office in the German Federal Republic.

The importance of the court is also reflected in its constantly increasing caseload. For the first years following its establishment, approximately 1,000 cases were filed annually with the FCC. Today, this number has increased to approximately 6,000. Because of this extreme increase, the Court is struggling to deal with its caseload. All cases are treated in a first round by a chamber (*Kammer*) constituted of three judges. The chambers, acting as access committees, dismiss about 95% of all claims of private actors (called *Verfassungsbeschwerde*). Just 1.9% of all *Verfassungsbeschwerden*, which amounts to 99.5% of all cases reaching the FCC, are successful.[77]

A judgment of the Federal Constitutional Court from December 2014 may illustrate its wide-reaching political influence today.[78] It has been mentioned above that one feature of German legislation is to facilitate the traditional German business culture. Although the FCC accepts and advocates this policy, the Court has recently extended its competences in review to the core of the legislature's task, namely establishing tax regulations. In this judgment, two provisions regarding dispensation from inheritance tax that favour small companies with less than 20 employees were declared unconstitutional. The FCC regarded the regulation of this specific field as a violation of the principle of equality as enshrined in the Basic Law.[79] The decision raises many interesting questions, e.g., regarding the scope of judicial review or the legislature's prerogative and discretion

73 Cf. BL Art. 21 (2), BVerfGE 2, p. 1: "Freiheitliche demokratische Grundordnung im Sinne des Art. 21 II GG ist eine Ordnung, die unter Ausschluss jeglicher Gewalt- und Willkürherrschaft eine rechtsstaatliche Herrschaftsordnung auf der Grundlage der Selbstbestimmung des Volkes nach dem Willen der jeweiligen Mehrheit und der Freiheit und Gleichheit darstellt. Zu den grundlegenden Prinzipien dieser Ordnung sind mindestens zu rechnen: die Achtung vor den im Grundgesetz konkretisierten Menschenrechten, vor allem vor dem Recht der Persönlichkeit auf Leben und freie Entfaltung, die Volkssouveränität, die Gewaltenteilung, die Verantwortlichkeit der Regierung, die Gesetzmäßigkeit der Verwaltung, die Unabhängigkeit der Gerichte, das Mehrparteienprinzip und die Chancengleichheit für alle politischen Parteien mit dem Recht auf verfassungsmäßige Bildung und Ausübung einer Opposition."

74 A study on the interrelationship between confidence and respect has been undertaken by Sebastian Sternberg, Thomas Gschwend, Caroline Wittig and Benjamin G. Engst, 'Zum Einfuss der öffentlichen Meinung auf Entscheidungen des Bundesverfassungsgerichts: Eine Analyse von abstrakten Normenkontrollen sowie Bund-Länder-Streitigkeiten 1974–2010' (2015) 56, Heft 4 *Politische Vierteljahresschrift*.

75 See https://www.bundesverfassungsgericht.de/EN/Homepage/home_node.html accessed 11 December 2019.

76 Haferkamp (2014) (n 12) 90.

77 See http://www.bundesverfassungsgericht.de/DE/Verfahren/Jahresstatistiken/2015/gb2015/AIV-2.pdf?__blob=-publicationFile&v=1 accessed 11 December 2019.

78 Judgment from 17. des. 2014 – 1 BvL 21/12.

79 BL Art 3.

as well as the legal method applied by the Court, etc. However, in this context the most interesting aspect is that this judgment illustrates that the FCC has the right and duty to supervise the activities of the legislature even when it comes to the legislature's core competences. In doing so, it is beyond doubt that the FCC is a political institution and not a merely legal one. In addition, this notion is emphasised by the fact that the FCC is the only court in Germany that publishes dissenting opinions alongside the judgment of the majority (*Entscheidungsgründe*).[80] All other court rulings, including those of the Supreme Courts, are unanimously given in the name of the people (*Im Namen des Volkes*) and contain no dissenting opinions.

2.5 Conclusion

In Germany legal conflicts are still resolved by a highly professional and specialised judiciary. Particularly important is the hierarchical structure of the court order with its functional and institutional deviation into different fields of law as well as internally divisions, chambers and senates, making the courts highly specialised bodies of conflict resolution. We shall see that the complex interrelation of the courts, the hierarchical order, and the constitutional review are important preconditions for both the courts' methodological approach, the role of case law as an element of legal method, the prevailing ideal of justice, and the expectation concerning the degree of specialisation of legal professionals.

3. Norm production

The main producers of norms in Germany are the Federal and the State Parliaments. Besides legislation, legal norms can occasionally be produced by the administration or the judiciary. A special feature of the German legal culture is the role of legal science in the creation of legal rules. We will consider all these sorts of norm production starting with legislation as the most important form of norm production.

3.1 Legislation[81]

The hierarchy of legal norms in Germany is a highly developed scientific construct, based on the supposition that the system of law contains an answer to every possible legal problem.[82] Its central element is legislation. The term 'legislation' has nevertheless not been narrowly defined by the legislature. 'Legislation' (*Gesetz*) is rather a reference

80 Cf. Bundesverfassungsgerichtsgesetz § 25 (4).

81 This subsection is partly based on Ingvill Helland, 'Introduction to German legal method' in Ingvill Helland and Sören Koch (eds), *Nordic and Germanic Legal Methods* (Mohr Siebeck 2014).

82 Reinhard Zimmermann, 'The German Civil Code and the Development of Private Law in Germany' (2006*) Oxford U Comparative L Forum 1*, IX ff., available at https://www.ouclf.iuscomp.org/.

to written law, including but not limited to Acts of Parliament.[83] It encompasses the constitutions of both the Federation and the individual states (*Länder*), and all other legislation from both the federal (*Bund*) and state (*Land*) level such as Acts of Parliament (*Gesetze*), by-laws (*Rechtsverordnungen*) and regulations (*Richtlinien*). EU law in the form of the founding treaties, regulations, and directives also falls under the scope of the concept *Gesetz.*[84]

The states (*Länder*) have a general legislative competence.[85] However, the Basic Law contains a number of provisions that provides the federal state (*Bund*) with the exclusive or a competing legislative competence.[86] Federal law regulates fields of law that are of importance for the legal, economic or not least the cultural unity of the federation. As a consequence, both criminal and private law are mainly governed by federal legislation.[87] However, the federal Parliament can often not issue legislation without the involvement of the states. The participation of the states in the legislative process depends on the character and the purpose of legislation to be enacted. Legislation directly concerning their interests needs their approval (*Zustimmungsgesetz*).[88] This approval has to be given by the second legislative organ on the federal level, the senate (*Bundesrat)*, which consists of representatives of all state-governments (*Länderregierungen*). In matters that only indirectly concern the interests of the states, the *Bundesrat* has to be heard before an Act of Parliament can be passed (*Einspruchsgesetz*). If the *Bundesrat* presents an objection, a procuration procedure has to be followed. Even though the federal parliament does not need a formal approval of the mediation panel (*Vermittlungsausschuss*) to adopt an *Einspruchsgesetz*, a compromise is normally agreed upon. Thus, as a general rule the legislative process contains an element of political compromise especially when the political majority in both houses is split. One of the main functions of this supervision is to safeguard that the new legislation does not cause any disharmony in the existing system of legislation, or at least to minimise such effects as far as possible.

---

83 Bruno Schmidt-Bleibtreu, Hans Hofmann and Axel Hopfauf, *Kommentar zum Grundgesetz* (Carl Heymanns Verlag 2011) Art. 20, 691 (mn. 91).

84 For a brief overview of German legal sources, see Gerhard Robbers, *An Introduction to German Law* (4th ed, Nomos 2006) 19 ff.; Hartmut Maurer, *Allgemeines Verwaltungsrecht* (18th ed, C.H. Beck 2011) 67, and for a more thorough presentation, see ibid 68 ff. See also Franz Bydlinski, *Juristische Methodenlehre und Rechtsbegriff* (2nd ed, Springer-Verlag 1991) 213 ff. He focused primarily on the Austrian legal method, but as demonstrated by Hinghofer-Szalkay (2014) (n 3), this corresponds in many respects to the one in Germany, and Bydlinski is also considered an authority by German legal scholars, although with some reservations. The references in this book refer to those parts of Bydlinski's writings which are considered equally valid for Germany.

85 Cf. BL Art. 70.

86 Cf. BL Art. 71–75.

87 The most important codes are: Civil Code = *Bürgerliches Gesetzbuch*; Penal Code = *Strafgesetzbuch*; Code of Commerce = *Handelsgesetzbuch*; all procedural codes are federal law as well, e. g., Civil Procedure Code = *Zivilprozessordnung*; Criminal Procedure Code = *Strafprozessordnung*; Procedural Code for Administrative Law = *Verwaltunggerichtgesetz*.

88 See BL Art. 74 containing an enumerative list of legal matters that the Constitution regards as in the direct interest of the states.

A special procedure has to be followed in case the parliament wants to change the Basic Law. Here the *Länder* have to be included also.[89] The constitution demands that 2/3 of all representatives in both houses consent to the modification. However, it also excludes some specific topics from modification (*Ewigkeitsklausel*).[90] The constitutional legislature is prohibited from abandoning the federal structure of the Republic, the principles that bind the State to protect human dignity (Art. 1), and basic democratic principles (Art. 20).[91]

Legislation in this broad sense of the term is without doubt the most important source of law in Germany. In a legislative period of four years, Parliament (Bundestag) adopts approximately 500 acts of federal legislation. The number of all applicable legislation in Germany on both the federal level, which alone is approximately 2,300, and on the state level can just be estimated and culminates at certainly over 70,000 individual acts. In addition, there have been more than 200,000 decrees and by-laws adopted in the same period.[92]

When it comes to legislation, Germany has a tradition to codify the main areas of law, such as civil law, penal law, and administrative law in comprehensive and systematic codifications. The most important codes are the Civil Code (*Bürgerliches Gesetzbuch*), the Penal Code (*Strafgesetzbuch*), and the Code of Commerce (*Handelsgesetzbuch*). Besides substantive law, procedural law is mainly covered by codifications as well, e.g., the Civil Procedure Code (*Zivilprozessordnung*), the Criminal Procedure Code (*Strafprozessordnung*), and the Procedural Code for Administrative Law (*Verwaltunggerichtgesetz*). There are, however, also areas of law which still can be characterised as more fragmented; illustrating examples of these are labour law and social welfare law. But in these areas of law the scientific and systematic approach to the law is also predominant. This does not mean, however, that the ideal of legislation is still to provide comprehensive regulation covering all imaginable set of facts, as had been the ideal of the Prussian Civil Code (*Allgemeines Preussische Landrecht*).[93] The structure and content of the BGB indicates that its fathers recognised a principle-based approach towards the regulatory nature of the civil law codification.[94]

Even though codifications are of central importance in German law, it is not uncommon to supply or even to modify the provisions of a code in limited areas of law by enact-

---

89 BL Art. 79 (1).

90 BL Art. 79 (3): "Eine Änderung dieses Grundgesetzes, durch welche die Gliederung des Bundes in Länder, die grundsätzliche Mitwirkung der Länder bei der Gesetzgebung oder die in den Artikeln 1 und 20 niedergelegten Grundsätze berührt werden, ist unzulässig."

91 The most precise concept for this bundle of principles is "*Rechtsstaatsprinzip*", which is not entirely identical with the concept 'rule of law'.

92 Alone 100,000 just concerning tax-matters. All numbers are based on the information from Parliament's website for the legislative period 2013–2017: https://www.bundestag.de/parlament/aufgaben/gesetzgebung_neu/gesetzgebung/weg-255468.

93 Zimmermann (2019) (n 1) 18.

94 See Joachim Rückert, 'Das BGB und seine Prinzipien: Aufgabe, Lösung und Erfolg' in Matthias Schmoeckel, Joachim Rückert and Reinhard Zimmermann (eds), *Historisch Kritischer Kommentar zum BGB*, Vol. I (Mohr Siebeck 2003) 34 ff.

ing statutes or ordinances. Here the principle of *lex specialis* is applied to solve potential conflicts. However, there is a tendency to implement new legislation into the existing codifications, as can be demonstrated by the implementation of consumer protection legislation into the Civil Code under a large reform of the law of obligations in 2002. The ideal for norm production is still that the democratically legitimised legislature issues acts that are prepared by lawyers in order to maintain concordance with both the constitutional order and the system of legal norms that form the framework of the German legal order as a whole. The same principles also apply for legislation produced on the state level.

3.2 Courts and administration as norm producers?

Legal norms are not just produced by the legislature, but occasionally also by courts and the administrative branch of government. However, in keeping with the principle of separation of powers, the Basic Law limits the competence of the German judiciary and the executive vis-à-vis the legislature.[95] BL Art. 97 (1) explicitly states that judges are exclusively bound by legislation (*nur dem Gesetz unterworfen*).[96] Originally this provision was merely regarded as a precondition and a safeguard for judicial independence.[97] Today, the emphasis is instead put on the judge's obligation to respect the democratic parliament's will.[98] BL Art. 20 (3) provides another constitutional limitation. The provision states that all courts, along with other state authorities, are bound by legislation and law (*Gesetz und Recht*).[99] This provision has to be read in conjunction with BL art. 1 (3) that likewise binds all three branches of government, including the judiciary, to observe the Basic Rights (*Grundrechte*) and thus the entire value system of the constitution.[100] Together they are considered an expression of the rule of law principle (*Rechtsstaatsprinzip*) and the manifestation of the principle of the separation of powers (*Gewaltenteilung*).[101] As mentioned before, the 'eternity clause' (*Ewigkeitsklausel*)

95 BL Art. 20 (3).

96 Cf. also § 1 Constitution of Courts Act of 1877 (Gerichtsverfassungsgesetz).

97 So still Karl Larenz, *Methodenlehre der Rechtswissenschaft* (Mohr Siebeck 1991), 352.

98 Rückert and Seinecke (eds) (2017) (n 11) 41.

99 BL Art. 20 (3): "...die vollziehende Gewalt und die Rechtsprechung sind an Gesetz und Recht gebunden."

100 BL Art. 1 (3): "Die nachfolgenden Grundrechte binden Gesetzgebung, vollziehende Gewalt und Rechtsprechung als unmittelbar geltendes Recht."

101 BL Art. 20 (3). 'Rule of law' is the common English translation both of the German term '*Rechtsstaat*' and its equivalent Norwegian '*rettsstat*'. However, despite being the closest available English term, the English concept covers only the technical part of the German concept. Both of these also have a substantive element: a state is only a *Rechtsstaat/rettsstat* if it respects certain fundamental values, among them human rights. On the German concept of *Rechtsstaat*, see Konrad Hesse, *Grundzüge des Verfassungsrechts der Bundesrepublik Deutschland* (20th ed, C.F. Müller 1999) 86 ff., especially 89; on the similar Norwegian *rettsstat*, see Jan Fridthjof Bernt and Synne Sæther Mæhle, *Rett, samfunn og demokrati* (Gyldendal 2007) 142 ff.; more recently Synne Sæther Mæhle and Ragna Aarli, *Fra lov til rett* (Gyldendal 2016) 121.

prevents the constitutional legislature from abandoning or modifying the fundamental principles laid down in Art. 1 and 20, including the binding force of *Gesetz und Recht*.[102]

Being bound to 'legislation and law' means, first of all, that the courts are obliged to base their decisions on legislation insofar as possible.[103] Furthermore, it means that the task of the courts is primarily the application of law.[104] Creating law is the domain of the legislature and consequently not the task of the courts. The constitution holds no provisions granting the courts such a competence, not even the federal courts are recognised as norm producers. However, a strict prohibition to do so, cannot be deduced from the abovementioned constitutional principles either.

Although written sources cover most legal issues in German law today, there still remain a few areas of law that have not been extensively regulated.[105] In contrast to Switzerland[106] and some other European countries,[107] we find no legal provisions regulating this situation.[108] Consequently, the norms applicable are based on unwritten customary law. According to these unwritten rules, where there is a gap (*Lücke*) in the existing legislation, the courts may fill the gap by establishing a new guideline for the solution of this type of case. This is called development of the law (*Rechtsfortbildung*). Only if the answer to a legal question does not follow from interpretation (including extensive and restrictive interpretation) of the relevant set of rules, may the courts fill the gap by creating new guidelines.[109]

At the same time, a lack of pertinent regulation does not necessarily imply that there is a gap, which judges are free to fill according to their own best judgment. Pursuant to BL Art. 20 (3), they are bound not only to 'legislation' but also to the 'law'. This means that before a judge may conclude that there is a gap in the law, he or she must investigate whether or not legal rules based on other sources exist. Customary law is one of these.

---

102 BL Art. 79 (3): "Eine Änderung dieses Grundgesetzes, durch welche die Gliederung des Bundes in Länder, die grundsätzliche Mitwirkung der Länder bei der Gesetzgebung oder die in den Artikeln 1 und 20 niedergelegten Grundsätze berührt werden, ist unzulässig." This Article is referred to as the "*Ewigkeitsklausel*".

103 To this effect, see i.e., Hesse (1999) (n 101) 87.

104 On when the answer can be said to follow directly from the wording of an Act, see Franz Bydlinski, *Grundzüge der juristischen Methodenlehre* (UTB 2005) 12 ff.; Hans-Peter Schwintowski, *Juristische Methodenlehre* (UTB 2005) 54 ff.

105 E.g. labour law see Heike Simon and Gisela Funk-Baker, *Einführung in das deutsche Recht und die deutsche Rechtssprache* (C.H. Beck 2009) 21.

106 Cf. Art. 1 (2) of the Swiss Civil Code (*Schweitzer Obligationen Recht*).

107 Cf. Italian Civil Code Art. 7; Spain Civil Code Art. 3.

108 The Constitution of Courts Act § 137 contains a general competence of the Supreme Courts and especially the Grand Senate to develop the law; this norm does, however, not manifest a specific approach to legal method, see Joachim Rückert, 'Die Schlachtrufe im Methodenkampf – Ein historischer Überblick' in Joachim Rückert and Ralf Seinecke (eds), *Methodik des Zivilrechts – von Savigny bis Teubner* (3rd ed, Nomos 2017) 590 para. 1475.

109 Bydlinski (1991) (n 84) 472 ff. brings a good overview of the different recognised approaches to establishing such guidelines. He mentions, *inter alia*, analogy, antithesis, teleological reduction, and universal principles of law as possible bases for a further development of the law. On how to identify a *Lücke* and how to deal with it once it has been identified, see also e.g., Karl Larenz and Claus-Wilhelm Canaris, *Methodenlehre der Rechtswissenschaft* (3rd ed, Springer-Verlag 1995) 187 ff.

Although its importance is declining as the scope of legislation continues to expand,[110] customary law remains part of the law (*Recht*) to which the courts are bound.[111]

However, the concept of *Recht* is broader than that. In this context of the Basic Law, *Recht* refers also to internal logic of the legal system and its general principles.[112] Even if these cannot be applied by means of induction or analogy, the judge is still bound to take these overriding principles into consideration when filling a gap in legislation (*gesetzesimmanente Rechtsfortbildung*). In theory, a judge who is confronted with such a gap is supposed to find a solution that safeguards the underlying principles of the legal order and its system and by doing so acting more as a legal scientist explaining the existing law *de lege lata* than the legislator when creating new law. In contrast to a legal scholar, the legislator has the freedom of *making*, and not just *suggesting*, policy decisions and can also take into account considerations that are not yet part of the legal order (*de lege ferenda*).[113] Against this background it makes sense that the preparatory works frequently state that a particular problem is supposed to be solved by the legal doctrine (*der Rechtswissenschaft überlassen*).[114] This is obviously not regarded to be the courts' task.

But what does that mean for the question whether case law is a formal source of law? Can case law have a normative force *erga omnes*? The majority of German jurists are reluctant to give an affirmative answer to this question.[115] The answer one will find most often, is that judge-made law is an important source to help lawyers interpret and understand the law (*Rechtserkenntnisquelle*). It is, however, not regarded as formal sources of law (*Rechtsgeltungsquelle*).[116] Only legislation and customary law possess the necessary normative quality to bind courts for the future.[117] This applies also for legal rules produced by the courts (mostly the five Supreme Courts) when developing the law, despite the fact that they are sometimes labelled as *de facto* sources of law. In contrast to courts in the common law tradition, German courts are not bound to their former legal practice. Accordingly, no theory of precedents is recognised.[118]

Pursuant to BL Art. 20 (3) courts are bound by law (*Recht*); that is the underlying system of law and the prevailing opinions in legal doctrine. Court driven development

---

110 Tomuschat (1972) (n 5) 39.

111 See Robbers (2006) (n 84) 22; Maurer (2011) (n 84) 75 ff.

112 BL Art. 20 (3).

113 For a different approach, see the methodological meta-norm in the Swiss Civil Code Art. 1 (2) which says that a judge in the absence of a written legal provision and pertinent customary law has to act as if she or he would be the legislator.

114 Zimmermann (2019) (n 1) 19.

115 See Larenz and Canaris (1995) (n 109) 187 f., Martin J. Schermaier, 'German Law' in Jan M. Smits (ed), *Elgar encyclopaedia of comparative law* (Edvard Elgar 2006), 283: "Despite the increasing importance of case law and the diminishing importance of oretical [Sic!] legal scholarship, the German legal system is not based on case law. Judgment does not bind either the supreme courts or lower courts."

116 Zimmermann (2019) (n 1) 48 rather clearly states: "The only formal source of law, of course, is legislation."

117 On the concept of source of law in Germany, see Helland and Koch (2014), 'Norwegian and German Legal Methods Compared' (n 6) 196.

118 Christian Kirchner, 'Methodiken für die juridikative Rechtsfortbildung im Zivilrecht' in Joachim Rückert and Ralf Seinecke (eds), *Methodik des Zivilrechts – von Savigny bis Teubner* (3rd ed, Nomos 2017) 503, para. 1295.

of the law (*richterrechtliche Rechtsfortbildung*) can therefore be relevant for other courts in subsequent rulings. However, it is not the *ratio decidendi* of a Supreme Court, but the abstract principle the decision is based on that becomes part of the law, and consequently binding.[119] This is a sophisticated, but crucial difference when comparing the function of case law *inter alia* with the common-law jurisdictions.

The lack of a formal theory of precedents in Germany also has consequences for the content and function of concepts like *ratio decidendi* and *obiter dictum*. In contrast to the common law tradition, where subsequent judgments confirm and refine what the *ratio* of a former case actually is, German courts tend to direct the reader's attention to the cases' *ratio decidendi* in separate headnote (*Leitsatz*) containing the essence of the legal norms applied in the case at hand. Those headnotes are an official part of a judgment (*amtlicher Leitsatz*) if they are provided by the ruling court.[120] Headnotes provided by editors of the publication channel (*Orientierungssatz*) are not part of the judgment.

On the other hand, *Obiter dicta* have mainly two functions. First, they give a court the opportunity to challenge a longstanding practice, which the court regards to be outdated.[121] The idea is that this might trigger lawyers to put forward cases that eventually can be decided contrary to the established but outdated opinion. Secondly, *obiter dicta* can be a tool to signal that the court is considering whether to deviate from its former opinion on a specific legal question. The Federal Court of Justice (*Bundesgerichtshof*) in particular has used *obiter dicta* to indicate changing an established doctrine. In such cases citizens cannot rely on the court maintaining its former practice.

We have so far established that the BL limits the judiciary's competence to produce legal norms, hence case law is not recognised as a formal source of law and there is no theory of precedent recognised in Germany. However, there are a few exceptions to the rule that case law is not binding *erga omnes*: pursuant to the Constitution of Federal Constitutional Court Act (*Bundesverfassungsgerichtsgesetz*) § 31 (1), the rulings of the FCC are binding for all state organs explicitly including the federal and state courts. Specific rulings even have the same quality as an Act of Parliament.[122] On average there are no more than 15, often less than 10, of such rulings published in the official law review (*Bundesgesetzblatt*) every year. The exceptional character of the provision and its

---

119 On the constitutional limits of '*Rechtsfortbildung*', see e.g., Frauke Kruse, *Die verfassungsrechtlichen Grenzen richterlicher Rechtsfortbildung* (Mohr Siebeck 2019). See also Larenz (n 97) 350 ff.

120 On the definition of an official headnote, see the ruling of the Federal Court of Justice of 21 November 1991 – I ZR 190/89: "Als amtlich verfaßt im Sinne des § 5 Abs. 1 UrhG ist ein Leitsatz dann anzusehen, wenn er von einem Mitglied des Spruchkörpers mit dessen Billigung formuliert und der Öffentlichkeit zugänglich gemacht worden ist. Unerheblich ist, ob eine dienstliche Verpflichtung zur Abfassung von Leitsätzen besteht. Entscheidend ist allein, ob der Inhalt der Verlautbarung erkennbar dem Gericht zuzurechnen ist, also vom Träger der öffentlichen Gewalt herrührt. („Leitsätze")."

121 Hans Lilie, *Obiter dictum und Divergenzausgleich im Strafrecht: Ein Spannungsfeld zwischen Revisionsrecht und Gerichtsverfassungsrecht* (Heymann Verlag 1993) 25; critical to the function of *obiter dicta* is the former president of the Supreme Court for Labour Law, Hans-Jürgen Dörner, 'Neues aus dem Befristungsrecht' (2007) Nr. 2 *Neue Zeitschrift für Arbeitsrecht* 57, 58. Rolf Lamprecht, 'Obiter dictum – Arabeske oder Ballast?' (1998) *Neue Juristische Wochenschrift* 1039, 1040.

122 See Constitution of Federal Constitutional Court Act § 31 (2) in conjunction with § 13 Nr. 6, 6a, 11, 12 and 14.

narrow scope of application proves that there is no general theory of precedent recognised in Germany.[123]

Another exception applies to longstanding case law, which, in addition, is widely accepted by legal scholars and implicitly accepted or at least tolerated by the legislator. However, due to comprehensive codifications and legislation in almost all areas of law, case-law-based customary law does in fact have very limited importance, even though it is still recognised as a formal source of law. Another reason for this is that the legislator has often implemented such customs into the codifications. Examples are the law on the violation of contractual duties (*positive Vertragsverletzung*) or the doctrine of frustration of contract (*Wegfall der Geschäftsgrundlage*).[124]

However, rules on causation or the extent of compensation for damages done, just to name two examples from the law of torts, have mainly been elaborated by the courts. These norms are not binding in the strictest sense of the word. They will, nevertheless, be applied in later cases unless a judge has very good reasons to depart from them. This will occasionally occur when the established doctrine in case law has been heavily criticised by legal scholars over a longer period of time or in case that the legal or social preconditions for such a norm have changed considerably, e.g., due to technical developments, etc.

Deviating from established case law is not an exclusive competence of the supreme courts. Once again, there is no theory of precedent. Consequently, judges on all levels of the court hierarchy can dissent even a longstanding practice of the competent supreme court.

Considering the role of courts for norm production in Germany depends, therefore, on the choice of perspective. From a constitutional and formal point of view, court-rulings are, with some very few exceptions, not sources of law and therefore not norm producers. From a functional and pragmatic perspective, however, lawyers and the administration especially treat Supreme Court judgments as if they were precedents. Trying to avoid one-dimensional categorisations, one may describe case law in Germany as an important interpretative factor with indirect normative force.

Due to the strict and formal theory of legal sources and the separation of powers, the practice of governmental agencies in Germany is not considered a source of law either. However, technical directives on critical values of pollution, noise, etc., are the domain of the administration and therefore cannot, or can only to a very limited extent be censored by the courts.[125] In light of the balance of power principle, the courts' right to review acts of the administration is further limited by the administration's scope in judgment evaluation (*Beurteilungsspielraum*). Furthermore, where the legislature has granted the administration discretion, the juridical review is restricted to the question of proportionality (*Verhältnismässigkeit*). In other words, the courts are not allowed to replace the administrative decision with a decision that the judges would have favoured. Instead, their competence is limited to deciding whether the use of discretion was in violation of the basic principle of proportionality.

---

123 See above (n 118).

124 Compare the German Civil Code (BGB) §§ 280 and 313 in the revised version of the Civil Code since 2002.

125 Maurer (2011) (n 84) 80.

3.3 Legal scholarship (*Rechtswissenschaft*)

Legal scholarship is another important factor when it comes to producing legal norms. Even though there is no constitutional or institutional basis for legal scholarship in Germany, the informal impact of legal scholars on legislation, the courts, and the application of law in practice is quite remarkable.[126] Both individual scholars and the profession of legal scholars have also traditionally contributed to shaping the German legal culture. A prominent example is Professor Carl Friedrich von Savigny. His writings had a tremendous influence on the general discussion on the issue of codification. Due to his criticism, the codification of civil law was postponed for almost 70 years, giving legal scholars the opportunity to develop a comprehensive system of law based on scientific ideals.[127] Another example was the famous scholar, Bernhard Windscheid,[128] who was in charge of the first committee that drafted the Civil Code. His methodological, philosophical, and ideological approach to law became a model for his contemporaries and is resembled in the structure and nature of the Civil Code. To this day, the Civil Code is widely recognised as a work of legal science (*Rechtswissenschaft*).[129] One of the prominent features of the scientific approach to law is its (alleged) unpolitical character. Safeguarding the inherent logic of a system of law is perceived as a main purpose of legal scholarship. At the end of the 19th century this also became an ideal for legislative technique and was applied by the drafting commission(s) (1874-1896). Particularly in the field of civil law, political and ideological considerations were regarded as disturbing factors in the process of norm production. The idea was to build a coherent system of norms and principles based on scientific rather than political preconditions. In the 20th century and especially after the Wold War II, the ideal of systematic coherence was transformed into a value-based judicial approach (*Wertungsjurisprudenz*).[130] This approach to law is still

126 Cf. Haferkamp (2014) (n 12) 92, concluding his article by stating: "Germany has remained the country of legal science."

127 On the impact of Savigny on the idea of codification, see Jan Smits, *The Making of European Private Law: Toward a Ius Commune Europaeum as a mixed legal system* (Intersentia 2002) 77 ff.

128 On his impact on the methodology-discourse, see Joachim Rückert, 'Methode und Zivilrecht bei Bernhard Windscheid (1817–1892)' in Joachim Rückert and Ralf Seinecke (eds), *Methodik des Zivilrechts – von Savigny bis Teubner* (3rd ed, Nomos 2017).

129 Emphasising the political neutrality of the Civil Code, Thomas Lundmark, *Charting the Divide Between Common and Civil Law* (Oxford University Press 2012) 133: "As the German code was understood to be the product of a logical process, it was seen as consisting of pure concepts that were politically neutral in content." Zimmermann (2019) (n 1) ch 1.05 underlines the flexibility of the scientific tradition, in which the Civil code was embedded: "The BGB was regarded as part of a tradition significantly shaped by legal scholarship. The phenomenon of scholarly 'development' of the law was quite familiar to the draftsmen of the code". Horst Heinrich Jakobs (*Wissenschaft und Gesetzgebung*, Rechts- und StaatswissenschftlicheVeröffentlichungen der Görres-Gesellschaft, Heft 38, 1983) characterised the BGB as a codification "which does not contain the source of law in itself but has its source in the legal scholarship from which it was created". The Civil code was designed to provide a framework for an organically progressive legal science. The idea of enacting a prohibition on commenting upon the BGB (as existed with regard to the Prussian Code of 1794) was alien to the draftsmen of the BGB: as alien as the equally outdated idea that it might be possible to lay down a specific rule for every imaginable situation.

130 For literature on the *Wertungsjurisprudenz*, see Rückert (2017), 'Die Schlachtrufe im Methodenkampf' (n 108) 607 f. for further references.

built on the idea that values can be analysed systematically. Accordingly, it is common to refer to the value system of the Basic Law. All this warranted the legal scholars' crucial influence on the development of law in Germany. Just recently in 2002, the comprehensive reformation of the law of obligations was closely monitored and discussed by prominent legal scholars. Law professors are frequently appointed to drafting committees or consulted to render their legal expertise by providing advisory opinions (*Gutachten*).

However, the impact of legal scholarship is not limited to the production of legislation. In addition, all kinds of academic writings are carefully monitored and taken into consideration by the administration, by practicing lawyers advising their clients and by judges.[131] Particularly important for the application of law in Germany are commentaries on legislation. These commentaries contain information on the purpose and background of an Act. Consequently, one of the first steps for German lawyers looking for a solution for a specific legal question is to consult a commentary on the relevant Act of Parliament. Legal doctrine becomes particularly influential in cases where a prevailing opinion (*herrschende Meinung/herrschende Lehre*) has been established.[132] In Germany preparatory works are often of minor interest because commentaries regularly contain similar information on the legislative intent, interpretation of abstract concepts, and the history of the rules and provisions. In contrast to preparatory works, commentaries, especially those on the Codes, are frequently updated and contain references to relevant case law. That they lack the remote democratic legitimacy of preparatory works is of minor concern in Germany due to the high reputation for law professors and other highly trained legal experts.

Finally, the German courts tend to quote legal scholarly writings to legitimise their verdicts. It is no precondition that a legal scholar to be quoted be either dead or particularly prominent.[133] The prevailing opinion in legal scholarship is perceived as being an influential or persuasive interpretative factor.[134] Supreme Courts developing the law (*Rechtsfortbildung*) will therefore heavily depend on academic writings when legitimising any new legal principle or abandoning an old one.

Legislative reforms are also often initiated, monitored and criticised by legal scholars. Recommendations of the Meeting of the Association of German Lawyers (*Deutscher Juristentag*) have on many occasions been the starting point of legislative projects. The Justice Department is traditionally headed by a politician with a legal background.

From a comparative perspective, the particularly close relationship between legal scholars and the judiciary is one of the most prominent characteristics of the German

131 Zimmermann (2019) (n 1) ch 1.10 E.

132 Christian Djeffal, 'Die herrschende Meinung als Argument – Ein didaktischer Beitrag in historischer und theoretischer Perspektive' *Zeitschrift für das Juristische Studium* 5 (2013) 463–466.

133 Zimmermann (2019) (n 1) 28.

134 For a comparative analysis of the relationship between legal scholarship and legal practice in Germany and France, see Johannes Masing, Matthias Jestaedt, Olivier Jouanjan and David Capitant (eds), *Rechtswissenschaft und Rechtspraxis. Ihr Verhältnis im Verfassungs-, Verwaltungs-, und Unionsrecht – Dokumentation des 7. Treffens des Deutsch-Französischen Gesprächskreises für Öffentliches Recht* (Mohr Siebeck 2019).

legal culture. We shall see that the scholarly and scientific approach to law is an important factor concerning also the intellectual elements of the legal cultural model.[135]

4. Ideal of justice[136]

As already mentioned above, the German legal order has traditionally had a strong focus on predictability and legal certainty. Producing predicable outcomes is still regarded as one of the legal system's main purposes.[137] This can also be seen as a logical consequence of the idea of equal treatment before the law. Comparable legal problems are supposed to lead to comparable legal solutions. The strong influence of legal science on German law has also contributed to this end. In the aftermath of the Kantian revolution and the abolishment of natural law as the prevailing theoretical basis for the law at the beginning of the 19th century, positive law and later especially legislation became main object of scholarly research. That, in turn, led to a specific systematic approach to law. Consequently, the idea of creating predictability by focusing on the inherent systematics of positive law and its written sources gained ground. This idea became even stronger when the claim for codification grow louder at the end of the 19th century.[138]

The legalistic and systematic approach to law, with its origin in the late 19th century, has been supplemented by a new component after the collapse of the judiciary under the Nazi regime. The prevailing ideal of justice, equal treatment before the law and consequently the idea of predictability got a new constitutional foundation. According to the Basic Law, all state authorities are bound by the constitutional order, including the rule of law, basic human rights and most importantly, the principle of equal treatment.[139] The importance of this fundamental constitutional principle is emphasised by the fact that these principles cannot be altered without abandoning the constitution itself.[140] This institutionalised modification of the constitutional order had enormous impact on the intellectual elements of the German culture, especially on legal method and the prevailing ideal of justice. In this subsection, I will focus on the latter one.

Even though the positivistic notion that it is the purpose of legislation to give guidelines to legally regulate and solve all imaginable sets of facts has long been abandoned in

---

135 For a different view see Schermaier, (2006) (n 115) 283 holds that the influence of legal scholars from the 1930s lost its impact on German law and that today the judiciary is developing the law.

136 This subchapter is based in part on Helland (2014), 'Introduction to German legal method' (n 81) 188 ff.

137 This becomes obvious when Josef Esser, an advocate for a hermeneutical approach to legal methods, admits that judicial interest is not primarily a hermeneutical one (*Verstehensinteresse*), but a systematic one (*Ordnungsinteresse*), see Josef Esser, 'Methodik des Privatrechts' (1972) in Peter Häberle and Hans G Leser (eds), *Wege der Rechtsgewinnung. Ausgewählte Aufsätze* (Mohr Siebeck 1990) 356 f.; see also Birgit Schäfer, 'Methode und Zivilrecht bei Josef Esser (1910–1999)' in Joachim Rückert and Ralf Seinecke (eds), *Methodik des Zivilrechts – von Savigny bis Teubner* (3rd ed, Nomos 2017) para. 789.

138 Haferkamp (2014) (n 12).

139 BL Art. 20 (3).

140 BL Art. 20 and Art. 79 (3).

Germany,[141] the starting point for the traditional form of conflict resolution doubtlessly was and still is to find solutions that can produce identical outcomes in cases based on similar facts. For the legitimacy of legal rulings, 'logically correct' application of law taking into consideration the inherent systematic of the positive legal order itself, is regarded a crucial precondition to achieve this goal.[142] Deducing legal consequences from legislation is regarded as a safeguard for outcome predictability. The focus on legislation is also supposed to provide substantive, and indirectly, individual justice. The underlying assumption is that legislation itself is produced based on scientific ideals of coherence, rationality, and justice. After the perversion of positive law under the Nazi regime, constitutional mechanisms have been established to warrant sufficient degree of accordance between Acts of Parliament and the values encompassed in the Constitution. Accordingly, applying law in accordance with the positive legal order is supposed to produce substantively just results as well.[143]

This applies even where a predictable outcome in an individual case may seem unfair, at least seen from a layman's perspective. In Germany, legal justice is a domain of highly educated professionals. Accordingly, providing justice does not connote finding the best solution for the individual case, nor a solution that is in accordance with former court practice, but a solution that is in accordance with the system of positive law and its underlying value system. This in turn requires a scientific approach to law and justice.

In its first chapter, the Basic Law contains an extensive catalogue of human and civil rights, called the Basic Rights (*Grundrechte*). These rights closely correspond to the value basis on which the German society and legal system have been built. Although the Basic Rights primarily concern the relationship between citizens and state authorities, and as such are in principle a part of public law, the Federal Constitutional Court established that these values can also have an indirect horizontal effect in private law.[144] Since the BL came into force, the values expressed in the Constitution and especially in its basic rights catalogue have constantly been referred to in order to adapt, modify or even to abandon outdated legislation or legal doctrines. Illustrative examples are the extension of tort claims in the case of non-pecuniary damages for infringements of the right of personality, the legal equalisation of same sex partnerships or the establishment of social rights in labour law.

As mentioned before, predictability primarily relies on legislative text in Germany.[145] The wording of each legal provision is interpreted in light of all the other provisions, in

141 See Zimmermann (2019) (n 1) ch 1.10 E with further references.

142 Larenz and Canaris (1995) (n 109) 187 ff., explicitly on 232.

143 This assumption is not uncontested in Germany, however, it can still be regarded the prevailing ideal.

144 BVerfGE 34, 269.

145 Obviously, not all legal provisions are sufficiently precise to provide a clearly predictable solution when seen in isolation, or even when considered in their systematic context. This is particularly true of constitutional provisions such as the Basic Rights, but is also the case with general clauses such as § 823 of the BGB. In these cases, the courts may rely on case law in order to achieve a more predictable application of the law. In the case of the Basic Rights, the case law of the Federal Constitutional Court will as a rule be decisive for the outcome, just as that of the BGH will normally determine the interpretation of general clauses in the Civil Code.

a cooperation between legislature and courts towards achieving a complete, consistent, and logically coherent system of written legal rules. In other words, the ideal is that the judge acts more like a scientist than as a legislator. Or as Gustav Radbruch once put it: "The law and its interpreter have to be even smarter than the legislator at the time the legislation was enacted."[146] Against this background, it is also understandable that one will find quite a lot of general clauses or clauses referring to good faith in German codifications. These are not regarded as threats to legal predictability because it is supposed that a trained lawyer applying such a clause will be able to find a solution that would be in coherence with the underlying system of legal rules.[147] Once again, in order to find a solution to a legal problem, the prevailing guideline for a legal practitioner is not primarily to contribute to individual justice or find the most pragmatic solution, but rather to present a solution that is seen as logical and systematic coherent from an intersubjective perspective.

This implies that legal terminology and legal concepts are highly important tools when it comes to the application of law. As a general rule, legal concepts have a narrow and clearly defined content. The competence to define the content of an abstract concept lies with the courts, unless the legislator itself has given an authentic definition (*Legaldefinition*). However, it is once again the task of legal science to safeguard that the court's interpretation is in keeping with the system of law and its scientific foundations. In order to legitimise their decisions in the eyes of the legal community, the courts therefore tend to apply a scientific approach to legal argumentation when explaining their verdicts.

The overall goal is to achieve predictability of outcomes, based on the ideal that each legal question has just one 'dogmatically correct' solution. A prominent feature of the scientific approach is to generate reproducible results. In contrast to Norway or England, the focus in Germany is consequently not so much on the predictability of a coherent application of law by the courts, but the predictability of outcomes they generate or, more precisely, are supposed to generate. This does not mean that there is no place for individual justice and fairness in the German legal culture. Fairness is a very important policy consideration and has been recognised as such in many provisions of the Basic Law.[148] However, when applying the law, fairness is not the only or even a prevailing consideration and has consequently to be balanced with other considerations such as systematic coherence and outcome predictability. On the other hand, justice is the guiding principle when producing legal norms, but this is, as we have seen, not the primary task of the courts.

Finally, the ideal of justice embedded in the constitution also impacts German lawyers' attitude towards the internationalisation of the national legal culture. We shall come back to this in more detail later.[149]

146 Gustav Radbruch, *Rechtsphilosophie* (4th ed, C.F. Müller 1999) 199 f.

147 Cf. Zimmermann (2006) (n 82) Chapter IX.

148 See Rückert and Seinecke (2017) (n 13) 50 f. para. 72 ff. who dedicate the last of their 12 method rules for practitioners to justice: "Vergiss nicht die Gerechtigkeit."

149 Cf. section 7.

5. Legal method[150]

5.1 The constitution determines core elements of legal method

As the ideal of justice in Germany, the legal method is to a great extent determined by the framework of the constitutional order. This is particularly important with regard to the courts' interpretation of legislation; pursuant to the principle of separation of powers, the courts are bound to legislation and law and consequently must respect the limits this constitutional rule implies. Taking into consideration that the Basic Law is *lex superior* to all ordinary legislation, an interpretation against the wording of an Act (*contra legem*) is prohibited unless fundamental principles of the Constitution itself support such an interpretation. In this case, an interpretation *contra legem* is not just possible but even mandatory. Furthermore, in cases where different understandings of a norm are possible, an interpretation in accordance with the Constitution has to be preferred (*verfassungskonforme Auslegung*).[151] This may in some situations require a restrictive and in other cases an extensive interpretation of the provision at hand. In other words, constitutional law not only restricts the possible sources of law, but also the scope for possible outcomes of interpretation and application of the law.[152]

5.2 Legal method and legal scholarship

As shown above, both norm production, conflict resolution and the ideal of justice are impacted heavily by ideals of legal science. The same applies when it comes to legal method. Significantly, one of the prevailing textbooks prevailing textbook on legal methods by Karl Larenz and Claus-Wilhelm Canaris is titled: *Methods of Legal Science* (*Methodenlehre der Rechtswissenschaft*).[153] The very rich literature on the topic promotes very different approaches and perspectives.[154] A common feature, however, is a strong focus on positivistic and constitutional framework and not so much on the application of law by courts and their argumentation.[155] As a consequence, argumentation theory is

150 See in more detail Helland and Koch (2014), 'Norwegian and German Legal Methods Compared' (n 6) and Helland (2014), 'Introduction to German legal method' (n 81).

151 Helland (2014), 'Introduction to German legal method' (n 81) 213; Larenz and Canaris (1995) (n 109) 232.

152 As regards the interpretation of the Basic Law, see Hesse (1999) (n 101) 29 f. (mn. 78) and 31 (mn. 80; on the limitations applicable to the interpretation of Acts of Parliament in conformity with the Basic Law). See also Helland (2014), 'Introduction to German legal method' (n 81) 211–212. Regarding interpretation of Acts of Parliament in general, see Larenz and Canaris (1999) (n 109) 138 f. (with regard to the interpretation of Acts of Parliament), 185 and 232 (as regards the development of the law by judges when there is a gap in legislation).

153 Larenz and Canaris (1999) (n 109) 188.

154 A comprehensive overview is provided by Rückert (2017), 'Die Schlachtrufe im Methodenkampf' (n 108).

155 See e.g., Josef Esser, *Vorverständnis und Methodenwahl in der Rechtsfindung* (2nd ed, Athenäum Verlag 1972). Such approaches are promoted also by scholars applying an economic analysis of law or theories of '*Institutionenökonomie*', see e.g., Heinz Dieter Assmann, Christian Kirchner and Erich Schanze (eds), *Ökonomische Analyse des Rechts* (Athenäum Verlag 1978); Rudolf Richter and Eirik Furubotn, *Neue Institutionenökonomik* (4th ed, Mohr Siebeck 2014).

mainly regarded a domain of legal philosophers and not perceived as pragmatic guidelines for practicing lawyers.[156] Empirical surveys on what judges actually do are rare exceptions.[157] Even the advocates of a hermeneutical approach to legal method, such as Josef Esser, state that the judge is bound by unwritten legal principles, which are as "communis opinion doctorum" part of the law (*Rechtsganzen*).[158] He explicitly regards it the task of legal science (more precisely legal scholars) to develop such principles on the basis of a systematic analysis of case law.[159]

An understanding of the contemporary discourse on legal methodology requires a brief historical presentation of the prevailing theoretical approaches. Commencing the establishment of the political union in 1871 and the enactment of the Civil Code, Philipp Heck (1858–1943) advocated the so-called '*Interessenjurisprudenz*' (an interpretative approach taking into consideration the interests underlying the law). His approach was anti-formalistic and based on the late Rudolf von Jhering's sociological ideas of law. After the Second World War, this theory was refined into the so-called '*Wertungsjurisprudenz*', focusing on the values underlying the law. With the *Lüth*-ruling,[160] the FCC became an important contributor in the debate, emphasising the need to balance interests and values in the light of the constitutional order (*Abwägungsjurisprudenz*).[161] This discourse has mainly two dimensions: an analytical scientific theoretic and a normative constitutional one.[162] These two dimensions still provide the framework for the great variation of theoretical approaches to legal method in Germany today. Important to note, however, is the highly abstract and theoretical nature of the debate, once again a result of and facilitating the specific scientific approach that characterises the German legal culture.

A result of this scientific approach is that the hermeneutical operation of legal argumentation (*Methodenlehre im engeren Sinne*) is separated from the mere academic question of what constitutes a legal source (*Rechtsquellenlehre*).[163] In other words, one has to distinguish between the way relevant legal arguments are actually applied in legal argumentation, and the question of what is relevant for legal argumentation.

156 The main focus on legal argumentation can be found in Robert Alexy, *Theorie der juristischen Argumentation* (Suhrkamp 1978); Ulfrid Neumann, 'Juristische Methodenlehre und Theorie der juristischen Argumentation' (2001) 32 *Rechtstheorie* 139; Ulfrid Neumann, 'Theorie der juristischen Argumentation' in Winfried Brugger, Ulfrid Neumann and Stephan Kirste (eds), *Rechtsphilosophie im 21. Jahrhundert* (Suhrkamp 2008). Rückert (2017), 'Die Schlachtrufe im Methodenkampf' (n 108) argued that: "Die Argumentationsjurisprudenz will also als Theorie gelesen werden, nicht als Dogmatik oder Politik und auch nicht als Methodenlehre."

157 The most prominent scholar promoting such an empirical-sociological approach is Günther Teubner, see 'Nach den Fällen: Paradoxien soziologischer Jurisprudenz' in Bertram Lomfeld (ed), *Die Fälle der Gesellschaft* (Mohr Siebeck 2017).

158 Josef Esser, *Grundsatz und Norm in der richterlichen Fortbildung des Privatrechts* (Mohr 1956) 24 f.

159 Ibid 311.

160 BVerfGE 7, 198.

161 For details, see Rückert (2017), 'Die Schlachtrufe im Methodenkampf' (n 108) 582 ff.

162 Ibid 585 para 1464.

163 See Schröder (2012) (n 10) 1.

5.3 Legal sources and other legal argument bases

The prevailing theory of legal sources still makes a distinction between sources of law, which are legally binding, and other relevant legal argument bases, which are not.[164] This distinction becomes crucial when determining the basis for a legal claim or action (*Anspruchsgrundlage*). Without such a basis, recognised in a formal source of law, this is mainly legislation,[165] or customary law,[166] no claim can be successfully filed. Consequently, arguments deduced from other than formal legal sources, such as court practice, the practice of the administration, an opinion in legal theory, and so forth may be relevant arguments in legal argumentation but cannot form the basis of a legal claim.[167] However, if over time, a consistent practice leads to the development of a corresponding prevailing opinion in legal literature (*opinio iuris*), case law can give rise to a binding legal rule, and eventually be recognised as customary law.

Elements not considered sources of law may hence be relevant for legal argumentation. Both the practitioner who wishes to advise his client on the content of the law, and the legal scholar researching a specific area of law in order to accurately describe the law *de lege lata*, can e.g., rely on case law and scholarly writings in order to determine what the law is.[168] At the same time, such elements are not considered to have any normative power in and of themselves, and it is entirely possible to maintain a legal opinion *de lege lata*, even when faced with more than five decades of consistent court practice to the contrary.[169]

This normative binding power is the main difference between arguments based on sources of law and arguments derived from other factors. In Germany a source of law is

164 See for example the explanation of the non-binding nature of case law that Robbers (2006) (n 84) 20 f. provides.

165 Simon and Funk-Baker (2009) (n 105) 21; Robbers (2006) (n 84) 19; Foster and Sule (2010) (n 20) 37.

166 Simon and Funk-Baker (2009) (n 105) 21; Robbers (2006) (n 84) 22; Foster and Sule (2010) (n 20) 38.

167 See Radbruch (1999) (n 145) 201.

168 Robbers (2006) (n 84) 20 f. on the role of case law in legal argumentation. See also Foster and Sule (2010) (n 20) 39 ff., who, in light of the *de facto* role of case law in legal argumentation find it hard "to completely ignore judicial law making as a source of law" (p. 42).

169 The ongoing debate concerning whether or not the European Convention on Human Rights, which was incorporated into German law through a *Zustimmungsgesetz* – a particular form of Act of Parliament – in 1952, is in fact constitutional law or "merely" on the level of ordinary legislation may serve as a helpful illustration. Although the Federal Constitutional Court has consistently maintained the latter opinion, voices in legal science continue to claim that the opposite is true *de lege lata*. See Jochen Abr. Frowein, 'Die Anforderungen der Europäischen Menschenrechtskonvention an den nationalen Rechtsschutz' in Jochen Abr. Frowein and Gerhard Ulsamer, *Europäische Menschenrechtskonvention und nationaler Rechtsschutz* (C.F. Müller 1985) 31 ff.; Thomas Giegerich, 'Wirkung und Rang der EMRK' in Rainer Grote and Thilo Marauhn (eds), *EMRK/GG Konkordanzkommentar* (Mohr Siebeck 2006) 82 ff.; Christof Grabenwarter and Katharina Pabel, *Europäische Menschenrechtskonvention* (C.H. Beck/Helbing Lichtenhahn/MANZ 2012) 19 ff.; Andreas Haratsch, 'Die Europäische Menschenrechtskonvention in der deutschen Rechtsordnung – Eine innerstaatliche Standortbestimmung' (2000) *MenschenRechtsMagazin: Themenheft "50 Jahre EMRK"* 62; Solveig Haß, *Die Urteile des Europäischen Gerichtshofs für Menschenrechte. Charakter, Bindungswirkung, Durchsetzung* (Peter Lang 2006) 113 ff.; Ulrike Heckötter, *Die Bedeutung der Europäischen Menschenrechtskonvention und der Rechtsprechung des EGMR für die deutschen Gerichte* (Carl Heymanns Verlag 2008) 92 ff.; Robert Uerpmann, *Die Europäische Menschenrechtskonvention und die deutsche Rechtsprechung* (Duncker & Humblot 1993) 78 ff. From an outsider's point of view, this does at times make it extremely difficult to separate between scientific discussions of the law *de lege lata* and *de lege ferenda*.

considered binding, which means that its content is compulsory. A source of law is not only one factor out of several, which must then be balanced with other equally ranked factors; instead the relevant source of law must be applied directly by the courts, the administration, other legal practitioners and everyone else it addresses.[170] It therefore makes sense that the German term *Rechtsregel* – legal rule – refers to that which is written down by the legislator. In contrast to Norway, where a legal rule marks the outcome of the application of law to the case at hand, a German legal rule marks the point of departure for the application of law.[171] However, since the German legislator must of course struggle with the same linguistic and human limitations, a *Rechtsregel* will usually be in need of interpretation. The outcome of interpretation is in Germany most commonly referred to as *Rechtssatz* or *Fallnorm.*[172]

5.4 Interpretation

What does a German lawyer actually look for when the process of interpretation begins? There are two possibilities: the aim of interpretation can either be the objective or the subjective will of the legislator. The objective will derives from the wording considered in a grammatical and systematic context by using a rational analysis of the text at hand, while the subjective will of the legislator refers to the historical legislator's original intention and can usually be found in the preparatory works. Considering the objective meaning by applying a rational analysis of a hypothetical will of the legislator makes it possible to include developments in society, which could not be foreseen by the historical legislator. However, the original intentions of the legislator are important as well, not least because the purpose of an Act may be relevant in determining its scope.[173] The FCC therefore has developed a theory combining both approaches with the aim of identifying the 'objectivised will of the legislature' as expressed through the Act.[174]

In Germany it is usual to differentiate between four types or modes of interpretation balancing the objective and subjective meaning of the legislative text. The starting

170 This is an important part of the reason why the judgments of the European Court of Human Rights are not considered *binding* beyond the scope of the adjudicated case (ECHR Art. 46). The FCC's demand in *Görgülü* (BVerfGE 111, 307) – that all German courts must take ECtHR judgments *into account* (para. 47 ff.) The mainstream German opinion is voiced by i.e. Haß (2006) (n 168) 167; Eckart Klein, 'Should the binding effect of the judgments of the European Court of Human Rights be extended?' in Paul Mahoney, Franz Mascher, Herbert Petzold and Luzius Wildhaber (eds), *Protection des droits de l'homme: La perspective européenne. Mélanges à la memoire de Rolv Ryssdal* (Carl Heymanns 2000) 706 ff.; Heckötter (2008) (n 168) 42–43. However, representatives of the opposite opinion can be found also in Germany, such as Anne-Christine Zoellner, *Das Verhältnis von BVerfG und EGMR* (Verlag Dr. Kovač 2009) 130 ff.

171 On the different contents of the German and Norwegian concept of legal rule, see Helland and Koch (2014), 'Norwegian and German Legal Methods Compared' (n 6) 270 f.

172 Larenz and Canaris (1995) (n 109) 71 ff. Although other terms exist, such as the term *Fallnorm* which is used by Wolfgang Fikentscher, *Methoden des Rechts in vergleichender Darstellung*, Vol. IV (Tübingen 1975) 202. As pointed out by Larenz and Canaris 254, however, Fikentscher's term *Fallnorm* is not entirely synonymous to *Rechtssatz.*

173 Thomas Henninger, 'Legal Culture and Common Principles of European Legal Method' in Ingvill Helland and Sören Koch (eds), *Nordic and Germanic Legal Methods* (Mohr Siebeck 2014) 432.

174 This approach is called "*Vereinigungslehre*", cf. BVerfGE 1, 299 (312), Leitsatz 2.

point is the natural understanding of the wording of the provision at hand. In case the wording of the provision is unambiguous, there is no need for further interpretation and the norm can be applied directly, unless there are serious doubts concerning the constitutionality of the outcome. If this is the case, the court dealing with the question has to postpone the trial and to submit the question to the FCC.[175]

In cases where the wording of the relevant provision allows for more than one understanding, further interpretation is necessary. For this purpose, the interpreter has three more modes of interpretation at his disposal: historical, systematic (logical) and teleological interpretation. This approach has roots far back in history. Savigny had pronounced a quite similar approach already in the early 19th century.[176]

The historical interpretation aims to reveal the original intent of the legislator when adapting the provision in question, in other words, the subjective will of the legislator. This includes the original meaning of the concepts used. Consulting preparatory works may provide relevant information. However, due to the abovementioned objections against a mere subjective interpretation in Germany, the historical argument has comparatively little weight in the application of law in practice.

Systematic or logical analysis is based on the underlying assumption that each provision is an integral part of a logical coherent system of norms. With the help of this mode of interpretation, it is possible to rule out any possible understandings that do not fit into the system, typically because they contradict the internal or external structure of the system. The internal system of norms refers to the inner logic of an Act and the composition and systematic placing of norms in an Act of Parliament. The external structure of the positive law takes other legislation in consideration as well.

Finally, teleological interpretation aims to discover the meaning of and purpose behind the provision being interpreted (*Auslegung nach dem Sinn und Zweck des Gesetzes*).[177] While the meaning refers clearly to an objective interpretation of the provision, the purpose has to be analysed by taking into account the will of the legislator. However, the interpreter is to some extent free to reconstruct the purpose both by assuming that the legislature wanted to adopt legislation in concordance to the Basic Law as well as other supreme international legislation and by reading the provision in the light of new developments in technology and society (see above *objektivisierter Gesetzgeberwille*).[178] Again, both purpose and meaning are to be considered in the light of the underlying system of law.

Consideration of fairness and equality can also be included when determining what the meaning and purpose of an Act is. Here one may find analysis of consequences based on empirical data or fictional evaluations. Teleological interpretation

175 Cf. BL Art. 100 in conjunction with §§ 80 ff. Constitution of the FCC Act (*Bundesverfassunggerichtsgesetz*).

176 On the importance of Savigny for adoption of a coherent theory on legal method in Germany, see Wolfgang Paul Reutter, *"Objektiv Wirkliches" in Friedrich Carl von Savignys Rechtsdenken, Rechtsquellen- und Methodenlehre* (Vittorio Klostermann 2011) 5 ff.

177 Examples for the teleological interpretation can be found in BGHZ 84, p. 381 (383); BGH ruling of 23. Sep. 1999, III ZR 322/98 (*Erbensucherfall*).

178 Cf. BL Art. 20 (3).

is thus a safety relief valve in cases where a deduction from concepts would lead to an outcome that would be incommensurable to fundamental legal principles of law. However, where the legislature had consciously decided to deviate from such a principle, e. g., when adopting a provision concerning the termination of contracts under certain circumstances in order to safeguard consumer rights, it would be of no help to refer to the general acknowledged principle *pacta sunt servanda.* General principles are therefore more often applied in order to support the individual outcome of a case and thus the rule applied by the court.

Even though case law is not considered a formal source of law in Germany, the four modes of interpretation are by analogy applied to court decisions as well. This applies particularly for rules in headnotes (*Leitsätze*), which contain the guiding principles and *Rechtssätze* applied by a court solving the case at hand. These headnotes are often formulated in an abstract and broad manner, comparable to abstract general norms in legislation. However, there are differences to the interpretation of legislation as well. The intent of the court is only relevant insofar as the rule has to be interpreted in the light of its specific context. Consequently, the technique of differentiation where the case at hand is compared with earlier case law in order to find differences and similarities is applied in Germany as well. However, because no formal doctrine of *stare decisis* has been established,[179] it is not essential to do so in order to deviate from earlier case law. The reason why judges apply this technique anyway is because they want to legitimise the outcome and safeguard their decision from being revoked by the appellate courts or the supreme courts. A deviation from well-established case law requires therefore *de facto* a more thorough explanation than a ruling in accordance with this legal practice.

After the content of the applicable (abstract) rules have been identified and determined by a court, the last step is to apply it to the facts of the actual case. This process is called *subsumption.* In theory, finding the applicable law and subsumption are two separate operations. However, in practice these two are strongly interconnected. The facts are decisive for the question of whether there is a relevant difference between the case at hand and the cases the legislator had in mind (subjective will of the legislature) or should have had in mind (objective will) when adopting the relevant provision. In addition, differences in the underlying facts may give rise to excluding the case at hand from the application of a rule set forth by earlier legal practice.

Conflicts between two or more legal provisions are in Germany, as in most other European countries, mainly solved by applying the *lex-principles.* However, these principles do not apply in case of a collision of norms of the Basic Law and those based on international law, especially the European Convention on Human Rights (ECHR). In several judgments the FCC has considered this situation without taking a clear position. Nevertheless, it is obvious that the *lex superior* principle is not applicable due to the fact that constitutional law and the Convention cannot be placed in a hierarchy of norms.

179 See Zimmermann (2019) (n 1) § 1.10 C, 27

They are instead two separate regimes with overlapping content, mainly complementing each other.[180] I will return to this problem below.[181]

5.5 Style of court-rulings

Even the style of court-rulings resembles the ideal of a scientific, objective and predictable application of law. All courts are obliged to give reasons for their verdicts and provide a brief summary of the facts. This aims to make judicial decisions transparent and reviewable, not least for legal scholars. Verdicts are rendered in the 'Name of the People', indicating the objectivity and impartiality of the judiciary. As a consequence of the idea that law should provide just one dogmatically correct answer to each legal question, court rulings do not contain dissenting opinions (with the exception of the FCC's rulings). Judgments are therefore drafted in rather impersonal and dispassionate style, avoiding the more personalised and subjective manner of reasoning typical of judgments in the common-law jurisdictions, but also in Norway. The '*Urteilsstil*' is based on a deductive operation, deriving legal consequences determined by the law. However, particularly the judgments of the Supreme Courts take conflicting opinions into account, discussing their merits and challenges. This allows for academic criticism. Indeed, these judgments are addressed to the legal community as much as the parties involved.[182]

6. Professionalisation

The way lawyers are educated is crucial for any legal culture.[183] Germany has traditionally been a country with an extraordinary high level of professionalisation in the field of law.[184] Ever since the late Middle Ages, law was taught at universities and other institutions focusing on education of administrative officials and noblemen.[185] Legal practitioners, lawyers, and legal scientists received at least some kind of legal education; initially this was as part of the study of theology, but soon separate law faculties emerged focussing on the study of Roman Law or natural law rather than canon law.[186] Local law became an independent subject at the universities especially after Christian Thomasius criticised Roman Law and argued for studying local legal traditions more

180 Rainer Grote, 'Internationalisation of the German Legal Method' in Ingvill Helland and Sören Koch (eds), *Nordic and Germanic Legal Methods* (Mohr Siebeck 2014) 334 ff. with further references.

181 Section 7.

182 See also Zimmermann (2019) (n 1) 28.

183 Ibid 36.

184 For a historical overview, see Thomas Rüfner, 'Historischer Überblick: Studium, Prüfungen, Berufszugang der Juristen in der geschichtlichen Entwicklung' in Christian Baldus, Thomas Finkenauer and Thomas Rüfner (eds), *Bologna und das Rechtsstudium* (Mohr Siebeck 2011) 3 ff. From a comparative perspective, see Stefan Vogenauer, 'Legal Scholarship' in Jürgen Basedow, Klaus J. Hopt, Reinhard Zimmermann and Andreas Stier (eds), *The Max Planck Encyclopaedia of European Private Law* (Oxford University Press 2012) 1077 ff.

185 E.g., *Ritterakademien*.

186 Rüfner (2011) (n 183) 5 f.

thoroughly.[187] The institutionalised structure of legal education can be traced back to the 18th century reforms in Prussia. At that point Prussia was a conglomerate of many and sometimes remote territories with highly diverse social and cultural background. In order to govern these territories efficiently, a body of highly and homogeneous educated lawyers was regarded as an essential precondition. Passing a university exam followed by a state-driven preparatory service became mandatory for all legal practitioners, judges, and notaries.[188] Today, the state is still in charge of the final examination (*Staatsexamen*) commencing the academic legal training at the universities and the preparatory service (*Referendariat*). Law professors are examiners in both exams.

Recently, however, the strict rules on practicing law have been relaxed, at least to some extent. In 2004, the FCC already had to decide a case regarding a retired judge's right to give legal advice. On grounds of the FCC's criticism of the applicable law, new legislation was passed in 2008.[189] In accordance with European law, everybody,[190] regardless of being an advocate (*Rechtsanwalt*) or having passed a legal exam, can give advice in legal matters. However, a distinction must be drawn between offering legal advice and the right to act before a court. In the latter regard, the applicable codes of procedure still contain certain restrictions. Nevertheless, judges still have to pass both the university exam and the following practitioner's exam. As a general rule, all participants in a lawsuit are educated lawyers, at least when it comes to proceedings at appellate and supreme courts.

As a consequence of the federal structure of Germany, the states (*Länder*) are in charge of legal training.[191] One could therefore expect that this feature of the German constitutional order would have a significant impact on the legal culture.[192] This, however, is not the case. The reason for this is twofold: first, the states have established a close cooperation with the goal of harmonising the legal education of lawyers, at least in terms of the basic structures.[193] Second, the legal sources and the legal methodology, which a German lawyer has to apply, are, disregarding some local administrative law specialities, fairly identical. This applies especially to fields like private law, criminal law or tax law where the pertinent regulations are mainly federal law.

The high esteem for a scientific background of lawyers is also likened to the notion that a doctoral degree is still regarded highly both in court and among legal practitioners alike. In addition, in Germany the title "Dr." is part of a person's name. Consequently,

187 Christian Thomasius, *Summarischer Entwurf der Grundregeln, die einem studioso juris zu wissen nöthig* (Halle 1699) Cap. I.

188 Cf. Gesetzes zur Verhütung von Mißbräuchen auf dem Gebiete der Rechtsberatung, enacted 13 December 1935 (RGBL I S. 1478).

189 Act on Legal Services (*Rechtsdienstleistungsgesetz*) enacted 12 December 2007.

190 Cf. EU Directive 2005/36 (ABL EG Nr. I. 255, S. 22).

191 Only a general framework is provided by federal legislation, cf. German Judiciary Act §§ 5 ff., Federal Lawyers' Act § 4; Federal Act on Notaries Public § 5.

192 Overemphasising the impact of federalism, Zimmermann (2019) (n 1) 39.

193 On the constant debate concerning reforms of the legal education see ibid 36 f. with further references.

misuse of an academic title is a criminal offence according to the Criminal Code.[194] However, as we have seen before, an academic degree is no formal requirement for practising law, but it is almost mandatory to become a law professor, still one of the most prestigious positions for lawyers.

On the other hand, the rules concerning advertisement for legal services are still very strict in Germany. Despite some minor amendments due to a European directive,[195] the Legal Service Act (*Rechtsdienstleistungsgesetz*) is very clear that a proper legal education is required to advertise legal services, and even for legal professionals, advertisement is permitted only within narrowly defined limits.[196] One reason for this is that studying law is still very popular in Germany and professional lawyers are thus anxious to exclude all other competition. Each year approximately 10,000 new law students attend the 46 legal education facilities in Germany.[197] Until 2000, the universities had a monopoly on the legal education of lawyers, however today more than 10% of the law students receive their training at colleges of higher education (*Fachhochschule*) or private universities. In 2012, 1,395 law professors were active; of these 1,168 men and 227 women.[198]

Law professors, other legal scholars (even law students), lawyers and judges produce a huge amount of legal literature each year. It is nearly impossible to measure the total number of publications related to juridical topics. In a survey on ranking of legal journals carried out by the University of Hamburg in 2012, 199 different legal journals were listed within Germany.[199] The real figures can be anticipated as being even higher. The estimated number of books published annually, which could also be classified as legal literature, is in the tens of thousands. In addition, thousands of judgments are published in specialised law reviews. Most of them are also available online today.[200] On this basis, case law is just a small share of the available legal argument bases. Taking into consideration that the German legal method does not recognise a *stare decisis* principle, but is based on the assumption that law consists of a system of norms, textbooks and legal commentaries or handbooks is often preferred as a starting point both in legal education and by practitioners when figuring out how to solve a case. To manage the vast amount

194 The criminal code (§ 134).

195 EU Directive No. 2005/36/EG.

196 Cf. Gesetz über außergerichtliche Rechtsdienstleistungen § 1 (1): "Dieses Gesetz regelt die Befugnis, außergerichtliche Rechtsdienstleistungen zu erbringen. Es dient dazu, die Rechtsuchenden, den Rechtsverkehr und die Rechtsordnung vor unqualifizierten Rechtsdienstleistungen zu schützen." This purpose has been criticised by Ulrich Everling, who in a report to the German confederation of lawyers (*Deutscher Juristentag*) claimed that Germany is the country with the strictest rules on exercising a legal profession. See *Gutachten C zum 58. Deutschen Juristentag*, München 1990, 69 ff., C 91. The majority of lawyers seem, however, to be of the opinion that the new rules are not strict enough, cf. e.g. Volker Römermann, 'Rechtsdienstleistungsgesetz – Die (un)heimliche Revolution in der Rechtsberatungsbranche' *Neue Juristische Wochenschrift*, Heft 42 2006, 3025 ff.

197 See http://de.wikiversity.org/wiki/Liste_der_juristischen_Fakultäten_in_Deutschland assessed 11. December 2019.

198 See Statistisches Bundesamt – Fachserie 11 Reihe 4.4 Bildung und Kultur – Personal an Hochschulen, p. 186.

199 The results of the survey are published by Marcel Gröls and Tanja Gröls. Ein Ranking juristischer Fachzeitschriften. Juristische Zeitschrift 17/2009 488 ff.

200 Court decisions and other legal materials including acts of parliament can be found in the database *Juris*, and the publisher *Beck* issues helpful manuals containing copies of all relevant legislation pertinent to a specific area of law.

of legal material, it has become necessary to apply a systematic approach, identifying first the legal problem at hand, then the pertinent legal provisions. When that has been achieved, the lawyer will carry on to consult relevant court practice. That does not, however, mean that court decisions do not play an important role in legal education. As a rule, a number of landmark decisions in each field of law are used to illustrate the main principle of law or the functioning of the legal system. Therefore, students sometimes tend to regard these decisions as precedents, even though they are not.

In addition, the German university-based education promotes mainly a systematic and scientific approach to the law. At the end of the academic training a very broad and at the same time detailed knowledge of substantive law, including legal doctrine, is required. Furthermore, the candidate has to master the highly formalised method of providing legal opinions on hypothetical cases. As pointedly stated by Professor Zimmermann:

> "This method is designed to ensure that the student considers the case under all relevant legal aspects, [...] Of central importance is the notion of an *Anspruch* ('claim') by means of which the leading 19th century scholar Bernhard Windscheid managed to remould the Roman *actio* into a term of substantive, rather than procedural law. [...] This way of thinking is designed to cure students of any temptation to approach the case with a naïve and unselfconscious sense of what is right and wrong. It nurtures a mental discipline that is widely regarded as a specific attribute of lawyers. It both requires and encourages a style of writing that is precise, detached and 'neutral'; or as may also be said, entirely colourless and devoid of any literary grace and personal flavour. And it possesses a sublime, if faintly pedantic, inherent logic."[201]

This changes, at least gradually, after the first state examination when the legal candidate enters into the last stage of this obligatory education. In the preparatory service (*Referendiat*), the candidate receives the necessary training that is required for practicing as a lawyer. Here, pragmatic considerations play a more important role than in the university education. Several months of obligatory apprenticeship in all sectors of the legal profession provide each lawyer with at least some practical experience before entering his or her first assignment. Despite some recent adjustments, *Referendariat* is still focused on the task of a judge.[202] Accordingly, no additional training is required for the few who are appointed as judges, nor is there any other requirement to become a judge than exceptionally good grades. Nevertheless, since judges are also appointed to one of the five court hierarchies, it is advisable to specialise, even while attaining the general education that all German lawyers have in common.

201 Zimmermann (2019) (n 1) 41.

202 Illustratively the German title for this exam is – *Richterexamen* or *Assessorexamen*.

7. Internationalisation

Germany is traditionally a country that had received strong impulses from international legal movements. Roman, canon, and natural law all have had enormous impact on the German legal culture.[203] However, after the major fields of law had been codified at the end of the 19th century, besides being exported to other legal cultures, German law became a more or less closed national system. Even though some international treatises made minor amendments necessary, these changes had little to no impact on the perception of German law as a mere national endeavour. This did not really change until the 1990s. After the fall of the Berlin Wall, international law came into focus once again, and legal science again played an important role. Driven by ideas of globalisation and general optimism regarding a real political and legal Union in Europe after the end of the Cold War, German scholars were engaged in various projects concerning the harmonising of law in Europe, and even a European Civil Code seemed in reach.[204] In 1991 Germany ratified the UN Convention on Contracts for the International Sale of Goods (CISG). This Convention has become highly influential particularly because it has produced a significant amount of case law.[205] At the same time, the influence of EU law on national legislation gradually increased and the case law of the Court of Justice of the European Union was recognised as important on the national level.[206] Students have to familiarise themselves with the basic principles of EU law and many law students are attending exchange programmes (Erasmus) in order to study abroad. At the same time the number of foreign students at German universities has considerably increased in recent years, often due to efforts by some law schools to obtain an international reputation and profile. Some faculties have established chairs for European Law Studies, European Private Law or European Legal History. However, most practitioners are still

---

203 Reinhard Zimmermann, *Roman Law, Contemporary Law, European Law: The Civilian Tradition Today* (Oxford University Press 2001) 3 ff.

204 See e.g. Martin Schmidt Kessel, 'European Civil Code' in Jürgen Basedow, Klaus J. Hopt, Reinhard Zimmermann and Andreas Stier (eds), *The Max Planck Encyclopaedia of European Private Law* (Oxford University Press 2012) 153 ff. with reference to the comprehensive literature on this topic; see also Ewoud Hondius, Arthur Severijn Hartkamp, Martijn Willem Hesselink and Carla Joustra (eds), *Towards a European Civil Code* (3rd ed, Kluwer 2004). Today the optimism has yielded to pragmatism or even total opposition. Nevertheless, the harmonisation projects have contributed to a large-scale consciousness of the common roots of the European legal cultures and promoted disciplines like legal history and legal comparisons. See also Zimmermann (2019) (n 1) 46. Arguing for academically supervised restatements of European Contract Law, Nils Jansen, *The Making of Legal Authority: Non-legislative Codifications in Historical and Comparative Perspective* (Mohr Siebeck 2012). The most recent discussion concerns a European Code of Commercial Law, cf. two leaders in (2019) Vol. 27 *Zeitschrift für Europäische Privatrecht.*

205 Zimmermann (2019) (n 1) 47.

206 *Zeitschrift für Europäische Privatrecht* contains regular reports on pertinent case law, the most recent is published in Vol. 27 (2019). From this volume, see Christian Kohler, Sibylle Seyr and Jean-Christophe Puffer-Mariette, 'Unionsrecht und Privatrecht - Zur Rechtsprechung des EuGH im Jahre 2017' 126 ff.; regarding new EU legislation: 'Rechtsakte der Europäischen Union auf den Gebiet des Europäischen Privatrechts 2018' 836; see also Vol. 25, 140 ff.

reluctant towards or even sceptical of internationalisation.[207] One important reason for this may be the impact international sources have on the carefully balanced 'scientific' national system of law.

Therefore it is often emphasised that Germany is a dualistic system, meaning that international law is considered a legal order separate from the national one.[208] The dualistic principle is expressed directly in the Basic Law.[209] According to the Basic Law only general principles of international law (*Die allgemeinen Regeln des Völkerrechts*) are automatically part of the German law;[210] all other rules based on international treaties and agreements have to be implemented by means of a special Act of Parliament called *Zustimmungsgesetz*, that is, law requiring approval.[211] This Act is at the same time regarded as implementation. The Basic Law also refers to the binding effect of a treaty within national law.[212] As an example of such an incorporation of international law into national law, one can refer to the enactment Act on implementation of the European Convention on Human Rights and Fundamental Freedoms passed by the parliament in 1952.[213] Since its incorporation via federal law (*Bundesgesetz*) the Convention is directly applicable law in all German courts.

A different question, however, concerns the ranking of the Convention in conjunction with other national legislation. Some consider the Convention as ranked equally to the Basic Law.[214] The Basic Law recognises human rights, which are inviolable and inalienable,[215] and constitutes the basis of all human society as well as peace and justice in the world.[216] They argue that this implies that all state authorities have to respect the human rights contained in the ECHR. The majority of legal scholars reject this view due to the fact that the legislature has no competence to restrict its own freedom to act for all posterity by means of an ordinary Act of Parliament (here the *Zustimmungsgesetz*

---

207 Zimmermann (2019) (n 1) 47 notes: "Yet, all these development shave not fundamentally changed the specifically German approach towards legal education, legal thinking, and legal writing. A comprehensive internationalisation is still one of the challenges faced by legal scholarship in Germany today." Significantly, Zimmermann regards handling the challenges of internationalisation a task for legal scholars, not primarily the legislator or the judiciary.

208 So explicitly in the ruling of the FCC in the *Görgülü*-case BVerfGE 111, 307, para. 34: "[...] shown by the existence and wording of Article 25 and Article 59 (2) of the Basic Law"; see for further details Ingvill Helland, *Rulings of the European Court of Human Rights as a Legal Argument – a comparison between German and Norwegian law* (PhD dissertation, Bergen 2012) 173.

209 BL Art. 25 and 59 (2).

210 BL Art. 25.

211 Cf. Art. 59 (2): "Verträge, welche die politischen Beziehungen des Bundes regeln oder sich auf Gegenstände der Bundesgesetzgebung beziehen, bedürfen der Zustimmung oder der Mitwirkung der jeweils für die Bundesgesetzgebung zuständigen Körperschaften in der Form eines Bundesgesetzes."

212 BL Art. 59. Emphasizing this difference is Helland (2012) (n 207) 173 ff.

213 Gesetz über die Konvention zum Schutze der Menschenrechte und Grundfreiheiten, Bundesgesetzblatt (BGBL) 1952 Vol. II, p. 685.

214 The different lines of argumentation are presented in more detail and with references in Helland (2012) (n 208) 177 ff.

215 BL Art. 1 (2): "Das deutsche Volk bekennt sich darum zu unverletzlichen und unveräusserlichen Menschenrechten als Grundlage jeder menschlichen Gemeinschaft, des Friedens und der Gerechtigkeit in der Welt."

216 BL Art. 1 (2).

of 1952).[217] A more moderate opinion treats the Convention as an instrument with intermediate constitutional rank over the Basic Law.[218] Proponents of this latter view argue that this general clause guarantees everyone to 'freely unfold their personality' and encompasses indirectly all rights and freedoms granted by the Convention.

Nevertheless, this opinion is not convincing due to the fact that it is much too vague to give a clear distinction. Another approach regards the Convention as semi-constitutional law. As already mentioned, universal rules of international law are directly applicable pursuant to the Basic Law.[219] However, even if not excluding international treaties from falling into the scope of "universal rules of international law", the FCC mainly refers to universally applicable international customary law, complemented by recognised fundamental principles of law.[220] While some provisions in the treaty may be regarded as universally applicable to international customary law, the ECHR as such does not fall within the scope of the Basic Law.[221] The German courts have therefore consistently rejected treating the Convention as constitutional or semi-constitutional law.[222] This is also in accordance with the prevailing opinion in legal science today.[223] However, since the Convention is a living instrument, its status has to be determined in each individual case. The main rule is still that it has no constitutional rank and consequently cannot, in case of a conflict, replace the fundamental principles of the Basic Law.[224]

In this context, the issue has been discussed whether the Convention would be superior to the national law even if this would affect that basic rights of the Basic Law.[225] The FCC has given its opinion several times on this highly controversial question. In the most recent rulings, the FCC argued for a synthetic approach giving the European Court of Human Rights (ECtHR) and the Convention high importance when determining the content of the basic rights in the German constitution. To avoid conflict with the protection of fundamental freedoms in the Convention, the national courts have to take the case law of the ECtHR into consideration. In the *Görgülü*-case from 2004, and even more elaborated in the *Preventive Detention* ruling from 2011, the FCC stated the following guidelines.[226] First, all German authorities must, as far as it lies in their competences, take into account the Convention and the case law of the ECtHR. When acts of these authorities, such as a court ruling, issuing new or modifying existing legislation, or executing an administrative order, have a direct impact on the rights of the Convention or the exercise of the Conventions rights, they are obliged to actively integrate the

217 Helland (2012) (n 208) 181 note 504 and 505.

218 BL Art. 2 (1). References in ibid 182.

219 BL Art. 25.

220 BVerfGE 23, 288 (317).

221 BL Art. 25. Helland (2012) (n 208) 186.

222 BVerfGE 74, 358 (370); BVerfGE 82, 106 (120) and lately acknowledged in BVerfGE 111, 307 para. 31.

223 For references, see Helland (2012) (n 207) 188 note 540.

224 This was emphasized once again in the *Görgülü*-case BVerfGE 111, 307 (headnote).

225 For a discussion of this problem in more detail, see Grote (2014) (n 180).

226 BVerfGE 111, 307 (321 ff.); BVerfGE 128, 326 (348 ff.).

convention as interpreted by the ECtHR into their reasoning and decision-making process.[227] However, in the very rare case that a Convention conformance interpretation cannot be achieved and the application of a ruling of the ECtHR would lead to an outcome that would be incommensurable to the fundamental values of the Basic Law, the latter has to take precedence.[228]

As a member of the European Union, Germany is also bound by the EU treaties. Actually, the Basic Law provides the basis for transfer of state power and sovereign rights to an inter-state institution such as the EU or NATO.[229] In consequence, the EU institutions have gained the competence to produce norms, which are applicable in Germany without any further acts of incorporation. Thus, EU regulations are directly applicable law in Germany.[230] In addition, Germany is obliged to implement EU directives. However, the Court of Justice of the European Union (CJEU) has consistently held that directives under certain circumstances can also produce direct legal effects within the member states. This applies especially when a member state has failed to implement the directive in time.[231] Even though initially the Federal Supreme Court dealing with tax-matters (*Bundesfinanzhof*) argued for a more restrictive approach, the view of CJEU was accepted by the FCC.[232]

Furthermore, the FCC stated that the CJEU has to be regarded 'lawful judge' (*gesetzlicher Richter*) in the sense of the Basic Law (art. 101 (1)).[233] This provision contains the constitutional guarantee of the right of a court hearing in all instances (*Garantie des rechtlichen Gehörs*). Pursuant to the Treaty on the Functioning of the European Union (TFEU), national courts are obliged to submit all questions concerning the compatibility of a national provision with Union law to an European Court.[234] Therefore, violating this obligation under TFEU contains as a general rule also a violation of the Basic Law.[235] Regarding the FCC, this applies to all cases where a national court deliberately or grossly negligent has ignored the obligation to consult the EU courts.[236]

Even if it is still controversial how to deal with conflicting competences, European institutions and their practices have been recognised as an integral part of the German legal system. In addition it is, at least in theory, accepted that interpreting the ECHR or EU-based legislation requires a different methodological approach than interpreting German national law.[237] In other words, internationalisation has also had an effect on

227 *Preventive Detention*-case BVerfGE 128, 326 (349).

228 BVerfGE 111, 307. On this specific issue from a Norwegian perspective, see Helland (2012) (n 208) 282 ff.

229 BL Art. 24: "(1) The Federation may by a law transfer sovereign powers to international organisations."

230 Cf. Art. 288 TFEU.

231 Since Case 148/78 *Pubblico Ministero v Ratti* [1979] European Court Reports (ECR) 1629.

232 *Bundesfinanzhof* ruling of 16 July 1981 [1982] 1 CLMR 527.

233 BVerfGE 73, 339 (366); 75, 223 (244 f.).

234 Art. 26 TFEU.

235 BL Art. 101 (1).

236 BVerfGE 75, 233 (245); regarding the guidelines put forward by the FCC concerning this issue, see Grote (2014) (n 179) 330 ff.

237 Axel Flessner, 'Juristische Methode und Europäisches Privatrecht' *Juristische Zeitschrift* 57 (2002) 14–23; Henninger (2009) (n 173), with further references.

the intellectual structure of the German legal culture, even if this impact is less obvious than at the institutional level. More difficult to evaluate is if the internationalisation has affected the idea of justice in Germany, and if so to what extent and direction.

These general tendencies have also impacted legal education. Teaching international law, especially EU law has been gradually more important in the last decade. Still, roughly 80% of the mandatory reading of a German student is exclusively related to national law. However, the impact of international law is often discussed within the courses and lectures given on national law. This is not surprising considering the great importance of the assumed logical coherence of the system of national law. Some German professors therefore regard international law as a threat to this coherence and present international sources in their fields of experience as disturbing factors. The reluctance regarding the Europeanisation of law and a common legal education can be demonstrated further by the strong resistance against establishing the Bologna system at German universities.[238] Due to this reluctance, the joint committee of justice ministers in Germany have decided to maintain the traditional model for legal education with two state examinations, instead of a master/bachelor degree.[239] Paradoxically, both the constitutional order and politics traditionally were quite open to extension of interstate cooperation and internationalisation of the law ever since the 1950s.[240] Against this background, the far-reaching influence of legal scholarship and its traditional focus on the systematic character of the law may prove an obstacle to a further internationalisation and harmonisation of the law. A critical supervision of this process may, on the other hand, contribute to safeguarding some of the unique features of the German legal culture that deserve to be protected.

238 Just some contributions to this debate in Germany: Heino Schöbel, 'Einführung des Bologna-Modells in der deutschen Juristenausbildung?' in Christian Baldus, Thomas Finkenauer and Thomas Rüfner (eds.), *Bologna und das Rechtsstudium* (Tübingen 2011) 253 ff.; Matthias Kilian, *Modelle der Juristenausbildung in Europa* (Deutscher Anwaltverlag 2010); Rainer Zaczyk, 'Rechtswissenschaft oder McLaw?' (2008) no. 1 *Bonner Rechtsjournal Sonderausgabe* 1 ff; Horst Konzen, 'Bologna-Prozess und Juristenausbildung' (2010) *JuristenZeitung* 241 ff.; Horst Konzen and Harald Schliemann, 'Bologna für Juristen – Gedanken zur Reform der Juristenausbildung' in Peter Hanau, Jens Thau and Harm Peter Westermann (eds.), *Festschrift für Klaus Adomeit* (Luchterhand 2008) 343 ff.; Christian Baldus, Thomas Finkenauer and Thomas Rüfner, 'Die Bologna-Reform aus Hochschullehrersicht' in Christian Baldus, Thomas Finkenauer and Thomas Rüfner (eds), *Bologna und das Rechtsstudium* (Mohr Siebeck 2011) 281 ff.; Deutscher Juristen-Fakultätentag (eds.), *Der "Bologna-Prozess" und die Juristenausbildung in Deutschland* (Boorberg 2007); Peter Huber, *Beiträge zu Juristenausbildung und Hochschulrecht* (Boorberg 2010); Gerfried Fischer and Thomas Wünsch (eds), *Der Bologna-Prozess an den juristischen Fakultäten* (Nomos 2006); Filippo Ranieri, *Juristen für Europa* (Münster 2006); Jan Ischdonat, *Die deutsche Juristenausbildung unter dem Einfluss des Bologna-Prozesses* (Optimedien 2010); Marcel Senn, 'Rechtswissenschaft nach der Bologna-Reform' (2010) *Rechtswissenschaft* 218 ff. Cf. for a very reluctant approach, Beschluss des 90. Juristenfakultätentags vom 3./4.6. 2010 (DJFT 2010/I); see also http://www.djft.de/ accessed 11 December 2019.

239 See http://www.justiz.de/justizministerkonferenz/index.php accessed 11 December 2019.

240 Cf. the first sentence of the Preamble to the BL: "Conscious of their responsibility before God and man, inspired by the determination to promote world peace as an equal partner in a united Europe, the German people, in the exercise of their constituent power, have adopted this Basic Law." Compare furthermore BL Art. 1 (2), above n 214.

8. Some concluding reflections

In this attempt to describe central features of the German legal culture, two fairly related features stand out: the exceptionally strong focus on legal science (*Rechtswissenschaft*) and the idea of law as a coherent system of norms. These notions have left traces and had impacts on the mechanisms of norm production, conflict resolution, the prevailing ideal of justice, legal method, and professionalisation. In addition, it could be demonstrated that these characteristics of the German legal culture have deep roots in the legal history and at the same time are a product of the specific legal and extra-legal preconditions upon which this culture is based. Reduced to its essence, one may state that German legal culture was, and still is, shaped to a greater extent than all other European legal cultures by legal science and its logic, methods, and purposes. The ongoing internationalisation in many ways is challenging the traditional structures of the German legal culture. However, German legal scholars are not leaving the field to European institutions but attempting to regain control over the process by identifying the historical roots and analysing the common core of European law and legal thinking. In order to further the systematisation of European law, several scientific research and study groups have been established to determine this common core, common principles, and a Common Frame of Reference especially within the field of private law. That German legal scholars are a driving force behind these enterprises cannot be surprising, taking into account the characteristics of the German legal culture. To what extent legal scholars can obtain a comparably strong influence on the European level depends to a great deal on the openness of legal science towards other legal cultures, and their specific institutional and intellectual characteristics, when forming new theories of law or models systematising it. This may explain the renewed interest in the disciplines of comparative law and legal history in recent years. One thing seems obvious: the scientific approach towards law and its application is the most distinct notion of the German culture.

The contemporary German Legal Culture	
Institutional structure	
Conflict resolution	*Norm production*
Multilayer court hierarchies on the state, federal and supranational level. Five separate court hierarchies each with a Supreme Court on the federal level. A federal Constitutional court on top (limited to constitutional review) High degree of specialisation regarding fields of law and in the internal structure of the courts.	Law-making on the state, federal and supra-national level by the EU, federal or state legislator, no theory of precedent, exception case law of the FCC. 'Law' (*Recht*) binds courts and the administration, therefore the case law of the Supreme Courts and legal doctrine contribute indirectly to the production of legal norms.

Intellectual structure			
Ideal of justice	*Legal method*	*Professionalisation*	*Internationalisation*
Outcome-predictability based on the idea that justice is reflected in and safeguarded by the system of positive law	Judges are constitutionally bound by legislation and law ("Gesetz und Recht" – Art. 20 (3) Basic Law). In practice: combination of deduction from legislation and induction from case law. Customary law and preparatory works are of secondary importance. Law is applied according to scientific standards of objectivity and transparency, impacting also the style of court decisions	High degree of professionalisation and specialization A scientific approach is still prevailing in the legal education but is also applied by legal professionals, in their argumentation, legal writings and verdicts.	High degree of internationalisation – still mostly positive attitude towards internationalisation as long as the international impulses do not threaten the system of law or fundamental values of the Basic Law.

9. Bibliography

Alexy R, Theorie der juristischen Argumentation (Suhrkamp 1978)

Assmann HD, Kirchner C and Schanze E (eds), *Ökonomische Analyse des Rechts*, (Athenäum Verlag 1978)

Baldus C, Finkenauer T and Rüfner T, 'Die Bologna-Reform aus Hochschullehrersicht' in Baldus C, Finkenauer T and Rüfner T (eds), *Bologna und das Rechtsstudium* (Mohr Siebeck 2011)

Battenberg F and Schildt B (eds), *Das Reichskammergericht im Spiegel seiner Prozessakten* (Böhlau 2010). DOI: http://dx.doi.org/10.7788/boehlau.9783412213176

Bernt JF and Mæhle SS, *Rett, samfunn og demokrati* (Gyldendal 2007)

Bieber R, Epiney A and Haag M, *Die Europäische Union – Europarecht und Politik* (11th ed, Nomos 2015)

Branahl U, *Justizberichterstattung. Eine Einführung* (VS Verlag für Sozialwissenschaften 2005). DOI: http://dx.doi.org/10.1007/978-3-322-80736-6

Bydlinski F, *Juristische Methodenlehre und Rechtsbegriff* (2nd ed, Springer-Verlag 1991). DOI: http://dx.doi.org/10.1007/978-3-7091-6705-2

—— *Grundzüge der juristischen Methodenlehre* (UTB 2005)

Collings J, *Democracy's Guardians: A History of the German Federal Constitutional Court. 1951–2001* (Oxford University Press 2015). DOI: https://dx.doi.org/10.1093/acprof:oso/9780198753377.003.0001

Esser J, 'Methodik des Privatrechts' (1972) in Häberle P and Leser HG (eds), *Wege der Rechtsgewinnung. Ausgewählte Aufsätze* (Mohr Siebeck 1990)

—— *Vorverständnis und Methodenwahl in der Rechtsfindung* (2nd ed, Athenäum Verlag 1972)

Decock W and others (eds), *Handbuch der Geschichte der Konfliktlösung in Europa. Vol. I–III* (Frankfurt am Main, forthcoming)

Deutscher Juristen-Fakultätentag (eds), *Der "Bologna-Prozess" und die Juristenausbildung in Deutschland* (Boorberg 2007)

Diedrichsen U, 'Das Bundesverfassungsgericht als oberstes Zivilgericht – ein Lehrstück der juristischen Methodenlehre' (1998) Vol. 198 *Achiv für die Civilistische Praxis* 171

Djeffal, C 'Die herrschende Meinung als Argument – Ein didaktischer Beitrag in historischer und theoretischer Perspektive' *Zeitschrift für das Juristische Studium* 5 (2013)

Dörner HJ, '*Neues aus dem Befristungsrecht*' (2007) Nr. 2 *Neue Zeitschrift für Arbeitsrecht* 57

Esser J, *Grundsatz und Norm in der richterlichen Fortbildung des Privatrechts* (Mohr 1956)

—— *Vorverständnis und Methodenwahl in der Rechtsfindung* (2nd ed, Athenäum Verlag 1972)

Fikentscher W, *Methoden des Rechts in vergleichender Darstellung*, Vol. IV (Tübingen 1975)

Fischer G and Wünsch T (eds), *Der Bologna-Prozess an den juristischen Fakultäten* (Nomos 2006)

Flessner A, 'Juristische Methode unde Europäisches Privatrecht' *Juristische Zeitschrift* 57 (2002) 14-23

Foster N and Sule S, *German Legal System and Laws* (4th ed, Oxford University Press 2010)

Freckmann A and Wegerich T, *The German Legal System* (Sweet & Maxwell 1999)

Haferkamp HP, 'Holy Roman Empire' in Basedow J, Hopt KJ, Zimmermann R and Stier A (eds), *The Max Planck Encyclopaedia of European Private Law* (Oxford University Press 2012)

—— Historical Conditions for the Contemporary Understanding of Legal Method in Germany' in Helland I and Koch S (eds), *Nordic and Germanic Legal Methods* (Mohr Siebeck 2014)

Haffner S, *Geschichte eines Deutschen – Die Erinnerungen 1914–1933* (Deutsche Verlags-Anstalt 2000)

Helland I, *Rulings of the European Court of Human Rights as a Legal Argument – a comparison between German and Norwegian law* (PhD dissertation, Bergen 2012)

—— 'Introduction to German legal method' in Helland I and Koch S (eds), *Nordic and Germanic Legal Methods* (Mohr Siebeck 2014)

—— 'The permissibility and (conditional) recommendability of *contra legem* interpretations in Norwegian law' (2014) Vol. 37 no. 1/144 *Retfærd* 17

—— and Koch S, 'Norwegian and German Legal Methods Compared: Similarities and Differences, their Reasons and Consequences' in Helland I and Koch S (eds), *Nordic and Germanic Legal Methods* (Mohr Siebeck 2014)

Henninger T, 'Legal Culture and Common Principles of European Legal Method' in Helland I and Koch S (eds), *Nordic and Germanic Legal Methods* (Mohr Siebeck 2014)

Hess B, *Intertemporales Privatrecht* (Mohr Siebeck 1998)

Huber P, *Beiträge zu Juristenausbildung und Hochschulrecht* (Boorberg 2010)

Frowein JA, 'Die Anforderungen der Europäischen Menschenrechtskonvention an den nationalen Rechtsschutz' in Frowein JA and Ulsamer G, *Europäische Menschenrechtskonvention und nationaler Rechtsschutz* (C.F. Müller 1985)

Giegerich T, 'Wirkung und Rang der EMRK' in Grote R and Marauhn T (eds), *EMRK/GG Konkordanzkommentar* (Mohr Siebeck 2006)

Grabenwarter C and Pabel K, *Europäische Menschenrechtskonvention* (C.H. Beck/Helbing Lichtenhahn/MANZ 2012)

Grote R, 'Internationalisation of the German Legal Method' in Helland I and Koch S (eds), *Nordic and Germanic Legal Methods* (Mohr Siebeck 2014)

Haratsch A, 'Die Europäische Menschenrechtskonvention in der deutschen Rechtsordnung – Eine innerstaatliche Standortbestimmung' (2000) *MenschenRechtsMagazin: Themenheft "50 Jahre EMRK"* 62

Haß S, *Die Urteile des Europäischen Gerichtshofs für Menschenrechte. Charakter, Bindungswirkung, Durchsetzung* (Peter Lang 2006)

Heckötter U, *Die Bedeutung der Europäischen Menschenrechtskonvention und der Rechtsprechung des EGMR für die deutschen Gerichte* (Carl Heymanns Verlag 2008)

Hesse K, *Grundzüge des Verfassungsrechts der Bundesrepublik Deutschland* (20th ed, C.F. Müller 1999)

Hinghofer-Szalkay SG, 'Twins or estranged Cousins? – Legal Methodology in Austria vis-à-vis Germany' in Helland I and Koch S (eds), *Nordic and Germanic Legal Methods* (Mohr Siebeck 2014)

Hondius E, Hartkamp AS, Hesselink MW and Joustra C (eds), *Towards a European Civil Code* (3rd ed, Kluwer 2004)

Ischdonat J, *Die deutsche Juristenausbildung unter dem Einfluss des Bologna-Prozesses* (Optimedien 2010)

Jachmann-Michel M, 'Art. 95' in Maunz T and Dürig G (eds), *Bonner Kommentar zum Grundgesetz* (8th ed, C.H. Beck 2019)

Jansen N, *The Making of Legal Authority: Non-legislative Codifications in Historical and Comparative Perspective* (Mohr Siebeck 2012). DOI: https://doi.org/10.1093%2Facprof%3Aoso%2F9780199588763.001.0001

Kämmerer JA, *Staatsorganizationsrecht* (2nd ed, Vahlen 2012)

Kilian M, *Modelle der Juristenausbildung in Europa* (Deutscher Anwaltverlag 2010)

Kirchner C, 'Methodiken für die juridikative Rechtsfortbildung im Zivilrecht' in Rückert J and Seinecke R (eds), *Methodik des Zivilrechts – von Savigny bis Teubner* (3rd ed, Nomos 2017). DOI: https://doi.org/10.5771%2F9783845272924-488

Klein E, 'Should the binding effect of the judgements of the European Court of Human Rights be extended?' in Mahoney P, Mascher F, Petzold H and Wildhaber L (eds), *Protection des droits de l'homme: La perspective européenne. Mélanges à la memoire de Rolv Ryssdal* (Carl Heymanns 2000)

Kohler C, Seyr S and Puffer-Mariette JC, 'Unionsrecht und Privatrecht - Zur Rechtsprechung des EuGH im Jahre 2017' (2019) Vol. 27 *Zeitschrift für Europäische Privatrecht* 126

Konzen H, 'Bologna-Prozess und Juristenausbildung' (2010) *JuristenZeitung* 241

—— and Schliemann H, 'Bologna für Juristen – Gedanken zur Reform der Juristenausbildung' in Hanau P, Thau J and Westermann HP (eds.), *Festschrift für Klaus Adomeit* (Luchterhand 2008)

Krüper J, Payandeh M and Sauer H (eds), *Konrad Hesses normative Kraft der Verfassung*, (Mohr Siebeck 2019). DOI: https://doi.org/10.1628%2F978-3-16-158238-7

Kruse F, *Die verfassungsrechtlichen Grenzen richterlicher Rechtsfortbildung* (Mohr Siebeck 2019). DOI: https://doi.org/10.1628%2F978-3-16-157618-8

Lamprecht R, 'Obiter dictum – Arabeske oder Ballast?' (1998) *Neue Juristische Wochenschrift* 1039

Larenz, K., *Methodenlehre der Rechtswissenschaft* (Mohr Siebeck 1991)

Larenz K and Claus-Wilhelm Canaris, *Methodenlehre der Rechtswissenschaft* (3rd ed, Springer-Verlag 1995). DOI: http://dx.doi.org/10.1007/978-3-662-08709-1

Lilie H, *Obiter dictum und Divergenzausgleich im Strafrecht: Ein Spannungsfeld zwischen Revisionsrecht und Gerichtsverfassungsrecht* (Heymann Verlag 1993)

Limbach J (ed), *Das Bundesverfassungsgericht. Geschichte – Aufgabe – Rechtsprechung* (C. F. Müller 2000)

Lundmark T, *Charting the Divide Between Common and Civil Law* (Oxford University Press 2012). DOI: http://dx.doi.org/10.1093/acprof:osobl/9780199738823.001.0001

Masing J, Jestaedt M, Jouanjan O and Capitant D (eds), *Rechtswissenschaft und Rechtspraxis. Ihr Verhältnis im Verfassungs-, Verwaltungs-, und Unionsrecht – Dokumentation des 7. Treffens des Deutsch-Französischen Gesprächskreises für Öffentliches Recht* (Mohr Siebeck 2019)

Maurer H, *Allgemeines Verwaltungsrecht* (18th ed, C.H. Beck 2011)

Mæhle SS and Aarli R, *Fra lov til rett* (Gyldendal 2016)

Neumann U, 'Juristische Methodenlehre und Theorie der juristischen Argumentation' (2001) 32 *Rechtstheorie*

—— 'Theorie der juristischen Argumentation' in Brugger W, Neumann U and Kirste S (eds), *Rechtsphilosophie im 21. Jahrhundert* (Suhrkamp 2008)

Oestmann P, *Ein Zivilprozess am Reichskammergericht* (Böhlau 2009)

Radbruch G, *Rechtsphilosophie* (4th ed, C.F. Müller 1999)

Ranieri F, *Juristen für Europa* (Münster 2006)

Reutter WP, *"Objektiv Wirkliches" in Friedrich Carl von Savignys Rechtsdenken, Rechtsquellen- und Methodenlehre* (Vittorio Klostermann 2011)

Richter R and Furubotn E, *Neue Institutionenökonomik* (4th ed, Mohr Siebeck 2014). DOI: https://doi.org/10.1628%2F978-3-16-151318-3

Robbers G, *An Introduction to German Law* (4th ed, Nomos 2006). DOI: http://dx.doi.org/10.5771/9783845262796

Römermann, V., 'Rechtsdienstleistungsgesetz – Die (un)heimliche Revolution in der Rechtsberatungsbranche' *Neue Juristische Wochenschrift*, Heft 42 2006, 3025

Rückert J, 'Das BGB und seine Prinzipien: Aufgabe, Lösung und Erfolg' in Schmoeckel M, Rückert J and Zimmermann R (eds), *Historisch Kritischer Kommentar zum BGB*, Vol. I (Mohr Siebeck 2003)

—— 'Die Schlachtrufe im Methodenkampf – Ein historischer Überblick' in Rückert J and Seinecke R (eds), *Methodik des Zivilrechts – von Savigny bis Teubner* (3rd ed, Nomos 2017). DOI: https://doi.org/10.5771%2F9783845272924-540

—— 'Methode und Zivilrecht bei Bernhard Windscheid (1817–1892)' in Rückert J and Seinecke R (eds), *Methodik des Zivilrechts – von Savigny bis Teubner* (3rd ed, Nomos 2017). DOI: https://doi.org/10.5771%2F9783845272924-120

—— and Seinecke R (eds), *Methodik des Zivilrechts – von Savigny bis Teubner*, (3rd ed, Nomos 2017). DOI: https://doi.org/10.5771%2F9783845272924

—— and Seinecke R, 'Zwölf Methodenregeln für den Ernstfall' in Rückert J and Seinecke R (eds), *Methodik des Zivilrechts – von Savigny bis Teubner* (3rd ed, Nomos 2017). DOI: https://doi.org/10.5771%2F9783845272924-38

Rüfner T, 'Historischer Überblick: Studium, Prüfungen, Berufszugang der Juristen in der geschichtlichen Entwicklung' in Baldus C, Finkenauer T and Rüfner T (eds), *Bologna und das Rechtsstudium* (Mohr Siebeck 2011)

Sahm P, 'Methode und (Zivil-)Recht bei Gunther Teubner' in Rückert J and Seinecke R (eds), *Methodik des Zivilrechts – von Savigny bis Teubner* (3rd ed, Nomos 2017). DOI: https://doi.org/10.5771%2F9783845272924-446

Schäfer B, 'Methode und Zivilrecht bei Josef Esser (1910–1999)' in Rückert J and Seinecke R (eds), *Methodik des Zivilrechts – von Savigny bis Teubner* (3rd ed, Nomos 2017). DOI: https://doi.org/10.5771%2F9783845259789_261

Schermaier, M J 'German Law' in Smits JM (ed), *Edgar encyclopaedia of comparative law* (Edvard Elgar 2006)

Schmidt-Bleibtreu B, Hofmann H and Hopfauf A, *Kommentar zum Grundgesetz* (Carl Heymanns Verlag 2011)

Schmidt Kessel M, 'European Civil Code' in Basedow J, Hopt KJ, Zimmermann R and Stier A (eds), *The Max Planck Encyclopaedia of European Private Law* (Oxford University Press 2012)

Schöbel H, 'Einführung des Bologna-Modells in der deutschen Juristenausbildung?' in Baldus C, Finkenauer T and Rüfner T (eds), *Bologna und das Rechtsstudium* (Mohr Siebeck 2011)

Schröder J, *Recht als Wissenschaft* (2nd ed., Mohr Siebeck 2012)

Schulze-Fielitz H, 'Art. 96' in Dreier H (ed), *Grundgesetz Kommentar*, Bd. 3 (2nd ed, Mohr Siebeck 2008)

Schwintowski HP, *Juristische Methodenlehre* (UTB 2005)

Senn M, 'Rechtswissenschaft nach der Bologna-Reform' (2010) *Rechtswissenschaft* 218. DOI: https://doi.org/10.5771%2F1868-8098-2010-2-218

Siems M, *Comparative law* (2nd ed, Cambridge University Press 2018). DOI: https://doi.org/10.1017%2F9781316856505

Simon H and Funk-Baker G, *Einführung in das deutsche Recht und die deutsche Rechtssprache* (C.H. Beck 2009)

Smits J, *The Making of European Private Law: Toward a Ius Commune Europaeum as a mixed legal system* (Intersentia 2002)

Sternberg S, Gschwend T, Wittig C and Engst BG, 'Zum Einfuss der öffentlichen Meinung auf Entscheidungen des Bundesverfassungsgerichts: Eine Analyse von abstrakten Normenkontrollen sowie Bund-Länder-Streitigkeiten 1974–2010' (2015) 56, Heft 4 *Politische Vierteljahresschrift*. DOI: https://doi.org/10.5771%2F0032-3470-2015-4-570

Sunde JØ, 'Champagne at the Funeral – An Introduction to Legal Culture' in Sunde JØ and Skodvin KE (eds), *Rendezvous of European Legal Cultures* (Fagbokforlaget 2010)

Teubner G, 'Nach den Fällen: Paradoxien soziologischer Jurisprudenz' in Lomfeld B (ed), *Die Fälle der Gesellschaft* (Mohr Siebeck 2017)

Thomasius C, *Summarischer Entwurf der Grundregeln, die einem studioso juris zu wissen nöthig* (Halle 1699)

Tomuschat C, *Verfassungsgewohnheitsrecht? – Eine Untersuchung zum Staatsrecht der Bundesrepublik Deutschland* (Carl Winter Universitätsverlag 1972)

Uerpmann R, *Die Europäische Menschenrechtskonvention und die deutsche Rechtsprechung* (Duncker & Humblot 1993)

Vogenauer S, 'Legal Scholarship' in Basedow J, Hopt KJ, Zimmermann R and Stier A (eds), *The Max Planck Encyclopaedia of European Private Law* (Oxford University Press 2012)

Weimann M, *Kollektiver Rechtsschutz – Ein Memorandum der Praxis [Collective Legal Protection: Notes from the Field]* (De Gruyter 2018). DOI: https://doi.org/10.1515%2F9783110609172

Wolff HA, *Ungeschriebenes Verfassungsrecht unter dem Grundgesetz* (Mohr Siebeck 2000)

Zaczyk R, 'Rechtswissenschaft oder McLaw?' (2008) no. 1 *Bonner Rechtsjournal Sonderausgabe* 1

Zimmermann R, *Roman Law, Contemporary Law, European Law: The Civilian Tradition Today* (Oxford University Press 2001)

—— 'The German Civil Code and the Development of Private Law in Germany' (2006) *Oxford U Comparative L Forum 1*, available at https://www.ouclf.iuscomp.org/.

—— 'Characteristic Aspects of the German Legal Culture' in Zekoll J and Wagner G (eds), *Introduction to German Law* (3rd ed, Wolters Kluwer 2019)

Zoellner AC, *Das Verhältnis von BVerfG und EGMR* (Verlag Dr. Kovač 2009)

9. An Introduction to Polish Legal Culture

Anna Klimaszewska, Anna Machnikowska, Sören Koch

1. Introduction[1]

1.1 A changing legal culture

The attempt to describe Polish legal culture at this very moment is a demanding task. From 1997 to 2015, its crucial elements remained more or less stable. Currently, it is a legal culture undergoing changes. After the elections of 2015, the ruling party (PiS) implemented many legal reforms, which have divided society and have been perceived differently by various groups. The relevant question for this contribution is whether these changes happen at the surface or are affecting deeper levels of law referring to Sunde's and Tuori's model of a legal sea.[2] On the surface level, one can easily determine the effect of political and legal changes by monitoring the tremendous amount of legislative amendments. Looking closer, it can be observed that at least some changes are driven by a change in deeper levels of the legal sea, impacting ideas and expectations of law. Whether they (will) affect the middle level of the unwritten general principles of law (guiding the application of law by lawyers) or reach the bottom level (of fundamental values) is more difficult to assess. Due to deep social division, their final direction is still not carved in stone. The engagement of EU institutions and careful monitoring by the international community and increasing resistance in Poland itself, are factors which have to be taken into account as well. Despite these challenges, this chapter will attempt to present the Polish legal culture and evaluate some aspects of recent changes.

---

1 This publication was prepared as part of the projects supported by funds from the National Science Centre (NCN), grant number UMO-2015/18/E/HS5/00762 and grant number UMO-2016/21/B/HS5/03221.

2 See Jørn Øyrehagen Sunde', 'Managing the Unmanageable – An Essay Concerning Legal Culture as an Analytical Tool' in this volume, chapter 2, 27.

1.2 The geographic, economic and social framework

The Republic of Poland is a unitary state located in Central Europe.[3] It is the ninth largest country in Europe in terms of the size of administrative territory and the sixth largest in the European Union in terms of population size (over 38 million people).[4] Its largest city and capital is Warsaw. Poland is the sixth largest EU economy and one of the most rapidly growing ones.[5] Its complicated political history has contributed to the fact that the Polish legal system, owing to its centuries-long experience of interweaving and mixing of various legal cultures, is a unique mosaic of solutions and institutions originating from different systems and cultures. The Polish legal identity, perhaps more so than any other in Europe, is strongly Europeanized.

When the Kingdom of Poland, founded during the reign of Bolesław I the Brave (992–1025), cemented its longstanding political association with the Grand Duchy of Lithuania by signing the Union of Lublin in 1569, the Polish-Lithuanian Commonwealth (or "the Republic of Two Nations") was established. It was one of the largest and most populous states in the Europe of the 16th and 17th century with a particularly liberal political system, which adopted the first written national constitution in Europe.[6] The partitioning of the country by the neighbouring states at the end of the 18th century sealed the loss of prosperity and prominence[7] and even the creation of the Duchy of Warsaw (1807–1815) under the French protectorate did not change this. However, this was also a time when many of the legal institutions that left a lasting mark on the Polish legal culture were established, e.g. stock exchange, a common court system, legal frameworks for commercial partnerships and companies, unrestricted ownership, and divorce.[8] Poland only gained political independence in 1918, but lost it again in 1939

3 Lonnie Johnson, *Central Europe: Enemies, Neighbours, Friends* (Oxford University Press 2011).

4 Cf. 'Concise Statistical Yearbook of Poland', *Central Statistical Office* 2018.

5 'The World Factbook', *Central Intelligence Agency*, available at https://www.cia.gov/library/publications/the-world-factbook/rankorder/2001rank.html; 'How Poland Became Europe's Most Dynamic Economy', *Bloomberg Businessweek*, available at https://multishoring.info/market-news/bloomberg-businessweek-%E2%80%9Ehow-poland-became-europes-most-dynamic-economy%E2%80%9D/. Cf. as well: 'Human Development Reports', *United Nations Development Programme*, available at http://hdr.undp.org/en/2018-update. All links accessed 15 November 2019.

6 Norman Davies, *Europe: A History* (Pimlico 1997) 554; Piotr S. Wandycz, *The price of freedom: a history of East Central Europe from the Middle Ages to the present* (Psychology Press 2001) 66.

7 Jerzy Jedlicki, *Jakiej cywilizacji Polacy potrzebują. Studia z dziejów polskiej idei i wyobraźni XIX wieku* (WAB – CIS 2002) 94.

8 More e.g.: Anna Klimaszewska, 'The Reception of the French Commercial Code in Nineteenth-Century Polish Territories – A Hollow Legal Shell' in Anna Klimaszewska and Michał Gałędek (eds), *Modernization, National Identity and Legal Instrumentalism: Studies in Comparative Legal History*, I (Brill 2019); Anna Klimaszewska, 'The Application of the 1807 French Commercial Code in Polish Territories: An Attempt to Establish an Anonymous Partnership in Lublin' in Marju Luts-Sootak and Frank L. Schäfer (eds), *Recht und Wirtschaft in Stadt und Land* (Peter Lang 2020) 89–109; Anna Klimaszewska, 'La responsabilité civile des associés des sociétés commerciales dans le droit polonais – les influences de la culture juridique française et les influences des autres cultures' in Zbigniew Hajn and Dagmara Skupień (eds), *La responsabilité civile en France et en Pologne* (WUŁ 2016); Katarzyna Sójka-Zielińska, *Kodeks Napoleona. Historia i współczesność* (LexisNexis 2008); Piotr Z. Pomianowski, *Rozwód w XIX wieku na centralnych ziemiach polskich. Praktyka stosowania Kodeksu Napoleona w latach 1808–1852* (Campidoglio 2018).

when World War II started and Poland was divided between Germany and the Soviet Union. In 1947, the Polish People's Republic was established as a satellite state under Soviet influence.[9] In 1989, Poland re-established itself as a presidential democratic republic.

2. Conflict Resolution

2.1 Introduction

In Poland, legal conflicts are solved either by mediating them or (more often) in courts of justice. We will start by looking at alternative forms of conflict resolution and their impact on the legal culture before focusing on judicial conflict resolution.

2.2 Alternative Dispute Resolution (ADR)

Recent attempts of the legislature, sociologists, and lawyers to popularize and strengthen the instruments of ADR (mainly mediation) have not been successful in Poland. Consequently, extra-judicial forms of conflict resolution have not yet affected Poland's legal culture on a deeper level. Recently, the reformers have strengthened the competencies of judges when referring cases to mediation, aiming to increase the number of mediations considerably.[10]

Some sociologists and lawyers have indicated that the reason why it is so difficult to convince the citizens to use mediation might be a very low level of social trust, ranging from 18 % (2002) to 23 % (2016).[11] Citizens do not trust one another.[12] This level of confidence has been one of the lowest in Europe for many years.[13] The lack of trust also affects mediation, its confidentiality and effectiveness, since the citizens trust neither the intentions of the other party participating in the mediation procedure nor the mediator's impartiality or professionalism.[14] Except for the situations when citizens have opposed political power, the culture of social cooperation in Poland has traditionally been underdeveloped. Since the Polish people regained freedom from the communist regime, individualism has been promoted, while support for the development of civil

9 Cf. Rafał Mańko, 'Demons of the Past? Legal Survivals of the Socialist Legal Tradition in Contemporary Polish Private Law' in Rafał Mańko, Cosmin Sebastian Cercel and Adam Sulikowski (eds), *Law and Critique in Central Europe: Questioning the Past, Resisting the Present* (Counterpress 2016).

10 Justification of the draft of the Code of Civil Procedure Amendment Act, version of 25 September 2018, 17–18, 28.

11 CBOS research communication no. 18/2016, available at www.cbos.pl.

12 Henryk Domański, 'Zaufanie między ludźmi' in Paweł B. Sztabiński, Franciszek Sztabiński (eds), *Polska – Europa. Wyniki Europejskiego Sondażu Społecznego 2002–2012* (IFIS PAN 2014) 8–17.

13 In 2002 it was the lowest in Europe, in 2016 Poles took the 4th place in the distrust ranking in Europe – results of a European public poll; available at https:// europeansocialsurvey.org. Cf. Paweł B. Sztabiński, Franciszek Sztabiński (eds), *Polska – Europa. Wyniki Europejskiego Sondażu Społecznego 2002–2016/2017* (IFIS PAN 2018).

14 Tadeusz Ereciński (ed), *Kodeks postępowania cywilnego. Komentarz* (Wolters Kluwer 2009) 523–525; Andrzej Marciniak (ed), *Kodeks postępowania cywilnego. Tom I (art. 1–205) Komentarz* (C.H. Beck 2019) 1140–1141.

society has been neglected. And thus participation in the formation of a new legal culture as a building block of social capital has been neglected as well.[15]

Another reason for the reluctance towards ADR might be the low level of experience with non-professional judges and informal procedures. This consolidated in the Polish legal culture the scheme of resolving legal matters in a formalised way, using professional courts of justice. Strikingly, the latest reforms mainly consist of strengthening the judges' procedural tools to overcome the parties' lack of trust in the settlement.[16]

The third reason for the failure to use mediation has a contemporary source. Those representing a public body or private company in such negotiations restrain from using settlements to avoid being held responsible for having sacrificed their employer's interests when entering into a compromise.[17]

2.3 Judicial conflict resolution

The most important mechanisms of conflict resolution are therefore organised in the court system that consists of ordinary and military courts under the supervision of the Supreme Court.[18] Administrative courts form a separate branch of the judiciary in Poland. The Constitutional Tribunal holds a special position in this court-structure:[19]

15 Monika Dorota Adamczyk, 'Kapitał społeczny czynnikiem konstytutywnym współczesnego ładu społeczno-gospodarczego' (2015) 2 *Roczniki Nauk Społecznych* 201; Ireneusz Krzemiński, 'Społeczeństwo obywatelskie i symbole wspólnoty' in Marek Drogosz (ed), *jak Polacy przegrywają? Jak Polacy wygrywają?* (GWP 2005).

16 Code of Civil Procedure Amendment Act of 4 July 2019; Dz. U. 2019; 1469.

17 See multiple conference lectures: *How to resolve a difficult economic dispute amicably*, Gdańsk 19 October 2018; *Marine economy dispute resolution specifics,* Gdańsk 6 July 2019; *Trade secret and compliance. Mediation in the labour law and business,* Gdańsk 23 May 2019; available at www.pcaim.org.pl.

18 For the purpose of this section, military courts are of minor interest and will not be discussed in detail.

19 From a formal point of view, the Constitution also provides for the existence of the Tribunal of State, but in practice it does not function. Cf. Zbigniew Landau and Bronisława Skrzeszewska, *Sprawa Gabriela Czechowicza przed Trybunałem Stanu – wybór dokumentów* (PWN 1961).

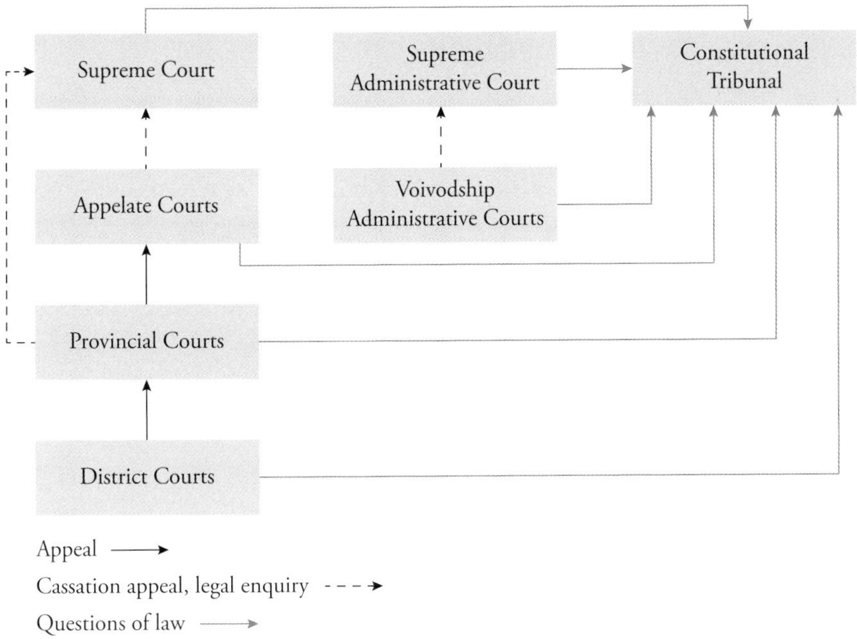

Fig. 1 The Polish Court System.

2.4 Ordinary courts

Art. 177 of Chapter VIII of the Polish Constitution of 2 April 1997 provides for the principle of presumed competence of ordinary courts: "The common courts[20] shall implement the administration of justice concerning all matters save for those statutorily reserved to other courts." Thus, they have the general competence to resolve all cases except for those vested in other special courts, such as administrative or military ones. These courts decide, among other things, on cases concerning criminal, civil, family, and juvenile law, commercial law, and labour and social security law. They also maintain land and mortgage registers.

The system of ordinary courts includes the district (*sądy rejonowe*), provincial (*sądy okręgowe*), and appellate courts (*sądy apelacyjne*). The jurisdiction of district courts usually covers an area of several communes.[21] The jurisdiction of provincial courts covers an area of several district courts and the appellate courts' jurisdiction covers a territory of at least two provincial courts. Currently there are 318 district courts, 45 provincial courts, and 11 appellate courts in Poland.[22] The Supreme Court supervises them. However, this

20 This term is used in the official translation of the Constitution of the Republic of Poland of 2 April 1997 – Dz. U. 1997, 78, 483, available at https://www.sejm.gov.pl/prawo/konst/angielski/kon1.htm. However, we stick to the terminology recommended by the European Commission, see https://e-justice.europa.eu/content_ordinary_courts-18-en.do.

21 The commune (*gmina*) – the basic unit of the administrative division of Poland.

22 'Statistical Yearbook of the Republic of Poland', Warsaw 2018, 162–163.

court is not regarded as part of the ordinary judiciary system.[23] As a rule, there is just one level of appeal.[24]

In 2018, there were 6,356 judges in district courts in total, 2,515 in provincial courts and 426 in appellate courts.[25] According to Table 3 (Appendix below), the number of judges on all levels has been reduced rather considerably in recent years. As we will explain in more detail below, this is one of the changes on the surface level, which might impact the legal culture on deeper levels.

The general rule is that district courts are courts of the first instance, and they handle most cases.[26] Provincial courts function as both first and second instance courts, handling more serious or complicated cases and appeals from district courts. However, this division is not very clear. Among other examples, provincial courts adjudicate in the first instance in cases: concerning property claims exceeding a value of PLN 75,000 (over EUR 17,160) with some exceptions,[27] concerning claims in respect of press law and certain non-property claims, and regarding preventing and countering unfair competition or compensation for damages caused by a final judgment contrary to law.[28] They also adjudicate cases concerning felonies and some misdemeanours specified by the law (e.g., money laundering,[29] euthanasia killing,[30] solicitation to and assistance in suicide[31]).[32] Also contrary to the general rule, provincial courts are courts of first instance in social security law cases,[33] which results in those courts having a higher number of proceedings than in the district courts.[34] The jurisdiction of district courts in social security matters is limited to a few specific types of cases.[35] Appellate courts are the second instance courts, handling appeals from provincial courts.

---

23 Cf. inter alia: Bogusław Banaszak, *Konstytucja Rzeczypospolitej Polskiej. Komentarz* (C.H. Beck 2009) 780; Dariusz Dudek (ed), *Zasady Ustroju III Rzeczypospolitej Polskiej* (Wolters Kluwer 2009) 247; Beata Stępień-Załucka, *Sprawowanie wymiaru sprawiedliwości przez Sąd Najwyższy w Polsce* (C.H. Beck 2016); Bogumił Szmulik, *Pozycja ustrojowa Sądu Najwyższego w Rzeczypospolitej Polskiej* (C.H. Beck 2008); Tadeusz Wiśniewski, *Przebieg procesu cywilnego* (Wolters Kluwer 2013) 17.

24 Andrzej Bałaban, 'Prawna pozycja władzy sądowniczej w III RP (ze szczególnym uwzględnieniem sądownictwa powszechnego)' in Ewa Gdulewicz, Wojciech Orłowski, Sławomir Patyra (eds), *25 lat transformacji ustrojowej w Polsce i w Europie Środkowo-Wschodniej* (WUMCS 2015) 211–222.

25 Data of the Statistical Information Management Department of the Ministry of Justice.

26 See Appendix, Table 1, below.

27 E.g. alimony cases, establishing separate property during marriage, infringement of possession. Cf. Art. 17, point 4 of the Act of 17 November 1964 (Code of Civil Procedure, hereinafter: CCP); Dz. U. [*Dziennik Ustaw* – Journal of Laws] 2018, 1360 as amended.

28 Art. 17 of the CCP.

29 Art. 299 of the Act of 6 June 1997 (Penal Code, hereinafter: PC); Dz. U. 2018, 1600 as amended.

30 Ibid Art. 150 § 1.

31 Ibid Art. 151.

32 Art. 25 § 1 of the Act of 6 June 1997 (Code of Penal Procedure, hereinafter: CPP); Dz. U. 2018, 1987 as amended. It is also the provincial court that issues safe-conducts (Art. 281 CPP) and the European Arrest Warrant (Art. 607a CPP).

33 Art. 477^8 § 1 of the CCP.

34 See Appendix, Table 1, below.

35 Art. 477^8 § 2 of the CCP.

Court proceedings have become increasingly longer in recent years, particularly in the second instance.[36] This rather dramatic development can be observed in many areas (criminal law is the least affected).[37] This is not only due to the enormous number of incoming cases every year (ca. 14–15 million).[38] but also caused by a broad competence in the ordinary courts and a small amount of cases settled through ADR. In addition, to judges handling too many cases, they have many additional office duties. Relatively low participation of professional representatives in court proceedings cause delays too, since parties without such an assistance often cannot act efficiently.

All ordinary courts are divided into specialised units (*wydziały*). Each district court contains at least one civil, criminal, family and juvenile division, as well as a land and mortgage registers unit. In some district courts, such as in Gdynia or Gdańsk-North, one can find two or even more units of the abovementioned types and then they can be even more specialised, since separate units adjudicate in e.g. litigious and non-litigious civil cases. However, other types of specialisation can be introduced as well; it depends on the needs of the court. In addition, some district courts have established specialised units for labour and social security as well as commercial law.

Each provincial court contains specialised units concerned with civil, criminal, labour and social security law. Sometimes there are several civil or criminal units, according to the specific needs of the region. Appeals and first instance cases are dealt with in separate units. In many provincial courts one can also find specialised units exclusively concerned with penitentiaries and supervision over execution of penal decisions. Some provincial courts also have commercial chambers. Finally, the Warsaw provincial court holds additional highly specialized units such as a division keeping a register of political parties, Competition and Consumer Protection Courts as well as a Community Trademark and Design Court.

Interestingly, when looking at the appellate courts, we can see a somewhat lesser degree of institutional specialisation. Each appellate court has civil, criminal, as well as labour and social security units. In some appellate courts, more than one civil unit has been established.

Considering the degree of professionalisation and specialisation of the ordinary courts, one has to take into account the composition of the judging bodies. As a very general rule, a single professional judge rules in the first instance.[39] On the second level, a panel of three professional judges is the rule.[40] However, the highly professionalised system of conflict resolution has some exceptions.[41] In Poland the lay judges, together with professional judges, are members of adjudication panels of first instance courts

36 More: Olga M. Piaskowska, Piotr F. Piesiewicz (eds), *Przewlekłość postępowania sądowego* (Wolters Kluwer 2018).

37 See Appendix, Table 2, below.

38 See Appendix, Table 1, below.

39 Art. 47 § 1 of the CCP; Art. 28 § 1 of the CPP.

40 Art. 367 § 3 of the CCP; Art. 29 § 1 of the CPP.

41 Cf. Art. 47 § 4 of the CCP; Art. 28 § 3-4 and Art. 29 § 2 and Art. 544 § 1 of the CPP.

in a narrowly defined group of civil and criminal cases.[42] In civil cases, lay judges are present e.g. in some labour law cases and cases involving damages in case of mobbing, as well as in some family law cases, including divorce and separation. In criminal cases, adjudicating panels with lay judges adjudicate in cases involving accusation of a felony, i.e. acts punishable by more than three years' imprisonment.

Note that between 2001 and 2017,[43] promotion of a judge was based on professional experience and merits alone. For many years, promotion to a higher judicial post required a judge to have previously held a post for several years in a lower court. This meant that judges in the highest courts had been gaining experience in stages and their work had been evaluated several times. The reform of 2017 changed the situation drastically. Even a district court judge can now be appointed to the Supreme Court.[44] Although the candidate is evaluated by judges, at the last stage decision is up to the National Council of the Judiciary, a body dominated by politicians. Moreover, it has become possible to perform the duties of a judge on the basis of delegation. The Minister of Justice, who is at the same time the Prosecutor General, can *ad hoc* appoint judges at each level of the court hierarchy. These procedural reforms concerning appointment and delegation are used to position judges loyal to the government in the higher courts. In this way, although the Minister of Justice has claimed that the reform of the courts has the purpose to democratize the judiciary and eliminate the judicial elite, he has created a new elite of judges, directly subordinate to and more seriously dependent on the Minister.

2.5 The Supreme Court

The Supreme Court has traditionally been at the top of the system of ordinary and special courts. However, the 1997 Constitution limited its role, transferring judicial supervision over administrative courts from the Supreme Court to the Supreme Administrative Court.

The primary duty of the Supreme Court is to exercise judicial supervision over ordinary and military courts.[45] It is the obligation of the Supreme Court to ensure compliance with the law and uniformity of judgment in those courts,[46] which guarantees a high level of legal certainty. The Supreme Court exercises its power in two ways. First, it reviews legal remedies against court rulings. The most common one is the cassation appeal against final and binding judgments, which can be filed only under certain circumstances. For example, it cannot be filed in civil cases where the value of the claim is less than appr. EUR 10,000, in alimony and support cases, divorces, tenancy rent,

---

42 Cf. Art. 47 § 2 of the CCP, Art. 28 § 2 of the CPP, Art. 7 § 2 of the of the PC. List of cases heard with the participation of lay judges cf. Artur Rycak (ed), *Metodyka pracy ławnika* (C.H. Beck 2011) 6 ff.

43 Act of 27 July 2001 – Law on the organisational structure of ordinary courts; Dz. U. 2001, 98, 1070.

44 Art. 64 and 77 of the Act of 12 July 2017; Dz. U. 2017, 1452.

45 Art. 183 para. 1 of the Constitution.

46 Art. 1 point 1 of the Supreme Court Act of 8 December 2017; Dz. U. 2019, 825.

for infringement of possession and many other cases that concern e.g. the family law, inheritance law or labour and social security law.[47] An appeal must also be filed within a short time limit.[48] This restriction aims to prevent destabilization of rulings on the lower level and thus warrants legal certainty.

An extraordinary appeal has recently been added to the catalogue of legal remedies.[49] This remedy is available when a ruling cannot be changed or revoked in any other procedure and when constitutional principles or human/civil rights or freedoms granted in the Constitution have been violated. An extraordinary appeal may be filed on the grounds of alleged misapplication of the law or erroneous factual finding. The time limit in such cases is generally longer than in case of cassation appeal.[50]

Second, in association with exercising supervision over ordinary and military courts, the Supreme Court may on request give an authoritative opinion concerning an interpretative question of general importance (legal enquiry). This happens when a court of second instance reviewing an appeal in an individual case comes across a legal issue that raises major doubts or requires a fundamental interpretation of a legal act.[51] A response is given in the form of a ruling passed by a panel of three or seven judges of the Supreme Court, and the ruling is binding on the court that reviews the specific case concerned, but not *erga omnes*.[52] However, because of the authority of the Supreme Court, judges in other courts frequently take such rulings into account. There were, e.g., a total of 142 legal enquiries submitted by the lower courts to the Supreme Court in 2018, and 152 in 2017.[53]

The Supreme Court may also comment on legal issues acting on its own initiative (when reviewing a cassation appeal) or on the initiative of one of the Presidents of the Supreme Court or competent state authorities, requesting the Supreme Court to rule on contradicting interpretations and opinions in the case law in an abstract procedure.[54] The latter requires a panel of seven judges. Under certain conditions, an entire chamber or joint chambers or even the whole Supreme Court (full panel) is involved. When these rulings become legal principles, they are regarded binding for Supreme Court judges.[55]

47 Cf. Art. 398^2 and 519^1 of the CCP. Limitations in criminal cases, cf.: Art. 523 and 439 of the CPP.

48 One month (criminal cases) or two months (civil cases) for the parties. Public authorities entitled to file a cassation appeal, like the Minister of Justice – Public Prosecutor General, Ombudsman, or Children's Ombudsman have a longer time limit. Art. 524 of the CPP and Art. 398^5 of the CCP.

49 Cf. Tadeusz Wiśniewski (ed), *Skarga nadzwyczajna w świetle systemu środków zaskarżenia w postępowaniu cywilnym* (Wolters Kluwer 2019).

50 Five years as a rule and when a cassation appeal was filed – one year from the judgment. Art. 89 § 3 of the Supreme Court Act. Moreover, under interim regulations, for the period of three years from the entry into force of the new regulations, an extraordinary appeal can be filed against every final and binding ruling issued in the last 21 years (after 17 September 1997). Ibid Art. 115 § 1. The Extraordinary Control and Public Affairs Chamber has been constituted to adjudicate these cases.

51 Art. 390 § 1 of the CCP and Art. 441 § 1 of CPP.

52 Art. 77 § 1 of the Supreme Court Act.

53 'Information of the Supreme Court activities in 2018', Warsaw 2019, available at www.sn.pl on p. 6.

54 Art. 82 and 83 of the Supreme Court Act.

55 The way a ruling receives the status of a legal principle is described in detail below, in the section on norm production.

However, they may be amended by a new ruling of a body at least of the same size or the whole Supreme Court.[56] In addition, the Constitution entrusts the Supreme Court to determine the validity of elections and national referendums.[57]

The function and organizational structure of the Supreme Court were reformed in late 2017.[58] However, the changes were challenged before the Court of Justice of the European Union (CJEU). Therefore, it is not yet possible to determine which of them will be maintained.[59] Currently, the Supreme Court has five chambers: Civil, Criminal, Labour Law and Social Insurance, Extraordinary Control and Public Affairs, and Disciplinary.[60] The last two are newly established entities. The adjudicating panels of the first three consist of only professional judges and the last two consist of both professional judges and lay judges, but professional judges constitute a majority of their respective panels.

Most controversial is the extensive autonomy granted to the Disciplinary Chamber and the reduced competences of the First President of the Supreme Court with respect to that Chamber, which disrupt the uniform structure of the Supreme Court. This chamber continues its work despite the fact that the method of appointing its members as well since the status and form of the new disciplinary procedure have been heavily criticized.[61] In addition, opponents of the reform emphasise that this new chamber is under the direct influence of the Minister of Justice – Public Prosecutor General.[62]

---

56 Art. 83 to 88 of the Supreme Court Act.

57 Art. 101, 125 para. 4, and 129 of the Constitution.

58 The first President of the Supreme Court Małgorzata Gersdorf expressed her criticism of the reform proposals in Grzegorz Borkowski (ed) *Granice niezawisłości sędziów i niezależności sądów?* (KRS 2016) 15–20.

59 According to the European Commission, the principles of the EU's rule of law were also violated. The act was amended after Poland lost the case before the CJEU. In particular, the First President of the Supreme Court and the other judges of the Supreme Court and Supreme Administrative Court were allowed to stay in office until the end of the term provided for in the Constitution (the new provisions also concern the judges of the latter court), whereas, according to the earlier version of the new provisions, due to the reduced retirement age, 1/3 of judges would have to resign in the middle of their term of office, as well as the First President of the Supreme Court, despite the fact that her term of office is explicitly defined by the Constitution (Art. 183 par. 3). Cf.: CJEU order of 19 October 2018, 15 November and 17 December 2018, respectively, CJEU judgment of 24 June 2019, C619/18, European Commission v. Poland; available at http://curia.europa.eu/juris/documents.jsf?oqp=&for=&mat=or&lgrec=pl&jge=&td=%3BALL&jur=C%2CT%2CF&num=C-619%252F18&page=1&dates=&pcs=Oor&lg=&pro=&nat=or&cit=none%252CC%252CCJ%252CR%252C2008E%252C%252C%252C%252C%252C%252C%252C%252C%252C%252Ctrue%252Cfalse%252Cfalse&language=en&avg=&cid=2644767 accessed 6 November 2019.

60 Art. 3 of the Supreme Court Act.

61 More in: Mirosław Granat, *Prawo konstytucyjne. Pytania i odpowiedzi* (Wolters Kluwer 2019) 411–413.

62 See n 59. Most members of the Chamber were public prosecutors, and they were appointed even though the Supreme Administrative Court ordered the appointment procedure to be suspended for the time of reviewing appeals filed against the procedure. Cf. also the influence of the Prosecutor's Office on judges' independence in case of Romania in CJEU: C-355/19 *Asociația "Forumul Judecătorilor din România" and Others*; Case C-127/19 *Asociația "Forumul Judecătorilor Din România" and Asociația Mişcarea Pentru Apărarea Statutului Procurorilor*; Case C-83/19 *Asociația "Forumul Judecătorilor Din România"*.

The recent changes concerning the Supreme Court in Poland have not only affected the domestic legal culture[63] but also resonate to the entire European Union. The European Commission and the CJEU reacted quickly to those changes, claiming to detect a violation of fundamental democratic principles such as the separation of powers, the independence of courts, and the rule of law.[64]

2.6 The Constitutional Tribunal

The Polish Constitutional Tribunal is a uniform body (no chambers) consisting of 15 judges, elected by the lower house of the Polish parliament (the Sejm) for a nine-year term.[65] This is an individual appointment, which means that the term of office of each judge is counted separately. The Constitution does not specify any requirements for the appointment of Constitutional Tribunal judges. "Distinguished legal knowledge" is sufficient.[66] However, precise regulation is established at the statutory level. According to Art. 3 of the Act on the Constitutional Tribunal, a candidate must have the same qualifications required for a Supreme Court or Supreme Administrative Court judge.[67] In practice, many judges of the Constitutional Tribunal are professors of law.

Constitutional Tribunal judges are elected by an absolute majority of votes in the Sejm.[68] The election has to take place in the term in which the mandate of the current judge of the Constitutional Tribunal expires.[69] An additional precondition is that the candidate's vow has been accepted by President of the Republic of Poland. These provisions of a mere formal character have proven to be problematic in the current crisis as they have been applied to prevent certain candidates to take office and to replace them by candidates favoured by the ruling party.

The functions of the Constitutional Tribunal are determined by the Constitution: 1) it controls the conformity of the lower ranking legal norms to higher ranking legal instruments, especially with the Constitution (including obligations arising from international treatises);[70] a special procedure for this review is the examination of constitutional complaints,[71] 2) it resolves competence disputes between central constitutional

63 Jakub Kościerzyński (ed), 'Justice under pressure – repressions as a means of attempting to take control over the judiciary and the prosecution in Poland. Years 2015–2019', available at https://www.iustitia.pl/images/pliki/raport2020/Raport_EN.pdf accessed 1 April 2020.

64 Fortunately, there was no situation similar to that in Hungary, where many judges, including the First President of the Supreme Court, were removed from office following reduction of the retirement age. That case was reviewed by the ECtHR only a few years after the law was amended, which is why the ruling of the ECHR did not influence the new regulations governing the court system in Hungary. See *Baka v Hungary* App no 20261/12 (ECtHR, 23 June 2016).

65 Art. 194 para. 1 of the Constitution.

66 Ibid.

67 Art. 3 of the Act on the Constitutional Tribunal.

68 Art. 31 para. 1 of the Sejm regulation.

69 Judgment of the Constitutional Tribunal of 3 December 2015, K 34/15.

70 Art. 188 points 1–3, art. 122 para. 3 and 4, art. 133 para. 2 of the Constitution.

71 Ibid Art. 79 and Art. 188 point 5.

organs of the state,[72] 3) it decides on the conformity to the Constitution of the purposes or activities of political parties,[73] and 4) it recognizes the temporary incapacity of the President to exercise his duties.[74]

The norm control is primarily of *a posteriori* nature, and it applies to normative instruments (legislation) that have already been enacted, are in force or are still in the *vacatio legis* period. Exceptionally, the review may have a preventive nature – *a priori*, and the only organ authorized to initiate such a procedure is the President of the Republic of Poland. The Tribunal does not rule on local legislation, nor does it rule on "vertical" competence disputes because it is not necessary due to the unitary structure of the state.[75]

The Constitutional Tribunal does not act on its own initiative but only on a motion. Some state-organs have the general authority to make application to the Constitutional Tribunal – e.g., the President, Marshals of the Sejm and Senate, the First President of the Supreme Court, the President of the Supreme Administrative Court, the Prosecutor-General (who is also the Minister of Justice), and the Ombudsman.[76] In some cases, the authority arises from the fact that the case falls within the applicant's scope of activity.[77]

However, some case proceedings are also initiated by individual subjects. Anyone who holds that he or she has received a verdict based on a provision which, in the applicant's opinion, is unconstitutional, has a right to a constitutional complaint.[78] The courts are also empowered to initiate constitutional review.[79]

From a systemic perspective, the constitution establishes the Constitutional Tribunal as a part of the judiciary, but functionally it is separated from the hierarchically-organised courts of justice.[80] The independent status of the Constitutional Tribunal is a distinguishing feature having important consequences for its judgments. According

72 Ibid Art. 189.

73 Ibid Art. 188 point 4.

74 Ibid Art. 131 para. 1.

75 Local government bodies may initiate proceedings before the Tribunal in the procedure of abstract review of norms, if the normative act concerns matters that fall within their scope of activity, however they are not allowed to lodge a constitutional complaint.

76 The entitled are also: the Prime Minister, the President of the Supreme Chamber of Control, as well as groups of 50 deputies or 30 senators, which in practice give the opposition access to initiation of review by the Constitutional Tribunal (Art. 191 para. 1 point 1 of the Constitution).

77 Ibid Art. 191 para. 1 point 2–5. E.g., in matters of the judiciary, the National Council for the Judiciary can file a motion, and in trade-related matters, national trade union bodies can do so as well, while in matters of freedom of religion, Churches and religious associations have the right to file motions.

78 The subject of the complaint may only be an allegation of non-compliance with the Constitution of a normative act on the basis of which a decision violating the applicant's rights was issued. The complaint may be directed only against the legal norm (and not e.g. the interpretation of the provision adopted in the process of applying the law), according to the narrow concept of the complaint adopted by the creators of the Constitution. For more, see Leszek Garlicki, *Polskie prawo konstytucyjne. Zarys wykładu* (Wolters Kluwer 2019) 412 ff.

79 Art. 193 of the Constitution. For an overview over the case load of the Polish Constitutional Tribunal, see Appendix, Table 4.

80 Pursuant to Chapter XX of the Polish Constitution, the judicial authority in Poland consists of two segments: the first are the courts constituting a hierarchical system of ordinary and specialised courts, and the second segment consists of two tribunals (Constitutional Tribunal and Tribunal of State) acting independently, in other words these tribunals are not part of the system of appeal and thus not part of the court system.

to Art. 190 para. 1 all its rulings are universally binding and final.[81] They have to be published immediately in the Journal of Laws or other proper official publication.[82] The unique status of the Tribunal between the legislative and the judicial branch of law, has been regarded as necessary to safeguard the constitutional order from short-term infringements by any parliamentary majority. It manifests the supremacy of the Constitution as a framework for the Polish legal culture.[83]

When the Tribunal was established in the 1980s, its importance was rather limited because the Sejm could block the effects of its rulings with a 2/3 majority. The existing restrictions were removed by the Constitution of 2 April 1997, followed by the Constitutional Tribunal Act of 1 August 1997, and its position was strengthened. After 18 years of stable functioning[84], the contemporary political changes have impacted its function and status tremendously. In 2015, the parliamentary majority of the old Sejm appointed some new judges for the Constitutional Tribunal. After the election, the new Sejm appointed different judges. The Venice Commission considered that to be unconstitutional.[85] Furthermore, the new President of the Republic of Poland did not accept the oath from judges elected by the previous Sejm, but only from judges who were elected by the new Sejm. Such and similar decisions by the President are constantly subject of controversy.[86] In addition, between 2015 and 2016 new provisions regarding the Constitutional Tribunal were enacted seven times. Some of them were very controversial.[87] The Tribunal itself found some of these amendments unconstitutional,[88] but the parliamentary majority questioned this assessment. Despite explicit constitutional instruction, these judgments were not published and the majority in Parliament treated them as "non-existing". The final character of the Tribunal's judgments and the principle of judicial review were thus informally challenged. Due to heavy criticism from the EU,

81 The verdicts of the Tribunal are therefore not subject to further appeal to any authority. See more: Piotr Winczorek, *Komentarz do Konstytucji Rzeczypospolitej Polskiej z dnia 2 kwietnia 1997 roku* (Wydawnictwo Liber 2008) 369.

82 Art. 190 para. 2 of the Constitution.

83 Cf. Monika Florczak-Wątor, *Horyzontalny wymiar praw konstytucyjnych* (WUJ 2014).

84 More: Marta Derlatka, Leszek Garlicki, Marcin Wiącek, *Na straży państwa prawa. Trzydzieści lat orzecznictwa Trybunału Konstytucyjnego* (Wolters Kluwer 2016).

85 In its opinion of March 2016, the Commission stated, among others, that "the current conflict over the composition of the Constitutional Tribunal originated from the actions of the previous Sejm" and that "both the previous and the present majorities of the Sejm have taken unconstitutional actions". See 'Opinion on Amendments to the Act of 25 June 2015 on the Constitutional Tribunal of Poland adopted by the Venice Commission at its 106th Plenary Session (Venice, 11–12 March 2016)' 21–22.

86 The Constitutional Tribunal in its previous composition concluded that the President had violated the regulations (judgment of the Constitutional Tribunal of 3 December 2015, K 34/1), in its new composition it decided that this activity was lawful (judgment of the Constitutional Tribunal of 24 October 2017, K 1/17).

87 Cf. Ewa Łętowska and Aneta Wiewiórowska-Domagalska, 'A '*Good*' *Change in the Polish Constitutional Tribunal*?' (2016) 1 *Osteuropa Recht* 79.

88 K 47/15.

the Venice Commission[89], and many lawyers in Poland, the newly introduced provisions were partly changed to give an impression that the situation has normalized.[90]

Questioning the Tribunal's constitutional status and function, and above all its justification, have had a serious effect on the Polish legal culture, and this could indicate that the relationship between law and politics is about to change.[91] Politicians of the ruling party explicitly stated that they had to establish some new rules for the functioning of the Constitutional Tribunal and appoint new judges, because they want the Constitutional Tribunal to interpret the Constitution differently than it did before. According to them, this is necessary to guarantee the freedom of the parliamentary majority in realizing the sovereign's will, and not the will of judges or parliamentary opposition.[92] The practical application of this argument has limited the independence of the Constitutional Tribunal and indicates that the legislative and executive authorities are no longer willing to fully respect the rule of law.

Introducing to the legal discourse the idea that the will of a simple majority of voters takes precedence over the Constitution indicates that populist notions and instrumental treatment of important legal institutions have already impacted the Polish legal culture on a deep level.[93] There has not yet been a profound change in the bottom level of the legal sea in Poland, but the mere fact of challenging the supremacy of fundamental constitutional principles shows a new dimension of the phenomenon. Marginalization, or even annihilation[94] of the Constitutional Tribunal was crucial for the government, since the Tribunal had the power to block unconstitutional reforms. The dramatic changes on the surface level may indicate an underlying change of ideas and expectations of law. Only the future will show to what extent they will change the institutional and intellectual structures of the Polish legal culture.

---

89 It clearly emphasized that "the Amendments of 22 December 2015, affecting the efficiency of the Constitutional Tribunal, would have endangered not only the rule of law, but also the functioning of the democratic system [...]. They [...] could lead to a serious slow-down of the activity of the Tribunal and could make it ineffective as a guardian of the Constitution". See 'Opinion on Amendments' (n 85) 24.

90 Since 2017, three acts regulate the organization and proceedings of the Tribunal and the status of its justices. Two acts of 30 November 2016: on the organization and procedure before the Constitutional Tribunal (Dz. U. 2019, 125) and on the status of judges of the Constitutional Tribunal (Dz. U. 2018, 1422), which, together with the Act of 13 December 2016 – Introductory provisions (to both of these acts; Dz. U. 2018, 849) determined the current shape of applicable provisions on the Constitutional Tribunal.

91 Cf. Grażyna Skąpska, 'Znieważający konstytucjonalizm i konstytucjonalizm znieważony. Refleksja socjologiczna na temat kryzysu liberalno-demokratycznego konstytucjonalizmu w Europie pokomunistycznej' (2018) 7/1 *Filozofia Publiczna i Edukacja Demokratyczna* 276–301.

92 Jarosław Kaczyński, the leader of the PiS party, clearly stated: "I am deeply convinced that the Tribunal (...) was to be that point, a kind of bastion [of opposition – AK, AM, SK] that could destroy all of our attempts to introduce reforms (...) not only in the administration of justice or in the media, but also such changes as PLN 500 per child" – statement in Radio Maryja, www.dziennik.pl accessed 31 December 2015.

93 Cf. the feuilleton of Ewa Łętowska under the title 'Tyranny of majority/Dictate of minority?', available at http://konstytucyjny.pl/tyrania-wiekszosci-dyktat-mniejszosci/ accessed 15 November 2019.

94 This term regarding the Polish Constitutional Tribunal was coined by Jacek Zaleśny, see 'Защита доминирующей роли конституции и разделение власти – спор о методах создания права в современных государствах' (2018) 48 *Political Science Studies* 79–80.

2.7 Administrative courts

This branch is based on sixteen voivodship administrative courts (*wojewódzkie sądy administracyjne*) – one in each voivodship (province) – adjudicating as first-instance courts, and the Supreme Administrative Court (*Naczelny Sąd Administracyjny*) adjudicating as a court of appeal, exercising judicial supervision over the case law of the voivodship administrative courts.

In 1997, the Constitution had already established the obligation to introduce a court proceedings system with at least two stages.[95] However, it was not until 2004, that the earlier one-stage proceedings before the Supreme Administrative Court were replaced by the two-stage proceedings based on the functioning of voivodship administrative courts and the Supreme Administrative Court as a court of appeal.[96]

The voivodship administrative courts are divided into divisions in terms of subject matter. The number of divisions depends on the needs of the particular court. Usually two to four were created, with the exception of the Warsaw voivodship administrative court with eight divisions.

The Supreme Administrative Court is divided into three Chambers: the Financial Chamber, the Commercial Chamber, and the General Administrative Chamber.[97] Each of the Chambers exercises supervision over the case law of voivodship administrative courts in cases falling within the jurisdiction of that Chamber.[98]

The essential task of the administrative judiciary is the control over acts/actions taken by the public administration in terms of their lawfulness. It includes the hierarchy-based control over the conformity of resolutions adopted by the bodies of local governments and normative acts adopted by the territorial bodies of government administration with statutory acts as well.[99]

---

95 Art. 176 para. 1 ("Court proceedings shall have at least two stages.") and Art. 236 para. 2 ("Statutes bringing Article 176 para. 1 into effect, to the extent relevant to proceedings before administrative courts, shall be adopted before the end of 5 years from the day on which the Constitution comes into force. The provisions relating to extraordinary review of judgments by the Supreme Administrative Court shall remain in effect until the entry into force of such statutes.") of the Constitution.

96 It was introduced by means of three acts of 2002: the Act of 25 July – Law on the System of Administrative Courts (hereinafter also as the LSAC), Dz. U. 2017, 2188 as amended; the Act of 30 August – Law on Proceedings before Administrative Courts (hereinafter also as the LPAC), Dz. U. 2018, 1302 as amended; and the Act of 30 August – Provisions implementing the Act – Law on the System of Administrative Courts and the Act – Law on Proceedings before Administrative Courts, Dz. U. 2002, 53, 1271.

97 Art. 39 § 1 of the LSAC.

98 Ibid Art. 39 § 2–4.

99 Art. 184 of the Constitution: "The Supreme Administrative Court and other administrative courts shall exercise, to the extent specified by the statute, control over the performance of public administration. Such control shall also extend to judgments on the conformity to the statute of resolutions of organs of local government and normative acts of territorial organs of government administration."

In the administrative courts, only professional judges, either as single judges[100] or as collective panels[101] adjudicate on both levels.[102] To become a judge of a voivodship administrative court, the candidate must not only complete law studies and earn a Master's of Law degree, but have a proper professional experience.[103] Layman participation is only allowed in mediation proceedings. Mediation procedures are provided for in the first instance.[104] Their purpose is to allow the parties to reach an agreement without conducting a hearing. However, this procedure, despite the latest amendments,[105] is getting increasingly unpopular. In 2018, just six cases were opened, and one was settled.[106] This can be explained by the speed and efficiency of examining cases in the ordinary mode. The voivodship administrative courts handled complaints within 3.95 months on average in 2017, and within 3.84 months in 2018.[107] The Supreme Administrative Court heard cases within an average of 12.3 months in 2017[108] and within 12 months in 2018.[109]

3. Norm Production

3.1 Introduction

Poland is a parliamentary republic with a parliamentary cabinet system. The executive authorities are the President of the Republic of Poland and the Council of Ministers heading the respective administrative bodies. The legislative body is the parliament that consists of two houses: Sejm (the lower house) and Senat (the upper house). The Parliament's main task is to produce legal norms. It has the exclusive authority to issue

100 Art. 16 § 2 of the LPAC.

101 Ibid Art. 16 § 1.

102 Ibid Art. 120. More about other exceptions: Zbigniew Kmieciak (ed), *Polskie sądownictwo administracyjne – zarys systemu* (C.H. Beck 2017) 176. In certain cases, a panel of seven judges, an entire chamber or a full panel of Supreme Administrative Court has to be gathered. See Art. 264 § 1 of the LPAC. The latter has happened only once. Cf. Resolution of the Supreme Administrative Court of 26 October 2009 – I OPS 10/09.

103 At least eight years as a judge, prosecutor, advocate, attorney-at-law or notary public; or ten years in public institutions, occupying positions involving the implementation or creation of administrative law. Art. 6 § 1 of the LSAC.

104 Is it regulated by articles 115–118 of the LPAC. More about the impact of the recommendations of the Committee of Ministers of the Council of Europe No. R (2001) 9 of 5 September 2001 on alternatives to litigation between administrative authorities and private parties: justification of the draft law of 22 October 2001, *Druk Sejmowy nr 19 Sejm IV kadencji*, 73–74.

105 Introduced by means of the Act of 7 April 2017 amending the act – Code of Administrative Procedure and some other acts (Dz.U. 2017, 935), which entered into force on 1 June 2017.

106 See Appendix, Table 8.

107 The Supreme Administrative Court of Poland, 'Annual Report 2017. Outline of activities of the Supreme Administrative Court and the Voivodship Administrative Courts in 2017' 8. The Supreme Administrative Court of Poland, 'Annual Report 2018. Outline of activities of the Supreme Administrative Court and the Voivodship Administrative Courts in 2018' 9.

108 The Supreme Administrative Court of Poland, 'Annual Report 2017' (n 107) 8.

109 The Supreme Administrative Court of Poland, 'Annual Report 2018' (n 107) 9.

ordinary acts and acts amending the Constitution.[110] However, in extraordinary circumstances such as being under martial law, but not in cases of state of emergency or natural disaster, Chapter XI of the Constitution allows the President to produce emergency regulations having the force of an act. However, so far there has not been a need to apply these provisions.

Since Poland is not a federal state, the Parliament has a very wide competence to regulate any area of social life as far as the constitution expressly limits the general competence to legislate on a specific topic. Some issues, such as the state budget, civic freedoms, rights and duties as well as other matters addressed directly by the Constitution, are mandatorily regulated by an Act as statutory matters.

Apart from Acts, another type of universally applicable written norms issued in Poland are regulations. They may be issued only by the bodies that are competent to do so pursuant to the Constitution, namely: the President,[111] the Council of Ministers,[112] the Prime Minister,[113] the ministers in charge of specific divisions of the government administration and chairs of certain committees[114], and the National Broadcasting Council (*Krajowa Rada Radiofonii i Telewizji*).[115] This list is exhaustive; no other body has the authority to issue regulations.[116] Regulations must always be implementing instruments, i.e. they may only be issued pursuant to statutory authorization that determines who may issue a regulation, on what matter and within which scope.[117] Local legal enactments issued by local government bodies and regional bodies of the central government administration must also be based on a competence given by a higher ranking norm, such as an Act of Parliament.[118]

Traditionally, the prevailing legislative technique was to produce systematically coherent codifications covering broader fields of law, such as civil or criminal law. However, codes do not have a special position within the legal hierarchy – formally, they are Acts of Parliament. For lawyers trying to find an answer to a specific legal question, searching for a legislative basis for a claim in these codes will nevertheless often be a starting point, and they do play important role in arranging the contents of the legal system. Many fields are covered by codified law. Examples are the Civil Code,[119] the

110 Changing the constitution requires a very complicated procedure provided for in Art. 235 of the Constitution. Since the entry into force of the current Constitution, i.e., since 1997, no act amending the Constitution has been passed.

111 Art. 142 para. 1.

112 Art. 146 para. 4 point 2.

113 Art. 148 para. 3.

114 Art. 149 para. 2 and 3.

115 Art. 213 para. 2.

116 In particular, entrusting certain tasks to a given body on the basis of the Constitution is not a premise for assuming that it can issue regulations for the purpose of carrying out these tasks, unless such a competence is expressly stipulated in the Constitution (Cf.: This was explicitly confirmed by the Constitutional Tribunal in its judgment of 2000, K 25/99).

117 Art. 92 of the Constitution.

118 Ibid Art. 94.

119 Act of 23 April 1964 (hereinafter: CC); Dz. U. 2019, 1145, as amended.

Family and Guardianship Code,[120] the Commercial Companies Code[121], the Labour Code[122], the Criminal Code[123], the Code of Offences[124], the Maritime Code,[125] as well as codes governing various kinds of procedures: the Code of Civil Procedure,[126] the Code of Criminal Procedure,[127] the Offences Procedure Code,[128] or the Code of Administrative Procedure.[129] However, Poland does not have a code governing the substantial administrative law. This field is rather covered by various other legal instruments.

The norms contained in over a dozen codes, as well as in other acts, often have a general and abstract character. However, there are also many legal instruments of a very detailed and highly technical character. As a rule, regulations that implement an Act are detailed. Consequently, the ideal of norm production is a mixture of general and highly abstract norms, specified by more technical legislation of lower rank. Taking into account that legislation is recognized as the only formal source of law in Poland, statutory law has to fulfil different functions and the different legal instruments are regarded as being suitable to the respective tasks.

Accordingly, custom and customary law are not listed in the Polish Constitution among the sources of law. Custom is, however, invoked a number of times in the Civil Code, which stipulates that "an act in law shall not only cause the consequences expressed in it but also those which result from, among other things, established customs",[130] or that "a declaration of intent shall be construed in a manner required by principles of social life and established customs, taking into account the circumstances in which it was made."[131] Custom is considered as a certain pattern of attitudes or behavior, determining the effects of legal acts or the content of declarations of will. An example are customs that exist among entrepreneurs. However, customary norms cannot repeal compulsory legal rules. In case of dispositive norms, custom can be treated as a criterion according to which the parties may, contrary to the indicated provision, establish and shape rights and obligations.[132]

In Poland, legal scholars do not play a special role in the production of norms. They may participate in norm production, if they are members of competent bodies, e.g. Parliament or Council of Ministers. However, no formal authoritative weight is attached

120 Act of 25 February 1964; Dz. U. 2019, 303, as amended.
121 Act of 15 September 2000; Dz. U. 2019, 505, as amended.
122 Act of 26 June 1974; Dz. U. 2019, 1040, as amended.
123 Act of 6 June 1997; Dz. U. 2019, 1950.
124 Act of 20 May 1971; Dz. U. 2019, 821, as amended.
125 Act of 18 September 2001; Dz. U. 2018, 2175.
126 Act of 17 November 1964; Dz. U. 2019, 1460, as amended.
127 Act of 6 June 1997; Dz. U. 2019, 150, as amended.
128 Act of 24 August 2001; Dz. U. 2019, 1120, as amended.
129 Act of 14 June 1960; Dz. U. 2019, 60, as amended.
130 Art. 56 of the CC.
131 Ibid Art. 65. Another example from the area of the civil law is Art. 69 of the CC: "If according to the custom established in the given circumstances or according to the content of an offer, it is not required that the other party's declaration on the acceptance of an offer reach the party making the offer, in particular where the party making the offer demands immediate performance of the contract, the contract shall become effective if the other party sets about performing it in an appropriate time; otherwise the offer shall cease to be binding."
132 E.g. Art. 394 of the CC.

to their opinion or interpretation, e.g. in commentaries to normative instruments or on judicial decisions. If they manage to influence the decisions of a legislative body, it is only by virtue of their intellectual authority and not due to the institutional position in academia. Legal science has a much greater impact on judicial decisions. Judges sometimes rely on and expressly quote doctrinal views established in academia in order to justify a specific argumentation or outcome.[133] Hence, the impact of legal scholars can be said to be only remote or indirect.

3.2 Judges as norm producers or controllers and interpreters?

From a formal point of view, judges' decisions are not regarded a source of law in the Polish legal culture. The main task of a judge is to apply the norms of legally binding statutory law. The obligation to apply relevant legislation has just one exception: when the judge is convinced that the provision is unconstitutional. In this case, he or she may initiate judicial review by bringing the question to the Constitutional Tribunal. When the Constitutional Tribunal finds a norm unconstitutional, it is no longer binding and cannot be the basis for other judgments in other courts. Furthermore, even earlier judgments based on an unconstitutional norm can be reviewed in a special procedure.[134] Obviously, the Constitutional Tribunal is not the only court that interprets statutes, but it is essential to emphasis that only its rulings are binding *erga omnes*. Verdicts of other courts including the Supreme Court and Supreme Administrative Court are not universally binding as a rule.[135] It should be added that in the years 1989–1997, the Constitutional Tribunal had the competence to issue general legal interpretations of statutes, but this prerogative was revoked by the current Constitution. Yet, since many judgments were delivered throughout this period, the legally binding judgments of courts and decisions issued by public authorities based on the Tribunal's interpretation were upheld.[136] Despite lacking a formal competence to issue general legal interpretations after 1997, in practice the Tribunal often delivered interpretations which *de facto* became as binding as the judgment itself.

The Supreme Court has the competence to settle legal enquiries submitted by the courts as well as to decide on divergences in the interpretations of law found in the decisions of ordinary courts, military courts, and the Supreme Court itself. In the event

133 71.8 % of judges pointed out the direct impact of legal scholarship on their own judgments – national survey in 2015–2016. Anna Machnikowska, *O niezawisłości sędziów i niezależności sądów w trudnych czasach. Wymiar sprawiedliwości w pułapce sprawności* (Wolters Kluwer 2018) 474; Iwona Rzucidło-Grochowska, Mateusz Grochowski (eds), *Uzasadnienia decyzji stosowania prawa* (Wolters Kluwer 2015); Maciej Wojciechowski, 'Sądowy dyskurs interpretacyjny dotyczący wykładni rozszerzającej' in Mikołaj Hermann and Sebastian Sykuna (eds), *Wykładnia prawa. Tradycje i perspektywy* (C.H. Beck 2016) 275–294; Ewa Łętowska and Krzysztof Sobczak, *Rzeźbienie państwa prawa. 20 lat później* (Wolters Kluwer 2012) 141–167, 340–341; Tomasz Gizbert-Studnicki, 'Prawda sądowa w postępowaniu cywilnym' (2009) 7 *Państwo i Prawo* 5.

134 E.g. Art. 401^1 of the CCP or Art. 145a of the Code of Administrative Procedure.

135 See below.

136 Art. 188 point 3 of the Constitution.

of legal issues that arouse serious doubts or cause divergences in case law, the case may be referred for examination by an expanded panel of this court: a panel of seven justices, an entire Supreme Court chamber, joint Supreme Court chambers, or the whole Supreme Court (full panel).[137] The ruling of the first type of panel may become a so-called legal principle when the judges of this panel decide to inscribe it to the book of legal principles. The rulings of the three latter types of panels automatically become legal principles.[138] Legal principles are, however, only binding upon all the judicial panels of the Supreme Court (and the lower court in a given case), and derogation from such a principle is only possible by way of adopting a new one.

The Supreme Administrative Court as well is competent to adopt rulings aiming to eliminate diverging interpretations by lower administrative courts and to determine questions of law that arouse serious doubts in a specific administrative court case. The Supreme Administrative Court can either provide abstract or concrete norm control and interpretation. The goal is to ensure the consistency of administrative court decisions. Both abstract and concrete rulings of a panel of seven justices, an entire Supreme Administrative Court chamber, or the whole Supreme Administrative Court (full panel) are binding in all administrative proceedings.[139]

The Supreme Administrative Court has no opinion-making or advisory competences of assisting the executive with legal advice, comparable to those enjoyed by the Council of State in France or in Belgium. In the course of the legislative process, it is treated on a par with the institutions that must be consulted as part of the general process of law-making.[140] Beyond that, the Supreme Administrative Court has no distinguished role in the production of administrative norms.

Moreover, the established procedure in Poland is that judgments of the Constitutional Tribunal, the Supreme Court, the Supreme Administrative Court, and of appellate courts are published, along with their justifications.[141] Judgments of the Constitutional Tribunal are published in the official journal and on its website.[142] Judgments of the

137 In 2018, there were a total 143 for example, and in 2017, 152 legal enquiries submitted by lower courts to the Supreme Court. In 2018, no rulings of the entire chamber or joint chambers, or all members of the Supreme Court were issued, only a few verdicts of seven judges were issued, but none of them received the rank of a legal principle. Cf. Article 390 of the Code of Civil Procedure and Article 441 of the Code of Penal Procedure, but also in the abstract procedure (Article 83 of the Act on the Supreme Court) – at the request of the First President of the Supreme Court, the Ombudsman, the Prosecutor General, and some other bodies may result in a legal principle.

138 Art. 87. § 1 of the Act on the Supreme Court of 8 December 2017; Dz. U. 2018, 5 as amended, consistent with Art. 61 § 6 of the Act on the Supreme Court of 23 November 2002, Dz. U. 2016, 1254 as amended.

139 Art. 269 of the LPAC. Cf. Tadeusz Woś, Hanna Knysiak-Sudyka and Marta Romańska (eds), *Prawo o postępowaniu przed sądami administracyjnymi. Komentarz* (Wolters Kluwer 2016) 1265 ff.

140 Resolution no. 190 of the Council of Ministers of 29 October 2013; Monitor Polski (hereinafter: MP) 2013, 979; Resolution of the Sejm of the Republic of Poland of 30 July 1992 – Standing Orders of the Sejm of the Republic of Poland, MP 2012, 32 as amended; resolution of the Senate of the Republic of Poland of 23 November 1990 – Standing Orders of the Senate of the Republic of Poland, MP 2002, 54, 741 as amended.

141 Cf. the website of the appellate court in Wrocław: http://orzeczenia.wroclaw.sa.gov.pl/ accessed 30 November 2019.

142 Judgments of the Constitutional Tribunal are published in Journal of Laws of the Republic of Poland (*Dziennik Ustaw Rzeczypospolitej Polskiej*) or in the official journal Monitor Polski and on the official website of Constitutional Tribunal: http://otkzu.trybunal.gov.pl/accessed 30 November 2019

Supreme Court or the Supreme Administrative Court are published in special official collections and on their websites as well.[143] Despite their lack of formal force as a source of law, in practice, courts of lower instances, state organs, and the general public use them as guidelines due to their inherent institutional and intellectual authority.

Due to the ongoing constitutional crisis in Poland, some legal scholars and judges have suggested that the presumption of constitutionality of issued legislation no longer holds.[144] This presumption was adequate under circumstances in which an independent Constitutional Tribunal functioned. The presumption of constitutionality is based on the idea that an independent Constitutional Tribunal forces the Parliament to restrain its legislative activities to meet the constitutional requirements. This is supposed to guarantee a decent quality of legislation. These claims were criticized by the current President of the Constitutional Tribunal, Julia Przyłębska, who holds that the preconditions of the presumption are met because the Constitutional Tribunal, in her view, is still independent.[145] Nevertheless, in the current situation it has been suggested that judges should apply the Constitution directly: an act should be presumed constitutional unless it is challenged by the courts based on Art. 8 para. 2 of the Constitution.[146] The right to perform judicial review is not a new competence of judges, since Article 8 has been in place since 1997, but it has never been used before. Despite these signals, practicing

143 Judgments of the Supreme Administrative Court are published in the official collection entitled *Orzecznictwo Naczelnego Sądu Administracyjnego i wojewódzkich sądów administracyjnych*, but are available as well at http://www.nsa.gov.pl/baza-orzeczen.php. Some important Supreme Court judgments are published in special official collections, however, many of them are available at http://www.sn.pl/orzecznictwo/SitePages/Baza_orzeczen.aspx. Both links accessed 30 November 2019.

144 E.g. Marcin Matczak, 'Dlaczego w Polsce nie obowiązuje już tradycyjne domniemanie konstytucyjności?', available at https://marcinmatczak.pl/index.php/2018/07/08/dlaczego-w-polsce-nie-obowiazuje-juz-tradycyjne-domniemanie-konstytucyjnosci/. Cf. also statements of Tomasz Pietrzykowski, 'Domniemanie konstytucyjności', available at https://www.academia.edu/20133667/Domniemanie_konstytucyjno%C5%9Bci. Both links accessed 6 November 2019. Cf. as well the opinion of A. Grabowski in '*Domniemanie konstytucyjności i reguła* lex superior *(w ujęciu argumentacyjnym kontroli konstytucyjności prawa)*', speech delivered at the conference: Pierwsze Krakowskie Sympozjum Konstytucyjne: *O problemach wykładni Konstytucji RP*, 7 October 2017. Cf. as well Aleksandra Dębowska and Monika Florczak-Wątor, 'Domniemanie konstytucyjności ustawy w świetle orzecznictwa Trybunału Konstytucyjnego', (2017) 2 *Przegląd Konstytucyjny* 5, 19 ff.

145 Cf. Interview with Julia Przyłębska to TVP INFO, available at https://www.tvp.info/37943917/prezes-tk-kwestionowanie-konstytucyjnosci-ustaw-prowadzi-do-anarchii accessed 6 November 2019.

146 Judges have signaled adopting such a course of action, among others in connection with the amendment of the Act on Public Gatherings, limiting the citizen's rights to gather in public, adopted in December 2016 and effective since the spring of 2017. Pursuant to this amendment, no other gatherings may take place at the time and place of gatherings organized by state authorities. Judge Waldemar Żurek, spokesman of the National Council of the Judiciary, openly stated (e.g., in an interview given to TVN24) that he would apply the Constitution directly in his judgments. Judge Łukasz Biliński invoked superiority of the Constitution over traffic regulations in his judgment acquitting a group of people who protested in front of the Sejm in December 2016, when the Speaker of the Sejm, a member of the ruling party, deprived the parliamentary opposition of the possibility to participate in voting on the Budget Act. Yet Judge Biliński does not replace acts with the Constitution; he simply organizes his arguments according to the constitutional order while applying statutory provisions. The most recent example (though connected with the direct application of a CJEU judgment) is the case of Judge Paweł Juszczyszyn, adjudicating in the provincial court in Olsztyn, who referred to the judgment of the CJEU of 19 November 2019 in his case regarding Poland, and for this reason was suspended as a judge, something that took place on 29 November 2019.

judges seem to be reluctant to make use of it, despite announcements that they may start doing so.[147]

4. Ideal of Justice

Polish legal culture is characterized by a very positivistic approach with a strong focus on the written sources of law. Another feature is the diverse origin of the content of the norms of positive law. They combine the achievements of distinguished European legal scholars with original Polish legal thought. The perception of law and justice in society is a particular kind of combination of trying to realise and protect the idea of individual freedom with the desire and expectation that daily life shall be regulated by a system of formalized norms, providing for both predictability and legal certainty. These factors determine the attitude of the majority of the Polish people towards law and justice and towards legal principles and institutions. This attitude is closely related not only to the formal catalogue of norms, which was discussed earlier, but also to the evolution of the Polish legal system.

Poland's loss of independence at the end of the 18th century led to the transition from a reality that was uncodified, particularistic and largely based on customary law, to externally imposed laws and codes, which were indeed often perceived as modern – especially in the case of German, French, and Austrian law – but at the same time seen as foreign to the local legal culture.[148] This was also the reason why the laws received were initially applied with great reluctance.[149] In addition, the authorities of the states that annexed the Polish territories further strengthened formalized solutions and limited social initiatives in order to exercise as much control as possible. Economic problems proved equally important for the Polish legal culture. Many developments, especially in commercial and contract law, took place with some delay compared to other central European countries. Restrictions on civil rights and liberties, enforced by the occupying powers, weakened not only the domestic capital but also the wider implementation of the principles of market liberalism into the legal order.

After Poland regained independence in 1918, restoration of national sovereignty required the establishment of unified legal institutions and the enactment of new substantive law. In the eyes of contemporary politicians and lawyers, this process demanded manifestation in the form of formalised and positive regulation. The need for new legislation was also caused by the demand to harmonise the fragmented legislation in the

147 Judges statements at the Extraordinary Congress of Judges Warsaw, 4 September 2016, own unpublished documentation. Cf. Krzysztof Sobczak, 'Gdy państwo prawa jest zagrożone, trzeba odwoływać się do konstytucji – „Sędzia a Konstytucja. Kryzys sadownictwa konstytucyjnego a rozproszona kontrola zgodności prawa z Konstytucją", konferencja w Katowicach, 3.03.2017 r.' (2017) 2 *Krajowa Rada Sądownictwa* 98 ff.

148 For more see: Juliusz Bardach and Monika Senkowska-Gluck (eds), *Historia państwa i prawa Polski. Od rozbiorów do uwłaszczenia* (PWN 1981) III. More about Polish legal culture up until the 18th century: Wacław Uruszczak, *Historia państwa i prawa polskiego, tom I* (966–1795) (Wolters Kuwer 2015).

149 Michał Gałędek and Anna Klimaszewska, 'A Controversial Transplant? Debate over the Adaptation of the Napoleonic Code on the Polish Territories in the Early 19th Century' (2018) 11 *Journal of Civil Law Studies* 269.

different parts of what had become the new Poland. At that time, some argued that an official recognition of custom as a source of law could cause obstacles in unifying the law and creating one legal system.[150] As in Germany in the 19th century, harmonizing the law was regarded a necessary precondition for social, political and economic integration. Representatives of the Polish legal academia, who were internationally educated and understood the new needs, implemented several spectacular reforms of the law.[151] Due to the very short period of independence (1919–1939), however, it was impossible to establish organizational and institutional preconditions and social attitudes in order to develop the Polish legal culture more holistically. The result was a widely fragmented tessellation of elements of different origin and ideological background.

The lost war in 1939 and the two parallel occupations – German and Soviet – lasting until 1945, reintroduced and facilitated the very formalistic attitude to law, especially when applying foreign law. The formal independence, which Poland regained after the end of the Second World War, contained no real sovereignty either. Poland entered the sphere of influence of the USSR and of the Soviet concept of state and law. This situation lasted for 45 years. Although a complete transfer of the communist legal ideology and system, which was alien to the Polish mentality, did not take place at that time, Poland's legal system and society were again under very strong pressure exerted by solutions typical of an authoritarian state. The development of a civil society and free economy was blocked once again and both were subordinated to central planning. As a consequence, the common experience with the law was still stigmatized by formalized procedures, casuistic content of norms, and their official interpretation.[152]

As a result of these circumstances, even though in the 19th and 20th centuries Poland was governed by very different ideologies and political systems, their common feature was the sometimes unofficial connection with the doctrine of legal positivism, in its version dating back to the 19th century.[153] This conception of law was very useful for both the foreign states that ruled over Poland's territory in the 19th century and to Polish governments, which in the second half of the 20th century conducted a legal policy that corresponded to the rules of an authoritarian ideology. The long experience of several generations that law is to be understood in terms of the aforementioned classical legal positivism still affects Polish legal thinking in the 21st century.[154] This stagnation took place despite the fact that Polish legal scholars were aware of the evolution of this doc-

---

150 Stanisław Wróblewski, *Komentarz do Kodeksu Handlowego części I (art. 1–13)* (Leon Frommer 1935) 11; Cf. Tadeusz Dziurzyński, 'Prawo zwyczajowe w przyszłej ustawie handlowej' (1929) 1–12 *Czasopismo Prawnicze i Ekonomiczne* 356; Leonard Górnicki, 'Przewodnie konstrukcje i pojęcia Kodeksu handlowego z 1934 roku' (2015) CI *Przegląd Prawa i Administracji* 75.

151 Leonard Górnicki, 'Kodyfikacja prawa prywatnego' in Marek Safjan (ed), *System Prawa Prywatnego* (C.H. Beck 2012) I.

152 For more, see Adam Lityński, *Historia prawa Polski Ludowej* (LexisNexis 2013).

153 Including Jellinek's views. Jarosław Kostrubiec, *Nauka o państwie w myśli Georga Jellinka* (WUMCS 2015) 10; A. Peretiakowicz, *Państwo współczesne* (ZZKiW 1928) 2–16.

154 Artur Kozak, *Myślenia analityczne w nauce prawa i praktyce prawniczej* (WUW 2010) 70–71; Jolanta Jabłońska-Bonca, *O szkolnictwie wyższym i kształceniu prawników* (WIWS 2020) 37–39, 211, 243.

trine (including: neo-positivism, Hart v Fuller debate, Hart v Dworkin, and R. Alexy's theory).[155]

The history of the Polish legal system also explains the attachment to a "culture of codes". First, the codes brought into the Polish territory were used to modernize the outdated legal system. Then, work on 'national' codes was considered a manifestation of national legal identity and an expression of autonomy. When Poland entered the sphere of influence of the communist ideology, the use of codes was not abandoned. The new codes, created in the 1960s, resembled to some extent the content and principles of the old codes, which were in force in the years 1919–1939. This was a result of the efforts of the Polish jurisprudence to preserve the identity of the Polish legal tradition in the socialist state.[156] On the other hand, the political authorities encapsulated them with many lower-order acts, through which they relativized the principles set forth in the codes. It also deprived the courts of hearing many civil cases and entrusted them to out-of-court bodies that mainly applied no-codex norms, often not complying with the content of the codes. In this way, although some traditional institutions were present in the legal order – e.g., courts and codes – in practice they did not play a crucial role in the legal system.

The centuries-old political perturbations were also an obstacle to stabilization of the justice system. This was accompanied by a lack of confidence in the courts, which is strongly rooted in the Polish legal culture. The feudal, non-uniform, and customary system of the Commonwealth was frequently perceived as unpredictable and arbitrary.[157] The changes introduced by the legislator in the 19th century, even though they often

---

155 Rafał Mańko, *W stronę krytycznej filozofii orzekania. Polityczność, etyka, legitymizacja* (WUŁ 2018); Maciej Pichlak, *Refleksyjność prawa. Od teorii społecznej do strategii regulacji i z powrotem* (WUŁ) 2019; Tomasz Barankiewicz, 'Inkluzywny pozytywizm prawniczy (geneza, rozwój, główne idee)' (2010) 1 *Państwo i Prawo* 10–24; Andrzej Grabowski, 'Inkluzyjny pozytywizm prawniczy (uwagi do aktualnej dyskusji)' (2011) 11 *Państwo i Prawo* 18–31; Jerzy Zajadło, 'Pięćdziesiąta rocznica debaty Hart-Fuller' (2008) 7 *Państwo i Prawo* 5–19; Tomasz Pietrzykowski, ' "Miękki" pozytywizm i spór o regułę uznania' in Jerzy Stelmach (ed), *Studia z filozofii prawa* (WUJ 2001) 97–121; Jolanta Jabłońska-Bonca, 'Wymiar sprawiedliwości a przemiany kultury prawnej w Europie' in Witold Morawski (ed), *Powiązania zewnętrzne. Modernizacja Polski* (Wolters Kluwer 2012) 296–313; Robert Alexy, 'W obronie niepozytywistycznej koncepcji prawa' (1993) 11–12 *Państwo i Prawo* 34–49, Herbert L.A. Hart, *Pojęcie prawa* Jan Woleński (trans) (PWN 1998), Jerzy Zajadło, *Przyszłość dziedzictwa: Robert Alexy, Ralf Dreier, Jürgen Habermas, Otfried Höffe, Arthur Kaufmann, Niklas Luhmann, Ota Weinberger: portrety filozofów prawa* (Arche 2008).

156 For more see: Adam Lityński, *Pół wieku kodyfikacji w Polsce. Wybrane zagadnienia (1919–1969)* (WSZiNS 2001); Witold Czachórski, 'Przebieg prac nad kodyfikacją prawa cywilnego PRL' (1970) *Studia Prawnicze* 26; Anna Stawarska-Rippel, *Elementy prywatne i publiczne w procesie cywilnym w świetle prac kodyfikacyjnych w Polsce (1918–1964). Studium historycznoprawne* (WUŚ 2015); Anna Machnikowska, *Prawo własności w Polsce w latach 1944–1981. Studium historycznoprawne* (WUG 2010); Anna Moszyńska, *Geneza prawa spadkowego w polskim kodeksie cywilnym z 1964 r.* (WNUMK 2019).

157 Cf. Jędrzej Kitowicz, *Opis obyczajów za panowania Augusta III (*Roman Pollak (ed), Zakł. im. Ossolińskich 2003), I, 205–225; Marcin Matuszewicz, *Diariusz życia mego (*Bohdan Królikowski and Zofia Zielińska (eds) PIW 1986), I–II, passim; Stanislas Auguste, *Mémoires* (Anna Grześkowiak-Krwawicz and Dominique Triaire (eds) IES – SHLP 2012), 41–46, 222, 267–268; Jerzy Michalski, *Studia nad reformą sądownictwa i prawa sądowego w XVIII w.* (Zakł. im. Ossolińskich 1958) I, 15–187; Zbigniew Naworski, *Szlachecki wymiar sprawiedliwości w Prusach Królewskich (1454–1772). Organizacja i funkcjonowanie* (WNUMK 2004); Adam Moniuszko, *Mazowieckie sądy ziemskie Organizacja-funkcjonowanie-postępowanie* (Campidoglio 2013) 62, 130–140, 160–175.

involved reforms of the judiciary, simultaneously introduced new, alien types of courts, instances, and procedures.[158] The judges were often foreigners or Poles associated with the authority of another state. In the 20 years of the interbellum period, overcoming the habits adopted by generation of lawyers, including the new judges could hardly be achieved. In addition, during the period of the Polish People's Republic, the justice system did not enjoy public confidence. The population perceived it instead as a system that served exclusively the political goals of the communist party.

The type of norms that were dominant in the legal system, the form of their regulation, and the tasks assigned to institutions of the justice system by the executive branch of government also affected the underlying principles of court proceedings. In addition, they determined the predominant ideal of law and justice in the Polish legal culture. The political authorities expected judges to strictly apply legal norms. When the communist system was introduced, Polish lawyers were still educated in accordance with the theory of legal positivism, because this doctrine required judges to strictly apply the rules. This ensured that the political power, which had created these provisions, had full control over the legal system. As a result, several generations of judges focused on the linguistic interpretation of laws, regarding law more as *lex* than *ius*. Therefore, non-professional judges were absent in the Polish court system. Moreover, the practice of out-of-court dispute resolution, e.g. through mediation and economic arbitration, was not strengthened. Consequently, in Poland throughout the 20th century there were no favorable conditions for the development of sources of law other than statutory law and the corresponding methods of interpreting law.

These intellectual and institutional preconditions facilitated a perception of judges who functioned more like court clerks. Judges themselves sometimes even share this view because of the rigid legislative framework. In addition, the very heavy workload prevents them from a broader and more creative interpretation of law. As a result, they cannot always provide solutions based on thoroughly balancing the considerations of individual justice and legal certainty. In a fast-changing and complex socio-economic reality they are instead forced to apply law in compliance with the letter of the law. Surveys have shown that only approximately 25 % of them regard maximization of usefulness for the parties the most important objective of court proceedings. Approximately 20 % regard a speedy solution as being the highest objective. No more than 13 % indicate that benefits for the society as a whole should be the main objective of conflict resolution.[159]

What is more, a majority of citizens today still perceive law as a command of state power, understood as a formalized, impersonal institution, and not as a result of social

158 For more, cf. Bardach and Senkowska-Gluck (eds) (1981) (n 148); Artur Korobowicz, *Sądownictwo Królestwa Polskiego 1876–1915* (UMCS 1995); Stanisław Płaza, *Historia prawa w Polsce na tle porównawczym, cz. 2, Polska pod zaborami* (Księgarnia Akademicka 2002); Władyław Sobociński, *Historia ustroju i prawa Księstwa Warszawskiego* (PWN 1964); Anna Klimaszewska, 'Commercial judiciary on the Polish territories in the 19th century – a repackaged French product or a mock-up?' (2019) *Revista da Faculdade de Direito da Universidade Federal de Minas Gerais*, special issue, Cristina Vano, Heikki Pihlajamäki and Ricardo Sontag (eds), 97.

159 Sociological research on a representative national sample of judges – Machnikowska (2018) (n 133) 482. This also applies to judges in criminal departments.

dialogue. Law is expected to provide legal security identified with the sense of certainty and equality before the law (strong egalitarian beliefs), and in recent years this is combined with the expectation of severe punishment for perpetrators of crimes and the demand for swift judgments in civil cases. As a consequence, courts composed of professional judges are still perceived as institutions that are best suited to achieve these objectives. The lack of confidence in the courts does not impede this point of view.

Not before the 1990's, were the preconditions finally met for an unrestricted development of the Polish legal culture. However, the long experience of several generations, who lived under rules that hindered the promotion of values that are necessary to establish and maintain a liberal democracy and the rule of law as fundamental for law and justice, had deeply affected ideas and expectations to law in society. Despite the change of the political system, a part of the political class and of the legal community had the expectation that in a liberal democracy, there is no need to internalize consciously and purposely the rule of law through education, dialogue, and everyday practice.[160] They assumed that the general legal awareness would develop automatically, along with other socio-economic changes. However, the correctness of this assumption seems rather questionable in the light of recent events.

Citizens have a strong expectation that the state and courts will act in accordance with the principles of social justice, despite the fact that positive law is expected to provide legal security. The main aspects of social justice are the absence of privileges in the legal system and state interventionism in the sphere of equal access to material goods, as well as access to free legal assistance for Polish citizens. Populists especially argue that except from the constitutionally guaranteed rights and freedoms, justice is determined by what the majority considers right and fair. The paradox is that, although the sense of belonging to a larger community is emphasized in relation to the concept of justice, in practice many citizens employ individualistic attitudes, which in turn have their basis in the lack of the joint activities strengthening the social legal awareness mentioned above. Moreover, the persistent mistrust concerns not only judges, but other citizens as well.[161] Therefore, social justice is more often associated with the expectation that state institutions operate more efficiently than solutions developed during social activities undertaken by citizens themselves or their various communities.[162]

A majority of judges also share the opinion that an important reason for social, political and legal tensions is caused by a lack of interest in the common good (93 %) and that the legal system should use the institution of mediation more frequently (88 %). Therefore, they seem to acknowledge the deficiencies of classical legal positivism. Furthermore, when asked about handling civil disobedience, more than 75 % declare that in their judgments they would act according to their conscience, 31 % would apply

160 Tadeusz Ereciński, 'O uwarunkowaniach, potrzebie oraz zakresie nowego kodeksu postępowania cywilnego' (2010) 1 *Polski Proces Cywilny*; Ewa Łętowska, 'Prawo w „płynnej rzeczywistości"' (2014) 3 *Państwo i Prawo* 1.

161 It has an impact on the very low rate of out-of-court proceedings. Cf. Conflict Resolution in this Chapter.

162 This is why it is so strongly expected, for example, that the legal system should severely punish criminals, rather than include further elements of rehabilitation.

extraordinary leniency, and 24.5 % would apply only the law in force, while 30 % would consider referring problematic provisions to the assessment of the Constitutional Tribunal.[163]

During recent years, Poland's political culture has once again changed dramatically. Politicians who declared "returning courts to citizens", including stricter and advocating for more severe punishment of criminals and stronger procedural protection for certain groups of civil cases, have already twice secured their victory in the parliamentary elections (2015, 2019). Currently, the ruling party (PiS) achieves its goals by formally increasing administrative influence over the courts and the legislative process. They are also critical to the idea of social negotiation and debate, claiming instead that the will of the parliamentary majority has priority over other liberal and pluralistic values.[164] Using terminology, which confirms that at least part of society has the goal to strengthen 'justice' and values such as legal security and democracy. By carrying out certain surface-reforms highly attractive for their voters, in fact at the deeper levels of legal culture, these changes might cause the opposite effect and weaken institutions and principles that are supposed to provide substantive justice. This applies particularly to the guarantee of fair legal treatment for those disagreeing with the ruling party.

Note that legal certainty and predictability are to be ensured primarily by legislative acts; case law is not regarded an instrument to safeguard a sufficient degree of legal security. On the other hand, legal acts in Poland, as everywhere else, require interpretation. The role of the Supreme Court and the Supreme Administrative Court is to provide uniform interpretations, thus indirectly contributing to predictable outcomes. In addition, their task is to develop the law in order to provide verdicts that hold a predictable solution for the future as well. The very positivistic approach is applied even by the Courts (see below) and does not allow for a considerable impact of equity and fairness.

The Constitutional Tribunal, whose basic task is to conduct judicial review, i.e., to decide on the compliance of lower-order acts with higher-order acts and especially with the Constitution of 2 April 1997, also used to contribute to maintain legal certainty. However, it is supposed to provide a value-based type of legal certainty. The concept of "constitution" cannot be limited only to its written text. Indeed, its content is determined not only in specifically expressed norms, but also in principles and values that are much less expressly stated in the Constitution and require judicial clarification. Some of them open up the system of positive law towards natural law and other external normative systems (e.g., Christian values). The Constitution therefore serves, on the one hand, as a point of reference for the control of constitutionality, and on the other hand, it is subject to a constant process of clarification in constitutional jurisprudence. The most typical example, but not the only one, is the evolution of case law on the interpretation of the principle of a democratic law-abiding state (Art. 2). From the very beginning, the Constitutional Tribunal has shown a tendency to treat it more broadly. It is understood as the collective expression of many principles and rules of a more detailed nature which,

163 Machnikowska (2018) (n 133) 487–492.
164 Machnikowska (2018) (n 133) 350–401.

although not explicitly enshrined in the Constitution, are derived indirectly from it.[165] An indispensable aspect of this set of principles is that legislation needs to be adopted by following a proper/decent procedure.[166] Equally important are the principles of proportionality and necessity as a precondition for any restriction of citizens' rights. The extent to which those unwritten principles can be said to have impacted the ideal of justice on a deeper level seems questionable. The ongoing political crisis may give an opportunity to verify the sustainability of the Constitutional Tribunal's *acquis*, particularly regarding the rule of law. Ordinary judges who would decide to apply the Constitution directly, bypassing some of the controversial provisions of the ordinary laws, might act as guardians of these principles.

Under such circumstances, the lawyers' perception of their own obligations towards the Constitution and towards the principles of protection of citizens' rights and freedoms might help to change the ideal of justice. Polish lawyers have recently directed public attention towards the importance of a functioning legal system, including but not limited to guarantees of legal certainty and predictability. History has witnessed how easily fundamental rights can be eliminated in the name of the people (or rather a majority). In such a situation the ability to warrant legal security by other elements of the legal system and the informal legal culture becomes highly important. However, even if resistance has been offered by the legal community (in the middle layer of the legal sea), the future of what will be the ideal of justice in Poland highly depends on which group manages to convince a majority of people of their interpretation of what the ideal justice should be based on: the tyranny of the majority or the values of the liberal democratic Constitution of 1997. Regardless of the outcome, one thing seems rather clear: the political crises triggered a discourse concerning the fundamental values and the perception of justice in Poland.

5. Legal Method

The legal method in the Polish legal culture is closely linked to a formalized catalogue of the sources of law contained in Chapter III of the Constitution.[167] Universally binding sources of law are the Constitution, statutes, ratified international agreements and regulations (in the following legal instruments).[168] The Constitution identifies not only formal sources of law, but also the principles for producing legal instruments.[169] Statutory law is organized into a hierarchical system, with the Constitution on top and all

165 E.g. judgment of the Constitutional Tribunal of 4 June 2013, P 43/11. Mirosław Granat, 'Trybunał Konstytucyjny. Osiągnięcie czy zadanie?' in Andrzej Szmyt (ed), *Trzecia władza: sądy i trybunały w Polsce: materiały Jubileuszowego L Ogólnopolskiego Zjazdu Katedr i Zakładów Prawa Konstytucyjnego, Gdynia, 24–26 kwietnia 2008 roku* (WUG 2008) 23–41.

166 See their review in the resolution of the seven judges of the Supreme Administrative Court of 12 March 2001, OPS 14/00, ONSA 2001/3, item 101).

167 Chapter III of the Constitution, Art. 87–94.

168 Art. 87 para. 1.

169 Art. 87–94 of the Constitution.

the other legal instruments subordinate to it. The application of law is highly formalistic since the Polish legal method is based on a doctrine of legal positivism. Accordingly, legal claims need a basis in a statutory provision.[170] However, the limitations to positivism following from the Radbruch's Formula have been widely accepted in legal theory.[171]

The Polish legal system is only to a very limited extent open to other non-formalized normative systems.[172] Customary law as such is not recognised as a source of law. On the other hand, a custom can be a foundation for rights and obligations under certain conditions. In order for that to happen, the custom has to be explicitly provided for by a norm in the statutory law (the norm in the statutory law should use the term "custom"). There are less than twenty such norms in the Polish legal order.[173] Nor do the provisions of the statutory law contain many general clauses that would enable using more diversified legal methods.[174] Procedural regulations sometimes enable courts to apply the principle of equity, but this only concerns the right of the court to increase or limit the scope of legal protection provided by the law.[175] In other words, equity is not decisive as to whether the court will consider or reject a claim in a particular case at all, because this depends only on the content of the statutory law.

---

170 The preamble of the Constitution speaks of justice and pursuant to Art. 45 para. 1, citizens have a right to have their cases fairly reviewed, however these concepts are not directly linked to the sources of law or its interpretation. The concept of justice (*iustitia*) used in the Constitution is not synonymous with the concept of equity (*aequitas)*. Cf. e.g. judgments of the Constitutional Tribunal of 27 June 1995, K 4/94; of 22 December 1997, K2/97; of 5 July 2010, P 31/09.

171 In Poland, the popularity of the academic analysis of Gustav Radbruch's Formula and the consequences of his approach to the contemporary legislation and case law may be attributed to J. Zajadło's publications. This is also due to the fact that, in the Polish legal system from before the political transformation in 1989, the law was very oppressive in some cases even though it aspired, undeservedly, to legality, taking advantage of the non-existence of a constitutional tribunal and the very limited independence of courts, Jerzy Zajadło, *Dziedzictwo przeszłości. Gustaw Radbruch: portret filozofa, prawnika, polityka i humanisty* (Arche 2007); idem, 'Formuła "Gesetz und Recht"' (2002) 1 *Ius et Lex* 39.

172 Cf. Bartosz Wojciechowski, 'Rozstrzyganie tzw. trudnych przypadków poprzez odwołanie się do odpowiedzialności moralnej' (2004) 70 *Studia Prawno-Ekonomiczne* 4; Marek Safjan, *Wyzwania dla państwa prawa* (Wolters Kluwer 2007) 204.

173 Cf. examples in given in the section on Norm Production.

174 Cf.: Zbigniew Radwański and Maciej Zieliński, 'Klauzule generalne w prawie prywatnym' in Marek Safjan (ed), *System Prawa Prywatnego, t. 1: Prawo cywilne – część ogólna* (C.H. Beck 2007) 335 ff; Agnieszka Choduń, Andrzej Gomułowicz and Andrzej Skoczylas, *Klauzule generalne i zwroty niedookreślone w prawie podatkowym i administracyjnym. Wybrane zagadnienia teoretyczne i orzecznicze* (Wolters Kluwer 2013); Tadeusz Zieliński, 'Klauzule generalne w nowym porządku konstytucyjnym' (1997) 11–12 *Państwo i Prawo* 134 ff.; Alina Wypych-Żywicka, 'Prawa podmiotowe w prawie pracy' in Krzysztof Wojciech Baran (ed), *Zarys systemu prawa pracy, t. 1: Część ogólna prawa pracy* (Wolters Kluwer 2017) 1359–1399; Leszek Leszczyński and Grzegorz Maroń, 'Pojęcie i treść zasad prawa i generalnych klauzul odsyłających. Uwagi porównawcze' (2013) 60/1 *Annales UMCS. Sectio G* 82 ff.; Tadeusz Zieliński, 'Klauzule generalne w procesie karnym' in Janina Czapska, Andrzej Gaberle, Andrzej Światłowski and Andrzej Zoll (eds), *Zasady procesu karnego wobec wyzwań współczesności. Księga ku czci Profesora Stanisława Waltosia* (PWN 2000) 786; Marian Zdyb and Jerzy Stelmasiak, *Zasady ogólne Kodeksu postępowania administracyjnego. Orzecznictwo Naczelnego Sądu Administracyjnego z komentarzem* (Lublin 1992) 47; Adam Szot, 'Klauzula generalna jako ponadgałęziowa konstrukcja systemu prawa' (2016) 63/2 *Annales UMCS. Sectio G* 291.

175 E.g. Art. 417^2 of the CC. Cf. also: Anna Drywa, *Odpowiedzialność odszkodowawcza za wydanie niezgodnej z prawem decyzji podatkowej* (Wolters Kluwer 2014) 28.

Legal argumentation is strongly influenced by the way judges argue their decisions. Legal practitioners apply the same type of reasoning when interpreting statutory law, and also when advising clients. This is because the vast majority of conflicts are resolved in courts (cf. Conflict Resolution). As judges predominantly use grammatical interpretation of legislation (simple legal syllogism), there is a high probability that the legal practitioners argue based on the same principles. For this reason, in view of a possible litigation, lawyers who negotiate contracts or advise clients on other matters, try to take into account interpretations of legal provisions applied by the courts.[176]

Since legal acts in Poland are of a very diverse nature, with norms that are sometimes very general and abstract and sometimes detailed and meticulous, literal analysis is sometimes not sufficient and a broader toolkit for interpretation is required. The judgments of the highest courts enjoy special authority, despite the fact that there is no theory of precedent in Poland and case law is not considered as a formal source of law by the Constitution.[177] From a formal point of view, judgments of the Supreme Court and the Supreme Administrative Court are binding only in the given case, unless they have received the status of a legal principle (cf. the section on Norm Production). However, even then, the Supreme Administrative Court's interpretation is binding only in all administrative proceedings and the Supreme Court's rulings are binding for the lower court in the particular case and the Supreme Court itself. Nevertheless, judges and other lawyers, in practice being familiar with these rulings, interpret a given provision in other cases in accordance with the methodological approach used by the Supreme Court.[178]

Case law, therefore, is considered in practice as a subsidiary source of law, which serves the purpose of finding a solution where it is impossible to conclude based on the wording of the pertinent provisions.[179] Lawyers pay less attention to other sources of legal knowledge, such as legal doctrine or legislative materials (preparatory works). However, in a court case the opinions of legal scholars with an eminent reputation in the field of law can be decisive. Furthermore, using non-legal scholarly opinions has

---

176 Therefore, databases with rulings occupy the second place (after databases with provisions of statutory law) in the statistics of using individual elements of legal information. In every legal profession they are a basic work tool. See Marcin Kokoszczyński and Grzegorz Wierczyński, *System informacji prawnej w pracy sędziego* (Wolters Kluwer 2011) 81.

177 Among the many judgments that assume the significance grounded in earlier court decisions, it is worth pointing out characteristic statements such as "in the jurisprudence of the Supreme Administrative Court, the application of the provision […] has been checked many times and currently the interpretation of this provision does not cause any doubts", judgment of the Supreme Administrative Court of 31 May 2000, I SA/Gd 102/98; "interpretation should be sought in court decisions", judgment of the voivodship administrative court in Opole of 4 April 2004, I SA/Wr 3918/01; "the explanations provided are consistent with the grounded case law of the Supreme Administrative Court", judgment of the voivodship administrative court in Warsaw of 16 June 2004, III SA 528/03. More: Agnieszka Bielska-Brodziak, *Interpretacja tekstu prawnego na podstawie orzecznictwa podatkowego* (Wolters Kluwer 2009) 81 ff.

178 In publications intended for judges regarding the methodology of their work, not only legal institutions are discussed, but the case law of the Supreme Court, which has shaped judicial practice, is strongly taken into account. Cf. Henryk Pietrzykowski, *Metodyka pracy sędziego w sprawach cywilnych* (Wolters Kluwer 2014).

179 Piotr Tuleja, 'Źródła prawa' in Paweł Sarnecki (ed), *Prawo konstytucyjne RP* (C.H. Beck 2014) 57; Józef Frąckowiak, 'Orzecznictwo i doktryna jako źródło prawa prywatnego' (2018) 112 *Przegląd Prawa i Administracji* 47.

been recommended when an evaluation of another area of knowledge is necessary to apply/interpret a specific legal solution.[180] Then, there is justification to use specialist opinions, such as court expert opinions, e.g. medical doctors witnessing on the state of mind of a person.[181]

Doctrinal interpretations of law including new concepts advocated by legal scholars gain significance only when the Supreme Court, the Supreme Administrative Court, or the Constitutional Tribunal refer to them in their rulings.[182] As an example, the high impact of John Rawls's concept of justice in Polish legal culture can be noticed, because the Constitutional Tribunal has referred to it several times.[183]

Despite the fact that the interest in the acquis of legal science has increased recently, a significant part of it still awaits wider application. This applies to the development of reasoning used in jurisprudence, which consists of applying logic, analysis, argumentation, and hermeneutics. In 2006, leading advocates of this trend, J. Stelmach and B. Brożek, proposed a paradigm of the jurisprudence model that dynamically incorporates various old and new fields of knowledge.[184] This gives an opportunity to adequately respond to the phenomenon of contemporary law, which requires research in the field of linguistics, sociology, psychology, and axiology, as well as a coherent application of these methods.[185] Scientific research aimed at analysing the interpretation applied in judicial

---

180 Maciej Zieliński, *Wykładnia prawa. Zasady – reguły – wskazówki* (Wolters Kluwer 2017) 299.

181 Olgierd Bogucki, 'Perspektywy rozwinięcia normatywnego ujęcia wykładni funkcjonalnej' in Mikołaj Hermann and Sebastian Sykuna (eds), *Wykładnia prawa. Tradycje i perspektywy* (C.H. Beck 2016) 218–219.

182 Marcin Romanowicz, 'Utrwalona linia orzecznicza jako argument z (własnego) autorytetu sądowego' in Tomasz Giaro (ed) *Rola orzecznictwa w systemie prawa* (Wolters Kluwer 2016) 173–200; Safjan (2007) (n 172) 15; Jadwiga Potrzeszcz, *Idea prawa w orzecznictwie polskiego Trybunału Konstytucyjnego* (Towarzystwo Naukowe KUL 2007); Granat, (2008) (n 165) 23–40. Cf also Piotr Tuleja, *Wyroki interpretacyjne Trybunału Konstytucyjnego* (Ars boni et aequi 2016); Florczak-Wątor (2014) (n 83).

183 Cf. Judgment of 22 December 1997, K 2/97, in which the Constitutional Tribunal emphasized that Rawl's concept of distributive social justice should be implemented in labour relations: „All social values—liberty and opportunity, income and wealth, and the social bases of self-respect—are to be distributed equally unless an unequal distribution of any, or all, of these values is to everyone's advantage."; John Rawls, *A Theory of Justice. Revised Edition* (Harvard University Press 1999) 54; Polish edition was cited by the Constitutional Tribunal: John Rawls, *Teoria sprawiedliwości* Maciej Panufik, Jarosław Pasek, Adam Romaniuk (trans) (PWN 1994) 89. The same reference was used in judgment of 2 December 2008, P 48/07. Cf. also judgment of 9 June 2003, SK 5/03, in which no specific publication of Rawl's was cited, just his authority was used by judge Marian Zdyb in his dissenting opinion: „As truth in knowledge systems – John Rawls used to say – so is justice first virtue of social institutions."

184 Jerzy Stelmach and Bartosz Brożek, *Metody prawnicze* (Wolters Kluwer 2006). English version: idem, *Methods of Legal Reasoning* (Springer 2006).

185 According to Ewa Łętowska: "First of all, the court must note the problem that requires interpretation. Contrary to what is commonly thought, for the court the need for interpretation is not a matter of ambiguity or lack of precision of the text, but above all an axiological matter. The beginning of the whole process takes place in sensitivity, which makes it possible to realize that there is an "interpretation deficit". The judge notices that the interpretation usually used so far is "bad", and this axiological discomfort becomes an impulse for interpretive searches. That is why – at least when it comes to interpretive innovation – progress is made not so much with hard cases as with axiological cases." See Ewa Łętowska, 'Boska sztuka interpretacji' in Adam Łopatka, Barbara Kunicka-Michalska and Stefan Kiewlicz (eds), *Prawo, społeczeństwo, jednostka. Księga jubileuszowa dedykowana Profesorowi Leszkowi Kubickiemu* (INP PAN 2003) 30.

decisions should also be noticed.[186] This helps in identifying developmental tendencies in the Polish legal system, and also forms the basis for a postulate, which is increasingly supported in legal science, that lawyers should make use of different forms of argumentation to a greater extent,[187] putting more emphasis on functional interpretation.[188] This applies to the recognition of so-called hard cases, which lawyers more frequently use even in courts of lower levels.[189] In recent years, this point of view has gradually found acceptance among judges who are slowly beginning to expand the scope of their legal reasoning. This, in turn, helps to transfer new theories to the application of law. This development is still in its early stages, but a new dynamic can be observed. Consequently, it can be expected that the legal method will become more heteronomic and open to new approaches.

Accordingly, principles of legal interpretation and their impact on legal methods have gained attention in recent years. This is the result of an increasing interest in legal methodology, which is facilitated by the internationalisation and globalisation of law, and the challenges this development has for judges and practitioners alike. The other reason is the judicial law reform enacted in Poland between 2015 and 2019, which has contributed to restructure the balance of powers in Poland. Prior to these reforms, the grammatical/linguistic interpretation was predominant. This is in line with the principles of legal positivism and its attitude to the text as a binding command by the legislature. If the outcome of such interpretation was unequivocal, ordinary courts could refer the case to the Constitutional Tribunal or, less frequently, to the Supreme Court, to replace the strict grammatical interpretation with a more functional one.

New methodological discussions, particularly concerning the way the Constitution and decisions by the Constitutional Tribunal should be treated, have also initiated a deeper reflection process regarding the need for institutional guarantees. The question arising is how to interpret not only the Constitution but other legal instruments as well, and what kind of methodology could be used to oppose or support the new populist policy in Poland. If the purpose of applying the law is to realise fundamental constitutional values instead of relativizing them, institutional and intellectual changes are inevitable.

6. Professionalisation

The degree of legal professionalisation in Poland is generally high. This is the result of the following factors: the path of legal education, the additional mandatory (with minor exceptions) apprenticeships required to practice and the system of central exams at different stages. Equally important is the mandatory affiliation of lawyers to corporations,

186 See Wojciechowski (2016) (n 133) 286–294.

187 Jerzy Stelmach, *Kodeks argumentacyjny dla prawników* (Zakamycze 2003); Katarzyna Budzyńska, *Logika a argumentacja,* available at http://www.calculemus.org/neumann/odczyty/budzynska.doc accessed 6 November 2019.

188 Mikołaj Hermann and Sebastian Sykuna (eds), *Wykładnia prawa. Tradycje i perspektywy* (C.H. Beck 2016).

189 Marcin Matczak, *Summa iniuria. O błędzie formalizmu w stosowaniu prawa* (WN Scholar 2007).

who monitor the way they conduct their profession and provide additional education. As mentioned before, lay judges are rarely used.

Admission to legal studies is possible only based on the results of national examinations held at the end of secondary education at the premises of secondary schools. Universities do not organize entrance exams. The majority of law students – about 82 % – study at state universities.[190] In 2019, an average of 3.43 persons applied for one available college place.[191] Currently, 40,500 law students are enrolled at Polish universities.[192] The legal studies are uniform master's studies lasting five years (there is no division into bachelor's and master's studies).

Universities have a relatively wide autonomy. They determine the content of the curricula and decide on their internal organization. They also conduct personnel policy by announcing competitions for vacancies. External experts provide evaluation of the education at universities. This evaluation takes place cyclically – once every few years. Each field of study, including legal studies, is subject to the assessment of the Polish Accreditation Commission (*Polska Komisja Akredytacyjna*). This institution operates on similar principles as accreditation institutions in other countries.[193] Polish universities are also members of international or EU organizations dedicated to the quality of education (e.g. EUCEN).

The main purpose of education in law faculties is to combine theory and practice. Students are prepared for independent professional activities and for active participation in the development of legal culture. Many assessments and teaching activities are dedicated to case studies. Students are required not only to know central Acts of legislation, but also to interpret them and combine legal knowledge with knowledge in the field of economics, politics, sociology and psychology. In most study programmes, around 50 % to 70 % of all subjects are compulsory, including logic, philosophy, Roman law, international law and EU legislation.[194] Constitutional, criminal, civil, financial, commercial and labour law are also compulsory.[195] Elective courses concern narrow branches of law or are very specialized. Increased importance is attached to shaping law students' ethical attitude. They become familiar with the ethics of individual legal professions and general

---

190 Data published by the Central Statistical Office (*Główny Urząd Statystyczny*): https://stat.gov.pl/obszary-tematyczne/edukacja/edukacja/szkoly-wyzsze-i-ich-finanse-w-2018-roku,2,15.html accessed 6 November 2019.

191 See https://www.rp.pl/Rankingi/306179997-Ranking-Wydzialow-Prawa-2019, data from the Information Processing Center of the National Research Institute (*Ośrodek Przetwarzania Informacji Państwowego Instytutu Badawczego*), accessed 6 November 2019.

192 See n 190.

193 More: Act of 20 July 2018 – Law on Higher Education and Science (Dz. U. 2018, 1668, as amended); Statute of the Polish Accreditation Commission; Annex to Resolution No. 4/2018 of the Polish Accreditation Commission of 13 December 2018 (consolidated text including changes introduced by the resolution of the Polish Accreditation Commission of 18 February 2019 No. 1/2019).

194 Cf. e.g. the programme of legal studies at the Jagiellonian University: https://wpia.uj.edu.pl/prawo/program-i-plan-studiow; at the University of Warsaw: http://strony.wpia.uw.edu.pl/zarzadzeniauchwaly/files/2017/02/Zal_1.pdf; and at the University of Gdańsk: https://prawo.ug.edu.pl/jesli_studiujesz/studenci/programy_studiow/program_studiow_-_prawo. All links accessed 6 November 2019.

195 Ibid.

principles, e.g., the CCBE Code of Conduct. Currently many universities particularly emphasize the role of the Constitution and its interpretation.

The legal education can be continued with an apprenticeship (*aplikacja*) that prepares law graduates for specific legal professions. Admission to the apprenticeship as well as its termination requires passing an additional state exam and passing this exam is difficult. There are usually about 8.5 persons who apply for one place at the judicial and prosecutor's apprenticeship (the number of places is determined in advance). In 2019, the success rate of examinations for other apprenticeships was as follows: 55 % for attorneys-at-law, advocates and notaries, and 29 % for bailiffs.[196] Apprenticeships for advocates, attorneys-at-law,[197] judges, and prosecutors last three years, for notaries 3.5 years, and for bailiffs two years. Completing the apprenticeship and passing the exams is necessary to practice as an advocate, attorney-at-law, notary, prosecutor, judge, or bailiff.

Legal corporations running their apprenticeships in centers located in many places in the country are in charge of the preparation to practice specific legal professions. An exception applies for education of judges and prosecutors. Common elements are entrance and final exams organized by the Ministry of Justice.[198] During the apprenticeships, theoretical knowledge is still required, but devoted to practical vocational training. The trainee remains under the supervision of his or her patron. Trainees are authorized to handle certain legal tasks already during apprenticeships.[199]

In Poland, advocates and attorneys-at-law provide legal services. Advocates may run their law firms themselves or with the participation of several advocates or with the participation of both advocates and attorneys-at-law. These law firms may operate in various legal forms – also as commercial law companies. State institutions or businesses are not allowed to employ advocates. Attorneys-at-law, who previously had a limited scope of competence compared to advocates,[200] can now plead in courts in any case, just like advocates do (civil, family law, criminal, and administrative law cases). What makes them different from advocates is that they are not restricted to conducting their business activity independently by running a law firm, but they may also be employed

196 See https://gov.pl/web/sprawiedliwosc/wstepne-wyniki-egzaminow-na-aplikacje-prawnicze-w-2019-r accessed 6 November 2019.

197 Up until October 2018, the official guideline was to translate *radca prawny* as a legal counsellor or legal adviser. Last year, however, the National Council of Legal Counsellors decided that this term does not reflect the scope of their competences and resolved that "attorney-at-law" will be more fitting, especially in light of the fact that there now exists a para-legal profession of legal adviser (*doradca prawny*, see below).

198 Act of 26 May 1982 Law on the Advocates' Profession (Dz. U 2019, 1513 as amended), Act of 6 July 1982 on Attorneys-at-Law (Dz. U. 2019, 730, as amended); Act of 23 January 2009 on the National School of the Judiciary and Prosecution Service (Dz. U. 2019, 1042); Act of 14 February 1991 Law on Notaries (Dz. U. 2019, 540 as amended); Act of 22 March 2018 on Court Bailiffs (Dz. U. 2019, 55 as amended).

199 For instance, after six months of apprenticeship, a trainee advocate may substitute an advocate at court, before organs of law enforcement, state authorities, self-government bodies and other institutions with the exception of the Supreme Court, Supreme Administrative Court, Constitutional Tribunal and Tribunal of State.

200 The existing division between advocates and attorneys-at-laws is currently deemed artificial and has mostly historical significance. In the 1960s, when Poland was a socialist country, legal counsellors (attorneys-at-law) were appointed to provide legal services to state enterprises, which was their domain until the end of the 1980s.

under a contract of employment in public institutions and private entities to provide legal services.

Notaries and bailiffs, on the other hand, have a complicated legal status. They also run their own firms and act as entrepreneurs by making a living from client fees, but at the same time they have the powers of public officials because they act on behalf of the state. This means that they are subordinate to both their own corporations and the supervision of Minister of Justice – Prosecutor General. In 2018, the government had significantly reduced the independence of bailiffs by thoroughly regulating this profession.[201]

A unique aspect regarding Poland is the career path of professional judges. The education of future judges is centralized and takes place in the National School of Judiciary and Public Prosecution (*Krajowa Szkoła Sądownictwa i Prokuratury*), which is a centralized institution responsible for the initial and continuous training of the judiciary and prosecution staff in Poland. Successfully passing the difficult exam gives the right to apply for a position of a judge, so the profession is open to candidates who have turned 29. The candidate does not need to have practical experience. This is different from many countries, where taking office as a judge is the crowning achievement of a legal career. The education in the judicial apprenticeship includes knowledge of EU case law and legislation. Those who wants to become a judge have to apply for an assessor position (trainee judge). Assessors perform the duties of a judge and have nearly the same competences.[202] After three years, they can apply for promotion to judge. The application requires that their work is evaluated positively. In voivodship administrative courts, two years of experience as a trainee judge is sufficient; however, an age limit (over 30 years) and several years of experience in one of the legal professions is required to become a trainee judge of a voivodship administrative court.[203] If their work is assessed positively, the trainee judge is appointed a judge by the President of the Republic of Poland.[204]

The institution of trainee judges is controversial. The main objection is that they are not truly independent, because they are not only supervised by other judges but also assessed by the National Council of Judiciary, which is partly controlled by politicians, including the Minister of Justice. Due to these concerns, the institution of a trainee judge was removed from the Polish legal system for several years;[205] however, it was restored in 2017. Trainee judges now represent less than 7 % of the total number of judges, but this figure will soon increase to around 10 %.[206]

---

201 See n 198.

202 Their competences do not only cover cases involving decisions on pre-trial detention and the handling of complaints against decisions not to open an investigation. Art. 2 § 1 of the Act of 27 July 2001 on the organizational structure of common courts; Dz.U. 2019, 52, as amended.

203 Art. 6 § 1 and Art. 6a § 1 LSAC.

204 Ibid Art. 106xa § 1-2.

205 After the judgment of the Constitutional Tribunal of 24 October 2007, which came into effect on 5 May 2009.

206 Own calculations based on announcements of the President of the Republic of Poland, see https://prezydent.pl/aktualnosc/nominacje accessed 6 November 2019.

The National Council of the Judiciary plays an important role in the appointment procedure. Before the reform of the judiciary in 2017, the Council came from elections held by judges themselves for the most part. Currently, it is elected by the Sejm by a simple majority of votes. As a result, the Council members are elected according to the will of the Prosecutor General – the Minister of Justice. Such a combination of competences in one person's hands raises objections and constitutional concerns. According to some representatives of the legal community and the European Commission, the current rules of electing the National Council of Judiciary violate the guarantees of the independence of judges, which is why this case was reviewed by the CJEU.[207] The CJEU found the Polish Supreme Court competent to assess this issue, at the same time providing interpretative guidelines. According the latest verdict of the Supreme Court, the Council in its current composition is not an impartial body, independent of the legislative and executive authorities.[208]

Judges and trainee judges, but also advocates, attorneys-at-law, notaries and bailiffs are subject to new rules on disciplinary liability which were introduced in 2018.[209] At that time, a new Disciplinary Chamber in the Supreme Court was established to act as a court of second instance and to rule on disciplinary matters concerning all persons practicing legal professions. Reformers claim that legal corporations have failed to properly perform control over the profession. The same was said about the internal control mechanisms for judges. Therefore, their competences had to be limited and transferred to the new institution. According to some lawyers and the European Commission, the procedure of appointing judges in the Disciplinary Chamber of the Supreme Court, as well as the new rules on disciplinary proceedings, lack transparency and allow the informal influence of politicians on this procedure. The character of the Disciplinary Chamber was questioned by the CJEU as well.[210]

Another way to acquire the right to perform the legal professions of a judge, a prosecutor, an advocate and an attorney-at-law is by obtaining the academic degree of a habilitated doctor of law or the title of a professor of law.[211] The two latter do not require an apprenticeship or passing the professional exams. Researchers with a PhD in legal science have the same privilege if they have previously performed some practical legal activities.[212] However, if the Doctor of Law has only scientific experience, he is exempt from legal apprenticeship, but he must pass a professional examination.[213]

Universities have the final decision on awarding a degree of doctor and habilitated doctor. However, a state institution, the Council of Scientific Excellence that consists of 141 members elected in nationwide secret elections by all scientists from various fields, including law, conducts the assessment procedure for habilitated doctors and law

207 The decision was issued on November 19, 2019. C-585/18, C 624/18 and 625/18.

208 Cf. Judgment of the Supreme Court of 5 December 2019, III PO 7/18.

209 Act of 8 December 2017 on the Supreme Court, Dz. U. 2019, 825, as amended.

210 See n 207.

211 E.g., Art. 25 para. 1 point 1 of the Act on Attorneys-at-Law.

212 E.g., ibid Art. 25 para. 1 point 5.

213 E.g., ibid Art. 25 para. 2.

professors. After the assessment of the candidate by the scientific council, the receipt of the highest academic title depends on the decision of the President of the Republic of Poland. Some presidents have refused to appoint certain candidates without justifying their decision. This issue was the subject of a legal dispute, which was settled by Polish courts. They considered that the President has a wide discretion.[214] He must reject appointing a person who has not received positive scientific reviews but may block the scientific promotion of a particular person for other reasons as well. This competence is regarded by some as a violation of the autonomy of the scientific community.

Alumni of faculties of law who graduated but did not complete any of the aforementioned apprenticeships or did not pass the final exam, may offer legal services as so-called legal advisers. This is a fairly new profession, which emerged following the Constitutional Tribunal's judgment issued on 26 November 2003. Here the Constitutional Tribunal stated that people with diplomas in law may conduct a private legal practice and that this may be justified by the interests of those social groups that cannot afford the highly-specialized services offered by advocates and attorneys-at-law.[215] Advisers may provide advice and draft letters; they can represent their clients in administrative proceedings (but not before administrative courts).[216]

Direct participation of citizens in the administration of justice does not have strong roots in the Constitution.[217] It only states that this matter is "provided for in a statute".[218] In Poland, lay judges co-judge in adjudication panels of first instance courts in a narrowly defined group of civil and criminal cases.[219] According to some scholars, the lack of lay judges in the judiciary has contributed to the low confidence in courts.[220]

Since 2019, certain procedures before the Supreme Court contain lay participation.[221] Before the last judiciary reform, the rule was that the most experienced judges and professors of law ruled in the Supreme Court. Now laymen participate (constituting a minority of the adjudicating panel) in disciplinary proceedings conducted against judges and representatives of other legal professions by the Disciplinary Chamber of the

---

214 *Per analogiam* to the inaction when appointing judges. Cf. Resolutions of the Supreme Administrative Court of 7 December 2017 – I OSK 857/17 and I OSK 858/17, as well as the Constitutional Tribunal's judgment of 5 June 2012, K 18/09.

215 Judgment of the Constitutional Tribunal of 22 November 2016, SK 22/02.

216 For other competencies see: Art. 87 para. 1 and Art. 87 para. 3,4,5,6 of the CCP.

217 Art. 182 of the Constitution.

218 Art. 182 of the Constitution.

219 In civil cases, lay judges are present e.g. in some labour law cases and cases involving damages in case of mobbing, as well as in some family law cases, including divorce and separation. In criminal cases, adjudicating panels with lay judges adjudicate in cases involving accusation of a felony, i.e., acts punishable by more than three years' imprisonment. Cf. Art. 7. § 2 of the PC. List of cases heard with the participation of lay judges cf. Rycak (ed) (2011) (n 42) 6 ff.

220 See e.g. Wojciech Zalewski, 'Why do people need courts? Adjudicating in the times of the trust crisis' in Anna Machnikowska (ed), *The Legitimation of Judicial Power* (Wyd. UG 2016) 213 ff.; Ryszard A. Stefański, 'Składy sądu w postępowaniu karnym' in Jolanta Jakubowska-Hara, Celina Nowak and Jan Skupiński (eds), *Reforma prawa karnego, propozycje i komentarze. Księga pamiątkowa Profesor Barbary Kunickiej-Michaskiej* (Scholar 2008) 435.

221 Act of 8 December 2017 on the Supreme Court.

Supreme Court,[222] and in considering a new legal remedy – the so-called extraordinary complaint.

In the explanatory note to this amendment, the reformers claimed that the new institution would help to remove unfair judgments. Ordinary citizens represented by lay judges would be a necessary precondition for that.[223] The reform was promoted under the slogan of democratization of the judiciary.[224] According to the official government policy, lawyers and their self-governments have become an elite that does not serve the general public.

In practice, however, the new regulations have not transferred significant power to the public. The actual purpose of the changes in the court system was to limit the independence of courts and judges. Particularly problematic is that the new competences were not transferred directly to citizens, but allowed politicians, including the Minister of Justice – the Prosecutor General to increase political influence. This critical opinion was shared by the vast majority of the representatives of the legal and scientific community, including Prof. E. Łętowska, F. Zoll, J. Zajadło, L. Garlicki, M. Matczak, R. Piotrowski,[225] as well as by deans and councils of many law faculties.[226]

To conclude, the degree of professionalisation in the Polish legal culture is high, even though there are some minor exceptions, concerning, among other things, legal advisors and lay judge participation in courts. Current political and legal changes are unlikely to change that. Even if the outcome is still open, these changes have triggered a discussion on the relationship between legal culture, principles of professional education of lawyers and the political status of courts and legal actors. Some of these reforms became the subject of CJEU rulings in 2019 and might even influence the European legal culture if they serve as role model for reforms in other countries.

7. Internationalisation

7.1 Dualistic or monistic approach?

As mentioned in the introduction, the Polish legal culture developed for centuries under the influence of foreign laws. Attempting to create the necessary legal terminology for a

---

222 Ibid Art. 59 § 1.

223 Cf. Paper no. 2003, Draft Act on the Supreme Court presented by the President of the Republic of Poland; paper no. 2071, Report of the Justice and Human Rights Committee on the draft law on the Supreme Court presented by the President of the Republic of Poland; paper no. 2071-A, Additional report of the Justice and Human Rights Committee on the draft law on the Supreme Court presented by the President of the Republic of Poland.

224 Ibid.

225 Including statements in the media by Prof. E. Łętowska, Prof. F. Zoll, Prof. J. Zajadło and Prof. M. Matczak (an interview for the online edition of *Die Welt* of 10 July 2019). More: Granat (2019) (n 61) 400–405, 422–425; Ryszard Piotrowski, 'The issue of the legitimation of the judicial power in a democratic state ruled by law', and Grzegorz Ławnikowicz, 'Judicial ethics in the time of the systemic transformation', both in Anna Machnikowska (ed), *The Legitimation of Judicial Power* (Wyd. UG 2016) 11–30, 85–102; Machnikowska (2018) (n 133).

226 Cf. Interview with Prof. J. Pisuliński: https://www.prawo.pl/prawnicy-sady/prof-pisulinski-po-skardze-nadzwyczajnej-niepewnosc-prawa,75048.html accessed 6 November 2019.

modern nation in the 19th century, Polish legal scholars and the legislator were inspired by the conceptual frameworks of France and Germany. In the first years of the new Millennium, new sources of inspiration were more international and supranational, particularly EU-law.

In terms of the relationship between international law and national law in Poland, some scholars have indicated that, "the dualistic approach, [although] in a less orthodox and more moderate manner, still better reflects the relationship between the international law and national law" in Poland.[227] Consequently, not all norms of international law become automatically part of the domestic legal order; however, the norms contained in ratified international agreements are a part. Hence the classic, Heinrich Triepel's dualism,[228] which does not assume points of contact and even excludes a collision of national and international law, does not reflect the state of affairs. On the other hand, it would be difficult to say that the Polish Constitution affirms pure monism. Nevertheless, it considerably incorporates international legal norms as directly applicable.

The opening up of the Polish legal system to international law has expressly been embraced in the Constitution of the Republic of Poland. In the very first chapter, in Art. 9, we find one of the principles of fundamental significance (a metarule) for the relationship between national and international law: "The Republic of Poland shall respect international law binding upon it".[229] Of all the constitutional provisions concerning international law, this is one of the most significant. The applied formula is broader than the principle of *pacta sunt servanda*, since this provision addresses all the sources of international law, not only international treaties but also generally recognized principles of international law and international customary law.[230] Thus, the constitutional legislator consciously decided that the system of law governing the territory of the Republic of Poland will comprise components of different origins. National and international law are supposed to coexist, based on mutually amiable interpretation and cooperation.[231] Accordingly, such a system can be called multicentric.[232]

In terms of international treaties, one can group them into three categories: treaties which are signed by competent bodies of the executive branch, treaties that have to be

227 Andrzej Wasilkowski, 'Prawo krajowe – prawo wspólnotowe – prawo międzynarodowe. Zagadnienia wstępne' in Maria Kruk (ed), *Prawo międzynarodowe i wspólnotowe w wewnętrznym porządku prawnym* (Wydawnictwo Sejmowe 1997) 15.

228 Heinrich Triepel, *Völkerrecht und Landesrecht* (Verlag von C.L. Hirschfeld 1899).

229 Official translation of the Polish Constitution. See https://www.sejm.gov.pl/prawo/konst/angielski/kon1.htm.

230 Jan Boć (ed), *Konstytucje Rzeczpospolitej oraz komentarz do Konstytucji RP z 1997 roku* (Kolonia Limited 1998) 157. Cf. Renata Szafarz, 'Międzynarodowy porządek prawny i jego odbicie w polskim prawie konstytucyjnym' in Maria Kruk (ed), *Prawo międzynarodowe i wspólnotowe w wewnętrznym porządku prawnym* (Wydawnictwo Sejmowe 1997) 19 and 24; Krzysztof Wójtowicz, 'Art. 9' in Marek Safjan and Leszek Bosek (eds), *Konstytucja RP. Komentarz* I (C.H. Beck 2016) 325; Małgorzata Masternak-Kubiak, *Umowa międzynarodowa w prawie konstytucyjnym* (PWN 1997) 200. Garlicki (2019) (n 78) 160.

231 Cf. Judgment of the Constitutional Tribunal of 11 May 2005, K 18/04.

232 Cf. Ewa Łętowska, 'Multicentryczność współczesnego systemu prawa i jej konsekwencje' (2005) 4 *Państwo i Prawo* 3–10.

ratified by the President[233] and those that have to be approved by Parliament before the President can ratify them. According to Chapter III of the Constitution, a so called approving act is only required for exactly specified types of international treaties, such as e.g. the North Atlantic Treaty.[234] The Constitution thus provides rules regulating the incorporation of international law and grants the Parliament a right to participate in the decision-making process concerning the scope of the international obligations of the State. The Constitution requires even stricter procedures before ratification when sovereign competences shall be transferred by virtue of international treaty. The leading example is the Treaty of Accession of Poland to the EU (16 April 2003, Athens). Passing such an approving act requires a qualified majority vote in both chambers of Parliament[235] or nationwide referendum. Upon ratification and publication of a treaty,[236] and under this very condition,[237] the provisions of the treaty become directly binding law. There is, therefore, a strong implication towards the monistic approach.

The division into ratified and non-ratified treaties is crucial because it determines the legal effectiveness of treaties in the domestic legal order. Although a non-ratified treaty cannot confer rights to individuals or impose obligations on them, it obviously binds the state in external relations, and it falls within the scope of Art. 9 of the Polish Constitution and sometimes – depending on its subject matter – requires implementation in national law.[238]

All ratified international treaties may contain provisions that are the source of generally applicable law; such provisions are part of the domestic legal order and are directly applicable. However, their position in the legal system differs depending on the ratification procedure applied, i.e., whether or not they were approved by the Parliament.

233 Art. 133 para. 1 point 1 of the Constitution.

234 Ibid Art. 89 para. 1. The approving act is required for treaties concerning: 1) peace, alliance, political pacts or military pacts; 2) civic freedoms, rights and obligations provided for in the Constitution; 3) membership of the Republic of Poland in an international organization; 4) major financial liabilities of the State; 5) matters governed by an act or for which the Constitution requires an act (Article 89 (1) of the Constitution). All the other international treaties do not require an approving act (however, the Sejm must be notified by the Prime Minister. Cf. Art. 89 para. 2).

235 Two-thirds in the presence of at least half of the statutory number of members of each chamber. Cf. Art. 90 para. 2 of the Constitution.

236 Cf. Judgment of the Constitutional Tribunal of 19 December 2002, K 33/02.

237 Cf. Judgment of the Constitutional Tribunal of 3 December 2009, K 8/09.

238 Anna Wyrozumska, *Umowy międzynarodowe: teoria i praktyka* (Wyd. PiPG 2006) 601; Małgorzata Masternak-Kubiak, *Przestrzeganie prawa międzynarodowego w świetle Konstytucji Rzeczypospolitej Polskiej* (Wolters Kluwer 2003) 203. Cf. also judgment of the Constitutional Tribunal of 19 December 2002, K 33/02. One of the methods of implementing the provisions of non-ratified treaties is the reference contained in the Constitution or in an Act of Parliament. E.g., the Supreme Administrative Court in a judgment of 26 August 1999 (V SA 708/99) granted the rights arising from the Geneva Convention of 28 July 1951 regarding refugee status (which, according to the Supreme Administrative Court, is a non-ratified treaty, however still binding upon Poland), the rank of constitutional rights, due to the reference to binding international treaties included in Art. 56 para. 2 of the Polish Constitution. According to Małgorzata Masternak-Kubiak, these norms should be directly applied in the internal legal circulation and do not require any additional (transforming) actions, see *Odesłania do prawa międzynarodowego w Konstytucji RP* (PiEBC 2013) 163.

Treaties ratified based on a consent expressed in an approving act have, by virtue of the Constitution, precedence over national Acts.[239]

The Constitution lacks explicit provisions determining the place of treaties ratified without a prior approving act. Legal scholars assume that such treaties can neither be superior to an Act of Parliament, nor have force equal to such an Act.[240] If such a treaty, based exclusively on the approval by the executive branch, had the force equal to an Act, it could amend or even abolish provisions of earlier Acts.[241] This would be regarded a violation of the Constitution's principle of separation of powers. Thus, treaties ratified without a prior approving act may, on the one hand, constitute a source of generally applicable law but, on the other hand, they are considered to be of lower rank than Acts of Parliament.[242]

7.2 Poland and the EU

Poland, being a Member State of the European Union since 2004, is bound by the same principles for applying EU law as all the other Member States: direct effect of EU law in the Member States, the primacy of EU law over domestic law in case of a conflict of norms and the obligation to contribute to interpret national law in accordance to EU law. Furthermore, Art. 91 para. 1 and 2 of the Polish Constitution states that EU treaties constitute part of the domestic legal order, are directly applicable (if possible), and have precedence over Acts of Parliament (and other sources of domestic law). In terms of the secondary law, Art. 91 para. 3 explicitly states that if this ensues from a treaty constituting an international organization ratified by the Republic of Poland, then the law established by it is applied directly, taking precedence in the case of conflict of laws.[243] In practice, there are no doubts in case of regulations, since they apply directly and constitute an independent legal basis for administrative and court decisions.[244] The question is rather what happens if the Polish government or Parliament does not or incorrectly implements a directive. If the deadline for implementing the directive has expired, and the legal norm can be precisely and unconditionally identified, this norm can be invoked by citizens against the state as failing to implement the directive correctly.[245] Detailed analysis of these issues, however, is beyond of the purpose of this section.

---

239 Art. 91 para. 2 of the Constitution. Cf. also Judgment of the Constitutional Tribunal of 4 March 2008, SK 3/07.

240 *A contrario* to Art. 91 para. 2. Cf. Garlicki (2019) (n 78) 164. Bogusław Banaszak, *Prawo konstytucyjne* (C.H. Beck 2004) 146. Cf. Art. 188 para. 2–3 of the Constitution.

241 Garlicki (2019) (n 78) 164.

242 Ibid.

243 Cf. e.g. judgments of ECJ in Case 14/83 *Von Colson and Kamann* [1984] ECR 1891; and Case C-106/89 *Marleasing* [1990] ECR I–4135 as well.

244 Cf. Judgment of the Constitutional Tribunal of 10 February 2015, SK 50/13.

245 Cf. e.g. ECJ judgments in the following cases: Case C-8/81 *Becker vs. Finanzamt Munster-Innenstadt* [1982] ECR 53; Case C-102/79 *European Commission v. Belgium* [1980] ECR 1473; Case C-41/74 *Van Duyn* [1974] ECR 1337; Case C-6/90 and C-9/90 *Francovich and others* [1991] ECR I-5357.

7.3 Principles of international law and international customary law

Insofar as international treaties are broadly discussed in the Polish Constitution, other sources of international law are not treated expressly, although the abovementioned Art. 9 of the Constitution explicitly states that the Republic of Poland observes the international law that is binding upon it. This metarule should be applied to all the sources of international law, not only international treaties but also generally recognized principles of international law and international customary law.[246] As L. Garlicki states, this does not *per se* include these norms in the domestic legal order, since the Polish Constitution provides for the inclusion of only some types of international treaties.[247] According to W. Sokolewicz, the rule expressed in Art. 9 has, however, a higher place in the internal hierarchy of constitutional norms and principles than the provisions of Chapter III – *Sources of Law*.[248] Consequently, one could assume that a judge, who is subject to the Constitution,[249] could apply Art. 9, if he/she states that Poland is bound by a specific norm of customary international law.[250] Furthermore, as B. Banaszak emphasised, generally recognized principles of international law and international customary law should have precedence over Act of Parliament, even if the Constitution lacks explicit provisions determining the place.[251]

From this provision follows also a duty to interpret the provisions of all Polish law as far as possible in accordance with Poland's international obligations.[252]

The binding force of judgments of the European Court of Human Rights in Strasbourg is also recognised in Polish law. The Helsinki Foundation for Human Rights has repeatedly pointed out backlogs concerning the implementation of the Courts rul-

---

246 See n 230.

247 Garlicki (2019) (n 78) 161.

248 Cf. Wojciech Sokolewicz, 'Artykuł 235' in Leszek Garlicki (ed), *Konstytucja Rzeczypospolitej Polskiej. Komentarz* II (Wyd. Sejmowe 2001) 16.

249 Art. 178 of the Constitution.

250 Anna Wyrozumska, 'Prawo międzynarodowe oraz prawo Unii Europejskiej a konstytucyjny system źródeł prawa' in Krzysztof Wójtowicz (ed), *Otwarcie Konstytucji RP na prawo międzynarodowe i procesy integracyjne* (Wyd. Sejmowe 2006) 39. Cf. resolution of the Supreme Court of 11 January 2000 (I PKN 562/99).

251 Banaszak (2004) (n 240) 149–150.

252 As it was emphasized in the opinion of the Advisory Legal Committee to the Minister of Foreign Affairs of 21 May 1999, resolutions of international organizations, after having met all the procedures required to obtain binding force in relation to the Republic of Poland, may be considered binding upon authorities of the Republic of Poland not only on the basis of effect of an international legal action, but also pursuant to Art. 9 of the Constitution of 1997. Private opinion cited after Andrzej Wasilkowski, 'Przestrzeganie prawa międzynarodowego (art. 9 Konstytucji RP)' in Krzysztof Wójtowicz (ed), *Otwarcie Konstytucji RP na prawo międzynarodowe i procesy integracyjne* (Wyd. Sejmowe 2006) 16. Cf. Wójtowicz (2016) (n 230) 332. In a judgment of 16 November 2011 (SK 45/09), the Constitutional Tribunal clearly emphasized that although the Constitution of the Republic of Poland has been clearly guaranteed the status of the highest law of the Republic of Poland, this regulation is accompanied by the "order to respect and favorable attitude towards properly shaped and binding regulations of international law in the territory of the Republic of Poland (Article 9 of the Constitution)." Cf. Also: Ewa Łętowska, 'A my w Krakowie wiemy swoje…' *Polityka* 23 May 1998; Andrzej Bałaban, 'Czy sędzia podlega umowie międzynarodowej', *Rzeczpospolita* 1 June 1998.

ings.[253] However in the last 19 years, e.g. the penal and civil procedure was amended several times, in order to comply with the ECtHR's interpretation of the ECHR.

7.4 Impact of Globalisation

Globalization has also impacted the Polish legal culture. For example, optional instruments devised by expert groups, such as the Principles of European Contract Law (PECL) or Principles of European Insurance Contract Law (PEICL) may be applied if the parties to the contract so choose. In respect of the latter, however, some legal scholars assume that they can serve as a point of reference for the reforms of the Civil Code.[254] INCOTERMS, created by the International Chamber of Commerce (ICC) in Paris, play a special role in relationships between entrepreneurs.[255] Direct references to INCOTERMS are contained in many different legal acts.[256] Also ordinary and administrative courts and the Superior Court invoke them.[257] FIDIC (Fr. *Fédération Internationale des Ingénieurs-Conseils*) standards are becoming increasingly popular and are used both in the public and private sectors. FIDIC contractual terms are used in Poland by way of incorporation into individual contracts. They are applied by public ordering parties in the system of public tenders, by international parties and financing banks, in highway investments, in contracts signed by the General Directorate for National Roads and Motorways, and in infrastructure projects financed by international institutions.[258] The national legal culture has consequently been impacted by and has to handle challenges of legal pluralism.

253 E.g. in a letter to the Speaker of the Sejm dated 20 January 2012.

254 Ewa Łętowska, 'Prawo zobowiązań a system prawa' in Ewa Łętowska (ed), *Prawo zobowiązań – część ogólna* (C.H. Beck 2006) 68–70; Dariusz Fuchs, 'Insurance Restatement jako europejski instrument opcjonalny służący regulacji umowy ubezpieczenia' (2010) Nr. 9 (2) *Rozprawy Ubezpieczeniowe* 126; Dariusz Fuchs, 'Nowelizacja kodeksu cywilnego w zakresie wybranych przepisów ogólnych o umowie ubezpieczenia w świetle przepisów ogólnych o umowie ubezpieczenia w świetle prac Project Group on a Restatement European Insurance Contract Law' (2007) 7–8 *Wiadomości Ubezpieczeniowe*.

255 It is established that they give rise to legal consequences stipulated in Art. 56 of the Civil Code, which states that "an act in law shall not only produce the consequences expressed in it but also those which result from, among others, established customs" and in Art. 65 of the CC: "§ 1. A declaration of intent shall be construed in such a manner as required by principles of community coexistence and established customs, with account of the circumstances in which it was made, § 2. When contracts are concerned, the concurrent intention of the parties and the purpose of the contract shall rather be examined than its literal wording."

256 Cf. Regulation of the Minister of Finance of 22 April 2004 on the detailed requirements that a customs declaration must satisfy (Dz. U. 2014, 94, 902); Ordinance of the Director General of State Forests no. 64 of 16 September 2015 on the rules applicable to the sale of timber at the State Forests National Forest Holding (B.I.LP. 2015, 10(274)).

257 Cf. Judgment of the Appellate Court in Szczecin of 23 December 2014 (I Aca 461/14); Judgment of the SC of 29 June 2010 (III CSK 255/09); Judgment of the Supreme Administrative Court of 22 June 2010 (I FSK 1114/09) and of 16 October 2014 (I GSK 1071/13); Judgment of the voivodship administrative court in Poznań of 30 July 2009 (I SA/Po 331/09); Judgment of the voivodship administrative court in Warsaw of 5 May 2009 (III SA/Wa 3448/08).

258 Janusz A. Strzępka and Wojciech Wyrzykowski, '*FIDIC* a umowa o roboty budowlane w Kodeksie cywilnym – wybrane problemy. Ogólna charakterystyka warunków kontraktowych *FIDIC*' in Joanna Kruczalak-Jankowska (ed), *Wpływ europeizacji prawa na instytucje prawa handlowego* (LexisNexis 2013) 402–411.

7.5 Mobilization of comparative law

Comparative law is recognised as an important field of law and has traditionally played an important role in Poland since the 19th century. The literature of the subject is permeated with references to doctrinal views, legal solutions and case law of other countries; currently it would be difficult to find an academic dissertation devoid of a comparative perspective.

Occasionally, the legislator applies such an approach. As an example, it may be pointed out that, as follows from the preparatory work to the 2016 tax ordinance, great emphasis was put on comparing legal mechanisms established in other countries.[259] Moreover, the Codification Commission of Maritime Law has analysed and used international case law besides regulations (mainly of the IMO and of the EU) and Polish judicial decisions. Direct references to these documents appear in preparatory works or opinions drafted by CCML members for the Commission's needs. The Maritime Policy of the Republic of Poland, adopted in 2015 by resolution 33/2015 of the Council of Ministers as a document providing guidelines for the Polish legislator concerning regulation of maritime law, contains references to the output of numerous global and regional organizations and forums.[260]

As regards Polish courts, the Constitutional Tribunal and the Supreme Courts traditionally refer to "external" examples frequently in their decisions. For example in its resolution of 20 July 2006, the Supreme Court analysed the position of the Irish High Court and of the Belgian Court of Cassation (the case concerned the European Arrest Warrant).[261] In its judgment of 2 June 2015, the Constitutional Tribunal found provisions of the 1991 Act on Labour Unions unconstitutional and incompliant with international agreements in respect of limiting freedom of association, based on a complaint submitted by the All Poland Alliance of Trade Unions, which invoked the opinion of the ILO Committee.[262] Another interesting example is the justification of the judgment issued by the Voivodeship Court in Łódź on 29 January 1997. The court invoked Protocol no. 6 to the European Convention on Human Rights, abolishing the death penalty in times of peace, which Poland had not ratified before 2000. Accordingly, comparative observations are sometimes utilised as an inspiration for both the legislator and the courts when developing the law.

259 Cf: Edward Juchniewicz, 'Общие принципы противодействия уклонению от уплаты налогов на примере Польши' in Anna Drywa, Jolanta Gliniecka, Edward Juchniewicz and Tomasz Sowiński (eds), *Prawo finansowe wobec wyzwań XXI wieku* (CeDeWu 2015).

260 See https://mgm.gov.pl/wp-content/uploads/2016/01/Polityka-morska-Rzeczypospolitej-Polskiej_uchw._Nr_33_RM_z_17_03_2015.pdf accessed 6 November 2019.

261 I KZP 21/06, OSNKW 2006, 9, 77.

262 K 1/13.

8. Conclusions

The phenomenon that has been taking place since the majority of seats in Polish Parliament was won in the 2015 election by the PiS party and their coalition partners is called abused constitutionalism.[263] In contrast to abusive constitutionalism, which consists in making use of mechanisms of constitutional amendment to erode the democratic order[264], the former manifests itself in introducing fundamental constitutional changes under ordinary laws in the absence of respect for the Constitution and the values expressed in it.

Consequently, by introducing changes, which theoretically are supposed to occur only on the surface of a legal sea, the government aims to (and in fact it does) affect its deeper layers. A parliamentary majority obtained by the PiS party is not enough to change the Constitution, however it allows them to pass every Act. As a consequence, it led to a number of fundamental reforms, including the annihilation of the Constitutional Tribunal, the subordination of the prosecutor's office and the courts to the political control, and the limitation of the self-government competencies, attempt to subordinate non-governmental organizations to political control, transformation of the public media into government agency and the right of assembly limitations. On the night of March 28, 2020, under the guise of fighting the Covid-19 pandemic, unconstitutional changes in electoral law were passed as well. These reforms are accompanied by ignorance of the current Constitution or by selective and instrumental reference to it (constitutional nihilism).[265]

Constitutional nihilism may lead to legal chaos, the first symptoms of which are already being felt in Polish legal culture. Legal acts which do not comply with the constitutional provisions or values expressed therein are adopted. They are also questioned at the European level. As a result, chaos then affects the middle level of the legal sea, because it permeates the processes of law application and touches the unwritten general principles of law guiding the application of law by lawyers. Judgments based on the Constitution and those based on Acts omitting it are issued, so there is a possibility for courts to issue contradictory and unpredictable judgments. As a result, legal certainty and predictability are endangered.

When analyzing Polish legal culture, it is worth remembering that, as Grażyna Skąpska noted, the fundamental system changes we experienced at the end of the last century were not through a bloody revolution and not as a result of the implementation of the ideas of philosophers, but by dint of social movements, citizens' initiatives, as well as through the use of law. The so-called peaceful revolution, not only in Poland but also in other countries of Central and Eastern Europe, therefore often took the form of

263 Skąpska (2018) (n 91).

264 Such a change is made while remaining faithful to the formal procedures for amending the constitution, and on the basis of democratic legitimacy, i.e. the support of a sufficient part of the electorate (constitutional majority) and its representation in the parliament. More: David Landau, 'Abusive Constitutionalism' (2013) 47/1 *UC Davis Law Review* 189–260. Landau gives among others Hungarian example.

265 Skąpska (2018) (n 91) 287 ff.

a "legal revolution", which meant the use of existing law by major actors of change to carry out essentially revolutionary political changes.[266] For several decades, these values seemed to have taken root in Polish legal culture and formed the bottom of a legal sea. The result of constitutional nihilism, however, is also a new version of the negative constitutional consensus consisting in the withdrawal of part of society from participation in the public sphere, failure to act in defense of the constitution and the rule of law in exchange for measurable benefits that the ruling party dispenses.[267] Polish society is admittedly currently extremely polarized, and the PiS party was enough to support the victory in the parliamentary elections in 2015 with just over 18 % of the total electorate.[268] However, if a considerable part of society agrees to violate fundamental values, the question arises whether these values really became fundamental during the "legal revolution" carried out a few decades ago.

The contemporary Polish Legal Culture	
Institutional structure	
Conflict resolution	*Norm production*
Two hierarchies of courts: ordinary/military courts under the supervision of the Supreme Court and administrative courts with the Supreme Administrative Court on the top. Special position of the Constitutional Tribunal. Extra-judicial forms of conflict resolution on a very low level. High authority in fact of the judgments of the highest courts, but no theory of *stare decisis*.	Law-making on the state, regional and supranational level by the EU, local government and regional bodies of the central government or state legislator. Legislation is recognized as the only formal source of law, however it may lose its binding force after an Constitutional Tribunal judgment. Exposed factual, but not formal position of codes. In addition, many other legal acts and instruments as well. No special role for legal scholars. Marginal references to custom. No theory of legal precedent. Norm interpretation produced by the Supreme Administrative Court binding in administrative proceedings.

266 Ibid, 277.

267 Grażyna Skąpska, *From 'Civil Society' to 'Europe'. A Sociological Study on Constitutionalism after Communism* (Brill 2011) 76. In Poland the phenomenon of "exchange of elites" is taking place. In practice it means that prestigious and lucrative positions in state administration, public media, nationalized banks and state-owned companies are filled based on political rather than substantive criteria, often based on family connections. In particular, positions in the managing and supervisory boards of state-owned companies are important. They make it possible to transfer profits from these companies to enterprises important for the government, including social programmes, as well as propaganda activities that are to ensure the favor of the electorate. Skąpska (2018) (n 91) 289.

268 37,58 % with an election turnout of 50,92 %.

Intellectual structure			
Ideal of justice	*Legal method*	*Professionalisation*	*Internationalisation*
Predictability and legal certainty safeguarded by the system of positive law combined with the protection of individual freedom, protected by courts composed of professional judges, despite increasing decline in confidence in courts and law.	Predominant positivistic approach in its classical form. Judicial interpretation traditionally focused mainly on the wording of legal acts respecting the authority of the highest courts and their interpretation of legal norms. However, the presumption of constitutionality of statutory law is being challenged. Courts' interpretation influences on lawyers' actions and advices as majority of cases are resolved in courts. Concepts of academia gains significance only if courts refer to them.	High degree of professionalisation, with minor exceptions, concerning legal advisors and lay judges. Long path of legal education, the additional mandatory (with minor exceptions) apprenticeships required to practice and the system of central exams at different stages. Mandatory affiliation of lawyers to corporations. Low level of practical experience needed to become a judge. Recent strengthening of the influence of the Minister of Justice on the system of judiciary and professional responsibility of lawyers.	Traditionally high degree of internationalisation. Polish legal system is neither a pure dualist system nor a pure monist one. Positive approach to international law emphasized in the Constitution with sector monistic for international law that originates from ratified international treaties. One of the highest number of cases among the complaints submitted to ECtHR relative to population size from Poland indicating that fundamental rights protection by the national judiciary is perceived as insufficient.

9. Bibliography

Adamczyk MD, 'Kapitał społeczny czynnikiem konstytutywnym współczesnego ładu społeczno-gospodarczego', (2015) 2 *Roczniki Nauk Społecznych*. DOI: https://doi.org/10.18290%2Frns.2015.7%2843%29.2-15

Alexy R, 'W obronie niepozytywistycznej koncepcji prawa' (1993) 11–12 *Państwo i Prawo*

Auguste S, *Mémoires* (Grześkowiak-Krwawicz A and Triaire D (eds), IES – SHLP 2012)

Bałaban A, 'Czy sędzia podlega umowie międzynarodowej', *Rzeczpospolita* 1 June 1998

—— 'Prawna pozycja władzy sądowniczej w III RP (ze szczególnym uwzględnieniem sądownictwa powszechnego)' in Gdulewicz E, Orłowski W and Patyra S (eds), *25 lat transformacji ustrojowej w Polsce i w Europie Środkowo-Wschodniej* (WUMCS 2015)

Banaszak B, *Prawo konstytucyjne* (C.H. Beck 2004)

—— *Konstytucja Rzeczypospolitej Polskiej. Komentarz* (C.H. Beck 2009)

Barankiewicz T, 'Inkluzywny pozytywizm prawniczy (geneza, rozwój, główne idee)' (2010) 1 *Państwo i Prawo*

Bardach J and Senkowska-Gluck M (eds), *Historia państwa i prawa Polski. Od rozbiorów do uwłaszczenia* (PWN 1981)

Bielska-Brodziak A, *Interpretacja tekstu prawnego na podstawie orzecznictwa podatkowego* (Wolters Kluwer 2009)

Boć J (ed), *Konstytucje Rzeczpospolitej oraz komentarz do Konstytucji RP z 1997 roku* (Kolonia Limited 1998)

Bogucki O, 'Perspektywy rozwinięcia normatywnego ujęcia wykładni funkcjonalnej' in Hermann M and Sykuna S (eds), *Wykładnia prawa. Tradycje i perspektywy* (C.H. Beck 2016)

Borkowski G (ed) *Granice niezawisłości sędziów i niezależności sądów?* (KRS 2016) 15–20

Budzyńska K, *Logika a argumentacja,* available at http://www.calculemus.org/neumann/odczyty/budzynska.doc accessed 6 November 2019

Choduń A, Gomułowicz A and Skoczylas A, *Klauzule generalne i zwroty niedookreślone w prawie podatkowym i administracyjnym. Wybrane zagadnienia teoretyczne i orzecznicze* (Wolters Kluwer 2013)

Czachórski W, 'Przebieg prac nad kodyfikacją prawa cywilnego PRL' (1970) *Studia Prawnicze*

Davies N, *Europe: A History* (Pimlico 1997)

Dębowska A and Florczak-Wątor M, 'Domniemanie konstytucyjności ustawy w świetle orzecznictwa Trybunału Konstytucyjnego', (2017) 2 *Przegląd Konstytucyjny*

Derlatka M, Garlicki L and Wiącek M, *Na straży państwa prawa. Trzydzieści lat orzecznictwa Trybunału Konstytucyjnego* (Wolters Kluwer 2016)

Domański H, 'Zaufanie między ludźmi' in Sztabiński PB, Sztabiński F (eds), *Polska – Europa. Wyniki Europejskiego Sondażu Społecznego 2002–2012* (IFIS PAN 2014)

Drywa A, *Odpowiedzialność odszkodowawcza za wydanie niezgodnej z prawem decyzji podatkowej* (Wolters Kluwer 2014)

Dudek D (ed), *Zasady Ustroju III Rzeczypospolitej Polskiej* (Wolters Kluwer 2009)

Dziurzyński T, 'Prawo zwyczajowe w przyszłej ustawie handlowej' (1929) 1–12 *Czasopismo Prawnicze i Ekonomiczne* 356

Ereciński T (ed), *Kodeks postępowania cywilnego. Komentarz* (Wolters Kluwer 2009)

—— 'O uwarunkowaniach, potrzebie oraz zakresie nowego kodeksu postępowania cywilnego' (2010) 1 *Polski Proces Cywilny*

Florczak-Wątor M, *Horyzontalny wymiar praw konstytucyjnych* (WUJ 2014)

Frąckowiak J, 'Orzecznictwo i doktryna jako źródło prawa prywatnego' (2018) 112 *Przegląd Prawa i Administracji*

Fuchs D, 'Nowelizacja kodeksu cywilnego w zakresie wybranych przepisów ogólnych o umowie ubezpieczenia w świetle przepisów ogólnych o umowie ubezpieczenia w świetle prac Project Group on a Restatement European Insurance Contract Law' (2007) 7–8 *Wiadomości Ubezpieczeniowe*

—— 'Insurance Restatement jako europejski instrument opcjonalny służący regulacji umowy ubezpieczenia' (2010) Nr. 9 (2) *Rozprawy Ubezpieczeniowe*

Gałędek M and Klimaszewska A, 'A Controversial Transplant? Debate over the Adaptation of the Napoleonic Code on the Polish Territories in the Early 19th Century' (2018) 11 *Journal of Civil Law Studies*

Garlicki L, *Polskie prawo konstytucyjne. Zarys wykładu* (Wolters Kluwer 2019)

Gizbert-Studnicki T, 'Prawda sądowa w postępowaniu cywilnym' (2009) 7 *Państwo i Prawo*

Górnicki L, Górnicki, 'Kodyfikacja prawa prywatnego' in Marek Safjan (ed), *System Prawa Prywatnego* (C.H. Beck 2012) I

—— 'Przewodnie konstrukcje i pojęcia Kodeksu handlowego z 1934 roku' (2015) CI *Przegląd Prawa i Administracji*

Grabowski A, 'Inkluzyjny pozytywizm prawniczy (uwagi do aktualnej dyskusji)' (2011) 11 *Państwo i Prawo*

Granat M, 'Trybunał Konstytucyjny. Osiągnięcie czy zadanie?' in Szmyt A (ed), *Trzecia władza: sądy i trybunały w Polsce: materiały Jubileuszowego L Ogólnopolskiego Zjazdu Katedr i Zakładów Prawa Konstytucyjnego, Gdynia, 24–26 kwietnia 2008 roku* (WUG 2008)

—— *Prawo konstytucyjne. Pytania i odpowiedzi* (Wolters Kluwer 2019)

Hart HLA, *Pojęcie prawa* Woleński J (trans) (PWN 1998)

Hermann M and Sykuna S (eds), *Wykładnia prawa. Tradycje i perspektywy* (C.H. Beck 2016)

Jabłońska-Bonca J, *O szkolnictwie wyższym i kształceniu prawników* (WIWS 2020)

—— 'Wymiar sprawiedliwości a przemiany kultury prawnej w Europie' in Morawski W (ed), *Powiązania zewnętrzne. Modernizacja Polski* (Wolters Kluwer 2012)

Jedlicki J, *Jakiej cywilizacji Polacy potrzebują. Studia z dziejów polskiej idei i wyobraźni XIX wieku* (WAB – CIS 2002)

Johnson L, *Central Europe: Enemies, Neighbors, Friends* (Oxford University Press 2011)

Juchniewicz E, 'Общие принципы противодействия уклонению от уплаты налогов на примере Польши' in Drywa A, Gliniecka J, Juchniewicz E and Sowiński T (eds), *Prawo finansowe wobec wyzwań XXI wieku* (CeDeWu 2015)

Kitowicz J, *Opis obyczajów za panowania Augusta III* (Pollak R (ed), Zakł. im. Ossolińskich 2003)

Klimaszewska A, 'La responsabilité civile des associés des sociétés commerciales dans le droit polonais – les influences de la culture juridique française et les influences des autres cultures' in Hajn Z and Skupień D (eds), *La responsabilité civile en France et en Pologne* (WUŁ 2016)

—— 'Commercial judiciary on the Polish territories in the 19th century – a repackaged French product or a mock-up?' (2019) *Revista da Faculdade de Direito da Universidade Federal de Minas Gerais*, special issue, Vano C, Pihlajamäki H and Sontag R (eds). DOI: https://doi.org/10.12818%2Fp.0304-2340.2019v74p97

—— 'The Reception of the French Commercial Code in Nineteenth-Century Polish Territories – A Hollow Legal Shell' in Klimaszewska A and Gałędek M (eds), *Modernization, National Identity and Legal Instrumentalism: Studies in Comparative Legal History*, I (Brill 2019)

—— 'The Application of the 1807 French Commercial Code in Polish Territories: An Attempt to Establish an Anonymous Partnership in Lublin' in Luts-Sootak M and Schäfer FL (eds), *Recht und Wirtschaft in Stadt und Land* (Peter Lang 2020)

Kościerzyński J (ed), 'Justice under pressure – repressions as a means of attempting to take control over the judiciary and the prosecution in Poland. Years 2015–2019', available at https://www.iustitia.pl/images/pliki/raport2020/Raport_EN.pdf accessed 1 April 2020

Kmieciak Z (ed), *Polskie sądownictwo administracyjne – zarys systemu* (C.H. Beck 2017)

Kokoszczyński M and Wierczyński G, *System informacji prawnej w pracy sędziego* (Wolters Kluwer 2011)

Korobowicz A, *Sądownictwo Królestwa Polskiego 1876–1915* (UMCS 1995)

Kostrubiec J, *Nauka o państwie w myśli Georga Jellinka* (WUMCS 2015)

Kozak A, *Myślenia analityczne w nauce prawa i praktyce prawniczej* (WUW 2010)

Krzemiński I, 'Społeczeństwo obywatelskie i symbole wspólnoty' in Drogosz M (ed), *jak Polacy przegrywają? Jak Polacy wygrywają?* (GWP 2005)

Landau D, 'Abusive Constitutionalism' (2013) 47/1 *UC Davis Law Review*

Landau Z and Skrzeszewska B, *Sprawa Gabriela Czechowicza przed Trybunałem Stanu – wybór dokumentów* (PWN 1961)

Leszczyński L and Maroń G, 'Pojęcie i treść zasad prawa i generalnych klauzul odsyłających. Uwagi porównawcze' (2013) 60/1 *Annales UMCS. Sectio G*

Lityński A, *Pół wieku kodyfikacji w Polsce. Wybrane zagadnienia (1919–1969)* (WSZiNS 2001)

—— *Historia prawa Polski Ludowej* (LexisNexis 2013)

Ławnikowicz G, 'Judicial ethics in the time of the systemic transformation' in Machnikowska A (ed), *The Legitimation of Judicial Power* (Wyd. UG 2016)

Łętowska E, 'A my w Krakowie wiemy swoje…' *Polityka* 23 May 1998

—— 'Boska sztuka interpretacji' in Łopatka A, Kunicka-Michalska B and Kiewlicz S (eds), *Prawo, społeczeństwo, jednostka. Księga jubileuszowa dedykowana Profesorowi Leszkowi Kubickiemu* (INP PAN 2003)

—— 'Multicentryczność współczesnego systemu prawa i jej konsekwencje' (2005) 4 *Państwo i Prawo*

—— 'Prawo zobowiązań a system prawa' in Łętowska E (ed), *Prawo zobowiązań – część ogólna* (C.H. Beck 2006)

—— 'Prawo w „płynnej rzeczywistości"' (2014) 3 *Państwo i Prawo*

—— and Sobczak K, *Rzeźbienie państwa prawa. 20 lat później* (Wolters Kluwer 2012)

—— and Wiewiórowska-Domagalska A, 'A '*Good' Change in the Polish Constitutional Tribunal*?' (2016) 1 *Osteuropa Recht*. DOI: https://doi.org/10.5771%2F0030-6444-2016-1-79

Machnikowska A, *Prawo własności w Polsce w latach 1944–1981. Studium historycznoprawne* (WUG 2010)

—— *O niezawisłości sędziów i niezależności sądów w trudnych czasach. Wymiar sprawiedliwości w pułapce sprawności* (Wolters Kluwer 2018)

Mańko R, 'Demons of the Past? Legal Survivals of the Socialist Legal Tradition in Contemporary Polish Private Law' in Mańko R, Cercel CS and Sulikowski A (eds), *Law and Critique in Central Europe: Questioning the Past, Resisting the Present* (Counterpress 2016)

—— *W stronę krytycznej filozofii orzekania. Polityczność, etyka, legitymizacja* (WUŁ 2018)

Marciniak A (ed), *Kodeks postępowania cywilnego. Tom I (art. 1–205) Komentarz* (C.H. Beck 2019)

Masternak-Kubiak M, *Umowa międzynarodowa w prawie konstytucyjnym* (PWN 1997)

—— *Przestrzeganie prawa międzynarodowego w świetle Konstytucji Rzeczypospolitej Polskiej* (Wolters Kluwer 2003)

—— *Odesłania do prawa międzynarodowego w Konstytucji RP* (PiEBC 2013)

Matczak M, *Summa iniuria. O błędzie formalizmu w stosowaniu prawa* (WN Scholar 2007)

—— 'Dlaczego w Polsce nie obowiązuje już tradycyjne domniemanie konstytucyjności?', available at https://marcinmatczak.pl/index.php/2018/07/08/dlaczego-w-polsce-nie-obowiazuje-juz-tradycyjne-domniemanie-konstytucyjnosci/ accessed 6 November 2019

Matuszewicz M, *Diariusz życia mego* (Królikowski B and Zielińska Z (eds), PIW 1986)

Michalski J, *Studia nad reformą sądownictwa i prawa sądowego w XVIII w.* (Zakł. im. Ossolińskich 1958)

Moniuszko A, *Mazowieckie sądy ziemskie. Organizacja-funkcjonowanie-postępowanie* (Campidoglio 2013)

Moszyńska A, *Geneza prawa spadkowego w polskim kodeksie cywilnym z 1964 r.* (WNUMK 2019)

Naworski Z, *Szlachecki wymiar sprawiedliwości w Prusach Królewskich (1454–1772). Organizacja i funkcjonowanie* (WNUMK 2004)

Peretiakowicz A, *Państwo współczesne* (ZZKiW 1928)

Piaskowska OM and Piesiewicz PF (eds), *Przewlekłość postępowania sądowego* (Wolters Kluwer 2018)

Pichlak M, *Refleksyjność prawa. Od teorii społecznej do strategii regulacji i z powrotem* (WUŁ) 2019

Pietrzykowski H, *Metodyka pracy sędziego w sprawach cywilnych* (Wolters Kluwer 2014)

Pietrzykowski T, 'Domniemanie konstytucyjności', available at https://www.academia.edu/20133667/Domniemanie_konstytucyjno%C5%9Bci accessed 6 November 2019

—— '"Miękki" pozytywizm i spór o regułę uznania' in Stelmach J (ed), *Studia z filozofii prawa* (WUJ 2001)

Piotrowski R, 'The issue of the legitimation of the judicial power in a democratic state ruled by law' in Machnikowska A (ed), *The Legitimation of Judicial Power* (Wyd. UG 2016)

Płaza S, *Historia prawa w Polsce na tle porównawczym, cz. 2, Polska pod zaborami* (Księgarnia Akademicka 2002)

Pomianowski PZ, *Rozwód w XIX wieku na centralnych ziemiach polskich. Praktyka stosowania Kodeksu Napoleona w latach 1808–1852* (Campidoglio 2018)

Potrzeszcz J, *Idea prawa w orzecznictwie polskiego Trybunału Konstytucyjnego* (Towarzystwo Naukowe KUL 2007)

Radwański Z and Zieliński M, 'Klauzule generalne w prawie prywatnym' in Safjan M (ed), *System Prawa Prywatnego, t. 1: Prawo cywilne – część ogólna* (C.H. Beck 2007)

Rawls J, *A Theory of Justice. Revised Edition* (Harvard University Press 1999)

—— *Teoria sprawiedliwości* Panufik M, Pasek J and Romaniuk A (trans) (PWN 1994)

Romanowicz M, 'Utrwalona linia orzecznicza jako argument z (własnego) autorytetu sądowego' in Giaro T (ed) *Rola orzecznictwa w systemie prawa* (Wolters Kluwer 2016)

Rycak A (ed), *Metodyka pracy ławnika* (C.H. Beck 2011)

Rzucidło-Grochowska I and Grochowski M (eds), *Uzasadnienia decyzji stosowania prawa* (Wolters Kluwer 2015)

Safjan M, *Wyzwania dla państwa prawa* (Wolters Kluwer 2007)

Skąpska G, *From 'Civil Society' to 'Europe'. A Sociological Study on Constitutionalism after Communism* (Brill 2011)

—— 'Znieważający konstytucjonalizm i konstytucjonalizm znieważony. Refleksja socjologiczna na temat kryzysu liberalno-demokratycznego konstytucjonalizmu w Europie pokomunistycznej' (2018) 7/1 *Filozofia Publiczna i Edukacja Demokratyczna*

Sobczak K, 'Gdy państwo prawa jest zagrożone, trzeba odwoływać się do konstytucji – „Sędzia a Konstytucja. Kryzys sadownictwa konstytucyjnego a rozproszona kontrola zgodności prawa z Konstytucją", konferencja w Katowicach,. 3.03.2017 r.' (2017) 2 *Krajowa Rada Sądownictwa*

Sobociński W, *Historia ustroju i prawa Księstwa Warszawskiego* (PWN 1964)

Sójka-Zielińska K, *Kodeks Napoleona. Historia i współczesność* (LexisNexis 2008)

Sokolewicz W, 'Artykuł 235' in Garlicki L (ed), *Konstytucja Rzeczypospolitej Polskiej. Komentarz* II (Wyd. Sejmowe 2001)

Stawarska-Rippel A, *Elementy prywatne i publiczne w procesie cywilnym w świetle prac kodyfikacyjnych w Polsce (1918–1964). Studium historycznoprawne* (WUŚ 2015)

Stefański RA, 'Składy sądu w postępowaniu karnym' in Jakubowska-Hara J, Nowak C and Skupiński J (eds), *Reforma prawa karnego, propozycje i komentarze. Księga pamiątkowa Profesor Barbary Kunickiej-Michaskiej* (Scholar 2008)

Stelmach J, *Kodeks argumentacyjny dla prawników* (Zakamycze 2003)

—— and Brożek B, *Methods of Legal Reasoning* (Springer 2006)

—— *Metody prawnicze* (Wolters Kluwer 2006)

Stępień-Załucka B, *Sprawowanie wymiaru sprawiedliwości przez Sąd Najwyższy w Polsce* (C.H. Beck 2016)

Strzępka J and Wyrzykowski W, '*FIDIC* a umowa o roboty budowlane w Kodeksie cywilnym – wybrane problemy. Ogólna charakterystyka warunków kontraktowych *FIDIC*' in Kruczalak-Jankowska J (ed), *Wpływ europeizacji prawa na instytucje prawa handlowego* (LexisNexis 2013)

Szafarz R, 'Międzynarodowy porządek prawny i jego odbicie w polskim prawie konstytucyjnym' in Kruk M (ed), *Prawo międzynarodowe i wspólnotowe w wewnętrznym porządku prawnym* (Wydawnictwo Sejmowe 1997)

Szmulik B, *Pozycja ustrojowa Sądu Najwyższego w Rzeczypospolitej Polskiej* (C.H. Beck 2008)

Szot A, 'Klauzula generalna jako ponadgałęziowa konstrukcja systemu prawa' (2016) 63/2 *Annales UMCS. Sectio G*. DOI: https://doi.org/10.17951%2Fg.2016.63.2.291

Sztabiński PB and Sztabiński F (eds), *Polska – Europa. Wyniki Europejskiego Sondażu Społecznego 2002–2016/2017* (IFIS PAN 2018)

Triepel H, *Völkerrecht und Landesrecht* (Verlag von C.L. Hirschfeld 1899)

Tuleja P, *Wyroki interpretacyjne Trybunału Konstytucyjnego* (Ars boni et aequi 2016)

—— 'Źródła prawa' in Sarnecki P (ed), *Prawo konstytucyjne RP* (C.H. Beck 2014)

Uruszczak W, *Historia państwa i prawa polskiego, tom I* (966–1795) (Wolters Kuwer 2015)

Wandycz PS, *The price of freedom: a history of East Central Europe from the Middle Ages to the present* (Psychology Press 2001)

Wasilkowski A, 'Prawo krajowe – prawo wspólnotowe – prawo międzynarodowe. Zagadnienia wstępne' in Kruk M (ed), *Prawo międzynarodowe i wspólnotowe w wewnętrznym porządku prawnym* (Wydawnictwo Sejmowe 1997)

—— 'Przestrzeganie prawa międzynarodowego (art. 9 Konstytucji RP)' in Wójtowicz K (ed), *Otwarcie Konstytucji RP na prawo międzynarodowe i procesy integracyjne* (Wyd. Sejmowe 2006)

Winczorek P, *Komentarz do Konstytucji Rzeczypospolitej Polskiej z dnia 2 kwietnia 1997 roku* (Wydawnictwo Liber 2008)

Wiśniewski T, *Przebieg procesu cywilnego* (Wolters Kluwer 2013)

—— (ed), *Skarga nadzwyczajna w świetle systemu środków zaskarżenia w postępowaniu cywilnym* (Wolters Kluwer 2019)

Wojciechowski B, 'Rozstrzyganie tzw. trudnych przypadków poprzez odwołanie się do odpowiedzialności moralnej' (2004) 70 *Studia Prawno-Ekonomiczne* 4

Wojciechowski M, 'Sądowy dyskurs interpretacyjny dotyczący wykładni rozszerzającej' in Hermann M and Sykuna S (eds), *Wykładnia prawa. Tradycje i perspektywy* (C.H. Beck 2016)

Woś T, Knysiak-Sudyka H and Romańska M (eds), *Prawo o postępowaniu przed sądami administracyjnymi. Komentarz* (Wolters Kluwer 2016)

Wójtowicz K, 'Art. 9' in Safjan M and Bosek L (eds), *Konstytucja RP. Komentarz* I (C.H. Beck 2016)

Wróblewski S, *Komentarz do Kodeksu Handlowego części I (art. 1–13)* (Leon Frommer 1935)

Wypych-Żywicka A, 'Prawa podmiotowe w prawie pracy' in Baran KW (ed), *Zarys systemu prawa pracy, t. 1: Część ogólna prawa pracy* (Wolters Kluwer 2017)

Wyrozumska A, 'Prawo międzynarodowe oraz prawo Unii Europejskiej a konstytucyjny system źródeł prawa' in Wójtowicz K (ed), *Otwarcie Konstytucji RP na prawo międzynarodowe i procesy integracyjne* (Wyd. Sejmowe 2006)

—— *Umowy międzynarodowe: teoria i praktyka* (Wyd. PiPG 2006)

Zajadło J, 'Formuła "Gesetz und Recht"' (2002) 1 *Ius et Lex*

—— *Dziedzictwo przeszłości. Gustaw Radbruch: portret filozofa, prawnika, polityka i humanisty* (Arche 2007)

—— 'Pięćdziesiąta rocznica debaty Hart-Fuller' (2008) 7 *Państwo i Prawo*

—— *Przyszłość dziedzictwa: Robert Alexy, Ralf Dreier, Jürgen Habermas, Otfried Höffe, Arthur Kaufmann, Niklas Luhmann, Ota Weinberger: portrety filozofów prawa* (Arche 2008)

Zaleśny J, see 'Защита доминирующей роли конституции и разделение власти – спор о методах создания права в современных государствах' (2018) 48 *Political Science Studies*

Zalewski W, 'Why do people need courts? Adjudicating in the times of the trust crisis' in Machnikowska A (ed), *The Legitimation of Judicial Power* (Wyd. UG 2016)

Zdyb M and Stelmasiak J, *Zasady ogólne Kodeksu postępowania administracyjnego. Orzecznictwo Naczelnego Sądu Administracyjnego z komentarzem* (Lublin 1992)

Zieliński M, *Wykładnia prawa. Zasady – reguły – wskazówki* (Wolters Kluwer 2017)

Zieliński T, 'Klauzule generalne w nowym porządku konstytucyjnym' (1997) 11–12 *Państwo i Prawo*

—— 'Klauzule generalne w procesie karnym' in Czapska J, Gaberle A, Światłowski A and Zoll A (eds), *Zasady procesu karnego wobec wyzwań współczesności. Księga ku czci Profesora Stanisława Waltosia* (PWN 2000)

10. Appendix

Table 1 Number of cases in ordinary courts in Poland:[269]

TYPES OF CASES BY LAW AREAS AND TYPES OF COURTS	INCOMING				
	2014	**2015**	**2016**	**2017**	**2018**
TOTAL	**14 649 495**	**15 156 076**	**14 910 884**	**15 782 479**	**15 049 054**
CRIMINAL CASES	**2 793 577**	**2 749 558**	**2 537 287**	**2 458 013**	**2 321 762**
Appellate courts	34 741	33 965	32 063	34 736	37 629
Provincial courts	380 913	371 978	354 002	368 815	364 406
District courts	2 377 923	2 343 615	2 151 222	2 54 462	1 919 727
CIVIL CASES	**9 856 760**	**10 378 225**	**10 378 421**	**11 127 035**	**10 764 222**
Appellate courts	41 183	43 681	44 166	46 061	43 221
Provincial courts	329 009	331 320	349 788	350 215	350 614
District courts	9 486 568	10 003 224	9 984 467	10 730 759	10 370 387
LABOUR LAW CASES	**156 572**	**105 728**	**82 102**	**71 911**	**127 926**
Appellate courts	1 076	1 000	994	955	1 052
Provincial courts	16 247	15 026	13 635	11 997	11 586
District courts	139 249	89 702	67 473	58 959	115 288
SOCIAL SECURITY LAW CASES	**213 015**	**192 612**	**175 751**	**154 588**	**173 513**
Appellate courts	24 982	25 938	23 700	21 362	22 800
Provincial courts	146 867	124 636	117 083	100 302	118 500
District courts	38 166	42 038	34 968	32 924	32 213
COMMERCIAL CASES	**1 629 571**	**1 729 953**	**1 737 323**	**1 970 932**	**1 661 631**
Appellate courts	14 150	10 751	11 505	11 479	13 126
Provincial courts	59 868	59 405	65 571	67 963	70 963
District courts	1 551 754	1 657 179	1 657 690	1 890 363	1 576 506
Cases in CCPC*	3 617	2 409	2 327	938	843
Cases in CTDC**	182	209	230	189	193

269 This table was prepared based on the data published by the Ministry of Justice in the annual statistical reports from the years 2014–2018, available at https://isws.ms.gov.pl/pl/baza-statystyczna/ accessed 22 November 2019.

TYPES OF CASES BY LAW AREAS AND TYPES OF COURTS	RESOLVED				
	2014	2015	2016	2017	2018
TOTAL	**14 848 936**	**15 101 482**	**14 192 052**	**15 835 956**	**14 914 999**
CRIMINAL CASES	**2 804 323**	**2 748 222**	**2 581 724**	**2 465 111**	**2 319 524**
Appellate courts	34 473	34 100	32 310	34 448	36 745
Provincial courts	382 723	375 441	352 597	366 690	361 745
District courts	2 387 036	2 338 681	2 196 817	2 063 973	1 921 034
CIVIL CASES	**10 030 243**	**10 321 768**	**9 708 373**	**11 206 617**	**10 648 531**
Appellate courts	38 971	41 287	42 190	44 371	43 871
Provincial courts	322 668	333 658	341 591	339 473	331 793
District courts	9 668 604	9 946 823	9 324 592	10 822 773	10 272 867
LABOUR LAW CASES	**141 000**	**124 368**	**88 129**	**74 622**	**124 182**
Appellate courts	1 009	997	937	948	1 129
Provincial courts	16 085	15 241	13 871	12 146	11 275
District courts	123 906	108 130	73 321	61 528	111 778
SOCIAL SECURITY LAW CASES	**203 886**	**202 698**	**191 279**	**165 587**	**149 374**
Appellate courts	29 070	24 806	24 948	21 815	21 883
Provincial courts	138 505	141 140	127 493	108 309	96 082
District courts	36 311	36 752	38 838	35 463	31 409
COMMERCIAL CASES	**1 669 575**	**1 704 426**	**1 622 547**	**1 924 019**	**1 673 388**
Appellate courts	11 508	11 636	12 434	15 117	9 297
Provincial courts	57 406	58 185	63 011	66 895	65 713
District courts	1 569 103	1 631 374	1544 698	1 840 083	1 596 705
Cases in CCPC*	31 338	3 045	2 181	1 734	1 492
Cases in CTDC**	170	186	223	190	181

TYPES OF CASES BY LAW AREAS AND TYPES OF COURTS	PENDING				
	2014	**2015**	**2016**	**2017**	**2018**
TOTAL	**2 244 765**	**2 299 497**	**3 018 336**	**2 964 885**	**3 098 944**
CRIMINAL CASES	**440 706**	**441 929**	**397 502**	**390 407**	**392 650**
Appellate courts	2 814	2 677	2 430	2 718	3 602
Provincial courts	39 786	36 323	37 728	39 854	42 515
District courts	393 106	402 929	357 344	347 835	346 533
CIVIL CASES	**1 408 463**	**1 464 878**	**2 134 926**	**2 055 358**	**2 171 054**
Appellate courts	9 395	11 787	13 763	15 452	14 802
Provincial courts	130 747	128 349	136 545	147 291	166 112
District courts	1 268 321	1 324 742	1 984 618	1 892 615	1 990 140
LABOUR LAW CASES	**58 061**	**40 422**	**34 396**	**31 685**	**35 429**
Appellate courts	297	300	357	364	287
Provincial courts	4 151	3 936	3 701	3 552	3 863
District courts	54 613	36 186	30 338	27 769	31 279
SOCIAL SECURITY LAW CASES	**123 865**	**113 781**	**98 253**	**87 255**	**111 394**
Appellate courts	15 205	16 337	15 089	14 636	15 553
Provincial courts	87 145	70 642	60 232	52 226	74 644
District courts	21 515	26 802	22 932	20 393	21 197
COMMERCIAL CASES	**212 670**	**238 487**	**353 259**	**400 180**	**388 417**
Appellate courts	5 539	4 654	3 723	84	3 913
Provincial courts	21 541	22 761	25 321	26 390	31 640
District courts	182 504	208 599	321 589	371 877	351 672
Cases in CCPC*	3 031	2 395	2 541	1 745	1096
Cases in CTDC**	55	78	85	84	96

* Competition and Consumer Protection Court

** Community Trademark and Designs Court

Table 2 Duration of court proceedings before ordinary courts (in months):[270]

		2012		**2013**		**2014**		**2015**		**2016**		**2017**		**2018**	
I INSTANCE	**TYPES OF CASES**	**DC**	**PC**	**DC**	**PC**	**DC**	**PC**	**DC**	**PC**	**DC**	**PC**	**DC**	**PC**	**DC**	**PC**
	Criminal cases	3.3	9.2	3.3	9.5	3.4	9.8	3.5	10.3	3.6	8.8	3.3	7.6	3.4	7.7
	Civil cases	4.3	6.8	3.9	6.9	4.7	7.4	4.0	7.7	4.6	7.3	5.7	7.5	5.5	7.8
	Social security law cases	7.4	7.3	7.8	8.0	8.5	8.4	9.1	9.2	10.3	9.6	10.9	8.9	10.7	8.8
	Labour law cases	6.3	9.9	7.0	10.4	6.9	11.0	8.4	14.0	9.4	13.3	9.5	13.7	8.7	12.4
	Commercial cases	4.0	5.9	4.1	5.4	4.6	7.9	4.5	9.0	5.6	8.7	6.5	9.2	6.7	9.0
II INSTANCE		**PC**	**AC**	**PC**	**AC**	**PC**	**AC**	**PC**	**AC**	**PC**	**AC**	**PC**	**AC**	**PC**	**AC**
	Criminal cases	2.2	1.9	2.4	2.0	2.6	2.3	2.6	2.4	2.7	2.8	2.9	3.0	3.0	3.6
	Civil cases	3.0	3.5	3.8	4.3	4.0	5.1	4.2	6.6	4.9	8.1	4.8	9.5	5.2	10.5
	Social security law cases	2.9	6.0	3.1	7.3	3.4	9.0	3.9	9.9	5.0	9.9	4.1	11.1	4.2	11.2
	Labour law cases	2.7	4.7	3.4	4.5	3.8	5.1	4.1	7.4	5.5	8.0	3.9	8.3	3.9	10.3
	Commercial cases	2.8	4.4	3.5	5.0	3.7	5.9	3.6	7.7	4.9	9.1	4.6	10.4	5.6	10.4

Table 3 Number of judges in ordinary courts in the given years:[271]

Type of courts	**2012**	**2015**	**2018**
Appellate courts	497	495	426
Provincial courts	2714	2783	2515
District courts	6694	6658	6356

270 Data of the Statistical Information Management Department of the Ministry of Justice. DC – district courts; PC – provincial courts; AC – appellate courts.

271 Data of the Statistical Information Management Department of the Ministry of Justice.

Table 4 Caseload of the Constitutional Tribunal:[272]

Number of judgments		1998	1999	2000	2001	2002	2003	2004
Norm review	A priori	4	5	0	5	1	2	2
	A posteriori: – abstract	42	34	44	50	46	48	40
	– concrete	3	9	15	13	15	20	19
Constitutional complaints	Total	168	184	200	181	195	210	224
	Accepted	5	18	25	26	27	28	50
Competence disputes		0	0	0	0	0	0	0
Political parties		0	0	1	0	0	1	0
Incapacity of the president to discharge the duties of office		0	0	0	0	0	0	0
Number of judgments		**2005**	**2006**	**2007**	**2008**	**2009**	**2010**	**2011**
Norm review	A priori	3	1	0	1	8	4	3
	A posteriori: – abstract	51	50	44	44	38	33	37
	– concrete	26	34	40	53	60	46	39
Constitutional complaints	Total	220	294	309	405	321	351	358
	Accepted	53	59	57	64	49	30	36
Competence disputes		0	0	0	1[273]	1	0	0
Political parties		0	0	3	0	0	2	1
Incapacity of the president to discharge the duties of office		0	0	0	0	0	0	0
Number of judgments		**2012**	**2013**	**2014**	**2015**	**2016**	**2017**	**2018**
Norm review	A priori	2	2	0	2	3	2	1
	A posteriori: – abstract	30	33	37	48	15	10	14
	– concrete	44	40	12	78	21	9	3
Constitutional complaints	Total	320	331	375	408	61	234	185
	Accepted	47	45	22	45	31	12	18
Competence disputes		0	0	0	0	0	1	0
Political parties		0	0	0	0	0	0	0
Incapacity of the president to discharge the duties of office		0	0	0	0	0	0	0

272 Prepared by Lech Garlicki on the basis of the *Informacja o istotnych problemach wynikających z działalności i orzecznictwa Trybunału Konstytucyjnego* [Information regarding significant problems resulting from the work and judgments of the Constitutional Tribunal"] reports, and for 2016, 2017, and 2018 on the basis of his own calculations. The *Informacja* report for 2016 was submitted to the Sejm with delay – on 21 February 2018, for 2017 – on 19 December 2018, and for 2018 it has not been submitted. Cf. Garlicki (2019) (n 78) 420–421. Ordinarily *Informacja* reports were published in the spring of the following calendar year.

273 The proceedings were discontinued – the Constitutional Tribunal refused to hear the case of a competence dispute.

Table 5 Complaints settled by voivodship administrative courts 2004–2018:[274]

YEAR	TOTAL NUMBER OF CASES TO RESOLVE (left from previous period + registered in given year)	NUMBER OF CASES RESOLVED (total)	CASES REMAINED FOR THE NEXT YEAR
2004	151,471	83,217	68,254
2005	131,163	87,383	43,780
2006	106,216	78,660	27,556
2007	86,184	66,942	19,242
2008	76,686	58,730	17,956
2009	77,058	59,500	17,558
2010	85,388	64,121	21,267
2011	91,118	69,281	21,837
2012	93,997	71,865	22,132
2013	103,766	75,696	28,070
2014	112,231	81,242	30,989
2015	114,520	81,353	33,167
2016	109,859	78,992	30,867
2017	103,293	77,567	25,726
2018	91,689	69,315	22,374

274 This table, as well as Table 5, 6 and 7, were prepared based on the data published by the Supreme Administrative Court in the annual reports presenting its activities and the activities of the voivodship administrative courts from the years 2004–2018, available at available at http://www.nsa.gov.pl/sprawozdania-roczne.php accessed 22 December 2019.

Table 6 Cassation appeals settled by the Supreme Administrative Court 2004–2018:

YEAR	TOTAL NUMBER OF CASES TO RESOLVE (left from previous period + registered in given year)	NUMBER OF CASES RESOLVED (total)	CASES REMAINED FOR THE NEXT YEAR
2004	6,167	2,918	3,249
2005	12,798	6,535	6,263
2006	16,700	8,788	7,912
2007	17,342	9,347	7,995
2008	18,114	9,389	8,725
2009	19,185	10,013	9,172
2010	20,848	10,922	9,926
2011	24,592	11,352	13,243
2012	28,260	12,276	15,984
2013	32,764	13,493	19,271
2014	37,058	14,994	22,064
2015	40,698	14,892	25,806
2016	44,653	16,829	27,824
2017	45,570	19,192	26,379
2018	46,608	18,959	27,649

Table 7 Rulings of the Supreme Administrative Court:

YEAR	**2004**	**2005**	**2006**	**2007**	**2008**	**2009**	**2010**	**2011**	**2012**	**2013**	**2014**	**2015**	**2016**	**2017**	**2018**
TOTAL	1	14	12	19	18	38	18	20	23	27	19	17	16	20	9
FINANCIAL CHAMBER	1	7	4	5	3	20	6	8	10	9	9	9	9	12	5
COMMERCIAL CHAMBER	0	0	1	11	7	6	4	3	5	4	4	2	3	2	0
GENERAL ADMINIS-TRATIVE CHAMBER	0	7	7	3	8	11	8	8	8	14	6	6	4	6	4
FULL PANEL OF THE SUPREME ADMINISTRA-TIVE COURT	0	0	0	0	0	1	0	0	0	0	0	0	0	0	0

Table 8 The number of mediations in administrative proceedings in 2004–2018:

YEAR	2004	2005	2006	2007	2008	2009	2010	2011	2012	2013	2014	2015	2016	2017	2018
OPENED CASES	679	204	172	87	36	21	11	23	25	8	10	8	8	1	6
SETTLED CASES	170	117	66	17	16	3	2	8	4	5	4	1	0	0	1

10. A Legal Cultural "Take" on the Legal System of England & Wales

Christian N.K. Franklin

"Let us now peruse our ancient authors, for out of the old fields must come the new corne."

[Coke, 4 Institutes of the Laws of England 109.]

1. Introduction

The present account aims at providing some insights into the legal system and culture of England & Wales. Had its objective been purely descriptive, then nothing could probably have been easier (or possibly duller). Yet the aim is more ambitious than that, in attempting to view this system through the particular legal cultural lens set out in the introductory chapter to this book. This is a task fraught with difficulty and several potential pitfalls. The English legal culture – admittedly, and presumably, like all others – is a highly complex and dynamic creature. As the founding father of the common law family, it has an incredibly rich and long history. The intricacies and peculiarities of the legal system itself are many and alien to most. The parameters set for this account are naturally too slight to do it full justice. So we have limited ourselves in the following to pursuing a few select strands of enquiry, focusing particular attention on the various aspects key to achieving the project's overall comparative aims.

By way of more general introduction, the United Kingdom of Great Britain and Northern Ireland (hereinafter "UK") is a constitutional monarchy with a parliamentary system of political governance based in the capital of London. The UK itself is made up of four constituent parts – England, Wales, Scotland and Northern Ireland – the latter three of which have all come to enjoy steadily increasing degrees of autonomy over the past few decades through the granting of certain, yet by no means unlimited, political and economic/fiscal powers.[1] This process of devolution as it is called is not to be confused with federalism, however, as the powers in question are transferred by

1 Wales was annexed by England by the Acts of Union of 1536 and 1543; Scotland and England were unified by treaty in 1707; and Ireland was to become part of the UK from 1801 until the secession of all bar Northern Ireland in 1922.

Parliamentary statute, meaning in turn that the process is not irreversible and may be retracted at any time by further statutory amendment.[2]

Looking at the UK economy, the industrial revolution of the 1700s was in many ways the historical catalyst for the rise of both the modern British economy and the Empire which it helped to build. For centuries, London has been regarded as one of the most important centres of international trade and commerce. The British Empire was the largest in history, at its height encompassing almost a quarter of the world's land mass. British influence may still therefore be observed in the language, culture, and legal systems of many of its former overseas territories and protectorates. Today, the highly globalized British economy constitutes the second largest in the EU (until January 2020) in terms of GDP and ranks in the top five worldwide. To what extent Brexit and the Corona-Crisis will affect these numbers, is still unclear.

It is important to note that the United Kingdom does not have a single, unified legal system. Whilst England and Wales have one joint legal system, the legal systems of Scotland and Northern Ireland are indigenous to those regions.[3] The hybrid nature of Scots law – which is usually said to enjoy the best of both common and civil law worlds – falls outside the scope of this chapter,[4] as does the more purely common law-oriented system in Northern Ireland. In 2018, the combined population of England & Wales was estimated at approximately 66 million people.[5]

2. Conflict Resolution

The English legal system belongs to the legal family or tradition known as the common law, as distinguishable to comparative lawyers from countries adhering to the Romano-Germanic civil law tradition, or some hybrid of the two. The very term "common law" is generally used to describe all legal rules created and developed by and through the courts. In order to understand the common law and how it works, we therefore need to understand the current structure and competences of the courts in England & Wales. And in order to fully understand the current court structure, we also need to know a bit about its history, and how it came into being. Since the history of the courts is central to the rise of the English common law system itself, it is also important for understanding the background of any common law system in the world.

2 Devolution trends have also extended to the regions of England. As part of the sweeping constitutional modernisation reform proposals instigated during the late 1990s and early 2000s (described in more detail below), the UK Parliament passed the Regional Assemblies (Preparations) Act in 2003, which made provision for holding referendums concerning the establishment of elected assemblies for the regions of England (excepting London, which already has its own Assembly). Plans for English devolution nevertheless lost their momentum following a (rather unexpected) "no" vote in the very first such referendum, which was held in the North East of England. The Act was later repealed by the Local Democracy, Economic Development and Construction Act 2009.

3 For simplicity's sake, and unless otherwise stated, reference will henceforth be made to the English legal system, rather than the legal system of England and Wales.

4 For an introduction to the Scottish legal culture, see instead the contribution by Andrew R.C. Simpson in this book.

5 'United Kingdom population mid-year estimate', *UK Office of National Statistics*, published 26 June 2019, available at http://www.ons.gov.uk/ons/index.html accessed 14 April 2020.

We shall therefore start in this section by looking at the gradual centralization of judicial power in England in the centuries following the Norman Conquest (section below). From here, we shall attempt to follow certain select historical lines and developments down to the present day. We shall see how several court hierarchies have come to exist. Which court to approach at first instance and/or appeal may vary greatly from one case to another, depending on several different factors – such as whether it is a civil or a criminal case, the gravity of the offence or harm caused, and the grounds of appeal relied upon to challenge the decision of a lower court.

Looking at the basic diagram (see Fig. 1 below), at the lower level we find the County Court, the Family Court and the Magistrates' Courts; at the next level we find the Crown Court and the High Court. As we shall see, the Crown Court, which enjoys predominantly criminal jurisdiction, and the High Court, which enjoys both criminal and civil jurisdiction, enjoy both an appellate and an original jurisdiction. If this might appear somewhat confusing to those approaching the English legal system for the very first time, matters are a bit more straightforward when it comes to the jurisdictions of the highest appellate courts – namely the Court of Appeal and the UK Supreme Court. For practical reasons (i.e. space), the several dozen tribunals with special jurisdiction to deal with certain types of cases will not be dealt with in this chapter.[6]

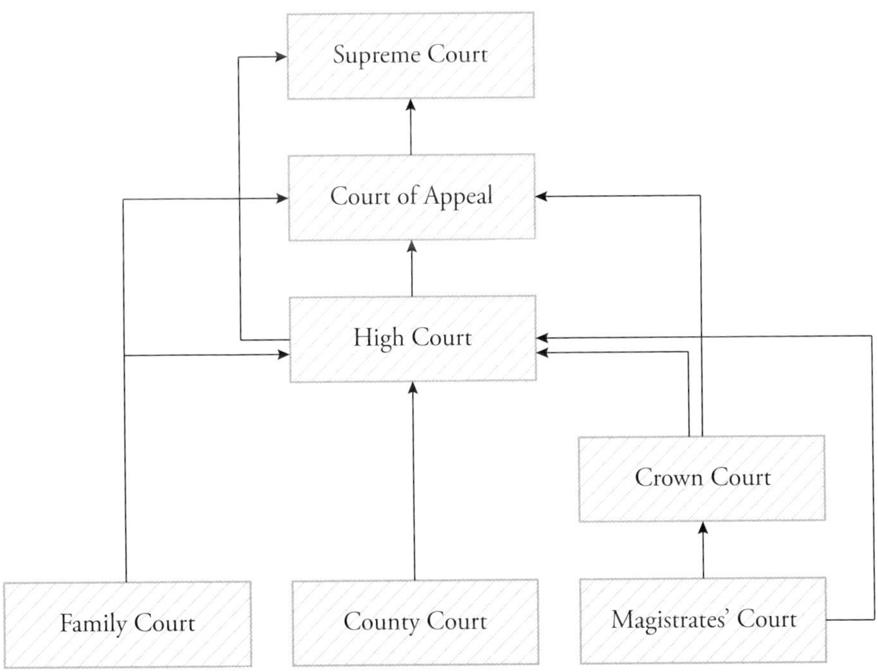

Fig. 1 Basic diagram of the court structure of England & Wales.

6 For more on these, see e.g. Peter Crane, *Administrative Tribunals and Adjudication* (Hart 2009).

2.1 The centralization of the courts

The process of centralization has many more facets than we are able to set out in this chapter. However, the two most important points to bear in mind are: (1) how it served to provide the very foundations for the development of the common law system in England, and (2) the role it played in shaping the court structure itself.

Central to English legal institutional history is the increasing and sweeping centralization of justice in the centuries following the Norman conquest of England in 1066, by Duke William II, also known as William the Conqueror. The overwhelming majority of customs and laws at this time were local, and could naturally differ rather greatly from one village, town, city or region to another. So too the "institutions" which convened to govern them – although one should be careful not to put too much into such a word; community gatherings would probably be more apt. From these ancient gatherings grew the first spires of what we today would call courts of law. There were several different types of courts, taking on many different names and forms, and exercising all manner of jurisdictional powers – sometimes indigenous to themselves, and sometimes concurrently with one another. The primary bodies for all kinds of governmental business were the vills (small land units, akin to a parish), the county courts and the courts of the Hundreds (geographical sub-divisions of the counties). These courts were in reality little more than routine meetings held at set intervals, attended by the more important landholders in a given area or their representatives, and representatives of communities of persons with lesser standing in society.[7] They enjoyed seemingly universal jurisdiction over all kinds of legal disputes raised before them. Other local courts of the time, enjoying more specialized (and in certain instances also competing) jurisdiction, include for example the ecclesiastical courts (or courts Christian), manor courts, courts of the cities and boroughs (urban equivalents to the county and Hundreds courts), and mercantile courts.[8]

The system which met the Norman invaders must have seemed rather bewildering to them, since they were used to more orderly administrative and governmental regimes. The years following the Conquest therefore marked the beginning of a slow, incremental process of centralization which would take centuries to complete. Indeed, well

7 For county courts, *Magna Carta* (1215) even contained a clause making clear that meetings were not to be held more frequently than once a month.

8 Manor courts enjoyed feudal jurisdiction over smaller communities of tenants (usually villages), not just of tenants of the same lord, but also their neighbours. As feudalism essentially embodied the economic structure of medieval society in England at the time, the feudal manor courts therefore had little to do with governmental matters as such. The essence of feudalism reflects the strong economic dimension behind the structure, which formed a pyramid: a superior (e.g. a lord) would allow measures of control to his inferiors (e.g. tenants), whose holdings he would undertake to protect in return for a tribute (money, chattels, fighting men, etc.). And so on down the scale to the bottom of the feudal pyramid structure itself. Three elements were largely present in the work of the manor courts: determination of property rights, sanctioning against those who failed in their feudalistic duties, compensation issues and petty crimes. Somewhat confusingly by today's standards, however, all such disputes could seemingly have been dealt with by the vills, or the county or Hundred courts, who enjoyed a concurrent jurisdiction over many of the same matters. Nevertheless, it would seem as though most disputes limited to tenants belonging to the same manor would be dealt with by the manor courts in practice.

into the 1300s, a two tier-structure continued to characterize the English legal system, with local courts at its base and the King above them. Of course, what mattered to the courts – as much then as presently today – was the resolution of specific disputes put before them. What mattered more to the King, however, was how to ensure an effective and ultimate control of the realm. Over time, proceedings before many of the Hundred courts therefore came to be presided over by a bailiff – a royal officer, who was sworn into office under oath. Enforcement powers in the regions were also kept increasingly under thumb, as the Shire-reeves (i.e. sheriffs) were made directly accountable to the King rather than local magnates in the exercise of their duties.[9]

Control over the country courts was also to slowly pass to the Regent, although in a slightly more convoluted way. Seen from the Crown's perspective, government in medieval England was primarily an issue of ensuring that it got what it was due. Forfeitures of land and other holdings ruled on by the local courts were often to be made directly to the King. Given his vested interest in knowing what the local courts were doing, it was perhaps inevitable that stronger mechanisms of control gradually came to be imposed. Local justiciars answerable to the King were, for example, required to take part in any proceedings before the county courts involving royal rights. Local institutions were further required to keep detailed accounts, which were audited by the Crown – firstly by the Coroners (the King's permanent, local accountants) and secondly (albeit more periodically) by the so-called Justices in Eyre, royal commissioners sent out from the Exchequer (i.e. the medieval Ministry of Finance) on circuit around the Kingdom to audit the accounts of the local institutions at second-hand.

What was essentially a penny-counting exercise nevertheless resulted in the first real step being taken towards the centralization of justice in England. The arrival of the Justices in Eyre in a county represented the coming of royal power to the regions, thus drawing the fullest assembly of local representatives to it. Why petition the local courts when one can approach the King's representatives directly for justice? Business before the Justices in Eyre was essentially split into two parts. The first orders of business were the so-called "pleas of the Crown". These covered a vast range of miscellaneous matters including: wardships, issues concerning franchises and markets, coroner's inquests into misadventure (i.e. unexplained deaths), alleged misdeeds of royal officials, such as the bailiffs or sheriffs, and any other matter of direct potential profit to the King and his coffers. The second part of business in the Eyre was known as the "common pleas", which was essentially litigation between private individuals, concerning mainly land disputes and other personal actions.[10]

---

9 For more on the history of the sheriffs of England, see e.g. William Alfred Morris, *The Medieval English Sheriff to 1300* (reprint edn, Manchester University Press 1968).

10 Although records show that a central Court of Common Pleas (also called the Common Bench) existed from the late 12th century to which private individuals could attempt to bring their cases, it would seem as though opting for that route was largely the exception to the general rule of seeking out the Justices in Eyre. The main reason for this most likely being that cases before the Common Bench required the issue of a writ (i.e. a special authorization to proceed with the case) which cost money. The writ system and the indelible mark it has left on the common law and legal culture of England & Wales is described further below.

The land actions seem particularly important to the growing centralization process. For example, legislative measures from the late 1100s had given rise to two frequently used new actions, the so-called "possessory assizes" of *novel disseisin and mort d'ancestor*, covering issues that had previously been determined largely by the local courts.[11] These actions brought many smaller property issues to be determined by royal inquest for the first time. Coupled with the development of an indictment system that allowed royal inquest into cases concerning the most serious wrongdoings, which in turn marked the starting development of criminal law as an indigenous field, it soon became apparent that more frequent gatherings of royal justices would be needed to handle the increased caseload – preferably at some fixed location.

Whilst the Justices in Eyre continued to be dispatched from the Exchequer until well into the 14th century to conduct financial audits in the regions, albeit much less frequently than in the past, their judicial jurisdiction was to gradually shift – in part to certain centralized authorities and their own commissioned representatives (such as for example Commissioners *nisi prius*, and Commissioners *oyer et terminer* – described in more detail below), and in part to permanent local commissioners appointed for each county, commissioned by the King to act at regular intervals, the so-called Justices of the Peace. As more and more people started to petition the King's representatives in the regions in more types of actions, however, this eventually gave way to the idea of sending representatives from the counties to petition the King at his place of being. Increasing demands for royal justice in turn led to the development of three centralized courts.

The first was the Court of the Exchequer, whose jurisdiction concerned mainly legal fiscal (i.e. revenue) matters. This Court grew from the administrative body of the Exchequer itself, which was the very financial centre of the State, and from which itinerant justice had previously been dispatched to the regions (i.e. the Eyre). Since the head of the Exchequer acted as regent in the King's absence (which was often), it therefore became a natural place for many to seek out royal justice directly.

The second centralized court was the Court of Common Pleas, also called the Common Bench, which grew as an off-shoot from the Exchequer, with a broad jurisdiction to provide royal justice in legal disputes between private parties. It was here that the common law would eventually come to be made, through the development of the writ system (i.e. orders allowing a case to proceed before it), and the different forms of action peculiar to it. Although merely confirming common practice at the time, *Magna Carta* (1215) had stipulated that all common pleas, bar the possessory assizes, should be heard in a fixed place.[12] It was largely from this that the Common Bench was to emerge as a court in the more modern sense of the word.

---

11 *Novel disseisin* was an action at common law designed to return land to a wrongfully dispossessed claimant, whilst *mort d'ancestor* was an action to recover lawfully inherited land taken by another before the heir was able to take possession. For more on these and their history, see e.g. Stroud Francis Charles Milsom, *Historical Foundations of the Common Law* (2nd edn, Butterworths 1981) 134–143.

12 *Magna Carta* (1215), c. 17; *Magna Carta* (1225), c. 11.

It is worth noting, however, that approaching the Common Bench was probably considered more of a luxury than an automatic right to start with. The normal route of access to royal justice in private disputes was to approach the Justices in Eyre on their tours about the Kingdom. In order to approach the Common Bench, one needed exceptional permission, which came in the form of a writ. Writs were essentially orders giving the Common Bench or the Court of Exchequer a warrant to proceed with a case, and were issued on application by the Chancery – a highly specialized body of clerks, performing mainly administrative, governmental duties, under the supervision of the Chancellor – one of the King's most trusted political advisers.[13] Writs cost money to obtain, yet were not required at all for proceedings commenced before the Eyre. Although access to the Common Bench was therefore more the exception to the general rule of seeking out royal justice locally, as more and more writs came to be sought over time, so the commonality of its jurisdiction and the very process of initiating legal proceedings before it (and the Exchequer) gradually came to be established.

The writ system and the various forms of action upon which it relied were to form the very basis for the continued development of the common law for centuries to come. During the 13th and 14th centuries, responsibility for issuing writs and entertaining pleas from applicants seeking to broaden the scope of existing writs to fit new types of situations as and when they might arise, continued to lie with Chancery. As such, this body played a vital role during the writ system's formative years of extending the scope of the common law itself. Over time, however, the powers of Chancery started to wane. Political struggles between the Crown and the nobility in the mid-1200s forced the King to concede several issues to his nobles under the Provisions of Oxford (1258), one of which effectively saw that no new types of writ would be made without the approval of Parliament. The Common Bench began to assert and develop its powers along these lines, reserving the right to quash or accept new types of writ issued by Chancery as it saw fit, thus rendering itself and Parliament as the ultimate arbiters of novel forms of action. In other words, although writs continued to be formally issued by Chancery, it seems as though the real decisions on the extension and development of the common law were to be decided by the Common Bench and Parliament jointly from this point onwards.

The third centralized court was the King's Bench. Under Henry II (1154–1189), it was decided that particularly difficult pleas which could not be solved by the Common Bench were to be referred to the King himself for determination. But the King and his direct court (the *curia regis*) were constantly on the move around the country – indeed, in the times of the crusades, the King himself was often abroad for years at a time. Cases referred from the Common Bench were therefore often left to be dealt with by others in his absence. From this gradually developed the King's Bench – an off-shoot of the King's Council – as an independent court of law based in Westminster, with not only jurisdiction in error (i.e. a form of appeal) from the Common Bench, but also juris-

13 Writs were not required (but could nevertheless be issued) for cases proceeding before the third of the centralised courts – the King's Bench (described directly below).

diction over pleas of the Crown of particular importance and/or other matters closely concerning the King.[14]

It is important to note here that the rigidity of the writ system itself, and the restraints placed on Chancery in developing it, meant that people with grievances falling outside the various forms of action had to seek out redress from other sources. Assuming that they were looking for royal justice (as opposed to local justice), there were several bodies which might be petitioned directly without the need for a writ: the King, the King's Council, the King's Bench – and even Parliament, which carried out a great deal of judicial work (see below). From this grew the separate branch of English law called equity – which quite literally means "fairness" – which we shall look at in more detail in Section 4 below.

The gradual centralisation process was key to the development of the common law system in England, but quickly proved rather costly compared to the time-worn local systems. Not only did it cost more for those seeking justice, who now had to purchase writs in order to proceed before the Common Bench and/or Court of the Exchequer, as well as travelling to the courts from the regions, but travelling costs were crippling jurors as well. When juries initially came to be used by the Justices in Eyre following the abolishment of several of the ancient modes of trial (described in more detail below), they performed their duties primarily in their home counties. But the development of the jury system before the Common Bench required jurors to attend the court at Westminster instead – almost always an expensive, and sometimes even physically impossible, task.

The establishment of the *nisi prius* system proved an important step towards preventing the continued impoverishment of the jurors, and also marked something of a return of judicial power to the regions. According to this system, whilst the legal issues in a dispute would be formed by the central courts at Westminster, they were subsequently put before a jury in the counties under the direction of centrally commissioned justices (i.e. Commissioners *nisi prius*). As time passed, it became more and more common to vest other competences in the same commission, such as for example the power of "*oyer et terminer*" (i.e. to hear and determine certain or all pleas of a particular kind in a particular county) and delivery to the jails. In this – and no doubt also inspired to some

14 Observant readers will note how the jurisdictions of the King's Bench and Common Bench could therefore often be deemed concurrent, i.e. as covering the same matters. For example, although trespass cases were ordinarily dealt with by the Common Bench, in cases involving aggravated trespass or in any event where Royal interests were concerned, the King's Bench was the correct venue. During the 1300s, the King's Bench also regularly tried to prevent ordinary writs of trespass from going to the Common Bench altogether, at times causing such cases to be diverted to its list. The jurisdictions of the Common Bench and the Exchequer also seemed to overlap in part, since the latter (up until 1300 – see 28 Edward I, Chapter 4) also enjoyed the power to hear certain common pleas, such as e.g. any case involving Exchequer officials, who owing to their privileged status could compel proceedings to be held on their home turf. Plucknett argues that this jurisdictional flexibility indeed was one of the early centralised courts' main strengths – allowing cases to flit back and forth between them, as required. See Theodore Frank Thomas Plucknett, *A Concise History of the Common Law* (5th edn, Butterworths 1956) 157. Viewed more subjectively, however, from the perspective of those approaching the courts at the time, it would probably have been considered a costly hardship for most – especially since the King's Bench at the time was still itinerant.

extent by the Eyre – we find the beginnings of the current circuit system in England today, whereby justices of the higher courts are sent out on tours of the regions to preside over certain types of cases proceeding before local courts (see further below).

As mentioned earlier, in addition to the travelling commissioners, it also became common to authorize local persons to act as Justices of the Peace. The Justices of the Peace were initially peacekeepers in a more literal sense, charged with all manner of policing duties, including the delivery of prisoners to the centrally commissioned Justices and sanctioning against abusive Sheriffs. By the mid-1300s, however, their powers had also been extended to trying certain prisoners for various wrongdoings – presumably those that were not considered serious enough to be dealt with by the travelling commissioners.[15]

In conclusion therefore, although a certain amount of judicial power was seen to return to the regions by virtue of mechanisms such as the *nisi prius* system and the Justices of Peace, the main difference from the pre-conquest era was now that most local jurisdictions derived their very existence from, and could be controlled to a certain extent by, a centralized judicial authority – namely the courts based in Westminster.

2.2 The County Court

Having provided the necessary backdrop, we now move on to consider the current court structure in England & Wales. Looking at the civil court system, at the lowest strata we find the County Court. Until recently, the county courts had remained very much a distant relative to the medieval system of local courts, expediting geographically limited civil jurisdiction at first instance.[16] This changed following sweeping judiciary reforms in 2014, which saw the county courts united for the first time under one jurisdictional banner and title as the County Court. Although justice is therefore still dispensed locally by the County Court in one of the 150-odd County Court hearing centres, the reform has removed previous geographical restrictions concerning the type of judge who may hear a case, thus making sure judges can sit where they are needed.[17]

The jurisdiction of the County Court is limited exclusively to civil law claims (e.g. actions in contract, tort, recovery of land, bankruptcy and insolvency, wills and trusts), and in many cases is concurrent with that of the High Court. Whether a case is to be heard by the County or High Court will sometimes be determined outright by the monetary value of the claim itself. For example, personal injuries claims under a value of £50,000 and consumer credit claims under £25,000 must be brought in a County Court, likewise any other claim below £100,000.[18] Claims above these values may pro-

15 During the reign of Edward III (1327–1377) – see e.g. 42 Edward III, chapter 6.

16 County Courts Act of 1846.

17 The Crime and Courts Act 2013 for example abolished the need for the Lord Chancellor to give his approval for High Court judges to hear cases at a County Court – see Section 5 of the County Courts Act 1984.

18 Sections 2.1 and 2.2 of Civil Procedure Rules Practice Direction 7A. Readers will nevertheless note an important exception in that any claim deemed suitable for inclusion on any one of the specialist court lists of the High Court (e.g. the Patent or Company Court), can always justify bypassing these monetary limits.

ceed before either court, with the choice usually dependent on the perceived public interest in the case, and/or whether it raises difficult or complex issues of fact and/or law.

All civil claims proceeding to court will be placed on a "track", according to the size of the case and the amount of case management that one assumes will be required. Track allocation is an important step, since it in turn will determine the detailed procedures by which the case will be handled, and also possibly influence which type of judge that will hear it. Claims of under £10,000 are placed on the "small claims track". Medium-sized claims between £5,000 and £25,000, which are capable of being disposed of by trial in one day, are allocated to the "fast track",[19] whilst larger claims over £25,000 go on to the "multi-track". Whereas small claims and fast track cases will usually be dealt with by one of the approximately 400 District Judges sitting alone, the more complex and weighty multi-track trials will usually be assigned to one of the more than 600 senior, roving Circuit Judges.[20]

In spite of it being a creature of statute, the County Court enjoys an (albeit somewhat limited) inherent jurisdiction – i.e. competence to determine its own procedure, essentially with a view to prevent it being used to achieve injustice.[21] The common law doctrine of inherent jurisdiction gives the court in question power to hear any matter that comes before it, unless a statute limits that power or grants exclusive jurisdiction to some other court or tribunal. In *Langley v. North West Water Authority*, the Court of Appeal therefore held that the County Court has the power to adopt local practice directions – i.e. supplemental guidelines concerning minor procedural matters issued by judges, designed to complement existing legislation, rules and regulations.[22] Approximately 1.5 to 2 million civil claims are raised before the County Court each year.[23]

2.3 The Family Court

The majority of family law proceedings – which depending on the civil or criminal nature of the case had previously been dealt with by either the County or Magistrate's

---

19 The use of the term "fast track" is actually something of a misnomer, given that directions for pre-litigation commence up to 30 weeks before the set trial date(!).

20 District judges are appointed by the Queen, following an open competition administered by the Judicial Appointments Commission, with a statutory qualification of five-year "right of audience" (i.e. the right of a lawyer to advocate in court) in relation to all proceedings in any part of the Supreme Court, or all proceedings in the County or Magistrates' Court. Circuit Judges must have more than 10 years right of audience and are usually expected to have previous experience as a Recorder or a District Judge. Circuit judges are appointed by the Queen, on the recommendation of the Lord Chancellor, following an open competition administered by the Judicial Appointments Commission.

21 As per Lord Diplock, in *Bremer Vulkan Schiffbau und Maschinenfabrik v. South India Shipping Corporation Ltd.* [1981] AC 909, [1981] 1 Lloyds Rep 253.

22 *Langley v. North West Water Authority* [1991] 3 All ER 610.

23 As mentioned previously, however, not all civil cases are dealt with at first instance by the County Court – certain particularly complex and/or substantial cases will go directly to the High Court (see further below).

courts (see section below) – are now determined by the Family Court.[24] All levels of judges are able to sit on the Family Court, which in turn allows for the possibility of an appeal from lower level judges assigned to a particular case (e.g. lay Magistrates) to more senior judges (i.e. circuit or High Court judges) within the Family Court itself.[25] Appeals may also be made in certain cases outside the Family Court, to either the High Court's Family Division or the Court of Appeal's Civil Division (both described further below). Family Court proceedings are usually held in County or Magistrates' court buildings, without juries. The number of cases filed at the Family Court averages at roughly 250,000 cases per year.[26]

2.4 The Criminal Courts: Magistrates' Court and Crown Court

The development of the criminal courts in England, and their organization, is inherently linked to the historical development of the various "wrongdoings" that eventually became subject to royal justice – the so-called "pleas of the Crown" (see section above).[27] As mentioned previously, the fact that the King stood to gain much financially from forfeiture and fines imposed on wrongdoers obviously gave him an increased interest in seeking to impose jurisdiction over such proceedings. Otherwise, they might just as readily have ended up in the hands of the local sheriffs and magnates. Following the Assize of Clarendon (1166), the itinerant (i.e. travelling) royal justices were therefore charged with dealing with such cases on their tours of the regions. This important jurisdictional change would in turn come to trigger the gradual revolution in the various modes of trial that a defendant might choose when his case was heard – a process which is described in more detail further below in this section. Suffice to say here that the development of a novel criminal procedure in the form of trial by jury during the middle-ages sowed the seeds from which the modern-day criminal courts of England & Wales were to sprout. Following the abolishment of the ancient trials by ordeal by Henry III in 1219, the King had left it to the Justices in Eyre to determine how matters of proof were to be ascertained according to their "own discretion and conscience".[28] After a short period of

---

24 Children and Families Act 2014; Crime and Courts Act 2013 section 17(3). According to these provisions, the Family Court has jurisdiction to deal with almost all family proceedings, except for a limited number of matters which are exclusively reserved to the High Court.

25 See the Civil Procedure Rules Family Practice Directions Part 30, as supplemented by Procedure Direction 30a on Appeals.

26 'Family Court Statistics Quarterly – October to December 2018' in *Ministry of Justice Statistics bulletin*, 28 March 2019.

27 Pleas of the Crown were not originally limited to what we would call criminal offences today, but also encompassed a number of civil claims in which lay a royal interest. By the 18th century, however, most of the civil claims had become removed from this heading in the books and reports dealing with such cases. There are several examples, such as e.g. for civil claims related to trespass, where the fine issued (i.e. the royal interest in such a case) eventually was rendered nominal.

28 Patent Rolls, Henry III, vol. 1 1216-1225, 186.

experimentation, trial by one's peers sitting in a jury became the norm.[29] Whether this was due to a feeling that this was the most justiciable solution, or whether it owed more to the mere convenience of having vast numbers of potential jurors ready at hand to pass judgment (i.e. the presentment parties of the vills and Hundreds who accompanied the Sheriff to the Eyre), is naturally difficult to say with any degree of certainty. In any event, it now fell to the representatives of the vills and Hundreds to not only present accused wrongdoers before the Justices, but also to assist in the Justices' inquisition as to a defendant's guilt or innocence in what came to be known as the "petty jury".[30] Of course, the (petty) juries of the medieval era bear little resemblance to what we recognize today in a jury – both with regard to their make-up (they could consist of any number of jurors the justices might fancy), and with regard to their role in proceedings (it was the justices who determined matters of guilt, the jury merely assisting in the inquisition itself, by positing sworn statements of "fact" based on what they either knew, had heard or – in the worst cases – merely supposed).

As we have already seen, this process of centralization of criminal jurisdiction was followed by a period of decentralization, which saw a steadily increasing amount of summary powers eventually passing back to the regions to be dealt with by the locally appointed Justices of the Peace – the main difference being that the actions of the local Justices were now naturally subject to greater control from the centralised courts at Westminster, as well as the King (and later Parliament). Royal commissioners would continue to travel the country on circuit to hear certain pleas of the Crown – usually, but not always, those that were too grave to be dealt with by Justices of the Peace, but not grave enough to warrant being tried before the King's Bench at Westminster. It is from the jurisdictions enjoyed by these local and travelling Justices – especially as developed

29 The laws of King Cnut (1016–1035) bear witness to the beginnings of a form of jury trial, although certain traces from the time before the Norsemen conquered Anglo-Saxon England also hint at similar mechanisms – such as King Ethelred's Law of Wantage from the end of the 900s. Of course, it is not only jury trial that we must thank the Scandinavian invaders for – the origin of the very word "law" is traceable to the Norse language(!).

30 Hundred Courts had for centuries dealt with a great many petty crimes and the like, and were well established long before the Conquest. In the mid-900s, King Edgar charged the Hundreds with capturing and trying thieves; and under King Cnut, no appeal to the King was made available unless justice could not be achieved before the Hundred. Local villages and townships were also often placed under a collective duty to report crimes and (preferably, if possible) present wrongdoers to the Hundred Courts'. This duty of presentment was carried out by the Sheriff and his four best men. Herein we can also spy certain traces of the modern criminal jury, since in several instances, the King's justices would call upon the sheriff and four best men of four or more neighbouring villages or townships to pass judgment on the guilt or innocence of a defendant. The modern civil jury for its part grew instead from the old criminal jury through the action of trespass, which as mentioned previously suffered a rather muddled past – being both a part civil and part criminal wrongdoing in nature (see e.g. Plucknett (1956) (n 14) 107). Whilst the collective policing and administrative duties of the Hundreds were steadily increased well into the 1800s, their importance as a judicial unit faced a rather abrupt decline: Sheriffs often controlled the Hundreds, appointing bailiffs under their control to steer proceedings; and many Sheriffs were kept firmly in the pockets of the larger landowners. Thus, many Hundreds were effectively under private control. That also meant that fines and forfeitures resulting from criminal inquiries – a lucrative source of revenue – could be (and probably often were) diverted from the King's coffers to local magnates. The Assize of Clarendon (1166), as later confirmed by *Magna Carta*, therefore served to remove the pleas of the Crown from the local courts' jurisdiction.

during the golden reign of the Tudors from the late 1400s to the early 1600s – that we find the origins of today's criminal courts. The Justices of the Peace for their part would for example hold two different types of gathering to hear disputes; the smaller "petty sessions", which saw two or more Justices of the Peace deal with minor wrongdoings by way of summary trial (i.e. without a jury), and the larger "quarter sessions", held four times a year, where grand juries were charged, presentments made and trials for most of the indictable offences held. Quarter sessions enjoyed an appellate jurisdiction over cases tried in petty sessions, and both were later made subject to the appellate jurisdiction of the King's Bench under the writ of *certiorari* (i.e. an order charging them to pass the case up). Proceedings held by the commissioned, itinerant Justices on tour in the main county towns were dubbed "courts of assize", where people accused of committing the most serious offences – such as murder, rape, robbery and forgery, and others who came within the scope of capital crime – were tried.

The petty sessions, quarter sessions and courts of assize were to remain a key feature of the English criminal judicial system for centuries to come, remaining substantially unchanged at least in form, well into the 19th century. As Parliament steadily added to the workload of these courts through statute, however, it became clear that changes were needed to help them cope. A major statutory reform in 1972 therefore made way for the criminal courts we find today.[31] Less serious offences that had previously been dealt with at the petty sessions are now handled by the Magistrates' Court in their entirety. The vast majority of criminal cases in fact start here and are heard by either two or three lay Magistrates sitting together, at times hailed by their historical title as "Justices of the Peace", or by one District Judge sitting alone. Whereas the District Judges are all legally qualified, full-time professionals, lay Magistrates are local volunteers who may or may not have any formal legal qualifications, but will have undertaken a training programme to develop the necessary skills to perform their duties. Magistrates are also offered sound legal and procedural advice during hearings by qualified clerks.

Magistrates' Courts meet with three kinds of criminal cases in practice. Firstly, the less serious "summary offences", for example motoring offences and minor assaults, for which the defendant is not usually entitled to trial by jury. Secondly, the so-called "either-way offences", for example theft or the handling of stolen goods. These offences can be dealt with either by the Magistrates or before a judge and jury at the Crown Court. A defendant accused of an "either-way offence" may insist on their right to trial in the Crown Court, and approximately one in ten of defendants do so. Whilst there can naturally be many possible reasons for doing so, the reason underlying the rule itself certainly appears connected to English notions or ideals of justice, and the right to be tried by one's peers (see Section 4 below). Magistrates can also decide that a case is so serious that it should be dealt with by the Crown Court, which has broader sentencing

31 For more on the background leading up to the passing of the Courts Act 1971, and the proposals of the Beeching Commission upon which it was largely based, see e.g. Fiona Cownie, Anthony Bradney and Mandy Burton, *The English Legal System in Context* (Oxford University Press 2007).

powers.[32] Thirdly, although "indictable-only offences" – such as murder, manslaughter, rape and robbery – must be heard at a Crown Court, the Magistrates' Court will generally decide whether bail is to be granted to the defendant, and other legal issues (such as e.g. reporting restrictions), before passing the case on.

From 2010–2019, a modernisation programme has seen 162 of the 323 Magistrates Courts in England and Wales closed, in order to save costs.[33] The remaining Magistrates Courts deal with somewhere in the region of 1.5–2 million proceedings against defendants per year. In addition to its broad criminal jurisdiction, Magistrates' Courts also enjoy a limited civil jurisdiction over certain types of cases (e.g. recovery of debts, licensing for gambling institutions and the sale of alcohol), but only as provided for by specific statutes – i.e. they enjoy no inherent civil jurisdiction as such.

More serious criminal cases are passed on to the Crown Court, as successor to the jurisdiction of both the quarter sessions and courts of assize before it. Cases may be passed up from the Magistrates' Court to the Crown Court either for a full trial with a judge and jury of 12, or for sentencing after the defendant has been found guilty before the Magistrates. In jury trials, the judge will be responsible for advising the jury as to the law, whilst the jury members make findings of fact and determine the guilt or innocence of the accused. The possibility in certain cases of being tried by one's peers goes in many ways to the very heart of English notions of justice and is often viewed as a beacon of political and civil liberty. The very fact that defendants in some cases will have a choice as to whether to have his/her case tried by a judge or by judge and jury may seem rather odd to some but must again be understood in light of history. The centre of English medieval criminal law revolved around issues of proof. If there was a witness to the crime, then trial by battle (literally!) was used to test whether the witness was speaking the truth.[34] In cases where there was no affirmative witness, the alleged offender's own word would need to be tested for its truth. This was done through a so-called "wager of law", which could be conducted in one of two ways – either by "compurgation", whereby the defendant would swear that he had not committed the act, and would be required to produce a certain number of trustworthy neighbours to ascertain his own credibility, or trial by ordeal of fire or water, which almost invariably resulted in death. The mere suspicions of one's neighbours were not enough to put a man to the ordeal – this required at the very least some material evidence that a wrongdoing had in fact taken place. However, this changed following the Assize of Clarendon in 1166, which stipulated that mere suspicion on the part of the Justices of the Peace should be enough to put a defendant to the ordeal, thereby sealing his (inevitably) dreadful fate. The ancient trial of ordeal was brought to an end at the beginning of the 13th century, however, as priests – who

32 Generally, according to Section 154 of the Criminal Justice Act 2003, defendants who either plead or are found guilty by the Magistrates may receive sentences of up to 12 months' imprisonment for a single offence (65 weeks in total for consecutive offences), or a fine of up to £5,000.

33 "Court Closures and Access to Justice", Debate Pack, CDP-0156, House of Commons Law Library, 18 June 2019, 4.

34 On a slightly different tangent, the mode of trial by battle in itself shows just how deeply entrenched the basic ideal of adversarial proceedings (and hence procedural law) really are in the English legal culture.

provided the very trigger upon which the procedure rested – were forbidden by the Church from taking any further part in its initiation.[35]

As touched upon previously, after a short period of experimentation by the Justices in Eyre, who ever since the Assize of Clarendon had been charged with dealing with pleas of the Crown, trial by one's peers sitting in a jury became the norm. The main problem with this ancient form of jury trial, however, was that it had to be *chosen* by the defendant. If the defendant did not choose to "put himself on the countryside" as it was termed, then he could not be convicted. And if he could not be convicted, his land and property would not be forfeit to the Crown. So, in cases where the defendant refused to choose jury trial, he would be incarcerated instead, and measures would be taken to persuade him to do so.[36] In most cases, this meant being tortured to death in prison, from which the term *peine forte et dure* stems. As claimed by Plucknett, "[u]nder such circumstances, a jury was just a newer sort of ordeal".[37] By the end of the 1700s, however, refusals to plea stopped being treated in this manner, and instead became automatic convictions. It was not until 1827 that the rule we recognize today of a plea of "not guilty" automatically being entered for those who refuse was finally introduced by statute.[38] But the choice as to mode of trial with regards to certain offences still remains even to this very day, integrally linked to the defendant's right to indicate a plea before such a decision is made – the modern day alternative to trial by jury being various modes of trial before the Magistrates.

The Crown Court also hears certain appeals against convictions and/or sentences of the Magistrates' courts and may consider matters of both law and fact in doing so. However, appeals made "by way of case stated" and applications for judicial review go directly to the High Court from the Magistrates (explained further just below). The Crown Court also enjoys a limited civil jurisdiction in its appellate capacity to rule over what might be termed quasi-criminal orders made by the Magistrates under various statutory instruments, such as for example Anti-Social Behaviour Orders, or Sexual Offender Orders. Such orders are quasi-criminal in the sense that they prevent offenders from doing whatever is set out in their terms, the breach of which may amount to a criminal offence in itself.[39]

Crown Court cases are presided over by Recorders (i.e. barristers/solicitors acting as part-time judges), Circuit Judges or High Court Judges, depending on the seriousness of the offence and/or complexity of the case. Judges of the Queen's Bench Division of the High Court (see section below) hear the most important criminal cases in the Crown Court and will travel around the country to do so – clear remnants of the dispensation of royal justice from Westminster to the regions in ancient times.

35 See e.g. Plucknett (1956) (n 14) 118–119.

36 Statute of Westminster I (1275), c. 12.

37 Plucknett (1956) (n 14) 125. By the 1670s, jury trial was still essentially medieval – indeed, wager by law not completely done away with until well into the 1800s.

38 Milsom (1981) (n 11) 411; as now set out in the Magistrates' Court Act 1980.

39 See further e.g. Alisdair Gillespie, *The English Legal System* (Oxford University Press 2015) 202–203.

In 2019, there were 77 fixed Crown Court locations across England and Wales, also called Crown Court Centres, dealing with approximately 150,000 cases sent for trial and/or sentencing by the Magistrates' Court each year.[40] Although Crown Court sessions may in fact be held at any location in England or Wales, hearing such cases at other venues rarely happens in practice.[41]

2.5 The mixed jurisdiction of the High Court

The High Court and the Court of Appeal (described in the next section) together form what are known as the Senior Courts of England & Wales. The High Court holds a rather unique place in the English legal system, its origins traceable all the way back to the first centralised courts at Westminster. Its place in the judicial hierarchy is rather complex, and difficult to explain to outsiders. Firstly, because it enjoys both a substantial appellate and original jurisdiction – i.e. sometimes hearing cases at first instance, and sometimes as an appellate body; secondly, because it also deals with both civil and criminal matters. The High Court's jurisdiction and procedures are governed by the Senior Courts Act 1981 (SCA 1981),[42] whose provisions are particularly broadly and loosely termed. This has left large gaps to be fleshed out in part by a statutory instrument called the Civil Procedure Rules (CPR), and in part by principles and rules developed by the High Court itself through its inherent jurisdiction. The inherent jurisdiction of the High Court derives primarily from the fact that it is the direct descendant of the ancient common law (and equity) courts discussed above (i.e. the Common Bench, the King's Bench, the Court of Exchequer and Chancery), and may only be ousted by the introduction of more recent statutory (i.e. legislative) rules covering the same subject matter. In this way, the High Court's jurisdiction is able to evolve and move with the times.

The High Court system of the middle-ages was significantly overhauled by judicial reforms in the late 1800s, largely in response to calls from leading industrial and commercial actors who found that complex commercial cases often required the attention of different branches of law in different courts. A series of Supreme Court of Judicature Acts did away with the old higher courts, creating a new Supreme Court of Judicature, consisting of the High Court of Justice and the Court of Appeal.[43] In 1873, the High Court was initially split into five divisional courts, based mainly on the old central court structure (i.e. King's Bench, Common Pleas, Exchequer, and Chancery), with the addition of a new Probate, Divorce and Admiralty division. The Common Pleas and Exchequer divisions were abolished in 1880, and their respective jurisdictions meted

40 'Criminal Court Statistics Quarterly, England and Wales – January to June 2014' in *Ministry of Justice Statistics Bulletin*, 25 September 2014; see also https://www.judiciary.uk/.

41 Section 78 of the Senior Courts Act 1981.

42 Formerly the Supreme Courts Act 1981.

43 This series of acts started with the Supreme Court of Judicature Act 1873, followed in quick succession by a further 14 orders and amending statutes leading up to the turn of the 20th century.

out amongst the other divisions, thereby providing much needed clarity to the appellate system and significantly reducing legal costs.

The jurisdiction of the High Court is today exercised by a tricephalous body – its three heads being the Queen's Bench Division, the Chancery Division and the Family Division. The Queen's Bench Division hears judicial review (a form of action seeking to establish whether governmental, administrative and/or judicial decisions have been made in the correct way), admiralty, and commercial cases. The Chancery Division deals essentially with cases related to realty, trusts, bankruptcy, intellectual property and company matters. The Family Division for its part does exactly what it says on the tin.[44] Sometimes, where a case spans the jurisdiction of several Divisions simultaneously, the claimant may choose the Division before which to proceed with his or her case.[45] In practice, most tort and contract claims go to the Queen's Bench Division, which enjoys the broadest jurisdiction of the three Divisions, and hence also deals with the most cases.[46] Certain specialized courts are also attached to both the Queen's Bench, such as the Commercial Court[47] and the Admiralty Court,[48] and the Chancery Division, such as the Companies Court and the Patents Court, to deal with cases concerning particular fields of the law. The setting up of specialized courts charged with dealing with specialized legal problems is certainly not new, and harks back to the age of the Tudors, and particularly the reign of Henry VIII. But it would be fallacious today to think of these specialized courts as entities separate from the High Court itself – what it really means is that High Court judges with particular expertise in such matters will usually deal with such cases.

Most cases which come before the High Court acting as a court of first instance are heard by a single judge.[49] Where the High Court acts in its appellate capacity, however, at least two judges will hear the case, sitting as so-called Divisional Courts.[50] The no more than 80 regular Justices of the High Court are called "puisne judges" (from the French *puisné*, meaning regular or junior), thereby demarking the difference in rank between them and the Lord Chief Justice, who is head of the judiciary and President of the Courts of England and Wales, in addition to being the President of the Criminal Division of the Court of Appeal, the Senior Presiding Judge, the President and Vice President of the

44 See Schedule 1 of the SCA 1981 for more details concerning the distribution of business at the High Court.

45 Such as e.g. concerning certain inheritance cases, which may be dealt with by either Chancery or the Family Division, according to the terms set out in the Inheritance Act 1975 and CPR 57.15.

46 Tort claims concern civil wrongs, such as wrongs against the person (e.g. defamation and libel), and/or against property (e.g. trespass; negligence and nuisance).

47 Business at the Commercial Court has a distinctly international flavour, dealing with a variety of claims relating more generally to the transactions of trade and commerce, such as e.g. commercial agreements, import and export, markets, carriage of goods, agency, insurance and reinsurance, banking and financial services, arbitration and competition matters.

48 The Admiralty Court enjoys jurisdiction over a number of maritime claims, such as the arrest of ships, mortgage and ownership claims, collisions and salvage.

49 Section 19(3) of the SCA 1981.

50 Section 66(3) of the SCA 1981. If only two judges hear an appeal and they disagree on the outcome, the judge agreeing with the order of the lower court will win the day – which would also serve to explain why criminal appeals at the High Court are in fact usually heard by three judges.

Queen's Bench Division, the President of the Family Division, and the Chancellor, who is the head of the Chancery Division.[51] Rather confusingly, certain cases in the High Court may on occasion also be heard by Circuit Judges or deputies. The reason for this is no doubt partly historical, given that the High Court itself is not bound geographically to one place, but may exercise its jurisdiction from several potential locations: High Court actions may be commenced in one of the diminishing number of local District Registries spread across the counties, and its business may in theory be conducted "at any place in England or Wales". Apart from all actions involving disputes based in London, most claimants may therefore choose whether a case is to be heard locally, usually the nearest Crown Court, or before the Royal Courts of Justice – the High Court's "headquarters" in London.

Whilst the Family Division of the High Court enjoys a broad appellate jurisdiction, hearing appeals concerning almost any family law matter from any lower instance, the civil appellate jurisdictions of both the Queen's Bench and Chancery Divisions are comparatively limited. Although the Queen's Bench has a relatively broad criminal appellate jurisdiction, empowering it to hear cases on appeal from both Magistrates and Crown Courts, the number of cases actually heard by way of appeal is rather limited. The primary reason for this is owing to the limited grounds for appeal from these courts to the High Court itself, which will only be entertained "by way of case stated" (i.e. claims that the original decision was either wrong in law or in excess of jurisdiction), or for judicial review (i.e. claims concerning procedural impropriety, unfairness or bias). No new evidence is adduced for appeals by way of case stated, where the lawyers argue solely on points of law. Appeals based on the facts of the case are generally dismissed out of hand, unless it concerns a finding of fact completely unsupported by the evidence, or one that no reasonable court or tribunal properly directed could have reached to begin with – such exceptional cases are then dealt with as an error of law, not fact.[52] Likewise appeals concerning sentences, which will only be admitted on the basis of case stated in highly exceptional circumstances, such as where a Magistrate passes a sentence that he or she clearly had no power to pass, or where a sentence given is so harsh that it might be considered made in excess of the lower court's jurisdiction.[53] Although oral hearings are sometimes dispensed with, most appeals procedures before the High Court will contain both written and oral stages.

---

51 Section 4(1) SCA 1981.

52 *Plowden v. The Director of Public Prosecutions* [1991] Crim LR 850.

53 For more on the powers of the High Court on appeal, see Section 6 of the Summary Jurisdiction Act 1857, which states that the High Court may affirm, reverse or vary the decision of the first instance court, make any order it deems fit, or send it back to the first instance court with its opinion attached. It may also order a rehearing of the case by the same (or different) judges.

2.6 The Court of Appeal

The first appellate mechanisms under the medieval English system – like so many of the historical threads of the common law – probably owe more to coincidence and pragmatism than concrete design. From the 13th century onwards, the justices of the centralized common law courts began to congregate to discuss particularly difficult cases together in a rather *ad hoc* plenary session, often held in a place called the Exchequer Chamber. Over the course of the 1400s, the practice settled into a mechanism of case referral from the Common and King's Benches, with the decision reached by the Exchequer Chamber passing back down to the referring court for final pronouncement. Referrals could not be demanded by the parties, however, and could only take place at the insistence of the judges hearing the case – as such, it represented only a more limited form of appeal. Nevertheless, the system thus created by exigency more than design came to do much of what would later be asked of more formalized appellate judicial structures.[54]

The monumental societal changes wrought by the industrial revolution in the UK in the 1700s led to a significant growth in the number and complexity of cases coming before the courts. There were many different courts enjoying jurisdiction to hear many different types of appeal – including the Exchequer Chamber. In short, the appeals system was a mess, and proved wholly inept to keep pace with the changing times and needs of an increasingly litigious nation. A report issued in 1869 by the Judicature Commission – which had been set up to examine the operation of the courts and make recommendations for its reform – therefore recommended the replacement of the existing courts with a new Supreme Court of Judicature, which was to be formed by a High Court and a new, single Court of Appeal above it. The main aim of the reform was to simplify and cut down on the numerous avenues and procedures of appeal in civil cases. Significantly, this included transferring the House of Lords' historical judicial competence to the Court of Appeal – which in turn would have seen the latter emerge as the highest (civil law) court in the land. Several political coincidences prevented the reform proposals on this particular point from ever entering into force (described in more detail directly below), leaving the Court of Appeal to adopt an intermediate position in the appeals system directly below the House of Lords (now the UK Supreme Court).

The Court of Appeal's original jurisdiction was primarily civil. Jurisdiction to hear criminal appeals took almost a century longer to secure. At the time of its establishment, criminal appeals were determined by the Home Secretary. The Criminal Appeal Act of 1907 saw the Home Secretary's jurisdiction transferred to an independent Court of Criminal Appeal, and in 1966 finally to the Court of Appeal itself.[55] Today, the Court of Appeal is split into two divisions – the Civil Division hears appeals from the County Court and High Court, whilst the Criminal division may entertain appeals from the

---

54 Other early examples of appellate jurisdiction include Parliament's jurisdiction in error over decisions from the King's Bench, discussed further below.

55 Criminal Appeal Act 1966.

Crown Court on all matters relating to trial on indictment and against any sentence imposed following a committal for sentence.[56]

Leave to appeal may be obtained from either the lower court or the Court of Appeal itself. Appeals will usually be on points of law, although the court may (re)open the facts and in particular cases, also allow new evidence to be admitted. The Lord Chief Justice is the President of the Criminal Division, while the Master of the Rolls is the President of the Civil Division. The Court is otherwise constituted of the President of the Queen's Bench Division, the President of the Family Division and Chancellor of the High Court, and 38 other permanent Lord and Lady Justices of Appeal – all of which may be called upon to hear cases in either Division.[57] Three judges usually sit on an appeal, whilst a single judge will usually hear applications for leave to appeal. In 2017, there were more than 5,000 applications for leave to appeal received by the Criminal Division, whilst 3,000 appeals were filed in the Civil Division.[58]

2.7 The Supreme Court

For many centuries, the highest court of England & Wales was the House of Lords. In addition to being judges, however, the 12 Law Lords were also life peers inducted into the second chamber of Parliament, and thereby also formally a part of the legislature. Schooled as we are on fundamental constitutional notions of the separation of powers, it might well seem strange for us today to imagine a body politic exercising any form of judicial competence whatsoever. Yet the Parliament of medieval times from which the current bicameral system later developed was quite a different body to the legislative assembly with which we naturally associate it today. As explained earlier, the writ system began to take a more rigid form following concessions won by the nobility over the Crown in the mid-1200s.[59] Unless one's case fell within one of the (admittedly rather many) existing forms of action, it became increasingly difficult to get a writ to proceed with one's case before the centralised courts.[60] This lack of flexibility in the writ system, which seemed to owe more to the ongoing power-struggle between the King and his Lords than anything else, effectively stunted the growth of the common law, by preventing novel types of claims from being addressed by the highest courts. Unsurprisingly in light of this situation, it became increasingly common to seek redress by way of direct petition to other centralized bodies. In many cases petitions would be made to Parliament. Such petitions were not only made in cases asking for redress at first instance,

56 The grounds for allowing and dismissing criminal appeals are currently set out in the Criminal Appeals Act 1995.

57 Certain High Court judges and senior Circuit Judges may sometimes be authorised to sit to hear cases in the Court of Appeal. Retired Lord and Lady Justices and current Justices of the UK Supreme Court appointed from England and Wales can also hear cases in either Division.

58 The Lord Chief Justice's Report 2018, available at https://www.judiciary.uk/wp-content/uploads/2018/11/lcj-report-2018.pdf accessed 14 April 2020.

59 Initially by the Provisions of Oxford (1258), as subsequently reaffirmed by the Provisions of Westminster (1259).

60 Chapter 24 of the Second Statute of Westminster (1285) did, however, empower Chancery to create new writs in narrowly defined circumstances, although this power certainly appears to have been used with extreme caution.

but also sometimes requesting that decisions of other courts be quashed. This should not come as too much of a surprise, however, as Parliament in its early days was more a gathering of prominent men summoned by the King to discuss any and all matters of law and state than an exclusively political institution as such.[61]

The judicial competence enjoyed by Parliament was first described in *Fleta* – a medieval treatise on the laws of England from the 1290s, whose authorship remains something of a mystery even to this day.[62] Here it was said that: "[T]he king has his court in his council in his parliaments (…) where doubts concerning judgments are resolved, new remedies are provided for newly arisen wrongs, and justice is done to everyone according to his deserts".[63] From this we can see that medieval Parliament enjoyed both an original and appellate jurisdiction, which was both civil and criminal. Further, that its jurisdiction was by no means ordinary but rather extraordinary in nature.[64] Indeed, although the establishment of the King's Bench in the early 1200s had in fact relieved Parliament of many of its judicial functions, it also furnished the latter with a novel appellate jurisdiction in error from this newly established court.[65]

The process by which Parliament's judicial competence eventually came to settle more firmly in the House of Lords requires a short explanation of how its bicameral structure came into being in the first place. It is important to remember here that Parliament had initially developed as an off-shoot from the King's Council, a fact which was also reflected in its make-up. In its early stages, it consisted primarily of various members of the nobility and the clergy. The reason for this was quite simple, since in a feudal system the King could not hope to get much done without their economic, military and spiritual backing and support. It therefore became customary for the King to consult representatives of the nobility and clergy ("the Lords temporal and spiritual") when important decisions of state needed to be made.[66] The consensual basis of the King's rule was gradually extended and further entrenched following the various concessions made to the nobility during the 1200s, and the Crown's ever-growing need for revenues. In order to ensure an efficient levying of taxes, the King needed to secure the backing of the local populous beyond that of his main tenants (i.e. the nobility). This in turn led to an

61 See e.g. Plucknett (1956) (n 14) 151.

62 Only one full manuscript of *Fleta* from the 1400s exists today and may be found in the British Library. The Selden Society has published edited versions of the treatise, translated from Latin under the steady hands of G.O. Sayles and H.G. Richardson; *Fleta – vol. ii. (Prologue, Books 1 & 2)* (1953) Vol. 72, Selden Society; *Fleta – Books 3 & 4* (1972) Vol. 89, Selden Society; *Fleta – Books 5 & 6* (1983) Vol. 99, Selden Society. *Fleta* is often said to be based largely on Bracton's earlier writings – an author who we shall return to touch upon briefly in Section 5 below.

63 *Fleta – vol. ii*, 2, § 1.

64 Plucknett (1956) (n 14) 201.

65 Later also confirming its jurisdiction in error from the Queen's Bench (Error from the Queen's Bench Act 1584) and more generally from lower common law courts (Error Act 1588).

66 Just as the pre-Conquest Anglo Saxon rulers of England were believed to have done at their Witans in (even more) ancient times. Like the early post-conquest Parliaments, the Witan was in no sense a popular assembly, but rather the council of the Anglo-Saxon kings. Its essential duty was to advise the king on all matters on which he chose to ask its opinion. Although its composition and time of meeting were determined at the King's discretion, they were usually attended by the greater nobles and bishops of the realm.

increasingly large body of less prominent men – local representatives from the shires and boroughs, referred to colloquially as "the commons" – being called for consultation in Parliament where taxes and levies were at issue. By the 1320s, the commons had become such an integral source of revenue for the Crown as to render it an indispensable part of Parliament. In order to accommodate both the nobility/clergy and commons under the system, Parliament was eventually split in two in order to conduct its business: whilst representatives of the nobility and clergy formed the House of Lords, representatives of the local communities (the commons) formed the House of Commons.

By the very end of the 14th century, as the House of Commons ceased (at its own request, one might add) to entertain petitions appealing decisions of other courts, so it eventually came to fall upon the House of Lords to exercise Parliament's judicial functions for the future. And following the high-profile spat with the House of Commons in 1667–1670 concerning *Skinner's Case*, the House of Lords' judicial competence came to be tacitly limited to its appellate jurisdiction alone.[67] Yet it was only following the Supreme Court of Judicature Act of 1875 and the Appellate Jurisdiction Act of 1876 that the House of Lords came to be fully recognised as the highest civil appellate authority of the land, and reporting of its decisions began in earnest.[68] The latter Act provided for appointing Lords of Appeal in Ordinary to the Appellate Committee of the House, meaning henceforth that cases would be decided by professional judges instead of hereditary peers. This proved a key move in confirming the position of the House of

67 18 Car. 2, 1666, 6 vol. 709; *Skinner v. East India Company* (1666) St. Tr. 710. Thomas Skinner had established a base for trade in the Far East, at a time when little regulation on such matters had existed. The East India Company subsequently took control in the area under state-sanctioned monopoly trade rights, confiscating Mr. Skinner's property in the process. He petitioned the King for relief, and the dispute was subsequently referred to the House of Lords, who decided in favour of Mr. Skinner. The East India Company in reply petitioned the House of Commons, claiming that the decision of the House of Lords had no merit as it should have first been dealt with by a court proper at first instance. The dispute between the Houses spiralled seemingly out of control, to the point where orders were made by the Commons for the imprisonment of Skinner, and by the Lords for the imprisonment of the East India Company's Chairman. Whilst the conflict eventually cooled off and was effectively abandoned by both Houses, it marked the House of Lords' final acceptance of a case under its original (civil) jurisdiction. Although it continued to hear e.g. indictments against peers, technically this was not at first instance, as such cases would first touch by the King's Bench before being referred up to the Lords – usually by the Lords' issuing of a writ of certiorari to it. For more, see e.g. Glenn Dymond, 'The Appellate Jurisdiction of the House of Lords' in *House of Lords Library note* (LLN 2009/010) 4.

68 As mentioned above (Section 2), the Judicature Act of 1873 had initially set out to do away with the House of Lords' judicial competence altogether – at least as far as cases originating in England were concerned. It would almost certainly have succeeded in doing so as well, had not the Gladstone (Liberal) government who introduced the bill to Parliament fallen due to its growing unpopularity during the following year, and thus before the 1873 Act had a chance to enter into force. The succeeding (Conservative) government passed two further acts in 1874 and 1875 – the first serving to suspend the entry into force of the 1873 Act, with the second abolishing it altogether. The very attempt to divest the House of its judicial powers was nevertheless rather unsurprising. Cases were at this point in time decided by all of its members – i.e. all of the Lords spiritual and temporal. The Lords proved often prone to high degrees of partisanship and capriciousness in their appraisal of the disputes that were brought before them. As such, the House of Lords' judicial decisions of the time – although growing steadily in number – enjoyed little respect by the people of the country or the Bar itself. For more generally on the role of the House of Lords in its judicial capacity following these events, see the remarkable book by Louis Blom-Cooper, Brice Dickson and Gavin Drewry (eds), *The Judicial House of Lords – 1876–2009* (Oxford University Press 2009).

Lords at the zenith of the judicial hierarchy and compelling respect of its decisions by the lower courts.[69] In 1907, the Criminal Appeal Act finally also established a right of appeal to the House of Lords in criminal cases (subject to Attorney General consent).[70]

The House of Lords' judicial competence was brought to an end following sweeping constitutional changes in the early 2000s – the removal of all judicial authority from the vestiges of Parliament and Government finally giving full voice to the adage that those who administer the law should not be involved in creating it, too. The Constitutional Reform Act of 2005 transferred the appellate jurisdiction of the House of Lords to a separate Supreme Court of the United Kingdom (UKSC), which opened on 1 October 2009. Judges appointed to the UKSC now become Justices thereof, with no automatic seat in the House of Lords, and may be removed from office by addresses from both Houses of Parliament.[71] The Act also modified the pivotal role of the Lord Chancellor, who had previously acted as both Head of the Judiciary, Speaker in the House of Lords, and also as a member of the Prime Minister's cabinet. Although the Lord Chancellor is still technically the head of the judiciary's administration and a Governmental minister (Secretary of State for Justice), he no longer acts in a judicial capacity as judge and his role in the House of Lords has been completely removed.[72] Judicial appointments to courts in England & Wales have also been removed from the Lord Chancellor's domain, and placed in the hands of an independent Judicial Appointments Commission.[73] As such, the Lord Chancellor has gradually become more part of the executive branch, with increasingly "ministerial" duties.

By securing greater independence for the highest appellate court in the land and reforming the office of Lord Chancellor, the reforms initiated by the Constitutional Reform Act of 2005 have certainly staked a path towards a clearer separation of pow-

69 The introduction of this statutory rule was in fact based on custom established some 30 years earlier in *O'Connell v. The Queen* (1844) 11 Cl. & Fin. 155, according to which lay members of the House of Lords (i.e. peers) were not to vote on appeals. It must no doubt have gone some way towards improving the standing of the House as a court of law in the eyes of the populous and the legal profession.

70 Dymond (n 67) 9. The House had in fact previously enjoyed jurisdiction in error in criminal cases, but it had virtually lapsed in practice at this point.

71 Sections 33 and 137 of the Constitutional Reform Act 2005. Although they rarely did so, the former Law Lords were able to vote on legislation as full Members of the House of Lords. In fact, in latter years, the Law Lords would only really be involved in certain committee work, especially in the EU Committee. The first Supreme Court Justices (as former Law Lords) remained Members of the House of Lords but were unable to sit and vote in the House. All new Justices appointed after October 2009 are directly appointed to the UKSC on the recommendation of a selection commission.

72 The idea of separating the political and legal roles of the Lord Chancellor was indeed not new, an attempt for example having been made 171 years earlier, in 1834, by the then Lord Chancellor (Brougham). The current reforms would no doubt also have pushed even further – doing away with many of his residual powers and distancing him even further from the legislature and judiciary. But many of these powers were statutory in nature, and the House of Lords' has proven highly reluctant to let go of some of the more ceremonial traditions vested in the office. For more, see e.g. Alexander Horne, 'The Role of the Lord Chancellor' in *House of Commons Library Standard Note* (SN/PC/2105 26 March 2015).

73 Appointments to the Supreme Court – which are primarily made on the basis of merit – are now governed by Sections 25 to 31 and Schedule 8, of the Constitutional Reform Act 2005, as amended by the Tribunals and Enforcement Act 2007 and the Crime and Courts Act 2013.

ers between the executive, legislative and judicial branches in the UK, leaving indelible marks on English constitutional history. Much debate has nevertheless ensued in the past few years as to whether the change to a Supreme Court was merely one of form and not substance. On one view, it might be thought that the new court would continue along exactly the same lines as the old court; on another, that its new-found independence might gradually lead to a more politically activist Court – a true(r) guardian of the British constitution – picking battles with the Government and/or Parliament in defence of individual rights and liberties, arguably in a way it had remained shy to commit itself to more fully in the past.[74] Time will no doubt tell as to which predictions (if any) prove correct, but there can be little doubting the symbolic virtue of the changes in making the Court's work more visible and accessible to the British public at large. Having lost its formal ties to the other two branches of State, attempts to maintain a constructive dialogue between the UKSC and the Government and Parliament in this new constitutional environment also seem particularly important.[75]

In any event, the formal jurisdiction of the UKSC is indeed essentially the same as that previously enjoyed by the Appellate Committee of the House of Lords, although it now also enjoys the former important, yet largely uncontroversial, devolution jurisdiction previously belonging to the Judicial Committee of the Privy Council.[76] As an appeal court, the UKSC cannot consider a case unless a decision has been made in a lower court. It hears appeals on arguable points of law of general public importance from both divisions of the Court of Appeal, and also sometimes directly from the High Court.[77] It also enjoys jurisdiction to hear appeals in civil (but not criminal) cases from the Scot-

74 Compare e.g. the views of Supreme Court Justice Lord Phillips of Worth Matravers, 'The Birth and First Steps of the UK Supreme Court' (2012) Vol. 1 Issue 2 *Cambridge Journal of International and Comparative Law* 9, with the views of Supreme Court Justice Lady Hale, as expounded at the Bryce Lecture 2015 ('The Supreme Court in the United Kingdom Constitution', Somerville College, Oxford, 5 February 2015): "The rule of law has always been the servant of Parliamentary sovereignty – the courts ensuring that public authorities stay within the bounds of the powers which Parliament has given them – but could it be that the rule of law is gradually taking over as the organising principle of our constitution?". See further Penny Darbyshire, 'The UK Supreme Court – is there anything left to think about?' (2015) Vol. 21 No. 1 *European Journal of Current Legal Issues.*

75 For a more recent example, see The Criminal Justice and Courts Act 2015, which amended Section 5 of the Constitutional Reform Act 2005 so as to allow the President of the Supreme Court to lay before Parliament written representations on matters of importance relating to the Supreme Court or to the jurisdiction it exercises.

76 See Section 40 and Schedule 9, Constitutional Reform Act 2005. The Judicial Committee of the Privy Council is the highest court of appeal for many Commonwealth countries, British Crown Dependencies and British Overseas Territories. Five judges – usually Justices of the Supreme Court (known as "The Board") – determine such cases. Whilst not binding as precedent on lower courts in England and Wales, the decisions of the Privy Council are nevertheless considered highly persuasive sources of law – unsurprising, perhaps, in light of the judges who usually decide the cases.

77 Section 63 of the Criminal Justice and Courts Act 2015 has recently broadened the range of appeals from the High Court that may "leapfrog" the Court of Appeal and go directly to the Supreme Court, thereby aiming at saving the cost and inevitable delay of the regular appeals procedure in cases which appear destined to end up before the UKSC in any event.

tish Court of Session.[78] Cases must be heard by an uneven number of Justices, at least three, and more than half of these must be permanent members of the Supreme Court.[79]

On allowing leave to appeal, the UKSC endeavours to concentrate on the cases of the greatest public and constitutional importance. The procedure in applying for leave to appeal is essentially the same today as it had been for the House of Lords. One big difference, however, was that leave to appeal was previously limited to granting by the Court of Appeal and/or the House of Lords.[80] Today, leave to appeal may also be granted by the High Court (subject to agreement by the UKSC) in so-called "leapfrog" appeals. In the event that the court appealed from refuses leave to appeal, the appellant can apply directly to the UKSC for permission. Such applications are generally decided on paper by a panel of three Justices, without an oral hearing. On average, the Supreme Court receives around 200 applications for leave to appeal each year, of which usually more than half are refused.[81]

Regarding the Supreme Court's substantive jurisdiction, it is worth noting that – just as with the House of Lords, and unlike many of the highest courts in other countries – it enjoys no power to nullify Acts of Parliament as unconstitutional. This follows from the key constitutional principle of Parliamentary sovereignty. The Supreme Court may nevertheless "disapply" (i.e. set aside) legislation in certain situations – notably as a result of UK obligations under EU law, and also the terms of devolution – thus achieving the same practical outcome in a given dispute as nullification would have.[82] But for the time being at least, and in spite of recent attempts to give fuller force to the rule of law, the principle of Parliamentary sovereignty seems destined to remain the keystone of the largely unwritten British constitution, effectively denying the courts the right to accept challenges to the legality of statutes.[83]

3. Production of legal norms & legal method

The following section is devoted to the various legal sources under English law. We shall see not only what rules there are and how they are made, but also how English lawyers seek to make use of the rules themselves when attempting to solve legal problems in

78 See Article XIX of the Act of Union with Scotland (1707); and *Bywater v. Lord Advocate* (1781) 2 Paton's ap. 564.

79 Section 42, Constitutional Reform Act 2005.

80 See the Administration of Justice (Appeals) Act of 1934.

81 Detailed figures from one year to the next are made public in the Supreme Court Annual Report and Accounts, available and free to download on the Supreme Court's website: https://www.supremecourt.uk/ accessed 14 April 2020.

82 The devolution settlements of the late 1990s saw competence to rule on the legality of actings of the Parliamentary Assemblies of Scotland, Wales and Northern Ireland fall to the Judicial Committee of the Privy Council. Following the Constitutional Reform Act 2005, the competence to rule on (and potentially strike down) such actings as incompatible with the powers granted to them by the UK Parliament, was transferred to the Supreme Court.

83 See the seminal ruling in *R (Jackson) v. Attorney General* [2005] UKHL 56, [2006] 1 AC 262. Although refuting the contention that they had power to strike down the controversial Hunting Act 2004, Lords Hope and Steyn and Lady Hale all hinted in *obiter dicta* to the potential limits of the principle of Parliamentary sovereignty; questioning whether Parliament could legislate so as to e.g. abolish judicial review by ordinary courts of law.

practice. Of course, legal method being more of an art than a science, we will have to limit ourselves (yet again) to a few particular aspects of it in the following – primarily those aspects that might help us to fulfil the comparative aims of the project. There are essentially four major legal sources: the common law, primary legislation (Acts of Parliament, or statutes), secondary legislation (delegated acts) and international (including European) law. These will be described in turn below.

3.1 The common law

As mentioned at the very outset of this chapter, the term "common law" is used to denote the legal rules created by and through the courts. The common law system of England & Wales may be regarded largely as a sedimentary by-product of the centralization of justice set out in the start of Section 2 above.[84] As such, much of the basis of English law has developed on a piecemeal basis over the centuries, owing a great deal to the mere (and arbitrary) accidents of litigation. As its very name suggests, the common law is exactly that – a common law for all of the country, built (originally, at least) on local customs. Yet customs tell us little more than how to resolve particular issues or questions at present – i.e. what should be done, and by whom. In order for there to be a system of legal norms produced by customs, they must become, or become seen as, binding. Yet any system based on custom lends itself inherently towards a rather dynamic evolution of the law itself. Times change, and society most often with it. As pointed out for example by Milsom, many (if not most) customs are formed by economic need. Yet economic need in itself makes for flexibility. In feudal times, custom for example provided that the greater the land tenure of the property-owning tenant, the more fighting men he was to provide to his Lord (ultimately, the Crown). As soon as the feudal structure lost touch with this economic reality, however, the custom – and hence, the law – changed accordingly. As such, it seems fair to say that:

> "The life of the common law has been in the abuse of its elementary ideas. If the rules of property give what now seems an unjust answer, try obligation; (…) If the rules on contract give what now seems an unjust answer, try tort. Your counterfeit will look odd to one brought up on categories of Roman origin; but it will work. (…) And so the legal world goes round."[85]

The binding nature of the customs forming the basis of the common law was to crystallise with the gradual establishment of a system of precedent. The vertical dimension of this principle of *stare decisis*, meaning to "let the decision stand", requires courts of lower status to treat the decisions of higher-ranking courts as legally binding. Following this logic, decisions of lower courts may accordingly be followed or overruled by courts of higher standing. Put in other words, decisions of lower courts are generally deemed per-

---

84 Milsom (1981) (n 11) 27.

85 Ibid 6.

suasive but not binding legal sources on higher courts. In light of this fact, the hierarchy of the court system (Section 2 above) becomes all the more important to bear in mind as a key element in shaping and developing the common law.[86]

The doctrine of precedent requires similar cases to be treated in a similar manner – not merely as this might seem desirable for example from the perspective of consistency or efficiency, or some innate notion of justice or fairness, but owing to a duty to do so. That does not mean, however, that everything that is said in a given court decision will be attached equal weight by other courts referring to it as authority for a particular point of law. Common lawyers are trained from the very outset of their legal studies to distinguish between the *ratio decidendi* of a case (i.e. the legal principle or rule and reasoning upon which the issue was decided, often referred to simply as the *ratio*) and statements which are made *obiter dicta* (i.e. any other pronouncements in the case on the law that deal with matters beyond the material facts of the case, and which are not wholly necessary to settle in order to determine the dispute in question). The *ratio* of a case is the part that binds other courts under the doctrine of precedent. *Obiter dicta* do not bind courts in future cases but may have persuasive value. As pointed out by Holland & Webb, it is important to bear in mind that in light of the evolutionary nature of the common law, one man's *obiter dicta* today may become another's *ratio* tomorrow.[87]

Identification of the *ratio* – not rarely a painstaking and difficult task in itself – is naturally key, as it is largely determinative of how far a particular case may carry as a future authority in practice; the wider the principle or rule in a decision is couched, the more future cases to which it might apply. The narrower it is, the more likely a case will be deemed limited to its own facts. Further difficulties arise in the event that a judgment contains more than one identifiable *ratio* – such as for example in the event that the court has presented several, concurrent lines of reasoning in its decision, or where several appellate judges agree on the outcome but present different legal arguments as to why this should be so.[88] Unlike many continental legal traditions, there is no culture for single judgments under the English legal system.

Once the *ratio* has been identified, a case may be treated in several different ways. As mentioned above, it may be followed by any court, or it may be overruled by a higher or the same court. In many cases, however, a decision will be distinguished. Doing so simply means that the court will rely on significant differences in the material facts or the reasoning used in the two cases as a basis for not applying the earlier authority.[89] Where a case is distinguished, this should not automatically be viewed as a criticism of the earlier ruling itself, but merely as a statement of its perceived (ir)relevance to the present case. The skill involved in arguing that a particular case should or should not

86 The inevitable discussion as to whether judges therefore create law or merely provide evidence as to what the law is, and the constitutional sensibilities it provokes, is naturally too big to deal with here. For a brief introduction to the discussion, see e.g. William Twining and David Miers, *How To Do Things With Rules* (Butterworths 2009).

87 James Holland and Julian Webb, *Learning Legal Rules* (7th edn, Oxford University Press 2010) 193.

88 In the latter case, however, it is common practice for later courts seeking to rely on an authority to endeavour to establish which of the varying opinions presented is the proper *ratio*.

89 Holland and Webb (2010) (n 87) 198.

apply to a case proceeding before the courts goes to the very heart of the common law method, and good advocates will often be able to render the binding effect of precedent as more apparent than real in practice.

It is worth emphasising that the doctrine of precedent is said to deal only with propositions of law, and not fact. If it was concerned with fact, then as pointed out by Lord Denning, the judges would surely have been crushed under the weight of their own reports.[90] On the one hand, by sticking to points of law alone, a solid platform is provided for ensuring a higher degree of consistency and uniformity in decision-making by the courts, in turn thereby strengthening legal certainty and predictability – and hence, ultimately, the rule of law.[91] On the other hand, however, it is easy to forget just how vexing a question the distinction between law and fact may actually be in a given case – especially in cases where facts are disputed, where the court will hear evidence to determine their validity; or where the case concerns issues of mixed law and fact. The courts themselves are also sometimes at a loss in drawing a consistent line in practice.[92]

Although one of the benefits of the system of binding precedent lies in its innate flexibility, and its ability to adapt to changing times and attitudes in society, it is a very slow-paced creature on the whole. In order to change the law, a case must naturally first be brought before the courts raising the particular issue.[93] In this sense, there is seldom any sense of immediacy in the common law – and certainly not in the sense offered by legislative reform – the most common vehicle for reform today, which is deliberately engineered to bring about changes to the law. One of the rather odd side-effects of the doctrine of precedent is also that it has inevitable, retrospective legal effects; when a court declares what the law is in a given case, it is also saying what the law was back at the time when the facts giving rise to the case occurred – and hence as applicable to all similar factual situations arising from that point in time onwards.[94] In the US, a doctrine of prospective overruling – i.e. stating that what the law is will not apply to the present case, but will to all future cases – is sometimes applied to mitigate the retrospective effects of precedent. Although the issue has been touched upon several times by the English courts – including the House of Lords and the UKSC – there seems to be no basis for claiming general acceptance of this doctrine under the English common law system today.[95]

The foregoing leaves one important question unanswered, namely whether the courts are bound to follow *their own* previous decisions. As far as the House of Lords/UKSC is

90 *Qualcast (Wolverhampton) Ltd. v. Haynes* [1959] 2 All ER 38.

91 As we have implicitly seen in earlier sections, drawing this distinction between law and fact is also important in other connections, such as e.g. in distinguishing between the functions of judge and jury, and in establishing general rights of appeal.

92 See further e.g. Ian Mcleod, *Legal Method* (Palgrave Macmillan 2005) 33–40.

93 Once a case *is* brought for determination by a court, however, then naturally changes to the law may prove much quicker than the process of law reform by Parliament.

94 An effect which the European Court of Human Rights has held to be compatible with Article 7 of the European Convention on Human Rights – see *S.W. v UK App no 20166/92 (22 November 1995) and C.R. v UK App no 20190/92 (22 November 1995).*

95 See e.g. *National Westminster Bank plc v. Spectrum Plus ltd and others* [2005] UKHL 41; and *Ahmed v. H.M. Treasury (no 2)* [2010] UKSC 5.

concerned, it certainly felt historically bound to do so. Following the issuing of a Practice Statement in 1966 by the House of Lords, however, it was apparent that the attitude of the court had changed.[96] The Practice Statement made clear that the court would not henceforth consider itself automatically bound by its earlier decisions. It was stressed that the Practice Statement only applied to the House of Lords, that it would not take a decision to depart from (i.e. in reality, overrule) a previous decision lightly, and that it was intent on proceeding cautiously. This was not altogether surprising, however, in light of the potentially significant retrospective effects that a change of precedent by the highest court of appeal might have – especially on legal titles to land, contract issues and in criminal cases. There are nevertheless several instances where the House of Lords/ UKSC has chosen to overrule its own previous decisions under reference to the Practice Statement – in both civil and criminal cases.[97]

The Court of Appeal, and the High Court at least when acting in its appellate capacity, will generally feel obliged to follow its own previous decisions, subject to three exceptions.[98] Firstly, in cases where the court encounters two (or more) conflicting decisions of its own, in which case only one must be followed. Secondly, in cases where it is satisfied that one of its own decisions was reached *per incuriam* – according to which a particular case that would otherwise be considered as binding precedent is not applied, under reference to the fact that the court dealing with that case had overlooked some earlier binding decision(s) or statute which undoubtedly would have led it to another conclusion. In these circumstances, the court will be bound to follow the earliest binding decision.[99] Thirdly, the Court of Appeal will not feel obliged to follow one of its own previous decisions if the UKSC, whilst not overruling the Court of Appeal's decision, delivers a subsequent judgment in which it indirectly calls the Court of Appeal's previous decision into question in some way. The (admittedly rebuttable) presumption nevertheless remains that the higher courts of England & Wales will normally see themselves as bound by their own decisions, unless particularly good reasons are present to warrant overruling them.

---

96 *Practice Statement (Judicial Precedent)* [1966] 3 All ER 77.

97 See e.g. *British Railways Board v. Herrington* [1972] 1 All ER 749, where the House of Lords overruled its previous decision in *Addie (Robert) & Sons (Collieries) ltd. v. Dumbreck* [1929] AC 358, thus creating liability in tort for damage caused to trespassers, where previously there had been none. Further in *R. v. Shivpuri* [1986] 2 All ER 334, where the House of Lords overruled its previous decision in *Anderton v. Ryan* [1985] 2 All ER 355, to the effect that even if it may not be possible to commit the full criminal offence in question because the factual basis is not present (in this case believing that one is handling drugs, which turn out to be a harmless white powder), if the facts had been as the defendant believed them to be (i.e. that he was in fact handling drugs), he can be charged with attempting to commit the offence in question.

98 As set out in *Young v. Bristol Aeroplane Co. ltd.* [1944] 2 All ER 293, and *Police Authority for Huddersfield v. Watson* [1947] 1 KB 842.

99 An exception to this exception is nevertheless deemed to apply as far as lower courts are concerned, as they are barred from disapplying decisions of higher ranking courts under reference to the *per incuriam* rule – see e.g. the Court of Appeal's attempt to do so in *Broome v. Cassell & Co. ltd.* [1971] 2 All ER 187, [1971] 2 W.L.R. 853, and the (rather harsh) subsequent rebuke by the House of Lord's on appeal in the same case ([1972] 2 W.L.R. 645, [1972] 1 All ER 801).

3.2 Statute – Acts of Parliament

Classifying England as a common law disciple does not mean that all, or indeed even most, law is created by and through the courts. That would pay scant regard to the fundamental constitutional principle of parliamentary sovereignty under English law, and the vast amounts of legislation passed by it over the centuries. History has seen several significant bursts of legislative (i.e. statutory) creation: during the reign of Edward I (1272–1307), in reaction to the on-going power struggle between Crown and nobility,[100] during the Reformation period under Henry VIII (1509–1547), in light of the settlement that resulted in the founding of the Church of England, which required a significant remodelling of the administrative courts, including the Privy Council,[101] following the Restoration in 1660 (i.e. the period following England's relatively short venture into republican rule, which saw the restoration of Charles II as King),[102] and following the end of the Napoleonic wars at the turn of the 19th century, which saw sweeping legislative reforms in the spirit of Bentham's singular devotion to parliamentary faith.[103]

The fundamental importance of statute as a source of law in any common law system should not therefore be underestimated. Even more recent changes in society – such as for example the emergence of the welfare state following the Second World War, the introduction of the Internet to the general public in the 1990s, and the financial crises of the early 2000s, leading to the still ongoing austerity drive in the UK (i.e. seeking to radically decrease public expenditure) – have led to vast amounts of reactionary statutory reforms being introduced.[104] Many areas of the law – such as social security law – also owe their entire existence to statute. It would nevertheless be fallacious to assume on the basis of what has just been said that courts are therefore more likely to shirk their duties under the doctrine of binding precedent under reference to the separation of powers, and merely leave amendments to the law to Parliament. Indeed, one could never be certain that a current or future Parliament would ever choose to introduce the necessary changes at all.

In the early 1300s, legislation was produced solely on the basis of royal initiative. As we have seen, however, the Lords (i.e. nobility and the clergy) and the Commons (i.e. representatives of local society) eventually put paid to the theoretical consensual

100 The most notable pieces of legislation include e.g. the Statutes of Westminster (I and II), and the Bill of exceptions. For more, see e.g. Plucknett (1956) (n 14) 27–31.

101 Ibid 44–46.

102 Indeed, the infancy of modern contract law can be traced to the Statute of Frauds (1677), which introduced regulation of more trade and commerce matters by requiring more formal methods of proof through written agreements than had hitherto been the case; and the Habeas Corpus Act (1679), which grew from the common law writ of the same name, and even earlier on from the practice of Royal command by the King to one of his officials.

103 Jeremy Bentham, *The Principles of Morals and Legislation* (Clarendon Press 1789). It was at this time that e.g. the wager of law was finally abolished as a method of proof in legal proceedings (see Section 2 above).

104 Indeed, the structural reforms to the judicial system brought about by the many legislative acts adapting, furthering and amending the Constitutional Reform Act 2005 no doubt also find a certain resonance in calls for increased austerity – although one should perhaps also be wary of the many challenges this might pose to upholding the rule of law, not least through access to justice and the courts as one of its primary virtues.

basis of the King's rule, thus forcing their will to enjoy a much greater influence over matters of state and government in practice. Over the course of the 14th century, Parliamentary assent – first from the Lords, then from the Commons – became an essential part of the legislative process. During this time, the Commons also began to present petitions of their own, formulating bills which targeted local (more than personal) grievances to which the King might answer by way of legislation. Which is not to say that all legislative power was thereby heroically wrenched out of the hands of the monarch at this stage – on the contrary, the petitions made were very much at the discretion of the King to accept or reject, and would often lead to counter-petitions from the King to steer his own political will through Parliament. We nevertheless see here the first vestiges of the representative system which would eventually stand up to – and ultimately, for the short while of the interregnum period in the mid 1600s, depose – the Crown, many centuries later.

Today, Acts of Parliament create new law or change existing law.[105] There are no general codes, like those found in most countries with civil law systems. New statutes (i.e. Acts of Parliament) are passed following the introduction of a legislative proposal (a "bill") from either the Government or an individual Member of Parliament. The most common types are public bills, which essentially seek to change the law as it applies to the general population. Whilst public bills must usually be passed in the same parliamentary year in which they are introduced, private bills (i.e. bills seeking to change the law only as it applies to specific individuals) may be carried over from one parliamentary session to another. Bills may be introduced to either the House of Commons or the House of Lords first but must crucially go through both in order to pass into law.

The procedure follows a number of stages. Having read out the title of the bill to the first House dealing with it (a formality known as the first reading), it is at the next stage where the main purpose of the bill itself will first be discussed and voted on (the second reading). If the bill passes this stage, it is moved on to be considered by a Committee, where it will be subjected to more rigorous and detailed scrutiny. When the bill is returned from the Committee, with or without any amendments, the whole House reviews it, adding any further amendments it sees fit. The third reading consists of a usually rather short debate followed by a vote on the bill as a whole – amendments may not usually be made at this stage.[106] If the bill passes, it will then proceed to the other House, which will follow the same process, making suggested amendments along the way.

If both Houses are in agreement, the bill will be presented for Royal Assent – the final stage whereby the bill becomes an Act of Parliament, and hence part of UK law. If the Houses are not in agreement, however, the situation becomes slightly more complicated. In the event that it was the Commons that dealt with the bill first and the Lords, which

105 Although Parliament changed from handwriting to printing the original Acts of Parliament back in 1849, they are still printed on vellum to this very day. Thankfully, the UK Government's website https://www.legislation.gov.uk/ukpga also makes all current Acts of Parliament and Statutory Instruments electronically available to the public.

106 By way of caveat, amendments may be made in the Lords at this stage, but only if the amendments themselves concern matters not previously debated and/or voted on at an earlier stage.

subsequently refused to agree on the text twice running, the bill may still be passed for Royal Assent. In these situations (less than 10 in the past 100 years), and in tune with fundamental democratic principles, the Parliament Acts of 1911 and 1949 ensure that the elected House (i.e. the Commons) has the power to overrule the appointed House (i.e. the Lords).[107] The effect of the Acts was to allow the House of Lords to merely delay bills it did not like, not to veto them altogether.

In terms of pure numbers, it would seem as though there has been something of a downward trend over the last 30 to 40 years, with 25–40 Acts passed each year since 2005.[108] This development should nevertheless also be viewed in the light of the steadily increasing numbers of delegated acts which have been passed in recent years.

Unlike many other European legal systems, the fundamental principle of parliamentary sovereignty under English law reflects and explains the absence of a general constitutional review mechanism for challenging the substantive validity of Acts of Parliament.[109] Although this principle would seem to suggest that judges therefore simply interpret the law and do not create it, such an assertion could not be further from reality – in truth, English judges create much law through interpretation. Judges will naturally also continue to develop common law rules and principles through case law – at least until and unless statutes are introduced to subsume such rules. A very important qualification to the principle of parliamentary sovereignty was nevertheless introduced following the UK's admission to the EEC (now EU) in 1972; Acts of Parliament may be "disapplied" if they conflict with directly effective provisions of EU law. It is no understatement to claim that this caveat has fundamentally changed the nature of the relationship between Parliament and the courts in practice (see further on international and European law below). It is important to note, however, that the very power to set aside an Act of Parliament in this way is itself set out in an Act of Parliament, and may therefore simply be amended by a new statute to such effect.[110] Notwithstanding this fact, there would appear to be certain matters that Parliament cannot change through legislation. Many have argued that certain statutes (such as for example the European Communities Act 1972 – see section below) are "constitutional" in nature, and therefore exempt from the doctrine of implied repeal. This doctrine refers to the situation whereby an earlier statute, although not expressly repealed, is found inconsistent with a later statute, and hence regarded as impliedly repealed under reference to a presumption of legislative

107 The situation is naturally more straightforward in democratic terms where the bill was first introduced in the House of Lords, and the House of Commons later refused to agree on the text – in these cases, the Commons would in any event always enjoy the last word.

108 Richard Cracknell and Rob Clements, 'Acts and Statutory Instruments: the volume of UK legislation 1950 to 2014' in *House of Commons Library Standard Note* (SN/SG/2911 19 March 2014).

109 Discounting (theoretical) situations where the formalities of the legislative procedure have not been adhered to – in such cases, judicial review of the validity of the Act may well be readily available.

110 Section 2(4) of the European Communities Act 1972.

intent on the part of Parliament that the later Act was to prevail.[111] Furthermore, it seems widely accepted that Parliament cannot bind future parliaments by passing unrepealable statutory provisions; as a matter of law, the courts therefore recognise Parliament as "omnipotent in all save the power to destroy its own omnipotence".[112]

More recently, several former Law Lords and current UKSC Justices have suggested that since the principle of parliamentary sovereignty is a construct of the common law itself, it might be open to even further qualification by the courts that created it in the future. As stated (*obiter*) by Lord Hope in the *Hunting Act*-case: "It is not entirely unthinkable that a government which has that power may seek to use it to abolish judicial review or to diminish the role of the courts protecting the interests of the individual. (…) The rule of law requires that the judges must retain the power to insist that legislation of that extreme kind is not law which the courts will recognise".[113] Staunch opponents would probably consider such an event as tantamount to a *coup*. Yet the very suggestion that the courts in such highly unlikely circumstances could strike down legislation on such grounds emphasises the rather delicate current relationship and balance between the rule of law and the principle of parliamentary sovereignty in practice.

Law students in the UK are invariably introduced to four basic canons of statutory interpretation during their first year of studies: the literal rule (i.e. understanding based on the plain, literal meaning of the words used), the golden rule (according to which if the plain, literal meaning would lead to an absurdity or inconsistency, then a contextual approach may be applied which seeks out the meaning of the words in light of the statute as a whole), the mischief rule (according to which the words are to be interpreted in light of the genetic cause of the very "mischief", i.e. the defect, in the common law which the legislature had sought to remedy by enacting the statute in the first place, with a view to suppressing the mischief and advancing the remedy), and the purposive rule (whereby rules are to be construed in light of the objectives sought to be achieved by the statute or provision in question). Although they are still taught and talked about as "rules" today, it is important to remember that they are not rules in the sense of having some binding force – as Lord Reid put it, "[t]hey are our servants, not our masters. They are aids to construction: presumptions or pointers."[114] They are in any event all used with a view to giving effect to what the courts believe to have been the intention of Parliament, and the true meaning not of what it meant to say, but rather of what it actually said.

111 The UKSC acknowledged in the seminal *HS2*-case that we can differentiate between "constitutional legislation" and "ordinary legislation" under UK law, thus challenging the traditional view and core of the principle of parliamentary sovereignty that all statutes of Parliament are legal equals (*R (HS2 Action Alliance Ltd.) v. Secretary of State for Transport* [2014] UKSC 3, [2014] WLR 324). As pointed out e.g. by Elliott, this decision has certainly done much to allow us to reimagine the UK constitutional landscape, and the constitutional setting within which the principle of parliamentary sovereignty is situated today, see Mark Elliott, 'Constitutional Legislation, European Union Law and the Nature of the United Kingdom's Contemporary Constitution' (2014) Vol. 10 No. 3 *European Constitutional Law Review* 379.

112 As per Sir Robert Megarry in *Manuel v. Attorney General* [1982] All ER 822.

113 *R (Jackson) v. Attorney General* [2005] UKHL 56.

114 *Maunsell v. Olins* [1975] 1 All ER 16.

In situations where a text seems open to more than one interpretation, and no contrary intention has been expressly stated by Parliament, the courts often work with a vast number of common law presumptions of legislative intent in seeking out its meaning – such as the presumption of compliance with international law (i.e. that Parliament should be presumed to not wittingly legislate at odds with the UK's international obligations), the presumption against retrospectivity (i.e. that Parliament would not generally enact laws which had retroactive effect), the presumption against deprivation of liberty in times of peace, the presumption against conferment of powers to remove rights to property without compensation, the presumption that penal rules will be construed strictly, and many more.

Another way of seeking out legislative intent is by recourse to preparatory legislative acts. It is common to find UK courts referring to reports or working papers of various law reform bodies, such as for example the Law Commission. Political documents such as White Papers have on rare occasions also been relied upon as interpretative tools, although the legitimacy of this approach has been questioned. Readers may therefore be surprised to find that the English courts– and notwithstanding the principle of parliamentary sovereignty – for a long time were prohibited from relying directly on statements made in Parliamentary debates as recorded in Hansard when interpreting statutes.[115] What better way to give effect to parliamentary intent than to spy and apply the very words of Parliament itself? The courts had nevertheless previously eschewed such an (essentially purposive) approach to statutory interpretation. This was to change, however, following the House of Lords' majority decision in *Pepper v. Hart*, in 1992.[116] The Court held here that in cases where legislation is ambiguous or obscure, or might lead to an absurdity, and the material to be relied upon consists of statements made by one of the promoters of the bill or a Minister, and those statements were clear, then reference to parliamentary materials set out in Hansard would be allowed. In spite of advocating caution in the use of Hansard, what was supposed to be an exceptional method of interpretation quickly appeared to become the norm. The danger in allowing the use of Hansard in all but the rarest of cases lay naturally in the fact that this might open any and all long-established rules or norms based on other methods of interpretation for re-examination through this new, purposive lens. In response, the House of Lords therefore added another condition to the test – that the statement relied upon must be "directed to the very point in question in the litigation".[117] A Practice Direction related to the use of Hansard was also introduced in 1995, and further consolidated over the years.[118] And in spite of the introduction of the Human Rights Act in 1998, which put added pressure on the courts to look to Hansard when evaluating potential incompat-

115 *De bene esse* arguments (whereby a judge allows a point to be argued in court "for what it's worth", yet without ruling on whether its weight or relevance will be accepted) might nevertheless naturally allow Hansard in through the backdoor, and there would in any event have been little stopping judges from actually looking into Hansard on their own time if they really wanted to.

116 *Pepper (Inspector of Taxes) v. Hart* [1992] 3 WLR 1032; [1993] 1 All ER 42.

117 *Melluish (Inspector of Taxes) v. BMI (N 3)* [1996] AC 454.

118 "Supreme Court Practice Direction (Hansard: Citation)" [1995] 1 WLR 192.

ibilities between UK law and obligations under the European Convention on Human Rights (ECHR), the picture in the last 20 years or so seems to be largely one of orderly retreat from over-use (or abuse) of Hansard in statutory interpretation.

3.3 Statutory Instruments – Delegated legislation

The practice of delegating statutory authority to governmental, local and other administrative bodies is widely used under the English legal system today, its beginnings traceable back to the middle-ages.[119] The power to issue delegated (or secondary) legislation usually stems from an existing Act of Parliament – also called a "parent Act". The scope of the measures which may be adopted will usually be set out in the parent Act itself, and may range from the purely technical, such as altering the level of a fine, to more detailed substantive rules. Whilst the main bulk of delegated legislation takes the form of Statutory Instruments, other measures are also sometimes used – such as for example Rules, Codes of Practice or byelaws.

The obvious advantages of using delegated legislation, which are no doubt common to all systems allowing such measures, lie in the speed and ease of passing them; Government can further implement and/or make changes to a law without having to push a completely new Act through Parliament. They are particularly helpful where swift responses are needed to meet emergency situations, such as pandemic outbreaks or imminent threats to national security. Yet the advantages must also be weighed against the possibility of abuse, for which judicial review before the courts will generally be available to challenge and potentially strike them down – typically based on *ultra vires* claims (i.e. that the adoption of the delegated legislation lay beyond the competence of those adopting it).

The House of Lords also plays a crucial role in supervising the use of delegated statutory authority. The Delegated Powers Scrutiny Committee (established in 1992) keeps under constant review the extent to which legislative powers are delegated by Parliament to the Government and examines all Bills with delegating powers which allow Statutory Instruments to be made. The Lords Secondary Legislation Scrutiny Committee further considers every negative and affirmative Statutory Instrument that a parent Act states must be laid before Parliament (approximately one thousand each year), with a view to determining whether the special attention of the House should be drawn to them. The flipside to this means in turn that 2/3 of the approximately 3,000 Statutory Instruments issued each year are not actively considered by Parliament at all, and simply enter into force on a specified date in the future.

119 Particularly noteworthy is the Statute of Proclamations of 1539, passed during the reign of Henry VIII, which formally provided the King and his Council with the prerogative (i.e. power) to issue proclamations having the force of acts of Parliament in cases of emergency – a power which appears to have been used moderately, however, and with little attempt to usurp the legitimate law-making powers of Parliament as such.

4. International and European law

The relationship between UK law and international law cannot be aptly described as either dualist or monist, since it clearly encompasses elements of both. It is dualist in the sense that treaties must be transformed into (i.e. made part of) UK law. Yet it also appears partially monist as regards reception of most rules of customary international law. This follows from the doctrine of incorporation, according to which international customary rules, once recognised as such, will automatically become a part of the English legal system and applied by the courts without an Act of Parliament.

The common law doctrine of incorporation can be traced back almost 300 years, and in spite of a few attempts to abandon it, is still considered to reflect the legal situation as it stands today.[120] It does not apply without certain qualifications, however, the most important of which is that a given rule of international customary law will not apply automatically where it contravenes an Act of Parliament. In the event of an irreconcilable conflict between an English statute and customary international law, or an international treaty for that matter, the principle of parliamentary sovereignty dictates that the statute will prevail. This is nevertheless mitigated in many cases by application of the presumption of compliance with international law (mentioned above), according to which courts – building on the presumed legislative intent of Parliament – will attempt to interpret statutes so as not to conflict with international law obligations.[121] Furthermore, at common law, the general rule is that customary international law cannot be incorporated if it would conflict with a decision of a higher court, as to do so would be in breach of the doctrine of *stare decisis* (explained in section above).[122] Significant exceptions are nevertheless made in situations where the previous decision of a higher court is rendered redundant thanks to more recent international law developments. Speaking in a case before the Court of Appeal, Lord Denning famously summed up the position: "If [the Court of Appeal] today is satisfied that the rule of international law on a subject has changed from what it was 50 or 60 years ago, it can give effect to that change – and apply the change in our English law – without waiting for the House of Lords [today the UKSC] to do it."[123]

One final qualification concerns crimes recognised in customary international law – although these may also be incorporated into UK law, they will not do so automatically, and will usually require transformation.[124]

As far as the relationship between UK and European law is concerned, the outcome of the Brexit referendum of 23 June 2016 – where 51.9 % voted in favour of leaving the EU – has understandably cast a long and murky shadow over the situation. There has also been serious talk in recent years of the UK withdrawing from the European Convention on Human Rights (ECHR), with former Prime Minister Theresa May

---

120 See e.g. *Playa Larga (Owners of Cargo Lately Laden on Board) v. I Congreso del Partido (Owners)* [1983] 1 AC 244.

121 This is sometimes referred to as "consistent" or "harmonious" interpretation in practice.

122 *Chung Chi Cheung v. The King* (1939) AC 160.

123 *Trendtex Trading Corporation v. Central Bank of Nigeria* [1977] 1 QB 529.

124 *R. v. Jones* (2006) UKHL 16.

advocating the (alleged) benefits of doing so on many occasions in the press.[125] At the time of writing, many questions remain unanswered as to exactly how the country will move forward, and just what the political and legal consequences of any such moves might truly be. Leaving the vagaries of future events to one side for now, there can in any event be no doubt as to the massive impact that European law has had on UK law since the country became party to the ECHR (in 1951) and joined the EU (in 1973).

The UK became a signatory to the ECHR in 1950, and Parliament ratified the Convention in 1951. Whilst individual petitions by British nationals to the European Court of Human Rights in Strasbourg (ECtHR) were finally allowed in the 1960s, this only applied in cases where all domestic remedies had been exhausted first – a costly and time-consuming affair. The true catalyst for "bringing rights home" was therefore the passing of the Human Rights Act in 1998, which allowed rights under the ECHR to be enforced directly in UK courts. The Act charges all national courts to interpret UK legislation so far as possible consistently with the rights laid down in the ECHR.[126] In doing so, they must take into account any case law of the ECtHR relevant to the case at hand, and also certain statements and decisions of the Commission and the Committee of Ministers.[127]

At first glance, Section 3 of the Human Rights Act would only seem to reflect what national courts were already required to do according to the principle of presumption of compliance with international law. Yet the manner in which this particular duty of consistent interpretation with ECHR law has been interpreted and developed by the courts has come to have a much more profound impact on traditional methods of statutory interpretation. As stated by the House of Lords in the seminal *Ghaidan* case, the obligation to interpret national law in line with the ECHR is particularly broad and far-reaching.[128] It went further than standard rules on statutory interpretation in many different ways: it did not require any ambiguity in the wording of the statute, it permitted departures from the strict and literal application of the words chosen by Parliament, it permitted the implication of words necessary to comply with the ECHR, and the precise form of words implied did not matter, either. Although limitations as to what might be deemed possible have also been identified by the courts, these are largely limited to either express statements by Parliament to such effect, which is an exceptionally rare occurrence, or where the interpretation in question would go against the "grain" or "thrust" of the legislation in question, thus giving courts an exceptionally

125 See e.g. Anuska Asthana and Rowena Mason, 'UK must leave European convention on human rights, says Theresa May' *The Guardian*, 25 April 2016, available at https://www.theguardian.com/politics/2016/apr/25/uk-must-leave-european-convention-on-human-rights-theresa-may-eu-referendum accessed 14 April 2020. Before taking office, the present Prime Minister, Boris Johnson, has nevertheless advocated in favour of remaining party to the ECHR.

126 Section 3 of the Human Rights Act 1998.

127 Section 2 of the Human Rights Act 1998.

128 *Ghaidan v. Godin-Mendoza* [2004] UKHL 30; [2004] 2 AC 557.

broad discretion.[129] Essentially, the broad construction by the English courts of this duty has rendered the possibility of not arriving at a consistent interpretation more illusory than real in practice.

Whether or not Section 3 of the Human Rights Act should ultimately be seen as extending the purposive rule or as adding a novel canon of statutory interpretation altogether, is of course open to debate. In any event, in situations where the court does not deem it possible to provide a harmonious interpretation, it may instead issue a so-called "declaration of incompatibility". It is important to note that such declarations do not invalidate the statute – that would amount to an effective usurpation of legislative authority, contrary to the fundamental principle of Parliamentary sovereignty. The practical consequence of such a declaration is to trigger a special fast-track statutory amendment procedure, leaving Parliament to remedy the wrong for the future.

The impact of the ECHR on English law can also be felt in many other ways, for example concerning reception of the principle of proportionality. The way this test appears to be applied by the ECtHR in its decisions would seem to require a more rigorous scrutiny of governmental action than traditionally required at common law when undertaking judicial review of public decisions – i.e. the so-called Wednesbury (un)reasonableness test.[130]

The Human Rights Act has been the subject of a great deal of praise and criticism since its entry into force in 2000. Some would argue that it served as a step up in terms of fundamental rights protection in the UK. Others would contend that it has merely served to subordinate the cardinal rule by which all judges decide cases – namely fairness, or equity – to that of overriding human rights standards, no matter how bizarre the results might be in certain cases. It is not my intention to weigh up the merits of either political view here in this chapter. From a legal point of view, however, it is important to stress that in the event that the Human Rights Act were to be repealed, the UK would still be a party to the ECHR. And in the event that the UK were to withdraw from the ECHR, this would probably not leave much by way of lacunae in fundamental rights protection in Britain either; whilst the adoption of a new British Bill of Rights might potentially fill such a void, there has also been a recent resurgence of reliance by UK

129 "An interpretation should not be adopted which is inconsistent with a fundamental or cardinal feature of the legislation since this would cross the boundary between interpretation and amendment." *Vodafone 2 v. Revenue and Customs Commissioners* [2009] EWCA Civ 446, with further reference to Lord Nicholls in *Ghadain*.

130 Wednesbury unreasonableness is a judge-made standard of reasonableness/rationality used by the courts when reviewing public decisions, according to which decisions that no reasonable person acting reasonably could have made will be quashed (*Associated Provincial Picture Houses Ltd. v. Wednesbury Corporation* (1948) 1 KB 223).

courts on human rights identifiable under the common law.[131] Regardless of the manner by which it is to be achieved, the overriding aim of this decidedly isolationist approach is still the same: attempting to bring legal developments in the field back under British sovereignty and control for the future.

The same objective applies with regards to the EU, at least as far as the champions of Brexit are concerned. Yet the obligations flowing from EU membership are much more invasive to the UK legal system than those stemming from the ECHR. Several fundamental EU principles – such as for example primacy and direct effect, and the direct applicability of EU regulations in the UK without further implementing measures – run entirely counter to the constitutional principle of parliamentary sovereignty. The entry and reception of EU law into UK law therefore had to be dealt with in a rather particular way, and differently to the way in which the ECHR was treated.

The statutory basis for giving effect to the EU Treaties in the UK is found in the European Communities Act 1972 (EC Act 1972), Section 2(1) of which states that:

> "All such rights, powers, liabilities, obligations and restrictions from time to time created or arising by or under the Treaties, and all such remedies and procedures from time to time provided for by or under the Treaties, as in accordance with the Treaties are without further enactment to be given legal effect or used in the United Kingdom shall be recognised and available in law, and be enforced, allowed and followed accordingly; and the expression "enforceable EU right" and similar expressions shall be read as referring to one to which this subsection applies."

Although the doctrine of direct effect was thus formally made part of UK law, it would take almost 20 years for its practical consequences to be fully felt: in the *Factortame* case, the House of Lords confirmed that in cases where there is a conflict between directly effective EU law and UK law, the former must prevail – regardless of the source of the UK law in question, and notwithstanding the principle of parliamentary sovereignty.[132] The decision was extremely significant in constitutional terms, since English courts had traditionally considered themselves unable to set aside or disapply Acts of Parliament under reference to obligations under international/European law. According to the Lords, the very primacy of EU law rested on a voluntary limitation of Parliament's sovereignty flowing from the EC Act 1972. The importance in emphasising this fact

131 In a series of judgments in the past few years, the UKSC has placed renewed emphasis upon the common law as a source of fundamental, constitutional rights – see e.g. *Osborn v. Parole Board* [2013] UKSC 61, [2014] AC 1115; *Kennedy v. Charity Commission* [2014] UKSC 20, [2014] 2 WLR 808; A v. BBC [2014] UKSC 25, [2014] 2 WLR 1243; and *R. (Evans) v. Attorney General* [2015] UKSC 21. Supreme Court Justice Lady Hale has suggested in the light of these cases that "there is emerging a renewed emphasis on the common law and distinctively UK constitutional principles as a source of legal inspiration", see Lady Hale, 'UK Constitutionalism on the March?', Constitutional and Administrative Law Bar Association Conference, 12 July 2014, available at https://www.supremecourt.uk/docs/speech-140712.pdf accessed 14 April 2020. For more on these developments, see e.g. Richard Clayton, 'The Empire Strikes Back: common law rights and the Human Rights Act' (2015) 1 *Public Law* 3.

132 *R. v. Secretary of State for Transport ex parte Factortame (N 2)* [1991] 1 AC 603; [1991] 1 All ER 70.

should not be underestimated, as it ultimately means that primacy of EU law is contingent upon continued acceptance and legitimation by Parliament; i.e. it rests on a domestic legal basis. This allowed primacy to be more easily squared away with the principle of parliamentary sovereignty, since primacy owes its recognition to and may ultimately be retracted by Parliament. As also mentioned previously, recent decisions of the UKSC have confirmed that the EC Act is to be considered a constitutional statute, meaning that it may not be impliedly – but only expressly – repealed by another, newer Act of Parliament.[133]

Reception of the EU principle of consistent interpretation has also had a significant impact on methods of statutory interpretation under English law. Section 2(4) of the EC Act – as read in context with Section 2(1) – provides the basis of the English courts' mandate to interpret national law consistently with EU law obligations: "(…) any such provision (of any such extent) as might be made by Act of Parliament, and any enactment passed or to be passed, other than one contained in this part of this Act, shall be construed and have effect subject to the foregoing provisions of this section (…)."

Whilst for many years English courts had interpreted this provision rather narrowly (i.e. similarly to application of the presumption of compliance with international law obligations), it has adopted a much broader understanding of the duty in more recent years. Much of this is owed to considerable developments of the underlying EU principle by the Court of Justice of the European Union in Luxembourg (CJEU), due regard to which is to be paid by UK courts according to Section 3 of the EC Act.[134] For example, whilst English courts had previously limited themselves to interpreting domestic statutes introduced specifically in order to transform EU law into UK law in this way,[135] later decisions of the CJEU also required statutes which pre-dated the EU law in question – and hence were not specifically designed to implement the latter – to be subjected, as far as possible, to consistent interpretations.[136] English courts have therefore subsequently changed their approach.[137]

More recent developments have also seen a remarkable cross-fertilisation between application of Section 3 of the Human Rights Act and application of the duty to perform interpretations consistent with EU law. Interestingly, whilst Section 3 of the Human Rights Act had initially been drafted based on the CJEU's understanding of the duty as it applied under EU law(!), the UKSC's broad interpretation of this provision in cases such as *Ghaidan* would in turn come to significantly influence application of the EU principle of consistent interpretation in practice. Today, the approach of UK courts to interpreting English law consistently with ECHR and EU obligations has therefore been

---

133 See e.g. the UKSC's decision in the *HS2*-case, discussed above.

134 Section 3 provides that: "For the purposes of all legal proceedings any question as to the meaning or effect of any of the Treaties, or as to the validity, meaning or effect of any [EU instrument], shall be treated as a question of law (and, if not referred to the European Court, be for determination as such in accordance with the principles laid down by and any relevant [decision of the European Court])."

135 See e.g. *Duke v. GEC Reliance Ltd.* [1988] AC 618.

136 See e.g. Case C-106/89 *Marleasing SA v. La Comercial Internacional de Alimentacion SA* [1990] ECR I–4135.

137 See e.g. *Pickstone v. Freemans plc.* [1988] 2 All ER 803, [1989] AC 66; and *Litster v. Forth Dry Dock and Engineering Co. Ltd.* [1989] 1 All ER 1134, [1990] AC 546.

largely assimilated. As mentioned previously, this means that courts will be allowed to depart from the strict and literal understanding of a statute, and effectively rewrite its provisions (i.e. implying words which are not there) so as to achieve a result compliant with EU obligations, as long as Parliament has not expressly forbidden this, or to do so would go "against the grain" of the legislation.[138]

From what has been seen above, in light of the reception of EU law into the English legal system, it would be difficult to say that the principle of parliamentary sovereignty has not been modified. It has clearly been watered down somewhat, at least and until such time as Parliament chooses to expressly repeal the constitutional statute (i.e. the EC Act) upon which the relationship hitherto has been based.

5. Ideal(s) of Justice – the rise of equity

Attempting to provide a picture of the notion or ideal of justice in a given legal system is an almost impossible task, as there are probably as many views on the matter as there are lawyers, if not to say people, in the world. The undertaking is made all the more difficult in light of the fact that our views on justice are more than likely to have evolved and developed significantly over time. The development of the law, and any ideal(s) of justice that it might be said to embody, is naturally closely linked to the development of society more generally. And as society changes, so our views of what might be considered just or unjust may well shift accordingly.[139]

There are naturally many different ways by which one might seek to illustrate how ideals or notions of justice have been incorporated into the English legal system. For example, one could look to the quintessential role played by procedural rules as vehicles for justice in England. The main and overriding principle in the Civil Procedure Rules (CPR), is that cases are to be dealt with justly (see Rule 1.1). This in turn reflects the fundamental notion that the primary purpose of the civil courts is to determine cases based on their merits, and not to cause injustices through procedural defaults. For example, CPR Rule 3.10 therefore provides that errors of procedure, such as a failure to comply

138 See e.g. *Jessemy v. Rowstock Ltd.* [2014] 3 CMLR 24; and *Vodafone 2 v. Revenue and Customs Commissioners* [2009] EWCA Civ 446.

139 Indeed, the axiom of medieval justice seemed to be "to each his own" (Plucknett (1956) (n 14) 31), and largely the product of the views of the Regent – by virtue of the divine right of the sovereign, and the centralization of the judiciary under his direct control. Yet these views naturally came to change as society developed. If the interregnum period between 1649–1660 without a King or Queen and the many experiments on various forms of government proposed during this time was to teach the English one thing, it was that the power to determine government ultimately lay in the hands of its people. And from this realization poured forth many new political theories of government, advocating many different forms of justice still taught today – such as those of Hobbes (advocating the virtue of the social contract between men, whereby justice is derived from the mutual agreement of everyone concerned), and Locke (who promulgated the virtues of justice as a part of natural law, according to which certain consequences will naturally derive from any given action). The changing ideals or notions of justice borne out of the English civil war are further reflected in the Act of Settlement of 1701, which finally cemented the complete independence of the lower rungs of the English judiciary, providing for the removal of judges from their posts only by decree of both Houses of Parliaments (i.e. the Commons and the Lords).

with a rule or practice direction. will not automatically invalidate steps already taken in the proceedings but will leave to the court to determine whether the error may be remedied or not. According to the CPR, dealing with cases justly includes (but is certainly not limited to) ensuring that the parties are on an equal footing, saving expense, dealing with cases in a proportionate manner according to the importance and complexity of the case and the financial position of each party, and ensuring that the case is dealt with expeditiously and fairly, particularly by actively managing the cases before them. Not only the courts but also the parties to the case are placed under an obligation to help ensure that the overriding objective is achieved, particularly by cooperating with each other in the conduct of proceedings (CPR Rule 1.3). Courts can also ensure that justice is done between the parties to a particular case by exercising their inherent jurisdiction to fill lacunae in the SCA 1981 and/or CPR, where the situation in question is not dealt with expressly in these instruments. Looking at the criminal procedural rules, as already noted above, a defendant prosecuted for a triable either-way offence may choose whether his case is to be heard before the Magistrates' or Crown Court. This very possibility again demonstrates how closely linked procedural rights are to notions of justice, and how integral such rights are perceived in the English legal system.[140]

Another example is the English system of judicial review, which provides an outlet for challenges against the exercise of state authority and judicial decisions. A highly developed system of internal control amongst the courts is important to English notions of justice, and especially so in a common law system, which naturally depends on the legitimacy of and faith in the courts for its existence. Under the system of judicial review for judicial decisions, the High Court controls activities of the lower courts in all matters not relating to trial on indictment. The High Court exercises its control by the use of so-called prerogative orders – *certiorari* (ordering a lower court to pass a pending dispute up to it), *mandamus* (compelling a lower court to act in cases where it should, but for some reason has not) and prohibition (requiring a lower court to stop acting in excess of its powers). *Certiorari* quashes the decision of the lower court(s) and will be issued for errors on the face of the record, certain acts made in breach of jurisdiction and for breaches of the rules of natural justice. As far as the latter is concerned, and deeply entrenched in the English legal system's soul, the Court is under a prevailing duty to act fairly. This means *inter alia* that judges must not decide cases that they have an interest in themselves, that they must hear both sides of any case, and that they must give reasons for their decisions.

We have also touched upon some very important examples of how ideals or notions of justice have been incorporated into the English legal system in the foregoing – such as trial by jury, often viewed as one of the keystones of English democracy and the

140 Procedural rights under English law have also had a marked influence on the development of procedural rights in other common law jurisdictions, and in the EU legal system – see e.g. Christian N.K. Franklin, 'The melting pot or the salad bowl revisited (again) – The meeting of legal cultures at the European Court of Justice' in Jørn Øyrehagen Sunde and Knut Einar Skodvin (eds), *Rendezvous of European Legal Cultures* (Fagbokforlaget 2010).

rule of law, and "the lamp which shows that freedom lives";[141] and the recent reforms introduced by the Constitutional Reform Act of 2005, which might be seen to serve as a catalyst for strengthening the rule of law, and hence justice, by securing the independence of the highest court in the United Kingdom through the creation of the UKSC (described above). Another example touched upon previously concerns the UKSC's ability to depart from its own previous decisions in order to do justice to particular cases, even if at the cost of legal certainty (Section 3 above).

To attempt to map out and exemplify the development of all of these, and other various notions or ideals of justice in England over the ages in more detail, would simply not be feasible in such a short chapter. In the following, we shall therefore limit ourselves to one of the select developments which has come to leave indelible marks on the English legal system and its ideals of justice – namely the rise of equity as a distinct branch of the law that evolved to mitigate the severity of the common law system.

The development of Chancery's equitable jurisdiction during the middle-ages in England is often viewed as a result of the transfer of decisions from God (i.e. the King, as sovereign by divine right) to man (i.e. the Lord Chancellor, as head of the Chancery).[142] Although the precise reason behind this jurisdictional shift is subject to a certain amount of conjecture, it is evident nonetheless from court records of the time. The rise of equity is probably largely unsurprising to all familiar with the age-old debate on the relationship between law and morals. Indeed, given the strong(er) societal ties between the church and the people of medieval England, when issues of conscience (arguably) played a more prevalent part in peoples' day-to-day lives than today, the rise of equity as a parallel system of law next to the common law seems all the more understandable. But we

141 Lord Patrick Devlin, *Trial by Jury* (Stevens & Sons 1956). It had not always been so, however: As jury trial quickly became the norm in the 1300s, it also came to be manipulated in many instances through bribery, stacking and intimidation. It is therefore not so difficult to imagine distrust of the juries being an important factor in the early popularity of equity courts (Plucknett (1956) (n 14) 178). Plucknett maintains further that the development of trial by jury can be seen as a reaction to (or dissatisfaction with) existing methods of proof; the obvious inclination being that any person presenting their own witnesses to swear as to their words and actions would more often than not be biased in their views. The juries themselves suffered under similar (and often decidedly warranted) accusations of bias in ancient times. Jurors were selected from the representatives of the vills and Hundreds presenting defendants to the itinerant Justices in Eyre. The very act of presentment of course entailed an accusation in itself – that the defendant had committed a wrongdoing. And as members of the presenting parties eventually came to be asked to determine matters of guilt as well, it was not that difficult to predict the likely outcome of their verdict – at least in those cases where they had presented the defendant to whom they were now to judge. The odds became even more firmly stacked against the accused over the course of the 1300s, as indictors risked being chucked in prison in the event of a subsequent acquittal. It was not until 1352 that a statute was finally introduced which allowed defendants to challenge jurors on the grounds of bias for also being part of the presenting party, and thus ensure some base modicum of justice in criminal proceedings (see 25 Edward III, stat. 5, c. 3). Over the course of the following century, it became possible to challenge the decision of juries in certain (and eventually all) civil trials for "attaint" – essentially a form of appeal to a new jury of 24 charged not only with rehearing the case but also with the issue of whether the initial jury had perjured itself. In criminal proceedings, the final act of ensuring a jury's impartiality was to arrive as late as in 1856, when an Act of Parliament was passed ensuring removal of certain cases from local jurisdictions to the Central Criminal Court in cases where bias might be feared (19 Vict., c. 16).

142 Milsom (1981) (n 11) 5.

shall also see that certain practical, institutional reasons no doubt played their part in its historical development as well.

It is worth noting from the very outset that equity itself can mean different things. The literal meaning is that which is fair or just, and it was certainly this meaning which the law of equity took in the beginning. In medieval times, the centralized courts in Westminster had initially enjoyed a great deal of discretion – particularly concerning what we today would term procedural matters – thus allowing them ample room to develop and adapt the common law to new situations. However, as the various forms of action and writs started to settle in the Common Bench, and gradually also in the King's Bench, the picture began to change. The Statute of Northampton (1328) for example significantly curbed the discretion of the courts, by obliging them to ignore royal commands that might disturb the course of the common law.[143] From the mid-1300s, one can therefore see signs of the central courts exercising remarkable judicial restraint – interpreting statutes more rigidly, and declining to deviate from age-old customs. This reining in of the courts was perhaps unsurprising and was no doubt illustrative of the growing power struggle between the Crown and nobility more generally; the Westminster courts were largely regarded as being the King's courts. The centralisation of judicial power had led to a reduction of local jurisdictions, which in turn meant diverting proceeds from forfeitures and fines from the nobility to the Crown. This might go some way at least in explaining the demands of the nobility in forbidding the creation of novel writs without the consent of Parliament, to which the Common Bench vigorously adhered over the course of the 14th century.

With significantly reduced chances of having new forms of action accepted, petitioners started to increasingly seek out justice from other sources, notably the King himself. The task of dealing with them was first delegated to the King's Council proper – i.e. the body of royal advisers from which the King's Bench first had sprung under the reign of Edward I (1272–1307) – and to Parliament. In this capacity, both of these bodies therefore appeared to wield an ample source of equitable and discretionary power. As the justice dispensed in equity outside the centralised courts continued to grow, however, the petitions eventually became too numerous to handle. Petitions made to the King's Council were therefore further delegated to Chancery.[144] As the sole and ultimate arbiter of all matters dealt with by Chancery, so the rise of the Lord Chancellor's discretionary, equitable jurisdiction – essentially allowing for relief in cases where the common law remained inflexible, or unable to provide a remedy – therefore seemed inevitable. And his jurisdiction in equity was clearly personal in the sense that it was not subject to precedent (i.e. how similar cases had previously been decided), but merely to his own

143 Plucknett (1956) (n 14) 158.

144 It is important to note, however, that Chancery's equitable jurisdiction was by no means made exclusive at this stage. A number of other courts, such as e.g. the Court of Exchequer, and the Councils of Wales and the North (the bodies set up to govern these troubled areas during the 1300–1400s), also exercised a considerable degree of equitable jurisdiction. Although the historical beginnings seem rather murky, it seems apparent from the rolls that the Exchequer also came to exercise a significant equitable jurisdiction in its own right, lasting from the early 1400s and all the way down to 1842, at which point its jurisdiction was transferred in its entirety to the Chancery.

whim. The very basis of equitable intervention was therefore that it was necessary on grounds of conscience. It became a common adage therefore to presume that equity – and hence justice – would and could often vary from one case and/or Chancellor to the next, according to the size of the incumbent Lord Chancellor's foot.[145]

In medieval England, the principal source of wealth and power was agriculture. The protection of rights connected to the ownership and use of land was therefore the paramount consideration in the development of the law and remained so for many centuries. Claims in equity largely concerned property rights, particularly the enforcement of the use of land. This led to the rather remarkable establishment of a novel, separate category of equitable property rights, which is probably best explained by way of example: if A was given land subject to an undertaking to hold it for the use and benefit of B – and there could be any number of practical reasons for doing so – the beneficial interest in the land belonging to B was called a "use" (the forerunner of the modern "trust").[146] Recognition of rights connected to the use (or trust) by the Lord Chancellor rendered B the owner in equity, in spite of the legal title belonging to A, which made A the owner in (common) law. New types of interest in land were thereby being created in equity, which were not possible under the common law.

The very fact that the trustee is considered the owner at law, whilst the beneficiary is the owner in equity, is one of the main oddities of ownership under the English law of trusts, which has survived to our very day. Concerning the nature of the equitable interest, in contrast to Roman law which classifies rights as either *in personam* (i.e. as being directed against the person) or *in rem* (i.e. as being directed against property), the beneficiary's right under English law is probably best understood as rooted in both. On the one hand, the beneficiary's remedy is clearly directed against the person of the trustee. The equitable remedies of specific performance – ordering the defendant to do a particular thing – and injunction – ordering the defendant to refrain from doing something – are decrees *in personam*, with any failure to adhere to them liable to lead to imprisonment or fines for contempt.[147] On the other hand, however, the beneficiary is also considered the owner of the equitable interest – which can be bought, sold, mortgaged etc. – and ownership is a right *in rem*. Determining the nature of the equitable interest is naturally important in the many situations where a trustee, as owner of the legal estate, sells land to which equitable interests are attached. The principle opted for in practice is that the

145 Edward Arber (ed), *John Selden – Table Talk 1689 – Reprint* (Alex. Murray & Sons 1868) 46.

146 The trust is a form of property holding under English law whereby the legal estate lies with the trustee and the equitable (i.e. beneficial) ownership is kept separate. The formation of trusts thus allows elaborate and complicated systems of beneficial interests to be created without complicating the legal title to a thing. Although it would naturally have been possible to achieve the same result using other mechanisms, the trust mechanism is viewed as a convenient (and today, pretty much the only) way of effecting complicated forms of property settlement under English law. Use of the trust has spread to other common law jurisdictions around the world, and guidelines for their recognition in other (i.e. civil) jurisdictions may be found in the suitably titled 1984 Hague Convention on the Law Applicable to Trusts and their Recognition.

147 The problems involved in securing that a defendant present himself to Chancery without the power of a common law writ also required new procedures to be established – notably the *subpoena*, requiring attendance on pain of a fine for contempt.

beneficiary's interest will be effective against everyone, except a *bona fide* purchaser of the land for valuable consideration (i.e. money or equivalent) who has no actual or constructive notice (i.e. information, or knowledge), of the equitable interest.[148]

Although the Lord Chancellor's equitable jurisdiction served to supplement rather than directly interfere with common law property rights, it did naturally encroach on the turf of the common law courts. Challenges to Chancery's equitable jurisdiction were therefore rather commonplace over the centuries, particularly during the troubled times leading up to the English civil war at the beginning of the 17th century.[149] The reason for this was mainly political rather than legal (i.e. jurisdictional). Chancery was a court dependent on the King's personal prerogative. There are numerous examples of the King both attending and presiding over proceedings before it, and also of determining jurisdictional disputes between Chancery and the other centralised courts in its favour.[150] Pro-royalists argued in favour of keeping Chancery, whilst their opponents argued in favour of its abolition. Yet getting rid of the court would probably have caused more harm than good at this stage. Successive Chancellors from the mid 1670s up to the late 1820s had in fact done much to transform equity from a jurisdiction based on personal conviction and conscience into a more predictable system of established rules and principles.[151] Equitable relief was also proving increasingly desirable and necessary in practice. The expansion of industry and the British Empire during the 18th and 19th centuries was presenting a host of entirely new societal needs, which could only be met effectively by the malleable trust mechanism; ultimately, Chancery was therefore to prevail.

By the mid-1850s, however, and in spite of steadily increasing the number of its judges from one to seven, the workload in Chancery had simply become too great to handle. The creation of the Supreme Court of Judicature by the Judicature Acts of 1873 and 1875 (see sections above) therefore finally vested in all branches of the High Court, the Court of Appeal, and the House of Lords jurisdiction both in equity and common law, allowing any point of law or equity to be dealt with in any of these courts.[152] In the event that common law and equity might lead to different results in a given case, it was decided that equity would always prevail.[153] The situation is different regarding conflicts

148 For more details, see e.g. Jill E. Martin, *Hanbury & Martin – Modern Equity* (15th edn, Sweet & Maxwell 1997) 32–38.

149 Attempts to curb the King's Council's equitable jurisdiction had for example been made by several Parliaments during the course of the 1300s.

150 See e.g. Plucknett (1956) (n 14) 192, 194.

151 Martin and others (n 148) 12–14.

152 This was not the first attempt at jurisdictional fusion. Sir Thomas More – who sat as Chancellor from 1529–1532 and was a lawyer trained in the common law – is for example known to have suggested to the Common Bench during his tenure that it adopt equity into its jurisdiction, and thereby do away with the need for discretionary injunctions. Needless to say perhaps, in light of what we shall see below, but his suggestion seemed to fall on deaf ears. See further Holdsworth (1924) 223–224; and Plucknett (1956) (n 14) 189–190.

153 Section 25 of the Judicature Act 1873; reproduced today in section 49(1) of the SCA 1981: "Subject to the provisions of this or any other Act, every court exercising jurisdiction in England or Wales in any civil cause or matter shall continue to administer law and equity on the basis that, wherever there is any conflict or variance between the rules of equity and the rules of the common law with reference to the same matter, the rules of equity shall prevail."

with statutory rules, however, since equity is bound in such situations by principle to follow the law.

Although all of the higher courts henceforth had jurisdiction to deal with both legal and equitable claims, this does not mean that equity and law were fused altogether. The modern law of trusts for example still distinguishes between legal and equitable rights. It is also still true to claim that equitable claims generally will only provide an equitable remedy. Thus, for example, innocent misrepresentations may be remedied by way of rescission of the contract in question – not by damages, which is the primary remedy for breaches of contract at common law, and available as of right. And although damages (i.e. compensation) in common law and compensation in equity both require causation to be proven, their requirements relating to remoteness of damage (i.e. foreseeability) differ in practice.[154]

Although not formally fused *per se*, equity and the common law have still come to influence each other in many different ways. Whilst for example damages (as just mentioned) are the primary remedy at common law for breaches of contract, equitable remedies (such as e.g. specific performance, rescission, or rectification) may in certain cases also be available to remedy both breach of contract and to enforce contractual rights. In this way, equitable remedies may be awarded to enforce both exclusively equitable rights and legal rights. They will only be granted at the court's discretion in accordance with the famed maxims of equity, however, and in any event only in cases where damages are proven inadequate to remedy the particular situation at hand. The term "maxims of equity" is used to describe the general principles on which the exercise of equitable jurisdiction is based in practice. We have already touched upon certain maxims already, e.g. that equity acts *in personam*, and that equity will not suffer a wrong to be without a remedy – the classic example of the latter being enforcement of the trust itself, for which the beneficiary had no remedy at common law. Other examples include the maxim that equity follows the law, which clearly provides that equity may not depart from statute, that he who seeks equity must come to it with clean hands, thereby making it impossible e.g. to obtain specific performance of a contract if one is already in breach of one's own obligations thereunder, and that equity will regard the intent and not the form (e.g. deeming a trust to exist even if the word itself is not used, or accepting a transaction to be a mortgage in substance – even if not so described – where property is transferred by way of security).

As we have seen over the course this section, if equity was taken at its literal meaning to start with, it has later come to take on a narrower legal meaning following the establishment of stricter rules for the application of its principles. The historical contrast between (common) law and equity as being between strict rules and discretion has therefore certainly faded over time. Yet whilst the solidification of equity as a separate branch of law has no doubt proven beneficial from the point of view of legal certainty, it would be wrong to assume that the discretionary and dynamic nature of equity has disappeared altogether. Far from it, in fact, since new equitable rights and remedies may

154 See e.g. *Target Holdings Ltd. v. Redferns* [1996] 1 A.C. 421, p. 438.

still be forged by the courts in practice. Two prevalent examples of this are provided by the so-called *Mareva* and *Anton Piller* injunctions, which may be ordered respectively to prevent a defendant's assets from being removed (i.e. a freezing order) or to prevent removal or destruction of evidence (i.e. a search order) – the latter being pronounced by Lord Denning as "the greatest piece of judicial law reform in my time".[155] In addition, statutory reforms are also constantly expanding the equitable jurisdiction of the lower courts in practice. For example, in spite of the almost exponential growth in housing prices in the UK over the last few decades, the maximum limit for the value of equity cases that could be dealt with by local courts had remained unchanged at £30,000 since the 1990s. Any cases above that level were required to go directly to the High Court, thus increasing its workload and creating long delays for claimants. Following the judicial reforms of 2014, the equitable jurisdiction of the County Court was therefore increased from £30,000 to £350,000.[156] The discretionary role of modern equity may therefore have taken on a different shape and significance today but is certainly far from obsolete.

6. Professionalisation

The process of centralization of justice mapped out in Section 2 above was the catalyst for true professionalisation of the legal vocation in England & Wales. Prior to this, the Justices in Eyre that were sent out to the regions to dispense royal justice were probably closer to what we today would call civil servants. Professional lawyers and judges in our modern sense did not exist. The establishment of the central courts in Westminster brought members of the legal profession together geographically for the very first time – an English counterpart of developmental trends previously seen in Roman law. By the end of the 13th century, all practice before the Common Bench was being conducted by so-called "serjeant counters" (later duped "serjeants-at-law") – persons licensed by the court, and instructed by an applicant to speak on his or her behalf.[157] This development was of great significance to the development of the common law itself as a distinct legal system, since serjeant counters were not versed in Roman and canon law, taught as it was in Latin at the places of learning on the continent well into the 1800's.

Practice before the Common Bench was conducted in French – the language of the English upper classes of the time. Since the work of the serjeant counters centred on pleadings under the writ system, and hence on adequately stating one's case in order to proceed before the central courts, they were trained at court. Indeed, as much had been decreed as early as in 1292 by Royal writ, instructing the best apprentices from the counties to attend the central courts to follow proceedings, to the exclusion of all others.[158] Had they been

155 Lord Denning, *The Due Process of Law* (Butterworths 1980) 134; *Anton Piller KG v. Manufacturing Processes* [1976] Ch. 55; [1976] W.L.R. 162; *Mareva Compania Naviera S.A. v. International Bulkcarriers S.A.* [1975] 2 Lloyd's Rep. 509.

156 Section 23 of the County Court Act 1984.

157 For more on the forerunners to the serjeant counters – the narrators – see Plucknett (1956) (n 14) 217.

158 *Rotulae Parliamentariaei*, i. 84.

trained at the universities instead, then the path of the English legal system might very well have been a different one, and far less removed from continental civil law traditions. It was the serjeant counters, as a very small and closed profession, who would eventually start to fill the Common Bench when new judges needed to be appointed.

This is much the same as we still see today, with the English judiciary employing new judges almost exclusively from the practicing Bar, as opposed to setting up a separate career service devoted to judges alone as is increasingly common in many other countries.[159] It is also worth noting that although the benefit of having many of the best and most experienced barristers on the bench is undoubtedly huge, one might well question the degree to which they have come to monopolise the courts. A strong argument can certainly be made that greater diversity among the judges would ensure greater public confidence in the judiciary, and hence in the rule of law.[160] Nevertheless, an equally strong counterargument could probably be made with reference to the many dissenting opinions published in decisions of the higher courts, which would seem to signify anything but homogeneity in the way in which English judges think about and approach the law.

The early 1500s marked the beginning of the gradual, albeit slow, decline of the serjeants' order. This was perhaps unsurprising, however, since the amount of cases being handled by the King's Bench and in Chancery was also growing dramatically in these years. The serjeants enjoyed no monopoly in these courts, and less emphasis was placed there on oral pleadings than before the Common Bench. These developments in turn made room for the rise of other legal actors, such as the solicitors, who were practicing especially in the courts of equity, and to whom a number of other quasi-legal tasks befell. The passing of the Judicature Act of 1873 proved the final nail in the coffin of the serjeants' order, and the rise of the barristers in their place. The differing roles of the barrister and solicitor (described further below) have converged somewhat over time, but still survive in various forms to this very day.

The more orderly state of affairs in governmental administration in the years following the Conquest saw a gradual transition from mere scraps of judicial and financial accounts to full-blown systematic court records. The process started with the Domesday Book, the oldest surviving public record, initiated during the reign of William the Conqueror – a two-volume, nationwide survey of all landholdings and stock, their value and owners, with a view to ascertaining rights of the Crown. Although the tomes were compiled essentially for financial purposes (i.e. taxation), records were later to become far more judicial in nature; the Exchequer's records contained both financial and judicial information, and were systematized under Henry I (1100–1135), thus giving us the "Great Rolls of the Pipe", which remained in use well into the 1800s. The Yearbooks provide us with the first real court reports as such, and started being compiled in the

159 For more on the serjeants and the beginnings of judicial recruitment from amongst their ranks, see e.g. John H. Langbein, Renée Lettow Lerner and Bruce P. Smith, *History of the Common Law – The Development of Anglo-American Legal Institutions* (Wolters Kluwer 2009) 155–162.

160 Se e.g. UKSC Justice Lady Hale, 'Appointments to the Supreme Court', speech delivered at Conference to mark the tenth anniversary of the Judicial Appointments Commission, University of Birmingham, 6 November 2015.

1200s. In these one finds reference to "apprentices", presumably apprentices to serjeant counters, who seemed to be learning their trade by watching others in court. By the 14th century, these apprentices, the medieval equivalent to today's barrister pupils, were living and learning together in the Inns of Court in London. The Yearbooks themselves became tools for systematically learning how to go about business at court – such as for example the making of counts and pleading, which still lay at the very heart of court procedure at the time, and which provided the ancient foundation for the present system of statements of claim that are used for initiating legal proceedings in civil cases.

Professional literature on the law was being propounded in England from the end of the 12th century onwards. Ranulf de Glanvill was Justiciar of the Exchequer during the latter part of Henry II's reign (1154–1189), and his commentary of the common law from 1187, which based itself around a commentary of the various writs, was to influence legal writing for centuries to come. Famed writers of the middle-ages leaving lasting impressions on the way in which English lawyers were trained and versed include Henry de Bracton, and his work *De Legibus et Consuetudinibus Angliae* (The Laws and Customs of England), of 1569. His treatise on the doctrine of the supremacy of law was to have a profound impact on Coke, and the coming conflict between Crown and Parliament that marked the House of Stuarts' reign in the early mid-1600s; according to Bracton, the King was subject not to other men, but to God and the law. Law was the basis upon which society was built, and all men – whether King or layperson – were subject to it. Of course, such thoughts, and the consequent decline of royal prerogatives over time for which they paved the way, seem second nature to most of us today. They were also embodied centuries earlier in *Magna Carta*, in all its versions and subsequent reaffirmations over the centuries. But for the sovereigns of the time, who reigned by divine right, it must nevertheless have still seemed somewhat preposterous – if not anathema – to suggest that the King be answerable to the law. The English civil war saw the eventual condemnation and execution of Charles I (1625–1649), and ultimately – in spite of the doomed Republican experiment of the Commonwealth during the interregnum period, and the Restoration of Charles II to the throne in 1660 – the beginnings of cementing Parliament's position as future policy dictator through the House of Commons. Until court reporting started in earnest, it was common for courts to treat the writings of the ancient authors as authoritative and binding. Today, the works of both ancient (and modern) authors are treated – although in many cases with a certain reverence – as merely persuasive indicators in identifying the law as it stood or still stands.

It is difficult to say how many law journals there are in the UK today, but the number must surely be somewhere in the hundreds, likewise, the number of books which are published each year devoted to various branches of the law. It is also difficult to get a full picture of the many outlets producing court reports – the successors to the earlier Yearbooks, recording decisions in cases before the courts and tribunals of England & Wales. Some courts publish all of their own decisions, both online and in hardcopy. But most reporting is in fact conducted by private publishing houses, and will usually be rather selective, both in terms of which courts they cover, and the amount of cases which are reported. The comprehensive Law Reports and Weekly Law Reports, published by the independent Incorporated Council of Law Reporters, are considered the most authoritative reports of cases in the UK, and began in 1865. The Reports include the most important judgments from the House of Lords/UKSC, the Privy Council, the Court of Appeal and the High Court. A rival publication called the All England Law Reports was started up in 1936, although these are considered less authoritative since they cover a more select body of case law.[161]

Today, undergraduate law programmes are taught at more than 100 higher educational establishments (universities, colleges etc.) in England & Wales, with almost 20,000 students accepted to begin law courses in 2018 alone. Most students take a Bachelor's Degree in Law (LLB), with postgraduate studies (i.e. a Master's Degree) usually only of interest to those contemplating future academic careers. Undergraduate and postgraduate legal studies in the UK are traditionally taught as academic (as opposed to vocational) disciplines. In order to practice law, further vocational courses therefore need to be completed. Two alternative routes are offered for those with qualifying law degrees: the Legal Practice Course (LPC) to become a solicitor, and the Bar Professional Training Course (BPTC) to become a barrister. These one-year, full-time courses are offered at certain Universities and specialist Law Schools and are almost exclusively taught by practitioners.[162]

It is also possible, and not entirely unusual, for non-law graduates to gain entry to the LPC or BPTC by taking a one-year conversion course on law first, known as the Common Professional Examination or Graduate Diploma in Law. This allows a very wide range of persons with knowledge in all manner of fields – such as e.g. natural sciences, engineering, architecture, geology, economics, etc. – to bring their skills and specialist knowledge to the legal profession. Although this might seem rather strange to some, to my mind it remains one of the most enriching features of the legal profession in the UK.

161 See the Practice Direction issued by Lord Woolf CJ in 2001, where he states in no uncertain terms how "both the High Court and the Court of Appeal require that where a case has been reported in the official Law Reports published by the Incorporated Council of Law Reporting for England and Wales it must be cited from that source. Other series may only be used when a case is not reported in the Law Reports." [2001] 1 WLR 194.

162 40 or so institutions currently offer the LPC to approximately 9,000 students per year; only eight offer the BPTC to approximately 2,000 students per year.

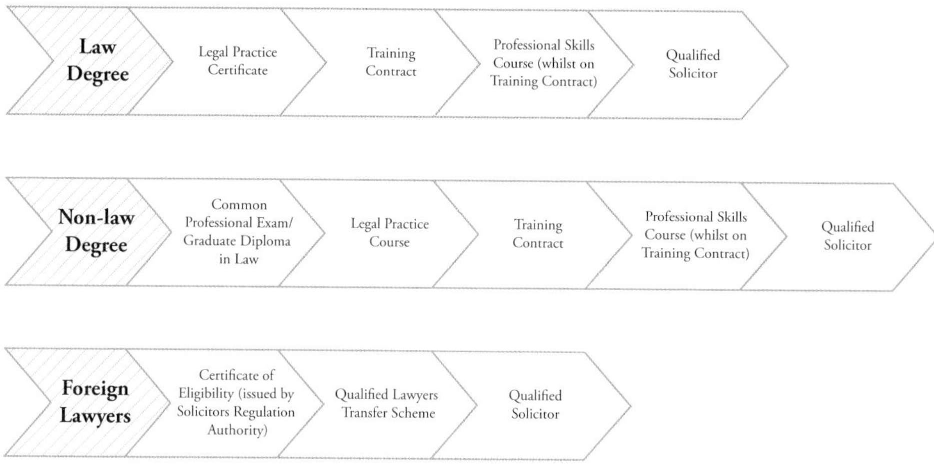

Fig. 2 Routes to becoming a solicitor.

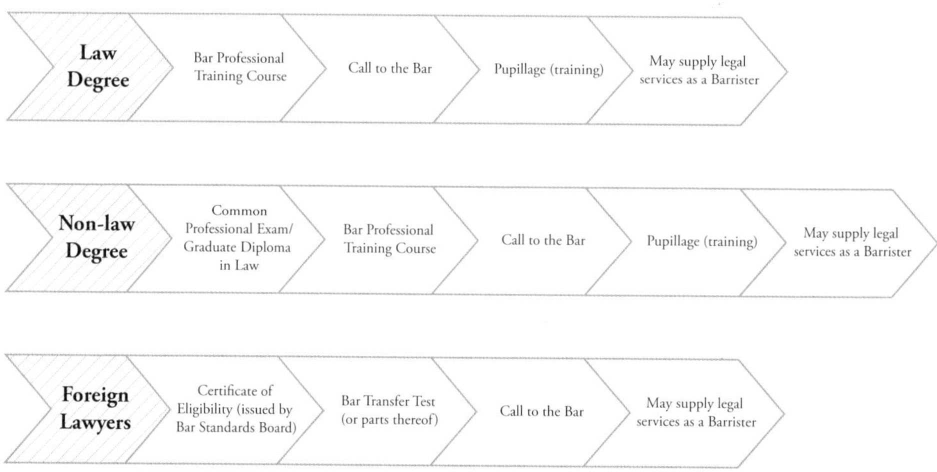

Fig. 3 Routes to becoming a barrister.

Whilst the LPC focusses on the core skills required for solicitors as general legal advisers, the BPTC focusses exclusively on the skills that barristers will need in their work as specialist advocates before the courts (i.e. procedural rules, advocacy, litigation, opinion writing & drafting, negotiation etc.). LPC graduates must complete a further two years of practical training under a training contract and a Professional Skills Course, building on knowledge acquired during the LPC, before they may apply for admittance to the Roll of Solicitors (i.e. receiving their licence to practice as solicitors in England & Wales). Competition for training contracts is fierce, with only around half of those completing the LPC being offered a place at law firms each year. The eye of the needle is even smaller for budding barristers: only approximately 1/3 of the 1,800 students completing the

BPTC gain pupillage (i.e. training contracts in barristers' Chambers) and go on to join the approximately 15,000 practicing barristers each year. By comparison, in 2017, there were approximately 140,000 active solicitors in England.[163]

The system of solicitors/barristers might seem rather alien to those fostered on different legal cultures and traditions but is known and used in many common law jurisdictions across the world today. The main historical difference between the two groups rested largely on the so-called "rights of audience" they enjoyed – i.e. before which courts they could argue cases. Solicitors have long enjoyed full rights of audience alongside barristers before Tribunals, Coroners, Magistrates' and County Courts. More recently, they have also gained the right to argue cases before the Family Court and European Courts. Until very recently, however, cases proceeding before the High Court, Court of Appeal or House of Lords/UKSC remained the exclusive domain of barristers alone. Solicitors, as the barrister's professional client, would therefore have to instruct a barrister to take their lay-client's case in order to proceed before one of these courts. Although the system ultimately guaranteed a larger degree of objectivity and expert opinion on the strengths and weaknesses of the case for the lay-client, and in many ways also provided an ethical filter for the courts by preventing many unwarranted claims from proceeding to trial, it goes without saying that instructing two lawyers is more expensive than only having one. Reforms have therefore been initiated in more recent times in an attempt to limit legal costs, amongst other ways by allowing solicitors to apply for higher rights of audience in proceedings before the Crown Court, High Court, Court of Appeal, and UKSC.[164] In spite of this, it is still common for solicitors to instruct barristers with their specialist knowledge and experience in and out of court to advise their clients – even for proceedings which solicitors can conduct themselves. Barristers are officers of the court. They are therefore placed in a rather peculiar situation as compared to many other lawyers hailing from other jurisdictions and must carefully balance and weigh their duties of care owed to the courts, their lay clients (who ultimately foot their bills), and also the solicitors who instruct them. Indeed, early and impartial advice from a barrister can often save clients the cost and worry of an unnecessary trial.

A programme of radical legislative reform concerning the regulation of the legal profession was initiated in 2004, following publication of the Clementi Report.[165] Prior to this, the education, training, qualification and disciplinary outlets for solicitors and barristers had been almost entirely self-regulatory, under the guise of the Law Society and the Bar Council and the further scrutiny of the judiciary. The Legal Services Acts of 2007 and 2010 did away with much of the old system, with regulation provided today by the independent, statutory Legal Services Board and a group of other Approved Regulators.[166] The main

163 According to numbers issued by the Solicitors Regulation Society, October 2017. Of these, approximately 2/3 work in private practice, with the rest working either in-house for large corporations (approx. 15,000) or for the local or central government (including approx. 2,000 for the Crown Prosecution Service).

164 See the Solicitors Regulation Authority's Higher Rights of Audience Regulations 2011, Part 2, Regulation 2.

165 David Clementi, *Review of the Regulatory Framework for Legal Services in England and Wales – Final Report* (2004), available at http://www.legal-services-review.org.uk/content/report/index.htm accessed 14 April 2020.

166 Such as e.g. the Solicitors Regulation Authority – an Approved Regulator charged with ensuring standards for education, training and qualification of solicitors, under the guise of the Legal Services Board.

objective of the Legal Services Acts is to support the principle of the rule of law, requiring regulation to be carried out in the public interest and with a view to promoting a strong, independent and diverse legal profession. Whether or not it lives up to such a billing will only be shown in time, since initial responses do seem to be somewhat mixed.

7. Conclusions

In this final, concluding section, we are asked to summarise our findings/observations by filling in a legal cultural model for our country:

The Legal Culture of England & Wales and its structures and structural elements					
Institutional structure		**Intellectual structure**			
Conflict resolution	*Norm production*	*Ideal of justice*	*Legal method*	*Degree of professionalisation*	*Character of internationalisation*
Several court hierarchies exist – which to use will depend on whether the case is civil or criminal, the gravity of the offence/harm caused, and the grounds of appeal available or relied upon.	No general codes – mix of common law, statute and international (including European) sources. Increasing amounts of secondary (i.e. delegated) legislation.	Equity crystalised into a distinct branch of law to mitigate the severity of the common law system. In situations of conflict, equity will prevail over the common law but must yield to statute.	Highly developed system of precedent (*stare decisis*). No constitutional review of statutes, but parliamentary sovereignty balanced out by broad presumptions of parliamentary intent (although mere exceptional use of Parliamentary debates) and increasing focus on purposive method.	Law traditionally taught as an academic discipline at University, but you do not need a University degree in law to practice the law; vocational training at Law School to become a solicitor or barrister may be pursued also by non-law graduates. Judges are not schooled but sourced primarily from the practising Bar.	Treaties must be transformed (dualism), customary int'l law mainly incorporated (monism). European law significantly impacts on parliamentary sovereignty (e.g. disapplication of national law where it conflicts with EU law) and methods of statutory interpretation (e.g. expanding method of purposive interpretation to avoid conflicts between ECHR/EU law and national law).

8. Bibliography

Arber E (ed), *John Selden – Table Talk 1689 – Reprint* (Alex. Murray & Sons 1868)

Bentham J, *The Principles of Morals and Legislation* (Clarendon Press 1789)

Blom-Cooper L, Dickson B and Drewry G (eds), *The Judicial House of Lords – 1876–2009* (Oxford University Press 2009). DOI: http://dx.doi.org/10.1093/acprof:oso/9780199532711.001.0001

Clayton R, 'The Empire Strikes Back: common law rights and the Human Rights Act' (2015) 1 *Public Law* 3

Cownie F, Bradney A and Burton M, *The English Legal System in Context* (Oxford University Press 2007)

Cracknell R and Clements R, 'Acts and Statutory Instruments: the volume of UK legislation 1950 to 2014' in *House of Commons Library Standard Note* (SN/SG/2911 19 March 2014)

Crane P, *Administrative Tribunals and Adjudication* (Hart 2009). DOI: http://dx.doi.org/10.5040/9781472560537

Darbyshire P, 'The UK Supreme Court – is there anything left to think about?' (2015) Vol. 21 No. 1 *European Journal of Current Legal Issues*

Lord Denning A, *The Due Process of Law* (Butterworths 1980)

Lord Devlin P, *Trial by Jury* (Stevens & Sons 1956)

Dymond G, 'The Appellate Jurisdiction of the House of Lords' in *House of Lords Library note* (LLN 2009/010) 4

Elliott M, 'Constitutional Legislation, European Union Law and the Nature of the United Kingdom's Contemporary Constitution' (2014) Vol. 10 No. 3 *European Constitutional Law Review* 379. DOI: https://doi.org/10.1017/S1574019614001291

Fleta – vol. ii. (Prologue, Books 1 and 2) (1953) Vol. 72, Selden Society (Sayles GO and Richardson HG tr.)

Fleta – Books 3 & 4 (1972) Vol. 89, Selden Society (Sayles GO and Richardson HG tr.)

Fleta – Books 5 & 6 (1983) Vol. 99, Selden Society (Sayles GO and Richardson HG tr.)

Franklin CNK, 'The melting pot or the salad bowl revisited (again) – The meeting of legal cultures at the European Court of Justice' in Sunde JØ and Skodvin KE (eds), *Rendezvous of European Legal Cultures* (Fagbokforlaget 2010)

Gillespie A, *The English Legal System* (Oxford University Press 2015). DOI: http://dx.doi.org/10.1093/he/9780198727217.001.0001

Holdsworth W S, *A History of English Law, vol. V.* (Little, Brown and Company 1924)

Holland J and Webb J, *Learning Legal Rules* (7th edn, Oxford University Press 2010)

Horne A, 'The Role of the Lord Chancellor' in *House of Commons Library Standard Note* (SN/PC/2105 26 March 2015)

Langbein JH, Lerner RL and Smith BP, *History of the Common Law – The Development of Anglo-American Legal Institutions* (Wolters Kluwer 2009)

Martin JE, *Hanbury & Martin – Modern Equity* (15th edn, Sweet & Maxwell 1997)

Mcleod I, *Legal Method* (Palgrave Macmillan 2005)

Milsom SFC, *Historical Foundations of the Common Law* (2nd edn, Butterworths 1981). DOI (1969 edn): http://dx.doi.org/10.1016/c2013-0-06206-8

Morris WA, *The Medieval English Sheriff to 1300* (reprint edn, Manchester University Press 1968)

Plucknett TFT, *A Concise History of the Common Law* (5th edn, Butterworths 1956)

Twining W and Miers D, *How To Do Things With Rules* (Butterworths 2009). DOI: http://dx.doi.org/10.1017/cbo9780511844959

Lord Phillips of Worth Matravers, 'The Birth and First Steps of the UK Supreme Court' (2012) Vol. 1 Issue 2 *Cambridge Journal of International and Comparative Law* 9. DOI: http://dx.doi.org/10.7574/cjicl.01.02.12

11. An Introduction to Scottish Legal Culture

Andrew R.C. Simpson[1]

1. Introduction

> "It seems to me that in truth Scots law has long been built by the working-out of doctrine in our case-law and that this is what gives strength to any statements of principle which may from time to time emerge... Scots law still remains that curious mixture of native, Roman and English elements. On the whole, if they thought about the matter at all, our predecessors do not appear to have worried too much about which element of the Scottish mixture they called into service at any particular moment, but rather let the law develop as seemed best suited to the demands and fashions of the times. We could do worse than follow their rather pragmatic example. If we do, then Scots law may never be perfectly coherent as a system, but it will respond to the needs of the times [and] enjoy the confidence of people in Scotland..."[2]

The late Lord Rodger was well aware that some elements of these views were controversial when he published them in 1996. That remains the case almost twenty-five years later, and it must be emphasised at the outset of this study of Scottish legal culture that not all academic writers would endorse his arguments. Nonetheless, his comments are representative of a vision of that culture which remains powerful today. More relevant here is that they serve to introduce many salient features of modern Scots law. The statement that Scots law has "long been built" through case law underlines the point that any attempt to discuss conflict resolution and norm production within Scottish legal culture must focus on the decisions of three courts in particular. The first two are the Court of Session, which deals with civil matters, and the High Court of Justiciary, which deals with criminal matters. The third, the United Kingdom Supreme Court

---

1 I am grateful to the late David Carey Miller, and to Malcolm Combe, John Ford, Greg Gordon, Tina Hunter and Eddie Simpson for their comments on the original version of this article; I am also grateful to the anonymous reviewer, Roddy Paisley and John Paterson for some thoughts on aspects of the present article. Any errors remain my own.

2 Alan Rodger, 'Thinking About Scots Law' (1996) Vol. 1 no. 1/4 *Edinburgh Law Review* 3, 11 and 23–24.

(UKSC), enjoys appellate jurisdiction in relation to the first two, albeit only in very limited circumstances in the case of the High Court of Justiciary. Of course, the authority of a statute promulgated by the British Parliament in London – commonly known as "Westminster" – overrides that of any decision of the Scottish courts. The same can be said for statutes passed by the Scottish Parliament in Edinburgh – commonly known as "Holyrood" – in so far as those statutes are consistent with various rights guaranteed by the European Convention on Human Rights. This will be explained further below, and at the same time the increasing importance of the Scottish Law Commission in shaping those statutes will be examined. Yet Scots law is still undoubtedly embedded in a legal culture structured around the decisions of the courts. So, there is no code of Scots law, albeit there are many statutes that codify large tracts of the law. This in turn raises important questions about the certainty, predictability and interpretation of the law in Scotland, referred to in this volume as falling within the "ideal of justice" within a legal culture. The ways in which Scots legal institutions attempt to balance the need to combine legal certainty with the need for flexibility in the adaptation of the law to new circumstances will be explored here. At the same time, the methods adopted by the courts for developing the law will be outlined. Law is certainly not deduced from a codified set of principles, according to a fixed set of interpretative rules; frequently it is declared by the courts, having been extracted from a range of authoritative sources. To some extent this can dovetail with the pragmatic approach to dispute resolution outlined by Rodger. The perceived role of two branches of the profession – advocates and solicitors – in realising these ends will then be discussed. Reference will also be made here to what one commentator has described as the "third branch of the profession" – academic lawyers specialising in Scots law.[3] Among other things, that "third branch" of the profession has helped to shape views about how appropriate it is to draw inspiration from traditions of legal ideas, such as those expressed in English law and Roman law. The academic debate in that regard has been intense, a point alluded to by Rodger in the passage quoted above. However, the debate has been complicated in many fields by the increasing importance of law produced outside of the Scottish jurisdiction. More than ever before, Scottish lawyers are required to consider laws promulgated in the European Union and by other international bodies.

When considering these matters here, it must be remembered that Scotland – and indeed, the whole United Kingdom, of which it is a part – is going through a period of great political and constitutional uncertainty and transition. In an independence referendum in 2014, a majority voted for Scotland to remain a part of the United Kingdom.[4] The apparent finality of this decision has been called into question by a subsequent

3 Kenneth G. C. Reid, 'The Third Branch of the Profession. The Rise of the Academic Lawyer in Scotland' in Hector L. MacQueen (ed), *Scots Law into the 21st Century. Essays in Honour of W. A. Wilson* (W. Green/Sweet & Maxwell 1996) 39–49.

4 While a majority of Scots voted to remain within the United Kingdom in a referendum September 2014, about 45% of the population voted in favour of independence; see http://www.scotlandreferendum.info/ accessed 7 November 2019.

referendum held at the United Kingdom level in 2016, in which 51.9% of those who participated voted to leave the European Union.[5] The result of this referendum has proven extremely controversial, including in Scotland, where 67.2% of those who participated voted to remain within the European Union. This, in turn, has made it possible to argue that Scotland is being taken out of the European Union against its will by the rest of the United Kingdom. As a result, the Scottish Government has previously sought to bring forward legislation to call a second independence referendum in 2020; but this cannot legally be done without the consent of the United Kingdom Government, and in any event the coronavirus crisis has now caused the Scottish Government to "pause" its stated aim of holding another vote.[6] By contrast, partly as a result of the Conservative victory in the General Election of December 2019, the United Kingdom Government is continuing to negotiate a trade deal with the European Union, following the British exit from the Union on 31 January 2020.[7]

Part of the challenge for Scots law over the next decade will be to demonstrate an ability to adapt to these new circumstances, and to adapt rapidly, given the speed of the political and social changes within which Scottish legal culture operates. Put another way, the existing legal system will be called upon to provide tools that are adequate to respond to the developing aspirations of the Scottish populace, in an atmosphere in which different forms and visions of internationalisation are already bringing great change to legal practice. The coronavirus crisis will only exacerbate the challenge facing

5 The Electoral Commission, 'Results and Turnout at the EU Referendum', available at https://www.electoralcommission.org.uk/who-we-are-and-what-we-do/elections-and-referendums/past-elections-and-referendums/eu-referendum/results-and-turnout-eu-referendum accessed 7 November 2019.

6 See 'Protecting Scotland's Future: the Government's Programme for Scotland 2019–2020', available at https://www.gov.scot/publications/protecting-scotlands-future-governments-programme-scotland-2019-20/pages/1/ accessed 7 November 2019; on the decision to pause the attempt to hold a second referendum, see also 'A letter from the Cabinet Secretary for Constitution, Europe and External Affairs, Michael Russell MSP, to the Chancellor of the Duchy of Lancaster, Rt Hon Michael Gove MP, setting out the Scottish Government's intention to pause work on holding an independence referendum in 2020 in light of the coronavirus crisis', available at https://www.gov.scot/binaries/content/documents/govscot/publications/correspondence/2020/03/coronavirus-covid-19---independence-referendum-cabinet-secretary-for-constitution-letter/documents/coronavirus-covid-19---independence-referendum-cabinet-secretary-for-constitution-letter/coronavirus-covid-19---independence-referendum-cabinet-secretary-for-constitution-letter/govscot%3Adocument/Mr%2BRussell%2Bletter%2Bto%2BCDL%2B-%2B18%2BMarch.pdf accessed 18 April 2020. As regards the legislation brought in to respond to the coronavirus crisis, see, for example, the Coronavirus Act 2020 (c.7), and the Coronavirus (Scotland) Act 2020 asp 7. It has not been possible in the present article to explore the effects these wide-ranging legislative changes may have on Scottish legal culture. One might be tempted to think that the effects of Brexit are somewhat eclipsed.

7 For the December 2019 election results, see https://commonslibrary.parliament.uk/parliament-and-elections/general-election-2019-the-results-so-far/ accessed 18 April 2020. For key provisions relevant to the British exit from the European Union, see the European Union (Withdrawal) Act 2018 (c.6) ss.1, 1A, 20; European Union (Withdrawal) Act 2020 (c.1) s.39; Agreement on the Withdrawal of the United Kingdom of Great Britain and Northern Ireland from the European Union and the European Atomic Energy Community O J L 29, 31.1.2020, p. 7–187. For a report of the UK Government's position that the Transition Period is not to be extended beyond 31 December 2020, see Sebastian Payne and Jim Brunsden, 'UK will refuse any EU offer to extend Brexit transition', *Financial Times*, 16 April 2020 https://www.ft.com/content/3c006614-767f-4447-8136-97987045517f accessed 18 April 2020.

Scottish legal culture, and indeed all legal cultures; while it is impossible to gauge the likely long-term effects at present, it does not seem an exaggeration to comment that the repercussions of coronavirus will be transformative in national legal systems across the globe.

Such matters will be considered further in the conclusion. For now, it will be helpful to begin by saying a little about Scotland and Scottish political history. Subsequently conflict resolution, norm production, the ideal of justice, the legal method, professionalisation and internationalisation within Scottish legal culture will be considered in turn.

2. Scotland

Just under five hundred kilometres north of London lie the River Tweed and the Solway Firth. Broadly speaking, the Tweed and the Solway mark the northern boundary of England. Almost all of mainland Britain beyond that boundary is Scottish. In turn, mainland Scotland can be separated into the Lowlands and the Highlands. Briefly put, the Lowlands are in the south and east. There are also hundreds of islands off the Scottish coastline. These can be divided into the Western Isles, from Lewis in the north to Islay and Jura in the south, and the Northern Isles, consisting of Orkney and Shetland. Shetland in the north is about as close to Norway as it is to mainland Scotland.

Most of the territories just mentioned were gradually united into one kingdom between the ninth and the twelfth centuries.[8] During the late 1100s, the relationship between the rulers of the Scottish realm, on the one hand, and their more powerful English neighbours, on the other hand, started to be redefined. Vague English royal claims to the overlordship of the British Isles began to crystallise into demands for recognition of feudal superiority, and these demands were resisted by successive Scottish dynasties from the early 1200s onwards. From this point onwards, the kings of Scotland claimed to recognise no superiors, and gave substance to that claim through diplomatic and military efforts.[9] Ultimately one of them, James VI (r. 1567–1625), inherited the English throne peacefully in 1603. In so doing, he initiated a process that would ultimately lead to the Union of the Parliaments of Scotland and England in 1707.[10] From the two countries the new sovereign nation of Great Britain emerged. Needless to say, a distinctive Scottish identity survived and developed following the Union of 1707. Contemporary movements for greater Scottish political autonomy resulted in the establishment of a devolved legislature by means of a Westminster statute in 1999.[11] This legislature is

8 See Alex Woolf, *From Pictland to Alba 789–1070* (Edinburgh University Press 2007).

9 See Richard Oram, *Domination and Lordship. Scotland 1070–1230* (Edinburgh University Press 2011); Dauvit Broun, *Scottish Independence and the Idea of Britain: From the Picts to Alexander III* (Edinburgh University Press 2013); Michael Brown, *The Wars of Scotland 1214–1371* (Edinburgh University Press 2004); Ranald Nicholson, *Scotland: The Later Middle Ages* (Edinburgh University Press 1978).

10 For the general political developments see Gordon Donaldson, *Scotland James V v James VII* (Edinburgh University Press 1971) 157–291.

11 See Ewan A. Cameron, *Impaled Upon a Thistle. Scotland Since 1880* (Edinburgh University Press 2010) 320–371.

the Scottish Parliament, and it sits next to Holyrood Palace, one of the old seats of the Scottish monarchs. It has a broad law-making competence, as will be explained further below. Nonetheless, legally Scotland remains a "part" of the United Kingdom in law, as it is frequently described in statute.[12] Furthermore, it is worth noting here that in any theoretical competition between laws promulgated at Westminster by the Queen in Parliament, on the one hand, and by Holyrood, on the other, the former would remain supreme.[13]

The population of the country at the date of the last national census in 2011 was about 5.3 million. The most populous Scottish city is Glasgow, with almost six hundred thousand inhabitants; by contrast, the population of the capital, Edinburgh, is less than half a million.[14] Both cities are within what is termed the Scottish "central belt", which roughly follows the lines of the River Clyde and the River Forth. The majority of Scots live in that part of the country.[15]

As might be expected at a time of political and constitutional flux, the nature and strength of the Scottish economy is the subject of much highly polemical debate. Nonetheless, a few points should be made about this. According to Scottish Government statistics, the national Scottish GDP in 2018 was estimated at £163.6 billion, or £30,100 per person, rising to £180.4 billion or £33,200 when oil and gas extraction from "Scottish waters" are taken into account.[16] In 2017, the five top Scottish export industries accounted for 52% of the national exports. These industries are, in order of economic importance: "manufacture of food products and beverages", "professional, scientific and technical activities", "manufacture of refined petroleum and chemical products", "mining and quarrying", and "wholesale and retail trade".[17]

3. Conflict Resolution

Having made these introductory remarks concerning Scotland and its geography, political history, population and economy, it is now possible to explore its legal culture. First conflict resolution and the court structure will be considered. One simple way to explain the court structure that exists today is to discuss its historical development; the histori-

12 See, for example, the House of Commons (Redistribution of Seats) Act 1944 (c. 41) Sch. 3 (which is no longer in force).

13 This is subject to the well-known convention that Westminster will not legislate in relation to devolved matters unless Holyrood permits it; see Hector L. MacQueen, The Rt. Hon. Lord Eassie and others, *The Law of Scotland by The Late W.M. Gloag KC LLD and The Late Candlish Henderson, QC, LLD* (14th edn, W. Green/Thomson Reuters 2017) (hereafter *Gloag and Henderson The Law of Scotland*) paras 1.29–1.30.

14 See Scotland's Census, available at https://www.scotlandscensus.gov.uk/ accessed 7 November 2019.

15 Office for National Statistics, 'Country Profiles: Key Statistics – Scotland, August 2012' 1, available at http://www.ons.gov.uk/ons/dcp171780_275330.pdf accessed 7 November 2019.

16 A National Statistics Publication for Scotland, 'GDP Quarterly National Accounts, Scotland, 2019 Quarter 2' 6, available at https://www2.gov.scot/Resource/0054/00548728.pdf accessed 7 November 2019.

17 A National Statistics Publication for Scotland, 'Export Statistics Scotland 2017' 7–8, available at https://www2.gov.scot/Resource/0054/00545619.pdf accessed 7 November 2019.

cal outline provided here will also prove useful as a reference point in later sections of this chapter.[18]

3.1 *Iudices*, Sheriff Courts, Justiciars' Courts and Parliament

The justiciar and the sheriff were two of the most important officials charged with the maintenance of the law in medieval Scotland. The remedies they gave litigants in disputes concerning feudal rights in land were known as "brieves", and were modelled on the English writs.[19] Their courts of the sheriff and the justiciar – also modelled on English equivalents – operated alongside those of the great magnates, the burghs and the church in administration of a wide range of legal remedies to different groups of litigants. There also existed individuals known as *iudices*, who seem to have been men who knew best the ancient laws and customs of their localities.[20] Their role gradually – and mysteriously – began to diminish over the centuries,[21] but the offices of the justiciar and the sheriff do have successors in the court structure today. While there was a great patchwork of courts in medieval Scotland, royal justice was increasingly asserting itself. By the fourteenth century, and arguably earlier than that, the king's writ was theoretically supreme across the kingdom.[22] Kings made statutes with parliaments to govern the realm, and so augmented the common law; the same parliaments had judicial functions, sitting "at the apex of a structure of royal courts" of the common law "providing litigants with remedies".[23]

3.2 The Conciliar Session and the College of Justice

In the mid-fifteenth century problems began to emerge with the common law courts of the sheriffs and the justiciars. One difficulty was that the procedures they applied to determine the outcome of disputes relied heavily on local knowledge as a means of ascertaining the relevant facts. As legal relationships and patterns of landholding became more complex, such local knowledge was often insufficient as a factual basis for reach-

18 On Scottish legal history generally, see John W. Cairns, 'Historical Introduction' in Kenneth Reid and Reinhard Zimmermann (eds), *A History of Private Law in Scotland Volume 1: Introduction and Property* (Oxford University Press 2000) 14–184; see also now Andrew R.C. Simpson and Adelyn L.M. Wilson, *Scottish Legal History Volume 1: 1000–1707* (Edinburgh University Press 2017).

19 On the brieves, see Hector L. MacQueen, *Common Law and Feudal Society in Medieval Scotland* (classic edn, Edinburgh University Press 2016); see also the critique of his thesis in David Carpenter, 'Scottish Royal Government in the Thirteenth Century from an English Perspective' in Matthew Hammond (ed), *New Perspectives on Medieval Scotland 1093–1286* (Boydell Press 2013) 117–159. See also now the highly significant contribution found in Alice Taylor's *The Shape of the State in Medieval Scotland* (Oxford University Press 2016).

20 On the *judices*, see now, above all, Taylor (2016) (n 19) 114–175.

21 But see W. David H. Sellar, 'Celtic Law and Scots Law: Survival and Integration' (1988) 29 *Scottish Studies* 1, 3–4.

22 See the debate emerging from MacQueen (2016) (n 19) 33–73 and Carpenter (2013) (n 19) 138–154.

23 A.M. Godfrey, *Civil Justice in Renaissance Scotland* (Brill 2009) 10–11.

ing a just result. Often legal learning and training was required to untangle complex disputes. Such learning was often not to be found in the courts of the sheriffs in particular – or so it would seem – in part because many of them held office by hereditary right. Furthermore, delay in the administration of justice was a problem, particularly in the justiciar's courts, which were peripatetic, and only appeared twice a year at best in each locality.[24]

Faced with these problems, litigants turned directly to the king and his lord of council to provide them with remedies. Among those who sat on the council were learned men with legal training, mostly in canon law and Roman law. Gradually, and only in so far as the common law permitted the council to accept jurisdiction in cases, its members began to develop new civil remedies to give justice to litigants. At first, they did not change the substantive common law, but rather created new procedural mechanisms to enforce it. It is unsurprising that the lords drew inspiration from the Roman law and canon law they knew so well in the process. Two procedural frameworks emerged – the old common law actions based on the English writs, and the newer actions, which were frequently handled and interpreted in light of the learned laws. The newer framework was increasingly popular with litigants, and ultimately the older simply withered away through disuse. At the same time, the lords of council found ways of circumventing the traditional restraints on their jurisdiction, so that by the late 1520s they possessed supreme *de facto* jurisdiction in Scottish civil matters.[25]

In 1532, James V (r. 1513–1542) reconstituted the session as a College of Justice; it was later known as the Court of Session. Fifteen lords of session sat in judgment in the court, over which presided the lord president. It was intended that the court would sit permanently in Edinburgh, which was by then the centre of royal government. More than ever before, it was expected that the judges would possess expertise in Roman law and canon law to aid them in reaching just decisions. As a result the feudal system of landholding that had been received from England was now interpreted, like the rest of the legal system, in light of the learned laws.[26] It should be noted that within this new structure the courts of the sheriffs continued to sit, but they were subordinate to the College of Justice. While reforms were introduced into the practices of the College of Justice in the sixteenth and seventeenth centuries, it retained its basic structure until the late-eighteenth century.[27]

24 See the discussions in MacQueen (2016) (n 19) 240–241, 257–259; Godfrey (2009) (n 23) 40–160; John W. Cairns, 'Revisiting the Foundation of the College of Justice' in H.L. MacQueen (ed), *Stair Society Miscellany Five* (vol. 52, Stair Society 2006) 27–50.

25 This is essentially the argument advanced in Godfrey (2009) (n 23) 40–160, 207–354; it is summarised at 441–453.

26 Godfrey (2009) (n 23) 40–160; Cairns (2006) (n 24).

27 See Cairns (2000) (n 18) 50–155.

3.3 The High Court of Justiciary and the Office of Lord Advocate

What of the justiciar's court? Its civil jurisdiction seems to have largely disappeared by the early sixteenth century, and in 1524 the justiciar "or his depute" was required to sit in Edinburgh permanently "to administer 'Justice in crimynale actiounis'". In 1672, the justice deputes were removed, and in their place five lords of session were appointed to sit as commissioners of justiciary together with the lord justice general and the lord justice clerk. The new court became known as the High Court of Justiciary. Its jurisdiction was at first limited by a variety of factors, such as the continued existence of the courts of great noblemen that had power to try crimes. But in time, it became the supreme court in criminal matters.[28] Today the High Court of Justiciary retains this position, subject to some minor exceptions.

It should also be noted here that from the early sixteenth century the office of king's advocate, or, as it came to be known, lord advocate, began to develop. The king's advocates helped to oversee the sale of remissions or pardons for crimes, and to pursue crimes (and financial forfeitures for crimes) in the king's name. Ultimately these officers grew in importance and acquired control of public prosecutions in criminal matters.[29] Today the holder of the office of lord advocate retains such responsibilities.[30]

3.4 The House of Lords

Article XIX of the Treaty of Union of 1706 between Scotland and England guaranteed the survival of the College of Justice and the High Court of Justiciary, and so the separate Scottish legal system. It was also provided in Article XVIII that the new Parliament of Great Britain would only be able to alter Scots Private law for the manifest utility of the people of Scotland.[31] Yet an important question concerning the authority of the College of Justice as a supreme court in Scottish civil matters following the Union was left unanswered. Prior to 1707 it had been possible, in certain circumstances, to challenge a decision of the Court of Session before the Scottish Parliament. After 1707, various litigants attempted to appeal decisions of the College of Justice to the new Parliament of Great Britain, and specifically to its judicial organ, the House of Lords. The House of Lords accepted jurisdiction. At first in Scotland the status of decisions of the House of Lords was not altogether clear. But in time the decisions of the House of Lords came to "be recognised as binding precedents of the highest authority".[32] The jurisdiction of the

28 For these points, see ibid 53, 62, 122–123, 147–149.

29 See John Finlay, *Men of Law in Pre-Reformation Scotland* (Tuckwell Press 2000) 170–205.

30 See the Court of Session Act 1988 (c. 36) s. 22; Timothy H. Jones and Ian Taggart (eds), *Criminal Law* (7th edn, W. Green 2018) para. 2.52.

31 Cairns (2000) (n 18) 112–118; J.D. Ford, 'The Legal Provisions in the Acts of Union' (2007) No. 1 *Cambridge Law Journal* 106.

32 See the discussion in J.D. Ford, 'Protestations to Parliament for Remeid of Law' (2009) Vol. 88 No. 1 *Scottish Historical Review* 57 (the passages cited are at 106–107).

House of Lords in civil matters has now been inherited by the United Kingdom Supreme Court (UKSC), as will be discussed below.

3.5 The Heritable Jurisdictions and the Reform of the Sheriff Courts, 1747

Significant reforms of the Scottish court system occurred during the eighteenth and nineteenth centuries. The civil and criminal jurisdictions of the great barons and nobles were transferred to the Court of Session, the High Court of Justiciary and the Sheriff Courts. Obviously, that meant that older limitations on the criminal jurisdiction of the High Court of Justiciary fell away; and it should be noted that appeals at this time were not brought from the High Court before the House of Lords. Hereditary sheriffs were also removed from office, and the Crown appointed sheriff deputes to preside over each sheriffdom. The sheriff deputes had to have legal training – they had to be advocates for at least three years. Furthermore, the sheriff deputes were given the power to appoint sheriff substitutes.[33]

3.6 Nineteenth Century Reforms of the Scottish Court System

Discussion of court reform in the late 1740s seems to have contributed to calls for reform of the Court of Session itself later in the century. At this time, it sat in what was known as Parliament House in Edinburgh, in two divisions – an Inner House and an Outer House. The Outer House was in Parliament Hall, which still stands today. The Inner House was an annexe attached to that Hall. Judges were selected from the fifteen lords of session to sit in the Outer House on rotation. They were appointed as deputies to deal with straightforward matters and also with the early stages of litigation before it proceeded to the Inner House. Furthermore, an individual lord ordinary could always report a difficult question to the Inner House to receive a decision on the point.[34]

In 1808 this basic structure was reformed, partly because litigants believed it had created a backlog of business, and partly because of the growing popularity of appeals from the Court of Session to the House of Lords. It was decided to split the court into two divisions with equal powers – the first division and the second division. Additionally, five junior lords of session were appointed as permanent Outer House judges, who sat alone. In 1814, a bill was laid before Parliament which successfully introduced civil jury trials into Scotland, relieving some pressure on the Court of Session.[35]

33 Cairns (2000) (n 18) 147–149.

34 Ibid 85–86; John Finlay, *The Community of the College of Justice: Edinburgh and the Court of Session, 1687–1808* (Edinburgh University Press 2012) 11–13; see also J.D. Ford, *Law and Opinion in Scotland during the Seventeenth Century* (Hart 2007) 6–7.

35 Cairns (2000) (n 18) 149–154, 178.

Significant reform of the High Court of Justiciary took a little longer, but in 1830 it was enacted in statute that the lord president of the College of Justice would always simultaneously hold office as lord justice general. Under the Criminal Procedure (Scotland) Act 1887, "the High Court of Justiciary was re-constituted to consist of the Lord Justice General, the Lord Justice Clerk, and all the remaining Lords of Session – every [Lord of Session] thus becoming a "Lord Commissioner of Justiciary".[36] This remains the position today.[37]

Other courts were also reformed in the early nineteenth century. For example, in 1811 it was provided that the sheriff substitutes – who, it will be recalled, were appointed by the sheriff deputes to carry out much of their work – could only be appointed if their qualifications for office were recognised by two of three senior judges, these being the lord president, the lord justice clerk and the chief baron.[38] In 1877, the power of appointing sheriff substitutes was removed from the sheriff depute and exercised directly by the Crown. During the course of the same century, the jurisdiction of the sheriff courts also expanded significantly, and by the mid-twentieth century, the sheriff had jurisdiction "in all civil cases except actions relating to status, actions of reduction and actions of proving of the tenor of lost documents; while in causes up to £50 in value... his jurisdiction [was] privative and final".[39]

These reforms established the "basic architecture"[40] of the Scottish court system that has recently been reformed. In general terms, and subject to certain caveats, throughout the twentieth century in civil matters a decision of a sheriff substitute – who came to be referred to simply as a sheriff – could be appealed to his sheriff depute – who came to be referred to as the sheriff principal. The decision of the sheriff, and indeed of the sheriff principal, could also be appealed to the first or second division of the Inner House of the Court of Session. Likewise, the decision of a lord ordinary sitting in the Outer House of the Court of Session could be appealed to the first or second division of the Inner House. Decisions of the Inner House could, in turn, be appealed to the House of Lords.[41] Furthermore, a series of statutes gradually increased the maximum number of judges that could be appointed to sit in the Court of Session. So, the Court of Session Act 1988 declared the number should be twenty-four; it is now thirty-five.[42]

The pattern was similar in relation to criminal law, albeit again subject to certain caveats. A decision of a sheriff in a criminal matter could be appealed to his sheriff

---

36 W. Croft Dickinson, 'The High Court of Justiciary' in Stair Society vol. 20, *An Introduction to Scottish Legal History by Various Authors* (Stair Society 1958) 408–412, 411.

37 A.M. Godfrey, 'The Courts of Scotland' in M.A. Mulhern (ed), *The Law* (European Ethnological Research Centre 2012) 143, citing the Criminal Procedure (Scotland) Act 1995 (c. 46) s. 1(2).

38 Cairns (2000) (n 18) 154.

39 C.A. Malcolm, 'The Sheriff Court: Sixteenth Century and Later' in Stair Society vol. 20, *An Introduction to Scottish Legal History by Various Authors* (Stair Society 1958) 356–362, 362.

40 Cairns (2000) (n 18) 178.

41 *Gloag and Henderson The Law of Scotland* (n 13) para. 2.01.

42 Court of Session Act 1988 (c. 36) s. 1, as amended by the Maximum Number of Judges (Scotland) Order 2016/423 (Scottish SI) art. 2.

principal or to the High Court of Justiciary; and a decision of the High Court of Justiciary, which retains privative jurisdiction in certain criminal matters, could be appealed to a larger bench of judges within same court sitting as a court of criminal appeal.[43] It should be borne in mind that the thirty-five judges who sit in the Court of Session are the same individuals as the Commissioners of Justiciary who have the authority to preside over criminal matters.

3.7 The Scotland Act 1998

The establishment of the Scottish Parliament should be considered here, because its establishment and its legislative activities have caused significant alterations to the structure of the Scottish courts. In 1999, a new Scottish Parliament was established by the Scotland Act of the previous year.[44] It came to be known as Holyrood, because of its ultimate location next to Holyrood Palace. It must be emphasised that the legislative powers possessed by this Parliament are devolved from Westminster, and the traditional view that the Queen in Parliament in Westminster remains sovereign is not undermined by devolution in itself. Westminster reserved many matters to itself – such as defence and foreign policy – and technically speaking, it is only by reason of a constitutional convention that it refrains from legislating on matters devolved to Holyrood.[45] Furthermore, the powers of Holyrood are restrained in another important way that is directly relevant to a discussion of conflict resolution in Scotland. The Scotland Act 1998 provides that Holyrood must not legislate in a manner inconsistent with either EU law or those rights established under the European Convention on Human Rights (ECHR) and protected by the Human Rights Act 1998 (a Westminster statute). Acts of the Scottish Parliament that are incompatible with these standards are *ultra vires*, and as such can be struck down by the Scottish courts.[46]

3.8 The Constitutional Reform Act 2005 and the UKSC

The appellate jurisdiction of the House of Lords in Scottish civil matters was transferred to the United Kingdom Supreme Court (UKSC) in London by virtue of the Constitutional Reform Act 2005.[47] Furthermore, the UKSC has jurisdiction over "devolution issues". Only a few of these issues needs to be considered here. For example, questions concerning the legislative competence of the Scottish Parliament are among a group of matters known as "devolution issues". Another devolution issue would arise if it were to be alleged that the Scottish Ministers, or certain legal officers, had acted in a manner inconsistent with the Scotland Act 1998. One of the officers in question is the Lord

43 Godfrey (2012) (n 37) 144.

44 See Cameron (2010) (n 11) 349–371.

45 *Gloag and Henderson The Law of Scotland* (n 13) para. 1.30; Scotland Act 1998 (c. 46) Sch. 4 Part 1 para. 2; Sch. 5.

46 Scotland Act 1998 (c. 46) s. 29.

47 Constitutional Reform Act 2005 (c 4) s. 40(3); see now the Courts Reform (Scotland) Act 2014 (asp 18) s. 117.

Advocate, who directs public prosecutions in Scotland. So, for example, if a prosecution were to proceed in a manner inconsistent with human rights protected under the Scotland Act 1998, then that would be a devolution issue.[48]

3.9 The Courts Reform (Scotland) Act 2014

Further major reforms to the court system have been implemented through the Courts Reform (Scotland) Act 2014, a statute of the Scottish Parliament.[49] One fundamental element of the appellate structure outlined above remains untouched. The sheriff courts remain subordinate to the Court of Session in civil matters, and to the High Court of Justiciary in criminal matters. However, in other ways the new structure is quite different, with the introduction of judges known as summary sheriffs, and a Sheriff Appeal Court, staffed by sheriff's principal.[50] Before outlining some details of these changes, it is helpful to reflect on the broad purpose of the reforms. Essentially the Court of Session has been heavily overburdened by litigation during the last few decades, and the purpose of the legislation is to transfer business to the sheriff courts and the Sheriff Appeal Court. The point can be illustrated with reference to one of the reforms. Prior to the enactment of the 2014 Act, if a sheriff court was competent to hear a civil action, then it had privative jurisdiction over that action at first instance *if* the value of the claim did not exceed £5000. In other words, actions worth more than £5000 – a comparatively small sum of money – could be initiated in the supreme civil court sitting in Scotland.[51] However, the Courts Reform (Scotland) Act 2014 altered this position. In cases where a sheriff court has jurisdiction, it has *privative* jurisdiction at first instance over claims worth up to £100,000. In other words, it is now generally impossible to initiate claims for less than £100,000 in the Court of Session.[52]

To reduce the burden on the Court of Session in other ways, the Courts Reform (Scotland) Act 2014 reformed the civil court structure as follows. In each sheriffdom new judges, known as summary sheriffs, have been appointed.[53] Summary sheriffs have a limited civil jurisdiction that nonetheless enables them to deal with routine matters. For example, they are able to grant decree for payment of some debts not exceeding £5000.[54] Furthermore, the 2014 act removed the right of appeal from a sheriff to his sheriff principal. In its place there is a right of appeal to a Sheriff Appeal Court. The new Court is empowered to hear appeals from the decisions of both summary sheriffs

48 Scotland Act 1998 (c. 46) Sch. 5–6.

49 Courts Reform (Scotland) Act 2014 (asp 18).

50 Courts Reform (Scotland) Act 2014 (asp 18) ss. 44–62.

51 The background to the reforms of the 2014 act is discussed in the 'Report of the Scottish Civil Courts Review' (2 volumes), Scottish Civil Courts Review, available at https://www.scotcourts.gov.uk/about-the-scottish-court-service/the-scottish-civil-courts-reform accessed 7 November 2019.

52 Courts Reform (Scotland) Act 2014 s. 39 (1–2).

53 Courts Reform (Scotland) Act 2014 ss. 5, 44–45.

54 Courts Reform (Scotland) Act 2014 s. 44; Sch. 1 para. 7.

and sheriffs.[55] The Sheriff Appeal Court is to be staffed with sheriffs principal drawn from across Scotland.[56] In some circumstances, it is possible to appeal the decisions of the Sheriff Appeal Courts to the Inner House of the Court of Session, and from there to the UKSC.[57]

Likewise, the 2014 act affected the criminal court structure. Summary sheriffs have a limited criminal competence,[58] and generally speaking, the Sheriff Appeal Court has the power to hear appeals in criminal matters formerly enjoyed by the High Court of Justiciary.[59] It is possible to appeal from the Sheriff Appeal Court to the High Court of Justiciary, but only if the latter gives its consent to the proceedings.[60]

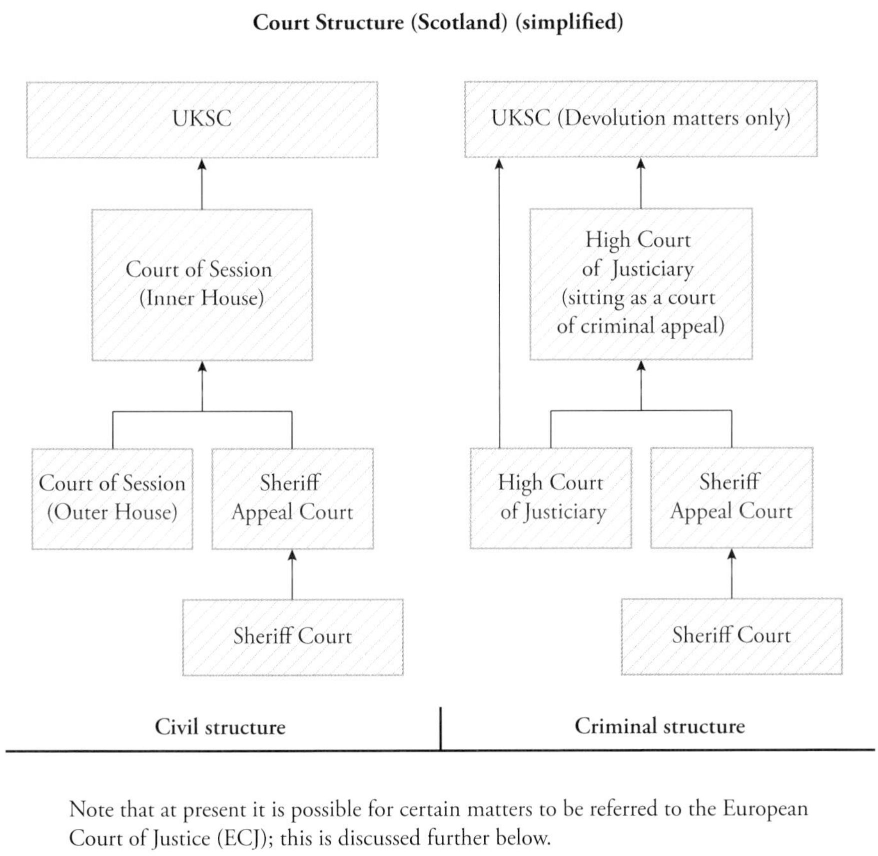

Fig. 1 The Scottish Court System.

55 Courts Reform (Scotland) Act 2014 ss. 109–111, 134.
56 Courts Reform (Scotland) Act 2014 ss. 46–62; 109.
57 Courts Reform (Scotland) Act 2014 ss. 112–117.
58 Courts Reform (Scotland) Act 2014 s. 45.
59 Courts Reform (Scotland) Act 2014 s. 118.
60 Courts Reform (Scotland) Act 2014 s. 119.

3.10 Other Courts

There are also a wide range of other courts that enjoy jurisdiction in a range of particular civil matters, which perhaps do not need to be considered in an introduction to Scottish legal culture. Among them are the Scottish Land Court and the Lands Tribunal.[61] It should also be noted that there are a range of tribunals set up to deal with particular civil matters. For example, there are Employment tribunals appointed to deal with employment disputes. Appeals can be brought from an Employment tribunal to the Employment Appeal Tribunal, and thereafter to the Court of Session.[62] Various elements of the tribunal system have been reformed through the Tribunals (Scotland) Act 2014.[63]

4. Norm Production

This account of the court structure contains the foundational knowledge required to understand the rest of Scottish legal culture, and in particular norm production. In the quotation given at the introduction of this article, Lord Rodger commented that "Scots law has long been built by the working-out of doctrine in our case-law", and in so doing he rightly underlined the centrality of the work of the courts in developing the law.[64] Nonetheless, other institutions that contribute to the development of Scottish legal culture from within Scotland are becoming increasingly important. The legislation promulgated by Holyrood is obviously having a major effect, and furthermore the role of the Scottish Law Commission (SLC) is highly significant. The SLC is a statutory body composed of five Scottish Law Commissioners, drawn from senior members of the legal profession and from academia. Its function is to make proposals for law reform to the relevant legislative bodies. Many of the recommendations of the SLC have received the support of the Scottish Parliament and have been enacted into law. Reflecting on this, Professor Reid, the Emeritus Professor of Scots Law at Edinburgh, recently commented that "the twenty-first [century] will surely be the age of the legislator". Consequently, he suggests, "[l]aw professors in pursuit of impact should pay less attention to judges: the new rulers of the universe are the members of the Scottish Law Commission."[65] This point will be considered further in due course. For now, it is helpful to consider the ways in which legal norms are generated at present. Reference will be made to the role of statute, case law, the distinctively Scottish sources known as the institutional

---

61 *Gloag and Henderson The Law of Scotland* (n 13) paras 2.20, 2.32. Questions of law must be referred from the Scottish Land Court to the Inner House of the Court of Session at the request of either party, but there is no appeal to the UKSC; see *Gloag and Henderson The Law of Scotland* para. 35.65. It is ultimately possible to bring an appeal from most types of cases begun in the Lands Tribunal before the Court of Session; for further details, see *Gloag and Henderson The Law of Scotland* para. 2.32.

62 Employment Tribunals Act 1996 ss. 20–21, 37; *Gloag and Henderson The Law of Scotland* (n 13) para. 2.30–2.31.

63 Tribunals (Scotland) Act 2014 (asp 10).

64 Rodger (1996) (n 2) 11.

65 Kenneth G C Reid, 'Smoothing the Rugged Parts of the Passage: Scots Law and its Edinburgh Chair' (2014) Vol. 18 No. 3 *Edinburgh Law Review* 315, 338–339.

writers, and equity, as it is understood in Scotland. The influence of norms produced outwith the jurisdiction will be discussed later in this essay, under the broad heading "Internationalisation".

4.1 Statutes

The earliest "statutes" were laws promulgated by Scottish kings in assemblies – later called parliaments – which were made up of representatives of the clergy, the nobility and the burgesses.[66] A few statutes of the pre-1707 parliaments of Scotland remain in force. A good example is the Leases Act 1449.[67] It is worth noting that a special rule applies to the pre-1707 statutes, in that they can be deprived of force due to the operation of the doctrine of desuetude and contrary common practice. For example, in 1913 the magistrates of Edinburgh attempted to rely on a statute of 1606 banning public gatherings without their consent. The Court of Session held that the 1606 act had fallen into desuetude, precisely because it had been disregarded in practice and because no reported case had given effect to it for a very long time.[68]

Only statutes of the pre-1707 parliaments are subject to desuetude. Statutes promulgated by Westminster or by Holyrood remain in force until they are repealed by a later act or – in the case of Holyrood statutes only – successfully challenged on the ground of incompatibility with the provisions of the Scotland Act 1998.[69] Holyrood can repeal Westminster statutes in so far as this is permitted by the Scotland Act 1998. Both Westminster and Holyrood are very active legislators. In 2018, the former legislature promulgated thirty-four public general statutes, of which twenty-four applied to Scotland.[70] In the same year, the latter enacted fifteen statutes.[71]

It should be noted here in passing that statute or "primary legislation" frequently permits government officials to exercise various powers by means of statutory instrument, also known as "secondary legislation". For example, a piece of primary legislation might empower a particular government minister to determine the date on which it is to come into force – which power he would exercise by means of a statutory instrument. Of course, a large range of powers can be exercised by statutory instrument – and also by Scottish statutory instruments, where the primary legislation emanates from Holyrood. Obviously, the use of these powers can be subject to judicial review.[72]

---

66 On the history of the parliaments of Scotland before 1707, see above all Keith M. Brown and Roland J. Tanner (eds), *Parliament and Politics in Scotland, 1235–1560* (Edinburgh University Press 2004); Keith M. Brown and Alastair J. Mann (eds), *Parliament and Politics in Scotland, 1567–1707* (Edinburgh University Press 2005); Keith M. Brown and Alan R. MacDonald (eds), *Parliament in Context, 1235–1707* (Edinburgh University Press 2010).

67 *Records of the Parliaments of Scotland* (*RPS*) 1450/1/6 in K M Brown and others (eds), *The Records of the Parliaments of Scotland* (St Andrews 2007–2017) http://www.rps.ac.uk/trans/1450/1/16 accessed 19 January 2017.

68 *McAra v Edinburgh City Council* (1913) 2 S.L.T. 110.

69 *Gloag and Henderson The Law of Scotland* (n 13) paras 1.29–1.30, 1.37.

70 See 'Legislation from 2014 Applicable to Scotland', available at http://www.legislation.gov.uk/2018/scotland accessed 7 November 2019.

71 See ibid.

72 *Gloag and Henderson The Law of Scotland* (n 13) paras. 1.29–1.30, 1.33–1.34.

To what extent, then, is the law expressed in statute? While there is no code of Scots Private law or Scots Criminal law, much of the law is declared in codifying statutes.[73] This is probably more true of Family law than of any other area of Private law, in part because legislative intervention was required to keep it in line with radically and quickly changing social expectations from the mid-twentieth century onwards. So the underlying principles of Family law – such as the duty to act in the best interests of the child when making residence or contact orders – are statutory.[74] By contrast, while large areas of property law are expressed in statute, many of its most basic distinctions and principles can still only be found in case law and the institutional writers. A good example is the distinction between real rights and personal rights, a real right being a power in a thing enforceable against the world, and a personal right being a power of exacting something due from another, enforceable only against that individual.[75] This is absolutely fundamental to Property law, and indeed the whole of Scottish Private law, and yet it is not enshrined in statute. Many of the principles of Contract law also remain uncodified, such as the rules concerning *consensus in idem*,[76] although of course much of the law governing specific contracts (such as sale of goods and insurance) is statutory – consider, for example, the Sale of Goods Act 1979.[77] In relation to Contract law, this process of codification is set to continue, with important work having recently been carried out on the subject by the SLC.[78] The law of intestate succession is largely to be found in the Succession (Scotland) Act 1964,[79] and in 2016 Holyrood promulgated a statute that reformed elements of the law of testate succession.[80] That said, codification of the whole of Succession law is not currently being planned; indeed in one area – rectification of wills – a statutory regime operates alongside the common law.[81] Much of this area of the legal system remains expressed in nineteenth-century case law.[82] Drawing upon such points, Professor Reid notes that "[f]rom the private law heartland, only delict and unjustified enrichment have been largely unaffected [by codifying statutes], at least in respect of general principles".[83]

Considering the developing role of legislation in shaping Scots Private law, Reid concludes that what is currently happening is "virtually codification by stealth", at least

73 For this point, and the discussion that follows, see Reid (2014) (n 65) 338–339.

74 Children (Scotland) Act 1995 (c. 36) s. 11(7)(a).

75 See the discussion in Kenneth G.C. Reid, *The Law of Property in Scotland* (Law Society of Scotland, Butterworths 1996) paras. 1–16.

76 *Gloag and Henderson The Law of Scotland* (n 13) para. 5.06.

77 Sale of Goods Act 1979 (c. 54).

78 See the Scottish Law Commission's law reform project 'Contract law in light of the Draft Common Frame of Reference (DCFR)', available at http://www.scotlawcom.gov.uk/law-reform/law-reform-projects/contract-law-light-draft-common-frame-reference-dcf/ accessed 14 November 2019; see also 'Report on Review of Contract Law: Formation, Interpretation, Remedies for Breach, and Penalty Clauses' (Scot Law Com No 252).

79 Succession (Scotland) Act 1964 (c. 41).

80 Succession (Scotland) Act 2016 (asp 7).

81 Succession (Scotland) Act 2016 (asp 7) ss. 3–4.

82 See, for example, *Gloag and Henderson The Law of Scotland* (n 13) paras. 39.01–39.37.

83 Reid (2014) (n 65) 339.

in some cases.[84] He is surely right, although the extent to which fundamental principles, distinctions and definitions continue to be left to develop at common law is also intriguing. In Private law, and also to some extent in Criminal law, the foundations of our Scottish statutory frameworks are still firmly embedded in case law and, to a lesser extent, the institutional writers.

4.2 Case law and Precedent

Individual decisions of the Scottish courts have not always enjoyed the force that they possess today. In the sixteenth and seventeenth centuries, most lawyers believed that the authority of an individual decision or "practick" of the College of Justice did not possess much weight. To explain, judges and advocates in this period, such as Thomas Craig of Riccarton (c 1538–1608), seem to have conceptualised the law fundamentally as "a body of learning fashioned through expert debate".[85] When expert Scottish lawyers drew upon their legal learning to reach consensus concerning the justice or equity of a particular proposition of law, then that proposition could acquire binding force. A practick on a particular point might reveal the first stage in the emergence of such consensus, which could then be reinforced by several consistent practicks concerning the same matter. Ultimately several such practicks could be taken as evidence of the emergence of customary law. That, at least, was one contemporary way of thinking about the authority of practick, as Professor Ford has shown.[86] Another seventeenth-century view, developed by the great Scottish jurist and lord president, James Dalrymple, Viscount Stair (1619–1695), sharply distinguished the learning inherent in the law from its authority, or binding force. He believed that the binding force of the law could be attributed to a series of consistent decisions of the lords of session on the basis that those lords participated in sovereignty.[87]

Both attitudes to the authority of a decision of the College of Justice are radically different from that held today. This does raise an important question – which is beyond the scope of this article – about how exactly the courts should handle the authority of an early modern decision when it is used in argument today. The problem does not arise often, but there are questions – such as the extent to which Scots law recognises acquisitive prescription of moveables – that can at present only be answered by making reference to early modern decisions of the session.[88]

The modern approach to the authority of decisions had begun to emerge by the end of the eighteenth century, at roughly the same time that many were seeking reform of the structure of the Court of Session. The reasons for this development merit further study; it suffices here to note the nature of the change. Prior to the 1790s, the decisions of the

84 Ibid.

85 Ford (2007), *Law and Opinion in Scotland during the Seventeenth Century* (n 34).

86 Ibid 181–246, 305–312.

87 Ibid; the argument is developed very clearly at 507–572, and a summary of the major distinction drawn here is at 539; a full explanation of this is beyond the scope of this article.

88 See the brief discussion in Andrew R C Simpson, 'Positive Prescription of Moveables in Scots Law' (2009) Vol. 13 No. 3 *Edinburgh Law Review* 445, 471–472.

lords of sessions were generally reported in a fairly standard form. The arguments of the parties would be presented in some detail, and then a few lines concerning sentence of the lords would follow. The individual opinions of the lords were generally not reported publicly. This began to change in the 1790s, when the reporter Robert Bell took the view that "it is the opinion of the judges, which ought to be preserved in our reports".[89] At first this met with some strong resistance from the judiciary.[90] But Bell's approach had become the standard attitude to law reporting by the beginning of the third decade of the nineteenth century, as it remains today. It is worth noting that the reporters published the decisions of both the majority and the dissenting judges. The published opinions of the judges rapidly became the most authoritative source of the law, second only to statute. The causes of this phenomenon are complex and require further study; yet there is no doubt that it was linked with Anglicisation of the law.[91]

At roughly the same period, broad rules crystallised concerning the authority of the decisions of the different courts in relation to one another. As a leading Scottish text on the subject puts it, "[t]he authority of a case depends upon the jurisdiction of the court by which it was pronounced".[92] So, broadly speaking, a decision of the UKSC in Scottish civil matters is binding on all Scottish courts. This means that if it resolves a legal problem in a particular way, then if that same problem arises again the solution laid down by the UKSC must be followed. House of Lords decisions remain binding on the other Scottish courts, regardless of how old they may be. Decisions of the Inner House of the Court of Session are binding on all inferior civil courts, including the Outer House and the Sheriff Courts. Note that a decision of a bench of seven within the Inner House is more authoritative than a decision of a bench of three, in the sense of the regard in which it is held. A decision of the Outer House is thought to be binding on a sheriff sitting alone.[93] Decisions of the Sheriff Appeal Court are binding on individual sheriffs and other inferior judges with civil jurisdiction.[94] In criminal matters, a similar hierarchy exists. So in devolution matters, the decisions of the UKSC must be followed by the High Court of Justiciary, and the decisions of the High Court are binding on the Sheriff Appeal Court and the Sheriff Courts.[95] Of course, this broad outline of the authority of decisions does over-simplify matters somewhat. This is because the decision of a higher court can sometimes be ignored by a lower court if the majority of the judges did not use the same reasoning in reaching a particular conclusion. Lawyers describe such decisions as having no binding *ratio*.[96]

---

89 Cairns (2000) (n 18) 172–177 (the passage quoted is at 174).

90 See R.G. Anderson, 'Introduction' in George Watson (ed), *Bell's Dictionary and Digest of the Law of Scotland* (reprinted edn, Edinburgh Legal Education Trust 2012) v–xlv, xx–xxiii.

91 Cairns (2000) (n 18) 172–177.

92 *Gloag and Henderson The Law of Scotland* (n 13) para. 1.54.

93 Ibid.

94 Courts Reform (Scotland) Act 2014 (asp 18) s. 48.

95 *Gloag and Henderson The Law of Scotland* (n 13) para. 1.54.

96 See, for example, *Burnett's Trustee v Grainger* 2002 S.C. 580 per Lord Hamilton at paras. 52–53.

Broadly speaking, the purpose of case law is to interpret and apply legislation, and also to declare the common law and refine the application of its principles. Consequently, even though judges are not legislators, they do possess considerable scope to develop the law.[97] The central role performed by case law in shaping the Scottish legal system at present will be discussed in more detail below when considering the Scottish ideal of justice and the Scottish legal method. Examples of the role and authority of precedent in practice will also be considered at that point.

4.3 Institutional Writings

In the early nineteenth century, at about the same time that the Scottish courts were being reformed and the modern system of law-reporting was emerging, Scottish lawyers began to recognise certain texts as highly authoritative in resolving legal disputes. These texts are now generally known as the works of the institutional writers.[98] The "canon" of institutional writers varies depending on which writer one reads.[99] But no one disputes the institutional status of various texts. In civil matters, perhaps the most frequently cited example is Viscount Stair's *The Institutions of the Law of Scotland*, which was first published in print in 1681, with a second edition appearing during the author's lifetime in 1693. So what does it mean to describe such texts, which were written for very different purposes, as "institutional writings"? Broadly speaking, it means that they have generally been treated as highly authoritative by members of the Scottish judiciary since the first half of the nineteenth century as repositories of common law rules and principles. The status is "a reflection of tradition and the attitude of the courts to various works". The relevant traditions surrounding the authority of these works emerged during the nineteenth century; and no further "institutional" works have been recognised since then.[100]

The authority of the institutional writers and their use in practice will be discussed below, in the sections headed "ideal of justice" and "legal method".

4.4 Equity

It is important to state at the outset that the limited role of "equity" in Scots law marks it off from the system of rules and principles known as "equity" in English law. The Court of Session possesses what is known as an "equitable" power to provide a remedy where no such remedy exists at common law and where it is thought that justice demands

97 *Gloag and Henderson The Law of Scotland* (n 13) paras. 1.27–1.53.

98 On the development of the "institutional" status of various texts, see John W. Cairns, 'Institutional Writings in Scotland Reconsidered' (1984) Vol. 4 No. 3 *Journal of Legal History* 76.

99 *Gloag and Henderson The Law of Scotland* (n 13) para. 1.54 lists the "chief" authorities as "Viscount Stair, Lord Bankton, Erskine and Bell" and "in the special sphere of criminal law" Hume and Alison. For a very high view of the authority of the writers, and a discussion of the canon, see T.B. Smith, *A Short Commentary on the Law of Scotland* (W. Green 1962) 32.

100 Cairns (1984) (n 98) 102–104; the passage quoted is at 103.

this. This power is called the *nobile officium*, and was described as follows in the case of *Humphries v. X and Y* (1982) by Lord President Emslie:

> "It may be exercised in highly special or unforeseen circumstances to prevent injustice or oppression. It cannot, however, be invoked in such a way as to defeat a statutory intention, express or implied, or to extend the scope of an Act of Parliament. When, on the other hand, the intention of a statute is clear but the necessary machinery for carrying out that intention in special circumstances is lacking, the power may be invoked to provide that machinery."[101]

4.5 Custom

It is possible for custom to be recognised as part of Scots law. In a case concerning the law applicable in Jersey, *Snell v Beadle* (2001), the Scottish judge Lord Hope commented that "[b]roadly speaking, custom may be said to be the product of generally accepted usage and practice. It has no formal sanction or authority behind it other than the general consensus of opinion within the community". He also pointed out that "as soon as custom is changed into formal or positive law by judicial decision or by statute it ceases to be custom. Authority is given to the law by the decision of the court or by the statute". These comments are treated as expressions of Scots law in a leading introductory work to the legal system, and probably can be taken as authoritative on the subject.[102] The same work points out that it is possible to recognise particular customs of trade as binding. For example, in *Wilkie v Scottish Aviation* (1956), Lord President Clyde accepted that a custom concerning remuneration of chartered surveyors might be recognised if it were found to be "reasonable, certain and notorious".[103]

5. Ideal of Justice

To some extent conflicting ideas of justice were at the heart of the decisions in *Sharp v Thomson* and *Burnett's Trustee v Grainger*, which interpreted different legislative provisions concerning the effects of insolvency. Exploring these cases sheds light on the extent to which one area of Scots Private law is designed to promote legal certainty. It also introduces some aspects of how the courts interpret statutes and other legal sources more generally.

101 *Humphries, Petitioner v X and Y* 1982 S.C. 79 at 83, per Lord President Emslie.

102 See *Gloag and Henderson The Law of Scotland* (n 13) para. 1.53, citing *Snell v Beadle* [2001] 2 A.C. 304 at 312, per Lord Hope.

103 *Wilkie v Scottish Aviation* 1956 S.C. 198 at 205 per Lord President Clyde.

5.1 A Difficult Legal Question: *Sharp v Thomson* (1997)

In 1984, a Scottish company known as Albyn Construction granted a floating charge over its assets – specifically, over its "property and undertaking" – in favour of the Bank of Scotland.[104] Put simply, a floating charge is a form of security for a loan; it was originally introduced into Scots law by the Companies (Floating Charges) (Scotland) Act 1961.[105] It is commercially useful because, unlike a pledge, it gives the creditor considerable security while allowing the debtor to retain possession of the security assets and to use them to raise the funds required to repay the loan. The charge "floats" over all of the assets unless the debtor becomes insolvent. At that moment the charge is said to "crystallise", meaning that it attaches to the assets. The creditor then acquires a real right to dispose of them and so recover the sum loaned.[106]

Sharp v Thomson arose because Albyn Construction owned a flat that was subject to the floating charge already mentioned. In 1989 Albyn entered into a contract – known as "missives" – to sell the flat to the Thomsons. The contract of missives constituted the first, contractual stage prior to the transfer of this immoveable or "heritable" property. At that point the Thomsons simply had a contractual right to force Albyn Construction to transfer ownership to them. In order to affect such a transfer, Albyn was required to deliver a deed known as a disposition to the Thomsons, detailing the nature of the transaction and the lands to be transferred. The delivery of the disposition constituted the second stage in the transfer of the flat. Yet it was commonly believed that the only way in which the real right of ownership in the flat could pass was through the registration of the disposition in the relevant land register – the third stage in the transfer.[107]

Unfortunately, Albyn did not deliver the disposition to the Thomsons for about a year. The company finally got around to doing this on 9 August 1990. A day later, on 10 August, Albyn Construction became insolvent, and the Bank of Scotland's floating charge crystallised over all of Albyn's assets. The Bank appointed Mr Sharp as the insolvency practitioner or "receiver" to realise the assets and recover the money owed. On 21 August 1990, the Thomsons registered the disposition transferring the flat to them.

The legal question seemed rather simple. When the floating charge crystallised, did it "catch" the flat? Specifically, was the flat within the assets – the "property and undertaking" – of Albyn Construction when the floating charge crystallised?[108] If this were so, then the real right in the flat would have passed to the Bank of Scotland as the holder of the floating charge. The bank would then have been entitled to sell it to satisfy the secured debt. Presumably the Thomsons at best would only have been left with an unsecured contractual claim to recover their losses from the insolvent estate of Albyn

104 The facts of the case were summarised in detail by Lord Hope in the Inner House; see *Sharp v Thomson* 1995 S.C. 455, at 457–458 per Lord President Hope.

105 Companies (Floating Charges) (Scotland) Act 1961 c. 46.

106 See *Gloag and Henderson The Law of Scotland* (n 13) para. 36.33.

107 See Kenneth G.C. Reid, 'Equity Triumphant' (1997) Vol. 1 No. 4 *Edinburgh Law Review* 464, 465.

108 See *Sharp v Thomson* 1995 S.C. 455 at 475–479, per Lord President Hope.

Construction.[109] Given that limited assets remained within that estate, it was unlikely that the contractual claim would be worth very much, even though the Thomsons had borrowed heavily to buy the flat in the first place. Yet it was recognised that those consequences – which seemed very harsh for the Thomsons – would only follow *if* the flat remained within the "property and undertaking" of Albyn when the floating charge crystallised. If that was *not* the case, then it followed that the Thomsons had acquired a real right of ownership when they registered their disposition on 21 August. Note that the question was, to some extent, one of statutory interpretation, because the words "property and undertaking" were ultimately lifted from the Companies Act 1985 s. 462(1).[110] This provided that "[a company may] create… a floating charge, over all or any part of the property… which may from time to time be comprised in its property and undertaking".[111]

5.2 Apparent Justice and Legal Certainty

The matter came before the Outer House, where it was held that the flat was still within the "property and undertaking" of Albyn Construction on 10 August, and consequently it was caught by the floating charge.[112] This judgment was approved on appeal to the Inner House in 1995. The (then) Lord President Hope delivered a judgment which affirmed what many lawyers thought to be the correct position in Property law. Faced with an argument that the Thomsons might have had some sort of intermediate right between a personal right and a real right that removed the flat from the "property and undertaking" of Albyn Construction, Lord Hope turned to the institutional works Stair, *Institutions* I.1.2 and Erskine, *Institute*, II.1.1 and III.1.2. He also relied upon the important academic analysis of Property law produced by Professor Reid in Volume 18 of the work known as the *Stair Memorial Encyclopaedia*.[113] His Lordship concluded on the basis of such sources that there was no "intermediate" right between a personal right and a real right in Scots law. The real right of ownership in heritable property could only pass on registration. That meant that on 10 August 1990 it was still within the "property and undertaking" of Albyn, and it had not passed to the Thomsons.[114] Lord Hope also discussed the history and development of floating charges in England to show that there was no warrant to give the words "property and undertaking" in s. 462(1) the narrow construction that would have favoured the Thomsons.[115] Consequently, it seems that at best they were left with a purely personal, contractual right against the estate of Albyn Construction.

109 Yet note the comments about such claims in *Burnett's Trustee v Grainger* 2004 S.C. 19 at 69, per Lord Rodger.

110 See *Sharp v Thomson* 1995 S.C. 455 at 475–479, per Lord President Hope.

111 Companies Act 1985 (c. 6) s. 462(1).

112 *Sharp v Thomson* 1994 S.C. 503.

113 Now published as Reid (1996), *The Law of Property in Scotland* (n 75).

114 *Sharp v Thomson* 1995 S.C. 455, at 461–475, per Lord President Hope.

115 *Sharp v Thomson* 1995 S.C. 455 at 477, per Lord President Hope.

The Thomsons then appealed to the House of Lords, where the leading speeches were given by the Scottish Law Lords at the time, Lord Jauncey and Lord Clyde.[116] As Professor Reid put it at the time, "[t]heir lordships were struck by the apparent unfairness of the result in the lower courts". This was because they perceived that "Albyn's receiver got both the price and the house; the Thomsons got nothing (other than, presumably, a claim against their solicitors)". In Reid's view, their lordships concluded that "Property law led to an unjust result", and they had two options open to them; to "rewrite" the law or to "ignore" it. Reid then pointed out that "Lord Jauncey chose the first course of action and Lord Clyde the second".[117]

Lord Clyde's solution turned upon the statutory interpretation of the words "property and undertaking" in s. 462(1) of the 1985 act. What did Parliament mean by those words? Lord Clyde began by stating that the "word 'property' is not a technical term of Scots law". He accepted that while "the holder of an unrecorded disposition" did not have a real right of ownership, it was nonetheless possible to consider him a proprietor in some circumstances. He cited several cases to establish this point (including *Heritable Reversionary Company Ltd v Millar*, *Thomas v Lord Advocate* and *Bowman v Wright*) and concluded that "'property' and feudal title may not be synonymous".[118] His Lordship also placed reliance on the fact that the charge extended to Albyn Constructions "property *and undertaking* [emphasis added]". He thought this served to "take one away from any exclusive concentration on the word property, to look to the variations in the identity of the property which may occur during the continuing course of the company's business". The rights of Albyn Construction in relation to the property were, Lord Clyde suggested, very limited, even though it retained what he called "bare title". Consequently, it was not sensible to hold that the flat remained within the "property and undertaking" of Albyn Construction following the delivery of the disposition to the Thomsons. As a result, Lord Clyde held that the flat had *not* been caught by the floating charge.[119]

Lord Jauncey agreed. Yet in the process he presented a view of Scots law which, as Professor Reid stated at the time, did "re-write" elements of Property law. Broadly, he determined that upon the delivery of the disposition to the Thomsons they acquired the "beneficial interest" in the flat. This beneficial interest was characterised as a personal right, and not a real right. Nonetheless, it was – apparently – a personal right that was effectively protected from the transferor's insolvency. For this reason, on a common-sense reading, the "property" in the flat had passed from Albyn Construction, which retained only the "bare title" – the real right recorded in the land register. This analysis did not come from nowhere; Lord Jauncey did cite case law drawn from the law of Trusts to support his views. Some nineteenth-century case law – including the decision in *Her-*

116 *Sharp v Thomson* 1997 S.C. (H.L.) 66.

117 Reid (1997) (n 107) 465.

118 *Sharp v Thomson* 1997 S.C. (H.L.) 66 at 80–81, per Lord Clyde, citing *Heritable Reversionary Company Ltd v Millar* (1892) 19 R. (H.L.) 43; *Thomas v Lord Advocate* 1953 S.C. 151 and *Bowman v Wright* 1877 4 R. 322.

119 *Sharp v Thomson* 1997 S.C. (H.L.) 82–85, per Lord Clyde.

itable Reversionary Company Ltd v Millar (1892)[120] – indicated that a trustee could hold a bare title to trust property while the right of ownership, in reality, was held by the beneficiary. Consequently, the beneficiary was protected from the trustee's insolvency. This account of the operation of the trust in Scots law had been seriously undermined by the time Lord Jauncey reached his decision in *Sharp*, in particular by the decision in *Inland Revenue v Clark's Trustees* (1939);[121] but nonetheless it provided a mechanism to enable the Thomsons to get the disputed flat. Thus, his Lordship attempted to transport beneficial interest out of the older law of Trusts into the modern general law of Property.[122]

Professor Reid argued that "the marked differences between the speeches of Lord Jauncey and Lord Clyde" left "the law in disarray".[123] He presented multiple objections to their analyses. One is particularly instructive for the purposes of the present section of this article. Scottish legal academics working in the field of Private law generally defend the view that real rights should be in some sense public. By this they usually mean that such rights should appear on public registers – a view that has been emphasised time and again in the common law, as will be explained shortly. The reason is that anyone who enters into transactions concerning a particular piece of heritable property ought to be able to trust the registers to give a near-complete picture of the rights affecting that land. So, a purchaser should be able to rely on the register when checking that a seller actually has title to transfer to him. A lender should be able to trust the register's declaration that land offered as security for a loan is actually owned by the debtor. The key point is that rights in land should be certain and should be public and patent to all. This is commonly referred to as the publicity principle. But by suggesting that the "property" or the "beneficial ownership" in land could – indeed, should – pass on the delivery of the disposition, and not on registration, Lord Jauncey threatened to undermine that principle.[124] No one could know that the Thomsons had acquired an effective right of property on delivery of the disposition to them; the act would have been private. As Professor Reid put it,

> "Lord Jauncey proposes uncertainty in place of certainty, and secrecy in place of publicity. The standard view is that ownership is indivisible and passes only with the public act of registration. Lord Jauncey divides ownership into two, in the English fashion. *Legal* ownership passes only with registration but *beneficial* ownership passes at some indeterminate earlier stage not vouched for by public act."[125]

On this analysis, two competing views of justice were at stake in the *Sharp* litigation. It seems difficult to avoid the conclusion that one sought to reach what was perceived

120 (1892) 19 R. (H.L.) 43.

121 1939 S.C. 11.

122 See *Sharp v Thomson* 1997 S.C. (H.L.) 66 at 68–77, per Lord Jauncey.

123 Reid (1997) (n 107) 469.

124 Ibid 468–469.

125 Ibid 466.

as a just result in the case of the Thomsons by adjusting certain very basic principles of Scots Property law – or, at the very least, by creating an exception to them, as Lord Clyde did in his analysis of s. 462(1) of the Companies Act 1985. The other approach, clearly favoured by Reid, sought to uphold established legal doctrine concerning the fundamental difference between real and personal rights, and also the publicity principle, so as to maintain legal certainty and faith in the registers. It is worth emphasising again that at the heart of the matter lay the question of how to interpret legislation. While the words "property and undertaking" in s. 462(1) were interpreted so as to enable the Thomsons to keep the flat, arguably it would have been better if they had been interpreted so as to uphold the publicity principle generally recognised at common law.

5.3 Burnett's Trustee v Grainger: Sharp Restricted

The decision in *Sharp v Thomson* created some confusion and drew sustained criticism from academic lawyers.[126] However, as *Sharp* was making its way through the courts, another very similar case arose. In *Burnett's Trustee v Grainger,* a certain Mrs Burnett entered into missives to sell a flat to one Rev. Grainger. The disposition was delivered soon after the sale, in November 1990, but was not registered – apparently due to the failure of Rev. Grainger's solicitors to protect his position. In the interim, Mrs Burnett was declared bankrupt. As a result, her estate was governed by s. 31(1) of the Bankruptcy (Scotland) Act 1985, which provided that "the whole estate of the debtor shall vest as at the date of sequestration in the permanent trustee for the benefit of the creditors".[127] (Note that sequestration refers here to the procedure used to transfer the debtor's estate to the "permanent trustee".) The permanent trustee – also known as the trustee in bankruptcy – was legally obliged to "recover, manage and realise" her estate, and to "distribute it among [her] creditors, according to their respective entitlements".[128] Given that Grainger's solicitors had not registered Mrs Burnett's disposition of the flat in his favour, her trustee in bankruptcy assumed that it still formed part of her "whole estate", within the meaning of s. 31(1). He then registered notice of title to the flat in December 1991 in the relevant land register. Note that he was duty-bound to do this, as he was legally obliged to ingather Mrs Burnett's remaining assets for the benefit of her creditors. A month later Rev. Grainger's solicitor finally registered the disposition that had been granted over a year earlier.[129]

The legal question can be put simply. Did the flat sold to Rev. Grainger form part of the "whole estate of the debtor" – i.e., Mrs Burnett – "as at the date of sequestration", or

126 See, for example, ibid; Robert Rennie, 'To Sharp v Thomson – an heir' 2000 S.LT. (News) 247–251; Scott Crichton Styles, 'Sharp pains for Scots property law: the case of Burnett's Trustee v Grainger' 2000 S.L.T. (News) 305–310; George L. Gretton, 'The integrity of property law and the property registers' 2001 S.LT. (News) 135–137.

127 Bankruptcy (Scotland) Act 1985 (c. 66) s. 31(1).

128 *Burnett's Trustee v Grainger* 2004 S.C. (H.L.) 19 at 42, per Lord Rodger, citing the Bankruptcy (Scotland) Act 1985 (c. 66) s. 3(1).

129 For these facts, see *Burnett's Trustee v Grainger* 2004 S.C. (H.L.) 19 at 39–41, per Lord Rodger.

did it not?[130] Counsel for Mrs Burnett's trustee argued that the flat had formed part of Mrs Burnett's "whole estate", and that consequently he had been entitled to complete his title to it. By contrast, counsel for Rev Grainger argued that in no meaningful sense could the flat be said to form part of her "whole estate" at the date of sequestration. It was pointed out that even though Mrs Burnett had retained the real right of ownership, she would not have been able to sell the flat again to another party without committing the crime of fraud against Rev Grainger. Because Mrs Burnett had no power to deal with the flat without committing a crime, it was argued, the same could be said of her trustee in bankruptcy.[131]

Lord Rodger gave a detailed and masterly judgment that secured the unanimous support of the House of Lords. He pointed out that it was quite acceptable, in principle, to interpret the phrase "the whole estate of the debtor" in s. 31(1) differently from the way in which the words "property and undertaking" had been understood in the context of the floating charge in *Sharp*.[132] He noted that the words "property and undertaking" had been lifted from s. 462(1) of the Companies Act 1985, and accepted that Lord Jauncey and Lord Clyde had been entitled to interpret them as they did in the earlier case:

> "The words which the House had to interpret in *Sharp* were relatively new, having first entered Scots law in the Companies (Floating Charges and Receivers) (Scotland) Act 1961 (cap 40). Since there was little prior authority to indicate how they should be interpreted in the circumstances of that case, the House was relatively free to adopt its own interpretation."[133]

Yet this was not the case in *Burnett's Trustee*:

> "Here, by contrast, the provision that the House has to interpret is only the latest embodiment of a measure with a history stretching back for 200 years or more. Moreover, the very wording of sec 31(1), which speaks of adjudication in implement of sale and adjudication for payment and in security of debt, imports by reference a body of law regulating these matters. In this case it is therefore simply not possible to interpret and apply the relevant words without regard to a considerable body of authority which underlies and surrounds the bankruptcy legislation."[134]

---

130 *Burnett's Trustee v Grainger* 2004 S.C. (H.L.) 19 at 42, per Lord Rodger.

131 *Burnett's Trustee v Grainger* 2004 S.C. (H.L.) 19 at 42–43, per Lord Rodger. A recent study of Lord Rodger's approach as a judge – which proved very helpful in writing the present article – can be found in Greg Gordon, 'The Exclusion of Consequential Loss in the Piper Alpha Case: A Study of Lord Rodger's Method of Textual Analysis' in Andrew R.C. Simpson, Scott Crichton Styles, Euan West and Adelyn L.M. Wilson (eds), *Continuity, Change and Pragmatism: Essays in Memory of Professor Angelo Forte* (Aberdeen University Press 2016) 434–465.

132 *Burnett's Trustee v Grainger* 2004 S.C. (H.L.) 19 at 44–45, per Lord Rodger.

133 *Burnett's Trustee v Grainger* 2004 S.C. (H.L.) 19 at 45, per Lord Rodger.

134 *Burnett's Trustee v Grainger* 2004 S.C. (H.L.) 19 at 45, per Lord Rodger.

His Lordship then proceeded to outline a detailed historical survey of the authorities that interpreted the measure that had come to be expressed in s. 31(1) of the 1985 act, many of which were produced during the eighteenth and nineteenth centuries. He showed that "for the last 200 years, in terms of the bankruptcy legislation, heritable property which the debtor has sold and disponed but on which the purchaser is not infeft [i.e. on which his title is incomplete] has been regarded as forming part of the debtor's estate that vests in the trustee in sequestration".[135] Lord Rodger also explained elements of the reasoning underpinning the law. One argument that had considerable force in the eighteenth-century law was essentially that personal deeds – such as unregistered dispositions – should not affect feudal rights. This was because such personal deeds were by their nature private, and absent from the public registers of land rights; and *all* creditors were presumed to lend on the faith of the contents of those registers, regardless of whether or not they actually consulted them at all.[136] Importantly, his Lordship also explained that even though Mrs Burnett herself could not have dealt further with the property without committing fraud, it was wrong to conclude that the same principle applied to her trustee in bankruptcy. This was because the same line of case law discussed by Lord Rodger made it abundantly clear that a trustee in bankruptcy does not "step into the shoes" of the bankrupt. He is *not* bound by all of the bankrupt's contractual arrangements. Rather the bankrupt's heritable property vests in him unburdened from such personal rights, so that it can subsequently be distributed to the creditors according to the bankruptcy regime.[137]

Lord Rodger concluded that the flat sold to the Graingers had formed part of the "whole estate of the debtor", and that Mrs Burnett's trustee had actually been legally obliged to complete title to it in so far as he was able to do so. This was because his duty was to protect the interests of the creditors. As his Lordship put it, "in this case the law of bankruptcy worked as it has been intended to work for at least 200 years…[w]hether that law is… 'in a condition altogether satisfactory' obviously involves fundamental issues of legal policy". Nonetheless, he told the House, such issues "are of a kind that must be left to the legislature. Your Lordships have to apply the existing law".[138] Thus, in broad terms, the holding in *Sharp* was distinguished and limited to the situations involving floating charges. Those who only have an unregistered disposition of property have nothing other than a personal right to complete title. Unless protected by the holding in *Sharp* they will lose the opportunity to complete title if an insolvency practitioner, like a trustee in bankruptcy, manages to do so first.

135 *Burnett's Trustee v Grainger* 2004 S.C. (H.L.) 19 at 62–63, per Lord Rodger; see generally his arguments at 53–66.
136 *Burnett's Trustee v Grainger* 2004 S.C. (H.L.) 19 at 54–60 (particularly at 59–60), per Lord Rodger.
137 *Burnett's Trustee v Grainger* 2004 S.C. (H.L.) 19 at 60–66, per Lord Rodger.
138 *Burnett's Trustee v Grainger* 2004 S.C. (H.L.) 19 at 69.

5.4 Conclusions from *Sharp* and *Burnett*

Sharp and *Burnett's Trustee* provide insights into the Scottish ideal of justice, at least in relation to statutory interpretation in the field of Property law. Lawyers working in that field tend to value legal certainty, and in particular the publicity principle, so as to enable parties to land transactions to proceed confidently on the faith of the registers. More broadly, *Sharp* and *Burnett* also serve to introduce the closely related topic of methods of legal interpretation. Lord Rodger's comments concerning the relative freedom of Lord Jauncey and Lord Clyde to interpret "relatively new" statutory words are intriguing. That is not to say that Lord Clyde and Lord Jauncey might, with respect, have been wise to interpret s. 462(1) so as to uphold the publicity principle recognised at common law. Yet Lord Rodger was also right to note the judicial freedom in this area of interpretation. It may not be going too far to say that a version of the same principle is currently being used to determine the meaning of the phrase "sustainable development" by the courts. This is a term that has appeared recently in Scottish legislation which promotes the use – and sometimes acquisition – of land for the purpose of such development. Its meaning is only gradually emerging in practice, as can be seen from the judgments of Lords Gill, Eassie and Malcolm in *Pairc Crofters Ltd v The Scottish Ministers* (2013).[139] Its significance is set to become greater given its role in the Land Reform (Scotland) Act 2016.[140]

Nonetheless, in Lord Rodger's mind – at least in *Burnett's Trustee* – there was a clear corollary of the principle of relative judicial freedom to interpret new statutory terms. This was that older legislative provisions that have been clad with a specific meaning over a long period of time by the courts should – generally speaking – continue to be interpreted in a consistent fashion. Lord Rodger's painstaking and rigorously researched reconstruction of the law underpinning s. 31(1) of the Bankruptcy Act 1985 as it had developed over the centuries constitutes a very fine example of exactly how this sort of work should be done. It should also be noted that this is not simply about the promotion of legal certainty. It is also – as Lord Rodger himself explained – a judicial duty to leave to the legislature any fundamental attempt to reform established interpretations of statute.

5.5 Principles of Interpretation More Generally

This discussion merely serves to introduce the complex ways in which statutory interpretation can be dealt with in Scots law. Other points can be drawn out from the cases considered. So counsel for Burnett's trustee said that the words "the whole estate of the debtor" in s. 31(1) should simply be given their normal, literal meaning.[141] In general, this is the rule followed by judges when attempting to discover Parliament's intention

---

139 *Pairc Crofters Ltd v the Scottish Ministers* 2013 S.L.T. 308, discussing the meaning of the words "sustainable development" in the context of the Land Reform (Scotland) Act 2003 (asp 2) Part 3.

140 Land Reform (Scotland) Act 2016 (asp 18) Part 5. I am grateful to Mr. Malcolm Combe for discussing this with me.

141 *Burnett's Trustee v Grainger* 2004 S.C. (H.L.) 19 at 42.

in a statute, unless this would result in a manifest absurdity.[142] Furthermore, the courts have laid down other general rules of interpretation in decided cases.[143] In an introductory survey of Scottish legal culture a few examples will suffice. An undefined word in a statute should be considered in light of the act as a whole; "[a] statute must, like any other continuous document, be read as a whole – *optimus statuti interpres statutum ipsum*".[144] In addition, if the statute provides a list of things to which it is to apply, the *eiusdem generis* rule makes it clear that it may also apply to things of the same type.[145] In *Henretty v Hart* (1885) betting was prohibited in "any house, office, room or other place"; but a racetrack was not considered *eiusdem generis* with these descriptive terms, and so excluded from the operation of the statute.[146] Furthermore, the ideal that some types of statutes should be interpreted broadly and others narrowly, found in Erskine, *Institute*, I.1.53, is now generally "discredited", save for the point that statutes that extend Criminal law are read strictly. Lord McCluskey explained in *Friel v Initial Contract Services Ltd.* (1994) that this was to ensure that "doubt or ambiguity" should "be construed in favour of the liberty of the subject".[147]

5.6 Conclusion

These are just a few examples of the interpretative principles that are scattered across many different Scottish cases. It must be admitted that Scots law lacks a rigorous, coherent and detailed academic study of those principles at present. Yet if, as seems likely, we now find ourselves in what Professor Reid terms the age of the legislator, it follows that we are also entering the age of the interpreter of legislation. Scots lawyers may find it necessary to reflect more critically on their interpretative practices. For now, rigorous interpretative approaches such as those of Lord Rodger – which honestly seek to uncover the meaning of statute, taking into account ways in which legislation had been interpreted in the past where appropriate – recommend themselves to attempts to foster clarity and legal certainty in practice.

6. Legal Method

The comments made above introducing Scottish norm production, ideals of justice and interpretative practices are also relevant to a discussion of legal method. A few further

---

142 *Gloag and Henderson The Law of Scotland* (n 13) para. 1.39.

143 Ibid 1.35–1.48.

144 *Magistrates of Buckie v Dowager Countess of Seafield's Trustees* 1928 S.C. 525 at 529 per Lord President Clyde, as discussed in *Gloag and Henderson The Law of Scotland* (n 13) para. 1.42.

145 *Gloag and Henderson The Law of Scotland* (n 13) para. 1.49.

146 *Henretty v Hart* (1885) 13 R. (J.) 9, as discussed in *Gloag and Henderson The Law of Scotland* (n 13) para. 1.49.

147 See *Gloag and Henderson The Law of Scotland* (n 13) para. 1.48 and footnote 302, discussing Lord McCluskey's views in *Friel v Initial Contract Services Ltd* 1994 S.L.T. 1216, 1221.

points will be made here concerning the sources used in legal arguments and the extent to which deduction from principle features in the formulation of such argument.

The sources used by lawyers in legal argument have already been explored, including statute, case law, the institutional writers, equity and custom. Reference has been made to the centrality of case law in legal development, and this has been explained through the examples of *Sharp* and *Burnett's Trustee*. It has also been explained that, in general terms, the authority of statute is greater than that of case law, and considerable attention has been given to the ways in which lawyers interpret statutes. As regards lawyers' approaches to the development of case law, subtly different attitudes can be detected. The ways in which academic lawyers are encouraging practitioners and judges to shape case law by deducing results from certain core principles has been illustrated. Reference has been made to Professor Reid's promotion of the publicity principle – which of course was already enshrined in the common law – as a means of criticising Lord Jauncey's speech. Indeed, the idea that Scots law favours – and should favour – deduction from a set of core legal principles as a methodological approach is well-established and has traditionally commanded the respect of a great number of lawyers.[148] Yet, as has also been seen from the decisions in *Sharp* and *Burnett's Trustee*, this approach operates alongside one that emphasises the role of comparing cases to find differences and similarities between them, facilitating a process of legal development by distinguishing precedents. So, Lord Rodger – while recognising the significance of the publicity principle – developed the law relating to the status of the unregistered disposition in insolvency proceedings in *Burnett's Trustee* by distinguishing *Sharp* and limiting its effects to cases involving floating charges.

In a treatment of Scottish legal method, it remains necessary to say something concerning the ways in which the institutional writers can be used in argument. Brief reference was made to the way in which Lord Hope used such sources in his judgment in the Inner House in *Sharp v Thomson*. Even though the judgment of the Inner House was overturned on appeal, a fuller examination of his Lordship's comments will prove instructive. It will be recalled that Lord Hope relied upon the institutional writers to establish a fundamental proposition of Scots law. This proposition is that there is no "intermediate, or incomplete, right which lies between the personal right on the one hand and the real right on the other".[149] In order to demonstrate this, he began by stating that at the heart of the questions raised in *Sharp v Thomson* lay a proper understanding of the "distinction between the law of property and the law of obligations".[150] He then noted that this "is one of the most fundamental of all the divisions which exist in our law".[151] Subsequently he justified that proposition with reference to a range of authori-

148 See, for example, T M Cooper, 'The Common and the Civil Law – A Scot's View' in T M Cooper, *Selected Papers 1922–1954* (Oliver and Boyd 1957) 201–209. Few (if any) would endorse all of the views found in this paper today, but it contains a very good (and influential) summary of the philosophical approach to law mentioned here.

149 *Sharp v Thomson* 1995 S.C. 455, at 463, per Lord President Hope.

150 *Sharp v Thomson* 1995 S.C. 455, at 461, per Lord President Hope.

151 *Sharp v Thomson* 1995 S.C. 455, at 461, per Lord President Hope.

ties, beginning with Stair's *Institutions*.[152] Next the work of another institutional writer, Professor Erskine, was cited to reinforce the point. He defined a real right as "the right of using and disposing of a subject as our own, except in so far as we are restrained by law or paction", whereas a personal right was stated to be "a legal tie, by which one is bound to pay or perform something to another".[153] Erskine went on to use this last observation to state the following general point:

> "A real right, or *jus in re*... entitles the person vested with it to possess the subject as his own... whereas the creditor in a personal right or obligation has only a *jus ad rem*, or a right of action against the debtor or his representatives, by which they may be compelled to fulfil that obligation..."[154]

Having quoted this passage, Lord Hope then proceeded to cite two leading academic works written in the twentieth century that concurred with these accounts of the distinction between real and personal rights. Finally, he then reached his conclusion, which was that "[t]he classification noted by the institutional writers provides no support for... [the]... argument that there is an intermediate, or incomplete, right which lies between the personal right on the one hand and the real right on the other". Of course, this tended to confirm the view that the holder of an unrecorded, unregistered disposition was left with nothing but a personal right, a point Lord Hope went on to develop with reference to other authorities.[155]

This illustrates two additional points about the sources used in legal argument, and the methods used in handling those sources. First, fundamental principles of Scots law can be deduced from the institutional writers. As one work puts it, "[t]he question whether a particular rule is recognised as part of the common law must be determined, except in the case where appeal is made to a custom or usage hitherto unrecognised, by consideration of the authorities", and the "authorities" include the institutional writers.[156] Of course, principles deduced from their works can be altered by statute, and developed and indeed re-worked in case law.[157] Second, leading academic commentaries of the modern era do have a certain status as persuasive authorities, but they are by no means binding on the courts.[158]

152 *Sharp v Thomson* 1995 S.C. 455, at 462, per Lord President Hope, citing Stair, *Institutions*, I.1.22.

153 *Sharp v Thomson* 1995 S.C. 455, at 462, per Lord President Hope, citing Erskine, *Institute* II.1.1 and III.1.2.

154 *Sharp v Thomson* 1995 S.C. 455, at 462, per Lord President Hope, citing Erskine, *Institute* III.1.2

155 *Sharp v Thomson* 1995 S.C. 455, at 463–465, per Lord President Hope; the passage quoted is at 463.

156 See *Gloag and Henderson The Law of Scotland* (n 13) para. 1.54.

157 See *The Laws of Scotland. Stair Memorial Encyclopaedia*, (Lexis Nexis) vol. 22 paras 439–441, available at https://www.lexisnexis.com/ accessed 14 November 2019.

158 See, for example, Smith (1962) (n 99) 33; *Stair Memory Encyclopaedia*, vol. 22, paras 442–445.

7. Professionalisation

High-quality legal reasoning and decision-making in the courts can of course be fostered through effective legal education and the existence of professional bodies. The Scottish legal system, like most others, recognises this to be true, and carefully regulates the teaching of law and those who go on to practise it. Here reference will be made to the rules governing entry to the profession, and also the various branches of that profession.

7.1 The LLB Degree and Entry to the Profession

In general, an LLB degree from a Scottish University is required for entry to the Scottish legal profession. That statement is subject to certain qualifications. For example, an applicant who possesses a certificate to the effect that he has completed a pupillage as a barrister in England may become an advocate in Scotland if he passes certain exams set by the Faculty of Advocates.[159] Yet most practitioners enter the profession having first obtained a Bachelor of Laws degree from a Scottish university. Ten universities offer such degrees – Aberdeen, Abertay, Dundee, Edinburgh, Glasgow, Glasgow Caledonian, Napier, Robert Gordon University (RGU), Stirling, and Strathclyde.[160] The Law Society, a professional regulatory body, requires each university to cover certain topics during the course of the LLB degree, and each institution does so slightly differently. Most of the teaching revolves around the exposition of the statutes and decided cases that shape each legal topic. Those studying for the Bachelor of Laws with Honours – the majority of students – are also required to take a number of "honours" subjects and to write a dissertation over the course of their third and fourth years. The resulting marks are used to calculate their degree classification. Honours students study topics of their choice in depth, and they are strongly encouraged to display original thought in engaging critically with the law.[161] Those who do so consistently and well generally receive first class honours degrees. Following the completion of the degree, students wishing to enter the profession are also required to complete the Diploma in Professional Legal Practice, a one-year qualification currently offered by Aberdeen, Dundee, Glasgow, Edinburgh, RGU, and Strathclyde.[162]

159 See Faculty of Advocates, 'Regulations as to Intrants', available at http://www.advocates.org.uk/media/2363/regulations-as-to-intrants.pdf accessed 14 November 2019. The exams in question are in Roman Law of Property and Obligations, Jurisprudence, Constitutional and Administrative Law, Scottish Criminal Law, Scottish Private Law, Commercial Law and Business Institutions, Evidence, International Private Law and European Law and Institutions.

160 See Law Society of Scotland, 'Where to study the LLB?', available at https://www.lawscot.org.uk/qualifying-and-education/qualifying-as-a-scottish-solicitor/llb-degree-in-law/where-can-i-study-the-llb/ accessed 14 November 2019.

161 See, for example, University of Aberdeen, 'Aberdeen University Calendar – Degrees in Law', available at https://www.abdn.ac.uk/registry/calendar/law.php. accessed 14 November 2019.

162 The Diploma Provides, 'The Law Society of Scotland', available at https://www.lawscot.org.uk/qualifying-and-education/qualifying-as-a-scottish-solicitor/diploma-in-professional-legal-practice/where-can-i-study-the-diploma/ accessed 14 November 2019.

7.2 Solicitors and Advocates

Those who complete the LLB degree and the Diploma may subsequently attempt to enter the profession. The profession can be divided into two major branches, the first of which is that of the solicitors. To become a solicitor – essentially a legal practitioner with authority to give formal legal advice, draft legal documents and appear in the lower courts – it is necessary to complete a two-year traineeship at a Scottish legal firm.[163] Under the Solicitors (Scotland) Act 1980, before a solicitor can practise he must be named on the roll of solicitors maintained by the Law Society of Scotland, and hold a practising certificate issued by the Council of that Society.[164] There are currently just under 12,000 solicitors qualified to practise in Scotland.[165] While the qualification to act as a solicitor is general, most specialise in particular areas of legal practice. Solicitors may join a number of local associations of practitioners in different parts of Scotland, many of which are hundreds of years old.[166] Note that some solicitors also choose to qualify as notaries public; among their functions include receiving certain oaths and affirmations and authenticating foreign documents.[167]

The Faculty of Advocates constitutes the second branch of the profession. Prior to 1990 a key factor that marked out advocates from the wider legal profession was that they enjoyed exclusive rights of audience in the Court of Session, the High Court of Justiciary and the House of Lords (now the UKSC).[168] The privilege emerged gradually, with the Faculty itself. When the old session was reconstituted as the College of Justice in 1532, ten men of law were given general licence to plead in all types of cases before the lords. Today there are about 450 advocates in practice. As stated above, the principal route to the bar is open to one who has obtained an LLB degree from a Scottish University and a Diploma in Professional Legal Practice. An individual must have completed a minimum of twenty-one months of a traineeship as a solicitor prior to commencing pupillage, or training to become an advocate. Pupillage lasts for about nine months, during which time the pupil shadows a practising advocate. Entrants are examined on "examination of witnesses, oral submissions, drafting pleadings and drafting a written opinion". If found competent, they are admitted to the Faculty.

---

163 See the 'Admission as a Solicitor (Scotland) Regulations 2019', Regulation 7, available at https://www.lawscot.org.uk/media/367853/admission-as-solicitor-scotland-regulations-2019.pdf, replacing (from 1 November 2019) the older 'Admission as a Solicitor (Scotland) Regulations 2011', Regulation 7, available at https://www.lawscot.org.uk/media/9330/admission-regulations-2011.pdf. Both links accessed 14 November 2019.

164 Solicitors (Scotland) Act 1980 s. 4.

165 See Law Society of Scotland, 'Annual Report 2018', available at https://www.lawscot.org.uk/about-us/strategy-reports-plans/annual-reports/annual-report-2018/ accessed 14 November 2019.

166 See 'The Society of Advocates in Aberdeen', available at http://www.socofadvocates.com/; 'The Royal Society of Procurators in Glasgow', available at http://www.rfpg.org/. Both links accessed 14 November 2019.

167 See Michael P Clancy, 'The Scottish Legal Profession (Except Advocates)' in Mark A Mulhern (ed), *Scottish Life and Society. A Compendium of Scottish Ethnology Volume 13: The Law* (John Donald 2012) 91–106, 101–103.

168 Godfrey (2012) (n 37) 139.

7.3 The Universities

It was said above that the Scottish legal profession is broadly divided into two branches. Nonetheless, Professor Reid has rightly drawn attention to the rise of the "third branch" of the profession, meaning academics who research and teach Scots law in the universities.[169] There are about one hundred professors – i.e., holders of chairs – scattered across the ten Scottish universities that offer law degrees.[170] Many other academics hold less senior posts within the universities, such as senior lecturer and lecturer.

Those applying for a position in academia are usually required to possess a law degree, but not necessarily a Scottish LLB. No teaching qualifications are required to secure appointment as a lecturer, although most universities offer in-house training in that regard. However, in most cases universities seek to appoint candidates who have either completed a doctorate of philosophy (PhD) or are close to doing so. A PhD is usually taken as a strong indication of research potential. One major problem with this development is that extremely able members of the legal profession who have practised for several years can find it difficult to enter academia if they do not possess a doctorate. Conversely, those with doctorates hoping to enter academia frequently do not complete professional qualifications, because these are not required by the universities. The result is a growing gap between academia and practice, which is surely regrettable.[171] One solution would be to provide academics with the opportunity to shadow practitioners, with a view to gaining some practical experience; the obvious problem is that such a proposal could have serious resource implications for the practitioners involved.

Nonetheless, the gap is still bridged, frequently to excellent effect. It is hoped that the various examples provided above of academics who have engaged in the development of the law over the past few years give some impression of the role that they continue to perform in shaping Scottish legal culture. Several have held appointments as Scottish Law Commissioners, and in that capacity they shaped – and continue to shape – legislation put before the Scottish Parliament. Perhaps one of the best examples is the Abolition of Feudal Tenure (Scotland) Act 2000, which completely reformed the structure of landholding in Scotland and emerged directly from the Scottish Law Commission *Report on the Abolition of the Feudal System* (1998).[172] Yet academics also seek to engage critically with the development of the law in less direct ways, for example through the dissemina-

---

169 Reid (1996), 'Third Branch' (n 3).

170 This information was been taken from the websites of the ten law schools accredited to offer LLB degrees, all last accessed 14 November 2019: http://www.abdn.ac.uk/law/; http://www.abertay.ac.uk/studentlife/schools/dbs/staff/; http://www.dundee.ac.uk/law/staff/; http://www.law.ed.ac.uk/; http://www.gla.ac.uk/schools/law/; http://www.gcu.ac.uk/gsbs/staff/; https://www.napier.ac.uk/people?fv=BE7C946393454607AD2CC3D91E65303F%7eBusiness+School%7c235A2CAF60FE4EF18E8582C32510E292%7eLaw&tab=1#rms; https://www.rgu.ac.uk/about/faculties-schools-anddepartments/aberdeen-business-school/law; https://www.strath.ac.uk/staff/?department=School of Law; http://www.stir.ac.uk/arts-humanities/staff-directory/.

171 See Reid (2014) (n 65) 339–340.

172 Consider the Abolition of Feudal Tenure (Scotland) Act 2000 (asp 5) and Scottish Law Commission, 'Report on the Abolition of the Feudal System' (Scot Law Com No 168), available at http://www.scotlawcom.gov.uk/files/1712/8015/2730/26-07-2010_1458_725.pdf accessed 14 November 2019.

tion of their research in the major Scottish legal journals, these being the *Edinburgh Law Review* and the *Juridical Review*. Shorter contributions to current debates are also often offered through *The Scots Law Times*, *The Journal of the Law Society of Scotland* and the *SCOLAG Journal* (the Journal of the Scottish Legal Action Group).

8. Internationalisation

8.1 The Influence of Comparative Law

One important aspect of Scottish legal culture has not been considered thus far, and it may be appropriate to consider it under the heading of "internationalisation" – although perhaps it belongs within a category of its own. During the course of the twentieth century there was a strong resurgence in interest in the civilian heritage of Scots law. Some judges and academics sought to defend many of the civilian elements of the legal tradition in the face of increasing Anglicisation. It was felt by some that the Anglicising trend was becoming so extensive that the survival of a separate Scottish legal system might be at stake. In order to develop the civilian heritage of Scots law in a modern context, it was frequently thought helpful to seek inspiration in other modern legal systems that were indebted to Roman law. This in turn facilitated the emergence of comparative law as a discipline within the Scottish universities.[173] In recent decades academics have frequently looked to various legal systems, including South African law, German law, the law of Louisiana and also the law of Sri Lanka when thinking about how Scots law might be augmented with ideas consistent with the civilian tradition.[174] Several of those legal systems – notably South African law – make particularly interesting comparators because they are, like Scots law, "mixed", in the broad sense that the civil law and the common law traditions both remain influential in their development.

Some Scottish academics are less willing to place such great emphasis on the continuing importance of the civilian tradition in Scots law today – at least if this is to the exclusion of the potential of other traditions of legal thought that might provide useful inspiration in the development of the legal system. The late Professor Forte for one was critical of any movement to ignore the potential value of English law. His work both in Commercial law and in legal history made him sensitive to the great debt Scots law owed to the common law tradition. Forte believed that the need to discover practical solutions to commercial problems had driven the reception of English legal ideas in the

173 These broad trends are discussed in various essays contained in Elspeth Reid and David L Carey Miller (eds), *A Mixed Legal System in Transition. T B Smith and the Progress of Scots Law* (Edinburgh University Press 2005), including Kenneth G C Reid, 'While One Hundred Remain: T B Smith and the Progress of Scots Law' 1–29; George L Gretton, 'The Rational and the National: Thomas Broun Smith' 30–43; Hector L MacQueen, 'Two Toms and an Ideology for Scots Law: T B Smith and Lord Cooper of Culross' 44–72; and John Blackie, 'T B Smith as a Legal Historian' 73–99.

174 See, for example, David L. Carey Miller, 'Three of a Kind? Positive Prescription in Sri Lanka, South Africa and Scotland' (2008) Vol. 12 *European Journal of Comparative Law*, available at http://www.ejcl.org/121/art121-3.pdf accessed 14 November 2019.

eighteenth and nineteenth centuries. Like Lord Rodger, he had little objection to the use of different traditions of legal ideas in practice if they produced pragmatic solutions to the needs of Scottish litigants.[175] Others, of course, express concern about the extent to which such an approach may compromise the systematic integrity of the law; the current system is seen not so much as a mixture as a muddle.[176] The debate continues, but the comments made here illustrate at least the openness of Scots lawyers to inspiration from systems of foreign law.

8.2 EU Law

More relevant to a discussion of the internationalisation of Scots law are international obligations and, of course, the role of EU law. As regards international obligations generally, the Scottish courts share the UK's dualist outlook.[177] As regards EU law, it has already been explained that under the Scotland Act 1998 the Scottish Parliament cannot legislate in a manner inconsistent with EU law.[178] More broadly now it is necessary to say something concerning the functioning of the European Communities Act 1972, recently repealed by the European Union (Withdrawal) Act 2018.[179] Under the former statute – by which the UK joined the European Economic Community – it was provided that rights arising from the Treaties of the EEC, and now the EU, would be enforceable in the British courts. While "most such provisions are intended to create obligations for, and so may be enforced against, the Member State" others "give rise to enforceable rights as between private persons".[180] Furthermore, the consequence of the 1972 Act was that EU regulations had to be enforced by the UK courts. It was explained by Lord Bridge in *R v Secretary of State for Transport, Ex p. Factortame Ltd (No. 2)* (1991), that "it [is] the duty of a United Kingdom court, when delivering final judgment, to override any rule of national law found to be in conflict with any directly enforceable rule of Community law".[181] The critical point of *Factortame* was that it enabled Community law to override a rule of national law expressed in a Westminster statute. Of course, if there were any doubt as to the meaning of EU law in a Scottish court, it might "sist proceedings and seek a preliminary ruling on the matter from the

175 Consider, for example, A.D.M. Forte, 'Scots law and Scottish national identity' in Gillian Fellows-Jensen (ed), *Denmark and Scotland: the cultural and environmental resources of small nations* (Kongelige Danske Videnskabernes Selskab 2001) 239–250.

176 Robin Evans-Jones, 'Receptions of Law, Mixed Legal Systems and the Myth of the Genius of Scots Private Law' (1998) Vol. 114 No. 2 *Law Quarterly Review* 228.

177 See, for example, the comments made by Lord Hodge in *Moohan and Another v Lord Advocate* 2015 S.C. (U.K.C.S.) 1, paras 29–30, 38.

178 Scotland Act 1998 (c. 46) s. 29(2)(d).

179 European Communities Act 1972 (c. 68) s. 2(1); European Union (Withdrawal) Act 2018 (c. 6) s.1.

180 *Gloag and Henderson The Law of Scotland* (n 13) para. 1.32. On the difficult questions regarding the horizontal direct effect of EU Directives, see Catherine Barnard and Steve Peers (eds), *European Union Law* (2nd edn, Oxford University Press 2017) 146–156. I am grateful to Dr Justin Borg-Barthet for this reference.

181 *R v Secretary of State, Ex p. Factortame (No. 2)* [1991] 1 A.C. 603 at 659, per Lord Bridge of Harwich.

European Court of Justice". Among courts the ECJ alone has the authority to declare an EU law invalid.[182]

The impact of EU law on Scots law and Scotland more generally is, of course, very great. Areas such as competition law, the law relating to equal pay, the free movement of workers and the right of establishment have all been influential.[183] Commenting on these developments, Forte, writing in 2001, also located them in part within the discourse of legal change driven by pragmatic considerations:

> "A further brake on legislative autonomy is represented by the European Union's long-term desire to create a European private law code, and its short-term objective of creating a European contract code, as adjuncts to the efficient functioning of the Single Market. Two things are worthy of comment. First, the driving force here is the facilitation of cross-border business. Second, the emphasis will be on solutions and not legal traditions. As we move into the twenty-first century, pragmatic realism and utilitarian functionalism will increasingly come to dominate legal developments both within Europe and beyond. This… represents an approach which is entirely consistent with Scottish success both past and present."[184]

It is hoped that everything that has been said thus far underlines the point that Forte's view is not representative of all participants in the development of Scottish legal culture, nor was his a lone voice. In many ways his arguments dovetailed with those of Lord Rodger cited at the beginning of this article.

For all the significance of EU law in the development of the Scottish legal system, its future role is unclear. This is the result of the referendum – already discussed above – on continued British membership of the EU in June 2016, which resulted in a vote to leave.[185] The UK subsequently left the EU on 31 January 2020, subject to an Implementation Period that will end on 31 December 2020, during which time the UK and the EU are seeking to negotiate a future trading relationship. It is worth noting that, during the Implementation Period, the law of European Union still largely applies to

182 See *Gloag and Henderson The Law of Scotland* (n 13) para. 1.32, citing Treaty on the Functioning of the European Union art. 267 and – on the authority of the ECJ – Case 314/85 *Foto-Frost v Hauptzollamt Lübeck-Ost* [1987] ECR I-4199.

183 See *Gloag and Henderson The Law of Scotland* (n 13) para. 1.32.

184 Forte (2001) (n 175) 248.

185 See The Electoral Commission, 'Results and Turnout at the EU Referendum', available at https://www.electoralcommission.org.uk/who-we-are-and-what-we-do/elections-and-referendums/past-elections-and-referendums/eu-referendum/results-and-turnout-eu-referendum accessed 7 November 2019.

the United Kingdom, in the terms discussed above.[186] The repercussions of the decision to leave the European Union will undoubtedly be highly significant within large tracts of the legal system.

8.3 The Role of the ECHR

The role of the European Convention on Human Rights (ECHR) was discussed above in passing. Under the Scotland Act 1998, Holyrood may not legislate in a manner inconsistent with the "Convention rights", as defined in the Human Rights Act 1998.[187] The Human Rights Act 1998 defines "the Convention rights" as Articles 2–12 and 14, Articles 1–3 of Protocol 1 and Article 1 of the Thirteenth Protocol of the ECHR; and it specifies that those provisions are to be read in light of Articles 16 and 18.[188] When interpreting the Convention rights, the courts are under an obligation to do so in light of the decisions of the European Court of Human Rights at Strasbourg.[189] The courts are also under an obligation to interpret primary and secondary legislation in a manner consistent with the Convention rights. If this is not deemed possible, and if the legislation in question proceeds from Westminster, then various courts – including, in Scotland, the Court of Session and the High Court of Justiciary sitting otherwise than as a trial court – are empowered to make what are known as "declarations of incompatibility". But that does not affect the duty of the courts to *apply* the Westminster statute to the case at hand.[190] It is then left to Westminster to decide what is to be done to remedy the situation.

The role of the Convention rights in shaping Scots law has been very great over the last few years; constraints of space make it impossible to explore this fully here.[191] Yet once again, the future of the Convention rights in the legal system of the UK is uncertain, because of the commitment of a recent Government to replace the Human Rights Act with a UK Bill of Rights.[192] Obviously the effects of such a change on the Scottish constitutional settlement would be enormous.

---

186 For key provisions relevant to the British exit from the European Union, see the European Union (Withdrawal) Act 2018 (c.6) ss.1, 1A, 20 (s.1A contains the saving provisions relating to the ongoing effects of EU Law in the UK during the Implementation Period); European Union (Withdrawal) Act 2020 (c.1) s.39 (which defines the Implementation Period as ending on 31 December 2020); Agreement on the Withdrawal of the United Kingdom of Great Britain and Northern Ireland from the European Union and the European Atomic Energy Community O J L 29, 31.1.2020, p.7–187. For a report of the UK Government's position that the Transition Period is not to be extended beyond 31 December 2020, see Sebastian Payne and Jim Brunsden, 'UK will refuse any EU offer to extend Brexit transition', *Financial Times*, 16 April 2020 https://www.ft.com/content/3c006614-767f-4447-8136-97987045517f accessed 18 April 2020.

187 Scotland Act 1998 (c. 46) s. 29(2)(d).

188 Human Rights Act 1998 (c. 42) s. 1(1).

189 Human Rights Act 1998 (c. 42) s. 2.

190 Human Rights Act 1998 (c. 42) ss. 3–4.

191 See, for example, Alan Boyle, Chris Himsworth, Hector MacQueen and Andrea Loux (eds), *Human Rights and Scots Law: Comparative Perspectives on the Incorporation of the ECHR* (Hart 2002).

192 See, for example, European Union Committee, 'The UK, the EU and a British Bill of Rights', 9 May 2016, HL 139 2015–16.

9. Conclusion

It is conceivable that future legal historians will think of the early twenty-first century as a time of transformation in the development of Scots law. Conflict resolution and the court structure have undergone radical changes as a result of the Courts (Scotland) Act 2014, the full effects of which are not yet apparent. Some commentators believe that the Scottish system of norm production is shifting, arguing that the twenty-first century will be the "age of the legislator", and drawing attention to the developing legislative role of the (relatively) new Scottish Parliament. Nonetheless, it must be emphasised that any developing role for the legislator will be complemented with a developing role for the interpreters of legislation – meaning the courts, and to a lesser extent academics.

Consequently, it is difficult to tell what effects the undoubted increase in codifying statutes will have on norm production. What has been argued above is that imitating the rigorous interpretative practices of judges like Lord Rodger will foster legal clarity and certainty and demonstrate exactly where the current law may be lacking, and where its principles may be sufficient to respond to current problems as they arise. Changes may also be evident in the Scottish ideal of justice – as defined within this volume – and to Scottish legal method. For example, in certain areas of the law academics are attempting to identify principles to guide interpretation. To what extent these activities will be successful is as yet unclear, albeit that they have undoubtedly shaped legislation indebted to the work of the Scottish Law Commission. What is certain, for now, is that the interpretation of Scots law will be shaped by the Convention Rights protected by the Scotland Act 1998. The legal profession too may face some restructuring as a result of the enactment of the Courts (Scotland) Act 2014, particularly as a result of the re-allocation of business from the Court of Session to the sheriff courts. Finally, bodies such as the EU are undoubtedly having a great impact on Scottish legal development. Yet if internationalisation is a force for change, movements to withdraw from international treaties may be equally significant in the future. The result of the referendum concerning the British exit from the European Union illustrates the point. Of similar importance will be whatever constitutional settlement eventually emerges to regulate relations between the different parts of the United Kingdom.

Regardless of the changes that may come, it is helpful, perhaps, to conclude by drawing attention to one point about Scottish legal culture that has been emphasised throughout this article. It should now be apparent that there is great diversity of opinion among lawyers and academics concerning the nature of Scots law, exactly what makes it distinctive, and what is to be celebrated about it – if anything. As one writer has put it, "[w]e appear today to be as divided as our predecessors were in our views on how the law of Scotland ought to operate in the context of the political unions that dominate the country's modern existence".[193] Yet perhaps this diversity of opinion constitutes some evidence of the vibrancy of the legal culture; the quality of the debate that resulted from the decisions in *Sharp* and *Burnett* tends to support that view. More rigorous reflection

193 J.D. Ford, 'Four models of union' (2011) No. 1 *Juridical Review* 45, 76.

on that culture than that which has been attempted here – particularly in a comparative context – may further clarify the parameters of the debates.[194]

The Scottish Legal Culture and its structures and structural elements	
Institutional structure	
Conflict resolution	*Norm production*
Several hierarchies of courts; two major examples are the civil and criminal hierarchies, complex structure due to its strong historical roots.	No general code. Increasing numbers of codifying statutes. Courts and to some lesser extent juristic works still important as norm producers.

Intellectual structure			
Ideal of justice	*Legal method*	*Degree of professionalisation*	*Character of internationalisation*
Broadly, interpretative practices are increasingly shaped by a desire for legal certainty. Note the role of the ECHR in informing interpretation.	A mixture of approaches, including deduction from legislation, distinction of precedents, deduction from general principles drawn from the common law.	High degree of academic-oriented education (LLB – 4 years) supplemented by a special practical training for those who want to practise law.	Dualistic system. Strong influences from EU/ECHR. Consequences of the vote in favour of the British exit from the EU are unclear. High degree of openness to international impulses.

10. Bibliography

Anderson RG, 'Introduction' in George Watson (ed), *Bell's Dictionary and Digest of the Law of Scotland* (reprinted edition, Edinburgh Legal Education Trust 2012)

Barnard C and Peers S (eds), *European Union Law* (2nd edn, Oxford University Press 2017). DOI: https://doi.org/10.1093%2Fhe%2F9780198789130.001.0001

Blackie J, 'T B Smith as a Legal Historian' in Reid E and Carey Miller DL (eds), *A Mixed Legal System in Transition. T B Smith and the Progress of Scots Law* (Edinburgh University Press 2005). DOI: https://doi.org/10.3366%2Fedinburgh%2F9780748623358.003.0004

Boyle A, Himsworth C, MacQueen H and Loux A (eds), *Human Rights and Scots Law: Comparative Perspectives on the Incorporation of the ECHR* (Hart 2002). DOI: https://doi.org/10.5040%2F9781472562654

Broun D, *Scottish Independence and the Idea of Britain: From the Picts to Alexander III* (Edinburgh University Press 2013). DOI: https://doi.org/10.3366%2Fedinburgh%2F9780748623600.001.0001

Brown KM and MacDonald AR (eds), *Parliament in Context, 1235–1707* (Edinburgh University Press 2010)

194 A similar – but by no means identical – point is made in ibid 74–76.

Brown KM and Mann AJ (eds), *Parliament and Politics in Scotland, 1567–1707* (Edinburgh University Press 2005)

Brown KM and Tanner RJ (eds), *Parliament and Politics in Scotland, 1235–1560* (Edinburgh University Press 2004)

Brown M, *The Wars of Scotland 1214–1371* (Edinburgh University Press 2004). DOI: http://doi.org/10.3366/edinburgh/9780748612376.001.0001

Cairns JW, 'Institutional Writings in Scotland Reconsidered' (1984) Vol. 4 No. 3/3 *Journal of Legal History* 76. DOI: http://doi.org/10.1080/01440368408530791

—— 'Historical Introduction' in Reid K and Zimmermann R (eds), *A History of Private Law in Scotland Volume 1: Introduction and Property* (Oxford University Press 2000)

—— 'Revisiting the Foundation of the College of Justice' in MacQueen HL (ed), *Stair Society Miscellany Five* (vol. 52, Stair Society 2006)

Cameron EA, *Impaled Upon a Thistle. Scotland Since 1880* (Edinburgh University Press 2010)

Carey Miller DL, 'Three of a Kind? Positive Prescription in Sri Lanka, South Africa and Scotland' (May 2008) Vol. 12 *European Journal of Comparative Law*

Carpenter D, 'Scottish Royal Government in the Thirteenth Century from an English Perspective' in Hammond M (ed), *New Perspectives on Medieval Scotland 1093–1286* (Boydell Press 2013)

Clancy MP, 'The Scottish Legal Profession (Except Advocates)' in Mulhern MA (ed), *Scottish Life and Society. A Compendium of Scottish Ethnology Volume 13: The Law* (John Donald 2012)

Cooper TM, 'The Common and the Civil Law – A Scot's View' in Cooper TM, *Selected Papers 1922–1954* (Oliver and Boyd 1957)

Dickinson WC, 'The High Court of Justiciary' in Stair Society vol. 20, *An Introduction to Scottish Legal History by Various Authors* (Stair Society 1958)

Donaldson G, *Scotland James V – James VII* (Edinburgh University Press 1971)

Evans-Jones R, 'Receptions of Law, Mixed Legal Systems and the Myth of the Genius of Scots Private Law' (1998) Vol. 114 No. 2/4 *Law Quarterly Review* 228

Finlay J, *Men of Law in Pre-Reformation Scotland* (Tuckwell Press 2000)

—— *The Community of the College of Justice: Edinburgh and the Court of Session, 1687–1808* (Edinburgh University Press 2012). DOI: http://doi.org/10.3366/edinburgh/9780748645770.001.0001

Ford JD, *Law and Opinion in Scotland during the Seventeenth Century* (Hart 2007). DOI: http://doi.org/10.5040/9781472560162

—— 'The Legal Provisions in the Acts of Union' (2007) no. 1 of 3 *Cambridge Law Journal* 106. DOI: http://doi.org/10.1017/s0008197307000050

—— 'Protestations to Parliament for Remeid of Law' (2009) Vol. 88 No. 1 of 2 *Scottish Historical Review* 57. DOI: http://doi.org/10.3366/e0036924109000584

—— 'Four models of union' (2011) No. 1/4 *Juridical* 45

Forte ADM, 'Scots law and Scottish national identity' in Fellows-Jensen G (ed) *Denmark and Scotland: The Cultural and Environmental Resources of Small Nations* (Kongelige Danske Videnskabernes Selskab 2001)

Godfrey AM, *Civil Justice in Renaissance Scotland* (Brill 2009). DOI: http://doi.org/10.1163/ej.9789004174665.i-488

—— 'The Courts of Scotland' in Mulhern MA (ed), *The Law* (European Ethnological Research Centre 2012)

Gordon G, 'The Exclusion of Consequential Loss in the Piper Alpha Case: A Study of Lord Rodger's Method of Textual Analysis' in Simpson ARC, Styles SC, West E and Wilson ALM (eds), *Continuity, Change and Pragmatism: Essays in Memory of Professor Angelo Forte* (Aberdeen University Press 2016)

Gretton GL, 'The integrity of property law and the property registers' 2001 S.LT. (News)

—— 'The Rational and the National: Thomas Broun Smith' in Reid E and Carey Miller DL (eds), *A Mixed Legal System in Transition. T.B. Smith and the Progress of Scots Law* (Edinburgh University Press 2005)

Jones TH and Taggart I (eds), *Criminal Law* (6th edn, W. Green 2015)

MacQueen HL, 'Two Toms and an Ideology for Scots Law: T B Smith and Lord Cooper of Culross' in Reid E and Carey Miller DL (eds), *A Mixed Legal System in Transition. T.B. Smith and the Progress of Scots Law* (Edinburgh University Press 2005)

—— *Common Law and Feudal Society in Medieval Scotland* (classic edn, Edinburgh University Press 2016)

Malcolm CA, 'The Sheriff Court: Sixteenth Century and Later' in Stair Society vol. 20, *An Introduction to Scottish Legal History by Various Authors* (Stair Society 1958)

Nicholson R, *Scotland: The Later Middle Ages* (Edinburgh University Press 1978)

Oram R, *Domination and Lordship. Scotland 1070–1230* (Edinburgh University Press 2011)

Reid KGC, *The Law of Property in Scotland* (Law Society of Scotland, Butterworths 1996)

—— 'The Third Branch of the Profession. The Rise of the Academic Lawyer in Scotland' in MacQueen HL (ed), *Scots Law into the 21st Century. Essays in Honour of W.A. Wilson*, (W. Green/ Sweet & Maxwell 1996)

—— 'Equity Triumphant' (1997) Vol. 1 No. 4/4 *Edinburgh Law Review* 464. DOI: http://doi.org/10.3366/elr.1997.1.4.464

—— 'While One Hundred Remain: T.B. Smith and the Progress of Scots Law' in Reid E and Carey Miller DL (eds), *A Mixed Legal System in Transition. T.B. Smith and the Progress of Scots Law* (Edinburgh University Press 2005)

—— 'Smoothing the Rugged Parts of the Passage: Scots Law and its Edinburgh Chair' (2014) Vol. 18 No. 3/3 *Edinburgh Law Review* 215. DOI: http://doi.org/10.3366/elr.2014.0227

Rennie R, 'To Sharp v Thomson – an heir' 2000 S.LT. (News)

Rodger A, 'Thinking About Scots Law' (1996) Vol. 1 No. 1/4 *Edinburgh Law Review* 3. DOI: http://doi.org/10.3366/elr.1996.1.1.3

Sellar WDH, 'Celtic Law and Scots Law: Survival and Integration' (1988) 29 *Scottish Studies* 1

Simpson ARC, 'Positive Prescription of Moveables in Scots Law' (2009) Vol. 13 No. 3/3 *Edinburgh Law Review* 445. DOI: http://doi.org/10.3366/e1364980909000584

—— and Wilson ALM, *Scottish Legal History Volume 1: 1000–1707* (Edinburgh University Press, forthcoming)

Smith TB, *A Short Commentary on the Law of Scotland* (W. Green 1962)

Styles SC, 'Sharp pains for Scots property law: the case of Burnett's Trustee v Grainger' 2000 S.L.T. (News)

Taylor A, *The Shape of the State in Medieval Scotland* (Oxford University Press 2016). DOI: http://doi.org/10.1093/acprof:oso/9780198749202.001.0001

The Law of Scotland by The Late W.M. Gloag KC LLD and The Late Candlish Henderson, QC, LLD (14th edn, W. Green/ Thomson Reuters 2017)

The Laws of Scotland. Stair Memorial Encyclopaedia, (Lexis Nexis) vol. 22

Woolf A, *From Pictland to Alba 789–1070* (Edinburgh University Press 2007). DOI: http://doi.org/10.3366/edinburgh/9780748612338.001.0001m

12. An Introduction to Belgian Legal Culture

Bruno Debaenst

1. Introduction

1.1 About Belgium

Belgium is a densely populated country, with a population of 11,431,406 legally residing inhabitants (2019) on a surface of 30.688 km², which equals to a population density of 378 inhabitants per km².[1] The majority of the population (6,589,069 or 57.6% in 2019) lives in Flanders (Dutch: "Vlaanderen", French: "La Flandre"), the Dutch-speaking North of Belgium, with a surface of 13,682 km². The South of Belgium is called Wallonia (Dutch: "Wallonië", French: "La Wallonie"). Wallonia has a surface of 16,844 km² but contains only 31.8% of the population: 3,633,795 French-speaking Belgians and 77,527 German-speaking Belgians in the East. The bilingual capital is Brussels (Dutch: "Brussel", French: "Bruxelles"), with 1,208,542 or 10.6% of the population, on a total surface of 161.4 km². Dutch, French and German are the three official languages in Belgium.[2]

In 2018, Belgium ranked 17th on the Human Development Index, with an index of 0.916.[3] It is a rather rich country, with an average GDP per capita of 34,300 Euro, but

1 For the population statistics, see https://statbel.fgov.be/en/themes/population/structure-population; for the land area, see https://bestat.statbel.fgov.be/bestat/crosstable.xhtml?datasource=b5c5eedc-95bf-4927-929e-d6395345a53a; for the population density, see https://www.populationpyramid.net/nl/bevolkingsdichtheid/belgië/2019. As for the land area, it was until recently calculated at 30,528 km2, see for example https://www.belgium.be/en/about_belgium/country/geography. The change can be explained by a new calculation method of Eurostat, which now also includes the beaches. All links accessed 31 March 2020.

2 This follows out of Article 4 of the Belgian Constitution: there are four language areas: the Dutch-speaking language area (Flanders), the French-speaking language area (most of Wallonia), the German-speaking language area (in the East of Belgium) and the bilingual (Dutch/French) Brussels area. The Constitution also stipulates in Article 30 that the use of languages in Belgium is free. For an analysis of the specific language situation in Brussels, see Laurence Mettewie and Rudi Janssens, 'Language Use and Language Attitude in Brussels' in David Lasagabaster and Ángel Huguet (eds), *Multilingualism in European Bilingual Contexts. Language Use and Attitudes* (Multilingual Matters 2007) 117.

3 http://hdr.undp.org/en/countries/profiles/BEL accessed 5 April 2019.

there are huge differences between the three regions.[4] Brussels is still the richest region, with a GDP of 63,300 Euro per capita in 2015, which can be explained by the large number of international companies who have their seat there. Flanders provides 58.8% of the Belgian GDP, which equals to 35,100 Euro GDP per capita, while Wallonia has a GDP per capita of only 24,600 Euro.[5] These differences in prosperity have resulted in enormous financial transfers within Belgium. According to a study published in 2017, in 2014 there was a net transfer of 7.1 billion Euro from Flanders to the rest of the country.[6]

More in general, one has to be careful with figures and statistics on Belgium, which are only averages hiding realities that are more complex. For instance, Belgium had an unemployment rate of 7.1% in 2017, but Flanders only had 4.4%, while Wallonia had 9.8% and Brussels even 15%.[7]

1.2 A historical perspective on the Belgian legal culture

The current Kingdom of Belgium is part of a region historically called "the Low Countries" (Dutch: "de Nederlanden", French: "les Pays-Bas"), situated at the North Sea in Western Europe and bordered by France in the South and Germany in the East.[8] The current division of the territories of the historical Low Countries in Belgium, the Netherlands, Luxembourg, (the North of) France, and (parts of the West of) Germany is the result of historical circumstances. Therefore, in order to understand the Belgian legal culture, one first has to study the complex historical development of the Low Countries.

In the Middle Ages, the Low Countries belonged partly to the Kingdom of France and partly to the Holy Roman Empire of German Nations.[9] It was a heterogeneous mix of counties (Flanders, Holland, Artois, Namur, Hainaut, and Zutphen), duchies

4 https://ec.europa.eu/growth/tools-databases/regional-innovation-monitor/base-profile/flanders accessed 5 April 2019.

5 For the regional GDP statistics, see https://ec.europa.eu/growth/tools-databases/regional-innovation-monitor/base-profile/brussels-capital; https://ec.europa.eu/growth/tools-databases/regional-innovation-monitor/base-profile/flanders; and https://ec.europa.eu/growth/tools-databases/regional-innovation-monitor/base-profile/wallonia. All links accessed 5 April 2019.

6 https://www.statistiekvlaanderen.be/sites/default/files/atoms/files/rapport-financiele-stromen-2000-2020.pdf p. 2, accessed 5 April 2019.

7 https://www.statista.com/statistics/528583/unemployment-rate-in-belgium-by-region/ accessed 5 April 2019.

8 The Romans called the inhabitants of the current Belgium and adjacent territories "*Belgae*" and their land "*Gallica belgica*". "*Belgica*" was also used as a synonym for the Seventeen Provinces, i.e., the Habsburg Netherlands between 1543 and 1585. When the North of the Low Countries became independent as the Dutch Republic ("*Republiek der Zeven Verenigde Nederlanden*"), its Latin name was "*Belgica Foederata*". In 1789–1790, the Austrian Netherlands declared independence as the United Belgian States (*Verenigde Belgische Staten/États-Belgiques-Unis*). During the French period, the word "Belgium" ("*België/la Belgique*") was used for the Southern Netherlands. In 1830, when the Southern part of the United Kingdom of the Netherlands revolted against the Dutch, they founded the Kingdom of Belgium.

9 With the Treaty of Verdun (843), the Carolingian Empire was divided into three kingdoms. The Low Countries were part of Middle Francia, ruled by Lothair I. With the treaties of Mersen or Meerssen (870) and Ribemont (880), the territories of Lotharingia were divided between West Francia (later France) and East Francia (later Holy Roman Empire of German Nations), leading to the division of the Low Countries.

(Brabant, Luxembourg, Limburg, and Guelders), bishoprics (Liège, Utrecht) and Lordships (Mechlin, Frisia, Groningen, Drenthe, and Overijssel). In 1384, the marriage of the Duke of Burgundy with the daughter of the Count of Flanders started the period of the so-called Burgundian Netherlands.[10] In the following decades, the Dukes of Burgundy managed to bring most of the territories of the Low Countries under their rule, by marriage, purchase, inheritance or military conquest. The Burgundian Netherlands slowly evolved from a sheer personal union to a more integrated state. In 1464 for example, Duke Philip the Good (1396–1467) for the first time gathered the States-General (Dutch: "Staten-Generaal"; French "États généraux") with representatives from the estates of all the different territories. In 1477, disaster struck: in his efforts to unite the two separate parts, Burgundy and the Netherlands, Duke Charles the Bold (1433–1477) was killed during the battle of Nancy. In the turmoil that followed, the original Burgundy territories were lost to France. Duchesse Mary of Burgundy (1457–1482) married the Habsburg Emperor Maximilian to secure her feeble position. When she died in 1482, her son Philip (1478–1506) inherited her territories. This was the official beginning of the Habsburg rule. [11]

Emperor Charles V (1500–1558), the most powerful ruler of the Habsburg dynasty, continued the unification of the Netherlands.[12] With the Burgundian Treaty of 1548, the Netherlands received a special status within the Holy Roman Empire.[13] The following year, Charles promulgated the so-called "Pragmatic Sanction".[14] In this edict, he streamlined the succession laws in all these territories and declared that only one heir would inherit them, this way reorganizing the Low Countries into an indivisible entity. By now, these Habsburg territories were known as the "Seventeen Provinces of the Netherlands".

In 1555, Charles V abdicated and his son King Philip II of Spain (1527–1598) inherited his mighty empire, with possessions in the Netherlands, Spain, Italy, and the Americas. Unfortunately, he also inherited the problems of the empire. Constant warfare led to high taxes, which weighed heavily on the rich Netherlands. In addition, these urbanized territories had been susceptible to the ideas of the reformation. This led to revolt in the Netherlands, which was the beginning of the Eighty-Years War (1568–1648). The

10 Bart van Loo, *De Bourgondiërs. Aartsvaders van de Lage Landen* (De Bezige Bij 2018) 560.

11 Benjamin Curtis, *The Habsburgs. The History of a Dynasty* (Bloomsbury 2013).

12 For instance, in 1531 he reorganized the central administration of the Netherlands. He installed three specific councils (the so-called *collaterale raden*). 1) The Council of State (*Raad van State/Conseil d'Etat*), consisting of 12 high nobles and competent for foreign affairs; 2) the Secret Council (*Geheime Raad/Conseil Secret*), a council with lawyers who dealt with matters of the interior and justice; and 3) the Financial Council (*Raad van Financiën/Conseil des Finances*), which dealt with financial matters.

13 With the Burgundian Treaty of 1548, ratified on 26 June 1548, the status of the Netherlands within the Holy Roman Empire was settled. It enlarged the Burgundian Circle within the Empire, so that it comprised all the Burgundian territories. In addition, these territories were no longer subject to the *Reichskammergericht*. Thomas Horn, *The Netherlands and the Holy Roman Empire at the Augsburg Reichstag, 1547–1548* (University of California 1956) 154.

14 On 4 November 1549, to be more precise. On the Pragmatic Sanction of 1549, see Lambert Surhone, Miriam Timpledon and Susan Marseken, *Pragmatic Sanction of 1549* (VDM Publishing 2010) 86.

result of these hostilities was a schism of the Netherlands. The (mainly) protestant North gained independence and prosperity as the Dutch Republic, also called the Republic of the Seven United Provinces of the Netherlands, while the South was reconquered by Spain and became homogenous Catholic once again (= the Counter-Reformation). These territories were called the Spanish Netherlands or the Southern Netherlands. In 1648, Spain formally recognized the independence of the Dutch Republic (today known as the Netherlands), in the Treaty of Münster.[15]

In the second half of the 17th century, the badly defended Southern Netherlands suffered repeated loss of territory to the French King Louis XIV (1638–1715).[16] From 1700 until 1714, the Wars of the Spanish Succession raged in the country. One result of this War was the changing hands of the Southern Netherlands to the Austrian branch of the Habsburgs.[17] The Southern Netherlands remained Austrian until 1793–1795, when the French revolutionary armies conquered these territories.

The French period (1795–1813) is a decisive period in the (legal) history of the Southern Netherlands. After the conquest, the French revolutionaries abolished the century-old political, administrative and legal institutions of the so-called "Ancien Régime" (i.e., the old regime) and the territories of the Southern Netherlands were simply annexed by France.[18] This included also the Prince-Bishopric of Liège, which had been a separate state in the Holy Roman Empire until then. In the following twenty years, the French radically erased all traces of the former Austrian and Spanish rule, by introducing French legislation, administration, judiciary, institutions, and education.[19]

After the defeat of Napoleon at the Battle of Leipzig in 1813, the French Empire collapsed and the Prince of Orange-Nassau William (1772–1843) filled the power vacuum in the Netherlands. With the London Protocol of 21 June 1814, the Allies awarded the Southern Netherlands to him and he became the first King of the United Kingdom of the Netherlands in 1815. For the first time in over three centuries, the Netherlands were again reunited. However, the long separation had left its marks and the marriage of the

15 Laura Manzano Baena, *Conflicting Words. The Peace Treaty of Münster (1648) and the Political Culture of the Dutch Republic and the Spanish Monarchy* (Leuven University Press 2011) 282.

16 Louis XIV made several military campaigns. In 1667, for instance he conquered the city of Lille, which was officially annexed in 1668 and is still French today. He also conquered other cities, such as Ieper, Veurne and Kortrijk, which were French for several decades, until he gave them back with the Treaty of Utrecht of 1713. They are now Belgian. In 1695, for instance he bombarded Brussels. When you visit the "Grote Markt" in Brussels, you can see that many buildings date from shortly after that bombardment.

17 This was settled with the Peace Treaty of Rastatt of 7 March 1714 between France and Austria. See Renger Bruin, Cornelis van der Haven, Lotte Jensen and David Onnekink, *Performances of Peace: Utrecht 1713* (Brill 2015) 288.

18 Jan Roegiers and Nicolaas Cornelis Ferdinand van Sas, 'Revolution in the North and South' in Johan Cornelis Hendrik Blom and Emiel Lamberts (eds), *History of the Low Countries* (Berghahn Books 2006) 269, see 289–296 on the French annexation in particular.

19 On the French era, see Emmanuel Berger, Dirk Heirbaut, Hervé Leuwers and Xavier Rousseaux, 'La justice avant la Belgique: tentatives autrichiennes, influences françaises et expériences néerlandaises (1780–1830)' in Margo De Koster, Dirk Heirbaut and Xavier Rousseaux (eds), *Deux siècles de justice. Encyclopédie historique de la justice belge* (Die Keure 2015) 26.

two countries was uneasy.[20] King William I reigned as an autocrat, and his religious, economic and language politics met heavy opposition in the South.[21]

In 1830 the tensions burst, and revolt broke out in the South.[22] The Belgian revolutionaries defeated the Dutch army and assembled in a National Congress. On 7 February 1831, they proclaimed the Belgian Constitution[23] and on 21 July 1831, Leopold of Saxe-Coburg-Saalfeld (1790–1865) took the oath as first king of the Belgians.[24] This day marks the end of the revolution and the beginning of the Kingdom of Belgium and serves therefore as Belgian National Day still today. In 1839, with the Treaty of London, the Dutch finally accepted Belgian independence. The Treaty also foresaw the establishment of the Grand Duchy of Luxembourg as an independent country.

National unity characterized the first years of the Belgian Kingdom. This relative peace would however soon be broken because of three major fields of tension in Belgian society. The first area of conflict is the confessional one, with on the one hand the Catholics and on the other the liberals, with fundamental discussions on the role of (the Catholic) religion in society (e.g., the role of the Church in education). The second is the socio-economic dispute, with the emergence of a proletariat opposed to the capitalist bourgeoisie. The third, communal field of tension relates to the different language/cultural identities in Belgium. Historically, the South of Belgium has always been French-speaking (Hainaut, Namur, parts of Brabant, Liège, and Luxembourg). The North of Belgium, however, has always been predominantly Dutch-speaking, divided into many dialects. It was mostly the French-speaking bourgeoisie that had been frustrated and suppressed in the United Kingdom of the Netherlands.[25] After the Belgian Revolution, they took over power. Soon, the whole public life in Belgium was French-speaking (parliament, higher education, administration, judiciary, etc.). This led to a reaction – commonly known as the Flemish Movement, which started fighting for the cultural rights of the Dutch-speaking majority of the population. In 1873, the first Language Act was enacted, allowing Dutch to be used in criminal procedures.[26] In 1878, the

20 Stefaan Marteel, *The intellectual origins of the Belgian Revolution. Political Thought and Disunity in the Kingdom of the Netherlands, 1815–1830* (Palgrave Macmillan 2018).

21 Roegiers and van Sas (2006) (n 18) 307–312.

22 On the Belgian political history from 1830 on, see Els Witte, Jan Craeybeckx and Alain Meynen, *Political History of Belgium from 1830 onwards* (ASP 2009).

23 On the Belgian Constitution, see Patricia Populier and Koen Lemmens, *The Constitution of Belgium. A Contextual analysis* (Hart Publishing 2015). On Belgian constitutional law, see André Alen (ed), *Treatise on Belgian Constitutional Law* (Kluwer 1992). The full, contemporary text of the Constitution can be consulted in English on the website of the Constitutional Court: http://www.const-court.be accessed 5 April 2019.

24 On the Belgian Kings and the historical role of the monarchy in Belgium, see Jean Stengers, *Koningen der Belgen van Leopold I tot Albert II* (Davidsfonds 1997).

25 King Willem had a language policy to install Dutch as official language in Flanders (education, judiciary, administration). This was a problem for the French-speaking bourgeoisie who did not speak Dutch. They were frustrated because they did not have career opportunities. Many of them were young lawyers who were also politically active by writing critical pamphlets. For this, they were often prosecuted and put in jail. See Bram Delbecke, 'The Political Offence and the Safeguarding of the Nation State: Constitutional Ideals, French Legal Standards and Belgian Legal Practice, 1830–70' (2013) Vol. 1 Issue 1 *Comparative Legal History* 45.

26 Act of 17 August 1878, Moniteur belge 26 August 1873.

second Language Act stipulated that the administrations in Flanders and Brussels had to be bilingual French/Dutch.[27] In 1898, the "*Gelijkheidswet*" ("Equality Act") finally accepted Dutch as an official language in Belgium, next to French.[28]

In the aftermath of the First World War, Belgium acquired a small German territory, Eupen-Malmédy, with some 75,000 German speakers. In the 1960s, there were growing tensions between the two main language groups, which slowly drifted apart.[29] In 1963, the language borders were finally fixed. Four language areas were established: Flanders (Dutch), Brussels (bilingual Dutch/French), Wallonia (French), and the German-speaking territories in the East. Student protests led to the split of the bilingual universities of Brussels and Leuven. In this period, all political parties also split along lines of languages. Both of the major language groups had a desire for more autonomy: the French-speaking wanted more economic autonomy, to face their specific problems, while the Dutch-speaking wanted more cultural autonomy, to defend their culture and language against the French-speaking dominance. These desires led to six successive reforms of the state.[30] The first one, in 1970, led to the establishment of three Cultural Communities (Flemish, French, and German-speaking), responsible for language and culture. The second one, in 1980, gave extra competences (personal affairs, such as healthcare and social assistance) to the communities and installed two regions: the Flemish and the Walloon region, competent for territorial affairs, such as the environment, spatial planning, and employment. Both the communities and the regions got their own government and parliament. The third state reform, in 1988, made the communities responsible for education, and installed a third region – Brussels. The fourth state reform, in 1993, turned Belgium into a federal state. The fifth one, in 2001, and the sixth one, in 2014, gave extra competences to the communities and regions.

These reforms caused Belgium to gradually evolve from a unitary state to a federal state.[31] As a result, the first article of the current Belgian Constitution states: "Belgium is a federal State composed of Communities and Regions." Belgium can serve as a model of managing cultural diversity in a peaceful way. However, the numerous political compromises that were necessary to safeguard this peaceful transition caused a rather complicated state structure, including fragmentation of competences and institutional responsibilities. Although the latest reform of the state only dates from 2014, there is already a call for a new, seventh reform of the state. For some politicians, the state reforms went too far, and they want to bring back some competences from the regional level to the national/federal level. There are, for instance, four different ministers competent for the environment or for energy, causing all kind of problems. Other poli-

---

27 Act of 22 May 1878, Moniteur belge 25 May 1878.

28 Act of 18 April 1898, Moniteur belge 15 May 1898.

29 See Martin Conway, 'Belgium's Mid-Twentieth Century Crisis: Crisis of a Nation-State?' (2005) 4 *Journal of Belgian History* 573.

30 On these reforms, see Populier and Lemmens (2015) (n 23) part III.

31 Godelieve Craenen, *The institutions of Federal Belgium: An Introduction to Belgian Public Law* (Acco 2001); See also Johan vande Lanotte, Geert Goedertier and Siegfried Bracke, *Belgium for Beginners: A Guide Through the Belgian Labyrinth* (Die Keure 2006).

ticians, such as the moderate Flemish nationalists, want to take the reform of the state a step further, by creating a confederal state.[32] This way, Flanders and Wallonia would agree on a limited number of competences that would remain shared, while all the other competences would go to the regional level.[33]

The three historic fields of tensions (confessional, socio-economical, and communal) are still present in Belgium, although in different forms.[34] As to the confessional, there are now growing tensions related to Islam, reviving old discussions on the role of religion in society. As to the socio-economical, there is the growing problem of the failed integration[35] of immigrants in Belgian society and the continuing problems with the economic reconversion in the South. Finally, regarding the communal tensions, one can see that Flemish and French-speaking communities have drifted apart considerably.[36] We can observe differences emerging regarding mentality, economic dynamics, politics, media, culture, etc. Flanders is economically prosperous and politically predominantly right-wing, while Wallonia is poor and predominantly left-wing. This has created growing difficulties in governing the country.[37] For instance, after the 2010 federal elections, it took 541 days to form a federal government. The outcome was a government with a minority

---

32 https://www.vrt.be/vrtnws/en/2019/01/13/a-belgian-confederation-is-our-highest-ambition/ accessed 25 March 2019.

33 https://www.vrt.be/vrtnws/en/2013/10/30/_belgium_must_becomeaconfederationoftwostates-1-1766725/ accessed 25 March 2019.

34 For an oversight of Belgian political history, see Witte, Craeybeckx and Meynen (2009) (n 22). For an short analysis of a number of developments in the Belgian legal culture, such as the consolidation of the Belgian *Rechtsstaat*, the linguistic problem, the socio-economical problem, the confessional problem, the emancipation of women, the problems regarding legal aid and the multicultural society, see: Koen Raes, 'Ontwikkelingen in de Belgische rechtscultuur. Een cultuurhistorische verkenning' in Dirk Heirbaut, Xavier Rousseaux and Karel Velle (eds), *Politieke en sociale geschiedenis van justitie in België van 1830 tot heden/Histoire politique et sociale de la justice en Belgique de 1830 à nos jours* (Die Keure 2004) 345.

35 For instance, immigrants perform worse in the labour market. In 2018, Belgium had the lowest employment rate (54%) of all EU member states for persons born outside the EU. See https://ec.europa.eu/eurostat/web/products-eurostat-news/-/DDN-20190529-1?inheritRedirect=true&redirect=%2Feurostat%2F. See also the following, taken from https://www.ilo.org/wcmsp5/groups/public/---ed_protect/---protrav/---migrant/documents/publication/wcms_222293.pdf p. 57: "If one looks at the labour market integration of the migrant population, Belgium is not performing well. Third-country nationals hold a worse labour market position compared to EU27 migrants and Belgian nationals. They have an unemployment rate that is more than double the unemployment rate of EU27 migrants and Belgian nationals." See also the following OECD report: http://www.oecd.org/belgium/41707374.pdf.

One of the causes of the high unemployment is the fact that these immigrants perform worse in school. See http://www.centrumvoorsociaalbeleid.be/ImPRovE/Working%20Papers/ImPRovE%20WP%201402_1.pdf. All links accessed 29 September 2019.

36 For an interesting analysis of this phenomenon, see: Robert Mnookin and Alain Verbeke, 'Persistent nonviolent conflict with no reconciliation: the Flemish and Walloons in Belgium' (2009) Vol. 72 Issue 2 *Law & Contemporary Problems*, 151.

37 These persistent problems made some Flemish and French-speaking academics (historians, sociologists) reflect on the possible future of Belgium: Bruno De Wever (ed), *What does history teach us about the future of Belgium's institutions* (Re-Bel e-book 2010), to be consulted through https://rethinkingbelgium.eu/wp-content/uploads/2019/08/Re-Bel-e-book-6.pdf accessed 14 April 2020

of Flemish represented. Since 2014, the situation is reversed, with only a small minority of French-speaking represented in the federal government.

The Belgian national (i.e., federal) state level has not only been weakened by the transfer of competences to the regional level, but also by an increasing impact of the international level. This process has started during the Second World War, with the foundation of the BENELUX.[38] This Union between Belgium, the Netherlands, and Luxembourg is a modern reminiscence of the historical Low Countries. The next step was the European Coal and Steel Community, established in 1951 by the Treaty of Paris, signed by Belgium, the Netherlands, Luxembourg, France, Germany, and Italy. From here, it was a small step to the European Economic Community, which led to the current European Union. As a small country with an open economy, Belgium has always been a partisan of European cooperation. Its capital, Brussels, also serves as the European capital, emphasizing the central position of Belgium in Europe. Just as the other member states, Belgium has delegated many competences to the European level.[39] This not only weakens the national level, but also adds an extra layer of complexity to the already complex institutional and intellectual components determining the shape of the Belgian legal culture.

1.3 The relativity of a "Belgian legal culture"

The "Belgian legal culture" is unique because of two reasons. To start with, the Belgian legal culture is predominantly French in origin. There are almost no traces left from the old, indigenous legal culture. After their conquest in 1795, the French started with a tabula rasa and transplanted their French legal culture onto Belgian soil (administration, judiciary, legal texts, etc.).[40] In the course of the following two centuries, much has changed, but it is fascinating to see that the core of the French legal culture is still intact. For instance, the 1804 Code Napoléon is still in force in Belgium,[41] the current provinces are the old *Départements*, and the judicial organization is still largely the same.

---

38 Some are pleading to revive the BENELUX: Jan Wouters (ed), *De Benelux: tijd voor een wedergeboorte* (Intersentia 2006)

39 There is not a specific provision in the Constitution allowing the national government to transfer sovereignty to the EU, but there is Article 167, § 1: "The King directs international relations, notwithstanding the competence of Communities and Regions to regulate international cooperation, including the concluding of treaties, for those matters that fall within their competences in pursuance of or by virtue of the Constitution." In Article 168 of the Constitution is written: "From the beginning, the Houses are informed of negotiations concerning any revision of the treaties establishing the European Community and the treaties and acts which have modified or complemented them. They receive the draft treaty before its signature."

40 Dirk Heirbaut and Jean-François Gerkens, 'In the shadow of France: legal acculturation and legal transplants in the Southern Netherlands/Belgium', in Eric Dirix and Yves-Henry Leleu, *The Belgian reports at the Congress of Washington of the International Academy of Comparative Law* (Bruylant 2011) 3

41 Dirk Heirbaut, 'Napoleons trouwste onderdanen, of waarom de Code civil na tweehonderd jaar nog steeds overeind staat in België' in Dirk Heirbaut and Georges Martyn (eds), *Napoleons nalatenschap. Tweehonderd jaar Burgerlijk Wetboek in België / Un heritage Napoléonien. Bicentenaire du Code civil en Belgique* (Kluwer 2005) 77.

After the independence, French legal culture continued to inspire Belgian lawyers.[42] On the other hand, although Belgium still uses the 1804 civil code, over half of the provisions have been altered through Belgian legislation or reinterpreted through Belgian case law and jurisprudence.[43] The result is some kind of a hybrid legal culture, with both original French elements and autochthon Belgian elements.

Secondly, the Belgian legal culture has been subject to a slow process of vaporization, following the disintegration of the Belgian state. Slowly but steadily, separate Flemish and French-speaking legal cultures are emerging.[44] One should not exaggerate this, since many competences and the judiciary are still national, but it is undeniable that the different languages, mentalities, and sources of inspiration, combined with growing regional competences, act as centrifugal forces. For instance, lawyers in both parts of the country consult different legal journals, which mainly publish case law and jurisprudence in their respective language.[45] They also have different sources of inspiration: Flemish lawyers tend to inspire themselves by looking towards Dutch and American law, while the main source of inspiration of French-speaking lawyers is still French law.[46] In Wallonia, there are more judges per inhabitant than in Flanders. This can be explained by a difference in legal culture: Walloon lawyers tend to be more elaborate and need more time to plea than their Flemish counterparts, who are more to the point.[47]

The ongoing discussions regarding juvenile law are a good example of illustrating the differences in mentality between Flemish and French-speaking.[48] Different views on how juveniles should be treated already led to the transfer of the competences regarding juvenile protection to the regions in 1980 and 1988, while the competence regarding juvenile delinquency remained a federal competence. As Flanders is more right-wing,

---

42 See Dirk Heirbaut and Matthias Storme, 'The Belgian Legal Tradition: From a Long Quest for Legal Independence to a Longing for Independence' (2006) *European Review of Private Law* 663.

43 In 2004, a cumulative edition of the 1804 Civil Code appeared, with a comparison of the contemporary and original text, including all the changes. See Dirk Heirbaut and Gustaaf Baeteman, *Cumulatieve editie van het Burgerlijk Wetboek: de huidige en de originele tekst met alle wijzigingen in België van 1804 tot 2004* (two parts, Kluwer 2004). On p. 2209–2032, there is a list with all the legislation that changed provisions of the Code. See also Dirk Heirbaut and Georges Martyn (eds), *Napoleons nalatenschap. Tweehonderd jaar Burgerlijk Wetboek in België / Un heritage Napoléonien. Bicentenaire du Code civil en Belgique* (Kluwer 2005); Dirk Heirbaut, 'Editing and Translating the Code civil in Belgium, 1804–2004' (2004) Vol. 72 Issue 3–4 *The Legal History Review* 215.

44 Dirk Heirbaut, 'The Belgian Legal Tradition: Does It Exist?' in Mark Kruithof and Walter De Bondt (eds), *Introduction to Belgian Law* (2nd ed, Wolters Kluwer 2017) see the pages 18–19.

45 For instance, the two main journals for private law are *Tijdschrift voor privaatrecht* (in Dutch) and *Revue Critique du Jurisprudence belge* (in French). The two main general journals are *Rechtskundig Weekblad* (in Dutch) and *Journal des Tribunaux* (in French). For a legal history of the legal periodicals in Belgium, see Sebastiaan Vandenbogaerde, *Vectoren van het recht: geschiedenis van de Belgische juridische tijdschriften* (Die Keure 2018).

46 Heirbaut (2017) (n 44) 1.

47 According to the president of the national order of magistrates in Belgium, in a newspaper interview in 2012. See https://www.nieuwsblad.be/cnt/dmf20120330_061 accessed 22 January 2019. Meanwhile the ministry of justice has started with so-called "*werklastmeting*", the measurement of workload, to get objective data, but there is not yet information available about this.

48 Sabien Hespel and Johan Put, *Jeugdsanctierecht voorgesteld: naar een constructief jeugdsanctierecht* (Larcier 2014); Geert Decock and Johan Put, *Jeugdsanctierecht gewikt en gewogen: toetsing van beleid en praktijk aan de principes van het jeugdsanctierecht* (Larcier 2012).

public opinion has been favouring (some) youngsters to be treated as criminals and to be locked away in juvenile prisons. In contrast, the more left-wing public opinion in the South regards juvenile delinquents primarily as minors, who should not be punished, but re-educated in specialized youth institutions. Because of the persisting different views in North and South, the sixth reform of the state in 2011 has allocated "material juvenile law" (i.e., what constitutes juvenile crimes, how they should be dealt with, etc.) to the regions, while "formal juvenile law" (i.e., the procedures, courts, etc.) has remained a federal competence (part of the judiciary, which still is federal). This way, Flemish and French-speaking can each pursue their own politics. Meanwhile, the Flemish parliament has indeed passed new, repressive legislation on the matter.[49]

This pattern is typical for the Belgian state reforms: there are ongoing disagreements between North and South on certain matters, until a state reform allocates the competence on (parts of) these matters to the regions. One should not underestimate the growing gap between the two main language groups. This is an ongoing process, without end in sight. To give one more example: during 1998–2002, the Flemish bars split away from the national Belgian order because of different views on the allocation of legal aid remunerations.[50] Not surprisingly, some Flemish lawyers are now asking for the complete split of justice in Belgium, so each part of the country could fully develop their own legal culture.[51] This would only be the formalization of an already existing situation. When asked, most Flemish lawyers will probably say that they feel first and foremost Flemish, while French-speaking will say they are Belgian. The only problem is that this "Belgian" identity only theoretically includes Flanders, since they mostly have no idea about the language, mentality, and (legal) culture on the other side of the language border.

Another factor that is changing the "Belgian" character of the Belgian legal culture regards the impact of the supranational level. Since the 1971 *Le Ski* case, the Court of Cassation has adhered to a monistic approach/theory, giving international law a supreme position in the Belgian legal order (see further, Section 7 on Internationalisation). As a result, European regulations have been increasingly replacing the original Belgian legislation. In addition, the case law of the Court of Justice of the European Union[52]

49 Decree of 15 February 2019 "betreffende het jeugddelinquentierecht", Moniteur belge 26 April 2019, accessed 4 December 2019, via https://jongerenwelzijn.be/assets/docs/ons/regelgeving/decreet_jdr.pdf.

50 There are now two bar associations in Belgium: the Flemish Bar Association OVB: https://www.advocaat.be/; and the Association of French-speaking and German-speaking Bars of Belgium OBFG: https://avocats.be/fr. Both links accessed 6 April 2019. On the rise and fall of the national bar association, see: Bart Quintelier, 'Opkomst en ondergang van de nationale orde van advocaten van België' in Georges Martyn, Greta Doncker, Sjoerd Faber and Dirk Heirbaut (eds), *Geschiedenis van de advocatuur in de Lage Landen* (Verloren 2009) 341.

51 One example is the former dean of the Law Faculty of the KUL (Catholic University of Leuven), Paul Van Orshoven, who pleaded for a split on the occasion of his inaugural lecture of the Francqui Chair at Ghent University. See https://www.gva.be/cnt/aid1334959/van-orshoven-wil-justitie-helemaal-naar-de-gemeenschappen accessed 22 January 2019.

52 See for instance about the influence of European Union Law on the Belgian judges and case law: Nicolas Cariat and Janek Tomasz Nowak (ed) *Le droit de l'Union européenne et le juge belge – Het recht van de Europese Unie en de Belgische rechter* (Larcier 2015); Gert Straetmans and Michel Rozie (ed), *Doorwerking van het Europese recht in de nationale rechterlijke praktijk* (Intersentia 2012)

and the European Court of Human Rights has a constantly increasing impact on the Belgian legal culture.

In the following sections, we will take a closer look at the six elements of the legal cultural model as presented in the second chapter of this book.

2. Conflict resolution in Belgium

The Belgian Constitution contains the framework for the Belgian judiciary. Firstly, Title III, Chapter V lays down the purpose and competence of Constitutional Court. Chapter VI deals with the ordinary courts. Finally, in Chapter VII, the organization and competences of the Council of State and administrative courts are determined. I will discuss them in the same order.

2.1 The Constitutional court[53]

The history of the Belgian Constitutional Court is directly linked to the reforms of the state.[54] The exclusive division of legislative competences (see below) created the problem of possible conflicts of competence. Therefore, with the second reform of the state in 1980, a Court of Arbitration *(Arbitragehof/Cour d'arbitrage)*[55] was created to decide on conflicts of competence between the national entity and the regional entities, or between the regional entities (that is, the first main competence).[56] In 1988, this court also received the competence to supervise the observance of the Articles 10, 11 and 24 of the Constitution, guaranteeing the principles of equality, non-discrimination and the rights and liberties regarding education.[57] In 2007, its name changed into the Constitutional Court (*Grondwettelijk Hof/Cour constitutionnel*).[58] The Constitutional Court has the competence to investigate the constitutionality of any legislative act and to review that there are no violations of the Articles 8 till 32, 143 §1, 170, 172 or 191 of the Belgian Constitution (that is, the second main competence).[59]

---

53 See http://www.const-court.be/public/brbr/e/brbr-2014-001e.pdf; see also Louis Paul Suetens, 'Judicial Review in Belgium' in Eivind Smith, *Constitutional Justice under Old Constitutions* (Kluwer 1995), 319; André Alen and David Haljan, *Constitutional law* (Kluwer Law International 2013).

54 On the history of the superior courts in Belgium, the Netherlands and Luxembourg see: Georges Martyn, 'Belgium, the Netherlands and Luxembourg Since 1800' in Alain Wijffels & Remco van Rhee (eds), *European Supreme Courts: a Portrait through History* (Third Millennium Publishing 2013) 218.

55 The term "arbitration" refers in this context to the role of "arbiter" between the different entities. At that time, the politicians did not want to introduce a Constitutional court – they only wanted an instance to settle disputes of competence that could arise because of the division of competences.

56 The Court of Arbitration was introduced in the Belgian legal system by the Act of 9 August 1980, published in the Moniteur belge on 15 August 1980, which added a new Article 107, *ter* in the Belgian Constitution (now Article 142). The Act of 28 June 1983, published in the Moniteur belge on 8 July 1983, dealt with the structure, competence and modus operandi of the new court.

57 This happened with the State Reform Act of 15 July 1988, published on 29 July in the Moniteur belge.

58 State Reform Act of 7 May 2007, published on 8 May 2007 in the Moniteur belge.

59 See Article 142 of the Belgian Constitution.

There are 12 judges in the Constitutional Court, equally divided over both main language groups.[60] One of the judges must also have an adequate knowledge of German.[61] The judges are appointed for life by the King from a list of two candidates proposed alternately by the House of Representatives and the Senate by a majority of at least two-thirds of the members present.[62] Half of the judges are appointed because of their legal experience (law professor, judicial officer at the Supreme Court or the Council of State, or legal secretary at the Constitutional Court), while the other half of the judges have a political background – they must have had at least five years of experience as Member of Parliament.[63]

The Constitutional Court judges on the constitutionality of a legislative act after receiving a request of annulment or a preliminary question.[64] A request of annulment has to be submitted within the period of six months after publication in the official journal.[65] There are two categories of actors who can make this request: the authorities designated by law (the federal government, the governments of the regions and communities, and the presidents of all parliaments, when two-thirds of the members of the parliament request this) and any person with a justifiable interest.[66] This last category comprises natural and legal persons, who have to prove that they are personally, directly and unfavourably affected by the legislative act they want to see annulled (= destroyed as if it never existed).[67] In exceptional circumstances, the Court can also order the suspension of an act (= putting it temporarily out of action).[68]

All other Belgian courts and tribunals have a constitutional duty to ask a preliminary question to the Constitutional Court when a question arises regarding a conflict of competence (see above) or the possible unconstitutionality of a legislative act.[69] This obligation is a consequence of the monopoly of the Constitutional Court to decide on the constitutionality of legislative acts.

The cases are generally decided by seven judges,[70] including the two presidents, but this number can be limited (to three)[71] or extended (to ten or twelve).[72] The procedures

60 See Article 31 of the Special Act 6 January 1989, published 7 January 1989. The English text of this Act can be consulted on the website of the Constitutional Court: http://www.const-court.be accessed 5 April 2019.

61 See Article 34 § 4 of the Special Act 6 January 1989, published 7 January 1989.

62 See Article 32 of the Special Act 6 January 1989, published 7 January 1989.

63 See Article 34 § 1 of the Special Act 6 January 1989, published 7 January 1989.

64 See Chapters 1 and 2 of the Special Act of 6 January 1989, published 7 January 1989. The judgments of the Constitutional Court are mostly in Dutch and French, but thanks to the Venice Commission, a number of judgments have been translated to English. They can be consulted on the website of the Constitutional Court.

65 See Article 3 of the Special Act 6 January 1989, published 7 January 1989.

66 See Article 2 of the Special Act 6 January 1989, published 7 January 1989.

67 See Article 2 of the Special Act 6 January 1989, published 7 January 1989.

68 See Articles 19 f. of the Special Act of 6 January 1989, published 7 January 1989.

69 See Chapter II of the Special Act of 6 January 1989, published 7 January 1989.

70 See Article 55 of the Special Act 6 January 1989, published 7 January 1989.

71 The limited chamber deals with a first control of the requests. See Article 69 of the Special Act of 6 January 1989, published 7 January 1989.

72 Article 56 foresees the extended composition of the Court when it has to judge matters foreseen in the Articles 37, 38, 42, 43, 44, 49, 50, 100 and 122 of the Special Act of 6 January 1989, published 7 January 1989.

are exclusively written. The Constitutional Court has to render a judgment within 12 months after having received the request of annulment or the prejudicial question. In 2017, the Constitutional Court rendered 151 judgments, thereby closing 232 cases.[73] In the same year, 229 new cases were brought to the Court. Four judgments dealt with a request for suspension, 102 answered a prejudicial question and 45 decided on a request for annulment. The Court found a violation in 47 of the 102 prejudicial questions[74] and it granted one-third of the requests for annulment (15 out of 45).[75] In the majority of the cases (128 out of 151), the Articles 10 and/or 11 of the Constitution were invoked.[76]

The consequences of the judgments of the Constitutional Court are the following. In the case of an annulment, the legislative act concerned is immediately wholly or partially invalid, with retroactive force. In other words, the Constitutional Court has the competence to control and overrule the legislator if an Act of Parliament violates the Constitution. In the case of a prejudicial question, the tribunal or court that has asked the question is strictly bound to follow the answer of the Constitutional Court on the prejudicial question. These decisions do not have effect *erga omnes* but are limited to the specific case at hand. However, the Act of 25 December 2016 provides the Constitutional Court with the authority to decide on the consequences of a legislative act that has been considered unconstitutional in such a prejudicial procedure.[77] In this case, the court can decide that certain provisions of the act will stay in force, for a determined or undetermined period. In addition, a new term of six months starts, during which a request for annulment can be filed.

Despite its relatively recent occurrence, the Belgian Constitutional Court has firmly acquired its position in the Belgian legal culture. It has a unique function as constitutional safeguard. Research has shown that the Belgian Constitutional Court is very careful in its decision-making, by taking many factors into account, such as the interpretation of the Constitution by the ordinary judges, the practice of the European Courts and of foreign constitutional courts, and the political interpretation of the Constitution by the executive and legislative branches.[78]

73 See http://www.const-court.be/public/jvra/n/jvra-2017n.pdf p. 71 f., accessed 4 December 2019.

74 See http://www.const-court.be/public/jvra/n/jvra-2017n.pdf p. 76, accessed 4 December 2019.

75 See http://www.const-court.be/public/jvra/n/jvra-2017n.pdf p. 74, accessed 4 December 2019.

76 Nine cases had to do with a conflict of competence. The following articles of the Constitution were also mentioned: Art. 12 (four times), Art. 13 (ten times), Art. 14 (three times), Art. 15 (two times), Art. 16 (ten times), Art. 19 (one time), Art. 21 (one time), Art. 22 (nine times), Art. 22 *bis* (two times), Art. 23 (22 times), Art. 24 (11 times), Art. 27 (six times), Art. 30 (two times), Art. 32 (one time), Art. 170 (six times), Art. 172 (11 times) and Art. 191 (two times).

77 Act of 25 December 2016, published on 10 January 2017 in the Moniteur belge.

78 Toon Moonen, *De keuzes van het Grondwettelijk Hof: argumenten bij de interpretatie van de Grondwet* (Die Keure 2015); see also Jan Erk, 'Why Multi-Ethnic Belgium's Constitutional Court Keeps Mum: The Constitutionalization of Ethnicity, Judicial Review, and 'Passive Virtues'' (2018) Vol. 3 *Constitutional Studies* 101.

2.2 Ordinary courts[79]

The Belgian judicial system is French in origin (see above). It has mainly preserved its French structure, characterized by a pyramidal structure, with hierarchy and division along competence and territoriality.[80] According to Article 144 of the Belgian Constitution, 'the ordinary courts have exclusive jurisdiction over disputes relating to civil rights'. Since 1948, administrative matters are judged by a newly established administrative court (see below).

At the bottom of the Belgian judicial pyramid are the justices of the peace (*vredegerechten/justices de la paix*) and the police tribunals (*politierechtbanken/tribunaux de police*).

There are 187 justices of the peace, with 229 seats. The justices of the peace have a general competence in civil matters for small disputes (up to 5,000 Euro, from 1 September 2018 on) and a series of special competences (rent disputes, conflicts between neighbours, etc.). Just like all the other professional magistrates, the justices of the peace are university-schooled lawyers (Masters' level). They handle an enormous amount of cases each year: in 2016, there were 433,619 new cases and 438,834 cases finished.[81] The procedures before the justices of the peace are written, with a possibility to plead the case.

There are 15 police tribunals in Belgium. Their main competence regards traffic violations. The police judges rendered 237,441 judgments in 2016.[82] Most of the procedures are very simple, with only a citation and an oral defense before the police judge, but some cases are more complex.

On the next level, we first find the *Rechtbanken van Eerste Aanleg/Tribunaux de première instance*, 13 in total. These tribunals occupy 53% of all the magistrates[83] in Belgium.[84] They first serve as courts of appeal for the justices of the peace and the police courts. They also have a general competency in civil and criminal matters. They are subdivided into civil tribunals *(burgerlijke rechtbank/tribunal civil)* for general civil matters,[85] criminal

79 For a recent overview of the Belgian judicial structure, see: Stefaan Voet, 'Belgium's new specialized judiciary' (2014) vol. 4 *Russian Law Journal* 129. See also https://www.tribunaux-rechtbanken.be/fr/tribunaux-et-cours accessed 4 December 2019. There are also pages in Dutch and German, but unfortunately not in English.

80 Piet Taelman and Claudia Van Severen, 'The Judicial System and Civil Procedure', in Marc Kruithof and Walter De Bondt (eds), *Introduction to Belgian Law* (Kluwer Law International 2017) 81.

81 See https://justitie.belgium.be/sites/default/files/jic_nl-2016.pdf p. 37, accessed 25 January 2019.

82 See ibid.

83 "Magistrate" ("*magistraat*"/"*magistrat*") is the generic term in Belgium for public prosecutors ("standing magistrates") and judges ("sitting magistrates"). Under the "civil law" systems of European countries, such as Belgium, France, Italy and the Netherlands, *magistrat* (French), *magistrato* (Italian) and *magistraat* (Dutch) are generic terms which comprise both prosecutors and judges, distinguished as the 'standing' versus 'sitting' magistrature, respectively.

84 See https://justitie.belgium.be/sites/default/files/jic_nl-2016.pdf p. 20, accessed 25 January 2019.

85 See https://www.rechtbanken-tribunaux.be/nl/rechtbanken-hoven/rechtbank-van-eerste-aanleg/burgerlijke-rechtbank accessed 22 January 2019.

tribunals (*correctionele rechtbank/tribunal correctionnel*) for criminal matters,[86] family tribunals (*familierechtbank/tribunal de la famille*) for family matters,[87] juvenile tribunals (*jeugdrechtbank/tribunal de la jeunesse*) for juvenile matters[88], and penalty tribunals (*strafuitvoeringsrechtbank/tribunal de l'application des peines*), that follow up the penalties that have been pronounced by the courts and tribunals.[89] In 2016, there were 118,653 new cases in civil, family and youth matters and 125,401 finished.[90] In 2014, there were 13,557 criminal cases pending, 51,810 new criminal cases started and 54,453 criminal cases finished.[91]

Further, there is a separate court for commercial matters (*ondernemingsrechtbank/tribunal de l'entreprise*, until 1 November 2018 called *rechtbank van koophandel/tribunal de commerce*). In 2016, 79,315 new cases were brought before these commercial tribunals.[92] Since 1970, there is also a separate court for social matters (labour law and social security law): the *arbeidsrechtbank/tribunal du travail*. In 2016, this tribunal welcomed 75,452 new cases and finished 77,115 cases.[93] Due to historical circumstances, both tribunals have lay judges: representatives respectively from the field of commerce and the field of labour (unions, employer organizations, etc.). Each chamber is presided by a professional magistrate, assisted by two lay judges. The procedure is both written and oral.

For the gravest crimes, such as murder, there is a special instance, the *hof van assisen/court d'assises*. This (temporary) court consists of three professional magistrates and a jury of 12 randomly selected citizens between 28 and 65 years old. It is the only Belgian judicial instance with a jury. It is used quite rarely: in the period 2011–2016, there were an average of only 82 cases a year.[94] The often-spectacular assize trials are highly mediatized, but also time consuming and costly, as they are completely oral. Moreover, in 2009, Belgium was convicted by the European Court of Human Rights for violation of Article Six of the ECHR.[95] Following this judgment, the Act of 21 December 2009 made a number of changes to the assize trial.[96] For instance, the professional judges now have to formulate the arguments underlying the decision, also in the case of an acquittal. Before, the jury only had to say "guilty" or "not guilty" on the charges presented by the

86 See https://www.rechtbanken-tribunaux.be/nl/rechtbanken-hoven/rechtbank-van-eerste-aanleg/correctionele-rechtbank accessed 22 January 2019.

87 See https://www.rechtbanken-tribunaux.be/nl/rechtbanken-hoven/rechtbank-van-eerste-aanleg/familierechtbank accessed 22 January 2019.

88 See https://www.rechtbanken-tribunaux.be/nl/rechtbanken-hoven/rechtbank-van-eerste-aanleg/jeugdrechtbank accessed 22 January 2019.

89 See https://www.rechtbanken-tribunaux.be/nl/rechtbanken-hoven/rechtbank-van-eerste-aanleg/strafuitvoeringsrechtbank accessed 22 January 2019.

90 See https://justitie.belgium.be/sites/default/files/jic_nl-2016.pdf p. 39, accessed 25 January 2019.

91 See ibid 40. I chose 2014 because the numbers of the other years were incomplete.

92 See ibid 38.

93 See ibid 38.

94 See ibid 44.

95 *Taxquet v Belgium* App no 926/05 (ECtHR, 13 January 2009).

96 Act of 21 December 2009 "tot hervorming van het hof van assisen", Belgisch Staatsblad 11 January 2010.

public prosecutor, without giving any arguments for their decision. Another element of the 2009 Act is the enlargement of the possibility to "correctionalize". This technique implies giving a lower qualification to the crime, so that it can be brought before the criminal tribunal ("*correctionele rechtbank*"/"*tribunal correctionnel*", hence the term), instead of the assize court. In 2016, the Minister of Justice generalized the possibility of "correctionalizing" to all the gravest crimes, virtually abolishing the assize court.[97] However, on 27 December 2018, the Constitutional Court partially declared this Act unconstitutional.[98] In order to abolish the assize court, one has to change the Constitution, which is in fact very hard.[99]

On the next level of the judicial pyramid, we find two institutions. For appeal in civil, criminal and commercial matters, there is the *Hof van Beroep/Cour d'appèl*, while for appeal in social matters, there is the *Arbeidshof/Cour du Travail*. Only professional judges sit on the first, generally in chambers with three, while the latter also has lay judges next to the professional judge who presides over the chamber. There are five of each of the appeal courts: in Ghent, Antwerp, Brussels, Liège, and Mons. The procedures are mainly written, with a limited possibility for pleading. As to the number of cases in appeal, there are the following numbers for 2016: labour cases – 6,463 pending, 4,534 new, and 4,574 settled – civil cases: 36,981 pending, 15,895 new, and 17,661 settled – criminal cases: 6,041 pending, 7,220 new, and 7,252 settled.[100]

On top, there is the Court of Cassation (*Hof van Cassatie/Cour de cassation*)[101], that only judges on the legality of judgments and does not rule on the facts. There are three chambers, for civil, criminal, and social matters. Each chamber has a Dutch-speaking and a French-speaking department. A chamber normally has five members. For simple matters, there are only three judges, while a full chamber has nine members. In 2017, the Court of Cassation rendered 2,660 judgments.[102]

Next to the division in competences, there is also a territorial division. In Belgium, there are 187 *kantons/cantons* (for the justices of the peace), 12 *arrondissementen/arrondissements* (for the police courts and the first instance courts), five districts (*ressorten/*

97 The so-called second "Potpourri Act". Act of 5 February 2016 "tot wijziging van het strafrecht en de strafvordering en houdende diverse bepalingen inzake justitie", Belgisch Staatsblad 19 February 2016.

98 Constitutional Court, Arrest of 21 December 2017, nr. 148/2017, see: http://www.const-court.be/public/n/2017/2017-148n.pdf accessed 25 January 2019.

99 The procedure to change the Constitution is stipulated in Article 195 of the Constitution: "The federal legislative power has the right to declare that there are reasons to revise such constitutional provision as it determines. Following such a declaration, the two Houses are automatically dissolved. Two new Houses are then convened, in accordance with Article 46. These Houses make decisions, in common accord with the King, on the points submitted for revision. In this case, the Houses can only debate provided that at least two thirds of the members who make up each House are present; and no change is adopted unless it is supported by at least two thirds of the votes cast."

100 See https://justitie.belgium.be/sites/default/files/jic_nl-2016.pdf p. 41–43, accessed 25 January 2019.

101 Jean-François van Droogenbroeck, *Cassation et jurisdiction. Iura dicit curia* (Bruylant 2004); Françoise Müller, *La Cour de Cassation belge à l'aune des rapports entre pouvoirs. De sa naissance dans le modèle classique de la séparation des pouvoirs à l'aube d'une extension de la fonction juridictionnelle 1832–1914/1936* (Die Keure 2011).

102 See https://justitie.belgium.be/sites/default/files/downloads/jaarverslag2017.pdf p. 202, accessed 25 January 2019.

resorts) for the courts of appeal, and the whole of the Kingdom for the Court of Cassation. The assize court is organized per province, of which there are 11.

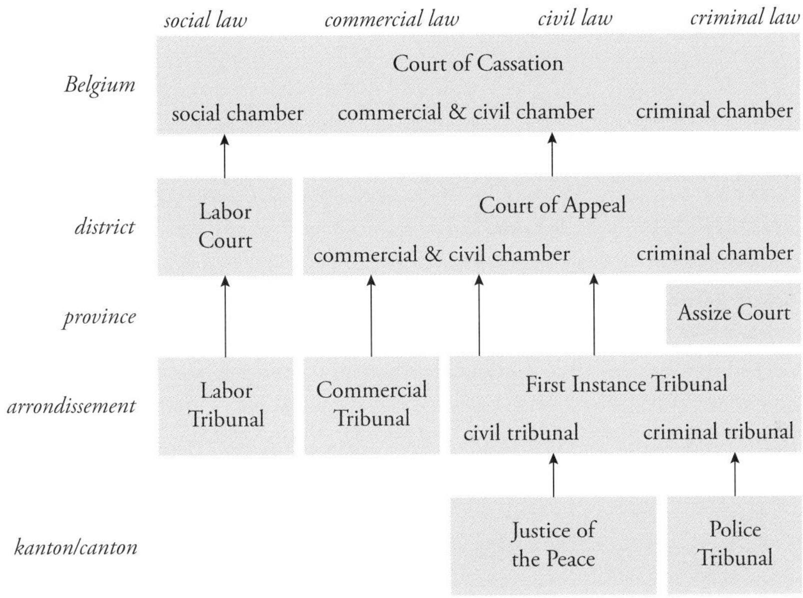

Fig. 1 The Belgian Court System.

2.3 Administrative courts

The Belgian administrative judicial organization is not as elaborate as the French one, which might be explained by its late development in Belgium. It took until 1946 before Belgium installed the *Raad van State/Conseil d'Etat*, modelled after the French State Council.[103] The Belgian Council of State has the power to censure, in proceedings for annulment, administrative acts vitiated by excess power, i.e. unlawful acts.[104] This is done by the administrative litigation section, but there is also a legislative section, which gives non-binding opinions on the preliminary drafts of legislation.

The Belgian Council of State comprises 44 members.[105] During the judicial year 2016–2017, 2,801 new cases were enrolled and in the same period, 3,339 judgments were delivered.[106] These last judgments can be divided into 3,084 judgments delivered in general litigation, 169 judgments delivered in litigation for the annulment involving

103 See http://www.raadvst-consetat.be accessed 22 January 2019.

104 Jacques Jaumotte, Jacques Salmon and Éric Thibaut, *Le Conseil d'Etat de Belgique* (Bruylant 2012), 2 volumes.

105 A first president, a president, 14 Chamber presidents, and 28 members.

106 See http://www.aca-europe.eu/en/eurtour/i/countries/belgium/belgium_en.pdf accessed 14 April 2019.

foreign nationals, and 86 judgments delivered in general litigation for annulment. Some 25% pertained to urban planning in the broad sense, 20% to civil service, and 13% to public procurement. At the end of 2016–2017, there were 4,261 pending cases. The average time to deliver a judgment is 17 months. When there is a conflict of competence between the State Council and the ordinary courts, the State Council settles this itself, but with a possibility of cassation by the Court of Cassation.

2.4 Mediation, arbitration and extrajudicial conflict resolution[107]

Most traces of mediation and conciliation in the Belgian judicial system are contributory to the French revolutionaries. For them, justice had to be fast, inexpensive and without the curse of procedural formalities. Citizens had to be judged by "*citoyens-juges*" (citizen-judges), who had to use equity and good sense rather than law. The best examples of this point of view are the justices of the peace who are still considered the most practical, down to earth and successful judicial instance in Belgium. Another relict of the French revolution in the Belgian judicial system is the great emphasis on conciliation. There is an obligatory conciliation phase in a number of specific procedures, such as rent disputes (justice of the peace) or divorces (first instance court – *rechtbank van eerste aanleg/tribunal de première instance*). More generally, the justices of the peace offer a handy possibility of conciliation: one only has to write a letter to the justice of the peace, with a short summary of the conflict and the data of the other party. Both parties are then formally invited to the courthouse, where the judge tries to conciliate them. If this succeeds, he makes up a minute (*proces-verbaal/procès-verbal*), which has binding force and can be directly enforced. The advantages of this conciliation procedure are multiple: free of costs, simple and accessible. Moreover, if parties do not reach an understanding and a judicial procedure has to be started afterwards, the parties appear before the same judge who has already tried to conciliate the parties.

Recently, mediation has found entry into the Belgian legal culture, under impulse of European regulation.[108] One can mention the Act of 19 February 2001 on mediation in family affairs[109] and the more elaborate Act of 21 February 2005 on voluntary and judicial mediation.[110],[111] It is based on the most recent version of the 1985

107 On mediation in Belgium, see: Piet Taelman and Stefaan Voet, 'Mediation in Belgium: a long and winding road' in Carlos Esplugues and Louis Marquis (eds), *New developments in civil and commercial mediation: global comparative perspectives* (Springer 2015) 89; On arbitration: Niuscha Bassiri and Maarten Draye (eds), *Arbitration in Belgium* (Kluwer 2016); Barbara den Tandt (ed), *The new Belgian arbitration law* (Die Keure 2015); Guy Keutgen, Georges-Albert Dal, Marc Dal and Gautier Matray, *L'arbitrage en droit belge et international* (Bruylant 2015).

108 Raf Van Ransbeeck (ed), *Bemiddeling* (Die Keure 2008); Bram Van Dael, 'Bemiddeling in België: justitie ge(re)medieerd?' in Remco Van Rhee, Dirk Heirbaut and M.L. Storme (eds), *De Code de procédure civile (1806) na 200 jaar: de traditie van het Frans civiel procesrecht in vergelijkend perspectief* (Kluwer 2008), 109.

109 Belgisch Staatsblad 3 April 2001.

110 Belgisch Staatsblad 22 March 2005.

111 Act of 24 June 2013, Belgisch Staatsblad 28 June 2013.

UNCITRAL Model Law on International Commercial Arbitration, as amended in 2006.[112] CEPANI,[113] the biggest Belgian Arbitration organization, settles some 100 cases a year.[114]

2.5 Some final considerations

Just like in other civil law systems, the Belgian court system has a comparatively high degree of specialisation. There are not only separate courts for different fields of law, but we can also find a high degree of specialisation within the individual courts. The caseload of the courts is quite high and among the highest in Europe. Constitutional review is a recognised and functional part of the system of conflict-resolution.

3. Norm production[115]

The federal and regional parliaments are regarded as the main producers of legal norms in Belgium. In addition, EU regulations and certain international law obligations are directly applicable in Belgium. These norms are as a rule organized in a hierarchy.

Belgium has a written constitution, which constituted the top of this hierarchy until 27 May 1971, when the Court of Cassation decided that international and supranational norms (including EU regulations) are above Belgian national legislation, the Constitution included.[116] The Belgian Constitution regulates the competences of and interaction between the legislative, the executive and the judicial branches of government. Commencing the reforms of the state, it also contains the general principles of the federal system. Furthermore, the Constitution contains a number of fundamental rights and freedoms. In addition to the text of the Constitution, there are a number of special acts containing further constitutional rules of the federal system. These acts were voted with a two-third majority and are therefore above ordinary legislation in the hierarchy of the norms.

When it comes to ordinary legislation, Belgium has, as many other civil law jurisdictions in Europe, a long tradition for organizing legal norms in systematic codifica-

112 See https://www.rechtbanken-tribunaux.be/sites/default/files/public/content/download/files/arbitrage.pdf accessed 24 January 2019.

113 See http://www.cepani.be/en accessed 24 January 2019.

114 There are no official numbers. These numbers are taken from the following newspaper article: http://www.standaard.be/cnt/dmf20180212_03354193 accessed 24 January 2019.

115 On the history of norm production in Belgium, see: Georges Martyn, 'De evolutie van de rechtsbronnen' in Dirk Heirbaut, Xavier Rousseaux and Margo De Koster (eds), *Tweehonderd Jaar Justitie : Historische Encyclopedie Van De Belgische Justitie = Deux Siècles De Justice : Encyclopédie Historique De La Justice Belge* (Die Keure 2015) 51.

116 *Fromagerie Franco-Suisse Le Ski vs. Belgische Staat*, Court of Cassation 27 May 1971, Arresten van het Hof van Cassatie 1971, 959. See further below (under section 7).

tions.[117] Since the 18th century, the prevailing idea of norm production is that legislation is the most effective way of legally governing a civil society.

Belgium inherited the French codifications: the Code civil (1804), the Code de procédure civile (1806), the Code de commerce (1807), the Code d'instruction criminelle (1808) and the Code pénal (1810). The civil code is still in force, albeit approximately half of the provisions have changed.[118] The commercial code has been gradually dismantled: parts have been subject to new legislation outside the existing code. Examples are the Company Code (*Wetboek van vennootschappen/Code des sociétés*) of 1999 and the Code of Economic Law (*Wetboek van Economisch Recht/Code de droit économique*) of 2013. In 2018, the old commercial code was finally abolished. Two codes have been replaced by a newer version: the criminal code in 1867 and the code of civil procedure one century later, in 1967. The code of criminal procedure is still the same but it received a new Preliminary Title in 1878.

These codifications may create the perception that there is a well-organized system of positive law in Belgium, but even if Belgian lawyers can make use of a number of codes, the vast majority of legislation is not codified. In theory, everyone is supposed to know the law (according to the principle *nemo censetur ignorare legem*), but this has become increasingly difficult. In 2005, there were some 25,000 statutes with a total of 1 million articles in force in Belgium.[119] The number of pages in the Belgian official journal (*Belgisch Staatsblad/Moniteur belge*) is skyrocketing each year: in 2018, it contained 108,622 pages.[120] Also, in theory, legislation is supposed to be abstract, with general principles that have to be applied to specific cases. In practice however, legislation is increasingly detailed, seemingly wanting to deal with all possible kinds of situations.

Ordinary legislation used to be made solely by the Belgian parliament, which consisted out of a bicameral system with a Chamber (*Kamer/Chambre*) and a Senate (*Senaat/Senat*). These statutes are called *wetten/lois*, which are executed by executive organs. The content, interpretation or application of legislation has traditionally been specified by royal decrees (*koninklijke besluiten/arrêtés royals*) and decrees of the state secretaries (*ministeriële besluiten/arrêtés ministériels*).

Since the reforms of the state, things have become more complicated. The state reforms have allocated a number of national legislative competences to the parliaments of the communities and the regions. At the level of the communities and of the Flemish and Walloon regions, the statutes are called *decreten/décrets*. Due to historical reasons,

117 Dirk Heirbaut, 'Codification in Belgium from Napoleon to Geens' in Harry Dondorp (ed), *De rebus divinis et humanis: essays in honour of Jan Hallebeek* (Vandenhoeck & Ruprecht 2019) 167.

118 Heirbaut and Martyn (2005) (n 43).

119 Herman Matthijs, Maarten Theo Jans and Hedwig de Koker, *Bestuurswetenschappen. De overheid. Instellingen en beleid* (Intersentia 2005) 19.

120 See http://www.standaard.be/cnt/dmf20181231_04071834 accessed 14 April 2019.

the Brussels legislation is called differently: ordinances (*ordonnanties/ordonnances*).[121] The regional statutes are executed by regulations and orders of the regional governments (*executieven/exécutifs*).

In contrast to other federal states such as Germany and the United States, the Belgian Constitution does not have a priority clause, giving federal law priority over regional law in case of conflict. In Flanders, for example, if a Flemish decree would be in violation of a provision issued on the federal level, the principle of *lex superior* would not be applicable. In other words, there is no hierarchy between national statutes or statutes issued by the regions and communities. In the case of conflicts of competence, it is the task of the Constitutional Court to settle these.[122] The Constitutional Court has, as mentioned above, the competence to annul, to declare unconstitutional or to suspend federal, regional and community legislation violating the constitution or any provision therein.[123] As a consequence, both the national (federal) and the parliaments of the territories are equally important producers of legal norms in Belgium.

On a lower level, there are provinces and municipalities, which enact their own provincial and municipal regulations and orders (*provinciale en gemeentelijke reglementen & verordeningen/règlements provincials & municipals*). The scope of application of these legal regulations are, however, strictly limited to the respective provincial and municipal communities.

The principle of legality applies to all the executive regulations and orders. The executive instances can only act insofar as empowered to do so by the Constitution or statutes by the federal, regional or community legislators. According to Article 157 of the Constitution, the ordinary courts have to refuse the application of executive acts that are in violation with the higher-ranking legal rules. The administrative section of the Council of State also has the power to annul regulations and orders in case of violation of the higher rules.

Since the Belgian legal culture is strictly legal positivistic, courts are not supposed to create law, only to interpret legislation. In reality however, the court decisions, especially

121 The Flemish were against Brussels as a separate region, while the French-speaking were pro. The explanation for this difference is simple: the French-speaking constitute the majority in Brussels. As a compromise, the Flemish agreed on Brussels as a separate region, but not on the same level as the two other regions. This was visualized in the terminology: Brussels legislation was called ordinances instead of decrees, which was considered inferior by the Flemish. On the contrary, the French-speaking always considered Brussels a full worthy region and ordinances equal to decrees. It is a typical example of a "Belgian compromise", in which both parties get what they want, through different interpretation of an agreement.

122 Patrick Peeters and Jens Mosselmans, 'The Constitutional Court of Belgium: Safeguard of the Autonomy of the Communities and Regions' in Nicholas Aroney and John Kincaid (eds), *Courts in Federal Countries: Federalists or Unitarists?* (University of Toronto Press 2017), 69.

123 Articles 8–32 (on the rights and freedoms of the Belgians), Article 143, §1 (the principle of federal loyalty), Articles 170 and 172 (legality and equality of taxes), and Article 191 (protection of foreign nationals).

of the highest courts, do have a certain normative power.[124] The judges also have a limited law making power, based on Article 5 of the Judicial Code, which states that there is denial of justice if a judge refuses to decide a case under any pretext, be it the silence, the obscurity or the incompleteness of the statute.[125]

4. Ideal of Justice

As mentioned earlier, Belgium has inherited the Napoleonic legal and judicial system. The French (Belgian) judiciary is a rational system, guided by three basic principles: "territoriality", "speciality" and "control".[126] These principles each reflect a different aspect of the ideal of law and justice in Belgium.

The first basic principle of "territoriality" refers to the geographic spread of tribunals and courts. In origin, the justices of the peace had to be within walking distance of each citizen, while the tribunals had to be reachable by horse.[127] Even today, there are still 187 justices of the peace, with 229 seats spread all over the country. The justices of the peace are supposed to be familiar with the particularities and specific needs of their district. They are also supposed to be easily accessible and provide the parties with the opportunity of an informal and free conciliation procedure (see above, under Mediation, arbitration and extrajudicial conflict resolution)[128]

One could say that the principle of territoriality is closely related to the ideal of "access to justice": justice has to be close to the citizens and accessible to anyone who needs it.[129] The poor in Belgium, for instance, have always had the possibility of free legal aid, by exempting the procedural costs for them and by obliging the advocacy to provide free legal assistance.[130] Still, during most of the twentieth Century, the realm of justice

---

124 See the recent PhD of Matthias Van Der Haegen, who has demonstrated this for the Court of Cassation. Formally, this Court only "finds" the law, but in practice, it is complementary to the legislator, by creating law in the case of legislative lacunae. Matthias Van Der Haegen, *Het Hof van Cassatie als lichtbaken van het Belgische rechtsbestel. Een theoretische en empirische toetsing* (unpublished PhD dissertation, Ghent University 2019).

125 This was the text of the old Article 4 of the Civil Code.

126 Georges Martyn, 'The Court system in the Low Countries (1800–2000)' in Marco Filho and Pedro Fonseca (eds), *Ciências penais e teoria do direito em perspectiva: estudos em homenagem ao professor Cláudio Brandão* (Editora D'Plácido 2017) 113.

127 On the history of the justices of the peace, see: Georges Martyn (ed), *Scènes uit de geschiedenis van het vredegerecht: verslagboek van de eerste dag van het internationaal colloquium 'De vrederechter in Europa', Gent-Rotterdam = Scènes de l'histoire de la justice de paix: actes de la première journée du colloque international 'Le juge de paix en Europe', Gand-Rotterdam* (Die Keure 2011); See also: Bruno Debaenst, 'L'Union fait la force! 125 Jaar verbondenheid van vrederechters in België' in Maria van Wilderode (ed), *125 Jaar Nabijheidsrechters : 125 Ans De Justice De Proximité* (Die Keure 2017) 31.

128 Kristiaan Rotthier (ed), *De vrederechter 'Tot uw dienst'* (Die Keure 2018) (see chapter 5, p. 35–38).

129 Access to justice has been accepted as a general principle of law in Belgian case law as part of the right to a fair trial. See https://fra.europa.eu/sites/default/files/fra_uploads/1522-access-to-justice-2011-country-BE.pdf accessed 14 April 2020.

130 Bruno Debaenst, 'Arme pro Deo? Enkele rechtshistorische impressies van het pro-Deo-systeem in België' in Georges Martyn, Greta Doncker, Sjoerd Faber and Dirk Heirbaut (eds), *Geschiedenis van de advocatuur in de Lage Landen* (Verloren 2009), 249.

was a separate universe, with its own habits and creatures, stuffed away in old-fashioned courthouses, in other words a more or less closed subsystem. Most people were not aware of or interested in what was going on there. And the other way around, the realm of justice was also not interested in opening up to the outside world. This changed dramatically in 1996, when Marc Dutroux was arrested on suspicion of having kidnapped, tortured and sexually abused six girls between age 8 and 19, of which four died. This horrible case caused huge public outrage when it became clear that many mistakes had been made in the judicial investigations. Also, after his arrest, several things went wrong. For instance, Dutroux managed to escape, only to be arrested shortly after by a forester. Public outrage led to what was called the White March, with over 300,000 people demonstrating in the streets of Brussels.[131] There was in general a loud cry for reform of the police and the judiciary, which indeed led to reforms. Consequently, public attention turned towards the system of justice and since then, many efforts have been made to restore the confidence of the citizens in the police and the judicial authorities.[132] For instance in 1999, the government installed specific instances in each judicial district, the "houses of justice" (*justitiehuizen, maisons de justice*), to provide first legal aid and general assistance with judicial matters. The same year, new "press magistrates" (*persmagistraat, magistrate presse*) were introduced, to communicate with the media.[133] Another example is the High Council of Justice, which was established in 2000 to improve the functioning of the judiciary in Belgium. Since 2002, this instance organizes surveys (*justitiebarometer/baromètre de la justice*) to investigate the attitude of the Belgian population towards justice. These surveys, which were organized in 2002, 2007, 2010, 2012 and 2014, show that the confidence of Belgians in their judicial system has increased since 2002. For instance, in 2014, the number of respondents who believed that justice improved went up from 20 to 25% in comparison with 2010, while the number of respondents who believed that justice became worse, went down from 49 to 40%.

Currently, the Belgians generally consider the judicial system as an effective one, but it suffers from bad communication. It also turns out that a substantial number of Belgians still believe that there is class justice,[134] even if most citizens believe that the system provides a fair trial by impartial judges. Another example of the renewed interest in justice is the federal funding of several projects since 2006 to study the history of

131 Xavier Rousseaux, 'Witte mars' in Aude Hendrick, Aude Musin, Xavier Rousseaux and Nathalie Tousignant (eds), *Het verhaal van justitie* (Snoeck 2017) 152.

132 Jolien Vanschoenwinkel, 'Vertrouwen' in Aude Hendrick, Aude Musin, Xavier Rousseaux and Nathalie Tousignant (eds), *Het verhaal van justitie* (Snoeck 2017) 184.

133 Randall Lesaffer, 'De justitie en de media' in Dirk Heirbaut, Xavier Rousseaux and Karel Velle (eds), *Politieke en sociale geschiedenis van justitie in België van 1830 tot heden/Histoire politique et sociale de la justice en Belgique de 1830 à nos jours* (Die Keure 2004) 357.

134 Kristel Beyens, 'Klassenjustitie' in Aude Hendrick, Aude Musin, Xavier Rousseaux and Nathalie Tousignant (eds), *Het verhaal van justitie* (Snoeck 2017) 160.

justice in Belgium.[135] In the recent years, new modern courthouses such as in Ghent (in use since 2007) and Antwerp (the "*butterfly palace*",[136] in use since 2005), have helped to support the idea of an open and transparent judiciary. Since 2011, there is also a television series, *De Rechtbank* ("*the court*"),[137] showing real life criminal and civil cases, which helps to span the gap between the realm of justice and the public. In conclusion, all these reforms aimed at making the judiciary and the law more transparent, and thus bringing people's ideas and expectations of law in concordance with institutionalised practices. This contributed to bringing the formerly closed legal system, with its own perceptions of justice, closer to the perceptions of justice shared by the majority of the people. This, in turn, might explain the increase in confidence into the justice system.

The second basic principle of the Belgian judiciary is "speciality", with different specialised institutions and procedures for civil, criminal, commercial and labour matters. The current situation not only reflects the original French model, but also the historical developments afterwards. In 1912 for instance, the growing need to have a specific instance for juvenile matters led to a new specialized court (*kinderrechtbank, tribunal de la jeunesse*) within the civil court system.[138] Another example are the labour courts, which are the successors of the industrial courts (*werkrechtersraden, conseils de prud'hommes*).[139] The latter had an autonomous development, until they were incorporated into the judicial system with the judicial reforms of 1967.[140] Recently, the criminal courts have been experimenting with specialized "drug chambers" (*drugsbehandelingskamer*), to deal with the specific problem of drug addict-related criminality.[141]

Another example of "speciality" in the Belgian judiciary is the preponderance of legal specialists: all professional magistrates, advocates, bailiffs and notaries nowadays need to have an academic law degree (see further). Lay judges are only to be found in the commercial and labour courts, but they are considered specialists in respectively commercial and labour matters. In other words, in Belgium it belongs to the ideal of justice that specialists staff the judiciary and deal with legal matters. In terms of the ideal of justice this is important since it demonstrates a general perception of law as the

135 See for instance the federal research project on the Sociopolitical History of Justice administration in Belgium (1795–2005). https://www.belspo.be/belspo/fedra/proj.asp?l=en&COD=P6%2F01, accessed 13 April 2020. This boasted the scientific research on the history of justice in Belgium. See for instance Dirk Heirbaut, Xavier Rousseaux and Margo De Koster (eds), *Tweehonderd jaar justitie: historische encyclopedie van de Belgische justitie* (Die Keure 2015).

136 See https://www.regiedergebouwen.be/nl/projects/justitiepaleis-1 accessed 13 April 2020.

137 See https://www.vier.be/de-rechtbank#afleveringen accessed 13 April 2020.

138 Filip Boudrez and Sylvie De Smet, *De jeugdrechtbank en rechtsvoorganger: organisatie, taken, bevoegdheid en archiefvorming (1912–2000)* (Algemeen Rijksarchief 2002).

139 Bruno Debaenst, 'Op zoek naar de leek in de werkrechtersraden' in Dave De ruysscher (ed), *Rechtspreken en lekenparticipatie. Noodzaak of traditie?* (Maklu 2013) 95.

140 Maarten Van Keersbilck, *Justitie in de steigers: gerechtelijke hervormingen in België. De moeizame weg naar het Gerechtelijk Wetboek* (Unpublished PhD Ghent University 2018–2019).

141 Freya Vander Laenen, Wouter Vanderplasschen, Ciska Wittouck, Anne Dekkers and Brice De Ruyver (eds), *Het pilootproject drugbehandelingskamer te Gent: Een uitkomstenevaluatie* (Academia Press 2013)

domain of highly professionalised specialists handling the challenges of an increasingly more complex society.

This has another important consequence: the principle of "speciality" refers to the underlying ideal that law and justice have to be "tailor made". Even the successive state reforms are guided by this idea. Flemish and French-speaking people historically had different needs and so the State was reformed accordingly. The communities are the tailormade answer to the Flemish need for cultural autonomy, while the regions reflect the Walloon demand for economic autonomy. Brussels and the German-speaking population have their own specific place within the state structure. In other words, the current Belgian state structure is "tailormade" to the different needs of its heterogeneous population.

The third basic principle in the Belgian judicial system is that of "control". As explained before, the Belgian judiciary is a pyramid. At the bottom are the justices of the peace. Under certain circumstances, their judgments can be appealed before the tribunals. The courts of appeal are the appeal instance for the tribunals. On top, is the Court of Cassation. The result of this hierarchy is a complex system of checks and balances that functions as follows.

All Belgian judges have to solve the cases brought before them according to the law, with the focus on legislation (see below on legal method). This gives democratic legitimacy to the Belgian judgments, since the judges are only applying the "volonté général" on individual cases. Further, according to Article 6 of the Belgian Judicial Code, a judicial decision always only applies to the case itself: "les juges ne peuvent prononcer par voie de disposition générale et réglementaire sur les causes qui leur sont soumises." This implies that formally, no theory of precedent is recognized in Belgium. Every Belgian judge has the full freedom to decide in the cases submitted to him/her and is not bound by the way any other court has solved a comparable problem previously.

Still, the Belgian judges will try to judge according to the consensus within the legal community, as can be found in earlier case law and doctrine. Within this consensus, decisions from the higher courts and especially the Court of Cassation have more weight than the decisions from lower instances. If the Belgian judge differs from that consensus, there is always the risk that the appeal instance will change the judgment or that the Court of Cassation will annul it. This system has a number of advantages. On the one hand, this system increases judicial harmony, legal certainty and predictability and uniformity of law, because the judges want to judge according to the general consensus. This offers extra legitimation to the Belgian judgments, since these are not only the result of the decision of an individual judge, but also mostly the outcome of the "opinio juris" of the Belgian legal community. On the other hand, there is still flexibility in the system because the judge always has the freedom to deviate from this consensus, if he/she finds this necessary or desirable in the light of the specific circumstances of the case at hand. Individual justice is thus safeguarded by judicial discretion vested in the courts. However, where the will of the legislator is sufficiently clear, the room for this discretion is very limited (see below). It is thus the positive law that provides for legal security and predictability in Belgium, not a principle of binding precedents.

In other words, the element of "judicial control" is not absolute, but rather a reflection of the ideal in Belgium that law and justice have to be "just", with the necessary "checks and balances". The interpretation of what is "just" has of course fundamentally changed throughout Belgian history. For instance, historically, the judicial system was a stronghold of the French-speaking bourgeoisie, who used it as a repressive instrument against the lower classes, minorities and the Dutch-speaking majority ("class justice").[142] Labourers on strike, for example, were prosecuted in the nineteenth century.[143] Street protests were violently suppressed by the gendarmerie and in 1886 even by the army. The Flemish, who constitute the majority of the population, were for a very long time confronted with (only) French-speaking judges. Women and children also had quite bad experiences with the judicial system, since the Napoleonic codifications were very unfriendly towards them.[144] A famous example is the Marckx case, which led to the conviction of Belgium by the European Court of Human Rights in 1979, because of the outdated, discriminatory legislation on illegitimate children.[145] Another example of the shifting ideal of "just" is the right to vote.[146] In 1831, only the richest Belgians could vote. In 1893, this changed to a system of voting duty for all adult Belgian men, although some categories received plural votes. In 1918, they introduced the "one man, one vote" system. Finally, in 1948, all Belgian adult citizens, men and women, got the right to vote. In 2020, law and justice imply a democratic society, with respect for human rights and the rights of minorities. The complex Belgian state structure actually contains numerous "checks and balances" to protect the minorities,[147] such as the French-speaking minority in Belgium, the Dutch-speaking minority in Brussels or even the minorities in some municipalities situated on the language border, the so-called "municipalities with language facilities" (*faciliteitengemeenten, communes à facilités*).

142 Stephan Parmentier, 'Meten met twee maten en twee gewichten. Van klassenjustitie naar justitie met klasse?' in Dirk Heirbaut, Xavier Rousseaux and Karel Velle (eds), *Politieke en sociale geschiedenis van justitie in België van 1830 tot heden/Histoire politique et sociale de la justice en Belgique de 1830 à nos jours* (Die Keure 2004) 369

143 Bruno Debaenst, 'Stakers gekraakt! Een uiterst beknopte rechtshistorische analyse van de strafrechtelijke repressie van stakers in de 19de eeuw in België' in Dirk Heirbaut, Xavier Rousseaux and Alain Wijffels (eds), *Histoire du droit et de la justice / Justitie- en rechtsgeschiedenis* (PUL 2010) 483

144 For the judicial treatment of women, see: Dirk Heirbaut, 'De vrouwen(on)rechtsgeschiedenis van Napoleon tot vandaag: een verhaal van voortdurende vooruitgang?' in Eva Brems and Liesbeth Stevens (eds), *Recht en gender in België* (Die Keure 2011) 25; for the judicial treatment of minors, see: Marie-Sylvie Dupont-Bouchat, Jenneke Christiaens and Charlotte Vanneste, 'Jeunesse et Justice (1830–2002)' in Dirk Heirbaut, Xavier Rousseaux and Karel Velle (eds*), Politieke en sociale geschiedenis van justitie in België van 1830 tot heden/Histoire politique et sociale de la justice en Belgique de 1830 à nos jours* (Die Keure 2004) 125

145 *Marckx v. Belgium*, App no 6833/74 (ECtHR, 13 June 1979); See also: Bruno Debaenst, 'Moeder Marckx maakt geen bastaard!' (2011) Vol. 14 *Pro Memorie* 97

146 See: Els Witte, Jean-Pierre Nandrin, Eliane Gubin and Gita Deneckere, *Nieuwe Geschiedenis van België* (Lannoo 2005), 3 volumes.

147 Patricia Populier and Catherine Van de Heyning, 'The Belgian Constitution: The Efficacy Approach to European and Global Governance' in Anneli Albi and Samo Bardutzky (eds) *National Constitutions in European and Global Governance: Democracy, Rights and the Rule of Law* (Springer 2019) 1225.

What we see here is that the Belgian legal culture adapts rather flexibly to changes in the perception of justice and law. However, because it concerns a civil law system, these changes are as a rule implemented by legislative changes, even though the courts are provided with and actually use the flexibility in the system to adapt the law to changing perceptions of justice.

In conclusion, when looking at the different facets of the ideal of justice in Belgium, a colourful picture emerges. In an ideal world, Belgian law and justice are accessible, tailormade, performed by specialists, just and subject to the necessary checks and balances.

5. Legal method

The Belgian legal culture is strictly legal positivistic. Legislation issued by one of the democratically elected Belgian legislators is regarded as the only binding source of law. Court decisions and jurisprudence are not binding, but still have some authority, since they influence the perception and interpretation of law in legal practice.

In Belgium, judges are supposed to apply the legislation to individual cases. Therefore, not surprisingly, the dominant interpretation theory is based on the maxim "*interpretation cessat in claris*" ("interpretation stops in the face of clarity").[148] This guideline indicates that a clear legal rule needs no interpretation; it only has to be applied. In practice however, the judges have gradually started using a pragmatic approach by playing a more active role when necessary.[149] An example is the Belgian principles and rules on extra contractual liability: in the Code civil, only five articles are dedicated to this.[150] During the 19th and 20th century, the judges developed this into a complete new branch of law, by spinning a complex web of case law, in interaction with the legal doctrine.[151] However, the legal basis of a tort-law claim will always be one (or more) of the articles 1382, 1383, 1384, 1385, 1386 or 1386bis of the Code civil.

When interpreting legislation, the Belgian judge uses the classical methods: the grammatical interpretation, the systematic or logic interpretation, the historical interpretation, the use of legislative preparatory works, and the teleological construction of statutes.[152]

Following the French tradition, Belgian judges generally provide rather limited argumentation in their judicial decisions. This is especially the case for the Court of Cassation, which simply states the correct interpretation and application of the law,

148 Mark Van Hoecke and Sebastiaan Vandenbogaerde, 'Basic Features of the Belgian Legal System' in Marc Kruithof and Walter De Bondt (eds), *Introduction to Belgian Law* (Kluwer Law International 2017) 28.

149 Martyn G, 'The Judge and the Formal Sources of Law in the Low Countries (19th–20th Centuries): From 'Slave' to 'Master'?' in Bryson WB and Dauchy S (eds), *Ratio decidendi. Guiding Principles of Judicial Decisions* (Duncker & Humblot 2006) 201.

150 Marc Kruithof, *Tort Law in Belgium* (Kluwer Law International 2018).

151 For a number of historical and contemporary examples, see Bruno Debaenst and Bram Delbecke (eds), *Vangnet of springplank? Het buitencontractuele aansprakelijkheidsrecht in een moderne samenleving (1804–heden)* (Die Keure 2014).

152 Bruno Debaenst, *Inleiding tot de rechtsmethodiek* (Die Keure 2012) 21–24.

rather than elaborating its underlying reasoning.[153] Judges will always try to link their argumentation to the authority of the legislator or to the decisions made by other, mostly higher courts. The higher the court, the stronger its argumentative power. Referring to the Court of Cassation, for example, is considered a very strong argument. Judges also sometimes refer to the general consensus about a particular interpretation or legal solution.

Doctrinal writings play an important role in the creation and development of law, even if they are only a non-binding and indirect source of law. They are only considered to be positive law if applied in court practice. However, since scholarly writings often offer a coherent description of applicable legislation and relevant court decisions, they are the most important source for "finding" the law.

Finally, two other sources of law can be mentioned here: customary law and general principles of law. Customary law only plays a marginal role, since almost all aspects of social life are ruled by legislation. Nevertheless, customs still play a certain role, especially in constitutional law. For instance, an outgoing government can only decide on the conduct of the "current affairs" and has to leave all the important decisions either to the parliament (if there is still one), or the next government. Another example is the confidentiality of the talks between the King and his ministers.[154] Finally, the courts have accepted a number of unwritten general principles of law, such as the principle of good faith or the reasonableness principle. The Court of Cassation has accepted that the breach of such a principle is a reason for annulment of a judicial decision.[155]

6. Professionalisation

The Belgian legal culture has always had a high degree of professionalisation. With the founding of Leuven University in 1425, the Netherlands had their own intellectual centre to provide academically schooled lawyers. They increasingly staffed the Burgundian and Habsburg central institutions, and in this way contributed to the state forming process (i.e., bureaucratization, judicialization, juridification). In the 15th century for instance, the Burgundy dukes installed a Supreme Court for the Netherlands[156] and in 1531, Emperor Charles reorganized the central institutions.[157] There were also many educated lawyers active in church, state, and city courts and administrations.[158] In 1531,

153 In addition, one can often find some more information in the advice of the public ministry (by *the advocaat-generaal/avocat-général*).

154 Van Hoecke and Sebastiaan Vandenbogaerde (2017) (n 148) 25–48 (36).

155 See judgment of 19 September 1983, where the Court of Cassation decided: "attendue que si le principe de l'exécution de bonne foi des conventions, consacré par l'article 1134 du Code civil…". Arr. Cass. 1983–84, 52.

156 In 1473, Duke Charles the Bold installed his judicial council in Mechlin, where it took the name "Great Council of Mechlin". His daughter Mary of Burgundy had to abolish it in 1477 on the occasion of the issuing of the Great Privilege, but it was reinstalled in 1504 by her son Philip the Fair. It was abolished during the French Revolution.

157 See above (n 12).

158 With "state", I refer to the different parts of the Netherlands (counties, duchies, etc.), which continued to exist until the end of the Ancien Régime.

Emperor Charles ordered the homologation of the local customs, which helped legal scholarship.[159] The Netherlands had many famous legal scholars, such as Filips Wielants (1441–1520), Joos De Damhoudere (1507–1581) and Hugo Grotius (1583–1645).

Belgium is part of the European continental legal tradition, where lawyers receive a mainly theoretical legal training at the university. When Belgium became independent in 1830, there were three law faculties, in the state universities of Ghent, Liège, and Leuven.[160] In 1834, the State University of Leuven was abolished, to be replaced the next year by the Catholic University.[161] The original language at the universities was Latin, but after the revolution, this soon changed to French. This remained the official language of the law curriculum until the 1930s, when the University of Ghent became officially unilingual Dutch and the universities of Leuven and Brussels bilingual Dutch/French. In the 1960s, Leuven and Brussels split into a Dutch-speaking and a French-speaking university. Nowadays, there are five Dutch-speaking law faculties (Leuven, Ghent, Brussels, Antwerp, and Hasselt) and the same number of French-speaking law faculties (Liège, Louvain-la-neuve, Namur, Mons, and Brussels).[162] The Flemish community governs the Dutch-speaking universities, while the French community governs the French-speaking ones. All these universities issue academic Bachelor's, Master's and PhD degrees in law. On 31 October 2017, there were 12,215 students inscribed in the Flemish law faculties – these numbers include law, criminology and notary students.[163] The female students were far in the majority: there were 7,997 female students and only 4,188 male students.[164] The law curriculum at the universities consists of three bachelor years and two master years. There are also a number of university colleges in Belgium,

159 The local customs were first written down and then inspected (and changed) by the central institutions. They were then issued as authentic legislation.

160 In 2017, the Universities of Ghent and Liège celebrated their 200th anniversary. For the commemoration book of the law faculties, see Marc Cools, Jean-Francois Gerkens, Geoffrey Grandjean, Dirk Heirbaut and Patrick Wautelet (eds), *Tweehonderd jaar rechtsfaculteiten Gent en Luik / Deux-centième anniversaire des facultés de droit de Gand et Liège* (Die Keure 2019).

161 The Catholic University had been founded in 1834 in Mechlin, but moved to Leuven in 1835. It considers itself the successor of the old Catholic university of Leuven, which was founded in 1425, but closed down by the French rulers in 1797.

162 To be more precise: Katholieke Universiteit Leuven (KU Leuven), Universiteit Gent (UGent), Vrije Universiteit Brussels (VUB), Universiteit Antwerpen (UA), Universiteit Hasselt (UHasselt), Université de Liège (ULiège), Université catholique de Louvain (UCLouvain), Université de Namur (UNamur), Université de Mons (UMons), and Université libre de Bruxelles (ULB).

163 See https://www.vlaanderen.be/nl/publicaties/detail/hoger-onderwijs-in-cijfers-2017-2018-1 accessed 24 January 2019.

164 The first female students started studying law at the end of the nineteenth Century, but they would remain a small minority until the last quarter of the twentieth Century. As can be seen in the figures, they are nowadays far in the majority. For an oversight of the feminization of the legal professions, see: Eva Schandevyl, 'De vervrouwelijking van de juridische beroepen', in Dirk Heirbaut, Xavier Rousseaux and Margo De Koster (eds), *Tweehonderd Jaar Justitie : Historische Encyclopedie Van De Belgische Justitie = Deux Siècles De Justice : Encyclopédie Historique De La Justice Belge* (Die Keure 2015) 578; for the history of women in the magistracy: Eva Schandevyl, 'Women and the Courts in Belgium: an Historical Perspective' in Sarah Kimble and Marion Roewekamp (eds), *New perspectives on European Women's Legal History* (Routledge 2016), 152.

which deliver professional bachelor degrees in law ("*rechtspraktijk*").[165] This professional bachelor programme is less theoretical and more oriented to the law practice. It lasts 3 years.

The high degree of professionalisation is reflected in the legal professions.[166] Currently, all legal occupations (magistrates, attorneys, bailiffs, notaries) require a Master's law degree. The only exceptions are the lay judges in the Labour and Commercial courts, but they are only temporarily appointed.[167]

A civil law notary (*notaris/notaire*) is a public officer, appointed by the King.[168] The notary has received a delegation of power from the State, in the following three main areas of law: real estate law (purchase and sale of real estate, mortgage loans, etc.), family law (marriage settlements, inheritances, donations, divorces, etc.), and business law (incorporation of companies, mergers, etc.). The notary has the authority to make "authentic deeds" – by authenticating agreements, the notary gives them a special value regarding evidence and enforceability that private contracts do not have. The notary is independent, impartial and bound by professional secrecy. In 2015, there were 1,546 notaries (485 women and 1,061 men) in Belgium, with approximately 7,500 collaborators.[169] They delivered in a total of 925,000 authentic deeds.

Next to the necessity of a university law degree, all legal occupations meanwhile have extra requirements: In order to become notary, one first has to obtain an additional specialized Master's degree (*master in het notariaat/master en notariat*).[170] There is also the obligation of an apprenticeship of three years and the passing of a written and oral exam. In the period 2001–2007, approximately one out-of-five candidates passed the exam.[171] The best 60 of those who passed the test are appointed candidate-notary. Since the number of notaries is limited, they can only be appointed as notary if there is a vacancy.

Similar rules apply for the bailiffs (*gerechtsdeurwaarder/huissier de justice*),[172] like the notaries, they are self-employed public legal officials. The State has delegated a share of official authority to them. Therefore, they cannot refuse to respond to a request to act. Bailiffs can take out-of-court measures, such as out-of-court recovery of debts or official

---

165 For an oversight of these colleges, see http://www.studyinflanders.be/ accessed 25 January 2019.

166 See https://e-justice.europa.eu/content_legal_professions-29-be-restore-en.do?member=1 accessed 6 April 2019. See also Georges Martyn and Bart Quintelier, 'Les professions juridiques' in Guy Vanthemsche and Patricia Van den Eeckhout (eds), *Sources pour l'étude de la Belgique contemporaine, 19e–21e siècles* (Commission royale d'Histoire 2017) 1122.

167 For an initial period of three years, which can be prolonged with five-year periods.

168 See https://www.notaris.be/other-languages/english/what-is-a-civil-law-notary accessed 24 January 2019.

169 See the year report of 2015, which can be downloaded here: https://www.notaris.be/nieuws-pers/jaarverslagen accessed 25 January 2019.

170 On the history of the notaries in Belgium, see: Fred Stevens, 'De Notarissen' in Dirk Heirbaut, Xavier Rousseaux and Karel Velle (eds), *Politieke en sociale geschiedenis van justitie in België van 1830 tot heden/Histoire politique et sociale de la justice en Belgique de 1830 à nos jours* (Die Keure 2004) 257

171 See http://bcn-not.be/sites/files/verslag2007.pdf accessed 25 January 2019.

172 See https://www.huissiersdejustice.be/ accessed 6 April 2019; on the history of this occupation: Sebastiaan Vandenbogaerde and Thierry Lemoine, 'Van deurwachter tot gerechtsdeurwaarder' in Dirk Heirbaut, Xavier Rousseaux and Margo De Koster (eds), *Tweehonderd Jaar Justitie : Historische Encyclopedie Van De Belgische Justitie = Deux Siècles De Justice : Encyclopédie Historique De La Justice Belge* (Die Keure 2015) 379.

findings of fact. For instance, there is always a bailiff present at the drawings of "*Lotto*", the Belgian lottery. They are also responsible for the enforcement of judicial decisions (i.e., "court measures").

Judges and public prosecutors have to pass a state examination, organized by the High Council of Justice. There are three types of exams.[173] The first is for young lawyers with limited professional experience (minimum 1 year). In 2017, there were 207 candidates for this exam, with 23% men and 77% women. Only 38 candidates passed the test (45% men and 55% women). The second exam is for experienced lawyers (with 5 years of experience for the public ministry and 10 years of experience for judges). In 2017, there were 381 participants for this exam (35% men and 65% women), of which only 38 passed (34% men and 66% women). Finally, there is also an oral exam for experienced lawyers (with at least 20 years of experience). In 2015, 20 persons (50% men and 50% women) took the exam, of which 4 passed (3 men and 1 woman). Once the candidates pass the exam, they have to do an apprenticeship of 18 months (public prosecutors) or 36 months (judges). After their apprenticeship, they have to be appointed upon a vacancy by the Minister of Justice. In 2018, there were 2,365 active magistrates in Belgium,[174] of which 54% were female.[175] In 2016, 46% were French-speaking and 54% Flemish.[176] Due to budgetary reasons, the Belgian judiciary is seriously understaffed: in 2019, only 83% of the positions were occupied, which equals to a shortage of 273 magistrates and 1,082 administrative collaborators.[177]

Attorneys (*advocaten/avocats*) have to do a three-year apprenticeship and pass an exam organized by the bar.[178] There are excessively many attorneys in Belgium: in 2014, there were 10,418 Flemish lawyers (5,931 male and 4,487 female)[179] and 7,756 French-speaking.[180] In Flanders, this comes down to 1 attorney per 774 inhabitants.[181] In 25 years, the numbers almost doubled and nowadays Belgium has the highest number of

173 For the numbers, see http://www.hrj.be/sites/default/files/press_publications/jaarverslag2017nl_0.pdf accessed 4 December 2019.

174 See https://www.koengeens.be/news/2018/03/20/justitie-die-ten-dienste-staat-van-de-mensen accessed 25 January 2019.

175 See https://www.hln.be/nieuws/binnenland/meerderheid-van-magistraten-is-vrouw~a93332b3/ accessed 25 January 2019.

176 See https://justitie.belgium.be/sites/default/files/jic_nl-2016.pdf p. 22, accessed 25 January 2019.

177 See https://www.vrt.be/vrtnws/nl/2019/03/19/gerechtelijke-wereld-trekt-aan-alarmbel-over-besparingen-273-m/ accessed 20 March 2019.

178 On the history of the advocacy in Belgium, see: Georges Martyn and Bart Quintelier, 'De Belgische advocatuur' in Dirk Heirbaut, Xavier Rousseaux & Margo De Koster, *Tweehonderd Jaar Justitie : Historische Encyclopedie Van De Belgische Justitie = Deux Siècles De Justice : Encyclopédie Historique De La Justice Belge* (Die Keure 2015) 330.

179 The female lawyers are today still in the minority, but given the fact that the majority of the law students are now female, this will probably change in the future. On the history of women in the advocacy, see: Patrick Humblet, 'De vervrouwelijking van de advocatuur en van het juridische werkveld' in Georges Martyn, Greta Doncker, Sjoerd Faber and Dirk Heirbaut (eds), *Geschiedenis van de advocatuur in de Lage Landen* (Verloren 2009) 227.

180 See https://www.ccbe.eu/fileadmin/speciality_distribution/public/documents/Statistics/EN_STAT_2015_Number_of_lawyers_in_European_countries.pdf p. 1, accessed 6 April 2019.

181 See https://jubel.be/het-advocatendilemma/. For the numbers in other European countries, see https://www.ccbe.eu/actions/statistics/. Both links accessed 25 January 2019.

attorneys per capita in Europe.[182] It is understood that this profession is facing some challenges, also because of new developments such as digitalization, competition from other occupations, etc. The ongoing internationalisation of law is challenging not just the judicial profession but the entire Belgian legal culture.

7. Internationalisation

Belgium is a small country, embedded in the heart of Western Europe. Before its independence in 1830, "Belgium" was always part of larger state entities (Burgundy, Spanish, Austrian, French, and Dutch states). Moreover, the Belgian territories always had an open, export-orientated economy, even since the Middle Ages.[183] It lies on the crossroad of cultures (English in the West, Dutch in the North, German in the East and French in the South). Therefore, it does not come as a surprise that Belgium has been very susceptible to internationalisation.

Until 1971, Belgian lawyers adhered to a dualistic vision, with the international and national level being two separate legal systems. A legal rule in an international treaty only became part of the national legal system if it was incorporated or implemented into national law. In 1971, the Court of Cassation left this approach for a monistic vision in the *Le Ski* case.[184] From that moment on, there is a supremacy of international law:[185] once the Parliament has given its consent to an international treaty, it becomes part of the Belgian legal order, without any need for incorporation.[186] Belgian courts have to apply international law over former and later acts of Parliament. The prevalence of international legal norms over domestic law is especially important in the field of human rights[187] and European Union law.[188]

182 See http://www.standaard.be/cnt/dmf20150427_01650585 accessed 25 January 2019; see also http://www.brusselstimes.com/belgium/2864/belgium-has-the-most-lawyers-per-habitant accessed 6 April 2019.

183 See for instance the case of the medieval commercial metropole Bruges: Jan Dumolyn and Andrew Brown (eds), *Medieval Bruges: c. 850–1550* (Cambridge University Press 2018).

184 *Fromagerie Franco-Suisse Le Ski vs. Belgische Staat* (n 116).

185 For an overview of the influence of international law in the Belgian legal culture, see: Jan Wouters and Dries Van Eeckhoutte (eds), *Doorwerking van international recht in de Belgische rechtsorde: recente ontwikkelingen in een rechtstakoverschrijdend perspectief* (Intersentia 2006).

186 Hervé Bribosia, 'Applicabilité directe et primauté des traités internationaux et du droit communautaire' (1996) Vol. 76 *Revue belge de droit international* 33.

187 Benoit Gors, 'Une cause de renvoi préjudiciel: la primauté de la convention Européenne sur la constitution' (2005) *Revue Belge de droit constitutionnel* 509; Luc Lavrysen and Jan Theunis, 'The Belgian Constitutional Court: a Satellite of the ECtHR?' in André Alen, Veronique Joosten, Riet Leysen and Willem Verrijdt (eds), *Liberae Cogitationes: Liber Amicorum Marc Bossuyt* (Intersentia 2013) 33.

188 European law has a huge influence on Belgian law; for private law, see: Ilse Samoy, Vincent Sagaert and Evelyne Terryn (ed.), *Invloed van het Europees recht op het Belgisch privaatrecht* (Intersentia 2012); for administrative law, see: Kris Wauters, Bram Delvaux and Bernard Vanheusden (ed) *Invloed van het EU-recht op het Belgisch bestuursrecht* (Die Keure 2014); for constitutional law, see regarding federalism: Stef Feyen, *Beyond Federal dogmatics: the Influence of Eu Law on Belgian Constitutional Case Law regarding Federalism* (Leuven university Press 2013).

Most of the provisions of the European Convention for the Protection of Human Rights and Fundamental Freedoms (ECHR) can be directly invoked by Belgian citizens before the courts. As a result, the ECHR has had a significant impact on several branches of law, such as family law and criminal procedure law. Famous examples are the *Marckx* case (see above)[189] and the *Salduz* case.[190] Because of the first, Belgium had to amend its civil code,[191] while the latter obliged the consultation of a lawyer before the first police hearing, for instance.[192] European Treaty law has also been superimposed on the Belgian legal system. The European Court of Justice ruled in 1964 that European Union law cannot be set aside by domestic norms of the Member States.[193] This reasoning was also accepted by the Belgian Court of Cassation in the already mentioned 1971 *Le Ski* case.

European directives are not directly applicable. They must be implemented into national law within the period set by the directive. If the period has lapsed, without the Member State having the directive implemented, self-executive provisions from the directive may be invoked against the negligent Member State.

This process of Europeanisation functions quite naturally in Belgium.[194] As said before, Belgium is a small country with a specific history. Belgians do not have a strong national feeling, so they accept the loss of national sovereignty without reservations. Belgians in general consider the European integration as a blessing for the country: in 2018, 67% were positive about the Belgian membership of the EU.[195]

One important consequence of the transfer of competences to the European level is the further dismembering of the Belgian national level. Some say the Belgian level is "vaporizing" between the European and regional levels. Soon there will be nothing left of Belgium, except the King and the national football team.

8. Conclusions

Belgium is a small, but complex country with an interesting and unique legal culture. The historical perspective is crucial to understand the contemporary Belgian legal culture. Together with the Netherlands and Luxembourg, Belgium is the heir of the old Burgundy and Habsburg Netherlands, which united most of the territories of the so-called "Low Countries". It inherited the French legal system from the period when it

---

189 *Marckx v Belgium* (n 145).

190 *Salduz v Turkey* App no 36391/02 (ECtHR, 27 November 2008).

191 Act of 31 March 1987, Moniteur belge 27 May 1987.

192 Act of 13 August 2011, Moniteur belge 5 September 2011.

193 This was in the judgment of the famous Case 6-64 *Costa v ENEL* [1964]; on the relationship between the Belgian courts and the European Court of Justice, see: Patricia Populier, 'Judicial Conversations in Multilevel Constitutionalism. The Belgian Case' in Monica Claes, Maartje de Visser, Patricia Populier and Catherine Van de Heyning (eds), *Constitutional Conversations in Europe* (Ius Commune Europaeum, vol. 107) (Intersentia 2012), 73.

194 See Dirk Heirbaut and Matthias Storme, 'The Belgian Legal Tradition: From a Long Quest for Legal Independence to a Longing for Independence' (2006) *European Review of Private Law* 663.

195 See http://www.europarl.europa.eu/belgium/nl/eurobarometer-één-jaar-voor-de-europese-verkiezingen-67-procent-van-de-belgen-denkt-dat-het-belgische-lidmaatschap-van-de-eu-een-goede-zaak-is accessed 25 January 2019.

was part of France (1795–1813). It broke free from the Kingdom of the Netherlands in 1830, to become the independent Kingdom of Belgium in 1831 – a constitutional monarchy with the most liberal constitution of its time. Just as Luxembourg and Switzerland do, it lies on the historical vault between Germanic and Romanic Europe, resulting in three different languages (respectively Dutch and German versus French) and two main populations, Flemish and French-speaking Belgians. In its origin a unitary state, half a century of successive state reforms has transformed the country into a federal state, with the new Constitutional Court as arbiter between the different entities who are all equal and without hierarchy. This in its turn, has resulted in two emerging subcultures that are slowly but steadily drifting apart. Internationalisation and Europeanisation adds another layer to the already complex mosaic of cultural diversity in this small jurisdiction in the very centre of Europe. Historically, as an offspring of the French legal culture, the Belgian legal culture belongs to the civil law family, with a set of (in origin Napoleonic) codifications and a rational judicial system. The organization of the judiciary and the application of law in many ways reflects the ideal of law and justice in Belgium: accessible, tailormade, specialised and sufficiently flexible to include considerations of individual justice, with the necessary checks and balances. Just as the French legal culture is, the Belgian one is strictly legal positivistic and with a high degree of professionalisation.

The Belgian Legal Culture	
Institutional structure	
Conflict resolution	*Norm production*
The Belgian judicial system is French in origin, characterized by a pyramidal structure, with hierarchy and division along competence and territoriality and with the Court of Cassation on top. Since 1946, there is a separate State Council for administrative matters. The state reforms created the need for a Constitutional Court that deals with (some) constitutional matters and with conflicts of competence between the national and regional entities, or between the regional entities.	The federal and regional parliaments are the main producers of legal norms in Belgium. In addition, EU regulations and certain international law obligations are directly applicable in Belgium. These norms are as a rule organized in a hierarchy.

Intellectual structure			
Ideal of justice	*Legal method*	*Degree of professionalisation*	*Character of internationalisation*
Legislation by the democratically elected Belgian legislators provides legal security and predictability in Belgium. Individual justice is safeguarded by judicial discretion vested in the courts.	The Belgian judges apply the legislation on the cases brought before them. By doing so, they try to judge according to the consensus within the legal community, as can be found in earlier case law and doctrine.	High degree of professionalisation and specialisation, with university schooled legal professions (magistrates, attorneys, bailiffs and notaries)	High degree of internationalisation, approved by the majority of the population. Since 1971 the Belgian legal culture adheres to a monistic vision, with a supremacy of international law.

9. Bibliography

Alen A (ed), *Treatise on Belgian Constitutional Law* (Kluwer 1992)

—— and Haljan D, *Constitutional law* (Kluwer Law International 2013)

Baena LM, *Conflicting Words. The Peace Treaty of Münster (1648) and the Political Culture of the Dutch Republic and the Spanish Monarchy* (Leuven University Press 2011). DOI: https://doi.org/10.2307%2Fj.ctt9qdxgt

Bassiri N and Draye M (eds), *Arbitration in Belgium* (Kluwer 2016)

Berger E, Heirbaut D, Leuwers H and Rousseaux X, 'La justice avant la Belgique: tentatives autrichiennes, influences françaises et expériences néerlandaises (1780–1830)' in De Koster M, Heirbaut D and Rousseaux X (eds), *Deux siècles de justice. Encyclopédie historique de la justice belge* (Die Keure 2015)

Beyens K, 'Klassenjustitie' in Hendrick A, Musin A, Rosseaux X and Tousignant N (eds), *Het verbaal van justitie* (Snoeck 2017)

Boudrez F and De Smet S, *De jeugdrechtbank en rechtsvoorganger: organisatie, taken, bevoegdheid en archiefvorming (1912–2000)* (Algemeen Rijksarchief 2002)

Bribosia H, 'Applicabilité directe et primauté des traités internationaux et du droit communautaire' (1996) Vol. 76 *Revue belge de droit international* 33.

Bruin R, van der Haven C, Jensen L and Onnekink D, *Performances of Peace: Utrecht 1713* (Brill 2015). DOI: https://doi.org/10.26530%2Foapen_613346

Cariat N and Nowak JT (ed) *Le droit de l'Union européenne et le juge belge – Het recht van de Europese Unie en de Belgische rechter* (Larcier 2015)

Cools M, Gerkens J-G, Grandjean G, Heirbaut D and Wautelet P (eds), *Tweehonderd jaar rechtsfaculteiten Gent en Luik / Deux-centième anniversaire des facultés de droit de Gand et Liège* (Die Keure 2019)

Conway M, 'Belgium's Mid-Twentieth Century Crisis: Crisis of a Nation-State?' (2005) 4 *Journal of Belgian History* 573

Craenen G, *The institutions of Federal Belgium: An Introduction to Belgian Public Law* (Acco 2001)

Curtis B, *The Habsburgs. The History of a Dynasty* (Bloomsbury 2013)

Debaenst B, 'Arme pro Deo? Enkele rechtshistorische impressies van het pro-Deo-systeem in België' in Martyn G, Doncker G, Faber S and Heirbaut D (eds), *Geschiedenis van de advocatuur in de Lage Landen* (Verloren 2009) 249

—— 'Stakers gekraakt! Een uiterst beknopte rechtshistorische analyse van de strafrechtelijke repressie van stakers in de 19de eeuw in België' in Heirbaut D, Rousseaux X and Wijffels A (eds), *Histoire du droit et de la justice / Justitie- en rechtsgeschiedenis* (PUL 2010) 483

—— 'Moeder Marckx maakt geen bastaard!' (2011) Vol. 14 *Pro Memorie* 97

—— *Inleiding tot de rechtsmethodiek* (Die Keure 2012)

—— 'Op zoek naar de leek in de werkrechtersraden' in De ruysscher D (ed), *Rechtspreken en lekenparticipatie. Noodzaak of traditie?* (Maklu 2013)

—— 'L'Union fait la force! 125 Jaar verbondenheid van vrederechters in België' in van Wilderode M (ed), *125 Jaar Nabijheidsrechters : 125 Ans De Justice De Proximité* (Die Keure 2017) 31

—— and Delbecke B (eds), *Vangnet of springplank? Het buitencontractuele aansprakelijkheidsrecht in een moderne samenleving (1804–heden)* (Die Keure 2014)

Decock G and Put J, *Jeugdsanctierecht gewikt en gewogen: toetsing van beleid en praktijk aan de principes van het jeugdsanctierecht* (Larcier 2012).

Delbecke B, 'The Political Offence and the Safeguarding of the Nation State: Constitutional Ideals, French Legal Standards and Belgian Legal Practice, 1830–70' (2013) Vol. 1 Issue 1 *Comparative Legal History* 45. DOI: https://doi.org/10.5235%2F2049677x.1.1.45

den Tandt B (ed), *The new Belgian arbitration law* (Die Keure 2015)

Dumolyn J and Brown A (eds), *Medieval Bruges: c. 850–1550* (Cambridge University Press 2018)

Dupont-Bouchat M-S, Christiaens J and Vanneste C, 'Jeunesse et Justice (1830–2002)' in Heirbaut D, Rousseaux X and Velle K (eds), *Politieke en sociale geschiedenis van justitie in België van 1830 tot heden/Histoire politique et sociale de la justice en Belgique de 1830 à nos jours* (Die Keure 2004) 125

Erk J, 'Why Multi-Ethnic Belgium's Constitutional Court Keeps Mum: The Constitutionalization of Ethnicity, Judicial Review, and 'Passive Virtues'' (2018) Vol. 3 *Constitutional Studies* 101

Feyen S, *Beyond Federal dogmatics: the Influence of Eu Law on Belgian Constitutional Case Law regarding Federalism* (Leuven University Press 2013)

Gors B, 'Une cause de renvoi préjudiciel: la primauté de la convention Européenne sur la constitution' (2005) Vol. 12 *Revue Belge de droit constitutionnel* 509.

Heirbaut D, 'Editing and Translating the Code civil in Belgium, 1804–2004' (2004) Vol. 72 Issue 3–4 *The Legal History Review* 215. DOI: https://doi.org/10.1163%2F1571819042872609

—— 'Napoleons trouwste onderdanen, of waarom de Code civil na tweehonderd jaar nog steeds overeind staat in België' in Heirbaut D and Martyn G (eds), *Napoleons nalatenschap. Tweehonderd jaar Burgerlijk Wetboek in België / Un heritage Napoléonien. Bicentenaire du Code civil en Belgique* (Kluwer 2005) 77

—— 'De vrouwen(on)rechtsgeschiedenis van Napoleon tot vandaag: een verhaal van voortdurende vooruitgang?' in Brems E and Stevens L (eds), *Recht en gender in België* (Die Keure 2011) 25

—— 'The Belgian Legal Tradition: Does It Exist?' in Kruithof M and De Strondt W (eds), *Introduction to Belgian Law* (2nd ed, Wolters Kluwer 2017) 1

—— 'Codification in Belgium from Napoleon to Geens' in Dondorp H (ed), *De rebus divinis et humanis: essays in honour of Jan Hallebeek* (Vandenhoeck & Ruprecht 2019) 167.

—— and Baeteman G, *Cumulatieve editie van het Burgerlijk Wetboek: de huidige en de originele tekst met alle wijzigingen in België van 1804 tot 2004* (two parts, Kluwer 2004)

—— and Martyn G (eds), *Napoleons nalatenschap. Tweehonderd jaar Burgerlijk Wetboek in België / Un heritage Napoléonien. Bicentenaire du Code civil en Belgique* (Kluwer 2005)

—— and Storme M, 'The Belgian Legal Tradition: From a Long Quest for Legal

Independence to a Longing for Independence' (2006) *European Review of Private Law* 663

—— and Gerkens J-F, 'In the shadow of France: legal acculturation and legal transplants in the Southern Netherlands/Belgium', in Dirix E and Leleu Y-H, *The Belgian reports at the Congress of Washington of the International Academy of Comparative Law* (Bruylant 2011) 3

——, Rousseaux X and De Koster M (eds), *Tweehonderd jaar justitie: historische encyclopedie van de Belgische justitie* (Die Keure 2015)

Hespel S and Put J, *Jeugdsanctierecht voorgesteld: naar een constructief jeugdsanctierecht* (Larcier 2014)

Horn T, *The Netherlands and the Holy Roman Empire at the Augsburg Reichstag, 1547–1548* (University of California 1956)

Humblet P, 'De vervrouwelijking van de advocatuur en van het juridische werkveld' in Martyn G, Doncker G, Faber S and Heirbaut D (eds*), Geschiedenis van de advocatuur in de Lage Landen* (Verloren 2009) 227

Jaumotte J, Salmon J and Thibaut É, *Le Conseil d'Etat de Belgique* (Bruylant 2012), 2 volumes.

Keutgen G, Dal G-A, Dal M and Matray G, *L'arbitrage en droit belge et international* (Bruylant 2015)

Kruithof M, *Tort Law in Belgium* (Kluwer Law International 2018)

Lavrysen L and Theunis J, 'The Belgian Constitutional Court: a Satellite of the ECtHR?' in Alen A, Joosten V, Leysen R and Verrijdt W (eds), *Liberae Cogitationes: Liber Amicorum Marc Bossuyt* (Intersentia 2013) 33

Lesaffer R, 'De justitie en de media' in Heirbaut D, Rousseaux X and Velle K (eds), *Politieke en sociale geschiedenis van justitie in België van 1830 tot heden/Histoire politique et sociale de la justice en Belgique de 1830 à nos jours* (Die Keure 2004) 357

Marteel S, *The intellectual origins of the Belgian Revolution. Political Thought and Disunity in the Kingdom of the Netherlands, 1815–1830* (Palgrave Macmillan 2018). DOI: https://doi.org/10.1007%2F978-3-319-89426-3

Martyn G, 'The Judge and the Formal Sources of Law in the Low Countries (19th–20th Centuries): From 'Slave' to 'Master'?' in Bryson WB and Dauchy S (eds), *Ratio decidendi. Guiding Principles of Judicial Decisions* (Duncker & Humblot 2006) 201

—— (ed), *Scènes uit de geschiedenis van het vredegerecht: verslagboek van de eerste dag van het internationaal colloquium 'De vrederechter in Europa', Gent-Rotterdam = Scènes de l'histoire de la justice de paix: actes de la première journée du colloque international 'Le juge de paix en Europe', Gand-Rotterdam* (Die Keure 2011)

——, 'De evolutie van de rechtsbronnen' in Heirbaut D, Rousseaux X and De Koster M (eds), *Tweehonderd Jaar Justitie : Historische Encyclopedie Van De Belgische Justitie = Deux Siècles De Justice : Encyclopédie Historique De La Justice Belge* (Die Keure 2015) 51

——, 'Belgium, the Netherlands and Luxembourg Since 1800' in Wijffels A and van Rhee R (eds), *European Supreme Courts: a Portrait through History* (Third Millennium Publishing 2013) 218

——, 'The Court system in the Low Countries (1800–2000)' in Filho M and Fonseca P (eds), *Ciências penais e teoria do direito em perspectiva : estudos em homenagem ao professor Cláudio Brandão* (Editora D'Plácido 2017) 113

—— and Bart Quintelier, 'De Belgische advocatuur' in Heirbaut D, Rousseaux X & De Koster M, *Tweehonderd Jaar Justitie : Historische Encyclopedie Van De Belgische Justitie = Deux Siècles De Justice : Encyclopédie Historique De La Justice Belge* (Die Keure 2015) 330

—— and Quintelier B, 'Les professions juridiques' in Vanthemsche G and Van den Eeckhout P (eds), *Sources pour l'étude de la Belgique contemporaine, 19e–21e siècles* (Commission royale d'Histoire 2017) 1122

Matthijs H, Jans MT and de Koker H, *Bestuurswetenschappen. De overheid. Instellingen en beleid* (Intersentia 2005)

Mettewie L and Janssens R, 'Language Use and Language Attitude in Brussels' in Lasagabaster D and Huguet Á (eds), *Multilingualism in European Bilingual Contexts. Language Use and Attitudes* (Multilingual Matters 2007) 117

Mnookin R and Verbeke A, 'Persistent nonviolent conflict with no reconciliation: the Flemish and Walloons in Belgium' (2009) Vol. 72 Issue *2 Law & Contemporary Problems* 151

Moonen T, *De keuzes van het Grondwettelijk Hof: argumenten bij de interpretatie van de Grondwet* (Die Keure 2015)

Müller F, *La Cour de Cassation belge à l'aune des rapports entre pouvoirs. De sa naissance dans le modèle classique de la séparation des pouvoirs à l'aube d'une extension de la fonction juridictionnelle 1832–1914/1936* (Die Keure 2011)

Parmentier S, 'Meten met twee maten en twee gewichten. Van klassenjustitie naar justitie met klasse?' in Heirbaut D, Rousseaux X and Velle K (eds), *Politieke en sociale geschiedenis van justitie in België van 1830 tot heden/Histoire politique et sociale de la justice en Belgique de 1830 à nos jours* (Die Keure 2004) 369

Peeters P and Mosselmans J, 'The Constitutional Court of Belgium: Safeguard of the Autonomy of the Communities and Regions' in Aroney N and Kincaid J (eds), *Courts in Federal Countries: Federalists or Unitarists?* (University of Toronto Press 2017) 69

Populier P, 'Judicial Conversations in Multilevel Constitutionalism. The Belgian Case' in Claes M, de Visser M, Populier P and Van de Heyning C (eds), *Constitutional Conversations in Europe* (Ius Commune Europaeum, vol. 107) (Intersentia 2012) 73

—— and Lemmens K, *The Constitution of Belgium. A Contextual analysis* (Hart Publishing 2015)

—— and Van de Heyning C, 'The Belgian Constitution: The Efficacy Approach to European and Global Governance' in Albi A and Bardutzky S (eds) *National Constitutions in European and Global Governance: Democracy, Rights and the Rule of Law* (Springer 2019) 1225

Quintelier B, 'Opkomst en ondergang van de nationale orde van advocaten van België' in Martyn G, Doncker G, Faber S and Heirbaut D (eds*), Geschiedenis van de advocatuur in de Lage Landen* (Verloren 2009) 341

Raes K, 'Ontwikkelingen in de Belgische rechtscultuur. Een cultuurhistorische verkenning', in Heirbaut D, Rousseaux X and Velle K (eds), *Politieke en sociale geschiedenis van justitie in België van 1830 tot heden/Histoire politique et sociale de la justice en Belgique de 1830 à nos jours* (Die Keure 2004) 345

Roegiers J and van Sas NCF, 'Revolution in the North and South' in Blom JCH and Lamberts E (eds), *History of the Low Countries* (Berghahn Books 2006) 269

Rotthier K (ed), *De vrederechter 'Tot uw dienst'* (Die Keure 2018)

Rousseaux X, 'Witte mars' in Hendrick A, Musin A, Rousseaux X and Tousignant N (eds), *Het verhaal van justitie* (Snoeck 2017) 152

Samoy I, Sagaert V and Terryn E (ed), *Invloed van het Europees recht op het Belgisch privaatrecht* (Intersentia 2012)

Schandevyl E, 'De vervrouwelijking van de juridische beroepen', in Heirbaut D, Rousseaux X and De Koster M (eds), *Tweehonderd Jaar Justitie : Historische Encyclopedie Van De Belgische Justitie = Deux Siècles De Justice : Encyclopédie Historique De La Justice Belge* (Die Keure 2015) 578

——, 'Women and the Courts in Belgium: an Historical Perspective', in Kimble SL and Roewekamp MV (eds), *New perspectives on European Women's Legal History* (Routledge 2016) 152

Stengers J, *Koningen der Belgen van Leopold I tot Albert II* (Davidsfonds 1997)

Stevens F, 'De notarissen' in Heirbaut D, Rousseaux X and Velle K (eds), *Politieke en sociale geschiedenis van justitie in België van 1830 tot heden/Histoire politique et sociale de la justice en Belgique de 1830 à nos jours* (Die Keure 2004) 257

Straetmans G and Rozie N (ed), *Doorwerking van het Europese recht in de nationale rechterlijke praktijk* (Intersentia 2012)

Suetens L P, 'Judicial Review in Belgium' in Smith E, *Constitutional Justice under Old Constitutions* (Kluwer 1995) 319

Surhone L, Timpledon M and Marseken S, *Pragmatic Sanction of 1549* (VDM Publishing 2010)

Taelman P and Voet S, 'Mediation in Belgium: a long and winding road' in Esplugues C and Marquis L (eds), *New developments in civil and commercial mediation: global comparative perspectives* (Springer 2015) 89

—— and Van Severen C, *Civil procedure in Belgium* (Wolters Kluwer 2018)

—— and Van Severen C, 'The Judicial System and Civil Procedure', in Kruithof M and De Bondt W (eds), *Introduction to Belgian Law* (Kluwer Law International 2017) 81

Van Dael B, 'Bemiddeling in België: justitie ge(re)medieerd?' in Van Rhee R, Heirbaut D and Storme ML (eds), *De Code de procédure civile (1806) na 200 jaar: de traditie van het Frans civiel procesrecht in vergelijkend perspectief* (Kluwer 2008) 109

Vande Lanotte J, Goedertier G and Bracke S, *Belgium for Beginners: A Guide Through the Belgian Labyrinth* (Die Keure 2006).

Vandenbogaerde S, *Vectoren van het recht: geschiedenis van de Belgische juridische tijdschriften* (Die Keure 2018)

—— and Lemoine T, 'Van deurwachter tot gerechtsdeurwaarder' in Heirbaut D, Rousseaux X and De Koster M (eds), *Tweehonderd Jaar Justitie : Historische Encyclopedie Van De Belgische Justitie = Deux Siècles De Justice : Encyclopédie Historique De La Justice Belge* (Die Keure 2015) 379

Van Der Haegen M, *Het Hof van Cassatie als lichtbaken van het Belgische rechtsbestel. Een theoretische en empirische toetsing* (unpublished PhD dissertation, Ghent University 2019)

Vander Laenen F, Vanderplasschen W, Wittouck C, Dekkers A and De Ruyver B (eds), *Het pilootproject drugbehandelingskamer te Gent: Een uitkomstenevaluatie* (Academia Press 2013)

van Droogenbroeck J-F, *Cassation et jurisdiction. Iura dicit curia* (Bruylant 2004)

Van Hoecke M and Vandenbogaerde S, 'Basic Features of the Belgian Legal System' in Kruithof M and De Bondt W (eds), *Introduction to Belgian Law* (Kluwer Law International 2017)

Van Keersbilck M, *Justitie in de steigers: gerechtelijke hervormingen in België. De moeizame weg naar het Gerechtelijk Wetboek* (Unpublished PhD Ghent University 2018–2019)

Van Loo B, *De Bourgondiërs. Aartsvaders van de Lage Landen* (De Bezige Bij 2018)

Vanschoenwinkel J, 'Vertrouwen' in Hendrick A, Musin A, Rosseaux X and Tousignant N (eds), *Het verbaal van justitie* (Snoeck 2017)

Van Ransbeeck R (ed), *Bemiddeling* (Die Keure 2008)

Voet S, 'Belgium's new specialized judiciary' (2014) vol. 4 *Russian Law Journal* 129

Witte E, Craeybeckx J and Meynen A, *Political History of Belgium from 1830 onwards* (ASP 2009)

Wauters K, Delvaux B and Vanheusden B (eds) *Invloed van het EU-recht op het Belgisch bestuursrecht* (Die Keure 2014)

Witte E, Nandrin J-P, Gubin E and Deneckere G, *Nieuwe Geschiedenis van België* (Lannoo 2005), 3 volumes.

Wouters J (ed), *De Benelux: tijd voor een wedergeboorte* (Intersentia 2006)

—— and Van Eeckhoutte D (eds), *Doorwerking van international recht in de Belgische rechtsorde: recente ontwikkelingen in een rechtstakoverschrijdend perspectief* (Intersentia 2006)

13. An Introduction to French Legal Culture

Sunniva Cristina Bragdø-Ellenes

1. Introduction – *La France*

The French republic covers 549,000 km^2 of mainland and includes five overseas (*outre-mer*) departments and regions (*les DOM-ROM*), Corsica, and five overseas communities (*collectivités d'outre-mer*). France is the second largest country in Europe after Russia, and the mainland, called *l'hexagone* due to its six sided shape, is characterized by vast and low plains; two thirds of its territory is below 250 meters.[1] Still, France is well known for its mountains on the borders to Switzerland, Italy (*les Alpes*), and Spain (*les Pyrénées*) and in the Auvergne-region (*Massif central*). Three of the country's six "sides" are coastlines, bordering the Mediterranean Sea, The English Channel (*La Manche*), and the Atlantic Ocean.

With a large surface and a population of 6 million on the mainland, France has a scattered population compared to Germany, Italy and Great Britain.[2] The principal religion is Catholicism. Mainly as a result of a large Maghrebin population,[3] Islam has become the second largest religion, before Protestantism and Judaism. The French state is secular, meaning that political and religious powers are separated and that the state is a neutral guarantor of the freedom to worship.[4]

The French language is spoken in all of France and Monaco, and in regions of Belgium, Switzerland, Luxembourg, and Italy – as well as in several other countries, mainly

1 *Les DOM-ROM* are Guadeloupe, Réunion, Mayotte, Guyane, and Martinique, situated in the Caribbean, South America and the Indian Ocean. The five *collectivités d'outre-mer* are French Polynesia, Saint-Barthélemy, Saint Martin, Saint Pierre and Miquelon, Wallis, and Futuna; The Constitution of 1958 Art. 73; *Dictionnaire Le Petit Larousse illustré. 2016. France (*Larousse 2015); http://www.vie-publique.fr/decouverte-institutions/institutions/collectivites-territoriales/categories-collectivites-territoriales/que-sont-departements-regions-outre-mer.html (accessed January 2019).

2 If the *DOM a*re included, the population is 67.3 million. See L'Insee, 'TEF, Tableaux de l'économie française', 11 and 14:/TEF2018.pdf (accessed January 2019). L'Insee is the French National Institute of Statistics and Economic Studies: http://www.insee.fr/en/.

3 From Maghreb, the northwest region of Africa.

4 The Constitution of 1958 Art. 1: "La France est une République indivisible, laïque, démocratique et sociale."

where France has or has had overseas territories. The French speaking population in the world, which counts about 274 million people on five continents, form *la francophonie*.

The French economy was ranked the world's sixth largest economy by gross domestic product, 2,181 billion euros in 2015, in Europe only behind Germany and Great Britain.[5] The country is ranked number 22 on the Human Development Index.[6] The leading industrial sectors are telecommunications, aerospace and defence, ship building, and pharmaceuticals. About 78 % of the country's electricity production comes from nuclear energy, where France is the world-leading country. Almost half of the total surface area in France is arable land and France is the overall largest European agricultural producer.[7] France received almost 83 million foreign tourists in 2015 and was the most popular tourist destination in the world.[8]

France's mainland is organized into thirteen *régions*, 96 *départements*, approximately 35,000 municipalities (*communes*), 330 *arrondissements* and 2,054 *cantons*. The number of municipalities is particularly high. Around 19,000 of them have a population of less than 500 each.[9] Though the country has several levels of regional and local administration, the country is reputed for centralisation, meaning that the influence of Paris, the capital, and its institutions dominate politics.[10]

French mayors and presidents of *départements* and regions were frequently also representatives on a national level (*le cumul des mandats*), which was considered to both strengthen the representative's position in national politics and be an efficient way of having a local influence on the institutions of the capital. The French parliament is composed of two chambers; the National Assembly (*Assemblée nationale*) and the Senate (*Sénat*).[11] In 2013, 236 (of a total of 577) members of the Assembly and 125 (of 348) of the members of the Senate were also mayors. From 2017, this "cumulating of

5 See http://data.worldbank.org/data-catalog/GDP-ranking-table (Accessed January 2019).

6 See http://hdr.undp.org/en/content/human-development-index-hdi (Accessed January 2019).

7 Chambres d'agriculture, 'French Agriculture. Key Figures', available at http://www.chambres-agriculture.fr/fileadmin/user_upload/National/002_inst-site-chambres/pages/infos_eco/FicheAgri_Anglais.pdf (Accessed January 2019).

8 The World Tourism Organization (UNWTO), 'Tourism highlights. 2014 edition' 6, available at http://www.dadosefatos.turismo.gov.br/images/pdf/estatisticas_indicadores/UNTWO_Tourism_Highlights_2016_Edition.pdf (Accessed December 2019). The UNWTO is the United Nation's agency responsible for the promotion of responsible, sustainable and universally accessible tourism.

9 L'Insee, 'TEF, Tableaux de l'économie française' (n 1) 14; *Dictionnaire Le Petit Larousse illustré. 2016* (n 1); Direction Générale des Collectivités Locale, 'Les chiffres-clés des collectivités locales 2018', available at https://www.collectivites-locales.gouv.fr/files/files/statistiques/brochures/chiffres_cles_2018_0.pdf (Accessed January 2019). On the municipalities' self-government, see Sigrid Stokstad, *Kommunalt selvstyre* (Akademika forlag 2012). See also Angélique Négroni, 'Il n'y a plus 36 000 communes en France', *Le Figaro* 7 January 2016, available at http://www.lefigaro.fr/actualite-france/2016/01/07/01016-20160107ARTFIG00005-il-n-y-a-plus-36000-communes-en-france.php (Accessed January 2019).

10 See the Constitution Art. 72 and following; Code général des collectivités territoriales concerning the administrative levels. Codes, statutes, case-law, and other sources of law (including some English translations) can be found at http://www.legifrance.fr/.

11 The constitution art. 24. The deputes are elected in a universal vote and seated in the Palais Boubon. The senators are indirectly elected in a universal vote and seated in the Palais du Luxembourg. See http://www.senat.fr/; http://www.assemblee-nationale.fr/ (Accessed 17 February 2020)

mandates" has been prohibited, in order to improve the representation of the mandates and renewal of the representatives.[12]

The president is elected by popular vote for a five-year period by absolute majority, meaning that if no candidate obtains more than 50 per cent in the first round, there will be a second round of election for the two candidates with the most votes. The executive power is shared between the president, the Prime Minister and the other ministers forming the government. The president appoints the prime minister, who in his/her turn selects and leads the other members of the government.[13]

France as a nation has developed since the monarchy of the Capet dynasty before year 1000,[14] known as "the old order" *(l'Ancien régime)* from the 15th century. Though violently abandoned during the revolution of 1789, monarchy (and empire) reoccurred for limited periods. Today France is a republic, and the present republic is counted as the fifth. The first Constitution was enacted by the constituent assembly (*l'Assemblée constitutante*) in 1791 and established a constitutional monarchy. A new Constitution in 1793 established France as a republic.[15] Depending on how one defines a constitution, France has had as many as fifteen. The symbolic significance of the Constitution is not as strong as in Norway or the United States, where it is attached to the nations' independence and identity.[16]

During the turmoil in the aftermath of the French revolution, Napoléon reigned as both *consul* and emperor, and marked the development of justice in many ways, especially by law reforms in the form of five codes: Code civil (or Code Napoléon, 1804), Code de procédure civile (1806), Code de commerce (1807), Code pénal (1810), and Code d'instruction criminelle (1811). The best known of the five codes, the Code civil, still remains in force, and brings together all the rules which determine civil rights (book I), goods and various changes in ownership (book II), different ways of acquiring property (book III), and suretyship (book IV). The Code civil has inspired law making in several other countries and regions, such as

12 Anders Lidström, *Kommunsystem i Europa* (Liber 2003) 84; Eivind Smith, 'Frankrike – ett konstitutionellt laboratorium' in Anders Melbourn (ed), *Författningskulturer. Konstitutioner och politiska system i Europa, USA och Asien* (Sekel bokförlag 2009) 77–78; Jean Girardon, *Les collectivités territoriales* (Ellipses 2011) 47–49; loi organique n° 2014–125 du 14 février 2014 interdisant le cumul de fonctions exécutives locales avec le mandat de député ou de sénateur; Anne Rovan, 'Vers la fin du député-maire', *Le Figaro* 5 July 2013, available at http://www.lefigaro.fr/politique/2013/07/05/01002-20130705ARTFIG00626-vers-lafin-du-depute-maire.php (Accessed January 2019); Le Nouvel observateur, 'Fin du cumul des mandats: ce que changera la loi', *Le Nouvel observateur* 21 January 2014, available at http://tempsreel.nouvelobs.com/cumul-desmandats/20140120.OBS3104/la-fin-du-cumul-des-mandats-ce-que-changera-la-loi.html (Accessed January 2019). One well known example is the conservative politician Alain Juppé, who during the years 1995–97 was prime minister and at the same time mayor of Bordeaux, a city of approximately 230,000 inhabitants.

13 The Constitution Art. 8 and 21; Catherine Elliott, Eric Jeanpierre and Catherine Vernon, *French legal system* (Pearson Education Limited 2006) 20. See also http://www.gouvernement.fr/.

14 Smith (n 12) 69–70.

15 Alain Wijffels, *Introduction historique au droit. France, Allemagne, Angleterre* (Thémis droit 2014) 261; *Dictionnaire Le Petit Larousse illustré. 2016* (n 1) 1503.

16 Smith (n 12) 69 and 70.

Monaco, The Netherlands, Spain, Portugal, and Latin America.[17] Napoléon also established *Le Conseil d'État*, at first an advisory organ for the head of state, later the government. *Le Conseil d'État* also developed into being an independent administrative court. Napoléon's codes, in a synthesis with the traditions from the autocratic period and the revolutionaries' reforms, are often presented as the platform for the present judicial organisation in France.[18]

2. Conflict resolution

2.1 The French court system

The French court system (see figures below) is characterized by a strong duality and a high degree of specialization. There are two main court hierarchies: a judicial one for civil and criminal cases, where *Cour de cassation* is the highest instance (*juridictions judiciaires*), and one hierarchy dealing with administrative law, headed by *Conseil d'État* (*juridictions administratives*). In addition there is a conflict tribunal (*Tribunal des conflits*), a constitutional court (*Conseil Constitutionnel*), a court of impeachment (*Haute Cour*), and the Court of Justice of the Republic (*Cour de Justice de la République*) treating cases of serious crimes or other major offences allegedly committed by a member of the Government in the holding of his/her office.[19]

Within both court hierarchies there are several general and specialized courts at the first level, for instance courts for land disputes, labour cases, and commercial cases. For criminal cases there are three first level courts for adults and three specialized first level courts for minors – depending on how severe the violation of the law is, the age of the minor and whether he/she is a recidivist. In civil cases there are two first level courts, depending on the economic value at stake in the case. For administrative cases, in addition to the general administrative courts, there are approximately 30 specialized first instance courts, as well as some specialized appellate courts.[20] These courts handle, amongst others, cases of professional discipline and asylum. Most cases start at first level, but some types are brought directly to the highest court, for instance disputes concerning *ordonnances* given by the President of the Republic or the French Authority of competition's decisions on prohibition of or limitations in companies' merger agreements.[21]

A French courts' field of jurisdiction can therefore be defined by the value at stake, the severity of the crime, the age of the defendant and/or the area of law from which the conflict arises. As a result of the highly specialized courts, judges often work with

17 *Dictionnaire Le Petit Larousse. Compact, France (*Larousse 1992) 1333 and 1340; Dominique Bureau, 'Codification' in Denis Alland and Stéphane Rials (eds), *Dictionnaire de la culture juridique (*Lamy 2003) 226.

18 Jean-Claude Farcy, 'Juridictions. Évolution du système français' in Denis Alland and Stéphane Rials (eds), *Dictionnaire de la culture juridique (*Lamy 2003) 873.

19 The webpages of the French Ministry of Justice contain information about (amongst other things) the justice organization and statistics, see http://www.justice.gouv.fr/.

20 René Chapus, *Droit du contentieux administratif (*Montchrestien 2008) 101; Roger Perrot, *Institutions judiciaires (*Montchrestien 2010) 237.

21 Code de justice administrative Art. R 311-1.

a limited area of law. But specialization may also result from the organization of the more general courts: Judges often work within divisions handling limited areas of law. The specialization obtained on the first level is secured on the level of appeal (*cour d'appel* and *cour administrative d'appel*) by specialized divisions there as well. For instance, the *Cour d'appel de Paris* has 74 specialized divisions. This is also the case on the highest level, the *Cour de cassation* and the *Conseil d'État*. The latter is divided into ten divisions, some are specialized, for instance in tax law, and some are general.[22]

The strong duality between civil/criminal and administrative matters in the French court system is also reflected in the law applied, the process, the legal education, and recruitment to the courts. The foundation of the law applied by the two systems is fundamentally different; whilst the judicial courts apply mostly written law, much of it codified, the administrative courts apply case-law, although the larger parts were codified (adopted as written law) in the last decades.[23] An example is the law of torts and damages where both judicial and administrative courts have competence, depending on the grounds for the claim.[24]

Particular French superior courts

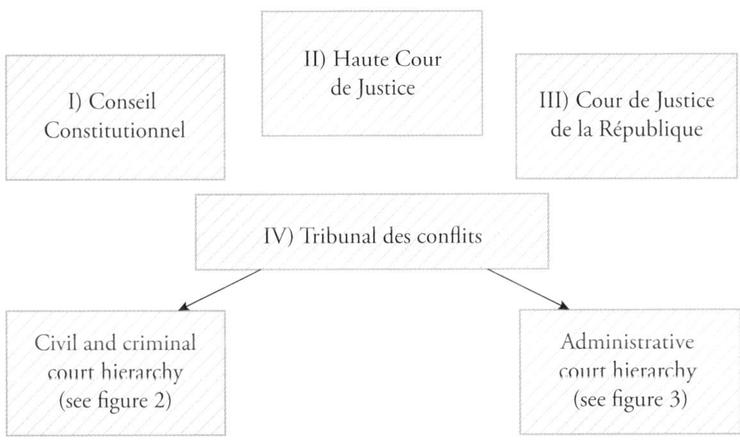

I *Conseil constitutionnel*: The constitutional council. **II** *Haute Cour de Justice*: A court of impeachment (the Parliament sitting as the High Court) treating the removal from office of the President of the Republic when accused of breach of his duties patently incompatible with his continuing in office. **III** *Cour de justice de la République*: This is also a court of impeachment, treating cases of serious crimes or other major offences allegedly committed by a member of the Government in the holding of his office.[25] **IV** *Tribunal des conflits*: Court of conflicts.

Fig. 1 Particular French superior courts.

---

22 *Cour d'appel de Paris:* http://www.ca-paris.justice.fr/index.php?rubrique=10977&ssrubrique=11057 (Accessed January 2019); *Cour de cassation:* https://www.courdecassation.fr/cour_cassation_1/organisation_cour_56/chambres_57/ (Accessed January 2019); *Conseil d'Etat:* http://www.conseil-etat.fr/Conseil-d-Etat/Organisation/Organigramme-du-Conseil-d-Etat (Accessed January 2019); Perrot (n 20) 101.

23 François Terré, *Introduction générale au droit (*Dalloz 2012) 16; Guy Braibant and Bernard Stirn, *Le droit administratif français (*Dalloz 2005) 89 and 95–96.

24 Marie-Louise Holle, *Hæftelsesansvar for selvstændigt virkende tredjemænd – med særlig henblik på offentlige oppgaver (*Karnov Group 2013) 224–225.

25 The *Conseil Constitutionnel,* see the Constitution Section VII; The *Haute Cour,* see Art. 68; The *Cour de justice de la République,* see Art. 68-1.

French civil and criminal courts

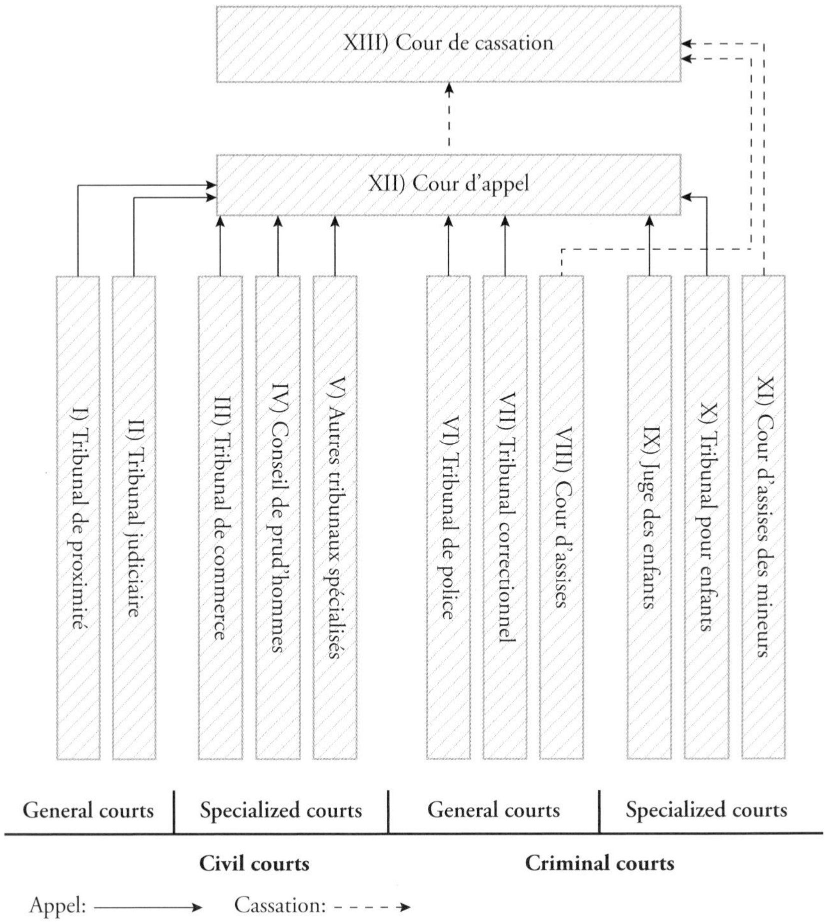

I *Tribunal de proximité*: First instance in disputes concerning values up to or equal to 10,000 euros and disputes about consumer credit.[26] **II** *Tribunal judiciaire*: First instance court in civil disputes concerning values of more than 10,000 euros, and some other cases (divorce, parental authority etc.). In all 161 such courts, thereof 16 with competence in commercial cases. **III** *Tribunal de commerce*: First instance in amongst others commercial disputes. **IV** *Conseil de prud'hommes*: First instance in certain labour disputes. In total 210. **V** Other civil law courts, for instance *Tribunal paritaire des baux ruraux*: Treat certain agricultural disputes.

VI *Tribunal de police*: First instance court in cases concerning fines of all degrees. **VII** *Tribunal correctionnel*: First instance court in criminal cases concerning crimes with a sentencing framework up to ten years (*délits*). VIII *Cour d'assises*: First instance court in criminal cases concerning serious crimes (*crimes*). Also organized as an appeal court, *cour d'assises d'appel*, in appeal cases from other cour d'assises. **IX** *Juge des enfants*: First instance in civil cases concerning children, for instance cases of parental neglect, and criminal cases concerning adolescents charged of offences. **X** *Tribunal pour enfants*:

26 The former first instance tribunals in civil cases *tribunal d'instance* and *tribunal de grande instance,* were recently reformed into the tribunal de proximité and tribunal judiciaire, see for instance https://www.gouvernement.fr/sites/default/files/contenu/piece-jointe/2018/03/dp_-_chantiers_de_la_justice.pdf (Accessed April 2020).

First instance court in criminal cases concerning minors (but see number XII). **XI** *Cour d'assises des mineurs*: First instance court concerning serious crimes (*crimes*) where the defendant is between 16 and 18 years.

XII *Cour d'appel*: Court of appeal in civil cases and in criminal cases, which are not appealed to the *cour d'assises d'appel*. In all of France there are 36 such courts.

XIII *Cour de cassation*: The highest instance in civil and criminal cases. Does not consider facts (*faits*), only law (*droit*), and will normally not give a decision on the merits of a case, but eventually quash it and send it back to another lower court for a new trial.

Fig. 2 French civil and criminal courts.

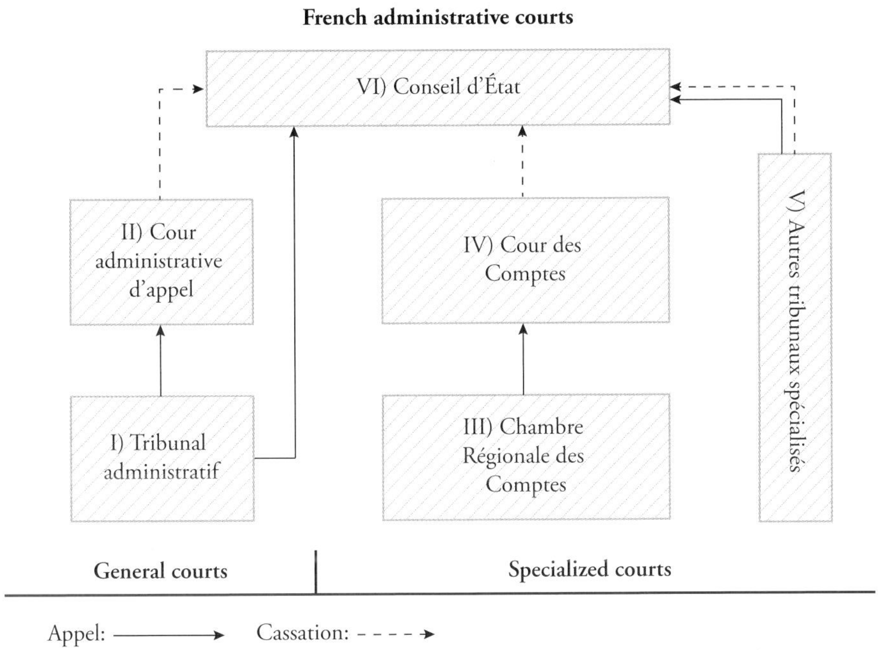

I *Tribunal administratif*: First instance administrative court. In total 42 such courts.[27] **II** *Cour administrative d'appel*: Administrative court of appeal. In total 8 such courts. **III** *Chambre Régionale des Comptes*: First instance specialized court in "audit cases" concerning public expenses. **IV** *Cour des Comptes*: Second and highest instance for cases from III.[28] **V** Other specialized administrative courts. In total approximately thirty, for instance the *Cour nationale du droit d'asile*, which is the national asylum court. **VI** *Conseil d'État*: Highest instance administrative court and advisory organ for the government.

Fig. 3 French administrative courts.

In 2017, there were made 2.6 million court decisions in civil and commercial cases, of these 20,268 in the *Cour de cassation* and 248,647 in the *cours d'appel*.[29] The most common types of disputes concerned (in decreasing order) work and social protection (*rela-*

27 On the mainland there are 31 first instance administrative courts. They have approximately 2.1 million inhabitants per court, and cover an average of 17,742 square kilometers. (In comparison, the 60 Norwegian *tingretter* have approximately 89,300 inhabitants per court and cover an average 5,068 square kilometers.)

28 For both levels, see https://www.ccomptes.fr/.

29 For all statistics, see Le Ministère de la Justice, 'Les chiffres-clés de la Justice 2018' (2018).

tions du travail et protection sociale), contracts (*droit des contrats*), and family law (*droit de la famille*). The average duration of processing, all cases included, was 13.3 months in the *cour d'appel*, 7.6 months in the *tribunaux de grande instance*, and 5.5 months in the commercial courts.

In 2017, there were 1,180,949 decisions in all in criminal cases. 7,906 criminal cases were handled by the *Cour de cassation*, 104,209 by the *cour d'appel*, and 63,383 by the *juge des enfants* or courts for minors.

In administrative courts, in 2017, a total 242,882 cases were decided;[30] 10,139 in the *Conseil d'État* (where the average time for each case (all cases included) to be decided was 5.5 months), 31,283 in the *cours administratives d'appel* (average time 11 months), and 201,460 in the *tribunaux administratifs* (9 months and 18 days). In 96 % of the cases, the definitive solution in the dispute corresponded to the one given in the first instance by *tribunaux administratifs*.[31]

2.2 Historical development

To explain the duality between the two hierarchies of judicial and administrative courts, it is useful to take a closer look at their historical development,[32] especially of the administrative courts that are newer. Their development is best comprehended in light of the revolutionaries' scepticism against the *parlements*, regional courts where the judges were known to be against reforms initiated by the central administration. Also, due to the influence of the eighteenth-century political philosopher Charles-Louis de Secondat de Montesquieu's doctrine of separation of powers, in 1790 the *Asssemblée constitutante* forbade the courts to review administrative acts.[33] Treating administrative disputes was therefore handed over to regional parts of the administration (*directoires de départements et de districts*). The head of the French state was the appeal-instance, and in some cases the only instance.

---

30 However, cases concerning neglect of children (which would be considered administrative cases in for instance Norway), are decided by the judicial courts and judges (like *juge des enfants)*. In 2017 these instances treated 367,083 cases concerning 119,973 minors "*en danger*" – in danger of neglect from parents. Also, the largest specialized administrative court, *La Cour nationale du droit de l'asile,* decided 47,814 cases in 2017.

31 See Le Conseil d'État, 'Le Conseil d'État et la justice administrative accompagnent les mutations de la société française. Bilan d'activité 2013' (2013) 2, 22; Le Conseil d'État, 'Rapport public 2018. Activité juridictionnelle et consultative des juridictions administratives en 2017' *33.*

32 See a detailed overview in Farcy (n 18) 872 ff.

33 There is a saying: "To judge the administration is also to administer." (*Juger l'administration, c'est aussi administrer.*) See Wijffels (n 15) 263–163; René Chapus, *Droit administratif général (*Montchrestien 2001) 748 with references to and quotes from loi des 16–24 août 1790 titre 2 Art. 13; Marie-Christine Rouault, *Contentieux administratif (*Meméntos LMD 2000) 71. Letting parts of the administration judge another part of the administration was not considered inconsistent with the doctrine of separation of powers. Montesquieu limited the field of the judicial power to crimes (*les crimes)* and private disputes (*les différends des particuliers)*; and not disputes between private persons and the administration. See Charles Louis de Secondat de Montesquieu, *Om lovenes ånd,* bog 11, kapitel 6 (first published 1748, Gad 1998) 168; Chapus, *Droit du contentieux administratif (*n 18) 40.

The administrative "self-control" did not function in a satisfying way, and already in 1799 independent organs with advisory functions were established by Napoléon; on the regional level the *conseils de prefecture* and on the national level the *Conseil d'État*. These authorities were part of the administration, but independent in the sense that their members were not part of the executive administration (*administration active*).[34]

Conseil d'État's mission was to give advice to the central administration, but with a few exceptions for Napoléon himself, the administration always followed the *Conseil*'s advice – which gradually became binding.[35] In 1806, a section for disputes (*Section du contentieux*) was established and over the years the *Conseil d'État* developed into an autonomous authority with court-like features. At the same time the council's other divisions (*sections consultatives*) gave advice on the preparation of statutes, governmental regulations (*règlements*), etc. Any citizen had the right to use this court and it considerably improved the position of the individual towards the administration. During the 20th century, local and regional administrative courts were established (from the *conseils de prefecture*) to reduce the *Conseil d'État*'s growing workload, and later named *tribunaux administratifs* and *Cours administrative d'appel*.[36]

2.3 Conflicts of jurisdiction between judicial and administrative courts

The divide which developed between judicial and administrative courts created possibilities for jurisdiction disputes between the two court hierarchies. In 1872, a jurisdiction disputes court, the *Tribunal des conflits*, was established as an independent tribunal. The court consisted of members from the two supreme courts, *Conseil d'État* and *Cour de cassation*, and the procedure is written.[37]

The rules defining the two court hierarchies' jurisdiction are to a certain extent regulated in statutes and are further developed in case-law.[38] When not statutory determined, one could say that in principle, administrative jurisdictions apply administrative law. They are competent for settling disputes where one of the parties is a public body and

34 Chapus, Droit administratif général (n 33) 749; Chapus, *Droit du contentieux administratif* (n 20) 39–40; Bernard Pacteau, *Contentieux administratif* (Puf 2005) 40; Rouault (n 33) 41.

35 The decisions were formally binding from 1872.

36 Braibant and Stirn (n 23) 573–576; Farcy (n 18) 875. The administrative courts also function as advisory organs for the executive authorities. For the lower instances, this advisory work is of a modest extent, but the *Conseil d'État*'s advisory missions for the government is one of the organ's two main roles (the other one being, of course, the highest administrative court). See organization-map (and information about the court, cases, studies etc.) here: http://www.conseil-etat.fr/.

37 Loi du 24 mai 1872 relative au Tribunal des conflits and décret n° 2015-233 du 27 février 2015 relatif au Tribunal des conflits et aux questions préjudicielles; Jean Waline, *Droit administratif* (Dalloz 2012) 604 ff; Rouault (n 33) 92–94, 100–105.

38 For instance, by law of 31.12.1957 all disputes arising from road traffic accidents – also those involving a public body or its agent – were transferred to the judicial courts. See Eva Steiner, *French law. A comparative approach* (Oxford university press 2018) 178.

the case concerns the application of public authority; the nature or purpose of the decision or act at issue is especially decisive. Examples are disputes arising in the area called *gestion privée des service*, such as a private law contract or a service from industrial and commercial public bodies (*service public industriel et commercial*), where the judicial courts are competent to settle the dispute.

The rules of the jurisdiction of the two court hierarchies have been complicated, and there are exceptions that are considered illogical, but many questions are now settled through the case-law of the *Tribunal des conflits*. The tribunal normally settles approximately 50 cases a year.[39] However, doubts about which tribunal to settle a dispute are considered an inconvenience.[40]

2.4 Procedures in the judicial and administrative courts

Procedures in judicial and administrative courts differ from one another, and they are different from legal procedures in many other countries. The procedure before the courts has been said to favour professional judges rather than lay personnel. Although, lay personnel (juge non professionnel) sit in commercial courts and labour courts, courts for minors and as jury in one of the criminal courts, Cour d'assises (and cour d'assies d'appel).[41] One of the judges drafts the motivation for the verdict.[42] The procedure in the courts is furthermore said to favour the use of inquisitorial rather than adversarial methods in the application of the process of justice. Both the preference of professional judges and inquisitorial methods can be explained partly by the notion of public service and identifying justice as being a part of this. Also the numerous procedural reforms in the aim of rationalizing the process and making it more effective can be seen as a result

39 Serge Guinchard, Gabriel Montagnier and André Varinard, *Institutions juridictionnelles* (Dalloz 2007) 402–403, 405; In 2017, 36 cases were decided. See Tribunal des Conflits, 'Rapport annuel d'activité du Tribunal des conflits pour l'année 2017'.

40 Perrot (n 20) 38–39; Braibant and Stirn (n 23) 530–537; Conseil d'État, 'La justice administrative en pratique' (2001) 23 ff. See also Chapus, *Droit administratif général* (n 33) 825 ff, 947 ff.

41 Code de procédure pénale art. 240 and 254; Code de l'organisation judiciaire art. L 251-3; Bell, Boyron and Whittaker (n 44) 62–63; European Commission for the Efficiency of Justice (CEPEJ) *Report on "European judicial systems – Edition 2014 (2012 data): efficiency and quality of justice"* (2014) 158. See https://rm.coe.int/cepej-report-on-european-judicial-systems-edition-2014-2012-data-effic/16807882a1

42 Code de procédure pénale art. 365-1.

of the same public service notion.[43] Further, this includes the principle of free access to justice, which is a heritage of the revolution; the state bears the costs of the justice system, but the parties bear the cost for legal counsel.[44]

Procedure, both before the judicial and administrative courts, is regulated in the respective procedural codes: *Code de procédure civile*, *Code de procédure pénale*, *Code de l'organisation judiciaire* and *Code de justice administrative*. In general, the French procedural system can be defined as more inquisitorial and less adversarial than in many other countries. Much of the work of preparing a case for trial is carried out by the judges, whilst these tasks in many other countries are the responsibility of the parties' lawyers.[45] The trials are often shorter than in some other countries, most certainly the Norwegian court process, partly because there is a stronger preference for documentary evidence, as opposed to oral evidence.[46]

Both in judicial and administrative courts, (attempts of) conciliation or mediation may be carried out throughout the proceeding. The initiative can come from one or both parties, or from the judge. In judicial courts, the conciliation can be performed by the judge, or the judge can appoint a conciliator. In the administrative courts, the mediator is a third party and the agreement reached by the parties must be within certain legal limits.[47]

---

43 Steiner (n 38) 193. The latest reform concerns several aspects of the justice system, see loi n°2016–1547 du 18 novembre 2016 de modernisation de la justice du XXIe siècle. There is also a large ongoing reform project concerning mainly improvement and simplification of civil and criminal procedure, digital processing, effectiveness of sentences, and adaptation of the judicial organization. See https://www.gouvernement.fr/conseil-des-ministres/2018-04-20/renforcement-de-l-organisation-des-juridictions-et-programma (Accessed January 2019) and https://www.gouvernement.fr/sites/default/files/contenu/piece-jointe/2018/03/dp_-_chantiers_de_la_justice.pdf (Accessed January 2019). See also some prepartory works: *Projet de loi de programmation 2018-2022 et de réforme pour la justice NOR: JUST1806695L/Bleue-2*, available at http://www.justice.gouv.fr/art_pix/20180420_pjljustice_.pdf (Accessed January 2019). Frequent reforms have also been "admitted" by the vice-president (who is the leader) of the *Conseil d'État*, Jean-Marc Sauvé: "Je l'ai dit: l'histoire de la juridiction administrative est scandée par les réformes; il n'est pas de décennie qui, depuis 1799, n'ait été une époque de changement et d'innovation." (I said it: the history of administrative jurisdiction is marked by reforms; there is no decade that, since 1799, has not been a time of change and innovation.) Quote taken from his lecture (written in collaboration with Chloé Szafran) during a conference about 'La réforme de la justice administrative', Faculté de droit de Poitiers, 28 November 2008, see: http://www.conseil-etat.fr/content/download/273/847/version/1/file/conf_fac_droit_poitiers_281108.pdf (Accessed January 2019).

44 John Bell, Sophie Boyron and Simon Whittaker, *Principles of French law* (Oxford university press 2008) 113–115; Steiner (n 38) 199. France has a system of legal aid (*aide juridictionnelle*) which covers parts or all of the litigants' fees for lawyers, depending on the applicant's income (the rates are progressive). In 2017 there were in civil, penal and administrative cases 985,110 admissions of legal assistance – of the total amount of 495.5 million. See Code de l'organisation judiciaire Art. L.111-2; Code de justice administrative Art. R. 441-1; décret no 91-1266 du 19 décembre 1991; See Le Ministère de la Justice, 'Demande d'aide Juridictionnelle' (Cerfa n° 51036#02); Bell, Boyron and Whittaker (2008) 282–283; Chapus, *Droit du contentieux administratif* (n 20) 449; See Le Ministère de la Justice, 'Les chiffres-clés de la Justice 2018' (2018) 5, 6. In many cases there is no obligation to be represented by a lawyer, but an ongoing reform aims to expand the obligation for the more complex cases, see Ministère de la justice, 'Chantiers de la justice. Les axes de la reforme' (2018) 7.

45 Kjølstad, Koch and Sunde, "An Introduction to the Norwegian Legal Culture", in this volume, chapter 5, 110 ff.

46 Chapus, *Droit du contentieux administratif* (n 20) 834; Steiner (n 38) 195.

47 Code de procédure civile art. 21, 127 – 131-15; Code de justice administrative art. L213-1 – L2113-10.

An example of an inquisitorial element in the French civil process is the judges' discretion to order legally appropriate investigative measures, for instance an expert, whilst questions of facts are considered to be the monopoly of the opposing parties in the case, and hence an example of an adversarial element in the process.[48] The procedure is – obviously – adversarial, and the principle is practiced, for instance by an obligation for the judge to hear all parties concerned, that the parties must disclose to one another for instance factual arguments, evidential means, and legal arguments, and that the judge may only take into consideration arguments, documents etc. that the parties have had an opportunity to discuss in an adversarial manner.[49]

Another distinct feature of French procedure is the collegiality of the courts. In first instance, civil and criminal cases are usually heard by three judges. In the first instance administrative courts there are usually three judges and a *rapporteur public* (se explanation below).[50] Nevertheless, many cases are decided by a single judge; in the administrative courts this has been a tendency in order to deal with the strongly increasing number of incoming cases.[51] An ongoing reform aims to expand the use of a single judge.[52]

A distinct feature of French procedure is the role of the Public ministry (*ministère public*). As will be explained in the chapter about recruitment and independence of judges, the notion "*juge*" is wide and refers to many different positions, for instance judges in the *ministère public*. These judges do not decide cases; their mission is to defend the interest of the *collectivité publique*. Before the *cours d'appel* they are called *procureurs généraux* and before the *tribunaux de grande instance* they are called *procureurs de la République*. In criminal cases, their role is to initiate and follow up the investigations (*déclencher et d'exercer les poursuites*), and in civil and commercial law to require what they consider to be the right application of the law in the case, and to present these observations before the judges who decide the case and who are not bound to follow the opinion of the *ministère public*.[53]

The procedure before the administrative courts is more inquisitorial and less party-driven than private law procedure. It has been said that "[t]here is almost a sense in which the procedure of the administrative courts is an investigation of administrative shortcoming, rather than litigation between parties."[54] The administrative procedure holds three main characteristics: it is adversarial, written, and inquisitorial. In practice, the procedures before administrative courts of first instance, the *tribunaux administratifs*, are led by the court (the judges in cooperation with the administrative personnel (*le*

48 Code de procédure civile Art. 10 and 12; Bell, Boyron and Whittaker (n 44) 102–103.

49 Bell, Boyron and Whittaker (n 44) 284.

50 Code de l'organisation judiciaire Art. L 212-1; Code de justice administrative Art. R. 222-18, see also for instance R. 222-20 on plenary compositions.

51 See Conseil d'État, 'Le Conseil d'État et la justice administrative en 2012' 30.

52 See Ministère de la Justice, 'Chantiers de la justice. Les axes de la reforme' (2018) 5, available at https://www.gouvernement.fr/sites/default/files/contenu/piece-jointe/2018/03/dp_-_chantiers_de_la_justice.pdf (Accessed Januray 2019).

53 Perrot (n 20) 42.

54 Bell, Boyron and Whittaker (n 44) 3.

greffe), which communicate documents between the parties, ensuring contradiction and the judge in charge's following up on the cases. The inquisitorial element is primarily the judge's capacity and responsibility to direct the development of the case (*instruction*) and of the law to be applied in the case. The parties do not communicate directly with one another, but through the court.[55] The judge has the capacity to order legally appropriate investigative measures (*prononcé de mesures d'instruction*), but is limited by the statement of claim (*conclusions*) and grounds (*moyens*) of the parties, which also sets the framework for what verdict can be pronounced.[56] Both the judge in charge (*rapporteur*) and normally also the *rapporteur public* consider the case. The *rapporteur public* plays a role that can be compared to the one of the *ministère public* in the judicial courts, but in the administrative courts he/ she is one of the judges in the court, except they do not take part in the decision of the case. The rapporteur public makes his/her report on the case independently and does not participate in the deliberation of the case. The *rapporteur public*'s report (called *conclusions*) is normally formulated in a more complementary and academic manner than the brief verdict.[57]

When the case is ready to be considered by the deciding judges, they will set a meeting to discuss the case (*séance d'instruction*) and later meet for the official hearing (*audience publique*), which is announced in most cases but not always carried out, since many

55 This part of the process (for instance which documents needs to be communicated) is regulated in Code de justice administrative Art. R. 611-1 and following and R. 612-6; Daniel Chabanol, *La pratique du contentieux administratif* (Litec 2013) 281; Corinne Lepage and Christian Huglo, *Code de justice administrative* (Litec 2013) 5 ff, 627 ff.

56 Code de justice administrative Art. R. 621-1 and following; Chapus, *Droit du contentieux administratif* (n 20) 831, 833 ff, 864 (no 988) ff; Lepage and Huglo (n 55) 659–660; Bernard Pacteau (n 34) 158 ff; Chapus, *Droit administratif général* (n 33) 790, 934 ff; Chabanol (n 55) 219–220. In French-Latin, the expression of the limitation of the judges' powers by the parties' claims etc., is expressed as a prohibition against judging *ultra petita* and *infra petita* (*interdiction de statuter ultra petita and infra petita*). In the civil courts this is expressed in Code de procédure civile Art. 464; Steiner (n 38) 141; Examples of requirements made by the judge are requests for more documentation from the parties (*demandes d'explications ou de documents*), view (*visite des lieux*), witness statement (*enquête*) or request the opinion of independent experts (*expertise*). A relatively recent decision from *Conseil d'État* gives precisions about the judges' responsibilities and limits during the process, see Conseil d'État, *La Lettre de la justice administrative* no 37 (January 2015) 2, with reference to the case: CE, Section, 1er octobre 2014, M B., No 349560: https://www.conseil-etat.fr/actualites/lettre-de-la-justice-administrative/lettre-de-la-justice-administrative/lettre-de-la-justice-administrative-n-37 (Accessed 6 De cember 2019).

57 Code de justice administrative Art. L. 7 and R. 222-23. The mission of the rapporteur public (formerly called *commissaire du gouvernement*) has been described like this in the case *Gervaise* CE Sect. 10 juillet 1957 and cited in Chapus, *Droit du contentieux administratif* (n 20) 901–903: "... le commissaire du gouvernement a pour mission d'exposer les questions que présente à juger chaque recours contentieux et de faire connaître, en formulant en toute indépendance ses conclusions, son appréciation, qui doit être impartiale, sur les circonstances de fait de l'espèce et les règles de droit applicables, ainsi que son opinion sur les solutions qu'appelle, suivant sa conscience, le litige soumis à la juridiction à laquelle il appartient." (...the role of the *commissaire du gouvernement* to set out the questions presented by each contentious appeal and to make known, by formulating his or her conclusions independently, his or her assessment, which must be impartial, on the factual circumstances of the case and the applicable rules of law, as well as his opinion on the solutions which, according to his conscience, call for the dispute submitted to the court to which he belongs.)

parties do not see the need to show up.[58] At each public hearing a number of cases are treated and the hearing of each case may last for approximately 5 minutes. After the hearing the judges deliberates.

2.5 Alternative conflict resolution

The French legal system contains numerous public or private alternatives to conflict resolution in courts, in addition to the possibilities to conciliate and mediate throughout a trial.[59] A well-established alternative, found worldwide, as arbitration (*arbitrage*), which is a court-like private dispute resolution, especially resorted to by private parties in commercial conflicts of a certain matter and value. Arbitrage means that the parties choose, normally one or three persons (*arbitre*) who are experts in the field the conflict arises from, and who decide the resolution of the conflict presented to them in legally binding decision (*sentence arbitrale*). Arbitration is normally quite expensive since the parties must pay the costs of the judges, in addition to the process.[60]

Less court-like conflict resolution mechanisms are mediation and conciliation outside the courts. First, conciliation or other attempts of amicable resolution of a dispute can be a necessary step before taking a dispute before a court. For certain administrative disputes, this includes a compulsory prior administrative appeal.[61] But conciliation (*conciliation*), mediation (*médiation*), and transaction (*transaction*) are also extrajudicial possibilities of ending a dispute, independently of a court trial.[62]

Mediation exists as private mechanisms, but also as (a part of) public institutions. The ombudsman-equivalent "Defender of rights" (*Le Défenseur des droits)* is regulated in the Constitution (art. 71-1) and is only accountable for his actions to the President of the Republic and to Parliament. The Defender's tasks are mainly to ensure due respect of rights and freedoms by state administrations, territorial communities, public legal entities, as well as by all bodies carrying out a public service.[63] There are several other mediation mechanisms, like the *médiation familiale* and the mediation procedure for

58 In 2013, 42 percent of the cases handled in first instance administrative courts were decided by a collegial composition of the court and 76 percent of the cases before the *cours administrative d'appel.* See Le Conseil d'État, 'Le Conseil d'État et la justice administrative accompagnent les mutations de la société française. Bilan d'activité 2013' (2013) 2.

59 Bell, Boyron and Whittaker (n 44) 52-54.

60 Arbitration is regulated in the Code the procédure civile, art. 1442-1503.

61 LOI n° 2016-1547 du 18 novembre 2016 de modernisation de la justice du XXIe siècle art. 4; Code des relations entre le public et l'administration, book IV: Dispute resolution with the administration (*Le règlement des différends avec l'administration*), articles L410-1 to L412-8; https://www.service-public.fr/particuliers/vosdroits/F2478 (Accessed 17 February 2020).

62 For more information, see: https://www.conciliateurs.fr/Qu-est-ce-que-la-conciliation-de-justice (Accessed 21 January 2020) See also code civil art. 2044-2052 on *la transaction*, which is a contract by which the parties, by reciprocal concessions, terminate a born dispute, or prevent an unborn dispute. For administrative disputes, see Code des relations entre le public et l'administration, book IV: Dispute resolution with the administration (*Le règlement des différends avec l'administration*), articles L410-1 to L424-1.

63 LOI organique n° 2011-333 du 29 mars 2011 relative au Défenseur des droits article 26; https://www.defenseurdesdroits.fr/fr/institution/moyens/protection / (Accessed 21 January 2020)

officials of the territorial public service and certain state services, which are mandatory before taking certain disputes to court.[64] Also, all consumers have the right to appeal free of charge to a consumer ombudsman for the amicable resolution of a dispute between them and a professional.[65]

2.6 Recruitment, independence and promotion in the two court hierarchies

Judges in the two hierarchies of courts do not share the same background, training, or status.[66] What both judges in the judicial and administrative courts have in common is that a large part of them are recruited directly after graduation from higher education (see Section 5 on judges' education) and devote their entire career to the judiciary. Being a lifelong judge, the rules of promotion are essential. Promotion is based on seniority or choice. The latter ensures the most apt for the vacant position, whilst the former prevents the interference from the executive power and is a guarantee for independence. Promotion by choice can moreover create a psychological subordination with regard to a superior.[67]

The rules of advancement are detailed and different in the two hierarchies of courts. In both court hierarchies, seniority plays a role for promotion, but it is especially important for advancement up to certain grades. Some judges are recruited directly to the corps of judges, for instance lawyers or civil servants. In the *Conseil d'État* this is referred to as a *tour extérieur* and the purpose is to make the corps of judges more heterogeneous and ensure a broader experience and background amongst the judges.[68]

Advancement within the court system is closely related to the question of judges' independence. In the judicial courts, the independence of the judges is protected by both the Constitution and law, whilst the legal protection of the independence of the judges in the administrative tribunals is weaker, at least formally.[69] The independence of the members of the *Conseil d'État* is protected by the precedents of the *Conseil constitutionnel,* which have established that their independence is a fundamental legal principle.[70]

---

64 See https://www.service-public.fr/particuliers/vosdroits/F34528 ; https://www.service-public.fr/particuliers/vosdroits/F34355 (accessed 21.1.20)

65 Code de la consommation art. L611-1 – L616-3; https://www.economie.gouv.fr/mediation-conso (Accessed 21 January 2020)

66 Steiner (n 38) 170.

67 Perrot (n 20) 303, 305; Code de justice administrative Art. L. 133-6 and L. 233-1 and following. Advancement in the *Conseil d'État* is formally decided by the *Conseil des ministres;* Code de justice administrative Art. L. 133-1 and following and L. 132-2. See more detailed regulation in Art. R. 134-1 and following.

68 Perrot (n 20) 288 ff, 295 ff; Code de justice administrative Art. L. 133-7, L. 233-3, L. 233-4; Guinchard S, Montagnier G and Varinard A, *Institutions juridictionnelles* (Dalloz 2007) 856–859. For a third type of recruitment, see Code de justice administrative Art. L. 233-7 and 233-8.

69 See ordonnance no 58-1270 du 22 décembre 1958 concerning the status of the judicial judges.

70 Decision from the *Conseil constitutionnel*: 119 DC du 22 juillet 1980; Guinchard, Montagnier and Varinard (n 68) 863.

Their status is regulated in the *Code de justice administrative*, which also regulates the regime of the judges in lower administrative courts.[71] For a long time, one of the most debated points of difference between the judicial and administrative judges was their irremovability, but this weakness in their independence was remedied by law in the 1980s, which limited the possibilities of moving the administrative judges to another service within the state without their consent.[72]

2.7 Some other characteristics of the two court systems

The physical appearance of court buildings within the two hierarchies is often quite different. The lower administrative courts occupy buildings that are often less stately than their judicial counterparts – where judges are surrounded by external signals of respect and status, and their impartiality is more established. The administrative judges do not wear robes and they appear more like civil servants than judges. Many administrative judges are quite conscious that they can be mistaken for being a part of the public administration and thus partial, and therefore emphasize their role as independent judges.

In the administrative courts, knowledge of the administration is considered valuable experience, and not a threat to the judges' independence or good judgment. This experience amongst the judges can help them reveal the administration's "tricks," and can also contribute to an easier acceptance of the courts' decisions by the administration.[73]

To conclude on the diversity in the French court system and to connect it to the French legal culture in general, one could say that "France is a multi-jural society with a variety of legal cultures that have some similarities and differences." The outcome seems to be that the law applied in the different courts has an impact on the legal culture partly because the law is designed for specific groups of people "who also form the body of judges who adjudicate on the application of those rules."[74]

71 Code de justice administrative, Art. L. 131-1 to L 136-2 and L. 231-1 to L. 236-3.

72 Code de justice administrative, Art. L. 231-3. But at the same time, the judges are not supposed to work for too long at the same court, and such limitations are considered to be according to the principle of irremovability. When changing court, judges will not lose his or hers place in the body of judges (*corps*). Code de justice administrative Art. L. 234-2 and R. 235-1 and 235-2; The Constitution Art. 64–65; ordonnance 58-1270 du 22 décembre 1958 Art. 4; Perrot (n 18) 298–300.

73 Perrot (n 20) 38; Braibant and Stirn (n 23) 514–515.

74 Bell, Boyron and Whittaker (n 44) 10.

3. Norm production – uncontested sources of law and case-law[75]

There is in French law a distinction between formal or uncontested and informal or contested sources of law. Formal sources are: the Constitution, EU law and international treaties, legislation (including government regulations), custom, and general principles of law. Influential or contested sources are case-law and legal writing (*la doctrine*) and a good lawyer will look at these for a reliable, but not binding, interpretation and statements of law. This division of law is anchored in Article 2 of the Constitution:[76] "government of the people, by the people and for the people," meaning that the formal sources of law have their origin, directly or indirectly, from decisions of the people, giving these sources legitimacy.[77]

3.1 Norm production from the parliament and the executive

The parliament and the government enact different types of norms, with different ranks (see Section 4 on the hierarchy of norms). Amendments to the Constitution, the norm with the highest rank, can be initiated by either the President of the Republic on the recommendation of the Prime Minister or by Members of Parliament, and are enacted by both houses of the Parliament, and can take effect after approval by referendum. However, a Government Bill to amend the Constitution shall not be submitted to referendum where the President of the Republic decides to submit it to Parliament convened in Congress, which is when the two houses sit together, where a three-fifths majority of the votes cast is necessary for the amendment to be approved.[78]

Under the 1958 Constitution, the power to enact legislation is divided between the Parliament and the government/the President. Statutes and government regulations (*règlements*) therefore have both an institutional and a material criterion. The institutional being that it is the work of the Parliament (*lois*) or the Executive (*règlements*) and the material that it must be within the limits of the Constitution, where the domains of parliamentary statutes are positively mentioned in Art. 34, 35, 53 and 72; whilst the area of government regulations is limited negatively in Art. 37, meaning that matters for government regulations are those not included in the domains of *lois*.

Article 34 of the Constitution distinguishes two categories of legislative domains. In the first, statutes shall *determine the rules* in the areas of, for instance, civil rights and

75 French sources of law (including contested "sources" and short explanations of the legal system) are found at https://www.legifrance.gouv.fr/.

76 Echoing Art. 2 of the Declaration of the Rights of Man and of the Citizen of 1789.

77 The Constitution Art. 2 last subsection: "Son principe est: gouvernement du peuple, par le peuple et pour le peuple."; Bell, Boyron and Whittaker (eds) (n 44) 14.

78 Catherine Elliott, Carole Geirnaert and Florence Houssais, *French Legal System and Legal Language. An introduction in French* (Longman 1998) 17–18; The Constitution Art. 89.

the fundamental guarantees granted to citizens for the exercise of their civil liberties: freedom, pluralism and the independence of media, determination of serious crimes, the base, rates and methods of collecting taxes and rules governing election-systems, fundamental guarantees granted to civil servants, and nationalization of companies. In the second category, statutes shall *lay down the fundamental principles* in the areas of: general organization of national defence, self-government, powers and revenue of territorial communities, education, preservation of the environment, systems of ownership, property rights and civil and commercial obligations, employment law, trade union law, and social security. In both areas, there is room for *règlements* completing statutes, and the division in Article 34 of the Constitution is of limited significance.[79]

The *Conseil constitutionnel* is exclusively competent to ensure conformity of parliamentary statutes with the Constitution, and also to decide cases concerning elections and referendums.[80] Prior to the promulgation of a law, the *Conseil* can control the constitutionality if initiated by the President, the prime minister, the president of the Senate, the president of the National assembly, or 60 members of the Parliament. After promulgation, a law's constitutionality can be controlled preliminarily (*la question prioritaire de constitutionnalité – QPC*) if the question is raised before a court, which in turn passes the question to the *Conseil constitutionnel* (via the *Cour de cassation* or the *Conseil d'État*).[81]

Besides the constitution there are different kinds of statutes:

a) *Lois organiques*, which supplement the Constitution in matters of organization of public powers.[82] These statutes are on a norm-level between constitution and ordinary *loi*.[83]
b) *Lois référendaires*. The President of the Republic may, on a recommendation from the Government or the National assembly and the Senate, submit to a referendum any Government Bill (*projet de loi*) which deals with, amongst other things, the organization of the public authorities, or reforms relating to economic, social or environmental policy.[84]
c) *Lois ordinaires*, which must be within the domain of Art. 34 of the 1958 Constitution (see above).
d) *Ordonnance*, which is provisionary law-making delegated by the assembly to the government in order for the latter to implement its program.[85]

---

79 Astrid Marais, *Introduction au droit* (Vuibert droit 2014) 106–107; Chapus, *Droit administratif général* (n 33) 68–69.

80 See http://www.conseil-constitutionnel.fr/conseil-constitutionnel/francais/le-conseil-constitutionnel/presentation-generale/presentation-generale.206.html (Accessed January 2019).

81 The Constitution of 4 October 1958 Art. 61 and 61-1; See Steiner (n 38) 6, 7; Perrot (n 20) 30–31.

82 See for instance Art. 6 of the Constitution regarding presidential elections and 65 regarding the status of judges.

83 Chapus, *Droit administratif général* (n 33) 80.

84 The Constitution Art. 11.

85 The Constitution Art. 38.

Lois ordinaires must be approved by both houses of the Parliament, the National assembly and the Senate, the former being the most important in a political perspective.[86] The President is in charge of promulgation of the statute within 15 days. The President can send the legislative proposal back for further consideration or ask the *Conseil constitutionnel* for a constitutional review. If the statute is passed, it enters into force following its publication in the official edition of statutes and decrees, the *Journal official. Lois et Décrets* (JO).[87] According to *Légifrance*, 80 statutes (*lois*) were published in 2013.[88]

Government regulations (*règlement*) can be categorized into two main categories, depending on whether they derive from the power held by the President and the Prime Minister according to the Constitution or from parliamentary delegation. Deriving from the Constitution (*règlements autonomes*), they are called *décrets* or *arrêtés*. The other form of *règlement* is given in relation to a parliamentary statute, to which it provides detailed rules necessary for their implementation (*règlements d'application*). They are also called *décrets*. These *règlements* can occur in both of the legislative domains listed in the Constitution Art. 34 – either because the Parliament ask for such regulation or because parliamentary statutes only define the fundamental principles, leaving the details to the government. At least in the field of administrative law, most statutes are prolonged by *règlements*.[89]

Ordonnances have the same legal force and effect as ordinary parliamentary statutes (*lois ordinaires*) when they are approved by Parliament. Prior to such approval they have status as *règlement*.[90] They can regulate the domain of power given to the Parliament (Art. 34). Another exceptional type of *règlement* regards certain decisions by the President of the Republic, in the event of a crisis, pursuant to Article 16 of the Constitution.[91] According to *Légifrance*, 24 *ordonnances* were published in 2013.[92]

The control of the compliance of *règlements* with legislation is ensured by the administrative courts and to some extent the judicial courts when necessary in criminal cases. If a question of the legality of a *règlement* is raised preliminary in a civil case, the ques-

86 Smith (n 12) 77.

87 The Constitution Art. 10, 24, 39–45 and 60, see http://www.journal-officiel.gouv.fr/.

88 74 in 2012, according to email from C. Garcia, La Direction de l'information légale et administrative (19 December 2014). In 2001, the estimated production of parliamentary statutes was 50–60 statutes per year, see Chapus, *Droit administratif général* (n 33) 70.

89 Marais (n 79) 107; Steiner (n 38) 9–13; Chapus, *Droit administratif général* (n 33) 67, 79–81. Read more about *règlements* on 649–695.

90 Steiner (n 38) 10; Chapus, *Droit administratif général* (n 33) 665 ff.

91 Between 1984 and 2006, 314 *ordonnances* were published – two thirds between 2000 and 2006. Some raised the question whether this was not an abuse of delegated legislation. See Marais (n 79) 108–109; Chapus, *Droit administratif général* (n 33) 82.

92 And 35 in 2012, according to email from C. Garcia, La Direction de l'information légale et administrative (19 December 2014).

tion must be passed to an administrative court.[93] *Règlements* must be consistent with all superior norms applicable in the French legal system.[94]

In 2007, there were 2,314 parliamentary statutes (*lois*) and 519 *ordonnances* with legislative rank in effect – representing a total of 22,505 articles. There were 23,883 *règlements* (with a total of 137,219 articles) in effect. The 69 applicable codes contained 33,742 articles of legislative rank, 57,080 articles *règlementaires*, and 11,415 articles in codes that do not distinguish between parliamentary legislation and government regulation.[95]

3.2 Codification *à la française*

> "Codification may take various forms ranging from mere compilations to full-fledged codification. This diversity is perhaps the major feature of codification today."[96]

A code can either be a coherent body of texts, which includes, according to a systematic plan, the whole of the rules in specific areas of law, and which are either the result of legislative works, or a *règlementaire* elaboration or a formal codification of pre-existing texts that are reclassified according to their origin: legislative or *règlementaire*. A code can also be a name given to a compilation of texts by a private publisher.[97] Consequently, there are several codification techniques.[98] An example of a code, which is both regrouping rules of administrative procedure, simplifying the law and codifying case-law, by *ordonnance* and *décret*, is new administrative code, *le Code des relations entre le public et l'administration.*[99] Examples of codes that were to a larger extent reformation of the law, are the Code civil (1804) and more recently the Code de procédure civile (1975) and

93 Marais (n 79) 117–118; Code pénal Art. 111-5; Perrot (n 20) 32; Braibant and Stirn (n 23) 528–529.

94 The control of the legality of *règlements autonomes* is more limited than the control of *règlements d'application*, see Chapus, *Droit administratif général* (n 33) 79, 28. See also 702.

95 Marais (n 79) 88.

96 French professor Tallon (1979), cited in Steiner (n 38) 30. See also Bureau (n 15) 225–230.

97 Gérard Cornu, *Vocabulaire juridique* (Puf 2001): "corps cohérent de textes englobant selon un plan systématique l'ensemble des règles relatives à une matière et issu, soit de travaux législatifs (Code civil, Code pénal), soit d'une élaboration réglementaire (Nouveau Code de procédure civile), soit d'une codification formelle (par décret) de textes préexistants et reclassés selon leur origine (partie législative, partie règlementaire etc. Ex. Code de l'organisation judiciaire, Code de la construction et de l'habitation, Code de l'administration communale etc.) … Nom donné à des compilations de textes publiés par un éditeur." (coherent body of texts encompassing according to a systematic plan all the rules relating to a matter and resulting either from legislative work (Civil Code, Criminal Code), or from regulatory development (New Code of Civil Procedure), or from a formal codification (by decree) of preexisting texts and reclassified according to their origin (legislative part, regulatory part etc. Ex. Code of the judicial organization, Code of construction and housing, Code of municipal administration etc.) … Name given to compilations of texts published by an editor.)

98 Bureau (n 15) 226.

99 Loi no 2013-1005 du 12 novembre 2013 habilitant le Gouvernement à simplifier les relations entre l'administration et les citoyens; Ordonnance n° 2015-1341 du 23 octobre 2015 relative aux dispositions législatives du code des relations entre le public et l'administration; Décret n° 2015-1342 du 23 octobre 2015 relatif aux dispositions réglementaires du code des relations entre le public et l›administration.

the Code pénal (1992). Especially the Code civil has had an important influence on the legal culture, illustrated by its longevity.[100] Approximately 60 % of the *lois* and 30 % of the *texts réglementaires* in force are codified.[101]

Modern codes, made by the (1989) *Commission supérieure de la codification,*[102] have little in common with the Napoleonic codes, like the Code civil mentioned above, which were reconsiderations of the law in a particular field. Modern French codes are more consolidations of pre-existing law.[103] The *Commission supérieure de codification* is an advisory body, set up with statutory existence and devoted to restatement of the existing law in codes – and not law reforms. Still, minor changes are allowed to be made on an informal basis, when contradictions are found between the provisions or to ensure the respect of the norm hierarchy.[104]

An important limitation in the content of these codes is that only statutes and regulations are codified. This excludes case-law, custom, international law, and EU law.[105] For instance, in the area of administrative law the codes don't cover all the dominant principles, since these are laid down by case-law, however, the new *Code des relations entre le public et l'administration* has undertaken, as part of the consolidation, the codification of case-law.[106]

The method used to create codes has taken place in a series of stages, usually by statute or *décret*. To accelerate codification, in 1999 the Parliament passed a statute allowing the government to edict a certain number of codes by *ordonnance* which was later given legislative status by the Parliament. For instance, this is the case for the *Code rural*, the *Code de l'éducation,* the *Code de commerce, and more recently the Code des relations entre le public et l'administration.*[107]

The numbering system in a code is logical, though not always easy to memorize. It consists of numbers (like in Code civil), but often the numbers are preceded by a letter: L for *Loi*, R for *décret en Conseil d'État*, D for *décret simple,* and A for *arrêtés*, for instance, Art. L121-2 to L121-3 on the *Conseil d'État*'s organization and functioning. Paragraphs containing government regulations (*règlementaire*) on the same topic have the same number and heading but start with R or D, in this case Art. R121-1 to R121-

100 Terré (n 22) 71-79.

101 Jean-Marc Sauvé, "25 ans de la relance de la codification" (Intervention lors du colloque organisé par l'Institut francais des sciences administratives (IFSA) au Conseil d'État. 13 October 2015), I B 2, available at https://www.conseil-etat.fr/actualites/discours-et-interventions/25-ans-de-la-relance-de-la-codification (Accessed 18 February 2020)

102 Décret n°89-647 du 12 septembre 1989 relatif à la composition et au fonctionnement de la Commission supérieure de codification. See also: https://www.gouvernement.fr/commission-superieure-de-codification.

103 Steiner (n 35) 30–31.

104 Loi n° 99-1071 du 16 décembre 1999 portant habilitation du Gouvernement à procéder, par ordonnances, à l'adoption de la partie Législative de certains codes; Bureau (n 17) 229; Bell, Boyron and Whittaker (n 44) 24.

105 Bureau (n 17) 230; But EU law has been incorporated in the Code civil.

106 Chapus, *Droit administratif général* (n 33) 85–87; Sauvé (n 101) II A 2.

107 Bureau (n 17) 226; See loi du 16 décembre 1999; Chapus, *Droit administratif général* (n 33) 85–87; Loi no 2013-1005 du 12 novembre 2013 habilitant le Gouvernement à simplifier les relations entre l'administration et les citoyens.

14. This way headings and article numbers correspond and are allocated in chapters, titles and books.[108]

3.3 Treaties and EU law

The French legal system is neither a purely dualist system, nor a purely monist system, but a sort of hybrid where there must be made a distinction between EU law and law arising under other international treaties. The Constitution (Art. 55) gives the impression of a monist system, declaring that "treaties or agreements duly ratified or approved shall, upon publication, prevail over acts of Parliament, subject with respect to each agreement or treaty, and to its application by the other party." Some treaties are signed by the President (Art. 52), but others require the approval of the Parliament (Art. 53). For treaties that need approval from the Parliament, the French system is more of a dualistic character.

The European Convention on Human Rights has been particularly important and influenced French law in several ways, mainly because the courts must disregard national law inconsistent with the Convention, and the legislator has to change such inconsistent statutes, as well as by being a source of inspiration of changes in French law.[109]

The Constitution contains a separate chapter on EU law.[110] EU law is considered to be part of international treaties that have been given supremacy over national legislation (between *le bloc constitutionnel* and statutes in the norm hierarchy, see Section 4) in Art. 55. As for all EU members, EU regulations have a direct effect in the French legal system when they are published in the *Journal officiel* of the European community. EU directives are binding in the result to be achieved but leave it to the member states to choose the form and method. In France the directives must be transpositioned to be effective and invoked before French courts and authorities.[111] Statutes' conformity with treaties (*contrôle de conventionalité*) is not controlled by the *Conseil constitutionnel*, but by the judicial and administrative courts.[112]

EU law has had a significant impact on French administrative law, for instance the principle of legitimate expectation and the principle of proportionality.[113] Cases from the European Court of Human Rights (ECHR) have led to for example changes in courts procedure: the *rapporteurs publics* in the administrative courts and the *ministère public*

108 Décret n°89-647 du 12 septembre 1989 relatif à la composition et au fonctionnement de la Commission supérieure de codification; Steiner (n 38) 38–39, 40-41; Bell, Boyron and Whittaker (n 44) 24. See also the annual reports of the *Commission supérieure de codification*, available at https://www.legifrance.gouv.fr/Droit-francais/Codification/Rapports-annuels-de-la-CSC (Accessed 6 December 2019).

109 Cf. Art. 55; Bell, Boyron and Whittaker (n 44) 17–19; Chapus, *Droit administratif général* (n 33) 133–134; Terré (n 23) 215–217.

110 Chapter XV – On the European Union.

111 Treaty on the Functioning of the European Union (TFEU) Art. 288; Chapus, *Droit administratif général* (n 33) 135; Bell, Boyron and Whittaker (n 44) 19–20.

112 Perrot (n 20) 31–32.

113 Steiner (n 38) 270.

in the judicial courts, have been excluded from participating in their respective court's deliberations. And before the administrative courts, the parties are, within reasonable time, informed of the *sens* of the report (*conclusions*) of the *rapporteur public*, and they are given the possibility to present their opinion orally or written (*note en délibéré*).[114]

3.4 Custom (*coutume*)

Since the Napoleonic codifications, custom has been a minor source of law, with the exception of some areas, such as contract, property, labour, and especially commercial law, where it is a significant element in determining what the law is. There are certain prerequisites for custom: a practice of long duration, a certain geographic expansion (a social environment, a group of professionals, for instance), a belief that the practice is obligatory, and consistency with the law.[115] An example is the local custom of cock-fights in some areas of France. Where this custom is uninterrupted, such practice is not considered indictable by the Code criminal.[116]

3.5 Case-law (*jurisprudence*) and the general principles of law (*principes généraux de droit*)

Although being a very influential source of law and despite its persuasive value for similar, future cases, case-law is not officially a binding source of law in the French legal system, and therefore courts are not producers of law *in a formal sense*. The reason is again to be found in the revolutionaries' scepticism against the regional tribunals at the time (*les parlements*), and their efforts to reduce these judges' influence on the administration.[117] Furthermore, influenced by Montesquieu's doctrine of separation of powers, judges were not allowed to interfere with the legislator's law-making function and their decisions could therefore not constitute binding precedents. The courts should only apply legislative texts. This rule was propounded in the Code civil Art. 5 and 1355, which taken together have been applied as a prohibition for the courts to determine in advance the

114 This practice has been considered to be in conformity with Article 6 of the Convention, see *Marc-Antoine v France* App no 54984/04 (ECtHR, 4 June 2013, decision); Jean-Marc Sauvé and Olivier Fuchs, 'Justice administrative et État de droit' (10 February 2014) 11, available at https://www.conseil-etat.fr/actualites/discours-et-interventions/justice-administrative-et-etat-de-droit#1 (Accessed 6 December 2019); Jean-Marc Sauvé and Stéphane Eustache, 'Perspectives sur la justice administrative' (6 October 2014) 3, available at https://www.conseil-etat.fr/actualites/discours-et-interventions/perspectives-sur-la-justice-administrative#_ftn1 (Accessed 6 December 2019); Steiner (n 38) 200-201.

115 Terré (n 23) 317–328; Bell, Boyron and Whittaker (n 44) 25; Steiner (n 38) 51; Elliott, Geirnaert and Houssais (n 78) 32.

116 Code pénal Art. 521-1; Marais (n 79) 128–129.

117 Torstein Eckhoff and Eivind Smith, *Forvaltningsrett* (10th ed, Universitetsforlaget 2018) 519.

outcome of subsequent similar litigation involving different parties.[118] But legislation, for instance Code civil and other legislative texts, cannot cover every question that will come up, and in some areas, as in the field of administrative law, for a very long time there were almost no texts. Administrative law is therefore fundamentally made out of case-law, parts of it being adopted as legislation. Consequently, French judges routinely make rules, as judges do in other legal systems.[119] The status of case-law can therefore seem a bit dishonest.[120] In the following, the status of case-law will be described first by drafting out the official status and secondly the more *de facto* point of view.

Formally, courts are only bound by legislation and general principles of law (*principes généraux de droit*). There are two exceptions: Decisions given by the *Conseil constitutionnel* are binding on public and administrative authorities and on all courts. Secondly, when the *Cour de Cassation* quashes for the second time a decision from a lower court (in the same case) for not having correctly applied the law, the *Cour de cassation*'s decision has a binding effect on the (third) lower court to treat the case. This does not happen often, as the second lower court usually follows the ruling of the *Cour de Cassation.*[121]

Keeping in mind these main principles, the law regarding French precedents has been summarized like this: precedents do not need to be followed in subsequent, similar cases. As a consequence, even the highest courts are not bound by their own previous decisions. Similarly, lower courts are not bound by the decisions of superior courts. Explicit reference by a court to its own precedents when giving a decision and more generally, citation of previous cases is not allowed when these are meant to serve as a legal basis for the court's decision.[122] As a consequence, failure by a court to follow a precedent cannot constitute a valid ground for appeal.[123]

However, from a more practical point of view, case-law is an important source of law. Although facts are not discussed and compared to prior decisions by the judges – courts rarely cite a single case as a legal authority – the counsel, *avocat général*, or a *rapporteur public* routinely refer to past precedents and the facts in those given cases, in

118 Smith (n 12); Steiner (n 38) 64–66; Elliott, Geirnaert and Houssais (n 78) 30; Code civil Art. 5: "Il est défendu aux juges de prononcer par voie de disposition générale et réglementaire sur les causes qui leur sont soumises." (*In the cases that are referred to them, judges are forbidden to pronounce judgment by way of general and regulatory dispositions.*) And Art. 1355: "L'autorité de la chose jugée n'a lieu qu'à l'égard de ce qui a fait l'objet du jugement. Il faut que la chose demandée soit la même; que la demande soit fondée sur la même cause; que la demande soit entre les mêmes parties, et formée par elles et contre elles en la même qualité." (*The authority of res judicata applies only to what was the object of a judgment. It is necessary that the thing claimed be the same; that the claim be based on the same cause; that the claim be between the same parties and brought by them and against them acting in the same qualities.*)

119 Steiner (n 38) 64.

120 Bell, Boyron and Whittaker (n 44) 31.

121 The Constitution Art. 62 and Code de l'organisation judiciaire Art. L 431-6; Marais (n 79) 135–136; Steiner (n 38) 64, 68–69.

122 It should be pointed out that what is liable to being quashed by the supreme courts is not the court's actual following of a precedent, but the explicit statement by the court that it is bound by a judicial precedent.

123 Steiner (n 38) 68–70. Eva Steiner is frequently referred to in this section. She is a Senior Lecturer at King's College London where she has taught French law for many years. She has been a practicing lawyer at the French Bar and has taught French law for undergraduate and postgraduate students at several of the universities of Paris, see the backing of the cover of her book *French legal method* (Oxford University Press 2002).

their arguments and submissions to court.[124] Furthermore, French administrative law, and to a lesser extent, French constitutional law, are considered "case-based systems, which operate in very similar ways to the common law, mainly because of the absence of codifications in the sense of a restatement of general principles."[125]

Two psychological and sociological reasons can explain why precedents are part of legal arguing before the courts and why French judges feel compelled to follow them: the "law of imitation" and "the law of continuity." Judges in lower courts find it expedient to follow a solution to a legal question that has been set out by a higher court. To follow the same model as a higher court also makes it less probable that the decision will be reversed if appealed. In general, continuity and consistency are considered desirable features in judicial decisions, and therefore the highest courts are less likely to overrule their own established precedents. The result is that French judges feel compelled to follow precedents.[126]

Bernard Stirn and the late Guy Braibant[127] have described the role of precedent as somewhat of a paradox, since it practically but not formally plays an essential role.[128] Some have gone as far as asking for a legislative intervention, which could give an official status to the creative power of the courts with the aim of clarifying the situation. It has

124 Steiner (n 38) 70–71; Catherine Elliott, Eric Jeanpierre and Catherine Vernon (n 13) 78.

125 Bell, Boyron and Whittaker (n 44) 7.

126 It has been suggested that they should feel even more compelled to do so than their common law counterparts, because French judges are not equipped with the same instruments to "escape" precedents. Steiner (n 38) 68–73; Terré (n 23) 295–296.

127 Respectively, former president of the *Conseil d'État*'s dispute section (*Section du contentieux*) and former president of the *Conseil d'État*'s *Section du rapport et des études*.

128 Braibant and Stirn (n 23) 281–282: "la jurisprudence n'est pas formellement une source de légalité, sauf dans le cas de la chose jugée qui occupe une place relativement peu importante dans l'ensemble des sources. On ne peut pas annuler un acte administratif parce qu'il est contraire à une décision de jurisprudence rendue quelques années auparavant dans une autre affaire. En ce sens, ce n'est pas théoriquement et juridiquement une source de légalité. Et pourtant, la jurisprudence joue un rôle essentiel dans cet ensemble des sources de la légalité: d'abord, parce que, souvent, il en précise la portée; ensuite, parce qu'il dégage et explicite les principes généraux du droit qui sont une source en eux-mêmes; enfin parce que c'est la jurisprudence qui a élaboré les théories des droits acquis et de la chose jugée. Par conséquence, à travers l'ensemble de ces sources, la jurisprudence joue un rôle essentiel, mais c'est un rôle pratique et non juridique." (Case-law is not formally a source of legality, except in the case of res judicata which occupies a relatively unimportant place in all of the sources. You cannot overturn an administrative act because it is contrary to a case-law decision made a few years earlier in another case. In this sense, it is not theoretically and legally a source of legality. And yet, jurisprudence plays an essential role in this set of sources of legality: first, because it often specifies its scope; second, because it identifies and explains the general principles of law, which are a source in themselves; finally because it is the jurisprudence which developed the theories of acquired rights and res judicata. Consequently, through all of these sources, case-law plays an essential role, but it is a practical and not a legal role.)

been suggested that case-law should be referred to as "*légisprudence*" instead of *jurisprudence*, and the judges "*jurislateurs*," since the courts in fact create law.[129]

Case-law has formed an officially acknowledged source of law, known as general principles of law (*principes généraux de droit*). These are authoritative rules of law established by the courts and binding upon them. Especially in the area of administrative law there are many of these principles, since this area of law has not been codified to the same extent as the civil law. For instance, the right to a hearing (*le droit de la défense*) was developed by the *Conseil d'État*, and in the area of private law, courts developed the principle of unjust enrichment (*enrichissement sans cause*), which led to the recognition of a separate remedy called the *action de in rem verso*, even though it was not contained in the Code.[130]

French jurisprudence is published in two main law reports. Approximately two-thirds of the decisions from the *Cour de cassation* are published in *Bulletin de la Cour de cassation*. About one-sixth of the decisions for *Conseil d'État*, and a few from lower administrative courts, are published in *Recueil des décisions du Conseil d'État*, called *Recueil Lebon*. It is also possible to find decisions on the Internet portals of each high court and on legifrance.fr.[131]

Decisions from the ECHR and the Court of Justice of the European Union (CJEU) are used directly before the courts in the sense that French judges apply this jurisprudence and make reference to it, but they do not apply them unless they are invoked by the parties.[132] Also decisions from other countries have been mentioned by the French judiciary, as an instrument of interpretation.[133]

---

129 Marais (n 79) 150. In the area of administrative law, this is particularly clear, and the late professor René Chapus expressed it like this, in *Droit administratif général* (n 33) 92–93: "Si la juridiction administrative ne faisait rien d'autre (comme c'est le cas, officiellement, des tribunaux judiciaires) qu'interpréter le droit écrit, son rôle dans la formation du droit administratif serait déjà remarquable. Mais elle fait beaucoup plus. … Parce que le droit administratif n'est pas codifié (au sens où l'est le droit civil), parce qu'aucune loi n'a jamais déterminé ses notions fondamentales et ses principes dominants, il est revenu au juge administratif de se faire, à proprement parler, jurislateur." (If the administrative jurisdiction did nothing else (as is the case, officially, of the judicial courts) than to interpret written law, its role in the formation of administrative law would already be remarkable. But it does much more. … Because administrative law is not codified (in the sense that civil law is), andbecause no law has ever determined its fundamental concepts and dominant principles, it is up to the administrative judge to be, strictly speaking, "jurislateur".)

130 Chapus, *Droit administratif général* (n 33) 92; Bell, Boyron and Whittaker (n 44) 32–33; Marais (n 79) 139–140; Steiner (n 38) 52; Some of *Conseil d'État*'s cases have been translated to English (and other languages), see http://english.conseil-etat.fr/Judging.

131 Bell, Boyron and Whittaker (n 44) 519–520.

132 See for instance a case decided by the *Conseil d'État*: Décision no 345103 (date de lecture: 30/12/2014) and a case before the *Cour de cassation*: Arrêt n° 1357 du 19 novembre 2014; Elliott, Jeanpierre and Vernon (n 13) 79; Marais (n 79) 102.

133 Elliott, Jeanpierre and Vernon (n 13) 79–80.

4. Legal method

Lord Justice Cooper, in a famous address delivered to Edinburgh University in 1950 stated:

> "The civilian naturally reasons from principles to instance, the common lawyer from instances to principles. The civilian puts his faith in syllogisms, the common lawyer in precedents; the first silently asking himself as each new problem arises, 'What should we do this time?' and the second asking aloud in the same situation, 'What did we do last time?'"[134]

4.1 Hierarchy of legal sources

As mentioned in Section 3, in French law there is an important distinction between formal sources of law and influential sources or contested and uncontested sources. Formal sources are the Constitution, the EU law and international treaties, legislation, custom and general principles of law. These sources are classified and hierarchized as shown in the pyramid below. The Constitution also includes in broader terms the 1789 Declaration of the Rights of Man, the social and economic rights listed in the preamble of the former 1946 Constitution, the fundamental principles recognized by the laws of the Republic as referred to in the 1946 preamble, and the rights and duties defined by the 2004 Charter of the environment; these are referred to as *le bloc de constitutionnalité*.[135]

Second from the top in the French norm-hierarchy we find treaties (international and EU). This rank is in accordance with the Constitution, which states their precedence over domestic parliamentary statutes (Art. 55).

Below treaties we find *lois*; the different types of French statutes have different rank. Between parliamentary statutes and government regulations (*règlements*) we find the general principles of law, as being deduced from *jurisprudence*.[136]

French norm hierarchy

Bloc de constitutionnalité

Treaties (international and EU)

Parliamentary statutes (*Lois organiques* are above *Lois ordinaires and ordonnances*)

Principes généraux de droit

Règlements

134 Lord Justice Cooper, in a famous address delivered to Edinburgh University (1950), cited in Steiner (n 38) 112.

135 The Constitution of 4 October 1958 Art. 61 and 61-1; See Steiner (n 38) 6, 7.

136 Chapus, *Droit administratif général* (n 33) 117: "Il est en effet établi que seule une loi (ou une convention internationale) peut tenir en échec un principe général du droit." See also 111–112; Perrot (n 20) 30.

4.2 Statutory interpretation

The starting point of statutory interpretation seems uncomplicated: When a statute is clear, it must be followed, and the text shouldn't be interpreted. This "rule" has exceptions: When the literal meaning of the text results in an absurdity in the case at hand, the judge can look for the legislative intent.[137]

Because French legislation is usually drafted in a rather general and open-textured manner, interpretation is often necessary, and there may also be a need to fill in gaps in the text. Different methods are used to interpret statutes; apart from a very few specific code provisions, these are not authoritative statements but the result of customary law, judicial practice, and legal writing. In addition to the starting point mentioned above (when a statute is clear, it must be followed), the principles of statutory interpretation have been expressed like this: When the language of the statute is obscure or ambiguous, one should construe it in accordance with its spirit rather than its letter. French judges are not tied too closely to the wording of a statutory text, and when diverging, they look to the legislator's purpose. Their approach to interpretation is traditionally fairly liberal and mainly purposive.[138]

Where there is a gap in the law or the statutory law is ambiguous, judges have a duty to rule in the case at hand (cf. Art. 4 Code civil). In such cases, judges are forced to make the rule and are thus given a normative function.[139] In a case concerning surrogacy, the *Cour de cassation* found surrogacy illegal based on Code civil Art. 1128 as it sounded until 2016, which forbade transactions with certain "things" (*choses*). The wording "things" does obviously not include a human being. Nevertheless, the court used this provision analogically to create a legal principle (*le principe d'indisponibilité du corps humain*).[140]

Lacunae may occur not only in the absence of a clear text, but also when a change in society has made the text inappropriate. In the case *Association des centres éducatifs du*

---

137 Steiner (n 38) 47–48; Marais (n 79) 204–205; Terré (n 23) 465–466.

138 Bell, Boyron and Whittaker (n 44) 33; Steiner (n 38) 45–47, 50. On 153: "As experience shows, it is extremely unlikely that judges will find an enacted rule or principle that corresponds exactly to a given set of facts. Legal rules, especially in a codified system as in France, do not provide for concrete facts; they only refer to categories of facts in a very abstract way. This frequently forces French judges to look for code provisions governing a class of situations capable of encompassing situations brought before them which have not been specially 'catered for'. In these circumstances, judges are very often faced with a choice between competing provisions, or even between competing interpretations of the same provision. The exercise of this choice will very often be dependent upon the specific nature of the case or upon comparisons judges can make with similar situations identified in earlier cases, which may be regarded as falling within the scope of the rule selected. A particulate choice between alternative rules may also be dictated by practical or policy-based arguments."

139 Code civil Art. 4: "Le juge qui refusera de juger, sous prétexte du silence, de l'obscurité ou de l'insuffisance de la loi, pourra être poursuivi comme coupable de déni de justice." (A judge who refuses to give judgment on the pretext of legislation being silent, obscure or insufficient may be prosecuted for being guilty of a denial of justice.); Marais (n 79) 138; Steiner (n 38) 46–47, 111–112; Maryse Deguergue, 'Jurisprudence' Denis Alland and Stéphane Rials (eds), *Dictionnaire de la culture juridique* (Lamy 2003) 885.

140 Code civil Art. 1128 as it sounded until 2016: "Il n'y a que les choses qui sont dans le commerce qui puissent être l'objet des conventions."; Marais (n 79) 140; Steiner (n 38) 52.

Limousin v Blieck, the *Cour de cassation* allowed an application of Code civil Art. 1384, now Art. 1242, to a new situation that the legislator of 1804 could not have foreseen: A centre for the handicapped, which had undertaken to look after a mentally handicapped person who had set fire to the plaintiff's property, was held liable for the damages although the wording in Art. 1384 was that "one" (*on*) could be held responsible for other people for whom one was answerable, and the examples in the provision included categories of persons, not a centre for handicapped people.[141]

When judges need to interpret statutes, they have several aids to construct the interpretation; especially important are preparatory works and to a lesser extent equity (*équité*). When there is a gap in statutory law the judges would normally use techniques of logical interpretation, and only exceptionally resort to custom and equity.[142]

4.3 Preparatory works (*travaux préparatoires*)

Preparatory works are not considered a formal source of law, but are a predominant external aid to interpretation, since it may help determine the meaning of a statute. The preparatory works are published in the *Journal official* and available online.[143] They include draft bills, statements made by the Minister or other promoter of the bill (*exposé des motifs*), reports made by official parliamentary committees, amendments, which were proposed and discussed, and the parliamentary debates.

The use of preparatory works is still limited. The judge may consult the preparatory works to interpret a statute, but not when the text is clear and therefore should be certain. A decision cannot be quashed on the basis of lack of reference to *travaux préparatoires* in interpreting the law. Further, recourse to parliamentary materials is of limited assistance when interpreting older statutes where circumstances have changed and the knowledge of the intention of the legislator is less relevant. French judges feel free to adapt older statutes to new situations without regards to the preparatory works. Since French judges hardly ever explicitly justify their decisions, the use of preparatory works must be assumed based on whether the court confirms an interpretation based on preparatory works proposed by a particular scholar, by the *rapporteur public* or *the avocat general.*[144]

---

141 See case D. 1991, 324 (89-15231). Code civil former Art. 1384, now Art. 1242 first subsection: "On est responsable non seulement du dommage que l'on cause par son propre fait, mais encore de celui qui est causé par le fait des personnes dont on doit répondre, ou des choses que l'on a sous sa garde." (We are responsible not only for the damage caused by our own act, but also for that which is caused by the acts of persons for whom we are responsible, or by things that are in our custody.); Steiner (n 38) 49–50.

142 Steiner (n 38) 47, 51. See also a quotation of the French comparative scholar René David from his *French law* (Baton Rouge 1972) in Bell, Boyron and Whittaker (n 44) 25: "In the absence of an applicable statute or custom, decisions can be based on principles of equity, reason, justice, or tradition." But see a more restrictive approach to equity in Terré (n 23) 287.

143 See for instance http://www.legifrance.gouv.fr/dossiers_legislatifs.jsp (Accessed January 2019). Statutes originating from the Parliament are *proposition de loi*, and statutes originating from the government are called *projet de loi*. Marais (n 79) 105; Steiner (n 38) 56–57.

144 Marais (n 79) 205; Steiner (n 38) 47–48, 57; Elliott, Jeanpierre and Vernon (n 13) 79.

4.4 The role of equity (*équité*)

"L'équité n'est pas une norme mais un procédé d'émergence de normes…"[145]

Equity is not considered a proper source of law and the application of *équité* in French law is limited. In the area of private law there are code provisions that the courts would rather interpret and apply for analogous situations, rather than turn to equity. This technique is facilitated by the frequent use of general statements of principles in many code provisions.

Further, equity does not have a good connotation in France; again, there is a connection with changes initiated by the revolutionaries, due to the pre-revolutionary society. French lawyers immediately associate it with the idea of arbitrary action. "God save us from the equity of the parliaments [pre-revolutionary courts]," is a formula that is often cited and continues to influence the thinking of lawyers and judges. Apart from a few exceptional cases where the legislator himself has referred to equity, a litigant has no chance of success if he simply argues the equity of his position before the judge. The French judge decides in law, not in equity.[146]

Recourse to equity has occurred first when the text allows it, for instance in Code civil Art. 565, 815–13, 1194, and 1579. Although courts cannot in principle rule in equity, equity can to a certain extent give room for fairness and avoid an unjust outcome in a case. An example is how courts have censored property owners' malicious use of their rights as owners, and also the doctrine of *enrichissement sans cause*, which is a pure creation of the courts and allows a person to recover money paid where there is no contract and another person has been unjustly enriched. The general principles of law are related to equity in the way that they have also been used to fill gaps in the law.[147]

Further, equity plays an important role in arbitration (*arbitrage*), where the parties in conflict may allow the arbitrator to settle the case not only on the basis of law, but also on the basis of equity – as a conciliator (*amiable-compositeurs*).[148] Finally, it should be mentioned that the French ombudsman equivalent, the *Défenseur des droits*, is allowed to apply equity – thus implicitly recognising that applying law without recourse to *équité* may lead to injustices.[149]

145 'Equity is not a norm, but a proceeding of emergences of norms…' Marjolaine Fouletier, *Recherches sur l'équité en droit public français* (L.G.D.J 2003) 251.

146 René David cited in Steiner (n 38) 51; Terré (n 23) 16, 287.

147 Steiner (n 38) 51–52; Marais (n 79) 247; Fouletier (n 145) 23–24; Terré (n 23) 15.

148 Terré (n 23) 16.

149 Steiner (n 38) 51–52; For references concerning the *Défenseur des droits*, see loi organique no 2011-333 du 29 mars 2011 Art. 6, 25 and 26.

4.5 Factors giving weight to precedents

When judges normally do not turn to equity to fill in gaps in the law, they search for more rational and solid solutions, which can be found in precedents.[150] There are certain specific factors giving weight to courts' decisions. Firstly, the rank of the court giving the judgment; obviously, the higher the rank of the court giving the decision, the more weight is carried by its decisions. Both the *Cour de cassation* and the *Conseil d'État* are the highest courts within each hierarchy. Whilst the former has the competence to quash cases, the latter, in addition to quashing cases (*cassation*), has quite a wide competence to settle cases (*appel*).[151] Within the two highest courts, many compositions of the courts' judges when deciding cases are possible, and these compositions do not have the same rank. In general, as the case becomes more important, more judges will participate in deciding it.[152]

Also decisions from lower courts can be authoritative, and this is especially the case when higher courts have not yet decided on a particular issue of law and when higher courts have delivered a decision on a particular question and lower courts follow this. It could also be the case when a legal question in a case is categorized as fact, which is left to the decisions of lower courts.[153]

Secondly, a decision will have more weight as precedent if it is attached to a consistent line of precedents. However, a single decision may also form precedent; this is the case when it represents an overruling of its own established *jurisprudence* (*revirement de jurisprudence*) and when it is considered a "leading case." Overruling cases have considerable importance attached to them and lower courts will in general follow them. There is more overruling now than earlier due to the development of the law and the need to make domestic law comply with new European law and case-law. The relatively limited number of leading cases, called *arrêts de principe*, where the court states clearly a principle of general application using broad terms, can also have important weight attached to them. The issues raised in these cases are often important, controversial, and/or new. They are widely commented on by legal authors.[154]

A final remark on judicial decisions should be made concerning a function of their drafting and legal certainty. Judges are required to state the grounds for their decisions

150 Terré (n 23) 287: "À défaut d'une solution d'équité, le juge doit donc fournir une solution rationnelle: il voudra se déterminer non pas au hazard, mais en se fondant sur des raisons solides, et parmi celles-ci, il y des décisions rendues antérieurement dans des cas identiques. Le juge s'appuiera sur les precedents judiciaires." (In the absence of a solution of fairness, the judge must therefore provide a rational solution: he will want to decide not at random, but on the basis of solid reasons, and among these, there are decisions rendered previously in identical cases. The judge will rely on the judicial precedents.)

151 Code de la justice administrative Art. L 321-1, L321-2, L 331-1 and R 321-1; Steiner (n 38) 71–72; https://www.courdecassation.fr/about_the_court_9256.html.

152 In the *Cour de cassation* they are called *l'assemblée plénière* and *chambre mixte*, and in *Conseil d'État, l'assemblée du contentieux* and *l'assemblée de section*, cf. Code de l'organisation judiciaire Art. L 431-5 and 431-6; Code de justice administrative Art. R. 122-18 and R. 122-20.

153 Steiner (n 38) 73–74.

154 Ibid 99–103.

and the judgments are drafted according to a deductive method where the final ruling is presented as the necessary outcome of a logical set of arguments.[155] The syllogism in setting out the grounds for the decision provides rules for dealing with similar cases in the future and facilitates consistency and predictability. It therefore leads to a greater degree of certainty within the legal system. However, the succinct style of the drafting of French judgments has the opposite function, since the judgment alone can sometimes make it difficult to predict how the judges will reason the next time they meet a similar factual situation. The judgments, especially those of the highest courts, are remarkably brief and the syllogism causes a peculiar logical and grammatical construction. The language is highly technical and chosen meticulously. The decisions do not contain any kind of policy or interpretative discussion and no expression of dissenting opinion.[156] They are drafted so elliptically that it is often only by reading the conclusions of the *rapporteur public*, which are published only in the most important cases, and the *ministère public* that one can discern the point in a case which determines the case (*ratio decidendi*). Commentaries to court decisions, made by authors with access to the case files, are therefore often studied.[157] The consequences especially for administrative law, are for instance that in practice, this field of law is accessible only for the initiates.[158] This way of drafting judgments is considered elegant and prestigious by some, whilst others have expressed concern, arguing that judgments should be drafted in a more accessible manner in order to ensure the confidence between the public and the courts.[159] A working group lead by the former president of the dispute section in *Conseil d'État, Bernard Stirn,* has recently developed a *Vade-mecum* giving directions for drafting judgments in a more comprehensible manner.[160]

155 Code de procédure civile Art. 455 first subsection: "Le jugement doit exposer succinctement les prétentions respectives des parties et leurs moyens. Cet exposé peut revêtir la forme d'un visa des conclusions des parties avec l'indication de leur date. Le jugement doit être motivé." (The judgement must set forth succinctly the respective claims of the parties and their grounds. Such presentation may take the form of a reference to the pleadings of the parties with the indication of their date. The judgement must be reasoned.)

156 Code de procédure civile Art. 455; Code de la justice administrative Art. L 9; Steiner (n 38) 111, 129, 131; Elliott, Jeanpierre and Vernon (n 13) 83.

157 See for instance Marceau Long, Prosper Weil, Guy Braibant †, Pierre Delvolvé and Bruno Genevois, *Les gands arrêts de la jurisprudence administrative* (Dalloz 2013); Steiner (n 38) 112, 120–122.

158 Chapus, *Droit administratif général* (n 33) 7, 125.

159 Steiner (n 38) 130. The vice-president of the *Conseil d'État* from 2006–2018, Jean-Marc Sauvé, mentioned accessibility and intelligibility of the judicial decisions, as one of the administrative courts' challenges. See Sauvé and Eustache (n 114) 6.

160 Conseil d'État, 'Vade-mecum sur la rédaction des décisions de la juridiction administrative', available at https://www.conseil-etat.fr/actualites/actualites/juridiction-administrative-nouveaux-modes-de-redaction-des-decisions (Accessed 12 December 2019).

4.6 Legal writing (*doctrine*)

The writing of jurists, academics and practitioners (like judges), is often referred to as *la doctrine,*[161] and is not considered a formal source of law. Legal writing cannot create law but can be influential in its capacity to construct law by guiding the judges, especially when it is recent and consistent. Certain authors have had a major influence on case-law. Legal writing can therefore be an important legal argument base. *La doctrine* is generally not cited in court decisions, but used both by judges and counsel, *Ministère public* and the *rapporteur public* when preparing for court hearings and judgments.[162]

The typical approach to a legal subject starts with *de lege lata* – a systematic view of statutes and codes as interpreted by the courts, and then proceeds to *de lege ferenda* – proposing how the deficiencies or gaps in the law should be remedied. An interesting type of legal writings concern jurisprudence, called *notes d'arrêts*, and are commentaries to court decisions. They started as a result of the need of further explanation of the brief judgments and are a form of extended footnotes to reported cases in law reports. The authors usually have access to the court's files through a personal connection or having worked with lawyers or judges involved in the case. The notes have two main functions, clarifying the meaning of judicial decisions and shaping precedent. Studying *notes d'arrêts* is an important part of the legal education.[163]

In 2013, there were 1,791 books classified as legal literature published, and there were 41 legal journals registered by the National library (*la Bibliographie nationale française*).[164]

4.7 Soft law (*droit souple/droit mou*)

A more recent development in French law concerns soft law. Both judicial and administrative courts apply soft law, and a similar development is to be found before the CJEU and ECHR, interpreting EU-law and the convention in light of non-binding instruments. The *Conseil d'État*'s annual report for 2013 is devoted to this topic, with the aim of creating a *doctrine* for public authorities' use of *droit souple*. In administrative court decisions, a *jurisprudence* concerning soft laws is "under construction." Many questions have yet to be addressed by the courts, for instance: the question of admissibility of disputes concerning soft law, the question of soft law's justiciability before the judge

161 But the word can also refer to the authors of legal writing (and even other definitions are possible). See Cornu (n 97) 304.

162 Marais (n 79) 150–152; Chapus, *Droit administratif général* (n 33) 28; Terré (n 23) 167; Bell, Boyron and Whittaker (n 44) 33.

163 Steiner (n 38) 149–155. Legal writings are often characterized as *traités* (complete views of a topic), *précis*, *thémis*, *manuels* (student textbooks), *mémentos* (short guides to a subject), and casebooks like *Les grands arrêts.* See Elliott, Jeanpierre and Vernon (n 13) 83; Bell, Boyron and Whittaker (n 44) 517–519.

164 According to email from Mathilde Koskas, Service de la Bibliographie nationale française – Livres, Département du Dépôt légal, Bibliothèque nationale de France (4 December 2014).

and how soft law should be taken into consideration in the motivations of the courts' decisions.[165]

Conseil d'État proposes a definition of soft law based on certain criteria: The instruments of soft law have the aim of modifying the behaviour of its recipients, evoking, as far as possible, their adherence. This criterion distinguishes soft law from opinions and other preparatory documents. Secondly, the instruments of soft law do not by themselves create rights and obligations for their recipients. This criterion marks the limit between soft law and hard law (*droit dur*). Thirdly, the instruments of soft law present, by their content and elaboration, a degree of formalisation and structure that relates them to law, and this final criterion distinguishes soft law from non-law.[166]

For instance, in private law, soft law can manifest itself as non-binding technical standards or non-binding norms for auditing. In administrative law, a kind of soft law can be found in conventions between the state and associates who cannot legally bind their constituents, for instance between the state and the *assemblées* ("parliaments") of the 96 *départements.* Soft law could also be found in more specific criteria for the use of the administration's discretionary powers. Soft law is in many areas an effective tool, and according to the *Conseil d'État* it is not desirable that it should escape control on the grounds that it is not binding.[167]

The development of soft law has provoked reactions. Some claim that it may lead to, amongst other things, a degradation of the legal clarity and certainty. Even though the extent of the requirements founded in soft law remain uncertain, in particular before the judge, one could also raise the question whether soft law is an extension of the judges' normative power.[168]

4.8 Practice of governmental agencies

Administrative authorities can give out *circulaires* and *réponses ministérielles* with the purpose of helping to interpret the law. The *circulaire*s can be either *impératives* or *non impératives*, and under certain conditions, the legality of the former can be controlled by the administrative judge. These *circulaires*, unless they are judged illegal, have a binding force for citizens and administrative courts, but not judicial courts.

The *réponses ministérielles* are written replies to questions posed to the ministries, by members of Parliament. Especially in some areas of public law, such as taxes and immigration, *circulaires* and *réponses ministérielles* represent a significant source for interpreta-

---

165 Conseil d'État, *Dossier de presse. Étude annuelle 2013. "Le droit souple." Le résumé*, 2, 9; *La lettre de la justice administrative no 33* (December 2013) 1.

166 Conseil d'État, *Dossier de presse. Étude annuelle 2013. "Le droit souple." Le résumé* 3, 4.

167 Jean-Pierre Sueur (Président de la Commission des lois du Sénat) in *La lettre de la justice administrative* no 33 (December) 2013, 1; Conseil d'État, *Dossier de presse. Étude annuelle 2013. "Le droit souple." Le résumé* 3, 9.

168 Jean-Pierre Sueur (Président de la commission des lois du Sénat) in *La lettre de la justice administrative no 33* (December 2013) 1; Conseil d'État, *Dossier de presse. Étude annuelle 2013. "Le droit souple." Le résumé* 3.

tion. They are not binding on the courts, but still increasingly relied on by judges and parties and published in the *Journal officiel*.[169]

5. Reflections on the ideal of justice

The French ideal of justice appears in some ways to be filled with paradoxes. Formally, and in an overall view, legal certainty is ensured through legislation and general principles of law. Judicial decisions are not binding officially. The judge is prohibited in making rules by determining in advance the outcome of subsequent similar litigation involving different parties. At the same time, the judge has a duty to rule, even if there is a gap in the law or it is ambiguous. When interpreting statutes, the starting point is that a clear text should not be interpreted in the light of other legal sources or legal argument bases. But the general and open-textured manner of drafting statutory texts, usually creates a need for interpretation. Here, case-law can provide the right tool to substantiate a certain interpretation. As a result, the judges are not too closely tied to the wording of a statutory text. In the field of administrative law, where codification (traditionally) has been modest, case-law plays a role more similar to common law-systems. In general, legal certainty and consistency is facilitated by the syllogism in forming the grounds for court decisions, but this again creates another paradox since the brief drafting of the judgments makes them rather inaccessible for those who does not understand fully this law. The often broadly formulated general clauses in the codes are in need of interpretation, opening for equitable adjustments in individual cases by taking into consideration the particular circumstances and facts. This enables judges to provide individually just and fair results without endangering the overall purpose to provide legal security. As the decisions of the courts apply only *inter partes*, with the exceptions mentioned above, this can be regarded as an acceptable balance between predictability and individual justice.

6. Professionalisation

6.1 Legal education

In 2013 there were 208,534 students of law in France, allocated in 68 faculties or other institutions teaching law. There were 2,724 professors and 6,038 *maîtres de conference* in law.[170] In large law schools, around 3,000 students are recruited annually. Entry into French universities is not selective, but the number of students drops considerably after the first year because of a high failure rate. The students are normally taught in large

169 Marais (n 79) 200–202; Terré (n 23) 273–276; Steiner (n 38) 4–5, 61-62.

170 Ministère de l'Éducation nationale, de l'Enseignement supérieure et de la Recherche, *Repères & références statistiques. Enseignement – formation – recherché* 231. And according to e-mails from Sophie Grassin, Département de la valorisation et de l'édition, Direction de l'évaluation, de la prospective et de la performance, Ministère de l'Éducation nationale, de l'enseignement supérieur et de la recherche and from Svein Hullstein, Utdannings- og forskningsråd, Direktør Norges hus, Kgl. norsk ambassade (both 19 January 2015).

groups (a thousand students in one lecture hall is not unusual the first year); interaction with the teachers, and student participation in the instruction are therefore difficult. Attending lectures is not compulsory but attending seminars (*travaux dirigés*) once or twice per week during the first year is. This class participation counts for the marks at the end of the year. In law, students usually have both written, oral, and multiple-choice exams.[171]

The law degree is structured into parts: *licence* (three years) and *master 1* (four years), *master 2* (five years), and *doctorate* (eight years). Students obtaining a licence may work in for example banking, public administration, insurance, as court personnel or estate agencies – but must in many cases join a training college which offers specialized education for each of these occupations.[172]

The content of the law degree is broad and includes other associated disciplines, such as economics, sociology and legal history. The law schools place a strong emphasis on theoretical knowledge (primarily the systematic exposition of existing rules and principles), analysis of main concepts to be found in codes and further developed by the courts, and argument based on a logical and formal analysis of legal problems.[173] Case-law is an important part of the law degree and students study *les grands arrêts de la jurisprudence* – the most important decisions from the highest courts. The interpretation of statutes is considered part of the basic teaching and is taught from a very early stage in the studies.[174]

6.2 Lawyers and judges

To become a lawyer, the students who have completed a four-year master degree (normally in law, but some other studies with a high content of law are considered equivalent) must continue their education at a *Centre régional de formation professionnel* for the professional stage of training that lasts for 18 months, the *certificat d'aptitude à la profession d'avocat* (*CAPA*). The students must pass an entrance exam and are tried in both written, practical, and oral tests.[175]

In 2018 there were 66,958 lawyers (*avocats*), and 123 lawyers with admission to plead before the *Conseil d'État* and the *Cour de cassation* – where a special permission is needed, and this group of lawyers are called *avocats aux conseils*.[176] In 2011, forty-seven percent of the lawyers were women. They were all organized in bars (*barreaux*), one for

171 Elliott, Jeanpierre and Vernon (n 13) 252–253.

172 Bell, Boyron and Whittaker (n 44) 73; Elliott, ibid 256.

173 Steiner (n 38) 156–165.

174 Ibid 65–66. And see for instance Marais (n 79).

175 Loi no 71-1130 du 31 décembre 1971 portant réforme de certaines professions judiciaires et juridiques Art. 11 and 12; Bell, Boyron and Whittaker (n 44) 73. See also https://www.cnb.avocat.fr/fr/lacces-la-profession-par-la-voie-normale-le-capa.

176 Le Ministère de la Justice, *Les chiffres-clés de la Justice 2018. Diffusion: Sous-direction de la Statistique et des Études* (2018) 35.

each first instance court in civil cases (*tribunal de grande instance*). For members of the bar, continual education is a requirement.[177]

Besides giving legal advice and drafting documents such as contracts etc., the main roles of French lawyers' main roles are giving assistance in pre-trial and trial court hearings. Much of the preparation for a case is done by the judge before the court hearing, such as interviewing witnesses and experts. The lawyers of the parties are normally present at these proceedings and make oral representation when necessary. The lawyers also draft pleadings and other written papers needed during the pre-hearing stage of the proceedings.[178]

In 2007 there were approximately 8,140 judges (*magistrats*) in the judicial courts, and as mentioned in Section 2, they have a number of functions. Most judges in the judicial courts are recruited from the *École Nationale de la Magistrature* (*ENM*),[179] which is a three-year continuing education preparing the students for many different types of work as a *magistrat*. About 80 % of the promulgated candidates from *ENM* are women.[180] To enter *ENM*, a master 1 (four-year university degree) is necessary, but this does not have to be a degree in law. Like other *grandes écoles*, the students must pass an entrance competition. The judges have several career possibilities besides the courts. Basically, they are divided into the *juge du siège* and *juge du parquet* (also called *ministère public* and *magistrature debout*), referring to their role during a court hearing (see Section 2).[181]

Judges in the administrative courts are not called *magistrats* in current language, but for instance members, councillors, etc. They are to a large extent recruited from the *École nationale de l'administration* (*ENA*),[182] which is another of the *grandes écoles* and a three-year continuing education. Entering this school requires four years of university and having obtained a licence, but most of the students have studied at the *Science Po* – a renowned Parisian school of political science. Students can also take courses to prepare them for the entering exams at the *ENA*. The education includes study, high-level seminars, and placements.

Both candidates from the *École nationale de la magistrature* and the *École nationale de l'administration* choose career possibilities based on their achievements leaving the school.[183] The candidates graduated from the *ENA* are recruited not only to the administrative courts, but also to public administration, and many of them fill influential roles in the state administration.[184] The best students can choose the most interesting and

177 Loi no 71-1130 du 31 décembre 1971 Art. 14-2; Pedro Estop Garanto, *La société Francaise. Une introduction* (Akademika forlag 2013) 119; Bell, Boyron and Whittaker (n 44) 73–74.

178 Elliott, Jeanpierre and Vernon (n 13) 243–245.

179 For more information about the school, see http://www.enm.justice.fr/.

180 Garanto (n 177) 118–119.

181 Bell, Boyron and Whittaker (n 44) 55–68; Steiner (n 38) 170; Perrot (n 20) 42.

182 For more information about the school, see https://www.ena.fr/.

183 This ranking and automatic transfer to vacant positions has been criticized. According to l'ENA (by mail from E. Doriry, 18 February 2014).

184 Chapus, *Droit du contentieux administratif* (n 20) 49; Smith (n 12) 74; Braibant and Stirn (n 23) 514–515.

prestigious positions, for instance in the *Conseil d'État* and the *Cour des Comptes*. Many of the judges in the lower administrative courts are recruited from the *ENA*, and all of the judges of the lowest degree at the *Conseil d'État*. In total, about 80 % of the members in the *Conseil d'État* are so called *énarques*.[185] In the courts, the freshly educated judges will make a career according to specific criteria of advancement (see Section 2).

7. Reflections on internationalisation

The French legal system is neither a purely dualist system, nor a purely monist system. Judgments from the ECHR and CJEU are directly applied in courts. International treaties applicable in French law are ranked above national legislation and under *le bloc constitutionnel*, and the Constitution contains a chapter on EU law and one on treaties and international agreements.[186] So, the principles of international law and European law have gradually spread into national law.[187] Also, French law is regularly changed to fit the demands of especially the ECHR and CJEU, which seem particularly influential in the internationalisation of the French legal system. As mentioned concerning international law, this has for instance been the case for the principle of legitimate expectation and the principle of proportionality.[188] As for cases from the ECHR, such have led to, for example, the exclusion of the *rapporteurs publics* (in the administrative courts) and the *ministère public* (in the judicial courts) from participating in their respective court's deliberations.

Historically, the French legal culture has been influenced but international legal regimes such as Roman law. Due to a long and proud tradition dating back to the enactment of the Code Civil, France was rather an exporter than a receiver of law. Today, as a member of the EU and as most other modern jurisdictions, France is governed by a plurality of legal regimes.

The Legal Culture and its structures and structural elements	
Institutional structure	
Conflict resolution	*Norm production*
Two hierarchies of courts: judicial and administrative. Many specialized courts in first instance. There are specialized appeal courts in the administrative hierarchy. Often specialization within the general courts also.	Aprox. 73 effective codes and several statutes. General principles of law and custom (especially in commercial law) are also considered official sources of law. *Jurisprudence* is de facto important.

185 Bruno Latour, *La fabrique du droit. Une ethnographie du Conseil d'État* (La Découverte 2002) 124.

186 Section VI – On treaties and international agreements and Section XV – On the European Union.

187 Jean-Marc Sauvé, "Le Conseil d'État et le droit européen et international" (Intervention l'Université de Tokyo, 26 October 2016), I A 2, available at https://www.conseil-etat.fr/actualites/discours-et-interventions/le-conseil-d-etat-et-le-droit-europeen-et-international (Accessed 18 February 2020)

188 Steiner (n 38) 270.

Intellectual structure			
Idea of justice	*Legal method*	*Degree of professionalisation*	*Character of internationalisation*
French judges are not tied too closely to the wording of a statutory text, which is usually drafted in a rather general and open-textured manner. Legal certainty within the legal system and consistency is facilitated by the syllogism in forming the grounds for a court decision.	Deduction from statutes which the judges are not tied too closely to, but a clear wording is to a large extent binding. Frequent need for interpretation of statutes, which is mainly based on the legislator's purpose. Some use of general principles of law as developed by the courts, especially in the administrative courts.	To practice as a lawyer, a 4-year university degree is required, in addition to 18 months of professional training. To work as a judge, there is a requirement of a four-year university degree in addition to a three-year continuing education at a *grande école*.	The French legal system is neither a pure dualist system, nor a pure monist system. Judgments from the ECHR and CJEU are directly applied in courts. French law is regularly changed to fit the demands of especially the ECHR and CJEU.

8. Bibliography

Bell J, Boyron S and Whittaker S, *Principles of French Law* (Oxford university press 2008)

Braibant G and Stirn B, *Le droit administratif français* (Dalloz, 2005)

Bureau D, 'Codification' in Alland D and Rials S (eds), *Dictionnaire de la culture juridique* (Lamy 2003)

Chabanol D, *La pratique du contentieux administratif* (Litec 2013)

Chapus R, *Droit administratif général* (Montchrestien 2001)

—— *Droit du contentieux administratif* (Montchrestien 2008)

Cornu G, *Vocabulaire juridique* (Puf 2001)

Deguergue M, 'Jurisprudence' in Alland D and Rials S (eds), *Dictionnaire de la culture juridique* (Lamy 2003)

Dictionnaire Le Petit Larousse. Compact, France (Larousse 1992)

Dictionnaire Le Petit Larousse illustré. 2016. (Larousse, 2015)

Eckhoff T and Smith E, *Forvaltningsrett* (Universitetsforlaget 2018)

Elliott C, Geirnaert C and Houssais F, *French Legal System and Legal Language. An introduction in French* (Longman 1998)

Elliott C, Jeanpierre E and Vernon C, *French Legal System* (Pearson Education Limited 2006)

Farcy JC, 'Juridictions. Évolution du système français' in Alland D and Rials S (eds), *Dictionnaire de la culture juridique* (Lamy 2003)

Fouletier M, *Recherches sur l'équité en droit public français* (L.G.D.J 2003)

Garanto PE, *La société Francaise. Une introduction* (Akademika forlag 2013)

Girardon J, *Les collectivités territoriales* (Ellipses 2011)

Guinchard S, Montagnier G and Varinard A, *Institutions juridictionnelles* (Dalloz 2007)

Holle ML, *Hæftelsesansvar for selvstændigt virkende tredjemænd – med særlig henblik på offentlige oppgaver* (Karnov Group, 2013)

Latour B, *La fabrique du droit. Une ethnographie du Conseil d'État* (La Découverte 2002)

Lepage C and Huglo C, *Code de jusitce administrative* (Litec 2013)

Lidström A, *Kommunsystem i Europa* (Liber 2003)

Marais A, *Introduction au droit* (Vuibert droit 2014)

Montesquieu CLS, *Om lovenes ånd*, bog 11, kapitel 6 (first published 1748, Gad 1998)

Pacteau B, *Contentieux administratif* (Puf 2005)

Perrot R, *Institutions judiciaires* (Montchrestien 2010)

Rouault MC, *Contentieux administratif* (Meméntos LMD 2000)

Sauvé JM and Fuchs O, *Justice administrative et État de droit* (Intervention. Institut d'études judiciaires. Université Panthéon-Assas)

Sauvé J-M and Eustache S, *Perspectives sur la justice administrative* (Discours à Versailles le 6 octobre 2014)

Sauvé J-M, 25 *ans de la relance de la codification* (Discours au Conseil d'État 2015)

Sauvé J-M, *Le Conseil d'État et le droit européen et international* (Intervention à l'Universiteé de Tokyo 2016)

Smith E, 'Frankrike – ett konstitutionellt laboratorium' in Melbourn A (ed), *Författningskulturer. Konstitutioner och politiska system i Europa, USA och Asien* (Sekel bokförlag 2009)

Steiner E, *French Law. A Comparative Approach* (Oxford university press 2018)

Stokstad S, *Kommunalt selvstyre* (Akademika forlag 2012)

Terré F, *Introduction générale au droit* (Dalloz 2012)

Waline J, *Droit administratif* (Dalloz 2012)

Wijffels A, *Introduction historique au droit. France, Allemagne, Angleterre* (Thémis droit 2014)

14. An Introduction to Austrian Legal Culture

Konrad Lachmayer and Niklas Sonntag

1. Introduction

The Republic of Austria was founded in 1918 as a successor state of the multi-ethnic Austrian-Hungarian Monarchy and the Federal Constitutional Act (*Bundes-Verfassungsgesetz*) of 1920 is still in force today. The First Republic (1918–1933) was followed by phases of authoritarian Austro-fascism and National Socialism (1938–1945) and eventually re-established as a democratic republic (Second Republic) as proclaimed on 27 April 1945. In 1955, Austria regained its sovereignty from the Allies in exchange for the guarantee of permanent neutrality. The same year, Austria became a member of the United Nations Organization, before joining the Council of Europe in 1956, the European Free Trade Association in 1960 and finally, after the fall of the Berlin Wall, becoming a member of the European Union in 1995.[1]

The Republic of Austria consists of nine constituent states, which are referred to as *Länder*, with the capital city of Vienna being the largest in terms of population. Since Austria is a federal state, the states play an important role. Nevertheless, from a legal perspective, the federal system in Austria can be characterised as highly centralised compared to other federal countries. The central government possesses many of the important powers in the federation, including significant judicial powers, responsibility for the police and military, control of public accounts as well as being in charge of (higher) education,[2] industry and the relevant infrastructure.

The Austrian Government is based on the principle of representative democracy.[3] Deputies to the federal and the state parliaments are elected at regular intervals (usually every five years). The federal parliament consists of two chambers, the National Coun-

1 A historic overview is given by Herbert Hausmaninger, *The Austrian Legal System* (4th edn, Manz 2011) 1 ff.; Wilhelm Brauneder, *Österreichische Verfassungsgeschichte* (11th edn, Manz 2009) 187 ff.

2 This is different from Germany, where higher education due to the federal structure is a competence assigned to the states.

3 See with regard to the Austrian Constitution, Manfred Stelzer, *The Constitution of the Republic of Austria* (Hart Publishing 2011) 32–36.

cil (*Nationalrat*), which is directly elected by the Austrian people every five years and the Federal Council (*Bundesrat*), consisting of deputies elected indirectly by the state parliaments. Elements of direct democracy, such as popular initiatives, referenda and consultations with the people complement this system.[4] In practice, the political parties traditionally play an important role in Austrian politics and the two major parties (Social Democrats and the conservative People's Party) usually formed the Federal government and dominated the parliament. The relevance of these two parties is on the decline, however, and the political landscape is increasingly becoming more plural. After a coalition government of the conservative party with the far-right Freedom party (2017–2019), a coalition government of the conservative party with the green party (2020–current) was formed for the first time in Austrian history.

The Head of State is the Federal President, who is directly elected by the people to serve a six-year term, has certain legal powers (e.g. formal commander-in-chief) but whose political relevance lies chiefly in his representative function. The Federal President appoints the Federal Government and can release it; moreover, the President has the power to dissolve the Federal Parliament.[5] At the moment, the Federal President is Mr. Alexander Van der Bellen, who has been a former leader of the green party.[6]

The Austrian population (8.8 mil. population) is generally quite homogenous regarding ethnicity and culture. About 83.8% of the population have Austrian citizenship. Non-Austrian residents come from Germany (2.17%), Serbia (1.37%), Turkey (1.32%), Romania (1.27%), Bosnia (1.08%), Hungary (0.93%), Croatia(0.90%) and other countries (7.19%, including immigrants from Syria [0.56%] and Afghanistan [0.5%]).[7] About 89% of the Austrian citizens have German as their mother tongue, this also being the official language of the Republic, while special constitutional provisions provide special language minority rights for the ethnic Hungarians, Croats and Slovenes living in Burgenland, Styria and Carinthia. In terms of religion, 57% of the Austrian population are Roman Catholics and about 8 per cent are Muslims. Immigration to Austria mainly originates from the EU member states of Germany, Romania, Poland and Hungary and the non-member Balkan states as well as Turkey. As the statistics above illustrate, relevant immigration took place from Syria and Afghanistan in the last years.

---

4 In the last years there has been, however, an increase in discussion on direct democracy, see the recent books by Theo Öhlinger and Klaus Poier (eds), *Direkte Demokratie und Parlamentarismus* (Böhlau 2015), and Peter Bußjäger, Alexander Balthasar and Niklas Sonntag (eds), *Direkte Demokratie im Diskurs* (New Academic Press 2014). It is, however, remarkable that politics is not using the constitutional possibilities of direct democracies in the same way (especially populistic) politics demands it (even when populists are in government). It can much more be observed that the Austrian legal system lacks a developed legal culture of direct democracy.

5 Austria adopted the German presidential model in 1929. While Germany dismissed the Weimar model of a Federal President after the Second World War, Austria set this model in force again in 1945. The political importance of the Federal President is, however, very modest. See with regard to the upset in the presidential elections in 2016, Konrad Lachmayer, 'The Austrian Presidential Crisis 2016', *Int'l J. Const. L. Blog*, 9 December 2016, available at http://www.iconnectblog.com/2016/12/the-austrian-presidential-crisis accessed 14 April 2020.

6 See https://www.bundespraesident.at/alexander-van-der-bellen/ accessed 14 April 2020.

7 See the website of the Statistik Austria available at https://www.statistik.at/ accessed 14 April 2020.

Austria is a small country (83,879 km2, 32,386 sq mi) and is economically dependent on the European Union and its neighbours, especially Germany. Although the banking and financial crises have seriously affected Austria, it can still be considered a wealthy country (GDP, nominal per capita $ 56,259 in 2019).[8]

2. Conflict resolution

2.1 Historical background

The present Austrian court system reflects a court model, which was developed during the monarchy and – roughly speaking – distinguishes between the ordinary courts, which pronounce on private law as well as labour and social lawsuits[9] and criminal charges, and the public law courts, which review administrative decisions. In the past, reviewing laws seemed to contravene the sovereignty of the monarch and it seemed inappropriate that various courts should be able to scrutinise laws the monarch had enacted with parliamentary consent. Nevertheless, it was suggested that scholars should establish a concentrated model of judicial review of laws.[10] This eventually resulted in the implementation of the centralised constitutional review by the Austrian Constitutional Court in 1920, which at that time was quite unique and served as a role model for various other countries.[11]

Initially, the Austrian Constitution set forth this separation between ordinary courts and administrative authorities only with respect to formal criteria, without explicitly leaving certain matters for ordinary courts to decide. While independent courts have handled all civil and criminal matters, administrative law cases were primarily addressed within the administrative authorities themselves, and unlawful administrative actions could only be appealed to the Administrative Court (*Verwaltungsgerichtshof*) as a court of last instance after all administrative appeals had been exhausted. This traditional Austrian dichotomy between ordinary courts and administrative authorities was challenged by the jurisdiction of the European Court of Human Rights (ECtHR), which demanded tribunals as instances of appeal instead of administrative authorities in a number of procedures. In light of this, the Austrian system of administrative review did not meet the requirements of Article 6 of the European Convention on Human Rights (ECHR) regarding the sepa-

8 See https://www.imf.org/external/pubs/ft/weo/2018/01/weodata/weorept.aspx?sy=2017&ey=2020&scsm=1&ssd=1&sort=country&ds=.&br=1&pr1.x=70&pr1.y=9&c=122&s=NGDP_RPCH%2CNGDPD%2CPPPGDP%2CNGDPDPC%2CPPPPC&grp=0&a= accessed 14 April 2020.

9 Within the structure of ordinary courts certain substructures exist, e.g. a separate commercial court or a labour and social court in Vienna. They are, however, part of the ordinary court system.

10 See in particular, Georg Jellinek, *Ein Verfassungsgerichtshof für Österreich* (Alfred Hölder 1885) 27 ff.

11 See Theo Öhlinger, 'The Genesis of the Austrian Model of Constitutional Review of Legislation' (2003) Vol. 16 No. 2 *Ratio Juris* 206. Christoph Bezemek, 'A Kelsenian model of constitutional adjudication' (2012) Vol. 67 *Zeitschrift für Öffentliches Recht* 115.

ration of powers between judicial and executive powers.[12] The dynamics in the last 25 years, including the accession to the European Union in 1995, finally led to the establishment of Administrative Courts of first instance in 2014, including a Federal Fiscal Court.

The present system of administrative courts is comparable to that in Germany or Sweden, insofar as these systems have also established administrative courts of lower instances to provide legal protection against administrative acts.

2.2 Basic structure of the Austrian Court System

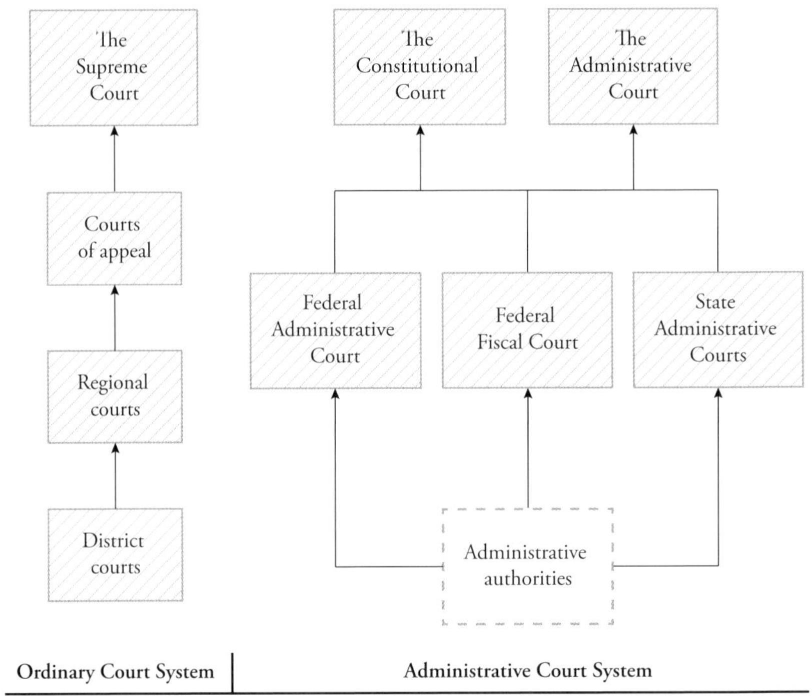

Fig. 1 The Austrian Court System.

12 Article 6 entitles everyone to have a claim regarding civil rights and obligations or criminal charges heard by an independent tribunal. A 1987 Constitutional Court ruling (VfSlg. 11.500/1987) then differentiated between core and peripheral areas of civil law, and held that decisions concerning the core area, including rights and obligations of citizens to one another, must be taken by the ordinary courts, whereas for matters of the peripheral area of civil rights, review by the Administrative or Constitutional Court would be sufficient. See Theo Öhlinger and Harald Eberhard, *Verfassungsrecht* (12th edn, facultas.wuv 2019) para. 647, and Stelzer (2011) (n 3) 178–185. Still, many areas of Austrian administrative procedure did not satisfy the above-mentioned requirements. In order to meet the standards set by Article 6 ECHR, special independent administrative bodies were established in 1991.

2.3 Ordinary court system

Ordinary jurisdiction in Austria is exercised on four levels. With regard to civil law cases, the 115 District Courts (*Bezirksgerichte*) have jurisdiction in all civil cases involving amounts up to 15,000 € and handle all matters of family law, regardless of the monetary value involved, as well as the land register.[13] All cases are heard by single judges. The 20 Regional Courts (*Landesgerichte*) function as courts of first instance in cases concerning sums above 15,000 Euros. Cases are usually heard by a single judge, except when the amount is over 100,000 Euros and the decision by a panel is requested by one of the parties. In this case, a panel of three judges makes the decision. The Regional Courts also rule as appellate courts in matters decided by the District Courts. The four Courts of Appeal (*Oberlandesgerichte*) in Graz, Linz, Innsbruck and Vienna function as Courts of Appeal for cases decided by the Regional Courts as trial courts. They hear cases in panels of three judges. Regarding review procedure, the Austrian Civil Procedure Code (*Zivilprozessordnung*) provides for an ordinary appeal against a judgment of a trial court and also for a second appeal against the decision of an appellate court. Usually, according to Article 90 of the Federal Constitutional Act, all proceedings have to be public and oral, although due to several changes over the last years, more and more procedural actions may be taken in written form, especially complaints against formal rulings and proceedings in second appeals.[14]

Regarding criminal charges, the District Courts have jurisdiction concerning all acts punishable by not more than one year of imprisonment – these trials are handled by single judges.[15] Regional Courts then function as appellate courts for decisions of the District Courts. Furthermore, the Regional Courts are courts of first instance for all capital crimes. Depending on the gravity of the offence, they decide as single judges, with special panels including one professional judge, along with two lay judges ruling in cases where the maximum sentence may exceed five years. Jury courts consisting of three judges and eight jurors who decide in criminal cases punishable by more than ten years and in all political crimes, whereas the decision on the penalty is made by the judges. Generally speaking, the value of what is at stake or the level of the impending punishment is decisive for the level at which a case starts. All proceedings regarding criminal charges have to be public and oral; judgments may only be based on facts established during an oral trial. The public can be excluded from certain cases, especially when privacy is required. Evidence is submitted in the respective court of first instance according to the rules outlined above. The Austrian criminal procedure consists of two

13 An overview is given by Hausmaninger (2011) (n 1) 208 ff.; see also Christoph Grabenwarter, 'Constitutional Law' in Christoph Grabenwarter and Martin Schauer (eds), *Introduction to the Law of Austria* (Wolters Kluwer 2015) 9 s.

14 See written and oral proceedings Georg E. Kodek and Peter G. Mayr, *Zivilprozessrecht* (4th edn, facultas.wuv 2018) para. 81–83.

15 An overview is given by Hausmaninger (2011) (n 1) 183 ff.

instances and generally it can be said that the appellate courts[16] do not decide on questions of evidence themselves but remit the case back to the first instance (cassation).[17] They only decide themselves in a few cases, especially those regarding the extent or type of punishment.

A total of about 2.9 million cases were handled by the Austrian courts in 2017, with the most being decisions on debt collections (about one million in 2017 decided by the District Courts). Regarding the hierarchy of courts, 2,573,619 civil and criminal cases were brought to the District Courts in 2017, 193,340 to the Regional Courts, and 121,439 to the Courts of Appeal. The Supreme Court decided 3,132 civil and criminal cases. In addition, there are about 550,000 criminal cases by public prosecution.[18]

As the highest tribunal in civil and criminal matters in Austria, the Supreme Court (*Oberster Gerichtshof*) is expressly established by the Constitution. It consists of a president, two vice-presidents, 13 panel presidents and 42 judges usually sitting in panels (*Senate*) of five. Three judges' panels may decide on certain formal matters and enlarged panels of eleven judges deal with legal questions of fundamental importance that may result in a departure from an established line of the Supreme Court's decisions. The Austrian Supreme Court decides in a written procedure in a non-public trial.[19] The Supreme Court also plays an important role in safeguarding constitutional law in the fields of its jurisdiction, which comprises most parts of civil and criminal law. Whenever the court seriously doubts whether a law is constitutional, it is obliged to file an application to the Constitutional Court, which may decide on this question. Since 2015, the parties from ongoing civil or criminal procedures have also had the right to do so, although only after a decision of a court of first instance.[20] Within the fields of criminal law, the Supreme Court has jurisdiction to rule on special fundamental rights applications by everyone who is detained on the order of a judge or a criminal court.

Specialised courts or panels are established to deal with matters of commercial law, antitrust law and labour and social law issues. They usually involve the participation of lay judges, who are appointed for three-year terms by the Ministry in commercial cases, or the employers' association in labour and social cases. In antitrust matters, the Vienna Court of Appeal functions as the Cartel Court for all of Austria. Appeals are decided by a special panel of the Supreme Court.

---

16 The concrete court depends on the competence in first instance – the Supreme Court is the appellate court in procedures of nullity appeal in all cases decided by jury and mixed courts, the court of appeals in all cases decided by the Regional Courts and ordinary appeals against decisions by jury and mixed courts and the regional court in all cases decided by the District Courts in first instance, see in detail Stefan Seiler, *Strafprozessrecht* (18th edn, facultas.wuv 2020) para. 94–116.

17 A cassatory judgment means that the court is (only) annulling the judgment of the lower court, but does not itself rule in the case. It is moreover up to the lower court to decide again in the light of the reasoning of the upper court, which annulled its decision.

18 According to the data published by the Ministry of Justice, see https://www.justiz.gv.at/ (in German) accessed 14 April 2020.

19 See § 509 of the Civil Procedure Code.

20 See recently Thomas Ziniel, 'Strengthening the Judicial Review System in Austria' (2014) *ICL Journal* 8, no. 4 437.

Overall 1,730 judges and 413 public prosecutors worked in the ordinary court system in 2018.[21] Since 1993 the Ministry of Justice started to promote gender equality. In 2018, 55% of the judges and 52% of the public prosecutors have been female. Several attempts have been made to avoid expensive trials. In civil law cases, many instruments of alternative dispute resolution play an important role, among them the possibility of settlement, such as a contract between the conflicting parties signed before the court. This is possible even before the case is brought before the court as what is called a "praetorian settlement" (*prätorischer Vergleich*) according to § 433 of the Civil Procedure Code, but of course also possible during the trial as a procedural settlement as regulated in § 204 of the Civil Procedure Code. In addition to this, arbitration and mediation have entered Austrian civil procedure during the last decades. Arbitration mechanisms have been established especially in various trade associations to avoid conflicts entering the courts, and in many laws regarding trade associations, as well as housing and incorporated associations, arbitration is obligatory before a civil trial is even possible.[22] Since 2004, mediation is obligatory in conflicts between neighbours; it is possible to take legal action only in cases where the attempts are unsuccessful.[23]

In criminal cases, special out-of-court settlements were established in Austria during the 1970s and 1980s, especially cases regarding drug addiction and juvenile delinquency. Since 2000, out-of-court measures (*Diversion*) have been laid down in the Austrian Criminal Procedure Act. The aim is to react to crimes without introducing a formal criminal procedure and to avoid stigmatization of criminals, especially in cases that have not caused serious effects on others and in which the delinquents are not dangerous. The assumption is that all circumstances are clear, no objections exist regarding general or specific deterrence and that the delinquent's guilt is not serious, meaning that reasons for mitigation exist. The catalogue of possible ways to avoid a trial in these cases include fees, reparation for their damages or welfare work. In cases where all requirements for the out-of-court conflict resolution are fulfilled, the judge has to make an offer, otherwise the accused can demand it. The solution then is not a judgment, which is important, for example, in order to meet the requirements according to Article 6 ECHR and is not included in any criminal record.[24]

Finally, the budgetary situation of the judiciary has been the focus of heated debate in recent years. In 2018, the presidents of the Courts of Appeal declared in a joint statement that budgetary cuts of the judiciary posed a threat to the rule of law in Austria.[25] In 2019 the Vice-Chancellor and Minister of Justice[26] of what was called the "transitional

21 https://www.justiz.gv.at/file/8ab4ac8322985dd501229ce2e2d80091.de.0/die%20%C3%B6sterreichische%20justiz%20stand%202018.pdf accessed 14 April 2020.

22 See e.g. §§ 39 ss. of the Austrian Rental Code and § 8 of the Law on Incorporated Associations.

23 See in detail Kodek and Mayr (2018) (n 13) para. 13–21, and Theodor Tomandl, *Rechtsstaat Österreich* (Manz 1997) 204 ff.

24 See Seiler (2020) (n 16) para. 685–723.

25 https://orf.at/v2/stories/2432134/2432133/ accessed 14 April 2020.

26 https://kurier.at/politik/inland/justizminister-jabloner-die-justiz-stirbt-einen-stillen-tod/400541399 accessed 14 April 2020.

government"[27] (after the Ibiza Scandal[28]) was even more explicit, when he diagnosed the "silent death" of the judiciary in a newspaper interview.

2.4 Administrative Adjudication

The 2012 Reform Act of Administrative Justice introduced a two-tiered system of administrative courts.[29] Each Austrian state now has its own State Administrative Court (*Landesverwaltungsgericht*) and, in addition, one Federal Administrative Court (*Bundesverwaltungsgericht*) has been established. Moreover, a specialised Federal Fiscal Court (*Bundesfinanzgericht*) focuses on questions of taxation. The new system began functioning in 2014 and changed the above-mentioned system of administrative review dating back to the monarchy. In present administrative procedure, decisions in the first instance are made by civil servants from federal, state or municipal authorities, depending on the distribution of competencies between the federation and the state. These authorities are usually bound by orders of superior organs and accountable to them in the exercise of their official functions. The decisions are subject to appeal before the State Administrative Courts or the Federal Administrative Court. Apart from that, the State Administrative Courts also decide upon complaints against acts of law enforcement as well as complaints for failure to make a timely decision. All administrative courts, including the State, the Federal and the Supreme Administrative Court consist of a president, a vice-president and numerous judges, who are nominated by the State Government (reg. State Administrative Courts) or the Federal Government (reg. Federal Administrative Courts) and appointed by the Federal President, and in both cases based on proposals submitted by the plenary meeting of the respective court. Decisions in administrative courts of first instance are usually made by a single judge.

The courts' decisions may be reviewed by the Administrative Court (*Verwaltungsgerichtshof*) as the supreme authority. This court also decides on cases of inaction of administrative courts and conflicts of responsibilities between them. The Administrative Court has a long tradition and was established back in 1867 as a court of last resort. The Administrative Court consists of its president and vice-president as well as 67 judges, including 13 panel presidents.[30] The Court makes its decisions in panels usually consisting of five

27 Even though this government was called a 'transitional government' by the press and the general public, it must be qualified as a regular government with full competences from a constitutional perspective because it was not constituted as such.

28 The Ibiza Scandal concerned the publication of a covertly filmed video, in which the then Vice-Chancellor of Austria Heinz-Christian Strache was shown discussing potential voter manipulation in exchange for public contracts with a pretended investor. The publication ultimately led to the collapse of the ÖVP/FPÖ government and premature reelections. See Konrad Lachmayer and Lukas Wieser, 'Entering into New Constitutional Territory in Austria', *Verfassungsblog*, 3 June 2019, available at https://verfassungsblog.de/entering-into-new-constitutional-territory-in-austria/ accessed 14 April 2020.

29 *Verwaltungsgerichtsbarkeits-Novelle 2012*, BGBl I 51/2012; for an overview see Anna Gamper, 'Administrative Law' in Christoph Grabenwarter and Martin Schauer (eds), *Introduction to the Law of Austria* (Wolters Kluwer 2015) 33 ff.

30 https://www.vwgh.gv.at/gerichtshof/richterinnen_und_richter/index.html accessed 14 April 2020.

members, while three-member panels decide on formal questions. Nine-member panels are required in cases of deviation from a firm line of decisions. The specific procedural rules of the Court are contained in the Administrative Court Act (*Verwaltungsgerichtshofgesetz*) of 1985. The petitioner and the responding administrative court are party to the proceedings, so decisions are made in the course of a contradictory procedure, although oral hearings are held only at the express request of one of the parties and rarely occur in practice. The court's function is basically cassatory as it annuls the unlawful ruling and remands the case to the respective administrative court of first instance. Only in cases of complaints about inaction of administrative courts does the court decide on the case *in merito*. In 2018, the Court decided in 8,000 cases. In 1,340 cases, the Administrative Court declared the underlying act of the administrative authorities as (partially) void.[31] The average duration for a case at the Administrative Court is 4.1 months. This has been decreasing in recent years due to the reform of the Court.

2.5 Constitutional Review

The Austrian Federal Constitution provides for a specialised Constitutional Court (*Verfassungsgerichtshof*) for constitutional review of statutes and the protection of constitutionally guaranteed rights. In 1920, Austria was the first state to effectively implement a system of centralised constitutional review, and the court can be described as a prototype also relevant for comparative purposes, since a large number of countries adopted a system similar to the one in Austria. Centralised constitutional review in Austria has a long tradition, as some powers of the Constitutional Court date back to the 19th century. The Imperial Court of the monarchy was re-named the Constitutional Court in 1919 and the Federal Constitution of 1920 extended its powers. The theoretical model of constitutional review by one specialised court was delivered and defended by the Austrian legal scholar Hans Kelsen during the 1920s.[32]

Today, the Constitutional Court consists of the president, the vice-president, twelve judges and six substitute judges. All of them must have completed law studies and worked in a legal profession for at least ten years. In practice, the judges are usually professors, lawyers or senior civil servants. With regards to the gender of the judges, equality has not been reached so far; in 2020 only four judges of the Constitutional Court (a female vice-president and three female judges) were women. All members of the Constitutional Court are appointed by the Federal President, who is bound to consider proposals made by the Federal Government and parliament. Despite several rules of incompatibility with political functions due to the procedure of selecting, a certain degree of political influence in the court is inevitable. Like judges in general, the

---

31 See the annual report of the Court to the parliament, available at https://www.vwgh.gv.at/ (in German) accessed 14 April 2020.

32 The theoretical background in particular is elaborated in Hans Kelsen, 'Wesen und Entwicklung der Staatsgerichtsbarkeit' in Hans R. Klecatsky, René Marcic and Herbert Schambeck (eds), *Die Wiener rechtstheoretische Schule* (Verlag Österreich 2010) 1485 ff.

constitutional courts' members enjoy the guarantees of independence and they cannot be bound by any instructions, nor removed from office or transferred to another post. Unlike other courts, the Austrian Constitutional Court does not sit permanently, but only meets four times a year in three-week sessions, although much of the work is done in the meantime as well. Moreover, there is no specific time limit for constitutional judges to serve, like 12 years in Germany. But there is, in contrast to the US Supreme Court, a retirement age, which is 70.[33]

Of course, its main function is the review of statutes, although the Constitutional Court is responsible for a large number of different functions, which are enumerated exhaustively in Article 137–145 of the Federal Constitution.[34] As mentioned, the court reviews an ordinary federal or state law to see whether it is in conformity with the Federal Constitution. Review of laws may take place on an abstract or concrete basis, depending on whether a law is reviewed without any case to decide or prejudicial in a concrete procedure; the Federal Government or one-third of the members of a state parliament may challenge a state law, a State Government or one-third of the members of the Federal Parliament may challenge a federal act of parliament. On a concrete basis, all ordinary and administrative courts may lodge an appeal against all kinds of laws that they have to apply in a certain procedure and whose constitutionality seems unclear. In 2018, a total of 13 statutes or at least parts of them were repealed.[35] Since 2015, parties of criminal or civil procedures have also been able to challenge a law when lodging an appeal against a decision in the first instance. The Constitutional Court itself may also review a law *ex officio* if the court deals with it in another procedure and doubts its constitutionality.

Other competencies of the Constitutional Court include the scrutiny of administrative regulations, state treaties and violation of international law,[36] as well as the control of the legality of elections, decisions on accusations against supreme functionaries and on pecuniary claims that cannot be settled in proceedings before ordinary or administrative courts. Interestingly, most of the cases decided by the Constitutional Court in recent years belong to its competence on reviewing decisions made by the Asylum Court, which existed between 2009 and 2014. In those years, the Constitutional Court was nearly flooded by applications of asylum seekers, with 2,475 cases in 2013 alone. The new system of administrative courts of first instance, now dealing with these cases, has changed these statistics.

33 See Konrad Lachmayer, 'The Austrian Constitutional Court' in András Jakab, Arthur Dyevre and Giulio Itzcovich (eds), *Constitutional Reasoning* (Cambridge University Press 2017) 85–87.

34 See Anna Gamper and Francesco Palermo, 'The Constitutional Court of Austria: Modern Profiles of an Archetype of Constitutional Review' (2008) Vol. 3 No. 2 *Journal of Comparative Law* 3 68, and Öhlinger and Eberhard (2019) (n 12) para. 991; compare also Grabenwarter (2015) (n 13) 12.

35 Data according to the 2018 annual report of the Austrian Constitutional Court, available at https://www.vfgh.at/ (in German) accessed 14 April 2020. The judgments are officially published and the repealed norms are additionally published in the federal and state law gazettes, mainly due to their normative character.

36 This competence of the Court does not include EU law, which is not understood as general international law by the Constitutional Court.

2.6 Interrelations of the highest courts

It has to be noted that all three highest courts mentioned in this chapter are of the same rank, with none of them being superior to the other. The relationship between them causes no particular difficulties, since the Federal Constitution precisely determines their respective functions. Some interesting relations between the courts may be mentioned, one being the decisions on the illegality of administrative rulings, which is normally done by the Administrative Court after the exhaustion of remedies. But in the case where a person feels violated in constitutionally guaranteed rights, he or she may lodge an appeal before the Constitutional Court. This distinction depends on the concrete case. In these cases, the Constitutional Court also serves as a supreme judicial body with regard to administrative rulings, but only concerning the review of fundamental rights. The Constitutional Court may somehow have a superior position in so far as it also decides on competence disputes between courts and administrative bodies.

In 2012 the Austrian Constitutional Court claimed that appeals on the grounds of violation of the EU Charter of Fundamental Rights have to be brought before the Constitutional Court (instead of the Administrative Court).[37] Through this judgment, the Constitutional Court extended its competence, while at the same time limiting the competence of the Administrative Court in matters regarding fundamental rights. It can therefore be seen as a shift of power between the courts.

This constitutional separation between the different court systems – constitutional court, administrative law courts, ordinary courts regarding civil action and criminal charges – has a significant impact on Austrian legal culture and legal methodology. In contrast to the German constitutional system, there is no possibility for a constitutional complaint against judgments of the Administrative Court or the Supreme Court to the Constitutional Court. Only the Administrative or the Supreme Court themselves can initiate a procedure to review a potentially unconstitutional statute at the Constitutional Court. The individual concerned cannot file a constitutional complaint against rulings of the Administrative or the Supreme Court at the Constitutional Court. The effect of this separation of courts is that the method of approaching legal interpretation differs to a certain extent between these different highest courts. Although the Constitutional Court is supreme to the extent that it decides on constitutional questions, the possibilities for the constitutional court to influence the decision-making of the other highest courts are limited.

3. Norm production

3.1 General characteristics

Like in many other jurisdictions, the distinction between public and private law is also quite important in the Austrian legal system, in particular with regard to legal action and

37 See VfSlg. 19.632/2012.

legal protection.[38] All legal acts by the state are categorised. Public law generally consists of constitutional, administrative, tax and criminal law, as well as all the procedural rules regarding the administrative and administrative court procedures. Private law typically covers all cases of contracts.[39] Private law is further differentiated into civil law, including family law, civil rights and obligations, as well as heritage and commercial law. Regarding the structure of the respective laws, as a rule in Austria every area is covered by one main code with special provisions included in several additional statutes. For example, the civil law is generally regulated by the Austrian General Civil Code (*Allgemeines Bürgerliches Gesetzbuch*), which was enacted in 1811. In addition to this, several statutes include special provisions, for example concerning marriage or consumers' rights. Criminal law also consists of the Criminal Code of 1974 (*Strafgesetzbuch*) on the one hand, and additional statutes regulating the rules regarding crimes in the fields of youth criminality, economy or food supply, on the other. The number of additional acts of parliaments is steadily increasing, and this has been particularly true in the last 20 years with regards to the implementation of EU law.

Whereas the structure in statutory law and codification is comparable to other countries, the structure of Austrian constitutional law deserves special attention.[40] Beyond the fact that the Federal Constitutional Act of 1920 is one the oldest constitutions in Europe still in force,[41] it should be noted that the Austrian Constitution is highly fragmented. Although the Federal Constitutional Act contains the essential parts of the constitutional law, a large number of federal constitutional laws exist to regulate matters on a single-issue basis. Moreover, it is possible to include 'constitutional provisions' in ordinary laws, which still requires a two-third majority in parliament but can be found in statutory law.[42] Due to this structure, constitutional law in Austria is not codified into one document but included in hundreds of different statutes covering all areas of law. As a consequence, the literature tells us that "Austrians never were nor will be able to have 'their' constitution presented in a handy little book".[43] Another characteristic of

38 The main provision on the differentiation is § 1 of the General Norm on Jurisdiction (*Jurisdiktionsnorm*) of 1895, according to which all civil cases are subject to ordinary courts' decisions. Some profound considerations on this question can be found in Franz Gschnitzer, *Allgemeiner Teil des bürgerlichen Rechts* (Springer 1966) 2 ff., and Hans Kelsen, *Reine Rechtslehre* (2nd edn, Verlag Österreich 1960) 284 ff.

39 There also exist public law contracts, which are, however, quite limited.

40 See Anna Gamper, 'Introduction to the Study of the Law of the Austrian Constitution' (2008) Vol. 2 No. 2 *ICL-Journal* 94.

41 Apart from the 1920 Federal Constitutional Act, several constitutional norms dating back to 1863 and 1867 are still in force.

42 This culture was started after the Second World War, when a grand coalition government (between the conservative People's Party and the Social Democrats) had a constitutional amending majority for a long time in parliament. Although in the late 1960s and the 1970s one of these two parties had an absolute majority in parliament but without a constitutional amending majority, the two grand parties still went on to amend the constitution regularly. This kind of political consensus was developed as a reaction to the deeply divided party system in the first republic in the 1920s. The post Second World War consensus of the two grand parties made possible this culture of amending the constitution on a regular basis to govern the country.

43 Stelzer (2011) (n 3) 22.

Austrian constitutional law is its flexibility.[44] It can partly be explained by the Austrian constitutional culture of amending the constitution on a regular basis with a two-third majority vote in Parliament.

Another structural distinction, which has dominated the Austrian legal system for a long time, is its specific approach to the hierarchy of norms (*Stufenbau der Rechtsordnung*), a hierarchical understanding of norms as a pyramid and their super and subordinate relationship to each other, theoretically established in detail by Austrian legal scholars like Adolf Merkl and Hans Kelsen.[45] Two criteria are used to decide on the rank of a norm, the first criteria being the requirements of the procedure it takes to create or amend the norm. As mentioned, a constitutional amendment needs a two-third majority in parliament, while an ordinary law is passed with a simple majority. Further, the constitution provides for specific procedures regarding 'total revisions' of the constitution, where a mandatory referendum is necessary. Such is the case when basic principles of the constitution – including democracy, abolishment of monarchy, federalism, rule of law, separation of powers and human rights – are heavily changed or abolished.[46] A second criteria for the hierarchical differentiation of norms is the determination from the constitutional level downwards, since the constitution determines ordinary laws and these are further specified in administrative ordinances and individual administrative or court decisions. According to this structural attempt, a legal norm may be abrogated only by norms of equal or higher rank. Nevertheless, in cases of contradiction in norm conflict, an unconstitutional statute remains in force until it is nullified by the Constitutional Court according to the procedures mentioned above.

3.2 Legislative process and democracy

The principle of legality, binding the administration to statutory law, is determined in Article 18, Paragraph 1 of the Federal Constitutional Act and its constitutional importance is very high. The production of norms in Austria usually falls within the sphere of legislation, although in some cases detailed ruling is left to administrative ordinances. According to the rule of law laid down in Article 18, Paragraph 2 of the Federal Constitutional Act, laws must have a clear and precise meaning and determine the actions of the executive power in detail. In cases where the norm production is transferred to administrative ordinances, the authorities are strictly bound to laws and must not issue regulations without legal authorization with exceptions only in certain emergency cases.[47] Legislation in Austria is allocated between the Federal and the state level, although all important legislative powers are concentrated in the Federation. The legal autonomy

44 See Konrad Lachmayer and Harald Eberhard, 'Constitutional Reform 2008 in Austria' (2008) Vol. 2 No. 2 *ICL-Journal* 115.

45 See in particular Adolf Merkl, 'Prolegomena einer Theorie des rechtlichen Stufenbaues' Hans R. Klecatsky, René Marcic and Herbert Schambeck (eds), *Die Wiener rechtstheoretische Schule* (Verlag Österreich 2010) 1071 ff.

46 See Lachmayer and Eberhard (n 44) 116–117.

47 Öhlinger and Eberhard (2019) (n 12) para. 597–611, and Gamper (2008) (n 40) 105 ff.; compare also Grabenwarter (2015) (n 13) 6.

of the states is very weak, leaving only land use, construction codes, environmental issues and hunting laws as exclusive state powers. This is a difference from Germany, where the states have wider legislative competences.

On the federal level, the parliament consists of two chambers, the National and the Federal Council, whereas the nine states' parliaments consist of only one chamber. After a vote in parliament, the laws are promulgated by the Federal President or the State Governors respectively. Regarding the recent norm production, 112 Federal laws were published in the *Federal Law Gazette* (*Bundesgesetzblatt*) in 2018, and 353 administrative ordinances.

Most of the initial drafts of bills derive from the respective Federal or State Government, which is the usual way in practice to introduce the legislative process, while in some cases laws are introduced directly by members of parliament.[48] Nevertheless, in both cases, the draft bills include extensive preparatory work and annotations regarding each paragraph changed or amended. Although not legally binding, the preparatory work plays an important role in the interpretation of the respective norm, as being one source of interpretation (objective-teleological considerations). They are usually part of the commentary literature and nowadays also electronically available with the laws published in the law gazettes on the internet.[49]

With regard to direct participation of the citizens in norm production, it should be noted that the democratic principle in Austria is strictly understood as a system of representative democracy, with elements of direct democracy being the exception. The Federal Constitution provides for the classic participatory instruments of people's initiatives, public consultations and referenda but all these are connected to parliament, since they are either dependent on a decision made by the parliament or may lead to actions by the parliament. No decisions in law-making are possible without the parliament getting involved.[50]

3.3 Other sources of law

Apart from statutes and administrative regulations, other sources of law also exist in Austrian legal culture, with at least customary law and decisions by the highest courts playing a role.

Regarding customary law as a general practice on a belief of legal obligation, some scholars deny its existence due to the fact that only the constitution regulates the authori-

---

48 The bills are usually drafted in the respective ministry. Thus, the influence on the draft is first a political one (with regard to the minister in charge) and second an expert one since the civil servants in the ministries will provide their knowledge of legislation.

49 See http://www.ris.bka.gv.at/ accessed 14 April 2020. On the role of preparatory work in interpretation, see Tomandl (1997) (n 23) 84 ff., and Hausmaninger (2011) (n 1) 31 ff.

50 See the decision made by the Constitutional Court: VfSlg 16.241/2001 and in detail Anna Gamper, 'The Principle of Homogeneity and Democracy in Austrian Federalism: The Constitutional Court's Ruling on Direct Democracy in Vorarlberg' in Peter Bußjäger and Anna Gamper (eds), *The Homogeneity of Democracy, Rights and the Rule of Law in Federal or Confederal Systems* (Braumüller 2003) 131 ss.

ties able to produce norms.[51] The Austrian Constitution does not mention custom or conventions as a source of norms. In private law, however, custom is accepted as a source of law due to some legal provisions that explicitly recognise it. For example § 549 of the Austrian General Civil Law Code, regarding the 'appropriate' funeral as the responsibility of the estate of a deceased person, and § 346 of the Austrian Commercial Code, regarding the consideration of customs in trade relations.[52] Beyond norms recognizing custom, some rules known as customary law in former times have been incorporated into statutory law with its codification, as happened for example with the right to enter public woods or provisions regarding inheritance between farmers.[53] In addition, some evidence for existing customary law in Austria can also be found.[54]

Judicial precedent as an acknowledged source of law is unknown in the Austrian legal system and § 12 of the General Civil Law Code expressly limits judicial decisions to individual cases with impact only *inter partes*. But to ensure legal certainty and predictability, it is agreed that an established line of decisions (case law) should not be abandoned without good reason.[55] The three Austrian highest courts in particular maintain uniformity in the decision-making regarding the respective legal area. The procedural rules for the Administrative Court and the Supreme Court in Austria also provide for safeguarding uniformity and continuity in decision-making.

Within the field of constitutionally guaranteed rights, the Constitutional Court plays an important role in clarifying the range of each fundamental right. This is necessary due to the heterogeneous sources of fundamental rights in Austria, with some provisions laid down in international treaties, others dating back to the 19th century and most of them formulated in a rather trivial way. The existing system of fundamental rights has mainly been established by the Constitutional Courts' rulings during the last four decades. For example, the equal protection clause includes obligations for the legislature as well as administrative authorities and might also lead to what is called a 'third-party effect',[56] meaning that private persons can also be bound to this under certain circumstances. Furthermore, special rules have been established due to Austria's accession to the European Union, which still challenges the range of equal protection. Nevertheless, the wording

---

51 Robert Walter, 'Die Gewohnheit als rechtserzeugender Tatbestand' (1963) 18 *Österreichische Juristen-Zeitung* 225.

52 The main theoretical positions on this question are outlined in ibid, and Gschnitzer (1966) (n 38) 18 ss. See also with regard to custom in Austrian Constitutional Law, Veronika Tiefenthaler, *Gewohnheit und Verfassung* (facultas. wuv 2012).

53 See § 33 of the Federal Forestry Code (*Forstgesetz*) and the provisions in the Farmers Inheritance Law (*Anerbengesetz*).

54 For example, the fact that the rather weak representation of the states in the Federal Council of the parliament is substituted by regular conferences of the State Governors not regulated in the constitution, but with a high political influence. In addition, the long-practiced principle of unanimity in decisions made by the Federal Government is not laid down explicitly, but can be understood as a constitutional convention. Regarding the acknowledged customary rules in international law, these are explicitly part of the Austrian legal system due to the transformation clause in Article 9 of the Federal Constitutional Act, see in detail Theo Öhlinger and Andreas Th. Müller, 'Art 9/1 B-VG' in Karl Korinek and Michael Holoubek et al. (eds), *Österreichisches Bundesverfassungsrecht* (Springer 2018).

55 Georg Kodek, '§ 12 ABGB' in Peter Rummel and Meinhard Lukas (eds), *ABGB* (4th edn, Manz 2014) para. 21 ss.

56 The Austrian concept refers to the German of 'mittelbare Drittwirkung der Grundrechte', see on this Sören Koch, 'An Introduction to German Legal Culture' in this volume, chapter 8.

of the Federal Constitutional Act remains the same as it was nearly one hundred years ago, still stating in Article 7 of the Federal Constitutional Act that 'All citizens are equal before the law', which shows the influence of the jurisdiction of the Austrian Constitutional Court on the development of Constitutional law itself.[57]

4. Ideal of Justice

4.1 General remarks

Hans Kelsen's scepticism towards an abstract idea of justice has led to a model of strong legal certainty; a strong belief in parliamentary democracy resulting in substantive predictability has been the prevailing ideal of justice. The constitutional approach followed a formal and procedural understanding of justice.

In Austria, all state powers including the legislative, administrative and judicial authorities are especially bound due to the hierarchy of norms mentioned above: legislative initiatives must always consider constitutional rules as well as the European Law and according to the rule of law, administrative authorities and courts are bound by the acts of parliament.

Nevertheless, a distinction has to be made between decisions by the administrative authorities and those by the courts. Due to historical reasons, administration in Austria is strictly bound to the law, which was usually founded on the democratic principle. The theory behind this idea was in particular established by Austrian legal scholars Adolf Merkl and Hans Kelsen and saw an interrelation between the democratic statute and decisions strictly bound to it. Today, administrative decisions and court decisions regarding criminal procedures are still subject to a strong dependence on the law, whereas civil law cases usually allow for more flexibility.

The statutes also differ regarding their structure and wording, with some being rather open to interpretation, whereas others include more detailed provisions. A distinction might be possible between the codifications of the 19th and 20th centuries, including the General Civil Law Code and the procedural laws for civil and criminal trials, of which some date back to the 19th century. The Civil Law Code in particular has passed the test of time, since many rules have remained unchanged to this day and are applicable to all kind of problems occurring before the courts. On the other hand, some of the more recent statutes occur on a single-issue basis or have been heavily modified during the last years, making it possible to regulate certain cases in detail, and not leaving any space for individual decision-making by the authorities.[58]

57 See Öhlinger and Eberhard (2019) (n 12) para. 760.

58 This is particularly the case in social welfare and tax law. The Austrian Social Security Act (*Allgemeines Sozialversicherungsgesetz*) of 1955 has been amended 295 times, the Austrian Income Tax Code (*Einkommensteuergesetz*) of 1988 has been amended 140 times, and in addition to this, 51, respectively 30 provisions of that law have been repealed by the Constitutional Court.

Civil law courts usually apply teleological reductions or extensions to take place as well as gap-filling strategies to ensure the idea of distributive justice in single cases. The General Civil Law Code offers flexibility, for instance regarding the interpretation of contracts with a limited variation of the good-faith clause as known from German civil law in some provisions, as well as the nullity of contracts according to a violation of public morals.[59] Moreover, some statutes provide more space for individual decisions, especially in case of penalties, where courts have a large arsenal of possible tools to meet the requirements of the case in question – this regards the question of guilt as well as the extent of punishment.[60]

4.2 The role of the courts

Regarding questions of legal certainty and equity, these are often the basis for laws on a single-issue basis or *ad hoc* amendments as mentioned above but are also developed through court decisions and precedent. Although the Austrian legal system knows no system of precedents, since court decisions are only effective *inter partes*, the decisions by the Supreme Court in particular enjoy high authority and courts usually follow them. From a comparative perspective, no significant difference can be found in the role of precedents as they occur practically in Austria as well. The arguments brought forward by the courts also often tend to be a general consideration of the individual case rather than references to concrete norms, although of course this depends on the extent of existing legal norms.[61]

With regard to fundamental rights, most of them have been developed by the Austrian Constitutional Court, establishing a system of human rights protection through precedents with hardly any changes in the legal norms.[62] Moreover, changing circumstances in society have effects on the character of fundamental rights as established by the Constitutional Court: for example, the obligatory attendance for women in a domestic science school in the state of Vorarlberg was in conformity with the equality clause in 1974. Nevertheless, when the court had to decide on the provision some twenty years later, it was repealed due to the equality clause in Article 7 of the Federal Constitutional Act, which itself remained unchanged, showing the dynamic in the court's case law.[63]

It is remarkable to see in a comparative perspective that the development of constitutional law by the Constitutional Court was based on the right to equal treatment and the principle of reasonability, which the Court qualified as inherent principle of the right to equal treatment. In its case law on equality, the Court also intensified its idea of distribu-

59 See in particular § 863 paragraph 2, § 879, and § 914 of the Austrian General Civil Law Code. See also Hausmaninger (2011) (n 1) 249 ff.

60 See §§ 32 ss. of the Austrian Criminal Code. See in detail recently Alois Birklbauer, 'Abwägungsentscheidungen im Strafrecht' in Lamiss Khakzadeh-Leiler, Sebastian Schmid and Karl Weber (eds), *Interessenabwägung und Abwägungsentscheidungen* (Verlag Österreich 2014) 107 ss.

61 See Tomandl (1997) (n 23) 146 ff.

62 See Stelzer (2011) (n 3) 208–215.

63 See the Constitutional Court's rulings VfSlg. 7.461/1974 and VfSlg. 13.917/1994.

tive justice instead of a mere formal approach to justice. The equal treatment of citizens is not limited to a procedural justice but to distributive justice in the particular context.

4.3 Balancing legal predictability and individual justice

To sum up, the Austrian legal system realises a model of strong legal certainty. However, different mechanisms exist that preserve individual justice in specific cases. Civil law courts usually apply teleological reductions or extensions to take place as well as gap-filling strategies to ensure the idea of distributive justice in single cases. The General Civil Law Code offers flexibility, for instance regarding the interpretation of contracts with a limited variation of the good-faith clause as known from German civil law in some provisions as well as the nullity of contracts according to a violation of public morals.

With regards to fundamental rights, the Constitutional Court has e.g. developed an interpretation of the principle of equality, that intensifies its idea of distributive justice instead of a mere formal approach to justice. The equal treatment of citizens is not limited to procedural justice but to distributive justice in the particular context. Furthermore, the principle of proportionality also opens up a margin of appreciation, which enables the courts to balance legal predictability and individual justice.

5. Legal Method

5.1 Legal interpretation

The Austrian legal system is based on a civil law approach, which first focuses on the statutes. Case law becomes important only in regarding the interpretation of the legislation. However, almost all legislation is in need of interpretation. The General Civil Law Code, enacted in 1811 and in force in 1812, contains short provisions on legal interpretation.[64] Sec. 6 of the General Civil Law Code states that the statute can only be interpreted with regard to the text and its system as well as the intention of the legislator, and Sec. 7 refers to teleological argumentation, analogy and general principles of law.[65]

Austrian constitutionalism started in 1848 and led to the first Austrian Basic Laws in 1867, which established fundamental rights for the citizens in the monarchy. However, it took until the end of monarchy and a new constitution that the Constitution became a relevant part of legal interpretation. The Austrian Administrative Court, which was established in 1876 developed considerable elements of administrative procedural law using a principle-based approach. This historical achievement of developing the principle of fair trial was turned into a statute in 1925, the General Administrative Procedural

64 Back then, Austria had neither a parliament nor a constitution. See on the relevance and dynamic of the Austrian General Civil Law Code, Constanze Fischer-Czermak and others (eds), *Festschrift 200 Jahre ABGB* (Manz 2012).

65 Stephan Hinghofer Salzey, 'Methodology in Austria vis-à-vis Germany' in Ingvill Helland and Sören Koch (eds), *Nordic and Germanic Legal Methods* (Mohr Siebeck 2014) 223, 225–6.

Act. The effect was that the Administrative Court became much more positivistic and legalistic in its approach than just being known for the development of new principles.

The Austrian Federal Constitution does not contain any explicit rule on legal interpretation; however, the principle of legality as mentioned in Article 18 of the Federal Constitutional Act became an important part of the understanding of public law in the second part of the 20th century. A formalistic approach towards the interpretation of law became an important part of the Constitutional Court and the Administrative Court.[66]

Since the 1970s and 1980s, the Constitutional Court has changed its overall approach towards a more open perspective of interpretation and towards judicial activism. The development of the Court was accompanied by the influence of the ECHR and since the 1990s by EU law.[67] Currently, the Constitutional Court uses a broad toolkit of interpretative measures. These include a great variety of methods from a historic teleological interpretation (with regard to the allocation of powers between the federation and the state), a principle-led interpretation (especially with regard to the rule of law principle and the democratic principle) and a human rights-based approach (especially regarding the right to equal treatment) to a European-friendly interpretation (especially with regard to EU law and the ECHR).[68]

The Austrian Supreme Court, dealing mainly with private law, always had a broader approach, which was not as legalistic as the public law courts. Thus, the Court also relied on teleological interpretation and equity arguments. The Court, however, struggled to integrate a human rights-based approach into its legal reasoning. In the last 20 years however, awareness of European human rights standards has increased, resulting in a change of the Supreme Court's understanding of its function. Whereas it had formerly understood itself as not responsible for human rights protection, the Court now sees its competence as including also the protection of human rights.[69]

5.2 Legal Sources

The Austrian legal system is still perceived as a hierarchical model. The Austrian Constitution represents the top of this pyramid but has two levels: the basic principles of the Austrian Constitution (including democracy, rule of law, human rights, federalism, republicanism and separation of powers), and ordinary constitutional law. Beneath the Constitution come the Acts of Parliament and ordinances by the Government and other administrative authorities.

Although, legally speaking, court decisions are only binding *inter partes,* the case law of the court is an important part of legal reasoning for the courts. The same applies to

---

66 Ibid 227–31.

67 Konrad Lachmayer, 'Eine Sprache, zwei Rechtskulturen: deutsches und österreichisches Verfassungsrechtsdenken' in Uwe Kischel (ed), *Der Einfluss des deutschen Verfassungsrechtsdenkens in der Welt: Bedeutung, Grenzen, Zukunftsperspektiven* (Mohr Siebeck Verlag 2014).

68 Lachmayer (2017) (n 33).

69 Lamiss Khakzadeh-Leiler, *Die Grundrechte in der Judikatur des Obersten Gerichtshofs* (Verlag Österreich 2011).

the doctrine by academia. It is not an official legal source, but an important part of legal reasoning by the courts. Soft law and custom play a certain role but are not acknowledged in the same manner as other sources of law.

This view of the Austrian legal system, however, ignores the impact of EU law, which can be understood as a further layer and affects all levels of the Austrian legal system.[70] The primacy of EU law and the principle to interpret domestic law in conformity with EU law have significant impacts on the Austrian legal system. Since Austria's accession to the European Union in 1995, which was understood in substantial constitutional terms as a total revision of the Austrian Constitution, all legal authorities have contributed to the consideration and implementation of EU law. EU Law did not only become a new layer of Austrian law, but also created new legal terminology, legal institutions and legal argumentation. Most prominently, the legalistic understanding of statutory law was complemented by the case law of the CJEU. The principle-based and case-by-case interpretation of the Court became very influential in Austria.

5.3 Legal principles and further elements of legal reasoning by the courts

Legal methodology is applied by courts, at the same time as they are the main actors to develop and advance legal methodology. The legal foundations in statutes regarding methods are very flimsy; the courts adapt and broaden the possibilities for legal interpretation themselves. They can refer to a case law that at least in certain areas of law dates back to the 19th century.

The Constitutional Court and the Supreme Court, including all other ordinary courts, use legal principles as part of their legal reasoning. However, the relevance of legal principles is less when it comes to the Administrative Court and the administrative courts of first instance, which established certain legal principles also used especially in the context of legal procedure or legitimate expectations.

The use of analogy as part of the reasoning by the courts is more common in the area of civil law than in constitutional or administrative law. A strict interpretation of the rule of law is not only common in criminal law but also in administrative law, which prohibits a broad application of the concept of analogy. Thus, *lacunas* of law are not always filled by analogy or the use of legal principles, but also by legislative activities of the parliament.

Finally, the facts of the case play a minor role when interpreting the legal sources.[71] The distinction of different cases by the facts of the case is not important since Austria does not follow a common law approach. The relevant interrelation is not between the different cases but between the statute and the case at hand. The courts will certainly take

70 Lachmayer (2014) (n 67) 85–89.

71 See e.g. Michael Potacs, ‚Richterliche Rechtsfortbildung und Verfassungsrecht' in Ulrich Torggler (eds), Richterliche Rechtsfortbildung und ihre Grenzen (Linde 2019) 63–76.

the existing case law into consideration, but they will not distinguish the case as part of legal reasoning. The consideration of the case law will be used as an affirmative reference or as a distinction from the existing case law. The distinction, however, will be found in the different interpretation of the statute but not in the facts of the case.

6. Professionalisation

6.1 The academic system of legal education

In Austria, seven law faculties are established in Vienna, Graz, Linz, Innsbruck, Salzburg and Klagenfurt, offering legal studies in the traditional sense of the word, meaning four years of studies to obtain the degree *magister iuris*. The system is, however, changing to the Bologna model, which includes the standardisation of university degrees (Bachelor's and Master's Degree) across Europe to further harmonization of the university sector and student mobility, step-by-step.

Moreover, the Vienna University of Economics and Business offers a Bachelor's and Master's Course in Law and Economics for an overall five years of studies. Since 2016 Sigmund Freud University in Vienna provides the first private university Bachelor and Master studies in law. It is necessary to practice as a lawyer or become a judge, etc. to have finished legal studies at a Master's Degree level.

Access to legal studies was free in Austria for all who completed the general qualification for university entrance until 2018. In 2019 entrance examinations were introduced, but so far have been only exercised at the Vienna University of Economics and Business. In addition, the University of Vienna (1,980 students) and the University of Graz (600 students) limited the number of students, who could start to study law on a "first-come, first-serve" model, which was acceptable as all applicants could still study law as long as they applied before the given deadline. At the state universities, there are no tuition fees for university in Austria. This overall situation led to a very high number of students in general: in 2018–2019, about 40,000 students (17,515 men, 21,849 women, 5511 international students) studied law in Austria.[72] Especially in Vienna, this situation means huge classes and exams in the first years. The university exams in the first year fulfil the function of student selection and lead to high dropout rates in the first year. The overall number of graduations in law in 2017–18 was 2,474.[73] It is obvious that most of the students starting a law study will never finish.

Until 2004, there was a unified concept of legal education in Austria, which since the autonomy of universities has diversified more and more. However, the curriculum of all universities contains certain core contents, which are also required by the Austrian Bar Association as a precondition for work as a lawyer. These include certain areas of law,

72 Data of 2018/19 according to Statistik Austria, available at https://www.statistik.at/web_de/statistiken/menschen_und_gesellschaft/bildung/hochschulen/studierende_belegte_studien/index.html accessed 14 April 2020.

73 Data of 2017/18 according to Statistik Austria, available at https://www.statistik.at/web_de/statistiken/menschen_und_gesellschaft/bildung/hochschulen/studienabschluesse/index.html accessed 14 April 2020.

especially criminal law and procedure, civil law and procedure, corporate law, public law, labour law, tax law, international and European law. Legal studies also include the teaching of certain foundational knowledge in legal history (including Roman law and German legal history), legal philosophy and methodology. Usually, comparative law is not an obligatory part of legal studies. Regarding legal skills, certain academic and research skills are taught. Law students usually have to write a master's thesis at the end of their studies.[74]

There are no specific statistics on law professors in Austria available. However overall in 2017, there were 2,377 university professors and 34,352 scholars working at university in all disciplines. More detailed numbers can be provided with regard to the University of Vienna, which has 452 professors overall (about 40 law professors), and 6,844 academic personnel overall (about 400 law school academic personnel). In conclusion, at the University of Vienna, the percentage of legal scholars is 7–10% of the overall personnel of academic scholars.

In Austria, there are about 100 journals established in the field of law. There is no reliable data on the publication figures for books in the field of law each year. However, an estimate of 300 and 500 books annually seems reasonable.[75] The numbers of journals and books have increased significantly in the last 20 years as the technological, and thus economic, barriers have been reduced by the introduction of IT in research. Most of the journals are not only run by academics but also by legal practitioners. The publication of books is also significantly related to lawyers in practice. Besides academic monographs and edited collections, commentaries on legislation and handbooks play an important role in the legal literature in Austria.

6.2 Legal professions and professional training

Certain traditional legal professions, such as judge, lawyer or notary, require specific professional training after the end of the legal studies.[76] To begin with, a seven-month period of work experience at the ordinary courts is an obligatory precondition for any of these legal professions. If one wants to become a judge, one has to apply within the first three months of the seven-month period to the Court of Appeals for a position as a judge on probation. There are highly selective exams that one has to pass successfully to reach this first step in the court system. After three years on probation, another demanding exam has to be passed to become a judge at an ordinary court. The exam also opens up the possibility of becoming public prosecutor.

The system of notaries is quite similar with the important difference that there is no entrance examination. Each notary has the possibility to select their own candidates. After finishing the three years on probation and the successful passing of the exam, there

74 The only exception is the Faculty of Law at the University of Vienna, where it is enough to write two seminar papers.

75 At least 300 books, which were published in Austria in 2018, are available at the library of the University of Vienna and are related to law.

76 An overview on legal professions in Austria is given by Hausmaninger (2011) (n 1) 107 ff.

is a long waiting list to become a notary, which can be achieved on average at the age of 40 to 45 years. There are about 500 notaries in Austria, who especially take care of notarization in corporate, real estate issues and probate proceedings.

The biggest group are the lawyers, of which there are more than 6000 in Austria. After finishing the seven-month placement at court, it is necessary to work as a candidate lawyer for three years. Again, it is necessary to pass a highly demanding bar exam to become a lawyer. Even after the exam, it takes up to two years to be put on the list of lawyers.

Lawyers, like graduates of other university studies, have the possibility of working as civil servants in public administration. A four-year period of professional training is concluded by an exam, which depends on the specific public authority and might be highly different in quality and difficulty. A specific exam is necessary to apply to the Ministry of External Affairs to become a diplomat. This highly selective exam is not just open to jurists, but a considerable number of jurists are considered.

In conclusion, the legal education and the access to legal practice is characterised in the following way: 1. free access to study law at university, 2. extreme selection in the first years, and 3. strong specification and narrow qualification after university studies including further education for some years in legal practice. While the access seems very liberal, the conclusion of legal education is very demanding.

7. Internationalisation

7.1 General remarks

The Austrian legal scholar Anna Gamper concluded that the Austrian approach towards law produced outside the jurisdictional borders was "Europe-friendly but not multicultural".[77] This conclusion is an adequate summary of the Austrian approach towards international and transnational law. Within the different legal layers beyond the state, it is necessary to distinguish between general international law, the European Convention of Human Rights, EU law and the relevance of comparative law.

7.2 The implementation of international law

Article 9 Paragraph 1 of the Federal Constitutional Act (F-CA) states that 'generally recognised rules of international law are regarded as integral parts of [Austrian] federal law.'[78] Moreover, the Austrian Constitution provides the framework of participation in international treaties (Article 50 and 65 F-CA) and international organizations (Article 9 Paragraph 2 F-CA). Usually, international treaties do not have a direct effect on the

77 See Anna Gamper, 'Austria: Non-cosmopolitan, but Europe-friendly – The Constitutional Court's Comparative Approach' in Tania Groppi and Marie-Claire Ponthoreau (eds), *The Use of Foreign Precedents by Constitutional Judges* (Hart Publishing 2013) 213. Anna Gamper is professor for public law at the University of Innsbruck.

78 See a similar provision in Article 25 of the German Basic Law.

Austrian legal system but have to be implemented by Parliament if they affect Austrian constitutional law.[79]

Overall, the Austrian constitutional order has tended to be rather permeable with regards to international law. This is mirrored in the case law of the Austrian Constitutional Court. Examples include the declaration of constitutionality of the ESM treaty[80] and the "six-pack" judgment[81]. However, in the "third runway" judgment 2017[82] the Constitutional Court deviated from this trend, declaring international treaties on the reduction of CO2 emissions not relevant for statutory interpretation.

7.3 The role of the European Convention of Human Rights

Austria joined the ECHR in 1958 and declared in 1964 that the ECHR was part of Austrian Constitutional Law.[83] Since the 1970s and up until today, the ECHR has fulfilled the function of a constitutional human rights catalogue with increasing importance. As part of Austrian constitutional law, the ECHR has had a huge impact on Austrian legal culture. First, the human rights of the ECHR affected constitutional law itself by significantly increasing the human rights available for people living in Austria. Second, the principle of proportionality and the development of the case law of the ECtHR had an important influence on the case law of the Austrian Constitutional Court.[84]

The ECHR and the case law of the European Commission of Human Rights led to constitutional changes in the Austrian administrative structure in the 1980s. Independent Administrative Senates were established, which met the requirement of a tribunal according to Article 6 ECHR. These developments finally led to the introduction of Administrative Courts of first instance in 2014, which substantially changed the Austrian system of administration.

The Austrian Constitutional Court did not always follow the case law of the ECtHR and started certain dialogues, e.g. on the understanding of civil rights and obligation in Article 6 ECHR or the principle of *ne bis in idem* in Article 4 of the Additional Protocol

79 See Stelzer (2011) (n 3) 134–136.

80 VfSlg. 19.750/2013.

81 VfSlg. 19.809/2013.

82 VfSlg. 20.185/2017.

83 See the amendment published in BGBl 59/1964.

84 See e.g. a statement by the former president of the Austrian Constitution Court in January 2015: "By being implemented by the Constitutional Court, the Convention and the case law of the European Court of Human Rights have become a major yardstick for the constitutionality of Austrian legislation. In many cases, judgments of the European Court of Human Rights or of the Constitutional Court concerning the interpretation of the Convention have caused Austrian legislation to be adjusted in the spirit of improving the safeguard of fundamental rights and freedoms. Recent judgments that highlight this influence concern medically assisted reproduction, the principle of non-discrimination with regard to sexual orientation as well as certain issues of asylum and immigration", available at http://www.echr.coe.int/Documents/Speech_20150130_Seminar_Gerhart_Holzinger_2015_ENG.PDF accessed 14 April 2020.

No. 7 to the ECHR. However, the constitutional court mainly adopted the case law of the ECtHR, e.g. regarding the non-discrimination of LGBT in recent years.[85]

The ordinary courts had more difficulty in adapting to human rights standards in civil and criminal law.[86] Although this has changed in recent years, the full establishment and awareness of human rights approaches in ordinary courts is still lacking. The successful political prohibition of the introduction of a constitutional complaint against Supreme Court judgments in 2015 illustrates that the Austrian legal culture is still divided between administrative law on the one hand and civil/criminal law on the other hand. This separation between the courts leads to the necessity for the Supreme Court, including all ordinary courts, to establish their own approach towards human rights. The ECtHR, which is also part of Austrian constitutional law, definitely offers an important contribution to that development, which still has high potential for improvement.

7.4 The overwhelming importance of EU Law

Austria's accession to the European Union in 1995 was prepared by the popular referendum in 1994. This referendum was necessary because Austrian constitutional lawyers were generally convinced that the accession meant a total revision of the Austrian constitution especially with regard to democracy, rule of law and federalism.[87] This total revision of the Austrian Constitution led to an immediate integration and implementation of EU law in the Austrian legal system and had a significant impact on Austrian legal culture. Austria is following a moderate monistic approach but acknowledges the dualistic preconditions.[88]

From the very beginning, not only the legislature but also the courts were willing to contribute to Austrian participation in European integration. All kinds of courts, including the three highest courts, most notably the Austrian Constitutional Court, were willing to start preliminary proceedings at the Court of Justice of the European Union (CJEU) in Luxemburg.[89] Although there is an obligation for courts of last instances to start preliminary ruling procedure when the interpretation of EU law is unclear or EU secondary law violates EU primary law, it was not self-evident at all over a long period

85 In 2015, the Austrian Constitutional Court e.g. opened up the possibility for adoption of children by homosexual partners. In 2017 the Constitutional Court declared the exclusion of same-sex couples from marriage as unconstitutional and in 2018 opened up the possibility of non-binary persons to declare themselves as belonging to a third gender on official documents.

86 See with regard to freedom of expression in recent years an overview available at https://blog.lehofer.at/2013/10/Artikel10-AT.html accessed 14 April 2020.

87 See Konrad Lachmayer, 'The Constitution of Austria in International Constitutional Networks: Pluralism, Dialogues and Diversity' in Anneli Albi and Samo Bardutzky (eds), *National Constitutions in European and Global Governance: Democracy, Rights, the Rule of Law* (Springer 2019) 1274–1275.

88 Michael Potacs, 'Das Verhältnis zwischen der EU und ihren Mitgliedstaaten im Lichte traditioneller Modelle' (2010) Vol. 65 *Zeitschrift öffentliches Recht* 117.

89 See e.g. VfGH 28.11.2012, G 47/12; 2.3.2001, W I-14/99; 12.12.2000, KR 1-6/00, KR 8/00; 10.3.1999, B 2251/97, B 2594/99; further information is available at https://www.vfgh.gv.at/rechtsprechung/referral_for_a_preliminary_ruling.en.html accessed 14 April 2020.

of time that domestic constitutional courts applied to the CJEU. Moreover, all highest courts in Austria use EU law directly as part of their legal reasoning.

This implementation of EU law had significant impacts on Austrian legal culture as a way of thinking that focused on case law, and general principles of law became more important in the legal reasoning of Austrian courts. By implementing EU directives, the legislature started to change the way of drafting bills using a more flexible understanding of the principle of legality, which gave courts again more flexibility in applying statutory law. However, the implementation of EU law means an ongoing struggle to implement into the Austrian legal system ideas, concepts and methods that are foreign and strange from an Austrian perspective. This challenge to the Austrian legal system has been taken up by Parliament as well as the administration and judiciary. It creates an ongoing process of adaption and developing strategies.

7.5 Foreign legal sources and comparative law in the Austrian legal system

The Austrian perspective towards foreign legal sources is still quite limited. The use of foreign precedents by the courts usually leads to Germany. The language, however, is not the only reason, because Swiss cases are hardly cited. The level of sophistication in German legal culture, the number of cases and the depth of legal analysis in academia have to be taken into account for this reason. These reasons, however, should not overshadow the fact that Austrian legal culture is – beside German influences – not very open towards legal developments in other countries, especially beyond Europe and the US. Although the relevance of other European countries and the US is already very limited in Austrian legal debate, hardly any further comparative exchange takes place, and this is limited to certain scholars or personal initiatives. While openness towards other legal cultures is little, the willingness to export Austrian legal culture is much greater. However, the success of this transfer of Austrian legal knowledge seems rather unconvincing. For historical reasons the transnational influence is mainly regional, especially with regard to Eastern Europe and the Western Balkans.

The Austrian Constitutional Court only refers explicitly to foreign courts in selected cases.[90] The main reference is to the German Constitutional Court; hardly any other constitutional or highest court is mentioned. In comparison, the Austrian Supreme Court quite often – about 450 times from 2000 to 2007 out of 28,868 – cites German Court decisions.[91] Otherwise, foreign court decisions are referred to only 40 times, with Switzerland, Italy or France among the countries mentioned.

90 See Gamper (2013) (n 76) 213.

91 See Martin Gelter and Mathias Siems, 'Language, Legal Origins, and Culture before the Courts: Cross-Citations between Supreme Courts in Europe' in (2013) No. 1 *Supreme Court Economic Review* 215; see also Martin Gelter and Mathias Siems, 'Citations to Foreign Courts – Illegitimate and Superfluous, or Unavoidable? Evidence from Europe.' (2014) Vol. 62 No. 1 *American Journal of Comparative Law* 35.

The role of comparative law in legal education is not very prominent either. Although the necessity for comparative knowledge and methodology is rising in practice, it is still a voluntary task for students to engage in comparative law.

8. Conclusion

In conclusion, Austria can be understood as a classic civil law country. The Austrian legal culture was strongly shaped by legal history and the establishment of legal education centuries ago. The traditional legal professions and their representatives also have an important impact on legal culture in Austria. The public administration also embodies legal knowledge; legal culture developed during the last 250 years. In the last decades, this traditional understanding has been shifting enormously towards a European approach. Austrian legal culture is first and foremost accommodating towards European law, including the ECHR as part of the Austrian Constitution and EU law. The case law of both the ECtHR and the CJEU is of major importance for the Austrian legal system. In this regard, the Austrian legal culture can serve as an example of the impact of case law oriented towards European law on civil law systems.

If one wants to characterise the Austrian legal culture, one has to take the three highest courts into consideration, which represent different pillars of Austrian approaches towards law. The Austrian Constitutional Court follows a human rights and value-based approach, which includes different forms of legal principles in its constitutional reasoning. The Administrative Court is based on a relatively strict understanding of the principle of legality and follows a more textual approach towards law. Finally, the Supreme Court is more open to teleological argumentation, analogy and general principles of law, but lacks a fully-fledged implementation of human rights in its case law.

With regard to general international law, the Austrian legal system is very open towards international influence. If one looks into the details, however, the Austrian approach is much more selective. Regarding comparative law and the transnational transfer of legal concepts, the German legal system has an overwhelming importance, while all other legal systems have a negligible impact. The Austrian academic system is changing only slowly towards a more international approach.

The Austrian Legal Culture and its structures and structural elements	
Institutional structure	
Conflict resolution	**Norm production**
Complex court system mainly dividing ordinary courts (dealing with civil actions and criminal charges) from administrative courts. Three highest courts (Constitutional Court, Administrative Court and Supreme Court).	Main focus on legislation, hierarchical legal system, high importance of the Constitution. Besides the statutes, case law is very important in practice, but no doctrine of strictly binding precedents has been introduced.

Intellectual structure			
Ideal of justice	**Legal method**	**Degree of professionalisation**	**Character of internationalisation**
The ideal behind the hierarchy of norms is a strict principle of legality and the importance of high legal certainty. In civil proceedings, substantive concepts of justice play a significant role. The Austrian Constitutional Court opened up its approach by using the principle of equality.	Legal methods can be distinguished between the different courts. The Constitutional Court is human rights oriented and value-based. The Administrative Court is restrictive and based on a strict understanding of the principle of legality. The Supreme Court takes teleological arguments, analogy and general principles of law into consideration, but lacks a full human rights-based approach.	1. Free access to study law at university 2. Extreme selection in the first years 3. Strong specification and narrow qualification after university studies including further education for some years in legal practice. While the access seems very liberal, the conclusion of legal education is very demanding.	The Austrian legal culture is Euro-friendly. The ECHR is part of the Austrian Constitution and has a major influence. EU law has an overwhelming impact on Austrian legal culture and courts are open-minded (e.g. regarding preliminary proceedings). Legal comparison mainly focuses on Germany but lacks a global and multicultural perspective.

9. Bibliography

Bezemek C, 'A Kelsenian model of constitutional adjudication' (2012) 67 *Zeitschrift für Öffentliches Recht* 115. DOI: http://dx.doi.org/10.2139/ssrn.1937575

Birklbauer A, 'Abwägungsentscheidungen im Strafrecht' in Khakzadeh-Leiler L, Schmid S and Weber K (eds), *Interessenabwägung und Abwägungsentscheidungen* (Verlag Österreich 2014) 107

Brauneder W, *Österreichische Verfassungsgeschichte* (11th edn, Manz 2009)

Bußjäger P, Balthasar A and Sonntag N (eds), *Direkte Demokratie im Diskurs* (new academic press 2014)

Damjanovic D, 'Soziale Grundrechte' in Heissl G (ed), *Handbuch Menschenrechte* (facultas.wuv 2009) 516

Fischer-Czermak C and others (eds), *Festschrift 200 Jahre ABGB* (Manz 2012)

Gamper, A, 'The Principle of Homogeneity and Democracy in Austrian Federalism: The Constitutional Court's Ruling on Direct Democracy in Vorarlberg' in Bußjäger P and Gamper A (eds), *The Homogeneity of Democracy, Rights and the Rule of Law in Federal or Confederal Systems* (Braumüller 2003) 125

—— 'Introduction to the Study of the Law of the Austrian Constitution' (2008) 2 no. 2 *ICL-Journal* 92

—— 'Austria: Non-cosmopolitan, but Europe-friendly – The Constitutional Court's Comparative Approach', in The Use of Foreign Precedents by Constitutional Judges, edited by Tania Groppi and Marie-Claire Ponthoreau, Oxford/Portland: Hart Publishing, 2013, 213–227. DOI: http://dx.doi.org/10.5040/9781472561312.ch-008

— — and Palermo F, 'The Constitutional Court of Austria: Modern Profiles of an Archetype of Constitutional Review' (2008) 3 no. 2 *Journal of Comparative Law* 64

— — 'Administrative Law' in Grabenwarter C and Schauer M (eds), *Introduction to the Law of Austria* (Wolters Kluwer 2015) 19

Gelter M and Siems M, 'Language, Legal Origins, and Culture before the Courts: Cross-Citations between Supreme Courts in Europe' (2013) 21 no. 1 *Supreme Court Economic Review* 215. DOI: http://dx.doi.org/10.2139/ssrn.1629169

— — 'Citations to Foreign Courts – Illegitimate and Superfluous, or Unavoidable? Evidence from Europe.' (2014) 62 no. 1 *American Journal of Comparative Law* 35. DOI: http://dx.doi.org/10.5131/ajcl.2013.0012

Grabenwarter C, 'Constitutional Law' in Grabenwarter C and Schauer M (eds), *Introduction to the Law of Austria* (Wolters Kluwer 2015) 1

Gschnitzer F, *Allgemeiner Teil des bürgerlichen Rechts* (Springer 1966)

Hausmaninger H, *The Austrian Legal System* (4th edn, Manz 2011)

Jabloner C, 'Das 'Denksporterkenntnis' des VfGH im Spannungsfeld von Verfassungsrecht und Rechtstechnik' in Bernd-Christian Funk and others (eds), *Staatsrecht und Staatswissenschaften in Zeiten des Wandels* (Springer 1992) 189.

Jellinek G, *Ein Verfassungsgerichtshof für Österreich* (Alfred Hölder 1885)

Khakzadeh-Leiler L, *Die Grundrechte in der Judikatur des Obersten Gerichtshofs* (Verlag Österreich 2011)

Kelsen H, *Reine Rechtslehre* (2nd edn, Verlag Österreich, 1960)

— — 'Wesen und Entwicklung der Staatsgerichtsbarkeit' in Klecatsky HR, Marcic R and Schambeck H (eds), *Die Wiener rechtstheoretische Schule* (Verlag Österreich 2010) 1485

Kodek GE, '§ 12 ABGB' in Rummel P and Lukas M (eds), *ABGB* (4th edn, Manz 2014)

— — and Mayr PG, *Zivilprozessrecht* (4th edn, facultas.wuv 2018)

Lachmayer K, 'Eine Sprache, zwei Rechtskulturen: deutsches und österreichisches Verfassungsrechtsdenken' in Kischel U (ed), *Der Einfluss des deutschen Verfassungsrechtsdenkens in der Welt: Bedeutung, Grenzen, Zukunftsperspektiven* (Mohr Siebeck Verlag 2014)

— — 'The Austrian Constitutional Court' in Jakab A, Dyevre A and Itzcovich G (eds), *Constitutional Reasoning* (Cambridge University Press 2017)

— — 'The Constitution of Austria in International Constitutional Networks: Pluralism, Dialogues and Diversity' in Albi A and Bardutzky S (eds), *National Constitutions in European and Global Governance: Democracy, Rights, the Rule of Law* (Springer 2019)

— — and Eberhard H, 'Constitutional Reform 2008 in Austria' (2008) Vol. 2 No. 2 *ICL-Journal*

Merkl A, 'Prolegomena einer Theorie des rechtlichen Stufenbaues' in Klecatsky HR, Marcic R and Schambeck H (eds), *Die Wiener rechtstheoretische Schule* (Verlag Österreich 2010) 1071.

Neudorfer S and Wernig C, *Implementation of International Treaties into National Legal Orders: The Protection of the Rights of the Child within the Austrian Legal System* (Max Planck Yearbook of United Nations Law Volume 14, Martinus Nijhoff Publishers 2010)

Öhlinger T, 'Art 9/1 B-VG' in Korinek K and Holoubek M (eds), *Österreichisches Bundesverfassungsrecht* (Springer 2002)

— — 'The Genesis of the Austrian Model of Constitutional Review of Legislation' (2003) 16 no. 2 *Ratio Juris* 16 206. DOI: http://dx.doi.org/10.1111/1467-9337.00233

— — and Eberhard H, *Verfassungsrecht* (10th edn, facultas.wuv 2014)

— — and Poier K (eds), *Direkte Demokratie und Parlamentarismus* (Böhlau 2015)

Potacs M, 'Das Verhältnis zwischen der EU und ihren Mitgliedstaaten im Lichte traditioneller Modelle' (2010) Vol. 65 *Zeitschrift öffentliches Recht* 117

—— 'Richterliche Rechtsfortbildung und Verfassungsrecht' in Ulrich Torggler (eds), Richterliche Rechtsfortbildung und ihre Grenzen (Linde 2019) 63–76.

Salzey SH, 'Methodology in Austria vis-à-vis Germany' in Ingvill Helland and Sören Koch (eds), *Nordic and Germanic Legal Methods* (Mohr Siebeck 2014)

Seiler S, *Strafprozessrecht* (18th edn, facultas.wuv 2020)

Stelzer M, *The Constitution of the Republic of Austria* (Hart Publishing 2011)

Tiefenthaler V, *Gewohnheit und Verfassung* (facultas.wuv 2012)

Tomandl T, *Rechtsstaat Österreich* (Manz 1997)

Walter R, 'Die Gewohnheit als rechtserzeugender Tatbestand' (1963) 18 *Österreichische Juristen-Zeitung* 225

Ziniel T, 'Strengthening the Judicial Review System in Austria' (2014) 8 no. 4 *ICL Journal* 437

15. An Introduction to Italian Legal Culture

Esmeralda Colombo and Lars Kvestad[1]

1. Introduction

In this chapter, legal culture is defined as "ideas of and expectations to law made operational by institutional(like) practices".[2] We construe law as a "symbolic normative phenomenon"[3] made of several elements and layers. With respect to elements, we follow the legal cultural model separating institutional elements (norm-production and conflict resolution) from intellectual elements (the ideal of justice, professionalization, internationalization, and the legal method).[4] With respect to layers, we apply the established understandings of legal orders as consisting of a surface layer of ever-new regulations and decisions, an intermediate layer that changes at a slower pace, and a bottom layer, which is more resistant to change.[5] Such layers relate to one another within the metaphor of a "legal" sea.[6]

As a general caveat, this chapter does not allow for the investigation of all possible interactions among the legal cultural elements. Moreover, our intermediary and general conclusions are not summaries, but rather critical remarks on the legal cultural model and Italian legal culture. In the legal cultural analysis, we begin with norm-production and conclude with the legal method. The starting point in norm-production origi-

---

1 The authors would like to express their gratitude to Prof. Sören Koch and Prof. Jørn Øyrehagen Sunde for their encouragement, guidance, and comments on earlier versions of this work. Heartfelt thanks to Prof. Michele Taruffo, Niels Graaf, Marius Mikkel Kjølstad, and an anonymous peer reviewer for having read and commented this work's manuscript. Deep gratitude goes also to Prof. Angelo Mattioni, Prof. Gabrio Forti, Prof. Angelo Giarda, and Prof. Luigi Paolo Comoglio, and many other faculty members at Università Cattolica del Sacro Cuore, Milan, for their wonderful teachings. Immense gratitude is owed to Judge Damiano Spera for having shown with wit and exactitude the normative universe of law in action.

2 See Jørn Øyrehagen Sunde', 'Managing the Unmanageable – An Essay Concerning Legal Culture as an Analytical Tool' in this volume, chapter 2.

3 Kaarlo Tuori, *Critical Legal Positivism* (Ashgate 2002) 40.

4 See Sunde (2020) (n 2).

5 Tuori (2002) (n 3) 154 ff.

6 Jørn Øyrehagen Sunde, *Speculum Legale: Rettsspegelen* (Fagbokforlaget 2005) 27–31.

nates from Italy's membership in the civil law tradition, where legislation is preeminent over case law. What materializes early, however, is the contribution of Italy's courts to norm-production through their case law, which is a feature peculiar to the common law tradition. Concluding this chapter with the legal method will offer the opportunity to explore the interactions that the legal method entertains with all other elements of the legal cultural model, which we deem a new, possibly heuristic, application of the legal cultural model. We believe that this approach clearly illustrates the most important elements of Italy's legal culture, and their interaction.[7]

2. Is there one Italian legal culture?

2.1 The Italian context

"Italy juts out into the sea from the almost crescent-shaped chain of the Alps".[8] It features an 8,962 kilometer-long coastline and its surface area covers 301,340 square kilometers. With regard to its political geography, Italy is divided into 20 regions and 93 provinces, but is known as the "land of cities" due to its 8,003 municipalities and 14 metropolitan cities.[9] Importantly, it has long provided the most accessible passage from east to west, notwithstanding the Alps in Northern Italy.[10] The Apennines, dividing the peninsula east- and west-ward, have contributed to the use of seaways for exchanges with foreign lands.[11] Encased within Italy are two independent states: the Republic of San Marino and Vatican City, which hosts the Holy See – the seat of the Pope's authority.

Due to its cultural history, the country encompasses a rich tapestry of languages and dialects.[12] With some variance based on regional autonomy, the official language is Italian. Its population of 59.4 million inhabitants[13] ranks Italy as the fourth most populous country in Europe – after Germany, France, and the United Kingdom[14] – and it features a high number of inhabitants per square kilometer (201 on average).[15] Projections show a population decrease in coming decades as Italy's fertility rate is the

7 On interactions, see also Sunde (2020) (n 2).

8 Pliny the Elder, *Historia naturalis,* Book III v.38.

9 *Territorio e ambiente* (Istituto Nazionale di Statistica, 2016) 6 and https://www.tuttitalia.it/province/popolazione/ accessed 27 February 2019. On the trope of Italy as a land of cities, see Edward Bispham, 'Pliny the Elder's Italy' (2007) no. 100 *Bulletin of the Institute of Classical Studies* 41, 43.

10 Ernesto Galli della Loggia, *L'identità Italiana* (Il Mulino 1998) 8–9.

11 Ibid 15.

12 E.g., French, German, Slovene, Croatian, Albanian Arbëresh, Greek, and Catalan, see https://www.britannica.com/place/Italy/Languages accessed 27 February 2019.

13 See http://hdr.undp.org/en/indicators/44206 accessed 27 February 2019.

14 See https://www.ined.fr/en/everything_about_population/data/europe-developed-countries/population-births-deaths/ accessed 27 February 2019.

15 *Territorio e ambiente,* Istituto Nazionale di Statistica (n 9) 5.

lowest in the EU, along with Spain (1.3 per woman).[16] Roughly 3.7 million non-EU citizens reside in Italy. The most represented nationalities among them are Moroccan, Albanian, Chinese, Ukrainian, and Filipino.[17] Compared to the previous year, in 2017 the authorities granted 16% more residence permits, of which 38.5% were for asylum and humanitarian protections.[18] The overall population's religious affiliations are Roman Catholic – nominal (55%), Roman Catholic – practicing (28%), Muslim (2%), and other (1%), whilst 14% of the population is non-religious or atheist.[19]

Italy is Europe's fourth largest economy.[20] Its labor force is divided between agriculture (7.5%), industry (23%), commerce (41.5%), and other services including public administration (28%). With arable land accounting for 22.44% of its territory,[21] Italy ranks first in the EU in terms of quality labels of food and beverages.[22] The industrial sectors that contribute most to GDP are the manufacturing, metallurgy, and machinery sectors.[23] Italy joined the G6, now G8, in 1975.[24]

2.2 A glimpse of Italian legal history

Italy's history resembles a kaleidoscope, constantly changing the peninsula's socioeconomic and political patterns and inclinations. This historical glimpse is meant to offer insights into the reasons behind the continuing debate over Italian "identity".[25]

Notwithstanding the legal legacy of Roman law before the fall of the Roman Empire, we follow Antonio Padoa Schioppa's partition of Italian legal history into six phases, starting with the intersection between ancient history and the Early Middle Ages, falling between the 4th and 6th centuries.[26] In particular, the decline of the Western Roman Empire in 476 A.D. did not coincide with a total loss of political power since the Eastern Roman (Byzantine) Empire kept some territories under its rule. But what defines this phase is that the Roman Empire centralized its law-production power under the authority of the Emperor.[27] The watershed in world legal history occurred with the issuance of the *Corpus Juris Civilis* by order of Emperor Justinian between 529–534 A.D.[28]

---

16 See https://data.oecd.org/pop/fertility-rates.htm accessed 27 February 19. Data refer to 2016, and assume no net migration and unchanged mortality. On Spain, see https://ec.europa.eu/eurostat/statistics-explained/images/0/0e/Fertility_indicators%2C_2016.png accessed 27 February 2019.

17 *Cittadini non comunitari: presenza, nuovi ingressi e acquisizioni di cittadinanza,* Istituto Nazionale di Statistica, 14 November 2018.

18 Ibid.

19 See https://www.britannica.com/place/Italy/Languages accessed 27 February 2019.

20 See https://ec.europa.eu/eurostat/web/products-eurostat-news/-/DDN-20180511-1?inheritRedirect=true accessed 27 February 2019.

21 See https://tradingeconomics.com/italy/arable-land-percent-of-land-area-wb-data.html accessed 27 February 2019.

22 'Agricultura' in *Annuario Statistico Italiano,* Istituto Nazionale di Statistica 2017, 450.

23 See http://dati.istat.it/Index.aspx?DataSetCode=DCCN_PILN accessed 27 February 2019.

24 See https://www.esteri.it/mae/en/politica_estera/g8/storia-del-g7-g8.html accessed 27 February 2019.

25 Galli della Loggia, *L'identità Italiana* (n 10) 59 ff.

26 Antonio Padoa-Schioppa, *Italia Ed Europa Nella Storia Del Diritto* (Il Mulino 2010) 21–29.

27 Ibid 22. The two sources of law were what we would now call case law (*rescripta)* and general law (*edicta).*

28 The Corpus Juris Civilis is a compilation of classical and late classical Roman law.

A second phase, between the 7th and 11th centuries, was marked by three conquests. The first was the conquest of the northern and central regions of the peninsula on behalf of the Longobards, a Germanic tribe. One Longobard regulation worth mentioning is pecuniary sanctions for criminal wrongs as a substitute for private *vendetta.*[29] The second occupation was effected by the Carolingians, who introduced feudal laws and institutions.[30] The third conquest was the Arab seizure of Sicily from the Byzantine Empire and the establishment of the Emirate of Sicily.[31] At the end of this phase, between the 11th and 12th centuries, a revolution commenced as one result of the revival and review of the *Corpus Juris Civilis* at the first Western university, Bologna University, which was founded by students in the second half of the 12th century.[32] At the same time in Bologna, canon law was collected in the *Decretum Gratiani,* which diffused its concept of equity among both students and scholars.[33] At this point in time, the Italian peninsula had no common political or legal institutions, except for those of the Church.

A third phase spanned the 12th to the 15th century – a true blossoming of the arts and the economy. The peninsula was characterized by a constellation of city-states, each establishing its own local legislation and institutions. Later, the political crisis of the city-states gave way to lordships in the 14th century, and principalities in the 15th century.[34]

A fourth phase, between the 16th and 17th centuries, could be identified as the "Spanish era", due to the great influence wielded by Spanish rule in both Northern Italy (e.g., the Duchy of Milan), and Southern Italy (e.g., the kingdom of Naples, Sicily, and Sardinia). Recognized for the rise of the aristocracy and courts of justice, this phase of Italian legal history was characterized by the quasi-legislative role of legal doctrine.[35]

A fifth phase spanned from the 18th century to Italy's unification in 1861. The Enlightenment finds one of its guiding lights in Beccaria, who harshly criticized the criminal system of his time. His fundamental objection to the death penalty persuaded the Grand-Duke of Tuscany, a member of the Hapsburg family, to abolish the death penalty in 1786, the first state to do so worldwide. Some years later, in 1796–1797, Napoleon's campaign in Italy not only contributed to his fame as a military commander, but also allowed for a unification under *one* administration and *one* body of laws in

---

29 Padoa-Schioppa (2010) (n 26) 23.

30 Ibid 23.

31 On the influence of the Arab legal method and jury on England through Sicily, see Lisa Watanabe, 'The Possible Contribution of Islamic Legal Institutions to the Emergence of a Rule of Law and the Modern State in Europe' in Nayef R. F. Al-Rodhan (ed), *The Role of the Arab-Islamic World in the Rise of the West: Implications for Contemporary Trans-Cultural Relations, (P*algrave Macmillan 2012) 74.

32 See James. A. Brundage, *The Medieval Origins of the Legal Profession: Canonists, Civilians, and Courts* (The University of Chicago Press 2008) 82.

33 On references to Roman law in the *Decretum Gratiani,* see Anders Winroth, 'Recent Work On The Making Of Gratians Decretum' (2008) 26 *Bulletin of Medieval Canon Law* 6.

34 Padoa-Schioppa (2010) (n 26) 24. Within this phase, the school of glossators started in Bologna, see Rafael Domingo, *Roman Law: An Introduction* (Routledge 2018), Chapter 6.

35 Padoa-Schioppa (2010) (n 26) 26. Within this phase, the school of commentators started in Bologna, see Domingo (2018) (n 35), Chapter 6.

Northern Italy and the Kingdom of Naples, respectively.[36] Without the Napoleonic influence, the period leading to the unification of Italy, known as the *Risorgimento,* and the very real unification of Italy in 1861 would have been unlikely.[37] Aided by France,[38] national unification was attained through the House of Savoy (Kingdom of Sardinia) and individuals in the Kingdom of the Two Sicilies, the sole "state" entities that Italy's history had hitherto featured.[39] This is a telling counterpoint to the history of urban polycentrism that had long characterized the rest of the peninsula.[40]

The sixth phase started with the unification of Italy in 1861 under the Savoy monarchy. Some of the legislation laid down in the Kingdom of Sardinia was maintained and a number of institutions were centralized,[41] but some territories remained external to the newly-born state. Two decades later, the first large-scale migration – the Italian diaspora as it was called – began, especially to the Americas.

In World War I, Italy joined the Allied powers. Gathering a number of disparate groups, including World War I veterans, the National Fascist Party took hold of the government in 1922, with no resistance on the part of either the King or the Parliament. The second so-called Italian diaspora started shortly thereafter. After siding with the Axis powers during World War II, the Fascist government collapsed and a part of Italy came under the protection of the Allies. September 8, 1943 marked the break of Italy's territorial unity, which was to be re-gained on April 25, 1945.[42] In 1946, the population voted in favor of creating a republic and for 556 constitutional drafters. Italy's constitution came into force in 1948, establishing a constitutional democracy. Since the introduction of the Italian constitution, Italy has had 62 governments in 70 years. Today an EU Member State, Italy is one of the founding members of the Council of Europe (1949) and the European Economic Community (1957).

2.3 Assessing Italian legal culture over time

2.3.1 Italian legal culture before 1861

Until 1861, the peninsula witnessed no common institution other than ecclesiastical bodies. Pursuant to the legal cultural models, the missing elements were thus institutions of norm production and conflict resolution. To argue for an Italian *legal culture* prior to unification is thus problematic. Commonality is, however, present in the common education on the *Corpus Juris Civilis,* as well as in the exchanges among professionals

36 Northern Italy was under the French influence from 1797 to 1814 with a blip from 1799 to 1801. Whilst Northern Italy was only formally independent from France, Naples was an independent republic in 1799 and kingdom from 1805 to 1815, often but not always under the influence of France.

37 Padoa-Schioppa (2010) (n 26) 42. Murat's *Proclama di Rimini* is often entwined with the beginning of *Risorgimento.*

38 Galli della Loggia (1998) (n 10) 61.

39 Ibid 62.

40 Ibid 77.

41 Ibid 59–84.

42 See http://www.treccani.it/enciclopedia/periferie-storico-identitatrie-e-costituzione-le-regioni-a-statuto-speciale_%28L%27Italia-e-le-sue-Regioni%29/ accessed 27 February 2019.

and merchants, aided by the common Italian language, which emerged as early as the 12th–13th centuries. One of the main exceptions to the experience of commonality is the Kingdom of Sicily under the Norman-Hohenstaufen monarchy (1130–1266),[43] which employed the *Liber Augustalis* (1231) as only one of many tools to consolidate its power.[44] The centralized approach embraced by the Norman-Hohenstaufen monarchy sets the Kingdom of Sicily apart from the polycentrism that characterized the city-states in the rest of the peninsula.

2.3.2 Italian legal culture after 1861

To establish whether one legal culture exists after 1861, this analysis will shed light on each element of the legal cultural model and their interaction (see *infra* 3-9). Before then, however, it would be remiss to ignore the role played by the 1948 constitution. Considering that the constitution and its principles have hitherto provided and maintained the premises for the legitimacy of the entire legal order,[45] we will briefly gauge some of its main traits as a framework for all elements in the legal cultural model.

The Italian constitution is supreme to all other legal sources.[46] With the victory of the republican form of government in 1946, the elected drafters – all drawn from anti-fascist parties – worked to reach a political agreement. In May 1947, however, with the ushering in of the Cold War, this agreement collapsed. Hence, Italy's constitution is marked by two elements: the lack of its full implementation, and the high number of informal avenues to adapt it to societal and political contexts.[47]

Undoubtedly, some constitutional principles have lain and will lie at the bottom of the legal sea, determining the deep structure of the legal culture. These are the principles based on the concept of personhood (personalist principle), equality,[48] the democratic principle,[49] the role of regions and the principle of subsidiarity,[50] as well as the pacifist, international, and republican principles.[51] Some of these core concepts are particularly interesting from the viewpoint of the legal cultural model. In addition to the "formal" constitution, Italy's Constitutional Court has clarified that there exists a "material" constitution, which consists of the "supreme values upon which the whole Constitution

43 Padoa-Schioppa (2010) (n 26) 37–38.

44 The *Liber Augustalis* is also called the Constitutions of Melfi. It was promulgated by Frederick II, then King of Sicily, King of Italy, and Holy Roman Emperor.

45 Giacomo D'Amico, 'Struttura ed effetti delle decisioni' in Elena Bindi, Mario Perini and Andrea Pisaneschi (eds), *I principi generali del processo comune ed i loro adattamenti alle esperienze della giustizia costituzionale* (Giappichelli 2008) 245.

46 On the doctrine of sources of law, see *infra* 3.2.1.

47 Tania Groppi and Irene Spigno, 'Constitutional reasoning of the Italian Constitutional Court' (2014) 4 *Rivista telematica dell'Associazione italiana dei costituzionalisti* 1, 3.

48 On the personalist principle and equality, see *infra* Section 5.

49 On the democratic principle, consider that the Constitution sets forth the requirement of democracy for both political parties and unions, which has not been implemented. On the democratic principle, see also *infra* 3.6 on referenda.

50 See *infra* 3.2.3.

51 On the republican principle, see in this sub-section. On the internationalist and pacifist principle, see *infra* 7.3.2.

is grounded in".[52] Of these, what emerges as an *explicit* value is the republican form of government. Pursuant to the very letter of the constitution, which is difficult to amend, the republican form of government is inviolable and unamendable.[53] Further supreme values, *implicitly* unalterable by constitutional amendment, are the fundamental principles of the legal order and the inalienable rights of each human being,[54] which are entwined with the personalist, equality, and democratic principles.

Although the constitution affects all elements of the legal cultural model, it is here worth laying the groundwork for the rest of the chapter by focusing on the interaction between constitutional principles and the legal method. It was Italy's Constitutional Court that pointed to the interpretation of the constitution in light of constitutional principles as the preferred interpretive method.[55] The underlying tenet rests with the "material" value of these principles and the tight connection among them. For this reason, interpreters ought to construe the constitutional principles systematically – i.e., within the context of other principles – so as to balance them reciprocally.[56] Even under the circumstances that some constitutional guarantees ought to be limited – even partially, the legislative power is altogether prevented from encroaching upon the core value of the guarantee.[57] The "inferiority" of all other sources of law to the constitution and its principles clears the way for permissive, rather than restrictive, judicial review.[58]

All in all, the constitution and its principles have hitherto provided and maintained the premises for the legitimacy of the entire legal order.[59] Anchoring the legal sea, they epitomize the historical watershed that occurred with the entry into force of the 1948 constitution.[60]

3. Norm production

3.1 Introduction

Norm production is one of the most problematic elements of Italy's legal culture, and at the same time one of the most important. In Italy, roughly 21 pages of new laws are passed every day.[61] The total number of laws is estimated to be 150,000, compared to

52 C.C. Decision 1146/1988 (authors' translation), para 2.1.

53 Italian Constitution, Article 139; Groppi and Spigno (2014) (n 47) 14.

54 C.C. Decision 1146/1988, para 2.1. This is known as the 'counter-limits' theory, which was first deployed by the Constitutional court vis-à-vis the European Communities. See C.C. Decision 183/1973 and *infra* 7.

55 Groppi and Spigno (2014) (n 47) 10 and C.C. Decision 7/1996.

56 C.C. Decision 1/2013. This type of interpretation is termed logic-systematic by Groppi and Spigno (2014) (n 47) 17.

57 See e.g. C.C. Decision 80/2010. Such construction mirrors the BVG's theory of *Wesensgehalt,* which is often recalled by the Italian doctrine. See Sören Koch, 'An Introduction to German Legal Culture' in this volume, Chapter 8.

58 See *infra* Section 4.

59 D'Amico (2008) (n 45) 245.

60 Groppi and Spigno (2014) (n 47) 10 and C.C. Decision 7/1996.

61 The reckoning includes ordinary laws, law-decrees, legislative decrees and regional laws; see Michela Finizio, 'Quanta lunga è una legge? Ecco il bilancio delle attivita' legislative' *Il Sole 24 Ore,* 20 April 2015. On these types of legislative instruments, see *infra* 3.2.

roughly 7,000 in France and 5,500 in Germany.[62] It is thus pivotal to begin our analysis of Italy's legal culture by turning to norm production.

3.2 Laws, decrees, and customs

3.2.1 The doctrine of sources in action

We must now enter the quicksand of the doctrine of legal sources. In not only Italy but also more generally in Europe, the doctrine of legal sources is experiencing a general crisis.[63] Within a legal culture, the doctrine of legal sources may mirror current practice (doctrine in action), or may not be updated according to current practice (doctrine in the books) as is the case in Italy today. One of the few legal cultures enshrining a written provision on the sources of law, the latter only lists laws, regulations, and usages, falling short of the doctrine of sources *in action.*[64] One of the possible explanations for such hiatus is the level of and attitude towards professionalization: manuals and university courses still privilege the "traditional" doctrine of legal sources,[65] yet they generally acknowledge that sources are much richer in practice. Accordingly, the following is a portrait of the doctrine of legal sources in action.

3.2.2 Constitutional laws, ordinary laws, and decrees with legislative status

The Italian Parliament is empowered to pass laws,[66] which can be either ordinary or constitutional. In either case, laws are passed by both chambers of Parliament, the House of Deputies and the Senate, which have for the most part the same functions.[67]

Within the general category of law, it is worth considering the "strange" case of the regulations of constitutional organs, which covers the internal organization of the Parliament, the Presidency of the Republic, and the Constitutional Court, including labor disputes between an entity and its employees. Such regulations are equivalent to constitutional laws since they can derogate from the constitution. Legal doctrine and the Court of Cassation have strongly criticized such regulative autonomy due to the lack of

62 Francesco Delzio, 'Il Paese delle leggi. E della rivoluzione possibile', *Avvenire,* 18 March 2017, available at https://www.avvenire.it/rubriche/pagine/il-paese-delle-leggi-e-della-rivoluzione-possibile accessed 27 February 2019.

63 See n 2. Giovanni Canzio, 'Nomofilachia e diritto giurisprudenziale' (2017) *Diritto penale contemporaneo* 1, 4.

64 Marinella Baschiera, 'Introduction to the Italian Legal System. The Allocation of Normative Powers: Issues in Law Finding' (2006) Volume 34, Issue 2 *International Journal of Legal Information* 279, 288 (fn. 26).

65 Provisions on the law in general (premised to the civil code), Article 1.

66 By law, we refer to either constitutional or ordinary law. We refer to ordinary laws, when non-constitutional laws are passed by the Parliament in the ordinary legislative process. We refer to law decrees and legislative decrees when non-constitutional laws are not passed by the Parliament in the ordinary legislative process, yet enjoy the same legislative status as ordinary laws.

67 Different types of voting procedures are available, with a variable degree of autonomy of the commission discussing the bills vis-à-vis the full chamber. Notwithstanding, both chambers represent the whole of the people, rather than regions or municipalities.

judicial scrutiny.[68] Autonomy, however, has been continuously reiterated by the Constitutional Court, the sole organ that could bring about any change. The Constitutional Court is, in this matter, *iudex in causa sua* (meaning, judge of its own cause).

Italy's constitution allows for encroachment on the "monism" of parliamentary legislation.[69] Unable to decide between two models of joint governmental and legislative activity, the drafters of the constitution decided to provide for both. These are the legislative decrees and the law-decrees, which enjoy legislative status – i.e., the same status as ordinary laws. Legislative decrees originate from Parliament and delegate the enactment of laws to the whole government. Parliament's delegation must include the guiding principles and criteria for exercising such power, as well as a circumscribed timeline and scope.[70] Law-decrees do not originate from a parliamentary delegation: the government is enabled to pass law-decrees solely under specific circumstances – extraordinary cases of necessity and urgency – and procedures by presenting Parliament with the decree on the very same day it is approved. Parliament has 60 days to approve the law-decree passed by the government, lest it ceases to produce effects.[71]

Law-decrees have proved one of the main causes of normative inflation. In fact, the government can circumvent the democratic process of ordinary parliamentary law. In reality, law-decrees have been deployed regarding matters unmarked by necessity or urgency. But law-decrees may create situations where the law is uncertain. If Parliament fails to convert the law decree within 60 days, all past and present effects lapse. To counter the lapse, the government historically would pass the same law-decrees and repeatedly present them to Parliament. It was solely in 1996, with the intervention of the Constitutional Court, that a more constitutionally sound practice was reinstated.[72] More than two-thirds of all legislative acts are now made of legislative decrees or decree-laws.[73]

Once approved, laws are promulgated by the President of the Republic, who controls the formal constitutional legitimacy of the law. If the President finds such legitimacy lacking, they can send the law back to Parliament with an explanation of their motivation. If the law is approved once again, the President has no power to send it back and is duty bound to promulgate it. All laws are published in a public issuance called *Gazzetta Ufficiale,* and they usually come into force after 15 days from their appearance in print, yet the law itself can determine a different timeframe, and law-decrees always enter into effect on the very day they are published.

68 On the violation of Article 6 of the *European Convention on Human Rights, Ets 5; 213 Unts 221,* due to the lack of independence and impartiality of the judicial section of the chamber of deputies in a particular labour dispute, see *Savino and Others v Italy* App no(s) 17214/05, 20329/05, 42113/04 (ECHR, 28 April 2009).

69 On monism in norm-production as a model, see Mario Comba, 'Constitutional Law' in Jeffrey S. Lena and Ugo Mattei (eds), *Introduction to Italian Law* (Kluwer Law International 2002) 47 ff.

70 Italian Constitution, Article 76.

71 Italian Constitution, Article 77.

72 C.C. Decision 360/1996 and Vittoria Barsotti, Paolo G. Carozza, Marta Cartabia and Andrea Simoncini, *Italian Constitutional Justice in Global Context* (Oxford University Press 2015) 166.

73 Ibid 165.

Italy is part of the international legal order and the EU legal order. Moreover, it is subject to the jurisdiction of the European Court of Human Rights (ECtHR). These matters are dealt with separately under the element of internationalization (*infra* 7).

3.2.3 Regional and provincial laws

Italy's Parliament, even in cooperation with the executive, holds no monopoly over norm-production.[74] Since Italy is a "regionalist" state,[75] regional laws lie at the same level as state law. The underlying tenet appears to be the need to devise a counterpower to the centralized power of the state.[76]

Albeit enshrined in the constitution, Parliament started implementing the provisions on regionalism solely in the 1970s. After a landmark reform in 2001,[77] Italy's constitution set forth three types of norm-production powers: i) exclusive legislative powers of the state, ii) concurrent legislative powers of the state and the regions, and iii) residual legislative powers of the regions. Whereas the first and third domains are not overly intricate,[78] concurrent legislative powers still pose a series of conundrums. Here, the state is responsible for passing either framework laws or principles for specific areas of legislation, and regions pass detailed laws within the confines set forth by the state.[79] When the state has not enacted framework statutes, nor laid down principles, in the domains that are concurrent, regions can generally pass laws including both principles and details.[80] Once the state enacts framework laws or lays down principles, however, regional laws shall be modified, or reinterpreted, accordingly. When the state has done so, yet a particular region delays passing detailed laws, the state's principles are still applicable and the state itself may pass detailed laws that would make for the *lacunae.*[81] Once the particular region enacts detailed laws, the state law passed to fill the *lacunae* would no longer govern the matter in that region.

---

74 Marco Macchia, 'The Incidental Legality Review of Regulations in Italy' (2013) Volume 2 *Italian Journal of Public Law* 261, 262.

75 See *supra* 2.3.2 on the constitutionalist principle of regionalism.

76 Marco Benvenuti, 'The Constitutional Distribution of Legislative Powers in Italy: Recent Judgments of the Constitutional Court' (2015) Volume 2 *Italian Journal of Public Law* 391.

77 Barsotti and others (2015) (n 72) 186 ff.

78 It should be recalled that regions are enabled to pass laws also in domains of exclusive state legislation, where the role of state legislation is to guarantee a baseline. See Paolo Stella Richter, 'I rapporti tra legislazione statale e legislazione regionale' 3–5, available at http://www.dsg.univr.it/documenti/Iniziativa/dall/dall353864.pdf accessed 4 March 2019. Similarly, exclusive state legislation at times needs to be so sweeping as to have an impact on both concurrent and residual legislation. This type of matters is called 'cross-cutting'. See Barsotti and others (2015) (n 72) 195 ff. Sweeping state legislation has been approved by the Constitutional Court also in matters that were concurrent in kind, where in principle the State can solely pass framework laws or principles. These are called 'catch-all' competences. See Barsotti and others (2015) (n 72) 197–198.

79 Interestingly, the provisions in the Constitution refer to fundamental principles to be set forth by the state (Article 117(3)). Truly, the Constitutional Court has allowed the State to set forth 'detailed principles', see Barsotti and others (2015) (n 72) 198–199.

80 Stella Richter, 'I rapporti tra legislazione statale e legislazione regionale' (n 78) 5–6.

81 Ibid 7.

A constitutional provision allows for the state to overrule regions when either EU law or international law are not complied with: in case of grave danger for public security, or when such substitution is warranted by either legal or economic unity, in particular when minimum protection levels are guaranteed for civil and social rights.[82] What appears to be decisive in this legislative power-sharing function is the very interpretation of the constitutional norms on legislative competence, which is undertaken by the Constitutional Court. Lately, the Constitutional Court has been criticized for leaning upon the state's determination of its competence remit.[83] One of the likely reasons for this approach is the economic and financial crisis that impacted Italy beginning in 2007.[84]

Nonetheless, the framework of power-sharing outlined above governs ordinary regions alone, whilst five regions with special charters can depart from the constitutional set up. For historical reasons, ever since its entry into force in 1948, the constitution has endowed special autonomy to five regions,[85] deemed "special" in light of their peripheral location, history, and identity.[86] The type of autonomy is determined by each region's charter, which the Italian Parliament passed as a constitutional law.[87] Besides possibly departing from the constitution, one of the practical effects of this special status is higher tax autonomy compared to ordinary regions.[88]

In light of the constitutional principle of subsidiarity,[89] autonomy is granted to small-scale forms of government, that is provinces, metropolitan cities, and municipalities. These, however, do not have legislative powers. The only exceptions are the autonomous provinces of Trento and Bolzano, which have had legislative powers ever since 1972, when an agreement was ushered in through the mediation of the United Nations.[90] The rest of Italy's provinces, metropolitan cities, and municipalities cannot legislate, but can pass local regulations that are lower in the hierarchy than laws. Since 2001, municipalities can exercise all administrative powers until higher instances of government intervene, which is warranted only for purposes of unity.[91]

---

82 Italian Constitution, Article 120. Such substitution power can be wielded also vis-à-vis metropolitan cities, provinces, and municipalities.

83 Stella Richter, 'I rapporti tra legislazione statale e legislazione regionale' (n 78) 14. See Barsotti and others (2015) (n 72) 194–195, who identify such a trend only lately.

84 Barsotti and others (2015) (n 72) 195.

85 Friuli Venezia Giulia, Sardegna, Sicilia, Trentino-Alto Adige, and Valle d'Aosta.

86 See http://www.treccani.it/enciclopedia/periferie-storico-identitatrie-e-costituzione-le-regioni-a-statuto-speciale_%28L%27Italia-e-le-sue-Regioni%29/ accessed 1 March 2019.

87 Ordinary regions have the power to lay down their charter, which in no way may be qualified as a constitution, as the charter itself needs to conform to the Italian Constitution, Barsotti and others (2015) (n 72) 190–191. Within regions, charters are hierarchically superior to the other norms passed by the regions. Regions ought to follow special procedures for the approval of charters, but the approval of the central government is not required.

88 Compare the two types of regions in https://temi.camera.it/leg17/temi/il_sistema_delle_entrate_degli_enti_locali accessed 1 March 2019.

89 See *supra* 2.3.2.

90 In 1946, a treaty was signed between Italy and Austria on the conditions of autonomy of Südtirol, which would nevertheless belong to Italy.

91 The level of government deploying administrative powers should be adequate and tailored to the capacity of the particular level of government, see Article 118 of the Italian Constitution.

Regional and provincial laws are published in the care of regional and provincial lawmaking bodies, respectively.

3.2.4 The "strange" case of decrees

In the hierarchy of legal sources, regulations have a lower status than laws. Regulations come under the heading of decrees and are passed by: i) the Council of Ministers, which is the government as a collegiate body; ii) the Prime Minister (called the President of the Council of Ministers); and iii) each Minister.[92] These decrees are promulgated by the President of the Republic as their own. Decrees are meant to specify and enable the implementation of the underlying law, but are also adopted when the Parliament delegates regulative power to the government. Parliament may do so when the subject matter is not governed, nor shall be governed, by laws or decrees with legislative status. Decrees are also enacted by state authorities, such as the Competition Authority.

According to some commentators, the government has abused its power to pass regulations, short of restraint on the part of the Parliament, which should be the "natural" counter-power, by the President of the Republic or the Constitutional Court.[93] In order to circumvent the ordinary participatory procedures and in the absence of a normed power of regulation, entities within the administrative organization have issued emergency orders in situations devoid of emergency character.[94] This political practice has undoubtedly contributed to normative inflation. A further element begetting normative inflation is the number of entities endowed with rule-making powers: among these are professional associations, e.g., lawyers, doctors, and engineers.[95]

3.2.5 Customs

According to the doctrine of legal sources on the books,[96] customs constitute one legal source for the Italian legal system. Owing to the vastness of legislative and regulatory norms, however, customs do not play a major role. Customs apply when they are recalled by laws or regulations on matters liable to be governed by laws,[97] or contract integration and interpretation.

With respect to customary international law, what is customary attains more importance. In fact, customary international law is automatically incorporated into Italy's legal order and carries the status of quasi-constitutional norms.[98] In relation to international customary law, Italy's legal system is thus monist.

---

92 One of the most important statute regulating the subject is Law n.400/1988.

93 See http://www.treccani.it/enciclopedia/regolamento-dir-cost_(Diritto-on-line)/ accessed 4 March 2019, and Macchia (2013) (n 74) 265. On the criticism of rule-making power as assigned to entities that are often remote from the citizens, such as the Ministers rather than municipalities, see Bernardo Giorgio Mattarella, 'Participation in Rulemaking in Italy' (2010) Vol. 2 *Italian Journal of Public Law* 339, 347.

94 Mattarella (2010) (n 93) 351.

95 Ibid 345.

96 See *supra* 3.1.

97 Disposizioni sulla legge in generale, Article 8.

98 Italian Constitution, Article 10.

3.2.6 Conclusions

As stressed at the beginning of this sub-chapter, norm-production is one of the most problematic among the elements of Italy's legal culture. The inflation of norm-producing entities and norm-production itself has hitherto led to a "normative crisis".[99] What is particularly staggering is the lack of norms regarding the power to issue decrees. If the role of regions was meant to bridle the ever-expanding rule-making powers of the central government, such potential has been hampered by the murky breakdown of legislative power-sharing throughout a series of constitutional reforms. Still open, and unsettled, is the issue of allowing for the representation of regions within one of the two parliamentary chambers.

3.3 Types of laws: Codes

Within the present discussion on norm-production, we shall center on codes, which are usually approved through the legislative process. Italy is a code-based jurisdiction: six general codes have been instituted, along with 17 codes regarding specific matters. For the most part, these 17 codes resemble more a collection of laws rather than a code. The six general codes include: the civil code (1942), the civil procedural code (1940), the criminal code (1930), the criminal procedural code (1988), the criminal military code in times of war (1941), and the criminal military code in times of peace (1941). Codes regarding specific matters are, for instance, the code of navigation (1942), the code of accounts-related justice (2016), and the code of civil protection (2018).

Having taken part in the "movement for codification and reform", which characterized continental Europe in the 19th century, Italy has for this reason been called paradigmatic of the civil law tradition.[100] Truly, Italy appears to have absorbed the two major codification styles of the 19th century, French and German, and to have added its own traits. By way of example, the civil code was influenced by the German Civil Code, *Bürgerliches Gesetzbuch* (BGB) (e.g., with respect to systematics and general clauses), the French *Code Civil* (e.g., in the regulation of consent as sufficient for the transfer of property), and the Swiss civil code (e.g., in some tort law provisions). One trait can be considered culturally Italian: the merging of civil law (contracts, quasi-contracts, torts, family law, succession law, and labor law) and commercial law. In this way, civil and commercial law were and still are grouped under one heading: the law of obligations.[101]

Similar to other European legal cultures, norm-production has swelled to such a degree that existing codes have been dwarfed by the bulk of further, so-called special

99 Literally, Padoa-Schioppa (2010) (n 26) 526 referred to "the deep crisis of the normative system" (authors' translation).

100 Michael A. Livingston, Pier Giuseppe Monateri and Francesco Parisi, *The Italian Legal System: An Introduction* (2nd ed, Stanford University Press 2015) 143–144.

101 Padoa-Schioppa (2010) (n 26) 522. The same author considers the architecture of the Italian civil code more harmonic and rational than the BGB and the Swiss Civil Code.

legislation.[102] This is the case of codes of substantive, rather than procedural, law. Yet, the general aspect of each code of substantive law still performs a pivotal function as an anchor for the interpretation and application of special legislation.

3.4 The role of courts

3.4.1 The Constitutional Court

3.4.1.1 Overview

The role that Italy's Constitutional Court (hereafter referred to as the "Court") plays in its legal culture can be understood through the lens of its norm-producing and conflict-resolving capacities. Here, we consider the Court's norm-producing capacity. Such a choice is determined by the Court's core business as an adjudicator of rights, which constitutes 90% of its activity, while only 10% is devoted to institutional dispute resolution.[103] Considering that it has rendered roughly 300–400 orders and decisions per year in the last decade,[104] the Court has had ample opportunity to shape the law. It does so by two modes: i) by re-modeling legislation in light of the constitution, and ii) by fostering or steering policymaking in a specific direction.[105]

As an "*ad hoc*" organ of constitutional justice, separate from the judiciary, the Court is made up of 15 judges. These are drawn from the higher courts of ordinary jurisdiction, law professors, and lawyers with more than 20 years of experience. Appointment is separately made by three bodies, each of whom can nominate five constitutional judges: the President of the Republic, the Parliament in joint session, by a three-fifths majority, and the upper echelons of the judiciary. Constitutional judges are in office for nine years and cannot be reappointed.

Modeled after the Austrian Constitutional Court and endowed with traits from the U.S. Supreme Court,[106] Italy's Constitutional Court is governed by the 1948 constitution and its laws of implementation. Due to the skepticism surrounding its role,[107] the necessary legislation to initiate the Court was delayed and the Court entered into full activity only in 1956. In the same year, it rendered its first judgment, the Italian *Mar-*

102 Livingston, Monateri and Parisi (2015) (n 100) 193.

103 On these categories, see Marta Cartabia, 'Of Bridges and Walls: the "Italian Style" of Constitutional Adjudication' (2016) Vol. 1 *Italian Journal of Public Law* 37, 42.

104 The amount of decisions and orders varies from year-to-year, from 592 (in 2000) to 276 (in 2015). See the time span 1997–2017 in Gioconda Verrengia, Ida Norelli and Maria Fierro, 'Giurisprudenza costituzionale dell'anno 2017. Dati quantitative e di analisi' (Extraordinary meeting of the Constitutional Court, 22 February 2018) 1, 7, available at https://www.cortecostituzionale.it/documenti/relazioni_annuali/grossi2018/dati_2018.pdf accessed 4 March 2019.

105 Baschiera (2006) (n 64) 324.

106 Cartabia (2016) (n 103) 38.

107 Ibid 39.

bury v Madison, which broke with both pre-Fascist and Fascist traditions.[108] Differently from what ordinary courts had maintained, especially the Court of Cassation, the Court declared that all constitutional provisions were immediately binding and justiciable, not only vis-à-vis the government, but also private parties. The Court took upon itself the power to review any laws allegedly in violation of the constitution.[109]

The Court steers a centralized system of judicial review of legislation that is concrete, rather than abstract. This means that when a judge adjudicating a particular case determines that a particular provision is applicable and the constitutionality issue is not manifestly unfounded, they are under an obligation to suspend the procedure and refer the case to the Court. By so doing, legislation can be reviewed indirectly. Once the Court has decided on the point of dispute or uncertainty, the judge resumes the case and makes a decision in accordance with the Court's judgment. When norms are declared unconstitutional, the Court's decisions unfold *erga omnes* effects and norms are null and void from the start.[110] Indirect review has developed to a quantitatively larger extent than in any other European state.[111]

This type of review concerns laws for the most part, except for particular cases.[112] Regulations and administrative acts can be directly annulled by administrative courts within a 60-day timeline, or "eliminated" by ordinary and administrative courts through incidental review even beyond this timeline.[113]

3.4.1.2 The Constitutional Court's style

Composed of legal experts, rather than political representatives, the Court's composition characterizes its judicial style. There exist two kinds of rulings: decisions and orders. While orders are interlocutory or procedural in kind, decisions hinge on the merits and are characterized by conceptually crafted legal language. The Court prefers to issue decisions, rather than orders, meaning that it is prone to decide a case on its merits. Inadmissibility orders ensue solely when the Court does not perceive itself able to strike "a reasonable balance between legislative discretion, constitutional review and concrete case solutions".[114]

The Court's activity has been deemed interpretatively creative and marked by activism, "which has facilitated the evolution of the Italian legal system with a view to the

---

108 Andrea Simoncini, 'The Success of a Constitutional Experiment: When History Matters. The Italian Constitutional Court in Global Context' (2016) Vol. 8 *The Italian Journal of Public Law* 79, 86, and C.C. Decision 1/56. As known, *Marbury v. Madison,* 5 U.S. 137 (1803) established constitutional judicial review on the part of the US Supreme Court and is one of the most paradigmatic decisions in judicial review matters.

109 Groppi and Spigno (2014) (n 47) 14. On *Drittwirkung,* see Baschiera (2006) (n 64) 291. See also Koch (2020), 'German Legal Culture' (n 57).

110 Macchia (2013) (n 74) 270

111 Alessandro Pizzorusso, 'Italian and American Models of the Judiciary and of Judicial Review of Legislation: A Comparison of Recent Tendencies' (1990) Vol. 38, Issue 2 *The American Journal of Comparative Law* 373, 381.

112 Macchia (2013) (n 74) 269

113 Ibid 283–284.

114 Paolo Zicchittu, 'The Italian Way to the "Political Question"' (2015) Vol. 1 *Italian Journal of Public Law* 222, 246.

establishment of a modern constitutional State in correspondence with the modernization of the Italian society".[115] Short of considering the full array of decisions molded by the Court,[116] it is here worth recalling some of its interpretive tenets. The Court rejects literal interpretation, "always a primitive method, and even more as far as constitutional interpretation is concerned",[117] even though the constitutional text is usually the first step in the interpretive process.[118] A further tenet rests on the tracing of a specific matter to the constitution, which should be regarded as an open text, to be progressively interpreted.[119] By so doing, the Court has shown "a level of judicial activism similar to judges in common law countries".[120] Albeit excluded by the "traditional" doctrine of sources, the court looks to parliamentary rules and common practice to supplement the text of the constitution.[121]

The Court's decisions generally serve as precedents; their precedential role does not derive from law,[122] but rather from practice in order to effectuate the Court's decisions. Precedents enjoy the same force as constitutional laws.[123] The Court refers to its precedents,[124] mostly as individual cases, but sometimes as the "permanent and coherent case law of the Court", followed by a list of references.[125] However, in the words of the Court's vice-president, "the Court does not disdain teleological interpretation, but also attaches great importance to its own precedents and to the coherence of its case law".[126] Hence, within the 40 most important decisions ever rendered by the Court, in no judgment did it distinguish from earlier cases,[127] yet it applied analogy-based arguments four times.[128] Because this distinguishing practice is not very popular, one of the techniques for overruling its own precedents is for the Court to hide this action; in practice, however, it criticizes its own precedents.[129] At other times, the Court re-reads its own precedents.[130]

---

115 Groppi and Spigno (2014) (n 47) 2.

116 For further depth, see Groppi and Spigno (2014) (n 47) 7; Zicchittu (2015) (n 114) 245–246; and Simoncini (2016) (n 108) 87.

117 C.C. Decision 1/2013, para 10. Groppi and Spigno (2014) (n 47) 28.

118 Groppi and Spigno (2014) (n 47) 16.

119 Ibid 28 and 34.

120 Ibid 34.

121 Ibid 13.

122 D'Amico (2008) (n 45) 239.

123 Ibid.

124 Groppi and Spigno (2014) (n 47) 19.

125 Ibid.

126 Cartabia (2016) (n 103) 52. See D'Amico (2008) (n 45) 231, who cautions against the risk that leaning on precedents may empty the particular decision of internal coherence. Until 2001, the Court has declared unconstitutionality for violation of its own case law six times, see D'Amico (2008) (n 45) 242–243 fn. 123.

127 Groppi and Spigno (2014) (n 47) 19–20.

128 Ibid 14–15.

129 Ibid 20.

130 Ibid 20. See also ibid 15.

Albeit frequent, reference to precedents is not the Court's *primary* interpretive style.[131] Most often, the Court's primary interpretive style is a reading of the constitution in light of its principles and with regard to the whole constitution, the so-called systematic interpretation.[132] In fundamental rights' judgments, this interpretive canon is usually joined with the unwritten principle of reasonableness, which has been molded by the Court itself.[133] The reasonableness test is an analogical judgment, initially grounded in the constitutional principle of equality. The test goes as follows: let us suppose that the law has regulated a case, A, to attain a specific goal, X. Considering X, is it reasonable that the law regulates a case, B, in a different or similar way regarding A?

The Court further applies the reasonableness test in matters entailing technical evaluations that are not covered by a political question, which is the theory that has developed in several apex courts in order to devolve politically-charged matters to the political branches.[134] In some situations where the Court appeared to recognize the political question,[135] a new type of decision emerged. The Court declared the particular provision unconstitutional and added a principle.[136] The role of the judge adjudicating a particular case is to apply the principle to the case, whereas the task for the legislature is to pass legislation in accordance with the principle, but still with some discretion.[137] From this, one can infer that the Court has been creative in molding the content and effects of its own decisions, similarly to other constitutional courts.[138]

Some areas are, at least formally, qualified by parliamentary discretion: substantive criminal law, immigration law, tax law, and procedural law.[139] Other subject matters, such as family law, have been particularly affected by the Court's norm-producing capacity.[140]

3.4.1.3 The entwining circle: Constitutional Court ↔ Court of Cassation and other courts

It is worth emphasizing that the Court has devised one of the most ingenious ways of keeping abreast of its case log by relying on lower courts. In principle, the Court has no leeway to filter its case log,[141] which can make for thousands of cases on the docket every

131 Ibid 28.

132 See *supra* 2.3.2. The systematic interpretation may be aligned with coherent interpretation in the German legal culture, see Koch (2020), 'German Legal Culture' (n 57).

133 Groppi and Spigno (2014) (n 47) 17 and 29. The subject is discussed twice in the paper.

134 Zicchittu (2015) (n 114) 242–243. See, however, Article 28, Law 87/1953 and Article 134 of the Italian Constitution, preventing the Court from exercising powers belonging to political institutions, as reported by Zicchittu 236.

135 Zicchittu (2015) (n 114) 248. The Court has also declined jurisdiction, most likely on a political question basis, see Zicchittu 230.

136 See for other strategies to cope with politically charged matters, ibid 233–234.

137 Ibid 250.

138 See also ibid 247. See also Koch (2020), 'German Legal Culture' (n 57) and Konrad Lachmayer and Niklas Sonntag, 'An Introduction to Austrian Legal Culture' in this book, chapter 14.

139 Zicchittu (2015) (n 114) 233.

140 Baschiera (2006) (n 64) 318–319.

141 Zicchittu (2015) (n 114) 252. The symbol ↔ points to the one-to-one correspondance between the two courts' functions, see bijective functions in Terence Tao, *Analysis I* (Springer 2015, third ed), 55.

year. Hence, the Court has developed the theory of consistent interpretation, whereby each adjudicating body is required to interpret legislation and regulation consistently with the constitution, even by stretching the literal meaning of the text.[142] These bodies act as gatekeepers,[143] a peculiar trait of Italy's legal culture.[144] As a result, the Court's language and conceptualization are quite technical: the Court addresses itself to other courts. If adjudicating bodies do not try to interpret the statute consistently with the constitution, their referral is dismissed on procedural grounds.[145]

A further consideration to be drawn from the doctrine of consistent interpretation concerns the *precedential* character of the Court's case law.[146] Precedents are needed because the case law of the Court ought to be coherent in order to be understood and applied to the specific posture of a particular case by lower courts. Applying the case law of the Constitutional Court may also provide lower courts with the upper hand. As we shall see later,[147] trial judges are culturally, albeit not formally, bound by an "attenuated" form of *stare decisis.*[148] Confined in their ability to criticize higher courts, they can do so by resorting to the Court's case law.[149] From a broader perspective, the doctrine of consistent interpretation and the *continuum* between the Constitutional Court and other adjudicating bodies has established the unity of the legal system, at least so far as constitutional interpretation is concerned.[150]

Beyond the doctrine of consistent interpretation, a further mode that the Court deploys to communicate with adjudicating bodies is to refer to the Court of Cassation. What is the interpretation to consider when a provision is challenged? The answer delivered by the Court has been: the "living law", which is the law developed by the Court of Cassation.[151] Even one ruling of the Court of Cassation can make for "living law",[152] whereas doctrine is excluded outright.[153] In an entwining circle, it appears that

142 Cartabia (2016) (n 103) 49 and Groppi and Spigno (2014) (n 47) 11. The theory of consistent interpretation was first made explicit in C.C. Decision 356/1996. See also C.C. Decision 23/2011; C.C. Decision 200/2012 and C.C. Decision 1/2013.

143 Piero Calamandrei, 'Il procedimento per la dichiarazione di illegittimità costituzionale' in *Opere Giuridiche,* vol. III (Morano 1965) 372.

144 Groppi and Spigno (2014) (n 47) 30.

145 Ibid 11.

146 See *supra* under the Constitutional Court's style.

147 See *infra* 4.

148 Mario Cappelletti, 'Doctrine of Stare Decisis and the Civil Law: A Fundamental Difference or No Difference At All?' in Herbert Bernstein, Ulrich Drobnig and Hein Kötz (eds), *Festschrift für Konrad Zweigert* (Mohr 1981) 381. Mauro Bussani, 'Constitutional Justice in Italy and Beyond: A Comparative (and Private) Law Perspective' (2016) Vol. 8 *Italian Journal of Public Law* 24.

149 Bussani (2016) (n 148) 24.

150 Groppi and Spigno (2014) (n 47) 11.

151 Simoncini (2016) (n 108) 88. Cartabia (2016) (n 103) 48–49. Cf. what appears to be an endorsement of the interpretation rendered by lower judges in C.C. Decision 33/1981, para 2.

152 See C.C. Decision 379/2000 and C.C. Decision 338/2011. See Luigi Salvato, 'La nomofilachia nella dialettica tra Corte costituzionale e Corte di cassazione' (2018) *Forum di Quaderni Costituzionali* 1, 4. Cf C.C. Decision 242/2008, where the Constitutional Court asserts to evaluate the constancy and repetition of the Court of Cassation's interpretation, but fails to define such features.

153 See Salvato (2018) (n 152) 3. Cf. reference to the case law and doctrine in Order n. 237/2001.

the Constitutional Court legitimizes the decisions rendered by the Court of Cassation as quasi-norms.[154] When a particular provision, as interpreted by the Court of Cassation, is unconstitutional, the Court declares it null and void on its face, rather than resorting to interpretive techniques.[155]

More generally, given the indirect type of review carried out, the Constitutional Court itself is affected by the conflict-resolution apparatus, especially by how the referring adjudicating body frames constitutional questions.[156]

3.4.1.4 The Constitutional Court's modes of operation in light of its functions

In light of the previous discussion, some of the specific modes of operation of the Court are now better grasped. The Court is prevented from rendering dissenting (or concurring) opinions and the decision-making process is secret. This mode of operation has been construed by scholars as motivated by the need to protect the Court from any political interference, as no judge should be required to justify their individual position outside of the Court.[157]

It is no mystery that the decision-making process is characterized by the broadest consensus.[158] The Court's President, elected for three-year terms by the other justices via secret ballot, nominates the *rapporteur*, namely the judge in charge of a specific case. Even dissenting and concurrent judges participate in drafting the decision,[159] which is officially authored by the drafting judge alone. One can infer that a judge is dissenting or concurring when the *rapporteur* and the drafting judge are not the same person. On account of these two modes of operation, it is understandable why, unlike many other constitutional courts, the Italian Constitutional Court never splits into chambers,[160] and is not affected by who holds the presidency of the Court. According to an unwritten rule, the President of the Court is chosen by seniority as a *primus inter pares* and does not play a predominant role.[161]

Most recently, in January 2020, the Constitutional Court amended its procedures in three notable ways. First, it allowed institutional bodies, professional associations, and non-governmental organizations to file *amici curiae* "[i]n line with the practice followed by the supreme and constitutional courts of many other countries".[162] Second, the Constitutional Court allowed itself to call in experts to be heard in chambers, with

154 On the *stare decisis* principle with regard to the Court of Cassation, see *infra* 3.4.2.

155 Cartabia (2016) (n 103) 85–86.

156 Zicchittu (2015) (n 114) 236.

157 Groppi and Spigno (2014) (n 47) 9.

158 Ibid 12.

159 Cartabia (2016) (n 103) 46.

160 Ibid.

161 Ibid 46–47.

162 Press of the Office of the Constitutional Court, *Press Release of 11 January 2020*, https://www.cortecostituzionale.it/documenti/comunicatistampa/Press_release_AC.pdf. It is important to note that the press release was in English, probably as a means of dialogue with other constitutional courts and the academia.

all parties present. Third, it made provisions for the intervention of each party with a valid, direct, and immediately relevant interest in the proceedings at a lower court on whether a specific constitutional matter should be sent to the Constitutional Court. Put differently, only the parties to the case and the President of the Council of Ministers previously had access to such proceedings.

3.4.1.5 Conclusions

One of the most striking features of Italy's legal culture is the role that the Constitutional Court has asserted for itself. Interacting with both norm-producing and conflict-resolving instances, the Court has been termed relational in character. According to some commentators, relationality is more generally the European style of constitutional adjudication.[163] What may appear to be a specific trait is the involvement of other adjudicating instances. Through this relationality, the Court has managed to i) decrease its caseload through the doctrine of consistent interpretation; ii) maintain the unity of the system, at least in terms of constitutionally-informed interpretation; iii) avoid political clashes; and iv) maintain its legitimacy.[164] Relationality has recently moved toward society at large, rather than only institutional actors, through three procedural amendments that the Constitutional Court carried out in January 2020.

The process of constitutional revision is presently a "marginal instrument for constitutional change".[165] Rather, the decisions of the Constitutional Court have contributed to an informal process of constitutional change.[166]

3.4.2 The Court of Cassation

3.4.2.1 Overview

As for the Constitutional Court, the role that Italy's Court of Cassation (hereafter called the CtC) plays in the legal culture can be understood through both its norm-producing and conflict-resolving capacities. We consider here the CtC's norm-producing capacity.

Italy's CtC is an apex court for courts of ordinary jurisdiction, in civil (including commerce and labor) and criminal matters. It is also an apex court for courts of special jurisdiction in tax and military matters. For other courts of special jurisdiction (admin-

163 On the relational character of the court, see Cartabia (2016) (n 103) 42. On relationality as the European style of constitutional adjudication, see Patricia Popelier, 'An Italian or a European Style of Judicial Review? Setting the Agenda for Comparative Research on Courts' (2016) Vol. 1 *Italian Journal of Public Law* 72, *passim.*

164 Tania Groppi, 'Giustizia costituzionale "Italian style"? Si, grazie (ma non qualche correttivo)' (2016) Issue 2 *Diritto Pubblico Comparato ed Europeo (Dpce online) 1*, 7. D'Amico (2008) (n 45) 246.

165 Tania Groppi, 'Constitutional Revision in Italy. A Marginal Instrument for Constitutional Change' in Xenophon Kontiades (ed), *Engineering Constitutional Change: A Comparative Perspective on Europe, Canada and USA* (Routledge 2012).

166 Groppi and Spigno (2014) (n 47) 2: "an important feature of Italian constitutionalism lies in the fact that constitutional change has largely taken place informally – that is, outside of the rules established for the enactment of formal amendments – in a variety of forms: ordinary laws with constitutional effects (such as electoral laws or the Standing Orders of each Chamber of the Parliament), constitutional conventions and practices, European law, and, last but not least, decisions of the Constitutional Court".

istrative courts and courts of accounts), it is an apex court solely on matters of jurisdiction. It scrutinizes decisions in terms of law, rather than fact. The CtC is divided into six "simple sections" having jurisdiction on civil law, including labor and tax law, and seven sections having jurisdiction on criminal law. The CtC deliberates in united sections when it has an eight-judge composition, presided over by the First President of the Court of Cassation. In civil law matters, the CtC adjudicates in united sections only the following: jurisdiction, power attribution, and questions of law where either the simple sections are split or the matter is of utmost importance, pursuant to the discretion of the CtC's First President. In criminal law matters, the CtC adjudicates in united sections only the following: a question that the simple sections believe has given rise to a split; and matters where the simple sections would need to follow the principle of law spelled out by the united sections, but do not agree.

Differently from other European supreme courts, the CtC renders a dizzying amount of rulings every year, roughly 83,000.[167] According to some commentators, the CtC features the highest productivity rate among all European supreme courts.[168] This circumstance, however, does not negate the dire straits in which the CtC presently finds itself, due to a number of factors of Italian legal history and culture that we are to consider.

Following unification in 1861, there were five different Courts of Cassation.[169] Court pluralism rendered any attempt at a unified interpretation implausible until one sole CtC was established in Rome in 1923. The practice of "attenuated" *stare decisis* has characterized the CtC ever since.[170] The unifying role was recognized in the midst of World War II, in 1941, when a royal decree bestowed upon the CtC had the function of ensuring "the exact compliance and uniform interpretation of the law, the unity of the objective national law".[171] The same decree maintained the CtC's other function as the supreme body of justice.

3.4.2.2 The Court of Cassation's style

Due to its norm-producing capacity, the CtC's style is quite explanatory. If the CtC's role concerned dispute settlement only, its decisions may have been more succinct, like those rendered by the *Cour de Cassation* in France, under which model the CtC was originally conceived.[172]

---

167 Canzio (2017) (n 63) 1.

168 Lucia Tria, 'La funzione di nomofilachia della Corte di cassazione alla luce dei principi del giusto processo di derivazione europea nonché del principio costituzionale di razionalità-equità' 21, available at http://www.europeanrights.eu/public/commenti/1%5E_Commento_Tria.pdf accessed 19 June 2019.

169 Pier Giuseppe Monateri, 'Shifting Frames: Law and Legal "Contaminations"' in Jeffrey S. Lena and Ugo Mattei (eds), *Introduction to Italian Law* (Kluwer Law International 2002) 21–30.

170 Ibid 28.

171 Article 65(1) Royal Decree 12/1941, n. 12 (authors' translation).

172 Tria, 'La funzione di nomofilachia' (n 168) 5.

3.4.2.3 The entwining circle: Court of Cassation ↔ Constitutional Court and other courts

Still in force, the previously mentioned 1941 royal decree clearly points to the current dual nature of the CtC. On the one hand, the CtC ensures unity of interpretation; on the other, it is the highest adjudicative instance in the court hierarchy for most courts. The constitution recognizes this second role[173] and adds one dimension: CtC judges are eligible to be nominated as judges to the Constitutional Court.[174]

In this context, it was for the Constitutional Court to clarify whether the CtC role of unifying the law is constitutionally relevant, which it confirmed in a series of rulings.[175] As noted earlier, further impetus to the "unifying" role of the CtC emerged when the Constitutional Court pointed to its interpretation as "living law".[176] By so doing, the Constitutional Court allowed the CtC to bridle the lower courts.[177] What the Constitutional Court endows the CtC with is not only the power, but also the duty, to flesh out the "living law".[178] But the Constitutional Court has (rarely) allowed itself to criticize the "living law" of the CtC, when the latter, "short of any criticism, takes upon principles that have been hammered out almost five decades before".[179] In fact, the unifying function of the Court of Cassation is one of fleshing out the "*living* law", that is in light of present-day societal needs and circumstances. Although the Constitutional Court is not preoccupied with the number of cases that should support "living law",[180] the CtC construes its unifying role as stemming from a stable case law of either one section or the CtC united sections.[181]

Legal doctrine has termed such unifying rule "nomophilachy", literally norm protection.[182] The Constitutional Court has itself recognized such a role as i) grounded in the constitutional principle of equality, pursuant to which similar cases ought to be adjudicated analogously as much as possible; and ii) endowing certainty onto legal relationships (*certezza del diritto)*.[183] The term nomophilachy has been endorsed also by Parliament, which deployed it for the first time in the title to a 2006 law.[184] Within

---

173 Italian Constitution, Article 135(1). The Constitution also mentions the CtC's apex offices, the First President and Attorney General. See Article 106(4) of the Italian Constitution. On the symbol ↔, see *supra* n 141.

174 See *supra* 3.4.1.

175 See, e.g., C.C. Decision 105/2018; Maria Acierno, Gaetano De Amicis, Enzo Vincenti and Mario Morelli, 'Il ruolo della cassazione: tradizioni e mutamenti' (2011) *Diritto Penale Contemporaneo* 1, 7; Salvato (2018) (n 152) 2. Cf. Giovanni Amoroso, 'Nomofilachia e Massimario', available at http://www.cortedicassazione.it/cassazione-resources/resources/cms/documents/Il_precedente_ed_il_ruolo_del_Massimario_s07.pdf accessed 4 March 2019, according to which the function is enshrined in Article 111(7) of the Italian Constitution.

176 See *supra* 3.4.1.

177 Salvato (2018) (n 152) 4–5.

178 Ibid 4.

179 C.C. Decision 336/2002, para 2.

180 See *supra* 3.4.1.

181 Cass. (Civil United Sections) 31 July 2012, n. 13620; Cass. 15 October 2007, n. 21553; Cass. 13 May 2003, n. 7355; Tria, 'La funzione di nomofilachia' (n 168) 3.

182 On the doctrinal origin of the term, see Canzio (2017) (n 63) 2. The term originates from Greek.

183 C.C. Order 149/2013.

184 Canzio (2017) (n 63) 2.

a series of laws, Parliament strengthened the CtC's nomophilachy.[185] For instance, no decision from a lower court can be challenged before the CtC in civil matters when the decision conforms to the established rulings of the higher courts and no grounds are apparent to modify them.[186] The CtC can also release the principle of law governing a case when the challenge has *not* been presented, when it has been withdrawn by the parties, or when the lower courts' decision cannot be challenged.[187]

Through law, the structure that has emerged within the CtC is hierarchical: when one chamber does not agree with the unifying rulings of the CtC's united sections, such chamber is under the duty to refer the matter to the united sections.[188] Any change in the case law of the united sections, overruling or *revirement,* is determined by the united sections themselves.[189]

The CtC has thus arisen as a court of precedents, steering a "system of precedents".[190] This system is quite different from proper *stare decisis.* It is not regularly based on analogy since it is a fact that the Court of Cassation has jurisdiction to scrutinize only the law, rather than the facts.[191] Also absent is a theory about the binding character and effect of precedents.[192] It is apparent that the "poignancy" of some precedents is higher under certain circumstances, especially when the line of precedents is "established", or consistent.[193] In contrast to *stare decisis* is also the fact that the CtC is no general court of precedents vis-à-vis some courts of special jurisdiction in certain matters.

Conclusively, it does not appear outlandish to follow eminent doctrine and former judges of the CtC in order to maintain that the current legal order is characterized by an "attenuated" form of *stare decisis,* close to common law systems,[194] and precedents are deemed a legal source for the practice of law.[195] Decisions of other higher courts (e.g., courts of appeals) may be cited, yet the CtC's precedents enjoy a higher status.[196]

---

185 Tria, 'La funzione di nomofilachia' (n 168) 4.

186 Article 360-bis(1) of the Civil Procedural Code. This has been called a 'filter', see Michele Taruffo, 'La Jurisprudencia Entre Casuística Y Uniformidad: Between Casuistry and Uniformity' (2014) Vol. 27, No. 2 *Revista de derecho (Valdivia)* 9, 12.

187 Article 363 of the Civil Procedural Code.

188 Article 374(3) of the Civil Procedural Code. See similarly in criminal matters, Article 610(2) of the Criminal Procedural Code. See further examples in Tria, 'La funzione di nomofilachia' (n 168) 4.

189 Article 374 of the Civil Procedural Code. See also Amoroso, 'Nomofilachia e Massimario' (n 175) 11.

190 Canzio (2017) (n 63) 2.

191 Michele Taruffo, 'Judicial Rulings with Prospective Effect in Italy' in Eva Steiner (ed), *Comparing the Prospective Effect of Judicial Rulings across Jurisdictions* (Springer 2015) 204.

192 Ibid 204.

193 Ibid 204.

194 Canzio (2017) (n 63) 6. It should be recalled that at the time of writing of this document, Giovanni Canzio was First President of the Court of Cassation. See also Amoroso, 'Nomofilachia e Massimario' (n 175) 8; Baschiera (2006) (n 64) 317 (fn. 103): "As for the principle in question, there is an increasing awareness of the path dependence to be traced in Italian case law; the phenomenon is multi-faceted and involves both elements of legal culture and of ideology, referring, with this latter term, to the confines marked (by legislator but also by academics and judges) for judicial interpretation within the legal system. Positive legal constraints and judicial standards of civil liability for the judge are also part of the framework that shapes path dependence in Italian case law".

195 Taruffo (2014) (n 186) 203.

196 Ibid 204.

Even though such characterization is liable to be criticized, particularly in light of some features of the Italian legal culture that we analyze in the following, it is worth acknowledging the perception that legal actors have of themselves and their legal order, which is *per se a* cultural feature. Being true to this self-characterization, which legal actors make of themselves and the legal order, is also poised to kindle an important discussion, especially in terms of comparisons with legal cultures where *stare decisis* is fully fledged.[197]

3.4.2.4 The Court of Cassation's modes of operation in light of its function

Deflating the backlog is a priority in the "judicial crisis" epitomized by the roughly 83,000 rulings rendered every year by the Court of Cassation. Yet, at a time of normative crisis, the "unifying" role of the CtC is all the more needed.[198] One of the CtC's modes of operation is to take pains to scrutinize other judges' motivations. Whatever adjudicative body intends to go astray from the CtC's rulings, the particular adjudicative body shall put forward new grounds.[199] A further mode of operation is the lack of dissenting and concurring opinions in the CtC's practice. This may be due to a cultural trait: there is no adjudicative instance featuring dissenting or concurring opinions in Italy.[200] But it may also be motivated by the high number of precedents.

Emphasis is thus on lesser but clearer principles of law. Even though the 1941 law defines the CtC's role with words of scientific exactitude, and the imperative of *uniform* interpretation,[201] such a demand is not realistic. Moreover, the degree of exactitude needs to be sacrificed when the CtC deems previous rulings outdated in terms of societal ideas and expectations of the law.[202] The CtC generally explains the reasons why it does not follow its precedents and overrules them with sole reference to a specific case, rather than prospectively.[203]

The CtC also relies on the solutions provided by doctrine[204] and lower judges, who are "the first to confront social fluidity".[205] Proof of this is how the Court of Cassation has allowed for unity in cases of lacunae by allowing for a "bottom-up" nomophilachy.[206] In adopting a lower court's solution that has proved flexible enough to accommodate the

197 Compare with *stare decisis* in England and Wales and in the United States in this book.

198 Tria, 'La funzione di nomofilachia' (n 168) 5, referring to the decreasing systematic character of legislation, and lack of clarity. This is due to the multiplying of norm-production sources, the difficulties of coordinating the existing sources and the worsening of the quality of black letter law in terms of formulations. On the normative crisis, see also *supra* 3.1.

199 Canzio (2017) (n 63) 6. Tria, 'La funzione di nomofilachia' (n 168) 4.

200 See *supra* 3.4.1 on the Constitutional Court.

201 See *supra* Royal Decree 12/1941, n. 12 and Canzio (2017) (n 63) 3.

202 On a dynamic type of nomophilachy, Canzio (2017) (n 63) 5.

203 Taruffo (2014) (n 186) 206. Ibid, this is also the way other courts go astray from precedents.

204 Canzio (2017) (n 63) 5. See the case law where doctrinal solutions are adopted by the CtC in Baschiera (2006) (n 64) 319.

205 Canzio (2017) (n 63) 5 (authors' translation).

206 E.g., Cass. 7 July 2011 n. 12408 and Damiano Spera, *Tabelle milanesi 2018 e danno non patrimoniale* (Giuffrè 2018) 49; Acierno and others (2011) (n 175) 6. On the need for a bottom-up nomophilachy, see Canzio (2017) (n 63) 5.

specifics of the case, the CtC is in the position to confer legitimacy to lower courts and decrease resistance. Within a drive for the fairness of the single case, lower courts have in fact criticized top-down solutions of the "one-size-fits-all" variety that the CtC has offered.[207] A further underpinning to the CtC's unifying role comes from international sources, which cannot deploy different effects before different courts,[208] lest Italy risk incurring international responsibility.

One of the practical modes for the court to exert its unifying role is to make available a series of maxims, which orient lower courts to understand whether the "principle of law" is relevant and applicable to the case under adjudication. In practice, lower courts rely highly on the maxims prepared by the maxims' office embedded in the CtC, which has the discretion to choose what ruling is worth instating as a maxim and is tasked with severing the "principle of law" from *obiter dicta.*[209] This body is made up of several judges who may be called to adjudicative functions upon the discretion of the CtC's President.[210] The maxims are written as summaries and are accessible through a database, *Italgiure,* which is widely available at lower courts. *Italgiure* has substantively facilitated access to precedents. For this reason, decisions usually refer to more than one precedent.[211]

Be that as it may, the unity of norm-production achieved through the CtC's unifying interpretation is threatened by three factors: i) the existence of some courts of special jurisdiction that are not subject to the CtC's full jurisdiction,[212] ii) the overwhelming case log,[213] and iii) dissent among different sections of the court.[214] While the first factor depends on Parliament, and partially on the Constitutional Court and CtC, the second factor can be better dealt with by introducing a higher threshold for review ("filter").[215] A real filter at review would sacrifice what may be termed as a culturally entrenched "right to litigate". The persuasive force of the reform lies in the equal protection of the law, which can be attained through a reduced case log where the CtC's role is more uni-

---

207 Acierno and others (2011) (n 175) 7. Taruffo (2015) (n 191) 205.

208 Acierno and others (2011) (n 175) 5.

209 Giulio Cataldi, 'Roulo e funzione della Corte di cassazione : il punto di vista del giudice d`apello' (2017) Issue 3 *Questione Giustizia 14*, 15. A precursor to the maxims' office emerged in 1924, but was explicitly regulated by law only in 1941. See Amoroso, 'Nomofilachia e Massimario' (n 175) 3. Compare with *Leitsätze* in Germany, see Koch (2020), 'German Legal Culture' (n 57).

210 Amoroso, 'Nomofilachia e Massimario' (n 175) 5.

211 Taruffo (2015) (n 191) 204, who refers to the importance of maxims as the most peculiar feature of the Italian system of precedents. Maxims and decisions/orders can be found on http://www.italgiure.giustizia.it/ accessed 13 February 2019.

212 See *infra 4*.5.

213 Tria, 'La funzione di nomofilachia' (n 168) 5. Franco Gaetano Scoca, 'Administrative Justice in Italy: Origins and Evolution' (2009) Vol. 2 *Italian Journal of Public Law 1*18, 152.

214 Amoroso, 'Nomofilachia e Massimario' (n 175) 6–7. See the constant number of 'dissents' at the level of the Court of Cassation itself, as provided in ibid 6. Dissents are higher in criminal law matters, ibid 6. On the contrasting decisions at the Court of Cassation, see Taruffo (2015) (n 191) 204–205.

215 Acierno and others (2011) (n 175) 6.

fying.[216] The third factor has not decreased through the years.[217] Under consideration now is the implementation of a label at the maxims' office that would term "certain" those CtC rulings that have been followed the most.[218]

3.4.2.5 Conclusions

The unifying role that the Court of Cassation has taken on, endorsed and strengthened by law and the Constitutional Court, has led to a system of "attenuated" *stare decisis* where norm-production is thus partly due to the CtC's principles of law. Former members of the Court of Cassation consider this function necessary to counter the uncertainty and fluidity of legal post-modernity,[219] notably the normative crisis of a burgeoning norm-production. Unity is secured through the hierarchy of courts with the Court of Cassation at the apex, at least in civil, criminal, and tax matters.

3.5 The role of individuals: Referenda

The constitution allows for popular referenda when requested by either 500,000 members of the electorate or five regional councils in order to fully or partially repeal a law. No referenda can be held on tax or budgetary laws, laws for amnesty or general pardon, or laws authorizing the ratification of international treaties.[220] The Constitutional Court decides on the admissibility of such referenda.

3.6 Conclusions

In some legal cultures, unity of law is mainly attained through the unity of courts, whereas other legal cultures dwell on unity of law through legislation. In Italy's legal culture, the first case better represents the current landscape. At a time when the codes are dwarfed by swelling legislation, where norm-producing capacities have been abused due to lack of normativity and control from countervailing instances, unity is attained through the case law of the Constitutional Court and the Court of Cassation. Whenever a legislative reform will increase the review threshold at higher courts (the so-called "filter"), the "attenuated" *stare decisis m*ay shore up its unity function.

216 Ibid.

217 Amoroso, 'Nomofilachia e Massimario' (n 175) 6–7.

218 Ibid 8.

219 Canzio (2017) (n 63) 4.

220 Article 75(2) of the Constitution. See Barsotti and others (2015) (n 72) 51.

4. Conflict resolution

4.1 Introduction

In Italy's courts, 1,509,856 cases were pending in criminal matters[221] and 3,488,596 cases were pending in civil and commercial matters in 2018.[222] From EU-wide statistics, it emerges that what is staggering is the high number of *pending* litigious civil and commercial cases,[223] whilst the number of incoming litigious cases does not stand out in comparison to the EU average.[224] The clearance rate, meaning the number of cases that are decided compared to those that are filed in a given time, has topped 120% in litigious civil and commercial cases,[225] but Italy's judicial proceedings in the first instance are the longest in the OECD area,[226] which has triggered the ECtHR's findings that Italy is in breach of the right to a speedy trial.[227]

The problem with tackling the present judicial crisis does not appear to rest with the allotted budget.[228] What is noticeable is: i) the low number of judges per 100,000 inhabitants compared to other EU countries,[229] ii) the low ability to identify early on long or problematic cases,[230] and iii) the restricted management responsibility of the chief justice.[231] Short of considering legal aid,[232] overall costs are the highest in the OECD area, which may be due to trial length.[233] Territorial differences, especially between the North

221 See https://www.giustizia.it/giustizia/it/mg_1_14_1.page?contentId=SST1288006&previsiousPage=mg_2_9_13 accessed 5 March 2019.

222 See https://www.giustizia.it/giustizia/it/mg_1_14_1.page%3Bjsessionid=sxIj1Zlin78R55XmVhDae1rJ?contentId =SST1287132&previsiousPage=mg_2_9_13 accessed 4 March 2019.

223 The European Commission, 'The 2017 EU Justice Scoreboard, Communication from the Commission to the European Parliament, the Council, the European Central Bank, the European Economic and Social Committee and the Committee of the Regions—COM(2017)' 11. Administrative cases appear to be no exception in comparison with EU average, see ibid. No data were provided for criminal cases.

224 Ibid 6.

225 Ibid 9.

226 OECD, 'Giustizia civile: come promuoverne l`efficienza?', *OECD Economics Department Policy Notes,* No. 18 June 2013, 2.

227 Paolo Ferrua, 'La ragionevole durata del processo tra Costituzione e Convenzione europea' (2017) Issue 1 *Questione Giustizia 1*09, 116–117.

228 The 2017 EU Justice Scoreboard (n 223) 25.

229 Ibid 26. The change in the number of judges from a society where 78% of the population was illiterate and practicing for the most agriculture (1865) to a more than doubled population in one of the most industrialized economies worldwide, where illiteracy has last been rated 2.1%, has been increased by roughly three/fifth, and only lately. See https://www.giustizia.it/resources/cms/documents/piante_organiche_magistratura_evoluzione_storica.pdf accessed 4 March 2019.

230 OECD, 'Judicial performance and its determinants: a cross-country perspective', *OECD Economics Department Policy Notes,* No. 5 June 2013, 24. Trial length tends to be lower in countries with good statistics, which Italy partly lacks. See ibid 25.

231 Ibid 28–29.

232 Legal aid is provided in all matters pursuant to the level of income. See the example provided by The 2017 EU Justice Scoreboard (n 223) 19.

233 OECD (2013), 'Judicial performance and its determinants: a cross-country perspective' (n 230) 15.

and the South, emerge in terms of litigation rate[234] and performance.[235] The appeal rate is not particularly high.[236]

4.2 Conflict resolution and its principles

The most important principle in terms of conflict resolution is the right to a fair trial, stipulated by the constitution.[237] The right to access justice applies to all courts. There is a constitutional right to review before the Court of Cassation, but not before appellate courts. Every person has a right to a "natural" judge, which equates to the right to a legal judge in the German legal order, meaning that no special judge can strip an individual of their rights, as is often the case in dictatorships. Judges are subject only to the law,[238] which is in line with the principle of the division of powers but also with the lack of a fully-fledged doctrine of *stare decisis.*[239]

The sole attribution of the Minister of Justice is to allow for the organization and functioning of the services of the justice system.[240] The government leaves the criteria for determining financial resources to the judiciary.[241] For this reason, the constitution establishes a self-governing body of judges, the Judicial Council, whose President is the President of the Republic.[242] Self-governing bodies for courts of special jurisdiction were established by law.[243] Independent from other powers, judges of ordinary or special jurisdiction shall also be autonomous from their peers and differentiated only by functions.[244] Moreover, each judge shall be impartial with respect to both the subject matter at issue and the parties who come before the court. To the general qualification of judges (*magistrati)* belong both adjudicating and prosecuting authorities.

---

234 Roberto Ippoliti, 'Efficienza Tecnica e Geografia Giudiziaria' (2014) *POLIS Working Papers no*. 217, Institute of Public Policy and Public Choice 23.

235 Silvia Giacomelli, Sauro Mocetti, Giuliana Palumbo and Giacomo Roma, 'La giustizia civile in Italia: le recenti evoluzioni', *Occasional Papers Banca D`Italia no*. 401 (2017) 6 and 23–25, available at https://www.bancaditalia.it/pubblicazioni/qef/2017-0401/QEF_401_17.pdf accessed 4 March 2019.

236 OECD (2013), 'Giustizia civile: come promuoverne l`efficienza?' (n 226) 9.

237 Italian Constitution, Article 111(1).

238 Italian Constitution, Article 101(2).

239 Salvato (2018) (n 152) 4.

240 Italian Constitution, Article 110.

241 The 2017 EU Justice Scoreboard (n 223) 26.

242 The first president and the first General Attorney of the Court of Cassation are members by law. On the clashes between the judicial council and the Minister of Justice, see Baschiera (2006) (n 64) 309.

243 The Council of the Presidency of Administrative Justice was established by law in 1982 as the self-governing body of administrative judges. The Council of the Presidency, established in 1988, is the self-governing body of accounting judges. The Council of the Presidency of Tax Justice, established in 1992, is the self-governing body of tax commissions. The Council of the Military Judiciary is the self-governing body of military judges.

244 Italian Constitution, Article 107(3). Judges cannot be members of political parties, see the Italian Constitution, Article 98(3); Legislative decree 109/2006, Article 3(1)(h); C.C. Decision 224/2009.

4.3 The Constitutional Court

The Constitutional Court is located in Rome. One of its conflict-resolving roles concerns conflicts of attribution, which can be either i) among powers of the central state, or ii) among subjects.[245] Within the first type of conflicts, the Constitutional Court determines which body is entitled to exercise a particular power. A typical case is a conflict of attribution brought by a judge against the Minister of Justice, or vice versa. Within the second type of conflict, two situations may arise: either i) the Constitutional Court is called on to determine whether the state or a particular region is entitled to exercise a particular power, or ii) the Constitutional Court is to determine whom should exercise a particular power among regions.[246]

Even though most of the Constitutional Court's activity belong to indirect review,[247] conflicts of attribution between the state and the regions have increased.[248] This may be due to the lack of a second parliamentary chamber representing regions,[249] as well as to the absence of flexibility rules or political fora where differences may be sorted out. The Constitutional Court hammered out the so-called principle of sincere cooperation in order to spur informal practices of cooperation.[250]

4.4 Courts of ordinary jurisdiction

4.4.1 Overview

Courts of ordinary jurisdiction consist of a hierarchical structure with the Court of Cassation at its apex. They have jurisdiction on civil, including commerce and labor, and criminal matters. Geographically, courts of ordinary jurisdiction are divided into offices of the justice of the peace and prosecuting lay judges, tribunals, and courts of appeals as first instance and second instance.

Offices of the justice of the peace are lay judges in a nuanced sense – in fact, they need to hold at least a Master's degree in law. They are first instance in either less egregious matters or matters where they substitute for tribunal judges. Tribunals encompass

---

245 For an overview of the subject, see Barsotti and others (2015) (n 72) 49 ff.

246 The autonomous provinces of Trento and Bolzano are also entitled to bring such type of claims. Law no. 87/1953 and Article 98(2) of the Regional statute of Trentino-Alto Adige. When the conflict concerns a legislative act, conflict resolution intermingles with norm production. The central government can challenge the constitutionality of a Region's Charter within 30 days from its publication and the Constitutional Court is called to carry out a direct review of constitutionality. The central government is also entitled to challenge the constitutionality of a Region's statute within 60 days from its publication, and a Region can do the same against a State's statute or another Region's statute. The effects of the decisions rendered by the Constitutional Court are not *erga omnes*, but solely unfold with regard to the specific conflict among regions or regions/state.

247 See *supra* 3.4.1.

248 Barsotti and others (2015) (n 72) 52.

249 See *supra* 3.2. Benvenuti (2015) (n 76) 393.

250 Ibid 394. Other conflict-resolving roles of the Constitutional Court revolve around i) deciding on charges against the President of the Republic when the latter is impeached by the Parliament sitting in joint session, and ii) deciding on the admissibility of referenda.

one office of the prosecutor, who may be aided by prosecuting lay judges. Each court of appeals encompasses one office for the prosecutor. Courts of appeals may also be aided by lay judges.

The Court of Cassation is located in Rome. The office of the public prosecutor of the Court of Cassation is established in both civil and criminal matters. The prosecutor's role is also related to the CtC's function of unifying the law as they can challenge judicial rulings from lower courts "in the interest of the law".[251] Within the CtC, a specialized prosecution office coordinates anti-mafia and terrorism investigations and prosecutions nationwide.

Since unification, the organizational framework has not changed significantly.[252] In 2011, a major reform set forth the premises for eliminating 30 out of 166 tribunals and offices of the prosecutors, all 220 sub-offices of tribunals, and 666 out of the 839 offices of the justice of peace.[253]

4.4.2 The conflict-resolving role of the Court of Cassation

Having considered the unifying function of the CtC, the emphasis here is on its other function – to adjudicate issues of law. The CtC adjudicates administrative and accounting matters (only jurisdiction), as well as civil, criminal, tax, and military concerns. In conflict resolution before the CtC, what is under scrutiny is not the judicial ruling itself, but rather the rationality of the argumentations.[254] The CtC's conflict-resolving role is generally deemed instrumental to its norm-producing role.[255]

4.4.3 Specialized units

First and second instance courts are organized into specialized units, which are determined by law, the size of the courts, or decisions by the head of the court.[256] The law has established units at both the first and second instance in the following matters: i) business matters (IP rights, competition, and other enumerated business law matters);[257] ii) bankruptcy; iii) agrarian matters; iv) labor matters; v) courts and offices for civil administrative and criminal matters concerning minors, including a discrete office for the prosecutor; vi) parole courts; and vii) assize courts for severe criminal cases.

---

251 Code of Civil Procedure, Article 363 (authors' translation).

252 Ippoliti (2014) (n 234) 1.

253 See Response to a request from Parliament Members (Justice Minister Andrea Orlando, 16 November 2016), available at http://www.senato.it/japp/bgt/showdoc/frame.jsp?tipodoc=Sindispr&leg=17&id=997629 accessed 4 March 2019; see also http://www.senato.it/japp/bgt/showdoc/frame.jsp?tipodoc=Sindispr&leg=17&id=997629. The reform is being gradually implemented, see ibid.

254 Cass. Decision (Criminal United Sections) 10 July 2002 n. 30328, para 9. It is worth noting that the decision was penned by Giovanni Canzio, who is often cited throughout this chapter.

255 Acierno and others (2011) (n 175) 5. Piero Calamandrei and Carlo Furno, 'Cassazione civile' in Antonio Azara and Ernesto Eula (eds), *Novissimo Digesto Italiano,* Volume II (UTET 1958) 1055.

256 Marco Fabri and Philip M. Langbroek, 'Is There a Right Judge for Each Case? A Comparative Study of Case Assignment in Six European Countries' (2007) Vol. 1, No. 2 *European Journal of Legal Studies* 1, 11.

257 Commercial tribunals had previously existed in Italy for two decades, from 1865 to 1888.

For the first instance there are specialized units for i) immigration, international protection, and the free movement of EU citizens; and ii) prosecuting offices having competence in anti-mafia and terrorism investigations and prosecutions.

Regional tribunals are in place for the public waters rule on administrative and civil matters concerning public waters and the occupation of land. The court of appeals to these regional tribunals is the superior tribunal of the public waters, located in Rome.

Procedural rules may vary. For example, the procedural rules applicable to labor matters have been deemed particularly effective,[258] providing a model for reforming ordinary proceedings. Specialization also varies. For example, the OECD has deemed specialization in Italy's business units medium-low.[259]

4.4.4 Lay judges

There exist two types of lay judges. One type identifies individuals holding a degree in law, but who did not sit for the state exam to become fully-fledged judges. The second type comprises judges that serve lay functions in a more proper sense – they do not need to hold a degree in law and are rather part of the adjudicative function due to their specific knowledge and representativeness.

With regard to the first type of lay judges, a recent reform, which has not yet been fully implemented, has expanded the role of the justices of the peace and prosecuting lay judges, and has increased their professionalization toward the adjudicating function. Yet, current law prohibits them from working as lay judges for more than two days per week, but allows them to work in a different capacity. They receive a minimum compensation, to which further compensation is added contingent on productivity. They hold a degree in law, and they receive practical training by judges and theoretical training at the Superior School of the Judiciary. They can be confirmed every four years for 16 years in total. A similar role is the one taken on by lay judges aiding courts of appeals, but their term does not extend beyond five years.[260]

The second type of lay judges can be found in several specialized units: minors' courts, parole courts, agrarian courts, and public water courts.[261] In these matters, lay judges contribute their specific knowledge, and not their legal expertise. These judges may thus be deemed "lay" in a fuller sense than justices of the peace, since they do not need to have studied law.

In assize courts, lay judges join two professional judges as members of assize court panels in order to decide the gravest crimes. Also called popular judges, they are drawn by lot from a list and do not need to have a legal background. Their role is more one of representing local society. They decide with the professional judges on an equal footing.

---

258 Tria, 'La funzione di nomofilachia' (n 168) 17.

259 OECD (2013), 'Judicial performance and its determinants: a cross-country perspective' (n 230) 27.

260 See https://www.csm.it/web/csm-internet/magistratura/onoraria/funzioni-onorarie?show=true&title=le%20diverse%20figure%20della%20magistratura%20onoraria&show_bcrumb=le%20diverse%20figure%20della%20magistratura%20onoraria accessed 5 March 2019.

261 Ibid.

4.5 Courts of special jurisdiction

4.5.1 Overview

Courts of special jurisdiction perform a judicial role but are not positioned within the judiciary, as opposed to courts of ordinary jurisdiction.[262]

Italy features a binary system, in line with France and Germany, whereby protection against the administration is divided into two different orders: the judge of ordinary jurisdiction and the judge of administrative jurisdiction. Administrative courts have a special jurisdiction based on general criteria – they adjudicate matters concerning legitimate interests, which are different from individual rights, and individual rights only in matters determined by law.[263] The administrative courts are organized in a two-tiered system. One administrative tribunal is present in each region. Decisions can be challenged before the Council of State, which is located in Rome. In Sicily, appeals are brought to the Council of Administrative Justice, according to Sicily's charter as a special region.[264] By national law, this body has been qualified as a sub-office of the Council of State.[265] The CtC is the apex court in matters concerning jurisdiction only, and has negated its jurisdiction to adjudicate the conformity of the Council of State's rulings to EU law.[266]

Another type of special jurisdiction is the one exercised by the judges of the Court of Accounts, which is spread into 21 sections across the territory and headquartered in Rome. Both at the regional and central levels, it features offices of the prosecutor. With regard to the Court of Accounts, the Court of Cassation plays the role of apex court on matters concerning jurisdiction only. Established by the constitution, the Court of Accounts checks: i) the legality of some governmental acts before they enter into force, ii) the accounting process after the state budget is spent, and iii) the financial management of the bodies to which the state generally contributes. It reports to the Parliament on these matters. It also adjudicates the liability of civil servants, treasurers, and employees in public administration.[267]

The case of tax jurisdiction is curious. Albeit this type of jurisdiction is special, the adjudicating judges are part of the judicial system, to which the courts of ordinary jurisdiction belong as well.[268] Ever since the Constitutional Court decision of 1974,[269] tax commissions are judicial, rather than governmental, bodies. They also feature lay judges with legal expertise. Tax commissions comprise first instance (at the provincial level) and appeals (at the regional level).[270] The Court of Cassation is the apex court.

---

262 This is the most common interpretation of the Constitution, see Scoca (2009) (n 213) 151.

263 Article 103 of the Constitution.

264 See *supra* 3.2.

265 Legislative Decree 24 December 2003, n. 373.

266 Cass. Decision of 17 January 2017 n. 956.

267 See http://www.corteconti.it/attivita/controllo/funzioni/ accessed 5 March 2019.

268 On the courts of ordinary jurisdiction, see *supra* 4.4. Administrative judges and the judges of the Court of Accounts do not belong to the judicial system, yet the main conflict-resolution principles are applicable to them. See Article 108(2) of the Constitution.

269 C.C. Decision n. 287 of 27 December 1974.

270 The system varies slightly with respect to Trento and Bolzano.

Military jurisdiction is established by the constitution.[271] It comprises nine first instance tribunals and a second instance court of appeal in Rome. It features also lay judges who serve in the army. The Court of Cassation is the apex court in these matters.

Having introduced these four special jurisdictions, it is proper to pause here. All four special jurisdictions appear historically entrenched and somehow makeshift. With regard to history, administrative courts were introduced in 1889–1890. The Court of Accounts has existed ever since 1862 and tax commissions can be traced back to 1864. A separate track for military jurisdiction has been in place since 1859. With regard to the makeshift feature, the constitution recognizes all jurisdictions, except the tax commissions. But the 6th transitional provision to the constitution tasked the newborn democracy with reorganizing special jurisdictions. This has not been done yet. The underlying rationale dwells with circumscribing special jurisdictions, which are "exceptions" to courts of ordinary jurisdiction. This rationale can be gleaned also from a provision in the constitution, which prohibits the establishment of special courts, different from those envisaged by the constitution.[272]

4.5.2 The Council of state, the Court of accounts, and the Court of Cassation

Before the image of a unifying Court of Cassation, some doubts surface due to the competing role of other courts. In fact, the Court of Cassation is the apex court for ordinary and special jurisdictions with two notable exceptions: administrative and accounting jurisdictions. Here, the Court of Cassation can adjudicate solely jurisdiction matters and the "unifying" role is played by the Council of State and the Court of Accounts, respectively.[273] Not only do these bodies decide controversies, but they also spell out "principles of law", similarly to the method applied by the Court of Cassation.[274]

In practice, the Council of State does not shrink from referring to both its own decisions and the decisions rendered by the Court of Cassation, thus legitimizing the "unifying" power of the latter even in administrative matters different from jurisdiction.[275] When contrasts in the dialectics arise, the Constitutional Court's interpretation is usually decisive.[276] This also occurs with regard to the Court of Accounts.[277]

271 Italian Constitution, Article 103(3).

272 Italian Constitution, Article 102. Mattarella (2010) (n 93) 341.

273 Giuseppe Barbagallo, 'Stile e motivazione delle decisioni del Consiglio di Stato' (1999) 52e Année No. 8 *La Revue administrative 1*16, 123–124, where it is found that the Council of State's reference to its own case law begins in 1930.

274 See *supra* 3.4.2 and 4.4. With respect to the Council of State, see Article 99 Legislative Decree 2 July 2010 n. 104. With reference to the courts of accounts, see Articles 114 and 117 Legislative Decree 26 August 2016, n. 174 (Code of accounts-related justice).

275 See https://www.giustizia-amministrativa.it/cdsintra/wcm/idc/groups/public/documents/document/mday/odq3/~edisp/e5qp24urzipodm6ot32lm32mwq.html accessed 4 January 2020.

276 C.C. Decision 254/2004.

277 Council of State – Appellate Division for Sicily, Decision 215/2018 (ECLI:IT:CONT:2018:215APPSIC).

An apt way to qualify the entwinements among the three courts is through the principle of functional unity. Asserted by both the Court of Cassation and the Constitutional Court, this principle can be particularly heuristic in devising the methodology for "unifying" the law – notwithstanding the lack of organizational unity.[278] In spite of this functional unity, the Council of State appears to have established a sub-culture within the wider Italian legal culture. It is interesting to note that, for no apparent reason, rulings are called *decisioni* instead of *sentenze: sentenze* is imbued with a "judicial" character and *decisioni* can be either judicial or non-judicial. The writing style is also different from the one applied by courts of ordinary jurisdiction, probably because the Council of State mainly addresses itself to the public administration in order to prompt it to conform its future behavior to law.[279]

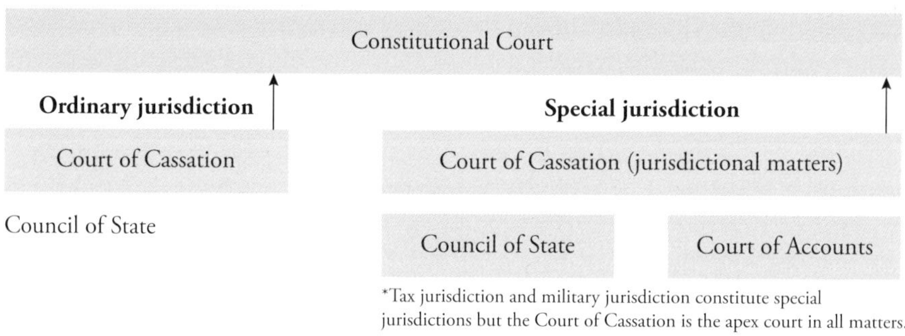

Fig.1 The Italian court system.

4.6 Ecclesiastical courts established by the Catholic Church

The ecclesiastical courts in Italy are due to the longtime presence and influence of the Catholic Church on Italian culture.[280] They are governed by the 1983 code for the Latin Church.[281] Existing in many other countries, ecclesiastical courts have been and are still partly influential on Italy's legal culture and may be qualified as a legal sub-culture. Through two international treaties between Italy and the Holy See, in 1929 and 1983, Italy's legal order recognizes the automatic effects of the Catholic rite of marriage. Besides few "secular" rules, the rite is regulated by canon law. When a marriage is declared null by the last instance tribunal, the Roman Rota, the decision can generally be recognized by the competent court of appeals. Italy's divorce law does not apply.

278 Scoca (2009) (n 213) 152.

279 Barbagallo (1999) (n 273) 117.

280 See *supra* 2.

281 Eastern Catholic Churches are governed by the 1990 Eastern Code.

4.7 Alternative dispute resolution (ADR)

Alternative dispute resolution mechanisms can be of two types: i) mechanisms outside of the official judicial system, which we here refer to as mediation; or ii) mechanisms attached to or secondary to official judicial mechanisms, which we here refer to as conciliation.[282] In arbitration, a dispute is submitted to one or more persons chosen by the parties.

The first practical ADR experiences as alternatives to judicial proceedings have emerged from below, mainly from the initiative of some chambers of commerce, municipalities, and courts. Being bound to implement directive 2008/52/CE on certain aspects of mediation in civil and commercial matters, the Italian Parliament introduced specific provisions,[283] including the obligation to refer specific matters to mediation before filing a case in court. These are enumerated civil and commercial matters. Lawyers are mediators by right but need to carry out continuing education to practice as mediators.

Labor matters are fairly different. In the 1970s, two statutes established voluntary mediation pathways. Since 1998, an attempt to mediate was obligatory to bring a labor matter before the courts. In 2010, a reform made such an attempt voluntary, except in few matters. A bill is under evaluation in order to usher in mediation also in criminal matters (restorative justice).

When judicial mechanisms have started, the proceedings are usually termed conciliation. Before 2013, some leeway existed for achieving conciliation in civil and commercial matters,[284] but there was no single way to account for the resolution of these cases. The possibilities of conciliation have increased since 2013 – the adjudicating judge in civil matters can now put forward a conciliation proposal before issuing the sentence.[285] Labor matters have been historically the most prominent for conciliation, which was implemented as early as 1893 but eliminated in 1928 during the Fascist era. Since 2005, a specific type of mediation has been in place for banking and financial matters. Available data point to a notable increase in mediation proceedings since 2011, probably due to its compulsory character in enumerated civil and commercial matters.[286] The subject areas where mediation is most practiced are banking contracts and rights *in rem.*[287]

Arbitration proceedings are governed in civil and commercial matters by the code of civil procedure, which provides for a claw-back regime in case the parties have not regulated the matters. Arbitration proceedings may end with either a contract or a decision. Contracts may be challenged pursuant to contract law, and decisions may be presented before a tribunal and their execution requested. Decisions are also partly challengeable before courts.

---

282 OECD (2013), 'Judicial performance and its determinants: a cross-country perspective' (n 230) 33, fn. 20.

283 Legislative Decree 28/2010.

284 See, e.g., Art. 37 Law-Decree 98/2001 and Article 696-bis civil procedural code.

285 See Art. 185-bis of the Civil Procedural Code.

286 See statistics in 'Mediazione civile, Statistiche del 2017', *Ministrero della Giustizia,* available at http://www.inmediar.it/wp-content/uploads/2018/03/Mediazione-Civile-Anno-2017.pdf accessed 5 March 2019.

287 Ibid.

The bottom line of ADR methods in Italy is promising, yet quite modest. Changing legislation has often produced a "chilling" effect. Unfortunately, legislation is not yet settled.[288] A further shortcoming lies in the fact that lawyers' professional bodies have long been critical of compulsory mediation.[289] Among the possible reasons, one may include the fear of being substituted by "non-lawyer" professionals. Moreover, it is unfortunate that the Judicial Council does not include an analysis of good practices in conciliation proceedings within its manual of good organizational practices and models.[290]

4.8 Conclusions

Italian legal culture is quite "court-oriented". This may be due to general features, for instance the culturally perceived right to litigate; or specific issues, for example the characterization of courts as the paramount, if not only, recourse to protect the individual from the public administration.[291] Still, the administrative justice system may not have responded to a sub-surface aspiration to full protection before administrative courts, for example due to the fact that the administrative judge is not empowered to issue injunctions.

5. The ideal of justice

The *ideal* of justice originates from the concept that the legal cultural model previously applied – the *idea* of justice. The transition from the *idea* to the *ideal* of justice occurred in the theorization of the model only in this edition of *Comparing Legal Culture,* short of ontological changes (*supra* Preface). Rather than defining how law is supposed to provide justice (the idea of justice), this latest theorization posits that justice is more germane to an ideal, encompassing different perceptions of justice. This broader concept of the ideal of justice is welcome. First, and most generally, it coheres with the post-modern reality of legal systems – lacking the gravitational force, hierarchy, and solid authority[292] to be able to spell out one definitive idea of justice. Second, and more specifically relating to the subject of this chapter, the Italian legal culture portrays justice as an aspiration rather

288 Giorgio Fabio Colombo, 'Alternative Dispute Resolution (ADR) in Italy: European Inspiration and National Problems' (2012) No. 29 *Ritsumeikan Law Review* 71, 80.

289 Giuseppe De Palo and Lauren Keller, 'Mediation in Italy: Alternative Dispute Resolution for All' in Klaus J. Hopt and Felix Steffek (eds), *Mediation: Principles and Regulation in Comparative Perspective* (Oxford University Press 2013) 264.

290 'Dalle buone prassi ai "modelli" Una prima manualistica ricognitiva delle pratiche de organizzazione più diffuse negli uffici giudiziari italiani' (Delibera CSM 7.7.2016), available at http://milanosservatorio.it/wp-content/uploads/2016/11/CSM-BUONE-PRASSI-LUGLIO-2016.pdf accessed 5 March 2019.

291 Mattarella (2010) (n 93) 340–341.

292 See e.g., Gunther Teubner, 'Breaking Frames: Economic Globalization and the Emergence of *Lex Mercatoria*' (2002) Vol. 5 *European Journal of Social Theory* 199. On solid and liquid authority, see Nico Krisch, 'Authority, solid and liquid, in postnational governance' in Roger Cotterrell and Maksymilian Del Mar (eds), *Authority in Transnational Legal Theory,* (Edward Elgar Publishing Limited 2016).

than an idea. Hence the metaphor used by the "father" of the Italian language, Dante. Dante described justice as the ocean floor that the eye cannot see when one is out on the water, but is nonetheless there, concealed by the deepest depths.[293] Having endorsed this latest theorization, some issues of interest rest with investigating: the main purpose of law and justice in the Italian legal culture, the institutions that are best suited to fulfill such purpose or goal, and the legal cultural features that contribute to realizing such purpose or goal. Some tentative answers emerge both in this sub-section and *infra* 8.3.3, which remarks on the legal method.

The ideal of justice belongs to the intellectual elements of a legal culture, but both shapes and is shaped by its institutional elements. Different approaches are available in order to identify the ideas and expectations around the ideal of justice. We consider a first approach, more entwined with the intellectual element of the legal method. A second approach is impacted by legal ideology, which is not yet an element within the legal cultural model that we apply.[294]

Within a first approach, the ideal of justice is related to the legal method. Legal sources are quite illuminating in this regard. Having considered the institutional elements of norm-production and how existing norms are applied in conflict-resolution mechanisms,[295] it is quite apparent that Italy is not oriented to predictability of outcome. The array of norms and the emphasis on dynamic, rather than textual, judicial interpretation,[296] does not allow for fully predicting the outcome of a controversy. Even though the certainty of the law has been pinpointed as an imperative by law and legal doctrine, as early as 1956 such certainty already appeared unattainable, especially due to the high quantity and low quality of legal norms.[297] On the other hand, the ideal of justice does not rest with continuity through precedents either – with regard to the Court of Cassation, we considered the above-mentioned multiple factors that factually decrease the precedential impact of its case law.[298]

What may be a specifically Italian trait in the conceptualization and practice of the ideal of justice is procedural predictability – *certezza processuale*[299] – which hinges on the predictability of procedures rather than outcomes. On the one hand, the predictability of procedures is entwined with the right to a fair trial, where fairness is construed as fair procedures. On the other hand, outcomes shall not necessarily be predictable. Through emphasis on interpretive evolution, the ideal of justice entails the need to adjust to societal values and practices, for which the adjudicating judge and the legislating

293 Dante Alighieri, *La Divina Commedia* (Hoepli 1932), Paradiso, Canto XIX, 58–63 (authors' translation).

294 On the ideal of justice as shaped by the institutional elements, see Sunde (2020) (n 2). On legal ideology, see ibid 23.

295 See *supra* 3 and 4.

296 See *supra* 3.4, most notably with regard to the Constitutional Court.

297 Giulio Lorenzi, 'La certezza del diritto' (1956) Vol. 79 *Il Foro Italiano* 73, 78.

298 See *supra* 3.4.2.

299 Cass. Decision (Criminal United Sections) 10 July 2002 n. 30328, para 6. Cfr. Marius Mikkel Kjølstad, Sören Koch and Jørn Øyrehagen Sunde, 'Introduction to Norwegian Legal Culture' in this volume, chapter 5, referring to procedural predictability as part of the ideal of justice in Norway's legal culture.

authority should be interpreters.[300] Procedural predictability is in fact complemented by fairness, meant as the justice done to the single case, by adapting, and even bending, the black letter law to the specificities of a particular case. Fairness appears to affect decisions where the Constitutional Court takes into account the context of the case,[301] for example "changes in public opinion and in the legal and social context".[302] These factors are considered to animate "the living constitution", but stop short of handing over the power of interpretation to popular sentiment.[303] This is not to understate the fact that the Constitutional Court has deployed outright non-legal, but rather moral, sociological, and economic, arguments.[304] Among the 40 most influential decisions ever rendered by the Constitutional Court, this type of argument appears in 12 judgments.[305] In this light, the procedural amendments that the Court has precipitated in January 2020 (*supra* 3.4.1) seem to point to a more inclusive empirical basis and decision-making process that allows for fairer results.

However, adjustments have emerged in order to attain some level of outcome predictability. For example, when the Court of Cassation overrules one of its precedents in an unpredictable way, anyone who had relied on the precedent does not incur the detrimental effects of the new ruling, pursuant to the CtC's case law.[306] Adjustments were also made to the idea of the "living constitution". Sometimes, the Constitutional Court's decisions do not purport the idea of a living constitution, but deploy a rather more neutral reasonableness test, by which the Constitutional Court emphasizes the need to avoid irrational contradictions "between the goals of the law and the content of its text".[307]

Predictability often characterizes systems of law, whereas fairness is more tied to the construction of the law as a living force in society.[308] The ideal of justice that infuses Italian legal culture thus appears to turn more on fairness. An explanation is not easy to find. Albeit a code jurisdiction, Italy's system of law may be difficult to navigate due to the number of provisions that are regularly passed outside of the code frameworks. Emphasis on the justice of a single case may be perceived as more important than maintaining a coherent system that is actually *not* there. Hence, in light of the pivotal role played by the right to a fair trial in Italy's legal culture, predictability attaches to the ideal of justice, but solely in terms of procedural predictability.

---

300 Cass. Decision (Criminal United Sections) 10 July 2002 n. 30328, para 4.

301 D'Amico (2008) (n 45) 232 fn 91.

302 Cartabia (2016) (n 103) 52.

303 Ibid.

304 Groppi and Spigno (2014) (n 47) 25. C.C. Decisions 15/1982; 361/1998; 172/1999; 102/2008; 80/2010 and 200/2012.

305 Groppi and Spigno (2014) (n 47) 25.

306 Tria, 'La funzione di nomofilachia' (n 168) 16.

307 Groppi and Spigno (2014) (n 47) 21.

308 Sören Koch, 'Sailing – using the LCM to analyse ideals of justice in Germany, England, and Norway' in this volume, chapter 20; Sunde (2020) (n 2).

Turning now to the second approach to the ideal of justice, one may wonder whether specific values embody the ideal of justice in Italy's legal culture. Not only norm-production and conflict resolution, but also legal ideology is implicated in this second approach.[309] As only one possible interpretation, the value of dignity may be pinned down as the value embodying the ideal of justice in Italy. One of the most influential constitutional provisions on dignity recalls "social dignity", which bridges the state's negative and positive obligations.[310] Dignity is also one of the limits to private economic initiative.[311] As opposed to the German constitution, a conceptualization of dignity in general and more Kantian terms is not present in Italy's constitution. Pursuant to the personalist principle and protection of inviolable rights, dignity is nonetheless implicitly recognized as inherent in each person.[312]

Even though a definition of dignity is unattainable, a specific trait of Italian legal culture is the implications that the Constitutional Court has drawn from the value of dignity. In dignity, the Court has grounded an array of interpretations where the law must adapt to the specific circumstances of individuals[313] – again, a conception nearing fairness. In a cultural sense, the idea that dignity rests on the chameleonic mutability of the human person mirrors the concept of dignity given in an influential work: *De Hominis Dignitate* by Giovanni Pico della Mirandola, an Italian humanist and philosopher.[314]

Although there may be several ideals of justice according to the different fields in which the law is applied,[315] it is worth emphasizing that both the first and second approaches appear to point to an ideal of justice hinging on fairness.

6. Professionalization

6.1 Introduction

Professionalization concerns the degree of legal expertise gained by the actors of a legal culture, which is instrumental for the rationality of law.[316] The typical legal professions

309 On legal ideology, see Sunde (2020) (n 2).

310 Italian Constitution, Article 3(1).

311 Italian Constitution, Article 41(2).

312 Angelo Mattoni, 'Profili costituzionali della dignità umana' (2008) Issue 2/3 *Jus* 251, 272. See *supra* 2.3.2 on the personalist principle. Anna Pirozzoli, *Il valore costituzionale della dignità. Un'introduzione* (Aracne 2007) 80–81. See, e.g., C.C. Decision 161/1985 and Decision 10/2010.

313 See, e.g., the need to 'individualize' the criminal sanction, Mario Bellocci and Paolo Passaglia, *La dignità dell'uomo quale principio costituzionale* (Quaderno predisposto in occasione dell'incontro trilaterale delle Corti costituzionali italiana, spagnola e portoghese, 30 September – 1 October 2007) 73, available at https://www.cortecostituzionale.it/documenti/convegni_seminari/STU_196_La_dignita.pdf accessed 5 March 2019.

314 Giovanni Pico della Mirandola, *De Hominis Dignitate (*1486) (Francesco Bausi ed, Fondazione Pietro Bembo 2003) cited by Pirozzoli (2007) (n 312) 23 and 29. See also Gabrielo Forti, *L'immane concretezza* (R. Cortina 2003) 277. Cfr. Zygmunt Bauman, *La società sotto assedio* (GLF Laterza 2011) 32.

315 See also Koch (2020), 'Sailing' (n 308); Koch (2020), 'An Introduction to German Legal Culture' (n 57); Sunde (2020) (n 2).

316 Tuori (2002) (n 3) 161.

in Italy are lawyers, judges, and notaries. Even though it does not neatly follow under legal professions, working as a legal scholar is another career pathway for law graduates.

In total, 47% of lawyers are men while 53% are women.[317] There exist four lawyers per 1,000 inhabitants.[318] The high number is often recalled in order to revive the legendary litigation rate of Italy's populace. While the finding of an exceptional litigation rate is not fully borne out by the statistics,[319] the number of lawyers in Italy is the second highest within the context of EU Member States[320] and the third highest compared to the population, after Lichtenstein and Spain.[321] In the last ten years, however, the number of people enrolled in law schools has decreased by 38%, with approximately 18,000 students enrolled in 2016–2017.[322]

Most often, there is no entry test, not even based on high school marks, to enter law schools at public universities. There exist 478 law schools at public universities,[323] and nine law schools at private universities.[324] The total number of judges fares medium-low in comparison to the rest of the EU, approximately ten per every 100,000 inhabitants.[325] The same ratio applies to notaries.

6.2 Education and qualifications

As we discussed above,[326] universities for legal studies developed in Italy in the 12th century with Bologna University as the epicenter. Already, legal education provided lawyers with a *habitus* and internalized mind frames to contribute to legal ideas and practices,[327] also through exchanges with students from across Europe. An international education is still valued in Italy, where almost 500,000 university students have participated in the Erasmus program since 1987.[328]

---

317 See statistics at https://www.versari.it/infografiche/distribuzione-numero-avvocati-italia-infografica/ accessed 5 March 2019.

318 See ibid and https://www.versari.it/infografiche/distribuzione-degli-avvocati-in-europa/ accessed 5 March 2019.

319 The 2017 EU Justice Scoreboard (n 223) 9. See a middle-high litigation rate, OECD (2013), 'Judicial performance and its determinants: a cross-country perspective' (n 230) 30. See on appeals OECD (2013), 'Giustizia civile: come promuoverne l'efficienza?' (n 226) 10.

320 The 2017 EU Justice Scoreboard (n 223) 28.

321 See statistics at links referred to in n 317 and 318.

322 Salvo Intravaia, 'Crollano gli iscritti a Giurisprudenza. E gli avvocati arrivano dall'estero', *laRepubblica.it* 9 January 2018.

323 Paolo Cirica, 'Ecco la classifica Censis delle migliori facoltà di Giurisprudenza', *Universityequipe* 12 April 2018, available at https://universityequipe.com/classifica-migliori-facolta-giurisprudenza accessed 5 April 2019.

324 Maria Russo, 'La Bocconi brilla nella classifica Censis di Giursiprudenza atenei private 2016', *Universita.it* 24 August 2016, available at https://www.universita.it/classifica-censis-giurisprudenza-atenei-privati-2016/ accessed 5 March 2019.

325 The 2017 EU Justice Scoreboard (n 223) 26.

326 See *supra* 2.2.

327 Tuori (2002) (n 3) 165.

328 Elena Maddalena, 'Mobilità studenti in Erasmus: cresce la partecipazione in Italia', *Erasmus+* 5 July 2018, available at http://www.erasmusplus.it/mobilita-studenti-in-erasmus-cresce-la-partecipazione-in-italia/ accessed 5 March 2019.

Some cultural features of legal education are remarkable. Interestingly enough, Roman law still ranks as one of the compulsory subjects in Italy's law schools, but its application in the case law has decreased. Citing the *Corpus Juris Civilis* was common in the Court of Cassation until 1880, but disappeared after 1900.[329] When it comes to the Council of State, these citations are generally absent.[330] Therefore, it appears that law graduates choosing to become either lawyers or judges refrain from using Roman law, whereas it is still studied at law school and in academia. Moreover, candidates are tested on Roman law in the oral exam to become ordinary judges. Equally noteworthy is the rise of comparative law in legal education. In 1971, there existed only one chair of comparative law; as of now, 197 full and associate professors have been appointed to teach and conduct research on private and public comparative law.[331] This blossoming of comparative law scholars and educators was enabled by two factors: the influence of such comparativist scholars as Rodolfo Sacco, and legal provisions designating comparative law a compulsory subject in legal education. In fact, since the 19th century, the Ministry of Education has determined the mandatory subjects for students enrolled in legal studies throughout Italy – within this normative framework, comparative law was introduced as a mandatory subject in 2005.[332] Similarly, international law scholarship is deeply rooted in Italian legal culture: in this vein, it was observed that, almost inadvertently, international law scholars have switched from Italian to English as their working language.[333]

To become a lawyer, a student obtains a five-year law degree and carries out an 18-month traineeship. To become a practicing lawyer in Italian courts, one has to take a bar exam. The Minister of Justice administers the exam, which is made up of a written test (two learned opinions and one document) and an oral test. Since 2018, the exam has become more selective and similar in kind to the exam to access the judiciary. To become a lawyer before the highest courts, further requirements need to be met, for example by either passing an exam or attending classes.

Italy portrays typically civil law notaries. They draft, receive, and record legal instruments for private parties in non-contentious proceedings, and are vested with authentication powers. To become a notary, a student is required to have a five-year law degree and enroll in an 18-month traineeship at a notary. The Ministry of Justice administers a state exam in Rome. The written test is practical, while doctrine and case law are important in the oral test.

Most lay judges need a law degree, and there is a preference for those with significant experience.[334]

329 Barbagallo (1999) (n 273) 123.

330 Ibid.

331 Francesca Fiorentini and Marta Infantino, "Context, Scope and Aim of the Book" in ibid, *Mentoring Comparative Lawyers: Methods, Times, and Places. Liber Discipulorum Mauro Bussani* (Springer 2020).

332 Ibid.

333 Giulio Bartolini, *The History of International Law in Italy* (Oxford University Press 2020) 477, 481.

334 See *supra* 4.

To become a judge in courts of ordinary jurisdiction, a student must acquire a five-year law degree and enroll in Schools of Legal Specializations, unless other circumstances are met.[335] The Ministry of Justice administers a centralized state exam in Rome. The written test is based on case law and doctrine (three learned opinions in civil, administrative, and criminal law). The oral exam revolves around case law and doctrine as well.

To become an administrative judge, a student needs a five-year law degree and usually accedes to another career in order to qualify for the state exam.[336] The Ministry of Justice administers a state exam in Rome. The written test is both practical and based on case law and doctrine. The same applies for the oral test.

To become judge of accounts, a student attains a five-year law degree and usually accedes to another career.[337] A positive evaluation of the CV is necessary to access the relevant state exam. The test is similar to that for administrative judges, albeit in somewhat different subjects.

To become a professor, the trajectory is a PhD – possibly post-doc positions or a position as temporary lecturer, temporary researcher, associate professor, or full professor. Universities are fairly autonomous.[338]

6.3 Conclusions

As described previously, the Italian legal culture counts on highly professionalized practitioners and scholars. Judges and notaries are selected through competitive exams and a recent reform is poised to make the bar exam for lawyers more challenging than it was. Traditionally open to internationalization, legal scholars have renewed their interest and centered legal education on comparative legal studies due to a ministerial reform in 2005. In its capacity as doctrine, scholarship often offers legal innovations that courts adopt in their case law – such osmosis occurs implicitly because courts are not allowed to cite scholarship (*supra* 4).

In light of the number of lawyers, a reform of the legal profession and the bar associations appears in order. Firstly, if judicial documents are not sufficiently clear and succinct, the right to a speedy trial may be violated. In order to enhance clarity and brevity, the First President of the Court of Cassation has issued a series of draft recommendations

335 There is no need to receive a degree from Schools of Legal Specializations if the candidate i) is already a lawyer, professor, leader in public administrations, administrative/accounts judge, or ii) has received a PhD in legal subjects, or iii) has been a trainee in courts or at the state advocates for 18 months.

336 Eligible to take the state exam are lawyers/public servants – including militaries, other types of judges, members of the Parliament or of the Secretariat for the Presidency of the Council of Ministries or Regional/Provincial/Municipal Councils, and the most qualified scholars.

337 Eligible to take the state exam are lawyers/public servants, other types of judges, state advocates/prosecutors, members of the Parliament or of the Secretariat for the Presidency of the Council of Ministries or EU institutions, and the most qualified scholars.

338 See https://www.eui.eu/ProgrammesAndFellowships/AcademicCareersObservatory/AcademicCareersbyCountry/Italy accessed 5 March 2019.

to the President of the National Bar Association.[339] Yet, local bar associations do not consider the National Bar Association to be their representative.[340] Secondly, lawyers' fees are approved by the Ministry of Justice. According to the OECD,[341] freely negotiated fees are associated with a lower litigation rate, but Italian lawyers' associations have generally blocked freely negotiated fees. Thirdly, there exists a deontological code, yet its specification can solely be found in the disciplinary case law of the local bar associations where publicity is nonetheless limited.[342] Fourthly, there exists no real incentive for lawyers to discourage frivolous claims, differently from elsewhere, for example the United States.[343]

7. Internationalization

7.1 Introduction

Italy's legal history is testament to early internationalization, due to the export of legal texts during the Roman Empire and the education provided at the peninsula's universities. Previously, it was shown how both comparative law and international law constitute vital areas of legal scholarship (*supra* 6). Moreover, internationalization has long been present in specific subjects and law reviews, for example in commercial law[344] and criminal law.[345] It is interesting to consider here how internationalization has affected the two institutional elements of norm-production and conflict resolution.

7.2 Internationalizing norm-production

It is quite intuitive to hold that the very history of Italy's constitution is entwined with a climate of international constitutionalism[346] in the aftermath of World War II. As seen earlier, Italy's legal system is monist with regard to international customary law.[347] It is dualist concerning treaty norms.[348]

---

339 Tria, 'La funzione di nomofilachia' (n 168) 10. On the need to enhance clarity and brevity in line with other courts in Europe, see 22.

340 Ibid 10–11.

341 OECD (2013), 'Judicial performance and its determinants: a cross-country perspective' (n 230) 31.

342 OECD (2013), 'Giustizia civile: come promuoverne l`efficienza?' (n 226) 8.

343 Baschiera (2006) (n 64) 314.

344 See the interest toward foreign decisions in one of the first reviews on Commercial law, Cesare Mozzarelli, 'L`annuario delle scienze Giuridiche, Sociali e Politiche (1880–1883)', *Quaderni Fiorentini, 16* (Giuffrè 1987) 11, fn. 12.

345 Internationalization is a methodical feature in the first criminal law review in late 1880, see Mario Sbriccoli, 'Il diritto penale liberale. La "rivista penale" di Luigi Lucchini 1874-1900', *Quaderni Fiorentini, 16* (Giuffrè 1987), 112–113.

346 Valerio Onida, 'The Constitution yesterday and today' (2012) Issue 1 *Italian Journal of Public Law 15*, 20.

347 See *supra* 3.2.5.

348 Italian Constitution, Article 11.

The European Convention on Human Rights (ECHR) has played an influential role in the interpretation of the constitution, as well as in its reform.[349] EU law has also been decisive for both interpreting Italian law in light of EU law and reforming existing law. An example is provided by the 2001 constitutional reform that modified the allocation of powers between the state and the regions, which turned the legal order of the EU into an explicit limit to legislation enacted by both states and regions, along with the constitution and international law.[350] As seen earlier, when EU law and international law are not complied with, states can substitute regions and other organizations.[351]

7.3 Internationalizing conflict resolution

7.3.1 Foreign law

The Court of Cassation does not usually refer to foreign law, notwithstanding notable exceptions.[352] Differently, the Constitutional Court is more explicit, even though a reference is often generic, mainly to the law of ECHR Member States, EU Member States, Germany, and the United States.[353] In the past, the Court has relied on an extensive analysis of foreign laws on the same subject (German, British, Finnish, Danish, American, French, Spanish, Portuguese, and Greek), but has ended up by explicitly pointing to the analysis in a cursory manner.[354] The Court may thus deploy strategies when referring to foreign law, by way of understating rather than emphasizing the impact that foreign law may have actually played on the decision. When no reference is made, the Court may engage with other courts in a "hidden" communication process by way of standards and principles, such as reasonableness and equality.[355] Differently, reference to foreign judgments is rare.[356]

If our attention turns to the Constitutional Court's organizational set up, we notice that two elements are signaling an ongoing internationalization within the court. Since the 1980s, the Court has a Foreign Law Department.[357] And since 2006, some decisions are available online in English.[358]

349 Onida (2012) (n 346) 22–23.

350 Article 117(1). Giacinto della Cananea, 'Legitimate expectations in European and Italian Law' (2009) Volume 1 *Italian Journal of Public Law* 1, 4–5, single PDF downloaded from http://www.ijpl.eu/assets/files/pdf/2009_volume_1/GdC%20-%20Legitimate%20expectations.pdf accessed 24 June 2019.

351 See *supra* 3.2.3.

352 Barsotti and others (2015) (n 72) 80. On the exception, see Cass. (Civil United Sections) 11 marzo 2004 ('Ferrini'), n. 5044, where the CtC referred to the United States' Foreign Sovereign Immunities Act. See also an end-of-life case where the CtC referred to the Supreme Court of New Jersey, the US Supreme Court, and the House of Lords, Civil Cass. Dec. 21748/2007.

353 Groppi and Spigno (2014) (n 47) 27.

354 Barsotti and others (2015) (n 72) 81.

355 Groppi and Spigno (2014) (n 47) 34.

356 Groppi (2016) (n 164) 5–6, on the basis of the 40 most important decisions.

357 Groppi and Spigno (2014) (n 47) 27.

358 Groppi (2016) (n 164) 2.

7.3.2 EU law

In 1973, one year before the landmark *Solange* decision rendered by Germany's Federal Constitutional Court, Italy's Constitutional Court broached the same theme and resolved it in a similar way. The theme was the relationship between the Italian legal order and the legal order of the then-European Communities (ECs). At the time, no protection of fundamental rights was enshrined in the treaties, nor was this an essential feature in the practice of European institutions. In fact, the Court of Justice of the European Communities (CJEC) had refused to review EU law in light of fundamental rights.[359] To this lacuna, Italy's Constitutional Court put forward the "counter-limits" theory, by which European treaty norms cannot override the "core principles of Italy's constitutional order or the inalienable rights of the human person".[360] The concept of counter-limits springs from the premise that Italy's adhesion to the EC's legal order is allowed by Article 11 of its constitution, which permits limitations of sovereignty that are necessary for securing peace and justice among nations. While European legislation generally prevails over national legislation,[361] the core principles of Italy's constitution or the protection of the inalienable rights of the human person bounce back as counter-limits to the limits of sovereignty.

The counter-limits theory has been reiterated several times.[362] While the Constitutional Court has never applied it, the Council of State did so.[363] Along the same lines, safeguards to some fundamental values have been put forward in Germany, France, Spain, and many of the Central and Eastern European countries that joined the EU in 2005.[364] Likely as a reaction to this national trend, the Treaty of Lisbon provides for Europe's constitutional pluralism.[365]

Interestingly, the Constitutional Court still refers to EU law as "interposed" norms, rather than fully incorporated norms: when applicable, these norms either prompt the adjudicating judge to "disapply" state or regional law, or integrate the Constitutional Court's parameters in the constitutionality review.[366] According to the Court's vice-president, the Court is in "direct dialogue" with the CJEU at least since 1984, but a preliminary ruling reference was only inaugurated in 2008.[367]

---

359 Case 1/58 *F. Stork & Cie v. High Authority of ECSC* [1959] ECLI:EU:C:1959:4. See, however, the inception of the CJEU theory on the integration of fundamental rights within the general principles of the Communities in its decisions Case 29-69 *Erich Stauder v City of Ulm – Sozialamt* [1969] ECLI:EU:C:1969:57; Case 4-73 *J. Nold, Kohlen- und Baustoffgroßhandling v Commission of the European Communities [*1974] ECLI:EU:C:1974:51.

360 C.C. Decision 183/1973 ('*Franchini*'). On the personalist principle, see *supra* 2.3.2 and 5.

361 Case 11/70 *Internationale Handelsgesellschaft* [1970] ECLI:EU:C:1970:114.

362 See e.g. C.C. Decisions 170/1984 ('*Granital*'), 284/2007, and 102/2008.

363 Council of State decision 4207/2005. Barsotti and others (2015) (n 72) 216.

364 Barsotti and others (2015) (n 72) 215.

365 Treaty on European Union (2009), Official Journal C 326, 26/10/2012 P. 0001 – 0390, Article 6(3).

366 C.C. Decision 102/2008 para 8.2.8.1.

367 Cartabia (2016) (n 103) 50.

7.3.3 ECHR Law

In the Constitutional Court's case law, the European Convention on Human Rights (ECHR), as interpreted by the European Court of Human Rights (ECtHR), constitutes an "interposed norm".[368] When applicable, they prompt the adjudicating judge to interpret state or regional laws consistently. When this interpretive method would turn into *intepretatio contra legem,* the adjudicating judge refers the question to the Constitutional Court.[369] Differently from what occurs with reference to EU norms, Italy's state and regional law cannot be "disapplied" by the adjudicating judge. The reason lies in the fact that the Constitutional Court does not recognize the primacy of ECHR law within Italy's legal order (dualistic approach). Hence, the adjudicating court ought to refer the question to the Constitutional Court, which may integrate ECHR law within its review parameters and declare the non-constitutionality of Italy's state or regional legislation, also in light of ECHR law.[370] This process is not automatic. The Constitutional Court perceives its function as one of striking a "reasonable balance" between compliance with international obligations, which is enshrined in the constitution, and the protection of other constitutional interests.[371] A further limit countering the porosity between ECHR law and Italy's legal order lies in "exceptional hypotheses where the treaty norm cannot integrate the parameter".[372]

7.3.4 International law

Since 2007, international law norms constitute interposed rules, as EU law and ECHR law.[373] An adjudicating judge cannot "disapply" national law for being in breach with international law, but shall rather refer the question to the Constitutional Court. Both international treaties and international customary law may integrate the parameters applied by the Constitutional Court in its review process.[374]

Until 2014, the theory of counter-limits was applied only vis-à-vis EU law. In the landmark decision 238/2014, the Court applied the theory of counter-limits also vis-à-vis international law. The controversy at hand originated from decisions rendered by lower judges and the CtC's united sections. In a case of deportation and forced labor during World War II, damages were awarded to Italian citizens who were recognized as victims of war crimes and crimes against humanity committed by the Third Reich,

368 C.C. Decisions 348/2007 and 349/2007. See also C.C. Decision 138/2010, para 10, even though the ECHR case law that the plaintiff invoked was not considered pertinent.

369 C.C. Decision 80/2011, para 1.

370 C.C. Decision 80/2011, paras 5.4 and 5.5. On the lack of primacy of ECHR law, see also C.C. Decision 348/2017, para 3.3 and Groppi and Spigno (2014) (n 47) 15.

371 C.C. Decision 348/2008, para 4.7 (authors' translation).

372 C.C. Decision 80/2011, para 2.

373 C.C. Decision 348/2007, para 3.3.

374 With regard to treaties, see C.C. Decision 348/2007. With regard to international customary law, see C.C. Decision 172/1999. See also Groppi and Spigno (2014) (n 47) 29.

when such conduct had occurred partially in Italy.[375] In such decisions, the customary international rule on foreign states' jurisdictional immunity from civil jurisdiction was construed as inoperative when conduct is characterized as an international crime, and when the state operates through its sovereignty (i.e., *de iure imperii).* Germany did not agree on this "dynamic" interpretation of foreign sovereign immunity and lodged a case with the International Court of Justice (ICJ) against Italy, where Greece intervened siding with Italy. In 2012, the ICJ supported Germany's interpretation of the international customary rule and maintained that Italian courts, hence Italy, had breached international law. Italy's Parliament passed a law to ensure that Italy's courts would comply with the ICJ's ruling. Some provisions of the law were brought to the attention of the Constitutional Court through indirect review. The Constitutional Court maintained that the law mandating Italy's courts to comply with the ICJ's ruling contravened the constitutional principle of access to justice for the protection of fundamental rights.[376] In the interpretation of the Court, the international customary rule of jurisdictional immunity does not warrant full immunity from jurisdiction in case of war crimes and crimes against humanity.[377] In light of this decision, the CtC's united sections has recently stated its jurisdiction over damages awarded against Germany.[378]

What this "textbook" case shows, is, firstly, that national courts significantly contribute to the development of international law – in this case, the Constitutional Court challenged the ICJ interpretation of the international rule of foreign sovereign immunity. Secondly, the case displays the tight entwinement and mutual legitimation between the Court of Cassation and the Constitutional Court. Not only did the Constitutional Court approve of the interpretation offered by the united sections on the matter, but the united sections applied the decision rendered by the Constitutional Court, which is in breach of international law as interpreted by the ICJ.

7.4 Conclusions

Due to internationalization, a number of fundamental rights are presently adjudicated by the CJEU and ECtHR. By the theory of consistent interpretation,[379] a wide array of questions is directly dealt with by adjudicating judges. It may be due to these two contingencies that the number of referrals by adjudicating judges to the Constitutional Court has decreased.[380]

---

375 See, *inter alia,* Cass. S.U. n. 5044/2004 ('*Ferrini*'). For a thorough comment, see Andrea Bianchi, 'Ferrini V. Federal Republic of Germany' (2005) Vol. 99, No. 1 *The American Journal of International Law* 242. The decision is particularly interesting for the systematic interpretation of the law of state immunity carried out by the CtC.

376 C.C. Decision 238/2014, para 5.1.

377 Ibid, para 3.5.

378 Civil Cass. Dec 15812/2016, para 9.

379 See *supra 3* and 4.

380 Groppi and Spigno (2014) (n 47) 5.

8. Legal method

8.1 Introduction

The legal method usually lies at the sub-surface levels of a legal culture.[381] It cannot possibly explain how a decision is arrived at, but it greatly illuminates the conditions that the deciding body has deemed proper to justify the decision, namely the legal argumentation of the decision.[382]

Addressing the multifaceted subject of the legal method as the "final" element of the legal cultural model may be particularly heuristic. Affecting and being affected by all other elements, the legal method may be analyzed by distinguishing its interactions with the model's institutional elements from its interactions with the model's intellectual elements. Pursuant to this mode, we will proceed.

8.2 Institutional elements affecting the legal method

8.2.1 Norm-production

One of the methodological elements of Italy's legal culture stems from the separation of powers principle. As seen earlier, in accordance with this principle, judges are subject solely to the law.[383] The subsumption-logical model is thus still predominant in legal interpretative processes. Subsumption is a type of syllogism by which the case and its extrinsecation (*fattispecie*) is brought under the applicable norms – the applicable norms are explained in the major premise and the case is stated in the minor premise. The conclusion leads to a logical "fit" between the major premise and the minor premise.[384]

Subsumption features in both civil law and common law traditions because the applicable norms may be case-law-based norms, or norms that are general and abstract. The process is deductive. The success of this method may be due to several endorsements. In the 18th century, Cesare Beccaria advocated its use and, in the early 20th century, Max Weber deemed it "an essential guarantee for the formal rationality of adjudication".[385] Subsumption, however, does not always apply. For example, in criminal law and proceedings, causation depends on scientific norms, which seldom offer a certainty of 100%.[386] In these cases, the Court of Cassation has pointed to an inferential-inductive legal method.[387]

---

381 Tuori (2002) (n 3) 167.

382 Ibid 168.

383 See *supra* 4.2.

384 For example, the major premise is: "the law prohibits securities fraud, namely the material misstatement of fact or omission of a material fact which made the statement materially misleading". The minor premise is: "in the posture of this case, enterprise X has not disclosed that it applied two proxy costs of carbon, which results in the omission of a material fact making the statement materially misleading". The conclusion is: "Enterprise X committed securities fraud".

385 Tuori (2002) (n 3) 167.

386 For example, in a case of medical malpractice, specifically negligence, we would inquire on the level of certainty allowing us to state that if the doctor had performed specific tests, the patient would not have died.

387 Cass. Decision (Criminal United Sections) 10 July 2002 n. 30328, para 6.

8.2.2 Conflict resolution

The lack of common institutions until 1861 may explain the role of doctrine, rather than courts, in shaping the legal method. Since the 12th century, the legal method revolved around comments on common texts.[388] Being widespread all across Europe, this method lost its sway in the 16th century, when other schools better responded to the need for: i) a critical approach to the *Corpus Juris Civilis,* ii) solutions to practical problems, and iii) the clarification of existing law through treatises.[389] Not even the philological and historical analysis of Roman law sources, which arose in the peninsula during the Renaissance (legal humanism), could fill the demand for a more "practical" legal method.[390]

Once common institutions arose in 1861, the legal method was particularly technical, purist, and ahistorical: –a form of "cultural agnosticism".[391] One of the avatars of cultural agnosticism was Arturo Rocco, who fathered the technical-juridical school in 1910 by positing the imperative for the interpreter to approach the law solely *de lege lata,* and never *de lege ferenda,* lest the loss of scientific merit; for itself, and short of the contribution of other disciplines, lest the loss of its purity.[392] It is worth recalling that Arturo Rocco's thought was instrumental in Fascist ideology and led the development of the 1930 criminal code, which is still in force, known as *Codice Rocco.* It is an understatement to hold that the technical-juridical method laid the groundwork for the interpreter's suspension of critical remarks toward the posited law, be it either liberal or Fascist.

Besides the doctrinal input, case law can also shape the legal method. After the unification in 1861, case law was long to emerge, especially in consideration of the lack of one Court of Cassation until 1923. Through the precedential value of its case law, the CtC transitioned the legal method to an analogical and systematic method, still present in today's "attenuated" *stare decisis.* Albeit not an official legal source, case law is generally seen as one of the "formants" of the law.[393]

The 1956 establishment of the Constitutional Court and its activism ever since have reinforced the core methodical tenets of the CtC.[394] As an addition to systematic interpretation, the Constitutional Court has allowed for the filling of *lacunae* by encouraging the use of *Drittwirkung (*third-party effect of fundamental rights) when legislation was lacking.[395] The Constitutional Court's own legal method has been characterized as

388 See *supra* 2.2.

389 Padoa-Schioppa (2010) (n 26) 26–27.

390 Ibid 34.

391 Livingston, Monateri and Parisi (2015) (n 100) 181.

392 Massimo Donini, 'Tecnicismo Giuridico e Scienza penale cent`anni dopo. La proclusione di Arturo Rocco (1910) nell`età europeismo giudiziario' (2010) No. 1 *Crimialia, Annuario di scienze penalistiche* 127, 128.

393 Baschiera (2006) (n 64) 317, referring to both systematic and analogical interpretive methods. On formants, see Rodolfo Sacco, 'Legal Formants: A Dynamic Approach to Comparative Law (Installment I of II)' (1991) Vol. 39 No. 1 *American Journal of Comparative Law* 1; 'Legal Formants: A Dynamic Approach to Comparative Law (Installment II of II)' (1991) Vol. 39 No. 2 *The American Journal of Comparative Law* 343; Canzio (2017) (n 63) 2.

394 On the mutual legitimation between the Court of Cassation and the Constitutional Court, see *supra* 3.4.1.

395 Baschiera (2006) (n 64) 291–292.

syncretic,[396] including systematic interpretation, interpretation in light of fundamental principles, and the balancing among different constitutional principles.[397] The preparatory works are not a source of law, and are rarely used to construe the law, albeit with notable exceptions.[398] Proportionality is rarely broached, probably because the Constitutional Court deploys it as reasonableness.[399]

The rising star of case law may have overshadowed the importance of doctrine. This is partly accurate. The decreasing influence of doctrine is, however, not due to case law alone, but also to legal provisions whereby judges cannot refer to doctrinal works. These provisions have been in place ever since 1865 in civil and criminal matters,[400] and ever since the Constitutional Court's very establishment in 1956 with regard to constitutional matters.[401] Doctrine can nonetheless play a major role, as it did in the compensatory framework for non-economic damages. The framework was first advocated by doctrine, applied by the justices of the peace, supported in trial and appellate courts, and legitimized by the Constitutional Court.[402]

The role of lay judges is still an open question. Most justices of the peace have a legal background, but lay judges in a fuller sense (without a legal background) participate in assize courts, parole courts, minors' courts, public water courts, and agrarian courts. Here, no legal sub-culture appears to have emerged. What is similarly unclear is how other features of conflict resolution interact with the legal method, such as: i) the lack of third-party intervention before the Constitutional Court,[403] ii) the lack of *amicus curiae* at the Constitutional Court,[404] iii) the lack of dissenting opinions in all courts, and iv) the full-length publication of decisions.

396 Groppi and Spigno (2014) (n 47) 28. Cartabia (2016) (n 103) 52.

397 On these and other methods, see Groppi and Spigno (2014) (n 47) 17.

398 C.C. Decision 138/2010.

399 Groppi and Spigno (2014) (n 47) 33.

400 Article 265 Royal Decree n. 2641 of 14 December 1865. Article 118(3) Implementing provisions to the Civil Procedural Code. See also Barbagallo (1999) (n 273) 124. In administrative courts, there exists no prohibition to refer to doctrinal works. See Article 47 Royal Decree 17 October 1889, n. 6516 and Article 65 r. d. 17 August 1907 n. 642. Yet, reference is not frequent and generally to the 'doctrine', short of specific authors.

401 Groppi and Spigno (2014) (n 47) 27. The rules of civil procedure apply to the Constitutional Court unless it derogates from them by laying down its own procedural rules. Still, the Constitutional Court has referred generally to the 'doctrine', see C.C. Decisions 15/82, 364/1988, 422/1995, 348/2007, 138/2010. According to a commentator, the Constitutional Court is recently less heedful of the suggestions put forward by the doctrine, D'Amico (2008) (n 45) 37.

402 Bussani (2016) (n 148) 26–27.

403 Groppi and Spigno (2014) (n 47) 34.

404 Groppi (2016) (n 164) 5. The *Conseil constitutionnel,* of which the Constitutional Court has assumed some of the procedural style, allows for *amicus curiae.*

8.3 Intellectual elements affecting the legal method

8.3.1 Professionalization

Considering that lawyers are highly professionalized, the legal method can be expected to be rather complex and technical, and only accessible to professionals.[405] This is accurate, but for Italian legal culture one may doubt that this is mainly due to lawyers' professionalization. One reason for the legal method's technical character may lie in the specialization of doctrine and courts, and the unifying role played by the Constitutional Court and the Court of Cassation. Moreover, the normative crisis renders a complex legal method necessary.[406]

The interaction between lawyers' high professionalization and the legal method surfaces in legal language, which non-lawyers cannot generally understand. Between 1905–1910, the Council of State solely used a common language,[407] a further element pointing to the existence of a sub-culture.[408] Yet, its language is presently quite technical. A legal historian, now a Constitutional Court judge, called the legal language in Italy's legal culture esoteric.[409]

8.3.2 Internationalization

We already evaluated how internationalization has influenced norm-production and conflict resolution, and some methodological profiles.[410] It is here interesting to consider how international influence has impacted the legal method through doctrine. Influence can be identified in French[411] and German doctrine, notably the pandectists.[412] Due to the influence of German legal culture, the post-unification years showcase the flourishing of what was dubbed "Italian" legal thinking,[413] and the institutional construction and practice of the new state as a collective endeavor.[414] Emancipation from international influences is also apparent,[415] notably in the anti-dogmatic tendency of commercial law.[416]

Currently, influence usually originates from the German and U.S. legal thinking.[417]

405 See also Kjølstad, Koch and Sunde (2020) (n 299).

406 On the normative crisis, see *supra* 3.1.

407 Barbagallo (1999) (n 273) 125.

408 *Supra* 4.5.2 on the subculture at the Council of State.

409 Paolo Grossi, 'Globalizzazione, diritto, scienza giurdica' (2002) Vol. 125 No. 5 *Il Foro Italiano* 151, 152.

410 See *supra 8.2*.

411 Monateri (2002) (n 169) 25. French doctrine also influenced the bureaucracy, as libraries of ministries used to receive French law reviews, see Guido Melis, 'La burocrazia e le riviste: per una storia della cultura dell'amministrazione' (1987) XVI *Quaderni Fiorentini* 47, 49.

412 Livingston, Monateri and Parisi (2015) (n 100) 188.

413 Padoa-Schioppa (2010) (n 26) 44.

414 Ibid 43.

415 Mozzarelli (1987) (n 344) 39–40.

416 Ibid 40.

417 Padoa-Schioppa (2010) (n 26) 47.

8.3.3 Ideal of justice

The interaction between the ideal of justice and the legal method is probably the most decisive. Previously, we concluded that the prevalent ideal of justice in Italy's legal culture is procedural predictability complemented by fairness.[418] How this ideal of justice is attained from a methodological viewpoint was explored in light of the interpretive techniques laid down by the Constitutional Court and the Court of Cassation. A further interaction can be explored by considering the power of equitable adjustment, called equity. Such power is regulated by law and is bestowed on both justices of the peace and professional judges in civil matters.

In the civil code and civil procedural code, equity needs to be informed by the guiding principles of the subject matter,[419] and can be either integrative or substitutive. When it is integrative, it allows the determination of *individual* economic elements, both in contract and tort. When it is substitutive, the *whole* decision is made on the basis of equity. For justices of the peace, substitutive equity *must* be deployed within cases where the amount in consideration is fairly low (€ 1,500) and *may* be applied when the law enables the judge to decide by equity.[420] Moreover, it *must* be applied by the first instance and appeals judge when the parties ask for it and the rights can be regulated by contract.[421] These decisions can be challenged on appeals on grounds that are more circumscribed than those available against non-equity-informed decisions.[422] The rationale behind such rulings can be found in the need of easing procedures for less important cases.

Judgments by equity are also warranted in case of lacunae. If no specific provision is applicable, the judge turns to analogous subjects or cases. If these are lacking, the judge turns to the general principles of the legal order.[423] If the decision is rendered by equity, such grounds shall be discussed in court,[424] and included in the reasoning.[425]

Judgment by equity is rarely asked for by the parties. This may be due to the fact that the judge is perceived as extraneous, whereas equity has historically characterized arbitral tribunals.[426] Equity can also be applied to decide arbitral disputes, when the parties have

418 See *supra* 5. This is the finding resulting from the first approach, based on the legal method, rather than the second approach, based on values.

419 This finding is inferable from the grounds of appeal in civil procedure, Article 339, co. 3 Civil Procedural Code.

420 No decision by equity is permitted when the case concerns template contracts and the opposition to decrees permitting execution by creditors. According to the Court of Cassation, cases that are devolved to the justices of the peace for subject-matter, rather than value, are not liable to be decided by equity. See Cass. Decision 26 October 2009, n. 22601; Cass. Decision 15 October 2009, n. 21926.

421 See Civil Procedural Code, Article 114.

422 Civil Procedural Code, Article 339(3).

423 Provisions on the law in general (premised to the civil code), Article 12(2).

424 Civil Procedural Code, Article 101(2).

425 Article 119(4) Implementing provisions to the Civil Procedural Code.

426 See http://www.treccani.it/enciclopedia/equita-giudizio-di_%28Diritto-on-line%29/ para 4.1, accessed 5 March 2019.

agreed upon such an arrangement[427] and so long as the law has not ruled out the possibility to render equitable arbitral awards.[428]

8.4 Conclusions

At a time of normative and judicial crisis, the demand for justice possibly increases. In order to flesh out the ideas and expectations around justice, a legal method is all the more decisive. In Italy's legal culture, the legal method has somewhat varied according to the fields of law and across time, yet at least two traits have been constant: i) the influence of the doctrine, especially in the past; and ii) its "evolutive", non-literal, interpretive techniques since unification. The legal method may appear quite complex in light of the intricacy of the legal system and sedimentation of cultures in Italy's legal history. Still, no sub-cultures appear in relation to the legal method.

9. General conclusions

After this short itinerary across time and space, the analysis of Italy's legal culture is apt to not only illustrate some fundamental interactions among the elements of the legal cultural model applied here, but also to shine the spotlight on several features common to liberal constitutional democracies: a burgeoning norm-production, judicial systems perceived as not fully efficient, an increasing demand for justice, incremental professional specialization, and the crisis of the doctrine of legal sources due to internationalization.

To respond to the inquiry posed previously, on the existence of a legal culture after Italy's unification in 1861 (*supra* 2), our tentative answer is positive. The analysis shows that Italy's legal culture has arisen in the aftermath of unification due to the establishment of common institutions and their practice. The analysis has also shown the unexpected resilience and stability of such culture, notwithstanding the lack of political stability. Even though Italy's political culture may be seen as standing somehow aloof from the country's legal culture, the institutionalized practice of law is nonetheless perceived for the most part in accordance with the prevailing ideas and expectations of law.[429] Albeit with some centrifugal spins, unity has been attained under the constitution and the interpretive practice carried out by the Constitutional Court and the Court of Cassation. Such practices have contributed to both the legal doctrine and lower courts.

Although Italy has historically emerged as the source of a civil law tradition,[430] the contingencies of the post-World War II era has made for a system of "attenuated" *stare decisis,* an ideal of justice hinging on procedural predictability and fairness, and a legal method that has gone astray from pure deduction. Rather than a "majoritarian" model

427 Civil Procedural Code, Article 822.

428 Article 829(4), n. 1–2, Civil Procedural Code; Article 36(1) Legislative Decree 17 January 2003 n. 5; Article 12 Legislative Decree 2 July 2010 n. 104; Article 209(14) Legislative Decree 18 April 2016, n. 5.

429 We are grateful to Professor Sören Koch for such precious two insights.

430 Livingston, Monateri and Parisi (2015) (n 100) 143–144.

of power-sharing, courts have tried to secure a "Madisonian"[431] model where justices, professionals, and doctrine are interpreters of societal changes and needs, often in opposition to a fragmented political system.

Italian legal culture					
Institutional elements		**Intellectual elements**			
Conflict resolution	*Normproduction*	*Ideal of justice*	*Legal method*	*Professionalization*	*Internationalization*
– Two types of courts: courts of general jurisdiction and courts with special jurisdiction; – unifying role of the Court of Cassation in jurisdictional matters; – overarching importance of the Constitutional Court.	– Legislation, mainly through laws and decrees; – a system of "attenuated" *stare decisis;* – the entwining circle of the Constitutional Court and the Court of Cassation.	– Procedural predictability (*certezza processuale)*; – social dignity (*dignita' sociale).*	– Subsumption (deduction from legislation); – high use of principles (implicit deduction from legal doctrine and explicit induction from case law); – high use of differentiation (induction from case law).	– Different professional paths and high degree of professionalization, with a strong focus on the case law of the Constitutional and Court of Cassation; implicit osmosis of legal innovations between legal doctrine and courts.	– Dualistic system (treaties) with monistic traits (customary international law); some exceptions concern the EU legal order (counter-limits theory); – student mobility.

10. Bibliography

Acierno M, De Amicis G, Vincenti E and Morelli M, 'Il ruolo della cassazione: tradizioni e mutamenti' (2011) *Diritto Penale Contemporaneo* 1

Alighieri D, *La Divina Commedia* (Hoepli 1932)

Amoroso G, 'Nomofilachia e Massimario', available at http://www.cortedicassazione.it/cassazione-resources/resources/cms/documents/Il_precedente_ed_il_ruolo_del_Massimario_s07.pdf accessed 4 March 2019

431 Alexander Hamilton, James Madison and John Jay, *The Federalist Papers,* No. 51 (Oxford University Press 2008).

Barbagallo G, 'Stile e motivazione delle decisioni del Consiglio di Stato' (1999) 52e Année No. 8 *La Revue administrative 1*16

Barsotti V, Carozza PG, Cartabia M and Simoncini A, *Italian Constitutional Justice in Global Context* (Oxford University Press 2015). DOI: https://doi.org/10.1093%2Flaw%2F9780190214555.001.0001

Bartolini G, *The History of International Law in Italy* (Oxford University Press 2020)

Baschiera M, 'Introduction to the Italian Legal System. The Allocation of Normative Powers: Issues in Law Finding' (2006) Volume 34, Issue 2 *International Journal of Legal Information 27*9. DOI: https://doi.org/10.1017%2Fs0731126500001499

Bauman Z, *La società sotto assedio* (GLF Laterza 2011)

Bellocci M and Passaglia P, *La dignità dell'uomo quale principio costituzionale* (Quaderno predisposto in occasione dell'incontro trilaterale delle Corti costituzionali italiana, spagnola e portoghese, 30 September – 1 October 2007) available at https://www.cortecostituzionale.it/documenti/convegni_seminari/STU_196_La_dignita.pdf

Benvenuti M, 'The Constitutional Distribution of Legislative Powers in Italy: Recent Judgments of the Constitutional Court' (2015) Volume 2 *Italian Journal of Public Law* 391

Bianchi A, 'Ferrini V. Federal Republic of Germany' (2005) Vol. 99, No. 1 *The American Journal of International Law* 242. DOI: https://doi.org/10.2307%2F3246103

Bispham E, 'Pliny the Elder's Italy' (2007) no. 100 *Bulletin of the Institute of Classical Studies* 41. DOI: https://doi.org/10.1111/j.2041-5370.2007.tb02463.x

Brundage JA, *The Medieval Origins of the Legal Profession: Canonists, Civilians, and Courts* (The University of Chicago Press 2008)

Bussani M, 'Constitutional Justice in Italy and Beyond: A Comparative (and Private) Law Perspective' (2016) Vol. 8 *Italian Journal of Public Law 2*4

Calamandrei, 'Il procedimento per la dichiarazione di illegittimità costituzionale' in *Opere Giuridiche,* vol. III (Morano 1965)

—— and Carlo Furno, 'Cassazione civile' in Azara A and Eula E (eds), *Novissimo Digesto Italiano,* Volume II (UTET 1958)

Cananea GC, 'Legitimate expectations in European and Italian Law' (2009) Volume 1 *Italian Journal of Public Law* 1, single PDF downloaded from http://www.ijpl.eu/assets/files/pdf/2009_volume_1/GdC%20-%20Legitimate%20expectations.pdf accessed 24 June 2019

Canzio G, 'Nomofilachia e diritto giurisprudenziale' (2017) *Diritto penale contemporaneo* 1

Cappelletti M, 'Doctrine of Stare Decisis and the Civil Law: A Fundamental Difference or No Difference At All?' in Herbert Bernstein, Ulrich Drobnig and Hein Kötz (eds), *Festschrift für Konrad Zweigert* (Mohr 1981)

Cartabia M, 'Of Bridges and Walls: the "Italian Style" of Constitutional Adjudication' (2016) Vol. 1 *Italian Journal of Public Law* 37

Cataldi G, 'Roulo e funzione della Corte di cassazione : il punto di vista del giudice d`apello' (2017) Issue 3 *Questione Giustizia 1*4

Cirica P, 'Ecco la classifica Censis delle migliori facoltà di Giurisprudenza', *Universityequipe* 12 April 2018, available at https://universityequipe.com/classifica-migliori-facolta-giurisprudenza accessed 5 April 2019

Colombo GF, 'Alternative Dispute Resolution (ADR) in Italy: European Inspiration and National Problems' (2012) No. 29 *Ritsumeikan Law Review* 71

Comba M, 'Constitutional Law' in Jeffrey S. Lena and Ugo Mattei (eds), *Introduction to Italian Law* (Kluwer Law International 2002)

D'Amico G, 'Struttura ed effetti delle decisioni' in Bindi E, Perini M and Pisaneschi A (eds), *I principi generali del processo comune ed i loro adattamenti alle esperienze della giustizia costituzionale* (Giappichelli 2008)

Della Cananea G, 'Legitimate expectations in European and Italian Law' (2009) Volume 1 *Italian Journal of Public Law* 1

Delzio F, 'Il Paese delle leggi. E della rivoluzione possibile', *Avvenire,* 18 March 2017, available at https://www.avvenire.it/rubriche/pagine/il-paese-delle-leggi-e-della-rivoluzione-possibile accessed 27 February 19

De Palo G and Keller L, 'Mediation in Italy: Alternative Dispute Resolution for All' in Hopt KJ and Steffek F (eds), *Mediation: Principles and Regulation in Comparative Perspective* (Oxford University Press 2013). DOI: https://doi.org/10.1093%2Facprof%3Aoso%2F9780199653485.003.0012

Domingo R, *Roman Law: An Introduction (*Routledge 2018)

Donini M, 'Tecnicismo Giuridico e Scienza penale cent`anni dopo. La proclusione di Arturo Rocco (1910) nell`età europeismo giudiziario' (2010) No. 1 *Crimialia, Annuario di scienze penalistiche* 127

Fabri M and Langbroek PM, 'Is There a Right Judge for Each Case? A Comparative Study of Case Assignment in Six European Countries' (2007) Vol. 1, No. 2 *European Journal of Legal Studies* 1

Ferrua P, 'La ragionevole durata del processo tra Costituzione e Convenzione europea' (2017) Issue 1 *Questione Giustizia 1*09

Finizio M, 'Quanta lunga è una legge? Ecco il bilancio delle attivita' legislative' *Il Sole 24 Ore,* 20 April 2015

Fiorentini F, Infantino M, "Context, Scope and Aim of the Book" in ibid, *Mentoring Comparative Lawyers: Methods, Times, and Places. Liber Discipulorum Mauro Bussani* (Springer 2020),

Forti G, *L'immane concretezza* (R. Cortina 2003)

Galli della Loggia E, *L'identità Italiana* (Il Mulino 1998)

Giacomelli S, Mocetti S, Palumbo G and Roma G, 'La giustizia civile in Italia: le recenti evoluzioni', *Occasional Papers Banca D`Italia n*o. 401 (2017), available at https://www.bancaditalia.it/pubblicazioni/qef/2017-0401/QEF_401_17.pdf accessed 4 March 2019

Groppi T, 'Constitutional Revision in Italy. A Marginal Instrument for Constitutional Change' in Kontiades X (ed), *Engineering Constitutional Change: A Comparative Perspective on Europe, Canada and USA* (Routledge 2012)

—— 'Giustizia costituzionale "Italian style"? Si, grazie (ma non qualche correttivo)' (2016) Issue 2 *Diritto Pubblico Comparato ed Europeo (Dpce online) 1*

—— and Spigno I, 'Constitutional reasoning of the Italian Constitutional Court' (2014) 4 *Rivista telematica dell'Associazione italiana dei costituzionalisti* 1

Grossi P, 'Globalizzazione, diritto, scienza giurdica' (2002) Vol. 125 No. 5 *Il Foro Italiano* 151

Hamilton A, Madison J and Jay J, *The Federalist Papers,* No.51 (Oxford University Press 2008)

Ippoliti R, 'Efficienza Tecnica e Geografia Giudiziaria' (2014) *POLIS Working Papers* no. 217, Institute of Public Policy and Public Choice

Krisch N, 'Authority, solid and liquid, in postnational governance' in Cotterrell R and Del Mar M (eds), *Authority in Transnational Legal Theory,* (Edward Elgar Publishing Limited 2016). DOI: https://doi.org/10.4337%2F9781784711627.00007

Livingston MA, Monateri PG and Parisi F, *The Italian Legal System: An Introduction* (2nd edn, Stanford University Press 2015). DOI: https://doi.org/10.11126%2Fstanford%2F9780804774956.001.0001

Lorenzi G, 'La certezza del diritto' (1956) Vol. 79 *Il Foro Italiano 73*

Macchia M, 'The Incidental Legality Review of Regulations in Italy' (2013) Volume 2 *Italian Journal of Public Law* 261

Maddalena E, 'Mobilità studenti in Erasmus: cresce la partecipazione in Italia', *Erasmus+* 5 July 2018, available at http://www.erasmusplus.it/mobilita-studenti-in-erasmus-cresce-la-partecipazione-in-italia/ accessed 5 March 2019

Mattarella BG, 'Participation in Rulemaking in Italy' (2010) Vol. 2 *Italian Journal of Public Law* 339

Mattoni A, 'Profili costituzionali della dignità umana' (2008) Issue 2/3 *Jus* 251

Melis G, 'La burocrazia e le riviste: per una storia della cultura dell`amministrazione' (1987) XVI *Quaderni Fiorentini 47*

Monateri PG, 'Shifting Frames: Law and Legal "Contaminations"' in Lena JS and Mattei U (eds), *Introduction to Italian Law* (Kluwer Law International 2002)

Mozzarelli C, 'L`annuario delle scienze Giuridiche, Sociali e Politiche (1880–1883)', *Quaderni Fiorentini,* 16 (Giuffrè 1987)

Onida V, 'The Constitution yesterday and today' (2012) Issue 1 *Italian Journal of Public Law* 15

Padoa-Schioppa A, *Italia Ed Europa Nella Storia Del Diritto* (Il Mulino 2010)

Pico della Mirandola G, *De Hominis Dignitate (*1486) (Bausi F ed, Fondazione Pietro Bembo 2003)

Pirozzoli A, *Il valore costituzionale della dignità. Un'introduzione* (Aracne 2007)

Pizzorusso A, 'Italian and American Models of the Judiciary and of Judicial Review of Legislation: A Comparison of Recent Tendencies' (1990) Vol. 38, Issue 2 *The American Journal of Comparative Law* 373. DOI: https://doi.org/10.2307%2F840104

Pliny the Elder, *Historia naturalis,* Book III

Popelier P, 'An Italian or a European Style of Judicial Review? Setting the Agenda for Comparative Research on Courts' (2016) Vol. 1 *Italian Journal of Public Law* 72

Press of the Office of the Constitutional Court, *Press Release of 11 January 2020*

Russo M, 'La Bocconi brilla nella classifica Censis di Giursiprudenza atenei private 2016', *Universita.it* 24 August 2016, available at https://www.universita.it/classifica-censis-giurisprudenza-atenei-privati-2016/ accessed 5 March 2019

Sacco R, 'Legal Formants: A Dynamic Approach to Comparative Law (Installment I of II)' (1991) Vol. 39 No. 1 *American Journal of Comparative Law* 1. DOI: https://doi.org/10.2307%2F840669

—— 'Legal Formants: A Dynamic Approach to Comparative Law (Installment II of II)' (1991) Vol. 39 No. 2 *The American Journal of Comparative Law* 343. DOI: https://doi.org/10.2307%2F840784

Salvato L, 'La nomofilachia nella dialettica tra Corte costituzionale e Corte di cassazione' (2018) *Forum di Quaderni Costituzionali* 1

Sbriccoli M, «Il diritto penale liberale. La "rivista penale" di Luigi Lucchini 1874–1900», *Quaderni Fiorentini,* 16 (Giuffrè 1987)

Scoca FG, 'Administrative Justice in Italy: Origins and Evolution' (2009) Vol. 2 *Italian Journal of Public Law* 118

Simoncini A, 'The Success of a Constitutional Experiment: When History Matters. The Italian Constitutional Court in Global Context' (2016) Vol. 8 *The Italian Journal of Public Law* 79

Spera D, *Tabelle milanesi 2018 e danno non patrimoniale (*Giuffrè 2018)

Stella Richter P, 'I rapporti tra legislazione statale e legislazione regionale' 1, available at http://www.dsg.univr.it/documenti/Iniziativa/dall/dall353864.pdf accessed 4 March 2019

Sunde JØ, *Speculum Legale – rettsspegelen* (Fagbokforlaget 2005)

Tao T, *Analysis I* (Springer 2015, third ed)

Taruffo M, 'La Jurisprudencia Entre Casuística Y Uniformidad: Between Casuistry and Uniformity' (2014) Vol. 27, No. 2 *Revista de derecho (Valdivia)* 9. DOI: https://doi.org/10.4067%2Fs0718-09502014000200001

—— 'Judicial Rulings with Prospective Effect in Italy' in Eva Steiner (ed), *Comparing the Prospective Effect of Judicial Rulings across Jurisdictions* (Springer 2015). DOI: https://doi.org/10.1007%2F978-3-319-16175-4_9

Teubner G, 'Breaking Frames: Economic Globalization and the Emergence of *Lex Mercatoria'* (2002) Vol. 5 *European Journal of Social Theory 1*99. DOI: https://doi.org/10.1177%2F13684310222225414

Tria L, 'La funzione di nomofilachia della Corte di cassazione alla luce dei principi del giusto processo di derivazione europea nonché del principio costituzionale di razionalità-equità' 1, available at http://www.europeanrights.eu/public/commenti/1%5E_Commento_Tria.pdf accessed 20 June 2019

Tuori K, *Critical Legal Positivism* (Ashgate 2002)

Verrengia G, Norelli I and Fierro M, 'Giurisprudenza costituzionale dell'anno 2017. Dati quantitative e di analisi' (Extraordinary meeting of the Constitutional Court, 22 February 2018) 1, available at https://www.cortecostituzionale.it/documenti/relazioni_annuali/grossi2018/dati_2018.pdf accessed 4 March 2019

Watanabe L, 'The Possible Contribution of Islamic Legal Institutions to the Emergence of a Rule of Law and the Modern State in Europe' in Al-Rodhan NRF (ed), *The Role of the Arab-Islamic World in the Rise of the West: Implications for Contemporary Trans-Cultural Relations,* (Palgrave Macmillan 2012). DOI: https://doi.org/10.1057%2F9780230393219.0007

Winroth A, 'Recent Work On The Making Of Gratians Decretum' (2008) 26 *Bulletin of Medieval Canon Law* 6

Zicchittu P, 'The Italian Way to the "Political Question"' (2015) Vol. 1 *Italian Journal of Public Law* 222

16. An Introduction to Romanian Legal Culture[1]

Cosmin Dariescu

1. Introduction

Romania is a state situated in Europe at the crossroads of Eastern, South-Eastern and Central Europe. It borders the Black Sea to the southeast, Bulgaria to the south, Serbia to the southwest, Hungary to the west, Ukraine to the north and the Republic of Moldova to the east. It has a total area of 238,397 square kilometers, being the 13th largest country in Europe and the 80th in the world. The river Danube flows through Romania and empties into the Danube Delta. The Carpathian Mountains cross Romania from north to southwest.[2] The highest peak is Moldovan, having an altitude of 2,544 m.[3]

Romania became a state in 1862, with the renaming of the United Principalities of Moldavia and Wallachia, established in 1859. It gained its independence from the Ottoman Empire in 1877. On 1 December 1918, Greater Romania was formed, uniting all the lands inhabited by Romanians, people speaking Romanian and generally adhering to the Orthodox faith.[4] In 1940, Greater Romania was torn apart by Hungary (which claimed the majority of Transylvania), by Bulgaria (which took the Southern Part of Dobruja, on the shores of the Black Sea), and by the USSR (which occupied Northern Bukovina and Bessarabia). Romania declared war on the USSR in 1941, joining the Axis Forces. Defeated in the Second World War, Romania lost the two provinces. The Communist Winter began. After the Revolution of 1989, Romania became a democratic republic.

---

1 This project is funded by the Ministry of Research and Innovation within Programme 1 – Development of the national RD system, Subprogramme 1.2 – Institutional Performance – RDI excellence funding projects, Contract no. 34PFE.

2 Ioan Mihăilescu, Mihai Ielinicz, Nicoleta Ionac, George Erdely and others (eds), *Romania. Geography and Tourism* (Royal Company Publishing House 2001) 7, 11.

3 Costel Coroban, *The Geography of Romania. Manual for Secondary Education* (Constanța 2013) 18.

4 Ioan Scurtu (ed), Theodora Stănescu-Stanciu and Georgiana Margareta Scurtu, *România între anii 1918–1940. Documente și materiale (*Ed. Universității București 2001) 3–10.

Romania became a member of the European Union on 1 January 2007.[5] The population of Romania is around 19,524,000 people.[6] The population density is approximately 91 inhabitants per square kilometer.[7] The capital of Romania is Bucharest, with a population of around 1,812,290 inhabitants.[8]

According to the Constitution of 1991, revised in 2003,[9] Romania is a unitary semi-presidential republic, the executive powers being shared between the President and the Government.[10] The country is governed on the basis of a multi-party democratic system and the separation of powers between the legislative, executive and judicial branches.[11]. The President of Romania is elected by citizens for a maximum of two terms of five years. The legislative branch of the government, known as the Parliament, consists of two chambers, the Chamber of Deputies and the Senate, with elected members. The Prime minister is appointed by the President from the ranks of the Parliamentary party that obtained the majority in elections. The Prime minister appoints the members of the Government.

The official language is Romanian. Romanian is part of the Eastern Romance sub-branch of Romance languages which was separated during the 5th-8th centuries from the Western Romance.[12]

While Christian Orthodoxy was named the state-religion in the Constitutions of 1866 and 1923, it was not in 1991. Romania has no state-religion today.[13] According to the results of the 2011 census, the main religious groups are: Christian Orthodox (16,307,004 out of 20,121,641), Roman Catholic (870,774), and Protestants

5 'EU member countries in brief', available at https://europa.eu/european-union/about-eu/countries/member-countries_en accessed 29 December 2019.

6 Romanian National Institute of Statistics, *Press Release no. 215/2018:* 'Resident population on 1 January 2018 decreased by 120, 7 thousand persons' [RO], available at http://www.insse.ro/cms/sites/default/files/com_presa/com_pdf/poprez_ian2018r.pdf accessed 29 December 2019.

7 Coroban (2013) (n 3).

8 'Bucharest Population 2019', available at http://worldpopulationreview.com/world-cities/bucharest-population/ accessed 29 December 2019.

9 An English version of the Romanian Constitution of 1991 is available at https://www.presidency.ro/en/the-constitution-of-romania accessed 29 December 2019.

10 Oana Șaramet, 'Powers of the President of Romania in Relationship with Government' (2016) no. 1 *Agora International Journal of Juridical Sciences* 23.

11 Provided for in Article 1 Paragraph 4 of the Constitution. Article 5 Paragraph 4 of the revised Romanian Constitution reads: "(4) The State shall be organised based on the principle of the separation and balance of powers – legislative, executive, and judicial – within the framework of constitutional democracy".

12 To distinguish it within that group, in comparative linguistics it is called Daco-Romanians as opposed to its closest relatives, Aromanian, Megleno-Romanian, and Istro-Romanian. Lucian Vasile Bâgiu, *Introduction in the Study of Romanian Language. A Textbook for Foreign Students (*Aeternitas 2018) 9, 10, 31–32, 36–37. On the similarities among Romanian and other Romance languages, see Daniela Gîfu, 'Diachronic Evaluation of Newspapers Language between Different Idioms' in Larry Brinbaum, Octavian Popescu and Carlo Strapparava (eds), *IJCAI 2016 Workshop. Natural Language Processing meets Journalism. Proceedings of the Workshop* (2016) 92–93; 'Lexical Semantics in Text Processing. Contrastive Diachronic Studies on Romanian Language', PhD thesis, "Alexandru Ioan Cuza" University of Iași, Romania, 2016.

13 'The Romanian Constitution' [RO], available at https://www.constitutia.ro/constitutiile-din-romania.htm accessed 29 December 2019.

(600,932).[14] Since all denominations have equal status in Romania, law and religion are strictly separated. Even the bishops and the officials of other denominations are treated as laymen from the legal point of view. However, their religious offices are grounds for special criminal jurisdiction rules, designed to involve more experienced judges and prosecutors.

According to the results of the 2011 census, the main ethnic minorities are: Hungarians with 1,227,623, Roma with 621,573, and Ukrainians with 50,920 persons of the total population. On 15 May 1995, Romania became party to the Council of Europe Framework Convention for the Protection of National Minorities. The Law on Education remains the main legislative basis for teaching in and of national minority languages. However, a policy to guarantee access to minority rights is still lacking and respect of rights of persons belonging to national minorities varies according to local conditions and the goodwill of the municipal or regional authorities. Negative attitudes and prejudice against the Roma and anti-Hungarian sentiment are of considerable concern, despite the efforts of the National Council for Combating Discrimination. The 2015 electoral law contains specific provisions on preferential seats for representatives of national minorities. These provisions allow election on a preferential basis of one representative from each national minority represented in the Council of National Minorities (CNM) [15]. It has to be noted, however, that the existing legal and administrative provisions on elections do not create favourable conditions for free and fair competition in the electoral process between different organizations representing national minorities.

The Romanian economy has a gross domestic product (GDP) of 211.9 billion US dollars and a gross domestic product per capita (GDPP) of 10,821 US dollars.[16]. From March 1996 to June 2019, Romania's GDP grew by an annual average rate of 3.9%.[17] In 2018, the main driver of growth was private consumption. Foreign investment – up to 0.5% of the GDP – underperformed despite the availability of EU funds. This situation was caused by political measures such as constant changes of tax legislation, increase of minimum wage as well as of old-age pensions combined with a low-rate of absorption of EU funds. The economic freedom score of Romania is 68.6 at present. Thus, the Romanian economy becomes the 42 unrestricted in the 2019 Index.[18]

---

14 'Population on sexes, according to religion, Macro-regions, Development Regions and Localities' [RO], available at http://www.recensamantromania.ro/noutati/volumul-ii-populatia-stabila-rezidenta-structura-etnica-si-confesionala/ accessed 29 December 2019.

15 ACFC/OP/IV (2017)005, Fourth Opinion on Romania – adopted 22 June 2017, published 16 February 2018, p. 6. Available at https://rm.coe.int/fourth-opinion-on-romania-adopted-on-22-june-2017/168078af76.

16 'The World Bank in Romania. Overview', available at https://www.worldbank.org/en/country/romania/overview accessed 29 December 2019.

17 'Romania Real GDP Growth', available at https://www.ceicdata.com/en/indicator/romania/real-gdp-growth accessed 29 December 2019.

18 'Romania', available at https://www.heritage.org/index/country/romania accessed 29 December 2019.

2. Conflict resolution

One may state that, despite its relatively low population and rather difficult economic preconditions, Romania has a comparably high degree of specialization in its court system. This applies to the internal specialization inside the courts. There are no specialized administrative courts in Romania.[19] The administrative cases are judged by specialized sections of ordinary courts. In Romania, there are no laymen participating at any level of the ordinary courts.

As a general rule, all Romanian courts consider both evidence and law whenever they hear a case as court of first instance or as an instance of appeal.[20] When acting as a court of review, the High Court of Cassation and Justice considers only law, while the courts of appeal and tribunals (in Civil Procedure) consider law to review the judgment and may consider both law and evidence if they keep the case to give a new solution on the merits.[21]

Romania has a single, four-tiered court hierarchy provided for in Article 126 of the Romanian Constitution and in Law No 304/2004 on judicial organization.[22] The Constitutional Court is an independent jurisdictional authority.[23] According to the Civil Procedure Code and the Criminal Procedure Code, written and oral procedures are combined in all Romanian courts.[24]

The following courts (see Fig. 1) constitute the judicial system.[25]

19 'Specialized Courts – Romania' [RO], available at https://e-justice.europa.eu/content_specialised_courts-19-ro-maximizeMS-ro.do?member=1 accessed 29 December 2019.

20 The High Court of Cassation and Justice can be court of first instance only in criminal procedures.

21 Ioan Leş, 'Consideraţii generale asupra căilor legale de atac' in Ioan Leş, Călina Jugastru, Verginel Lozneanu and others (eds), *Tratat de drept procesual civil. Vol. II* (Universul Juridic 2015) 11; Ioan Leş and Sebastian Spinei, 'Recursul' in Ioan Leş, Călina Jugastru, Verginel Lozneanu and others (eds), *Tratat de drept procesual civil. Vol. II* (Universul Juridic 2015) 124–126; Ion Neagu and Mircea Damaschin, *Tratat de procedură penală. Partea specială (*Universul Juridic 2015) 383.

22 Claudia Şerban Cernat, *Organizarea profesiilor juridice. Ediţia a II-a revizuită şi completată (*Braşov 2017) 10–11.

23 Provided for in Title V of the Constitution. 'Access to Justice in Europe – Thematic study: Romania' 1–2, available at https://fra.europa.eu/sites/default/files/fra_uploads/1542-access-to-justice-2011-country-RO.pdf accessed 29 December 2019.

24 Articles 15, 63, 68, 77, 148–150, 194, 205, 209, 231–233, 235, 401–402 and 424–426 of the Civil Procedure Code and Articles 97, 110, 111, 123, 286, 289, 295, 309, 314, 327–328, 345, 347, 370, 390 and 400–404 of the Criminal Procedure Code.

25 'Courts. Courts of Appeal, tribunals and district courts', available at http://www.justitia-romana.org/lista-instante accessed 29 December 2019.

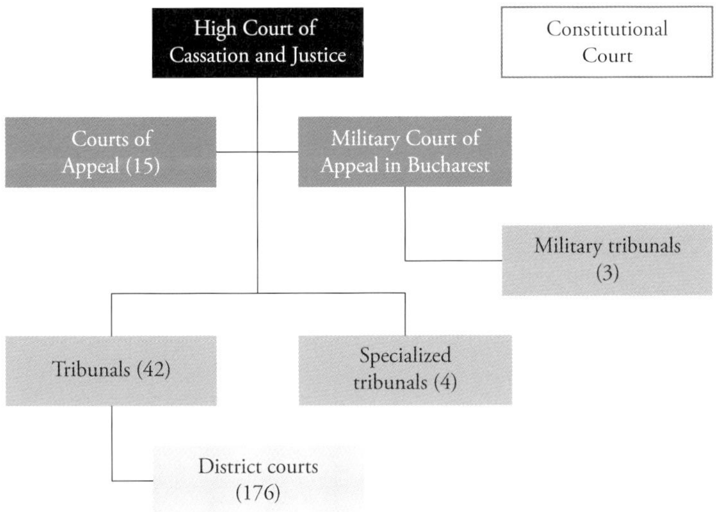

Fig. 1 The Romanian Judicial System.

2.1 The High Court

The High Court of Cassation and Justice (*Înalta Curte de Casație și Justiție* – abbr. High Court) functions as the Supreme Court in Romania. It ensures that the law is uniformly interpreted and applied by the other courts. In order to achieve that goal, the court applies the procedures know as 'Review in the interest of law'[26] and 'Request for preliminary ruling'.[27] The High Court of Cassation and Justice has four independent sections with their own jurisdiction: Criminal Section, Civil Section, and Administrative and Tax Litigation Section[28]. Furthermore, there are other sections established with special jurisdiction, such as the four Panels of Five Judges, the Joint Sections, the Panel on Reviews in the Interest of Law, and the Panel on Clarifying Certain Legal Matters.

The Panels of Five Judges represent an expedient that replaces the United Sections of the High Court in the cases provided by the law. They have jurisdiction both in civil and in criminal matters. In civil matters, they judge on: applications for review against disciplinary action decisions of the Higher Council of Magistrates, conflicts of jurisdiction between two Chambers of the High Court of Cassation and Justice, applications for review in cases against decisions to waive a claimed right, in cases against decisions

26 'Introduction to Romanian's judicial system. Ordinary courts', available at https://e-justice.europa.eu/content_ordinary_courts-18-ro-en.do?init=true&member=1 accessed 29 December 2019.

27 'Jurisdiction – Panels for Clarification of Legal aspects', available at http://www.scj.ro/en/1085/Jurisdiction accessed 29 December 2019.

28 Article 2 of the Regulation of 24 September 2004, available at http://www.scj.ro/CMS/0/PublicMedia/GetIncludedFile?id=5268 accessed 29 December 2019.

ascertaining obsolescence, against revision of decisions for contrariety between decisions, and in cases when such revision was settled by one of the Chambers of the High Court. In the criminal field, these panels rule in applications for review against decisions given in the first instance by the Criminal Chamber of the High Court and in challenges against court resolutions given in the first instance during the trial by the Criminal Chamber of the High Court.[29] The Joint Sections, or United Chambers, convene to settle the motions on the changes of the jurisprudence of the High Court, to notify the Constitutional Court to check the constitutionality of laws prior to enactment, or to communicate to the Ministry of Justice the cases where an improvement of law is required[30].

The Panel on Reviews in the Interest of Law decides legal issues settled differently by final court decisions in lower courts in order to unify law.[31] The proceedings before this panel can be instituted only by four authorities: the Prosecutor General of the Prosecutors' Office attached to the High Court of Review and Justice, the Management Collegium of the High Court of Review and Justice, the collegial management of Courts of Appeals, as well as the Ombudsman.[32]

The Panel on Clarifying Certain Legal Matters rules on requests filed in order to achieve preliminary judgments clarifying specific legal aspects, in both Criminal and Civil Law.[33] The Panel is restricted to rule only on unclear matters. The clarification of legal aspects is binding for the court having requested such clarification as of the date the judgment was returned and for other courts as of the date the judgment is published in Part I of the Official Gazette of Romania.

In order to deal with civil cases of Private Law litigations, The High Court has two sections: the First Chamber and the Second Chamber. They have no specialised jurisdiction. They decide applications for review: against judgments handed down by courts of appeal, motions for revisions in cases set by law, nullification, case transfer applications, conflicts of jurisdiction and applications for review against non-final judgments or judicial acts of any nature which cannot be appealed by any other means and in case

29 'Jurisdiction – 5-Justice Panels/the 9-Justice Panels', available at http://www.scj.ro/en/558/Jurisdiction accessed 29 December 2019.

30 'Jurisdiction – The United Chambers', available at http://www.scj.ro/en/580/Jurisdiction accessed 29 December 2019.

31 'Jurisdiction – Panels for the Settlement of Appeals in the Intertest of Law', available at http://www.scj.ro/en/604/Jurisdiction accessed 29 December 2019.

32 The Romanian Ombudsman (People's Advocate) is provided for in Articles 58, 59 and 60 of the Constitution as well as in Law no. 35/1997 (consolidated). The People's Advocate Institution is a national independent institution for the promotion and protection of human rights of natural persons in relation with public authorities. The Ombudsman is appointed by the Parliament for a five-year term. He/she has deputies that are specialised in different fields. There are 18 territorial offices of this institution. For more details on the Romanian Ombudsman, see http://www.avp.ro/index.php?option=com_content&view=article&id=56:structuraavp&catid=2&lang=ro-ro&Itemid=164 accessed 29 December 2019.

33 'Jurisdiction – Panels for Clarification of Legal Aspects', available at http://www.scj.ro/en/1085/Jurisdiction accessed 29 December 2019.

of which legal proceedings before a court of appeal have been interrupted.[34] The Administrative and Tax Litigation Section has jurisdiction similar to civil sections, limited to Administrative and Tax Law.[35]

The Criminal Section will hear cases and applications involving people holding particularly high offices. Thus, offences committed by senators, deputies or Members of the European Parliament, offences committed by members of the Government or by judges of the Constitutional Court, by marshals, admirals, generals, etc. are brought before this section. As a court of review, the Criminal Section of the High Court of Cassation and Justice checks the legality of judgments rendered for serious crimes and for crimes perpetrated by high state officials or by members of the high clergy. Thus, it hears the following cases: applications for review against criminal judgments rendered, at first instance, by a court of appeal or by the Military Court of Appeal, applications for review against criminal judgments on appeal given by a court of appeal or by the Military Court of Appeal, applications for review against criminal judgments, at first instance, given by the Criminal Section of the High Court, and other cases provided for by law [36]. In total, the High Court had 104 judges in 2019. The Civil Section I had 18 judges[37], the Civil Section II had effectively 22 judges[38], the Criminal Section, 33 judges[39], and the Administrative and Tax Law Section, 31 judges.[40] All the other panels of the High Court are composed of the aforementioned judges.[41]

In order to be promoted to the High Court, a judge or a prosecutor must have at least three years of experience in a court of appeal, with no disciplinary punishment and a 'very good' rating in the last three evaluations – also, he/she has to be declared 'admitted' at a competitive examination organized by the Superior Council of Magistracy by means of the National Institute of Magistracy. The examination has three stages: the evaluation of the judicial activity of the candidate, an interview in front of the Superior council of Magistracy, and a written paper with practical questions.[42]

According to the Romanian Ministry of Justice, the High Court decided 19,220 cases in 2016, 12,535 cases in 2017, and 17,028 cases in 2018.[43] In 2018, the First Civil Chamber decided 4,251 cases, the Second Civil Chamber 5,355 cases, and the

---

34 'Jurisdiction – the First Civil Chamber', available at http://www.scj.ro/en/468/Jurisdiction; 'Jurisdiction – the 2nd Civil Chamber', available at http://www.scj.ro/en/492/Jurisdiction accessed 29 December 2019.

35 Article 21 para. 1 of Law no. 304 of 2004. 'Jurisdiction – the Administrative and Tax Litigation Chamber', available at http://www.scj.ro/en/536/Jurisdiction accessed 29 December 2019.

36 'Jurisdiction – Criminal Chamber', available at http://www.scj.ro/en/514/Jurisdiction accessed 29 December 2019.

37 'Judges – First Civil Chamber', available at http://www.scj.ro/en/471/Judges accessed 29 December 2019.

38 'Judges – Second Civil Chamber', available at http://www.scj.ro/en/495/Judges accessed 29 December 2019.

39 'Judges – Criminal Chamber', available at http://www.scj.ro/en/517/Judge accessed 29 December 2019.

40 'Judges – Administrative and Tax Litigations Chamber', available at http://www.scj.ro/en/539/Judges accessed 29 December 2019.

41 See for example 'Judecătorii - Completele de 5 judecători / Completul de 9 judecători', available at http://www.scj.ro/561/Judecatorii?culture=en accessed 29 December 2019. All judges of the High Court can be members of the Panel on Reviews in the Interest of Law and of the Panel for Clarifying Certain Legal Aspects.

42 Cernat (2017) (n 22) 29.

43 According to the data provided in Notice No. 27427/28 March 2019 of the Ministry of Justice.

Administrative and Tax Litigation Section handled 4,656 cases, while the Criminal Section dealt with 2,628 cases. The Panel of Five Judges decided 428 cases. The Panel on Reviews in the Interest of Law decided 25 cases and the Panel on Clarifying Certain Legal Matters 104 cases.[44]

2.2 The courts of appeal

The 15 appellate courts (*curți de apel*) have two or three tribunals and specialized tribunals from several districts under their jurisdiction. These courts are both courts of appeal and courts of first instance, the latter for important administrative, financial and criminal litigations. In civil matters, the courts of appeal hear, as courts of first instance, applications relating to administrative and tax disputes, in accordance with special legal provisions. As courts of appeal, they hear appeals against judgments given by tribunals at first instance.[45] As courts of review, they hear the reviews[46] declared against decisions given by the tribunals in appeal or against judgments given in the first instance by tribunals, which according to the law are not subject to the appeal as in any other cases expressly provided by the law. Appellate courts are forums of second degree for Civil Litigations. For Administrative and Tax litigations, they act as first instance when central authorities are involved.

In criminal matters, the courts of appeal act as both courts of appeal and courts of first instance (the latter when the Criminal Procedure Code provides it). They hear, as courts of first instance, cases on for instance treason, espionage, conspiracy, subversion of state authority or of the national economy, and offences against Romania's national security. They also have jurisdiction over offences committed by:

1) judges of a district court or a tribunal,
2) prosecutors of the prosecutors' offices attached to those courts,
3) lawyers, notaries, judicial enforcement officers or auditors of the Court of Accounts,
4) leaders of religious denominations organized in accordance with the law and other high-ranking religious figures,
5) assistant magistrates of the High Court of Cassation and Justice,
6) judges of a court of appeal or the Military Court of Appeal, or prosecutors of prosecutor's offices attached to those courts,
7) the President of the Legislative Council, or
8) the Ombudsman.

---

44 High Court of Cassation and Justice, 'Centralizing Statistical Table. January 01 – December 31, 2018', available at http://www.scj.ro/CMS/0/PublicMedia/GetIncludedFile?id=20565 [RO] accessed 29 December 2019.

45 On the role of mini-supreme courts played by the courts of appeal, see Codru Vrabie, 'Rolul CSM, ICCJ Și MP Față De Politicile Publice Din Justiție.', 2014, p. 3, available at www.onoratainstanta.ro accessed 29 December 2019.

46 The main difference between appeal and review in Romanian Civil Procedure consists on the grounds for exercising them. In appeal, the judgment is revisited for both the interpretation of fact and legal rules applicable, while in review it is possible to consider only the correct application and interpretation of legal rules.

As courts of appeal, they hear appeals against criminal judgments given by tribunals at first instance. As courts of review, they hear applications for review against criminal judgments given by district courts, at first instance, excluding those that are within the jurisdiction of tribunals, and other cases specifically referred to by law. The courts of appeal also decide on conflicts of jurisdiction between tribunals or between district courts and tribunals within their area of jurisdiction or between district courts within the jurisdiction of different tribunals in a court of appeal's area of jurisdiction. Furthermore, the courts of appeal decide on requests for the extradition or transfer abroad of convicted persons.[47] In order to be promoted in a court of appeal, the judge or the prosecutor must have six years of experience in a tribunal, with a good conduct and with a 'very good' rating at the last evaluation – also, he/she has to pass a competitive examination organized by the Superior Council of Magistracy by means of the National Institute of Magistracy.[48]

According to the Romanian Ministry of Justice, in 2016, the Courts of Appeal decided 153,036 cases, in 2017, 170,961, and in 2018, 163,071.[49] In 2018, the new cases brought to justice in front of the courts of appeal were: administrative and tax law 30%, criminal law 24%, employment law 11%, civil law 11%, social security litigations 9%, litigations among professionals 7%, bankruptcy 7%.[50] Of all these cases, 45% were procedurally treated as appeals, 33% as reviews and 13% were first instance cases.

2.3 The tribunals

The 42 legal tribunals (*tribunal*) are established at district level and in the capital of Bucharest. They are located, as a rule, in the main town of each district – called *Județ*. They are both courts of first instance and courts of appeal for less significant civil or criminal cases. The tribunals have separate sections or panels specialized in: civil cases, criminal cases, cases involving children or family matters, administrative cases or tax disputes, cases related to labour disputes, social insurance, companies, the Trade Register, insolvency, unfair competition, and other matters and cases involving maritime or fluvial matters.

In civil matters, the tribunals hear, as courts of first instance, all applications which does not fall within the jurisdiction of other courts. As courts of appeal, they hear appeals

47 'Introduction to Romania's judicial system. Ordinary courts', available at https://e-justice.europa.eu/content_ordinary_courts-18-ro-en.do?init=true&member=1 accessed 29 December 2019.

48 Cernat (2017) (n 22) 25–26.

49 According to the data provided in Notice No. 27427/28 March 2019 of the Ministry of Justice.

50 Superior Council of Magistracy, 'Report on the state of justice 2018', p. 14, available at: https://www.csm1909.ro/267/3570/Rapoarte-privind-starea-justi%C5%A3iei [RO] accessed 29 December 2019.

against judgments given by district courts at first instance.[51] As courts of review, they hear cases specifically provided for by the law. In criminal matters, the tribunals hear, as courts of first instance, serious offences against life or corporal integrity and health, offences against personal freedom, sexual offences, property offences, and other offences provided for in Article 36 of the Criminal Procedure Code. As courts of review, they hear applications for review against judgments given by district courts in cases set by law. The tribunals decide, also, on conflicts of jurisdiction between district courts within their area of jurisdiction and on other cases specifically provided for by law.

In order to be promoted to justice in a tribunal court, the judge or the prosecutor must have five years of experience in a district court, with good conduct and with 'very good' rating at the last evaluation, and has to pass a competitive examination organized by the Superior Council of Magistracy with the help of the National Institute of Magistracy.[52]

According to the Romanian Ministry of Justice, in 2016, tribunals decided 462,542 cases, in 2017, 503,476, and in 2018, 462,636 cases. In 2018, new cases brought into tribunals were: administrative and tax law 23%, criminal law 21%, civil law 19%, litigations among professionals 11%, employment law 8%, bankruptcy 7%, minors and family 6%, and other legal matters 5%[53]. 56% of the cases were brought in the first instance and 34% in appeal.

2.4 District courts

There are 176 district courts (*judecătorii*) under the jurisdiction of tribunals; each tribunal supervises the judicial activity of several district courts. In civil matters, they hear the cases provided for in Article 94 of the Civil Procedure Code. District courts also hear appeals against decisions of the local public administration authorities with local jurisdiction and other bodies with such jurisdiction, and in cases provided for by the law. In criminal matters, district courts hear cases on all types of offences, with the exception of those that are to be heard at first instance by the tribunals, the courts of appeal or the

51 In Romania, the complexity of the case or the value of what is on stake is decisive for the level of the court seized. For instance, according to Articles 94 and 95 of the Civil Procedure Code, the tribunal is the common civil court to be seized, with the exception of litigations provided for district courts. As mentioned above, the jurisdiction of district courts, as courts of first instance, includes eleven types of litigations, including those with a pecuniary object evaluated up to and including RON 200,000 (approximately 41,993 Euro), regardless of whether or not the parties have the status of professionals. Nine articles of the Civil Procedure Code (Articles 98 to 106) provide in detail the manner in which the patrimonial object of the litigation should be assessed in accordance with the type of litigation. In criminal procedure, district courts have general jurisdiction (Article 35 of the Criminal Procedure Code), while tribunals, courts of appeal and the High Court of Cassation and Justice have jurisdiction only on serious crimes specified by law (Articles 36, 38, 40 of the Criminal Procedure Code). Law no. 135 of 1 July 2010 of the Criminal Procedure Code is available in English at http://legislatie.just.ro/Public/Acasa) accessed 29 December 2019.

52 Cernat (2017) (n 22) 25–26.

53 Superior Council of Magistracy, 'Report on the state of justice 2018' 21–22, available at: https://www.csm1909.ro/267/3570/Rapoarte-privind-starea-justi%C5%A3iei [RO] accessed 29 December 2019.

High Court of Cassation and Justice.[54] District courts are the starting point in a magistrate career, be it judge or prosecutor. After the final examination, the trainee, judge or prosecutor, is appointed to a district court.[55]

In 2016, district Courts decided 1,088,992 cases, in 2017, 1,484,837, and in 2018, 1,501,578 cases. In 2018, 63% of the new cases brought into district courts were civil cases, 21% were criminal cases, while family and minors cases represented 7%. Litigations among professionals increased to 7%, while other matters made up 2% of the total case load.[56]

2.5 Specialized tribunals

There are four specialized tribunals in the Romanian court system. They function as separate courts for cases involving minors and family law and for specific commercial cases.[57] They have territorial jurisdiction only at the district level. Thus, the Tribunal for Minors and Family in Brașov hears the cases on crimes committed by minors or against minors and civil cases concerning family matters. The three specialized tribunals for commercial cases are: the Specialized Tribunal in Cluj, the Specialized Tribunal in Mureș, and the Specialized Tribunal in Argeș. They hear litigations among professional actors in commerce. All persons owning an enterprise are considered professionals.[58]

In 2018, the specialized tribunals decided 9,629 cases, compared with 8,530 cases in 2017. The Specialized Tribunal in Cluj decided 4,723 cases in 2018, the Specialized Tribunal in Mureș 2,520 cases, the Specialized Tribunal in Argeș decided 1,152 cases, and the Tribunal for Minors and Family in Brașov decided 1,234 cases.[59]

54 District courts have general criminal jurisdiction. But they cannot interfere with the criminal jurisdiction of tribunals, courts of appeal and the High Court. Depending on the type of crime and the social position of the alleged perpetrator, the case must be heard by the court of competence, according to the Criminal Procedure Code. So, district courts never handle cases that other courts handled as first instance. See 'Introduction to Romanian's judicial system. Ordinary courts', available at https://e-justice.europa.eu/content_ordinary_courts-18-ro-en.do?init=true&member=1 accessed 29 December 2019.

55 Cernat (2017) (n 22) 24.

56 Superior Council of Magistracy, 'Report on the state of justice 2018' 32, available at https://www.csm1909.ro/267/3570/Rapoarte-privind-starea-justi%C5%A3iei [RO] accessed 29 December 2019.

57 'Presentation of the court. Juvenile and Family Tribunal' [RO], available at http://portal.just.ro/1372/SitePages/prezentare.aspx?id_inst=1372 [RO] accessed 29 December 2019. The Ministry of Justice's Order for establishing the Specialized Commercial Tribunal in Mureș is to be found at http://portal.just.ro/1371/SiteAssets/SitePages/prezentare/Ordinul%20ministrului%20Justitiei.PDF [RO] accessed 29 December 2019.

58 'Specialized courts – Romania' [RO], available at https://e-justice.europa.eu/content_specialised_courts-19-ro-maximizeMS-ro.do?member=1 accessed 29 December 2019; 'Presentation of the Romanian judicial system' [RO], available at https://www.csm1909.ro/271/Prezentarea-sistemului-judiciar accessed 29 December 2019.

59 Superior Council of Magistracy, 'Report on the state of justice 2017, pp. 29–30, available at https://www.csm1909.ro/267/3570/Rapoarte-privind-starea-justi%C5%A3iei accessed 29 December 2019.

2.6 Military courts

There is a military Court of Appeal in Bucharest (*Curtea Militară de Apel*) and four military tribunals (*tribunale militare*) in the cities of Bucharest, Cluj, Iași, and Timișoara.[60] Altogether, there are 18 military judges.[61] In 2018, the Military Tribunal in Bucharest decided 315 cases, the Military Tribunal in Iași decided 157 cases, the Military Tribunal in Cluj-Napoca 139 cases, and the Military Tribunal in Timișoara decided 109 cases.

Each of the military tribunals is considered a military unit and Annex 2 of Law no. 304 of 2004 on judicial organization provides each territorial jurisdiction.[62] The Military Court of Appeal decides over conflicts of jurisdiction between military tribunals and on other cases specifically provided for by law.[63] A person who meets the conditions stipulated by law for entering the magistracy may be appointed as judge or military prosecutor if she/he obtains the Ministry of National Defence's approval on the fulfilment of the legal conditions for acquiring the status of active officer in the Army.[64] Their promotion as magistrates is supervised by the Superior Council of Magistracy. Military judges and prosecutors are active military personnel and have all the rights and obligations arising from this quality.[65] The persistence of the military justice in democratic Romania is justified by specific requirements of the military life that are unknown to many civil magistrates, especially in a country where the compulsory military service was abolished in 2003.

2.7 The Constitutional Court

The constitutional court (*Curtea Constituțională*) was established by the Constitution of 1991 and is the unique authority of constitutional jurisdiction in Romania. It is independent of any other public authority, in the sense that the executive and legislative powers contribute to the formation of the court by appointing a group of judges, but, after this moment, all the three powers in the state have to comply with its decisions.[66] Therefore, in the framework of the three branches of government, it can be placed between the legislative and the judicial branch.

The Constitutional Court is composed of nine judges, appointed for a nine-year term that cannot be renewed nor prolonged[67]. Three judges are appointed by the Chamber

---

60 Their jurisdiction is provided for in the Criminal Procedure Code, Articles 37 and 39.

61 For the organisational chart of each of the military courts, consult the Ministry of Justice Portal of the Courts by selecting the siege at http://portal.just.ro/SitePages/acasa.aspx [RO] accessed 29 December 2019.

62 Provided for in Annex 2 of Law no. 304 of 2004 on judicial organization. See 'Military Courts' [RO], available at https://www.csm1909.ro/271/3585/Instan%C5%A3e-militare accessed 29 December 2019.

63 Law no. 135 of 1 July 2010 of the Criminal Procedure Code is available in English at http://legislatie.just.ro/Public/Acasa accessed 29 December 2019.

64 Article 32 of Law no. 303 of 2004.

65 Article 74, para. 4 of Law no. 303 of 2004.

66 'The Court's Role and Powers', available at https://www.ccr.ro/en/Rol-i-atribuii accessed 29 December 2019.

67 The nine-year-mandate of judges of the Constitutional Court is mandatory. Of course, if a judge becomes unable to complete his/her term, he/she is replaced with a new judge who has to finish his/her predecessor's term. Afterwards, the new judge can be elected for a full term of nine years.

of Deputies, three by the Senate, and the other three by the President of Romania. The constitutional judges elect by secret vote a President of the Constitutional Court for a three-year term. A third of the judges of the Constitutional Court are renewed once in three years.

The competences of the Constitutional Court are determined by Constitution[68] and by Organic Law no. 47 of 1992.[69] The most important of the Constitutional Court competences are: 1) adjudicating the constitutionality of ordinary laws (in a general sense) before promulgation, 2) establishing the unconstitutionality of ordinary laws (in a general sense) brought before courts by individuals or by the Romanian Ombudsman, 3) adjudicating the constitutionality of treaties,[70] 4) supervising the procedure of the presidential election in Romania, and 5) authenticating the results and solving constitutional conflicts between public authorities.[71]

Judgments of the Constitutional Court can be invoked as precedent, because, if an article of law has been declared unconstitutional, another exception of unconstitutionality on it is rejected by the Constitutional Court. Moreover, according to Article 31 paragraph 3 of Law no. 47 of 1992 consolidated, decisions of the Constitutional Court, through which the exception of unconstitutionality is admitted, have a repealing effect on the unconstitutional article of law.[72] This is true only if the Parliament does not replace the unconstitutional article within 45 days after the publication of the judgment. The judgment of the Constitutional Court only amputates the law without providing new articles of law to replace the unconstitutional ones. For instance, on 25 October 2018, some of the recent alterations of the provisions of the Criminal Code of 2009 concerning embezzlement and the abuse in office were declared unconstitutional[73].

These judgments are mandatory for every public authority in Romania. Even the Parliament, when amending the unconstitutional law, is compelled to enforce the Court judgments.[74] Therefore, these judgments are highly influential for the legal argumentation, having both practical and doctrinal effects, since they have always been enforced. The Constitutional Court decided 795 cases in 2016, 859 cases in 2017, and 877 cases

68 Articles 142–147.

69 According to Merriam-Webster Dictionary, an organic law is one of the laws that make up a body that is part of the original foundation of a government or a law that regulates civil rights and liberties (criminal laws for example). See https://www.merriam-webster.com/legal/organic%20law accessed 29 December 2019.

70 'Specialized Courts – Romania' [RO], available at https://e-justice.europa.eu/content_specialised_courts-19-ro-maximizeMS-ro.do?member=1 accessed 29 December 2019.

71 'The Court's Role and Powers', available at https://www.ccr.ro/en/Rol-i-atribuii accessed 29 December 2019. The procedure concerning the settlement of constitutional conflicts among public authorities is described in Mihaela Simion, 'Constitutional Legal Disputes between the President of Romania and Other Public Authorities in the Case law of the Constitutional Court of Romania' (2017) no. 2 *AGORA International Journal of Juridical Sciences* 89–90.

72 Mihail Niemesch, *Teoria generală a dreptului (*Hamangiu 2014) 114–116.

73 Adelina Săhlean, 'Curtea Constituțională: Codul penal este parțial neconstituțional', available at https://newsweek.ro/justitie/judecatorii-ccr-codul-penal-este-partial-neconstitutional accessed 29 December 2019.

74 See Constitutional Court Decision no. 466 of 29 July 2019 [RO] p. 33, available at http://www.ccr.ro/download/decizii_de_admitere/Decizie_466_2019.pdf accessed 29 December 2019.

in 2018.[75] The judgments of the Constitutional Court are always enforced. However, there are two examples of delaying the enforcement of these decisions. In one, the President delayed the dismissal of the chief-prosecutor of the National Anti-Corruption Directorate and in another, a decision declaring the unconstitutionality of some provisions of the Law on the election of the President was published after a month in order to allow the first round of the presidential elections of 2019 to unfold.[76]

2.8 Alternative dispute resolution

In Romania, there are three ways to settle a legal dispute outside the court system: alternative dispute resolution on consumer rights (ADR), mediation, and arbitration. Consumer rights are protected in both domestic and cross-border disputes by the ADR procedure carried out according to Government Ordinance no. 38 of 2015, by the ADR entity organized within the National Authority for Consumer Protection. The trader who violates the consumer rights has to be based in Romania. For consumer disputes on banking services, there is a special ADR entity called Centre for Alternative Disputes Resolution in Banking Field.[77] For disputes concerning financial services other than banking, there is SALFIN[78]. On 2 July 2018, the ADR entity organized within the National Authority for Consumer Protection was recognized as such by the European Commission. After this, the ADR entity organized within the National Authority for Consumer Protection decided nine cases.[79] Thus, in 2018, the Centre for Alternative Disputes Resolution in Banking Field received 1,293 complaints, compared with 505 in 2017.[80] 550 of them became cases and were decided, compared with 214 in 2017.[81] SALFIN received 232 complaints in 2018, compared to 197 in 2017, and decided 140 of them.[82]

75 Constitutional Court of Romania, 'Centralizing Statistical Table Decisions per Attribution', available at https://www.ccr.ro/statistica/ [RO] accessed 29 December 2019.

76 Decision no.66 of October 1, 2019 on the appeal filed against the Decision of the Central Electoral Bureau no. 32 / D of September 27, 2019 regarding the application of the provisions of art. 17 para. (1) lit. c) the first thesis of Law no. 370/2004 for the election of the President of Romania. Text published in the Official Gazette, Part I no. 907 of November 8, 2019.

77 'Alternative Dispute Resolution', available at https://www.eccromania.ro/en/information/ask-the-expert/alternative-dispute-resolution/#1484175468582-4d2fc8a0-734a accessed 29 December 2019.

78 'Attributions', available at http://www.salfin.ro/secretariatul-tehnic/ [RO] accessed 29 December 2019.

79 National Authority for Consumer Protection, 'Activity Report 2018' 18–19, available at https://anpc.ro/galerie/file/544/2019/raport_anpc_2018.pdf [RO] accessed 29 December 2019.

80 CADRBF Activity Report at 31 December 2017, available at https://csalb.ro/rapoarte-csalb/raport-anual-csalb-31-12-2017/ [RO] accessed 29 December 2019.

81 CADRBF Activity Report at 31 December 2018, available at https://csalb.ro/rapoarte-csalb/raport-de-activitate-csalb-la-31-12-2018/ [RO] accessed 29 December 2019.

82 SALFIN Activity Report 2018, p. 6, available at http://www.salfin.ro/wp-content/uploads/2019/03/Raport-privind-activitatea-desf%C4%83%C8%99urat%C4%83-de-entitatea-SAL-Fin-%C8%99i-de-Colegiul-de-Coordonare-a-acesteia-%C3%AEn-anul-2018.pdf [RO] accessed 29 December 2019.

Mediation is possible in any dispute on civil, commercial, family or penal matters, in the consumer protection sector, in labour cases, and in any other matters[83]. In criminal matters, mediation can decide the case only for crimes where the criminal action is brought to justice by a prior complaint, or where reconciliation removes criminal liability. In this field, the mediation agreement should be concluded before the reading of the bill wherein the case was sent to trial.[84] There are few statistical records on mediation. In criminal matters, in the first semester of 2017, there were 70 mediation agreements and 48 cases were decided by mediation.[85] In the first semester of 2018, in criminal matters, there were 53 mediation agreements and 42 cases decided by mediation.[86] In 2018, there were 50 cases of medical malpractice pending in the mediation procedure.[87]

Arbitration is provided for in the Romanian Civil Procedure Code. Romania is party to the most important conventions on the matter.[88] There are specialized arbitration courts, such as the Court of International Commercial Arbitration, attached to the Romanian Chamber of Commerce and Industry of Bucharest,[89] or the arbitration courts of the local chambers of commerce. All these courts have the same arbitration procedure, provided for in the Rules on Arbitral Proceedings of the International Court of Commercial Arbitration.[90] The decisions delivered by ADR entities or by arbitrators can be challenged before the ordinary courts in a fixed term, while the mediation agreement can be enforced only if it is approved by a notary public or by an ordinary court.

For the moment, the Romanian public is reluctant to use extrajudicial conflict resolution on a large-scale in spite of information campaigns. The general trend towards ordinary

83 For more details, see 'Mediation Romania', available at https://gettingthedealthrough.com/area/54/jurisdiction/73/mediation-romania/ accessed 29 December 2019. Mediation is regulated by Law No. 192/2006 and the Mediation Council is an autonomous legal entity that organizes and supervises this activity.

84 Ilie Dorin and Parascheva Dorin, 'Efectele Deciziei CCR privind acordul de mediere penală. De lege ferenda', available at https://www.juridice.ro/457306/efectele-deciziei-ccr-privind-acordul-de-mediere-penala-de-lege-ferenda.html accessed 29 December 2019.

85 Notice No. 1919/C/282/2017 of the Public Ministry, 'Prosecutor's Office attached to the High Court of Cassation and Justice. The statistical situation regarding the mediation agreements and the cases resolved as a result of their conclusion on units of public prosecutors, in the first semester of 2017', p. 2, available at: https://www.cmediere.ro/page/1879/b-situatia-statistica-privind-acordurile-de-mediere-si-a-cauzelor-solutionate-ca-urmare-a-incheierii-acestora-pe-unitati-de-parchet-in-semestrul-i-2017- [RO] accessed 29 December 2019.

86 Notice No. 1920/C/42/2018 of the Public Ministry. 'Prosecutor's Office attached to the High Court of Cassation and Justice. Statistical situation regarding mediation agreements and cases resolved as a result of their conclusion on units of public prosecutors, in the first semester of 2018' 2, available at: https://www.cmediere.ro/page/2102/b-va-comunicam-situatia-statistica-privind-acordurile-de-mediere-si-a-cauzelor-solutionate-ca-urmare-a-incheierii-acestora-pe-unitati-de-parchet-in-semestrul-i-2018- [RO] accessed 29 December 2019.

87 Mugur Bogdan Mitroi, 'Crește numărul cauzelor de malpraxis medical soluționate prin intermediul medierii', available at https://www.cmediere.ro/page/2076/b-creste-numarul-cauzelor-de-malpraxis-medical-solutionate-prin-intermediul-medierii- accessed 29 December 2019.

88 'Arbitration Romania', available at https://gettingthedealthrough.com/area/3/jurisdiction/73/arbitration-romania/ accessed 29 December 2019.

89 Established by Law no. 335 of 2007.

90 These rules are available at the Court of International Commercial Arbitration: http://arbitration.ccir.ro/arbitration-rules/ accessed 29 December 2019.

litigation can be explained by the novelty of ADR in Romania as well as by the historical tradition, by the confidence in the effectiveness of judgments compared with arbitral awards or with mediation agreements and sometimes by pecuniary consideration.

3. Norm production

3.1 Legislation

Romanian law is part of the Romano-Germanic legal tradition. That means that codified law plays the key role among the legal sources.[91] The most notable codified laws are the Civil Code, the Criminal Code, the Civil Procedure Code, and the Criminal Procedure Code[92].

The Civil Code (Law no. 287 of 2009) replaces the former Civil Code of 1864, The Family Code (1954) and the Commercial Code (1887), as well as the Private International Law Act no. 105 of 1992.[93] This Code is a legal source for civil law, family law, business law, and private international law (Book VII). It is inspired by the Civil Codes of Quebec, Brazil, Switzerland, and Germany.[94]

The Criminal Code (Law no. 286 of 2009) replaces the Criminal Code of 1969, though it keeps its structure.[95] It is inspired by the criminal law legislation in Germany, Spain, Portugal, France, and Holland.[96]

The Civil Procedure Code (Law no. 134 of 2010) replaces the Code of 1865. Its provisions cover the civil, business, employment, family, as well as international litigations. It holds special provisions for arbitration, both national (Book IV, Articles 541–621)

---

91 For the differences between Common Law and Romano-Germanic Law, see Ismail Jama, 'On the differences between Common Law & Romano-Germanic Law (Civil Law)', available at https://www.academia.edu/9381113/On_the_differences_between_Common_Law_and_Romano-Germanic_Law_Civil_Law_ accessed 29 December 2019.

92 The Criminal Procedure Code (Law no. 135 of 2010) replaces the Code of 1969. It is inspired by the criminal procedure acts of Germany, Italy, France, Spain, Belgium, and Greece, as well as from the relevant jurisprudence of the European Court of Human Rights against Romania. The principles of the new Criminal Procedure Law are studied in Costin-Ion Udrea, 'The Principles of New Criminal Procedure Code' (2015) no. 3 *Journal of Law and Administrative Science 124*. For details, see the Explanatory Memorandum of the Code of Criminal Procedure [RO], pp. 1, 4, 13, 14, and 23, available at https://www.juridice.ro/wp-content/uploads/2015/07/Expunere-de-motive-Proiectul-Legii-privindCodul-de-procedura-penala-forma-transmisaParlamentului.doc accessed 29 December 2019.

93 Daniel Buda, 'The Administrative Reform in Romania: The New Civil Code and the Institution of Marriage' (2012) no. 36E *Transylvanian Review of Administrative Sciences* 28, 28.

94 Explanatory Memorandum of the Law on the Implementation of the Civil Code [RO] p. 11, available at https://www.juridice.ro/wp-content/uploads/Cod-civil-expunere-de-motive.doc accessed 29 December 2019.

95 On the changes introduced in the Romanian Criminal Law by the new code, see Mihai Adrian Hotca, 'The New Romanian Criminal Code-Changes Suggested in the General Part', pp. 49–59, available at http://cks.univnt.ro/uploads/cks_2012_articles/index.php?dir=01_legal_sciences%2F&download=cks_2012_legal_sciences_art_007.pdf accessed 29 December 2019.

96 Explanatory Memorandum of the Criminal Code [RO], pp. 4, 9, 17, and 27, available at https://www.avocatnet.ro/articles/download/27594dd98162e6a0f16f508136c53140 accessed 29 December 2019.

and international (Title IV of Book VII).[97] It was inspired by relevant jurisprudence of the European Court of Human Rights against Romania, by EU regulations and by the civil procedure codes of Italy, Finland, Switzerland, Germany, and Holland, as well as by the Latin America Draft for a Civil Procedure Code (Latin America Institute for Civil Procedure) and by the Principles of Transnational Litigation (American Law Institute and UNIDROIT).[98]

Ordinary laws and government emergency orders are important legal sources for regulating all other aspects of Romanian society. Sometimes, government emergency orders are used as an expedient in order to modify organic laws, such as the codes, especially the Criminal Code and the Criminal Procedure Code. However, according to Article 115 of the Constitution, these orders are subjected to the approval of the Parliament by virtue of law and to the restrictions provided for them in Paragraph 6 of the same Article. They cannot regulate in fields concerning constitutional laws, the essential institutions of the state, constitutional rights and liberties, etc. On 8 October 2019, there were 2,171 emergency orders in force.[99]

The possibility to regulate by special laws and by Government emergency orders has triggered a legislative effervescence. For instance, during the year 2018, in the Official Gazette, Part I, 348 statutes were published, which is nearly a statute per day.[100] On 8 October 2019, there were 6,898 statutes in force.[101]

The preparatory works of the Romanian sources of law are not publicly available (for instance, the preparatory works for the Civil Code – Law no. 287 of 2009 have not been published so far)[102]. Therefore, jurists do not use them as supplements for legislation.

3.2 Court rulings

Belonging to the Romano-Germanic legal tradition, case law is not considered a legal source. However, as discussed below (in the section on the degree of internationalisation), Romanian law gives priority to EU law and is regularly amended in order to comply with the case law of the European Court of Human Rights and of the Court of Justice of the European Union. Being party to the European Convention on Human Rights,[103] Romania is obliged to comply with the case law of the European Court of

97 Articles 1111–1133 of the Civil Procedure Code.

98 Explanatory Memorandum of Law no. 134 of 2010, Code of civil Procedure [RO], p. 18, available at https://www.juridice.ro/wp-content/uploads/2011/05/Expunere-de-motive-proiect-LPA-CPC.doc accessed 29 December 2019.

99 In Romania there are 2,171 GEOs in force, 6,898 laws, and 1,015 simple ordinances, see https://www.g4media.ro/statistica-vedem-just-in-romania-sunt-in-vigoare-2-171-de-oug-uri-6-898-legi-si-1-015-ordonante-simple.html [RO] accessed 29 December 2019.

100 According to Notice No. R547/29 March 2019 of the Legislative Council.

101 Cfr. n 99.

102 For details, see Mădălin Niculeasa, 'Despre contextul noului Cod civil (I). Nevoia de context', available at https://www.juridice.ro/165466/despre-contextul-noului-cod-civil-nevoia-de-context-i.html accessed 29 December 2019.

103 Ratified by Law no. 30 of 18 May 1994.

Human Rights.[104] The decisions of this court are directly binding and can be used as a legal source directly in Romanian courts, even if they do not directly concern Romania.[105] Moreover, since 1 January 2007, European Union law has become mandatory, surpassing Romanian law.[106] In order to ensure the uniform interpretation and enforcement of European Union law, the case law of the Court of Justice of the European Union can be used directly in Romanian courts.

Judgments of the Constitutional Court enjoy the legal status shown above. That means that Romanian laws have to be learned and enforced in accordance with the interpretation offered by these judgments. Therefore, summaries of such judgments are published in small letters beneath the corresponding article of law. However, Constitutional Court judgments only amputate the law. They do not provide new articles of law to replace unconstitutional ones. Only the Parliament can make new rules, in accordance with the guidelines stated in the judgment. However, Constitutional Court judgments have a repealing effect on laws when their provisions violate the Constitution and if the Parliament does not replace the unconstitutional provision within 45 days after the publication of the judgment.

Concerning other Romanian national laws, Art. 1 of the Civil Code does not provide for precedent as a legal source of civil law. However, certain court practice is used when interpreting the vagueness of statutes. E.g. the judgments of the High Court given in the procedural form of review in the interest of law or as a preliminary ruling in clarifying certain legal aspects must be taken into account by subordinated courts. This means that the interpretation of an article of law given by the High Court, object to review or clarification of certain legal aspects, is binding for all courts as of the date the judgment is published in Part I of the Official Gazette of Romania.

When an article of law is differently interpreted by courts and enforced in a contradictory way, that provision must become the object of a review in the interest of law. That means that the High Court is summoned to offer a uniform interpretation of that provision. This interpretation then becomes mandatory for all other Romanian courts. The judgment given in the review in the interest of law has no retroactive effect.[107] The review in the interest of law is triggered on the request of the Ministry of Justice, the General Prosecutor of the Prosecutor's Office attached to the High Court, the collegial management of the High Court or of a certain court of appeal, and of the Ombuds-

104 See 'Country Profile: Romania', available at https://www.echr.coe.int/Documents/CP_Romania_ENG.pdf; and Law no. 30 of 18 May 1994 [RO], available at http://www.cdep.ro/pls/legis/legis_pck.htp_act_text?idt=14340 accessed 29 December 2019.

105 Mihai Șandru, 'Despre traducerile hotărârilor Curții Europene a Drepturilor Omului (CEDO): paradoxul accesibilității' 2, available at http://beta.ier.ro/documente/arhiva_evenimente_2013/Jurisprudenta_CEDO_diseminare_IER_8_feb.pdf accessed 29 December 2019.

106 See EU Law, available at https://e-justice.europa.eu/content_eu_law-3-en.do?init=true accessed 29 December 2019.

107 Liana Gabriela Gheorghiu, 'Recursul în interesul legii-izvor de drept. Aplicarea deciziilor interpretative în timp' 5, available at http://revcurentjur.ro/old/arhiva/attachments_200634/recjurid063_48F.pdf accessed 29 December 2019.

man[108]. In the context of the enforcement of four new important codes of laws, reviews in the interest of laws are numerous. The decisions are published in the Official Gazette of Romania, and their abstracts are introduced as appendices to the text of the statute, so that citizens be able to find out the correct interpretation. If such an interpretation of the law is overlooked by a court, the judgment of that court can be overturned in appeal or in review, constituting an error in the enforcement of law.

The procedure of preliminary rulings in clarifying certain legal aspects is triggered by a panel of the High Court, of a court of appeals or of a tribunal competent to settle the case as a last resort. The clarification of legal aspects is binding for the court having requested such clarification as of the date the judgment was returned and for other courts as of the date the judgment is published in Part I of the Official Gazette of Romania.[109] These judgments are considered by the Romanian legal doctrine an auxiliary legal source,[110] which means that they might shed light on the issue but they do not have any binding character.

3.3 Customary law

According to Article 1 Paragraphs 2-6 of the Civil Code of 2009, custom is considered a legal source only in case the situation is not regulated by a written law, an increasingly rare occasion considering the legislative inflation.[111] Where the case is regulated by legislation, the custom applies only by the delegation of the written statute. Only customs that are compatible with public policies and good practices will be considered as relevant by the civil courts. The interested party is obliged to prove the custom, apart from customs published in the collected works of the authorized entities in that field of activity. The custom can be overturned by a contrary proof. Furthermore, custom is considered a legal source only in commercial relations among professionals.

In the context of the recent enactment of the four important codes, doctrine has gained more importance. It has many ways of expression: treatises or courses, commentaries, alphabetical or systematic repertoire of case law, monographs, studies, and papers. Currently, doctrine is considered an indirect source of law.[112] Moreover, the influence of legal doctrine on legislation is often an indirect one. The members of the legislative body, called upon to enforce the statutes have been trained and influenced by the doctrine.

---

108 'Review in the interest of law', available at https://legeaz.net/dictionar-juridic/recurs-in-interesul-legii [RO]; 'Jurisdiction – Panels for the Settlement of Appeals in the Interest of Law', available at http://www.scj.ro/en/604/Jurisdiction. Both accessed 29 December 2019.

109 Jurisdiction – Panels for Clarification of Legal aspects, available at http://www.scj.ro/en/1085/Jurisdiction accessed 29 December 2019.

110 Niemesch (2014) (n 72) 116; Marius Andreescu, 'Aspecte privind constituționalitatea recursului în interesul legii și a deciziilor pronunțate în această procedură.', available at https://www.juridice.ro/90021/aspecte-privind-constitutionalitatea-recursului-in-interesul-legii-si-a-deciziilor-pronuntate-in-aceasta-procedura.html accessed 29 December 2019.

111 Marilena Uliescu, 'Despre legea civilă' in Marilena Uliescu (ed), *Academia Română. Institutul de Cercetări Juridice. Departamentul de Drept Privat "Traian Ionașcu". Noul Cod civil. Studii și comentarii* (Universul Juridic 2012) 43.

112 Niemesch (2014) (n 72) 126.

Their admission to a legal profession was allowed after a serious exam during which the ability to operate with the main ideas of the legal doctrine played a major role. Sometimes, doctrine exercises a direct influence on legislation. This was the case when the four codes were drafted by a group of experts.[113] However, all the four codes and many other Romanian statutes suffer greatly from the absence of a general responsible editor who can spot the discrepancies and the gaps and ask the authors to reach an agreement or to fill the gaps.

The practice of governmental agencies is not considered a source of law in Romania. On the contrary, it is subjected to judicial control through the procedure of administrative contentious. However, it could be considered a party to an element of the factual evidence base that must be proven using an expert. As such, the practice of governmental agencies can influence the decision of the pending case, but it will not influence the resolution of other similar cases. This practice is not mandatory for Romanian courts. Generally, governmental agencies are compelled to adapt their practice to the judicial interpretation of law.

4. Ideal of justice

In this article, the concept of ideal of justice contains two main elements: legal certainty – especially predictability of law – and individual justice.

Romanians have many sayings on justice. Three of them are revealing for the folks' ideal of justice: "The poor man's justice does not hang, as it is very light"; "Where justice is lacking, there, robbery reigns"; and "Justice is such as gentlemen want".[114] So, for Romanians, true justice means protecting the rights of the poor and feeble against the rich and powerful. Traditionally, Romanians considered that only the Prince – Vodă in Romanian – was able to prevent the noblemen from oppressing the paupers. Therefore, systematically-structured legislation has been perceived as a safeguard for individual justice. There is a saying: "Where there is law, there are no negotiations". In the Romanian collective mind, the ideal of justice means legal certainty which in turn guarantees individual justice. The Romanian historical tradition confers the role of providing justice to the State through the legislator and appointed judges.[115]

Justice is considered an important value of the Romanian state, along with human dignity, citizens' rights and liberties, free development of human personality, and the multiparty system. Romania is a state governed by the rule of law. According to the Romanian Constitution "the observance of the supremacy of the Constitution and the

---

113 Mircea Duțu, 'Noul Cod civil - o etapă importantă în dezvoltarea dreptului privat român' in Marilena Uliescu (ed), *Academia Română. Institutul de Cercetări Juridice. Departamentul de Drept Privat „Traian Ionașcu". Noul Cod civil. Studii și comentarii (*Universul Juridic 2012) 25.

114 'Sayings about Justice', available at https://www.portal-info.ro/proverbe/proverbe-despre-dreptate.html [RO] accessed 29 December 2019.

115 The role of state judges in the administration of individual justice is stressed by the saying: "If you have a judgment (a writ), you will be right".

laws is obligatory for all state bodies".[116] Thus, the constitutional principles of legality, including the principle of legality of incrimination,[117] of the citizens' equality before law and authorities[118], as well as the magistrates' duties to obey the law, to be impartial,[119] and to avoid creating binding precedents[120] are the main features of the Romanian legal culture that aim to realize the goal of legal certainty.

However, assuring certainty in the context of a legislative inflation is quite a difficult to achieve, as the relevant jurisprudence of the Constitutional Court testifies.[121] Three entities have engaged in this legal battle: the High Court through the abovementioned review in the interest of law and the request for preliminary ruling, the Legislative Council and the Constitutional Court. The Legislative Council is a consultative body of the Parliament.[122] It has two main purposes: to check the conformity of projects of normative acts – like laws, emergency orders of the Government, orders of the Government, etc. – and to keep track of the Romanian legislation.[123] In accomplishing these tasks, the Council enforces the provisions of Law no. 24 of 2000 on the legislative technique for the elaboration of normative acts. According to Article 2 Paragraph 1 of this Act, the Legislative Council ensures the systematization, unification and coordination of legislation, as well as the appropriate legal content and form for each normative act. Legislative technique rules are mandatory for draft laws promoted by the Government, legislative proposals belonging to deputies, senators or citizens, in the exercise of the right to legislative initiative, the elaboration and adoption of ordinances and decisions of the Government, as well as for the elaboration and adoption of normative acts by other authorities with similar functions (Article 3 Paragraph 1 of Law no. 24 of 2000). The law on legislative technique is enforced through the constitutionality check carried out by the Constitutional Court.

However, all three entities have only a small chance to win the battle against legal uncertainty without extensive help from all authorities concerned by the legislative process.[124] Thus, we can say that legal certainty is assured in a relative way, by law – reviewed

116 Article 1 para. 3 and 5 of the Romanian Constitution.

117 Articles 23 para. 12 of the Constitution.

118 Article 16 of the Constitution.

119 Article 124 of the Constitution for judges and 132 of the Constitution for prosecutors.

120 Article 126 paragraph 3: The High Court of Cassation and Justice shall provide the other courts of law with a unitary interpretation and implementation of the law, according to its competence. Article 5 paragraph 4 of the Civil Procedure Code.

121 Marieta Safta, 'Valorificarea normelor de tehnică legislativă în controlul de constituționalitate' (2016) no. 2 *Buletin de informare legislativă;* Ion Predescu and Marieta Safta, 'Principiul securității juridice, fundament al statului de drept. Repere jurisprudențiale' 9, available at https://www.ccr.ro/uploads/Publicatii%20si%20statistici/Buletin%20 2009/predescu.pdf accessed 29 December 2019.

122 This council, provided for in Article 79 of the Constitution, was established 1 April 1996 according to Law no. 73 of 1993.

123 'Legislative Council – Description', available at http://www.clr.ro/InfoPublic/Home.aspx [RO] accessed 29 December 2019.

124 Safta (2016) (n 121) 22.

by the Legislative Council and the Constitutional Court – as well as by the relevant jurisprudence of the Constitutional Court and the High Court.

On the other hand, considerations of individual justice have a prominent place in the Romanian legal system as well. E.g. Bona fides is a fundamental concept of the Romanian Law, see Article 14 Paragraph (1) of the Civil Code, according to which every person - natural or legal – is obliged to exercise her/his rights and fulfil her/his obligations with bona fides (good faith), complying with public order and good manners.[125] Legal doctrine as well as jurisprudence considers that bona fides (good faith) is presumed in any legal matter, being a principle of Civil Law.[126] As such, the principle of bona fides governs the formation of contract, its interpretation as well as its performance.[127] Bona fides is also a principle governing the exercise of civil procedural rights and obligations.[128]

As shown above, legal certainty is the central pillar of justice for Romanians. Therefore, legislative technique is regarded as the main safeguard of individual rights and liberties. In general, Romanian legislation is a mix of casuistic rules, offering limited possibilities of interpretation and general norms using broad terminology. Especially since 2009 when the new codes were drafted, the tendency to enact laws written in a language comprehensible for lay persons has been noticeable. For instance, Article 1080 Point 3 of the Civil Procedure Code contains the easily comprehensible definition of a consumer, when dealing with the exclusive international jurisdiction of the Romanian courts over consumer contracts concluded in Romania. The articles of the Civil Code on succession use the concept of deceased,[129] while the legal doctrine recommended the Latin concept of *de cuius*, etc. However, general provisions have been enacted as well, using broad concepts in need of interpretation. For instance, the choice-of-law rule in Article 2626 of the Civil Code on the law applicable to public record formalities concerning trade of goods implies broad legal concepts such as: public record formalities, goods, place of the performance of the formalities, legal ground of birth, conveyance and termination of rights in rem and law. Another example is the extensive use of the concept of habitual residence as a connecting factor in the choice-of-law rules of the Civil Code or in the international jurisdiction rules of the Code of Civil Procedure. However, the high number of laws has caused contradictions due to a lack of coordination in the legislative process. Therefore, the need for interpretation and disambiguation of legal texts is so urgent.

Furthermore, international law has influenced the ideal of justice in Romania. This impact has facilitated the idea that law shall be fair next to being predictable. How-

---

125 Article 57 of the Constitution and Article 14 paragraph (1) of the Civil Code.

126 Andreea Claudia Agapie, 'Quo vadis bona fides? Unde începe și unde se încheie buna-credință?', available at https://www.juridice.ro/433915/quo-vadis-bona-fides-unde-incepe-si-unde-se-incheie-buna-credinta.html accessed 29 December 2019.

127 Lucia Uță, 'Buna credință în negocierile precontractuale', available at http://www.nos.iem.ro/bitstream/handle/123456789/232/Uta%20Lucia.pdf?sequence=1&isAllowed=y accessed 29 December 2019.

128 Wolters Kluwer Blog, 'Opinii esențiale despre buna credință în reglementarea noului Cod de procedura civilă', available at https://blog.wolterskluwer.ro/opinii-esentiale-despre-buna-credinta-in-reglementarea-noului-cod-de-procedura-civila/ accessed 29 December 2019.

129 See Article 954 Paragraph 2 or the choice-of-law rule of 2633

ever, this impact is of a more indirect nature. Article 20 of the Constitution as well as Article 4 of the Civil Code and Article 3 of the Civil Procedure Code provide for the interpretation of the constitutional (civil) rights and liberties according to the Universal Declaration of Human Rights, with the covenants and other treaties to which Romania is a party. Where any inconsistencies exist between the covenants and treaties on fundamental human rights Romania is a party to on one side, and internal laws on the other, international regulations shall take precedence. The decisions of the ECHR are directly binding. Often, Romanian legislation is amended in order to keep it in line with the decisions of the ECHR. Article 5 of the Civil Code as well as Article 4 of the Civil Procedure Code provide for the priority of European Union law on the matters already regulated by Romanian legislation. Therefore, human rights and liberties as well as European Union regulations are considered general principles of Romanian law. Importing the advanced legal concepts of EU law on individual rights and fairness was regarded as a considerable improvement of Romanian Law, which was governed by a totalitarian legal regime 30 years ago.

Aiming to increase legal certainty, the Romanian legislator enacted many new laws. However, right-based conception of fairness became a source of justice too. New general principles of law, based on the prevailing legal doctrine, were established and codified. One of those were the presumption of innocence, which is provided for in the Constitution[130] and in the Criminal Procedure Code.[131] Another one is the principle of good faith or the consequences of the abuse of rights.[132] Since legal science constitutes one of the main safeguards of equity and justice in Romania, many of the *de lege ferenda* proposals made by the legal scholars have been enacted in the new codes, for instance, the criminal responsibility of legal entities[133] and the use of electronic evidence in Criminal and Civil Procedures.[134]

5. Legal method

The sources of Romanian Law are internal and international.[135] We shall start with the national sources, because they are the natural starting point for the application of law in what concerns internal conflicts. Thereafter, we will consider international law, since the Constitution defines the binding force of international treaties. However, these are treated in a special section of this paper reserved for the international legal sources. Romanian sources of law are organised hierarchically, and their legal power is proportional to their position in the legal hierarchy.

---

130 Art. 23 paragraph 11.
131 Art 4.
132 Cf. Civil Code art. 14 and 15.
133 Art. 135 to 151 of the Criminal Code.
134 Art. 138 to 147, 152 and 154 of the Criminal Procedure Code and art. 272 to 281 of the civil Procedure Code.
135 'Romania', available at https://e-justice.europa.eu/content_member_state_law-6-ro-en.do?member=1 accessed 29 December 2019.

The Constitution is Romania's supreme law. It regulates the structure of Romania as a national, unitary and indivisible State, the relations between the executive, legislative and judicial power, and between State bodies, citizens, and legal persons. All other pieces of legislation and norms must comply with the Constitution.

As explained above, an organic law is one of the laws that make up a body, which is part of the original foundation of a government or a law that regulates civil rights and liberties. Organic laws regulate areas of high importance to the State, such as the organization of Government bodies, political parties, Romanian citizenship, the rights of individuals harmed by a public authority, property and inheritance regulations, the organization and holding of referenda, criminal offences, sentences and rules on the serving of sentences, the organization and functioning of the Superior Council of Magistracy,[136] of the courts, of the Public Prosecution Service, national defense, etc. The Parliament adopts such laws by qualified majority.

Ordinary laws regulate all other areas which are not covered by organic laws. An ordinary law cannot amend or modify a norm of higher importance, such as an organic law or the Constitution, but it can be an important tool to interpret the former and can contain important elaborations. The Parliament adopts such laws by a simplified majority.

In special cases (Parliamentary recesses), certain areas – as determined by the Parliament and based on a legislative delegation – can be regulated by government orders. According to the Constitution[137], such orders are issued on the basis of a special act of empowerment, within the limits and under the conditions laid down by that act. In emergency situations, the Government can issue emergency orders in any area if considered necessary.

Government decisions determine the way laws are to be effectively implemented and other organizational aspects of their implementation. The Constitution defines these decisions as normative acts issued to organize the execution of laws.[138]

Legislative acts issued by the central government administration – orders and instructions – are issued only on the basis of and in order to implement laws, Government decisions and Government orders. Legislative acts issued by local government administration – County Councils, Local Councils, Bucharest General Council – regulate areas that fall within the competence of local government authorities. As stated above, all these laws and decisions have to comply with the rules of legislative technique provided for in Law no. 24 of 2000. Often, many legislative acts are still enacted trespassing these provisions.

---

136 The Superior Council of Magistracy is the authority that, under Articles 133 and 134 of the Constitution, is supposed to ensure the independence of justice. Furthermore, it has to ensure the observance of law and of the criteria of competence and professional ethics in the exercise of the professions of judges and prosecutors. The disciplinary court of judges and prosecutors and the entire career of a magistrate (judge or prosecutor) depends on this council. For details, see Ann Johnson and Bianca Radu, 'The Effect of E.U. Anti-Corruption Measures on the Romanian Judiciary' (2013) *International Journal of Court Administration* 1–2; see, moreover, 'Short history. Presentation', available at https://www.csm1909.ro/262/Prezentarea-consiliului accessed 29 December 2019.

137 Article 108 para. 3 of the Constitution.

138 Article 108 para. 2 of the Constitution.

Romanian law is part of the Civil Law tradition. Therefore, the main legal source is the statutory law which operates with abstract concepts. In order to find the specific statutory rules applicable to a certain case, Romanian lawyers have to make a classification. First, they have to evaluate the facts of the case in order to select, according to them, one or several statutory provisions that presumably regulate the case. Second, they have to interpret the concepts of the presumable relevant provisions in order to check whether they are applicable to the case, an operation labelled deduction. So, the facts of the case are of utmost importance both in selecting the relevant provisions and in allocating meaning to them.

Legal provisions on the interpretation of laws are scarce. According to Article 9, the creator of the civil legal rule has the power to officially interpret it. The interpretative rule produces effects only for the future. The court's interpretation of a legal rule is made only in order to apply it to the case the court has to decide. Article 10 of the Civil Code forbids the analogy of a law that derogates from the general rule by confining civil rights or which provides for civil punishments. These exceptions are of strict interpretation, being valid only for the cases provided by the rule itself. Therefore, the legal doctrine provides the interpretative tools used by Romanian jurist in order to assure fairness in the enforcement of laws. Any lecture of The General Theory of Law or of Introduction into Civil Law deals with them.[139] The interpretative methods are, from the point of view of legal texts, intrinsic – grammatical interpretation,[140] logical

139 Carmen Marilena Popa, *Teoria generală a dreptului. Manual pentru uzul studenților la forma de învățământ la distanță* (Ed. Universității "Lucian Blaga" din Sibiu 2009) 91–94.

140 Grammatical or literal interpretation is based on the processes of morphological and syntactic analysis of the text, starting from the grammatical meaning of the words used. This involves the previous clarification of legal terminology. The meaning of some terms and expressions used in a legal text may be the same as in the ordinary language or it may be different.

interpretation,[141] extrinsic – systematic interpretation,[142] historic interpretation,[143] teleological interpretation,[144] and analogy.[145]

The gaps of law are filled by legal doctrine, analogy and case law of the Constitutional Court and the High Court, given by the latter in the review in the interest of law and in the request for preliminary ruling.

Romanian doctrine distinguishes between two categories of analogy: first, analogy of rule – applying the rule to similar cases not covered by legislation and second, analogy of law – using legal principles in order to regulate a case for which no other existing rule could be applied using analogy.[146] Analogy should be used only as an interpretative method of a particular statute, in order to cover an unintended gap in legislation and not as a creative method meant to repair the defects of the written law. Otherwise the interpreter would infringe the upon the domain of the legislator. In Civil law, the analogy is allowed in both forms.[147] However, even in this field, the analogy of a law that derogates from the general rule, by confining civil rights, or which provides for civil punishments, is forbidden (Article 10 of the Civil Code). In criminal law, the doctrine is not unitary on the matter. Some consider that analogy is forbidden, because it violates the principle of legality.[148] Others consider that analogy is allowed only in favour of the defendant, for instance in case of mitigating circumstances.[149]

---

141 Logical interpretation is based on the application of rules of formal logic.

142 Systemic/systematic interpretation is based on establishing the meaning of some rules on their correlation with other norms, either belonging to the same legal institution or branches of law or belonging to different institutions or branches. The need to apply the systemic method arises from the systemic character of the law of a state, constituting not a mere sum of rules, but a unit made up of interdependent parties.

143 Historical interpretation is based on research of historical, social-political conditions, etc. that determined the adoption of a normative act (*occasio legis*) and according to the conditions on the determination of the goals pursued by the legislator (*ratio legis*). This involves the study of the sources of documentation, of the preparatory materials for the adoption of the act, of the explanatory statement, of discussions that took place during the debate on the respective act in the parliament, the press, or the specialized papers. If the normative act has a preamble and an introduction, these in themselves provide the information necessary in order to establish the causes and purposes of the elaboration of the act.

144 Teleological interpretation is based on the purpose of the normative act interpreted. This requires the creativity of the interpreter. By its nature, the teleological method demands its use in parallel with others, because the legislator's intention can also be found by corroborating the norm with other norms and by analysing the context of its adoption and referring to its letter.

145 Niemesch (2014) (n 72) 150–152; Carmen Lazăr, 'Sinteza: Metodele de interpetare din teoria generală a dreptului', available at https://codfiscal.net/1000/sinteza-metodele-de-interpretare-din-teoria-generala-a-dreptului accessed 29 December 2019.

146 For details, see Maria Irina Grigore-Rădulescu, 'Analogia legii și analogia dreptului. Aspecte teoretice și consecințe practice' (2014) no. 6 *Pandectele române 37*.

147 Articles 1 paragraph 2 of the Civil Code and Article 5 paragraph 3 of the Civil Procedure Code.

148 Mihai Adrian Hotca, 'Aspecte teoretico-practice privind principiul legalității incriminării', available at http://www.hotca.ro/index.php/blog-post/aspecte-teoretico-practice-privind-principiul-legalitatii-incriminarii/ accessed 29 December 2019.

149 Ibid; Ana Maria Sângeorzan, 'Drept penal general' 2, available at http://www.hotca.ro/index.php/blog-post/aspecte-teoretico-practice-privind-principiul-legalitatii-incriminarii/ accessed 29 December 2019; Constantin Sima, 'Principiul legalității-fundamentul dreptului penal modern' (2016) no. 1 *Revista Pro Lege*, available at http://revistaprolege.ro/principiul-legalitatii-fundamentul-dreptului-penal-modern/ accessed 29 December 2019.

The jurisprudence of the Constitutional Court and of the High Court that are considered secondary sources of law, interpret the statutes, filling their gaps or removing the unconstitutional provisions. Accordingly, the central function of the Romanian legal method is to allocate legal provisions to the facts of the case. Therefore, interpreting the law, using sometimes analogy and sometimes definitions offered by the High Court or the Constitutional Court plays a major role in deciding a case. It is worth mentioning that preparatory works are not considered sources of law and there is no doctrine of *stare decisis*, since case law is not considered a binding source of law.

6. Professionalisation

In order to practice law in Romania a 4-year university degree in law is required.[150] Academic legal studies are just one requirement for practicing law in Romania; the more important ones are to pass the admission exam and to accomplish the training period provided by law for each legal profession. Because of the great number of graduates in law, these exams are very difficult to pass.

After the Revolution of December 1989, legal studies have become the backbone of private universities. Well-paid jobs available at the time in the legal field along with the strict admission exams of traditional public universities made many choose to study law in private universities that were newly established. Therefore, in 2011, there were 42 law faculties in the country, 40 of them being ranked by the Ministry of National Education according to the confidence their legal curricula inspired by accomplishing strict legal criteria.[151] At present, four of the law faculties ranked are in liquidation.[152]

It is worth mentioning that, according to Government Decision no. 115 of 2018, on the academic year 2018-2019, all the 36 faculties of law are allowed to enroll students in the first year of study, thus totaling 12,150 students. Trying to get an image of the

---

150 This requirement is provided for in Law no. 303 of 2004 on the status of judges and prosecutors (Article 14), in Law no. 51 of 1995, consolidated (Article 12) for the organization and practice of the profession of lawyer, in Law no. 514 of 2003 for the organization and practice of the profession of legal adviser (Article 8), in Law no. 36 of 1995 consolidated (Article 16) for notaries public, in Law no.188 of 2000, consolidated, on legal enforcement officers (Article 15) and in Law no. 567 of 2004 for clerks of the court (Article 33). For the latter legal profession, the university exam in law is required only for hearing clerks, statistician clerks and research clerks. Even legal assistants can be appointed but only if they have a university degree in law (Article 2 of Government Decision no. 616 of 2005).

151 The hierarchy of curricula organized by accredited universities in the national education system according to art. 193 of the National Education Law no. 1/2011 and the provisions of Government Decision no. 789/2011 regarding the approval of the Evaluation Methodology for the Classification of Universities and the Ranking of Study Programmes' [RO], 33 and 34, available at http://chestionar.uefiscdi.ro/docs/programe_de_studii.pdf. See, moreover, Ioana Vlad, 'Vrei să studiezi Dreptul? De ce facultăți să te ferești', available at https://www.avocatnet.ro/articol_26446/Vrei-sa-studiezi-Dreptul-De-ce-facultati-sa-te-feresti.html accessed 29 December 2019.

152 'Accredited private higher education institutions', available at https://www.edu.ro/institutii%20de%20inv_superior%20particulare%20acreditate [RO] accessed 29 December 2019. The fact that in 2018 four faculties were in liquidation is attested by Government Decision no. 115 of 2018, Annexes 3 and 6.

popularity of legal education in Romania, the reader is invited to focus on the first four faculties of Law benefiting from the highest reputation, according to the Ministry of National Education: the faculties of the University of Bucharest, of Alexandru Ioan Cuza University in Iași, of Babeș-Bolyai University in Cluj, and of Lucian Blaga University in Sibiu.

In the academic year 2016-2017, the Faculty of Law of the University of Bucharest had 3,150 students in the Bachelor degree programme, and 539 in the Master programme.[153] At present, the Faculty of Law of the University of Iași has 1,952 students in all the programmes of study.[154] The Faculty of Law Simion Bărnuțiu of Babeș-Bolyai University had in the academic year 2017–2018, 2,268 students, while in the academic year 2016-2017, it had 2,243 students[155]. The Faculty of Law Simion Bărnuțiu of the University Lucian Blaga in Sibiu has, in the academic year 2018–2019, 1,037 students – 907 enrolled in the Bachelor's degree programme and 130 in the Master's programme.[156]

On the matter of law professors, the situation is also complicated. The existing 42 faculties of Law have many professors, some being involved in several private universities. The total number is unknown at present, and we shall hence focus on the number of professors teaching in the first four faculties mentioned above. Thus, Faculty of Law of the University of Bucharest has 73 full tenured professors and 64 non-tenured professors.[157] The Faculty of Law of the University of Iași has 36 full-tenured professors, while the non-tenured professors are 63 in number.[158] The Faculty of Law of Babeș-Bolyai University has 43 full-tenured professors[159]. The Faculty of Law Simion Bărnuțiu of the University Lucian Blaga of Sibiu has 45 professors, including non-tenured professors.[160]

All of these faculties have admission exams comprising an evaluation of the Romanian language level and the grade obtained to the final exam of the high school (*baccalaureate*) is taken into account.

Bachelor studies have a duration of four years. The Master programme comprises one year. PhD studies have a duration of three years. PhD education is a prerequisite in order to work in academia. Magistrates and other jurists paid by the state are encouraged to

153 University of Bucharest. Faculty of Law, 'Self-Assessment Report 2016–2017', Annex no. 4, available at https://drept.unibuc.ro/dyn_doc/despre-noi/Raport%20autoevaluare%202016-2017.pdf [RO] accessed 29 December 2019.

154 According to the Faculty of Law, see http://www.uaic.ro/en/studies/faculties/faculty-law/ accessed 29 December 2019.

155 According to Notification No. 299/22 April 2019 of the Faculty of Law of "Babeș-Bolyai" University of Cluj.

156 These data were obtained through the courtesy of Adrian Circa, Associate Professor of the Faculty of Law "Simion Bărnuțiu" of the University "Lucian Blaga" of Sibiu.

157 University of Bucharest. Faculty of Law, 'Self-Assessment Report 2016–2017', Annex no. 4, available at https://drept.unibuc.ro/dyn_doc/despre-noi/Raport%20autoevaluare%202016-2017.pdf [RO], corroborated with the counting of individual professors mentioned in the lists provided at https://drept.unibuc.ro/Departamentul-de-drept-public-s16-ro.htm; https://drept.unibuc.ro/Departamentul-de-drept-privat-s17-ro.htm; and https://drept.unibuc.ro/Departamentul-de-drept-penal-s18-ro.htm, both accessed 29 December 2019.

158 'Faculty of Law' at http://www.uaic.ro/en/studies/faculties/faculty-law/ accessed 29 December 2019.

159 According to Notification No. 299/22 April 2019 of the Faculty of Law of "Babeș-Bolyai" University of Cluj.

160 These data were obtained through the courtesy of Adrian Circa, Associate Professor at the Faculty of Law "Simion Bărnuțiu" of the University "Lucian Blaga" in Sibiu.

complete the PhD education by a monthly allowance granted to holders of PhD titles in the amount of 50% of the minimum gross basic salary.[161] Therefore, the appeal of PhD studies for lawyers, notaries public and judicial enforcement officers is considerable smaller.

Courses are generally taught in the form of lectures. The Socratic Method is considered insufficient, because of the need to transmit strict provisions of different laws. At the moment, Romanian law professors struggle to strike the correct balance between the Socratic method and the need for legal exactitude. Every lecture is accompanied by seminars. The attendance to seminars is mandatory in order to be accepted to the corresponding exam. During seminars, case law is debated, papers written by students on designated matters are presented, and students' theoretical knowledge is tested.

Undergraduate studies are accomplished by a four-hour final exam in criminal law, criminal procedure, civil law and civil procedure. Students who pass this exam have to defend their Bachelor thesis.

Professors consider jurisprudence as an important auxiliary material in teaching the main concepts of a certain branch of Romanian Law. In addition, they use case law during tutorial classes in order to train their students to apply theoretical knowledge. In writing their articles or papers, legal scholars pay considerable attention to case law, criticizing or praising certain trends. Students are eager to learn the algorithm of landmark cases because difficult and sometimes ambiguous cases are part of admission exams in almost all legal professions. However, the amount of case law is influenced by the branch of law which is studied.

At present, each major branch of law has its own legal journal. The majority of these journals, with the exception of the two bulletins of jurisprudence (of the High Court of Cassation and of the courts of appeal) are also eager to publish papers written by foreign legal scholars.

A brief survey of the websites of the major legal publishing houses, such as Universul Juridic, Hamangiu, C.H. Beck or Wolters Kluwer, shows that the Romanian legal literature is quite rich.[162]

At the beginning of his/her practice within the profession, a lawyer must perform a 2-year training, during which he/she has the status of trainee lawyer.[163] The conditions in which the training is performed, the rights and obligations of the trainee lawyer, as well as the bar to which he/she belongs are regulated by the by-laws of the profession. The trainee lawyer is compelled to attend the lectures of the National Institute for Training and Further Training of Lawyers.[164] The trainee lawyer's practice in district courts or tribunals is supervised by a qualified lawyer having at least six years seniority in that capacity and enjoying

161 'Minimum Gross Basic Salary in the Country Guaranteed in Payment in 2019' [RO], available at http://www.mmuncii.ro/j33/images/Date_lunare/s1-2019.pdf accessed 29 December 2019.

162 For Universul Juridic, see https://www.ujmag.ro/; for Hamangiu, see https://www.hamangiu.ro/noutati-editoriale; for C.H. Beck, see https://www.beckshop.ro/; for Wolters Kluwer (who is focusing on building digital legal libraries and databases), see https://wolterskluwer.ro/. All links accessed 29 December 2019.

163 Law no. 51 of 1995 consolidated (Article 18).

164 Article 289 of the Regulation of lawyers' profession. For details, see the Institute website at http://www.inppacentral.ro/despre-noi-2/ accessed 29 December 2019.

an intact professional reputation.[165] After the training, the trainee lawyer will undergo the final examination, where court practice plays a major role. A trainee lawyer rejected three times at the final examination will be automatically excluded from the profession.

Judges and prosecutors, too, have to complete two practice-based training periods. After passing the admission exam organized by the National Institute of Magistracy (I.N.M. in Romanian), the student becomes an auditor of justice.[166] The auditor has to perform a 4-year training comprising a one-year theoretical training and a three-year practical training. After graduating from the National Institute of Magistracy, auditors have to choose from the available positions of trainee judge or trainee prosecutor.[167] The trainee judge or prosecutor has to perform another two-year training under the guidance of a senior judge or prosecutor. During this training period, practice plays the major role.[168] After the training, the trainee judge or prosecutor will undergo the final examination where her/his practical skills are verified. A trainee judge or prosecutor rejected two times at the final examination will lose the position and she/he will be compelled to refund the stipend cashed as auditor of justice.[169] All these exams are organized by the National Institute of Magistracy. The advancement of judges and prosecutors is possible only through a national examination organized by the National Institute of Magistracy on behalf of the Superior Council of Magistracy.[170]

We can conclude by stating that the degree and attitude towards professionalisation in the Romanian legal profession is relatively high. Legal education focuses on law as formed by the legislative framework and legal doctrine. Case law is studied in order to understand the underlying legal principles when applying the law, but not as an authoritative source of law.

7. Internationalisation

Historically, foreign legal sources played a major role in teaching law in Romania. In the 17th century, the Byzantine Law along with Prospero Farinacci's writings were extensively used in two collection of laws printed by Metropolitan bishops at the order of princes of Moldavia and Wallachia: 'The Romanian Book of Learning from the Imperial Laws and Other Judicial Authorities' (Moldavia, 1646) and the 'Guidance of the Law by God That Has All the Canon and Imperial Judicial Authorities on All the Priestly and Secular Crimes' (Walachia, 1652).[171] In the 18th century, Roman-Byzantine law was adapted to the reality of the time in the Law Manuals by Mihail Fotino Photinopoulos (1765, 1766, 1777), Dumitrache

165 Article 19 of Law no. 51 of 1995.

166 Article 16 of Law no. 303 of 2004.

167 Article 21 of Law no. 303 of 2004.

168 Article 23 of Law no. 303 of 2004.

169 Article 25 of Law no. 303 of 2004.

170 Cernat (2017) (n 22) 26–29.

171 Cosmin Dariescu, *Istoria statului și dreptului românesc din antichitate până la Marea Unire* (C.H. Beck 2008) 109; Cosmin Dariescu and Nadia Cerasela Dariescu, 'Incrimination of Ravishment in 17th Century Walachia' 5, available at https://uaic.academia.edu/CosminDariescu accessed 29 December 2019.

Panaiotache Catardzi-Fotiade (1793) or by Toma Carra (1806). In the 19th century, Byzantine Law inspired Andronache Donici in his legal handbooks published in 1814,[172] while the French Civil Code of 1804 and the French doctrine, especially J. A. Rogron's writings, were used by Ioan Bărbătescu in his book entitled 'Course of Romanian Civil Law' in order to explain the choice-of-law rules used in Wallachia around 1849.[173] In the 20th century, professor Dimitrie Alexandresco used many examples from foreign law in his monumental work 'Theoretical and Practical Explanation of the Romanian Civil Code' in 12 volumes[174] and in 'The Principles of Romanian Civil Law' in four volumes.[175]

At present, the use of foreign legal sources in Romanian legal education differs depending on the branch of law that is studied. Thus, for public international law,[176] EU law, private international law,[177] constitutional law,[178] etc., legal sources from abroad are considered to a great extent, while their role is negligible for teaching domestic branches as criminal law,[179] civil law,[180] family law, etc.

The Romanian Constitution of 1991 provides that the Romanian State has to fulfil as such and in good faith its obligations deriving from all international treaties, enacted by the appropriate body.[181] Treaties ratified by Parliament, according to the law, are part of national law. Thus, international treaties must be incorporated into law by the Parliament. In other words, Romania follows the dualistic approach to international law.

Covenants and treaties on fundamental human rights to which Romania is a party have a special effect. Where any inconsistencies exist between them and internal laws, international regulations shall take precedence.[182]

---

172 Dan Constantin Mâță, 'The Development of Romanian Legal Science (1814–1940)' in Zoran Pokrovac (ed), *Rechtswissenschaft in Osteuropa. Studien zum 19. und fruhen 20. Jahrhundert* (Vittorio Klostermann 2010) 213–215.

173 Cosmin Dariescu, 'Private International Law Principles of Walachia in the First Half of the 19th Century (Principii de drept internațional privat valah din prima jumătate a secolului al XIX-lea)' (Romanian) (29 April 2009). A XVIII-a Conferință Științifică Anuală cu Participare Internațională "Tradiție și Reformă în Dreptul Românesc", Iași, May 29–31, 2008. Available at SSRN: https://ssrn.com/abstract=1396608 or http://dx.doi.org/10.2139/ssrn.1396608 accessed 29 December 2019.

174 The book was republished by Universul Juridic Publishing House in 2018. See https://www.ujmag.ro/drept/drept-civil/pachet-explicatiunea-teoretica-si-practica-a-dreptului-civil-roman-set-14-titluri-12-tomuri accessed 29 December 2019.

175 Mâță (2010) (n 172), 259–260.

176 Carmen Moldovan, *Drept internațional public. Principii și instituții fundamentale* (Hamangiu 2017) 74–104.

177 Adrian Circa, 'Eficacitatea hotărârilor străine' in Ioan Leș, Călina Jugastru, Verginel Lozneanu and others (eds), *Tratat de drept procesual civil. Vol. II* (Universul Juridic 2015) 890–893 and 957–980; Cosmin Dariescu, *Fundamentele dreptului internațional privat*. Ediția a V-a revăzută și adăugită (Universul Juridic 2018) 79–97, 167–173, 177–180 and 211–216.

178 Marius Bălan, *Drept constituțional și instituții politice. Vol. 1. Teoria generală a statului și a constituției. constituția română în context european (*Hamangiu 2015) 186–187 and 342, etc.

179 Ancuța Elena Franț, *Întreruperea cursului sarcinii. Repere juridice și etice* (Universul Juridic 2016) 424.

180 However, even in these branches, some foreign legal sources are studied. For instance, EU law is presented in Carmen Tamara Ungureanu, *Drept civil. Partea generală. Persoanele (*Hamangiu 2012) 21–22 or in Luiza-Cristina Gavrilescu, *Drept civil. Partea generală* (Universul Juridic 2015) 23.

181 Article 11 of the Constitution.

182 Article 20 paragraph 2 of the Constitution.

Being a member of the Council of Europe since 1993, Romania has to comply with the case law of the European Court of Human Rights.[183] The decisions of this court are directly binding and can be used as legal source directly in courts[184]. Especially in criminal law cases, ECtHR judgments are often cited. They are seldom used in civil cases, and particularly here in procedural matters.

Romania has been a member of the European Union since 1 January 2007. Therefore, the European Union law has become an integral part of the Romanian legal culture.[185] Citizens of the European Union member states can invoke rights provided for by EU law in Romanian courts. Also, EU law prevails over Romanian law.[186] Article 148 of the Constitution provides for the precedence of EU law and compels the Parliament, the President, the Government, and the judicial authorities to enforce this priority.

The jurisprudence of the Court of Justice of the European Union can be used directly in Romanian courts in order to ensure the application and uniform interpretation of European Union law.[187] Regularly, Romanian law is changed in order to fit the demands of the European Court of Human Rights and of the Court of Justice of the European Union. Sometimes these changes can stir up internal troubles on the violation of the ECHR in terms of detention conditions. A law was enacted that allows prisoners held in crowded prisons to apply for a reduction of detention days. Thus, many prisoners have been released. Unfortunately, this law has boosted recidivism.[188]

8. Conclusion

Romania is a civil law country, with codified legislation which is the primary source of law. Case law has persuasive but not binding authority. However, the case law of the Constitutional Court, of the High Court (in the review in the interest of law or as preliminary ruling) and the jurisprudence of the ECtHR and CJEU have binding effects in national courts, meaning that the court is not allowed to set aside international law even if it contradicts a clear wording of a national provision.

183 Ratified by Law no. 30 of 18 May 1994. See 'Country Profile: Romania', available at https://www.echr.coe.int/Documents/CP_Romania_ENG.pdf, accessed 29 December 2019; and Law no. 30 of 18 May 1994 [RO], available at http://www.cdep.ro/pls/legis/legis_pck.htp_act_text?idt=14340, accessed 29 December 2019.

184 See Article 20 of the Constitution (that gives precedence to the ECHR) and Șandru (n 105) 2.

185 See Article 148 of the Constitution (that provides for this precedence and compels the Parliament, the President, the Government and the judicial authority to enforce this priority) and 'EU Law', available at https://e-justice.europa.eu/content_eu_law-3-en.do?init=true accessed 29 December 2019.

186 See 'International Law', available at https://e-justice.europa.eu/content_international_law-10-en.do accessed 29 December 2019.

187 For more details on the changing position of the Romanian Constitutional Court on the prevalence of EU Law, see Viorica Viță, 'The Romanian Constitutional Court and the Principle of Primacy: to Refer or Not to Refer?' (2015) vol. 16, issue 6, *German Law Journal* 1623.

188 See the Pilot Decision in *Rezmives and Others v Romania* App. No. 61467/12 *et al.* (ECtHR, 25 April 2017).

Romanian Legal Culture and its structures and structural elements					
Institutional structure		**Intellectual structure**			
Conflict resolution	**Norm production**	**Ideal of justice**	**Legal method**	**Degree of professionalisation**	**Degree of and attitude towards internationalisation**
A single hierarchy of general courts with specialized sections or panels. There are only four specialized tribunals. A Constitutional Court, separated from the court hierarchy, with jurisdiction limited to constitutional review and conflict resolution among state powers.	A hierarchical system of statutes, with the Constitution on top. Four codes of law accompanied by a great number of special laws. Mandatory force of the jurisprudence of the Constitutional Court and of the High Court (in the review in the interest of law or as preliminary ruling).	Romania is a rule of law. Legal certainty is difficult to achieve in the context of legislative inflation. Good faith is a fundamental concept. Fairness is assured by the priority of the Constitution, of international legal sources on human rights, as well as of EU law.	First, evaluation of the facts of the case in order to select some statutory provisions. Second, interpretation of the concepts of the relevant provisions (deduction). The legislation is interpreted by intrinsic and extrinsic interpretation methods. The gaps of the law are filled by legal doctrine, analogy, and the case law of the Constitutional Court and of the High Court of Cassation and Justice.	To practice law in Romania, one needs a 4-year university degree and has to pass a difficult admission exam. To practice as a lawyer, one has to perform a 2-year training and undergo a final exam. To practice as a judge/prosecutor, one has to complete two training periods: a 4-year training period, at the I.N.M., and a 2-year training period as a trainee judge/prosecutor and undergo a final examination.	The Romanian legal system is dualist. The covenants and treaties on fundamental human rights to which Romania is a party take precedence over internal law. European Union law is mandatory and prevails over internal law. Judgments from ECtHR and CJEU are directly applied in courts. Regularly, Romanian law is changed in order to fit the demands of the ECHR and ECJ. The use of foreign legal sources in legal education differs depending on the branch of law that is studied.

9. Bibliography

Agapie AC, 'Quo vadis bona fides? Unde începe și unde se încheie buna-credință?', available at https://www.juridice.ro/433915/quo-vadis-bona-fides-unde-incepe-si-unde-se-incheie-buna-credinta.html accessed 29 December 2019.

Andreescu M, 'Aspecte privind constituționalitatea recursului în interesul legii și a deciziilor pronunțate în această procedură.', available at https://www.juridice.ro/90021/aspecte-privind-constitutionalitatea-recursului-in-interesul-legii-si-a-deciziilor-pronuntate-in-aceasta-procedura.html , accessed 29 December 2019.

Bălan M, *Drept constituțional și instituții politice. Vol.1. Teoria generală a statului și a constituției. constituția română în context european* (Hamangiu 2015).

Buda D, 'The Administrative Reform in Romania: The New Civil Code and the Institution of Marriage' (2012) no. 36E *Transylvanian Review of Administrative Sciences* 28.

Cernat CS, *Organizarea profesiilor juridice. Ediția a II-a revizuită și completată* (Brașov 2017).

Circa A, 'Eficacitatea hotărârilor străine' in Ioan Leș, Călina Jugastru, Verginel Lozneanu and others (ed), *Tratat de drept procesual civil. Vol. II* (Universul Juridic 2015).

Coroban C, *The Geography of Romania. Manual for Secondary Education* (Cambridge School of Constanța 2013).

Dariescu C, *Istoria statului și dreptului românesc din antichitate până la Marea Unire* (C.H. Beck 2008).

—— 'Private International Law Principles of Walachia in the First Half of the 19th Century (Principii de drept internațional privat valah din prima jumătate a secolului al XIX-lea)' (Romanian) (29 April 2009). A XVIII-a Conferință Științifică Anuală cu Participare Internațională "Tradiție și Reformă în Dreptul Românesc", Iași, May 29–31, 2008. Available at SSRN: https://ssrn.com/abstract=1396608 or http://dx.doi.org/10.2139/ssrn.1396608 accessed 29 December 2019.

—— *Fundamentele dreptului internațional privat.* Ediția a V-a revăzută și adăugită (Universul Juridic 2018)

—— and Dariescu NC, 'Incrimination of Ravishment in 17-th Century Walachia', available at https://uaic.academia.edu/CosminDariescu accessed 29 December 2019.

Dorin I and Dorin P, 'Efectele Deciziei CCR privind acordul de mediere penală. De lege ferenda', available at https://www.juridice.ro/457306/efectele-deciziei-ccr-privind-acordul-de-mediere-penala-de-lege-ferenda.html accessed 29 December 2019.

Duțu M, 'Noul Cod civil - o etapă importantă în dezvoltarea dreptului privat român' in Uliescu M (ed), *Academia Română. Institutul de Cercetări Juridice. Departamentul de Drept Privat "Traian Ionașcu". Noul Cod civil. Studii și comentarii* (Universul Juridic 2012).

Franț AE, *Întreruperea cursului sarcinii. Repere juridice și etice* (Universul Juridic 2016).

Gavrilescu LC, *Drept civil. Partea generală* (Universul Juridic 2015).

Gheorghiu LG, 'Recursul în interesul legii-izvor de drept. Aplicarea deciziilor interpretative în timp', available at http://revcurentjur.ro/old/arhiva/attachments_200634/recjurid063_48F.pdf accessed 29 December 2019.

Gîfu, D, *Lexical Semantics in Text Processing. Contrastive Diachronic Studies on Romanian Language*, PhD thesis, "Alexandru Ioan Cuza" University of Iași, Romania, 2016.

Gîfu D, 'Diachronic Evaluation of Newspapers Language between Different Idioms' in Larry Brinbaum, Octavian Popescu and Carlo Strapparava (eds), *IJCAI 2016 Workshop. Natural Language Processing meets Journalism. Proceedings of the Workshop* (2016)

Grigore-Rădulescu MI, 'Analogia legii și analogia dreptului. Aspecte teoretice și consecințe practice' (2014) no. 6 *Pandectele române* 37

Hotca MA, 'Aspecte teoretico-practice privind principiul legalității incriminării', available at http://www.hotca.ro/index.php/blog-post/aspecte-teoretico-practice-privind-principiul-legalitatii-incriminarii/ accessed 29 December 2019.

—— 'The New Romanian Criminal Code-Changes Suggested in the General Part', available at http://cks.univnt.ro/uploads/cks_2012_articles/index.php?dir=01_legal_sciences%2F&download=cks_2012_legal_sciences_art_007.pdf accessed 29 December 2019.

Jama I, 'On the differences between Common Law & Romano-Germanic Law (Civil Law)', available at https://www.academia.edu/9381113/On_the_differences_between_Common_Law_and_Romano-Germanic_Law_Civil_Law_ accessed 29 December 2019.

Johnson A and Radu B, 'The Effect of E.U. Anti-Corruption Measures on the Romanian Judiciary', (2013) *International Journal of Court Administration*.

Lazăr C, 'Sinteza: Metodele de interpretare din teoria generală a dreptului', available at https://codfiscal.net/1000/sinteza-metodele-de-interpretare-din-teoria-generala-a-dreptului accessed 29 December 2019.

Leş I, 'Consideraţii generale asupra căilor legale de atac' in Leş I, Jugastru C, Lozneanu V and others (eds), *Tratat de drept procesual civil. Vol. II* (Universul Juridic 2015).

—— and Sebastian Spinei, 'Recursul' in Leş I, Jugastru C, Lozneanu V and others (eds), *Tratat de drept procesual civil. Vol. II* (Universul Juridic 2015).

Mâță DC, 'The Development of Romanian Legal Science (1814–1940)' in Pokrovac Z (ed), *Rechtswissenschaft in Osteuropa. Studien zum 19. und fruhen 20. Jahrhundert* (Vittorio Klostermann 2010).

Mihăilescu I, Ielinicz M, Ionac N, Erdely G and others (eds), *Romania. Geography and Tourism* (Royal Company Publishing House 2001).

Moldovan C, *Drept internaţional public. Principii şi instituţii fundamentale* (Hamangiu 2017).

Neagu I and Damaschin M, *Tratat de procedură penală. Partea specială* (Universul Juridic 2015).

Niculeasa M, 'Despre contextul noului Cod civil (I). Nevoia de context', available at https://www.juridice.ro/165466/despre-contextul-noului-cod-civil-nevoia-de-context-i.html accessed 29 December 2019.

Niemesch M, *Teoria generală a dreptului* (Hamangiu 2014).

Popa CM, *Teoria generală a dreptului. Manual pentru uzul studenţilor la forma de învăţământ la distanţă* (Ed. Universităţii "Lucian Blaga" din Sibiu 2009).

Predescu I and Safta M, 'Principiul securităţii juridice, fundament al statului de drept. Repere jurisprudenţiale', available at https://www.ccr.ro/uploads/Publicatii%20si%20statistici/Buletin%202009/predescu.pdf accessed 29 December 2019.

Safta M, 'Valorificarea normelor de tehnică legislativă în controlul de constituţionalitate' (2016), no. 2, *Buletin de informare legislativă*.

Săhlean A, 'Curtea Constituţională: Codul penal este parţial neconstituţional', available at https://newsweek.ro/justitie/judecatorii-ccr-codul-penal-este-partial-neconstitutional accessed 29 December 2019.

Şandru M, 'Despre traducerile hotărârilor Curţii Europene a Drepturilor Omului (CEDO): paradoxul accesibilităţii', available at http://beta.ier.ro/documente/arhiva_evenimente_2013/Jurisprudenta_CEDO_diseminare_IER_8_feb.pdf accessed 29 December 2019.

Sângeorzan AM, 'Drept penal general', available at http://www.hotca.ro/index.php/blog-post/aspecte-teoretico-practice-privind-principiul-legalitatii-incriminarii/ accessed 29 December 2019.

Şaramet O, 'Powers of the President of Romania in Relationship with Government' (2016), no. 1 *Agora International Journal of Juridical Sciences* 23.

Scurtu I (coordinator), Stănescu-Stanciu T and Scurtu GM, *România între anii 1918–1940. Documente şi materiale* (Ed. Universităţii Bucureşti 2001).

Sima C, 'Principiul legalităţii-fundamentul dreptului penal modern' (2016) no. 1, *Revista Pro Lege*, available at http://revistaprolege.ro/principiul-legalitatii-fundamentul-dreptului-penal-modern/ accessed 29 December 2019.

Simion M, 'Constitutional Legal Disputes between the President of Romania and Other Public Authorities in the Case-Law of the Constitutional Court of Romania' (2017), no. 2, *AGORA International Journal of Juridical Sciences*.

Udrea CI, 'The Principles of New Criminal Procedure Code' (2015), no. 3, *Journal of Law and Administrative Science* 124.

Uliescu M, 'Despre legea civilă' in Uliescu M (ed), *Academia Română. Institutul de Cercetări Juridice. Departamentul de Drept Privat "Traian Ionașcu". Noul Cod civil. Studii și comentarii* (Universul Juridic 2012).

Ungureanu CT, *Drept civil. Partea generală. Persoanele* (Hamangiu 2012).

Uță L, 'Buna –credință în negocierile precontractuale', available at http://www.nos.iem.ro/bitstream/handle/123456789/232/Uta%20Lucia.pdf?sequence=1&isAllowed=y accessed 29 December 2019.

Vasile Bâgiu L, *Introduction in the Study of Romanian Language. A Textbook for Foreign Students* (Aeternitas 2018).

Viță V, 'The Romanian Constitutional Court and the Principle of Primacy: to Refer or Not to Refer?' (2015), vol. 16, issue 6, *German Law Journal* 1623.

Vlad I, 'Vrei să studiezi Dreptul? De ce facultăți să te ferești', available at https://www.avocatnet.ro/articol_26446/Vrei-sa-studiezi-Dreptul-De-ce-facultati-sa-te-feresti.html accessed 29 December 2019.

Vrabie C, 'Rolul CSM, ICCJ Și MP Față De Politicile Publice Din Justiție', 2014, available at www.onoratainstanta.ro accessed 29 December 2019.

10. Official notices

1. Notice No. 27427/28. 03.2019 of the Ministry of Justice.
2. Notice No. R547/29.03.2019 of the Legislative Council.
3. Notice No. 299/22.04.2019 of the Faculty of Law of "Babeș-Bolyai" University of Cluj.
4. Notice No. 1919/C/282/2017 of the Public Ministry. Prosecutor's Office attached to the High Court of Cassation and Justice. Statistical situation regarding mediation agreements and cases redecided as a result of their conclusion on units of public prosecutors, in the first semester of 2017. https://www.cmediere.ro/page/1879/b-situatia-statistica-privind-acordurile-de-mediere-si-a-cauzelor-solutionate-ca-urmare-a-incheierii-acestora-pe-unitati-de-parchet-in-semestrul-i-2017-.
5. Notice No. 1920/C/42/2018 of the Public Ministry. Prosecutor's Office attached to the High Court of Cassation and Justice. Statistical situation regarding mediation agreements and cases resolved as a result of their conclusion on units of public prosecutors, in the first semester of 2018. https://www.cmediere.ro/page/2102/b-va-comunicam-situatia-statistica-privind-acordurile-de-mediere-si-a-cauzelor-solutionate-ca-urmare-a-incheierii-acestora-pe-unitati-de-parchet-in-semestrul-i-2018-.

17. A View of the Legal Culture of the United States of America

Lloyd T. Wilson, Jr.

1. Introduction

From the outset, the topic of *the* legal culture of the United States presents a problem of perspective. On the one hand, the American system of federalism means that instead of one legal culture, there are at least fifty-one legal cultures – the culture of the national legal system and the culture of the legal systems of the fifty states, each of which exercises sovereignty.[1] At the same time, however, even as the dual legislative systems, dual executive systems, and dual judicial systems operate separately, they also operate in reference to each other. In that sense, the fifty-one separate legal cultures form a single legal culture. As this chapter will attempt to show, both perspectives – fifty-one legal cultures and a single legal culture – are accurate. Understanding both perspectives is indispensable for understanding *the* legal culture of the United States.

Geography, demographics, history, and government structure make up the wider context for the legal cultural landmarks of the United States. Geography and demographics help provide an understanding of the people who participate in the legal culture of the United States and are served by it. History and the structure of our government explain the complexity of our legal culture.

1.1 Geography and Demographics

Geographically, two facts stand out. The first is size. The U.S. is the third largest country in the world comprising 9.8 million square km. The distance from the eastern shore of Maine to the western coast of Washington State is approximately is 4,414 km; the

1 The reference here to "states" actually understates the situation with regard to the existence of separate legal systems as the District of Columbia, which is not a state, and five territories – American Samoa, Guam, the Northern Mariana Islands, Puerto Rico, and the U.S. Virgin Islands – are part of the larger legal system of the United States. See https://www.uscourts.gov/about-federal-courts/court-role-and-structure accessed 11 April 2020. The special circumstances of the District of Columbia and the territories are not discussed in this chapter, but additional information can be found in "Developments in the Law" (2017) Vol. 130 *Harvard Law Review* 1617.

1.2 History

Understanding a country's contemporary legal culture requires an appreciation of that country's past.[16] History is relevant to the legal culture of the United States because of the laws, practices, and concepts inherited from Great Britain or developed in response to colonial rule by Great Britain.[17] In broad outline, early U.S. history can be divided into two phases, the colonial period and the period following independence.

The Anglo-centric version of U.S. history begins with the founding of the first English colony in Jamestown, Virginia in 1607. Over the next century, additional colonies were authorized by royal charter, with all but one of the thirteen original colonies being founded in the 17th century. During the colonial period, people living in the colonies considered themselves to be subjects of the British monarch. When the colonists drafted documents for colonial government, they expressly utilized English models, including principles set forth in the Magna Carta. When tensions arose between the colonies and Great Britain, the relief sought by many colonists was not separation but instead was recognition of their rights as British subjects. Only when such recognition and equal treatment were denied did separation assume primacy, resulting in the Declaration of Independence on July 4, 1776.[18]

Prior to 1776, the status of the thirteen colonies is clear – they were colonies of Great Britain. What may be less obvious is the status of the former colonies after independence. It is easy to view a former colony, Virginia for example, as transitioning from colony to "state," as in one of the fifty states that currently make up the United States. This view misstates the situation. The "United States" as we think of it today did not assume its current government and legal structure until ratification of the Constitution on June 21, 1788, with government under that document commencing on March 4, 1789. An earlier attempt at creating a national government began with approval of the Articles of Confederation by the First Continental Congress on November 15, 1777. The weaknesses of the national government as it was established by that document led to the 1789 Constitution, which created the government and legal structure of the U.S.

---

16 For books about American history from a broader perspective, consider Eric Foner, *The Story of American Freedom* (W.W. Norton & Co. 1998); Ted Morgan, *Wilderness at Dawn: The Settling of the North American Continent* (Simon & Schuster, Inc. 1993). For an accessible and insightful account of U.S. history, especially from the first settlements to the early 20th century, written by a non-American, see Winston Churchill, *The Great Republic: A History of America* (Random House 1999). For an extended narrative and analysis of four great waves of immigration to the U.S. from Great Britain and their impact on American culture, both in general and legal, see David Hackett Fischer, *Albion's Seed: Four British Folkways in America* (Oxford University Press 1989). The four waves voluntary immigration are the immigration of Puritans to Massachusetts (1629 to 1641), Cavaliers and indentured servants to tidewater Virginia (1642 to1675), Quakers to Pennsylvania and the Delaware River basin (1675 to 1725), and English and Scots from the borderlands to the backwoods regions of Virginia and North Carolina (1717–1775).

17 A volume that focuses on the development of law in the U.S. is Lawrence M. Friedman, *A History of American Law* (4th ed., Oxford University Press 2019).

18 Anthony Arlidge, *The Lawyers Who Made America: From Jamestown to the White House* (Hart Publishing 2017), Preface ("Those who opposed the actions of the British government started by claiming their rights as British subjects. This was not surprising – The Virginia Charter was drawn by English lawyers and all the early colonies insisted they remained British subjects."); 76 ("Like other revolutionaries [Thomas Jefferson's] initial claim was to his rights as an Englishman; independence was not his starting point.").

that remains in place today. However, an important question remains: what was the legal status of the former colonies between independence and the Articles of Confederation?

The answer is that the former colonies were indeed "states" but in the sense of nation-states, each with sovereignty and independence – from each other and from all other nation-states – equal to that enjoyed by other nations in the world. The treaty signed with Great Britain at the end of the War for Independence provided that the "British government relinquished all authority over the territories in America" and that "the 13 American states were recognized as sovereign nations."[19] This fact is crucial because the "aboriginal existence" of the states is the source and explanation of the distinctive brand of federalism practiced in the U.S. Because the states existed first, it is the states that created the national government, and it is the states that determined the powers the national government would have and would not have. This relationship is known as vertical federalism and will be seen to be a defining force in the topics discussed in this chapter.

Upon independence, the states "received" English common law as the basis for their own legal systems.[20] In doing so, the American states began their existence with the benefits of a legal system that had developed and matured over centuries and included high respect for law, for the lawyers and judges who practiced it, and for the academics, like Blackstone, who studied it. Of course, the American states also introduced some dramatic innovations.

1.3 Government Structure

The complexities of the legal culture of the United States have their origin in the structure of government established by the Framers of the Constitution.[21] Because of their retained sovereignty, each state makes its own laws, executes its own laws, and adjudicates its own laws independent of each other and largely independent of the national government. At the same time, the national government carries out similar law-making, law-executing, and law-adjudicating functions. Thus, one might be tempted to conclude that it is not possible to talk about *a* government structure for the U.S. However, there is indeed a structure, but it is not unitary or vertically arranged. Instead, the structure is both disaggregated and overlapping.

When the states designed the government structure for their new union, perhaps the most central issue was power. How would power be allocated and distributed? The Framers of the 1789 Constitution devised two mechanisms to answer this question: fed-

19 Ibid. 72 (referring to the Treaty of Paris, 3 September 1783, that concluded the American war for independence.)

20 For the history of the common law in both Great Britain and the U.S., including the reception and recasting of English legal principles in America, see John H. Langbein, Renee Lettow Lerner and Bruce P. Smith, *History of the Common Law: The Development of Anglo-American Legal Institutions* (Aspen/Walters Kluwer 2009).

21 "Framers" is a term used to describe the leaders involved in debating the issues involved in establishing an independent American government and in drafting the crucial documents, such as the Declaration of Independence, the Constitution, and the Federalist Papers.

eralism and separation of powers.[22] Both are indispensable to understanding American legal culture. In fact, one could reasonably assert that all significant legal questions in the U.S. can be connected to these two concepts.

Federalism comes in two forms – horizontal federalism and vertical federalism. Horizontal federalism describes the relationships among the fifty states, each of which is sovereign and independent of the others. Vertical federalism describes the relationship between the federal government[23] and the governments of the states. Horizontal federalism cannot be ignored, especially with regard to the Full Faith and Credit Clause, found in Article IV, § 1 of the Constitution, which requires each state to recognize and enforce the official acts of all other states, but the impact of horizontal federalism has received less scholarly inquiry than the impact of vertical federalism.[24]

An important impact of vertical federalism is that the Constitution confers only limited legislative power on Congress. Article I, § 8 of the Constitution, known as the Enumerated Powers Clause,[25] lists seventeen specific subjects about which Congress is authorized to make law. Many of these subjects relate to actions one would expect to be taken by a national government, such as levying and collecting taxes, coining money, establishing a postal service, providing for an army and a navy, protecting patents, conducting diplomatic affairs, and regulating commerce with foreign nations and among the states.

However, many legal subjects are not found in the Enumerated Powers Clause, which means those subjects are within the authority of the states. Subjects absent from the Enumerated Powers Clause, and thus beyond Congress' direct authority, include

---

22 Neil M. Gorsuch, Associate Justice of the U.S. Supreme Court, makes the structures and organization established by the Framers and the resulting allocation of power the central topics of his book, *A Republic, If You Can Keep It* (Crown Forum 2019).

23 The relationship between the national government and the states under vertical federalism is often described in terms like "friction" and "counterbalance to power." In "The Benefits of Regulatory Friction in Shaping Policy" (2016) Vol. 71 Issue 2 *Food and Drug Law Journal* 228, Diana R. H. Winters says that friction is often said to be undesirable because it is viewed through a "lens of adversity." Professor Winters argues that friction is also beneficial since the strata of regulation made possible by vertical federalism create a space of foment for policy change and for democratic engagement and allows the national government and the states to strengthen each other by filling gaps. The counterbalance aspect of vertical federalism is discussed in Ronald D. Rotunda, "Vertical Federalism, the New States" Rights, and the Wisdom of Crowds' (2016) Vol. 11 *Florida International University Law Review* 307.

24 Horizontal federalism has begun to attract an increasing amount of scholarly attention in recent years. For example, Heather K. Gerken and Ari Holtzblatt, "The Political Safeguards of Horizontal Federalism" (2014) Vol. 113 Issue 1 *Michigan Law Review* 88 offers a "trans-substantive" account of horizontal federalism by which the "ineluctable friction" arising from the "spillovers" that arise when the effect of one state's law intruding on another state is resolved by political as opposed to judicial means. In a similar vein, see Heather K. Gerken, "The Taft Lecture: Living Under Someone Else's Law" (2016) Vol. 84 Issue 2 *University of Cincinnati Law Review* 377. A systematic scrutiny of horizontal federalism is the goal of Allan Erbsen, "Horizontal Federalism" (2008) Vol. 93 Issue 2 *Minnesota Law Review* 493.

25 Even though Congress may not have authority to directly legislate in an area outside the enumerated powers, Congress can exert immense indirect influence on the states by way of a principle known as "conditional spending." This principle means that the federal government pledges to disburse large sums of money to the states provided the states enact laws consistent with Congressional wishes. Conditional spending explains why the states have uniform laws on seat belt use and on the minimum age to consume alcohol. In both matters, conformity with Congressional wishes was a pre-condition to the disbursement of federal funds.

matters relating to tort law, contract law, property law, domestic relations law, business organizations law, and law regulating professions (including the legal profession).

Because each state is independent of the others, one effect of federalism on the legal culture of the United States is the variation, often significant, in law from state-to-state. As Supreme Court Justice Louis Brandeis famously observed, this variation enables a situation in which states function as "laboratories of change."[26] Individual states can experiment with legislative or judicial responses to social issues. If a state's experiment is unsuccessful, only that state is affected, and other states know not to try the same response. If a state's experiment is successful, other states can emulate it. In this independence to experiment, one can see an advantage of horizontal federalism. Recently, Judge Jeffrey S. Sutton of the Sixth Circuit Court of Appeals noted the benefits of the states' ability to act independently in terms of vertical federalism. Specifically, Judge Sutton analyzes cases in American legal history in which state supreme courts have surpassed the federal courts in recognizing and protecting citizens' rights. He compared such jurisprudential leadership with what he sees as the all-to-prevalent practice of state courts following the federal courts in lockstep, thereby abdicating the authority and responsibility state supreme courts have under state constitutions. Ultimately, Judge Sutton advocates that rights protection is a responsibility shared by federal and state courts since neither court system alone is sufficient for the task. This idea is the source of the book's title, *51 Imperfect Solutions*.[27]

The weight of vertical federalism is felt by the judicial branch of the federal government in the form of a limitation on the subject matter jurisdiction of federal courts, which is set forth in Art. III, § 2 of the Constitution. This topic is discussed in detail in the section below on conflict resolution. In short, just as Congress has limited legislative competence, the federal courts have limited judicial competence, since federal courts are authorized to hear only two kinds of cases.

In addition to limiting the powers granted to the federal government in Articles I and III, the states also emphasized their retained sovereignty in the Bill of Rights.[28] The 10th Amendment provides that "[t]he powers not delegated to the United States by the Constitution, nor prohibited by it to the States, are reserved to the States respectively, or to the people." However, even as the states reserved wide-ranging powers, they also delegated significant power to the federal government. The Supremacy Clause, found in Article VI of the Constitution, states:

> "This Constitution, and the Laws of the United States which shall be made in Pursuance thereof; and all Treaties made, or which shall be made, under the Authority of the

26 "It is one of the happy incidents of the federal system that a single courageous State may, if its citizens choose, serve as a laboratory, and try novel social and economic experiments without risk to the rest of the country." *New State Ice Co. v. Liebmann*, 285 U.S. 262, 311 (1932) (Brandeis, J., dissenting).

27 Jeffrey S. Sutton, *51 Imperfect Solutions: States and the Making of American Constitutional Law* (Oxford University Press 2018).

28 The Bill of Rights is the name given to the first ten Amendments to the Constitution.

> United States, shall be the supreme Law of the Land; and the Judges in every State shall be bound thereby, any Thing in the Constitution or Laws of any State notwithstanding."

The complexity of the American government structure, and hence of the American legal culture, should now be becoming apparent. The picture that emerges is one of a legal culture consisting of: (1) legislative, executive, and judicial branches of government existing concurrently at the federal and state levels, (2) some law-making powers placed exclusively in the federal government, (3) extensive law-making powers retained by the individual states, and (4) the opportunity for conflicts between state and federal law in areas where federal law and state law overlap.

1.4 Separation of Powers

The second foundational principle of government organization and thus of American legal culture is the doctrine of separation of powers, also known as the system of checks and balances. As with vertical federalism, the issue behind the system of checks and balances is the distribution and diffusion of power. The Constitution assigns certain duties and powers to each branch of government. The system of checks and balances is designed to ensure that no branch exceeds its allocated powers and that the branches are kept "in their proper places."[29] This is done by giving each branch "power over" the other two branches.

Vertical federalism and separation of powers are the two most important landmarks of American legal culture. However, these landmarks have not remained static since the Constitution was ratified by the states. In fact, these principles exhibit dramatic activity, with the balances struck by vertical federalism and separation of powers trending in different directions at different times, always dynamic and in dialectic tension. Contemporary manifestations of that tension are felt throughout the American legal system.

2. Conflict Resolution

Conflict resolution is everywhere a principal function of courts. For federal courts in the U.S. legal system, however, conflict resolution is the only function, since these courts are constitutionally limited to acting on "cases or controversies," which means actual disputes between parties who have a direct stake in the outcome of a dispute.[30] As a result, federal courts are prohibited from rendering advisory opinions, including opinions about whether legislation or administrative action would be unconstitutional if enacted or executed. Some state courts operate under a similar restraint; other state constitutions do not contain a cases-or-controversies limitation; in still other states, courts use a "standing" requirement

29 James Madison, "The Federalist No. 51" in *The Federalist Papers* (Isaac Kramnick Ed., Penguin Books 1963) 319. Because the governments of the fifty states are likewise organized into three branches of government, the principles of separation of powers and checks and balances are also observed by the states.

30 The origin of the cases or controversies requirement is Art. III, § 2 of the U.S. Constitution. The requirement of "standing" can also be used to the same effect in state courts.

or similar principle as a basis for refusing to render advisory opinions. Conflict resolution does not occur only in the courts, however. Increasingly, parties resolve disputes in the U.S. using various methods that come under the umbrella term of alternative dispute resolution (ADR),[31] a topic discussed at the end of this section.

Understanding conflict resolution within the court systems of the U.S. requires discussion of three topics: competency, organization, and procedure. Competency refers to the kinds of cases a particular court is authorized to hear, i.e., a court's subject matter jurisdiction. Organization refers to the hierarchy of courts and their interrelationship. Procedure includes two additional landmarks of American legal culture – the adversary system and the jury system.

2.1 Competence of Courts

Any discussion of the competence of courts in the United States runs headlong into the doctrine of vertical federalism. Because the states retained a significant portion of their aboriginal sovereignty, each state has its own court system separate from the federal court system. For the purposes of this chapter, the existence of both state and federal court systems has two repercussions. First, the federal and state court systems must be discussed separately since they are fundamentally different. That is the nature of vertical federalism. Second, the variations among the court systems of the states mean that any discussion of state courts must necessarily involve generalizations. The generalizations made about the state court systems below are valid, but any reader who delves deeper into the court system of any particular state should expect to find differences. That is the nature of horizontal federalism.

The first thing to note about the competence of courts in the United States is that federal courts are "courts of limited jurisdiction" while state courts are "courts of general jurisdiction." Understanding these labels begins with Article III, § 2 of the Constitution. This section provides that federal courts are competent to hear only two kinds of cases: (1) cases based on "federal question jurisdiction," which includes cases that "arise under" the U.S. Constitution, an act of Congress, a regulation issued by a federal administrative agency, or a treaty with another nation, cases affecting ambassadors, public ministers and consuls, and cases of admiralty and maritime jurisdiction, and (2) cases based on "diversity of citizenship jurisdiction," which exists when a dispute is between citizens of different states or between a citizen of a state and a foreign national.[32] Unless one of those two bases for jurisdiction exists, the federal courts are not available to resolve conflicts. Instead, the litigants must utilize the state court system.

31 The American Bar Association identifies twelve processes of Alternative Dispute Resolution. The most well-known are arbitration, mediation, early neutral evaluation, and mini-trial. See https://www.americanbar.org/groups/dispute_resolution/resources/DisputeResolutionProcesses/ accessed 15 July 2019.

32 Congress has placed a limitation on the availability of diversity jurisdiction by imposing a threshold requirement that the amount in controversy must exceed $75,000. 28 U.S.C. § 1332. The federal courts have imposed a second limitation in the requirement of "complete diversity" among all plaintiffs and all defendants. These requirements evidence voluntary limitations on federal court authority not demanded by Art. III, § 2.

While federal courts are courts of limited jurisdiction, state courts are courts of general jurisdiction. Unless the case relates to one of the small number of areas where federal courts have exclusive jurisdiction,[33] state courts can hear any kind of case. Accordingly, state courts are competent to hear cases based not only on state law but can also hear cases based on federal law, including cases based on the federal Constitution.[34]

2.2 Organization and Hierarchy of Courts

Unlike the fundamental distinctions between federal and state courts with regard to competence, the two court systems share many similarities with regard to organization, hierarchy, and functions. Both systems generally consist of three levels of courts: a trial court, an intermediate appellate court, and a final appellate court. The names attached to these courts vary somewhat between the federal and state systems, and among the systems of the various states, but those variations do not impair the validity of the three-tier model outlined below.

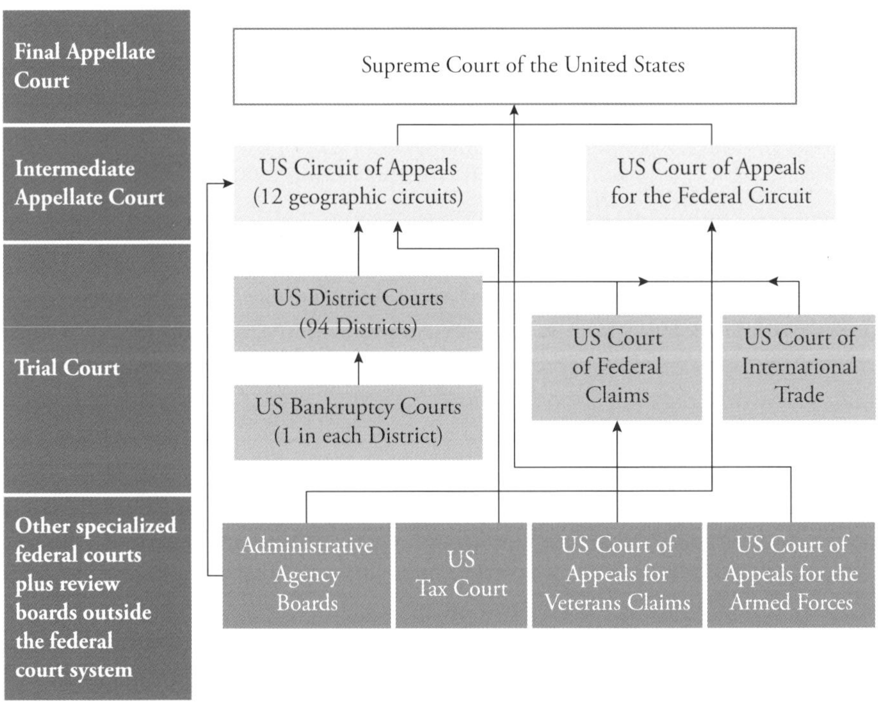

Fig. 1 The Federal Court System.

33 Federal courts have exclusive subject matter jurisdiction over a limited number of specified areas of law, including cases involving admiralty, antitrust, bankruptcy, federal crimes, intellectual property (patent and copyright), securities regulation, disputes between States, disputes involving ambassadors, and other cases specified by federal statute.

34 As noted by Samuel P. Jordan, "Reverse Abstention" (2012) Vol. 92 Issue 6 *Boston University Law Review* 1771, 1772, fn 1, state courts also are called upon to decide cases based on the law of other states and even based on international law.

2.2.1 Federal Court System – Organization

In the federal court system, the trial courts are called District Courts. The territorial boundary of each District Court is defined by a particular region within the boundaries of a state. This fact is reflected in the court's full name, e.g., United States District Court for the Southern District of Indiana, which has jurisdiction over cases originating in the southern two-thirds of that state. There are ninety-four District Courts in the federal court system. The number of District Courts in each state tends to reflect population and therefore case load. California, the most populous state, has four districts, and there are sixty-one active status judges in District Courts in that state. Twenty-six states have a single federal district. The smallest number of federal District Court judges in a state is two.[35]

Judges in the federal District Courts are generalists and are called upon to decide all manner of cases, both civil and criminal.[36] Trials in the District Courts are to a single judge or to a single judge supplemented by a jury. In addition to the general model of federal trial courts, there are two specialized trial courts in the federal system – the Court of International Trade,[37] which addresses cases involving international trade and customs laws, and the U.S. Court of Federal Claims,[38] which deals with most claims seeking money damages from the U.S. government.

The intermediate appellate court in the federal system is called a Circuit Court of Appeals. There are thirteen federal Circuit Courts of Appeals. The territorial boundary of eleven of the circuits is defined geographically by the boundaries of multiple states, ranging from three to nine. These courts are identified by number, e.g., the United States Court of Appeals for the Tenth Circuit, which hears appeals from District Courts in the states of Colorado, Kansas, Oklahoma, New Mexico, Utah, and Wyoming. The boundary of a twelfth Circuit Court of Appeals coincide with the boundaries of the District of Columbia. The thirteenth federal appellate court is the Court of Appeals for the Federal Circuit, which hears appeals from all federal District Courts in the nation concerning international trade, government contracts, patents, trademarks, certain money claims against the United States government, federal personnel, veterans' benefits, and public safety officers' benefits claims.

---

35 Data pertaining to the U.S. District Courts can be found at the official U.S. Courts website and associated links, beginning with https://www.uscourts.gov/about-federal-courts/court-role-and-structure accessed 14 November 2019. For the U.S. District Courts, an informative site is https://www.uscourts.gov/about-federal-courts/federal-courts-public/court-website-links accessed 16 July 2019. This site contains a map showing the geographic jurisdictional boundaries of the U.S. District Courts and the federal Circuit Courts of Appeal. It also contains a chart showing the number of District Courts in each state. Data for the number of judgeships authorized in each federal judicial district are found at https://www.uscourts.gov/sites/default/files/districtauth.pdf. accessed 16 July 2019.

36 In the U.S., the term "civil cases" includes all non-criminal cases, including cases brought against the national government and the governments of the states. This terminology differs from the practice in many countries where administrative cases are designated as a separate category.

37 The home page of the U.S. Court of International Trade is http://www.cit.uscourts.gov/ accessed 16 July 2019.

38 The home page of the U.S. Court of Federal Claims is http://www.uscfc.uscourts.gov/ accessed 16 July 2019.

The federal Circuit Courts hear appeals in collegial panels of three judges. Occasionally, a Circuit Court of Appeals will sit *en banc*, which means all members of the Court participate in deciding the case. For the reasons given below with regard to the function of each level of court, juries are not used in the Circuit Courts. As with federal trial courts, the number of judges in the federal Circuit Courts varies from circuit-to-circuit. The total number of authorized Circuit Court judges is 179. The Ninth Circuit has the largest number of judges, twenty-nine; the First Circuit has the fewest, six.[39]

There is one final appellate court in the U.S. – the United States Supreme Court.[40] The Supreme Court hears appeals from all federal Circuit Courts of Appeals. The Court also hears appeals of cases decided by state supreme courts where those courts decided a question of federal law or where a criminal defendant invokes federal *habeas corpus*[41] rights following conviction of a crime in a state court. The United States Supreme Court has nine justices. All appeals before the Supreme Court are heard *en banc*.

2.2.2 State Court Systems – Organization

State trial courts are generally organized on a county level, which is a political subdivision between a state and cities or towns. The number of trial courts in the states varies widely, with the number of trial courts reflecting population in the geographic region within a court's jurisdiction.

There are more than 30,000 judges in state trial courts. This number is approximately forty-four times the 678 trial judges in the federal system. The disparity in number of judges mirrors the disparity in the number of cases filed annually in each system – an estimated 83 million in state trial courts in 2017[42] versus 376,762 cases filed in the federal trial courts in 2019.[43] These numbers support the observation that state trial courts conduct "95 % of all judicial activity in the U.S."[44] This result should not be surprising given two facts: many areas of civil law are reserved to the states and the vast majority of criminal law in the U.S. is state-made.

---

39 Data pertaining to the U.S. Circuit Courts of Appeals can be found at the official U.S. Courts website and associated links, beginning with https://www.uscourts.gov/about-federal-courts/court-role-and-structure/about-us-courts-appeals. Data for the number of judgeships authorized for each Circuit are found at https://www.uscourts.gov/sites/default/files/appealsauth.pdf. The home page for the Court of Appeals for the Federal Circuit is http://www.cafc.uscourts.gov/the-court/court-jurisdiction. All links accessed 16 July 2019.

40 The homepage of the U.S. Supreme Court is https://www.supremecourt.gov/ accessed 16 July 2019.

41 *Habeas corpus* (Latin for "You have the body") is the "name given to a variety of writs (…) having for their object [the bringing of] a party before a court or judge (…) The primary function of the writ is to [obtain a] release from unlawful imprisonment." *Black's Law Dictionary* (5th ed., West Publishing Co. 1979) 638. The reader will encounter writ of *habeas corpus* again in the discussion of the place of international law in the American legal system.

42 National Center for State Courts, available at http://www.courtstatistics.org/~/media/Microsites/Files/CSP/Overview/CSP%202017%20Data%20-%20Spreads%20for%20viewing.ashx) accessed 11 April 2020.

43 See https://www.uscourts.gov/statistics-reports/federal-judicial-caseload-statistics-2019 accessed 11 April 2020. See also William Burnham, *Introduction to the Law and Legal System of the United States* (6th ed., West Publishing Company 2016).

44 "Court Statistics Project", *National Center for State Courts*, available at http://www.courtstatistics.org/ accessed 17 July 2019.

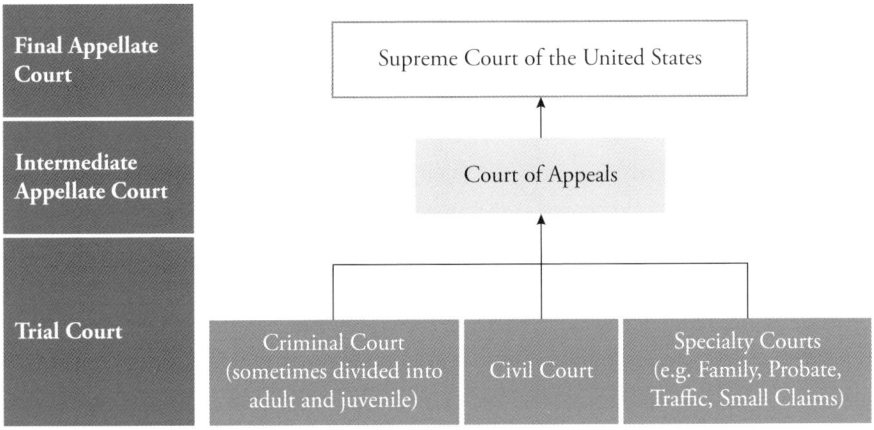

Fig. 2 The State Court Systems.

Many trial court judges are generalists and hear both civil and criminal matters. However, in urban areas trial courts may be divided into separate civil and criminal divisions. In addition, there can be specialized courts to handle cases involving landlord-tenant disputes, domestic relations issues, and probate of estates. Trials in state courts are to a single judge or to a single judge supplemented by a jury. As a general matter, neither the level of complexity of a case nor the monetary value at stake is relevant for determining the subject matter jurisdiction of a state trial court. However, a low monetary value at stake may permit the case to be heard by an inferior form of court, often called a "small claims" court. The jurisdictional limit for such courts varies, but a cap of $5,000 in dispute is typical. Procedures before small claims courts are informal and rules of evidence are not strictly observed, with the goal that involvement by lawyers is unnecessary.

In the states, an intermediate appellate court is often called the Court of Appeals. Forty-one states have an intermediate appellate court; nine states omit that layer and have only a final appellate court. There are 1,008 judges in the state intermediate appellate courts.[45] Appeals are heard by collegial panels of three judges. Due to the function of state intermediate appellate courts, which is described below, a jury is not used.

The final appellate court in the states is usually called the Supreme Court. State supreme courts hear appeals from the intermediate appellate court of appeals but in special circumstances can also hear appeals directly from state trial courts. Examples of direct appeal include cases involving a declaration by a trial court that a law is unconstitutional under the state's constitution and cases involving capital punishment. There

45 "Number of Appellate Judges", *National Center for State Courts*, available at http://data.ncsc.org/QvAJAXZfc/opendoc.htm?document=Public%20App/SCO.qvw&host=QVS@qlikviewisa&anonymous=true&bookmark=Document\BM82 accessed 18 July 2019. Data for entries identified as "not answered" were obtained from the official websites of the relevant courts. This number and the number of state supreme court justices includes the fifty states but does not include the judiciary in American Samoa, Guam, Northern Mariana Islands or Puerto Rico, each of which is included in the U.S. judicial system.

are 316 justices in the state final appellate courts.[46] The number of justices on a state supreme court varies from state-to-state, although the number is usually five, seven, or nine. Appeals before the state supreme courts are heard *en banc*, as in the federal Supreme Court. Juries are not used in proceedings before a state supreme court.

2.3 Functions and Procedures of Courts at the Various Levels in both Systems

The functions and procedures of courts at the various levels within the federal and state court systems are fundamentally similar and may be discussed together. To facilitate a unified discussion, functional names for each level of court will be used rather than formal names. At each level, the procedures used by a court reflect the court's function.

The function of a trial court in the U.S. is to resolve disputes, which a court does by taking testimony from witnesses, by examining various forms of physical evidence, and by listening to opposing arguments of attorneys. In the context of the adversary system (discussed below) the trial judge or the jury (also discussed below) determines the facts and applies the law to reach a decision.

Every litigant can appeal the trial court's decision as a matter of right. An intermediate appellate court cannot refuse to consider an appeal. The principal function of an intermediate appellate court is to correct errors of law that occurred at the trial court. This function has several implications for procedure in these courts. First, an appeal in U.S. courts – both federal and state – is not a "trial of the second instance." No new testimony or other forms of evidence is submitted on appeal. Instead, an intermediate appellate court examines the Record of Proceedings[47] and reads briefs filed by the appellant and appellee. Oral argument can occur but is not routine. When oral argument is permitted, the time allotted to the parties is short, perhaps twenty minutes per side. These procedures are explained by the function of an intermediate appellate court – to correct errors of law. It is not the court's main role to correct conclusions about facts, and its authority to do so is quite limited, especially if the facts were determined by a jury.[48]

A final appellate court will correct errors of law if they are present, but that is generally not seen as the court's primary focus, which is to determine public policy and to guide the development of law. The reasons for involving a court in establishing public policy are discussed below in the section on norm production. Given its role, a final

46 Ibid.

47 A Record of Proceedings is a transcript of all proceedings that occur in a trial court. "The official collection of all the trial proceedings, exhibits, orders, and word-for-word testimony that took place during the trial." *Black's Law Dictionary* (n. 41) 1145.

48 Although precise formulations of the standard of review that binds an appellate court when reviewing a finding of fact will differ from one jurisdiction to another, it is generally accurate to say that even if the appellate court disagrees with a finding of fact made by a judge in a bench trial, the finding made at trial can be reversed only if it can be deemed "clearly erroneous." For a finding of fact made at trial by a jury, the appellate court's authority is even more limited since it can reverse the finding "only if there is a complete absence of any substantial credible evidence to support it." Burnham (2016) (n. 43) 170.

appellate court does not hear testimony or receive evidence. Instead, a final appellate court reviews documents, including the Record of Proceedings from the trial court, the opinion issued by the intermediate appellate court, and the appellate briefs filed by the parties, which will now include arguments directed at the intermediate appellate court's reasoning and decision. The reasons for these procedures are the same as for the intermediate appellate court. An appeal is not a "trial of the second instance," and there is little basis for the final appellate court to displace the findings of fact made at trial by the judge or jury.

Another difference between an intermediate appellate court and a final appellate court involves access to the final court. Unlike an appeal from the trial court to an intermediate appellate court, which either party may exercise as a matter of right, an appeal to the final appellate court is a matter of discretion. The final appellate court can accept or decline to accept an appeal based on the court's evaluation of the importance of the case to public policy and to the development of law.[49]

In fact, the number of appeals accepted by final appellate courts is very low. In a given year, approximately 7,000 to 8,000 requests for permission to appeal are filed with the U.S. Supreme Court. Of these petitions, the Court agrees to provide plenary review for approximately eighty cases—about 1 %.[50] Comprehensive statistics for appeals to final courts of appeal in all states are more difficult to obtain, but an example will convey the point. In 2017, the Indiana Supreme Court granted 55 of 693 petitions to appeal, an acceptance rate of about 7.9 %.[51]

2.4 The Adversary System

The adversary system of litigation is based on three fundamental principles: (1) the existence of an impartial decision maker, (2) the effective development, organization, and presentation of all information necessary for the decision maker to resolve the dispute, and (3) the existence of impartial procedures.[52] These principles are commonly found in all mature legal systems, and nothing about them requires the adversary system as opposed to the inquisitorial system. Where the adversary system in the U.S. diverges from the inquisitorial system is with regard to the means used to realize these principles.

49 The discretionary nature of acceptance of appeals by the U.S. Supreme Court and the factors that would affect the Court's decision to accept or refuse to accept an appeal are stated in Rules of the Supreme Court of the United States, Rule 10, available at https://www.supremecourt.gov/filingandrules/2017RulesoftheCourt.pdf accessed 11 April 2020.

50 See https://www.supremecourt.gov/about/courtatwork.aspx accessed 11 April 2020. The Supreme Court also disposes of approximately 100 cases each year without plenary review.

51 Annual Report of the Indiana Supreme Court, 2017–2018, available at https://www.in.gov/judiciary/supreme/files/1718report.pdf accessed 14 July 2019; statistical data also provided by Indiana Supreme Court Justice Steven David (on file with the author).

52 For an excellent and concise discussion of the fundamental principles and implementing mechanisms of the adversary system, see Burnham (2016) (n. 43) 80–85. The discussion in this section and the section on the jury system utilizes Burnham's analytical framework.

The principles listed above are implemented in the American adversary system through four mechanisms: (1) a neutral and passive decision maker, (2) the discovery, organization, and presentation of evidence exclusively by the parties, (3) proceedings that are concentrated and uninterrupted, and (4) equal opportunities for the parties to present evidence and to make arguments. The first two of these mechanisms will be the focus of this chapter. These mechanisms are both independent and interrelated.

It is often noted that one of the major differences between the adversary system and the inquisitorial system concerns the role of the judge. Judges in an inquisitorial system are described as active participants in the proceedings, including having the authority to investigate facts and examine witnesses. Judges in the adversarial system, on the other hand, are characterized as passive. They are prohibited from having any involvement in gathering facts and in presenting evidence. Instead, the role of a trial judge in the U.S. – at least until the parties have concluded their cases – is limited to listening to the evidence and to ruling on legal matters, such as the admission or exclusion of evidence.

The passivity of trial judges in the U.S. is valued because it is thought that passivity helps prevent the judge from engaging in "preliminary theorizing" about the outcome of the case before all evidence has been presented. The goal of "keeping an open mind" throughout the case is not unique to American judges. What is significant in American legal culture is the extent to which the problem posed by preliminary theorizing is recognized and the structural supports that the adversary system provides to minimize the problem.[53]

Party control of the discovery, organization, and presentation of evidence is valued because it is thought that party incentives produce the maximum quantity of evidence for the decision maker. No one has more incentive to discover, organize, and present evidence than the party who will be directly impacted by the result of the case. The maximum quality of evidence is believed to result from party control by way of the "adversarial clash." The adversarial clash acknowledges that each party will present evidence in a way most beneficial to that party's position. It is possible, therefore, to say this goal leads not to the pursuit of truth but instead to the pursuit of only truths helpful to a party. The adversarial clash counters this concern by giving the opposing party an

53 Among many insightful conclusions is this, "the ostensible irrationalities and frustrating inefficiencies of the American legal system – and its virtues as well – flow from fundamental features of the American *political* system." The problem of preliminary theorizing can be linked to the psychology of decision-making, especially cognitive "shortcuts" such as the availability heuristic (a tendency to form an opinion based on a limited amount of data, which is the case when a judge has heard only a small amount of evidence early in a trial), the anchoring heuristic (a tendency to hold fast to an initial impression rather than to admit an error of judgment), and the ordering heuristic (a tendency to emphasize new data that is consistent with data previously received and to marginalize data that is inconsistent). Each of these heuristics can lead a judge to engage in premature theorizing about the outcome of the case. The trial process itself, with alternating opening statements of counsel, alternating examination and cross-examination of witnesses, and alternating closing statements, is designed to counteract preliminary theorizing. See Burnham (2016) (n. 43) 81–85. For a book-length engagement with the many facets of the adversary system, see Robert A. Kagan, *Adversarial Legalism: The American Way of Law* (2nd ed., Harvard University Press 2019).

equal opportunity to present contradictory evidence. Under this "marketplace of ideas" concept, the decision maker is able to identify the truth.[54]

2.5 The Jury System

No discussion of dispute resolution in American legal culture would be complete without recognizing the jury system. Like the adversary system, the jury system is a deeply rooted part of American legal culture. The importance of the jury system is displayed by the fact that the jury right is mentioned four times in the U.S. Constitution,[55] far more than any other right.

A jury consists of citizens randomly selected from the community, and it is a fundamental principle that trial by a jury involves a trial by a jury of one's peers. To meet this requirement a jury must represent a cross-section of the community. A jury in a criminal trial includes twelve people, and in the federal court system the jury's decision must be unanimous. Unanimity is also common in criminal trials in state courts, but it is not required in all states. The situation is similar with regard to civil cases, with the federal courts requiring unanimous verdicts and some states permitting verdicts by super majority vote. There are few qualifications to serve on a jury: a juror must be at least eighteen years old, must be of sound mind, must be able to communicate in English, and must be a citizen of the state where the trial is being held. There are no education requirements. Jurors are assumed to be untrained in law.[56]

Even though the right to a trial by jury is highly valued in the U.S.,[57] that right does not extend to all cases. In criminal cases, there is no right to a jury for "petty offenses," with pettiness often defined as crimes punishable by fine only or by imprisonment for less than six months. In civil cases, trial by jury is not available if the plaintiff seeks injunctive relief or in proceedings where recovery of monetary damages is not the

---

54 The effectiveness of the adversary system as a truth-seeking process has critics as well as supporters. For selected criticisms of the adversary system and responses, see Burnham (2016) (n. 43) 115–20. Another skeptic of the "grip of the adversary system on the American legal mentality" is Richard A. Posner. In *Divergent Paths: The Academy and the Judiciary* (Harvard University Press 2016) 140, Posner notes shortcomings with judicial passivity and concludes it is time to "bury the umpireal analogy."

55 Article III, § 2 (right to a jury trial of "all Crimes"), 5th Amendment (requirement of indictment by grand jury), 6th Amendment (right in criminal prosecutions to a "speedy and public trial by an impartial jury"), and 7th Amendment (right to trial by jury in civil actions "at common law, where the value in controversy shall exceed twenty dollars.") The twenty dollar amount remains unchanged since ratification in 1791.

56 The qualification requirements to serve on a jury in the federal court system are listed at https://www.uscourts.gov/services-forms/jury-service/juror-qualifications accessed 14 April 2020. The listed requirements may be seen as quite basic. Juror qualifications in the states tend to resemble the federal model, but some states may add, delete, or rephrase the qualifications. See, e.g. the qualifications for California: https://www.juryduty101.com/states/california, and the qualifications for Cumberland County, Pennsylvania: https://www.ccpa.net/2395/Qualifications-Exemption-from-Jury-Servi. Both links accessed 14 April 2020.

57 The jury system is also subject to several meaningful criticisms, including lack of competence to decide complex cases and overt and implicit biases. See, Drury R. Sherrod, *The Jury Crisis: What's Wrong with Jury Trials and How We Can Save Them* (Rowman & Littlefield, 2019); Dennis Hale, *The Jury in America: Triumph and Decline* (University of Kansas Press 2016).

focus.[58] Where trial by jury is available, it is important to identify the proper functions of the jury and the balance of authority between the jury and the judge. In general, it is appropriate to say the function of the judge is to decide issues of law and to say the jury has two functions: to decide issues of fact and to determine the outcome of the dispute by applying the law (as instructed by the judge) to the facts.

The classic exposition of American legal culture is found in Alexis de Tocqueville's *Democracy in America*. Although his observations are wide-ranging, de Tocqueville was especially insightful with regard to the jury system. Even though he observed that the jury functions as both a judicial and a political institution, he dwells on the latter, writing that "[t]he jury is, above all, a political institution, and it must be regarded in this light in order to be truly appreciated."[59] As a political institution, he continues the jury "places the real direction of society in the hands of the governed (…) and not in that of the government (…) The institution of the jury consequently invests the people (…) with the direction of society."[60] Accordingly, he concludes, "The jury system as it is understood in America appears to me to be as direct and as extreme a consequence of the sovereignty of the people as universal suffrage."[61]

De Tocqueville was especially impressed by the impact of the jury system on the American people. The jury, he writes, "imbues all classes with a respect for the thing judged and with the notion of right" and becomes "associated with the idea of justice itself."[62] As a result, the jury

> "invests each citizen with a kind of magistracy; it makes them all feel the duties which they are bound to discharge towards society and the part which they take in its government. By obliging men to turn their attention to other affairs than their own, it rubs off that private selfishness which is the rust of society."[63]

In the balancing of the perceived benefits and perceived drawbacks of the jury system,[64] it is the over-arching values identified by de Tocqueville that explain the durability of the jury system in American legal culture.

---

58 One of the features of English law carried over into American law, albeit with modification over time, is the distinction between suits "at law" and suits "in equity". In the former, the plaintiff seeks money damages; in the latter, the plaintiff seeks a non-monetary remedy, often an order compelling the defendant to do something or to refrain from doing something. Although trial courts in the U.S. have the authority to award both forms of remedy, the distinction remains important as trial by a jury is not available in suits in equity.

59 Alexis De Tocqueville, *Democracy in America* (Vol. 1, first published 1835, Alfred A. Knopf 1972) 282.

60 Ibid.

61 Ibid. 283.

62 Ibid. 284.

63 Ibid. 285.

64 For a concise discussion of benefits (e.g., diversity of life experiences, collective wisdom, civic participation, populist check on state power) and criticisms (e.g., questionable competence in complex civil litigation, increased litigation cost, excessive size of jury awards), see Burnham (2016) (n. 43) 85–91. For a study that rebuts the claim that juries are prone to awarding excessive amounts of money, see Neil Vidmar, "The American Civil Jury for Ausländer" (2003) Vol. 13 Issue 3 *Duke Journal of Comparative & International Law* 95.

The jury system also includes an interesting phenomenon called jury nullification. The principle of jury nullification involves the relative powers of the jury and the trial judge, specifically the insulation of a jury's verdict from the ability of a judge to set aside the jury's decision. On an even more fundamental level, jury nullification raises issues concerning the powers allocated to government and powers retained by the people.

More specifically, jury nullification refers to the ability of a jury to issue a verdict in contravention of the law as enacted through the legislative process. As a preliminary matter, it is important to note that jury nullification is possible only in criminal cases and only when the jury returns a verdict of not guilty. In that situation, the judge is powerless to alter the verdict, no matter how contrary to law it may be. Furthermore, the state is powerless to appeal the "incorrect" verdict, because an appeal would violate the guarantee of the 5th Amendment that no person "shall (...) be subject for the same offense to be twice put in jeopardy of life or limb." The jury's pronouncement of "not guilty" is the final law and supersedes any statutory provision enacted by the legislature and signed into law by the executive. By contrast, if a jury in a civil case issues a verdict inconsistent with the law, the trial judge has the power to correct the jury's erroneous action.

Jury nullification sounds scandalous and heretical to readers accustomed to a legal system based on legislative supremacy and almost certainly leads to the question of why the principle is permitted in the U.S. First, it should be noted that jury nullification is presumed to occur rarely.[65] The vast majority of juries seek to follow the law. In those instances where jury nullification is suspected, it tends to occur in cases that involve sensitive social issues, especially where public sentiment runs counter to a formal legislative position or where a particular criminal trial calls up social discontent.[66]

---

65 Reliable empirical data about the incidence of jury nullification are not obtainable because jurors are under no obligation to provide a reason for their verdict, and a finding of "reasonable doubt" may have more than one motivation. In the absence of empirical evidence, we must rely on anecdotal evidence. The following is illustrative: "Even though most courts adamantly refuse to inform juries of their powers to reach an independent verdict, there clearly exists a large group of cases in which juries not infrequently reject the written law in favor of a merciful verdict based on their own concepts of justice and equity. When the defendant has already suffered enough, when it would be unfair or against the public interest for the defendant to be convicted, when the jury disagrees with the law itself, when the prosecution or the arresting authorities have gone 'too far' in the single-minded quest to arrest and convict a particular defendant, when the punishments to be imposed are excessive or when the jury suspects that the charges have been brought for political reasons or to make an unfair example of the hapless defendant, the jury is likely to refuse to convict." See Clay S. Conrad, *Jury Nullification: The Evolution of a Doctrine* (Cato Institute 2013).

66 Perhaps the first and most famous case of jury nullification in the U.S. is the case of John Peter Zenger in 1735 in New York. In the face of indisputable evidence that Zenger had published political attacks against the colonial governor, considered libelous at the time, a jury acquitted him of the charges. The verdict was characterized as an act to safeguard liberty, baffle tyranny, and expose arbitrary power. See Alfred H. Knight, *The Life of the Law: The People and Cases that have Shaped our Society, from King Alfred to Rodney King* (Crown Publishers, Inc. 1996) 105. Cases involving acquittals for possession of small amounts of marijuana and assisting the suicide of people with terminal illnesses are often considered to be examples of jury nullification. An argument has been made that the acquittal of O.J. Simpson for the murders of his ex-wife and her friend is an example of jury nullification prompted by a history of racial discrimination by police in Los Angeles.

This power of a jury to issue a verdict contrary to enacted law might also seem anti-democratic. After all, a statute of criminal law enacted by the duly elected representatives of the people has been ignored by twelve people. It can be proposed, however, that jury nullification is a supremely democratic action. If "the people" are the source of all political and legal power, by acquitting a defendant, "the people" have spoken and have exercised a form of democracy in addition to the form of democracy exercised at the ballot box. Perhaps it is the enacted law that is out-of-step with society and not the jury.

2.6 Conflict Resolution outside the Court Systems – Alternative Dispute Resolution

Alternative dispute resolution (ADR) methods are a major part of the legal culture of conflict resolution in the U.S.[67] ADR comes in multiple forms, including voluntary mediation, court-ordered mediation in conjunction with a pending lawsuit, summary jury trial, arbitration, and early neutral evaluation. Among these, contract-based arbitration is particularly prevalent, since an arbitration clause will be found in nearly every commercial contract, whether between merchants or between a merchant and a consumer.

The stated advantages of ADR are speed, expertise of the arbitrator, informal procedures, lower expense compared to litigation (as a result of speediness), avoidance of uncertainty associated with judicial proceedings, especially those involving a jury, and confidentiality.[68] Arbitration has its limitations and drawbacks, however. First, arbitration clauses can be oppressive when there is an imbalance of power between the contracting parties, a risk perhaps especially relevant to minorities, women, the poor, and other disadvantaged people.[69] Second, use of arbitration necessarily involves a waiver of one's right to have a dispute resolved by a jury. Third, confidentiality can enable a wrong-

67 Deborah R. Hensler, "Our Courts, Ourselves: How the Alternative Dispute Resolution Movement is Re-Shaping Our Legal System" (2017) Vol. 122 Issue 1 *Dickinson Law Review* 349, provides a comprehensive history of the dispute resolution movement in the U.S. and shows that the ADR movement has enjoyed some success in changing views about the best way to resolve legal disputes.

68 Often stated advantages of arbitration and mediation can be found in many places, including websites maintained by the American Bar Association: https://www.americanbar.org/groups/dispute_resolution/resources/DisputeResolutionProcesses/ accessed 15 July 2019; and by the American Arbitration Association: https://www.adr.org/aaa-panel accessed 15 July 2019.

69 The increased use of ADR despite these risks and despite studies showing that disempowered people achieve better results in litigation as opposed to ADR is considered in Richard Delgado, "The Unbearable Lightness of Alternative Dispute Resolution: Critical Thoughts on Fairness and Formality" (2017) Vol. 70 Issue 3 *Southern Methodist University Law Review* 611. With regard to traits like ethnicity and gender on outcomes in ADR, Charles B. Carver, "Do Alternative Dispute Resolutions Disadvantage Women and Minorities?" (2017) Vol. 70 Issue 4 *Southern Methodist University Law Review* 891 concludes that such traits are largely irrelevant today, while Gilat J. Bachar and Deborah R. Hensler, "Does Alternative Dispute Resolution Facilitate Prejudice and Bias? We Still Don't Know" (2017) Vol. 70 Issue *4 Southern Methodist University Law Review* 817, after identifying 388 qualitative efforts to test empirically the hypothesis that mediation and arbitration create systematic differences in outcomes by gender, ethnicity, and socio-economic stratum, say the data are inconclusive and the issue requires more investigation.

doer to prevent the public, including persons who experience problems similar to those alleged in a dispute, from knowing about the existence of a defective product or undesirable practices. Lastly, unlike litigation, an arbitration award does not result in a judicial opinion, which impairs growth of the common law. The place of ADR in a legal culture involves an ongoing balancing of free will notions of contracting against protection of social interests. Nevertheless, given the data on the number of disputes resolved by ADR, there is no doubting the importance of ADR in contemporary American legal culture.[70]

3. Norm Production

The discussion in this section addresses formally created legal norms, specifically norms that are produced by legislation, executive action, judicial decisions, and legal scholarship.

3.1 Legislatively Created Norms

With regard to legislatively created norms, it is important to note that there is no comprehensive civil code in the United States. Although codes exist to define procedural rules for both civil and criminal litigation and to regulate highly specialized areas such as taxation, legislative norms are otherwise produced by way of individual statutes enacted on an *ad hoc* basis. While many legal topics in the U.S. are governed by the common law, the number of enacted statutes has increased dramatically in the past several decades.

At the federal level, in the 115th Congress (January 3, 2017 to January 3, 2019) 13,556 bills and resolutions were introduced, of which 443 bills were enacted and 758 resolutions were passed.[71] Federal statutes are collected and published in the United States Code, which consists of fifty-four titles. As of the end of 2018, the length of the United States Code is 79,150 pages.[72]

The authoritative status of work done prior to enactment of a statute, known as legislative history, must be considered separately for the federal and state systems. Legislative history in the federal system includes many sources, such as prior drafts of bills, House and Senate committee reports, transcripts of committee hearings, and statements made by legislators on the floor of the House or Senate. These sources are available to federal courts when called upon to interpret a statute; however, whether and how to use them can depend on a judge's preference among philosophies of interpretation, such as textualism, purposivism, or consequentialism.

70 The American Arbitration Association boasts 5,807,332 "cases administered" since 1926 and 168,923 "cases resolved" between 1 January and 15 July 2019. See https://www.adr.org/ accessed 15 July 2019.

71 Rundown of House of Representatives Oversight Activities, "Statistics and Historical Comparison", available at https://www.govtrack.us/congress/bills/statistics accessed 18 July 2019.

72 United States Code, Office of the Law Revision Counsel, House of Representatives, available at https://uscode.house.gov/detailed_guide.xhtml accessed 18 July 2019. This number excludes indexes, tables, and similar items.

The status of legislative history in the states varies widely. Some states operate like the federal government; other states do not maintain or give legal effect to any form of legislative history. States that give legal effect to legislative history do so because they find probative value in the process by which a statute is enacted. States that do not give effect to legislative history often give at least two justifications. First, many statutes undergo significant evolution between first introduction and final passage, so comments made early in the process may no longer be relevant. Second, legislators voted only on the final version of the bill, and only the final version is law.[73]

3.2 Administratively Created Norms

The principal function of the executive branch is to execute laws enacted by the legislature. In addition, the executive has the power to create legal norms in two ways: through administrative agencies by delegation of power from the legislature and by executive order.[74]

The executive branch of the federal government consists of fifteen administrative agencies that operate under the leadership of the President.[75] These agencies were created by Congress and derive their norm-making authority from Congress. The process of delegating authority to the executive branch generally involves three steps, commonly provided in an enabling statute. First, Congress identifies a matter in need of regulation; second, Congress notes that this matter requires on-going and specialized attention beyond the institutional capacity of the legislature; and third, Congress delegates rule-making authority over the matter to the executive branch. In response to this delegation of authority, executive branch agencies enact administrative regulations. In addition to this legislative function, executive branch agencies also use the delegation of power to enforce regulations by monitoring compliance and by imposing sanctions for non-compliance. Lastly, agencies establish their own administrative tribunals to adjudicate disputes between the regulating agency and people or business organizations subject to regulation.

The scope of regulatory authority and the number of administrative regulations have both expanded dramatically since the 1970s. For example, one study states that between 1995 and the end of 2016, federal agencies issued 88,899 rules and regulations, a number that represents an average of twenty-seven rules for every law enacted by Congress over that decade.[76] Federal regulations are published in *Code of Federal Regulations*

---

73 Gorsuch (2019) (n. 22) 129–144 discusses competing theories about the use of legislative history as a tool of statutory interpretation, including the positions taken by those who favor textualism, purposivism, and consequentialism.

74 The delegation of power from the legislative branch to the executive branch occurs in a similar fashion in the governments of the states. The governors of the states also have the power to issue executive orders similar to the President. Because the principles are similar, this section will refer only to the national level of government.

75 There are fifteen federal agencies: The Departments of Agriculture, Commerce, Defense, Education, Energy, Health and Human Services, Homeland Security, Housing and Urban Development, Justice, Labor, State, Interior, Treasury, Transportation, and Veterans Affairs.

76 Clyde Wayne Crews, Jr., "How Many Rules and Regulations do Federal Agencies Issue?", *Forbes* 15 August 2017, available at https://www.forbes.com/sites/waynecrews/2017/08/15/how-many-rules-and-regulations-do-federal-agencies-issue/#428e5b5b1e64 accessed 6 December 2019.

(CFR). As of the end of 2018, there were 182,300 pages in the fifty titles of the CFR.[77] These facts have led to the assertion that "in today's America, most binding rules come (…) from agencies (unelected) rather than from lawmakers."[78] This quote signals two issues in contemporary American legal culture. One issue relates to the great increase in the number of administrative regulations, which critics say impose costly burdens that impede commerce. Others say the increased number of regulations merely reflects the increasing complexity of modern life. The second issue relates to the political unaccountability of administrative rule makers. Critics complain about the rise of an "administrative state." Although agency heads serve at the pleasure of the President, agency bureaucrats do not. This fact has led to claims that a "deep state" exists within federal agencies that is insulated from voter control and is capable of taking positions contrary to those of the President. Finally, while this section establishes the fact of administrative norm making, thorny legal problems abound, including separation of powers issues relating to judicial review of the delegation by the legislature and the interpretation of the delegation by the executive. These issues are considered in the section below on the relationship among norm producers.

Binding norms can also come from the executive branch in the form of the President's inherent power as chief executive to issue executive orders. An executive order is a directive from the President, which he most often uses to manage the operations of the executive branch of government. Executive orders are recorded in the Federal Register and have the power of federal law. Several landmark moments in American history arose from executive orders, including the Emancipation Proclamation by Abraham Lincoln.[79] Every President in U.S. history has issued executive orders, but their use has become more commonplace in modern times.[80] Presidents are inclined to use executive orders when one or both houses of Congress is controlled by the opposing party, since executive action may allow the President to achieve policy changes where legislative approval cannot be obtained.[81] In such cases, the system of checks and balances comes into play, since the President's action may be subject to reversal by judicial review. Executive orders have

77 "Code of Federal Regulations", *U.S. Government Publishing Office*, available at https://www.govinfo.gov/app/collection/cfr/2019/ accessed 18 July 2019.

78 Crews, Jr. (n. 76).

79 The Emancipation Proclamation is identified as Proclamation 95, a number assigned by the Department of State. The National Archives maintains an On-Line Exhibit of the Proclamation in President Lincoln's handwriting as well as a transcription at https://www.archives.gov/exhibits/featured-documents/emancipation-proclamation accessed 13 April 2020.

80 For a list of total executive orders issued by each President from George Washington through the first 2.4 years of the Trump Administration, see "Executive Orders", *The American Presidency Project (University of California Santa Barbara)*, available at https://www.presidency.ucsb.edu/statistics/data/executive-orders accessed 15 July 2019.

81 Edward G. Carmines and Matthew Fowler, "The Temptation of Executive Authority: How Increased Polarization and the Decline in Legislative Capacity Have Contributed to the Expansion of Presidential Power" (2017) Vol. 24 Issue 2 *Indiana Journal of Global Legal Studies* 369, contend that increasingly polarized politics and approximately equal strength of the political parties results in gridlock in Congress have contributed to a shift in the balance of power between the executive and legislative branches and have encouraged Presidents to act unilaterally via executive orders.

received much attention in recent years, with scholars exploring such topics as whether executive orders usurp democratic norms and thus are a fundamental challenge to the rule of law,[82] the extent to which executive orders allow a President to circumvent the public notice-and-comment process that an administrative agency is obliged to follow if executive power is exercised pursuant to Congressional delegation,[83] and whether, for purposes of the standard of judicial review, courts should treat executive orders like other executive branch actors or like other elected policy makers.[84]

3.3 Judicially Created Norms

As a common law country, legal norms are also produced in the U.S. by judges, who in applying the common law rely on principles of *stare decisis* and precedent. The place of common law in the hierarchy of laws in America and the method for using precedent are discussed below in the section on Legal Method. In terms of norm production by the courts (as opposed to norm implementation), it is important here to consider two questions: what qualifies as common law and who is bound by common law precedent.

The starting place for determining what qualifies as common law begins with the recognition that common law is law made by judges. However, that statement is incomplete, since judges in the U.S. make law in two different contexts. One context is statutory interpretation. It is possible to say that a judge does not make law when he or she interprets a statute but instead merely applies the statute to the facts presented by each case. From an American perspective, that is the orthodox explanation of a judge's role in civil law countries. On the other hand, it is also possible to say that every interpretation makes a substantive addition to the statute and thus involves judicial lawmaking.

An important feature of judicial interpretation of statutes in the U.S. legal system is the place of that interpretation in the hierarchy of laws. A judicial interpretation of a statute is treated as having the same authority as the statute itself. This is important because it means the only way to alter a judicial interpretation of a statute is to amend the statute. When it is a constitutional provision that has been interpreted, the impact is even greater as the only way to alter a judicial interpretation of the Constitution is to amend the Constitution itself.[85] Amending the federal Constitution is extraordinarily difficult. Only twenty-seven amendments have been ratified since 1789. Because ten of those amendments were added only two years after the ratification of the Constitution and were part of negotiations that led to ratification, there have been only seventeen amendments since 1791. The difficulty

82 David M. Driesen, "President Trump's Executive Orders and the Rule of Law" (2019) Vol. 87 Issue 3 *University of Missouri-Kansas City Law Review* 489.

83 Adam J. White, "Executive Orders as Lawful Limits on Agency Policymaking Discretion" (2018) Vol. 93 Issue 4 *Notre Dame Law Review* 1569.

84 David M. Driesen, "Judicial Review of Executive Orders' Rationality" (2018) Vol. 98 Issue 4 *Boston University Law Review* 2013.

85 It is also possible for the Supreme Court to overrule an interpretation of the Constitution made by that court in the past. Because such reversals are not common they are especialy noteworthy.

involved in amending the Constitution[86] solidifies the significance of a judicial interpretation of the Constitution in the hierarchy of laws.

Even though judicial interpretation of regulations, statutes, and constitutions may involve judicial lawmaking, such interpretation is generally not considered to be common law. The classic conception of common law involves judicial lawmaking in the absence of legislative activity.[87] Common law is predominantly state law and is the basis of many areas of law, including tort law, contract law, and property law. Federal common law is comparatively rare, and it is conventional to say federal common law is possible only when as part of legislation, Congress has specifically authorized federal courts to develop principles because peculiarly federal interests are implicated.[88]

The second inquiry for this section is identifying who is bound by the common law courts create. The binding nature of precedent is generally determined vertically. In both the federal and state court systems, precedent is produced by appellate courts. In both court systems, a decision of the final appellate court is binding on all lower courts in the same jurisdiction. However, this vertical view of binding precedent must be supplemented by geography, i.e., by the territorial limitations of appellate court jurisdiction. A decision by an appellate court is binding only on lower courts in the same jurisdiction. In the federal court system, a decision by the United States Supreme Court is binding on all intermediate appellate courts and all trial courts in the federal court system. If the Supreme Court has not spoken on an issue, a decision by one federal Circuit Court of Appeals is technically binding only on federal trial courts in that circuit. Even though federal Circuit Courts of Appeals and federal District Courts in other circuits are not technically bound by an out-of-circuit decision, such decisions may be treated as persuasive authority. Nonetheless, federal Circuit Courts sometimes disagree, and different interpretations of law can exist among federal circuits.

---

86 The process for amending the national Constitution is fertile ground for scholarly inquiry. Should constitutional change be structured to be corrective or elaborative or to "dismember" by repudiation the essential characteristics of a constitutions? In other words, does a constitution exist to express enduring principles or to serve as a fundamental expression of political policy of the day? These are questions considered in Richard Albert, "Constitutional Amendment and Dismemberment" (2018) Vol. 43 Issue 1 *Yale Journal of International Law* 1; how does the constitutional amendment process spur social improvement but also hold fast in the protection of fundamental institutions is a problem analyzed by Ernest A.Young in "Against Amendments" (2018) Vol. 13 Issue 2 *Duke Journal of Constitutional Law & Public Policy* 149; because the constitutional amendment process is a "dead end," courts have "rescued" a polity that would otherwise be in perpetual thrall to principles of the 18th century but at the expense of the constitutional rule of law is the position of Richard S. Kay in "Updating the Constitution: Amending, Tinkering, Interpreting" (2019) Vol. 67 Issue 4 *Drake Law Review* 887.

87 One example is the decision of the Florida Supreme Court in 1973 to shift from the long-standing tort concept of contributory negligence to the concept of comparative fault. *Hoffman v. Jones*, 280 So. 2d 431 (Fla. 1973). No legislation was involved in this paradigm shift in the law. See Burnham (2016) (n. 43) Appendix A. It is not uncommon, however, for a legislature to later codify a common law decision.

88 The theoretical bases for, and proper scope of, federal common law are explored in articles such as Caleb Nelson, "The Legitimacy of (Some) Federal Common Law" (2015) Vol. 101 Issue 1 *Virginia Law Review* 1 and Alexander Volokh, "Judicial Non-Delegation, the Inherent-Powers Corollary, and Federal Common Law" (2017) Vol. 66 Issue 6 *Emory Law Journal* 1391.

The same territorial limitations on precedent exist in the state court system. Courts in one state are not bound by decisions made by appellate courts in other states. Again, even though courts are free to ignore decisions by out-of-state courts, such decisions may be considered. Sometimes out-of-state decisions are given persuasive effect; other times, such decisions are rejected because of policy differences between the states. Appellate opinions in casebooks in U.S. law schools often include opinions where, to resolve a case of first impression, the final appellate court in one state examines decisions on the same issue by courts of other states in which those courts reached contradictory outcomes.

A final point about the binding nature of precedent should be mentioned. When a federal trial court decides a case where subject matter jurisdiction is based on diversity of citizenship, the federal court must apply state law.[89] In such a case, both the federal trial court and the federal intermediate appellate court are bound to follow state court precedent. If state law does not exist or is unclear, in all states but one (North Carolina) a federal court can "certify" the issue to the state's final appellate court and thereby obtain guidance.[90] This procedure may be valuable, but its use is subject to limitations imposed by the supreme courts of the states. Although states have authorized the certification process, they retain the discretion whether to act on the federal court's request.[91]

3.4 Relationship among Legislatively, Administratively, and Judicially Created Norms

The existence of multiple norm producers in the U.S. requires that there be policies and procedures to govern relationships among them. Vertical federalism is, once again, relevant because legal norms are produced by the federal government and by the governments of the states. As discussed below in connection with the hierarchy of laws in the U.S., pursuant to the Supremacy Clause of the U.S. Constitution, norms produced at the federal level and within the powers granted to the federal government take precedence over conflicting norms produced at the state level. In areas of law reserved to the states, state-level norms prevail because, by definition, no federal law is possible.

The relationship among norm producers must also be viewed with regard to the branches of government that produce them – the legislative branch via statutes, the executive branch via regulations and executive orders, and the judicial branch via the power of judicial review. In other words, the relationship among norm producers involves the

89 This rule arises from one of the most famous decisions of the U.S. Supreme Court, *Erie Railroad Co. v. Tompkins*, 304 U.S. 64 (1938). Many scholarly articles about federal common law use *Erie* as the starting place for analysis.

90 The certification process is set forth in Rule 10 of the Rules of the Supreme Court of the United States, https://www.supremecourt.gov/filingandrules/2017RulesoftheCourt.pdf, accessed 14 April 2020.

91 See, for example, Rule 6-8 of the Supreme Court and Court of Appeals of Arkansas: "The Supreme Court may, in its discretion, answer questions of law certified to it by order of a federal court of the United States …", available at https://casetext.com/rule/arkansas-court-rules/arkansas-rules-of-the-supreme-court-and-court-of-appeals/article-6-special-proceedings/rule-6-8-certification-of-questions- accessed 14 April 2020.

principle of separation of powers. Because the separation of powers principle is similar for the federal government and the governments of the states, one discussion is sufficient.

Just as vertical federalism is a mechanism for allocating and distributing power between the national government and the governments of the states, the separation of powers doctrine allocates and distributes power among the three branches of government. Separation of powers is implemented by a system of checks and balances, by which each branch of government exerts power over the other branches and at the same time is subject to powers exerted over them by the other branches.

The relationship between norms produced by the legislative branch via statutes and norms produced by the executive branch via agency regulations is governed by hierarchy of laws rules – statutes are a higher source of authority than administrative regulations.[92] The relationship between norms produced by those branches of government and judicially created norms is more complicated and often generates significant debate in American legal culture.

The relationship between the judiciary and the other branches of government is based on the power of judicial review. Pursuant to this power, courts in the U.S. can invalidate legislative or executive action by declaring it to be unconstitutional. The concept of legislative supremacy, common in many countries, does not exist in the U.S. The power of judicial review is not explicitly mentioned in the federal Constitution, but the U.S. Supreme Court declared the existence of the power in 1803 in the case of *Marbury v. Madison*.[93] In that case, the Court found the power of judicial review to be implicit in the framework of the Constitution. The Court reasoned that the Constitution intended to create three branches of government that are not only separate but are also co-equal. For this to be possible, the judicial branch must have a power similar to the President's power to veto bills passed by Congress and similar to Congress' power to override a Presidential veto. Judicial review is that power. Controversy arises because it is difficult to identify the line separating an appropriate exercise of judicial review and an apparently excessive exercise, often labeled "judicial activism."[94]

---

92 The sources of law in the U.S. are discussed below in the section on Legal Method.

93 *Marbury v. Madison*, 5 U.S. 137 (1803).

94 The meaning of and views toward "judicial activism" vary widely. Bruce A. Green and Rebecca Roiphe in "Judicial Activism in Trial Courts" (2018–2019) Vol. 74 *New York University Annual Survey of American Law* 365, 365 say "Judicial activism has no fixed meaning (…) beyond the predominant understanding that judicial activism is bad – a transgression of the judge's role." In addition they argue that when "judicial activism" is considered in terms of a judge's active use of discretion in engagement with a case instead of bias, activism is a good thing, perhaps especially for judges in trial courts; Warren S. Grimes in "Judicial Activism in the First Decade of the Roberts Court: Six Activism Measures Applied" (2019) Vol. 48 *Southwestern Law Review* 37, notes that the term "judicial activism" is used whenever a judge votes in a way one dislikes. In other words, a judge rules "properly" when a ruling is favorable and engages in "activism" when a ruling is unfavorable. Substantively, Grimes argues that structural reforms for the Supreme Court are necessary to correct ideological activism, including changes to control of the Court's docket and changes in the appointment process for Supreme Court Justices to permit regular turnover on the Court; Jack M. Balkin in "Why Liberals and Conservatives Flipped on Judicial Restraint: Judicial Review in Cycles of Constitutional Time" (2019) Vol. 98 Issue 2 *Texas Law Review* 215 notes the intersection of personal interest and judicial ruling when applying the label of "activism" and identifies structural reasons that explain why the allegation is made at different times by liberals and conservatives; Clint Bolick in "The Proper Role of 'Judicial Activism'" (2019) Vol. 42

An important separation of powers issue concerning norm production arises when legislation delegating power to an administrative agency has gaps or is ambiguous. In such a situation, the interpretive task will fall initially to the agency. However, that fact calls up the question of who – agency administrators or judges – is best situated to provide the interpretation and the question of who is constitutionally authorized to interpret the enabling legislation. The balance struck by the Supreme Court is complex and evolving. One of most well-known expressions of this balancing is known as *Chevron* deference, named after the case in which the principle was announced. In general, the Supreme Court said in *Chevron* that courts should defer to agency interpretations in situations where the legislature has not directly spoken to the issue involved and the agency's interpretation is a permissible and reasonable construction.[95]

Proponents of a relationship that would defer to interpretations by administrative agencies contend that, compared to courts, agencies are more accountable to the public, can more easily alter interpretations to respond to changes in circumstances, are more familiar with the broader regulatory scheme, can more readily establish uniform interpretations, and have greater expertise.[96] Proponents of a more vigorous role for the judiciary in the interpretation of enabling statutes say that deference is unconstitutional since it violates Art. III by limiting the interpretive power of courts to say what the law is, violates the non-delegation doctrine of Art. I, § 1 of the Constitution, which vests all legislative powers in Congress and prohibits delegation of that power, and is inconsistent with the Administrative Procedures Act, which directs federal courts to review statutes *de novo*.[97] It is obvious that the relationship among norm makers with regard to administratively created norms is complicated and is being re-evaluated while the branches of government search for the right balance of duties and powers under the Constitution.

Legal research in the United States occurs both within and across identifiable doctrinal areas. Theoretical inquiry is important because it searches for abstract concepts with explanatory power. Legal research within doctrinal fields is also valued since it seeks to develop effective policies to address social needs and improve the application of law and

---

Issue 1 *Harvard Journal of Law and Public Policy* 1 contends that rather than too much judicial activism, there is too little, especially with regard to protecting individual rights from governmental transgression. For an analysis of the level of judicial activism appropriate for (newer) teleological constitutions versus the level appropriate for (older) structural constitutions, see Jorge M. Farinacci-Fernos, "Constitutionally Required Judicial Activism: Re-Examining the Role of Courts in Modern Constitutional Adjudication" (2018) Vol. 28 Issue 1 *Kansas Journal of Law & Public Policy* 36.

95 *Chevron U.S.A., Inc. v. Natural Resources Defense Council, Inc.*, 467 U.S. 837 (1984).

96 F. Andrew Hessick, "*Remedial Chevron*" (2018) Vol. 97 Issue 1 *North Carolina Law Review* 1, 4–5.

97 Ibid. 3 (Hessick supports deference to agency interpretations and proposes a solution to the constitutional objections by restructuring *Chevron* from an interpretation doctrine that limits judicial review to a remedial doctrine that restricts what courts can do about interpretations made by agencies); see also, Michael Kagan, "Loud and Soft Anti-*Chevron* Decisions" (2018) Vol. 53 Issue 1 *Wake Forest Law Review* 37 (noting that inconsistency in the Supreme Court's application of the *Chevron* doctrine signals lurking problems and doubts about it); Yoav Dotan, "Deference and Disagreement in Administrative Law" (2019) Vol. 71 Issue 4 *Administrative Law Review* 761 (proposing the difference between "disagreement deference" and "avoidance deference" as key for understanding developments in administrative law). Gorsuch (2019) (n. 22) 75–83 offers a vigorous rejection of a presumption of deference.

seeks to establish accessible norms out of the vast resources and diversity inherent in the common law and across state-level variations in other forms of law. These research-based objectives can be seen in the Restatements of Law, Model Laws, and scholarly publications.

Restatements of Law are treatises devoted to specific doctrinal areas and are published by the American Law Institute (ALI), an organization made up of leading judges, practicing attorneys, and legal academics. Currently there are twenty-one treatises covering thirteen topics.[98] While the Restatements are frequently consulted in American legal culture and can have persuasive influence, the Restatements are not law and are not binding authority. The original goal of the Restatements was to examine the myriad of judicial decisions that constitute the common law and to distill those decisions into principles that could be used by lawyers and judges in the application of law to future cases. This goal can be seen in the mission statement of the Restatement [First] of Contracts, which provided that "[t]he function of the Institute is to state clearly and precisely in light of the [courts'] decisions the principles and rules of the common law."[99] The mission of the ALI has evolved over time. Currently, in formulating "restatements" of common law, the ALI also looks at trends in case law and applies normative considerations. According to the ALI, its members "have the opportunity to influence the development of law in both existing and emerging areas."[100]

Model laws are proposed by the Uniform Law Commission (ULC), also known as the National Conference of Commissioners on Uniform State Laws.[101] The ULC has produced 152 model statutes it says are "ready for enactment in your jurisdiction."[102] As with the Restatements of Law, uniform laws written by the ULC are not law. Instead, they are proposals directed at the legislatures of the states.

ULC members include practicing lawyers, judges, legislators and legislative staff personnel, and law professors. The reader will recall that the Constitution reserves many areas of law to the states. Because the federal government cannot legislate in these areas, uniformity in laws cannot be imposed within a top-down model. If uniformity is to be achieved, it must occur as a result of concerted effort by the states. However, even if two states adopt a model law with no changes (or with identical changes), uniformity is still not assured. The supreme courts of those states may interpret identically worded laws in different ways. The ultimate result is meaningful but not complete uniformity. To know "the law" in areas reserved to the states means to know the law of the state that has jurisdiction over the parties and their activities.

---

98 For a list of published volumes of Restatements of Law, see https://www.ali.org/media/filer_public/f2/9a/f29a6aa8-e61a-4ea8-9adf-06c35d9cf72a/2019-checklist.pdf accessed 15 July 2019. The ALI homepage is https://www.ali.org/ accessed 17 July 2019.

99 Herbert Weschler, "The Course of the Restatements" (1969) 55 *American Bar Association Journal* 147, 156.

100 Ibid.

101 The mission and projects of the Uniform Law Commission can be found at its homepage: https://www.uniformlaws.org/home accessed 17 July 2019.

102 See https://www.uniformlaws.org/acts/catalog/current#&&StartRowIndex=0 accessed 15 July 2019.

As noted below in the section on professionalism, there are several thousand professors in U.S. law schools, and most of them are expected to conduct legal research and to write books and articles. Thus, there is a plentiful supply of scholarly publications,[103] some of which have meaningful impact and advance theoretical understanding.[104] At the same time, there is a debate in the U.S. about the value of legal scholarship, especially value as measured in terms of usefulness to American courts. One school of thought marginalizes the contribution of legal scholarship to norm production in the U.S. Outspoken representatives of this school include the prestigious federal appellate judges Harry T. Edwards[105] and Richard A. Posner. U.S. Chief Justice John Roberts has also been identified as being sympathetic with this view.[106] Perhaps the most fundamental and fruitful place to begin engaging with this school of thought – and to provide a point of comparison with the place of legal scholarship in norm production in other countries – is with Judge Posner's distinction between jurisprudence that is viewed conceptually and universally and jurisprudence that is viewed pragmatically and contextualized. With this distinction in mind, Judge Posner concludes that attempts to define law are "futile, distracting, and illustrative of the impoverishment of traditional legal theory."[107] Posner and critics of similar thought perceive legal scholarship as being produced by academics who have only a weak identification with the legal profession and therefore produce scholarship that is relevant only to similarly situated colleagues in academia

103 Paul Campos, "Is Legal Scholarship Worth Its Cost" (2017) Vol. 88 Issue 2 *University of Colorado Law Review* 377 cites an empirical study for the statement that "American law school professors are now publishing about 8,000 law review articles per year." The cited study is Jeffery L. Harrison and Amy R. Mashburn, "Citations, Justifications, and the Troubled State of legal Scholarship: An Empirical Study" (2015) Vol. 3 Issue 1 *Texas A&M Law Review* 45, 84.

104 See John N. Drobak, "Beyond Stamp Collecting: Ronald Coase and 'Scientific' Legal Scholarship" (2017) Vol. 53 *Washington University Journal of Law & Policy* 21 (noting the contributions of both doctrinal and theoretical scholarship); Kristen K. Tiscione, "How the Disappearance of Classical Rhetoric and the Decision to Teach Law as a Science Severed Theory from Practice in Legal Education" (2016) Vol. 51 Issue 2 *Wake Forest Law Review* 385 (discussing the recursive relationship between theory and experience).

105 Judge Edwards is noted for commentary such as, "[S]ome of the worst effects of the problems that I see in legal education [are]: faculty hiring that is tilted in favor of 'impractical' scholars; inattention to written work, clinical training, and ethics; an increasing number of law teachers who hold the profession in disdain; a proliferation of legal scholarship that does not aim to serve the profession; and a growing inattention to the needs of the disadvantaged." Quoted in Ronald K. Collins, "On Legal Scholarship: Questions for Judge Harry T. Edwards" (2016) Vol. 65 Issue 3 *Journal of Legal Education* 637, 637.

106 See, Tamara R. Piety, "In Praise of Legal Scholarship" (2017) Vol. 25 Issue 3 *William and Mary Bill of Rights Journal* 801, 801.

107 Richard A. Posner, *Law and Legal Theory in England and America* (Clarendon Press 1996). Within a discussion of the jurisprudential theories of H.L.A. Hart and Ronald Dworkin, Posner writes that he "ha[s] nothing against philosophical speculation. But one would like it to have some pay-off; *something* ought to turn on the answer to the question "What is law?" if the question is to be worth asking by people who could use their time in other socially valuable ways. Nothing does turn on it. I go further: the central task of analytical jurisprudence is, or at least ought to be, not to answer the question "What is law" but to show that it should not be asked, because it only confuses matters." Ibid. 3 (emphasis in the original).

but is irrelevant, unhelpful, and inaccessible to the judiciary.[108] Other commentators defend the value of legal scholarship produced in the U.S.,[109] including publications that offer quantitative proof that courts do indeed consider scholarly research when deciding cases.[110] These contrasting views are a part of American legal culture.

4. Ideal of Justice

4.1 A Dialectic – Certainty and Flexibility

The framework provided for the chapters in this book approaches the ideal of justice in terms of a dialectic between "legal certainty and equity."[111] This framework is valuable because it captures two basic interests of a healthy legal system. Certainty recognizes the value of stability, which enables people to order their affairs secure in the knowledge that their expectation interests will be protected. On the other hand, equity – let's call it legal flexibility – is necessary for a legal system to respond to social change and, by responding, to achieve just results not attainable under pre-existing rules. As American legal scholar Karl Llewellyn put it: "Our society is changing, and law, if it is to fit society, must also change. Our society is stable, else it would not be a society, and law which is to fit it must stay fixed. Both truths are true at once."[112]

To state the dialectic is to beg the questions of how certainty is maintained and how flexibility is introduced. As noted in the section on norm production, the U.S. has many statutes – on both the federal and state levels – but the American legal system is not based on systematic and comprehensive codes. As a result, to the extent that stability is achieved through the legislative process, it occurs by way of individual statutes directed at augmenting existing legal frameworks. Similarly, statutes and the administrative regulations issued under them are adapted to changed conditions by way of legislative or administrative revision in response to democratic input. Statutes are also adapted to changed conditions by judicial interpretation. While the process of judicial interpretation is explained more fully in the following section on legal method, it is appropriate

108 See Posner (2016) (n. 54). Caustic criticisms of American academic legal scholarship can be found throughout this book. See, e.g., p. 33 (Academic "'scholarship' would strike most judges as frivolous, even narcissistic") and p. 44 ("[A]t present, increasingly, academic legal scholarship, especially that practiced in the elite law journals, is inaccessible to outsiders, including I fear most judges.").

109 See Erwin Chemerinsky and Catherine Fisk, "In Defense of the Big Tent: The Importance of Recognizing the Many Audiences for Legal Scholarship" (1999) Vol. 34 *Tulsa Law Review* 667. Although the article's scope is broad, it includes a response to Judge Edwards' claims; Edward L. Rubin, "The Practice and Discourse of Legal Scholarship" (1988) Vol. 86 Issue 8 *Michigan Law Review* 1835, analyzing and exemplifying theoretical legal scholarship.

110 See Lee Petherbridge and David L. Schwartz, "An Empirical Assessment of the Supreme Court's Use of Legal Scholarship" (2012) Vol. 106 Issue 3 *Northwestern University Law Review* 995. Other citations to articles on both sides of the argument can be found in Posner (2016) (n. 54) 26–29, fns. 21–27.

111 See Jørn Øyrehagen Sunde, "Managing the Unmanageable – An Essay Concerning Legal Culture as an Analytical Tool" in this volume, Chapter 2, 32.

112 Karl Llewellyn, *The Bramble Bush: On Our Law and Its Study* (first published 1930, Oceana Publications, Inc. 1996) 72.

here to consider the certainty-flexibility dialectic in terms of the attitude with which American judges traditionally approach statutory law.

One judicial approach is to treat statutes and regulations as statements of broad principles that courts can use to germinate rules for application to specific situations. This is not the approach used in the U.S. legal system. Instead, the traditional American approach is found in the principle that "a statute in derogation of the common law must be strictly construed."[113] In other words, courts traditionally restrict the application of a statute to its express terms and refrain from germinating any additional content. One impact of this approach is that statutes in the U.S. tend to be long and very detailed. Legislators know that if they do not specifically include terms in a statute, courts will not infer additional content. At the same time, American courts recognize an obligation to interpret statutes to clear up ambiguity and to fill lacunae. Statutory interpretation can also be said to involve a consideration of contemporary public values.[114] The strict construction approach promotes a form of certainty while the allowances found in purposive and consequential approaches to statutory interpretation introduce flexibility.

Legal certainty and flexibility are accomplished in the common law by way of analogical reasoning applied to precedent cases. The reasoning process itself is described more fully in the following section. For the purpose of this section on the ideal of justice, it is the "strict" and "loose" approaches to precedent that are relevant. As Professor Llewellyn explains,[115] a judge's ability, within bounds, to consider a precedent case to be analogous and binding, thereby dictating stability, or to consider that same case to be distinguishable and non-binding, thereby facilitating flexibility, provides the judicial mechanism by which the common law is able to meet both needs of a healthy society.

4.2 Underlying Values – Due Process and Equal Protection

The concepts of certainty and flexibility are necessary to the ideal of justice, and mechanisms for implementing each within the American legal system have been identified. However, it seems that a further task remains, which is to identify principles that guide the choice between certainty and flexibility in a given situation. The principles of due process and equal protection, which have come to the forefront of American jurisprudence in the past half century, may be seen as values that underlie the ideal of justice in the U.S. Due process and equal protection guarantees arise from the 5th and 14th Amendments to the U.S. Constitution. The 5th Amendment, which applies to the national government, provides that "No person shall be (…) deprived of life, liberty or property, without due process of law." The 14th Amendment, applicable to the states

113 Karl N. Llewellyn, "Remarks on the Theory of Appellate Decision and the Rules or Canons about How Statutes are to be Construed" (1950) Vol. 3 *Vanderbilt Law Review* 395, 401 (Canon Number Two).

114 An example of an analysis of "public values" in statutory interpretation theory is William N. Eskridge, Jr., "Public Values in Statutory Interpretation" (1989) Vol. 137 Issue 4 *University of Pennsylvania Law Review* 1007.

115 For a detailed discussion of Professor Llewellyn's analysis of judicial approach to precedent, see the section on Application of Common Law below.

since 1868, provides, "No State shall (...) deprive any person of life, liberty, or property, without due process of law; nor deny to any person within its jurisdiction the equal protection of the laws."

Due process, in its procedural sense, promotes justice by requiring the existence of processes to implement law that can be evaluated objectively to ensure that law makers in fact adhere to them. Substantive due process promotes justice by recognizing the existence of rights, even when not expressly stated in the Constitution. Equal protection promotes justice by requiring equal application of law free from arbitrary distinctions among people. These concepts have become dominant because the Supreme Court has applied them to an increasing number of matters. Procedural due process concerns underlie important principles relating to notice of government action, to an opportunity to be heard in opposition, and to an impartial decision maker. Substantive due process has given rise to the inference of a right to privacy. Equal protection concerns are at the heart of numerous decisions that now define U.S. law, including cases eliminating racial segregation in public schools and barring discrimination based on gender. In these and many other circumstances, due process and equal protection principles have provided flexibility for law to keep pace with social change and sometimes, in the interest of justice, to lead that change.

Perhaps the conclusion to be drawn from the concepts identified above – strict construction of statutes and statutory interpretation methodologies; strict and loose views of precedent; adherence to notions of fairness and equality – is that the ideal of justice in the U.S. is an on-going dialectic of stability and equity, with neither interest permitted to exclude the other. Indeed, certainty and flexibility operate as mutual checks. Certainty is generally desirable because it promotes stability and fulfills expectation interests. However, stability can become a detrimental force when it serves to entrench the interests of dominant groups in society or to perpetuate outdated social assumptions or biases. In such situations, flexibility in law is necessary to act as a corrective force. Similarly, flexibility is generally desirable, but unchecked flexibility can engender unpredictability, which in too great a measure becomes instability. Neither entrenchment nor instability is consistent with an ideal of justice.

Indeed, if the ideal of justice involves an on-going balancing of certainty and flexibility, guided by cardinal principles like due process and equal protection principles, the certainty/flexibility dialectic furnishes an explanation for many of the apparent oppositions at work in the American legal system as it seeks justice.

5. Legal Method

This section on legal method and the section on norm production are closely related, with some discussion suitable for inclusion in either section. As noted in the initial sentences on norm production, that section focusses on the contributions made to norm production by legislation, administrative regulation, judicial decision, and scholarship. As such, the section on norm production addresses the question of how and by whom norms are produced. This section dwells on processes that implement those norms. The former can be seen as including perceptions of justice in the surrounding society and the relationship of norm production to those perceptions; the latter lies more within the province of legal professionals as they bring norms into effect.

5.1 Hierarchy of Laws

A discussion of legal method in the U.S. appropriately begins with identifying the sources of American law and by placing them in a hierarchy. As a general matter, the sources of law in the U.S. are constitutions, treaties, statutes, court rules, administrative regulations, and common law. This generalization should be seen as preliminary, however, since it requires significant nuancing.

Identifying the hierarchy of laws begins with two principles. First, the Supremacy Clause elevates federal law above conflicting state law. Second, statutory law displaces conflicting common law. These two principles would seem to settle the hierarchy between federal and state law and between enacted and common law in the following order: (1) the federal Constitution, including judicial interpretations of the Constitution, (2) statutes enacted by Congress, including federal court interpretations of those statutes, court rules created by federal courts, and treaties,[116] (3) administrative regulations issued by federal agencies and agency interpretations of those regulations, and (4) federal common law followed by (5) the constitution of each state, including judicial interpretations, (6) statutes enacted by state legislatures, including state court interpretations, and court rules created by state courts, (7) administrative regulations issued by state agencies, including agency interpretations of those regulations, and (8) state common law.

In fact, the accuracy of this hierarchy is significantly impacted by vertical federalism, i.e., by the relative authority of the federal government and the governments of the states established by the Constitution. Article VI states clearly that federal law is supreme and conflicting state law is invalid. However, there is a crucial limitation. For federal law to be supreme, the federal government must be capable of creating law, a capacity that for Congress is limited by the Enumerated Powers Clause.

The point of the Enumerated Powers Clause is that if a power is not listed in Article I, § 8, Congress is incompetent to make a law. In turn, this means law making authority could not be delegated to a federal agency, which in turn precludes that agency from promulgating regulations and interpretations. As previously noted, many fundamental areas of law are not mentioned in the Enumerated Powers Clause. For each of these areas, there is no directly governing federal law in the U.S. Subject to the "constitutionalization of law" principle discussed below, substantive law in these areas is state law. In those areas, the eight levels listed above becomes shortened to the four sources (items

116 These four sources of law are listed together because they are treated as having the same level of authoritativeness. The authoritative equivalence of federal statutes and international treaties may be surprising to non-American readers. The importance of that equivalence is discussed in detail below in the section on Internationalization.

five through eight) applicable in the states. Viewed from the perspective of daily life in the U.S. – that is from a functional as opposed to a formalistic approach – the hierarchy originally presented is out of order.

However, even if the formalistic hierarchy were inverted to reflect the functional view, further nuancing would be necessary. First, inversion is not possible in those limited areas of law solely within the lawmaking authority of the federal government, such as bankruptcy, federal taxation, patent protection, immigration, and treaty making.

Furthermore, two important developments in U.S. law have significantly affected vertical federalism – the division of power between the national government and the states – since they have expanded the scope of lawmaking power of the national government. One development relates to the interpretation of the kinds of activity that constitute interstate commerce, which would authorize federal lawmaking even within the construct of the Enumerated Powers Clause. As the U.S. transitioned from an agrarian and localized nation to an urban, industrial, and interconnected economy, more and more transactions naturally came within the scope of the Commerce clause and thus of federal regulation. In addition, interpretations by the U.S. Supreme Court have generally expanded the scope of the Commerce Clause, although in recent years there has been a retreat from the most expansive interpretations.[117]

The second development is described by the phrase "constitutionalization of law." This term describes the process by which matters once thought to be exclusively within the lawmaking power of the states have been brought under the power of the federal government through the due process and equal protection clauses of the 14th Amendment. A recent example, involving same sex marriage, is illustrative.[118] Many states had statutes or constitutional provisions that defined marriage as the union of one man and one woman. Because the Enumerated Powers Clause does not mention domestic relations, Congress could not enact a federal marriage law. However, once the issue came to be seen in light of equal protection of the law – treating heterosexual and homosexual couples equally – the 14th Amendment became applicable, and the Supremacy Clause ended any dispute about which law prevails. As a result, we are left with an ongoing tension. While states remain the primary creators of law in many areas of life, the states' powers are subject to the overarching guarantees of the federal constitution.

---

117 For an example of an expansive view of the federal government's power under the Commerce Clause, see *Wickard v. Filburn,* 317 U.S. 111 (1942) (U.S. Supreme Court concluded that Congress could apply national quotas to wheat grown on a farmer's own land for his own consumption, because the total of such local production and consumption could potentially affect the overall national goal of stabilizing prices). For an example of a more restricted view, see *United States v. Lopez*, 514 U.S. 549 (1995) (U.S. Supreme Court declined to expand the scope of the Commerce Clause and effectively convert "congressional authority under the Commerce Clause to a general police power of the sort retained by the States.").

118 *Obergefell v. Hodges*, 135 S. Ct. 2584 (2015). Also accessible at https://www.supremecourt.gov/opinions/14pdf/14-556_3204.pdf accessed 12 July 2019.

5.2 Application of Statutory Law – Judicial Interpretation

Statutory law is carried out by the executive branch through administrative agencies. The task of ensuring that the administration of statutes and regulations is constitutionally proper falls to the judicial branch, and involves two tasks.

First, through its power of judicial review, courts can invalidate statutes or regulations that violate the Constitution, either because they violate a constitutionally protected right or because they exceed the authority vested by the Constitution in the legislature or executive. The second task is the courts' responsibility to interpret ambiguities in statutory language and to fill lacunae. The polestar principle of statutory interpretation in American legal culture is that courts should seek to give effect to the intent of the legislature. Although cited ubiquitously in statutory interpretation cases, it should be clear that "determining legislative intent" is an end and not a means. To determine legislative intent, courts have developed a set tools, often called canons of statutory interpretation.[119] Interpretation tools include: (1) plain meaning, (2) legislative history, (3) social purpose, (4) language context, (5) linguistic assumptions, and (6) a variety of presumptions, including in civil cases a presumption against any interpretation that would produce an illogical or unconstitutional result, and in criminal cases where the meaning of the law is in doubt, a presumption in favor of leniency for the accused.

Perhaps surprisingly, there is no hierarchy to these canons. Multiple canons can apply to any particular case, and it is recognized that the canons can lead to conflicting results. In fact, it has been asserted that "there are two opposing canons on almost every point."[120] Because the canons are indeterminate, some skeptics view them as justifications for a desired result. Others view them as the best tools available for ensuring proper application of statutes or regulations that are ambiguous or incomplete.

One principle of statutory interpretation has special importance because it flows from separation of powers concerns. That principle, mentioned above in the section on norm production, is expressed in the maxim that "statutes in derogation of the common law are to be strictly construed."[121] In essence, this phrase means statutes that conflict with established common law principles should "be made to mean as little as they can be made to mean."[122] The result of this judicial approach to statutes is that courts traditionally construe statutory language narrowly and thus limit the effect of the statute to its express language. Judges often justify this constrictive approach to statutory interpretation by noting that the legislature could have expressly identified additional situations it intended a statute to cover. In the absence of such express instruction, judges can say it is improper for them to expand the scope of the statute by inference, because to do so would inject the court into the act of legislating and violate the separation of powers principle. This approach is less evident in opinions by judges who utilize purposive or

119 Llewellyn (1996) (n. 112).

120 Ibid. 401–406. Lewellyn lists twenty-eight canons of statutory interpretation and a corresponding twenty-eight conflicting canons.

121 Ibid.

122 Ibid. 89.

consequentialist approaches than in opinions written by judges who take a textualist approach. In what would seem to be an acknowledgment of the continuing viability of a strict reading of statutes, state legislatures include in some statutes a direction for the courts to give the statute a "liberal implementation."[123]

5.3 Application of Common Law: Analogizing and Distinguishing Precedents

Prior to discussing the application of common law at the level of a judge's engagement with the facts of a particular case, it is beneficial first to look at the broader topic of the way judges in the U.S. generally conceive the law and their approach to it, in other words in terms of jurisprudential theory. The prevailing jurisprudential concept of and approach to the common law in contemporary America is a pragmatic form of realism. The Legal Realism movement of the 1920's and 1930's displaced more formalistic theories previously in use[124] and gave rise to the critical theories much used today by judges and scholars, such as critical legal studies, feminist legal theory, law and economics, and critical race theory.[125] In basic terms, legal pragmatism states that judicial decision making should include consideration of social interests and public policy and not simply depend on abstract rules.[126] Legal pragmatism, which is often contrasted with legal formalism, has been described as

> "blurring the distinction between form and substance, which is to say between doctrine and fact. The formalist views fact through the lens of doctrine, which is primary to him. The realist forms a preliminary assessment of the best decision in the case by an assessment of the facts (…) and the values and policies promoted or retarded by the facts and

123 The statute governing limited liability companies in Kansas is a representative example. The first sentence of this act, K.S.A. 2019, 17–76,1334, states: "Construction and application of act and operating agreement. (a) The rule that statutes in derogation of the common law are to be strictly construed shall have no application to this act."

124 Brian Leiter, "Legal Realism and Legal Doctrine" (2015) Vol. 163 Issue 7 *University of Pennsylvania Law Review* 1975, 1975 concludes that "[w]hat the Legal Realists taught us is that too often the doctrine that courts invoke is not really the normative standard upon which they *really* rely, and it was central to Legal Realism to reform the law to make the actual doctrine cited by courts and treatise writers correspond to the *actual* normative standards upon which judges rely." (emphasis in the original); another contribution of Legal Realism is that "it stands for the conception of law as an ongoing institution distinguished by the difficult accommodation of three constitutive yet irresolvable tensions: power and reason, science and craft, and tradition and progress." Hanoch Dagan, "Doctrinal Categories, Legal Realism, and the Rule of Law" (2015) Vol. 163 *University of Pennsylvania Law Review* 1889, 1890. Additionally, "Realists insist that the main roles of doctrinal categories are to consolidate people's expectations and to express law's ideals with respect to distinct types of human interaction." Ibid. 1891.

125 Richard Delgado and Jean Stefancic, "Southern Dreams and a New Theory of First Amendment Legal Realism" (2015) Vol. 65 Issue 2 *Emory Law Journal* 303, 304.

126 The noted scholar Lon L. Fuller connects the theory of legal realism with the dialectic of certainty and flexibility (see the section on Ideal of Justice) by stating, "Legal certainty for the layman is not predictability of judicial decision, it is *congruence between legal rules and the ways of life*." See Lon L. Fuller, "American Legal Realism", (1934) Vol. 82 Issue 5 *University of Pennsylvania Law Review* 429, 432 (emphasis in the original).

> then asks whether the case can be decided on the basis of that assessment without undue violence to legal doctrine."[127]

The concept of judicial reasoning according to legal pragmatism is perhaps best explained in the words of distinguished jurists and scholars, since their explanations have themselves become part of American legal culture. U.S. Supreme Court Justice Oliver Wendell Holmes, Jr. provides an often-quoted insight:

> "The life of the law has not been logic: It has been experience. The felt necessities of the time, the prevalent moral and political theories, intuitions of public policy, avowed or unconscious, even the prejudices which judges share with their fellow men, have had a good deal more to do than the syllogism in determining the rules by which men should be governed. The law embodies the story of a nation's development through many centuries, and it cannot be dealt with as if it contained only the axioms and corollaries of a book of mathematics. In order to know what it is, we must know what it has been, and what it tends to become."[128]

Such pragmatism finds methodological expression in the common law's manipulation of precedent and *stare decisis*. As discussed in the section on the ideal of justice, the common law achieves stability by ensuring that cases with similar facts are decided similarly. At the same time, the common law utilizes flexibility to keep pace with social change. The process that enables the coexistence of stability and flexibility is vividly described by Professor Llewellyn who identifies "strict" and "loose" approaches to precedent. Under the strict approach, "a later court can reexamine the [precedent] case and can (…) through examination of the facts (…) narrow the picture of what was actually before the [previous] court and can hold that the ruling made requires to be understood as thus restricted."[129] By "confining the [precedent] case to its particular facts," the precedential value of the prior case is "whittled away" and the court is freed from it.[130] By this process, a judge can avoid "unwelcome" precedents and can introduce flexibility to achieve justice for the case at hand. On the other hand, through a loose view of precedent a court can find similarity by viewing facts from a level of generality. At a sufficiently high level of generality, the current case can be found to be similar to a previous one. "This is a device for capitalizing welcome precedents" and for preserving stability.[131] The crucial point is that "[w]ithin the law (…) rules *guide*, but they do not *control* decision. There is no precedent the judge may not at his need either file down to razor thinness or expand into a bludgeon."[132] In reality, the doctrine of precedent

127 Posner (2016) (n. 54) 83.

128 Oliver Wendell Holmes, *The Common Law* (first published 1881, Little, Brown & Co. 1963) 5.

129 Llewellyn (1996) (n. 112) 72.

130 Ibid. 73.

131 Ibid. 74.

132 Ibid. 180 (emphasis in the original).

> "is two-headed. It is Janus-faced. That it is not one doctrine, but two, and two which, *applied at the same time to the same precedent, are contradictory to each other*. That there is one doctrine for getting rid of precedents deemed troublesome and one doctrine for making use of precedents that seem helpful. That these two doctrines exist side-by-side. That the same lawyer in the same brief, the same judge in the same opinion, may be using the one doctrine, the technically strict one, to cut down half the older cases that he deals with, and using the other doctrine, the loose one, for building with the other half. [In this way one can see] how it is possible for law to change and develop, and yet to stand on the past."[133]

These descriptions of common law reasoning may seem to imply that an American judge is free to do as he or she pleases. In fact, this is not seen as a significant risk in American legal culture as judges exercise their power within several constraints. One constraint is found in the practice of written judicial opinions, in which judges engage precedent cases and explain the reasoning supporting the decision in the current case. The length and detail customary in written opinions is a significant institutional limit on judicial discretion. Another institutional limitation is the practice of publishing judicial opinions, since judges know their opinions will be scrutinized by other judges, including the possibility of reversal on appeal, and by academics. Further, the propriety of adhering to precedent and to making changes only incrementally is inculcated in the minds of law students from the beginning of their legal education. Lastly, the power of precedent is based on respect for the thoughtful work of legal professionals of the past that is now present as accumulated wisdom.

Despite all of its perceived value, the method of common law reasoning does create a conceptual quandary known as the retroactivity problem. The retroactivity problem refers to the fact that when a judge announces an alteration of an existing common law rule or creates a new common law rule, that altered or new rule will adversely affect one of the parties – often the defendant. This is true even though the new rule did not exist at the time of the conduct that gave rise to the dispute. In other words, at the time when the defendant engaged in the conduct that is the subject of the lawsuit, the defendant did not know to conform his or her behavior to the rule the judge announces at the conclusion of the subsequent litigation.

The unfairness of this situation is patent, and it is a problem that would impair the justness of the common law if left unaddressed. Fortunately, the common law has at least two mechanisms to handle the problem. The first mechanism is to give the newly announced rule prospective application only. This approach is used where the alteration or creation of a new rule works a significant change in the law. Prospective application of the newly announced rule protects a defendant's reliance interest while still allowing the law to keep pace with social change.

The second mechanism allows retroactive application of the new rule, but only in situations where the rule change is small. Most changes to common law occur in incre-

133 Ibid. 74–75 (emphasis in the original).

mental steps and involve facts that can be seen as analogous to the facts of precedent cases. The closeness of the analogy means that a defendant's reliance interest is not unfairly impacted since the defendant could reasonable have expected his conduct would result in legal liability, even in advance of the newly announced rule.

A final avenue for appreciating the culture of the American legal method is to compare descriptions of legal reasoning within the common law system as practiced in the U.S. with descriptions of legal reasoning in a civil law system. Many jurists and legal scholars in the U.S. have sought to capture the essential nature of legal reasoning in our system through such comparisons. Judge Roscoe Pound identifies the different strengths of the common law and civil law systems in this way: "[T]he strength of the common law is in its treatment of concrete controversies, as the strength of its rival, the modern Roman law, is in its logical development of abstract conceptions."[134] Professor Llewellyn echoes this idea:

> "Now this ad hoc approach to logic [of the common law], this building up of major premises out of a group of cases not so much to find what is in them as to decide a case in hand – this is of the essence of our case law system. It is not so of every legal system, even of every system built on case law. The classical jurists of Rome, though they worked case by case, seem to have built up a strangely systematic whole; the French and German writers before the Codes had gone a great distance further on that road. *Elegantia juris* is the Latin for it: *form* in the law, in whole and in each part. Our sin is lack of elegance and even taste; our virtue is a sturdy, earthy common-sense."[135]

Lastly, Alfred Knight invokes creative imagery to describe the essence of the common law and the roles judges and lawyers play in it:

> "Walk into any law library, and you will find yourself in the presence of countless individual stories about human beings in every conceivable circumstance of risk, dishonesty, bad luck, greed, carelessness, nobility, and passion. These stories were told, tested, denounced, and urged by lawyers, and the endings were written by judges. The constantly accumulating judge-endings are what we call law, and they are used to predict the probable outcomes of similar future conflicts. Contrary to popular belief, the law is not mechanistic, and the lawyers and judges who write it are neither mechanics nor, usually, charlatans. They are, in their own philistine way, a breed of artists painting on living canvases. The law is not an 'it,' it is a becoming, and like everything that is dynamic, it either grows or dies."[136]

Holmes, Pound, Llewellyn, and Knight all point to core characteristics of the common law in American legal culture. The common law is organic, grounded in experience,

134 Roscoe Pound, *The Spirit of the Common Law* (first published 1921, Beacon Press 1963) 2.
135 Llewellyn (1996) (n. 112) 82.
136 Knight (1996) (n 66) 1.

informed by common sense, and is the flexible medium judges and lawyers use to achieve justice and to keep law in step with society.

6. Professionalization

The professionalism of actors in the American legal culture is highly developed. Professionalism begins with the legal education of students preparing to become lawyers and is extended by the continuing legal education that lawyers and judges are required to obtain after they become members of the bar.

6.1 Status of Lawyers and Judges

Lawyers and judges are generally held in high regard in the U.S. and enjoy high social status, a fact that has been true throughout our history. Following his tour of the U.S. in 1830, Alexis de Tocqueville wrote:

> "In America there are no nobles or literary men, and the people are apt to mistrust the wealthy; lawyers consequently form the highest political class and the most cultivated portion of society (…) If I were asked where I place the American aristocracy, I should reply without hesitation that it is not among the rich (….) but that it occupies the judicial bench and the bar."[137]

De Tocqueville further observed that lawyers "are naturally called upon to occupy most of the public stations. They fill the legislative assemblies and are at the head of the administration; they consequently exercise a powerful influence upon the formation of the law and upon its execution."[138] This observation remains true, and the legal profession remains disproportionately represented in political life. The role of attorneys in the founding of the nation is well documented, with lawyers drafting the constitutions of the colonies and later of the states.[139] In addition, twenty-five of the fifty-six signers of the Declaration of Independence were lawyers as were thirty-two of the fifty-five Framers of the Constitution. Twenty-five of forty-five U.S. Presidents were lawyers.[140] As of 2018, thirty-eight percent of the Members of the U.S. House of Representatives and

137 De Tocqueville (1972) (n. 59) 278.

138 Ibid. 279.

139 Anthony Arlidge (2017) (n. 18) 3–4.

140 Of the forty-four people who have been elected President, twenty-five (57 %) were lawyers. See Norman Gross, *America's Lawyer-Presidents: From the Law Office to the Oval Office* (Northwestern University Press 2004). Even though there have been forty-five presidencies, forty-four persons have occupied the office since President Grover Cleveland served two non-consecutive terms.

fifty-seven percent of U.S. Senators have law degrees.[141] The view of law as a noble profession and of lawyers as respected members of society is a staple of American literature, television, and movies.

One positive aspect of the legal profession that is probably not well known among non-lawyers is the commitment of the legal profession to social responsibility. Not only do lawyers "give back" to the community by voluntarily providing pro bono legal services on behalf of public interest groups and people with low income, the profession recognizes pro bono service as a moral obligation of attorneys, an obligation set forth in the Model Rules of Professional Responsibility promulgated by the American Bar Association (ABA).[142] Nurturing the spirit of providing pro bono services begins in law school, since "94 law schools reported that 18,411 law students in the [graduating] class of 2017 contributed more than 3.9 million hours in legal services as part of their legal education."[143]

6.2 Legal Education

There are 203 law schools in the United States accredited by the American Bar Association[144] and thirty-two non-accredited law schools.[145] For the fall 2018 term, 111,561 students were enrolled in J.D. programs.[146] In that year, U.S. law schools employed

141 In the 115th Congress (2017–2018), 165 Members of the U.S. House of Representatives (37.8 %) have law degrees. The presence of lawyers is even more pronounced in the U.S. Senate as 55 of the 100 Senators (55 %) have law degrees. See "Membership of the 115th Congress: A Profile" 5, *Congressional Research Service*, available at https://fas.org/sgp/crs/misc/R44762.pdf accessed 15 July 2019.

142 ABA Model Rule of Professional Responsibility 6.1, available at https://www.americanbar.org/groups/professional_responsibility/publications/model_rules_of_professional_conduct/rule_6_1_voluntary_pro_bono_publico_service/ accessed 16 July 2019. Following the ABA's lead, states have enacted similar rules that encourage pro bono service. See Rule 6.1 of the Rules of Professional Conduct of New York. Indiana professional responsibility rules include a mandatory reporting requirement for pro bono work as part of the annual attorney registration process. Indiana Rules of Professional Responsibility, Rule 6.1 and 6.7, available at https://www.in.gov/judiciary/rules/prof_conduct/index.html#_Toc461714698 accessed 16 July 2019.

143 Association of American Law Schools Survey, Law Class of 2017, cited in "Pro Bono & Justice", a publication of the AALS Section on Pro Bono and Public Service Opportunities, March 2018, available at https://www.aals.org/wp-content/uploads/2018/09/March-newsletter-2018.pdf accessed 7 November 2019. As part of its role as regulator of legal education, the ABA encourages law schools to "promote opportunities for law student pro bono service that incorporate the priorities established in Model Rule 6.1". See ABA Interpretation 303-3, available at https://www.americanbar.org/content/dam/aba/publications/misc/legal_education/Standards/2018-2019ABA-StandardsforApprovalofLawSchools/2018-2019-aba-standards-chapter3.pdf accessed 6 December 2019. At the Indiana University McKinney School of Law alone (the author's law school), students in the 2018-19 academic year contributed over 20,000 hours of pro bono service to legal, civic, and charitable organizations. Supporting statistics on file with the Office of the Dean, Indiana University McKinney School of Law.

144 See https://www.americanbar.org/groups/legal_education/resources/aba_approved_law_schools/ accessed 18 July 2019. One of the 203 schools is "provisionally approved."

145 See the Law School Admission Council website: https://www.lsac.org/choosing-law-school/find-law-school/non-aba-approved-law-schools accessed 18 July 2019.

146 See https://www.americanbar.org/content/dam/aba/administrative/legal_education_and_admissions_to_the_bar/statistics/2018-509-enrollment-summary-report.pdf accessed 18 July 2019. The term "J.D. program" refers to the course of study that leads to the Doctor of Jurisprudence degree in American law schools. The J.D. is the degree

6,700 full-time professors and 16,300 part-time professors.[147] Adjunct professors are often practicing lawyers who have developed an expertise in a specialized area of law or are judges from all levels of courts. Adjunct professors usually teach one course in an academic year and are not required to produce legal scholarship.

Law schools sponsor one or several law journals. The total number of journals for all U.S. law schools in 2018 was 650.[148] A typical journal will publish up to four volumes per year. In addition, there are 156 peer-reviewed journals.[149] Journals published by law schools are mentioned here because a significant majority of journals published by law schools are managed by students. A faculty member is appointed to serve as an advisor to the student-managers, but it is the students who decide which scholar-authored articles will be published and how they should be edited.[150] Election to a law journal is a high honor, and for students fortunate enough to be selected, service on a journal is a key element of their legal education.[151]

---

that enables a graduate to sit for a bar exam and upon passage engage in the practice of law. The J.D. degree is the first degree in law in the U.S. legal education system. For nearly all law graduates, the J.D. is the only law-related degree they will obtain. The J.D. is a graduate level degree, since all J.D. students must have earned a bachelor's degree at the undergraduate level. There is no undergraduate degree in law in the U.S., nor is there any required course of study leading to admission to law school. One hundred sixty-four U.S. law schools also offer the LL.M. (Legum Master) degree. To obtain an LL.M. degree, an American student must first obtain the J.D. degree. Few American students seek an LL.M. degree, since it is not seen as contributing to the skills used by practicing lawyers. Most students who obtain an LL.M. degree in the U.S. are foreign nationals. Such students must have a first degree in law, but for students from most countries that means an LL.B. degree. Fifty U.S. law schools also offer the S.J.D. (Doctor of Juridical Science) degree. The S.J.D. degree is the terminal degree in law in the U.S. and is directed at people who aspire to a career in legal academia. The S.J.D. is analogous to the PhD degree. The PhD degree in law was historically not offered in the U.S. However, three U.S. law schools now confer a PhD degree in law. An LL.M. degree is generally a prerequisite for the S.J.D. degree. Students in S.J.D. programs in U.S. law schools include both Americans and foreign nationals. A fourth degree offered by a growing number of U.S. law schools is the M.J. (Master of Jurisprudence) degree. The M.J. program is designed for non-lawyers who are typically already engaged in a non-legal career. Completion of the M.J. program does not enable the graduate to sit for a bar exam. Instead, the program is intended to enable a graduate to appreciate the impact of law on the graduate's non-legal employment. For complete data on post-J.D. degrees offered in U.S. law schools, see "LL.M. and Post-J.D. Degrees by School", *The American Bar Association*, available at https://www.americanbar.org/groups/legal_education/resources/llm-degrees_post_j_d_non_j_d/programs_by_school/ accessed 7 November 2019.

147 See the Center for Legal Education Excellence website: http://analytix.accesslex.org/DataSet accessed 18 July 2019.

148 "Law School Rankings", *Washington and Lee School of Law*, available at https://managementtools4.wlu.edu/LawJournals/ accessed 18 July 2019.

149 Ibid.

150 Although student-managed law reviews play an important role in legal scholarship and have defenders, there is also criticism. A critical engagement with the student-management model is Barry Friedman, "Fixing Law Reviews" (2018) Vol. 67 Issue 7 *Duke Law Journal* 1267.

151 The following description of the student-edited law journal at the University of Washington Law School is illustrative: "Student scholarship through participation on law journal editorial boards is an important academic opportunity for law students. All journals are student-run, and each publishes articles by law professors and legal practitioners from across the country and around the world. Exceptional law student articles are also published in each journal. Being part of a law journal staff is an excellent way for law students to critically engage in current legal issues and to collaborate closely with other students to study the nuances of contemporary legal scholarship. The experience enhances writing, editing and citation-checking skills." See https://www.law.uw.edu/academics/student-journals accessed 12 April 2020.

Legal education in the U.S. occurs at the graduate level, and completion of undergraduate education resulting in a bachelor's degree is a prerequisite for admission to law school. Even though an undergraduate education is necessary, there is no required major or course of study.[152] Law students have undergraduate majors that range from the social sciences to the hard sciences to music and the arts.

As might be expected with the existence of 235 law schools, variations in the course of study exist from one law school to another. At the same time, there is significant continuity, especially with regard to compulsory courses. J.D. programs require a student to complete ninety credit hours of course work. Ordinarily, the length of study for students in a full-time program is three years. A four-year, part-time program with classes conducted in the evening is offered at sixty-nine law schools.[153] The first-year curriculum usually consists of required courses and tends to be dominated by the common law. A typical first-year law student will take courses on contract law, tort law, property law, civil procedure law, criminal law, constitutional law, and a course on legal research and writing. These courses are traditionally taught using textbooks that consist primarily of collections of appellate court opinions. The second year of study may include a few additional required courses, but in their second and third years of study students generally choose from numerous elective courses.

Instruction in U.S. law schools is known for its use of the Socratic Method of teaching. There are many variations in the implementation of the Socratic Method,[154] but the general outlines can be identified. First, a professor asks a student to summarize a case as described in a published opinion issued by a court. This summary consists of: (1) describing the relevant facts and procedural history of the case, (2) identifying the legal issues raised by the case, (3) stating the legal arguments advanced by the opposing parties, (4) stating the court's resolution of the legal issue, and (5) explaining the reasoning used by the court to reach its decision. After the student completes the summary, the professor will then lead a discussion that proceeds by way of asking "question after

---

152 The ABA's position on "Preparing for Law School" states: "The ABA does not recommend any undergraduate majors or group of courses to prepare for a legal education. Students are admitted to law school from almost every academic discipline." See https://www.americanbar.org/groups/legal_education/resources/pre_law/ accessed 12 April 2020.

153 "Best Part-time Law Programs", *U.S. News & World Report*, available at https://www.usnews.com/best-graduate-schools/top-law-schools/part-time-law-rankings accessed 18 July 2019.

154 Scholarship about the Socratic Method is as varied as its implementation. See Jeannie Suk Gersen, "The Socratic Method in the Age of Trauma" (2017) Vol. 130 Issue 9 *Harvard Law Review* 2320, a reflection on connections and contradictions between inherited pedagogical traditions, the desires and needs of students in a diverse law school, and aspirations for law graduates in a changing world; Jamie R. Abrams, "Reframing the Socratic Method" (2015) Vol. 64 Issue 4 *Journal of Legal Education* 562, appearing in a volume dedicated to innovations in legal teaching and to identifying unique dimensions of the method that could be better leveraged to strengthen other reforms and innovations. For a comparative analysis that may be of special interest to readers of *Comparing Legal Cultures*, see Erin Ryan with Xin Shuai, Yuan Ye, You Ran and Li Haomei, "When Socrates Meets Confucius: Teaching Creative and Critical Thinking across Cultures through Multilevel Socratic Method" (2013) Vol. 92 Issue 2 *Nebraska Law Review* 289, reporting on a case study of adapting the Socratic Method to teach critical-thinking skills underemphasized in Chinese universities and group competency skills underemphasized in U.S. law schools.

question."[155] Based on the answers given by the student, the professor will ask follow-up questions intended to enable the student to appreciate the persuasive power of a different analysis or explanation. Often the professor will challenge the student's analysis by asking if it would remain valid under other facts or circumstances. Through such questioning, the professor leads the student to a self-discovery of doctrine and analytical process.

The goal of the Socratic Method of teaching is to help students "think critically about their ideas and refine their beliefs."[156] Such critical thinking involves engaging with "one's own arguments and those put forth by others, and to understand the effect of the law on those subject to it. Such discourse requires participants to articulate, develop and defend positions that may at first be imperfectly defined."[157]

Experiential learning and skills development courses are also important components of legal education in the U.S. One form of experiential learning is an externship, which involves placing students in law firms, legal departments of corporations, or government agencies where they work on legal issues under the direction of an attorney. Another form of experiential learning is offered in legal clinics. Many law schools operate one or even several clinics, which are administered by professors who are also admitted to practice before local courts.[158] These clinics are often called "live client" clinics because students represent (under supervision of the professor) real people in real cases in the courts. Clients of clinics are usually persons of low income who are unable to afford a lawyer. In this way, law school clinics both further a law student's education and instill a sense of responsibility to the community by emphasizing that lack of money should not bar access to justice.

American law schools do not offer separate tracks of study based on a student's intended career path, such as one path for students who want to represent clients and another path for students who want to become judges. A feature of American legal culture is the "unitary law degree," which means there is one first degree in law – the Doctor of Jurisprudence (J.D. degree) – and upon earning the J.D. degree a person is qualified to engage in any career in the legal profession, including private practice (with no barrister/solicitor distinction), in-house corporate counsel, government attorney, or serving as a judge.

A final point to be made about legal education in the United States is that the predominant force in the regulation of legal education in the U.S. is a non-governmental

---

155 "What is the Socratic Method that Law School's Use?", *U.S. News & World Report*, 4 April 2019, available at https://www.usnews.com/education/best-graduate-schools/top-law-schools/articles/2019-04-04/what-is-the-socratic-method-and-why-do-law-schools-use-it accessed 7 November 2019.

156 Ibid.

157 Elizabeth Garrett, "Becoming Lawyers: The Role of the Socratic Method in Modern Law Schools", available at https://www.law.uchicago.edu/socratic-method accessed 7 November 2019.

158 The Indiana University McKinney School of Law is home to nine live-client clinics: the appellate clinic, the child advocacy law clinic, the civil law practice clinic, the criminal defense clinic, the conservation law clinic, the disability law clinic, the health and human rights clinic, the immigration law clinic, and the wrongful conviction clinic. Students perform meaningful work in each of these clinics. For example, using DNA evidence, the wrongful conviction clinic obtained the release in 2001, 2016, 2017, and 2020 of a total of five persons wrongfully incarcerated for crimes they did not commit.

organization – the American Bar Association. The ABA has established comprehensive standards that regulate education in America's law schools.[159] The goal of these standards is to ensure that law students receive appropriate preparation to become legal professionals. ABA accreditation is crucial because, in many states, graduation from an ABA accredited law school is a requirement for eligibility to take the bar exam. In recent years, the ABA has become increasingly involved in defining the curriculum, and thereby the basic mission, of law schools in the U.S. Under direction from the ABA, law schools now offer an increasing number of courses designed to develop the skills students will use after graduation in the practice of law.[160]

State supreme courts may impose some additional educational requirements. Although court-imposed requirements are binding, they are small in number compared to ABA regulations. The national government plays no direct role in regulating legal education. Regulation of the legal profession, like the regulation of other professions, is not included in the tasks allocated to the federal government in the Constitution.

6.3 Regulation of Admission to the Bar

Regulation of admission to the bar is another part of legal culture that has traditionally been controlled by the states, and historically there has been no bar admission process that would enable a person to practice law on a nationwide basis. There is no national regulation of admission to the bar in America for the same reason there is no national regulation of legal education. Instead, government regulation occurs at the state level, usually under the direction of a state's supreme court, which determines all prerequisites for admission to the bar in that state and oversees a commission of administrators called a State Board of Bar Examiners or similar name.

With admission to the bar determined on a state-by-state basis, practicing law in multiple states is a difficult process because it involves passing the bar exam of each state in which a lawyer wants to work.[161] Although a small number of lawyers undertake

---

159 The ABA Standards of Rules and Procedures for Approval of Law Schools is available at https://www.americanbar.org/groups/legal_education/resources/standards/ accessed 12 July 2019. Although the ABA is the direct regulator of law schools in the U.S., the federal government exerts its influence through the Department of Education's power to "certify" bodies that regulate education. For more on this form of indirect control see https://www.americanbar.org/content/dam/aba/publications/misc/legal_education/2016_accreditation_brochure_final.authcheckdam.pdf accessed 19 June 2020.

160 The ABA's Standards for the "Program of Legal Education" establish competency in "professional skills needed for competent and ethical participation as a member of the legal profession" as one of four educational objectives expected from ABA accredited law schools. Means for obtaining this objective include experiential courses, law clinics, field placements, and pro bono legal services. The professional skills objective is found in ABA Standards 301 to 304 and in accompanying Interpretations.

161 ABA Model Rules of Professional Conduct 505(b) states: "A lawyer who is not admitted to practice in [a] jurisdiction shall not (…) establish an office or other systematic and continuous presence in [the] jurisdiction for the practice of law; or hold out to the public or otherwise represent that the lawyer is admitted to practice in [the] jurisdiction." Rule 505 has been adopted by all of the states, see https://www.americanbar.org/groups/professional_responsibility/publications/model_rules_of_professional_conduct/alpha_list_state_adopting_model_rules/ accessed 12 April 2020.

this chore and become admitted to practice in two states, especially when they live in a metropolitan area that encompasses contiguous states, the vast majority of lawyers are licensed to practice law in only one state. Within this state-oriented framework, it is possible for a state to enter into reciprocity agreements with other states, which would allow a person admitted to practice in one state to be eligible to practice in the consenting states. However, such agreements often apply only to attorneys who have been engaged in the practice of law for a prescribed period, such as five years, and not all states recognize reciprocity with all other states.[162]

Over the past few decades, this traditional model of bar admission has been undergoing significant reform in the U.S., especially with regard to standardizing the content of bar examinations for all states. In a first phase of reform, two parts of the bar examination were standardized by the states' adoption of a multistate examination over certain substantive law topics and a multistate professional responsibility examination. However, states continued to administer a third part that examined students' knowledge of state-specific laws. [163]

The phase of reform currently in progress is toward a standardized examination administered uniformly across the U.S. and when passed would be accepted in each state for purposes of bar admission. This standardized test is the Uniform Bar Examination (UBE), and it is becoming the prevailing method for determining competence sufficient for admission to the profession. Thirty-four states, plus the District of Columbia and the U.S. Virgin Islands, have adopted the UBE.[164] Other states are considering adoption of the test.[165] The UBE consists of three parts: (1) the MBE (Multistate Bar Exam), which is a six-hour, 200 question, multiple-choice examination covering contracts, torts, constitutional law, criminal law, evidence, and real property, (2) the MEE (Multistate Essay Exam), which includes six, thirty-minute essay questions from nine subject areas and is given over one-half of a day, and (3) the MPT (Multistate Performance Test), which consists of two ninety-minute skills questions covering legal analysis, fact analysis, problem solving, resolution of ethical dilemmas, organization and management of a lawyering task, and communication. Applicants for admission to the bar must also pass a fourth test, the MPRE (Multistate Professional Responsibility Exam), which is a two-hour, sixty question, multiple choice examination intended to measure awareness of professional responsibility considerations and ethical rules within a given fact situation. However, this test is administered separately from the MBE.

---

162 Admission to the bar of this type is call admission on motion. The National Conference of Bar Examiners publishes a chart summarizing the availability of, and conditions required for, admission on motion in the states. See http://www.ncbex.org/pdfviewer/?file=%2Fassets%2FBarAdmissionGuide%2FCompGuide2020_021820_Online_Final.pdf#page=54 accessed 21 April 2020.

163 For background information about the evolution of bar examination procedures in the U.S., including examination of state-specific laws, see Margo Melli, "Passing the Bar: A Brief History of Bar Exam Standards" (1990) Vol. XXI No. 1 *Grăgule* 3.

164 National Conference of Bar Examiners, available at http://www.ncbex.org/exams/ube/ accessed 13 April 2020.

165 States at some stage of considering adoption of the UBE include Indiana, Nevada, and Oklahoma.

The major institutional actor in the development of the UBE has been the National Conference of Bar Examiners (NCBE). The NCBE was founded in 1931 and arose from activities within the American Bar Association directed at improving the bar examination process. The NCBE's interest in standardizing the bar examination on a national basis gained little traction for nearly fifty years, with the states holding fast to their control. Given the statistics cited above, it is clear the tide is shifting. There are two principal explanations. First, exclusive state regulation of the bar examination restricts the employment options of lawyers, as they are limited to working only in a state where they have taken and passed that state's bar examination. Second, state-by-state admission does not reflect the contemporary practice of law, which is often multi-jurisdictional in the sense that a lawyer's client may have a presence in multiple states and in the sense that many law firms have offices in multiple states.[166] However, the widespread use of the UBE does not equate to universal or unqualified acceptance. Sixteen states, including states with large legal markets such as California, Florida, Michigan, and Virginia, have not adopted the UBE. One of the criticisms made of the UBE is that it fails to adequately test an applicant's knowledge of the law of the state in which he or she will predominately or even exclusively practice. In this sense, retaining state-level control of the bar examination promotes the interests of consumers of legal services by ensuring competence in matters of state law. Further, there are variations in the UBE even among states that have adopted it, including the ability of states to include additional testing and to determine the score necessary to pass the exam.[167]

The emergence of the UBE is a significant development and merits reflection on its impact on some of the landmarks of legal culture in the U.S. Principally, the UBE can be seen as augmenting the trend toward standardization that is also visible in the discussion above concerning the Restatements of Law and Uniform Laws. In this regard, one can wonder about the effect of homogenization on notions of state individuality and sovereignty, in other words on notions of horizontal and vertical federalism.

6.4 Selection and Removal of Judges

Because the U.S. does not use a career judiciary training model, the topic of professionalism in American legal culture must include a discussion of the manner in which judges are selected and removed. The processes for selecting and removing judges in the federal and state judicial systems are strikingly different. As a result, the two systems must be addressed separately. Before taking up the differences, the two court systems concur with regard to steps taken prior to a person's decision to pursue a position as a judge. Notably, there is no separate education path by which law students prepare specifically for a career as a judge. Lawyers typically spend several or even many years practicing law

166 For a collection of essays on the benefits of the UBE, see "Essays on a Uniform Bar Examination", (2009) Vol. 78 No. 1 *The Bar Examiner* 6.

167 The National Conference of Bar Examiners lists eleven different policies concerning the UBE that states continue to establish on an independent basis. See http://www.ncbex.org/exams/ube/ accessed 13 April 2020.

before they become a judge. Further, there is no civil service-like career path for judges once they take the bench. In other words, there is no systematic process for moving "up the ladder" of judicial positions. In fact, there is no ladder at all. The vast majority of judges spend their entire careers in the same position.

All judges at every court level in the federal judicial system are selected and removed in the same way.[168] To become a federal judge a person must be nominated by the President, and the nomination must be confirmed by a majority vote in the United States Senate. Once confirmed, all federal judges hold their positions "during good behavior." In practice, this phrase means "for life." The rationale for lifetime tenure is that it insulates judges from political changes and from the passions of the day and permits them to focus exclusively on the law.

When choosing a nominee for an opening on a federal District Court, it is traditional for the President to seek recommendations from that state's two Senators. This is appropriate because the boundary of a federal District Court's jurisdiction lies within the boundaries of a state and because a federal judge hearing a case based on diversity of citizenship is required to apply the law of that state. Because the boundary of each federal Circuit Court of Appeals includes multiple states, the President traditionally consults with the Senators from each relevant state. This rationale does not apply to nominees for appointment to the United States Supreme Court, which of course hears appeals from across the nation.

In recent decades, the judicial confirmation process has become increasingly politicized.[169] While nominations to become a judge at the District Court or Circuit Court of Appeals level generally do not generate the same level of heated debate and charged emotions as nominations for appointment to the Supreme Court, partisan politics can still play a significant role. Senators tend to support the confirmation of nominees when the Senator and the President are members of the same political party and tend to oppose the confirmation when the Senator and the President are from opposing parties. Given the importance of federal judges in norm production and the fact that federal judges receive lifetime appointment and thus can remain on the bench for decades, the politicization of the appointment process is not expected to diminish.

Just as federal judges are selected in only one way, they can be removed in only one way – by impeachment. Impeachment of a federal judge is handled procedurally in

168 This statement is true of all "Article III" judges in the federal system. Article III judges are judges appointed to the U.S. District Courts, the Circuit Courts of Appeals, and the U.S. Supreme Court. They are so-called because these judicial positions are authorized by Article III of the Constitution. Other federal judges, including federal magistrate judges and federal bankruptcy judges, are called Article I judges because the positions are legislatively created. Article I judges are appointed by Article III judges; they are not subject to the Presidential nomination and Senate confirmation process. Article I judges also do not have lifetime appointment; instead, they are appointed for a term of eight years. All discussion of federal judges in this chapter refers to Article III judges only.

169 The nomination of Robert Bork in 1987 and the Senate's vote to deny confirmation is cited as an example of politicization. The confirmation hearings for Justice Brett Kavanaugh in 2018 show the height (or depth) of politicization. A simple internet search will produce scores of links to heated assertions of persons supporting and opposing the nomination. The status of the situation prompted the Public Broadcasting System to ask: "Is the new hyper-partisan Supreme Court confirmation process 'the new normal'?" See https://www.pbs.org/newshour/nation/is-the-hyper-partisan-supreme-court-confirmation-process-the-new-normal accessed 13 April 2020.

a two-step process, the same as with impeachment of a President. The process begins when a majority of Members of the House of Representatives votes to issue articles of impeachment. Following that vote, a trial is conducted in the Senate. A vote of two-thirds of Senators is required to impeach. Impeachment of a sitting federal judge has occurred only fifteen times in U.S. history, with only eight of those impeachments resulting in conviction and removal from office.[170]

The processes for selecting judges differ widely among the states. A state may use one process to select trial court judges and a different process to select appellate court judges. Some states even have multiple methods for selecting trial court judges.[171] Thus, the best way to describe the selection and removal of judges among the state court systems is to speak of categories of processes. Five processes can be identified: (1) partisan elections, (2) nonpartisan elections, (3) legislative elections, (4) gubernatorial appointment, and (5) assisted appointment.[172] One method for selecting judges for state trial courts and one method for selecting judges for state appellate courts are summarized below. These methods are chosen because they are widely used and because they illustrate the interests of democratic input and merit recognition a state must balance when deciding how to select its judges.

A common method for selecting state trial court judges is by partisan election. In other words, trial court judges are elected by popular vote in general elections along with candidates seeking election to other public offices. This means judges seek election by affiliation with a political party. Even though candidates for a judicial position in the partisan election model run for office against a candidate of the other party, they are not permitted to campaign in the same way as candidates for offices in the legislative or executive branches. Candidates for office in the political branches usually spend a great amount of time making promises to voters about the things the candidate will do if elected. Such promise-making is inappropriate for judicial office seekers because promising to decide a legal issue in advance violates a judge's duty of impartiality. In general, candidates for a judicial position simply display signs bearing their names and the office they seek. They may also distribute highlights of their legal education and experience.

Some states also use the popular election model to select appellate court judges. Other states select appellate court judges by way of gubernatorial appointment. There

---

170 "Impeachment of Federal Judges", *The Federal Judicial Center*, available at https://www.fjc.gov/history/judges/impeachments-federal-judges accessed 12 July 2019.

171 For example, at least four different methods are used to select trial court judges in the state courts of Indiana: partisan election, non-partisan election, and merit selection (also called assisted gubernatorial selection), and a hybrid process. These four methods contain even further differentiations, such as procedures for filling a vacancy on the bench. Summary of Judicial Selection Methods in Indiana, Memorandum from Indiana Supreme Court Justice (Retired) Frank Sullivan, Jr., on file with the author. This situation exemplifies the diversity of judicial selection processes in the state court systems. See State of Indiana, Judicial Branch website: https://www.in.gov/judiciary/5245.htm accessed 12 July 2019.

172 See the National Center for State Courts websites: http://www.judicialselection.us/ accessed 12 July 2019.

is a third model, called the Missouri Plan, used by two-thirds of states.[173] This approach involves a bipartisan judicial nomination commission created for the purpose of screening applicants for state appellate court judgeships. After the commission reviews the applications and interviews the candidates, it selects three and sends their names to the governor, who makes the final decision. Proponents of this assisted appointment model contend that it ensures a merit-based decision as only the most qualified applicants receive bipartisan recommendation and avoids cronyism since the governor's appointment discretion is limited to the people selected by the commission.

State court judges, whether at the trial level or at the appellate level, do not have lifetime appointments like their colleagues in the federal courts. Instead state court judges serve for a stated term of office and can be removed from office by voters at the next election. State court judges can also be removed during their term of office by impeachment in the state legislature or for disciplinary reasons by the state supreme court.

7. Internationalization

The term "internationalization" is widely used in contemporary American legal culture, especially in three contexts: cultural engagement, commercial transactions, and the status of international treaties in American law, including their enforceability in American courts. In the context of cultural engagement with regard to law schools, internationalization can be seen in the great expansion of the number of U.S. law schools that recruit and admit foreign nationals in J.D., LL.M., and S.J.D. programs.[174] Another indicator of the value placed on engagement is the emphasis American law schools put on establishing institutional and personal collaborations with foreign law schools and law professors.

Internationalization is also embraced in American legal culture in the context of commercial transactions. Cross-border business transactions, and the disputes that result, have become an important component of the work of many American law firms. In addition, commercial legal culture in the U.S. puts great emphasis on the use of international treaties to protect intellectual property rights, such as the TRIPS agreement,[175] and to resolve commercial disputes between Americans and foreign nationals through arbitration via the New York Convention.[176]

173 Ibid. See the "Method of Selection" heading for the Supreme and Appellate courts in each state. The non-uniform terminology used by the states to identify their selection processes complicates the task of determining how many states use the Missouri Plan. Available at http://www.judicialselection.us/judicial_selection/methods/selection_of_judges.cfm?state= accessed 12 July 2019.

174 LL.M. programs in American law targeted at foreign national students are offered at ninety-two U.S. law schools. "LLM Programs in American Law", *LLM Guide*, available at https://llm-guide.com/schools/usa/concentration/american-law-us-law accessed 18 July 2019. For definitions of the J.D., LL.M., and S.J.D. degrees and programs, see n. 146 above.

175 Agreement on Trade-Related Aspects of Intellectual Property Rights, 1869 UNTS 299; 33 ILM 1197 (1994).

176 Convention on the Recognition and Enforcement of Foreign Arbitral Awards, 330 UNTS 38; 21 UST 2517; 7 ILM 1046 (1968).

Outside the sphere of commercial transactions, the reception of internationalization in the American legal system is mixed and is the subject of significant debate and disagreement, especially with regard to the enforceability of international treaties in American courts. That issue was resolved by the U.S. Supreme Court in the 2008 decision in *Medellín v. Texas*,[177] an opinion authored by Chief Justice John Roberts. Because of the importance of that decision, it is discussed at length below.

7.1 The Place of International Law in the Hierarchy of Laws

There are three sources of international law in the U.S. legal system: treaties, customary international law, and general principles of law.[178] International law is referenced in the 1789 Constitution in Article I, § 8, which delegates to Congress the power to "define and punish (…) Offenses against the Law of Nations." The term "law of nations" is taken to mean "underlying principles of right and justice among nations." In 1900, the Supreme Court declared that "[i]nternational law is part of our law, and must be ascertained and administered by the courts of justice of appropriate jurisdiction."[179]

These propositions establish basic principles. The task remains to determine the place of international law within the context of the American legal system. The first relevant principle is that in the American legal system a treaty is considered to be on the same hierarchical level as a federal statute. As a result, treaties are subject to the same "later in time" principle as statutes, i.e., even after a treaty has been ratified, "Congress could pass and the President could sign legislation that rendered the treaty ineffectual – or Congress could do it alone by mustering a two-thirds majority sufficient to override a presidential veto."[180] Application of the "later in time" principle to international treaties can be seen as problematic. As one author has observed, the fact that a "simple statute can abrogate a duly signed and ratified treaty with a foreign State (…) might not appear to be the best arrangement for the orderly conduct of international relations."[181] The second principle is that by occupying the same hierarchical status as a statute, an international treaty is subject to the provisions of the U.S. Constitution. This statement of relative authority may sound implausible to some, especially to persons not familiar with the "internal logic" of the Constitution, which places responsibility for treaty observance in the political branches of government that are responsible to democratic principles.[182]

177 *Medellín v. Texas*, 552 U.S. 491 (2008).

178 *Restatement (Third) of Foreign Relations Law of the United States § 102* (American Law Institute 1987).

179 *The Pacquete Habana*, 175 U.S. 677, 700 (1900).

180 Burnham (2016) (n. 43) 696.

181 Ibid. 698.

182 Before delving into the facts, analysis, and outcome of the *Medellín* case, it is appropriate to identify at least a few academic treatments of the larger issues involved with regard to the place of international treaties in U.S. law, such as Oona A. Hathaway, Sabria McElroy and Sara Aronchick Solow, "International Law at Home: Enforcing Treaties in U.S. Courts" (2012) Vol. 37 Issue 1 *Yale Journal of International Law* 51 (identifies three ways other than direct enforcement that the three branches of the federal government can strengthen enforcement of international law); John F. Coyle, "The Case for Writing International Law into the U.S. Code" (2015) Vol. 56 Issue 2 *Boston College Law Review* 433 (advocating, in view of a judicial retreat from international law, that the Congress and the President

7.2 The Dualist Framework for Treaties

An additional inquiry, closely related to the two principles noted above, is whether international law in the form of a treaty becomes federal law so that, pursuant to the Supremacy Clause, the terms of the treaty become the "supreme law of the land" and therefore binding on the national courts, including the courts of the states, or whether international law is to be viewed solely as an "international commitment," with compliance or non-compliance left to the judgment of the political branches of government. The difference is inherent in the principle that "not all international law obligations automatically constitute binding federal law enforceable in United States courts."[183] Determining whether a treaty has binding effect in U.S. courts begins with a distinction between treaties that are self-executing and those that are not.

The U.S. Supreme Court "has long recognized the distinction between treaties that automatically have effect as domestic law, and those that – while they constitute international law commitments – do not by themselves function as binding federal law."[184] The Supreme Court has also held that "a treaty is 'equivalent to an act of the legislature,' and hence self-executing, when it 'operates of itself without the aid of any legislative provision.'"[185] By contrast, when

> "[treaty] stipulations are not self-executing they can only be enforced pursuant to legislation to carry them into effect" (…) In sum, while treaties 'may comprise international commitments (…) they are not domestic law unless Congress has either enacted implementing statutes or the treaty itself conveys an intention that it be 'self-executing' and is ratified on these terms."[186]

7.3 The Enforceability of Treaties by U.S. Courts: The Impact of Federalism and Separation of Powers – the *Medellín* Decision

Against this background, the place of international treaties in the U.S. legal system may best be illustrated by examining the Supreme Court's decision in *Medellín v. Texas* since

---

enact domestic statutes that incorporate international law rules); Austin L. Parrish, "Fading Extraterritoriality and Isolationism: Developments in the United States" (2017) Vol. 24 Issue 1 *Indiana Journal of Global Legal Studies* 207 (noting recent decisions by U.S. courts that belie the conventional narrative that the U.S. judiciary has disengaged from the broader world and instead signal an increasing receptiveness of a role for domestic courts that is consistent with foundational principles of international law; Anthea Roberts, "Comparative International Law? The Role of National Courts in Creating and Enforcing International Law" (2011) Vol. 60 Issue 1 *International and Comparative Law Quarterly* 57 (noting that the increasing importance of domestic judicial decisions on the development and enforcement of international law which creates a basis for a study of international comparative law).

183 *Medellín*, 552 U.S. at 504.

184 Ibid.

185 Ibid. 505 (quoting *Foster v. Neilson*, 2 Pet. 253, 315 (1829)).

186 Ibid. (quoting *Whitney v. Robertson*, 124 U.S. 190, 194 (1888)).

that case states the issues treaties encounter because of the structure of the American government and legal systems.

The *Medellín* case involves the Vienna Convention on Consular Relations (VCCR), Apr. 23, 1963, [1970] 21 U.S.T. 77, T.I.A.S. No. 6820, and the Optional Protocol Concerning the Compulsory Settlement of Disputes, Apr. 24, 2963, [1970] 21 U.S.T. 325, T.I.A.S. No. 6820. Article 36 of this Convention provides that if a person detained by a foreign country "so requests, the competent authorities of the receiving State shall, without delay, inform the consular post of the sending State" of such detention, and "inform the detainee of his rights," including the right to request assistance from the consul.[187]

The facts of the *Medellín* case are these. José Ernesto Medellín was a Mexican national who had lived in the U.S. since he was a child. As a member of a gang, Medellín raped and murdered two girls, age fourteen and sixteen. He was arrested by Houston police. The police read the *Miranda* rights to Medellín but did not inform him of his rights under the VCCR.[188] Following a trial in a Texas state court, Medellín was convicted of murder. The conviction was affirmed on appeal by the Texas Court of Criminal Appeals.[189]

Medellín subsequently filed a petition for post-conviction relief and, for the first time, alleged that his conviction was improper because he was not informed of his VCCR rights. The Texas trial court rejected this claim on the basis of the "procedural default" rule. This rule states that claims or defenses not asserted at trial cannot be asserted for the first time on appeal. The rule promotes efficiency by requiring all claims or defenses to be asserted at one time and promotes finality of judgments by preventing sequential assertion of claims or defenses in multiple proceedings. The Texas Court of Criminal Appeals rejected Medellín's argument and affirmed the trial court's ruling.[190] Medellín then filed a *habeas corpus* petition in federal District Court, which denied the petition, concluding that Medellín had forfeited the defense as a matter of Texas criminal procedure law by failing to raise the VCCR issue at trial.[191]

While Medellín's appeal of the District Court's rejection of his *habeas* petition was pending before the Fifth Circuit Court of Appeals, the International Court of Justice (ICJ) issued a decision in the *Case Concerning Avena and other Mexican Nationals (Mexico v. U.S.)* ["*Avena*"].[192] The ICJ concluded that "the United States had violated

187 Art. 36(1)(b), 21 U.S.T. at 101.

188 *Medellín*, 552 U.S. at 501. "*Miranda* rights" are the rights of a person suspected of committing a crime to be informed, prior to any police interrogation, that the person has the right to remain silent, the right to be informed that anything the suspect says can and will be used against the suspect in court, the right to an attorney, and if the suspect cannot afford to pay an attorney, the right to have one appointed at no charge. The U.S. Supreme Court established these rights, and the corresponding duties of police, in *Miranda v. Arizona*, 384 U.S. 436 (1966). The basis of the rights is the 5th Amendment of the U.S. Constitution.

189 *Medellín v. State,* No. 71,997 (Tex. Crim. App., May 16, 1997).

190 *Ex Parte Medellín*, 223 S.W.3d 315 (2006).

191 *Medellín v. Cockrell,* 2003 WL 25321243 (S.D. Texas 2003). *Habeas corpus* is defined in note 41.

192 2004 I.C.J. 12 (Judgment of 31 March).

Article 36(1)(b) of the Vienna Convention by failing to inform (…) Medellín of [his] Vienna Convention rights."[193] The ICJ ruled that the U.S. was obligated to review and reconsider Medellín's conviction and to do so without regard to the procedural rules of the State of Texas.[194] The Fifth Circuit Court of Appeals subsequently denied Medellín's petition, and Medellín appealed that denial to the U.S. Supreme Court.

To complicate matters further, after the Supreme Court agreed to hear Medellín's appeal from the Fifth Circuit Court of Appeals but before the Supreme Court heard oral argument, President George W. Bush signed a Memorandum to the U.S. Attorney General, which stated:

> "I have determined, pursuant to the authority vested in me as President by the Constitution and the laws of the United States of America, that the United States will discharge its international obligations under the decision of the International Court of Justice in [*Avena*], by having State courts give effect to the decision in accordance with general principles of comity in cases filed by the 51 Mexican nationals addressed in that decision."[195]

The majority opinion in *Medellín* says the Supreme Court accepted Medellín's appeal to decide two questions:

> "*First*, is the ICJ's judgment in *Avena* directly enforceable as domestic law in a state court of the United States? *Second*, does the President's Memorandum independently require the States to provide review and reconsideration of the claims of the 51 Mexican nationals named in *Avena* without regard to state procedural default rules."[196]

A majority of Justices said no to both questions, concluding that "neither *Avena* nor the President's Memorandum constitutes directly enforceable federal law that preempts state limitations on the filing of successive habeas petitions."[197] Accordingly, the effect of Supreme Court's decision was to uphold the decisions of the trial court and the Texas Court of Criminal Appeals, which had rejected Medellín's claim that application of the procedural default rule violated the VCCR.[198]

The Supreme Court's decision in *Medellín* is a significant statement of American legal culture because the reasoning is based on three fundamental concepts: (1) separation of powers among the branches of government, with the accompanying checks and balances, (2) vertical federalism, and (3) the role of the Supreme Court in determining what laws are, and are not, enforceable in the U.S. The separation of powers issue is based on the framework established in the Constitution for making treaties. According

---

193 Ibid. 502.

194 *Medellín*, 552 U.S. at 498.

195 Memorandum for the Attorney General, (Feb. 28, 2005), quoted in *Medellín*, 552 U.S. at 503.

196 *Medellín*, 552 U.S. at 498 (italics in the original).

197 Ibid.

198 Ibid. 498–99.

to this framework, the treaty power is allocated to the President, who is authorized to negotiate treaties, and to the Senate, which must provide advice and consent. In this way, the decision to enter into a treaty, the content of a treaty, and the decision to abide by a treaty (or waiver from it) after ratification are left to the political branches of government. The judicial branch does not have a role in the process, other than to decide, when there is uncertainty, whether the President and the Senate intended the treaty to be self-executing. In *Medellín,* the Supreme Court held that no such intent could be found with regard to the VCCR or Article 94(1) of the United Nations Charter, 59 Stat. 1051. T.S. No. 993 (1945).[199] Concerning the nature of proof required to establish that a treaty is self-executing, the Court noted that Congress "knows how to accord domestic effect to international obligations when it desires such a result."[200] Accordingly, for a treaty to have domestic effect, it seems Congress must "plainly provide" for self-execution.

Separation of powers and checks and balances are also involved in the Supreme Court's treatment of President Bush's Memorandum. On this issue, the Court acknowledged that "the President's constitutional role 'uniquely qualifies' him to resolve sensitive foreign policy decisions that bear on compliance with an ICJ decision"[201] and said that by issuing his Memorandum, President Bush sought "to vindicate United States interests in ensuring the reciprocal observance of the Vienna Convention," interests that the Court labeled "plainly compelling."[202]

Even so, the Court concluded that such considerations "do not allow us to set aside first principles," including the requirement that "[t]he President's authority to act (…) 'must stem either from an act of Congress or from the Constitution itself.'"[203] On this matter, the Court noted that non-self-executing treaties must be implemented by Congress, not the President. The Court found President Bush's Memorandum to be an improper attempt to exceed his constitutional role by "unilaterally converting a non-self-executing treaty into a self-executing one."[204]

The *Medellín* decision also required the Supreme Court to examine the impact of vertical federalism on the enforceability of international treaties in U.S. courts. The basis for Medellín's appeal was that by precluding him from raising a VCCR claim for the first time on appeal, Texas criminal procedural law violated his rights under the VCCR, which he contended, and the ICJ agreed, must be enforced in U.S. courts. The difficulty with this position is that if Medellín's claim and the assertion of the ICJ were accepted, Congress and the President through a treaty would exert a power not authorized in the Constitution, which is to dictate criminal procedure laws to the states despite their retained sovereignty. In this sense, the question becomes whether Congress and

199 Ibid. 509–11.
200 Ibid. 522.
201 Ibid. 523–24.
202 Ibid. 524.
203 Ibid.
204 Ibid. 525.

the President can indirectly exercise power through international treaties they are not authorized to exercise directly. The Supreme Court said they cannot.

This issue is of vital importance to the American structure of government because a treaty properly made and that is either self-executing or implemented by Congressional action becomes the "supreme law of the land" and pursuant to the Supremacy Clause in Article VI preempts contradictory state law. If Congress and the President through a treaty could make federal law in areas not delegated to the federal government in the Constitution, the balance of power between the national government and the governments of the states established by the Framers would be fundamentally and improperly altered.

The majority opinion clearly recognized this impact, stating that a judgment by the ICJ, which would "of its own force constitute binding federal law that preempts state restrictions on the filing of successive habeas petitions (…) would be extraordinary, given that basic rights guaranteed by our own Constitution do not have the effect of displacing state procedural rules."[205] To hold as Medellín and the ICJ advocated would produce "the improbable result of giving the judgments of an international tribunal a higher status than that enjoyed by 'many of our most fundamental constitutional protections.'"[206] In short, the limited power granted to the federal government by the states cannot be expanded by an international treaty.

The third important aspect of the *Medellín* decision is the question of who has the final word in determining what matters will be enforceable in the courts of the United States – the Supreme Court or an international body, such as the ICJ. In *Medellín*, the Court unequivocally said the final word rests with it – "[W]hether the treaties underlying a judgment are self-executing so that the judgment is directly enforceable as domestic law in our courts is, of course, a matter for this Court to decide."[207]

Three Justices dissented from the majority's opinion. The dissent would have found the VCCR to be self-executing and thus the judgment of the ICJ to be controlling law in Medellín's appeal.[208] Justice Stephen Breyer, author of the dissent, asserts that the *Medellín* case "considers when Congress must, and when it needn't, enact a law to make a treaty's provisions enforceable in American courts."[209] In his view, "[t]he majority opinion reads texts and describes standards in a way that makes automatic incorporation of such provisions more difficult"[210] than is necessary or proper.

In another context, Justice Breyer also notes that the issue of self-execution is inseparable from the broader issue of "how the United States – and similar constitutional democracies – shall reconcile the expansion of international regulation with the pro-

205 Ibid. 523.

206 Ibid.

207 Ibid. 519.

208 Ibid. 539 (Breyer, J., dissenting).

209 Stephen Breyer, *The Court and the World: American Law And the New Global Realities* (Alfred A. Knopf 2015) 215.

210 Ibid.

cedural and substantive safeguards that domestic law typically provides."[211] He clearly perceives a dilemma:

> "If, through treaty, we delegate too much rule-making authority to unsupervised international bodies, what becomes of the assurances of fairness that the Constitution provides or, for that matter, of the "legislative" power that the Constitution grants to Congress? But if we severely restrict the power to enter into treaties or other international agreements that delegate rule-making power to international bodies, how can we cooperate with others? How can we coordinate, for example, the enforcement actions of different nations? How can we possibly solve the international problems of environment, trade, and security that so directly affect us but which we cannot solve alone?"[212]

Justice Breyer does not resolve the dilemma but expresses a hope that a resolution lies in "work[ing] out what bodies, national or international, should review the fairness, transparency, and legality of findings of international regulators."[213]

The opinions written by Chief Justice Roberts and Justice Breyer evidence a conversation taking place in the United States concerning the status of international law in U.S. legal culture. Even so, the *Medellín* decision confirms that international law is subject to the "first principles" expressed in the Constitution, including separation of powers, checks and balances, vertical federalism, and protections guaranteed by the Constitution. The unique structure of the American system of government is not applied only to domestic matters with some other structure applied when international matters are involved.

8. Conclusion

The introduction to this chapter addressed the importance of perspective, particularly the process by which fifty-one separate legal cultures at the same time form one legal culture. It seems four conclusions can be drawn that are valid from both perspectives – the separate and the cumulative. First, American legal culture, like the American governmental and legal systems, is complicated. The culture values and the legal systems evidence a diffusion and allocation of power among multiple makers, implementers, and evaluators of law. Second, the culture and the legal systems are dynamic as both affirmatively promote an exchange of competing ideas and ideologies. Third, the culture and the legal systems give expression to dialectic tensions about law and law's relation to society. The result of such tensions is an ebb and flow of ideas, constantly testing and correcting each other. Lastly, the culture and the legal systems of the United States exhibit a commitment to the first principles of our Constitution as the best way to promote justice. Infused with creative tension may be a way to describe American legal culture.

---

211 Ibid. 233.
212 Ibid. 235.
213 Ibid.

The Structures and Structural Elements of the Legal Culture of the United States of America	
Institutional Structure	
Conflict Resolution	*Norm Production*
The federal court system and the judicial systems of the states operate concurrently. Subject to a few exceptions, state courts have general subject matter jurisdiction over all types of cases, whereas federal courts have limited subject matter jurisdiction and have authority to hear only two kinds of cases. Overlapping subject matter jurisdiction is possible, which means a case could be heard in either federal or state court. The federal court system is characterized by a three-tiered hierarchy of non-specialized courts, although there are a small number of specialized federal courts. The majority of court systems in the states are organized similarly, but specialized courts exist with more frequency in the state court systems, especially in urban areas. In both court systems, there is a right to one appeal from the trial court to an appellate court. That appeal is not a "trial of the second instance." Instead, it is based on a written transcript of the proceedings conducted at the trial court plus appellate briefs, occasionally supplemented by limited oral argument. In the federal court system and in states that have three levels of courts, further appeal from the intermediate appellate court to the final appellate court is discretionary, with the exception of a limited number of issues that are appealed directly from the trial court to the final appellate court. Use of arbitration and other extra-judicial methods for dispute resolution has increased dramatically in recent decades.	With the exception of the federal tax code, no systematic and comprehensive law code exists at the national level or in the states. Instead, Congress and state legislatures produce norms by situation-specific statutes. The President and the governors of each state produce norms through individual regulations promulgated by administrative agencies and also by executive orders. Judges in the federal and state court systems produce norms by interpreting constitutions, statutes, and regulations and in the state courts by creating common law. A substantial amount of legal scholarship is produced each year, including both theoretical and doctrinally focused research. The relevance of academic legal scholarship to the legal system is both valued and marginalized.

Intellectual Structure			
Ideal of Justice	*Legal Method*	*Degree of Professionalization*	*Character of Internationalization*
The implementation of existing law and the development of new law involves a dialectic between stability, which recognizes reliance interests, and flexibility, which recognizes the need for law to keep pace with social change. This dialectic is demonstrated in the malleable approach the common law takes to the principles of stare decisis and precedent. In the past fifty years, the constitutional principles of equal protection and due process have been important implementers of the ideal of justice in the U.S.	Legal analysis is generally pragmatic, as opposed to formalistic, especially with regard to both case law reasoning in judge-made common law. The pragmatic method is derived from the legal realism movement, which gave rise to a variety of contemporary theories of critical analysis.	There is a high degree of inculcation of professional values and problem-solving skills in graduate-level (JD degree) legal education. A high degree of professionaliza tion of attorneys and judges is maintained through mandatory continuing legal education. The requirements for legal education and admission to the bar are determined by a non-governmental body, the American Bar Association, and by the Supreme Courts of each state.	The U.S. considers international law in a dualist framework. Treaties are considered to be self-executing only if so indicated in the language of the treaty itself or accompanied by other Congressional implementation The dualist framework reinforces separation of powers principles, since the Constitution allocates foreign relations to the "political bodies," not to the courts. The dualist framework also reinforces federalism, since unchecked implementation of international law by federal courts could exceed the limited powers of the federal government and intrude on the retained sovereignty of the states. As a result, decisions by international organizations are not automatically enforced by U.S. courts.

9. Bibliography

Abrams, JR, "Reframing the Socratic Method" (2015) Vol. 64 Issue 4 *Journal of Legal Education* 562.

Albert, R, "Constitutional Amendment and Dismemberment" (2018) Vol. 43 Issue 1 *Yale Journal of International Law* 1. DOI: https://doi.org/10.2139%2Fssrn.2875931

Arlidge, A, *The Lawyers Who Made America: From Jamestown to the White House* (Hart Publishing 2017).

Bachar, GJ and Hensler, DR, "Does Alternative Dispute Resolution Facilitate Prejudice and Bias? We Still Don't Know" (2017) Vol. 70 Issue *4 Southern Methodist University Law Review* 817.

Balkin, JM, "Why Liberals and Conservatives Flipped on Judicial Restraint: Judicial Review in Cycles of Constitutional Time" (2019) Vol. 98 Issue 2 *Texas Law Review* 215. DOI: https://doi.org/10.2139%2Fssrn.3423135

Black's Law Dictionary (5th ed., West Publishing Co. 1979).

Bolick, C, "The Proper Role of 'Judicial Activism'" (2019) Vol. 42 Issue 1 *Harvard Journal of Law and Public Policy* 1.

Breyer, S, *The Court and the World: American Law and the New Global Realities* (Alfred A. Knopf 2015).

Burnham, W, *Introduction to the Law and Legal System of the United States* (6th ed., West Publishing Company 2016).

Campos, P, "Is Legal Scholarship Worth Its Cost?" (2017) Vol. 88 Issue 2 *University of Colorado Law Review* 377.

Carmines, EG and Fowler, M, "The Temptation of Executive Authority: How Increased Polarization and the Decline in Legislative Capacity Have Contributed to the Expansion of Presidential Power" (2017) Vol. 24 Issue 2 *Indiana Journal of Global Legal Studies* 369. DOI: https://doi.org/10.2979%2Findjglolegstu.24.2.0369

Carver, CB, "Do Alternative Dispute Resolutions Disadvantage Women and Minorities?" (2017) Vol. 70 Issue 4 *Southern Methodist University Law Review* 891.

Chemerinsky, E and Fisk, C, "In Defense of the Big Tent: The Importance of Recognizing the Many Audiences for Legal Scholarship" (1999) Vol. 34 *Tulsa Law Review* 667.

Churchill, W, *The Great Republic: A History of America* (Random House 1999).

Collins, RK, "On Legal Scholarship: Questions for Judge Harry T. Edwards" (2016) Vol. 65 Issue 3 *Journal of Legal Education* 637.

Conrad, CS, *Jury Nullification: The Evolution of a Doctrine* (Cato Institute 2013).

Coyle, JF, "The Case for Writing International Law into the U.S. Code" (2015) Vol. 56 Issue 2 *Boston College Law Review* 433.

Crews, Jr., CW, "How Many Rules and Regulations do Federal Agencies Issue?", *Forbes* 15 August 2017.

Dagan, H, "Doctrinal Categories, Legal Realism, and the Rule of Law" (2015) Vol. 163 *University of Pennsylvania Law Review* 1889.

Delgado, R, "The Unbearable Lightness of Alternative Dispute Resolution: Critical Thoughts on Fairness and Formality" (2017) Vol. 70 Issue 3 *Southern Methodist University Law Review* 611.

Delgado, R and Stefancic, J, "Southern Dreams and a New Theory of First Amendment Legal Realism" (2015) Vol. 65 Issue 2 Emory Law Journal 303.

De Tocqueville, A, *Democracy in America* (Vol. 1, first published 1835, Alfred A. Knopf 1972).

"Developments in the Law" (2017) Vol. 130 *Harvard Law Review* 1617.

Dotan, Y, "Deference and Disagreement in Administrative Law" (2019) Vol. 71 Issue 4 *Administrative Law Review* 761. DOI: https://doi.org/10.2139%2Fssrn.3097742

Driesen, DM, "Judicial Review of Executive Orders' Rationality" (2018) Vol. 98 Issue 4 *Boston University Law Review* 2013.

Driesen, DM, "President Trump's Executive Orders and the Rule of Law" (2019) Vol. 87 Issue *3 University of Missouri-Kansas City Law Review* 489.

Drobak, JN, "Beyond Stamp Collecting: Ronald Coase and 'Scientific' Legal Scholarship" (2017) Vol. 53 *Washington University Journal of Law & Policy* 21.

Erbsen, A, "Horizontal Federalism" (2008) Vol. 93 Issue 2 *Minnesota Law Review* 493.

Eskridge, Jr., WN, "Public Values in Statutory Interpretation" (1989) Vol. 137 Issue 4 *University of Pennsylvania Law Review* 1007.

"Essays on a Uniform Bar Examination", (2009) Vol. 78 No. 1 *The Bar Examiner* 6.

Farinacci-Fernos, JM, "Constitutionally Required Judicial Activism: Re-Examining the Role of Courts in Modern Constitutional Adjudication" (2018) Vol. 28 Issue 1 *Kansas Journal of Law & Public Policy* 36.

Fisher, DH, *Albion's Seed: Four British Folkways in America* (Oxford University Press 1989).

Foner, E, *The Story of American Freedom* (W.W. Norton & Co. 1998).

Friedman, B, "Fixing Law Reviews" (2018) Vol. 67 Issue 7 *Duke Law Journal* 1267. DOI: https://doi.org/10.2139%2Fssrn.3011602

Friedman, LM, *A History of American Law* (4th ed., Oxford University Press 2019). DOI: https://doi.org/10.1093%2Foso%2F9780190070885.001.0001

Fuller, LL, "American Legal Realism", (1934) Vol. 82 Issue 5 *University of Pennsylvania Law Review* 429. DOI: https://doi.org/10.2307%2F3308406

Gerken, HK, "The Taft Lecture: Living Under Someone Else's Law" (2016) Vol. 84 Issue 2 *University of Cincinnati Law Review* 377. DOI: https://doi.org/10.2139/ssrn.2822404

Gerken, HK and Holtzblatt, A, "The Political Safeguards of Horizontal Federalism" (2014) Vol. 113 Issue 1 *Michigan Law Review* 88.

Gersen, JS, "The Socratic Method in the Age of Trauma" (2017) Vol. 130 Issue 9 *Harvard Law Review* 2320.

Gorsuch, NM, *A Republic, If You Can Keep It* (Crown Forum 2019).

Graefe, DR, De Jong, GF, Hasanali, SH and Galvan, C, "Immigrants, Place, and Health: Destination Area Health Contexts and Routine Physician and Dental Care for Children of Mexican Immigrants" (2019) Vol. 53 Issue 2 *International Migration Review* 369. DOI: https://doi.org/10.1177%2F0197918318789128

Green, BA and Roiphe, R, "Judicial Activism in Trial Courts" (2018–2019) Vol. 74 *New York University Annual Survey of American Law* 365.

Grimes, WS, "Judicial Activism in the First Decade of the Roberts Court: Six Activism Measures Applied" (2019) Vol. 48 *Southwestern Law Review* 37. DOI: https://doi.org/10.2139%2Fssrn.3012339

Gross, N, *America's Lawyer-Presidents: From the Law Office to the Oval Office* (Northwestern University Press 2004).

Hale, D, *The Jury in America: Triumph and Decline* (University of Kansas Press 2016).

Harrison, JL and Mashburn, AR, "Citations, Justifications, and the Troubled State of legal Scholarship: An Empirical Study" (2015) Vol. 3 Issue 1 *Texas A&M Law Review* 45. DOI: https://doi.org/10.2139%2Fssrn.2569499

Hathaway, OA, McElroy, S and Solow, SA, "International Law at Home: Enforcing Treaties in U.S. Courts" (2012) Vol. 37 Issue 1 *Yale Journal of International Law* 51.

Hensler, DR, "Our Courts, Ourselves: How the Alternative Dispute Resolution Movement is Re-Shaping Our Legal System" (2017) Vol. 122 Issue 1 *Dickinson Law Review* 349.

Hessick, FA, "*Remedial Chevron*" (2018) Vol. 97 Issue 1 *North Carolina Law Review* 1. DOI: https://doi.org/10.2139%2Fssrn.3131018

Holmes, OW, *The Common Law* (first published 1881, Little, Brown & Co. 1963).

Jordan, SP, "Reverse Abstention" (2012) Vol. 92 Issue 6 *Boston University Law Review* 1771.

Kagan, M, "Loud and Soft Anti-*Chevron* Decisions" (2018) Vol. 53 Issue 1 *Wake Forest Law Review* 37.

Kagan, RA, *Adversarial Legalism: The American Way of Law* (2nd ed., Harvard University Press 2019). DOI: https://doi.org/10.4159%2F9780674242678

Kay, RS, "Updating the Constitution: Amending, Tinkering, Interpreting" (2019) Vol. 67 Issue 4 *Drake Law Review* 887.

Knight, AH, *The Life of the Law: The People and Cases that have Shaped our Society, from King Alfred to Rodney King* (Crown Publishers, Inc. 1996).

Kooragayala, S, "Preschool for All: *Plyler v. Doe* in the Context of Early Childhood Education" (2019) Vol. 15 Issue 1 *Northwestern Journal of Law and Social Policy* 98.

Llewellyn, KN, "Remarks on the Theory of Appellate Decision and the Rules or Canons about How Statutes are to be Construed" (1950) Vol. 3 *Vanderbilt Law Review* 395.

Llewellyn, KN, *The Bramble Bush: On Our Law and Its Study* (first published 1930, Oceana Publications, Inc. 1996).

Langbein, JH, Lerner, RL and Smith, BP, *History of the Common Law: The Development of Anglo-American Legal Institutions* (Aspen/Walters Kluwer 2009).

Leiter, B, "Legal Realism and Legal Doctrine" (2015) Vol. 163 Issue 7 *University of Pennsylvania Law Review* 1975.

Madison, J, "The Federalist No. 51," *The Federalist Papers* (Isaac Kramnick Ed., Penguin Books 1963).

Mead, JF and Page, MA, "Building a Wall around the Schoolhouse: Education and Immigration in the Trump Age" (2019) Vol. 48 Issue 4 *Journal of Law and Education* 449.

Melli, M, "Passing the Bar: A Brief History of Bar Exam Standards" (1990) Vol. XXI No. 1 *Gargoyle* 3.

Morgan, T, *Wilderness at Dawn: The Settling of the North American Continent* (Simon & Schuster, Inc. 1993).

Nelson, C, "The Legitimacy of (Some) Federal Common Law" (2015) Vol. 101 Issue 1 *Virginia Law Review* 1.

Parrish, AL, "Fading Extraterritoriality and Isolationism: Developments in the United States" (2017) Vol. 24 Issue 1 *Indiana Journal of Global Legal Studies* 207. DOI: https://doi.org/10.2979%2Findjglolegstu.24.1.0207

Petherbridge, L and Schwartz, DL, "An Empirical Assessment of the Supreme Court's Use of Legal Scholarship" (2012) Vol. 106 Issue 3 *Northwestern University Law Review* 995.

Piety, TR, "In Praise of Legal Scholarship" (2017) Vol. 25 Issue 3 *William and Mary Bill of Rights Journal* 801.

Posner, RA, *Law and Legal Theory in England and America* (Clarendon Press 1996).

Posner, RA, *Divergent Paths: The Academy and the Judiciary* (Harvard University Press 2016). DOI: https://doi.org/10.4159%2F9780674915596

Pound, R, *The Spirit of the Common Law* (first published 1921, Beacon Press 1963).

Price, PJ, "Immigration Policy and Public Health" (2019) Vol. 16 Issue 2 *Indiana Health Law Review* 235. DOI: https://doi.org/10.18060%2F23297

Restatement (Third) of Foreign Relations Law of the United States (American Law Institute 1987).

Roberts, A, "Comparative International Law? The Role of National Courts in Creating and Enforcing International Law" (2011) Vol. 60 Issue 1 *International and Comparative Law Quarterly* 57. DOI: https://doi.org/10.1017%2Fs0020589310000679

Rotunda, RD, "Vertical Federalism, the New States' Rights, and the Wisdom of Crowds" (2016) Vol. 11 *Florida International University Law Review* 307. DOI: https://doi.org/10.25148%2Flawrev.11.2.5

Rubin, EL, "The Practice and Discourse of Legal Scholarship" (1988) Vol. 86 Issue 8 *Michigan Law Review* 1835.

Ryan, E with Shuai, X, Ye, Y, Ran, Y and Haomei, L, "When Socrates Meets Confucius: Teaching Creative and Critical Thinking across Cultures through Multilevel Socratic Method" (2013) Vol. 92 Issue 2 *Nebraska Law Review* 289.

Sherrod, DR, *The Jury Crisis: What's Wrong with Jury Trials and How We Can Save Them* (Rowman & Littlefield, 2019).

Sutton, JS, *51 Imperfect Solutions: States and the Making of American Constitutional Law* (Oxford University Press 2018).

Tiscione, KK, "How the Disappearance of Classical Rhetoric and the Decision to Teach Law as a Science Severed Theory from Practice in Legal Education" (2016) Vol. 51 Issue 2 *Wake Forest Law Review* 385.

Vidmar, N, "The American Civil Jury for Ausländer" (2003) Vol. 13 Issue 3 *Duke Journal of Comparative & International Law* 95. DOI: https://doi.org/10.2139%2Fssrn.460222

Volokh, A, "Judicial Non-Delegation, the Inherent-Powers Corollary, and Federal Common Law" (2017) Vol. 66 Issue 6 *Emory Law Journal* 1391.

Weschler, H, "The Course of the Restatements" (1969) 55 *American Bar Association Journal* 147.

White, AJ, "Executive Orders as Lawful Limits on Agency Policymaking Discretion" (2018) Vol. 93 Issue 4 *Notre Dame Law Review* 1569.

Winters, DRH, "The Benefits of Regulatory Friction in Shaping Policy" (2016) Vol. 71 Issue 2 *Food and Drug Law Journal* 228.

Young, EA, "Against Amendments" (2018) Vol. 13 Issue 2 *Duke Journal of Constitutional Law & Public Policy* 149.

10. Principal cases

Case Concerning Avena and other Mexican Nationals (Mexico v. U.S.) 2004 I.C.J. 12
Chevron U.S.A., Inc. v. Natural Resources Defense Council, Inc., 467 U.S. 837 (1984)
Erie Railroad Co. v. Tompkins, 304 U.S. 64 (1938)
Hoffman v. Jones, 280 So. 2d 431 (Fla. 1973)
Marbury v. Madison, 5 U.S. 137 (1803)
Medellín v. Texas, 552 U.S. 491 (2008)
Miranda v. Arizona, 384 U.S. 436 (1966)
New State Ice Co. v. Liebmann, 285 U.S. 262 (1932)
Obergefell v. Hodges, 135 S. Ct. 2584 (2015)
The Pacquete Habana, 175 U.S. 677 (1900)
United States v. Lopez, 514 U.S. 549 (1995)
Wickard v. Filburn, 317 U.S. 111 (1942)

18. An Introduction to Australian Legal Culture

Tina Soliman Hunter

1. Introduction

The legal culture of Australia is truly unique. Certainly, on first blush one might think that Australia's legal culture is similar to that of other settled colonies that received common law, such as Canada, the USA or India, under Blackstone's principles of Settled Land.[1] Or perhaps one might assume that the legal system was received into Australia as a result of conquest, such as in South Africa. Yet Australia is none of those things. Rather the legal system and its resulting legal culture are truly unique, reflective of the unique nature of the country. Australia is a vast country, the breadth of the contiguous United States, yet with a population of barely 25 million.[2]

Australia was neither settled nor conquered. Instead, Australia's legal culture has been shaped by the perception of occupation of the land. Firstly, Australia was not a conquered land, like many other countries that received common law. Rather, it was seen as an empty land, even though aboriginal people with a rich culture and legal system inhabited it.[3] Justice Blackburn eloquently iterated this concept in *Millirrpum v Nabalco* from 1971:

1 For a discussion on the distinction between settled land and conquered land according to Blackstone's Principles, see Australian Law Reform Commission, *Recognition of Aboriginal Customary Laws* (1986), Australian Law Reform Commission Report No. 31, Chapter 5 'The Settled Colony Debate', available at https://www.alrc.gov.au/publications/report-31 accessed 30 December 2018.

2 As at November 2019. See 'Australian Population', *Worldometer*, available at https://www.worldometers.info/world-population/australia-population/ accessed 22 November 2019.

3 The prevailing view of aborigines at the time is typified by the report of James Matra on the Endeavour, who wrote in his report *A Proposal for Establishing a Settlement in New South Wales* that it was "peopled only by a few black inhabitants, who, in the rudest state of society, know no other arts than such as were necessary to their mere minimal existence, and which was almost entirely sustained by catching fish." See James Matra, *A Proposal for Establishing a Settlement in New South Wales* (1783), available at http://nzetc.victoria.ac.nz/tm/scholarly/tei-McN01Hist-t1-b2-d1-d1.html accessed 10 December 2018. The indigenous legal system will be addressed in section 4 where a consideration of indigenous legal norms is made.

> "There is a distinction between settled colonies, where the land, being desert and uncultivated, is claimed by right of occupancy, and conquered or ceded colonies. The words 'desert and uncultivated' are Blackstone's own; they have always been taken to include territory in which live uncivilized inhabitants in a primitive state of society. The difference between the laws of the two kinds of colony is that in those of the former kind all the English laws which are applicable to the colony are immediately in force there upon its foundation. In those of the latter kind, the colony already having law of its own, that law remains in force until altered."[4]

Thus, the settlement that occurred on this *terra nullius*, or empty land, was not that of the free. Rather, unlike any other country in the world, Australia began life as an English prison, where the so called "dregs of society" – the thieves, the forgers and the swindlers – were sent for periods typically of seven or fourteen years, but which effectively meant a life sentence. Thirdly, and perhaps more importantly, the culture of Australia from its outset, was individualistic, both on a personal and a community level.

On a larger scale, this individualism arose with the establishment of separate colonies. Commencing with the colony of New South Wales (NSW), there existed a legal tradition, which continues today, of the establishment of different colonies with different rules, arising from the origins of the colony.[5] After the establishment of this first colony, there was a rapid expansion and establishment of penal settlements in Van Diemen's Land (which from 1803 was an outpost of the NSW Colony until becoming an independent colony in 1825),[6] Port Phillip (Melbourne) in 1802, and Moreton Bay (Brisbane) in 1824. Later, free settlements were established in Perth (Swan River Settlement) in 1829, and South Australia in 1836. Although both colonies were established as free settlements rather than penal settlements, Perth received 9,721 convict offenders between 1850 and 1868, to alleviate the severe shortages of labour.[7] These convicts – mainly juvenile – were used as labour for the fledgling colony, which had been established to prevent the French from founding a colony.[8] On the other hand, the settlement of South Australia was without convict labour, and was comprised of all free settlers, initially primarily from Britain,[9] but later continental Europe, especially Germany.

---

4 *Millirrpum v Nabalco Pty* Ltd (1971) 17 FLR 141, 201.

5 The origins and legal traditions of each colony will be addressed in Section 2 below.

6 Hamish Maxwell-Stewart, 'The State, Convicts and Longitudinal Analysis' (2016) 47 No. 3 *Australian Historical Studies* 414.

7 *Convict Discipline and Transportation. Further correspondence on the subject of convict discipline and transportation*, House of Commons Parliamentary Papers Online, 251; I. H. Vanden Driesen, *Essays on Immigration Policy and Population in Western Australia 1850–1901* (University of Western Australia 1986) 67.

8 For an account of French interest in Perth (and Western Australia) see Peter Johnston, 'The Tale of Two Coins: France's eighteenth-Century Claim to Western Australia' (2015) Vol. 39 (2) *University of Western Australia Law Review* 25.

9 South Australia Land Company, *Proposal to His Majesty's Government for Founding a Colony on the Southern coast of Australia* (1831), available at https://openlibrary.org/books/OL20440157M/Proposal_to_His_Majesty's_Government_for_Founding_a_Colony_on_the_Southern_Coast_of_Australia accessed 1 January 2019.

The unique settlement of Australia, either as a penal or free settlement, has had a major influence on the legal culture of Australia, which pervades to this day. Of special importance is that the Australian legal system commenced as a series of colonies, some of which developed their own legal systems independently, and all were based on the reception of English common law into each jurisdiction, and united in 1901 when Australia became a Federation. The Australian Commonwealth Government (the Commonwealth/Cth) acts as the centralized federal power, each Australian state acts in a legal manner similar to a country, and on top of that you have the territories that also enjoy a great deal of legal freedom. It is against this backdrop of the unique nature of the establishment of Australian legal system that's its legal culture is considered.

2. Historical background and overview of Australian legal culture

2.1 Legal system and culture during the colonial period

As noted in the introduction above, Australia was founded as a prison colony, with six separate colonies established by the middle of the nineteenth century.[10] Consequently, the history of Australia's legal system, and hence its legal culture is unorthodox. If one examines the history of Britain's legal system, there is a clear evolution, where the influence of invasion, war and monarchy has had a marked influence on the development of the legal framework, real property law, and equity. Australia's legal history, and hence legal culture is completely different. Rather than evolving, England's legal system was thrust upon European settlers and their convicts under the concept of *terra nullius* (or empty land), rather than recognizing the indigenous Aboriginal Australians as first occupiers.

The first Australian court was constituted on 11 February 1788, a mere 15 days after arrival. Given that the penal colony was established under military law rather than common law, it is logical that the first court would also be a military court. Three Naval officers and three Marines sat along with the Judge Advocate General in the Court of Criminal Jurisdiction.[11] The colony was governed by military rulers until 1822,[12] with the Governor the sole arbitrator of authority. There was a perception by some early settlers and soldiers that some governors were acting outside their authority, implementing military ordinances that conflicted with English law. The conflict between the military and society came to a head in 1808 in the 'Rum Rebellion', where the New South Wales

10 New South Wales, Moreton Bay (Brisbane, and later to become Queensland), Port Phillip (Melbourne, to become Victoria), Van Diemen's Land (Tasmania), Adelaide (South Australia), and Perth (Western Australia).

11 Prosecution Project, *New South Wales Court: Early Justice* (2017), available at https://prosecutionproject.griffith.edu.au/other-resources/new-south-wales-courts/ accessed 22 April 2020.

12 Governors are Captain Arthur Phillip (1788–1792); Captain John Hunter (1795–1800); Captain Phillip John Gidley King (1800–1806); Captain William Bligh (1806–1808 – removed from office by the NSW 'Rum' Corp; Colonel Lachlan Macquarie (1810–1821).

Corps and associated leading land-owners took over government house, arrested the governor and governed the colony themselves for the following two years.[13] Legal order was restored by the incoming Governor, and the transition from military colony with military justice to a civil society with a civil government began.

Objection to the ruling of the colony and judicial system persisted. In 1823 the New South Wales Act 1923 (Imp),[14] repealed the Court of Criminal Jurisdiction and established the Legislative council of New South Wales, the establishment of Van Diemen's Land as a separate colony, and the establishment of the Van Diemen's Land Parliament and Supreme Court. Upon its termination in five years, The Australian Courts Act 1828 (Imp) clarified the extent to which common law and statutes of England applied to the colonies of New South Wales and Tasmania, strengthened the role of the supreme court in these colonies, and removed the ability of a case to be appealed from the Supreme Court to the governor. This, as well as the establishment of a legislative council in each jurisdiction, had the desired effect of diluting the power and role of the governor, and strengthened the legal and civil standing of legislative and judicial institutions in each colony. In addition, the Australian Courts Act 1828 (Imp) clearly enunciated the colony of Van Diemen's land as a civil colony, and therefore English law was applied.[15] Further legislation, the Colonial Laws Validity Act 1865, delineated the legislative power of British statutes in line with other colonies.[16]

As the move from convict government to responsible government occurred in the colonies in the second quarter of the nineteenth century, the rule of law had an importance influence. Particularly the growth in trade, commerce and free settlement during this period and beyond demonstrated a need for the implementation of local laws suited to the developing colonies. Recognizing this need, the English Imperial Parliament enacted the Colonial Laws Validity Act 1865 (Imp), which recognized colonial laws, and clarified that should a colonial law be repugnant to the provisions of an Act of the British Parliament, the colonial law would be void.[17]

---

13 State Library of New South Wales, *From Terra Australis to Australia: The 1808 'Rum' Rebellion* (n.d), available at https://www.sl.nsw.gov.au/stories/terra-australis-australia/1808-rum-rebellion accessed 22 April 2020.

14 Act to provide for the administration of justice in New South Wales and Van Diemen's Land, and for the more effectual government thereof. "Imp" is the standard abbreviation for Imperial in citing legislation, and refers to legislation passed by the British parliament as Imperial Parliament.

15 Section 24.

16 It is important to note that during this period the colonies of Victoria and Queensland had not yet been established and were still part of the colony of new south Wales. Victoria became a separate colony in 1851, and Queensland in 1859. Therefore, since they were part of the colony of New South Wales at the time of the Australia Courts Act in 1828, broadly the reception of English statute law into these jurisdictions dates back to 1828, with the reception of common law in 1788, the same as New South Wales and Van Diemen's Land. The date of establishment of the Western Australian Colony (1 June 1829) is deemed to be the date of reception of both common law and statute law, as set out under s73 of the Interpretation Act 1984 (WA). Similarly, s3 of the 1872 Act (SA) recognized 28 December 1836 as the date of founding of the Province of South Australia, and therefore the date of reception of English common law and English statute law into South Australia.

17 Sections 2,3 and 4 of the Colonial Laws Validity Act 1865 (Imp).

2.2 Federation

By 1865, the last of the Australian colonies had undergone separation and transformation to fully-fledged independent colonies. Furthermore, the Colonial Laws Validity Act 1865 (Imp) had established clear boundaries for colonial laws and had determined when laws would be valid. The impetus behind both the political and legal changes were complex, but largely driven by trade and commerce. During the 1850s to 1870s, the Australian colonies were largely inwardly focused, with each colony focusing on its own internal concerns and challenges. For the newer colonies such as Western Australia and Queensland, their sheer size, the establishment of infrastructure, and exploring their territory was a priority.

However, by the early 1880s, attentions began to be focused outwith by the individual colonies. The establishment of the Australian Colonies Duties Act 1873 (UK) enabled different colonies to set different tariff rates to protect local industries,[18] fuelling protectionism. It is this issue of protectionism that drove colonies to debate the issue of a possible federation in the years around the 100th anniversary of the establishment of the colony of New South Wales. A Convention in Sydney considered the question of federation, ultimately recommending the establishment of a limited federal authority. This authority was considered by all colonies with the exception of New South Wales, as well as Fiji. The member colonies made a request to the British government for formal recognition of the Authority, resulting in the Federal Council of Australasia Act 1885 (UK) and the establishment of the Federal Council of Australasia in 1886, without New South Wales, with a mandate to meet at least every two years, and bestowed limited legislative authority.[19]

A change in government in New South Wales meant that by 1895, New South Wales supported Federalism, however by then the north, south and central areas of Queensland were unable to agree on aspects of federation. A third national convention was held in 1898, and again aspects of various bills were not agreeable to some colonies, particularly New South Wales' objective to equal state representation on the senate, as well as fiscal clauses which favoured the smaller states. However, amendments to the Constitution Bill were agreed on, and a referendum for an Australian constitution and federation was held in 1899, which was successful in all colonies except Western Australia where the

18 It is important to note that colonies' industries differed. New South Wales and Western Australia were largely wheat/sheep producers, with gold mining beginning to play some part in the economy towards the end of the century. Meanwhile, Victoria had established a strong manufacturing base.

19 Such legislative authority is outlined in s2 of the Federal Council of Australasia Act 1885 (UK) and includes laws relating to letters patent, the naturalization of aliens of European descent, the status of corporations and joint stock companies, the recognition of supreme court decisions from other colonial jurisdictions in Australia and compelling the Supreme Court of a colony to produce a document.

referendum was not held at that time.[20] Finally the Australian Constitution Act 1900 passed the House of Commons and House of Lords, receiving Royal Assent on 9 July 1900, and the New Federation of Australia came into being on 1 January 1901.

In seeking to implement a form of responsible government that would be accepted by six disparate colonies, the Australian constitution is unusual in that it takes elements from the UK's Westminster system as well as elements from the US federal system (division of powers, federal court to solve state disputes, and the implementation of a senate and house rather than house of lords). This system of government has often been referred to as the "Washminster Mutation"[21] since it draws on Washington and Westminster in its construction. Academics have argued that this system was necessary since it enabled Australia to meet the specific needs of the British colonial masters as well as providing a workable arrangement between the colonies and the Commonwealth.[22]

2.3 Australian territories

Aside from the six historical colonies that became states, Australia has a number of territories, which can be divided into internal territories and external territories.

2.3.1 Internal Territories

2.3.1.1 Northern Territory (NT)

At the time of federation, the Northern Territory did not exist. Although the British government issued letters patent to establish a colony of northern Australia as a settlement for former convicts, a change of government meant that this did not go ahead.[23] Rather, the northern area of Australia was annexed by South Australia by letters patent in 1863,[24] leading to the sale of land in the northern territorial area of south Australia. A successful northern settlement was established in 1869.[25] By the early 20th century, low population – non-aboriginal less than 8,000, aboriginal approximately 50,000 – and the loss of customs and immigration control meant that South Australia continued to incur financial losses relating to the Northern Territory. It was proposed that South Australia

20 Hence the reason why the Constitution Act 1900 of the Commonwealth of Australia's preamble, as part of the Commonwealth Constitution which received assent on 9 July 1900, reads: "Whereas the people of New South Wales, Victoria, South Australia, Queensland and Tasmania, humbly relying on the blessing of almighty God, have agreed to unite in one indissoluble Federal Commonwealth under the Crown of the United Kingdom of Great Britain and Ireland." Note that Western Australia is not mentioned in the preamble, although s3 of the Constitutions includes Western Australia (if Her Majesty is satisfied that the people of Western Australia have agreed).

21 Elaine Thompson, 'The Constitution and the Australian System of Limited Government, Responsible Government and Representative Democracy: Revisiting the Washminster Mutation' (2001) Vol. 24 (3) *University of New South Wales Law Journal* 657.

22 Ibid.

23 Alistair Heatley and Graham Nicholson, *Select Constitutional Documents on the Northern Territory* (Darwin 1989) 27.

24 Northern Territory Act 1863 (SA).

25 As well as several failed attempts of settlement in 1824, 1828, and 1838.

divest itself of NT and the Commonwealth to take over the legislative and financial responsibility of NT in accordance with the Australian constitution.[26] In December 1907 an agreement was executed for the transfer of the NT, and Commonwealth formal responsibility for the administration and debt of Northern Territory occurred from 1 January 1911.

The Commonwealth government administered the NT from 1911 until the grant of self-government in 1978. Even though it has devolved self-government to the Territory, the Commonwealth has full legislative power over it if it chooses to exercise it under s122 of the Australian constitution.[27] This Commonwealth legislative power has been exerted many times, including during the Second World War, the aboriginal intervention of 2007,[28] and for the mining of uranium in Kakadu National Park.[29]

2.3.1.2 Australian Capital Territory (ACT)

The ACT was established in 1911 as a separate administrative division, under the Seat of Government Acceptance Act 1909 (Cth) and the Seat of Government Surrender Act 1909 (Cth),[30] which transferred the Crown Land to the Commonwealth, and provided for the acquisition of private land.[31] The role and purpose of the ACT is that of a national capital, named Canberra. The site was chosen due to its location between Sydney and Melbourne, far enough inland to avoid ship cannons.

The two 1909 Acts provided the legal basis for the Commonwealth governing of the ACT and the ACT Police department was established in 1927 when the Commonwealth government located to the ACT. In December 1988, the enactment of the Australian Capital Territory (Self-Government) Act 1988 established a framework that enabled the ACT to transition to self-government. The elections of the ACT Legislative Assembly were held in March 1989, and Self-government commenced in May 1989. As part of self-government, a new judicial system was established in the ACT.

---

26 Section 122.

27 "S" is the standard abbreviation for section when citing legislation.

28 The *Northern Territory National Emergency Response* was an alteration to the law and provision of welfare services, and land tenure in response to an alleged increase in sexual abuse and neglect in the Northern Territory, although no cases of sexual abuse have been prosecuted. It included bans on alcohol, pornography and quarantining of welfare payments. Most worrying, it removed customary law and cultural practice considerations from criminal bail applications and sentencing hearings.

29 The commonwealth government and the Northern Land Council reached an agreement on mining in Kakadu in the 1970s, with the first mine opening in 1980, and the national park in 1981.

30 "Cth" is the standard abbreviation for Commonwealth in citing legislation.

31 Section 125 of the original Australian Constitution stated: "The seat of Government of the Commonwealth shall be determined by the Parliament, and shall be within territory which shall have been granted to or acquired by the Commonwealth, and shall be vested in and belong to the Commonwealth, and shall be in the State of New South Wales, and be distant not less than one hundred miles from Sydney. Such territory shall contain an area of not less than one hundred square miles, and such portion thereof as shall consist of Crown lands shall be granted to the Commonwealth without any payment therefor. The Parliament shall sit at Melbourne until it meets at the seat of Government".

2.3.2 Australian External Territories

2.3.2.1 Non-self-governing occupied external territories

Australia has two occupied non-self-governing external territories: Christmas Island, and Cocos (Keeling) Island all located in the Indian Ocean, northwest of Australia. As a result of the Territories Law Reform Act 1982 (Cth), the legal framework applying to these territories is Commonwealth law, with a Western Australian based legal system introduced and administered by Western Australia. Western Australian Courts have jurisdiction, subject to laws relating to each territory that were in existence prior to 1 July 1982.

2.3.2.2 Non-occupied external territories

Australia has a number of external territories that are not occupied on a permanent basis: Ashmore and Cartier Islands, Coral Sea Islands, Heard Island, Macquarie Island, and Australian Antarctic Territory. In limited circumstances, Commonwealth law applies to these territories when so expressed in the Commonwealth law. However, the main sources of law are Ordinances from the governor General of Australia, which may be made for the "peace, order and good government" of a particular territory.

2.3.2.3 Self-governing territory – Norfolk Island

An oddity in Australian territorial, political and legal culture is Norfolk Island, which is located in the Pacific Ocean east of Brisbane. Originally a penal settlement, it received the descendants of Fletcher Christian and his crew from Pitcairn Island in 1856. Today it has a population of approximately 1,750 people. Although an external territory of Australia, it was granted self-governance in 1979 by the Norfolk Island Act 1979 (Cth), which continued until 2015. During this period taxation, immigration and social security laws differed from mainland Australia. As a result of different immigration status, it was necessary for an Australian citizen to present a passport to gain entry to Norfolk Island. In 2010, the Island announced a desire to voluntarily surrender its self-government, which was revoked in 2015 by the Norfolk Island Legislation Amendment Act 2015 (Cth). Upon abolishment of self-government, it became Norfolk Island Regional Council, part of New South Wales' local council system but the financial responsibility of the Commonwealth. All Norfolk Legislation passed during self-rule converted to New South Wales legislation from 1 July 2016. In addition, the NSW court system also now applies to Norfolk Island.

2.3.2.4 Administrative Authority – Lord Howe Island

Lord Howe Island is a set of 28 islands and islets, located in the Pacific Island South of Norfolk Island. It contains a small population of less than 400 people as well as a tourist destination of limited numbers. The statutory authority Lord Howe Island Board was established in 1953 by the Lord Howe Island Act 153 (Cth). This enables a high level of autonomy without conferring self-government. Since the administration is through a Statutory Authority administered by New South Wales on behalf of the Commonwealth, the judicial system of NSW applies.

2.3.2.5 Principality of Hutt River (Hutt River Province)

In 1970, the micronation of Hutt River Province in Western Australia was proclaimed by Leonard Casley in an attempt to secede from Australia over wheat production quotas. Casley then began styling himself as "Prince Leonard", abdicating the throne for his son in 2017. Although Casley died in February 2019, the principality continues. Even though the Province issues currency and passports it has no legal status in or outwith Australia, and is subject to Australian law, including taxation.[32]

3. Dispute Resolution

3.1 The courts

As discussed in Section 2 above, at the time of Federation to establish the Commonwealth of Australia, there were six clearly established colonies, that became known as states. Each of these has a well-developed and separate legal system that has developed as the colonies developed. The legal system Queensland and Victoria were all based upon that of NSW, since these two states were part of the former colony of NSW until independence. Meanwhile, the legal system of Tasmania developed from early on after being granted separate colony status under the New South Wales Act 1923 (Imp).[33] The Western Australian and South Australian legal system also developed separately since they were established as separate colonies. In addition, there are separate legal systems for the two internal territories, Northern Territory and the Australian Capital Territory.

Until the time of Federation, each legal system was completely independent, since each colony was independent of the others. Upon Federation, these independent courts remained independent, with judicial decisions in one state having no binding legal effect in another state. However, the Australian Constitution established a High Court of Australia with original jurisdiction,[34] and the appellate jurisdiction of the High Court.[35] This enables the High Court to hear and determine appeals from any decision of the High Court in original jurisdiction, or appeals from any other Federal, State or Territory

32 In 2007, Casley sought leave to appeal to the high Court of Australia over a taxation decision in the Federal Court, which had ruled that Hutt River Province was not separate to Australia and was subject to Commonwealth taxation. See *Casley v Commissioner of Taxation* [2017] HCA Trans 590 (4 October 2017); *Deputy Commissioner of Taxation v Casley* [2017] WASC 161.

33 Act to provide for the administration of justice in New South Wales and Van Diemen's Land, and for the more effectual government thereof.

34 Section 71. Under s75 of the Australian Constitution, original jurisdiction confers upon the court jurisdiction over all matters arising in relation to treaties, disputes between states or states and the Commonwealth, and consular matters.

35 Section 73.

Court.[36] In addition, the Australian Constitution enables the establishment of other federal courts,[37] and to vest federal (Commonwealth) jurisdiction in any state court.[38] There was a presumption that state jurisdiction could be similarly vested in the Federal Court; however, in *Re Wakim,* the court found that cross-vesting of state justification in the Federal Court was unconstitutional.[39]

3.1.1 State and territory court systems

There are ten separate court systems in Australia: six state systems, three territory systems, and the Federal system. Each is a separate legal jurisdiction. The state court systems are characterised by a hierarchy of lower courts: magistrates or country courts, and then district court, with the Supreme Court at the apex in each jurisdiction. The exception to this is Tasmania, which has only two levels of court: the Magistrates court and the Supreme Court. The court system of each jurisdiction is illustrated in Figure 1. Each state also has a Supreme Court of Appeal, where cases for the Supreme Court and lower courts are heard on appeal, with either a single judge or the full bench sitting. Most states and territories also have specialised courts, which vary from state-to-state and reflect the interests of the state. These specialised courts may be related to a class of persons, e.g. a Children's Court, or may be attached to a function, such as a Planning and Environment Court, a Mine Warden's Court, a Coroner's Court, or a Drugs Court.

Setting aside the specialised courts, typically in each jurisdiction there are clear parameters for each level of court. The lowest court, the Magistrates, Local or County Court, typically hears minor civil matters and some criminal matters. The limit of civil matters heard is usually delineated by the amount claimed. For example, in NSW the Local Court deals with civil claims up to $100,000. All criminal cases are heard in the Local Court in the first instance, then summary offences remain at the Local Court, while more serious offences are referred to the district of Supreme Court. The District Court of NSW hears civil claims of $100,000 to $750,000, and indictable criminal offences with the exception of murder and treason. The Supreme Court has unlimited civil jurisdiction, hearing claims of more than $750,000. In its criminal jurisdiction, the Supreme Court tries only the most serious cases, that of murder and treason. This structure is repeated in each state jurisdiction, with only the monetary value of civil claims at each court level varying.

Each state has a Court of Appeal, which hears civil appeals from lower courts, as well as specialised courts and some tribunals, depending on the jurisdiction. In order for a case to be heard in the Supreme Court of Appeal, an application for leave to appeal must be made, and leave granted. The Court of Appeal generally sits as a bench of an odd number of judges and may be a partial bench (e.g. three of five judges sit) or a full bench (all five judges of the court sit), depending on the importance of the case. In all instances

36 Australian Constitution, s73(ii).

37 Australian Constitution, s77(i) and (ii).

38 Australian Constitution, s77(iii).

39 *Re Wakim; Ex Parte McNally* (1999) 198 CLR 511.

the majority view prevails, and there is no requirement for a unanimous decision. In addition, each state has a Supreme Court of Criminal Appeals, which hears criminal appeals from Magistrates and District Courts (Magistrates Court only in Tasmania). In NSW, the Court of Criminal Appeals also hears select cases from the Land and Environment Court where criminal conduct is involved.

Territory court systems are similar to that of the state court systems, with lower courts and a Supreme Court. The Northern Territory (NT) comprises two levels of courts: Local Court (formerly Magistrates court) and Supreme Court. Both courts hear civil and criminal cases. Similar to Local/Magistrate /County Courts in the states, civil claims less than $100,000 are heard in the Local Court. For criminal matters, all cases are initially heard in the Local Court, with most offences tried in the Local Court, and committal hearings for serious offences such as murder, robbery and sexual assault are heard and then referred to the NT Supreme Court. The NT Supreme Court has original and appellate jurisdiction, with a Court of Appeal for civil cases and a Court of Criminal Appeal for criminal cases. Like the state Courts of Appeal, cases from these courts can be appealed to the High Court of Australia.

The ACT Court System is similar to that of the NT, with the exception that civil disputes up to $250,000 are heard in the lowest court, the Magistrates Court. All others are heard in the Supreme Court, which also has an appeals court. Interestingly, the ACT Court system also has a specialised indigenous court, the Ngambra Circle Sentencing Court, which sentences indigenous offenders who plead guilty to an offence. This is not a court of trial, but rather only a court of sentencing.

Norfolk Island also has its own court system. The general court system comprises the lower court of Petty Sessions and the Supreme Court. In addition, there is a specialised Coroners Court. There are three specialist tribunals (Employment, Mental Health and Administrative Appeals), as well as a Commonwealth Administrative Appeals Tribunal. The Supreme Court of Norfolk Island has unlimited jurisdiction, where matters are heard before a single judge. In addition, it also has jurisdiction over the Coral Sea Islands Territory, as conferred under the Coral Sea Islands Act 1969 (Cth).

Appeals from state Courts of Appeal – both civil and criminal – can be made to the High Court of Australia in its appellate function. Appeals from the territory courts go to the full Court of the Federal Court in the first instance, and then the High Court of Australia.

In addition to a court system, each state and territory has a system of tribunals that are part of the judicial framework, feeding into the court system. Many of these tribunals deal with minor matters, including minor civil disputes, residential tenancy disputes and consumer disputes of $5,000 or less. These tribunals are also often associated with lower courts such as magistrates or county courts, and can either be general, such as a Civil Tribunal, or specialised, such as a Mental Health Tribunal.[40]

3.1.2 The Commonwealth Judicial System

The establishment of a Commonwealth judicial system is enunciated in Chapter III of the Australian Constitution. Therefore, federal courts are referred to as Chapter III bodies.

3.1.2.1 High Court of Australia

Section 71 of the Australian Constitution establishes the supreme court of Australia, to be known as the High Court of Australia (HCA). It was formally constituted in 1903 with the appointment of the first judges under the Judiciary Act 1903 (Cth). It originally comprised three justices, expanding to five in 1906. It again increased in 1913 to seven judges and continues to comprise seven judges. Normally a case will be heard by the Full Bench of the HCA, unless a justice recuses due to conflict of interest.[41]

It holds an appellate function, as set out by the Australian Constitution,[42] whereby any case from a federal, state or territory court can be heard by the HCA. However, a case cannot be heard as a matter of right. An appellant must seek leave to appeal for the case to be heard in the High Court. Leave to appeal will only be granted where hearing the appeal will be relevant to the public interest rather than the personal interest of the party. In accordance with the Constitution, the judgment of the HCA shall be final and conclusive. Under this appellate function, cases could be appealed to the UK's Privy Council. This practice ceased in 1988, 200 years after the establishment of the Colonisation of Australia, through the enactment of the Australia Act 1986 (Cth), and the Australia Act 1986 (UK). In addition, until 1963 the HCA regarded the decisions of the UK's House of Lords as binding, thus leading to substantial uniformity between Australian and English common law until this time.

The HCA holds original jurisdiction under the Australian Constitution,[43] hearing matters related to national issues such as interpretation of treaties and conflict between

40 The Tribunals are numerous for each jurisdiction. For example, in Tasmania tribunals include: Anti-Discrimination Tribunal, Asbestos Compensation Tribunal, Health Practitioners Tribunal, Mental Health Tribunal, Mining Tribunal, Motor Accident Compensation Tribunal, Resource Management and Planning Appeal Tribunal, and Workers Compensation and Rehabilitation Tribunal. In addition, most jurisdictions have a 'general' Tribunal that hears petty civil matters, for example the Queensland Civil and Administrative Tribunal (QCAT), Administrative Decisions Tribunal (NSW), Victorian Civil and Administrative Tribunal (VCAT), South Australian Civil and Administrative Tribunal (SACAT), State Administrative Tribunal (WA), and the Administrative Appeals Tribunal (Tas).

41 The decision to recuse lies with the judge. There have been a number of instances where a justice has recused himself, such as Justice Stephen Gaegler in the case *Commonwealth v Australian Capital Territory* (2013) 250 CLR 441. In addition, there have been arguments where a justice was accused of apprehension of bias and requested to recuse himself: after controversy and public debate, Justice Ian Callinan recused himself from the Hindmarsh Island Bridge Act Case (*Kartinyeri v The Commonwealth* (1998) 195 CLR 337).

42 Section 73.

43 Section 75.

states and the Commonwealth. Throughout the history of the Court there have been critical decisions, which have established a strong body of precedent. In addition, the HCA in its original jurisdiction establishes the extent of the power of the Commonwealth in relation to the Australian Constitution. Both of these features will be considered more closely in section 4.1 below.

3.1.2.2 Federal Courts

The federal judicial system sits alongside the state and territory court systems. It comprises the Federal Court of Australia, the Federal Circuit Court of Australia, and the Family Court of Australia.

The lowest court system, the Federal Circuit Court of Australia (formerly the Federal Magistrates Court of Australia) was established in 1999 as a result of the Federal Magistrates Act 1999 (Cth). It was renamed the Federal Circuit Court in recognition of its role as an intermediate court in regional centres of Australia. It has jurisdiction over matters in ten general areas: family law and child support, administrative law, admiralty law, bankruptcy, copyright, human rights, industrial relations, migration, privacy, and trade practices. Generally, most cases in these areas are held in this court in order to free up the Federal Court of Australia. In addition, it hears appeals from Commonwealth tribunals.

The Federal Court of Australia was established in 1976 by the Federal Court of Australia Act 1976 (Cth), at a time when a raft of Commonwealth legislation (especially the Trade Practices Act 1974 (Cth)). Since it was the first general federal court, its mandate was to hear federal (Commonwealth) civil and criminal cases, although many have now been moved to the lower Federal Circuit Court of Australia. The Federal Court of Australia hears cases in the first instance with a single judge, but also has an appellate division, known as the Full Federal Court, which comprises three judges. In addition to Federal jurisdiction, the Federal Court of Australia hears appeals from the Supreme Court of Norfolk Island. In limited circumstances, as set out by the Federal Court Act 1976,[44] the Federal Court of Australia can hear appeals from states and internal territories exercising federal jurisdiction.

The Family Court of Australia was established in 1975 by the Family Law Act 1975 (Cth) to adjudicate family law matters under the newly established Family Law Act 1975 including divorce applications, parenting disputes, and division of wealth. Originally the only court dealing with family matters, much of the work of the Family Court of Australia was delegated to the Federal Circuit Court of Australia upon its establishment, due to the high number of matters. Now it only determines cases of complex law and facts, and intractable family cases. It also hears family law appeals from the Federal Circuit Court of Australia. In addition to hearing cases in its original jurisdiction, the Family Court of Australia has an Appeals Division, which is constituted by the full Family Court bench. An appeal from the Full Bench can only be heard by the High Court of Australia where special leave is granted.

44 Section 37.

In 1975, Western Australia declined to have family law matters heard by the Family Court of Australia, and instead established the Family Court of Western Australia. Interestingly, a review of the Family Court of Australia in 2008 proposed that the governance and delivery of judicial hearing of family law cases by the Family Court of Australia and the Federal Circuit Court of Australia be altered to a new model, similar to that of the Family Court of Western Australia. In May 2018, the Australian Attorney General announced that new legislation[45] would be introduced to effect structural changes, bringing together the Federal Circuit Court and the Family Court of Australia into the Federal Circuit and Family Court of Australia in 2019.[46] This established two divisions: Division 1 for family court, and Division 2 preserving the Federal Circuit Court. The legislation was considered by the Senate Committee on Legal and Constitutional Affairs and, subject to minor amendments, recommended the bill be passed.

3.1.2.3 Tribunals

The first Commonwealth tribunal, the Administrative Appeals Tribunal (AAT), was established in 1975. It was established to review a broad range of government decisions, including matters related to social security, veterans, migration, taxation, and freedom of information. As its workload expanded, a number of specialist tribunals were subsequently established, including the Social Security Appeals Tribunal and the Migration and Refugee Review Tribunal.

Unlike most countries, Commonwealth tribunals are not part of the judiciary. This is attributable to the separation of powers in the Australian Constitution. Chapter III of the Constitution establishes the Judicature as being that of the High Court of Australia and other courts under it.[47] In the *Wheat* Case from 1915, the HCA held that judicial power can only be vested in a court described in Chapter III of the constitution, and no other body can exercise judicial power, such as a Royal commission (a Chapter IV body, which was the case in this instance).[48] This was extended by the *Boilermakers* Case,[49] which held that a court cannot discharge arbitration and judicial powers, since it would breach the separation of powers. Because Commonwealth tribunals are established under Chapter II, The Executive, they are not judicial bodies. As such, they cannot exert judicial functions.

3.2 Alternative dispute resolution (ADR)

The use of ADR in Australia is wide-reaching within the judicial system. It is generally viewed as a viable alternative to litigation, thereby freeing the courts of increasing levels

45 Federal Circuit and Family Court of Australia Bill 2018 (Cth).

46 Australian Government Attorney-General's Department, 'Structural Reforms of the Federal Courts', 2018, available at https://www.ag.gov.au/LegalSystem/Courts/Pages/Structural-reform-of-the-federal-courts.aspx.

47 Section 71 and 77.

48 *New South Wales v Commonwealth* (1915) 20 CLR 54.

49 *R v Kirby; Ex parte Boilermakers' Society of Australia* (1956) 94 CLR 254.

of litigation. The requirement to engage in some form of ADR has been stipulated by both the court system and statute.

3.2.1 Alternative Dispute Resolution in the Courts

The use of ADR in Australia is well established, with reference to its use going back to the 1980s. Today most state and federal courts make provisions for ADR as part of the judicial process, and most often it is compulsory. Such use of ADR is usually stipulated under court rules, such as in the federal court, or a referral made by the court.

At the federal level, the Federal Court Rules 2011 (Cth),[50] enables mediation and arbitration processes to be employed in federal judicial proceedings. In each of the federal courts, parties are required under the Civil Dispute Resolution Act 2011 (Cth) to file a "genuine steps" statement, outlining the steps that have been taken to genuinely resolve a dispute, which will include mediation.[51] In addition, Practice Direction No. 1 of 2019 of the Federal Circuit Court of Australia sets out the arrangements for conducting Judicial Mediations in family law proceedings. Article 3 of the Practice Direction stipulates that "[i]t is expected that practitioners and parties will exhaust all mediation alternatives, prior to judicial mediation".

As noted by Mack, "most Australian courts now have legislation and/or rules of court that give explicit authority for the court to refer eligible matters to some form of ADR, and there is relatively little restriction on the ability of courts make such referrals."[52] Such referral includes the District Court of Queensland Act 1967 (Qld)[53] and the Supreme court of Queensland Act 1991 (Qld).[54] Similarly, the Western Australian Rules of the Supreme Court 1971 recognise the value and need for ADR. In NSW, the Supreme Court has the discretionary power to mandate mediation once proceedings are initiated, introduced under the Supreme Court Amendment (referral of Proceedings) Act 2000 (NSW). In addition, most lower courts have provisions for mediation, albeit on a voluntary basis.

3.2.2 ADR in statute

The implementation of ADR into statute commenced in the 1990s with the NSW Farm Debt Mediation Act 1994 (NSW),[55] which required creditors and farmers to undertake ADR (mediation) to resolve famer debt. It is a structured negotiation process that assists farmer and creditor in communicating to resolve debt matters. The success of this legislation is demonstrated in its introduction into other jurisdictions, including

50 Part 28.

51 Section 6.

52 Kathy Mack, *Court Referral to ADR: Criteria and Research* (2003) 7, see https://www.ag.gov.au/LegalSystem/AlternateDisputeResolution/Documents/NADRAC%20Publications/Court%20Referral%20to%20ADR%20-%20Criteria%20and%20Research.PDF.

53 Section 97(4). "Qld" is the standard abbreviation for Queensland in citing legislation.

54 Section 102(1).

55 "NSW" is the standard abbreviation for New South Wales in citing legislation.

Victoria (2011) South Australia (2018), New Zealand (introduced as a Bill in 2018), and Canada (1997).

ADR in statute is now commonplace and applies to many areas of law. For instance, the requirement for a Land Access Agreement under the Land Access Code in Queensland sets out the use of mediation if the parties cannot agree, prior to the use of judicial proceedings. Part IIIB and Part VII of the Family Law Act 1975 (Cth) set out the court's role in relation to ADR, including the court's role in relation to mediation and arbitration.

4. Norm production

4.1 Constitution

The Australian Constitution is the source of norm production, delineating the scope of power of the Commonwealth, state and territory governments. In the development of Federation,[56] the proponents made it clear that a Constitution with a clear separation of powers was desirable. As such, the Australian constitution is constructed in Chapters. Importantly, Chapter I concerns the Parliament, Chapter II the Executive, Chapter III the Judicature, Chapter IV Finance and Trade, Chapter V the States, and Chapter VI the New States. Under the Australian Constitution, certain powers are reserved for the Commonwealth Parliament and are enunciated within the Constitution.

Section 51 of the Australian Constitution outlines the legislative powers of the Commonwealth Parliament, which includes trade and commerce, taxation, postal and other services, military defence, quarantine, fisheries beyond territorial limits, currency, corporations,[57] social benefits, marriage and divorce, immigration, external affairs, indigenous peoples, matters referred to the Commonwealth by the states,[58] and any matters incidental to the execution of any power vested by the constitution in any House of Parliament, the Executive, or the Judicature.[59] Furthermore, by virtue of the Australian Constitution, the "Commonwealth Parliament may make laws for the government of any territory surrendered by any state to and accepted by the commonwealth (…) or otherwise acquired by the Commonwealth".[60] The Commonwealth Parliament has at times exerted its right to make laws, such as the overriding of the Rights of the Terminally Ill Act 1995 (NT) (Euthanasia Act) by the Euthanasia Laws Act 1997 (Cth), which also prevented the establishment of euthanasia laws in the ACT and Norfolk Island.

56 See Section 2.2 above for an overview of federation.

57 The case *New South Wales v Commonwealth* (1990) 169 CLR 482 confirmed that the 'Corporations Power' extends only to those corporations that have already been formed. Therefore, the regulation of the formation of Corporations fell to the States.

58 Section 51(xxxviii) of the Constitution – for example the formation of Corporations was referred by each state to the Commonwealth, to be regulated alongside the 'corporation Power', and the Corporations Act was created in 2001.

59 Section 51(xxxix) of the Australian Constitution.

60 Section 122.

Any powers that are not defined in the Australian Constitution are reserved for the states/territories, enabling them to make laws. Each state's Constitution enables that state to "make laws for the peace, welfare and good government" of that state.[61] Generally, if the area is not enunciated in the Commonwealth Constitution,[62] it will fall under the jurisdiction of the state. This includes matters such as schools, hospitals,[63] roads, public transport, utilities, mining, agriculture, forestry, community services, police, prisons, and ambulances. Where the Commonwealth and states/territories make laws with respect to the same matters, such as roads and health, and there is an inconsistency between a state and Commonwealth law, the Commonwealth law will override the state law to the extent of the inconsistency.[64]

The respective powers of the Commonwealth and the states were considered by the HCA in 1920 in the *Engineers* Case,[65] which considered the extent of the Commonwealth's power under the Australian constitution.[66] The HCA also considered the broader issue of constitutional interpretation, sweeping away the earlier, more narrowly construed doctrines[67] of implied intergovernmental immunity and reserved state powers. As noted by Chief Justice Sir Anthony Mason in 2003:

> "The combination of literal interpretation and a broad construction of Commonwealth powers led to the Commonwealth assuming a dominant position in the Australian federation vis-a-vis the states. The Engineers case ushered in a period of literal interpretation of the Constitution. Literal interpretation and legalism (of which Sir John Latham was the chief exponent) were characteristic of the Court's constitutional interpretation for the greater part of the 20th century."[68]

Hence, since the *Engineers* Case, the balance of power between levels of government, shifted from the Founding Fathers' vision of co-ordinate power, where the Commonwealth and states were financially independent and their own spheres of influence, to an increasing system of co-operative federalism that commenced with the *Engineers* Case and grew during the Second World War when taxation was taken over by the Commonwealth. This financial inequality is addressed through system of horizontal fiscal

---

61 For example, s2 of the Constitution of Queensland 2001 (Qld), and s5 of the Constitution Act 1902 (NSW).

62 Sections 51 and 52 of the Australian Constitution.

63 Although the provision of medical services is regulated by the state, there is a Commonwealth health system (Medicare) that was established under s51(xxiiiA), an alteration to the Commonwealth constitution by referendum in 1946. This enables the Commonwealth to establish and operate the Medicare Scheme, but not the operation of hospitals throughout Australia.

64 Section 109 of the Australian Constitution.

65 *Amalgamated Society of Engineers v Adelaide Steamship Co Ltd* (1920) 28 HCA 129.

66 Section 51(xxxv) of the Australian Constitution.

67 *D'Emden v Pedder* (1904) 1 CLR 91; *Deakin v Webb* (1904) 1 CLR 585; and *Federal Amalgamated Government Railway and Tramway Service Association v NSW Rail Traffic Employees Association* 1906) 4 CLR 488 (*Railway Servants Case).*

68 Anthony Mason, 'The High Court of Australia: A Personal Impression of its First 100 Years' (2003) 27 *Melbourne University Law Review* 864.

equalisation and adjudicated through the Commonwealth Grants Commission which was established in 1933.

The scope and limits of Commonwealth power under the Australian Constitution has been developed over the last 120 years and is characterised by several landmark cases.[69] Such developments in Commonwealth power and the importance of the Constitution in norm production can be demonstrated by a consideration of two critical Commonwealth powers: the trade and commerce power[70] and the external affairs power.[71]

The scope of the trade and commerce power was broadly construed in *W & A McArthur Ltd v Queensland*,[72] which extended the scope of the power to transportation as a direct and necessary scope of trade and commerce, as well as peripheral matters such as employment conditions. The domestic scope of the power was extended in *Wragg v New South Wales*[73], where the HCA held that a distinction is maintained between interstate and intrastate trade, although this distinction is not absolute, as considered in *Airlines of New South Wales Pty Ltd v New South Wales* (No. 2).[74] The scope of the overseas component of the trade and commerce was confirmed in the *Murphyores* Case,[75] where the HCA ruled that the Environment Protection (Impact of Proposals) Act 1974 (Cth) was valid, thereby providing the Commonwealth Minister with wide discretion to regulate the export of materials and to prohibit altogether the export of some goods. Furthermore, in *Murphyores*, Justice Murphy stated that in considering an application for export, the Minister may use regard to national policies not only in trade and commerce, but in other areas such as the economy, foreign affairs, defence, and, as in this case, the environment.[76] The principles eschewed in *Murphyores* remain valid, and the trade and commerce power continues to be widely interpreted.

Similarly, the scope and limits of the external affairs power has continued to expand, but with its scope not recognised as encompassing three areas: relations with other countries, matters external to Australia, and implementation of treaties. In the matter of relations with other countries, the decision of the *HCS in R v Sharkey*[77], the HCA found that external affairs extended to relations with other countries, not just Commonwealth Dominions. The scope was extended in *Koowarta*[78] to include international legal persons, including the United Nations and its specialised agencies. Regarding matters external to Australia, the scope was extended in *Polyukhovich v Commonwealth*[79] when the majority of the HCA concluded that the external affairs power contained a sufficient

69 Section 51.

70 Specified in the Australian Constitution 51 (i) as trade and commerce with other countries and among the states.

71 Sections 51(xxix) of the Australian Constitution.

72 *W & A McArthur Ltd v Queensland* (1920) 28 CLR 530.

73 *Wragg v New South Wales* (1953) 88 CLR 353.

74 *Airlines of New South Wales Pty Ltd v New South Wales (No. 2)* (1965) 113 CLR 54.

75 *Murphyores Incorporated Pty Ltd & Anor v The Commonwealth of Australia & Anor* (1976) 136 CLR 1.

76 *Murphyores Incorporated Pty Ltd & Anor v The Commonwealth of Australia & Anor* (1976) 136 CLR 1.

77 *R v Sharkey* (1949) 79 CLR 121.

78 *Koowarta v Bjelke-Peterson* (1982) 153 CLR 168.

79 *Polyukhovich v Commonwealth* (1991) 172 CLR 501.

grant of power to support a law to identify and prosecute war crimes committed during the Second World War. This was reaffirmed in *XYZ v Commonwealth*,[80] which held that sex crimes perpetrated by Australians in overseas jurisdictions can be prosecuted in Australia. The scope of the external affairs power in relation to treaties was tested in the *Sea and Submerged Lands* Case,[81] where Australia sought to implement the 1958 Geneva Convention on the Continental Shelf, with the Commonwealth claiming sovereignty over the Territorial Sea and the Continental Shelf.

4.2 Judicial decisions and precedent

Given that Australia is a common law system, courts play a critical role in the development of legal norms through the production of common law or case law. Fundamental to the system of common law in Australia is the concept of precedent, where previous judicial decisions are binding upon an inferior court or court of the same level. Annually, the HCA receives approximately 3,000 applications for special leave,[82] with the HCA typically hearing and deciding 50–70 cases per annum.[83] This binding nature of judicial decisions is known as *stare decisis*, with the theory articulated by Baron Parke in 1833 when he stated:

> "Our Common Law system consists in the applying to new combinations of circumstances those rules of law which we derive from legal principles and judicial precedents; and for the sake of attaining uniformity, consistency, and certainty we must apply those rules, where they are not plainly unreasonable and inconvenient, to all cases which arise…"[84]

In establishing precedent, judges apply the method of inductive reasoning, where broad generalisations can be made from specific observations. In this way, when the facts of a case are encountered again, the previous solution, as precedent, can be applied. Under this thinking, a series of decisions in the same pattern will ultimately lead to a general rule, which is the fundamental, philosophical nature of judicial reasoning. Alongside this sits the concept of judicial restraint, which is grounded in the idea that each branch of government will stick to its own defined function, and not step outside these responsibilities.[85] This concept dominated the thinking of most of the Justices born in the first half of the twentieth century, and therefore the development of precedent in Australia.

80 *XYZ v Commonwealth* (2006) 227 CLR 532.

81 *New South Wales v Commonwealth* (1975) 135 CLR 337.

82 Almost 3,200 applications for special leave were lodged in 2019. Special Leave refers to an application to the HCA for a case to be heard. The HCA does not hear every case that is sent to the HCA, and applications for Special Leave (both Civil and Criminal) are usually heard by a panel of three Justices.

83 The HCA decided 53 cases in 2016, 56 cases in 2017, 64 cases in 2018, and until 22 November 2019, had decided 41 cases in 2019.

84 See Jim Corkery, *Starting Law* (2nd ed, Scribbler 2002) 134.

85 Michael Kirby, *Through the World's Eye* (The Federation Press 2000) 101.

It is the role of the judiciary to uphold the binding nature of precedent. In Australia, given the ten legal systems, the binding nature of precedent applies only to that jurisdiction, where the decision of the highest court is binding on its lower courts. However, the decision of any court, even the Supreme Court of Appeal, is not binding on any court of another jurisdiction. For example, a decision of the full Bench of the NSW Supreme Court of Appeal is only binding on the lower NSW courts, including the Supreme Court and a single judge in the Supreme Court of Appeal. It is not binding, although persuasive, on the courts – Supreme Court or otherwise – of another jurisdiction. In addition, technically the decisions of the full bench of the Supreme Court of Appeal are not binding on itself, although there would need to be an exceptionally good reason for deviation from a decision to occur. All supreme courts are bound by the decisions of the HCA in both its original and appellate jurisdictions, under the concept of *stare decisis*.

The High Court of Australia has been given original jurisdiction in "all matters arising under the Constitution or involving its interpretation",[86] hearing and determining constitutional questions, often in proceedings regarding the validity of an exercise of Commonwealth enumerated powers.[87] In addition, in its appellate jurisdiction, it acts as the appellate court for the state and territory court systems, as well as the federal court system. Throughout Australian judicial history since Federation, justices of the High Court have applied judicial reasoning to the decision-making process of the court to create precedent. It is the justices of the High Court who, in developing the common law, give meaning to the constitution in a society that has experienced immense political, social and economic change throughout the first century of Federation.[88] These issues which face the Justices were aptly articulated by Lord Porter in the *Bank Nationalisation* Case, which stated that "the problem to be solved will often not be so much legal as political, social or economic. Yet it must be solved in a court of law."[89]

Where the highest court makes a decision, it is not bound by its decision, but would require good reason to not adhere to previous decisions, although this does happen. As considered in Section 4.1 above, limitations were imposed on state and federal powers, with the State and federal Governments prevented from intruding in each other's affairs, and reinforced with the Doctrine of Immunity.[90] Whilst this Doctrine was not spelled out in the constitution, the members of the HCA established this as precedent through judicial decision early into their tenure, to give common law support to the goal of coordinated federalism[91] that the participants had contemplated. Secondly, early decisions were less concerned with legalistic decision-making, than with the establishment of the relative roles of the state and federal governments in the new federation of states. However, rather than a narrow interpretation of later decisions, an altered

86 D.F Jackson, 'The Australian Judicial System' (2001) 59 *University of NSW Law Journal* 1.

87 Ibid.

88 George Williams, 'The High Court and the Mass Media' (1999) 1 *UTSLR* 1.

89 *Commonwealth v Bank of NSW* (1949) 79 CLR 497 at 639.

90 *D'Emden v Pedder* (1904) 1 CLR 91.

91 Gwynneth Singleton, Don Aitkin and Brian Jinks, *Australian Political Institutions* (7th ed, Pearson Education 2003) 45.

HCA composition enabled a wider view on issues of constitutional interpretation in the *Engineer's* Case. In this decision the HCA ruled that federal arbitration power could be extended to awards of state governments. In this judgment, the reasoning in *D'Emden v Pedder* was distinguished, federal legislative powers were substantially broadened, and the balance of state/federal power considerably tipped in favour of the Commonwealth. [92] This decision has had a profound and lasting effect on the doctrine of precedent in Australia. Rather than an adherence to a narrow interpretation, the Constitution was subsequently construed as being given a wide and literal effect. Such was the effect of the judgment of the case that a leading newspaper of the time reported: "This is a judgment of momentous importance, providing new principles of interpretation (…) the judgment of D'Emden v Pedder is overthrown, and all decisions based on it. People must wonder how long this new interpretation will last."[93] High Court Justice Lionel Murphy noted that, when referring to entrenched statutory or precedent, hard cases reveal that new law, statutory or decisional precedent, is required. [94] Such was Justice Murphy's commitment to the issue of hard cases, that he uttered his famous interpretation of the Doctrine of Precedent:

> "then there is the Doctrine of Precedent, one of my favourite doctrines. I have managed to apply it at least once a year since I have been on the bench. The doctrine is that whenever you are faced with a decision, you always follow what the last person who was faced with the same decision did. It is a doctrine eminently suitable for a nation overwhelmingly populated by sheep. As the distinguished chemist, Cornford, said, 'the doctrine is based on the theory that nothing should ever be done for the first time."[95]

Furthermore, Justice Murphy noted that when both judiciary and the legislature are out of step with the deeper moral conscience of the community they serve, it is the duty of the judges, as much as the legislature, to be radical. In its decision-making and establishment of precedent, Justice Murphy's view came at a time when Australia's judicial thinking was beginning to shift away from the positivist, rule-dominated formal law that arose in the 19th century and maintained throughout the first half of the 20th century.

An illustration of the HCA not bound by its own decisions is in the area of s92 of the Australian Constitution – trade and commerce between the states shall be absolutely free. This area was first tested in 1909,[96] and again in 1936,[97] with the HCA firmly entrenching the individual rights theory of s92 in the 1949 decision of the *Bank Nationalisation* Case.[98] This view of s92 firmly held by the courts in the 1976 decision

92 *Amalgamated Society of Engineers v Adelaide Steamship Co. Ltd* (1920) 28 CLR 129.

93 *Argus* 1 September, 1920.

94 Richard and Jean Ely, *Lionel Murphy: the Rule of Law* (Akron Press 1986) 114.

95 Lionel Murphy, 'The Responsibility of Judges' in Gareth Evans (ed), *Law, Politics and the Labor Movement* (LSB 1980) 6.

96 *Fox v Robbins* (1909) 8 CLR 115.

97 *James v Cowan* (1936) 47 CLR 386, although overturned on appeal to the Privy Council.

98 *Commonwealth v Bank of New South Wales (*1949) 79 CLR 497.

of *Buck v Bavone*,[99] maintaining the precedent established in the *Bank Nationalisation* Case, although Justice Murphy in dissent enunciated that the doctrine of individual rights was highly artificial and was only being maintained through the adherence to bad law.[100] Justice Murphy's dissenting view was accepted by the court in 1988 in the pendulum decision view of the s92 case of *Cole v Whitfield*.[101] In the judicial version of a double back-flip with a twist, the High Court reversed eighty years of individual rights theory, embracing the early s92 interpretation found in *Fox v Robbins*,[102] and turned its back on the previous Criterion of Operation formula:

> "In truth the history of the doctrine is an indication of the hazards of seeking certainty of operation of constitutional guarantee through the medium of an artificial formula. Either the formula is consistently applied and subverts the substance of the guarantee, or an attempt is made to achieve uniformly satisfactory outcomes and the formula becomes uncertain in its application."[103]

Such straying from the Doctrine of Precedent in Australia is rare, although more likely during the HCS period of judicial activism during the 1970s-early 1990s.[104] In the era of a conservative HCA today, the observance of precedent prevails, and is the cornerstone of judicial decision-making.

4.3 Statutes

As a traditional common law jurisdiction, historically the dominant source of law has been precedent. However, in the modern era statutes – legislature-created law – dominate the law-making process in all Australian legal jurisdictions.[105] It is the production of statutes that produce, by far, the vast majority of legal norms in Australia. Statutes are created in the parliament of each jurisdiction, and over the last thirty years, the volume and complexity of statutes has increased markedly. For example, in 2018 alone, 274 new statutes were passed by the Commonwealth parliament, representing over 35,000 new pages of legislation.[106]

Australian Commonwealth statutes are notoriously cumbersome. For example, the taxation law is so voluminous and difficult that Paul Gerber noted that "I suspect if a million monkeys were put in front of a million typewriters, by Wednesday one of them would come up with an improved version of the Income Tax Assessment Act".[107]

---

99 *Buck v Bavone* (1976) 135 CLR 110.
100 Ibid 132.
101 *Cole v Whitfield* (1988) 165 CLR 360.
102 *Fox v Robbins* (1909) 8 CLR 115.
103 *Cole v Whitfield* (1988) 165 CLR 360 at 402, per Mason J.
104 See Section 6.2 for a consideration of judicial activism in Australia.
105 States and territories, although no longer Norfolk Island.
106 Source: Austlii Database: Commonwealth Legislation (calculated by Author).
107 Quoted from Joan Priest, *Sir Harry Gibbs: Without Fear or Favour* (Scribblers Publishing 1995) 170.

Statutes in Australia are typically prescriptive or rule-based and can run to hundreds or thousands of pages. This trend to ever more lengthy and complex legislation is typified by tax statutes. The Income Tax Assessment Act 1936 (Cth) ran at less than 800 pages, a behemoth in that era. Yet currently, the superseding Act, The Income Tax Assessment Act 1997 (Cth) is almost 9,000 pages by 2005, before being reduced to over 6,000 in 2008. Similarly, the Current Australian Offshore Petroleum and Greenhous Gas Storage Act 2006 (Cth) runs to three volumes and over 1,400 pages.[108]

Such statutory excess is not only confined to Commonwealth legislation. There has been an increase in the length and volume of legislation in all state jurisdictions. The Queensland Petroleum and Gas (Production and Storage) Act 2003 (Qld) runs to over 800 pages, with thousands of amendments and almost 100 reprints.[109] Today legislation has become so much "fatter and uglier", as typified by Queensland in the period between 1988 and 2006, where the Parliament enacted five times more legislation than was enacted in the 135 years from 1828 to 1962.[110] Not all jurisdictions have fat and ugly legislation. In South Australia, there has been a purposive attempt to streamline legislation, seeking to implement objective-based regulation that is shorter and more precise. In 2000, South Australia implemented the Petroleum and Geothermal Energy Act 2000 (SA), the equivalent of the Petroleum and Gas (Production and Storage) Act 2003 (Qld). Being objective-based, this Act is only 79 pages long, covering all of the aspects of the Qld act, as well as geothermal resource production.

In the Australian legal system, statutes overrule common law (cases) where both apply to an area of law. This means that either statute and common law principles sit side-by-side, or statute completely replaces an area of common law. This is the government's attempt to control future activity. However, often a statute is unable to formulate every scenario leading to legislative amendments. Furthermore, the ambiguous nature of a statute may require judicial interpretation. Interpretation of statutes may be made applying the rules of statutory interpretation: the literal rule (only taking what the statute says on its face), the golden rule (where the statute is interpreted in a way that takes the ordinary meaning of the words of a statute in order to avoid absurdity), or the mischief or purpose rule (where the statute is interpreted in accordance with the intention of the maker). The purposive approach dominates, and in 1981 this approach was inserted into the Acts Interpretation Act 1901 (Cth), stating that

> "in the interpretation of a provision of an Act, a construction that would promote the purpose or object underlying the Act (whether that purpose or object is expressly stated

---

108 Professor Terrence Daintith described the predecessor to the Offshore Petroleum and Greenhous Gas Storage Act 2006 (Cth), the Petroleum (Submerged Lands) Act 1967 (Cth), a small 630-page tome) as "old, fat and ugly, and not likely to score highly in a legislative beauty contest", see Terrence Daintith, 'A critical evaluation of the *Petroleum (Submerged Lands) Act* as a regulatory regime' (2000) *2000 AMPLA Yearbook* 91, 92.

109 A list of reprints is found on pages 716–720 of the Legislation. For example, the legislation was reprinted in January, March, April, May, June, July and September 2011.

110 Transcript of Proceedings, Supreme Court of Queensland 22 September 2006, 14–15.

> in the Act or not) shall be preferred to a construction that would not promote that purpose or object."[111]

In addition, extrinsic materials, such as reports from a Royal Commission or Law Reform Commission, Explanatory Memorandum or Parliamentary Speeches, can be considered in the interpretation of a statute.[112] This use of extrinsic material is not confined to the Commonwealth, but rather is used by the states and territories.

4.4 Codes

A hallmark of the common law is the reliance on precedent in the formation of legal norms. However, since common law jurisdictions increase the use of statutes, it is argued that common law systems are coming closer to their civil law brethren, with much of the common law codified into statute. Usually such codification is generally seen as the passing of statute. However, in many Australian jurisdictions, criminal law has been codified. The first to codify was Queensland[113] and Western Australia[114] at the beginning of the 20th century. Such codification was also implemented by Tasmania,[115] the Northern Territory,[116] the ACT,[117] and the Commonwealth.[118] The use of such codes in Australia is confined to criminal law only, whereas the common law continues to play a significant role in the development of civil law in the common law.

4.5 Legal writing and other minor forms of norm production

Unlike civil law jurisdictions, legal writing by eminent publicists has little impact on norm production in any jurisdiction in Australia. On occasions eminent justices, such as High Court and Supreme Court justices, will deliver speeches such as their commencement speech, or at a significant event.[119] Whilst not in itself producing legal norms, such speeches provide some insight into the thinking and reasoning of the particular justice.

111 Section 15AA.

112 Acts Interpretation Act 1901 (Cth) s15AB.

113 Criminal Code Act 1899 (Qld).

114 Criminal Code Act 1902 (WA) and the Criminal Code Act Compilation Act 1913 (WA).

115 Criminal Code Act 1924 (Tas).

116 Criminal Code Act 1983 (NT).

117 Criminal Code Act 2002 (ACT).

118 Criminal Code Act 1995 (Cth).

119 As an example, for selected speeches of the current Chief Justice of the High Court of Australia, Susan Kiefel, see http://www.hcourt.gov.au/publications/speeches/current/speeches-by-justice-kiefel accessed 26 November 2019.

4.6 Indigenous law norms

Aboriginal customary law was first considered in the 1986 Australian Law Reform Commission Report number 31: Recognition of Aboriginal Customary Laws. At the heart of the issue was the debate over Australia as a settled colony or whether there was conquest, and therefore the laws of the indigenous peoples should be recognised. Certainly, indigenous customary law as a system of law was recognised in 1992 in the case of *Mabo v Commonwealth* (No. 2).[120] In this landmark decision, the HCA held that the doctrine of *terra nullius* did not apply where there were already inhabitants, even where the inhabitants appeared "uncivilised". Therefore, existing indigenous customary laws that were present at the time of colonisation survived the reception of English law. More specifically, the customary law of indigenous land title was not extinguished in certain circumstances and prevails. Subsequent to the *Mabo* judgment, the Native title Act 1993 (Cth) established indigenous customary law in statute, outlining what indigenous title over land is and how such title is determined.[121]

5. Ideal of justice and legal method

5.1 Rule of law and separation of powers

The doctrines of the rule of law and the separation of powers are the cornerstone of the Australian Constitution, establishing the federalist system under which Australia is governed. The Australian constitutional system is very much a hybrid system, incorporating many of the nuances of the Westminster system, as brought to the Australian shores upon colonization. It also embraces features of the American constitutional system, primarily due the existence of numerous Australian colonies at the time of Federation, analogous to the system of United States of America.

In establishing the Washminster system of democracy, the founding fathers of Federation clearly sought to retain the rule of law, with a separation of powers as outlined in the Constitution. This system of government has been preserved to this day, with the High Court playing an ever-increasing role in the interpretation of the constitution, in both the separation of powers, such as in the case of *Re Wakim*, but also in the exercise of Commonwealth and State power throughout the 20th century.

As the court has gone about applying judicial reasoning and interpretation to delineate the boundaries of commonwealth and state powers, the court has clearly upheld the concept of the rule of law, as well as itself embarking on a journey, delineating the boundaries of its own powers and processes. This delineation includes its role within the separation of powers, and the process by which the High Court arrives at a judicial decision, especially the judicial reasoning process "fundamental to the system is that the validity of all legislation and executive action is judged by the courts, not legislature

---

120 *Mabo and Others v Commonwealth (No. 2)* (1992) 175 CLR 1.

121 Section 223 and 225.

or executive."[122] The separation of powers purports to be just that – a distinct delineation of the judiciary from the other two arms of the government, where the role of the court from Federation is to determine the constitutional validity of the laws enacted and executed by the two arms of the government, in an independent manner, through Chapter III of the Australian Constitution.[123]

That the High Court is involved in the exercise of political power may appear to conflict with the notion of the separation of power espoused by John Locke and Charles Montesquieu.[124] This is especially questionable since there is an overlap between the judiciary and the executive branch of government. The judges are chosen by the Parliament, appointed by the executive, and may be dismissed by the Governor-General on address from both Houses of the Parliament in the same session on the grounds of proved misbehaviour or incapacity as defined in the Constitution.[125]

Since Federalism, the High Court has interpreted the constitution as providing a separation of powers, and in *Dignan's* Case,[126] the court considered and ruled on the nature of separation of powers between the legislature and the executive.[127] In this judgment, both Justice Evatt and Dixon support the separation of powers, daring to provide substantive argument regarding the separation of powers, with Evatt further venturing to discuss the issue at length.[128] Evatt accepts there is a separation of judicial powers, based on the High Court decisions, and that "judicial functionaries should be free from any interference from the legislative or the executive, the special nature of judicial power and the elaborate provisions of chapter III."[129]

Since *Dignan's* Case, and beyond, the High Court has formally adhered to the separation of powers doctrine, reiterated by the court in 1956 with the *Boilermakers* Case,[130] where the High Court ruled that the body established to exercise the Commonwealth's power to conciliate and arbitrate industrial disputes could not also operate as a court of the kind the Commonwealth parliament may create under Chapter III of the Constitution.

5.2 Equity

The concept of equity arose in England during the reign of early kings, and by the 14th century the Chancery operated as a court, granting remedies where the application of the strict common law writ system provided a harsh remedy or no remedy to a plaintiff who deserved better. By the end of the 17th century, the system of equity was well

122 *Australian Capital Television v Commonwealth* (1992) 177 CLR 106.

123 Jackson (2001) (n 86) 1; Australian Constitution, s71, s73, ss75–6.

124 David Soloman, *The Politics of the High Court* (Allen & Unwin 1992) 7.

125 Section 72.

126 *Victoria Stevedoring & General Contracting Co. Pty Ltd v Dignan* (1931) 46 CLR 73.

127 Haig Patapan, *Judging Democracy: the New Politics of the High Court* (Cambridge University Press 2000) 157.

128 Ibid 157–8.

129 *Victoria Stevedoring & General Contracting Co. Pty Ltd v Dignan* (1931) 46 CLR 73 at 115–6.

130 *R v Kirby: Ex parte Boilermakers' Society of Australia* (1956) 94 CLR 254.

developed, with lawyers appointed as Chancellor to dispense equitable relief through the Court of Chancery. It was this law that was received into the Australian colonies in the 19th century as they became established.

Judicature reforms in the 1870s under the Judicature Acts of 1873 and 1875 saw the fusing of the split systems of common law and equity in England and Wales, thereby removing the existence of two separate systems. After this time, on hearing a case, a Court could grant both common law and equitable relief in the same hearing. The granting of an equitable relief remained discretionary, relying on the applicant meeting the requirements of the equitable maxims, particularly laches (delay) and clean hands.

The reception of the Judicature Acts was slow in some of the colonies. Whereas the Queensland Judicature Act 1876 (Qld) established that equity and common law relief could be administered at the same time, it was not until 1970 that the separate equity jurisdiction in the NSW Supreme court was fused with the common law system under the Supreme Court Act 1970 (NSW). Today, the NSW Supreme Court maintains an equity division for the hearing of cases, including corporations and commercial law, admiralty, probate and real estate issues. It is able to make orders in both equity and common law.

5.3 Good faith

Although commonly regarded as an equitable concept, there is also the common law concept of good faith.[131] Its place in the common law has been reaffirmed by the English High Court in *MSC Mediterranean Shipping Co v Cottonex Anstalt* (*MSC Mediterranean*),[132] which considered Canadian jurisprudence in *Bhasin v Hrynew*.[133] Essentially, *MSC Mediterranean* reaffirmed that good faith "underpins and informs more specific rules and doctrines of common law contract law".[134] It has also increasingly found a place in statute, where there is a requirement for good faith. An excellent example of that is the Native Title Act 1993 (Cth), which requires that negotiations are undertaken in good faith.[135] Other examples include the Fair Work Act 2009 (Cth)[136] and the Farm Debt Mediation Act 1994 (NSW).[137]

131 Found in Clause 1 of the Magna Carta.

132 *MSC Mediterranean Shipping Co v Cottonex Anstalt* [2015] EWHC 283 (Comm) 12 February 2015.

133 *Bhasin v Hrynew (2014)* SCC 71.

134 Claus Peter Berder and Thomas Arntz, 'Good Faith as a 'general organizing principle' of the Common Law' (2016) Vol. 32 (1) *Arbitration International* 167, 167.

135 Section 31(1)(b).

136 Workplace bargaining must meet the good faith requirements required in Division 8 of the *Fair Work Act 2009* (Cth), and is an overarching principle of the legislation, as set out in the Objects s 3 of the Act.

137 Section 18E of the *Farm Debt Mediation Act 1994* (NSW) requires the parties to engage in mediation in good faith.

5.4 Rights

Unlike the US Constitution, the Australian Constitution contains no bill of rights. In addition, there is presently no Commonwealth rights act. The closest that the commonwealth comes to a rights act is the establishment of the Human Rights Commission under the Human Rights Commission Act 1986 (Cth). Instead, rights are protected under a series of acts that seek to protect discrimination and breaches of human rights in public life from the Commonwealth executive. These include the Racial Discrimination Act 1975 (Cth), the Sex Discrimination Act 1984 (Cth), the Disability Discrimination Act 1992 (Cth), and the Age Discrimination Act 2004 (Cth). Importantly, there is no specific act protecting against religious discrimination, which is allegedly protected under the Fair Work Act 2009 (Cth). The Ruddock Review on Religious Freedom was handed down in 2018, recommending that either the Racial Discrimination Act 1975 (Cth) be amended to include discrimination based on religious belief or activity, or that a new religious discrimination act be enacted.[138] The Australian Government has committed to introduce a Religious Discrimination Bill into the parliament,[139] although it has yet to do so, and the issue formed part of the Liberal Coalition election platform in 2019.[140]

There is some constitutional protection of rights in Australia. For instance, there is the explicit protection of the right to vote and the right to jury for federal crimes, respect of relation, no discrimination due to state of residence, the right that compulsorily acquired property can only be done so on just terms, and the right to challenge a decision made by the executive. Through the development of the common law, there is also an implied constitutional freedom of political communication, and freedom to discuss the government to participate effectively in elections. Other common law freedoms include the right against self-incrimination, the right to sue for false imprisonment, the presumption of innocence in criminal trials, and the presumption that the standard of proof in criminal cases is that of beyond reasonable doubt. However, it is important to note that the passing of legislation can override these common law rights.

The need for, and creation of a single documents protecting rights in Australia (a Bill of Rights) has been debated for decades. The Australian Government has long argued that rights are adequately protected in the Constitution, statutes, and common law. However, many still believe that a single document outlining the rights of individuals is critical, particularly at a time where laws pertaining to terrorism, asylum seekers, detainment, and sedition are proliferating. As noted by Branson,

---

138 Phillip Ruddock, *Religious Freedom Review: Report of the Expert Panel* (2018), available at https://www.pmc.gov.au/domestic-policy/religious-freedom-review 5, accessed 22 April 2020.

139 Australian Government, *Australian Government Response to the Religious Freedom Reviews* (2018), available at https://www.ag.gov.au/RightsAndProtections/HumanRights/Documents/Response-religious-freedom-2018.pdf 4, accessed 22 April 2020.

140 Matthew Doran, 'Religious Discrimination Act to form part of Coalition Election Platform', *ABC News* 13 December 2018, available at https://www.abc.net.au/news/2018-12-13/religious-discrimination-act-to-form-part-of-coalition-election/10613608 accessed 22 April 2020.

> "My experiences as a judge left me persuaded, as they did my predecessor the Hon. John von Doussa QC, that in Australia we have legislatures that are insufficiently rights-conscious and bureaucracies that are insufficiently rights-sensitive. I don't mean to suggest that our government is on a mission to breach human rights principles. But I most certainly mean to suggest that, currently, human rights are hardly at the forefront of the thinking of many of our lawmakers and decision-makers. It would be a very good thing if that changed."[141]

This need for a Bill of Rights has been recognised in Victoria and the ACT, with both enacting a Bill of Rights – Human Rights Act 2004 (ACT) and the Charter of Human Rights and Responsibilities Act 2006 (Vic).

5.5 Judicial interpretivism and judicial activism

In Australia there were many philosophical influences on the development of the constitution, particularly Locke, Hobbes, and Montesquieu, and their contribution to the rule of law and separation of powers in a federal constitution. These social contractarian philosophies were 18th century in origin, arising in a time of the return of natural law and its influence on the judicial decision-making process. Whilst these influences had a profound effect on the development and reasoning of the government of the USA, our British convict history and the time of the development of federation ensured that positivist law and its legal reasoning would have a profound influence on Australian High Court Justices.

The concept of judicial restraint in interpreting the law is grounded in the concept of the rule of law, where each branch of government will stick to its own defined function, and not step outside these responsibilities.[142] For the first half of the century there is no doubt that the HCA was influenced by the judicial reasoning process related to rule-based reasoning and its connection with Jeremy Bentham,[143] and later H. L. A. Hart. In this positivist view of legal reasoning, public decision-making authorities need to give guidance to lower courts, future legislators, and citizens through clear, abstract rules laid down in advance of actual applications.[144] This positivist view treats the law as a body of rules, where judicial decisions are concerned with the application of rules, the value of formal justice, and factual, non-moral criteria.[145]

This rule-based legal system served Australia well for the first seventy years of the Court, applied by a body of men well versed in classical positivist legal reasoning theory. However, the legal positivist Hart admitted that there are difficult (or penumbral)

141 Catherine Branson, *Envisaging a Fairer Australia: Everyone, Everywhere, Everyday* (2008), available at https://www.humanrights.gov.au/news/speeches/envisaging-fairer-australia-everyone-everywhere-everyday accessed 22 April 2020.

142 Michael Kirby, *Through the World's Eye* (The Federation Press 2000) 101.

143 Cass R Sunstein, *Legal Reasoning and Political Conflict* (Oxford University Press 1996) 10.

144 Ibid 10–11.

145 Ibid 90.

cases that defy formal justice and the rules of recognition in interpreting the law. These penumbral cases, as Hart described them, sat outside of the rule-based system of formal justice, defying the ability to classify and catalogue.[146] Justice Murphy, in his analysis of the rule of law, noted that hard cases (when referring to entrenched statutory or precedent law), make "bad law",[147] and hard cases reveal that new law, statutory or decisional (precedent) is required. Furthermore, Murphy noted that when both judiciary and the legislature are out of step with the deeper moral conscience of the community they serve, it is the duty of the judges, as much as the legislature, to be radical.[148] Murphy's view came at a time when Australia's judicial thinking was beginning to shift away from the positivist, rule-dominated formal law that arose in the 19th century and maintained throughout the first half of the 20th century to more principle-based natural law.

This new, principles-based natural law developed predominantly in the USA, with the likes of John Finnis, John Rawls and Lon L. Fuller considering morality and law together seriously for the first time in over 150 years. However, the definitive work was that of Ronald Dworkin,[149] who defined the important roles of principles, policies and rules in judicial reasoning. In developing his Rights Thesis, where rights are like trumps, Dworkin considers Harts penumbral cases, and approaches these cases by the application of legal principles.[150] Furthermore, Dworkin urges that the idealistic application of the principle theory is the development of a justice who is an infinitely resourceful and patient judge who approaches the application of the law as one of integrity, judgments of fit and political morality – in essence Justice Hercules![151] This notion of judicial reasoning, with judicial activism at its core, was to dominate the High Court for the last three decades of the 20th century.

There are many opinions regarding the role of the judge in judicial decisions, both from commentators, and from the justices themselves. Perhaps the most modern opinion comes from Australia's greatest dissenting judge, Justice Michael Kirby. In a formative address in 2003, Justice Kirby assessed the judicial reasoning foundations of Australia, changes in judicial reasoning, and the current backdrop of judicial reasoning within which the High Court sits. He identified a desperate need for judicial activism, considering policy, principle and rules in judicial decision-making to ensure that judges interpret laws to meet the needs of the community they serve.[152]

The concern and controversy regarding judicial activism centres on whether the judiciary exceeds their role in the separation of powers. Whether this modern judicial reasoning upholds the doctrines of rule of law and separation of powers has been a contentious issue, debated by judges and commentators alike. What can be substantiated is

146 Ibid 26.

147 Ely and Ely (1986) (n 94) 114.

148 See above (n 95), 114.

149 Ronald Dworkin, *Taking Rights Seriously* (Harvard University Press 1977) Ch 3.

150 Ibid.

151 Sunstein (1996) (n 143) 48–50.

152 Michael Kirby, *Judicial Activism: Authority, Principle, and Policy in the Judicial Method* (The Hamlyn Lectures, Fifty-Fifth Series 2003) Lectures 1–4.

that judicial reasoning in Australia over the last 100 years has altered, as a consequence of both intrinsic and extrinsic factors. The issue raised by judicial activism is simple. In the very nature of judicial activism – utilising principle, policy and rule to achieve judicial decisions – is the separation of powers compromised? Certainly, the issue of rule of law is paramount, with even the most active of judicial decision-makers, Michael Kirby, advocating control on judicial activism:[153]

> "we need a middle ground that reflects the pragmatic character of the Common law in contemporary times. The extremes of unbound judicial creativity and invention will be tamed. But so too will be the extreme of mechanical application of old law without considering the context in which it must operate and its justice and conformity to basic principle."[154]

The decade from the late 1970s was perhaps one of the most judicially active since Federation, an era unlikely to be seen again for some time. This rise in judicial activism can be attributed to many factors, some interrelated, some isolated, which together coalesce to form a force that altered the reasoning process of Justices and therefore the High Court of Australia and influenced the reasoning process of High Court justices at the same time.

Many fundamental constitutional issues decided by the HCA in the last four decades, encompassing many areas of constitutional law, were interpreted in a manner of judicial activism. Perhaps the greatest illustration of this was the 1983 *Tasmanian Dams* Case,[155] which epitomized the new mode of thinking of the court, established Commonwealth powers in the areas of external affairs,[156] customs and excise,[157] acquisition of property on just terms,[158] and limited the Commonwealth corporations power. Quite simply, it was a remarkable decision by a court that a decade before had been influenced by judicial restraint.

Another landmark decision was that of *Mabo* in 1992.[159] Whilst it did not challenge or alter the course of any enumerated federal constitutional power, it accomplished something even more fundamental, rewriting 200 years of Australian history by altering the Australian position on *terra nullius,* thereby establishing native title rights to indigenous Australians. This decision was a reversal for the court, given that only twenty years previously in *Millirrpum v Nabalco Pty Ltd,*[160] the court was reluctant to consider the land rights issue, and certainly conceded no legal gains to the indigenous applicant.

---

153 Ibid lecture 3, 1.

154 Ibid 3.

155 *Tasmania v Commonwealth* (*The Tasmanian Dam Case*) (1983) 158 CLR 1.

156 Section 51(xxix).

157 Section 90.

158 Section 51(xxxi).

159 *Queensland v Commonwealth* [no. 2] (1992) 175 CLR 1.

160 *Millirrpum v Nabalco Pty Ltd* (1971) 17 FLR 141.

As noted earlier, the decision in *Cole v Whitfield*[161] was the judicial pendulum swing of the century. Rather than the court deciding for the first time on some area of law, this case reversed well established and theoretically grounded precedent and reasoning that had prevailed in the highest court of the land for over 80 years. A survey of commentaries regarding this era of judicial activism[162] noted a global common law paradigm shift toward judicial creativity and away from the strict legalism that had dominated the court since the Second World War. A number of prominent judiciaries pointed to events in the fifties and sixties that shifted the judicial goalposts, particularly decisions from the Warren Court of the United States.[163] These decisions enabled the Warren Court and its judicial activism to permeate the Australian High Court, ultimately influencing fundamental decisions in the original jurisdiction.

In his swearing in speech, Chief Justice Gleeson noted two particular issues in the 1980s that affected the High Court's role forever:[164] the first was the abolition of appeals to the Privy Council in 1988. The second relatively recent change affecting the appellate work was the implementation of the Special Leave, which is application for an appeal, rather than the hearing of a case in the HCA as a matter of right. Leave is granted or refused according to such considerations as whether the case involves a question of law of public importance, or whether the High Court is required to resolve differences between other courts as to the state of the law.[165]

Many justices of the court at the time of judicial creativity had been students of Professor Julius Stone, and therefore exposed to his exposition of appellate decision-making at a time when judicial legalism was the order of the day. In this form of judicial decision-making, "the judge remains a judge, working within the constraints of the law, but the task is better and more honestly done if the leeways are acknowledged."[166] Stone's form of judicial reasoning was heresy when Justice Mason joined the Court in 1972, but close to accepted reality in 1995 when he left.[167] Justice Mason commenced his judicial service on the High Court by espousing restraint in judicial reasoning: "change, especially major change, should be left to the Parliament."[168] His early decisions such as that in *Trigwell* were entirely orthodox reflections of Sir Owen Dixon's "strict and complete legalism". Yet his decision in *Teoh*[169] encompassed a healthy dose of judicial activism,

161 *Cole v Whitfield* (1988) 165 CLR 360.

162 As defined by Kirby (2000) (n 85) in Chapter 8 "Judicial Activism" 96.

163 Such decisions included *Brown v Board of Education of Topeka* (1954) 347 US 483; and *Miranda v Arizona*, (1966) 384 US 436.

164 Chief Justice Gleeson, 'Ceremonial Sitting – Swearing in of the Chief of Justice the Hon. Anthony Murray Gleeson CJ Ac COO/1998', 25 March 2004, available at http://www.austlii.edu.au/cgi-bin/disp.pl/au/other/hca/transcripts/1998/C00/3.html?query=%7e+swearing+in+gleeson.

165 Ibid 4.

166 Michael Kirby, 'Julius Stone and the High Court of Australia' (speech marking the Fiftieth Anniversary of the Publication of *Province and Function of Law*) (1997) Volume 20(1) *UNSW Law Journal* 239, 245

167 Kirby (2000) (n 85), in Chapter 8 Judicial Activism 120.

168 *State Government Insurance Commission v Trigwell* (1979) CLR 617, at 633, per Justice Mason.

169 *Minister for Ethnic Affairs v Teoh* (1995) 183 CLR 273.

with the incorporation of international human rights developments, and a willingness to see those rights reflected in Australia's legal and constitutional principles.[170]

Another student of Julius Stone on the HCA Bench during the judicial activist era, Justice Deane, straddled the middle ground in the judicial road to activism. He expressed the function of a judge in the highest court as one of reserve, not held back by the strict legalism that had previously pervaded, nor judicially active to the point of compromising the Rule of Law:

> "the primary duty of any judge in a society governed by the rule of law is the application of legal authority. But often legal authority is unclear. The constitution of statute may be ambiguous. The presented cases may not be readily stretched by the tools of analogical reasoning to afford a solution to the case in hand. Then, the judge in the tradition of the English Legal system may call in aid legal policy and legal principle."[171]

Justice Deane's just and guiding hand in judicial decision-making provided a rudder for the High Court in time of change, being neither reactive nor judicially active. Another student of Julius Stone, Justice Brennan's steady approach to the law in this period of judicial activism was articulated amidst his peers at the occasion of his swearing in ceremony as Chief Justice on 21 April 1995:

> "this Court is not a parliament of policy; it is a court of law. Judicial method is not concerned with the ephemeral opinions of the community. The law is most needed when it stands against popular attitudes, sometimes engendered by those with power, and when it protects the unpopular against the clamour of the multitude. But judicial method is concerned with the equal dignity of every person, his or her capacity to participate in the life of the community, to contribute to society and to share in its benefits; it is concerned with the powers entrusted to governments and the manner in which those powers are exercised. Judicial method starts with an understanding of the existing rules; it seeks to perceive the principle that underlies them and, at a deeper level, the values that underlie the principle. At the appellate level, analogy and experience, as well as logic, have a part to play. Judgments must be principled, reasoned and objective, as Sir Anthony Mason said yesterday. And, most significantly, each step in the reasoning must be exposed for public examination and criticism."[172]

At his swearing in speech in 1996, Justice Kirby, a former student and ardent supporter of Julius Stone, set the scene for a continued judicially active and open court, publicly criticising and rejecting Chief Justice Dixon's strict reasoning:

---

170 Ibid, at 288 per Chief Justice Mason and Justice Deane.

171 *Fay v Ocean Sun Line Special Shipping Company* (1988) 165 CLR 195 at 252 per Deane J.

172 Chief Justice Brennan 'Ceremonial Sitting – Swearing in of Brennan CJ Coo/1995', available at http://www.austlii.edu.au/cgi-bin/disp.pl/au/other/hca/transcripts/1995/C00/2.html?query=%7e+brennan+swearing+in accessed 31 December 2018.

There will be no returning to the social values of 1952 when Sir Owen Dixon spoke, still less those of 1903 when this Court was established. It falls to each generation of Australian lawyers, led by this Court, to fashion new principles of the Constitution, common law, and of equity, which will contribute wisely to the good governance of the Australian people… Judges are now more candid about this aspect of their function. Without a measure of creativity how else would the common law have survived seven centuries, from feudalism to the space-age? How else would it have endured in so many lands after the sun had set on the British Empire?[173]

From this public declaration of judicial creativity, Justice Kirby embarked on a path of judicial modernisation, incorporating judicial activism in his decisions,[174] backed up by some of the most controversial and policy-oriented judicial commentaries in Australia, such as his dissent in *Henderson's* Case.[175] Despite the many strengths and visions demonstrated in Justice Kirby's judgments, some commentaries see Kirby's vision of law as inherently flawed:

> "he accepts the notion of parliamentary sovereignty which regards parliament as able to make any laws it wishes, providing technical (including constitutional) requirements are met. For Justice Kirby there are no deeper human goods which [transcend] and ultimately [control] the law."[176]

One hundred and ten years after the establishment of the High Court of Australia, a decade of conservative government appointments to the High Court has rendered a shift from the judicially active era of the 1970s to the 1990s. Instead there has been a return to judicial conservatism. Justice Hayne supported traditional jurisprudence, with its roots embedded in rules and precedent.[177] Similarly, Justice Callinan on previous occasions openly criticised the judicial activism exhibited by the High Court,[178] advocating a return to strict legalism in the tone of Dixon in the 1940s and 1950s. In particular, Justice Callinan has been vocal on the Court's position on freedom of speech: "I fear that an enlarged constitutional 'right' of freedom of speech has the potential simply to produce an oppressive, even more powerful media, unlikely to lead to the sort of better-informed society that the High Court may be contemplating."[179] Similarly, Justice Heydon's views on judicial activism is clear: "Radical legal change is best effected by professional politi-

173 Michael Kirby, 'Speech on the Occasion of his swearing in and welcome as a Justice of the High Court of Australia', available at http://www.austlii.edu.au/cgi-bin/sinodisp/au/other/speeches/kirby_swear.html?stem=0&synonyms=0&query=~%20swearing%20in%20kirbyaccessed 23 February 2019.

174 Michael Kirby (2003) (n 152) lecture 3, 1.

175 *Re Residential Tenancies Tribunal of NSW; Ex parte Defence Housing Authority* (1997) 190 CLR 410.

176 Simon Travers, 'Justice on trial in the High Court', available at http://pandora.nla.gov.au/pan/10449/19960630/member12/HCOURT1.HTM AT 18.3/2004.

177 Justice Kenneth Hayne, 'Letting Justice be done Without the Heavens Falling' (2001) 27 *Monash Law Review* 12, 13.

178 Ian Callinan, 'An Over-Mighty Court?' (Paper presented at the Fourth Conference of the Samuel Griffith Society, Brisbane, 29–31 July 1994), available at http://www.samuelgriffith.org.au/papers/html/volume4/v4chap4.htm accessed 4 January 2019.

179 Ibid 3.

cians who have a lifetime's experience of assessing the popular will. They might not be an ideal class, but they are [better] fitted than the courts to make radical legal changes."[180]

Only time will tell whether or not judicial activism is a threat to the rule of law. However, what is clear is that the period of judicial activism on the Australian High Court has been tempered by more conservative appointments since 1996. Given the tenuous political situation in Australia, where the last nine years has been characterised by almost as many Prime Ministers, it is difficult to imagine that judicially active justices will be appointed to the High Court any time soon. This means that the judicially active approach of the HCA that arose during the tenure of Julius Stone devotees has receded, and a more conservative High Court bench will remain.

6. Professionalisation

6.1 Barrister and solicitor

The professionalisation of the legal profession in Australia has been heavily borrowed from England, with the splitting of the legal profession into two sections – solicitors and barristers. A legal professional is usually either a solicitor or a barrister, and is admitted as both a solicitor and barrister, with the exception of Queensland, which has a separate bar. In addition, NSW requires barristers to have a separate practising certificate. The remaining state and territory jurisdictions have a fused profession as well as an independent bar for lawyers who only practice as barristers. According to the Law society of New South Wales, as of 2018 there were 76,303 solicitors in Australia, with women comprising 52% of all solicitors.[181]

Solicitors generally aggregate into legal practices, some of which are large firms which may have national and international branches. The role of a solicitor is to advise clients, draft legal letters and documents, and prepare cases for court, including the gathering and ordering of evidence. In addition, they can undertake civil work, including preparation of contracts, leases, wills and the like. It is important to note that solicitors generally do not run court cases. Instead, a solicitor will brief a barrister about a case, and prepare the evidence and witnesses for trial. On limited occasions, a solicitor may appear in the court for hearings, but not for trials.

Conversely, only barristers ever practice alone, although they will often form Chambers, which are loose associations with other barristers, where some facilities such as libraries, meeting rooms and secretarial services may be shared, with each barrister paying a portion of the costs for such services. Barristers serve as advocates, running court cases, both civil and criminal. They are required to take cases in their field of knowledge, known as the 'cab rank' principle, unless they have a sound reason not to. Barristers are also expected to donate their services for pro bono work, similar to the expectation for solicitors.

---

180 Justice Dyson Heydon, 'Judicial Activism and the Death of the Rule of Law' (2003) Vol. 47(1) *Quadrant* 9.

181 Law Society of New South Wales, *2018 National Profile of Solicitors* (2019), available at https://www.lawsocietywa.asn.au/wp-content/uploads/2015/10/2018-National-Profile-of-Solicitors-Final-Report.pdf accessed 26 November 2019.

6.2 Requirement for admission as a legal practitioner

There are nine jurisdictions for the practice of law in Australia: the states, internal territories, and the Commonwealth jurisdiction. In order to practice law in Australia it is necessary to be admitted as a lawyer by the Supreme Court of that jurisdiction. To be admitted to practice law as a solicitor, an applicant must be a "fit and proper person" and have completed a recognised law degree – either Bachelor of Laws (undergraduate) or the postgraduate Juris Doctor. In addition, it is necessary to complete some form of practical legal training, as required by the relevant jurisdiction. This will vary from practical legal training degree/diploma, or in-situ training through article clerking, or a combination of both. Generally, there is a move away from article clerking to a combined practical legal training/practice experience model, but this varies from state-to-state. To be admitted as a barrister, similar to a solicitor, a recognised law degree is required. The trainee barrister must take a bar course and exam and will also need to undertake a period of 'pupillage' from a senior barrister for a required period. Generally, a barrister will specialise in different areas of law.

Once solicitor or barrister training is completed, admission to legal practice can occur. Applications must be made to the Supreme Court and completed within five years of graduation from a recognised law degree. In addition, an applicant's admission needs to be "moved" by a legal practitioner. Admission can be made to any of the state or territory Legal Practitioner's Admission Board, and once admitted to a jurisdiction, a legal professional will also be admitted to the High Court of Australia. Once admitted, a legal professional must hold a practice certificate.

6.3 Study of law

There are thirty-nine universities in Australia, and at present there are thirty-eight law schools, graduating approximately 7,500 law graduates per annum.[182] Most law degrees offered are conducted on campus, although several universities offer an online law degree.[183] Universities in Australia are divided into the group of 8 "sandstone" universities,[184] and the remaining universities. The first law school was established in 1855 at the University of Sydney, and the most recent at Charles Sturt University in 2016. The eligible law degree can either be undergraduate or the graduate Juris Doctor degree. Some law schools, such as the University of Melbourne and the University of Western Australia, only offer the Juris Doctor Program, in line with the structure of

182 Council of Australian Law Deans (CALD), *Data regarding law school graduate numbers and outcomes* (2017), available at https://cald.asn.au/wp-content/uploads/2017/11/Factsheet-Law_Students_in_Australia.pdf accessed 26 November 2019.

183 Such as Central Queensland University and University of Southern Queensland.

184 A "sandstone university" is an old, traditional university in Australia, with initial buildings usually constructed from sandstone, hence the name. The sandstone universities are the University of Sydney, University of Melbourne, Australian National University, University of Queensland, University of Western Australia, University of Adelaide, Monash University, and University of New South Wales.

the USA. Others, such as Bond University and the University of Sydney, offer both the undergraduate Bachelor of Laws (LLB) and the post graduate Juris Doctor (JD).

Law Schools in Australia generally have an excellent reputation, and are ranked highly on World Rankings Tables, particularly the sandstone universities. According to the 2019 Times Higher Education Rankings, four Australian law schools are ranked in the top 50 in the world.[185] In order to be eligible to be admitted as a legal practitioner in any Australian jurisdiction, it is necessary to study set areas of law, known as the "Priestley 11": Administrative Law, Civil Procedure, Company Law, Contracts, Criminal Law and Procedure, Equity and Trusts, Ethics and Professional Responsibility, Evidence, Constitutional Law, Property Law, and Torts. These subjects are only taught as part of a recognised LLB or JD program. The study of a taught master or research master or a PhD in an Australian Law school will not qualify the holder for admission to practice.

Most law schools also offer a taught master's degree (LLM). This may either be a general master's degree or can be a subject specialist master's degree. For instance, Bond University offers on-campus master's specialisations in corporate and commercial law and practice, family dispute resolution, international business and finance law, dispute resolution, and Canadian law and practice.[186] Increasingly, law schools are offering master's degrees online, as more postgraduates seek higher degrees in specialised areas but are often unable to attend on-campus courses. Specialisations are increasingly popular, particularly given that barristers are expected to specialise in an area of law.

Legal academics usually follow the academic structure of the UK – Lecturer, Senior Lecturer Reader and Professor – although more law schools are adopting the term Associate Professor rather than Reader. A handful of law schools have adopted the US academic hierarchy, using the terms Assistant Professor, Associate Professor and Professor. In addition, the University of Western Australia had adopted the term "Winthrop Professor", which refers to a full professor at other universities.[187] This system of academic titles was withdrawn in 2015 in favour of the more traditional UK-based Australian approach.

It is typical for law academics to be a generalist teacher as well as having an area of speciality. The amount of generalist teaching will depend on the area of specialty but is often tied to the area of specialty wherever possible. For instance, an academic may be a professor in natural resources law, but teach administrative, constitutional and property law, since the area of specialty encompasses many of these in general. In other instances, an academic may only teach in his area of specialty if it is a major area of law, such as torts or property law.

---

185 The University of Melbourne Law school is ranked 7th in the world, University of NSW ranked 31, University of Sydney ranked 33, and Australian National University ranked 42; Times Higher Education, *World University Rankings* (2019), available at https://www.timeshighereducation.com/world-university-rankings/2019/world-ranking accessed 26 November 2019.

186 See Bond University, 'Masters of Laws' (2019), available at https://bond.edu.au/intl/program/master-laws accessed 26 November 2019.

187 A Professor at the University of Western Australia was equal to an Associate professor at other Australian Universities, an Associate Professor was equivalent to Senior Lecturer, Assistant Professor equal to Level B Lecturer. See http://www.news.uwa.edu.au/201502127345/academic/academic-titles-uwa.

7. Nationalisation and Internationalisation

7.1 Nationalisation and legal harmonisation

It is important to remember that as six states, two internal territories and a number of external territories, Australia is a union, acting in a manner very similar to the European Union. Individual states act very much like individual EU countries, while the Commonwealth government acts in a manner similar to the EU parliament, with areas of power set out clearly. If crime occurs in one jurisdiction and the perpetrator flees to another jurisdiction, extradition is required. The power to extradite between states and territories of Australia is conferred under the Australian constitution,[188] through the service and execution throughout the commonwealth of the civil and criminal processes and the judgments of the courts of the States. The execution of extradition is governed by the Service and Execution of Process Act (Cth).

The judicial system of each state is separate. This means that the doctrine of precedent does not apply from one state to another. There have been attempts to harmonise the law in certain areas, such as in criminal law, mining health and safety, and conveyancing. However, other vital areas of society, such as Torrens title real property system, vehicle licensing and registration, and sale of goods, remain state-based and individual.

7.2 Internationalisation

The internationalisation of Australia's legal system has occurred relatively recently, from the mid-1970s when the Racial Discrimination Act 1975 (Cth) implemented Australia's international obligations under the International Convention on Civil and Political Rights. As a dualist state, in order for an international treaty to have effect in Australia, it is required to be implemented into national law, since "international law as such can confer no rights cognisable in the municipal courts. It is only insofar as the rules of international law are recognized as included in the rules of municipal law that they are allowed in municipal courts to give rise to rights and obligations."

The implementation of international law into national law has been the subject of a number of HCA cases. Indeed, Justice Murphy referred to Australia's international law obligations in several constitutional cases (e.g. *Koowarta v Bjelke-Peterson*),[189] as well as prominent in rejecting the narrow construction of the external affairs power in the *Tasmanian Dams* Case.[190] In these cases the legal issues were perceived by the High Court from a human rights perspective, with an open mindedness about the need to reject the old doctrine when it no longer accorded to the social conditions and community attitudes of justice and fairness in modern Australia.[191] In the landmark *Mabo* decision,[192] Justice

---

188 Section 51(xxiv).

189 *Koowarta v Bjelke-Peterson* (1982) 153 CLR 168.

190 Kirby (2000) (n 85), in Chapter 8 "Judicial Activism" 137.

191 Ibid 139.

192 *Queensland v Commonwealth* [Mabo No. 2] (1992) 175 CLR 1.

Brennan referred to the International Covenant on Civil and Political Rights, noting that international law is a legitimate and important influence on the development of common law, especially when international law declares the existence of universal human rights.[193]

In addition to the incorporation of international law into national law through statute, there has been some attempt by High Court of Australia justices to utilise principles of international law in judicial decisions. Prior to the case of *Minister for Immigration v Teoh* (*Teoh*),[194] principles of international law had little effect on Australian domestic law with principles used as a guideline for developing the common law. However, *Teoh* confirmed that it is possible for judges to bring part of a treaty into effect through the exercise of their powers, as long as they do not bring the entire treaty into effect in an illegitimate manner. The decision in *Teoh* was an important development in Australia's legal culture relating to internationalisation, with the majority of the justices stating that ratification of a Convention "is an adequate foundation for a legitimate expectation, absent statutory or executive indications to the contrary."[195]

One of Australia's greatest activist justices, Michael Kirby, provided extensive commentary on the concerns for sovereignty and democracy and the need for courts to consider international law, noting that referring to international human rights law does not undermine either principle, since international law should be referred to when there is an ambiguity in the law, and therefore the action of the court should be considered an application of sovereignty. For instance, Justice Kirby has incorporated the Bangalore Principles of international law into judgments wherever possible. Part of Kirby's justification of this path comes from an unusual source:

> "In my own way I have been endeavouring to carry on this important legacy.... "I confess that, at first, I regarded his [Justice Murphy's] attitude of internationalism in the law as unorthodox, and even heretical...I now acknowledge that I was wrong. Lionel Murphy merely saw a great truth before most others did."[196]

In a number of instances, Australian cases have been taken to United Nations Committees.[197] The first was the case of *Toonen*,[198] who challenged Tasmanian laws that criminalised consensual homosexual acts that occurred in a private home. The UN Human Rights Committee found that this violated the International Covenant on Civil and Political Rights,[199] recom-

193 Kirby (2000) (n 85) 137.

194 *Minister for Ethnic Affairs v Teoh* (1995) 183 CLR 273.

195 Andrew Edgar and Rayner Thwaites, 'Implementing Treaties into Domestic Law: Translation, Enforcement and Administrative Law' (2018) Vol. 19(1) *Melbourne Journal of International Law* 24, 37; *Minister for Ethnic Affairs v Teoh* (1995) 183 CLR 273, 291.

196 Kirby (2000) (n 85) 138.

197 See for instance *Rogerson v Australia* (2002) UN Human Rights Committee Communication No. 802/1998 (CCPR/C/74/802/1998) and *Madafferi v Commonwealth* (2004) UN Human Rights Committee Communication No. 1011/2001 (CCPR/C/81/D/1011/2001).

198 *Toonen v Australia* (1994) UN Human Rights Committee Communication No. 488/1992 (CCPR/C/50/C/488/1992).

199 Article 9 (1).

mending that the offending law be repealed. The Commonwealth implemented a repeal through the introduction of the Human Rights (Sexual Conduct) Act 1994 (Cth), forcing Tasmania to abolish the law as it fell afoul of the Australian Constitution.[200]

The Australian Legal Culture	
Institutional structure	
Conflict resolution	*Norm production*
Nine sets of hierarchical courts in nine jurisdictions (six states, two territories plus the federal court structure) with specialist courts in federal jurisdiction. Apex court for all courts is the High Court of Australia, which has a dual role as appellate court for all jurisdictions plus its own original jurisdiction for constitutional matters. Tribunals handle specialist matters, especially administrative appeals and small claims.	Legislation through statutes (acts and regulations) in all jurisdictions, with the federal government able to override legislation in the territories by virtue of s122 of the Constitution. Precedent arises from the apex court in each jurisdiction, which is binding only on that jurisdiction, while decisions from the High Court are precedent for all courts.

Intellectual structure			
Ideal of justice	*Legal method*	*Degree of professionalisation*	*Character of internationalisation*
Predictability through statutes is the starting point, with points of law clarified by binding precedent. International law only applied if implemented.	Pragmatic approach to legal argumentation based on a flexible balancing-model taking into account a variety of legal argument bases, including legislation, case law, and policy considerations.	Four-year bachelor's degree in law is required to practice as a lawyer, supplemented by a legal training certificate for solicitor or barrister. Large increase in the output of law graduates, especially in the last 10 years, even though the job market has remained steady. Judges are only appointed from barristers' component of the profession, never from academia or solicitors.	Dualistic system – implementation required into domestic legislation. Federal authority to do so under s51(xxix) of the Constitution.

200 Section 109.

8. Bibliography

Berder CP and Arntz T, 'Good Faith as a 'general organizing principle' of the Common Law' (2016) Vol. 32(1) *Arbitration International* 167

Börzel TA and Risse T, 'Who is Afraid of a European Federation?' (2000) *Harvard Jean Monnet Working Paper (Symposium),* part of Jean Monnet Working Paper No.7/00, Symposium: Responses to Joschka Fischer, 1

Branson C, *Envisaging a Fairer Australia: Everyone, Everywhere, Everyday* (2008), available at https://www.humanrights.gov.au/news/speeches/envisaging-fairer-australia-everyone-everywhere-everyday

Callinan I, 'An Over-Mighty Court?' (Paper presented at the Fourth Conference of the Samuel Griffith Society, Brisbane, 29–31 July 1994), available at http://www.samuelgriffith.org.au/papers/html/volume4/v4chap4.htm accessed 4 January 2019

Corkery J, *Starting Law* (2nd ed, Scribbler 2002)

Daintith T, 'A critical evaluation of the *Petroleum (Submerged Lands) Act* as a regulatory regime' (2000) *2000 AMPLA Yearbook* 91

Dworkin R, *Taking Rights Seriously* (Clarendon Press 1994)

Edgar A and Thwaites R, 'Implementing Treaties into Domestic Law: Translation, Enforcement and Administrative Law' (2018) Vol. 19(1) *Melbourne Journal of International Law* 24

Ely R and Ely J, *Lionel Murphy: The Rule of Law* (Akron Press 1986)

Gleeson M, 'Ceremonial Sitting – Swearing in of the Chief of Justice the Hon. Anthony Murray Gleeson CJ Ac COO/1998', 25 March 2004, available at http://www.austlii.edu.au/cgi-bin/disp.pl/au/other/hca/transcripts/1998/C00/3.html?query=%7e+swearing+in+gleeson

Hayne K, 'Letting Justice be done Without the Heavens Falling' (2001) 27 *Monash Law Review* 12

Heatley A and Nicholson G, *Select Constitutional Documents on the Northern Territory* (Darwin 1989)

Heydon D, 'Judicial Activism and the Death of the Rule of Law' (2003) Vol. 47(1) *Quadrant* 9

Jackson DF, 'The Australian Judicial System' (2001) 59 *University of NSW Law Journal* 1

Johnston P, 'The Tale of Two Coins: France's eighteenth-Century Claim to Western Australia' (2015) Vol. 39 (2) *University of Western Australia Law Review* 25

Kirby M, 'Julius Stone and the High Court of Australia' (speech marking the Fiftieth Anniversary of the Publication of *Province and Function of Law*) (1997) Volume 20(1) *UNSW Law Journal* 239

—— *Through the World's Eye* (The Federation Press 2000)

—— *Judicial Activism: Authority, Principle, and Policy in the Judicial Method* (The Hamlyn Lectures, Fifty-Fifth Series 2003)

Leben C, 'A Federation of Nation States or a Federal State' (2000) *Harvard Jean Monnet Working Paper (Symposium),* part of Jean Monnet Working Paper No.7/00, Symposium: Responses to Joschka Fischer, 1

Mack K, *Court Referral to ADR: Criteria and Research* (2003)

Mason A, 'The High Court of Australia: A Personal Impression of its First 100 Years' (2003) 27 *Melbourne University Law Review* 864

Matra J, *A Proposal for Establishing a Settlement in New South Wales* (1783), available at http://nzetc.victoria.ac.nz/tm/scholarly/tei-McN01Hist-t1-b2-d1-d1.html accessed 10 December 2018

Maxwell-Stewart H, 'The State, Convicts and Longitudinal Analysis' (2016) 47 No. 3 *Australian Historical Studies* 414

Murphy L, 'The Responsibility of Judges' in Evans G (ed), *Law, Politics and the Labor Movement* (LSB 1980)

Patapan H, *Judging Democracy: The New Politics of the High Court* (Cambridge University Press 2000)

Singleton G, Aitkin D and Jinks B, *Australian Political Institutions* (7th ed, Pearson Education 2003)

Soloman D, *The Politics of the High Court* (Allen and Unwin 1999)

Storey T and Turner C, *Unlocking EU Law* (Routledge 2005)

Sunstein CR, *Legal Reasoning and Political Conflict* (Oxford University Press 1996)

Thompson E, 'The Constitution and the Australian System of Limited Government, Responsible Government and Representative Democracy: Revisiting the Washminster Mutation' (2001) Vol. 24 (3) *University of New South Wales Law Journal* 657

Travers S, 'Justice on trial in the High Court', available at http://pandora.nla.gov.au/pan/10449/19960630/member12/HCOURT1.HTM AT 18.3/2004

Vanden Driesen IH, *Essays on Immigration Policy and Population in Western Australia 1850–1901* (University of Western Australia 1986)

Williams G, 'The High Court and the Mass Media' (1999) 1 *UTSLR*1

19. An Introduction to Chinese Legal Culture

Jiang Dong

1. An overview of China: Culture, history, landscape, politics and economy

The official language in China is Standard Chinese (普通话), also known as Mandarin, serving as one of the five official languages used by the United Nations. As one of the oldest known written languages, the Chinese writing system is a unique phenomenon in the modern world of alphabet scripts. Instead of a few dozen letters, it has developed thousands of complex signs or 'characters' that represent morphemes and words. Its history reaches back to over 4,000 years ago.[1] It is hard to guess how many dialects exist, but they can be roughly classified into seven large groups. Even though they are mutually unintelligible, the fact that they share the common writing system and have a common cultural background, supports the argument that they are dialects of the official Chinese language, Mandarin. This language is spoken mostly by the Han people. The 55 ethnic minorities in China, except for the Chinese-speaking Hui (回, a Muslim ethnic group in China) and Manchu (满), each have their own language. The other 53 ethnic groups speak over eighty languages,[2] spoken by around 6 % of the population, and 30 of them have written forms.

The People's Republic of China is situated in eastern Asia on the western shore of the Pacific Ocean, with an area of 9.6 million square kilometres. China is the most heavily populated country in the world. In 2017, the Chinese population was about 1.39 billion, 58.52% of which live in urban areas.[3] China is also the third largest country in the

1 The Romanized phonetic spelling system created in the 1950s for Mandarin, is a way to write Mandarin Chinese with 25 letters in English except "V".

2 Those languages spoken by comparatively large minority groups are Tibetan (藏), Uighur (维吾尔), Kazakh (哈萨克), Mongolian (蒙), Korean (朝鲜), Zhuang (壮), Yi (彝), Miao (苗), Buyi (布依), Dong (侗), Hani (哈尼), Bai (白), Dai (傣族), Li (黎), and Yao (瑶)).

3 'Population and Its Composition', available at http://www.stats.gov.cn/tjsj/ndsj/2018/indexeh.htm accessed 31 December 2019.

world by landmass, after Russia and Canada. Today, China is bordered by 14 different countries that range from small nations like Bhutan to very large ones like Russia and India.[4] With a borderline stretching over 22,800 kilometres and a coastline extending over 18,000 kilometres, its shape on the map is like a rooster. Its vast sea surface is studded with more than 7,600 islands. China has 34 provincial authorities, including four municipalities directly under the central government,[5] 23 provinces, five autonomous regions[6], and two Special Administrative Regions, namely Hong Kong and Macau.[7]

A united and multi-ethnic country since ancient times, Chinas Central government has so far identified 56 different ethnic groups. Since the majority of the population belongs to the Han (汉) ethnic group,[8] China's other 55 ethnic groups are customarily referred to as the national minorities.[9] Ethnic minorities in China live in every province, autonomous region and municipality directly under the Central Government, and in most county-level units, two or more ethnic groups live together.[10] China's ethnic groups live together over vast areas, although some live in individual concentrated communities in small areas. In some cases, minority peoples can be found living in concentrated communities in areas inhabited mainly by the Han people, while in other cases the situation is the other way around. This distribution pattern has taken shape throughout China's long history as the ethnic groups migrated and mingled.

4 The 14 countries bordering China are: Afghanistan, Bhutan, Burma, India, Kazakhstan, Kyrgyzstan, Laos, Mongolia, Nepal, North Korea, Pakistan, Russia, Tajikistan, and Vietnam.

5 Up to now, there are four municipalities directly under the central government, namely Beijing, Shanghai, Tianjin, and Chongqing. See 'Administrative Division', available at http://english.www.gov.cn/archive/china_abc/2014/08/27/content_281474983873401.htm accessed 31 May 2015.

6 According to the Chinese Constitution, self-government is exercised – under unified national leadership – in areas heavily resided by ethnic minorities. Organs of self-government in these areas administer the right of self-government. In principle, the administrative status of areas where self-government of ethnic autonomy is exercised is decided according to the geographical size and population of the areas (Article 4). Autonomous regions enjoy the same status as provinces (Article 30).

7 According to the NPC-drawn Hong Kong Basic Law of Special Administrative Region and Macau Basic Law of Special Administrative Region, both Hong Kong and Macau are part of the People's Republic of China. However, they have a high degree of self-government and maintain the previous capitalist system and way of life unchanged for 50 years. They enjoy executive, legislative and independent judicial power, including that of final adjudication. Laws drawn by the NPC and its Standing Committee may not be enforced in special administrative regions, except those which concern national defense, foreign affairs and involve national unification and territorial integrity and which do not concern the scope of self-government in special administrative regions. The central and local government shall not interfere in the affairs of self-government by special administrative regions according to law. In addition, the Central Government neither collects taxes in Hong Kong and Macau, nor do these regions turn over their revenues.

8 According to the 1 % National Population Sample Survey in 2015, Han Chinese accounts for 91.46 % of China's overall population. See The Bulletin of the Major Statistics of the 1 % National Population Sample Survey in 2015 (2015年全国1 %人口抽样调查主要数据公报), available at http://www.stats.gov.cn/tjsj/zxfb/201604/t20160420_1346151.html accessed 31 December 2019.

9 According to the 10th Population Census, the overall population of the 55 minority peoples is about 120 million, accounting for 8.04 % of the Chinese population. See *China's Ethnic Statistical Yearbook 2012* (China Statistics Press 2013) 624.

10 The State Council Information Office and The China International Publishing Group, 'A United Multi-Ethnic Country', available at http://www.china.org.cn/e-white/4/4.1.htm accessed 31 May 2015.

In order to curb the growth of its massive population, China imposed the one-child rule in 1978, hoping to relieve the pressure exerted by the large population on various social, economic and environmental issues. The statistics show that the policy has been a success in the sense that 400 additional births has been prevented,[11] and the life expectancy has increased from 36.3 years in 1960 to 75.6 in 2011.[12] However, the population of the City of Beijing, the capital of China, is approaching 22 million.[13]

The power in the People's Republic of China belongs to the people and the organ for the people to exercise state power is the National People's Congress (NPC) and local people's congresses at all levels. The NPC and local people's congresses are established through democratic elections, responsible to and supervised by the people. State administrative, judicial and procuratorial organs are created by, responsible to and supervised by the people's congresses. The NPC is the highest organ of state power. Local people's congresses are local organs of state power.

The NPC:

1) exercises the state power of amending the Constitution and supervising the enforcement of the Constitution,
2) enacts basic laws of the state,
3) elects and decides on the choices of the leading personnel of the highest state organs of China, including the President and Vice President, the choice of the Premier of the State Council and other component members of the State Council,
4) elects the Chairman of the Central Military Commission and decides on the choice of other component members of the Central Military Commission,
5) elects the President of the Supreme People's Court and the Procurator-General of the Supreme People's Procuratorate,
6) examines and approves the plan for national economic and social development and the report on its implementation,
7) examines and approves the state budget and the report on its implementation,
8) and makes decisions on other important issues in national life.

11 National Health and Family Planning Commission of PRC, 'The Progresses of China's Family Planning Policy', available at http://www.chinadaily.com.cn/m/chinahealth/2014-07/16/content_18955539.htm last updated 16 July 2014, accessed 31 May 2015.

12 'China Life Expectancy History' at http://www.worldlifeexpectancy.com/country-health-profile/china accessed 31 May 2015. See also http://data.worldbank.org/indicator/SP.DYN.LE00.IN. China's family planning has always included the two aspects of controlling the population size and improving the population quality in terms of education and health. While making efforts to control the population at an appropriate size, the Chinese government has devoted great attention to developing educational, medical and other services in order continuously to improve the quality of life in terms of education and health. See Information Office of the State Council of the People's Republic of China（国务院新闻办公室), 'Family Planning in China' (中国的计划生育) (August 1995), available at http://www.scio.gov.cn/zt2008/gxb2zn/06/200812/t249351.htm last updated 8 September 2000, accessed 31 May 2015.

13 The resident population of Beijing was about 21.148 million in 2013. See Beijing Statistical Information Net, 'How Much You Should Know About the Population in Beijing' (北京人口知多少), available at http://www.bjstats.gov.cn/rkjd/ accessed 31 May 2015.

The NPC is elected for a term of five years. It meets in session during the first quarter each year and is convened by the NPC Standing Committee. As the permanent organ of the NPC, the Standing Committee is endowed with extensive legislative and supervisory rights under the constitution.[14]

The Chinese political system is different from the present European ones. The foundation for the political system in China is the multi-party cooperation and political consultation under the leadership of the Communist Party of China (CPC). The system means that the CPC is the only party in power in China. While under the precondition of accepting the leadership of the CPC, the eight other political parties participate in the discussion and management of state affairs, in cooperation with the CPC. Political consultation means that under the leadership of the CPC, all parties, mass organizations and representatives from all walks of life take part in consultations on the country's basic policies and important issues in political, economic, cultural and social affairs before a decision is adopted, and in the discussion of major issues in the implementation of the decisions.[15]

The Chinese People's Political Consultative Conference (CPPCC) is the organ implementing cooperation and political consultation. As a political advisory body, the CPPCC consists of delegates from a range of political parties and organizations, as well as independent members. The proportion of representation of the various parties is determined by established convention, negotiated between the parties. The relationship between the CPPCC, the NPC and the government is that the CPPCC conducts consultations before policy decisions are made while the NPC votes on policy decisions after the consultations are finished and the government carries them out after policy decisions are made. Under the leadership of the CPC, the CPPCC, the NPC, and the government assume their own responsibilities respectively according to laws and their charters, coordinate their work efforts, perform their own functions, and complement each other. The National Committee of the CPPCC is elected for a term of five years.

---

14 According to Article 67 of the Chinese Constitution, the Standing Committee of the NPC has the right: to enact and amend statutes, to interpret the Constitution and laws, to supervise the enforcement of the Constitution, to supervise the work of other state organs (such as the State Council, the Central Military Commission, the Supreme People's Court, and the Supreme People's Procuratorate), and to annul those administrative rules and regulations, decisions or orders of the State Council that contravene the Constitution or the statutes of the state. It also has the right: to appoint and remove high-ranking officials such as the ministers in charge of ministries or commissions or the Auditor-General and the Secretary-General of the State Council according to the nomination by the Premier of the State Council, vice-presidents and judges of the Supreme People's Court and deputy procurators-general and procurators of the Supreme People's Procuratorate. It is also responsible for other major issues in state affairs, such as: deciding on the ratification and abrogation of treaties and important agreements concluded with foreign countries, deciding on the proclamation of a state of war when the state faces armed encroachment, and examining and approving partial adjustments to the plan for national economic and social development and to the state budget that prove necessary in the course of their implementation when the NPC is not in session. The Chinese Constitution is available in full text here: http://www.npc.gov.cn/englishnpc/constitution2019/201911/1f65146fb6104d-d3a2793875d19b5b29.shtml accessed 17 December 2019.

15 The State Council Information Office, 'Section IV. The System of Multi-Party Cooperation and Political Consultation' in 'China's Political System' http://china.org.cn/features/political/2006-11/08/content_1029034.htm accessed 31 May 2015.

Plenary sessions are the highest form of consultation by the CPPCC. The Standing Committee of the CPPCC National Committee calls and presides over a plenary session. Meetings of the Standing Committee are the main form of the CPPCC's performance of its functions when a plenary session is not in session.[16]

Even though China does not have a counterpart to the western-moulded separation of powers,[17] the Chinese government is divided into different bodies of function. In China, the State Council, or the Central People's Government, is the executive body of the highest organ of state power and the highest organ of state administration. The State Council exercises unified leadership over local state administrative organs at various levels throughout the country and regulates the specific division of power and function of the state administrative organs at the central level and the provincial, autonomous regional and municipal levels. The Premier assumes overall responsibility for the work of the State Council and is responsible to the NPC and its Standing Committee on behalf of the State Council.

In 2018, the structure of Chinese government witnessed an overhaul through the amendment of the Chinese Constitution,[18] in which one of the most profound changes is the establishment of the National Supervisory Commission and the supervisory commissions at the provincial, city, and county levels, which share offices and work together with CPC's disciplinary inspection commissions. Under the leadership of the National People's Congress,[19] the National Supervisory Commission functions as the state anti-corruption organ, on an equal footing with the State Council, the Supreme People's Court, and the Supreme People's Procuratorate. The supervisory commissions will independently exercise their power of supervision and not be subject to interference by any administrative organ, public organization or individual, for the purpose of ensuring that

16 The National Committee of the CPPCC, 'The Main Ways in Which the CPPCC Does Its Work' http://www.cppcc.gov.cn/zxww/2012/07/03/ARTI1341301557218109.shtml accessed 31 May 2015.

17 Article 1 of the Chinese Constitution provides that The People's Republic of China is a socialist state under the people's democratic dictatorship. In China, based on Article 2 of the Constitution, the National People's Congress is more than a legislature. It is the organ through which the people exercise state power, while all administrative, judicial and procuratorial organs of the State, according to Article 3, are created by the people's congresses to which they are responsible and by which they are supervised.

18 For a brief history of the amendments made to the Chinese Constitution and the process of the 2018, see 'China's national legislature adopts constitutional amendment', *China Daily* 11 March 2018, available at http://www.chinadaily.com.cn/a/201803/11/WS5aa4e2cba3106e7dcc140e40.html accessed 10 January 2019. For the specific amendments, see http://www.fdi.gov.cn/1800000121_39_4866_0_7.html accessed 10 January 2019.

19 Article 62 (7) of the Chinese Constitution sets forth that the National People's Congress is empowered to elect the Chairman of the National Supervisory Commission; and according to Article 63 (4) of the Chinese Constitution, the National People's Congress has the power to remove the Chairman of the National Supervisory Commission; Article 67 (6) of the Chinese Constitution grants the Standing Committee of the National People's Congress the power to oversee the work of the National Supervisory Commission.

supervision covers everyone in the public sector who exercises public power.[20] Supervisory commissions will be given responsibilities, powers, and means of investigation in accordance with law.

China's rich and extensive recorded history can date back to as early as 4000 BC, spanning more than 5,000 years. Historians divide Chinese history into categories of traditional China and modern China. Traditional China saw its rule switch from dynasty to dynasty among 18 dynasties in total. The founding of China's first dynasty, the Xia (夏) Dynasty, in the 21st century BC marked a change from a primitive society to a slave society. In the third dynasty, the Zhou (周) Dynasty, especially in the era of the Spring and Autumn Period (770 BC–403 BC) and the Warring States Period (403 BC–221 BC), the struggle for survival among warring regional lords motivated the unprecedented reform and flourishing of new ideas, leading to the cultural prosperity known as the 'schools of thought contended' (百家争鸣), in which a great number of thinkers and philosophers emerged, most famously Confucius. In 221 BC, Qin Shi Huang (秦始皇), the first emperor of the Qin (秦) Dynasty, established a centralized, unified, multi-national imperialist state. The Qin Dynasty was short-lived, because the cruel practices based on the philosophy legalism (法家) led to a revolt. This gave way to the Han Dynasty, which was named after the members of the ethnic majority in China, the 'people of Han'. Confucian ideals of government were adopted as the canon of the Han Empire and Confucian scholars gained conspicuous status as the core of the civil service. During the Han Dynasty, the Silk Road was formally established, which started from Chang'an (today's Xi'an), the capital of the Western Han Dynasty, extending 6,000 kilometres to the eastern Mediterranean Sea. Chinese imperial civilization peaked during the Tang (唐) Dynasty (618 AC–907 AC), when Tang people traded with people all over the world. The Tang Dynasty also exerted a powerful cultural influence over neighbouring states such as Korea, Japan, and Vietnam.[21]

Under the Tang rule, the Imperial Examination (科举), the Civil Service Examination system of recruiting civil officials based on merit rather than family or political connections was improved and made more effective. As an important vehicle of social mobility, it played an especially central role in Chinese social and intellectual life until its abolition in 1905. This competitive procedure of selecting state bureaucracy through examination on classical Confucian literature and philosophy functioned to draw the best talents into government, serving as high ranking officials such as the prime minister (宰相) to the grass-roots magistrate. The imperial examinations facilitated the able men from almost any social stratum to fulfil their aspirations of climbing up the social ladder. Aristocracy-

---

20 The supervisory powers are very broad, as manifested by Article 15 of the National Supervision Law. Article 15 stipulates that the supervision powers will be imposed on: civil servants, personnel engaged in public affairs at organizations managing public affairs upon authorization by laws or regulations or lawful entrustment by state organs, managers of state-owned enterprises, personnel engaged in management in public entities (in education, scientific research, culture, health care, and sports, among others), personnel engaged in management at basic-level self-governing mass organizations, and other personnel who perform public duties in accordance with the law.

21 Chinese residing overseas often call themselves "*Tang Ren*" (唐人), or the People of Tang, and the Chinese term for Chinatown bears the dynastic title "*Tangrenjie*" (唐人街), or The Tang People's Street.

by-examination had another far-reaching consequence. A high degree of national stability was ensured despite changes of emperor and dynasty because the civil service, fuelled by the exam system stemming from persistently dominant Confucianism, could continue independently of the imperial regime. The period of imperial society continued until the Opium War in 1840. During these 2,000 years, China's economy and culture continued to develop, leaving a rich heritage of science and technology, literature and the arts.

In 1840, anxious to continue its opium trade in China, Britain started the Opium War against China. After the war, the big foreign powers forcibly occupied 'concessions' and divided China into 'spheres of influence'; thus, China was transformed into a semi-colonial, semi-feudal society. In 1912, the bourgeois democratic Xinhai Revolution, (辛亥革命) led by Sun Yat-sen (孙中山), overthrew the last Dynasty of China – the Qing (清) Empire – ending the 2,000-year-long imperial rule and starting the republic regime through the establishment of the Republic of China. In 1949, the Chinese Communist Party founded the People's Republic of China, replacing the Republic of China. In 1978, China adopted the Open Up and Reform Policy, aimed at integration with the global economy. In 2001, China's access to WTO as its 143rd member brought China into a new era to further open up, a key step forward in its unprecedented strategy to catch up with the advanced industrial world by means of market socialism. Since initiating market reforms in 1978, China has shifted from a centrally-planned to a market-based economy and experienced rapid economic and social development, with GDP growth averaging about 10 percent a year.[22] China is now the world's second largest economy by nominal GDP, and the world's largest economy by purchasing power parity, according to the IMF.[23]

2. Conflict Resolution

The Chinese legal system is a socialist system of law based primarily on the Civil Law model. The Organic Law of the People's Courts of 1980 and the Constitution of the People's Republic of China of 1982 established China's four-tiered court system: the Supreme People's Court at the centre, the Higher People's Courts at the provincial level, the Intermediate People's Courts at the municipality level and the Basic People's Courts at counties or city districts level. Further down at the local level of individual towns, municipalities and autonomous communities, the Basic People's courts have people's tribunals. In practice, these tribunals are usually called 'outpost tribunals' (派出法庭), in case the jurisdictional area of the Basic Courts cover a dense population or vast geographical space.[24] According to the statistics of 2010, the Basic People's Courts are comprised of more than 3,000 courts at the county or city district level, which are further subdivided into about 20,000 smaller people's tribunals located in towns and

22 The World Bank, 'China Overview' http://www.worldbank.org/en/country/china/overview accessed 31 May 2015.

23 See http://www.imf.org/external/pubs/ft/weo/2014/02/weodata/weorept.aspx?pr.x=79&pr.y=11&sy=2012&ey=2019&scsm=1&ssd=1&sort=country&ds=.&br=1&c=924%2C111&s=NGDPD%2CPPPGDP%2CPPPSH&grp=0&a= accessed 31 May 2015.

24 Article 124 of the Constitution; Article 2 and Article 19 of the Organic Law of the People's Courts.

villages. There are 406 Intermediate People's Courts and 31 Higher People's Courts located in the provinces.[25]

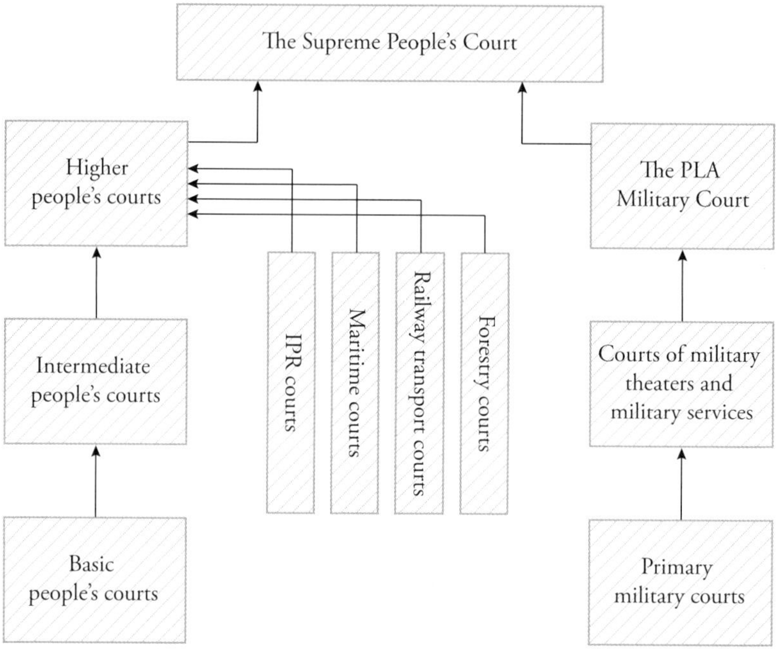

Fig. 1 The Court Structure of the People's Republic of China.

Outside the main court system are the special courts, namely, military courts, railway transport courts, forestry courts, and maritime courts. They enjoy limited subject matter jurisdictions as their names suggests.[26] Though they focus on specific issues, their decisions can be appealed to the Supreme People's Court as well.[27] China also considers establishing new types of special courts as an important approach to push forward the judicial reform initiative. In August 2014, the Supreme People's Court issued the *Provisions on the Establishment of Intellectual Property Courts in Beijing, Shanghai and*

25 The Supreme People's Court of China, *Guardian of Equality and Justice: The Supreme People's Court of the People's Republic of China* 32–33; In addition, the HK Basic Law and Macau Basic Law provide that Hong Kong and Macau have distinct and separate court systems, British and Portuguese-based respectively. The basic laws also empower the HK and Macau courts to hold the power of final adjudication.

26 See The State Council Information Office and The China International Publishing Group, 'The National Court Organizations' http://english.gov.cn/archive/china_abc/2014/08/23/content_281474982987258.htm accessed 31 May 2015.

27 Maritime courts have no jurisdiction over criminal cases. Cases of appeals against the judgments and orders of a maritime court are handled by the higher people's court in the locality where the maritime court is located. The railway transport courts comprise basic and intermediate courts. Cases of appeals against the judgments and orders of a railway transport court are handled by the higher people's court in the locality where the railway transport court is located.

Guangzhou,[28] and already in December 2014, the Beijing Intellectual Property Court came into operation as the first specialized court for intellectual property issues. The Court hears civil and administrative lawsuits regarding patents, new plant varieties and technological knowledge, layout design of integrated circuits, technological secrets, and computer software. However, the intellectual property courts have not yet been given any jurisdiction over criminal matters.

Specialization of the judicial function makes up one of the driving forces for Chinese judicial reform, showcased by the innovation of the first internet court worldwide. With 800 million internet users and counting the largest netizen population in the world, China has got its hands full with online disputes between citizens. Therefore, in the 36th meeting of the Central Leading Small Group on Comprehensively Deepening Reform (中央全面深化改革领导小组) held on 26 June 2017, the Scheme for Establishing the Hangzhou Internet Court was approved (《关于设立杭州互联网法院的方案》). Hangzhou was considered an appropriate location as Hangzhou is a stronghold of e-commerce domestically and internationally. It is also the location of the headquarter of Alibaba – the Chinese counterpart of Amazon. The company has an annual income of hundreds of billions of dollars. The Court opened on 18 October the same year.[29] One month later, it was followed by Bejing Internet Court and Guangzhou Internet Court. The internet courts' subject matter jurisdiction mainly covers online business-related cases, including contract disputes arising from online shopping, service and small loans, copyright and infringement lawsuits, and domain name disputes. They also handle internet defamation and some administrative lawsuits. The first year's caseload of the Hangzhou Internet Court was around 9,600 cases and the average duration of litigation is 38 days, 50 percent shorter than conventional courts.

Another newly established special court is the Shanghai Financial Court inaugurated on 20 August 2018.[30] It is responsible for commercial cases such as disputes involving securities, futures, insurance, bills, and financial lending. It will also deal with bankruptcy cases where financial institutions are the debtors and administrative cases with financial regulators as defendants. Appellate trials of finance-related cases first heard by grassroots-level courts in Shanghai also fall into the court's jurisdiction. In 2017, courts in Shanghai heard more than 179,000 finance-related cases in the first instance. The number of such lawsuits in Shanghai grew by an average of 51 percent annually from 2013 to 2017.

At the very top of the court system, the Supreme People's Court can review the decisions of all lower courts and has jurisdiction over all regular and special courts. The president of the Supreme People's Court is elected by the NPC and its Standing Com-

28 See http://www.lawinfochina.com/display.aspx?id=18117&lib=law accessed 31 May 2015.

29 Hangzhou Internet Court provides a comprehensive online case filing service, boasting of filing a lawsuit in 5 minutes. See https://www.netcourt.gov.cn/portal/main/en/index.htm.

30 The establishment of the court is based on the Decision of the Standing Committee of the National People's Congress on Forming the Shanghai Financial Court (《全国人大常委会关于设立上海金融法院的决定》), which came into force on 28 April 2018. The website of Shanghai Finance Court is http://shjrfy.hshfy.sh.cn/jrfy/English/index.jsp.

mittee. His term of office is five years and he may serve for no more than two consecutive terms. The NPC Standing Committee appoints or dismisses vice-presidents, heads and associate heads of divisions, and judges. Generally, the Court has jurisdiction over the following cases: cases of first instance assigned by law and other cases that it considers it should try itself, appealed and protested cases against judgments and other orders of higher courts and specialized courts, and protested cases filed by the Supreme People's Procuratorate. The Supreme People's Court has two case-filing divisions. The case-filing divisions of the Supreme People's Court are responsible for receiving and approval of hearing of cases filed to the Supreme People's Court. They also handle jurisdiction disputes and review applications for retrial of legally effective judgments made by the courts at all levels. The Court has five criminal divisions. They assume their respective responsibilities based on the types of cases and geographical jurisdictions and can hear cases of first and second instance. Another important function is to review and approve the death penalty. The Supreme People's Court also has four civil divisions,[31] an administrative division, an adjudication supervision,[32] an enforcement department, an office of the state compensation, and a research department.[33] It may also establish such other divisions as it deems necessary. In 2015, the Supreme People's Court accepted and heard 15,985 cases of various types, up by 42.6 % over 2014, and concluded 14,135 cases, up by 43 %.[34]

The Supreme People's Court also gives interpretations on questions concerning specific application of laws and decrees in judicial proceedings. In reality, the practice of interpreting laws and decrees by the Supreme People's Court has developed in recent years to an extent that is called 'judicial legislation'. This was not previously defined in the constitutional law. However, the legislation does require guidance in order to fill gaps and to solve conflicts and some vagueness among the laws so that effective enforcement can be carried out by the judicial branch.

---

31 The Civil Division I of the Supreme Peoples' Courts hears cases of first and second instance related to marriage and family, labour dispute, unjust enrichment, voluntary service, torts, and real estates. The Civil Division II hears contract and tort cases arising from corporations, cases of securities, futures, commercial instruments and bankruptcy and cases of application for withdrawal of domestic arbitration. The Civil Division III is the IPR Division, responsible for hearing first and second instance cases of copyright, trademarks, patents, scientific and technological achievements and new plant varieties, cases of technological contracts, and unfair competition. The Civil Division IV hears the maritime cases and cases involving parties from foreign countries or Hong Kong, Macau and Taiwan.

32 The adjudication supervision division of the Supreme People's Court is responsible for retrial *de novo* of cases filed by an unsatisfied party or parties against legally effective judgments made by the Supreme People's Court itself or by all lower level courts (maritime and IPR cases excluded). It also hears cases challenged by the Supreme People's Procuratorate. Any death penalty made in the retrial proceeding should go through the review of this division.

33 The research department of the Supreme People's Court assumes the responsibility of drafting judicial interpretations, takes part in the legislative activities, solicits and analyses opinions on drafts of laws, regulations and rules, and produces judicial statistics.

34 *Report on the Work of The Supreme People's Court of 2016* (Law Press 2016) 50.

The establishment of the trans-regional court, nominally the circuit court (巡回法院), marks the latest effort of China's judicial reform.[35] With the robust growth of market economy and rapid increase of administrative lawsuits, the number of judicial cases involving different administrative regions and the amount of money involved in these cases have risen enormously. As a result, local officials paid growing attention to such cases and some even took advantage of their posts to meddle in particular cases within their jurisdiction. The innovation of the trans-regional court thereby aims to eliminate interference from local officials and ensure judicial independence, by establishing courts and procuratorates beyond the limits of administrative regions.[36] These circuit courts are satellites of the Supreme People's Court, depriving the local government of the power of filling and funding the bench as they do to the local courts.

In addition, the circuit courts can accept and hear appeals from different provincial-level higher courts. The circuit courts act on behalf of the Supreme People's Court and render judgments that have the same rank as those by the Supreme People's Court. There is therefore no possibility of further appealing to the Supreme People's Court. Prior to the establishment of permanent circuit courts, the jurisprudence of circuit trials would typically be presented on a case-by-case basis.[37] By setting up permanent courts, one hopes to facilitate case filing and improve the peoples' access to justice by reducing the possibility of local government interference. The first two circuit courts, one in the southern Chinese city of Shenzhen and one in Shenyang, the capital of northeast China's Liaoning Province, opened in January 2015. The two courts, whose locations were chosen for the two regions' advanced economic status and greater demands for judicial trials, will primarily handle major administrative, civil and commercial cases

35 On 2 December 2014, the Chinese legislature passed the Supreme People's Court's Pilot Plan for Establishing Circuit Courts (《最高人民法院设立巡回法庭试点方案》) and the Pilot Plan for Establishing Trans-regional People's Courts and People's Procuratorates (和《设立跨行政区划人民法院、人民检察院试点方案》) on the Seventh Session of the National Development and Reform Commission of the Communist Party of China Central Committee (中共中央全面深化改革领导小组第七次会议). It also recommended the implementation of the Plans according to relevant approval procedures after further modification. It is a remarkable step towards the separation of the judiciary and the administrative powers.

36 'China to explore establishing trans-regional courts procuratorates', *Xinhuanet*, available at http://www.chinadaily.com.cn/china/2014-10/28/content_18817423.htm accessed 31 May 2015.

37 Article 135 of the Civil Procedure of the PRC provided that a people's court could, as needed, try civil cases in a circuit manner and on the spot. The circuit court functioned as an outpost tribunal of the people's court. It aimed at facilitating the litigants to get access to justice in places where the traffic conditions were poor. Instead of letting the litigants appear in the regular forum, the circuit court would travel to and hold the trial at a venue easy for the litigants and the audience to reach. The circuits would be regularly or randomly itinerant based on the caseloads.

filed locally and from neighbouring regions.[38] In 2015, they concluded 1,653 cases in total.[39] As the "experimental units" of the judicial reform, the two courts paved the way for the Supreme People's Court to open on December 28–29, 2016 four additional circuit courts in the east (the No. 3 Circuit Court, sitting in Nanjing, Jiangsu), central (the No. 4 Circuit Court, sitting in Zhengzhou, Henan), southwest (the No. 5 Circuit Court, sitting in Chongqing) and northwest (the No. 6 Circuit Court, sitting in Xi'an, Shaanxi) China respectively.[40] The combined caseload handled by the six circuit courts was about 17 thousand in 2018.[41]

As for the inner structure of the courts, each Chinese people's court consists of several divisions, such as civil, criminal, administrative, and enforcement divisions. A court has one president and several vice-presidents, a division has one chief and several associate chiefs. Within a court, the collegial panels function as the basic units to adjudicate. They are neither permanent bodies, nor inflexible in their composition; instead, their members are appointed on a case-by-case basis. A collegiate panel consists of at least three judges or a combination of judges and People's Assessors, and the members must be an odd number. However, a single judge can hear simple civil cases, economic cases, minor criminal cases, and cases that are otherwise provided for in the law.

Cases going up to the appellate court must be heard by a collegial panel of three or five judges.[42] The president judge of the panel (审判长) is appointed by the president of the court or the division chief. When the president of the court or the division chief attend a case themselves, they serve as president and judge concurrently. When assessing a case, the collegiate panel should follow the principle of simple majority. The opinions of the minority, however, should be recorded in the court log and published with signatures of the members of the panel.

---

38 On 28 January 2015, the same date as the first circuit court was inaugurated in Shenzhen, the Supreme People's Court issued a judicial interpretation titled Regulation about the Trial of Circuit Courts (《最高人民法院关于巡回法庭审理案件若干问题的规定》). The regulation contains the circuit court's establishment place, circuit area, institutional nature, scope of accepted cases, and procedures of submission of materials by litigants, among other matters. According to the interpretation, the jurisdiction of the first circuit court in Shenzhen covers the three provinces of Guangdong, Guangxi, and Hainan, and the second circuit court in Shenyang covers Liaoning, Jilin, and Heilongjiang. The original jurisdiction of the circuit court includes civil, commercial and administrative cases with national significance. They also hear appeals of civil, commercial and administrative cases from the provincial level higher courts and review the cases appealed from the higher courts through the adjudicative supervision procedure. For the criminal cases, they review the cases appealed to them through the adjudicative supervision procedure with its jurisdiction.

39 *Report on the Work of The Supreme People's Court of 2016* (n 34) 67.

40 'China issues white paper on judicial reform of Chinese courts', available at http://www.chinadaily.com.cn/china/2017-02/27/content_28361584_3.htm htm accessed 31 December 2019.

41 Zhou Qiang, 'The Work Report of the Supreme People's Court', delivered 12 March 2019 at the Second Session of the 13th National People's Congress (周强：最高人民法院工作报告 – 2019年3月12日在第十三届全国人民代表大会第二次会议上), available at http://www.xinhuanet.com/politics/2019-03/19/c_1124253887.htm accessed 31 December 2019.

42 Article 178 of the Criminal Procedure Law sets forth that trials of first instance cases in the Higher People's Courts or the Supreme People's Court shall be conducted by a collegial panel composed of three to seven judges or of judges and people's assessors totaling three to seven.

Both the trial courts and the court of appeal can deal with issues of facts and law.[43] The right to question is granted to the litigants in the trial of first instance, the appeal and the review in the adjudicative supervision procedure.[44] The questioning is mainly done orally in the court hearing, e.g., the cross examination of the witnesses, but the defendant's answer to the plaintiff's complaint is also subject to questioning. The litigants can question both the factual issues and the application of law orally or in writing. Procedural issues, like the jurisdiction of the court, can also be questioned.

A local people's court will usually hear cases at first instance.[45] Its judgment at the conclusion of a case will explain the cause of action, the laws applied in the case, the facts and causes affirmed by the judgment, the final judgment of the court, the costs and the parties responsible for them, and the procedure for filing a timely appeal. The unsatisfied party may bring a right of appeal only once to the people's court at the next higher level. In 2016, the caseload for the first instance criminal cases, civil cases and administrative cases was respectively 1,116,000, 6,738,000 and 225,000.[46]

The court of appeal can decide not to grant leave to appeal if deeming a court session unnecessary after looking over the case file, investigating the litigants and consequently finding no new facts, evidence or reason submitted. If granted leave to appeal, the court of appeal will review the case *de novo* with a public trial considering both law and facts. After hearing the appeal cases, the court of appeal, can dismiss the appeal and uphold the trial court's original judgment. If the trial courts have made an incorrect fact ascertain-

---

43 Both the Civil Procedure Law (Art. 167) and the Criminal Procedure Law (Art. 222) provide that "the people's court of second instance shall review the facts and application of law in relation to the claims in appeal." Article 67 of the Civil Procedure Law and Article 52 of the Criminal Procedure Law also grant the court the authority to investigate and collect evidence from the relevant entities and individuals, and the relevant entities and individuals shall not refuse such investigation and collection of evidence.

44 Article 12 of the Civil Procedure Law sets forth that "when a people's court tries a civil case, the parties shall have the right to debate". The Criminal Procedure Law has no such articulate provision, but its Article 193 provides that in the trial of first instance "in a court session, any fact or evidence related to conviction or sentencing shall be investigated and debated." For the case of the second instance, Article 223 prescribes that "where a people's court of second instance decides not to hold a court session to hear a case, it shall arraign the defendant and hear the opinions of other parties, defenders, and litigation representatives. A people's court of second instance may hold a court session to hear an appellate case at the place of occurrence of the case or the place where the original trial court is located."

45 As for the civil cases, Article 17 and 18 of the Civil Procedure Law set forth that the intermediate people's courts shall exert original jurisdiction over important foreign-country-party-involved cases, cases which have a major impact within their respective jurisdictions or cases which are under the jurisdiction of the intermediate people's courts as determined by the Supreme People's Court. Similarly, higher people's courts can hear first instance cases of major impact within their jurisdiction. If a case has nationwide significance, the Supreme People's Court shall be the trial court. In addition, the Supreme People's Court can hear any case as the first instance court once it deems it necessary. The intermediate people's courts, the higher people's court, and the Supreme People's Court also have the original jurisdiction over criminal cases. Article 20 of the Criminal Procedure Law empowers the intermediate people's court to hear cases of first instance concerning national security or terrorist activities, or punishment up to life imprisonment or death penalty. According to Article 21 and 22, a higher people's court and the Supreme People's Court shall have the original jurisdiction upon cases respectively significant in its jurisdiction and significant nationally.

46 China Law Society, *Annual Report on Promoting the Rule of Law in China* (2016), available at http://english.legalinfo.gov.cn/2017-06/15/content_29761256_4.htm accessed 31 December 2019.

ment or application of law, the court of appeal can reverse, revoke or modify the original judgment. The court of appeal can also remand the case to the trial court due to unclear finding of the basic facts or serious violations of statutory procedures, such as omitting a party or illegally entering a default judgment.[47]

The litigant cannot appeal against the decision rendered by the court of appeal. China practices a system of courts characterized by four levels and two instances of trials. This means the court of the second instance will deliver the final judgment. The exceptions are cases involving the death penalty, while other cases take legal effect immediately upon announcement.[48] Any judgments and orders rendered by the Supreme People's Courts as the court of the first instance, however, shall become immediately binding.

However, through the regime called 'adjudicative supervision' – a discretionary post-final decision review – a limited number of both civil and criminal cases may, according to the Civil Procedure Act and the Criminal Procedure Act, be heard for a third time. The procedure law empowers the court, the procuratorate and the litigant concerned to initiate an adjudicative review to challenge the second-instance court's effective decision.[49] After reviewing the complaint, the president of the higher court may ask the judicial committee to make a decision to accept or reject the appeal for review. Under no circumstances does the review initiated by trial supervision procedure suspend the enforcement of the effective judgment that is challenged. Where the president of a court finds a definite error in its own effective judgment that should

---

47 To correct the irregular practices in the procedures regarding retrial of remanded cases, the Civil Procedure Law was amended in 2012 to revise and improve the procedure for the retrial of such cases. The new provisions clearly state that if the litigant makes an appeal after the trial court makes its ruling in the retrial of a remanded case, the people's court of second instance shall not send the case back for a retrial (Article 170 (4)).

48 According to Chapter 4 of the Criminal Procedure Law (Procedure for Review of Death Sentences), a death sentence must always be reviewed by a higher people's court and approved by the Supreme People's Court. In addition, if an intermediate people's court has sentenced a defendant to death, but at the same time has imposed a two-year suspension of the execution (死刑缓期两年执行), a higher people's court must approve the suspension. Ultimately, collegial panels of three judges at the higher people's court or the Supreme People's Court will review death sentences or suspensions. After its review, the Supreme People's Court will issue a ruling either approving or rejecting the death sentence. If it rejects the sentence, the court may remand the case or revise the sentence itself. Article 240 of the Criminal Procedure Law requires the Supreme People's Court to speak with the defendant during its review of his or her death sentence. The defense lawyer may also speak with the court, if he or she so requests. The Supreme People's Procuratorate can also choose to submit an opinion on the sentence.

49 Article 200 of the Civil Procedure Law sets forth the detailed reasons for the litigant to file a petition for retrial: new evidence is found which suffices to overturn the original judgment or ruling; basic facts were missed to support the original judgment; the primary evidence admitted in the original judgment was forged or was not cross-examined; the people's court failed to investigate and gather the primary evidence necessary for the trial, which a party is unable to gather and has applied in writing for the court to do; the original judgment has incorrectly applied the law; the collegial panel was not legally composed or any judge disqualified in accordance with law failed to be disqualified; a party's right to debate was illegally denied; a party, if as a person without competency, had no legal representative representing him in the litigation or a party failed to appear in the trial where he should be present, due to reasons not attributable to the fault of the party or the legal representative; a default judgment is entered against a party which has not been subpoenaed; the original judgment or ruling omitted claims or exceeded the claims of the parties; the legal instrument on which the original judgment is based has been revoked or modified; the judge making the original judgment was found not impartial due to corruption in the hearing.

lead to a review, he must submit it to the judicial committee to determine whether the review should be done or not.

Chinese courts at all levels set up judicial committees as the most authoritative body – the highest judicial organ – in the court,[50] tasked with summing up judicial experience and discussing important or difficult cases and other issues relating to judicial work.[51] These committees are institutions peculiar to the Chinese courts and critical to their operation: besides hearing cases, they review and rule on the most complicated, controversial and significant cases. The catalogue of cases mandatorily submitted to the judicial committee for deliberation and decision, mainly covers the death penalty cases. In addition, it contains the final approval of the imposition of the death penalty that has been brought back to the Supreme People's Court – cases of life imprisonment, wrongly decided cases to be retried, cases of acquittal, important and complicated cases to be transferred to the people's courts at higher levels for trial, and difficult cases in which it is proposed that the court ask the higher court for instructions. In certain other cases, the collegial panel may, in its discretion, submit the case to the court president for discussion by the judicial committee. In addition, the collegial panels may submit the following cases to the court presidents to decide whether the judicial committees should review them:

1) if the collegial panel has major differences and is having difficulty in reaching a decision,
2) if relevant legislation is unclear or there are difficult issues in the application of law,
3) if the results of the case may have a major effect on society,
4) and if a new type of case will set an example for future cases.

Members of judicial committees of local people's courts at various levels are appointed and removed by the standing committee of the People's congress at the corresponding level, upon the recommendation of the presidents of these courts. The presidents of the people's courts preside over the meeting of the judicial committees.[52] Other members of the judicial committee include the vice presidents, division chief and senior judges who are more experienced but lack a specific title within the court structure. In case of differing opinions, the majority's opinion shall be adopted.

As in other civil law countries, China has a procuratorate system that parallels the court system but is independent from both the courts and the Ministry of Justice and it

50 Some scholars refer to it as an 'adjudication committee'.

51 Curiously enough, the Criminal Procedure Law is the only law out of the three procedure laws (criminal procedure, civil procedure, and administrative procedure) that outlines the basic mode by which judicial committees operate by providing that "with respect to a difficult, complex, and major case, regarding which the collegial panel considers it difficult to make a decision, the collegial panel shall refer the case to the president of the court, for him to decide whether to submit the case to the judicial committee for discussion and decision. The collegial panel shall implement the decision of the judicial committee."

52 There is no specific requirement as to the number of members in the judicial committees, but the number should be odd.

is responsible for the supervision of the judicial system. In China, the procuratorate is an active player in the adjudication system.[53] The Supreme People's Procuratorate, the higher, intermediate and grassroots local people's procuratorates, and special procuratorates like the military procuratorates exercise the power of prosecution. The Supreme People's Procuratorate directs the prosecution work of the local and special procuratorates. But China's procuratorate is rather unique compared to its western counterparts, since it has a dual role in the criminal process: both prosecution and adjudicative supervision as mentioned above.[54] The procuratorate can initiate an adjudicative review referred to as a 'protest'. They may also launch a protest against a civil case, where besides a protest challenging the court's decision based on the discovery of definite errors, the procuratorate can request the court to make a retrial in case the decision will infringe upon the national interest or public interest. In a civil action, a litigant may petition the procuratorate for procuratorial recommendations or appeal: if the court either dismisses a petition for retrial or fails to issue a ruling regarding a petition for retrial within the prescribed time limit, or if the judgment or the ruling rendered after retrial is clearly erroneous, the procuratorate shall, within three months, examine the party's application and make a decision to offer or not to offer its recommendations, or make a decision, to file or not to file an appeal. But the litigant shall not apply for the second time to acquire the procuracy's intervention. The adjudicative supervision of the procuratorate can also be achieved through its recommendations to the court or by requesting the procuratorate at the next higher level to file an appeal with the people's court at the corresponding level.

The judicial reform and China opening up to the world, led to a litigation boom. In 1978, 613,000 cases were tried by the courts at all levels,[55] while the number of cases accepted in 2011 and 2013 increased to 12,215,570 and 14,217,000 (among which 11,489,0120 and 14,217,000 were closed),[56] showing an increase of 20 times in 35 years. Another indicator, the civil litigation rate, i.e. the number of civil cases tried by

---

53 The procuratorate system parallels the four-tier hierarchy of the court structure from the top down: The Supreme People's Procuratorate, the Higher People's Procuratorate, the Intermediate People's Procuratorate, and the Basic People's Procuratorate. Article 130 of the Constitution provides that the PRC establishes the Supreme People's Procuratorate, local people's procuratorate at different levels, the military procuratorate and other special people's procuratorate.

54 Article 129 of the Constitution and Article 1 of the Organic Law of the People's Procuratorates stipulate that "the people's procuratorates of the People's Republic of China are state organs for legal supervision." This means that, in addition to the function performed similarly in most countries like deciding which cases will be prosecuted, the procuratorates oversee investigation and trial, supervision of the legal activities of the people's courts, the execution of judgments, and the activities of prisons. In 2013, the procuratorates protested against 6,345 criminal cases that were deemed wrong cases and corrected 42,873 cases of unlawful execution of punishments. In terms of legal supervision of civil and administrative actions, they delivered 15,538 protests against effective judgments and mediation documents or procuratorial suggestions for retrial, 18,398 procuratorial suggestions for law violations in trials, and 41,069 suggestions for law violations in the enforcement of civil cases. See China Law Society, *Annual Report on Rule of Law Construction in China (2013)* (Xinhua Press) 112–114.

55 Zhu Jingwen, 'Behind More Litigation: Positive and Negative Impacts' (2014) 9 *Frontier of Law in China* 105, 106.

56 See China Law Society, *Annual Report on Rule of Law Construction in China (2011)* (Xinhua Press) 107; China Law Society, *Annual Report on Rule of Law Construction in China (2013)* (n 54).

the courts in the first instance per 10,000 population also witnessed a dramatic increase, growing from 31.5 in 1978 to 435.6 in 2010.[57] In 2013, the people's courts at all levels heard and closed 3,554,000 civil cases of first instance, tried and closed 537,000 cases related to personal injuries, labour and employment, education, medical service, housing and consumption, 203,000 cases concerning the right of usage of land, homestead and wage disputes, and 1,612,000 cases related to family and marriage disputes. As for the criminal adjudication, China's courts heard and closed 954,000 criminal cases of first instance in 2013, resulting in sentencing 1,158,000 criminals. 250,000 cases were heard and closed against serious crimes such as homicides, robbery, kidnapping, explosions, raping, abducting and selling women and children. For offences against property, the caseload was 303,000.[58]

In terms of the caseload, China has comparatively a small number of judges. There are altogether 189,000 judges in China, of which 7,000 are in the high people's courts, 36,000 in the intermediate people's courts and 146,000 in the primary people's courts. Among them, 23.86 % are female.[59]

China has a several thousand year-old tradition for mediation and every year close to 8 million cases are mediated. More than half of them are mediated by the People's Mediation, which is grass root community-based mediation. There are more than 4 million people's mediators in China and they are an affordable means of conflict resolution, which has not lost popularity parallel to the immense growth in the judicial sphere of Chinese society. Mediation has been modernized, and in 2017 an online dispute resolution platform was launched.[60]

3. Norm production

Both republican China and imperial China have had a body of statutory laws. During China's 5000 year history, codified system of laws sprotued with roots reaching back to the Spring-, Autumn- and Warring states periods.[61] It was during the Han dynasty when Confucianism became the dominant political ideology, and became the primary influence on the traditional Chinese view of law that an individual should be guided by *Li* (礼, ritual or propriety) rather than by *fa* (法, the law). As an ethical system, Confucianism seeks to teach the proper way for all people to behave in society. The cornerstone of Confucianism is filial piety (孝), or respect for elders. Benevolence (仁), the fundamental concept of Confucianism is to treat our peers humanely. Under the sys-

57 Jingwen (2014) (n 55) 105, 109.

58 China Law Society, *Annual Report on Rule of Law Construction in China (2013)* (n 54).

59 The Supreme People's Court of China, *Guardian of Equality and Justice: The Supreme People's Court of the People's Republic of China* 33.

60 https://weinsteininternational.org/mediation-in-china/ accessed 4 May 2020.

61 China had its first statutory law in 536 BC. It was called the "penal law inscribed on bronze tripods" (刑鼎), because it was cast in the bronze tripod and disclosed to the public. Comparatively, the first statutory law in the West, the Twelve Tables in ancient Rome, was enacted between the 3rd century BC and the 1st century AD, that is, 200–500 years later than the first Chinese statute.

tem of *Li*, Confucianism designs the society to be organized in a hierarchy of superior/inferior relationships: the rulers to the subjects, parents to children, men to women. If every person performs his or her role, stability and social order will be sustained. Because Confucians believed in the fundamental goodness of man and advocated rule by moral persuasion in accordance with *Li*, Confucians held that codified law was inadequate to provide meaningful guidance for the human activities, even though they were not against using laws to control the most unruly elements in the society.[62] The teachings of Confucius have had an enduring effect on Chinese life and have provided the basis for the social order through much of the country's history.

Legalism, a competing school of thought during the Warring States period, maintained that man was by nature evil and had to be controlled by strict rules of law, harsh penal punishment, and uniform justice. In China, the first criminal code was promulgated in the early period of the Warring States Period as a product of this legalism.[63] Legalist philosophy had its greatest impact on the codification of the first imperial dynasty, the Qin (221–207 BC).

From Qin, each Chinese dynasty used *Lü* (律, code) as the fundamental law, which was a body of criminal rules promulgated by the Emperor. Even though the Han dynasty (206 BC–220 AD) overthrew the Qin, the Han retained the basic legal system established under the Qin. The Code of Han modified some of the harsher aspects in line with the Confucian philosophy of social control based on ethical and moral persuasion, kicking off the Confucianisation process of the ancient Chinese legal system. The Tang Dynasty (618–907 AD) accomplished the hundred-year-long Confucianisation of the law with the great work of the Code of Tang (唐律), which was passed on and developed in the following feudal dynasties until the collapse of the last Dynasty of Qing, and which strongly influenced the development of the criminal laws in other East Asian Countries.[64]

The guiding philosophy of The Tang Code is "the moralities and rites are the essence of the political administration while criminal punishments are its application" (德礼为政教之本，刑罚为政教之用). *Li* then became the fundamental spirit of the jurispru-

62 The relationship between *Li* and law or punishment in Ancient China can be characterized by "what will be excluded by *Li* will be punished by the penal law. *Li* and law then interact", see *B Biography of Chen Chong of The Book of Han* ("礼之所去，刑之所取，失礼则入刑，相为表里也"。《汉书·陈宠传》).

63 The first actual reference to a code is to one supposedly compiled in the fourth century BC by a certain Li K'uei (李悝), who was considered the founding father of the Legalism. It is stated that Li, who was the tutor to Marquis Wen of Wei (魏文公, reigned 427-387 BC in the Warring States Period), brought together the laws of all the states existing at that time and formed them into a code, the Canon of Laws (*fajing*, 法经). See Wallace Johnson (tr), *The T'ang Code* (Princeton University Press 1979) 7. To be specific, Li's code has six parts, namely盗(containing rules on crimes against property), 贼(containing rules on crimes against personal rights), 囚(containing rules on adjudication and imprisonment), 捕(containing rules on arrest), 杂(containing miscellaneous rules on punishment of crimes that could not be classified in any of the categories were listed), and 具(containing rules to punish severely or leniently).

64 See William C. Jones, 'Trying to Understand the Current Chinese Legal System' in C. Stephen Hsu (ed), *Understanding China's Legal System: Essays in Honor of Jerome A. Cohen* (New York University Press 2003) 8.

dence and was applied as the standard to judge laws.[65] Thus, *Lü* aimed at establishing a legal order under the doctrine of *Li*, resulting in introducing provisions that dealt with the private concerns of individuals such as a man or his wife addressing abusive language to his grandparents or parents, which would be a severe violation of *Li* – the superior/inferior relationships of parents and children – and would be considered a crime with a punishment of being strangled if the abused grandparents or parents themselves complained to the magistrate and had themselves heard the abusive language.[66]

Since the Confucian teaching laid the foundation for the overall legal system, the classically trained local Confucian gentry played a crucial role as arbiters and handled all but the most serious local disputes. Even a dispute that went up to the magistrates, the administrative officers as well as the judiciary (who were trained in Confucian philosophy and literature and selected through the civil service exam thoroughly steeped in the Confucian classics) would usually be guided by the Confucian teachings to solve the disputes, even though they had to follow the provisions of the Code.

Different from the rights-centred *Corpus Juris Civilis*, the primary concern of the traditional Chinese *Lü* was to make it clear to the magistrate what activities had to be punished, and precisely what penalties he was to impose. Moreover, the majority of the provisions were not the only part of *Lü* addressed to magistrates to enforce as part of their administrative duties; these also concerned the behaviour of officials on the job. In essence, *Lü* was significant to the activities of the government or Emperor. An offense was regarded as a disruption of society that had to be restored by punishment. *Lü* also reflects an attempt by a centralized, bureaucratic state to extend and protect its power throughout all of China. This is certainly another reason why the local magistrate was permitted no discretion at all in the sentencing of cases. For each case, he had to provide some relevant article of the Code, the Statutes, the Regulations or the Ordinances to justify his decision. Failure to do so would result in being punished himself.[67]

In fact, imperial China had large bodies of written laws, in which *Lü*, the Criminal Code, was the major form of law. For example, in the Tang Dynasty, other divisions of law included *Ling* (令, ordinance), *Ge* (格, injunction), and *Shi* (式, standard). *Ling*, literally referring to ordinance or order, but formally and functionally as statutes summarizing general administrative rules for the central government, was the most important of the three. In order to prevent and punish the unlawful and evil acts not covered by *Lü* or *Ling*, *Ge* was introduced as a means through which new provisions and rulings would be drawn up as supplements to *Lü* and *Ling*, while *Shi* seemed to be detailed

65 For example, for the item "improper act", it was annotated in "Za *Lü*" (杂律, miscellaneous rules) that it referred to "those acts that are not prohibited by the legal provisions, but still should not be done according to the principles of '*Li*' (rites)". (《唐律疏议·杂律》"不应得为"条（总第450条）：诸不应得为而为之者……谓律、令无条，理不可为者).

66 《大清律例•刑律•骂詈》(总第329条)："凡骂祖父母、父母及妻妾骂夫之祖父母、父母者，并绞。". See Sir George Thomas Staunton, *Ta Tsing Leu Lee; Being the Fundamental Laws and A Selection from the Supplementary of the Penal Code of China* (original edition printed for T. Cadell and W. Davies 1810, Ch'eng-Wen Publishing 1966) Article 330, 'Book IV Abusive Language, Sixth Division: Criminal Law, Penal Code of Qing' 357.

67 See Jones (n 64) 12.

measures of different government departments to perform their duties in limited areas of law, in contrast to *Ling*. In addition to the Criminal Code of *Lü*, the emperor of the Tang Dynasty also codified the administrative law into *Liu Dian* (六典, The Six Statutes of Tang), which specified the duties and functions of the central and local governments and created the template for the *Liu Dian* of the Ming and the Qing Dynasty.

It is quite fair to say that imperial China had a legal system of statutory laws. Even though cases played a certain part in the adjudication, they cannot be considered the Chinese counterpart of common law precedents. The Chinese cases, *Li* (例), a word usually translated as 'sub-statute', though 'codified precedent' might be better, were detailed rules that were normally based on decisions or interpretations by officials at the highest level of the central government, and were printed following the article of *Lü* to which they referred.[68]

After the Opium War broke out in 1840, efforts were made to transplant some notions of the rule of law from modern Western countries to China. Legal reform was undertaken so that China could ask the treaty powers to abolish extraterritoriality. In the final years of the Qing Dynasty, reform advocates in the government implemented certain aspects of the modernized Japanese legal system. These efforts made up the movement of law amendment (清末修律). Even though the introduction into China of the modern civil law system did not save Qing Dynasty from collapse, it surely sparked the modernization of the Chinese legal system.[69]

---

68 Ibid 10. The court should not directly render their decisions based on the cases. In the Qing Dynasty, in which the sub-statute style cases were affiliated to the articles of *Lü* (the code) to clarify the application of the comparatively abstract statutory language, the Ministry of Justice (the department of the central government for judicial and penal processes, 刑部) submitted to the emperor the analytical opinion of important cases reported from the local governments. On the approval of the opinion, the cases turned into leading cases (成案). The court, after reporting to the Ministry of Justice and getting the approval of the Emperor, could cite the leading case in the adjudication. If the application of a leading case became a practice for a number of years, it would be codified into the code as a sub-article (条例), functioning as an interpretation of how an article should be applied in the real cases. Unlike the articles of the code, a sub-article could be altered in the course of time and according to the circumstances. The sub-articles' kind of "precedent" became more and more important in the daily business of the Qing courts, since the inflexible code enacted at the birth of the dynasty could not adequately solve the new issues constantly emerging during the 200-year life of the dynasty.

69 In the decade-long law amendment movement in the late Qing Dynasty, China for the first time established a civil law code system like that of Japan. The late Qing borrowed legislation from Japan in such areas as the Constitution, civil laws, criminal laws, commerce laws, and bankruptcy laws. On 27 August 1908, the late Qing enacted the first constitutional document in Chinese history – The Outline of the Imperial Constitution (钦定宪法大纲). This was a copy of the Japanese constitution, generally speaking. Other important laws include the Organization Law for Central Judicial Office (大理院审判编制法), the Criminal Code of Qing (大清新刑律), the Draft of Civil Code of Qing (大民律草案), the Draft of Criminal Procedure Law (刑事民事诉讼法草案), and the Draft of Civil Procedure Law (民事诉讼法草案). These achievements laid down, for the first time in China, the principle of judicial independence, separation of civil laws from criminal laws, and the creation of the procuratorate. A law school, a new system of courts, and a Ministry of Justice were also established. The fact that the late Qing reformed its legal system based on pragmatic considerations – to rescue the Qing Dynasty from the crisis and difficulties under the disguise of taking back the judicial sovereignty, rather than to follow some kind of universally applicable general principles – led to its final failure. But the step of modernizing the Chinese legal system under the civil law system has never been stopped since then.

After the fall of the Qing dynasty in 1911 and the turmoil of the early Republic of China (中华民国), the Kuomintang (国民党, the Nationalist Party) established the Nationalist government, which unified the country in 1928. The government began a series of legal reforms which continued until the outbreak of the Sino-Japanese War in 1937. During this period, the Nationalists codified all the major civil, criminal, and commercial laws of China.[70] Although many of these laws were patterned after the codes of Germany, Switzerland, France, and Japan, the Nationalists tried to retain traditional values, which they believed were consonant with the goal of modernization. For example, a suspect who voluntarily surrendered to the authorities before the crime was discovered would automatically receive a reduction in sentence.

In 1949, the People's Republic of China was founded and the Kuomingtang's laws were abolished. The Chinese government then started to establish a socialism legality, which was brought forward in the early 1950s by the creation of the first three laws of the People's Republic of China, namely the Marriage Law of 1950, the Land Reform Law of 1950, and the Constitution of 1954 (1954年宪法). Since then, and especially since 1978, when the reform and opening up were initiated, the construction of the legal system in the PRC entered a new period.

After more than three decades of continuous work on the rule of law, China now exercises uniform yet multi-tiered legislation. The hierarchy of law in China includes from the top to the bottom: the Constitution, laws (法律), regulations (规章) or provisions (条例), rules (规则), detailed rules (细则), methods or measures (办法), decisions (决定), resolutions (决议), and orders (命令). The Constitution is enacted or amended by the National People's Congress (NPC). Since 1949, China has drawn up four Constitutions: in 1954, 1975, 1978 and 1982. The 1982 Constitution has been amended five times, in 1988, 1993, 1998, 2004. And 2018. A law (法) is a statute that has been enacted by the NPC or its Standing Committee. Law serves as basic statutes in the national sphere of government, such as the criminal law and civil law as well as organic laws on state organs and other matters, which could be partially supplemented and amended when the NPC is not in session by the Standing Committee of the NPC, provided that the basic principles of these laws are not contravened. In accordance with the Legislation Law of the People's Republic of China, laws on the following affairs must be made exclusively by the NPC and its Standing Committee:

1) affairs involving state sovereignty,
2) the formation, organization as well as the functions and powers of state organs,
3) the system of regional ethnic autonomy,
4) the system of special administrative regions,

70 The main legal system of the Nationalist Republic of China then was referred as Six Law Pandects (六法全书), including the constitution, the civil law, the criminal law, the civil procedure, the criminal procedure, and the administrative procedure. It consisted of codes (such as the civil code, criminal code, civil procedure code, and criminal procedure code, but the administrative procedure was not codified), but also of special laws made in the abovementioned six areas of law.

5) the system of sel f-government of people at the grassroots level,
6) criminal offences and their punishment,
7) deprivation of citizens' political rights,
8) mandatory measures and penalties involving restriction of the freedom of the person,
9) expropriation of non-state-owned property,
10) the basic civil system,
11) the basic economic system,
12) basic systems of finance, taxation, customs, banking and foreign trade,
13) and systems of litigation and arbitration.

Usually, laws will adopt the form of comprehensive legislation covering its subject matter. The latest legislative achievement is the codification of the civil law. The Civil Code of the People's Republic of China was published on May 28 of 2020 and will come into force on January 1 of 2021.[71] The General Provisions of the Civil Code, which will be the first Book of the Civil Code, have allready been adopted at the 5th Session of the 12th National People's Congress and promulgated the same day. It went into force on 1 October 2017. The General Provisions include general principles applied across the board unless special exemptions are later made in the code under specific topics. The other five Books of the planned Chinese Civil Code are

1) Real Rights,
2) Contract,
3) Personality Rights,
4) Torts,
5) Marriage and Family,
6) and Inheritance.

Regulations (规章), also translated as 'provisions' or 'measures', are the national level administrative rules designed to implement a law or policy and are usually issued by the State Council. In contrast, a lower-level agency can also issue regulations to address a narrower question. Under the Constitution and the Legislation Act, at the local level, the people's congresses or their standing committees of the provinces, autonomous regions (自治区) and municipalities directly under the central government may enact local regulations covering their jurisdiction and approve the larger cities' regulation. The four special economic zones authorized by the State Council[72] are also endowed with regulation-making power. In addition, the people's congresses of the ethnic autonomous areas (自治地方) under the autonomous regions have the power to enact their regula-

71 China's Civil Code published, http://www.chinadaily.com.cn/a/202006/02/WS5ed616e9a310a8b24115a570.html

72 They are Shenzhen (深圳), Zhuhai (珠海) and Shantou (汕头) of Guandong Province (广东省) and Xiamen (厦门) of Fujian Province (福建省). All of them are port cities located in the Southeast coast of China. Shenzhen and Zhuhai border with Hong Kong SAR and Macau SAR respectively.

tions on the basis of the political, economic and cultural conditions of the local ethnic group(s).

A set of rules (规则, *guize*) or detailed rules (细则, *xize*) are usually issued by a ministry or a commission of the State Council within the limits of their competences, and often contain specific rules of interpretation or explanation of a law or a regulation. Moreover, the provincial level governments and the larger cities may also enact rules for their jurisdiction.

Other statutory sources of law include methods or measures (办法), which are rules or regulations that are more detailed and seek to address a narrow issue. An administrative decision (决定) for explanatory purposes may also have the force of law. In addition, state organizations, political parties, and social organizations adopt resolutions (决议), which have little prescriptive legislative value but record common concerns and opinions expressed at a particular meeting or forum. An order (命令) refers to a proclamation issued by a state organization that is intended to prescribe legal standards.[73]

In China, another source of law comes from the court and the procuratorate. The Supreme People's Court and the Supreme People's Procuratorate bear the authority to issue nationally enforceable Judicial Interpretations (司法解释) as guidelines to the trials.[74] The interpretations by the Supreme People's Court are more voluminous, comprehensive and pervasive than the laws they intepret and therefore, constitute a significant part in the hierarchy of Chinese law. Judicial interpretations issued by the Supreme People's Court may be made in four forms, namely, 'interpretation' (解释), 'provision' (规定), 'reply' (批复), and 'decision' (决定). An 'interpretation' deals with general issues of the law application, such as whether a certain law should be applied or how a law should be applied to a certain category of cases or a certain kind of legal issues. Judicial interpretations that formulate the norms or opinions to guide the trial work stemming from the legislative intent shall be made in the form of a 'provision'. A 'reply' shall be made to give instructions on the application of law to specific issues on the request of the higher people's courts or the Military Court. The amendment or abolishment of judicial interpretations shall be made in the form of a 'decision'. A noteworthy phenomenon about the judicial interpretations is that the articles of a judicial interpretation will out-

73 James M. Zimmerman, *China Law Deskbook: A Legal Guide for Foreign-Invested Enterprises Paperback* (2nd edn, ABA Section of International Law 2005) 65–66.

74 Their authority of interpreting laws and regulations is derived from the Resolution of the Standing Committee of the National People's Congress Providing an Improved Interpretation of the Law (《全国人民代表大会常务委员会关于加强法律解释工作的决议》), issued on 10 June 1981. Its Article 2 sets forth that the Supreme People's Court shall make interpretations of application of laws and decrees at trial, just as the Supreme People's Procuratorate does in the procuratorial work. If their interpretations are in conflict, they shall be submitted to the Standing Committee of NPC for final decision. Article 33 of the Organic Law of Courts provides that the Supreme People's Court gives interpretations on questions concerning specific application of laws and decrees in judicial proceeding. On 18 January 2012, the Supreme People's Court and the Supreme People's Procuratorate jointly issued a Notice on Prohibiting Local People's Courts and People's Procuratorates from Formulating Documents of a Nature of Judicial Interpretation (《最高人民法院、最高人民检察院关于地方人民法院、人民检察院不得制定司法解释性质文件的通知》), strengthening and clarifying their exclusive power to make judicial interpretations.

number that of the statute it construes. This can explain to some extent its importance in the adjudication.[75]

The judicial interpretations' practice has witnessed the growth of its two actual functions: one is to concretize rules with factual data within a particular social framework, and the other, usually through the 'provision' kind of judicial interpretations, is to change the scope or even the meaning of the rules to meet new situations or new social demands. The latter aroused quite many concerns and controversies, since it blurred the function of the court and the legislature in terms of law-making. The Constitution prescribes that the NPC enjoys complete sovereignty and courts have no power to review legislations, let alone the power to change or modify legislation. But scholars hold that rapid social changes make the court's law-making function necessary and inevitable against the transitional nature of current Chinese society.[76]

However, even though judicial interpretations can be defined as a function of law-making, these follow a different approach than judge-made law in the common law countries. Generally speaking, the production of a judicial interpretation cannot be triggered on a case-by-case basis. Judicial interpretations derive neither from the hearing of a concrete case nor the dealing with a specific issue at a trial. They are made at the initiation of the Supreme People's Court or the Supreme People's Procuratorate, as general rules to provide detailed analysis, clearer definitions or gap-filling rules for statutes either shortly after their promulgation or at any time the Supreme People's Court or the Supreme People's Procuratorate feels that there is a need for an interpretation. Therefore, the strictly labelled 'judicial interpretation' is not a kind of judicial discretion for individualized justice in particular cases, but another form of legal rules with general nature. In addition, the judicial interpretations are not made by one or two individual judges in the process of adjudication, but by the Judicial Committee of the Supreme People's Court or the Supreme People's Procuratorate through deliberation.

China has recently taken a new remarkable measure to place more weight on using cases in the judicial work. In 2011, China established the system of 'guiding cases' (指导性案例) through announcing the first set of such cases: two civil law cases and two criminal cases, a decisive achievement to implement the second Five-Years Reform Outline for the People's Court (2004–2008), issued on 26 October 2005, which aims to ensure the unified application of legislation. Proposal Number 13 of the Reform Outline set the tone for the guiding cases systems:

---

75 For example, the General Principles of the Civil Law has 156 articles, while its judicial interpretation – Opinions of the Supreme People's Court on Several Issues concerning the Implementation of the General Principles of the Civil Law (《最高人民法院关于贯彻执行《中华人民共和国民法通则》若干问题的意见》) – has 200 articles. The article numbers of the Civil Procedure Law (modified in 2012) and its judicial interpretation – Interpretation of the Supreme People's Court on the Application of the Civil Procedure Law, issued 30 January 2015 (《最高人民法院关于适用中华人民共和国民事诉讼法的解释》) – are respectively 284 and 552.

76 See Wang Chenguang, 'Lawmaking functions of the Chinese Courts: Judicial Activism in a Country of Rapid Social Changes' (2006) 1 *Frontiers of Law in China* 524, 545–546.

> "Guiding cases should play the role in unifying the application of legislation by directing the lower courts' operation, enriching and developing their jurisprudence and so on. The Supreme People's Court shall formulate opinions normative for making the guiding cases, define the standard form and the process of case-selection and set the way of releasing the guiding cases and guiding rules and so on."

A guiding case is an judgment selected by the Supreme People's Court from its own jurisprudence or that of the lower level courts. The Supreme People's Court will single out guiding cases from the following five types of cases: (1) cases that have attracted broad social attention, (2) cases where terms of the legislation applied in the case are broad, (3) cases where the type of dispute is paradigmatic, (4) cases that bring difficult, complicated, or new legal issues, or (5) other cases that have a guiding function.[77] The Case Guidance Office of the Supreme People's Court is established to compile guiding cases each year. A guiding case will consist of five components:

1) key points of the judgment,
2) relevant legal provisions,
3) basic facts,
4) the judgment,
5) and the judgment's reasoning.

As of 25 February 2019, the Supreme People's Court had issued 102 guiding cases in 21 batches.[78]

The guiding case system has far-reaching consequences for the Chinese civil law legal system. Compared with judicial interpretations, guiding cases resemble more closely the doctrine of precedent of the common law system. Can the adoption of the guiding cases system represent the introduction of precedent into China? If so, how should the statutory source of law be harmonised with the case law in the adjudication? The Supreme People's Court does not mention whether or not the guiding cases are binding, instead, the Supreme People's Court gives the guiding cases the power of reference for people's courts at all levels when adjudicating similar cases.[79] The guiding cases are not therefore, in themselves, authoritative. In other words, the *ratio decidendi* of guiding cases cannot be the legal ground for the lower court's judgment, but it can be cited as a reason for explaining the judgment. In 2015, the Supreme People's Court issued the Detailed Rules for the Implementation of the

77 See Article 2 of The Work Rule of the Supreme People's Court on Issuing the Case Guidance (《关于案例指导工作的规定》), issued by the Supreme People's Court on 26 November 2010.

78 All the guiding cases and the notice of issuing a newly issued batch of guiding cases can be found at http://www.court.gov.cn/shenpan-gengduo-77.html accessed 31 December 2019.

79 Article 7 of The Work Rule of Supreme People's Court on Issuing the Case Guidance.

Provisions of the Supreme Peoples' Court Concerning Work on Case Guidance,[80] which stipulates that lower courts "should quote the Guiding Cases as a *reason* for their adjudications, but not cite them as the basis of their adjudication." In other words, guiding cases should be invoked not as an independent source of law but as a necessary aid to judicial reasoning. Thus, the provisions from 2015 did much to legitimate the use and citation of guiding cases in lower court decisions, while still supporting the view that guiding cases were binding *de facto* but not *de jure*.[81] The possible legal bases of a judgment were not expanded: the text of the statutes is still the only binding legal authority. The judgment of guiding case is more like an interpretation of specific provisions, through which the higher courts clarify vague provisions and fill in legal loopholes. The guiding case system attempts to preserve the feature of the Chinese legal system, whilst giving some power to shape the law to the judicial branch. In other words, the new system is an effort to secure the advantages of both the common law and civil law systems. However, an obvious challenge is how the lower courts will use the guiding cases issued. Normally, judgments handed down by Chinese courts are very brief, and this is also true of the judgments of the guiding cases.[82] The Supreme People's Court does not issue, attached to the guiding cases, a detailed guideline to determine which guiding cases to follow and what significance these cases should be given, creating practical difficulties for a judiciary that has been trained in the context of civil law.[83]

Yet another feature of the guiding case system could make it more similar to the common law precedents. The higher people's courts can also issue "reference cases" within their respective jurisdictions, even though they cannot use such titles as "guiding cases" or "guidance cases", in order to avoid confusion with guiding cases. However, they have to report in a timely manner and on a level-by-level to the Supreme People's Court any problems encountered in the implementation of the guiding cases and referencing cases.

---

80 Detailed Rules for the Implementation of the Provisions of the Supreme People's Court Concerning Work on Case Guidance（《最高人民法院关于案例指导工作的规定实施细则》), issued by the Judicial Committee of the Supreme People's Court on 13 May 2015. See http://www.lawinfochina.com/display.aspx?id=19290&lib=law accessed 31 December 2019.

81 Mark Jia, 'Chinese Common Law? Guiding Cases and Judicial Reform' (2016) Vol. 129, No. 8 *Harvard Law Review* 2213, 2224.

82 Each case of the first set of four guiding cases issued on 20 December 2011 has an average length of about of 1,200 thousand Chinese characters (about 900 English words). They have four parts: key points of the judgment, basic facts, judgment, and reasoning.

83 The Supreme People's Court articulates principally in Title II – "Effectively using guiding cases" – of the Notice of the Supreme People's Court on Issuing the First Set of Guiding Cases（《最高人民法院关于发布第一批指导性案例的通知》) on 20 December 2011, that courts at all levels shall thoroughly and accurately understand the spirit and significance of guiding cases, strengthen the consciousness of using guiding cases and properly hear similar cases in light of advanced judicial concepts, so as to further improve the quality and efficiency of case handling, ensure the unity of the legal effects and social effects of adjudications, and guarantee social stability and harmony.

This implies that the lower courts cannot issue any reference cases in conflict with the guiding cases of the Supreme People's Court.[84]

In essence, guiding cases constitute a persuasive and a legal argumentation base, rather than binding precedents. Judges cannot cite them directly in the judgment as the applicable law. However, they can use the guiding cases as reference in the legal reasoning. The increasing use of guiding cases may help push forward the ongoing efforts of reforming the style of legal opinion through strengthening the part of reasoning. In China, like in some other civil law countries such as France, the typical decision is short, concise and devoid of explanation or justification. Its briefness may not give sufficient explanation about how to understand the law and how it should be applied, causing unnecessary confusion among the litigants and even the judges. The reasoning added in a guiding case's legal opinion will greatly enhance the clarity of laws applied. At the moment, the requirement for court decisions is that they must analyse: objectivity, lawfulness and relevance of evidence, the reasons or grounds for admissible and inadmissible evidence and the meanings and application of legal provisions interpreted and explained in combination with the facts of cases.[85] Through reference to the reasoning of a guiding case and the analogy of its facts, judges can produce a decision with not only a sufficient, but also an easily comprehended basis supporting the decision. The purpose of the guiding cases system is the enhancement of the reasonableness of the legal opinions. In addition, the reference to guiding cases in the legal opinion will also prop up the consistency of the application of the law, since these set up a concrete example of how a legal provision has been interpreted and applied in similar situations.

The following description can provide an overview of the sources of law in China until May 2015: there were 284 statutes, 716 regulations, 5654 provincial level regulations, 2,790 regulations issued by the larger cities, 301 by special economic zones and 894 regulations issued by the autonomous areas. The total number of judicial decisions was 462, including 374 from the Supreme People's Court, 42 from the Supreme People's Procuratorate and 46 jointly issued by the two institutions. As for rules issued by a ministry or a commission of the State Council and the local governments, the number of the former is 3,016 and the latter is 8,990.[86]

84 However, there is still a huge difference between the guiding cases and the precedents in common law systems. The guiding cases, even though selected and issued by the Supreme People's Court, are usually from the lower level courts, to which the higher-level courts will have to take reference in the adjudication. In this regard it differs from the doctrine of *stare decisis*, which requires the lower level courts to abide by the decisions of the higher-level courts rather than the reverse scenario.

85 See Notice of the Supreme People's Procuratorate on Issuing the Opinions of the Supreme People's Procuratorate on Strengthening the Reasoning of Prosecutorial Legal Documents (for Trial Implementation) (《最高人民检察院关于印发最高人民检察院关于加强检察法律文书说理工作的意见(试行)的通知》), issued on 9 August 2009.

86 See http://www.chinalawindex.cn/ accessed 31 May 2015.

Before the adoption of the General Provisions of the Civil Law, custom was not considered a general source of law.[87] To be specific, the General Principles of the Civil Law do not grant custom the status of source of law, because Article 6 provides that civil activities must be in compliance with the law; where there are no relevant provisions in the law, they shall be in compliance with state policies, thus depriving custom of general enforceability in the civil law.[88] However, custom appears in the specific clauses in a few statutes. For example, Article 85 of the Property Law provides that local customs can be used to resolve disputes of contiguous relationship where no legal provision exists. In Contract Law, the customary business practice could decide whether an act could lead to a valid acceptance, as an exception of acceptance generally made in the form of a notice.[89] In the criminal law area, serious encroachment on the customs or habits of minority nationalities by the workers of the state agencies is a crime punishable up to two years in prison.[90] Generally, customs of ethnic minorities have been most frequently introduced into the law to protect the minorities' rights, usually in the statutory language like "respect for the minorities and their ethnic mores and customs".[91] Whilst according to Article 10 of the General Provisions of the Civil Law, resolution of a civil dispute shall be in compliance with the law; where there are no relevant provisions in the law, the custom shall be applied on the condition it does not conflict with good public order and good faith. In an era where the nets of law are tightly woven, how custom will be applied to fill in the loopholes deserves much attention.

Even though custom does not automatically transcend into the customary law through judicial acceptance, some of it can be binding through the judicial interpretations dealing with a particular kind of legal issue. For example, in the judicial interpretation regarding how to apply contract law, the Supreme People's Court explained the criteria for a business practice to be a custom judicially accepted as: without any conflict with law or regulation, it shall be universally adopted at the place of transaction or in a certain field or sector, shall be known or should be known by the other party to the transaction when the contract is concluded, and shall be often used by both parties. The claimant shall bear the burden of proof on a customary business practice.[92] A judicial

87 However, in the Civil Code of the Republic of China, custom earned the status of the power of source of law. Its article stipulated that if there was no applicable act for a civil case, the case should be decided according to customs. If there was no such custom, the case should be decided according to the jurisprudence.

88 The General Principles of the Civil Law (《民法通则》) was passed by the National People's Congress on 12 April 1986 and entered into force on 1 January 1987. It serves as the foundation of the civil acts and regulates the fundamental issues of the civil law, such as civil rights, civil liability, legal persons, natural persons, limitations, the agency, the guardianship, etc. The full version can be found at http://www.wipo.int/wipolex/zh/text.jsp?file_id=182628.

89 Article 22 of the Contract Law.

90 Article 251 of the Criminal Law.

91 For example, Article 14 of the Law on the Protection of Consumer Rights and Interests provides that in purchasing and using commodities or receiving services, consumers shall be entitled to human dignity, respect for their ethnic mores and customs, and legal protection of personal information.

92 Article 8 of the Interpretation II of the Supreme People's Court of Several Issues concerning the Application of the Contract Law of the People's Republic of China (《最高人民法院关于适用中华人民共和国合同法若干问题的解释(二)》), issued on 24 April 2009.

interpretation can give a more concrete explanation about what kind of specific business practice the court can accept as a basis for adjudication. For example, according to the interpretation about sales of goods, ordinary invoices can be a valid proof for a valid enforcement of payment if both parties treat them customarily as a proof of payment in the course of prior transactions.[93] In the adjudicative process, the court will have the discretion to decide whether a practice should be treated as a custom for the guidance to enter into the judgment, even though they usually will not utilize it in most cases where law and regulation has very clear provisions.[94]

However, unlike the status of custom in the Chinese legal system, policies can be a general source of law, usually included in the statutes. As mentioned above, Article 6 of the General Principles grants the state policies binding force in case no legal rules can be applied. Policies reflect the goals and intent of the government and serve as the guidance for administration and adjudication. They play a special role in China's new era, which has a theme of reform and social transition; China initiates political, economic, and social change mostly through the issue of policies. The August 1997 Notice Concerning Further Stabilizing and Perfecting the Rural Land Contracting Relationship (《中共中央办公厅、国务院办公厅关于进一步稳定和完善农村土地承包关系的通知》) can serve as an example. This policy stood alone for almost a year before the Land Management Act was passed to put the policy's intent into law. Development of formal legislative processes over the past thirty years has made Chinese state institutions the source of most formal legislation. Whereas reforms appear necessary to change the unsatisfactory *status quo* in certain social areas, legislation typically follows the issuance of a precursor policy statement, as a mature manifestation of such policy. The abovementioned Land Management Act reflects how the formal legislation follows on the heels of an earlier-issued state policy.

In practice, policies will usually be transformed into regulations and judicial interpretations. For example, on 27 November 2014, the State Council issued the Notice on Reviewing and Regulating Preferential Policies for Taxation and Other Aspects, which stipulated general requirements and the mechanism in principle of effectively regulating taxation preferential policies. Judicial interpretations are another tool for the policy's integration into the legal system, since they give concrete explanation about policies with a high level of generality. For example, the Supreme People's Court clarified in a judicial interpretation which crimes should be treated leniently and which should be

93 Article 8 of the Interpretation of the Supreme People's Court on Issues Concerning the Application of Law for the Trial of Cases of Disputes over Sales Contracts (《最高人民法院关于审理买卖合同纠纷案件适用法律问题的解释》), issued on 20 May 2012.

94 In an auction case, the court rendered the judgment with the reference to the practice of the 'Threetime Quotation Method' as a judicially accepted custom. See ZengYilong v. Jiangxi Goldhorse Auction Co., Ltd., Bank of China Limited, Shangrao Branch, and XuShengju (《曾意龙与江西金马拍卖有限公司、中国银行股份有限公司上饶市分行、徐声炬拍卖纠纷案》), from the Supreme People's Court on 19 October 2005.

treated rigidly, echoing the government's new criminal policy of Combining Leniency with Rigidity.[95]

Where there is no pertinent legal provision, polices amount to a direct source of law, meaning that citizen and governmental conduct must comply with the relevant state policy. For example, before the enactment of the General Provision of the Civil Law in 1986, the policies issued by the Supreme People's Court served as the important legal basis for handling civil cases. They are namely the 1962, 1979 and 1984 version of Opinions about the Implementation of the Civil Policies. The 1984 version still remains effective, but along with the enactment of the General Provision of the Civil Law, the Property Act, the Contract Act, the Torts Act and other civil law statutes, it can be rarely used in adjudication.

4. Legal Method and Ideal of Justice

In short, China is by nature a civil law country. Lawyers therefore usually start from a legal norm contained in legislation, and by means of deduction make conclusions regarding the actual case. The role of judges is to establish the facts of the case and to apply the provisions of the applicable code. Unlike common law courts, Chinese courts deal with cases apart from any precedence value. They generally decide cases using legislated provisions on a case-by-case basis, without reference to other judicial decisions.

The legal reasoning based on deduction demands a correct premise, that is, a clear and unambiguous statement of a legal rule, which the statutory language may not provide all the time. The interpretation of the statutes accordingly turns out to be inevitable and necessary. In China, the legislative and the judicial interpretations function to clarify the meaning of the statute. The power to make legislative interpretation, which is termed 'legal interpretation' in the Legislation Act, is vested in the Standing Committee of the NPC, which will establish the meaning of the law if a specific provision needs to be further defined or a newly occurred situation demands further explanation as to how the law should be applied.[96] History shows that the legal interpretation generally lies dormant, and was rarely triggered to construe the meaning of the foundational laws such as criminal law, criminal procedure, Hong Kong and Macau Basic Laws, etc.[97] The Stand-

95 Notice of the Supreme People's Court on Issuing Some Advice on Implementing the Criminal Policy of Combining Leniency with Rigidity (《最高人民法院印发关于贯彻宽严相济刑事政策的若干意见的通知》), issued on 20 August 2010. To facilitate the implementation of the policy, the Supreme People's Court then issued the Three Model Cases on People's Courts' Implementation of the Criminal Policy of Combining Punishment with Leniency Published by the Supreme People's Court (《最高人民法院发布三起人民法院贯彻宽严相济刑事政策典型案例)》 in February 2013.

96 Article 45 of the Legislation Law, enacted on 1 July 2000 and amended on 15 March 2015.

97 The search engine for Chinese source of laws – http://www.pkulaw.cn – reveals that the Standing Committee of the National People's Congress only produced 24 legal interpretations from 1995 to 2014. By contrast, in 2013, the Supreme People's Court and the Supreme People's Procuratorate jointly issued nine judicial interpretations. The former also issued 19 judicial interpretations independently and the latter issued 4 judicial interpretations. See China Law Society, *Annual Report on Rule of Law Construction in China (2013)* (n 54) 116.

ing Committee's latest effort was made in 2014. For the first time, it exerted the power of legal interpretation under the request of the Supreme People's Court, which petitioned for further explanation of the rules concerning the right to a name. Article 99 (1) of the General Principles of the Civil Law bestows on people the right to determine, use or change their personal names, and according to Article 22 of the Marriage Act a child may take the surname of either the father or mother. But could a child take a surname other than that of her father or mother? The Standing Committee of the NPC replied in its legal interpretation that people may take the surname of either the father or mother; however, one can also select the surname of a senior lineal relative by blood, the surname of a guardian if he was raised by a guardian, or another surname that is justified and does not go against public order and good customs. The Standing Committee harmonized the possible collision between the inertia of the traditional culture and the new rule of law conforming to the constant change in social life. On one hand, the surname in a name traditionally reflects consanguinity, ethical order and cultural traditions, and citizens' selection of surnames thus involves public order and good customs. On the other hand, the freedom to choose one's own name is a basic individual right in the modern society.[98]

In practice, even though legislative interpretations and judicial interpretations play a tremendous part in filling in statutory gaps and interpreting statutory language, they cannot wholly eliminate the possibility of judges' involvement in the statutory interpretation.[99] Here is an example: Through the extensive interpretation in the application of Article 120 of the General Principles of the Civil Law, which stipulates that the infringement upon the right of name, portrait, reputation or honour will lead to compensation for losses, judges introduced into Chinese legal system compensation for the infliction of emotional distress caused by any tortuous acts. This judicial invention finally entered into the 2009 enacted Tort Law, where Article 22 stipulates that any harm caused by a tort to a personal right or interest of another person inflicts a serious mental distress on the victim of the tort, the victim of the tort may require compensation for the infliction.

Judges in China are generally equipped with the methodologies of statutory interpretation including literal interpretation, teleological interpretation, systematic interpretation, etc. Such skills play an important role in dealing with the general clauses on good faith.[100] Courts extend the meaning of the statutory language through interpreta-

98 Interpretation of the Standing Committee of the National People's Congress on Paragraph 1 of Article 99 of the General Principles of the Civil Law and Article 22 of the Marriage Law of the People's Republic of China (《全国人民代表大会常务委员会关于中华人民共和国民法通则第九十九条第一款、中华人民共和国婚姻法第二十二条的解释), issued on 1 November 2014.

99 In theory, Chinese judges do not have the power to interpret the statutes, for the statutory interpretation was granted in the ways of legislative interpretation exercised by the Standing Committee of the National People's Congress (Article 67 of Chinese Constitution and Article 42 of the Legislation Law), or the statute-like judicial interpretation. Neither the Constitution, the Legislation Law nor the Judge Law grant judges expressly the power to interpret the statutes case-specifically. However, in practice, it is inevitable for judges to clarify the meaning of the statutory languages in case of ambiguity or vagueness, especially in applying the general principles like good faith, fairness, etc.

100 Article 4 of the General Principles of the Civil Law stipulates that in civil activities, the principles of voluntariness, fairness, making compensation for equal value, and good faith shall be observed. The principle of good faith can also be found in Article 6 of the Contract Law and Article 13 of the Civil Procedure Law.

tion guided by the principle of good faith. In a guiding case, the court held that unfair competition activities were not limited by those listed in Article 5 to Article 15 of the Anti-Unfair Competition Law. By contrast, the court utilized the good faith doctrine to determine whether unlisted activities constitute unfair competition, on the condition that they violate the business ethics and damage the lawful rights of other business operators.[101] The application of the good faith principle can clarify the meaning of the statutory language. In Guiding Case No. 30 issued by the Supreme People's Court, the responsible court produced an interpretation with the help of the good faith clause to further articulate the meaning of unfair competition under the Anti-Unfair Competition Act. The court explained that under the principle of good faith provided by Article 2 of the Anti-Unfair Competition Act, unfair competition means activities made by business operators who damage the others' legal rights and interests, disturb the order of social economy and violate the provisions of the Anti-Unfair Competition Act. In addition, business operators refer to legal persons, other economic organizations and individuals who engage in commercial business or profitable service (commodity in this Act hereafter includes service). Therefore, the protection given by the Anti-Unfair Competition Act was not limited to the business operators who engage in specific or direct competition, nor that they operate in the same industry.[102] The general clause of good faith is also used by the court as the basic reason to apply the method of analogy. In Guiding Case No. 15, the court held that, based on the principle of good faith, the nature of claimed harmful consequences is similar to circumstances as provided in Paragraph 3, Article 20 of the Company Act, and therefore the joint defendants should assume liability in accordance with Paragraph 3, Article 20 of the Company Act.[103] However, the courts will not apply the general clauses such as the good faith doctrine unless ambiguities or blanks in the statutory language necessitate them to do so.

Unlike the common law jurisdictions such as in the United States or England, there is no doctrine of *stare decisis* in China. Hence, Chinese judges do not have to decide if a case is sufficiently different from earlier cases, which would otherwise have set a precedent. Nevertheless, it is inevitable for judges to deal with the facts of a case. They need to work with facts to make the legal rules meaningful for concrete cases. In a word, the adjudication is the process of the application of the rule to the fact. However, not

---

101 The Guiding Case No. 45 of Beijing Baidu Netcom Science and Technology Co., Ltd. v. Tsingtao Osun Network Technique Co., Ltd. et al. (北京百度网讯科技有限公司诉青岛奥商网络技术有限公司等不正当竞争纠纷案) in Notice of the Supreme People's Court on Issuing the Tenth Group of Guiding Cases (《最高人民法院关于发布第十批指导性案例的通知》), issued on 15 April 2015.

102 The Guiding Case No. 30 of Lan Jianjun and Hangzhou SUREMOOV Auto Maintenance and Repair Technology Co., Ltd. v. Tianjin SUREMOOV Auto Maintenance and Repair Service Co., Ltd. et al. (指导案例30号：兰建军、杭州小拇指汽车维修科技股份有限公司诉天津市小拇指汽车维修服务有限公司等侵害商标权及不正当竞争纠纷案) in Notice of the Supreme People's Court on Issuing the Seventh Group of Guiding Cases (《最高人民法院关于发布第七批指导性案例的通知》), issued on 26 June 2014.

103 Guiding Case No. 15 of Xuzhou Construction Machinery Group Co., Ltd. v. Chengdu Chuanjiao Industry and Trade Co., Ltd., et al. (Sales contract dispute) (指导案例15号：徐工集团工程机械股份有限公司诉成都川交工贸有限责任公司等买卖合同纠纷案) in a Notice of the Supreme People's Court on Issuing the Forth Group of Guiding Cases (《最高人民法院关于发布第四批指导性案例的通知》), issued on 31 January 2013.

everything that happens will amount to be *fait juridique*, a fact of legal relevance. The facts of the case function to connect the abstract rule of law prescribed in the statutes and the different situations in each individual case. Judges need to make the distinction between ordinary facts and legal facts proved by the evidence. For a rule in the form of general clause, judges may have more discretion to decide whether a fact falls within the ambit of the rule. Common sense, public virtue and the desire for public order will help them to make the decision, for example, whether a particular business practice should be considered in good faith. As for specialized rules, which account for the majority of the statutory provisions, it is impossible to completely write out all the leeway for the judges have to interpret them in the light of facts. A crime enumerated in the criminal law prescribes that a type of act should be punished. The decision that an act constitutes torts implies that judges have categorized it as tortious rather than contractual, which is in essence differentiating the legal rule of torts and contract. Hence, judges are actually interpreting the rule through selecting what fact should be within its ambit; but they will not do it arbitrarily. They are restrained by the legislative intent, and the utilization of analogy and syllogism, to some degree, will technologically constrain their discretion.

In China, the role of judges has generally been limited to "the straightforward and mechanical application of the law to identify the correct solution", which involves little legal reasoning or judicial discretion.[104] However, discretion cannot be wholly wiped out. Since the last resort of the judiciary is to ease the tension between the formal laws and the concept of individualized justice, the discretionary power equips Chinese judges to handle the gap between rhetoric and reality in the legal system. What characterizes the Chinese practice of judicial activism is the idea of achieving the "social effect". Many scholars have commented upon the concrete meanings of this concept, almost all of which have emphasized that according to the requirement of achieving social effects and promoting social stability, the judges are not required to provide judgments based purely on the application of law, but may balance the application of law with the parties' needs, considering past and potential disputes associated with the current case, with the intention of avoiding future disputes.[105]

The discretionary power of the judiciary mainly rests upon the application of the general clauses in the statutes, which reflect highly the value of fairness, voluntariness, honesty, public interests, etc.[106] Judges will use the ideal of equity to satisfy those basic values. Courts will nullify or modify a contract once it burdens the debtor with a duty to pay an extravagant price compared with the prevailing market practice. In cases of an unpredictable changed circumstance, the contract could be terminated to avoid

---

104 Daniel C.K. Chow, *The Legal System of the People's Republic of China: In A Nutshell* (West 2003) 204. But other scholars have observed from the practice of Chinese courts that the judicial discretion is extensive. See Ji Weidong, 'The Judicial Reform in China: The Status Quo and Future Directions' (2013) Vol. 20, No. 1 *Indiana Journal of Global Legal Studies* 185.

105 Yang Qin, *The Current Situation of Chinese Judges: Lost in a Cloud of Conflict and Confusion* (ZChinR 2011) 244.

106 For instance, Article 4 of the General Principles of the Civil Law stipulates that civil activities should abide by the principles of voluntariness, fairness, making compensation for equal value, honesty and credibility. In addition, Article 6 of the same law requires the observation of the public interests.

any unfair liability for the party due to the impact of the changed situation. Once the designated amount of liquidated damages either failed to provide sufficient compensation or eventually amounted to a windfall, it will be modified under the request of the interested party. The litigants can petition the courts to reduce the price if the quality of the subject matter does not meet the representations. Equity is also a very important element for judges to determine the duty of compensation. In a tort case, if neither party is negligent or intentionally liable for the financial loss or physical injuries, the better-off party might make certain compensation to the victim – usually a socially disadvantaged party. Some areas of law illustrate how the ideal of equity "with Chinese characteristics" can help courts balance the interests of the litigants. Marriage is one such area. If the marital agreement provides that husband and wife separately own the property they respectively obtain during the existence of the marriage, judges could still grant a party certain compensation from the other party, if he or she has spent considerably more effort in supporting the children, taking care of the elderly or assisting the other party in work, etc.; thus, judges would render a divorce decision requiring a party to render appropriate assistance from his or her personal property, in case the other party suffers from difficulties in life. An illustrating example is a divorce judgment ordering one party to accommodate the other party in one room of his or her house, if the other party cannot afford to buy or rent a shelter.[107]

5. Professionalisation

Without high quality legal education, no qualified judges or lawyers will be produced. Although legal education in China has a history almost as old as the political history of China,[108] modern legal education in China did not start until the beginning of last century. The first government-sponsored modern legal education institute was the Beijing College of Law (京师法律学堂), established in 1906 as part of the legal reform in the late Qing Dynasty.[109] The establishment of the Republic of China further boosted legal

107 An old Chinese saying goes: a day together as husband and wife means endless devotion the rest of your life (一日夫妻). It will help to understand the Chinese Style Divorce (中国式离婚). Anyway, every culture advocates the ideal of equity, but its meaning and contents could be at least slightly different in different cultural background.

108 In ancient China, the study of law was called "律学" (Science of Code). It focused on the analysis of the statutory provisions, the application of the penalties and the relation between Li (rite) and punishment. The legal skills were predominantly taught in private schools through the apprenticeship. However, in some dynasties, the central government established specific positions –律博士 (Doctor of Law or Code) or institutions –律学馆 (Institution for Science of Code) to carry out the "legal education". Doctor of Law numbered from two to a dozen in different dynasties.

109 Prof. W.W. Blume from the University of Michigan Law School served as the second Dean of the Soochow University Law School (东吴大学法学院) in the early 20th century. In an address delivered at the third annual meeting of the International Bar Association in 1923, he said that "one of the first institutions in China undertaking to teach modern law was the Pei-yang University at Tientsin (天津北洋大学). Law subjects were placed in the curriculum as early as 1895, and on the reorganization of the school in 1905 a department of law was established. It was not until 1915 or 1916, however, that the department was built up to the standards of a modern law school". See Hugh Chan (Chen Sheau), 'Modern Legal Education in China' (1936–1927) 9 *China Law Review* 142.

education. Before the Japanese Invasion, there were 16 government law schools and 17 private law schools. The course of study leading to the LL.B. degree at first covered three years and was later extended to four years. The first year was, however, more or less devoted to the studies of social sciences, languages, and elementary courses on law.[110]

In the early years of the People's Republic of China after 1949, legal education was reformed on the soviet model, with the emphasis on developing specialized institutes. Five colleges of political sciences and law (政法学院) were then officially established: Beijing, Southwest (西南), East China (华东), Central Southern China (中南), and Northwest (西北). At the same time, law departments were established in four universities including Peking University, Renmin University, Wuhan University, and North China University (now Jilin University). According to the national strategy, the political-legal colleges cultivated judicial personnel and the law departments in universities produced legal scholars. The period of study was five years in the university and four years at a law college. After the beginning of the reform and opening period in 1979, law schools began to flourish. Currently, more than 600 institutions, including faculties of law under comprehensive universities or universities of political science and law,[111] offer bachelor's degrees in law. The law major student population amounts to nearly 300,000 per year.[112] More than 300 law faculties or social science research institutes were entitled to confer master's degrees in law. In addition, more than 30 of the abovementioned institutes were entitled to confer degree of PhD in law.

Since China adopts the statutory law system, the lecturing pedagogy dominates legal education in China. Different from the Socratic method in American law schools, Chinese law professors usually do not analyse cases or raise questions in class. However, they tend to start by introducing and explaining concepts, theories, and certain systems, and then try to illustrate the underlying key points by commentary and analysis of legal theories. 16 key courses are mandatory to acquire the LL.B. degree. They are:

1) Jurisprudence,
2) Chinese Legal History,
3) Constitutional Law,
4) Administrative Law and Administrative Procedure,
5) Criminal Law,
6) Criminal Procedure,
7) Civil Law,
8) Civil Procedure,

110 Ibid.

111 They develop from the college of political science and law. Beijing College of Political Science and Law is now China University of Political Science and Law, Southwest is Southwest University of Political Science and Law, East China is East China University of Political Science and Law, Central Southern China is Zhongnan University of Economics and Law and Northwest is Northeast University of Political Science and Law East China.

112 The structure of the legal education institutions changed hugely in the new era: the number of law colleges has not increased, but the law schools under the comprehensive universities has boomed from a dozen to around 600 hundred.

9) Economic Law
10) Intellectual Property,
11) Commercial Law,
12) International Law,
13) International Private Law,
14) International Economic Law,
15) Environmental and Resource Protection Law,
16) and Labour and Social Security Law.

The LL.B. program lasts four years; LL.M. is achieved after two or three years of additional study, and a PhD in Law usually takes three to six more years of work.

Reform strikes a consistent note in China during the last four decades. Legal education is no exception. Two U.S. inspired transplants highlight the legal education reform. The first was the introduction of the Juris Master (JM) professional degree influenced by the model of the U.S. Juris Doctor (JD). In 1996, the Ministry of Justice introduced the JM degree to gradually become the main professional degree for the study of law. The goal of the JM degree is to produce practice-oriented legal professionals and the objective of the experimental pedagogies is to specifically develop critical and analytical thinking skills as a central criterion for being a lawyer. Unlike the conventional legal education model of an undergraduate major in a comprehensive university, JM programs are carried out as a professional training in the post-graduate school, with most of the students having a non-law bachelor degree.[113] Up to 2014, there were JM programs at 186 universities.

The second noticeable legal education reform was the introduction of clinical legal education, which started in 2000 in seven universities with the help of the Ford Foundation.[114] This effort has been motivated by a strong desire to change how students learn and think about the law, aiming to expose them to legal aid work and to give them the tools with which to apply theories learned in the traditional classroom to everyday realities. Therefore, the clinical program emphasizes "learning from practice", advocating the new ideology of encouraging law students to learn legal theories, professional skills, and professional ethics from practice. It plays an active role in Chinese legal education reform and consequently has been integrated into the curricula of many law schools.[115]

---

113 In recent years, students with an LLB degree can also apply for the JM program, during which they will pursue the JM degree in two years. By contrast, the non-law undergraduates will get the JM degree in three years.

114 Peking University, Tsinghua University, Renmin University of China, Wuhan University, Zhongnan University of Economics and Law, East China University of Political Science and Law, and Fudan University.

115 The Law school curriculum requires students to spend a two or three-month internship (*shixi*, 实习) period in a judicial office or law firm. Most law schools implement it during the student's last semester of the four-year LL.B. program (when they are particularly anxious about their graduate theses and prospects for finding a job) and set no clear standards for how the internships should be conducted. Hence, the two or three-month internship period often becomes a mere break for the students from their ordinarily frenzied class schedules. Participating in the clinics will exempt students from the internship.

Clinical legal education focuses on filling in the gaps between the traditional indoctrination-modelled legal education and the more participatory and interactive model. Law students, under the guidance of clinical professors qualified to be attorneys at law, provide legal advisory services for those in need, diagnose their problems and give prescriptions to furnish them with methods of resolution and legal aid. Needless to say, this model combines theoretical study with legal practice. Clinical legal education has achieved four transitions: 1) students transitioning from passive to initiative/active learning, 2) professors transitioning from lecture-centred to interactive teaching, 3) classroom activities transitioning from listening and note-taking activities to open discussions, and 4) the legal pedagogy transitioning from a commentary, lecture-oriented method to a practical, skill-oriented method.

Clinical legal education also aims to help in building up the law students' sense of social responsibility. Clinical students apply their efforts to offering legal aid services, especially to the disadvantaged, in response to strong public demands for social justice. The clinics not only provide students with a place to deal with real cases and to practice legal professional skills and ethics, but they also offer a good opportunity for law students to gain a better understanding of society and the importance of justice and fairness.

Professional legal qualifications are prerequisites for persons to become lawyers, judges, prosecutors, and other judicial personnel (paralegals). In accordance with the Judge's Act and the Procurator's Act – adopted in 1995 and amended in 2001 – general qualifications for judges and procurators include: 1) Chinese nationality, 2) to have reached the age of 23, 3) to endorse the Chinese Constitution, 4) to have a fine political and professional quality and to have good conduct, and 5) to be in good health. The professional qualifications, particularly the requirement of academic degrees and work experience have been increased: to become a judge for LL.B. graduates or non-law graduates with a bachelor's degree but possessing professional knowledge of law, candidates must have worked in the legal field for two years. For those who will work at a Higher People's Court or the Supreme People's Court, three years of legal working experience is required. For those graduates with a Masters or PhD degree, one year of working experience is required.[116] In addition, entry-level judges and procurators will be selected from those who not only meet the above requirements, but also have passed the National Judicial Examination. However, the Judge's Act and the Procurator's Act allow the exception in the minority regions, where the qualification can be reduced to three-year training certificates (大专) in law from colleges or universities within a certain time limit, subject to examination and determination by the Supreme People's Court.

The qualifications for lawyers are stipulated in Article 2 of the Lawyer's Act – adopted in 1996 and amended in 2007 – which defines a lawyer as a practitioner who has acquired a lawyer's practice certificate and provides legal services to the public. The admission to the Bar requires passing the national bar examination and a one-year apprenticeship. To sit for the bar exam, the applicant should have a Bachelor's degree, whether this is as

116 Article 9 of the Judge's Law and Article 10 of the Procuratorate's Law.

a law major or not.[117] The Ministry of Justice is responsible for administering the annual exam, usually held in mid-September. The Supreme People's Court and the Supreme People's Procuratorate join the Ministry of Justice to form a national judicial examination coordination committee to discuss the major issues concerning the exam. The bar exam will test theoretical jurisprudence, applied jurisprudence, current legal provisions, legal practice and legal professional ethics.[118] At the end of 2013, more than 14,000 law firms in China accommodated 250,000 lawyers, 225,000 of which were full-time and more than 10,000 part-time.[119]

6. Internationalisation

The State Council of the People's Republic of China is responsible for concluding treaties and agreements with foreign states. The Standing Committee of the NPC shall ratify and abrogate of treaties and important international agreements.[120] In general, domestic laws shall not be in conflict with treaties signed and entered into force. For example, according to the General Principles of the Civil Law and the Civil Procedure Law, an international treaty shall apply if it differs from civil laws or civil procedures.[121] However, the constitutional law of China and relevant constitutional legislation do not define an explicit prescription as to what domestic implementation approach shall make treaties an organic component of the legal system, that is, whether treaties should be directly incorporated into the domestic legal system, or be transferred into domestic law through domestic legislation, even though treaties acceded or ratified by China should be treated legislatively and judicially as part of Chinese legal system. In practice, the most likely scenario is that treaties can be enforced directly in China, reflected by the above-mentioned general principle of treaties' superiority over domestic law in civil laws and manifested by judicial interpretations, such as the Provisions of the Supreme People's Court on Several Issues Concerning the Hearing of International Trade Administrative Cases. Its Article 9 states that once a specific clause of the law or administrative regulation faces two or more reasonable interpretations when applied in an international trade administrative case, the court should adopt the one consistent with the relevant provisions of the international treaty. Treaties can also gain the force of law through the method of transformation into legislations. In 1992, the NPC passed the Women's

117 From 2008, the fourth-year undergraduate can also apply for the bar exam. See Notice of Ministry of Justice on Issues Concerning the 2008 National Bar Exam (《司法部关于2008年国家司法考试有关事项的公告》), available at http://www.moj.gov.cn/organization/content/2009-05/31/ldgg_8218.html accessed 31 May 2015.

118 The two-day-long bar exam includes three half days of multiple choice tests covering the key courses, the judicial system and professional responsibilities, and the rest of the last half day is case analysis on jurisprudence, constitutional law, administrative law and administrative procedure, criminal law, criminal procedure, civil law, commercial law and civil procedure.

119 Article 12 of the Lawyer's Law stipulates that the faculty at the law school or law researcher in the social science academy, if passing the bar exam, can work as a part-time lawyer, with the consent of their employer.

120 Article 3 of the Law of the People's Republic of China on the Procedure of the Conclusion of Treaties.

121 Article 142 of the General Principles of the Civil Law and Article 235 of the Civil Procedure Law.

Rights Securing Law of the People's Republic of China, incorporating relevant contents of the Convention on the Elimination of All Forms of Discrimination against Women.

7. Conclusion

In essence, China has a legal system primarily based on the continental law mode, for in the 2,000 years-long imperial era, each dynasty had its own penal code as the basic law. The modernization of the Chinese legal system from the midst of the 19th century was dominated by the transplantation of continental European laws.[122] But China's legal system has its own characteristics.[123] Unlike the separation of powers in the western countries, China centralized the state power into the NPC, which not only enacts legislation but also appoints and supervises administrators and the judiciary. In the process of adjudication, to guarantee a fair trial, the 'protest' system empowers the people and the procuratorate to supervise the courts. To apply the statutory laws, courts have the quasi law-making power to issue judicial interpretations.

The establishment of new specialized courts, the promulgation of the trans-regional courts, the implementation of the guiding cases, just to name a few features, are the results of the latest development of China's striving to build up a legality with Chinese characteristics. The accumulated experiences in the last four decades of rule of law momentum have accelerated the steps of the legality modernization. In the next few years, China will enact and amend dozens of laws to fit in with the new domestic and international situations. Big hopes rest on the formulation of the civil code.[124]

---

122 China also introduced certain common law rules into its legal system. For example, even though the Contract Law is mainly patterned after the civil law provisions, the doctrines of anticipatory breach of contract (Article 108) and the doctrine of undisclosed agency are borrowed from the common law. The Contract Law also adopts some rules from the CISG. See Wang Liming, 'CISG's Impact on the Enactment and Improvement of the Contract Law of China' (2013) Vol. 5 *Global Law Review* 119. (王利明：《联合国国际货物销售合同公约与我国合同法的制定和完善》，载《环球法律评论》2013年第5期，第119–131页。)

123 In 2008, China published the White Book on Rule of Law titled Promoting the Rule of Law in China (《中国的法治建设》), claiming that China has built up the legislation and legal system with Chinese characteristics. It points out that the legal system of China accords with the principle of universality for the development of human political civilization, and conforms to the basic conditions of the primary stage of socialism in China. It is in line with the basic tasks of socialism, and has distinctive Chinese characteristics. The essence of this legal system is to put people first, reflect the common will of the people and guarantee the fundamental interests of the people. It is in line with the economic development and social progress of China, and provides legal safeguards for scientific, harmonious and peaceful development of the country. China's socialist legal system with Chinese characteristics is open and developing. As China is at a stage of social transformation, its legal system is still being implemented and forward-looking. It will continue to promulgate new laws and revise present ones, so as to develop and improve the legal system. See http://news.xinhuanet.com/newscenter/2008-02/28/content_7687281.htm accessed 31 May 2015.

124 The Annual Legislation Plan of 2018 of the NPC Standing Committee (全国人大常委会2018年立法工作计划), see http://www.npc.gov.cn/npc/c30834/201804/1c1b9070eb574282b8ef6d2f33615383.shtml accessed 31 December 2019. The draft of the General Principles of the Civil Code for soliciting opinions (《中华人民共和国民法典•民法总则专家建议稿（征求意见稿）》) is available at http://www.civillaw.com.cn/zt/t/?29169 accessed 31 May 2015.

Reform and innovation characterises the 21st century's China. China and China's legal system is facing great challenges, for human history has never witnessed a country with billons of people transforming from a semi-colonial, semi-feudal society to a nation not only with modernity but also its own features. There is no model to emulate. "As a systematic approach, to comprehensively promote the rule of law is also a far-reaching and profound revolution".[125]

The Chinese Legal Culture and its structures and structural elements	
Institutional structure	
Conflict resolution	*Norm production*
China has a four-tier courts system, where the second instance is final. Except for a few specialized courts, the courts have general jurisdictions and are divided into several divisions to handle different subject matters. Recently, China has established the trans-regional circuit courts as the satellite tribunals of the Supreme People's Court to prevent localism in the judicial process.	The hierarchy of law in China is patterned after the continental system. The statutes and regulations are the basic binding source of law. The statute-like judicial interpretations made by the Supreme People's Courts and Supreme People's Procuratorate are also a valid source of law and very useful in practice. The newly developed guiding cases system will help China to accommodate some common law elements, even though the guiding cases are in effect referential.

125 See Decision of the CPC Central Committee on Major Issues Pertaining to Comprehensively Promoting the Rule of Law (中共中央关于全面推进依法治国若干重大问题的决定), http://news.xinhuanet.com/politics/2014-10/28/c_1113015330.htm accessed 31 May 2015.

Intellectual structure			
Ideal of justice	*Legal method*	*Degree of professionalisation*	*Character of internationalisation*
Laws are the only formal source of justice. Judges are required to apply laws strictly. Without express empowerment of law, judges in practice can de facto interpret statutory provisions case-specifically in accordance with legislative intent and social needs	The deductive reasoning based on syllogism is the basic tool of adjudication. The statutory languages are open to interpretation and judges virtually exercise interpretation discretion in case of ambiguity or vagueness, especially dealing with the general principles.	A national bar exam is the requisite for the admission to the legal profession as lawyers, judges and public prosecutors, while the absence of legal education will not disqualify the applicant as long as they have a bachelor degree of whatever major. Legal education is held at the universities through 4 years of LL.B., 2–3 years of LL.M. and 3–6 years of PhD in Law. One-year apprenticeship is required to become a practitioner.	A hybrid of monism and dualism due to lack of clear provisions in the Chinese Constitution. Most treaties will be applied directly, while some should be incorporated into domestic legislation under the requirement of Chinese laws.

8. Bibliography

Biography of Chen Chong of The Book of Han (“礼之所去，刑之所取，失礼则入刑，相为表里也”。《汉书・陈宠传》).

Chan H (Chen Sheau), ‘Modern Legal Education in China’ (1936–1927) 9 *China Law Review* 142

Chenguang W, ‘Lawmaking functions of the Chinese Courts: Judicial Activism in a Country of Rapid Social Changes’ (2006) 1 *Frontiers of Law in China* 524

China Law Society, *Annual Report on Rule of Law Construction in China (2011)* (Xinhua Press)

China Law Society, *Annual Report on Rule of Law Construction in China (2013)* (Xinhua Press)

China's Ethnic Statistical Yearbook 2012 (China Statistics Press 2013)

Chow DCK, *The Legal System of the People's Republic of China: In A Nutshell* (West 2003)

Jia M, ‘Chinese Common Law? Guiding Cases and Judicial Reform’ (2016) Vol. 129, No. 8 *Harvard Law Review*

Jingwen Z, ‘Behind More Litigation: Positive and Negative Impacts’ (2014) 9 *Frontier of Law in China* 105

Johnson W (tr), *The T'ang Code* (Princeton University Press 1979)

Jones WC, ‘Trying to Understand the Current Chinese Legal System’ in Hsu CS (ed), *Understanding China's Legal System: Essays in Honor of Jerome A. Cohen* (New York University Press 2003)

Laiyun S (chief editor), *China Statistical Yearbook – 2013* (China Statistics Press 2013)

Liming W, ‘CISG's Impact on the Enactment and Improvement of the Contract Law of China’ (2013) Vol. 5 *Global Law Review* 119

Qin Y, *The Current Situation of Chinese Judges: Lost in a Cloud of Conflict and Confusion* (ZChinR 2011)

Staunton Sir GT, *Ta Tsing Leu Lee; Being the Fundamental Laws and A Selection from the Supplementary of the Penal Code of China* (original edition printed for T. Cadell and W. Davies 1810, Ch'eng-Wen Publishing 1966)

Weidong J, '*The Judicial Reform in China: The Status Quo and Future Directions*' (2013) Vol. 20, No. 1 *Indiana Journal of Global Legal Studies*

Zimmerman JM, *China Law Deskbook: A Legal Guide for Foreign-Invested Enterprises Paperback* (2nd edn, ABA Section of International Law 2005

20. Sailing – Analysing Ideals of Justice in Germany, England, and Norway

Sören Koch

1. Introduction

This last chapter provides an example of how to compare legal cultures by using the Legal Cultural Model in combination with the COMPASS formula on the *macro* comparative level. In other words, how to sail the legal cultural ocean. It attempts to illustrate how similarities and differences regarding the 'ideal of justice' can be identified, contextualised, explained, analysed and compared by applying both the legal historical and the comparative dimension of the model.[1] The reason for picking this very abstract and often misunderstood element of the LCM is to show how it can be concretised and instrumentalised in order to understand differences among the intellectual structure of legal cultures but also to understand the internal interdependence of legal institutions, the application of law and law in the minds. The aim is to provide an example of how ideas and expectations have been made operational in institutional(-like) practice.

As explained above, the specific research question depends on the comparatists epistemological interest.[2] The overall interest of this paper is to provide knowledge and a deeper understanding of how different ideals of justice based on ideas and expectations of law have impacted the institution(-like) practice of law, in short how the ideal of justice interacts with other legal cultural elements in different legal cultures. Since the 'ideal of justice' is an abstract concept, we need to define its content in order to formulate a sufficiently precise research question. Several contributors in this volume have identified legal certainty, in particular predictability and individual justice as two

1 For a legal theoretical approach on this topic Sen Amartya, *The Idea of Justice* (London: Allen Lane 2009).

2 See Chapter 4 above.

central values of justice in their legal cultures.[3] There can occur tensions between both ideals. Predictable outcomes are not necessarily identical with individually just ones. To illustrate that let us imagine the following situation. The retired teacher A owns an old house in a very popular area of a major town. Her tenants pay a humble rent which has not been raised for years. She has put all her savings into the renovation of the house, which she intended to lend out claiming a 30% increased rent. The raise is necessary to compensate for her investments and to provide her with a pension. The new rent would be at the average level of rent paid for an accommodation of the same standard in this area. Before she finds a new tenant, the local government enacts a decree prohibiting raising the residential rent for a period of five years by more than 1.3% annually.[4] The aim of the rule is to stop rental prices going through the roof and making it impossible for persons with low income to pay the constantly increasing rents. Let us assume that the legislation provides no reliefs or exceptions which could help A.[5] Applying the letter of the law will in this case certainly provide a predictable outcome. However, taking the particular circumstances of A's situation into consideration, the result might appear unjust. In all legal cultures there are mechanisms to solve such dilemmas. The degree to which the one or the other value is favoured as well as the institutionalised mechanisms to achieve them may vary considerably. Occasionally remedies are contained in legislation, or it is the task of the judiciary or the administration to remedy the hardest consequences of the strict application of law. Accordingly, the research question could be phrased broadly as: how do legal cultures balance predictability and individual justice. We could further specify the question by distinguishing between the extent to which lawyers of different legal cultures attempt to realise both of these values and which mechanisms are applied to solve potential conflicts between them.

Following the COMPASS formula, the next step is to choose the objects, purpose, and method of the study. To show variations among different legal cultures but at the same time to limit the empirical material, a main focus on three legal cultures with rather different characteristics seems appropriate.[6] I have chosen the national legal cultures of Norway, Germany and England and Wales (in the following just England). We take

---

3 Thomas Lundmark, *Charting the Divide between Common and Civil Law* (Oxford University Press 2012) 96–128, who uses exactly the same dichotomy between predictability and individual justice in his survey based on interviews of legal philosophers from both legal traditions. See also Åse B. Grødeland and William L. Miller, *European Legal Cultures in Transition* (Cambridge University Press 2015) 90 ff. having found that English and Norwegian respondents tend to prefer principles or pragmatic approaches to law, while Bulgarian, Polish and Ukrainian respondents indicate to prefer detailed legislation applied literally. The survey explores the attitudes and perceptions of the general public and law professionals in five European countries: England, Norway, Bulgaria, Poland, and Ukraine.

4 An example for such a regulation is § 3 of the Act on limitation of residential rent in Berlin (Gesetz zur Neuregelung gesetzlicher Vorschriften zur Mietenbegrenzung, MietenWoG Bln – Febr. 11th 2020) https://www.berlin.de/sen/justiz/service/gesetze-und-verordnungen/2020/ausgabe-nr-6-vom-22-2-2020-s-49-56.pdf accessed 30.04.2020.

5 Cf. §§ 7 and 8 of the above-mentioned Act, providing very narrowly defined exceptions for renovations and modernization (§ 7) and allowing an application for remedies in cases of unjust burdens for the owner (§ 8).

6 Note however, that all these cultures share some philosophical heritage, which can be said to be the foundation of a common European legal tradition, see Franz Wieacker, 'Foundations of European Legal Culture' (1990) Vol. 38 *The American Journal of Comparative Law* 1. They are all part of the Western-legal tradition.

a closer look at the general attitude towards the values of predictability and individual justice and the institutionalised mechanisms to realise these values in the respective countries. The information provided by respective chapters in this book will serve as basis and a point of departures for the study. Each of these chapters contains a section on the ideal of justice. Studying these sections will allow developing a general idea on the degree to which the legal cultures maintain different stereotypes of predictability. This will also allow us to evaluate the extent to which legal security has to yield to considerations of individual fairness. Establishing the intellectual preconditions and having studied the theoretical frameworks ('law in books'), is necessary but not sufficient. Further we need to show that these ideals have influenced the application of law ('law in action'). In other words, we need find out how the ideal of justice has impacted the institutional elements of the legal culture, i.e. norm production and conflict resolution. Analysing legislative texts and the style of court judgments in the supreme courts will provide us with a better understanding of how the prevailing ideals of justice have impacted the institutionalised practice of law in the respective countries. Comparing the results allows us to identify some crucial similarities and differences between England, Germany, and Norway. Both the historical and legal cultural dimensions of the LCM will be used to explain them contextually. Finally, we need to systematise the findings. A table at the end of the article displays four categories (degree of outcome predictability, mechanisms to achieve outcome predictability, degree of individual justice and mechanisms to warrant individual justice) in all three countries. Based on these findings we can provide an (tentative) answer to the initial research question.

2. The intellectual framework – different theoretical approaches to justice

2.1 Legal security and predictability

When comparing these national legal cultures, we can observe that they provide, like almost all Western legal cultures, measures to safeguard legal certainty and predictability. This is important for both their inhabitants and foreign investors.[7] Legal security is guaranteed by fundamental procedural and substantive legal principles. The most basic principle is that similar cases should be treated alike. The prohibition of discrimination is also related to this ideal. Presentations of the Goddess Justitia show her as a rule blinded to emphasise the impartiality of law and justice. Law is supposed to be objective and

7 On the central importance of 'legal certainty' for modern legal systems and different ways of how to warrant legal predictability, see Mathias Siems, 'Comparative Legal Certainty: Is there a Common-Civil Law Divide?' in Mark Fenwick, Mathias Siems and Stefan Wrbka (eds), *The Shifting Meaning of Legal Certainty in Comparative and Transnational Law* (Hart Publishing 2017); Lundmark (2012) (ibid.) 92; see also Sören Koch, 'An Introduction to German Legal Culture' in this volume, Chapter 8, 248 ff.; Christian N.K. Franklin, 'A Legal Cultural "Take" on the Legal System of England & Wales' in this volume, Chapter 10, 373 ff.; Marius Mikkel Kjølstad, Sören Koch og Jørn Øyrehagen Sunde, 'Introduction to the Norwegian Legal Culture', in this volume, Chapter 5, 121.

intersubjective, that is to provide solutions regardless of the person seeking justice or the subjective preferences of judges. This implies that the discretion of the judges must have limits. They cannot be bound by their consciences only. Furthermore, under the rule of law, citizens should be able to understand their rights and duties. To avoid social, economic, and legal conflicts but also to guide social behaviour, outcome or result predictability is therefore an essential prerequisite.

Looking more closely at the legal cultures of England, Germany, and Norway reveals that the way of how they try to achieve this goal may differ at least to some extent, often most significantly regarding the underlying legal *theoretical* approaches. Indeed, it seems that different legal cultures have a rather different focus on or promote different stereotypes of predictability. Furthermore, they have developed quite different legal mechanisms to facilitate predictability.

In England, for example, traditionally the *stare decisis* principle as the core element of the theory of precedents provides predictable outcomes in all legal matters where relevant case law exists.[8] Making case law binding for commencing decisions in lower courts and courts at the same level helps lawyers predict the outcome of actual legal problems by looking at how comparable cases have been solved in the *past*.[9] An English lawyer will therefore look at the way judges have treated situations similar to the case at hand. Where the *ratio decidendi* of the former case promotes a favourable solution, the lawyer will build her arguments on the principle extracted (induced) from this decision.[10] The explanation for the development of this mechanism for safeguarding legal security must be seen as a result of the comparatively organic development of the English legal system,[11] with its roots back to the medieval period and dominated by courts as the main actors in the development of the law.[12]

In Germany, on the other hand, systematically coherent legislation (enacted in accord with the prevailing opinion in legal doctrine) is perceived as being the best way of achieving the same goal: to produce outcome-predictability.[13] An important function of legislation is to avoid that legal conflicts occur or, where this already has happened, to provide dogmatically sound and intersubjective solutions. In a perfectly rational world,

8 Rupert Cross and James W. Harris, *Precedent in English Law*, 4th ed. (Oxford: Clarendon Press 1991), 97; Colin Manchester, David Salter and Peter Moodie, *Exploring the Law: The Dynamics of Precedent and Statutory Interpretation*, 2nd ed (London: Sweet & Maxwell 2000), 13; Franklin (2020) (n 7) 358 f.

9 On the stare-decisis principle and its historical development, see Sir John Baker, *An Introduction to English Legal History* (5th ed, Oxford University Press 2019) 210. On the contemporary function, see Manchester et al. (2000) (ibid.) 13 ff. emphasising the role of the *ratio decidendi*.

10 In case the potential precedent promotes an unfavourable outcome, he or she will use the technique of distinguishing in order to argue that differences in the underlying facts ban the use of the former decision as a precedent. If the precedent contains a dissenting opinion the lawyer may argue that the principle contained here suits much better the facts of his or her case.

11 Manchester, Salter and Moodie (2000) (n 8) 3 ff.; Franklin (2020) (n 7) 336 ff.; see also Baker (2019) (n 9) 1–240.

12 Baker (2019) (n 9) Chapter 2–9; Lloyd T. Wilson, Jr., 'A View of the Legal Culture of the United States of America' in this volume, Chapter 17, 638.

13 Reinhard Zimmermann, 'Characteristic Aspects of the German Legal Culture' in Joachim Zekoll and Gerhard Wagner (eds), *Introduction to German Law* (3rd ed, Wolters Kluwer 2019) 57; Koch (2020) (n 7) 248 ff.

this would make courts virtually redundant. However, legislation is always in need of interpretation in order to provide a solution for the individual cases. This leaves the lawyer room to manoeuvre. Still, she is not entirely free. She is instead bound by the underlying system of law; in other words, the law scientifically reconstructed in light of the intention, purpose and function of all positive law including the basic rights established by the constitution (*Grundgesetz*). Therefore, the question a German lawyer asks is how should we solve the problem in accord with the system of law and not, as his English colleague would do, how did we solve the problem last time?[14]

The underlying ideal (an utopia) in Germany is that the *pre-existing* system of law provides one 'dogmatically correct' answer to each legal problem and it is the lawyer's task to find this correct solution by applying a scientific inspired method of interpreting statutory law.[15] Consequently, the natural starting point for a German lawyer is to find a relevant legal provision in a code or statute and interpret it in light of its wording, the legislative intention, and its position in the system of law. Consulting commentaries on the relevant legislation will provide help to identify the intention of the historical legislator and the prevailing doctrinal opinions on the controversial elements of the law. These commentaries will also contain explanations of abstract concepts. As a rule, the scholar providing the commentary will support his or her interpretation of the legislative provision by referring to court practice from supreme courts and if necessary, also from appellate courts or even courts of first instance. However, the legal foundations for claims, rights or duties is not the *ratio decidendi* of a court ruling or any legal principle therein. To wit, ordinary courts lack the competence to produce strictly binding precedents.[16] Still, court practice can be a highly persuasive factor when interpreting the law and thus help to create outcome predictability, but in a different way than in England.[17] That is, not due to its institutionalised function as source of law, but rather by helping the lawyer to understand abstract concepts and rules, thereby indirectly discovering the system of law that holds the solution. Applying a scientific approach to law is supposed to enable the lawyer to identify the presumably predictable solution for any legal question.

In Norway a combination of different mechanisms is in place to safeguard predictable outcomes in the application of law. On the one hand, the ideal of regulating society

14 Lord Justice Cooper, in a famous address delivered to Edinburgh University (1950), see full quote in Sunniva Cristina Bragdø-Ellenes, 'An Introduction to French Legal Culture' in this volume, Chapter 13, fn 134.

15 See e.g. Jannis Lennartz, *Dogmatik als Methode* (Mohr Siebeck 2017) 6, defining legal method as: "[…] die Summe der Regeln, mit denen wir feststellen, was das positive Recht abstrakt oder angewandt auf einen Sachverhalt aussagt". See also 36; Karl Larenz and Claus-Wilhelm Canaris, *Methodenlehre der Rechtswissenschaft* (3rd ed, Mohr Siebeck 1995) 322; Ingvill Helland, 'Introduction to German legal method' in Ingvill Helland and Sören Koch (eds), *Nordic and Germanic Legal Methods* (Mohr Siebeck 2014) 219; Zimmermann (n 13) 75; Koch (2020), 'German Legal Culture' (n 7) 238, 252.

16 Koch (2020) (n 7) 254.

17 Heike Simon and Gisela Funk-Baker, *Einführung in das deutsche Recht und die deutsche Rechtssprache* (Munich: Beck 2009) 21; Lennartz (2017) (n 15) 25 ff.

through legislation has deep roots in the Norwegian legal culture.[18] On the other hand, precedents produced by the supreme court enhance the possibility for citizens to understand their rights and duties. Furthermore, when pondering different solutions to a legal problem the lawyer is supposed to choose the alternative which produces predictable results over any solution that would not or to a lesser degree do so. In other words, predictability is an important policy consideration (*reelle hensyn*), and hence recognised as source of law in Norway.[19] In this regard it seems important to emphasise that outcome predictability addresses laymen, (in other words, it is the outcome a person without a legal education would most likely regard as fair) while in Germany and England the predictability of outcomes is based on complex judicial considerations (identifying the ratio decidendi, distinguishing, systematic and teleological interpretation) which as a rule are the domain of legal professionals.

We can thus conclude that both the English, German, and Norwegian legal culture have developed mechanisms to warrant *outcome*-predictability but apply (at least in theory) very different mechanisms to realise this ideal.[20] The presentation of these theoretical points of departure are of course just a rather incomplete reflection of reality.[21] In Germany, court practice from the supreme courts has become a highly relevant factor for interpretation of statutory law and has contributed considerably to facilitate the ideal of outcome-predictability by determining the content of law quite similar (but not identical) to precedents. Colombo and Kvestad argued in their contribution that case law has become so important in the Italian legal culture that one can claim that an "attenuated principle of *stare decisis*" has been widely accepted.[22] Taking into account that Italy is traditionally considered a civil law system, this statement shows that dynamic changes in legal cultures can challenge the classification into different legal traditions that was developed in the 20th century. The LCM, even though it just roughly maps legal cultures, can thus also explain developments, challenges and inconsistencies which remain undetected using the classical categorisations into legal traditions and legal families.

On the other hand, in England, the amount of legislation and statutory law has increased considerably in the late 20th and 21st century not least due to the influence of the European Union.[23] The principle of parliamentary sovereignty demands that the courts obey the will of the Westminster Parliament at least as far as this will has been put forward clearly. Accordingly, legislation and statutory interpretation have become

18 Jørn Øyrehagen Sunde, 'Daughters of God and Counsellors of the Judges of Men: Changes in the Legal Culture of the Norwegian Realm in the High Middle Ages' in Stefan Brink and Lisa Collinson (eds), *New Approaches to Early law in Scandinavia* (Brepols 2014) 139–141.

19 Kjølstad, Koch and Sunde (2020) (n 7) 122 f.; Ingvill Helland and Sören Koch, 'Introduction to Norwegian Legal Method' in Ingvill Helland and Sören Koch (eds), *Nordic and Germanic Legal Methods* (Mohr Siebeck 2014) 121.

20 Martin Brenncke, *Judicial Law-Making in English and German Courts – Techniques and Limits of Statutory Interpretation*, (Cambridge: Intersentia 2018) 26.

21 See on the LCM's limitation to resemble the full complexity of real life, Jørn Øyrehagen Sunde, 'Managing the Unmanageable – An Essay Concerning Legal Culture as an Analytical Tool' in this volume, Chapter 2, 23 ff.

22 Esmeralda Colombo and Lars Kvestad, 'An Introduction to the Italian Legal Culture' in this volume, Chapter 15, 554 ff.

23 Franklin (2020) (n 7) 368.

increasingly important as factors facilitating predictability. Despite Norwegian legislation in theory being only one of at least seven equally ranged legal sources (*rettskildefaktorer*), deviation from the clear wording and intention of an Act of Parliament requires extraordinarily persuasive arguments.[24]

Accordingly, the attitudes towards predictability seem rather different in theory, but they might be of less importance when applying the law in practice. Still, for understanding the way lawyers argue and think, the different approaches to provide predictability may prove valuable, not least from a pedagogical point of view.

2.2 The Degree of Individual Fairness

Unjust legislation is not law (*lex injusta no est lex*).[25] This quote can be found in large letters on a stone outside of the Federal Supreme Court of Germany. It is said to originate with St. Augustine and has been referred to by Thomas Aquinas.[26] In the 20th century, legal philosophers strongly associated with natural law theories, such as Gustav Radbruch, John Finnis and Lon Fuller, applied the motto to emphasise that the ultimate aim of law should be to provide justice.[27] According to Radbruch, an act of legislation, even if enacted according to the relevant constitutional procedures, cannot be treated as law if its only purpose is to establish injustice. As example he refers to the systematically discriminating race-legislation enacted by the Nazi-regime between 1933 and 1945.[28] Legal positivists have challenged such statements as a confusion of law and morals.[29] Still, the idea that law is supposed to provide justice seems rather widely accepted. But what is justice? Trying to give a concise definition seems difficult and may depend on the perspective and preferences of the one asking the question. Nevertheless, it seems fair to state that different legal cultures have developed different perceptions of justice. In the following we will focus on some characteristics of judicial justice, which is the way lawyers tend to determine elements of justice. I will ask the following questions: In the eyes of a lawyer, what are foundations of justice and what kind of justice should the legal system provide?

In earlier times justice was perceived as a quality of God. Accordingly, acting in accord with God's precepts was seen as an appropriate guideline to justice.[30] All state law

---

24 Kjølstad, Koch and Sunde (2020) (n 7) 125 ff.; Helland and Koch, 'Introduction to Norwegian Legal Method' (n 19) 121.

25 David Dysenhaus, *Redrafting the Rule of Law: the Limits of Legal Order*, (Hart Publisher 1999) 41.

26 Norman Ketzmann, Lex Iniusta non est lex: Laws on trial in Aquinas' Court of Conscience, 33 American Journal of Jurisprudence (1988).

27 Brian Brix, *Jurisprudence: Theory and Context* (Sweet&Maxwell 2009) 70.

28 Gustav Radbruch, 'Gesetzliches Unrecht und Übergesetzliches Recht, Süddeutsche Juristenzeitung (1946) 105–109 reproduced in Gustav Radbruch, *Rechtsphilosophie,* (9th ed. Mohr Siebeck 2012) 45.

29 Herbert Lionel Adolphus Hart, 'Positivism and the Separation of Law and Morals', (1958) Harvard Law Review 593 ff.

30 Wim Decock. *Theologians and Contract Law, The moral Transformation of the IUS COMMUNE* (ca. 1500–1650) (Nijhoff Publishers 2013) 22 ff.

in conflict to the divine precepts could be ignored.[31] In later periods, justice was constructed in accord with basic principles of natural law, derived from general principles such as keep promises, do not harm others and provide everybody with what is theirs.[32] In the 19th century, more positivistic theories of law challenged those perceptions that were based on a close connection between law and morality. However, customs and constitutions were now regarded as the foundation for central values that determined what was accepted as just.[33] In the 20th century, ideas of legal realism promoted the idea that what is just had to be determined by those applying the law, in particular the judges in the highest courts.[34] Recently, justice has become increasingly internationalised and even globalised through standards established by international treatises and customs particularly related to human rights.[35] In the relationship between the state and its citizens these rights have a strong focus on the individual. Concerning the interaction of citizens, the different conceptions of justice can be observed.

The egalitarian social structure in Norway, in combination with a fragmentary legislation, a lack of legal scholarship and a traditionally strong pragmatic approach to law facilitated a turn towards legal realism in the 20th century.[36] Law was perceived as what lawyers do, the supreme court Judges in particular.[37] Accordingly, their perception of law, developed with regard to specific factual situations, would be highly relevant when determining what was just and fair.[38] The aim is to find the best and most pragmatic solution for the case at hand.[39] Consequently, individual justice has a strong standing even in cases where the Supreme Court produces precedents. The Norwegian concept of justice is flexible and takes developments in society into account as well. Accordingly, a popular perception of justice based on the present moment of the decision is decisive. The relatively high degree of lay participation in the courts seems to further facilitate the importance of individual justice.[40]

In Germany, the realistic approach to law was rejected in legal theory and never manged to replace the more dogmatic and scientific approach to law.[41] The system of law is supposed to provide justice, since legislation should be produced and applied in accordance with the system of values established by the constitution. Pursuant to BL. Ar. 20 III, judges are bound by legislation and law (*Gesetz und Recht*).[42] Hence, applying the system of law is supposed to produce just results. In other words, justice is embedded

31 Bernd Mathias Kremer, *Der Westphälische Friede in der Deutung der Aufklärung*. (Mohr Siebeck 1986) 40.

32 David Johnston, *A brief History of Justice*, (Wiley-Blackwell 2011), 142.

33 Ibid. 167 ff.

34 Ibid. 196 ff.

35 Ibid. 223 ff.

36 Kjølstad, Koch and Sunde (2020) (n 7) 126.

37 Ibid.

38 Ibid. 127.

39 Ibid.

40 Ibid.

41 Koch (2020) (n 7) 246 f.

42 Ibid. 242.

in the system of law.[43] This means the emphasis is not so much on the individual case but rather on a more principle level. The dogmatically correct solution is supposed to provide the highest possible degree of just results for the individual and all similar cases. It might therefore be appropriate to characterise the German approach as facilitating systematic justice.[44]

Traditionally in England, justice was the domain of the judiciary.[45] The legislator acted rather as a corrective if the common law provided solutions which were perceived as unjust in the light of the development of society. Still, in contrast to Norway, judges are to a higher degree bound by the *stare decisis* principle. What is perceived as just is determined with a strong focus on the past. On the other hand, the idea that justice is part of a system of law was never accepted in England.[46] Finally, England lacks a written constitution, which makes it difficult to relate to constitutional values in the same way this is possible in Germany or Norway. A medium level of lay participation in court facilitates considerations of individual justice, but to a lesser extent than in Norway.

2.3 Mechanisms for balancing Predictability and Individual Justice

The commencing question is how the chosen legal cultures tend to balance the demand for legal security with the perception that law is supposed to produce just and fair results in individual cases.[47] The discussion about how to balance individual justice (*equity/ æquitas*) and predictability can be traced back to the very foundations of all European legal cultures – the philosophy of Aristoteles.[48] But once more, we can observe that different cultures have developed different ways to establish this balance.[49] Using the LCM as an analytical tool can again provide interesting insights.

When in England the system of writs, which for centuries had been decisive for legal procedure, became too rigid at the end of the Middle Ages, the old common law had to be supplemented by a new legal order based on equity.[50] Equity became a separate legal

43 Ibid.

44 Ibid. 250.

45 Franklin (2020) (n 7) 336 f.

46 Ibid. 358 ff.

47 Martin Brenncke, *Judicial Law-Making in English and German Courts – Techniques and Limits of Statutory Interpretation*, (Intersentia 2018) 242 compared attitudes of professional judges in Germany and England when exercising discretion while interpreting legislation. He distinguished between formal and material justice. For statutory interpretation Brenncke concluded that there does not exist 'a large legal cultural distinction' (245); rather he observes a converging of judicial reasoning in Germany and England.

48 Sunde (2014) (n 18) 148 ff., Roger Cotterrell, 'Is it so bad to be different? Comparative Law and the Appreciation of Diversity' in Esin Örücü & David Nelken (eds), *Comparative Law a Handbook* (Oxford: Hart Publisher 2007) 133.

49 The discussion has left traces in the medieval dispute between Baldus (*jus strictum*) and Martius (*ius aequium*); as well as in the legislation of the late medieval codes in Catalonia (*Las Siete Partidas,* 1265) and Norway (King Magnus the Lawmender's Code of the Realm, 1274), cf. Book IV Chapter 18. See Jørn Øyrehagen Sunde, *Speculum Legale* (Fagbogforlaget 2005) 117 ff.; Sunde (2014) (n 18) 139 ff.

50 Franklin (2020) (n 7) 373; Baker (2019) (n 9) 105 ff.

system but was merged into the common law court system in the 19th century.[51] However, as a separate branch of law,[52] even now it provides particular remedies in certain fields of law.[53] Still, we must not make the mistake to think that equitable remedies are less formalised and institutionalised than common law principles.[54] Consequently, it would be wrong to state that the prevailing ideal of justice in the English legal culture is to promote individual justice because one of its branches is labelled "equity". This term must be understood in light of its historical context. Today it has almost completely lost its original function: to provide equitable remedies for an outdated and inflexible common law system of writs.[55] The reason why one can argue that English law is more open to considerations of individual justice is the very fact that legal norms and principles developed by the courts always arise from particular cases in which the deciding court has to invent a new legal rule for the specific situation. In absence of another applicable legal rule, the precedent will (at least to some extent) have to be based on considerations of (individual) justice.[56] Consequently, the *ratio decidendi* which lawyers induce from the precedent will also be based on considerations of individual justice.

In Germany, lawyers and philosophers such as Pufendorf, Wolff, and Savigny had a rather different problem to solve. They had to figure out how to create legal unity and predictability in a nation without a centralised court system and without a political authority that could regulate society comprehensively with the help of codifications. They were faced with legal pluralism and law consisting of many, often conflicting, regimes, such as local or regional law and norms based on Imperial, Roman, Canon or Natural law.[57] Despite all ideological differences between the universal regimes of law, they had two things in common. First, the idea that law must be assessable and predictable for its subjects (the citizens). Second, to achieve this aim it had to be organised in a system that could be used by deducing legal consequences from abstract rules, principles, and maxims. Even if Pufendorf, Wolff and Savigny had very different ideas about the legal philosophical foundations of this system (natural law, deductive logic, peoples' customs [*Volksgeist*]), they all extracted most of these rules and principles from the same scholarly discourse that had been dwelling in the continental law faculties for hundreds of years.[58] The result was a rather systematic approach to justice. Not the facts and circumstances of the particular case should be decisive, but the question whether the legal rule applied to one particular case will provide a just solution also in similar cases or problems. Such a systematic approach to justice and law requires a high degree of academic education and professionalisation.

---

51 Baker (2019) (n 9) 122.

52 Franklin (2020) (n 7) 374 ff.

53 Ibid.

54 Baker (2019) (n 9) 124.

55 Brenncke (2018) (n 47) 245.

56 Stefan Vogenauer, *Die Auslegung von Gesetzen in England und auf dem Kontinent* (Mohr Siebeck 2001) 1315 ff.

57 Franz Wieacker, *Privatrechtsgeschichte der Neuzeit* (2nd ed, Vandenhoeck & Ruprecht 1967) 301 ff. and 377 ff.

58 Jan Schröder, 'Zur Vorgeschichte der Volksgeistlehre. Gesetzgebungs- und Rechtsquellentheorie im 17. und 18. Jahrhundert' (1992) Vol. 109 *Savigny Zeitschrift für Rechtsgeschichte (Germ. Abt.)* 1, 23 ff.

Accordingly, in Germany legal justice is strongly dependent on and impacted by the views of legal scholars and professional lawyers and their scientific approach towards the law. In England, the sophisticated use of precedents and the method of distinguishing these also requires a specialised legal education, but of a more practical and less scientific nature.

Compared to Germany and England, in Norway outcome-predictability may more easily be replaced by considerations of equity and individual justice.[59] The Norwegian legal culture has developed a rather unique mechanism to balance predictability and individual justice. The pragmatic way of applying the law in combination with the high degree of confidence in the courts has contributed to the idea that the courts' task is to find "the best (expressly including the "fairest") result for the case at hand".[60] As long as the Norwegian judges do not violate the general precepts of legal method they have a very wide discretion in deciding what the best solution might look like.[61] In other words, if a court or other legal practitioner bases a decision on a methodologically sound argumentation, the result will be regarded acceptable and legitimate even if it was almost impossible for the involved parties to foresee the specific outcome. Consequently, in Norway it seems more appropriate to talk about achieving "methodological and procedural predictability" than to achieve outcome-predictability when talking about the prevailing ideal of justice.[62]

This concurs to some extent with what Wilson in his contribution on the US legal culture calls judicial "flexibility".[63] Legal cultures that traditionally have been based on case-law-driven norm production will as a rule leave judges more room for "flexible" solutions than codification-based systems do.[64] This applies also for the situation where a judge wants to deviate from former case law in order to avoid an unjust outcome. Both in the USA and in England, judges are provided with the competence to decide if the abstract principle which is inherent in the precedent's *ratio decidenti* has a narrow or wide scope of application.[65] Interpreting the scope of a potential precedent narrowly may cause the precedent to lose some of its function to provide outcome-predictability, but provides the judge with the flexibility to find a fair solution in the individual case. Often, the scope of a principle is determined by several subsequent decisions.[66] The wider previous case law treated the scope of a principle inherent in a precedent, the narrower was the discretion of a judge to not apply it. Legal principles applied and produced in this way, therefore, have their origin in a very specific situation but can develop into

59 Kjølstad, Koch and Sunde (2020) (n 7) 123; Helland and Koch (2014) (n 19) 105.

60 Erik Monsen, *Innføring i juridisk metode og oppgaveteknikk* (Cappelen Damm 2012) 55; Ragna Aarli and Synne Sæther Mæhle, *Fra lov til rett* (2nd ed, Gyldendal 2017) 201, speaking of "reasonable results".

61 Helland and Koch (2014) (n 19) 134.

62 Kjølstad, Koch and Sunde (2020) (n 7) 124 f.

63 Wilson (2020) (n 12) 657 ff.

64 For an overview on the newly revived discussion on the constitutional limits of judge made law in Germany, see Kruse (2019) (n 78) with further references.

65 Franklin (2020) (n 7) 360 f.; Wilson (2020) (n 12) 658 ff., 666 ff.

66 Ibid.

highly sophisticated principles or even doctrines.[67] The technique of "distinguishing" provides the judge with an additional tool to correct the hardest consequences of the *stare decisis* principle and consequently enables them to balance predictability and individual justice.[68]

A legislator, on the other hand, tries to avoid or regulate future conflicts by formulating general and abstract norms which are applicable to a range of similar situations regardless of minor deviation regarding the underlying facts. That these norms may produce unjust results in a small number of individual cases seems acceptable in legal cultures where *systemic justice* is regarded higher than *individual justice*. From a formal point of view, the latter always contains an element of arbitrariness and subjectivity. The lack of confidence in ordinary courts in many civil law cultures like Germany but also France, Romania, and Poland can explain the reluctance concerning a wider discretion for judges.[69] The prevailing opinion is (often even supported by the judges themselves)[70] that giving judges too much discretion would inevitably lead to the misuse of power and consequently to unjust judgments.[71]

3. Manifestation of ideals of justice in court practice and legislation

3.1 Style of court judgments

In all three countries both institutional and intellectual legal cultural features, particularly the ideal of justice, manifest in the composition and style of court rulings.

In Germany, courts provide their judgments in the name of the people (*im Name des Volkes*).[72] In other words, the verdict appears to be based on pre-existing law and not the subjective opinion of individual judges. Consequently, the judge, acting on behalf of the people, has just one task: applying the law to the case at hand. German judgments have, as a rule, no easily recallable names. Rather they are cited by using a technical reference code, e.g. V ZR 11/18.[73] Occasionally, the superior courts formulate official headnotes

---

67 Cross and Harris (1991) (n 8) 39 ff.; Patricio Fernandez and Giacomo Ponzetto, 'Stare Decisis: Rhetoric and Substance' *Journal of Law and Economics and Organization* 28 (2010) 313–336, 332.

68 Ibid. 333.

69 Koch (2020) (n 7) 226; Bragdø-Ellenes (2020) (n 14) 486; Cosmin Dariescu, 'An Introduction to Romanian Legal Culture' in this volume, Chapter 16, 615 ff.; Anna Klimaszewka, Anna Machnikowska and Sören Koch, 'An Introduction to Polish Legal Culture' in this volume, Chapter 9, 277 ff.

70 Ibid.; see also Brenncke (2018) (n 47) 2, which references to judges both in England and Germany.

71 From a historical perspective Bernd Rüthers, *Die Unbegrenzte Auslegung*, 8th ed. (Mohr Siebeck 2017) 35 ff.

72 Koch (2020) (n 7) Subsection 2.

73 Judgment of the Federal Court of Justice – V. Civil Senate from 14.02.2020. The reference-code contains the abbreviation for the deciding body (5th Civil Senate = V), the number of the case entered into the court chronologically (11) and the year of entry into the register (2018 = 18).

(*Leitsätze*) containing the case's *ratio decidendi*.[74] These headnotes are phrased in general terms deliberately abstracted from the particular facts of the case.

The judgment begins with the verdict (*Urteil*). The reasons follow and are introduced by the formula "Von Rechts wegen" (according to law), once again stressing the objectivity of the law. The facts (*Tatbestand*) are briefly presented, whereby the focus is on legally relevant aspects, often including the wording of pertinent legal provisions. The reasoning in the judgments is highly technical and presented in an impersonal style resembling the objectivity of the law.[75] One will therefore not find any dissenting opinions or subjective statements of individual judges.[76] To support the reasoning, courts tend to cite both previous court practice and scholarly works.

Historically this objective and scientific approach to law and legal reasoning has deep roots in the intellectual foundations of the German legal culture dating back to the reception of Roman, Canon and Natural law in the Middle Ages and the Early Modern Period.[77] In addition, the experience of judges misusing their power to interpret German law in accord with the race doctrine of the Nazi-regime has facilitated a general scepticism towards the free discretion of judges. The constitutional limitations of judges' competences pursuant to Art. 20 III and 95 have further contributed to the perception that the judge is bound by legislation and law.[78] The style of judgments in ordinary courts in Germany reinforces the impression that judges apply the law rather than developing it according to the facts of the individual case. Law appears to be a pre-existing but sufficiently flexible system of norms. All of this helps to create the *impression* that German law provides a high degree of (outcome-)predictability.

In England, the structure and style of judgments are rather different. The title of a ruling is plainly 'Judgment'.[79] The names of the parties including their role in the proceedings are stated next. This enables to precisely identify individual cases, which makes it easier to use them as precedents. After that, the names of the judge or judges hearing the case are listed followed by the date of the decision. The author of the judgment (and the dissenting opinions) are not the court as a collective organ, but individual judges, e.g. Lord Hodge.[80] The ruling starts with a comprehensive presentation of the facts followed by a discussion of the legal issues involved.[81] A personal (often almost literary)

74 Gerhard Robbers, *An introduction to German Law* (4th ed, Nomos 2006) 21.

75 Zimmermann (2019) (n 13) 28 and 41; Koch (2020) (n 7) Subsection 5.

76 Koch (2020) (n 7) Subsection 2. Different however to some extent concerning the verdicts of the FCC, see for the historical reasons for that Ruth Katharina Weber, *Der Begründungsstil von Conseil constitutionnel und Bundesverfassungsgericht. Eine vergleichende Analyse der Spruchpraxis* (Mohr Siebeck 2019) 218 ff.

77 Explaining the long historical developments Jan Schröder, *Recht als Wissenschaft* (2nd ed, Mohr Siebeck 2012); with concise presentation of central contributors, Joachim Rückert and Ralf Seinecke, *Methodik des Zivilrechts – von Savigny bis Teubner* (3rd ed, Nomos 2017) 53–488.

78 Frauke Kruse, *Die verfassungsrechtlichen Grenzen richterlicher Rechtsfortbildung. Zur Gesetzmäßigkeit der Rechtsprechung unter dem Grundgesetz* (Mohr Siebeck 2019) 45.

79 See e.g. *Aspen Underwriting Ltd and others v. Credit Europe Bank NV*, UKSP Judgment 1. April 2020; https://www.supremecourt.uk/cases/docs/uksc-2018-0229-judgment.pdf.

80 Ibid.

81 The English method of distinguishing requires a comprehensive presentation of the underlying facts.

style including individual and (in case of dissenting opinions) diverging assessments of law, provide English judgments with subjective elements that lack in German rulings. Still, the English judge is also not free to decide according to his or her conscience. The binding effect of relevant case law limits the discretion of the judges considerably, but in a rather different way than the system of law restricts the discretion of German judges.

This more individualistic judgment style has been shaped over centuries in the rather organically developing English legal culture. It resembles the common law tradition in which courts were recognised early on as a main producer of legal norms. Case law has been and still is an important source of law. Individual judges have contributed to create and develop the body and principles of common law.[82] Recognising their voices is a precondition for creating intellectual and legal authority on which the legitimacy of case law rests. References to legal scholars or the system of law are unusual. Consequently, law is recognised as a dynamically changing and constantly developing body of rules and principles. The essential role of judges, both for providing justice and predictability, is evident.

In Norway, a ruling is headed by the title of the institution providing it, e.g. "Norges Høyesterett".[83] The date of the decision and its nature (e.g. *Kjennelse*, *Dom*, *Beslutning* etc.) is followed by the names of the judges hearing the case. In the national database (*Lovdata*) a summary of the case and its *ratio* is provided, but in contrast to the German headnotes, this is not an official part of the ruling. An individual judge (*førstvoterende*) introduces the facts and the history of the proceedings including the parties' legal evaluations before giving his or her assessment of the law related to the case at hand. If one or several judges disagree with this assessment, they provide dissenting opinions. The verdict is given at the end of the judgment and the majority determines the outcome. The style of argumentation contains subjective notions ("In my view…") but traditionally, legislation is the natural starting point for the application of law.[84] However, there are also other legal sources recognised, which in theory can be used to interpret or if necessary set aside the wording of a pertinent legislative provision in a particular case.[85] The judgments of the Norwegian Supreme Court are recognised as "binding" legal sources, even though they are not as strictly binding as precedents in England. Therefore, one frequently finds references to the case law of the supreme court but rarely to legal scholarly works. Judges often consider different arguments and ponder alternative solutions in a balancing process. The individual facts of the case are decisive. Systematic considerations are rather scarce. A high degree of (outcome) predictability has been recognised as one of the value-based assessments or policy considerations (*reelle hensyn*),[86] which are regarded a source of law in its own right. Still, it is regarded that the main task of the courts is to find the best solution for the case at hand, if necessary by developing the

82 Franklin (2020) (n 7) 358 ff.

83 See e.g. Norwegian Supreme Court ruling (Grand Chamber) from 27 March 2020, HR-2020-661-S.

84 Kjølstad, Koch and Sunde (2020) (n 7) 125; Helland and Koch (2014) (n 19) 121.

85 Helland and Koch (2014) (n 19) 109 ff.

86 Monsen (2012) (n 60) 57; Helland and Koch (2014) (n 19) 110; Kjølstad, Koch and Sunde (2020) (n 7) 122 ff.

law. The idea of a pre-existing system of law has found little support in Norway where lawyers traditionally had a rather pragmatic and realistic perception of law. The role of individual judges in the application and development of law is less prominent in Norway than in England, but clearly more visible than in Germany.

3.2 Legislation

In England the ideal of governing the country with the help of legislation never gained ground to the extent to which the ideal of legislation became prevalent in the continental European legal cultures already in the early modern period.[87] In England, legislation was often used to amend outdated common law rules and principles or to realise a specific policy related to a narrowly defined field of law.[88] England has not adopted modern comprehensive and systematic codifications.[89] Areas governed by legislation are regulated rather comprehensively and casuistically, leaving the law applier little room for interpretation.[90] The implementation of EU law has increased the importance of statutory law relative to judicial law-making. Both factors have contributed to increases the outcome predictability of legislation.

In Germany, codification is regarded as the ideal form of legislation. The abstract concepts of codifications are ideally said organised in a systematic manner that allow the reader to interpret the provisions of the code in light of the underlying system of law.[91] The general abstractly framed provisions in codes are in need of interpretation. Legal consequences for a specific case have to be extracted from the wording of legislation in the form of a deductive process.[92] The underlying system of law provides guidance and at the same time limits the lawyer's discretion. In addition, the lawyers build their arguments in accordance to the prevailing opinion in legal doctrine even though it does not bind them formally. Departing from the established opinion in legal literature ('*herrschende Meinung*') will therefore require an extraordinary argumentative effort.[93] Finally, court practice is frequently used to identify the meaning of abstract concepts and to support legal dogmatic and systematic considerations. Despite the rather abstracts terms used in legislation, a combination of a systematic interpretation, legal doctrine, and court practice contribute to create predictable outcomes when determining the applicable law.

In Norway, a combination of different legal source factors offers guidance to a solution. The democratic legitimacy of legislation determines the law to a greater extent than the other legal sources. However, compared to Germany and England, the fragmentary character of legislation, broadly framed statutory provisions and the often very wide

87 Ibid. 115 f.
88 Brenncke (2018) (n 20) 28 ff.
89 Franklin (2020) (n 7) 362 f.
90 Ibid.
91 Koch (2020) (n 7) Subsection 3.
92 Ibid. subsection 5.
93 Ibid. 247.

scope of discretion provided by the legislator make it more difficult to predict the outcome of individual cases and to establish the applicable law. The traditionally pragmatic way of applying the law favours the idea that the aim is to find the best solution for the case at hand. In the light of the legal realistic approach to law, producing predictable outcomes based on systematic or authoritative considerations has been less important. Consequently, legislation furthers the ideal of outcome predictability to a lesser degree compared to Germany and England.

It seems appropriate to illustrate these still rather abstract considerations with an example. Let us take a look at the way the three countries have regulated the tort liability of children. The Norwegian Act on Compensation for Damages (Skadeserstatningsloven 1969) contains in § 1-1 the following provision: "Children and young persons under the age of 18 are obliged to compensate for damages which they have caused negligently or intentionally, in so far as this seems fair considering their age, development, the relevant behaviour, economic or other considerations." The Norwegian Supreme Court held in a recent decision that the decision should be based on a comprehensive evaluation of all relevant factors (*en bred helhetsvurdering*).[94] The Norwegian legislator has provided very broad categories, the very last even unspecified ("other considerations"). Based on such a provision the outcome of an individual case seems hardly predictable. The legislator provides the law applier with a rather broad opportunity to reduce the liability of the underaged tortfeasor; even the economic situations of the offender must be taken into account. The preparatory works maintain that a reduction of the compensation should be the rule rather than the exception.

In Germany, the legislator has regulated the same question differently. Pursuant to § 828 III of the Civil Code, the young tortfeasor between the age of 7 and 18 is reliable for the damage, except for cases where the ability to understand the consequences of the action are lacking. There are no other considerations mentioned that can be used to remedy the liability. According to German law the economic situation of the tortfeasor is irrelevant (cf. § 249). The German legislator allows a much lesser degree for considerations of individual justice and fairness. On the contrary CC § 829 allows a claim of compensation even if the tortfeasor lacks the capacity to act reasonably. This norm attempts to strike a balance between the interests of the child and the victim of the tortious act.[95] In England, courts have developed a liability-test. This test does not contain any consequences for the minor tortfeasor. In this respect minors and adults are treated alike. We can thus conclude that the Norwegian legislator has provided a wider access to considerations of equity that can be found in German and English law.

94 HR-2018-1014-A para 30. In the case at hand a 15-year-old boy had intentionally committed two murders. The judges at the Supreme Court ruled that the tortfeasor had to pay full compensation and in addition a compensation for pain and suffering. In a different case from 2004, another 15-year-old boy was regarded as responsible for committing gross negligent harm to another boy of 16 with fireworks. Interestingly, in both cases the judges were acknowledged to have a broad discretion but seemed to have been rather reluctant to use the wide discretion provided by the legislator.

95 Miquel Martin-Casals, *Comparative Report, Children in Tort Law. Children as Tortfeasors* Vol. I (Springer 2006), 16 ff.

4. Conclusion

We have seen that different legal cultures, despite recognising the demand for legal security, have developed different approaches and mechanisms to safeguard predictability. Applying the LCM enables us to understand that we can distinguish between different types of predictability prevailing in different legal cultures. In Germany the systematic and scientific approach to law facilitates the ideal of outcome-predictability. Legislation and legal doctrine are regarded to provide solutions for present and future legal problems, while the court's function is to apply the law in accord with the system or where the legislation has gaps to develop solutions fitting into the framework of the system. In England outcome-predictability is provided by looking at how courts have solved similar cases in the past, supported by the increasing amount of often rather casuistic legislation. In Norway the pragmatic approach to law allows for a combination of both mechanisms to provide outcome-predictability. However, the less stricter binding character of case law (no *stare desicis*), in combination with a general realistic approach to legal method and a high degree of confidence in the court, promotes the impression that Norwegian lawyers value procedural and methodological predictability higher than outcome predictability. This impacts also the perceptions regarding the role of individual justice. In Norway value-based assessments including considerations of individual justice are explicitly recognised as a legal source. This allows for adjusting the law to the fact of an individual case if necessary. In England, individual justice is an inherent part of the production of legal norms in form of precedents, but just in the limits set by the principle of *stare decisis*. In Germany it is regarded the purpose of the legislation to provide both outcome predictability and justice, but in a systematic and scientific sense, therefore to a lesser degree dependent on the individual circumstances of the case at hand. In conclusion the following figure might provide a highly abstract (and therefor necessarily imprecise) presentation of essential perceptions of justice and mechanisms to realise them.

Ideal of Justice	Degree of outcome-predictability as an ideal of justice	Mechanisms of achieving outcome-predictability	Degree of individual justice/flex-ibility	Mechanism for achieving individual justice
Germany	High	Legislation and system of law	Low –	General clauses, justice as part of the system
England & Wales	Medium-high	Strictly binding precedent and statutory legislation	Medium –	Precedents contain elements of ind. justice
Norway	Medium-low	Combination of fragmented legislation and Supreme Court judgments that must be taken into account (not formally binding)	High –	Considerations of fairness recognised as legal source (*rettskilde-faktor*)

Fig. 1 Comparison of Ideals of Justice in Germany, England & Wales, and Norway.

Returning to the initial research-question, we have seen that different ideals of justice are a product of both the historical preconditions and their development as well as the internal interplay between the different legal cultural elements of the LCM on both the institutional and intellectual level. The three legal cultures under investigation warrant outcome-predictability to a different degree and have developed different mechanisms to realise the underlying values.

5. Bibliography

Aarli R and Mæhle SS, *Fra lov til rett* (2nd ed, Gyldendal 2017)

Amartya S, *The Idea of Justice* (Allen Lane 2009)

Baker J, *An Introduction to English Legal History* (5th ed, Oxford University Press 2019)

Brenncke M, *Judicial Law-Making in English and German Courts – Techniques and Limits of Statutory Interpretation* (Intersentia 2018)

Cotterrell R, 'Is it so bad to be different? Comparative Law and the Appreciation of Diversity' in Örücü E & Nelken D, *Comparative Law a Handbook* (Hart Publisher 2007)

Cross R and Harris JW, *Precedent in English Law*, 4th ed. (Clarendon Press 1991)

Decock W, *Theologians and Contract Law, The moral Transformation of the IUS COMMUNE* (ca. 1500–1650) (Nijhoff Publishers 2013)

Fernandez P and Ponzetto G, 'Stare Decisis: Rhetoric and Substance' *Journal of Law and Economics and Organization,* Vol. 28 No. 2 (Oxford University Press 2010) doi:10.1093/jleo/ewq006

Grødeland ÅB and Miller WL, *European Legal Cultures in Transition* (Cambridge University Press 2015)

Hart, HLA 'Positivism and the Separation of Law and Morals' (1958) Harvard Law Review Vol. 71, No. 4 (Feb., 1958)

Helland I, 'Introduction to German legal method' in Helland I and Koch S (eds), *Nordic and Germanic Legal Methods* (Mohr Siebeck 2014)

—— and Koch S, 'Introduction to Norwegian Legal Method', in Helland I and Koch S (eds), *Nordic and Germanic Legal Methods* (Mohr Siebeck 2014)

Kruse F, *Die verfassungsrechtlichen Grenzen richterlicher Rechtsfortbildung. Zur Gesetzmäßigkeit der Rechtsprechung unter dem Grundgesetz* (Mohr Siebeck 2019)

Larenz K and Canaris C-W, *Methodenlehre der Rechtswissenschaft* (3rd ed, Mohr Siebeck 1995)

Lennartz J, *Dogmatik als Methode* (Mohr Siebeck 2017)

Lundmark T, *Charting the Divide between Common and Civil Law* (Oxford University Press 2012)

Manchester C, Salter D and Moodie P, *Exploring the Law: The Dynamics of Precedent and Statutory Interpretation*, 2nd ed. (Sweet & Maxwell 2000)

Miquel Martin-Casals, *Comparative Report, Children in Tort Law. Children as Tortfeasors* Vol. I (Springer 2006)

Monsen E, *Innføring i juridisk metode og oppgaveteknikk* (Cappelen Damm 2012)

Robbers G, *An introduction to German Law* (4th ed, Nomos 2006)

Rüthers B, *Die Unbegrenzte Auslegung*, 8th ed. (Mohr Siebeck 2017)

Rückert J and Seinecke R, *Methodik des Zivilrechts – von Savigny bis Teubner* (3rd ed, Nomos 2017)

Schröder J, 'Zur Vorgeschichte der Volksgeistlehre. Gesetzgebungs- und Rechtsquellentheorie im 17. und 18. Jahrhundert' (1992) Vol. 109 *Savigny Zeitschrift für Rechtsgeschichte (Germ. Abt.)* 1

—— *Recht als Wissenschaft* (2nd ed, Mohr Siebeck 2012)

Siems M, 'Comparative Legal Certainty: Is there a Common-Civil Law Divide?' in Fenwick M, Siems M and Wrbka S (eds), *The Shifting Meaning of Legal Certainty in Comparative and Transnational Law* (Hart Publishing 2017)

Simon H and Funk-Baker G, *Einführung in das deutsche Recht und die deutsche Rechtssprache* (Beck 2009)

Sunde JØ, *Speculum Legale – rettsspegelen* (Fagbokforlaget 2005)

Sunde JØ, 'Daughters of God and Counsellors of the Judges of Men: Changes in the Legal Culture of the Norwegian Realm in the High Middle Ages' in Brink S and Collinson L (eds), *New Approaches to Early law in Scandinavia* (Brepols 2014)

Vogenauer S, *Die Auslegung von Gesetzen in England und auf dem Kontinent* (Mohr Siebeck 2001)

Weber RK, *Der Begründungsstil von Conseil constitutionnel und Bundesverfassungsgericht. Eine vergleichende Analyse der Spruchpraxis* (Mohr Siebeck 2019)

Wieacker F, *Privatrechtsgeschichte der Neuzeit* (2nd ed, Vandenhoeck & Ruprecht 1967)

Zimmermann R, 'Characteristic Aspects of the German Legal Culture' in Zekoll J and Wagner G (eds), *Introduction to German Law* (3rd ed, Wolters Kluwer 2019)

List of contributors

The Outset – How to Learn Sailing the Ocean of Legal Cultures
Sören Koch, Professor University of Bergen (Norway), Anwalt (Germany)

Managing the Unmanageable – An Essay Concerning Legal Culture as an Analytical Tool
Jørn Øyrehagen Sunde, Professor University of Oslo (Norway)

Legal Culture and Comparative Law – Diving into the Ocean
Sören Koch, Professor University of Bergen (Norway), Anwalt (Germany)

From Mapping to Navigation – a COMPASS Formula for Conducting Comparative Analysis
Sören Koch, Professor University of Bergen (Norway), Anwalt (Germany)

An Introduction to Norwegian Legal Culture
Marius Mikkel Kjølstad, PhD Candidate University of Bergen (Norway)
Sören Koch, Professor University of Bergen (Norway), Anwalt (Germany)
Jørn Øyrehagen Sunde, Professor University of Oslo (Norway)

An Introduction to Finnish Legal Culture
Anna Nylund, Professor University of Tromsø (Norway)

An Introduction to Estonian Legal Culture
Merike Ristikivi, Associate Professor University of Tartu (Estonia)
Andreas Kangur, Lecturer University of Tartu (Estonia)
Irene Kull, Professor University of Tartu (Estonia)
Katre Luhamaa, Lecturer University of Tartu (Estonia)
Marin Sedman, PhD Candidate University of Tartu (Estonia)
Hesi Siimets-Gross, Associate Professor University of Tartu (Estonia)
Age Värv, Associate Professor University of Tartu (Estonia)

An Introduction to German Legal Culture
Sören Koch, Professor University of Bergen (Norway), Anwalt (Germany)

An Introduction to Polish Legal Culture
Anna Klimaszewska, Assistant Professor University of Gdańsk (Poland)
Anna Machnikowska, Professor University of Gdańsk (Poland)
Sören Koch, Professor University of Bergen (Norway), Anwalt (Germany)

A Legal Cultural "Take" on the Legal System of England & Wales
Christian N.K. Franklin, Professor University of Bergen (Norway), Barrister (Gray's Inn) (UK, England)

An Introduction to Scottish Legal Culture
Andrew R.C. Simpson, Professor University of Edinburgh (UK, Scotland)

An Introduction to Belgian Legal Culture
Bruno Debaenst, Professor Uppsala University (Sweden)

An Introduction to French Legal Culture
Sunniva Cristina Bragdø-Ellenes, Associate Professor University of Agder (Norway)

An Introduction to Austrian Legal Culture
Konrad Lachmayer, Professor Sigmund Freud University Vienna (Austria)
Niklas Sonntag, Civil servant Constitutional Service of the Austrian state of Tyrol (Austria)

An Introduction to Italian Legal Culture
Esmeralda Colombo, PhD Candidate University of Bergen (Norway)
Lars Kvestad, Associate Professor Western Norway University of Applied Sciences (Norway)

An Introduction to Romanian Legal Culture
Cosmin Dariescu, Associate Professor University Alexandru Ioan Cuza (Romania)

A View of the Legal Culture of the United States of America
Lloyd T. Wilson, Jr., Professor Indiana University (USA)

An Introduction to Australian Legal Culture
Tina Soliman Hunter, Professor Macquarie University (Australia)

An Introduction to Chinese Legal Culture
JIANG Dong, Associate Professor Renmin University of China (China)

Sailing – Analysing Ideals of Justice in Germany, England, and Norway
Sören Koch, Professor University of Bergen (Norway), Anwalt (Germany)